SEARCHING FOR PEACE
IN EUROPE AND EURASIA

EUROPEAN
CENTRE
FOR
conflict prevention

A project of the European Centre for Conflict Prevention
(Utrecht, The Netherlands) in cooperation with the
Center for Conflict Management (Almaty, Kazakhstan), the
Center for Nonviolent Action (Sarajevo, Bosnia & Herzegovina), and
the International Center on Conflict & Negotiation (Tblisi, Georgia)

Financially supported by
the Ministries of Foreign Affairs of the Netherlands and Denmark,
Department for International Development (DfID) of the UK, and
the Karl Popper Foundation, Switzerland

SEARCHING FOR PEACE IN EUROPE AND EURASIA

An Overview of Conflict Prevention and Peacebuilding Activities

edited by
Paul van Tongeren, Hans van de Veen,
and Juliette Verhoeven

LYNNE
RIENNER
PUBLISHERS

BOULDER
LONDON

Published in the United States of America in 2002 by
Lynne Rienner Publishers, Inc.
1800 30th Street, Boulder, Colorado 80301
www.rienner.com

and in the United Kingdom by
Lynne Rienner Publishers, Inc.
3 Henrietta Street, Covent Garden, London WC2E 8LU

Library of Congress Cataloging-in-Publication Data
Tongeren, Paul van.
    Searching for peace in Europe and Eurasia : an overview of conflict
    prevention and peacebuilding activities / edited by Paul van Tongeren,
    Hans van de Veen, and Juliette Verhoeven.
    Includes bibliographical references and index.
    ISBN 1-58826-054-2 (alk. paper)
    ISBN 1-58826-079-8 (pbk. : alk. paper)
    1. Peaceful settlement of international disputes. 2. Reconciliation.
3. Human rights. 4. Conflict management. 5. Peaceful change (International
relations) 6. Civil society. 7. Europe—Politics and government—1989–
8. Asia, Central—Politics and government—1991– I. Veen, Hans van de.
II. Verhoeven, Juliette. III. European Centre for Conflict Prevention. IV. Title.
JZ5597 .T66 2002
327.1'7—dc21   2001048935

British Cataloguing in Publication Data
A Cataloguing in Publication record for this book
is available from the British Library.

Printed and bound in the United States of America

The paper used in this publication meets the requirements
of the American National Standard for Permanence of
Paper for Printed Library Materials Z39.48-1984.

5 4 3 2 1

Contents

Part 3 Directory

Foreword:
Searching for Peace in Europe and Eurasia

Max van der Stoel

Early action should follow early warning. Early warning relies on good information. This book not only makes that point, but also provides the raw materials. Searching for Peace in Europe and Eurasia *is a vital handbook for anyone interested in conflict prevention and crisis management.*

The European Platform for Conflict Prevention and Transformation has developed a reputation for networking and providing valuable information on conflict indicators. This book describes some of its lessons learned and points out some possible troubles ahead. Through its conflict surveys, list of contacts, and information-packed appendixes, it is a handy reference for those of us who are searching for peace in Europe and Eurasia.

From personal experience as high commissioner on national minorities for the Organization for Security and Cooperation in Europe (OSCE) between 1993 and 2001, I know the value of reliable information and a good network of contacts. One cannot only count on official sources or the media. It is important to go behind the scenes to see the root causes of conflicts, the positions of the parties, the context of discussions, and the systemic factors that can all have a bearing on how situations evolve. This book provides such insights.

Conflicts seldom erupt in isolation. In an increasingly interdependent world, it is vital to understand the regional context of situations. One cannot fully understand developments in Abkhazia or Chechnya without looking at the broader security, political, and economic factors in the Caucasus. Interethnic tensions in Macedonia and the Presovo Valley have a great deal to do with a spillover of the conflict in Kosovo. And developments in the Ferghana Valley stem from a number of local and regional factors, including developments in Uzbekistan, Afghanistan, and Tajikistan. This book helps to explain the regional dynamics that affect violent conflict in Europe and Eurasia.

More often than not, the types of conflicts we are looking at start as small-scale issues that slowly accumulate. The key to heading them off is to tackle them at an early stage and to ensure that mechanisms, laws, or projects are put in place to reduce the likelihood of future tensions. This book gives some food for thought on how that can be done by providing policy recommendations.

The main strength of *Searching for Peace in Europe and Eurasia* is its analytical chapters, particularly the Conflict Surveys. The focus is the whole OSCE area. Some conflicts (such as those in Western Europe or the Balkans) are well known, while others (in Nagorno Karabakh or the Ferghana Valley) may seem more exotic. Sadly, many of these situations only show up on our radar when there is a problem. Who had heard much about Chechnya or Kosovo until a few years ago? When there is only low-level conflict, people are not interested. Once a crisis erupts, it is often too late to effectively intervene. We must do more to generate interest and involvement in tensions at an early stage so that they do not develop into violent conflicts later on. We must do more to ensure that early information is followed by decisive early action.

Organizations such as the European Platform for Conflict Prevention and Transformation can play a key role. They can be the eyes and ears of the international community in gathering information on potential conflict situations and raise the alarm when there are signs of smoke. The better integrated the network, both among its members and in relation to international organizations, the greater the impact of the information that is collected. A coordinated, targeted, and informed approach will strengthen the credibility of the information and give it a better chance of being channeled into the policymaking pipeline.

In that regard, it is worth noting that this book is not a static resource. It is the crystallization of the European Platform's work in recording, describing, and analyzing prevention and management efforts in the main violent conflicts in Europe and Eurasia. But it is also part of an ongoing process to contribute to the process of de-escalating conflicts. It is up to you, the reader, to make the most of it so that we may all continue our search for peace.

Former Dutch minister of foreign affairs Max van der Stoel served as high commissioner on national minorities for the Organization for Security and Cooperation in Europe between 1993 and 2001.

Acknowledgments

This book is the outcome of a project of the European Platform for Conflict Prevention and Transformation that started three years ago. Numerous individuals and organizations from all over the world contributed to the effort by providing advice and support in developing the project, participating in seminars, commenting on the draft texts, and contributing articles for the publication. Without their valuable contributions, this publication would not have been possible. Here we would like to express our gratitude for this constructive cooperation.

Several representatives of the member organizations of the European Platform have been instrumental in developing the Searching for Peace program from the start. We would like to thank in particular Kevin Clements (International Alert), Mari Fitzduff (Incore), John Marks (Search for Common Ground), Anne Palm (KATU), Norbert Ropers (Berghof Research Center), and Valery Tishkov (Eawarn).

We are very much indebted to the Ministries of Foreign Affairs of Denmark and the Netherlands, the Department for International Development of the United Kingdom, and the Karl Popper Foundation for providing financial support for this project. Former Danish ambassador Michael Wagtmann enabled the start of this project by his timely support.

The goal of this book is to provide a concise overview of the conflict prevention and peacebuilding efforts in Europe, the Caucasus, and Central Asia. Our own staff conducted part of the research, but we relied heavily on the expertise of several practitioners and scholars. We benefited greatly from the intellectual advice and guidance provided by Gregg Austin, Yll Bajraktari, Mient Jan Faber, Gevork ter Gabrielian, George Khutsisvili, Mathilde Lub, Madeleine Rees, Mirjam Struyk, Stefan Vassilev, Franklin de Vrieze, Tom Woodhouse, and Dubravka Zarkov. In particular, we thank Jonathan Cohen for his constructive recommendations and great help in shaping the project.

The book itself is the collective effort of a large group of practitioners and scholars with long-term expertise on specific conflicts or issues. Many of the authors wrote on conflicts in the area where they live, and we greatly appreciate their outstanding efforts in presenting a balanced view of conflicts in which they are, inevitably, involved. We hope their analyses will help a broad audience to better understand the situation. All authors had their draft texts reviewed by a broadly composed group of experts and practitioners. We are very grateful for the willingness and flexibility shown by the authors in revising and updating material quickly. When we realized that some additional pieces and updates were needed, most authors produced high-quality articles at a very late stage. Thank you for that.

To ensure the accuracy and objectivity of the analysis in the surveys, we organized several meetings of practitioners, scholars, and other experts to discuss the draft texts. The meetings proved to be very useful, and local input was further ensured by this consultative process. We thank Tobias Debiel from the Peace and Development Foundation for co-organizing a meeting in June 2000 in Bonn, Germany, to discuss the draft surveys of the conflicts in the Caucasus. We are very grateful to the experts who participated and provided us with relevant comments and critical questions about the surveys (naming just those not mentioned above): Bruno Coppieters, Paula Garb, and Liana Kvarchelia. We would also like to gratefully acknowledge Anna Matveeva's readiness to write draft texts in a very early stage of the project and her flexibility in revising and updating the texts.

Together with Conciliation Resources, we organized a meeting in London in December 2000 where we discussed the draft surveys of conflict prevention for Central Asia. At this meeting the participants provided us with many more insights into today's issues and problems. We are very grateful for the extremely useful comments and suggestions provided by Kamolludin Adbullaev, Shirin Akiner, Vicken Cheterian, Luigi De Martino, Jonathan Goodhand, Heinz Krummenacher, Elena Sadovskaya, Randa Slim, and Anara Tabyshalieva. We are also grateful to Catherine Barnes from Conciliation Resources for co-organizing the meeting and helping us to shape the project in relation to Central Asia.

We also organized a three-day regional seminar in Sarajevo in April 2000 to discuss the role of NGOs in conflict prevention and the draft surveys about conflicts in the Balkans. We greatly appreciate the participation of the many practitioners from throughout the region, their presentations, and their critical feedback to the draft texts, which undoubtedly contributed to qualitative improvements at large. Thank you (again, just those previously unmentioned) Kalin Babusku, Laura Davis, Michael Doyle, Iskra Evrosimovska, Arben Fetahi, Ivana Franovic, Katarina Kruhonja, Vladimir Maric, Gordana Miljevic, Goran Lapcevic, Filip Pavlovitz, Yannick du Pont, Dennis Sandole, Christina Schweitzer, Albana Shala, Robert Stallaerts, Daliborka Uljarevic, and Nenad Vukosavljevic. Furthermore, we thank Eran Fraenkel and Sally Broughton from Search for Common Ground in Macedonia for their support in shaping the program for the meeting. Subsequently, we organized a follow-up meeting to further discuss the surveys of the Balkans. Yll Bajraktari, Raymond Detrez, Dragan Lakicevic, Filip Pavlovic, and Franklin de Vrieze all came to the Netherlands to participate, and we thank them for that.

In the end of November 2001 we organized a regional seminar in Almaty, Kazakhstan, bringing together participants from the five Central Asian republics to discuss the potential role of NGOs in peacebuilding and conflict prevention. We are very grateful for the beneficial input from the participants on the chapters dealing with Central Asia. The lively discussions ensured a realistic and up-to-date view of the situation in the region. Among the many people who we would particularly like to thank for their useful input are Mavlyuda Abduhalimova, Atirkul Alicheva, Akmal Gafurov, Gulnaz Hidoyatova, Abdudjabor Hotamov, Raya Kadyrova, Alla Kuvatova, Mariya Lisizina, Ahmet Muradov, Rano Kuldasheva, Madina Najimova, Parviz Mullodjanov, Azizi Rahimulla, Dodarbek Saidaliev, Igor Savin, John Schoeberlein, Olga Sosnina, Elena Voronina, Evgeni Zhovtis, and Tatyana Zlobina. We are very grateful to Svetlana Bekmambetova, Elena Sadovskaya, and Lada Zimina for their excellent assistance in co-organizing the event.

We want to express our sincere gratitude to the Center for Conflict Management in Kazakhstan, the Center for Nonviolence in Bosnia and Herzegovina, and the International Center on Conflict and Negotiation in Georgia. These organizations worked extremely methodically to compile the directory of organizations for the Balkans, the Caucasus, and Central Asia. Without their invaluable collaboration it would not have been possible to provide profiles of organizations in these regions that are not well known internationally. In particular we thank Ivana Franovic, George Khutsishvili, Lada Zimina, and Elena Sadovskaya for their constructive work and beneficial comments on the development of the project.

We are most grateful to Jan ter Laak, who directed us through the project and provided useful advice and suggestions.

Many people from different backgrounds have contributed to this book. The journalists of Bureau M&O—Environment and Development Productions in Amsterdam provided an invaluable service in writing the organization profiles, as well as in editing the chapters and surveys. We thank Esther Bakker, Annemieke Horst, Jos Havermans, Niall Martin, Bram Posthumus, and Jim Wake. Karel Meyer of MMS Grafisch Werk developed all the maps.

This book would not have been possible without the Herculean efforts of the staff of the European Centre for Conflict Prevention. We express our sincere appreciation to Joost Janmaat for his useful research assistance, as well to student assistants Eric Boessenkool, Madeleine Clarin, Aleksej Scira, Olena Tochyslovska, Emmy Toonen, and Iris Wielders. In particular we thank Mats Lundström for his extremely consistent compilation of the directory of European organizations. We are very grateful for his solid work, valuable assistance, and involvement in this project. Further we thank Guido de Graaf Bierbrauwer for his research assistance and beneficial knowledge about politics in the Balkans and we owe him much gratitude for his flexibility.

While thankful for all the support we have received, we assume full responsibility for this publication.

—*The Editors*

Introduction

Paul van Tongeren, Hans van de Veen, and Juliette Verhoeven

Several of the lessons that the richer part of the world is slowly but surely learning in the aftermath of the September 11 events are precisely the lessons hard won from the soils and by the peoples of the marginalized areas. Perhaps the most important is that security is not linked primarily to the size and quantity of weapons. Much more, security is linked to the quality of our relationships with other people, how we view each other, and how we care for each others' needs. Security in the world is connected to the inclusion of people in gaining a voice and access to the basic resources necessary for a peaceful global community.

Giving a voice to people who try to build peace, locally and internationally, was one of the main ideas behind the establishment of the European Platform for Conflict Prevention and Transformation in 1997. The Platform—presently a network of more than 150 organizations working in the field of prevention and resolution of violent conflicts in the international arena—aims to provide comprehensive information and support for the conflict prevention and transformation activities of the different players in the field. The European Platform also strives to stimulate networking and improved coordination. Connecting local with international NGOs, practitioners, academics, donor agencies, policymakers, and media provides a useful vehicle for sharing experiences and views from various perspectives. Creating such interdisciplinary and interregional platforms serves the discussion about effective conflict prevention and peacebuilding strategies. One of the main problems confronting people and organizations working for peace today is the lack of information about the many initiatives currently being undertaken and the people and institutions that have gained expertise in this field. There is also an increasing need for clearer insights into what does and what doesn't work and how to raise political and public interest in conflict prevention and peacebuilding.

This book should be seen in this light, offering a unique combination of background information, detailed descriptions of ongoing activities, and assessments of future prospects for conflict prevention and peacebuilding. The European Centre for Conflict Prevention, which acts as the secretariat of the

European Platform, started the Searching for Peace program three years ago, aiming to record, describe, and analyze conflict prevention and peacebuilding efforts in the main conflicts in the world. The present publication is the second in a series, following the 1999 publication of *Searching for Peace in Africa.*

The first objective of the Searching for Peace program and publications is to provide basic information on who does what, including hundreds of organizations, as well as important publications, resources, contacts, websites, and databases. The second objective is of a more evaluative nature. The surveys in this volume offer insight into the varying approaches used in conflict prevention and peacebuilding in different situations, which can help organizations to better attune and harmonize their activities and work together in order to develop more effective policies. The third objective is to give a voice to local NGOs; the potential of these organizations to act as intermediaries between civil society in the conflict areas and international organizations should be taken into account much more than it typically is. A further objective is to act as a bridge between NGOs and networks from different regions, academic institutions, and international organizations such as the OSCE. We use a regional approach to underscore the international context of situations and the possible spillover effects. The transnational characteristics of violent conflicts, such as the flow of refugees, the illicit trade in natural resources and weapons, and the transit of armed forces across borders, tend to sustain conflicts and can destabilize neighboring countries.

The overall objective of the Searching for Peace program—to contribute peacefully to the transformation of violent conflicts—is even more crucial after the September 11 events. The causes and background of violent conflicts should be better understood. Long-term involvement in peacebuilding and the transformation of violent conflicts is needed, even after peace agreements are signed and the international media have left the place. At the same time it is even more important than before to dedicate our attention to the lesser-known violent conflicts, such as in the Ferghana Valley and Georgia/Abchazia.

The book is organized in three parts. The chapters in Part 1 provide a contextual framework for a better understanding of the conflicts in Europe, the Caucasus, and Central Asia. Part 2 presents regional surveys, including general chapters that describe the dynamics and political developments in each region and policy chapters that focus specifically on policy options and future perspectives for the region and reflect on conflict prevention and management tools that have been applied. The surveys in Part 2 provide a brief background analysis of 18 of the major violent conflicts in Europe and Eurasia. The primary focus of each survey is the activities of the key local and international actors working to resolve the conflict. The selection of the conflicts was based on the list of High-Intensity and Low-Intensity Conflicts identified by the *World Conflict and Human Rights Map 2000,* produced by the Interdisciplinary Research Programme on Causes of Human Rights Violations (PIOOM); the annual *States in Armed Conflict* published by the Department of Peace and Conflict Research at the Uppsala University was also consulted.

Part 3 of the book is a directory of more than four hundred organizations in Europe and Eurasia in the field of conflict prevention and peacebuilding. For each organization, both a short profile and practical contact information is provided.

Putting all this information together has been a Herculean labor in which many people from all over the world have participated. Many practitioners, scholars, and other experts have been consulted and have commented on draft versions of this volume. Seminars were organized in the different regions to bring together local experts and international practitioners and scholars to discuss the main issues, the balance of the text, and inclusiveness of all actors. However, we recognize that there are still gaps in the information and we therefore see this undertaking as an ongoing process. Parts of the book and additional information are available on the website of the European Platform (www.conflict-prevention.net) and will be updated regularly.

Our purpose is to fill in the gaps in information about conflict prevention and peacebuilding activities in the violent conflicts in Europe and Eurasia and to contribute to the discussion about effective measures for conflict prevention. Furthermore, we hope with this book to build a bridge between practitioners, scholars, policymakers, media, and the donor community, thus enhancing the capacity for the prevention of violent conflicts.

PART I

Reflections

I

Conflict Prevention
and the European Union:
A Potential Yet to Be Fully Realized

Paul Eavis and Stuart Kefford

Southeast Europe and the countries of Central Asia are becoming increasingly important economically and politically for the European Union (EU). Addressing instability and underdevelopment in these regions has now become a central issue for the EU. Important programs to address instability and promote development are already in place in both regions, but the EU's role in peacebuilding is yet to be fully realized.

The enlargement of the European Union will make stability in the Balkans and the Caucasus even more important to the EU. Many Southeast European countries hope to join the EU and its enlarged borders may well extend to the Black Sea. Furthermore, preaccession talks with Turkey raise the prospect of the EU coming into direct contact with the Caucasus, and closer to Central Asia. Stability in the whole region is crucial to reduce the risk of conflict spilling over into the Union, and is a key requirement for developing successful economic and trading links. The presence of natural resources, specifically oil in the Caucasus and Central Asia, increases the strategic importance of the region to the EU.

The high level of instability in Southeast Europe and Central Asia means that peacebuilding is a difficult task. However, the EU occupies a strong position to help play an important role in conflict prevention in the region. The EU is a major donor of development assistance to the region; it also has the biggest single market, and carries influence in a number of prominent bodies addressing world affairs (UN agencies and the Security Council, the G-8, World Trade Organization, and others). This chapter gives an overview of the different policy instruments and programs that the EU has in the region for preventing conflict and building peace.

Approaches to Addressing Violent Conflict

The EU has voiced support for conflict-prevention measures from the mid-1990s. A number of significant policy documents and resolutions have been published and agreed upon that identify root causes of conflict and the role that EU instruments can play to help address them.[1] To date, these approaches have not been effectively implemented to prevent conflicts from becoming violent. Instead, the EU has prioritized crisis management policies, focusing on developing an international military and police capacity to respond to and manage conflicts. The EU's emphasis on promoting measures to enhance military and civilian crisis management are important, but efforts to balance this approach with more effective preventive action are long overdue. The EU must broaden its focus, and attach attention to long-term preventive action to prevent crises from occurring in the first place.

Recent developments in EU circles have indicated a welcome move in this direction. A series of initiatives has been brought to the fore of late that have raised the profile of conflict prevention to the level of heads of state. For example, the high representative of the Common and Foreign Security Policy, Javier Solana, and commissioner for External Relations, Chris Patten, presented a paper at the Nice summit on the effectiveness of EU action in the field of conflict prevention.[2] The European Commission (EC) followed this up by publishing a communication on conflict prevention. These initiatives indicate an improved political will to pursue preventative action. These were followed by the agreement at the Gothenburg Summit (June 2001) on a conflict-prevention Programme of Action.

The EU's main instruments for implementing these conflict-prevention policies fall within the Common and Foreign Security Policy (CFSP) and development cooperation policy.

Common Foreign and Security Policy

The CFSP was established in 1993 by the Maastricht Treaty to "preserve peace and strengthen international security,"[3] implying conflict prevention as a central theme. However, the capacity for planning, implementing, and monitoring the CFSP was inadequate, and the member states recognized that it could not function effectively. New initiatives formed in 1999, under the Amsterdam Treaty, aimed to revitalize the CFSP.

These developments have the potential to enhance the EU's conflict-prevention capacity. They included:

1. The creation of the position of high representative of CFSP, taken up by Javier Solana, to represent the EU externally
2. The establishment of the Policy Planning and Early Warning Unit (PPEWU) to enhance the capacity for monitoring potential conflict situations and policy planning
3. The strengthening of defense links between the EU and the Western European Union (WEU), and
4. The mandating of the WEU to deal with the so-called Petersberg tasks of humanitarian and rescue missions, peacekeeping, and crisis management including peacemaking

The EU has taken a number of practical CFSP initiatives aimed at conflict prevention that have either been focused on Central and Southeast Europe, and Central Asia, or have the potential to be applied there. These include the original Stability Pact, the development of a civilian crisis-management capacity, and initiatives to control small-arms proliferation.

Stability Pact (the Balladur Plan)

The Stability Pact was the first initiative in the field of CFSP, adopted by the EU in 1993, to encourage the countries of East and Southeast Europe to resolve mutual historical grievances regarding ethnic minorities and frontiers. This was, and remains, a necessary precondition for EU membership. The Stability Pact aimed to promote good neighborly relations between countries, to promote peace, and stability. The EU considered the Stability Pact a useful mediating tool in the quest for regional stability, and it achieved some positive results.

However, the initiative highlighted poor coherence at the EU level in the planning and execution of programs, with one commentator noting that "where activities . . . have been mutually reinforcing, this has seemed to resemble an accident or piecemeal effort rather than a well planned and implemented strategy."[4] Experience pointed to the need for greater coherence between different aspects of EU policy.

Civilian Crisis-Management Capacity

Recent moves to develop the EU's civilian crisis-management capacity have important relevance to Southeast Europe and the Caucasus as these are likely to be two of the regions where the proposed rapid reaction force (RRF) may be deployed. The Feira Summit in April 2000, during the Portuguese EU presidency, identified civilian crisis management to include the four areas of policing, rule of law, civilian administration, and civil protection. Member states set an initial target, reinforced during the Swedish presidency, that by 2003 they should provide up to 5,000 police officers (1,000 of which could be deployed in thirty days) and 200 officials in the area of rule of law, for international missions in conflict prevention and crisis-management situations. The numbers involved will be clarified when member states announce their contributions at the Police Capabilities Commitment Conference taking place in the end of 2001. Currently there are 3,500 European police officers already mobilized for international missions, within the framework of the UN, the Organization for Security and Cooperation in Europe (OSCE), and the WEU.

The police RRF could play two major roles: implementing programs to strengthen local police and substituting for local police in nonstabilized situations. Where local structures are failing, the EU will have the capacity to substitute for local police with a Rapid Reaction Police Force, similar to the UN force deployed in Kosovo. In a violent crisis, police missions will form part of a military operation that can be deployed to establish overall control on the ground, followed by a transitional phase to restore public security, and then be involved in postcrisis reconstruction and institution building. This would include training programs to bring local police capabilities up to acceptable standards relating to ethical practice and adherence to human rights, and providing assistance and advice to local counterparts on ethical behavior in the field of law enforcement. This focus on building police capacity and security-sector reform will be an important issue in the countries of Southeast Europe and the Caucasus.

During the Swedish presidency of the EU, member states identified a Police Action Plan for the planning and conduct of policing operations within the area of civilian crisis management. This plan covers several areas for the EU to develop relating to the planning and conduct of police operations, systems for the command and control of police, a legal framework for missions to work within, a program of basic and specialized training, and modalities for financing operations. This final area has not yet been fully addressed in all areas of civilian crisis management. The Swedish presidency initiated work on identifying principles for applying finances for operations with defense and security implications, which supports substitute police in nonstabilized situations. However, financing arrangements for other areas of civilian crisis management—increasing local police capacity, strengthening the rule of law, and providing civil protection—still need to be worked out.

Strengthening the rule of law and providing civilian protection is vital for preventing conflict and consolidating peace. The task of the EU is to build a database of experts in these areas and provide the expertise to implement effective rule of law in areas where it is needed. To address this area adequately the EU must overcome a significant difficulty in "extracting" experts from their permanent engagements within member states and tailoring their expertise to match local needs. Difficulties have been experienced recently in Kosovo, where some recent cases presided over by internationally appointed lawyers have ended in a welter of recriminations often due to judges with an "unfamiliarity with local legislation."[5] Nevertheless the EU must focus on developing the capacity of a sufficiently large number of member-state officials and experts to support measures to strengthen the rule of law. To satisfactorily achieve the 2003 targets, there must be a pre-identification of capacity and functions needed, and programs implemented to develop common training modules for officials to ensure complete familiarity with their tasks.

Parallel to the policing and judicial aspects of civilian crisis management, the EU must develop a pool of experts in civilian administration to carry out advisory, training, and monitoring activities to set up or ensure the existence of a functional administrative apparatus. The EU has committed to creating a pool of experts in this area. Their mandate would involve assisting the transition to local ownership of administrative bodies at the appropriate time to allow sustainability.

It is vitally important for the EU to maintain their support to military and policing intervention in areas of instability. However this must not reduce the focus on less high-profile support in terms of developing local policing capacity and supporting the development of the rule of law and civilian administration institutions. The political will to support these areas is needed to signify the EU's intent in implementing fully the capacity of civilian crisis management. The targets set must be adhered to, in order to provide the optimum chance of supporting peace and preventing future conflict in Southeast Europe and Central Asia.

Joint Action and Resolution to Control Small Arms

One of the factors undermining programs to build peace and stability in Southeast Europe and the Caucasus is the proliferation of small arms and light weapons in the region. In December 1998 the member states agreed on a "Joint Action on the European Union's Contribution to Combating the Destabilizing Accumulation and Spread of Small Arms and Light Weapons." The Joint Action works in two ways to address the problems of small-arms proliferation: preventive measures to limit the potential for accumulation of small arms such as establishing effective export controls and a national inventory; and reactive measures to help reduce existing accumulations of small arms such as removing surplus stock and destroying it. Alongside the Joint Action, the EU also agreed on a "Development Council Resolution on Combating the Destabilizing Accumulation and Spread of Small Arms and Light Weapons." The resolution encourages countries to eliminate surplus weapons, and additionally calls for international cooperation to combat illicit trafficking and challenges the culture of violence.

Effective implementation of the EU Joint Action in the region is vital. In Southeastern Europe and the Caucasus, the problem of small-arms proliferation is acute. For example, in Albania, official stockpiled weapons, including 600,000 Kalashnikov rifles, 200,000 Simonov guns, and hundreds of tons of explosives went missing after storage bunkers across the country were broken into during unrest in March 1997. Two programs in South Ossetia and Albania have so far received EU support, but this support needs to be increased if the issue is to be effectively addressed.

EU Institutional Developments in Support of Conflict Prevention

During recent years there have been a number of important institutional developments in the EU that have the potential to enhance its capacity for conflict prevention. The EU's new PPEWU functions as an advisory body to the Council of Ministers on potential crises, their impact on the EU, and appropriate strategies to be implemented. However, the PPEWU's potential to provide early warning of potential conflict situations and coherently plan a response has not been realized, partially due to a lack of personnel.

Not only is the unit short on personnel, it also doubles up as the cabinet of Solana, with a significant amount of time dedicated to planning Solana's schedule, writing speeches, and carrying out other duties diverting them from their intended task. This lack of capacity is compounded by political pressures, which press the unit to concentrate on short-term crisis management, rather than taking on long-term preventive approaches. To date, the Balkans has been a major focus of the PPEWU, but attention has also been given to the Caucasus. The unit prepared a paper in advance of a Troika visit to the Caucasus in February 2001, outlining the role the EU could play to promote stability and development in the region, and concluding that "the Troika favored looking for new ways for the Union to back efforts to *prevent* and resolve conflicts and carry out post-conflict rehabilitation."[6]

Also, significantly, nongovernmental organizations (NGOs) were consulted in the development of this policy paper, showing a welcome move toward listening to independent experts and actors "on the ground." This is all positive, but the PPEWU needs enhanced capacity to fully carry out its mandate, not only in the Balkans and the Caucasus but in other regions of the world that have been relatively neglected, such as sub-Saharan Africa.

The EC's new policy toward "deconcentration" of authority into the hands of country delegations also has the potential to enhance the EU's capacity to target policies to prevent violent conflict. The delegates are in a position to exercise informed judgment over the content of EC-funded programs, and have the potential to take appropriate action against potentially inflammatory situations and prevent escalation. It is essential, though, that suitably qualified and experienced staff make up the delegations to ensure accurate readings of conflict-risk situations to enable appropriate preventive approaches to be taken. It is also vital that they work closely with local NGOs to seek local expertise and views on appropriate responses to potential conflict situations.

Another EU tool with the potential to play a role in peacebuilding is Common Strategies (CS). These were established from the Amsterdam Treaty and aim to ensure consistency of EU external policies across the EU institutional framework. CS was designed to set out a comprehensive and coherent approach to a particular country, region, or issue. The first CS was planned for Russia, Ukraine, the Balkans, and the Mediterranean, with a key objective to ensure stability and security via regional cooperation. However, other policy instruments already existed in these areas (Partnership and Cooperation Agreements, Stability Pact), which limited the added value of Common Strategies. CFSP High Representative Solana published a damning paper in December 2000 describing this new instrument as simply resembling an inventory of existing policies, rather than producing anything new.

A further criticism was the choice of high-profile locations to implement CS and the transparency used in the internal documentation, which was well suited for diplomacy purposes but less useful for approaches to sensitive issues, which the EU would prefer to keep confidential. The high-profile nature of this approach, and the openness with which it was carried out, led to an avoidance of politically sensitive topics and consequently to an evasion of issues that really matter—for example, the CS for Russia failed to address the specific issue of Chechnya. The shortcomings of this approach led to a planned CS for the Balkans not being implemented. Much more work is needed to address Solana's criticisms and revamp CS to use their full potential to increase coherence across EU policies in a long-term peacebuilding approach to conflict-affected regions or issues.

The Role of EU Development Assistance

EU development assistance potentially has an important role to play in helping prevent violent conflict. Experience demonstrates that violent conflict is most likely in countries that are poor, divided by identity and gross disparities in wealth, and lack the political and legal systems necessary to manage change while avoiding violence. If development assistance is targeted to address the root causes of conflict, then the EU's developmental approach has the potential to build peace and stability in conflict-threatened regions such as Southeast Europe and the Caucasus. Assistance to the region is channeled through various programs aimed at promoting economic prosperity and developing more transparent and democratic government practice.

Partnership and Cooperation Agreement and Europe Agreement

Partnership and Cooperation Agreements (PCAs) and Europe Agreements are legal frameworks that development programs work within. The agreements are bilateral country-specific agreements signed and ratified by the EU and the partner country. The difference between the two agreements is in the geographical coverage. PCAs concentrate on Southeastern Europe and the Caucasus, and have been taken up by nine of the Eastern European and Central Asian countries,[7] whereas the Europe Agreements concentrates on East Europe and has been signed by ten countries of this region.[8] Both agreements carry the same objectives to strengthen stability and security with partner countries by promoting democracy, instilling respect for human rights, and providing support for the introduction of the market economy.

The areas covered by the agreements are defined in very general terms and cover education, transport, consumer protection, the fight against money laundering and drug trafficking, and development of a tourist industry, ensuring a mix of proactive measures for growth and approaches to curb organized crime and other hindrances to growth. The particular emphasis on different areas is dependent on the specific agreement signed by the EU and the partner country, though support for economic growth is a key point. It is accepted that economic development, reducing economic disparity, and reducing poverty are important precursors to building stability and preventing the escalation of violence in volatile areas, and growth has been evident in the economies of the Newly Independent States (NIS),[9] many supported by PCA programs. Imports to EU countries from the NIS have grown significantly. Since 1989, imports to the European Community from the NIS have increased by 33 percent, while EC exports to the NIS have grown by 25 percent over the same period.

In addition to the economic benefits that partnership and cooperation can bring, a core objective of PCAs and Europe Agreements is the promotion of regional political cooperation to help harness democratic practice and the emergence of accountable government, a key issue in preventing the escalation of violence.

TACIS and PHARE

The more developmental-based TACIS (Technical Assistance for the Commonwealth of Independent States) and PHARE (Poland and Hungary: Action for Rehabilitating the Economy) programs both work within the legal framework outlined by PCA or Europe Agreements respectively. PHARE has now been extended to cover fourteen countries throughout East and Southeast Europe and is targeted specifically to prepare them for accession to the EU, whereas TACIS focuses on the newly independent states formed following the breakup of the Soviet Union.

The programs have been in force since 1991, and share similar aims: providing financial and technical assistance to support the transition to a market economy, and providing institutional support to aid the growth of a democratic society.

TACIS and Central Asia

After seventy years of communism, the countries of the Caucasus faced a major readjustment of policy to successfully integrate into the international economy. Programs focusing on training and transfer of know-how are important for these countries' successful economic transition. Along with this, TACIS promoted practical measures such as providing low-interest loans aimed at specific sectors, allowing local entrepreneurs to become owners of their means of production and thus central to the country's economic development.

The programs are regional, not country-specific. Within TACIS, the Inter-State and Cross Border Cooperation Programme is a direct attempt to encourage regional cooperation and establish a relationship between countries where they work together to rehabilitate their economy and society. It is equally held that cooperation and dialogue help resolve conflict and prevent tensions from escalating. For example, the TRACECA (Transport Corridor Europe Caucasus Asia) Programme aims to develop a trade corridor from Central Asia through the Caucasus to Europe, to encourage trading links with the EU countries, and help bring the Central Asian countries into the international economy.

The emphasis on improving regional relations has been significant in developing intergovernmental cooperation among the countries of Central Asia. TACIS's regional cooperation approach was seen to be significant in bringing together the heads of state of Armenia and Azerbaijan in 1999, for the first time since the outbreak of the Nagorno Karabakh conflict in 1988. Similarly, mutual regional interest in a new border crossing between Azerbaijan and Georgia brought senior political representatives together to pursue common interests. Such movements are essential for developing regional trade, cooperation, and prospects for regional stability.

PHARE and Southeastern Europe

PHARE concentrates on providing assistance to preaccession countries to help bring them up to the economic, democratic, and environmental standards expected from the EU. The PHARE program for 2000–2006 concentrates on institution building and financing investment. The links between economic development, encouraging democratic practice, and an anticipated increase in stability are a feature of PHARE programs. A method of increasing the economic developmental aspects of both PHARE and TACIS programs is to fully involve the private sector with economic aspects of the programs and highlight the importance of stability to the potential growth of the economy.

Engaging Private-Sector Business

As conflict has a damaging impact on the economic development of most private-sector business, there is an argument that contributing to conflict prevention is a genuine business interest. Programs such as TRACECA are vital in helping develop the regional economy, but a further area of potential is to engage private companies as partners to develop EU initiatives and conflict-prevention objectives. A move to support the UN's Global Compact and create a legally binding framework to regulate the operations of EU transnational corporations in developing countries could signify a proactive commitment to cooperate with the private sector in addressing the root causes of conflict. Given the key role of oil companies in the Caucasus region, this is an important area for action.

PHARE and TACIS Democracy Programme

Whereas TACIS and PHARE work to promote cooperation to strengthen economic ties, the specific PHARE and TACIS Democracy Programme (PTDP) provides support for developing knowledge and practices relevant to democratization and the rule of law. The emphasis on local cooperation is vital to this process. PTDP directly encourages the development of NGOs and specifically works with them, complementing the PHARE and TACIS programs, which work essentially with national governments. Associations with the nongovernment sector have been integral to promoting democratization by influencing the authorities to ensure the materialization of a democratic system.

PTDP works on developing partnerships and networks between European NGOs and local NGOs in various sectors to enable input into parliamentary activity, ensure more transparency in the government sector, promote an independent media, and to monitor human rights, among other things. There is a definite preference for supporting small NGOs in Eastern and Southeastern Europe. The "small projects program" is seen as an important tool for improving regional relations at the grass-roots level. Programs tend to be based on the transfer of know-how and have included training journalists and the media sector, improving election monitoring, and teaching methods for effective human-rights monitoring.

A successful example of a project that PTDP has supported was run by the British organization VERTIC (Verification Technology Information Centre), which collaborated with the Caucasian Institute for Peace and Democracy in South Ossetia to train journalists in the ideology of a free press. Similar transnational approaches in civil-society building facilitated by the Helsinki Citizens Assembly have brought about the liberation of prisoners of war.

Emergency Assistance

On first impression it may seem paradoxical to use humanitarian assistance as a tool of conflict prevention. It is the norm to call on such assistance in response to acute crises, rather than before they occur. However, emergency assistance can be used as a measure of preparedness to mitigate against disasters and their consequences. This type of assistance can be used continuously as a safety net, rather than purely as a response, to cushion populations against unexpected shocks causing discontinuity in the development process and resultant instability. The PCA framework allows exceptional aid to be provided to mitigate against the effects of sudden shocks to a system that could otherwise have severe economic repercussions.

For example, in response to the downturn in the Russian economy during the 1997 economic crisis, assistance in the form of food aid and medical supplies to vulnerable groups helped maintain social and political stability in what could have been a crisis. This assistance was provided by the European Community Humanitarian Office, who still maintain a presence in the Caucasus providing health-care services and assistance to vulnerable groups. This type of aid, and the provision of food security assistance unquestionably has a stabilizing effect on society, and such assistance must remain a key component in helping to prevent crisis situations from escalating.

Stability Pact

Another major route through which EU assistance is channeled to Southeast Europe is the Stability Pact. This is a quite different tool than the previous Stability Pact (or Balladur Plan), which was a program planned and implemented by the EU. This new Stability Pact was initiated in June 1999 on the initiative of the EU, but is not directly an EU tool. It is supported by over forty nations, regional bodies, and international organizations all working in partnership, and operates under the auspices of the OSCE, though the EU carries influence as a substantial donor for supporting the body's long-term conflict-prevention strategy.

The three working principles of the Stability Pact address democracy building and human-rights violations, building infrastructure to rehabilitate society, and promoting reform of the security sector for more accountable, transparent rules of law enforcement. Within these approaches, the Stability Pact intends to develop a free-trade area in Southeastern Europe to strengthen the regional economy. As an independent organization outside the EU infrastructure, the Stability Pact has 244 projects planned, 80 percent of which are operational now.

Conclusion

The EU has a number of useful tools at its disposal for addressing the issue of conflict prevention, and the countries of Southeastern Europe and Central Asia provide an important challenge for putting EU policies into practice.

To date, the EU's attempts at development have tended to concentrate mainly on implementing programs that support economic growth, with problems of instability addressed almost as a by-product. Present practice has shown a much more focused attempt to link economic growth to strengthening democracy. This is reflected in the PCAs and PHARE program where promoting democracy is a stated goal, along with supporting the introduction of a market economy. Mainstreaming conflict prevention into the EU's development assistance programs is essential to providing the maximum potential for addressing instability successfully.

Improved coherence across EU bodies and policies is also vital. Short-term measures aimed at managing "at risk" situations, such as the police RRF, must be linked to long-term objectives. Thus, for example, providing a substitute military or police force in areas of instability must be complemented with support for the development of an accountable domestic police force, together with a strengthening of the rule of law and building administrative institutions to support the development process. These measures can strengthen national security and promote democracy, but they must be allied to other policies such as halting the proliferation of arms into civilian hands, and measures to integrate developing countries into the global economy and enable growth with equity.

The EU has the capacity to make this happen, and recent developments during the Swedish presidency demonstrate that the political will may now exist. The test will be whether the EU can implement these initiatives in a coherent and comprehensive effort to address the root causes of conflict and help build peace in Southeast Europe and the Caucasus.

Since 1995, Paul Eavis has been the director of Saferworld, the independent think tank working to develop and publicize more effective approaches to preventing armed conflict. Between 1990 and 1995 he was research director of Saferworld. Over the past ten years, Mr. Eavis has written and/or edited numerous reports and briefings on European arms-export controls, small-arms proliferation, and security-sector reform. He is on the management committee of the International Action Network on Small Arms (IANSA) and the Steering Group of the European NGO Platform for Conflict Prevention and Transformation.

Stuart Kefford holds an M.A. in development studies from the University of Leeds and has been working as the media officer with the conflict and arms team at Saferworld since March 2000.

Notes

1. Conclusions on "Preventative Diplomacy, Conflict Resolution, Conflict Resolution and Peace-Keeping in Africa" (General Affairs Council, 4 December 1995); Communication from the Commission to the Council on "The European Union and the Issue of Conflicts in Africa: Peace-Building, Conflict Prevention and Beyond"

(6 March 1996); Resolution on Coherence of the EC's Development Cooperation (included within the Council Conclusions to the Dutch Presidency in June 1997); EU Approach to Peace-Building, Conflict Prevention and Resolution (included in the Development Council Conclusions of December 1998).

2. Javier Solana and Christopher Patten (December 2000), *Improving the Coherence and Effectiveness of EU Action in the Field of Conflict Prevention,* report presented at the EU summit, Nice.

3. Maastricht Treaty, Article J.1(2), 1993.

4. Reinhardt Rummel, *Common Foreign and Security Policy and Conflict Prevention.* London: Saferworld and International Alert, May 1996.

5. Michael Hartmann, international prosecutor in "International War and Peace Reporting Crisis Report No. 265."

6. The Troika represents the EU externally and is made up of the current president of the EU, assisted by the high representative for Common and Foreign Security Policy, and the upcoming member state to hold the presidency "if need be." Quote is from European Union (February 2001), *Council Conclusions on the Southern Caucasus,* from <http://europa.eu.int/abc/doc/off/bull/en/200101/p106104.htm>, Brussels.

7. The countries are Armenia, Azerbaijan, Georgia, Kazakhstan, Kyrgyzstan, Moldova, Russia, Ukraine, and Uzbekistan.

8. The countries are Bulgaria, the Czech Republic, Estonia, Hungary, Latvia, Lithuania, Poland, Romania, Slovakia, and Slovenia.

9. The NIS include all former states of the Soviet Union except the Baltic states and Tajikistan.

2

The OSCE:
Uniquely Qualified for a
Conflict-Prevention Role

Wolfgang Zellner

The Organization for Security and Cooperation in Europe has been one of the world's fastest growing international governmental organizations in field operations, staff, and budget. This chapter deals with two questions: First, it asks which political qualities enable the OSCE to perform crisis-prevention tasks and examines the limits of the organization. Second, it gives an overview of the most important prevention instruments, namely the high commissioner on national minorities and OSCE field activities.

The Organization for Security and Cooperation in Europe (OSCE) is the successor to the Conference on Security and Cooperation in Europe (CSCE) established in 1975 with the signing of the Helsinki Final Act. Whereas the CSCE, before 1990, consisted of a loose series of conferences, the OSCE is an international governmental organization (IGO) that currently boasts twenty-one different field operations with about 4,400 staff members (1,100 international and 3,300 local) in Central, Eastern, and Southeastern Europe, the Caucasus, and Central Asia.[1] Nearly 90 percent of the OSCE's budget of approximately 208 million euro in 2000 was spent on field activities. In 1993, the OSCE's budget totaled only 12 million euro and it employed only a few dozen staff members in field missions.[2]

Five closely interrelated political characteristics qualify the OSCE for conflict prevention tasks:

1. Since the Charter of Paris in 1990, the OSCE has a common and comprehensive value base including human and minority rights, democracy, the rule of law, and a market economy. This unique normative groundwork is the basis for all its practical activities. However, in spite of the fact that the fifty-five participating states voluntarily have agreed on these politically binding norms in a series of documents, many states frequently disregard their OSCE commitments. This is not only true for transition states in Eastern and Southeastern Europe,

the Caucasus, and Central Asia; even certain states in the Euro-Atlantic context do not fully comply with their commitments, especially when it comes to minority rights.

2. The OSCE follows a comprehensive and inclusive approach in more than one sense. On the one hand, this applies to the three tightly interlinked issue areas dealt with by the organization: security and stability, economic and environmental issues, and democracy and human rights—the three "baskets" of the 1975 Helsinki Final Act. On the other, the OSCE is inclusive in the sense that all of its participating states have, at least in principle, equal rights and must fulfill their commitments. From this follows the principle of consensus in decisionmaking and the organization's cooperative approach in assisting its participating states in living up to their commitments. While the consensus principle works for the organization's major political decisions (i.e., mission mandates or budgets), many operational decisions are taken by a rather narrow circle of participating states including the acting chairman-in-office and the so-called Big Five (the United States, the Russian Federation, France, Germany, and the United Kingdom). By providing personnel (the vast majority of OSCE international staff is "seconded" and paid for by its participating states) and "voluntary contributions," the larger and richer states have considerable means for structuring the organization's activities according to their interests. The Russian Federation and other transition states are not the only ones that have objected to these varying degrees of influence and unequal access to information. On the occasion of the establishment of the Rapporteur Mission to Belgrade in December 2000, the Netherlands stated to the Permanent Council: "We deplore the total absence of transparency. . . . The essence of consensus is the right to participate in the decisionmaking process, and, even more, the right to know what is going on. We feel more and more left out of that process."[3]

3. Because of its common value base and inclusive approach, the OSCE enjoys a high level of legitimacy that enables the organization, at least in principal, to intervene in the domestic affairs of its participating states in a limited and cooperative way. The 1992 Prague Document stated "that appropriate action may be taken by the Council . . . , if necessary in the absence of consent of the state concerned, in cases of clear, gross and uncorrected violations of relevant CSCE commitments."[4] This ability to "intervene cooperatively" is the very basis of the OSCE conflict-prevention potential, but in practice, there are a number of factors that tend to limit the exercise of OSCE conflict-prevention applications. Powerful states can afford to keep the OSCE out when they feel that this is serving their interests. For example, the chairperson-in-office has been negotiating for the return of the OSCE Assistance Group to Chechnya for over a year now without success. Some western states have managed to keep OSCE activities out of their countries even though violent conflicts and violations of human and minority rights have occurred there. The Russian Federation and other eastern states have criticized this approach, arguing that it creates a "double standard." The unilateral misuse of the OSCE's cooperative approach is very damaging to the OSCE image. The most prominent recent

example is the Russian Federation's perception of the OSCE Kosovo Verification Mission as "a cloak or cover for certain activities of NATO states that were part of the preparations for war."[5] Thus, the Kosovo and Chechnya cases mark a deterioration of the OSCE's legitimating base and thus its potential for preventive action.

4. The OSCE cooperates with a wide range of other IGOs and international and local NGOs. The programmatic basis for doing this has been summarized in the Charter for European Security adopted at the 1999 OSCE Istanbul Summit. The charter mainly deals with cooperation with IGOs but also mentions NGO cooperation: "Non-governmental organizations (NGOs) can perform a vital role in the promotion of human rights, democracy and the rule of law. . . . We pledge ourselves to enhance the ability of NGOs to make their full contribution to the further development of civil society and respect for human rights and fundamental freedoms."[6] A variety of OSCE meetings and seminars are open to NGO participation. The OSCE's Office for Democratic Institutions and Human Rights (ODIHR) has a specific NGO unit that has developed an NGO strategy clearly focused on the Caucasus and Central Asia. Related projects with local and regional NGOs primarily aim at fostering dialogue between state and NGO actors and raising public awareness of human rights.[7] Among the OSCE institutions, the representative on freedom of the media, Freimut Duve, has been especially active in cooperating with NGOs. Every OSCE field mission maintains its own NGO activities. The OSCE cooperates with various international NGOs including Human Rights Watch, Interkeerkelig Vreedensverband, the International Committee of the Red

ECCP

Mitrovica, Kosovo: Roma refugee camp

Cross, the International Press Institute, Médecins Sans Frontières, the Open Society Institute, Reporters Sans Frontières, the Soros Foundation, and several humanitarian NGOs.[8] By taking advantage of the synergies ensuing from better interlocking of track-one and track-two diplomacy, the OSCE is in a position to increase its conflict-prevention potential considerably in the long term.

5. A more organizational feature of the OSCE is its flexibility and cost effectiveness. It is difficult to find another IGO that spends nearly 90 percent of its budget on field activities, and this figure does not even include the rather substantial amount of money spent by participating states on "seconded" personnel. It is also impressive that although it had no previous experience, the organization's learning curve has gone up dramatically through the deployment of over twenty field operations within less than a decade. The fact that the participating states have designed the OSCE in such a lean manner means, however, that the organization's resources are always taxed to the limit.

If one considers these features as a whole, the potential of the OSCE for conflict prevention is less based on static characteristics than on a series of dynamic contradictions between common principles and the specific interests of the different participating states. What the OSCE can do in a specific conflict depends mainly on the political will of its major participating states.

OSCE Field Activities: A Brief Overview

According to the Conflict Prevention Network of the European Commission, four stages of the conflict cycle are discernible: stable peace, unstable peace, high tension, and open conflict.[9] This is true both for the preconflict and postconflict phases, when conflict intensity diminishes after an open conflict from high tension to stable peace. "Each of these stages differs in terms of the kinds of causes that are present, their associated features, the turning points or thresholds that mark the transition from one phase to another, and the type of international engagement that is most emphasized."[10] Because violent conflicts are by their inherent logic nonlinear and contingent events, this model cannot be used mechanically. Transitions from one stage to another may differ in terms of shape and speed. Conflict prevention is possible at the unstable-peace and high-tension stages before *and* after an open conflict; at the stage of stable peace it is superfluous; and during an open conflict it is impossible or at best very difficult. Conflict prevention may emerge from very different sources and use a wide array of instruments. Generally, one can distinguish between general and special prevention. General prevention aims at tackling the root causes of potentially violent conflicts such as economic inequality and deficient democracy, as well as exclusive state- and nation-building strategies. Within the framework of the OSCE, they are mainly dealt with by the ODIHR, which provides a broad scope of programs ranging from election observation and assistance in drafting and implementing of election laws and systems to assistance in establishing democratic institutions, strengthening the rule of law, fostering the establishment and continued existence of NGOs, and the functioning of civil societies. Special prevention, on the other hand, always contains specific measures aimed at a specific conflict at a certain stage. The OSCE has two main instruments for this purpose at its disposal: the high commissioner on national minorities (HCNM) and the missions and other field activities.

The High Commissioner on National Minorities

Many observers regard the HCNM as *the* success story of the OSCE. Initiated by the Netherlands, the 1992 CSCE Helsinki Summit adopted the HCNM mandate, which states that "the High Commissioner will provide 'early warning' and, as appropriate, 'early action' at the earliest possible stage in regard to tensions involving national minority issues, which have not yet developed beyond an early warning stage, but, in the judgement of the High Commissioner, have the potential to develop into a conflict within the CSCE area, affecting peace, stability or relations between participating states."[11] The high commissioner has a double task: on the one hand, he or she is charged with mediating in majority-minority conflicts as long as this is possible, and on the other he is responsible for warning the international community when a conflict threatens to get out of hand. As the designation—high commissioner *on* (and not for) national minorities—clearly indicates, the HCNM is not an ombudsman for minorities but an instrument of conflict prevention. Thus, the HCNM embodies the primarily political approach of the OSCE, compared with the more legal approach of the Council of Europe. Of course, the HCNM works on the basis of OSCE commitments and other international minority-rights documents, but the logic of his methods indicates the reverse approach: the HCNM can be seen as an instrument of a strategy that petitions the observance of minority rights because this is an indispensable condition for peace and stability.

The OSCE mandate gives the high commissioner considerable room to maneuver: he is not dependent on consensual decisions by any OSCE body but can act according to his own assessments, and does not even require authorization from the chairman-in-office. His only obligation is to consult the chairman and to provide him with confidential reports on specific activities. Thus the high commissioner is by far the most independent institution within the OSCE. The only restrictions imposed on the high commissioner through his mandate are that he is neither allowed to deal with individual cases nor to "consider national minority issues in situations involving organized acts of terrorism." The latter clause was inserted at the behest of Western states such as the United Kingdom, Turkey, and Spain seeking to impede the HCNM from intervening in conflicts in their countries.

In December 1992, the former Dutch foreign minister, Max van der Stoel, was elected as the first high commissioner.[12] On taking office in January 1993, he had a very small staff, almost no budget, and no working procedures at all. Today the HCNM's office in The Hague consists of about fifteen people and his standard annual budget is around 2 million euro. In order to raise additional funds for minority-related projects, the high commissioner established an NGO, the Foundation on Inter-Ethnic Relations. His biggest achievement, however, was the development of working methods, on which his mandate is not very precise.

In order to resolve majority-minority conflicts, the HCNM travels to the countries involved—he has been active in around fifteen countries—and has face-to-face conversations with the highest representatives of both the majority and minority parties, such as prime ministers and other ministers, party and parliamentary leaders, and occasionally NGO representatives. Some countries, such as Lithuania, have only been visited once, while others have been visited frequently—Macedonia, for example, has been visited over twenty times. The HCNM's conversations are confidential; he only delivers press statements in rare cases, and in these cases primarily with the consensus of all parties concerned. The HCNM's talks may lead, but do not necessarily have to lead, to written recommendations in the form of a letter to the foreign minister of the country involved. This instrument of recommendations has been developed into one of the most important working instruments of the HCNM. To date, recommendations of this kind have been developed for thirteen countries as well as two reports on the situation of the Roma and Sinti. Recommendations are not binding and Van der Stoel repeatedly turned down proposals to make them binding, arguing that only consensus and not compulsion would lead to sustainable solutions.

Van der Stoel quickly discovered that the existing international minority-rights documents were too general to be applied to specific situations. In order to bridge this gap, he asked the Foundation on Inter-Ethnic Relations, with the assistance of international experts, to draft three sets of specific recommendations: the Hague Recommendations on Education Rights of National Minorities (1996), the Oslo Recommendations on Linguistic Rights of National Minorities (1998), and the Lund Recommendations on Effective Participation of National Minorities in Public Life (1999).[13] Although these documents do not represent OSCE commitments—the HCNM has no mandate to create new OSCE norms—they have had considerable impact on the thinking of key players in a number of countries. However, not even the Lund Recommendations were incorporated into the 1999 Istanbul Summit document and thus none have been made an OSCE commitment.

How successful has the HCNM been with his approach on cooperative "soft intervention"? There have been successes in Estonia and Latvia, where the main issue was access for a sizeable Russian-speaking minority to citizenship. In these two countries, which regained their sovereignty in 1991, citizenship was not granted to all residents but only to the citizens of the interwar republics and their descendants. Others (more than a quarter of the population) had to complete lengthy and complicated naturalization procedures in order to gain citizenship. In both cases the high commissioner succeeded in obtaining a considerable liberalization on language tests, fees, treatment of stateless children, etc., which altered the basic construction of the citizenship laws to a certain degree. In Slovakia, after the nationalistic prime minister Meciar left office, the high commissioner helped to effect the adoption of a minority-language law that entitled persons belonging to national minorities to communicate with local authorities in their mother tongue in those municipalities where they represented at least 20 percent of the population. This law also paved the way for the Slovak Republic to accession talks with the European Union by fulfilling an important EU Copenhagen accession criterion. It is significant that all these three cases involve EU accession candidates. And indeed, the high commissioner has consulted closely with the European Commission on whether the minority-rights accession criteria have been fulfilled.

However, the HCNM has also been successful in countries whose accession to the EU is a long-term prospect. In the case of the Crimean quest for autonomy, the high commissioner was instrumental in de-escalating tensions between the Ukrainian government and the Crimean authorities, and in introducing new lines of thinking, which taken together contributed considerably to a final constitutional solution. The Crimean Tatars had been expelled under Stalin and started to return to Crimea after the Ukraine gained independence. The HCNM has been the leading institution in directing the attention of the international community to the Tatars' miserable economic and social situation.

The high commissioner has contributed decisively to a solution to the highly contentious issue of an Albanian-language university in Macedonia. He not only convinced the Macedonian government and parliament to amend its education law to permit private universities to offer instruction in languages other than Macedonian, but also succeeded in raising more than US$20 million for the establishment of the private South Eastern Europe University in Tetovo, in which courses will be offered, inter alia, in Albanian and English. The new university opened its doors on 1 October 2001. Since the beginning of armed clashes between Albanian secessionists and the Macedonian security forces in mid-March 2001, the effective operation of this institution has become even more important because it represents a major element of a strategy aimed at a political solution to the conflict and the isolation of terrorist forces.

In sum, the high commissioner is an example par excellence of both a highly effective and cost-effective institution for conflict prevention.

OSCE Missions and Other Field Activities

Mandates and budgets for OSCE missions and other field activities must have the consensus of the participating states, and a host country must consent to the presence of a mission. Operational control is the chairman's responsibility, but the chairman does not always have the means to deal with every mission in the same way. Therefore the Heads of Missions have considerable room to maneuver. In nearly every host country, conflicts are dealt with not only by the OSCE, but also by other IGOs, states, and NGOs.

The OSCE currently fields ten operations that are explicitly designated as missions in Bosnia and Herzegovina, Croatia, the Federal Republic of Yugoslavia, Kosovo, Macedonia (the Spillover Mission to Skopje), Estonia, Latvia, Moldova, Georgia, and Tajikistan. There are four other missions that have been given other labels for diplomatic reasons, in Albania, Belarus, Chechnya, and

Nagorno Karabakh. The OSCE also has offices in Baku and Yerevan, and centers in Almaty, Ashgabad, Bishkek, and Tashkent. The OSCE Missions of Long Duration in Kosovo, Sandjak, and Vojvodina, and the Kosovo Verification Mission, were both closed because of the political situation in Yugoslavia, and the Mission to the Ukraine was closed in 1999 and replaced by a project coordinator.[14]

All missions conduct their work in Central, Eastern, and Southeastern Europe, the Caucasus, and Central Asia; none are active in EU or NATO member states. Twelve of the fourteen active missions deal with ethnopolitical conflicts. The exceptions are Belarus, where the mission deals with grave deficiencies in democracy and human rights, and Albania, where a general collapse of state structures occurred in 1997. Classifying missions according to levels of escalation is to a certain degree arbitrary because the dividing lines between the stages are blurred and, especially, because situations change over time. For example, the Spillover Mission to Skopje may have operated in a situation somewhere between unstable peace and high tension at the time of its establishment (1992), and later on it was clearly at the stage of unstable peace, whereas today, it is operating at a stage close to open conflict.

If one looks at the five missions that are or were active at the level of unstable peace and/or high tensions *before a conflict* (Skopje, Estonia, Latvia, Ukraine, Belarus) it is evident that they are all rather small, comprising four to eight mission members, mostly diplomats or specialized scholars. Missions of this type employ the classical instruments of crisis prevention: collection of information, monitoring the situation, reporting to the OSCE bodies, talking with government officials as well as with representatives of (minority) parties and NGOs, advising governments, making efforts to start a dialogue between majority and minority, working with NGOs, etc. In those four countries where ethnopolitical issues were on the agenda, the high commissioner has also been active. In addition, these missions serve as the eyes and ears of the HCNM. In countries where the situation is relatively stable, governments usually strive to have missions withdrawn because they are considered a "stigma" impeding integration into Western structures. The Ukraine, a large country, has already been successful in this regard, and the missions to Estonia and Latvia may be closed by the end of 2001 if these countries live up to certain conditions. In contrast, it is quite striking to see that the Spillover Mission to Skopje has failed to contribute much to a situation in which high tensions have been transformed into open conflict. Despite the fact that mission staff was doubled to sixteen in March 2001, other actors such as the EU and NATO were in fact the more influential players. This clearly shows that OSCE preventive capabilities fade away when the situation approaches open armed conflict.

The cases in situations of *open conflict and thereafter* are quite different. One subgroup is the so-called frozen conflicts where fighting has stopped, and cease-fire is in place, but no final solution to the conflict has been reached (Moldova, Georgia, and Nagorno Karabakh).

Accordingly, the mission agendas are broader and the number of mission members usually higher. Prevention tasks to avoid a new escalation are mixed with conflict resolution, and missions make efforts to promote negotiations in which other actors, including both IGOs and states, are also involved. Another task is monitoring cease-fires and borders, between Georgia and Chechnya, for example. If political solutions are reached for this type of conflict in the future, the OSCE will most probably have to field multifunctional missions including light peacekeeping elements (military observers) to monitor and facilitate the implementation of these agreements.

The OSCE presence in Albania, the mission to Tajikistan, the assistance group to Chechnya, and the Kosovo verification mission may be considered to form another group in the sense that they have all been deployed *during a conflict*, though the conflicts themselves have nothing in common. Comparing these four cases, one can conclude that the lower the level of violence, the shorter the period of fighting, and the smaller the country involved, the more successful the OSCE is in conflict prevention. Albania is a special case because what happened there was not an outright civil war but the violent follow-up of a complete breakdown of state structures. Additionally, the broad OSCE mandate allowed this mission to deal with almost every issue and to function as a coordinator of the other IGOs involved. In Tajikistan, a peace accord was only adopted after a five-year civil war with over 100,000 victims and a half million refugees. This accord was initially implemented by UNMOT (UN Mission of Observers to Tajikistan) and after its dissolution in May 2000, is being executed by UNTOP (UN Tajikistan Office of Peacebuilding) in close cooperation with the OSCE mission. In the case of Chechnya, the OSCE assistance group was able to achieve some minor results in the first round of this war in 1995, but later had to leave the region for security regions. Currently, the Russian government does not seem interested in a resumption of the group's work, even on a limited basis. This clearly shows that the more powerful states have sufficient means at their disposal to block OSCE conflict prevention or resolution if it is not in their interest. In the case of Kosovo, it is doubtful whether the OSCE verification mission was ever up to the task of monitoring a cease-fire that was quickly undermined by both sides.

A third category includes cases going from the stage of tension or high tension to unstable peace *after a conflict*, the classical peacebuilding environment. These operations are in sovereign states (Croatia), and in de facto protectorates (Bosnia and Herzegovina and Kosovo) where mission work has to be protected by a robust military force. The number of staff members ranges from slightly below 200 (Croatia, Bosnia and Herzegovina) to almost 700 international mission members (Kosovo, plus 1,400 local staff members).[15] Together these three missions consume nearly 80 percent of the total OSCE budget. All three are entrenched in a larger international context, the most sophisticated example being the OSCE Mission in Kosovo (OMIK) which provides one of the three pillars of the United Nations Interim Administration Mission in Kosovo (UNMIK). OMIK is responsible for institution building in the following areas: human resources capacity building, including the training of the new Kosovo police force; democratization and governance, including the development of a civil society, NGOs, and political parties; organization of elections; and media affairs. A substantial share of UNMIK's and OMIK's tasks are those of sovereign states. Under these conditions, conflict prevention in the sense of peacebuilding amounts to the administration of a protectorate.

Conclusion

OSCE conflict-prevention activities vary tremendously when it comes to the use of instruments, deployment of resources, and determination of when the organization intervenes in the conflict cycle. While classical wisdom advises that conflict prevention be initiated—in the words of the HCNM's mandate— "at the earliest possible stage" of a *potential conflict*, reality shows a remarkable shift to large peacebuilding activities *after conflicts have manifested themselves.* Dealing with manifest conflicts will remain necessary, but we should not forget the dangers arising from the fact that states and IGOs including the OSCE are still reluctant to initiate action and spend money before conflicts have reached the stage of open violence. This unresolved contradiction between better insight and the ongoing tradition of only reacting to manifest conflicts is highly important when considering the chances for successful conflict prevention. Without neglecting the pressing task of peacebuilding, the OSCE should direct more of its efforts toward classical conflict prevention. Necessary steps in this direction include:

1. Establishing an analytical unit in the OSCE Secretariat
2. Elaborating realistic regional strategies for the Caucasus and Central Asia and further developing the regional strategy for Southeastern Europe
3. Improving the cooperation between the different conflict prevention instruments inside and outside the OSCE; and
4. Strengthening a project-oriented approach by providing for a specific conflict-prevention fund

Because effective conflict prevention requires considerable resources, it is up to the OSCE's participating states to act upon Max van der Stoel's fundamental insight that "capital invested in conflict prevention (and it is with intention that I say 'invested' and not merely 'spent') is capital well and meaningfully invested. Conflict prevention, after all, is cheaper than peacekeeping measures, which, in turn are cheaper than war."[16]

Wolfgang Zellner is deputy head of the Centre for OSCE Research (CORE) at the Institute for Peace Research and Security Policy at the University of Hamburg. From 1984 to 1991 he worked as an assistant to a member of the German Bundestag dealing with issues of security, military policy, and European arms control. In 1993 he finished his Ph.D. thesis on the negotiations for the Conventional Armed Forces in Europe Treaty.

Notes

1. For an overview of OSCE field activities see: <http://www.osce.org/field_activities/field_activities.htm>, 25 March 2001.

2. Cf. <http://www.osce.org/general/budget/index.htm>, 14 March 2001.

3. PC.JOUR/313, 7 December 2000, Annex, Statement by the Delegation of the Netherlands, in: <http://www.osce.org/docs/english/pc/2000/journals/pcoej313.htm>, 20 February 2001.

4. CSCE, Second Meeting of the Council, Prague, January 1992, Prague Document on Further Development of CSCE Institutions and Structures, in: <http://www.osce.org/docs/english/1990-1999/mcs/2prag92e.htm>, 14 March 2001.

5. Alexander Matveev, "The OSCE Identity Crisis," in Institute for Peace Research and Security Policy at the University of Hamburg / IFSH (ed.), *OSCE Yearbook 1999,* Baden-Baden: Nomos Verslagsgesellschaft, 2000, p. 63.

6. OSCE, Charter for European Security, Istanbul, November 1999, par. 27, in: <http://www.osce.org/docs/english/1990-1999/summits/istachart99e.htm>, 14 March 2001.

7. Cf. Office for Democratic Institutions and Human Rights, NGOs in the Caucasus and Central Asia: Development and Cooperation with the OSCE, Human Dimension Implementation Meeting, October 2000, Background Paper 2000/1, in: <http://www.osce.org/odihr/docs/bp00-1-ngo.htm>, 12 May 2001.

8. See <http://www.osce.org/docs/english/misc/anrep00e_org.htm>, 23 March 2001.

9. See Stiftung Wissenschaft und Politik/Conflict Prevention Network (eds.), *Peace-Building and Conflict Prevention in Developing Countries: A Practical Guide* (principal contributors: Michael Lund and Andreas Mehler), CPN Guidebook (Draft Document), Brussels: Ebenhausen 1999, pp. 19–23.

10. Ibid., p. 19.

11. CSCE 1992 Summit, Helsinki, 9–10 July 1992, CSCE Helsinki Document 1992, The Challenges of Change, III CSCE High Commissioner on National Minorities, in: <http://www.osce.org/docs/english/1990-1999/summits/hels92e.htm>, 24 March 2001.

12. Van der Stoel's term of office ended on 30 June 2001. His successor is the Swedish diplomat Rolf Ekéus.

13. See: <http://www.osce.org/hcnm/documents/index.htm>, 13 March 2001.

14. See footnote 1 and: <http://www.osce.org/publications/survey/index.htm>, 25 March 2001.

15. See: <http://www.osce.org/kosovo/index.php3>, 25 March 2001.

16. Max van der Stoel, "Democracy and Human Rights: On the Work of the High Commissioner on National Minorities of the OSCE." Speech at the Institute for Peace Research and Security Policy at the University of Hamburg, 17 March 1997, Hamburg, Germany, in Max van der Stoel, *Peace and Stability Through Human and Minority Rights, Speeches by the OSCE High Commissioner on National Minorities,* edited by Wolfgang Zellner and Falk Lange, Baden-Baden: Nomos Verslagsgesellschaft, 1999, p. 139.

3

History and Legacies of the USSR: The Demise of a Multiethnic Experiment

Valery Tishkov

In spite of being relatively peaceful, the dissolution of the Union of the Soviet Socialist Republics generated a lot of social and ethnic tension as well as violent clashes and internal wars. What was the nature of this multiethnic state and of the Soviet ethnic engineering, and what were the reasons for the breakup? What are the legacies of the USSR that embedded painful memories, old and new cleavages, and potential conflict?

By the end of the nineteenth century, Russia spanned 22.5 million square kilometers of territory, peopled by 128.2 million inhabitants with a rich cultural mosaic, and with ethnic Russians comprising less than a half of the population (Table 3.1). This multiethnicity has evolved over the course of historic territorial expansion through military conquests, colonization, and development of new lands carried out by the state. But the major agents of colonization were those who sought to escape serfdom, tyranny, and lifelong military service—peasants, religious dissidents, individual entrepreneurs, etc. The dominant ethnic component of the state was Eastern Slavs, whose cultures were to give rise to the ethnic identities of Russians, Ukrainians, and Belorussians. From the early times, the population of Russia also included Finns, Balts, Turkic, and other non-Slavic groups. The ethnic mosaic grew particularly complex after the sixteenth-century annexation of the Volga area and the colonization of Siberia. In the seventeenth century, the state added the Ukraine, West Siberia, and a part of the Caucasus; in the eighteenth to nineteenth centuries, East Siberia, Caucasus, and Central Asia were included. With respect to non-Orthodox people, the policy of the Russian monarchy was that of social oppression and cultural assimilation. Appropriation of lands inhabited by indigenous peoples was widely practiced. A system of various taxes and levies was applied to this category of the population, as well as the practice of nonequivalent goods exchanges.

Unlike the classic colonial empires, Russia's metropolis was not so geographically distant from the colonized peripheries, whose population was extremely diverse with respect to levels of modernization and political consolidation. The so-called indirect-rule method was applied: many of the areas and cultural communities in the territory were granted differing degrees of autonomy and self-government. Serfdom and compulsory military service applied mainly to the ethnic Russian population. Several centuries of interethnic contacts resulted in a high degree of mutual cultural influence and integration, especially between the Slavic and Turkic peoples. In the second half of the nineteenth century, the periphery of the empire saw the growth of nationalist movements echoing in spirit the East European social democratic movements that embraced the peoples within the three major imperial entities: the Austro-Hungarian, Ottoman, and Russian.

After the overthrow of the monarchy in February 1917, Finland and Poland acquired their political independence from Russia. In the early years of the Bolshevik rise to power, independence was proclaimed by the Ukraine, the Transcaucasian republics (Georgia, Armenia, Azerbaijan, Abkhazia), and the Baltic countries (Lithuania, Latvia, and Estonia). Movements for autonomy sprang up among other regions of Russia.

Table 3.1 Major Ethnic Groups of the Russian Empire, 1897

Ethnic Group[a]	Number (in thousands)	Percentage of Total
Russian	55,670	43.4
Ukrainian	22,380	17.5
Pole	7,930	6.2
Belorussian	5,890	4.6
Jew	5,060	3.9
Kazakh	3,800	3.0
Finn	2,660	2.1
Tatar	2,230	1.7
German	1,790	1.4
Uzbek	1,700	1.3
Lithuanian	1,660	1.3
Azerbaijani	1,480	1.2
Latvian	1,435	1.1
Georgian	1,350	1.1
Bashkir	1,320	1.0
Moldavian	1,120	0.9
Mordva	1,025	0.8
Estonian	1,000	0.8
Chuvash	845	0.7
Kirgiz	600	0.5
Udmurt	420	0.3
Tajik	350	0.3
Total	128,200	100%

Note: a. This list of modern names was projected on tribal, cultural, and religious groups and regional identities that existed in 1897.

The Bolshevik Experiment

In contrast to their political opponents who advocated "one and indivisible Russia," the Bolsheviks supported political movements among the non-Russian peoples, viewing them as allies in the struggle against absolutism. The Bolsheviks' declarations received an enthusiastic response from nationalist activists in the periphery and provided the new power with support from the non-Russian population. At this point, in declaring itself to be an internationalist movement, Marxism in Russia actually included in its program the doctrine of ethnic nationalism. This doctrine can explain the rise to power experienced by the Bolsheviks all over the country and their victories in the civil war. Two postulates were particularly attractive to the multiethnic country:

1. The doctrine recognized that a nation as an ethnic group has a set of inalienable characteristics, including its own territory, common language, and a distinct sociopsychological mentality
2. The doctrine established that a necessary condition for the existence and development of a nation was the existence of an ethnic group declared to be an "indigenous nation" within their "own" statehood

Once the Soviet power consolidated, it then proceeded to eliminate the right to secession from their practice. The Bolsheviks realized the right to national self-determination within the borders of a single state. Such a state was to be built on the principles of "socialist federalism" as opposed to "bourgeois federalism," in that the internal division of the state was to be based not on the principle of administrative territories, but on the principle of "national statehoods." But the principles and norms of federalization were not defined, or at least not publicly proclaimed. The ethnic policy of the Soviet Union was designed on an improvised basis partly to meet the serious challenges issuing from the regions and ethnic peripheries of the Russian Empire, and partly to meet ideological aspirations. However, this ideology of ethno-nations necessitated social engineering to put the idea into practice—or, more precisely, to construct realities that could correspond to political programs. The first task of this project was an inventory of ethno-nations. After all, in many Soviet regions the cultural mosaic did not conform to strict boundaries, and ethnicity was overshadowed by other forms of identity. But the state proclaimed the right of self-determination for "formerly oppressed nations" and introduced ethnic federalism; thus it became crucial to count not languages, but ethnic groups per se. For that purpose, the first Soviet census of 1926 asked citizens to indicate their ethnic belonging ("nationality"). This produced the result of some 190 different identities displaying varying sorts of particularism, from locality to clan affiliation.

Lobbying for Borders and Status

The early history of Soviet ethnic policy shows a mixture of missionary projects and local rivalries, reflecting momentous power dispositions. Motives behind major decisions on granting autonomy and establishing republics were determined by political raison d'être rather than by any conscious "nation killing" strategy. That is why this policy seemed to have so many inconsistencies. There was a combination of aspirations to reward formerly "oppressed nations" and to keep the state under Soviet rule. These motives lay behind the unification of Armenia, Georgia, and Azerbaijan into the Trans-Caucasian Federation in 1922 after they were "sovietized" in 1920–1921. A tense situation developed in the case of the Armenian enclave in Azerbaijan–Nagorno Karabakh. Long and heated debates about its affiliation were resolved by the Caucasian Bureau of the Central Committee of the Russian Communist Party in 1920 after the head of the government of Azerbaijan, Nariman Narimanov, threatened to stop the deliveries of kerosene from Baku.

Because the number of claimants to "their own" statehood proved to be greater than the Bolsheviks had probably supposed, one more innovation of the "socialist federalism" was born—a kind of hierarchy of ethno-national units of the Russian *matrushka*-doll type. In some areas, the ethnic principle could not be strictly observed, particularly where the more powerful basis for a collective identity was religion, dynastic or regional belonging, or where the ethnic mosaic was too complex to draw up administrative lines. Such was the situation in Central Asia and North Caucasus. In 1918 in the North Caucasus, the Soviet Terskaya *oblast* (Tersk region) was established with territories inhabited by the Tersk Cossacks, Kabardin, Ingush, Chechen, and others. In 1921 the Terskaya *oblast* was reorganized into the Gorskaya autonomous

Grozny, Chechnya: A women's work brigade paid by the
Russian federal authorities to sweep the streets of the war-ravaged city center

republic from which separate autonomous Kabardino-Balkarian and Chechen *oblast*s were detached almost immediately. In 1924 the Gorskaya republic was dissolved and its remaining territory was divided into the North Ossetian and Ingush autonomous *oblast*s and Sunzhenskii *okrug* (territory) with one administrative center—the city of Vladikavkaz. In 1928, within the limits of Stavropol *krai* (territory), the Cherkess autonomous *oblast* was set up. In Transcaucasus, the Abkhazian autonomous republic joined Georgia under the Treaty of 1921. Two more autonomies emerged within Georgia: South Ossetia and Adjaria. The establishment of Soviet power in Central Asia and in North Caucasus was accompanied by cruel repression and mass migrations of the indigenous population. Several hundred thousand people, mostly representatives of the aboriginal elites and participants of the resistance *basmatch* and *mokhadjir* movements, were forced to leave their homelands.

In December 1922 the Union of the Soviet Socialist Republics (USSR) took shape; and in 1924 the first Soviet constitution was adopted. But the process of territorialization of ethnicity in the form of titular statehoods was not finished. The 1920s saw the continued imposition of ethnoterritorial borders in Central Asia. New republics with redefined borders drawn closer to ethnic lines was formed for the Kazakhs, Kirgiz, Tajiks, Turkmen, and Uzbeks. Up to 1936, their status and territories changed several times, especially in the Ferghana Valley. However, attempts to achieve ethnic homogeneity failed. A significant portion of the Uzbeks remained in Kirghizia and Tajikistan, and the Uzbek-populated rural regions around the predominantly Tajik cities of Bukhara and Samarkand were included in the Uzbek Republic. Because of economic considerations, vast territories with a predominantly Russian population were included in the Kazakh Republic when its status was elevated to a constituent union republic in 1936.

The Soviet Constitution of 1936 registered the state's structure as consisting of eleven union republics and twenty autonomous republics. The 1939 Molotov-Ribbentropp Pact enabled Stalin to annex western Belarus and western Ukraine, as well as Bessarabia. In 1940 the three Baltic states were annexed to the USSR and in 1944 Tuva, by the headwaters of the Yenitsei River in southern Siberia, was annexed. By the time of its demise, the USSR included fifty-three national-state entities: fifteen union and twenty autonomous republics, eight autonomous *oblast*s, and ten autonomous *okrug*s. These were peopled by representatives of 128 ethnic groups, numbering from a few hundred to several million (see Table 3.2).

The Policy of Repression

Large-scale ethnic engineering within a single state proved possible because of its totalitarian regime. Stalinism was ruthless, showing no mercy to any manifestations of unsanctioned initiative. The late 1920s put an end to any discussion of nationality issues in the country and ushered in a long period of repression against leaders in the republics. Victims of this repression included many outstanding political and cultural figures of the Ukraine, Caucasus, and

Table 3.2 Ethnic Composition and Demographic Growth of the USSR's Population, 1959–1989

Main Ethnic Group	Number in Thousands			Percentage Increase 1959–1989	Percentage of Total	
	1959	1979	1989		1959	1989
Russian	114,114	137,397	145,155	127.2	54.6	50.8
Ukrainian	37,253	42,347	44,186	118.6	17.8	15.5
Uzbek	6,015	12,456	16,698	277.6	2.9	5.8
Belorussian	7,913	9,463	10,036	126.8	3.8	3.5
Kazakh	3,622	6,556	8,136	224.6	1.7	2.8
Azerbaijani	2,940	5,477	6,770	332.3	1.4	2.4
Tatar	4,918	6,185	6,649	135.2	2.4	2.3
Armenian	2,787	4,151	4,623	165.9	1.3	1.6
Tajik	1,397	2,898	4,215	301.7	0.7	1.5
Georgian	2,692	3,571	3,981	147.9	1.3	1.4
Moldavian	2,214	2,968	3,352	151.4	1.1	1.2
Lithuanian	2,326	2,851	3,067	131.9	1.1	1.1
Turkmen	1,002	2,028	2,729	272.4	0.5	1.0
Kirgiz	969	1,906	2,529	261.0	0.5	0.9
German	1,620	1,936	2,039	125.9	0.8	0.7
Polish	1,380	1,151	1,126	81.6	0.7	0.7
Chuvash	1,470	1,751	1,842	125.3	0.7	0.6
Latvian	1,400	1,439	1,459	104.2	0.7	0.5
Bashkir	989	1,371	1,449	146.5	0.5	0.5
Jew	2,177	1,762	1,378	63.3	1.0	0.5
Mordva	1,285	1,192	1,154	89.8	0.6	0.4
Estonian	989	1,020	1,027	103.8	0.5	0.4
Chechen	419	756	957	228.4	0.2	0.3
Udmurt	625	714	747	119.5	0.3	0.3
Mari	504	622	671	113.1	0.2	0.2
Avar	270	483	601	124.5	0.1	0.2
Osset	413	542	598	114.9	0.2	0.2
Total	208,827	262,085	285,743	136.8%	100.0%	100.0%

Central Asia. At the same time, the government adopted a program of measures to develop the economy and culture in the republics, and to expand the political representation of non-Russian nationalities, as well as making several other positive decisions. That was especially true with relation to the so-called *korenizatsiia* (nativization) policy. This policy, as well as further related programs, provided resources and guarantees for education development and for training managerial workers, civil servants, and intelligentsia from the ranks of the "indigenous nationalities." This gave an enormous boost to modernization and social improvements. But the same policy served as a tool for the system of indirect governance and for imposing communist indoctrination under strict control from the center. Thus, through this dual use of repression and privileges the regime was able to exercise control over the periphery for many decades.

The most terrible acts of genocide were committed in the form of deportations and organized hunger in the campaign against the *kulaks* and to effect mass collectivization. Realized in the late 1920s and early 1930s, this policy mostly affected the Ukraine, southern Russia, and Kazakhstan. In 1932–1933,

2 million people were deported from the Kuban area alone, with its relatively prosperous rural population. During the period of forced collectivization of 1931–1932 in Kazakhstan, over 2 million Kazakhs died of hunger or left their homes because of the destruction of the traditional nomadic economy and social order.

Immediately after the "total victory" of collectivization from the mid-1930s, purely ethnic deportations began. On many occasions the aims could hardly be explained by anything else but geopolitical fantasies of Stalin and his maniacal distrust. The first ethnic deportation was carried out against the Korean minority of the Far East, who was moved to Kazakhstan in 1935. In 1937 many Kurds and Turks were deported from the Transcaucasian republics; and in 1939–1940 mass deportations began from the newly annexed areas of Bessarabia, West Ukraine, West Belarus, and the Baltics. The outbreak of war with Nazi Germany served as the excuse to deport the Germans living in the Volga region and other areas. Similar arguments of "collaborationism" were used for further deportations during the 1941–1945 war. Completely deported from the North Caucasus were the Karachai, the Ingush and Chechens, and the Balkars. In 1943, the Kalmyks were deported, in May 1944 the Crimean Tatars, and in November 1944 the Meskhetian Turks from Georgia. The territorial autonomies of "punished" peoples were abolished and new administrative units were established.

By the time of Stalin's death in 1956, the total number of deportees constituted 2.7 million people, including 1.2 million Germans, 316,000 Chechens, 84,000 Ingush, 165,000 Crimean Tatars, 100,000 Lithuanians, 81,000 Kalmyks, 63,000 Karachai, 52,000 Greeks, 50,000 Meskhetian Turks, 45,000 Moldavians, 40,000 Letts, and 20,000 Estonians. These figures do not include those imprisoned or shot, or those who died of hunger or disease. Other sources indicate that 3.5 million people were forcefully removed from their homelands between 1936 and 1956.

The living conditions of the deportees were hard and humiliating. The most severe restriction that survived up to 1957, and for some peoples (Crimean Tatars, Ingush) up until very recently, was that they were forbidden to return to their former homes. Most other deportees were allowed to return to their native places soon after 1956. The Checheno-Ingush, Karachai-Cherkess, Kabardino-Balkar, and Kalmyk autonomous republics were reinstituted, although not with their previous borders. Part of the Kalmyk territory remained within the limits of the Astrakhan *oblast,* and part of the Ingush territory within North Ossetia.

During the Stalinist period, the repressed peoples had to experience tremendous physical and emotional trauma that, along with some territorial problems, has carried directly over into the political situation today, serving as a major cause of interethnic tension and conflict. The problem of these peoples was aggravated by slow and limited rehabilitation measures, and, in some instances, because of counteraction against these measures on the part of authorities and the local population. It was not until 1989 that the Supreme Soviet of the USSR adopted the declaration "On Recognizing as Unlawful and Criminal the Repressive Acts Against the Peoples Subjected to Forced Resettlement." On 22 April 1991 the Supreme Soviet of the Russian Federation adopted the law "On Rehabilitation of the Repressed Peoples." Both acts were important steps toward democratization, but ironically the latter law has caused more problems than it resolved because it legitimized local territorial claims and demands for exclusive material compensation for members of deported groups.

The Policy of Prestige

Although guided by motives of prestige and propaganda, the Soviet regime invested a great deal of effort and resources in substantiating its declaration about a "solution of the nationality question." In the republics and among the smaller indigenous peoples, the development of education was strongly encouraged (written languages and textbooks were developed for fifty-seven ethnic groups). Culture in its professional forms (music, theater, literature, cinema) as well as other attributes of national statehood (academies of sciences, professional unions of creative workers, media and publishing, university education) were supported and paraded to demonstrate the success of the system. Local intelligentsia and managerial personnel, as well as influential party bureaucracy, were formed already in the prewar period through the nativization policy among major Soviet nationalities.

The 1960s–1980s were an important period in the history of Soviet nationalities. The gap that had existed in social structures of main ethnic groups was practically eliminated as a result of social mobility, together with quotas and preferences in the sphere of education. Average educational standards in the ethnic republics—in particular, the percentage of those holding university diplomas and scholarly degrees—grew considerably higher than the average national indices, outstripping the corresponding figures for the Russian majority. Rising social expectations and the growing power of the peripheral elites were accompanied in some cases by serious demographic shifts; the numerical growth among non-Russians (or, more exactly, non-Slavic and non-Baltic peoples) was much higher than that of the Russians, Ukrainians, Belorussians, and the Balts. From 1979 to 1989, the Russian population in the USSR increased by 5.6 percent. During the same period, population growth among the Azerbaijanis was 24 percent, Uzbeks and Turkmens 24 percent, Kirgiz 32 percent, and Tajiks 45 percent. In contrast, the natural growth among Latvians and Estonians was the lowest in the country (1.4 and 2.4 percent respectively)—which subsequently provided a powerful argument for exclusive local nationalism to "restore the demographic balance." In most republics, the 1970s were marked by the emerging process of ethnic homogenization in favor of the titular nationalities. The main reason for this development was the migration of ethnic Russians from areas of Central Asia and the Transcaucasus. Meanwhile, in such republics as the Ukraine, Kazakhstan, Belarus, Latvia, and Estonia, the proportion of Russians increased. In Estonia and Kazakhstan, the changing demography resulted in growing anxiety among the titulars about losing the dominant majority in their "own" republics and becoming subject to an even greater degree of Russian acculturation.

The economic policy of the Soviet state exerted a contradictory influence on the ethnic situation. From the very first years of Bolshevik government there was an official goal to eliminate the economic backwardness of the national republics. In the predominantly rural areas, industrial enterprises were built specifically for the purpose of ensuring the growth of the working class, which the regime saw as its main stronghold, and to improve social conditions. After World War II, modern industrial enterprises were established in the republics to help accelerate the urbanization of the population. However, such measures did not prevent the introduction in some republics of a monocultural agrarian economy, with grave repercussions on natural environments and health conditions. A specific case in point was the massive cotton-growing economy of Central Asia. In total, Soviet economic policy led to a high degree of economic interdependence between all union republics, with the Russian Republic providing large subsidies to other republics, supplying cheap energy and raw materials.

The unitary strategy of development and the imposition of Russian-language ideological presentations from the center resulted in the formation of similar socioprofessional structures and common cultural and value orientations among the various Soviet nationalities. The emergence of the "one community of Soviet people" doctrine in the country was no accident: the overwhelming majority of Soviet citizens shared the same (or very similar) social, political, and even cultural values. On the other hand, differences in cultural traditions, industrial development, demographic behavior, and political culture managed to survive all through the Soviet period. But the model that seeks to explain disintegration by reference to developmental levels and by the "winners and losers" dichotomy fails to explain the situation that existed, and contradicts the fact that it was the most advantaged and well-off republics that initiated the disintegration of the USSR. Even more difficult to accept is the thesis that cultural differences between republics stem from the very nature of their civilizational character, and that such differences could never coexist in the bosom of a single state.

While the Soviet central power was strong enough to control the local administrations, and at the same time suppress any attempts at organized nationalist movements, it was also in a position to secure the tolerance and consent of key social actors through the notion of a single multiethnic state. But as soon as the power and unified ideology weakened, the very foundation of the nationalities policy lost its hold. Ethnicity as a basis of group solidarity, and ethnic nationalism as a political doctrine, challenged the status quo.

The Fight for Sovereignty

In spite of a dominant explanatory model for the breakup of the USSR as a "triumph of nations," there was no explicit revolt or insurrection on the part of non-Russians. Mass rallies and demonstrations were full of praise—for *perestroika,* for Mikhail Gorbachev personally or in combination with particular demands like keeping a longtime party boss in office (Kazakhstan, December 1986), annexation of a territory (Armenia, January-February 1988), and environmental and cultural demands (Baltic republics, Moldova, Georgia in 1988–1989). What was taking place was a reassertion of individual and collective dignity, irrespective of ethnic meaning. Ethnic revolt as a stand was to be learned later; it could be traced as such only in the Baltic republics and in peaceful forms. In a situation of political liberalization, weakening state institutions, and rising local initiatives, ethnic unrest in the USSR started not as a major political cleavage but as interethnic riots and communal clashes directed mainly toward vulnerable "double minorities" in national republics. Examples are the anti-Armenian pogrom in Sumgait, Azerbaijan, in February 1988; the expulsion of Meskhetian Turks from the Fergana region of Uzbekistan in June 1989; anti-minorities riots in the Tajik capital of Dushanbe in February 1990; and other similar events. Not all major cases of conflicting ethnicity were directed at the Russian imperial center, even in the Baltic, where there were far greater reasons and legitimacy for political upheaval.

The most important influence in this course of events was to be found behind Kremlin walls. The first Congress of People's Deputies elected in 1989 could boast a remarkable representation of major Soviet nationalities. The most eloquent and flamboyant figures were sent first to the all-union parliament to speak out on the country's problems as well on the concerns of the republics and regions. The first serious challenge to Gorbachev's gradual top-down liberalization and economic reforms came from the Baltic republics— where the need for sociocultural improvements was in fact less urgent than elsewhere in the USSR. But the Baltic republics were smaller polities with articulate Westernized elites quick to grasp the opportunities of the opening society. The Balts also enjoyed relatively higher standards of living—and these they wanted to keep and to strengthen, rather than lose them through the slow movement of the larger Soviet society. Along with this reassertion came the image of the "occupied nation," which became the core of the reemerging Baltic identity.

The programmatic context of so-called national movements in the USSR was diffuse and rapidly changing. Few of the leaders of the periphery linked their position with Gorbachev and his program. Many more switched loyalties and doctrinal baggage to become nationalists. Ethnic nationalism was attractive to former communists because its vision of a uniform and disciplined society in which leaders define what constitutes the popular will mimics the totalitarian pretensions of Stalinism.

The center proved ill-prepared to conduct negotiations or make the concessions necessary to meet these challenges. Its reaction was directed primarily at the policy of force and punishment. While some Communist Party leaders and academic experts were trying to transform the official policy toward the periphery, adherents of force were suppressing the rising local opposition in Tbilisi (April 1989), Baku (January 1990), and Vilnius (January 1991). There was a strikingly limited arsenal of arguments and appeals that central authorities could use to confront the newly permitted expressions of long-accumulated complaints and expectations. Such an inconsistent policy served to provoke greater dissatisfaction, destroying illusions about the ability of the center to provide responsible governance and freedoms to the nondominant nationalities and peripheral territories.

The ethnic policy of the *perestroika* period proved a failure, exploited by Gorbachev's opponents in Moscow and by opponents of Moscow in the periphery as the main argument to abolish the Soviet Union. The demise of the state could at the same time be considered a great achievement of the leaders of the main non-Russian groups who were able to realize their aspirations peacefully. The irony of the situation is that the initiator of this disintegration was in fact the Russian Federation and its leader, Boris Yeltsin, who was brought to power by radical democratic groups and could register significant victories in the Russian republican elections of 4 March 1990. On 12 June 1990, the Russian Congress of People's Deputies adopted the Declaration of Sovereignty for this largest and most powerful of the Soviet republics. The political meaning of this document was explicitly directed against Gorbachev and the USSR's power structure.

This could be interpreted as a clash of two strategies and of two political blocs on the question of how to proceed with reforms and democratization. But it was also a power struggle between Yeltsin and Gorbachev. Yeltsin undertook radical steps to expel Gorbachev and his other former Politburo compatriots from the Kremlin. He rejected the compromise economic-reform plan adopted by the Supreme Soviet in October 1990. Russia's Supreme Soviet reaffirmed the primacy of its own legislative acts for the territory of this republic. The leadership of the Russian Republic blocked all efforts of the union center to reorganize the structure of the entire country. Other republics followed suit.

On 16 July 1990, the Supreme Soviet of Ukraine passed its Declaration of Sovereignty, which called for full autonomy and for a separate army. Declarations of sovereignty and the supremacy of the authorities of the various republics were announced and established throughout much of the union. Periphery leaders urged skepticism and disregard for the efforts of Gorbachev and the All-Union Supreme Soviet to work out a new Union Treaty. In spring 1991, Gorbachev initiated the Novo-Ogarevo process to keep together at least those parts of the country where leaders were ready to negotiate a new and looser formula for the union. Three meetings were held in Novo-Ogarevo (near Moscow) in May, June, and July where republican leaders and leaders of ethnoterritorial autonomies (such as Abkhazia in Georgia, Tatarstan and Bashkiria in Russia) bargained fiercely for their own interests amidst efforts to work out the text of the new treaty. The dialogue resulted in the agreed text of a new Union Treaty—which, however, did not prevent the Russian Republic from recognizing the independence of Lithuania a week later.

The August 1991 coup was an attempt to reestablish Communist rule in the country. It was also a question of the ongoing disintegration of the country, viewed by conservative, nonreformist forces as an unacceptable price for liberalization. The territorial integrity of the Soviet state was actually the main issue of the coup. This was to become a painful reality after Russia took the lead in the process of dissolving the Soviet Union. After that time, the political focus shifted from the nearly accomplished Baltic secession to the complete breakup of the Soviet polity.

The coup failed, leaving in its wake a high degree of political enthusiasm among the winning Russian democracy. Yeltsin, indeed, not only played the central political role in defeating the coup, but used the opportunity in effect to mount a countercoup, usurping the powers of the union president and other central institutions. Thus it was Russia that was the key actor in the demise of the USSR. Even Baltic independence could have been questionable without the support it got from the Russian democratic movement. The demise of the Soviet Union was a political improvisation not preceded by any assessment of the decision and its possible consequences. But basically it was to the good.

Valeri Tishkov is professor of History and Anthropology and director of the Institute of Ethnology and Anthropology at the Russian Academy of Sciences, and former minister of nationalities in the Yeltsin government. He is the author of many books on indigenous people, minorities, nationalism, and conflict, including Ethnicity, Nationalism and Conflict in and After the Soviet Union *(London: Sage, 1977) and* The Anthropology of War-Torn Society: The Case of Chechnya *(University of California Press, forthcoming). He edited two encyclopedias (in Russian):* The Peoples of Russia *(1994) and* The Peoples and Religions of the World *(1999).*

4

Minority Issues in Southeastern Europe: A Future of Ethnically "Pure" States?

Hugh Poulton

States that harbor only one ethnic or linguistic group inside their borders are rare. Even Western Europe, which has produced some of the most ethnically homogeneous states anywhere in the world, is having to deal with growing local or imported minorities. But in the Balkans, ethnically "pure" states have started to emerge in the wake of the civil wars that accompanied the breakup of Yugoslavia: Croatia, for example, or the Republika Srpska inside Bosnia and Herzegovina. Events in Kosovo appear to point in a similar direction. In spite of the rhetoric that would suggest otherwise, these developments have been sanctioned or encouraged by the international community. From a historical perspective, mixed populations inside a country's borders have been overwhelmingly the norm in the Balkan region. There were various ways in which minority issues were treated in the past and these methods can be traced back to the days of the two great empires that used to straddle this region: Hapsburg and Ottoman. Presently, the main challenges for those Balkan states that remain ethnically mixed are minority representation in the security apparatuses, the role of the media, and minority education.

The new states that emerged in the nineteenth century from the decaying Ottoman and Habsburg Empires claimed long histories. In classic nationalist fashion, they looked back to a mythologized "golden era" in the past. But these states were not old; they were born out of the very new creed of modern nationalism. Upheld as ethnic states, each based on one dominant nation, the new states suffered from two problems. On the one hand, there was irredentism (the idea that all speakers of one language should be living in the same country). On the other, there was tension between majority and minority populations. In areas that had been under the control of the Ottoman Empire, tension was particularly evident in the relations between the new Orthodox Christian rulers and their Muslim minority populations, which were seen as undesirable relics from the Ottoman past. In many of these areas the legacy of the Ottoman millet system has remained to the present day. (The millet system classified the population by religion rather than ethnicity or language.) Although the ideology of nationalism, which traveled to the Balkans from Western and Central Europe, was essentially secular, its impact in the region has produced a close correlation and often confusion between religion, identity, and modern citizenship that persists until today.

This tendency to see themselves as being ethnic states bore little relation to the actual situation in the area where mixed populations were often the rule. But the idea fitted in to some extent with the prevailing spirit of the times. At the time of their emergence in the nineteenth and early twentieth centuries, the concept of the nation-state as the ideal was widespread and illustrated by U.S. president Wilson's attempts at redrawing along ethnic lines the post–World War I map of Central and Southeastern Europe.

The various treaties that recognized the post–World War I states in Southeastern Europe contained provisions relating to minorities. In practice, these provisions existed mainly on paper only and were often flagrantly ignored. The international community failed to adequately protect minority rights in the period between the two world wars and Hitler used the issue of minorities for revanchist ends, which directly led to World War II. After the war, a situation emerged whereby minority rights were effectively ignored in favor of emphasis on individual ones; until the 1990s, Article 27 of the ICCPR (the International Covenant on Civil and Political Rights of 1966) was the only international measure specifically dealing with guaranteeing minority rights.

A partial exception to this process was the situation in the Soviet bloc where, in accordance with Lenin and Stalin's views, there was often a measure of state support for minority cultures within the rigid Marxist-Leninist framework. This was summed up in the phrase "nationalist in form but socialist in content." Even here, with the exception perhaps of the former Yugoslavia where no one group had an outright numerical majority, there were pressures to assimilate to the majority culture. These pressures intensified throughout the region as Marxism-Leninism progressively lost its legitimacy and the regimes began to openly espouse nationalism. In the end, Communist Eastern and Southeastern Europe became "socialist in form but nationalist in content."

When in the late 1980s the Cold War ended and the Soviet bloc collapsed, minority rights once more came on the international agenda. Since then, the international community has moved toward a standardization and codification of minority rights. This led to the 1990 Copenhagen document of the Conference on Security and Cooperation in Europe (CSCE), and the UN Declaration on the Rights of Persons Belonging to National or Ethnic, Religious and Linguistic Minorities, adopted by the UN General Assembly as Resolution 47/135 of 18 December 1992. This has in turn been followed by various regional declarations, the most important of which for this study has been the Council of Europe's Framework Convention for the Protection of National Minorities, which entered into force on 1 February 1998. The Framework Convention followed on from the European Charter for Regional or Minority Languages of October 1992. In this document, the value of protecting the regional or minority languages of Europe was emphasized. It was noted that some languages were in danger of eventual extinction, and the charter saw "the right to use a regional or minority language in private and public life" as an "inalienable right." The Framework Convention is the first legally binding international instrument devoted to the plight of minorities and it calls on states to overcome the corrosive effects of "benign neglect"—whereby assimilation to the dominant culture tends to occur over a few generations. It encourages states to take active steps to allow minority cultures to develop. For the states of Southeastern Europe, adequate application of the new standards is seen as one prerequisite for joining the European Union, to which ultimately they all aspire: a country such as Greece would not today be allowed to join the EU without radically changing its internal minority policies.

A key factor of the evolving situation is the ending of the central state's past monopoly on the means of propagating culture. In the past, the early modern state usually centralized education and media and used them to instill cultural norms on often culturally diverse populations. This is changing due to the "communications revolution"—especially the expansion of satellite television ownership and other means of transnational communication that has occurred in the last few years and is beginning to penetrate Southeastern Europe as well. Similarly privatization means that diverse groups can fund their own publications. This trend will surely continue despite recent efforts by previous centralist authoritarian governments such as Milosevic's Serbia and Tudjman's Croatia to hinder it.

Another factor is the greater freedom of movement that has seen the creation of new minorities in states. The Framework Convention does not require people who belong to national minorities to be citizens of that nation. An enduring feature of the region is a tendency to classify the population into defined "historical" groups, sometimes enumerated as such in constitutions. This does not take into account the modern world. Greece, for instance, is now home to large numbers of Roman Catholics from Southeast Asia who have come as domestic helpers. There are also numerous Muslim Albanians in Greece, a country with an overwhelming Orthodox majority.

Irredentism and Expansion

Many of the new states that emerged in the nineteenth century had large numbers of their co-nationals living as minorities in neighboring states. Indeed, the initial rational for the first Greek and Serbian states was to expand and incorporate their perceived co-nationals into the "mother" state. Similar incorporation occurred in Bulgaria and Romania later in the century and in Central Europe in the 1930s, where the existence of German minorities was used by Hitler during his rise to power. In Southeast Europe, the post–World War I "losers" such as Hungary and Bulgaria explicitly followed policies aimed at redrawing boundaries at the expense of the "winners" such as Greece, Romania, and the first Yugoslavia. Within the latter, the dissatisfaction of the Croats and Albanians was used by Mussolini to try and destabilize the state, leading to the destruction of Yugoslavia in World War II.

Where this issue of dissatisfaction with borders has remained, minority issues have become potentially more conflict-ridden than those where this is not so. The final acceptance by Germany of her eastern borders, for example, has done much to assuage Polish fears of German revanchism and this has been reflected in improved conditions for Poland's German minority. Similarly, Hungary's acceptance that Transylvania will remain part of Romania has helped allay Romanian fears about Hungarian designs and has confirmed the ultimate loyalty of Romania's Hungarians, who have since played a constructive role in Romania's governments. Macedonia's recognition by the international community was based on changing its constitution to remove threats of irredentism against Greece and Bulgaria. Conversely, Serbia's initial refusal to accept the new borders in the breakup of Yugoslavia in the 1990s and its attempts to incorporate the large Serb minorities into a Greater Serbia resulted in wars and the genocide in Bosnia and Herzegovina. The same can be said of Tudjman's Croatia, whose attitude to Herzegovina was ambivalent to say the least.

At the time of this writing, the most dangerous conflict concerns the position of ethnic Albanians in Kosovo, southern Serbia, and Macedonia. There are strong currents among Albanians outside of Albania, who refuse to accept the "truncated" Albania of 1912–1913 and are willing to fight for a Greater Albania. Within Albania itself this does not appear to be a high priority, but the problem is that the Albanian state is extremely weak and not in a position to reassure its neighbors that their borders are safe. The easy access to firearms following Albania's meltdown in 1997 is a further factor.

Inclusion and Exclusion: Assimilation and Expulsion

The new states of the nineteenth century tended to be made up of a patchwork of different ethnic groups utilizing diverse languages/dialects and predominantly living in small agrarian communities with distinct localized cultures. The nationalist intellectual elites of the new states were faced with problems of removing the old local/religious loyalties of the bulk of the peasant populations and replacing them with loyalties to the new nation-state. (In places such as the Rhodope Mountains straddling Greece and Bulgaria, this process is still continuing.) People who were seen as being unable to do this were viewed as essentially alien and encouraged or forced to leave. Today, we would call this "ethnic cleansing." This was especially the case for Muslims in the Orthodox successor states of the Ottoman Empire, and for Christians in the new Turkey of Ataturk.

The two world wars saw massive loss of life, ethnic slaughter, and mass population movements. Serbia lost up to a quarter of its population in World War I. During World War II, the occupation by Axis forces (Germany and Italy) of large parts of Southeastern Europe saw further mass murder of specific groups—especially Jews and Roma (gypsies). The bulk of the region's

Jews were murdered in the death camps with the exception of the Jewish community in Bulgaria. In the Ustashe puppet state of Croatia during World War II (which incorporated much of Bosnia and Herzegovina) Serbs, Jews, and Roma were systematically massacred along with Muslim and Croatian opponents of Ante Pavelic's regime. Following the war, ethnic Germans from Yugoslavia were expelled en masse and the majority of Jewish survivors in the region emigrated to the new state of Israel.

The exodus of Muslims from the Balkans to Anatolia following the dissolution of the Ottoman Empire has continued to the present day. The largest such movement was in 1989 from Bulgaria. This was caused by the repressive policies of the Zhivkov regime, which resulted in some 310,000 fleeing the country. Many among those who took part in the original great exodus of 1989 did not stay in Turkey but went back to Bulgaria. Nevertheless, mass emigration to Turkey has continued, spurred on by a severe decline in the former host country; after all, many ethnic Bulgarians have also left for economic reasons.

Ethnic-cleansing measures, initially carried out on a large scale by Serbs against Bosniaks and Croats, became widespread in the Yugoslav wars and affected many different groups. When the military balance changed, many Serbs opted to move or were coerced into moving to areas under Serb control rather than be minorities in their traditional homes in Croatia and what is now the Federation of Bosnia and Herzegovina. The Dayton agreement largely sanctioned this by recognizing the ethnic Serb entity in Bosnia and Herzegovina as a separate unit—possibly a dangerous precedent. The return of the refugees to their original homes remains an aim to which at least lip service is paid by the international community, but just how many return remains in doubt. Such returns may occur in Croatia and Bosnia and Herzegovina, where nonnationalist political forces have grown in strength, but it seems very unlikely that Serbs will return to Albanian-controlled areas in Kosovo.

Thus, throughout the region, ethnic cleansing has a long history. This practice has frequently gone hand in hand with attempts at ethnic restructuring by the central authorities. This is done through the settlement of large numbers of a particular ethnic group (usually the majority) with a view to change the ethnic structure of a particular region. In addition to this sorry tale of ethnic intolerance and attempted homogenization, there have been and continue to be massive movements of "economic migrants."

Back in the nineteenth century, there were also people living in the new states who perhaps may not have been regarded as "pure" but who shared crucial markers: Orthodoxy, for instance, in states such as Greece or Bulgaria, or Islam, as with the Kurds in Turkey. They were seen as potential members of the nation even though other crucial markers were missing. Perhaps their mother tongue was not the state language. These people were subject to assimilation. In order to instill a unitary state-sponsored nationalism, the communication and educational monopoly of the centralized bureaucracies was used. If necessary, there were punitive sanctions against, for example, speaking the "wrong" language. This method was an imitation of the French model

Djakovica, Kosovo: The picturesque center with typical Albanian architecture was renovated in the 1970s. It was systematically burnt down by Serbs once the NATO bombing campaign started (June 1999).

of nation building whereby internal minorities are negated and the state imposes a uniform culture. Elements of this remain and lead to a refusal to recognize certain minorities by certain states, in spite of the fact that this constitutes a violation of basic rights. The Bulgarian authorities remain wary of recognizing an ethnic Macedonian minority separate from Bulgarians, while in Greece expressions of a non-Greek ethnic consciousness by Orthodox Slav Macedonians remain taboo and a source of conflict.

Citizenship and Population

The breakup of Yugoslavia saw the creation of a number of new states, all of whom had to introduce criteria for citizenship that were often highly restrictive and blatantly biased in favor of supposed ethnic kin living outside the new states. This occurred at the expense of perceived aliens inside the state boundaries. Many people in former Yugoslavia moved, often from an area where their language and ethnicity was the majority to one where they became minorities. The reverse also happened. When the state collapsed, many people found themselves residing in territories that were their birthplaces or natural homelands, but had become different countries. Denying citizenship to such people effectively makes them illegal aliens in their own homes. The ethnic component on granting citizenship has also been used against groups seen as undesirable. This especially applies to Roma, who tend not to be welcome anywhere in the region, but also to other groups seen as potentially hostile to the state. These groups include Serbs in Croatia and Albanians in the Federal

Republic of Yugoslavia and in Macedonia. Large numbers of people have been denied citizenship in one new country on the grounds that they were born elsewhere in former Yugoslavia and do not belong to the dominant ethnic group. Roma and Albanians are not dominant groups in any of the former Yugoslav states on whose territories they were born, although for Albanians the quasi-state of Kosovo now to some extent plays that role. They are often denied citizenship, resulting in large numbers of stateless people.

This ties in with the issue of numbers, always a contentious point in Southeastern Europe. Censuses have become heavily politicized, often with minority groups such as the Albanians claiming far greater numbers than officially credited. Here a crucial factor for the future is the very high birthrate of the Albanians and the Roma in comparison with other groups—especially majority groups who have followed Western European trends of small families and even negative birthrates. This was a key factor in Kosovo in the 1980s and plays a similar role in Macedonia currently with the possible scenario of ethnic Albanians even becoming a majority in the future. The "numbers game" is further complicated by the Roma: due to their low status, they traditionally register themselves as members of more dominant groups so that their official numbers are always far below their real figure. (This is known as "ethnic mimicry.")

The Roma
The situation of the Roma merits special mention. Everywhere in the region they constitute a significant minority and in places such as Hungary they are the largest minority. However, they are without a "mother state." Unlike other transnational minorities, such as the Vlachs, who have been successful in integrating into their wider respective communities, the Roma continue to be a virtually separate stratum of society. They are subject to extreme discrimination and prejudice from virtually all other groups. Their economic and social condition is often dire in the extreme (although the Roma should not be seen as a monolithic whole; some sections of Roma have been economically successful). All the states in the region need to combat and overcome deep-seated anti-Roma prejudices among the general population, prejudices that are shared by local members of the executive, if not central, state organs.

Religion and Threats to Religious Minorities
There is a noticeable difference between states that were part of the Ottoman Empire for a long period and those that were under the Habsburgs. The Ottoman millet legacy, with its emphasis on religion as a primary focus of identity, greatly contributes to state and social pressure against religious minorities. This is especially the case with hitherto unrecognized religious groups and occurs especially in states with an Orthodox majority. It is very apparent in Greece where in the late nineteenth century a nationalist emphasis on Orthodoxy was an essential component of "Greekness," leading to a continuing confusion of Orthodoxy, ethnicity, and citizenship. In Greece, the Muslim populations continue to be regarded as suspect and are not considered as true

citizens of the state. This has also applied to non-Orthodox Christian groups such as evangelical Protestants, Roman Catholics, and Jehovah's Witnesses. The Orthodox Church remains a significant factor in modern Greek politics and individual bishops can exert considerable pressure in minority situations. The Simitis government has shown a welcome break with this past practice but obstruction from local bureaucracy remains.

The other states with a long Ottoman millet heritage display similar characteristics. In Bulgaria, despite guarantees on freedom of religion, the constitution characterizes Orthodox Christianity as the "traditional" religion. The government provides financial support for it and the other major religious bodies, the Muslim and Jewish communities. Other groups, however, are treated with suspicion and hostility, especially proselytizing ones such as Jehovah's Witnesses, Mormons, Word of Life, Baha'is, and others who have been denied registration. Police have broken up meetings of such groups, who have also been subjected to physical attacks by local political forces without interference from the authorities.

In Macedonia, the constitution specifically provides for freedom of religion for the Macedonian Orthodox Church and other religious communities and groups. A law of July 1997 on religious communities classifies the Macedonian Orthodox Church, the Islamic community, and the Roman Catholic Church as "religious communities" while all others are classified as "religious groups." The law requires registration before any group can carry out religious functions. There have been complaints, especially by Protestants, that they have been refused registration and prevented from holding religious meetings outside of church premises. Arguments over recognition from other Orthodox churches remain, particularly with regard to the Serbian Church, which prior to the founding of the Macedonian one in 1967 controlled Macedonia's Orthodox churches.

The case in Albania is different, due in part to the severe persecution of the Hoxha era. The abolition of religion in 1967 was followed by the extreme persecution of all religious groups, the virtual extinction of religious personnel, and the destruction of almost all places of worship, whether they were Sunni Muslim, Orthodox, Catholic, or Bektashi. When this period of blanket intolerance came to an end, the main religious communities were faced with huge problems. They have been helped by increased religious toleration and even mutual help. However, even here the millet heritage with its correlation of Orthodoxy and ethnicity is evident. The Greek minority is mainly concentrated in the south and is almost wholly Orthodox. Ethnic Albanians make up the majority of Albania's Orthodox community, which in the 1923 census—the last to note religious affiliation—amounted to some 20 percent of the population. Neighboring Greece tends to view the entire Orthodox minority as Greek. After the Hoxha era, the lack of trained personnel led to the appointment of Greek bishops in 1992 to fill the vacuum. This provoked strong protest in Albania. The expulsion of Archimandrite Chrysotomos in 1993 for allegedly advocating cession to Greece fuelled the controversy. However, archbishop

Anastasios Yanoulatos, a Greek citizen, has been exemplary in avoiding exacerbating interethnic tension. Protestant religious groups and other groups such as the Baha'is have also been very active, although many were attacked during the spring 1997 anarchy reflecting the general regional distrust of new religious groups.

In Federal Yugoslavia, there is no official state religion. But there has been a reemphasis on Orthodoxy as an integral component of Serbianism, aggravated by the Yugoslav wars, which has seen preferential treatment to the Serbian Orthodox Church by the authorities in the form of access to state-run television for major religious events. However, due to the Habsburg legacy in significant areas like the Vojvodina, Federal Yuoslavia does not have the same intensity of millet heritage as Greece or Bulgaria. Indeed, despite the all-out Serb/Muslim fighting in Bosnia and Herzegovina, the large Serbo-Croat–speaking Muslim population in the Sandzak straddling Serbia and Montenegro (many of whom now refer to themselves as Bosniaks) have not been religiously persecuted.

The situation in Bosnia and Herzegovina was similar but has been severely affected by the recent war. The millet legacy was evident, especially in the genesis of the Muslim or "Bosniak" nation since the 1960s. However, the Habsburg legacy, the lack of a majority group, and the largest group being Muslim by custom if not religious practice, have led to a remarkable religious diversity and tolerance in the area. Despite the recent events, this tolerance has survived in cities such as Sarajevo and Mostar, which are proud to point out that places of worship belonging to Jews, Catholics, and even Orthodox—the "Serb aggressors"—remain undamaged. This is not the case in the areas occupied by Serbs and those currently in the Republika Srpska, where mosques and Catholic churches have been systematically destroyed as part of the ethnic cleansing. Similarly, in other parts of Bosnia and Herzegovina, Croat forces engaged in struggle for territory with Muslims have destroyed mosques.

This contrast between the Ottoman millet heritage and the Habsburg one is clear in Hungary and Romania, where religious intolerance is not an issue. It is further shown in Croatia, which despite the close association of Roman Catholicism with "Croatness" does not officially put obstacles in the way of minority religious practice. However, the Serb/Croat war has given rise to anti-Orthodox sentiment that has spawned acts of violence on Orthodox property, especially in the formerly Serb majority Knin area. There has been little sanction by the police. The Ustashe heritage, with its anti-Jewish aspects, has also resurfaced with the desecration of Jewish cemeteries such as the May 1997 daubing of fascist insignia on tombstones in Karlovac.

Minority Representation and Minority Education

Key issues that can potentially lead to conflict initiated by both sides concern minority representation and minority education. A common feature is the centralized nature of the states in the region and the issue of local government in places such as Istria and the Vojvodina may not primarily be a minority issue.

However, the two are often intimately combined. In areas where ethnic minorities make up sizeable percentages or even majorities, the ethnic composition of the local executive—especially the police force—is a key factor. Typically, ethnic minorities are severely underrepresented in the security forces and in such circumstances "simple" law-and-order issues can escalate into interethnic conflict. In successor states to the former Yugoslavia, where the risk of large-scale fighting remains, this can be combined with the issue of sovereignty. In southern Serbia and western Macedonia, for example, sections of the majority ethnic Albanian minority appear to be aiming for their areas to become essentially international protectorates, similar to Bosnia and Herzegovina and Kosovo. They would prefer these territories to be policed by outside "peacekeepers" rather than remain under the control of security forces, which are dominated by what they perceive as members of the hostile majority. Whether this "losing of sovereignty" is problematic remains an open question—the current Macedonian authorities, for example, also appear to welcome international troops to police its long and problematic border with Albania and Kosovo.

Minority-language education, especially up to university level, is another potential conflict issue, as shown by past clashes in Tetovo over the nonrecognized Albanian University. The closure of the separate Hungarian Bolyai University in Cluj and its merger with the Romanian-language Babes University by the Communists in the 1950s remains a source of friction.

In the media, the European Charter on Regional and Minority Languages requires governments to define exactly which kinds of access to the electronic media the minority groups will have. Its Article 11 presents a shopping list of options from which states must chose; they must also specify which provision will apply to which language groups and over which territory. As noted above, modern telecommunications has to a large extent ended the central state's monopoly on broadcasting, allowing minorities, among others, greater access to the electronic media.

However, measures that give minorities greater access to local government, education, and the media run the risk of a nationalist backlash from sections of the majority group. In a number of countries there have been street demonstrations against granting perceived "privileges" to minorities. Here, it is possible to differentiate between the reactions of the authorities: they can either try and use such expressions of xenophobia for populist political aims, or they can ignore this temptation and practice more responsible government. The former option was chosen by Milosevic's regime in Serbia. In the latter camp we find the Bulgarian authorities when they were faced with the declaration by Bulgarian nationalists of a "Bulgarian Republic of Razgrad" in 1990 and calls for "ethnic municipalities" in 1997 in Kardzhali. The Macedonian authorities can also be included in this camp, when they had to respond to virulently nationalistic protests by ethnic Macedonian students against legislation allowing the use of Albanian in the pedagogical faculty in Skopje. Where racist attitudes to the Roma are concerned, local executives can run counter to central government. This was shown in Cluj in Romania, where the notorious nationalist mayor Gheorghe Funar promised in January 2001 not to enforce a new draft law on administration, which would require local authorities to provide for employees who speak either majority and/or minority languages in areas where minorities reach 20 percent.

Hugh Poulton is a specialist on the Balkans and Turkey. From 1984 to 1991 he was Amnesty International's researcher on Eastern Europe. He is currently a consultant on the Balkans for the Minority Rights Group, and on Turkey, Azerbaijan, and Central Asia for Article 19: The Global Campaign for Free Expression. His publications include The Balkans: Minorities and States in Conflict; Who Are the Macedonians?; Top Hat, Grey Wolf and Crescent: Turkish Nationalism and the Turkish Republic; *and he was coeditor and major contributor of* Muslim Identity and the Balkan State.

5

NGOs Versus Political Parties: Combatting Xenophobia and Racism in Western Europe

Harlan Koff

Western Europe has seen a steady flow of immigrants from the south and the east since the beginning of the 1990s—and with it a rise in far-right political parties and an increase in racist attacks on immigrants. To some extent, restrictive immigration policies adopted by the EU may have exacerbated the situation. Although, as racist incidents have increased, the European Union, Western European governments, and mainstream political parties have taken action to combat racism, and antiracist legislation has been enacted, the most effective responses to xenophobia in Western Europe have originated with nongovernmental organizations.

The fall of communism in 1989 began a new era for Europe, one that was supposed to be devoid of major conflicts. The reunification of the continent at the end of the Cold War was seen as a victory for democracy and peace. Even though Europe is more stable politically at the start of the twenty-first century than it was during most of the twentieth, conflict still exists, albeit in a different form. Many scholars correctly argue that liberal democracy, while the dominant ideology in European politics, has not monopolized the political arena nor ended ethnic conflict. In fact, this school argues that globalization and the spread of liberal democracy fundamentally changed domestic politics and has resulted in a cultural backlash and a revival of nationalism. As EU enlargement becomes a reality, adherence to human-rights standards and the equal treatment of ethnic minorities have been included in the membership criteria. However, the recent rise of xenophobia is not exclusive to those Eastern European states experiencing democratization. A similar trend is found in Western Europe itself.

Democratic systems are characterized and based on citizen participation in politics, either directly or indirectly. In modern democracies, political parties have provided an institutionalized channel through which preferences are expressed. However, in recent times parties have often been accused of representing undemocratic values such as elitism and nonresponsiveness. In fact, many have suggested that political parties are currently suffering from a crisis of confidence in European politics. As a result, many Europeans have turned to the nongovernmental sector to articulate their interests, as an alternative to parties. One area where this trend is visible is the field of immigration or, more precisely, integration politics. During the last decade, radical-right parties have moved from the margins of European party systems into the mainstream, and their nationalist platforms have often forced governing parties to adopt more nativist positions concerning immigration and ethnic inclusion. Those who oppose the recent rise of xenophobia and nationalism in Western Europe have most effectively responded to the renaissance of the extreme right through activity in the nongovernmental sector.

Radical-Right Parties and the Rise of Xenophobic Populism

At the conclusion of World War II, the radical right was effectively marginalized from European party systems. These parties had been decapitated, as their leaders were politically discredited and often imprisoned as Nazi or fascist collaborators. Moreover, neofascism was paying the consequences for changes in international politics. Following the Nuremberg trials and the adoption of the Universal Declaration of Human Rights, the first international human-rights system was erected. Obviously, radical-right party platforms were inconsistent with this change in political values. Furthermore, the Cold War put extreme-right parties in a compromised position. The United States and the Soviet Union both combated neofascism in Western Europe due to its ideological opposition to both democracy and communism. These factors effectively froze European party politics, creating a system that pitted secular or Christian conservative parties against various parties of the left. The radical right remained a negligible force, achieving modest results in postwar elections despite the rise of immigration and the implementation of the guest-worker system caused by the massive economic reconstruction of Western Europe.

During the past twenty years, two significant developments in European politics and society greatly improved the fortunes of the radical right and led to a renaissance of nationalism. Increased access to transportation, the unequal international distribution of wealth, and the rise of ethnic conflict in the Balkans have all led to a rise in mass migration to Western Europe. While non–European Union immigration slightly increased in traditional immigrant societies, such as France, Germany, and the United Kingdom, the most significant demographic changes occurred in southern Europe, where mass migration transformed previous emigration societies—most notably Italy, Spain, and Portugal—into new immigration states. This trend is illustrated in Table 5.1.

These demographic developments were accompanied by the political revolution caused by the end of the Cold War, which thawed European party systems. According to many scholars of Western European party politics, party systems were characterized by dealignment, evidenced by lower rates in voter turnout, ideological shifts within the established party families of the left and center-right, and the appearance of new parties such as the Greens and the radical right.

The combination of these two factors opened a window of opportunity for new xenophobic and authoritarian parties of the radical right. According to P. H. Merkl, "ultra-nationalist feelings and movements are back with a vengeance, like genies in the bottles in which they were so long confined."[1] The increased migration flows have led to an increase in racism in Western European society, based on both economic and cultural fears, paving the way for electoral gains by extreme-right parties. As Herbert Kitschelt explains:

> Whereas racism and ethnocultural parochialism were contingent phenomena in fascism that were in some movements replaced by militarism and nationalism, they are central components of the NRR [New Radical Right] appeal. While racist dispositions probably are always present in certain population groups, they become politically virulent for the contemporary NRR precisely because of the historical conjuncture of a rapidly changing occupational structure and an increasing international vulnerability of economic sectors in industry and services. On the level of direct economic interests, they are fueled by the fear of less-skilled workers and marginal small producers that they will be displaced by immigrants and foreign competitors producing with cheaper labor. On a deeper level, the multiculturalization of European societies offends individuals whose authoritarian dispositions and experiences harbor little tolerance for cultural and ethical difference and nonconformism. European fascist movements emerged before the advent of European multicultural societies; the NRR is in part the product of this process of multiculturalization.[2]

When the radical right enjoyed its first electoral gains in the 1980s, many scholars argued that it represented a protest vote against established political parties. The success of these parties in Western Europe throughout the 1990s

Table 5.1   Immigration in the European Union, 1985–1998

Country	Immigrants present 31 December 1985	Immigrants present 31 December 1998	Percentage variation 1985–1998
Austria	308,800	739,837	139.6
Belgium	860,600	864,616	0.5
Denmark	117,000	256,267	119.0
Finland	17,000	85,060	400.4
France	3,594,000	3,970,786	10.5
Germany	4,512,700	7,365,833	63.2
Greece	111,100	161,148	45.0
Ireland	91,300	111,100	21.7
Italy	318,700	1,250,214	292.3
Luxembourg	101,600	152,900	50.5
Netherlands	552,500	662,372	19.9
Portugal	79,600	177,774	123.3
Spain	293,200	719,647	145.4
Sweden	390,800	532,000	36.1
United Kingdom	1,785,000	2,120,600	18.8
European Union	13,133,900	19,170,163	46.0

Source: Caritas, *Immigrazione Dossier Statistico 2000*, Rome: Anterem, 2000.

demonstrates that they represent more than just a protest vote. In fact, radical-right parties have thrived on nationalist attitudes that have become part of the Western European political landscape. Recent opinion polls clearly illustrate significant levels of xenophobic and anti-immigrant attitudes in Western Europe. In 1991, Eurobarometer surveys reported that 51 percent of the respondents agreed with the statement, "There are too many non-EC nationals in the EC." The highest rates of agreement were found in Italy (64 percent), France, Belgium (56 percent), Germany (55 percent), and the United Kingdom (54 percent).[3] These sentiments have been confirmed by recent polls at both the European and national levels. A Eurobarometer survey conducted at the end of 1997 showed that 33 percent of those interviewed considered themselves to be "very racist" or "quite racist." National surveys reflect similar trends.[4] In France, two-thirds of those who responded to a poll conducted in 2000 claimed that there were too many North Africans in the country. In Italy, a survey that same year found that 73.5 percent of those who participated agreed that "the presence of immigrants increases crime rates."[5]

Xenophobic attitudes in Western Europe have also been highlighted by an increase in racist violence. In countries where statistics on antiforeigner, anti-Semitic, or extreme-right violence are kept, such as France, Greece, Denmark, and Spain, a clear increase of such crime is evident. The three most prominent cases are Belgium, the United Kingdom, and Germany. In Belgium, 919 complaints were registered in 1999, of which 101 were directed against the police or the gendarmerie. In England and Wales, more than 7,000 verbal and physical attacks attributed to extremist right-wing groups were reported. In Germany, neo-Nazi activity continues to be a pressing concern. The number of neo-Nazis increased to 9,000 in 1999 and the violent crimes they committed increased by 5 percent.[6] In 2000, after the German government began its campaign to ban neo-Nazi political parties, extreme-right violence erupted. Far-right crime increased to 998 offenses. Anti-Semitic crimes rose by 69 percent to 1,378, and 3,594 crimes against foreigners were registered, a 57 percent increase. The total number of right-wing crimes in Germany, including the display of nazi symbols and the distribution of propaganda, reached its highest level in the postwar period: 15,951 offenses, an increase of 59 percent over 1999.[7]

Due to this spread of nationalism and the fear of economic globalization, radical-right parties thrived in the 1990s. After early successes in Scandinavia on antitaxation platforms, a new radical right emerged in Western European politics mixing liberal economic-policy positions with ethno-nationalism. Piero Ignazi correctly divides the extreme right into two camps: traditional extreme-right parties versus postindustrial ones. This classification is illustrated in Table 5.2. Parties with traditional ties to fascism or nazism have been unable to overcome their ideological and historical baggage. These parties have never won more than 5–6 percent of the vote. Conversely, the postindustrial parties have filled the emerging spaces on the right of contemporary Western European party systems and have won significant shares of the vote. Most notably, the Austrian Freedom Party won 27 percent of the vote in the 2000

Table 5.2   Classification of Extreme-Right Parties

The Old Traditional Extreme Right-Wing Parties

Italy	MSI	(*Movimento Sociale Italiano*—Italian Social Movement)
Germany	NPD	(*Nationaldemokratische Partei Deutschlands*—German National Democratic Party)
Great Britain	BNP	(British National Front)
Netherlands	CP'86	(*Centrumpartij'86*–Center Party '86)

The New, Postindustrial Extreme-Right Parties

Austria	FPO	(*Freiheitliche Partei Österreichs*—Austrian Freedom Party)
Belgium	VB	(*Vlaams Blok*—Flemish Bloc); FNB (*Front National Belge*—Belgian National Front)
Denmark	FRPd	(*Fremskridtsparteit*—Progress Party)
France	FN	(*Front National*—National Front)
Germany	REP	(*Die Republikaner*—The Republicans)
Italy	LN	(*Lega Nord*—Northern Leagues)[a]
Netherlands	CD	(*Centrumdemocraten*—Center Democrats)
Norway	FRPn	(*Fremskrittspartiet*—Progress Party)

Source: Piero Ignazi, "The Extreme Right in Europe: A Survey," in *The Revival of Right-Wing Extremism in the Nineties,* edited by Peter H. Merkl and Leonard Weinberg. London: Frank Cass, 1997.

Note: a. Added to list by author.

general election, becoming that country's second party. In France, before the split of the National Front (FN), it received 10–15 percent of the vote between 1984 and 1998. In Italy, both the nationalist National Alliance (formerly the MSI) and the ethnoregionalist Northern League have attracted around 10 percent of the national vote. In certain regions, the Northern Leagues received more than 30 percent of ballots cast. Similarly, the Vlaams Bloc received more than 15 percent of the vote in Flanders (Belgium).[8]

One of the greatest perceived differences between traditional radical-right parties and the new extreme right is the willingness of the new parties to work within democratic structures and collaborate with mainstream parties. Mickenberg states, "They are 'extreme' not in terms of being against or outside the existing constitutional order but in terms of being extreme within that order."[9] However, this trait alone does not qualify new radical-right parties as "democratic." Hainsworth accurately refutes this notion on the basis that

> an anti-system party "abides by a belief system that does not share the values of the political order within which it operates" (Giovanni Sartori, *Parties and Party Systems*). Thus, espousal of narrow ethnically based, exclusionary representations of the nation, combined with authoritarian political perspectives, renders such parties as extremist, intolerant and suspect participants in the realm of constitutional politics.[10]

In fact, one cannot argue that the relationship between the radical right and constitutional democracy is one-dimensional. The recent success of these parties has profoundly affected these same systems. Many scholars note that the international liberal regime pressures countries to open borders, and adopt broader notions of citizenship, based on democratic values rather than ethnic affiliation. This obviously has not yet occurred in Western Europe. The radical right has forced mainstream political parties to adopt more protectionist immigration and refugee policies. This is most evident in France, Italy, Spain, and the United Kingdom. While mainstream political parties often publicly contest the radical right, they have been forced to shift their platforms toward positions made popular by these new parties. Their strategic shifts of position on immigration issues, influenced by the constraints placed on them by voters, demonstrate their limited ability to challenge the radical right and popular xenophobia.

The European Union's
Response to Immigration and Racism

For many years, the European Union was severely criticized, especially by those in the nongovernmental sector, for its lack of responsiveness to racism in Western Europe. Many critics even accused the EU of contributing to the rise of xenophobia. In fact, the EU did help create a negative atmosphere surrounding immigration politics through the establishment of the so-called Fortress Europe. In 1994, after the passage of the Schengen agreement, which abolished most of the EU's internal border controls, the European Council passed legislation severely limiting the immigration of non EU nationals. This measure restricted legal migration to Europe. However, its greatest impact on European migration politics may have been its symbolic value, framing immigration as a public security issue, with the subsequent result of "criminalizing" migrants. Moreover, it did force many immigrants into precarious social positions because they bypassed national controls and entered EU member states illegally. This further increased public fear of immigration and provided radical-right parties with ammunition for their nationalist agendas.

While such criticisms of EU policy are valid, they are not surprising given the traits of internal EU politics. The European Parliament (EP) has issued opinions and resolutions on racism in Europe since the 1970s. Most significant were the EP resolutions passed in 1995 (27 April and 26 October) on racism, xenophobia, and anti-Semitism, which outlined a program recognizing a need for EU action in the fight against racism and xenophobia. However, within the EU, the European Council is the most powerful institution and the EP is relatively weak. Because the council is composed of the leaders of EU member states, it is more responsive to national interests than it is to European ones. For this reason, the political and legal restriction of migrants in the EU reflected the domestic political climates described above.

Moreover, having come into existence as an economic institution, the EU had neither the legal structures nor the political culture necessary to adequately defend human rights or address racism within the EU. Until 1998, when the Treaty of Amsterdam was signed, there was no legally binding document in the EU that directly addressed either of these questions. EU "policy" in these fields was based on decisions made by the European Court of Justice and was limited in both scope and application.

Since 1995, the EU immigration agenda has slowly shifted. The external barriers to migration remain and have even been reinforced due to the harmonization of EU refugee and migration policies. This was especially evident during the recent crises in the Balkans, as less than 10 percent of the asylum seekers from the Balkans were granted asylum. However, the EU has begun to react to racism and xenophobia within its borders. In 1995, the European Commission and the European Council issued important resolutions on racism and xenophobia in employment, social affairs, and education. In 1996 a joint declaration against racism was issued by the Council, Commission, and Parliament. EU involvement in antiracist strategies became more concrete in 1997, officially declared the European Year Against Racism, as numerous initiatives were organized to combat xenophobia in the EU. The most significant of these was the establishment of the EU Monitoring Center for Racism and Xenophobia in Vienna, which opened its doors in April 2000.

The year 1998 was a watershed in EU antiracism politics. With the introduction of antidiscrimination clauses in the Treaty of Amsterdam, legal recognition of racism was finally adopted into law, permitting the Council, after the ratification of the treaty, "to take appropriate action to combat discrimination based on sex, racial or ethnic origin, religion or belief, disability, age, or sexual orientation," on the basis of proposals from the Commission. In addition, an EU action plan against racism was adopted by the Commission based on:

- Legislative initiatives to be based on the Amsterdam Treaty
- Integrating the fight against racism into community policies and programs
- Developing and exchanging new models in the fight against racism
- Strengthening information and communication work

Thus, whereas EU immigration policies once reflected the nationalist tendencies of domestic politics in Western Europe, they now include measures that combat xenophobia. This change in direction could have a major impact on the work of NGOs in this sector.

NGOs: Fighting Racism from Below

Western European governments have slowly begun to take action against the rise of racism and the radical right in Europe. However, these measures have already proven to be relatively ineffective. The most prominent example is the EU member states' failed boycott of Austria after the inclusion of the Freedom Party in the national government. On the domestic level, the German government has moved to ban the NPD for its ties with neo-Nazi groups. This well-intentioned measure has been criticized as "undemocratic" and, as mentioned above, it has led to mobilization of neo-Nazis. Many EU countries, such as Germany, France, Belgium, and the Netherlands, have passed specific antiracism laws. However, their impact has been limited due to uneven enforcement.

Government reaction to the rise of racism in Western Europe has been recent and limited compared to the activity of nongovernmental organizations in this field. NGOs have been more effective than governments in combatting racism and mediating conflict for three reasons. First, their organizational flexibility allows them to quickly implement social and educational programs, combating racism at its roots. Second, their grass-roots nature puts them in contact with local citizens, giving their work more legitimacy than government-sponsored initiatives. Third, NGOs are not constrained by voter preferences, providing freedom of action that governments do not enjoy. Moreover, their activities at the national and local levels are complementary. Locally, NGOs usually act as conflict mediators. Nationally, their work consists in lobbying against racism.

Local NGOs: Creating Communities

NGOs have been the most effective agents of ethnic integration at the local level in Western Europe. Their activities have focused on the cultural and economic fears that cause xenophobia. On a material level, NGOs provide basic services such as housing, legal assistance, and health care to recent migrants, especially those with irregular legal situations. However, the real value of NGOs has been their ability to construct communities and create channels of communication between migrants and local polities and societies.

Most studies of the radical right demonstrate that these parties reflect a negative perception of economic and cultural globalization. These factors have radically transformed the economic and social orders of European cities. The decline of industrialism and the shift toward technological and service economies has resulted in fractures in many European cities and increased unemployment in urban areas. Simultaneously, globalization has led to increased tourism and immigration that have, in the eyes of many, led to the degradation of local cultures.

NGOs have targeted their programs on these two issues. First, many NGOs have instituted programs aimed at economic integration. Cooperatives or social entrepreneurs offer job training and experience in the form of short-term employment, providing a bridge between the unemployed and local companies. Other NGOs offer business advice in order to promote entrepreneurship within marginalized segments of the population. NGOs also focus on urban regeneration, attempting to improve the social conditions of certain neighborhoods, in order to attract private investment. Along with these initiatives, NGOs have instituted educational and cultural programs aimed at interethnic communication. Through such initiatives, NGOs attempt to institutionalize social interaction, leading to constant cultural exchange and mutual respect.

It must be noted that these activities often call for partnerships between NGOs and local authorities, which create opportunity structures that influence the effectiveness of NGOs. In statist countries such as France, NGOs are usually restricted by rigid government regulations. Because the French government enforces detailed guidelines on NGO activity, the ability of the nongovernmental sector to react to conflict is reduced. Furthermore, because French policy does not recognize ethnicity, instead defining projects by neighborhood, NGO activity is limited on a geographic level. Many NGO representatives complain that initiatives are restricted to these zones of urban poverty, when social programs should focus on exposing youth to the possibilities available outside these areas.

In Italy, NGOs have been negatively influenced by the inefficiency of local government and the lack of state support. NGOs enjoy much more freedom than their French counterparts but also receive fewer economic and political resources from the state. This has led to fragmentation and competition within civil society, which has impeded program efficiency.

NGOs and National Politics

On the national level, NGOs have been active as political lobbies, and the recent increase in government attention to xenophobia can be viewed as a victory for nongovernmental activity. German NGOs have been protesting against neo-Nazi violence for years. In 2000, anti–neo-Nazi marches that attracted thousands of participants were organized in several cities, including Berlin, Dortmund, and Frankfurt. Similarly, the success of the Freedom Party in Austria led to a protest in Vienna that mobilized 200,000 people.

While such rallies demonstrate the organizational capabilities and political responsiveness of NGOs, their work cannot be reduced to such simple protest. NGOs have played key roles in ethnic mobilization and the creation of multicultural citizenship in Western Europe. In France, groups such as SOS Racisme, MRAP, and CIMADE have fought for immigrant rights since the late 1970s. Other groups, such as the Comite de Soutien des Sans Papiers and France Plus have provided migrants a means of expression in French politics and have openly challenged the republican model of citizenship. Such groups have also led the resistance to xenophobic nationalism, specifically, that espoused by the FN. Scholars of French politics correctly observe that French NGOs have met the political challenge of the FN through the use of similar symbols and tactics.

In Italy, NGO activity has greatly influenced immigration legislation passed in 1990 and again in 1998. Previously, Italian immigration law focused on public security and labor regulation. The 1990 legislation recognized the need to protect migrants from racist attacks, and to offer access to social services. The 1998 legislation expanded immigrants' rights and introduced tougher measures against discrimination. Italian NGOs, especially Caritas, also monitor ethnic tensions in the country. They publish annual studies on the situation of migrants in Italy and provide the government's Commission on Integration with information.

NGO activity has been essential to conflict mediation in Western Europe. At the local level, NGOs have played intermediary roles, acting as bridges between local migrant populations and native citizens and governments. At the national level, the nongovernmental sector has lobbied for tougher stances on racism and the defense of migrants' rights. With the expansion of the role of the EU, NGOs have even begun to organize on a European level in order to adopt broader tactics in the fight against racism.

Conclusion

The recent rise of anti-immigrant xenophobia has led to violent conflict in Western Europe. In just the first five months of 2001, there were three race riots in England, and numerous racially motivated killings in Scandinavia, Italy, and Germany. One of the factors that has perpetuated this climate of ethnic tension in Western Europe has been the recent success of the radical right in Western European party politics. Many studies have shown that the new radical right is not a single issue (anti-immigration) party. In fact, most of its support comes from more general antiglobalization reactions against perceived dislocation caused by international economic forces and, in many cases, the "Americanization" of European cultures. NGOs already address these fears in the local and national arenas. However, in order to improve their effectiveness, it is important that they globalize their efforts by participating more in EU politics.

In the past, NGO-EU relations were most frequent in the Parliament and the Commission. This limited the impact of NGOs on EU immigration politics because policy was made by the Council. Since 1997, the nature of this relationship has begun to change. The EU Monitoring Center on Racism and Xenophobia has been given the responsibility of coordinating the European Racism and Xenophobia Information Network (RAXEN). More than six hundred organizations are already collaborating with the Monitoring Center. The Commission and Council also have attempted to further include NGOs in the policymaking process and have increased funding to more than 10 million euros.

There are three major challenges that need to be overcome in order to solidify a working relationship between the EU and NGOs in the field of immigration politics. First, the EU has to improve its record on transparency. In order to improve the effectiveness of EU antiracism politics, they need to be made more public. Andrew Geddes correctly argues that the EU's democratic deficit "assesses the capacity of the Union in this policy area and notes a developing EU capacity for immigration and asylum controls, but a relatively underdeveloped capacity to deal with the problems of racism and xenophobia."[11] NGOs can provide valuable aid in this arena by monitoring and contributing to EU policymaking. If the EU is to become a continental political system, then the democratic deficit must be overcome and points of access for citizen participation must be opened. NGOs have already proven at the local and national levels that they can effectively mediate government-citizen relationships in the social sector.

Second, if NGOs are to collaborate more in EU politics, then a coordinated European third sector must be developed. Under the current system, NGOs often act as lobbies in competition for the same funding. These divisions have weakened the ability of NGOs to influence EU immigration politics. Because the EU has given priority to cross-national projects, some international cooperation already exists. However, the recently established networks of NGOs in Europe must be nurtured and consolidated if NGOs are to gain leverage in political competition at the EU level. Participation in networks such as the Council of Immigrant Associations in Europe, which includes representatives of over 2,500 immigrant associations, would also contribute to the formation of a European identity that would support the transition of political power to the EU and, consequently, combat the parochialism that is the foundation of radical-right support.

Finally, the approach utilized by many NGOs in the field of antiracism politics must be modified. Many NGOs working in this field follow what is known as the "human rights approach." This course of action is based on a strategy of publicly denouncing human-rights abuses and discrimination. Obviously, it is important that the public be informed of these issues and that pressure be exerted on violators. However, NGOs must also, at times, adopt a more "diplomatic approach," especially with the EU and member-state governments. By utilizing informal diplomacy or liaison diplomacy with national governments and leaders, it could be possible to further institutionalize antiracist and prointegration measures. In this way, mainstream party leaders could be persuaded to extend the rights of migrants at the national and European levels. If NGOs can institutionalize their already substantial efforts in the field of ethnic relations in Western Europe, they would be in a much stronger position to mediate conflict resulting from immigration. If NGO-government relationships are antagonistic, then efficiency suffers.

This conflict has had a significant impact on Western European democracies. Even though political parties are generally considered one of the bases of democratic systems, they have contributed to the xenophobia that is negatively affecting these systems. NGOs could play a more substantial role in strengthening European democracy at the local, national, and EU levels. The importance of these organizations in solidifying Eastern European political systems has been recognized by Western European leaders in the form of foreign aid. Their contribution to democratic stability and peace in Western Europe could be equally significant.

Harlan Koff is a Ph.D. candidate at the department of political science at Duke University (Durham, North Carolina) and teaches political science at Syracuse University's Center for European Studies in Strasbourg, France. Mr. Koff is the coordinator of the Ethnobarometer Research project on the integration of migrants in selected European cities.

Notes

1. Peter H. Merkl, "Introduction," in *The Revival of Right Wing Extremism in the Nineties,* edited by Peter H. Merkl and Leonard Weinberg. London: Frank Cass, 1997, p. 6.

2. Herbert Kitschelt, *The Radical Right in Western Europe,* Ann Arbor: University of Michigan Press, 1995, pp. 31–32.

3. Hans-Georg Betz, *Radical Right Wing Populism in Western Europe,* New York: St. Martin's Press, 1994, p. 82.

4. European Commission Report, *Racism and Xenophobia,* Eurobarometer Opinion Poll no. 41.1, December 1997.

5. Caritas, *Immigrazione: Dossier Statistico 2000,* Rome: Anterem, 2001, p. 207.

6. EU Monitoring Center on Racism and Xenophobia, *1999 Report*, pp. 20–21.

7. CNN.Com, "Race Crime Protests in Germany," 3 March 2001.

8. Paul Hainsworth, "Introduction," in *The Politics of the Extreme Right,* edited by Paul Hainsworth. London: Pinter Press, 2000, p. 2.

9. Ibid., p. 7.

10. Ibid., p. 7.

11. Andrew Geddes, "Immigrant and Ethnic Minorities and the EU's 'Democratic Deficit,'" *Journal of Common Market Studies* 33 (2), June 1995, p. 198.

6

The FRESTA Approach: Stimulating Cross-Border Connections in Civil Society

Michael Wagtmann

Peacebuilding in the Balkans moves ahead in starts and stutters, but even with much frustration, there are initiatives that provide examples of successful approaches that could be more widely applied in the Balkans and elsewhere. One of these approaches is the FRESTA initiative, from the Danish words freds *and* stabilitetsrammen—*peace and stability.*

The FRESTA initiative provides support to democratic institutions and structures, endeavors to strengthen civil society, works specifically in support of concrete reconciliation activities, and promotes cross-border collaboration. In the Balkans, FRESTA provides support to organizations in civil society addressing four targeted priorities: media, refugees, human rights, and youth. To achieve the cross-border collaborations that are central to the approach, it has established a number of networks that serve to promote and facilitate the exchange of information, training, provision of services, and collaborative activities among the network members. Because the situation is difficult and the dynamics are constantly changing, one of the most fundamental tenets of the approach is flexibility. And longer-term viability depends on the cultivation, at the earliest possible stage, of a sense of local ownership.

Regional Cooperation as a Prerequisite for Peace
In 1999, the Danish government established the FRESTA fund. At that time, it was decided that during the initial phase, special emphasis would be given to Southeastern Europe, but the FRESTA initiative is, in principle, global. The FRESTA initiative was launched against the backdrop of the continuing and prolonged conflicts in Southeastern Europe. Toward the end of the 1990s there was an increased awareness of the need for more emphasis on conflict prevention and peacebuilding, in addition to the focus on crisis management with humanitarian assistance and military involvement. Kosovo, for example, can be viewed as a conflict with vast human and material costs, which might well have been avoided if the right instruments had been applied in due time.

One aspect of the initiative was to draft a Danish Strategy for Conflict Prevention and Peace Building to cover all Danish activities by all branches of government and NGOs during all phases of conflict—conflict prevention, crisis management, and peacebuilding. The strategy is being developed with due attention to similar currently ongoing activities undertaken by the UN, the EU, NATO, and other countries. One of the most important objectives of the strategy is to be able to react in a timely and appropriate manner in such a way as to maximize the synergy between those Danish and international actors involved.

Southeastern Europe has been the scene of all the various phases of conflict for many years now, and the recent events in Macedonia indicate that there will be a need for conflict prevention and peacebuilding for a long time to come. From events in the region, it is clearly apparent that the root causes of the violent conflicts are complex, interrelated, and often of a regional nature.

The FRESTA initiative is based on four guiding principles of conflict prevention and peacebuilding—guiding principles that are being applied in Southeastern Europe and elsewhere. First, projects should support democratic institutions and structures, since democracies only very rarely wage war against each other. Second, lasting peace and stability can only be achieved by strengthening civil society. The establishment of democracy as such is not enough for the development of a pluralistic democratic culture in the population at large. Third, in civil societies that have been divided by propaganda and abuse of power, a reconciliation process must take place, but reconciliation can only be achieved through concrete, targeted activities. And fourth, regional cross-boundary civil-society collaboration is seen as a key to the achievement of lasting peace and stability, because of the regional nature of problems in connection with potential and manifest violent conflicts. To sum up: in Southeastern Europe, the FRESTA fund provides regional activity-oriented support to civil society—efforts that can pave the way for true democratic development, and peace and stability.

The FRESTA South East European Programme

The FRESTA South East European Programme facilitates civil-society collaboration across boundaries—geographical, religious, political, or professional. Civil society is relatively new in many parts of Southeastern Europe, but regional cooperation is not. Prior to the Balkan wars of the 1990s, regional cooperation was well established. The program, inter alia, aims to revitalize this cooperation by making it possible for civil-society organizations to meet within network structures. It supports activities in the priority areas of media, refugees, human rights, and youth.

The reasons for selecting these four specific areas are their direct relevance to civil society and conflict prevention/peacebuilding, and also the fact that Denmark has well-established civil-society organizations within these areas—organizations that are able to act as partners in assisting the networks. The Danish partner organizations are: the Danish School of Journalism, Baltic Media Centre (media), the Danish Refugee Council (refugees), the Danish Centre for Human Rights (human rights), the Danish Association for International Co-operation, and Danish Youth Council (youth).

The activities are coordinated within the network structures, which consist of civil-society institutions and NGOs. Many activities cover more than one area of priority—maintaining the ability to support activities that span these various priorities is seen as very important. Addressing refugee problems, for instance, involves media components (e.g., local radio broadcasts) to communicate with large groups of displaced persons. Moreover, securing proper living conditions and basic rights of returnees is both a refugee matter and a human-rights matter.

Flexibility in the South East European Programme is also of major importance. Within the network structures, new thoughts and ideas are being developed all the time—some of these ideas evolve into projects and end up being part of the actual program. This aspect of the program partly explains why the local participating actors have a real sense of ownership of the network processes. Local ownership is seen as fundamental, if the networks are to have real and positive effects, and it is, therefore, ultimately a prerequisite if the networks are to actually promote peace and stability. As soon as possible, the networks themselves should become self-sustaining, in effect gradually taking over coordination and facilitation of the supported activities.

The new situation in Serbia following the fall of Serbian president Slobodan Milosevic is an example of a positive development that requires flexibility and the ability to react swiftly and with the right partners to be able to support consolidation of democratic forces. The FRESTA fund has supported independent media both before and since the recent political changes in Serbia. Recently, within the human-rights area, the FRESTA fund has provided support to strategic reforms in the Serbian police and justice sectors.

FRESTA supports six networks in Southeastern Europe. There are three media networks—Professionalisation of the Media; Public Broadcasters; and Private Broadcasters, and one network within each of the other three areas of priority—a Human Rights Network, a Refugee Assistance Network, and a Youth Twinning Network. In the remainder of this chapter, the activities within these networks will be discussed. Since the recent developments in the Serbian Republic have created a mixture of new and ongoing activities that, taken together, best exemplify the FRESTA approach, examples from Serbia that have relevance for the region as a whole will be highlighted.

The Media

For years the combination of state control, censorship, lack of journalistic training, and poor working conditions made it difficult for the media in Southeastern Europe to provide balanced and nonbiased reporting to the public. Often, the media instead played a leading role in promoting hatred, intolerance, and nationalism. Control of the media in Southeastern Europe was tight, and as a result many skilled journalists fled their profession. Others established independent media outlets, which together constituted a significant platform for the process of democratization in most countries in the region. Because an independent media is a relatively new phenomenon, the majority of the people working in the independent media are young. Most of them share enthusiasm and dedication,

Albania:
Sunday morning in Tirana—going over the Socialist Party paper

but they only have limited formal training in journalism and little knowledge of professional ethics. Approximately 70 percent of those engaged in journalism today have worked in the media for seven years or less.

Previously only very few journalists had the opportunity to interact with colleagues in countries outside their own. The consequence of this professional isolation was the inability of journalists to put domestic issues into a regional context. The process of creating new media legislation and setting up independent regulatory bodies is now under way in most countries in the region. There is a need for cooperation among media institutions in the region, as well as a change in the mentality within political and media circles. The FRESTA program supports three networks that address media-related problems and challenges in a regional context: one network for professionalization of the media, which is involved in the training of journalists, and additional networks of public and of private broadcasters, each involved in the exchange of programs, among other things. The network of private broadcasters consists of local radio stations that serve as vital sources of information for both refugees and displaced persons, and for the general population.

Support to Serbian Independent Media
The support to Serbian media institutions was initiated well before the fall of the Milosevic regime. The network organizations invited independent Serbian press and media institutions to take part in the cooperation. Support was given to media and grass-roots organizations because of their potential to bring about democratic change. As a result of earlier connections, the institutions

that had benefited from the support were positioned in such a way as to exert considerable influence during the drafting of new Serbian media laws. These laws should facilitate the restructuring of state radio and television, provide for the training of journalists, and address the issues of professional ethics in journalism. Partly due to FRESTA funds, it has been possible to support and help consolidate a positive development at an opportune moment.

Human Rights

Building a culture conducive to respect for human rights is one of the major challenges facing Southeastern Europe. Recent history has witnessed atrocities and genocide, and the instability of the region has made entire ethnic groups vulnerable to violent persecution. There is a widespread lack of awareness of human rights, both among ordinary citizens and among upholders of law and order, and this lack of knowledge constitutes a threat to the democratic development that is slowly unfolding in the region. In this respect, human-rights organizations have a vital role to play by serving as positive examples for governments to follow in terms of cooperation across boundaries and ethnic differences.

The Balkan Human Rights Network focuses on the training of journalists, judges, lawyers, policemen, and other state officials. By providing education and raising awareness, the network believes it is possible to create a new culture of human rights that contributes to democratic development. Trainers are taught at the regional level to enable them to subsequently pass on their skills to the respective professional groupings at the national level. In addition, "human rights schools" are being organized by the network to bring human-rights standards to the attention of tertiary students, the future decisionmakers of Southeastern Europe. To further enhance ordinary people's access to and knowledge of human rights and responsibilities, public campaigns have also been undertaken, and a network database has been established.

In order to influence legislation at national and regional levels, the Balkan Human Rights Network focuses particularly on lobbying and advocacy work. The experience gained in this regard is of interest to all other networks supported by the FRESTA program. The Balkan Human Rights Network cooperates specifically with the South East European Network for Professionalisation of the Media by training journalists, editors, and others on human-rights issues.

Support to Reform the Serbian Police and Justice Sectors

A particularly relevant initiative within the human-rights area is the support for strategic planning for the reform of the Serbian police and justice sectors, which is effected by means of cooperation between the Serbian Ministries of the Interior and Justice and the Danish Centre for Human Rights. In addition, support is provided to begin the review and refinement of draft legislation on juvenile justice, and to assure the continued activities of the independent Belgrade Centre for Human Rights. In the current political situation in Serbia, there is now a unique opportunity to initiate reform processes at a time when a very real possibility exists to advance democratic development and to influence long-term positive prospects for peace and stability in Serbia, the Federal Republic of Yugoslavia, and the wider Balkans region.

Refugees

After a decade of civil war, millions of people in Southeastern Europe have been forced to leave their homes either as refugees or as internally displaced persons. In addition to the social and psychological problems for the people involved, the refugee crisis poses a threat to the economic development of the entire region. It is therefore of vital importance that the refugee problem be solved in order to achieve lasting peace and stability at a regional level.

A regional approach to the refugee problem is essential since displaced persons are often living in each other's homes, thus preventing return from taking place. Moreover, settlement of the refugee problem is impeded because the living conditions for the returnees are not secure, and there is inadequate information on services to meet basic needs such as health and education for children. To prevent instability related to the return of refugees, it is also essential to bring about reconciliation and to assure the economic self-reliance of the refugees.

The Refugee Assistance Network consists of more than twenty organizations active in repatriation assistance, promotion of self-reliance, provision of psychosocial assistance, and lobbying for and monitoring the adherence of refugee-related legislation to international standards. An important part of the activities of the network is to facilitate the free flow of information about the refugee and security situation between countries in the region. This information is not only important for the network itself, but also serves as a tool that can be used to influence public opinion. For this purpose a Refugee Radio Network has been established.

The Triangle Cooperation

Within the refugee network it soon became evident that there was a need for specific, targeted cooperation between NGOs in Croatia, Bosnia-Herzegovina, and Serbia on the repatriation of Serbian refugees. This so-called triangle cooperation was made possible with the change of government in Croatia in January 2000. With the support of the Danish Refugee Council, the participating organizations coordinated a dialogue along three main tracks: (1) the exchange of information, (2) the training of organizations in lobbying, and (3) the provision of legal counseling to returning refugees. In this way, the Refugee Assistance Network made it possible for organizations with a common interest in repatriation to engage in a practical dialogue. And with this dialogue, the possibilities to make a start on the return of Serbian refugees to Croatia have been significantly improved. The importance of a multidisciplinary approach to problem solving in Southeastern Europe is underlined by the fact that organizations and experts from the Human Rights Network have been involved in discussions on the legal rights of returning refugees. In addition, a media component (local radio) has been included in this work to broadcast relevant information to refugees.

Youth

The involvement of young people in the major changes taking place in Southeastern Europe is vital to ensure the consolidation of lasting peace and stability. Young people are not only the decisionmakers and heirs to the future—they also have the potential to contribute significantly to the process of overcoming the psychological and physical traumas of war. Because they are young, they are not as deeply rooted in bias, fear, and mistrust as older generations. Building on this potential is an essential component of FRESTA's South East European Programme.

In addition, the young people of Southeastern Europe experience many of the same kinds of problems, related to drugs, sex, AIDS, etc., as young people experience all across Europe and other parts of the world. There is a need to help the young to create space in their societies to deal with these issues alongside other issues. The South East European Programme supports a Youth Twinning Programme whose aim is to build the capacity of youth organizations in Southeastern Europe by twinning them with like-minded organizations in Denmark, thus creating new links between young activists across the region and in Europe.

The Youth Network aims to bring young people together, and to engage them actively in exploring and defining new democratic values and approaches. One of the core activities of the program is leadership training. The network offers young people in Southeastern Europe a chance to move to another part of their region to live and work for a period of time. The exchange program also provides the possibility for exchange between young Danes and Southeastern Europeans. Support is also given to regional work camps and the linking of these camps to the international work camp exchange system. In association with the program, support is provided to additional sporting and cultural activities.

Open Fun Football Schools

A very successful initiative within the youth sphere, though not directly sponsored by the Youth Network, is the Open Fun Football Schools project. The aim of this project is to create football schools in which children and young people can engage in sport together, across ethnic, political, and social divides, and in that way contribute to a general normalization of the situation and the reestablishment of confidence and tolerance between the different populations. The Football School project was initiated in 1998 in Bosnia-Herzegovina, and later also in Macedonia. During 2001, the project will be enlarged to embrace Montenegro and Serbia, including Vojvodina. Since its beginning, the project has enjoyed widespread local support at all levels, from the grass roots to the governmental level. So far, more than 13,000 children and 1,100 voluntary trainers have participated in the activities.

Interdisciplinary Activities

In dealing with the postconflict environment in Southeastern Europe, it has proven useful to be able to support activities that involve more than one of the four priority areas. This is especially evident within the refugee area, where the Refugee Assistance Network has developed activities cutting across the dividing lines between the priority areas and established relationships with most of the other networks in the FRESTA program. Examples include cooperation with one of the media networks on the exchange of news and programs among local radio stations. The Refugee Assistance Network also cooperates with the Human Rights Network in coordinating a refugee repatriation project, and in a project on national/regional legislative standards and practices, and the provision of legal advice at the local level. Another example of such interdisciplinary activity is the cooperation between the Refugee Assistance Network and the Youth Network in developing an initiative focusing on information, communication, and reconciliation.

Looking Ahead

The FRESTA program is based on a strong belief that the development of true democracy in Southeastern Europe must grow out of a strong, active, and regionally engaged civil society. The collaboration between FRESTA and the six networks in Southeastern Europe is still in its early stages, and at this point it is not possible to predict how the program will unfold in the years to come. Much depends on the developments taking place in the region. Accordingly, flexibility will remain an essential feature of the FRESTA approach.

Michael Wagtmann is head of the Secretariat for Peace and Stability Fund (FRESTA) of the Danish ministry of foreign affairs. The FRESTA fund supports civilian conflict prevention and peacebuilding measures. Prior to his present assignment, Michael Wagtmann served as ambassador to the Czech Republic. He has also been head of the Policy and Planning Department of the Danish International Development Agency (DANIDA).

7

Calling for a Broad Approach to Conflict Resolution[1]

Hugh Miall, Oliver Ramsbotham, and Tom Woodhouse

A broad conflict-resolution approach requires prevention, management, and transformation of deadly conflicts. Interventions across international frontiers are valuable, but the key goal should be strengthening the conflict-resolution capacity of societies and communities within conflict areas.

Conflict resolution as a defined specialist field has come of age in the post–Cold War era. The development of the field started to accelerate in the 1950s and 1960s, at the height of the Cold War, when the development of nuclear weapons and the conflict between the superpowers seemed to threaten human survival. A handful of people in North America and Europe began to establish research groups to develop new ideas, part of which derived from experience with conflict management in industrial relations and from community mediations. These people's efforts were not taken very seriously, but nevertheless, the new ideas attracted interest. The field began to grow and spread. Scholarly journals in conflict resolution were created. Institutions to study the field were established. By the 1980s, conflict-resolution ideas were also increasingly making a difference in existing conflicts, such as in Northern Ireland, where groups inspired by the new ideas had set up community-relations initiatives that were reaching across community divides.

By the closing years of the Cold War, the climate for conflict resolution was changing radically, which had a huge impact on the field. As a result of improved relations between the superpowers and a sharp rise in the number of ethnic and other types of internal conflicts, a climate arose in which the attention of scholars of international relations and comparative politics turned to exactly the type of conflict that had preoccupied the conflict-resolution thinkers for many years. A richer cross-fertilization of ideas developed between conflict resolution and the traditional fields.

A Wider View

One of the most outspoken new developments that surfaced in the post–Cold War era has been the shift of focus from international wars to internal conflicts. In response there has been a differentiation and broadening in the scope of third-party intervention. Whereas classical conflict resolution was mainly concerned with entry into the conflict itself and with how to enable parties in violent conflict to resolve the issues between them in nonviolent ways, the contemporary approach is to take a wider view of the timing of intervention. It suggests that efforts to resolve conflict should begin before armed conflict has started. They should be maintained even in the heat of battle and are applicable to peacekeeping and humanitarian intervention. Efforts also include assisting parties to settle violent conflicts. And conflict-resolution approaches continue to be relevant into the postsettlement phase, when peacebuilding must address the continuing issues in conflict.

More Attempts

As the concept of conflict resolution has gained currency, many more conflict-resolution attempts are being made. They involve different kinds of agencies, address different groups, and vary in form, duration, and purpose. Although the primary responsibility for responding to contemporary conflicts no doubt lies within the affected state, outsiders are inevitably involved as they often are part of the cause of a conflict or are affected by it. A large part of the outsiders'

UNICEF-sponsored class on landmine awareness. Showing a leaflet that describes different kinds of landmines in the village school of Zupa, near Dubrovnik, Croatia. Through the program, children have identified 6,500 landmines planted in the area, without a single casualty.

involvement in conflicts concerns third-party mediation by governmental actors, including the UN. It is ironic, however, that contemporary conflicts that, in an overwhelming amount of cases, reflect a weakening of state structures, the collapse of sovereignty, and a local breakdown in the state system, primarily rely on involvement of international institutions that are still based on precisely the system of sovereignty and noninterference that the new conflicts undermine. It is not surprising that the international community struggles to find effective means of response.

The United Nations has made several efforts to increase its role as a prime instrument through which the international community attempts to defuse crises and de-escalate conflicts, but the post–Cold War experience has been mixed, with notable successes (Namibia, Cambodia, El Salvador, and Mozambique) alongside dismal failures (Somalia, Bosnia, and Rwanda). The vital factor distinguishing success from failure has usually been not so much the UN institutions, but rather the policies of the major powers on the Security Council and the intractability of the conflicts themselves.

The UN's Agenda for Peace, issued in 1992, proposed that the UN should be involved in peacekeeping, peacemaking, and peacebuilding from the earliest stage of conflict prevention to the stage of postconflict reconstruction. The scope of UN action has certainly enlarged and, for all its weaknesses, the UN remains the only institutional expression of the international community as a whole in its conflict-resolution capacity. Regional organizations make up a second tier of external agents in contemporary conflict resolution. The member states of the Organization for Security and Cooperation in Europe have gone farthest in accepting a role for their regional organization in reviewing the human-rights and security practices of member states. The charter of the Organization of African Unity (OAU) precludes interference in the affairs of member states and has therefore been reluctant to involve itself in internal conflicts. However, in 1993 it set up the OAU Mechanism for Conflict Prevention, Management and Resolution (MCPMR) to provide assistance to states affected by war.

Indigenous Traditions

It is an undisputed fact that there are gaps in the coverage of internal conflicts by the official arms of the international community. This leaves space for humanitarian agencies and nongovernmental organizations to play a larger role. Agencies such as the International Committee of the Red Cross have taken on an enhanced profile in internal conflicts. NGOs have also become more important. The number of NGOs involved with conflict resolution increased rapidly in the 1980s, as development agencies, aid donors, and governments became willing to fund their activities.

Whatever the constraints on individual NGOs, as a whole, given their multiplicity and variety, they have the advantage of flexibility and adaptability. They are able to work with local protagonists without the worry of thereby conferring official recognition, and can operate at the grass roots as well as at some higher levels. NGOs have played a significant role in a number of peace-making breakthroughs, although in individual cases the appropriateness and effectiveness of particular NGO initiatives have been criticized.

The current trend in NGO interventions is moving away from entering into the conflict situations by outsiders, and toward training people inside the society in conflict in the skills of conflict resolution, and combining these with indigenous traditions.

Criticism

An increased presence and visibility of the conflict-resolution field over the past decade, along with a greater degree of impact, has also brought greater scrutiny on the theoretical level. Realists criticized conflict resolution as soft-headed and unrealistic. From a different angle, neo-Marxists and radical thinkers from development studies saw the conflict-resolution enterprise as misconceived, since it attempted to reconcile interests that should not be reconciled and failed to take sides in unequal and unjust struggles. Other critics were skeptical of overblown claims made for the field by conflict-resolution proponents. This latter group also questioned whether the models of conflict resolution that were developed during the Cold War still had application to post–Cold War conflicts.

This last criticism is the most challenging. Are we witnessing a fundamentally new kind of conflict, to which previous ideas do not apply? If modern conflicts are becoming neomedieval struggles between warlords, drug barons, mercenaries, and militias who benefit from war and have made it their only means of making a living, of what value will be efforts to resolve conflicts between them peacefully? Can conflict resolution apply in situations such as those that have prevailed in Bosnia, where ethno-nationalist leaders whipped up ethnic hatred and courted war in order to serve their own political purposes?

Appreciating the Role of Internal Parties

These questions led to new discussions and the taking of new positions in the field. We argue that the developing tradition of thinking about conflict and conflict resolution is all the more relevant as the fixed structures of sovereignty and governance break down. All over the world, societies are facing burdens from population growth, structural change in the world economy, migration into cities, environmental degradation, and rapid social change. Societies with institutions, rules, or norms for managing conflict, and well-established traditions of governance are generally better able to accommodate peacefully to change; those with weaker governance, fragile social bonds, and little consensus on values or traditions are more likely to buckle. Strengthening the capacity of conflict resolution within societies and political institutions, especially preventively, is a vital part of the response to the phenomena of warlordism and ethno-nationalism.

We approve of a shift from seeing third-party intervention as the primary responsibility of external agencies toward appreciating the role of internal third parties or indigenous peacemakers. Instead of outsiders offering the fo-rums for addressing conflicts in one-shot mediation efforts, the emphasis should be on the need to build constituencies and capacity within societies and to learn from domestic cultures how to manage conflicts in a sustained way over time. This implies supporting domestic peace constituencies, developing domestic institutions, and eliciting from those in conflict what approaches are socially and culturally acceptable.

Behind all this lies an increased sensitivity to the culture question in gen-eral and the hope that if the conflict-resolution field has in the past been too narrowly Western, it may in the future become the truly cooperative cross-cul-tural venture that its founders conceived it to be. We emphatically argue that although the theories and practices of conflict resolution we deal with spring from Western roots, every culture and society has its own version of what is, after all, a general social and political need. The point is not to abandon con-flict resolution because it is Western, but to find ways to enrich Western and non-Western traditions through their mutual encounter. It is in the encounter with local traditions that important lessons about conflict resolution are being learned, particularly about the limitations of the dominantly Euro-American model. In his study of the Arab Middle East, for instance, Salem has noted a "rich tradition of tribal conflict management [that] has thousands of years of experience and wisdom behind it."[2] Such perspectives are now beginning to emerge in current understandings and practices of conflict resolution.

A Broad Approach

We also argue for a broad understanding of conflict resolution. It would be wise to include not only mediation between the parties but also efforts to address the wider context in which international actors, domestic constituencies, and intra-party relationships sustain violent conflicts. The implication of this broadening of scope and applicability of conflict-resolution approaches has been to see the need for a complementary range of third-party interventions. They should be multitrack instead of just Track I (governmental) or Track II (NGOs, churches, civil society, etc.), and address both elites and the grass roots.

A broad view of conflict transformation is necessary to correct the mis-perception that conflict resolution rests on an assumption of harmony of in-terests between actors, and that third-party mediators can settle conflict by ap-pealing to the reason or underlying humanity of the parties. On the contrary, conflict transformation requires real changes in parties' interests, goals, or self-definitions. These may be forced by the conflict itself, or may come about because of intraparty changes, shifts in the constituencies of the parties, or changes in the context in which the conflict is situated. Changes in the context in which a conflict is embedded may sometimes have even more dramatic ef-fects than changes within the parties or in their relationships. The end of the Cold War—to give an example—is the prime recent context transformation that has shown to unlock protracted conflicts in South Africa, Central Amer-ica, and elsewhere.

Robust Interventions

In line with the necessity of a broad view, conflict resolution should concern itself not only with the issues that divide the main parties, but also with the social, psychological, and political changes that are necessary to address root causes, the intraparty conflicts that may inhibit acceptance of a settlement, the context that affects the incentives of the parties, and the social and institutional capacity that determines whether a settlement can be made acceptable and workable. In other words, a multitrack approach is necessary, relying on interventions by different actors at different levels.

Looking back on recent history, one can safely say that some interventions and negotiated settlements are more robust than others. Although generalization is treacherous, successful settlements are thought to have the following characteristics: first, they should include the affected parties. The parties are more likely to accept a settlement if they have been involved in the process that reaches it; this argues for inclusiveness and against imposed settlements. Second, settlements need to be well crafted and precise, especially as regards details over transitional arrangements—for example, demobilization assembly points, cease-fire details, and voting rules. Third, they should offer a balance between clear commitments and flexibility. Fourth, they should offer incentives for parties to sustain the process and to participate in politics, for example through power sharing rather than winner-take-all elections. Fifth, they should provide for dispute settlement, mediation and, if necessary, renegotiation in case of disagreement. And sixth, they should deal with the core issues of the conflict and bring about a real transformation, incorporating norms and principles to which the parties subscribe, such as equity and democracy, while at the same time creating political space for further negotiations and political accommodation.

Hugh Miall is lecturer at the Richardson Institute of Peace studies, Department of Politics and International Relations, University of Lancaster. Oliver Ramsbotham is senior lecturer in Peace Studies, University of Bradford. Tom Woodhouse is codirector of the Centre for Peace Studies, also at the University of Bradford.

Notes

1. This is an authorized summary of *Contemporary Conflict Resolution* by Hugh Miall, Oliver Ramsbotham, and Tom Woodhouse, Oxford: Polity Press/Blackwell Publishers, 1999.

2. Paul Salem (ed.), *Conflict Resolution in the Arab World: Selected Essays.* New York: American University of Beirut, 1997, p. 95.

8

The State of the Art of Conflict Transformation

Kevin Clements

The field of conflict resolution/conflict transformation is still in a dynamic stage of evolution. It is an evolving sphere or interdisciplinary endeavor that has both theoretical and practical implications. This chapter will begin with a map of the field and an assessment of the state of the art. It will then analyze and assess these schools of thought by identifying trends or themes within the different perspectives. This will be followed by a critique of the field and recommendations for improving the theory and practice of conflict transformation.[1]

Conflict resolution as a field is divisible into four general theoretical and practical schools:

1. Alternative dispute resolution (ADR)
2. Political and public policy conflicts
3. Analytical conflict resolution
4. Forgiveness and reconciliation

These schools operate at different levels and with different major actors. The ADR and political and public policy schools, for example, normally focus on community and national levels in countries with stable political and economic systems. The analytic and reconciliation schools normally concentrate on intractable conflicts in countries or regions with unstable political and economic systems.

There are two major types of intervening actors. Track I actors are official, diplomatic, and governmental, while Track II actors are informal and unofficial academic, voluntary, or nongovernmental actors. Track I interventions range from official and noncoercive measures such as "good offices," "fact-finding missions," "facilitation," "negotiation/mediation," and "peacekeeping" to coercive measures such as "power-mediation," "sanctions," "peace enforcement," and "arbitration." Track II activities refer to all noncoercive and nonofficial measures such as "facilitation," "informal consultation processes," interactive "problem solving," and the generation of safe spaces for dialogue between conflicting parties.

An Overview of the Schools

Whatever the level or type of operation, the underlying theoretical assumptions of each theory are good predictors of general orientations to change and transformation. The ADR school, for example, is not aimed at changing basic social institutions but simply making them work better. It fulfills useful purposes in society and is used to develop specific skills and processes of mediation and arbitration. Many within this school refer to their work as conflict management. ADR practitioners focus their efforts primarily on negotiation, mediation, arbitration, ombudsmanry, and negotiated rule making.[2] Although the intentions of ADR practitioners may differ, usually this school simply reinforces the sociopolitical status quo. It does not challenge accepted values or established institutional arrangements.

The school that deals with political and public-policy disputes embraces the idea that the promise of conflict resolution can best be realized in the realm of social engineering by making public-policy processes more transparent, more accessible, and therefore better. It is based on incorporating all relevant stakeholders into decisionmaking processes and argues that pragmatic incremental reform (based on inclusive and collaborative relationships) is the best method for resolution. This consensus-based model for public-policy disputes grew exponentially during the 1980s, partly as a response to the turbulent social debates and policymaking failures of the 1960s and 1970s and partly by the recognition that adversarial winner-takes-all approaches to public-policy conflicts were not the best way of solving complex economic, social, and environmental problems.[3]

The perspective of analytical conflict resolution and problem solving argues that each minor or major conflict (especially those that are violent) represents an invitation to explore better and different ways of organizing social and political relationships. It suggests that each conflict represents broken or traumatized personal, social, community, and political relationships. As such, the role of the conflict analyst, in conjunction with the parties, is to analyze the origins of the conflict and then jointly determine the most satisfying solution(s) for all parties. Sometimes this might be a permanent separation of the parties, while other times it might involve the reconstitution of problematic relationships so that they cease being dysfunctional and become functional for the development of human community. This perspective normally concentrates on deep-rooted and intractable conflicts and, unlike ADR and the public-policy approach, is deliberately transformational.

This orientation unequivocally views conflict analysis as a critical force in sociopolitical transformation. It seeks to change attitudes, behavior, and contexts so that individuals can realize their own potential in collaboration with, rather than in opposition to, each other. Of course this perspective only works if it takes into account a variety of different structural and proximate causes of conflict and seeks ways and means of dealing with both. The challenge facing the analytical problem-solving school is nothing less than that of dealing with both direct and indirect sources of conflict. This is a challenge because of the complex nature of most violent conflict. As recent commentators have argued:

> Economic, political and cultural sources [of violent conflict] are intertwined; economic stagnation or collapse, especially when coupled with large disparities among groups (horizontal inequality) and individuals (vertical inequality), spur political discontent, which leaders use to mobilize people to support their struggles for power, thus deepening and exploiting perceived cultural differences. Group differences, based on differences in ethnicity, race, religion, caste or class, are reinforced, and sometimes created, by the conflict. While these differences are not the primary cause, they acquire an independent force that makes peacemaking difficult. Moreover, in war, collective action is the consequence of individual decisions. Individuals' political and economic aims may be served by war. Such motivation fuels and may even cause conflict.[4]

The challenges facing analytical problem solvers, therefore, are those of separating all the diverse needs that individuals, groups, and larger collectivities have; ascertaining whether or not these are being satisfied (and by whom); and then identifying satisfiers acceptable to all parties.[5] John Burton, who is an exemplary figure in this school, argues very strongly that there is a need to develop new ways of not only solving "puzzles" (which are prima facie solvable) but also solving "problems" (which are prima facie not necessarily solvable). The latter require much more explicit attention to questions of process, power, and relationships.

The assumptions that underlie the forgiveness and reconciliation school are slightly harder to define. Scholars debate whether this perspective is essentially a set of techniques, a political philosophy, an analytic perspective, a systemic vision for peace, or a spiritually inspired utopia. The reconciliation school represents an acknowledgment that conflictual relationships will only become cooperative if there is a commitment to the pursuit of peace, justice, compassion, forgiveness, and sustainable development. These aspirations are profoundly religious and critical components of most utopic and religious visions. In the Bible, for example, the Psalmists look forward to the time "love and faithfulness meet together and righteousness and peace kiss each other" (Psalm 85). In the religious traditions of Buddhism, Islam, and Hinduism there are equally strong commitments to peace and justice. The concepts of paradise and nirvana, for example, all have strong connotations of justice, harmony, nonviolence, and union. These aspirations are religious ways of saying that most people in most communities and cultures—confronted with choices between order/chaos; peace/war; harmony/disharmony; structural stability/instability; equality/inequality; inclusion/exclusion; justice/injustice; tolerance/intolerance; abundance/poverty—will, wherever possible, choose the former over the latter.

The reconciliation perspective, therefore, is both religiously inspired and potentially transformative but not in the narrow political or Track I diplomatic sense. Rather it is transformative in the sense of a tectonic shift in consciousness and behavior that will take a multitrack or systemic approach to really build sustainable peace. The reconciliation school, therefore, will only fulfill its total promise if all goals are pursued simultaneously and conjunctively.[6]

Theory and Practice

As can be seen from these perspectives, the field of conflict resolution has both conservative and radical utility. Where agreement exists about central social values and institutions, then ADR, as the utilization of conflict-resolution techniques to make basically sound institutions work better, is perfectly acceptable. Where there is disagreement on the central values and institutions, then an application of ADR or public-policy techniques may be inappropriate, or worse, prevent the transformation of relationships that need to change if human security is to be achieved. The field can, therefore, be divided into those that see their role in largely therapeutic terms and those with more structural transformational orientations.

The disciplines of psychology, counseling, education, philosophy, religion, and social work inform the therapeutic model. The underlying assumption is that changing individuals is the goal, and that by transforming their attitudes, behavior, and orientations, society will be transformed.

The structural model, on the other hand, assumes that individuals choose conflicts in order to optimize favorable outcomes for themselves or the groups of which they are a part. The disciplines that inform the structural model are political science, sociology, international relations, systems engineering, physics, economics, and business. Within this model, individuals and groups have to believe that they are politically effective and can make a difference to the structural sources of conflict. This may mean incremental social engineering or deliberate efforts to achieve just social change and reconciliation. Reconciliation between formerly warring parties is the place where peacemaking, long-term peacebuilding, and conflict resolution come together.

What is clear is that the field has been diffident about separating therapeutic from structural perspectives since good structural transformation needs to be processually sensitive and vice versa.

For those who imbed their analysis and practice in conflict-and-change theory, more weight, however, is given to processes of empowerment and liberation from dependent and unequal exchange processes. Those who understand both power and the economy will ensure that peacebuilding is as much about unmasking the sometimes latent sources of power and equalizing unequal relationships as it is about solving manifest problems.[7] This is an important antidote to those who see their role in more therapeutic and establishment terms. Construed in this way, conflict resolution is radical and should be aimed at enhancing freedom, justice, and autonomy. This perspective is very worrying to establishment-oriented conflict resolvers concerned more about preserving harmony and order than achieving justice and peace.

This general division into therapeutic and structuralist perspectives is reflected in different professional conflict-resolution training programs. There are currently over two hundred programs that provide conflict-resolution training both inside and outside of university settings.[8] They come in many forms, but three basic distinctions can be made between programs that are (1) religiously informed, (2) international in focus, and (3) dispute-resolution oriented. Each of these groups has specific theoretical foundations that inform their work.

Approximately eighty programs approach peace and conflict resolution from a religiously informed perspective.[9] Although the religious denominations of the universities that have such programs are quite diverse, a number are associated with the historic peace churches, the Quakers and Mennonites. Some examples are Eastern Mennonite University, Earlham and Haverford Colleges (Quaker), Notre Dame University (Roman Catholic), and Brandeis University (Jewish). The programs that have religious affiliations seem to be conducive to the schools of reconciliation and analytical conflict resolution discussed above. Their "peace with justice" orientation results in structural perspectives that challenge and are aimed at transforming fundamental economic and political processes.

Those programs focused on international conflict resolution draw theory from interdisciplinary sources such as human needs, consensus building, social change, and analytical problem-solving workshops. Primary programs within this group are George Mason University's Institute for Conflict Analysis and Resolution, Syracuse University, University of Colorado–Boulder, and American University. The Carter Center in Atlanta is a practitioner-based organization that also works to transform conflict through a combination of direct intervention in crises alongside structural prevention of the underlying causes of conflict and violence.

Analytical conflict resolution and reconciliation programs are mainly focused on analyzing the deep roots of intractable conflicts and on challenging the political, economic, and social systems that give rise to and perpetuate conflict cycles.

Programs in the dispute-resolution category are informed by traditional negotiation and bargaining theory, legal processes, and Track I diplomacy. Not unsurprisingly, they are located at well-established universities such as Harvard, Stanford, Boston University, and MIT. With the rapid professionalization of the conflict-resolution field, it is the institutions in this dispute-resolution group that are most visible. This category of programs emerges from a general ameliorative/therapeutic framework and is more interested in bettering the existing political and economic structures than in reinventing them.

Peacebuilding strategies, on the other hand, seek to address the underlying causes of violent conflicts and crises either to prevent violent conflict or to ensure that violence will not recur. Nafziger Stewart, and Vayrynen argue that preventive policies need to be applied to all countries vulnerable to conflict, which includes all countries exhibiting sharp horizontal inequalities, all low income countries, all countries with negative growth and countries which have had serious conflict over the past quarter of a century. Preventive action needs also to be concerned with countries in which the state is fragmenting and cannot govern the society in a legitimate manner.[10]

Long-term peacebuilding strategies, therefore, have a strong preventive character to them and aim at meeting basic needs for security and order, shelter, food and clothing, and for recognition of identity and worth. It is the foundational basis of conflict transformation and occurs at all levels of activity.

Analytical problem-solving workshops address many of these issues by focusing on unsatisfied human needs.[11] They have, however, been preoccupied largely with political issues rather than issues of justice—although the two are linked. Relatively few problem-solving workshops assign primacy to economic- and social-development issues as a means to resolving political and military conflicts. By not paying attention to economic and social issues, many problem-solving workshops, therefore, deal with symptoms rather than the underlying economic and social asymmetries that underpin many modern conflicts.

On the other hand, therapeutically oriented peace processes between warring parties in the Caucasus, for example, are often undermined because they do not rest on solid economic and social foundations. This means that efforts to build trust and confidence or generate political and military security within the region are subverted by elite corruption and minimal attention to the role of the public sector in rectifying horizontal and vertical inequalities.

Some theorists argue that a concentration on economic and political factors is insufficient and that equal attention should be given to the religious dimensions of conflict resolution and social engineering. This is because religious or humanitarian values can prompt people to make the sacrifices necessary to build and rebuild peaceful communities for the future.

In all of these perspectives, conflict theorists underline the importance of holistic analysis and holistic solutions. Efforts to resolve conflicts by simple attitudinal, behavioral, or situational changes alone will never result in either their resolution or transformation. Most of the conflicts in the new war zones have to be linked firmly to sustainable economic development and democratization strategies if they are to be dealt with adequately.

Selecting the Best Approaches

The theoretical classifications outlined above integrate often disparate and even contradictory assumptions, but we are still left with a question about whether the field offers any overarching themes or visions. Namely, what is the promise and what are the essential ingredients of conflict resolution and transformation?

1. Conflict resolution and transformation aim to channel the energy generated by conflict in constructive and nonviolent ways rather than destructive

and violent directions. Its aim is not to eliminate conflict but to utilize conflictual processes for generative and positive change (which may be relatively spontaneous or directed). In this way, conflict transformation works to develop resilient personal and social systems where human security is enhanced by the quality of community relationships.

2. Conflict transformation occurs when violent conflict ceases and/or is expressed in nonviolent ways, and when the original structural sources of the conflict (economic, social, political, military, and cultural) are changed in some way. The propensity for violence is diminished by democratization, demilitarization, de-alignment, socioeconomic development, and expansion of human rights, humanitarian law, and sociocultural openness.

3. Conflicts can be transformed by normal sociopolitical processes (incremental changes over time), by the parties acting alone, by expert third-party intervenors and parties acting together, or by judicious advocacy and political intervention. Depending on whether the conflicts are personal, national, regional, or global, the intervenors can be governmental, intergovernmental, or nongovernmental. Good conflict resolution should incorporate a wide cross-section of political decisionmakers, citizens, aid and development agencies, religious organizations, businesses, and social movements. Too often in the past, conflict transformation has been conceptualized largely as a political problem. It has to be cast as a social and economic problem as well if structural change is to occur and sustainable peace and development is to ensue.

4. Conflict resolution and transformation can take place at any stage of the escalatory cycle. Ideally, before there is any hint of an escalating problem, effective peacebuilding should remove the conditions for violence and war. If this does not happen in the early stages of an evolving conflict, conflict-management processes may simply take the form of an early warning system and apply suitable preventive measures. As the conflict escalates (especially if it turns violent), its transformation may depend on some kind of crisis management or intervention. Later, it may require conciliation, mediation, negotiation, arbitration, and collaborative problem-solving processes. In the end, any lasting conflict transformation involves processes of resolution, reconstruction, and reconciliation.

Analysis and Critique of the Field

The field of conflict analysis and resolution/transformation has now reached a point in its development when it can be evaluated both in terms of its theoretical development and also its contribution to the peaceful nonviolent solutions to problems. At a theoretical level, the results are mixed. The field continues to be strongly influenced by a variety of social-science disciplines. Both psychology and communications theories, for example, have contributed a good deal to the emergence and refinement of negotiations and bargaining theory. International relations and political science have also made their own distinctive contributions to the field.

What is lacking, however, is a synthetic theory that combines these different disciplinary perspectives into a separate interdisciplinary field of inquiry. There are a number of reasons why this has not happened. The field itself is a new one and most of its theorists have come out of specific social-science disciplines. It is natural, therefore, that the initial work should have a disciplinary base. Second, because the field can be divided, for heuristic purposes, into ameliorators and transformers, there is little agreement on the central theoretical assumptions of the field. Those who adopt a transformative perspective tend to rest their analyses on human needs and/or sociopolitical structural theory, for example, whereas those who are primarily interested in integrative or distributive bargaining base their analyses and actions on rational-choice models of behavior. Those who see their role therapeutically tend to adopt psychological or counseling models. The theorist who comes closest to developing an integrated model of the field, John Burton, argues that conflict resolution should be the basis of a new nonadversarial political philosophy.[12]

By and large, however, there have been few attempts to synthesize micro and macro theories of conflict resolution. There have also been few studies of the ways in which microprocesses (e.g., confidence-building workshops, safe spaces for dialogue and mediation, etc.) articulate to the wider macroprocesses (e.g., official negotiations, macroeconomic strategy, and coercive capacity).

The combination of psychological, social-psychological, and interpersonal-communications theories with political, economic, and social structural theories is critical if conflict resolution is to fulfill its nascent promise.[13] Perhaps one of the reasons this has not occurred so far has been an uneasy tension within the field itself between theorists and practitioners.

While there is no denying that processes of recognition, affirmation, and sensitive listening are critical to the success of macro development and reconstruction processes, it is also clear that they are not sufficient to deal with indirect structural violence or even direct violence flowing from collapsed economic and political systems. For this to occur, greater attention must be paid to the structural sources of violent conflict in order to identify alternative pathways.

Chris Mitchell bridges the micro-macro split in the field by emphasizing the triangular nature of all conflicts and the importance of identifying the interrelationships between social, political, and economic situations, individual and collective attitudes, and specific behavior.[14] Only by understanding how these different dimensions interact with each other will we have any chance of understanding what changes need to be made to the political, economic, or social systems within which the conflicts are taking place. What is becoming more obvious as the field evolves, however, is that structural location of conflicting parties and whether the adversaries are equal or unequal in terms of position and resources—not to mention questions about the number of issues at stake and the length of time that they have been on the table—all have powerful effects on the possibility of short- and long-term solutions to conflict. The major challenge facing both theorists and practitioners is how to engage these complexities in ever more creative ways.

1. This probably means a closer relationship between theorists and practitioners. Theorists need to be challenged by practitioners about which of their theories best helps explain violent situations and which best helps them design processes for dealing with them. Practitioners interested in helping parties to devise durable solutions to their problems also need to be informed about which practices work and which do not and what is likely to reinforce or undermine agreements. The challenge to theorists, therefore, is working out ways of ensuring that their micro and macro explanations are connected to the daily dilemmas of intervenors in the field. The challenge to practitioners is to imbed their daily work in a theoretical and research context that enables them to gain a wider perspective on their problems than they might otherwise receive simply by applying tried and tested techniques to conflicts.

2. The evolution of the field of conflict resolution requires an acknowledgment of its dual role as an agency of both control and change. Both of these tendencies need to be held in tension. Transformation without some sense of how to maintain order and continuity will generate anarchy. The maintenance of order without some sense of how to alter dysfunctional relationships and institutions in a positive direction will generate repressive and oppressive conditions. The challenge facing conflict resolutionaries is how to facilitate changes that will eliminate the root causes of conflict by handling contradictory and conflictual relationships in a nonviolent and generative fashion. Thus conflict transformation, of which peacebuilding and problem-solving processes are two critical elements, is primarily about social and economic change and a quest for justice and peace by peaceful means. Genuine conflict resolution or problem solving always involve some implicit or explicit agreement about the notion of justice. Ignoring concepts of justice will not result in positive or durable agreements.

3. The third prerequisite for enhancing conflict-resolution theory and practice is the application of an ethical framework that ensures that movement toward peace and justice will be by peaceful and just means. There is no agreement within the conflict-resolution field, for example, of anything comparable to the fundamental principles of the International Red Cross and Red Crescent movements, although organizations such as International Alert and the Berghof Institute, for example, have developed codes of conduct to guide their own practice in field situations. An internationally agreed code of ethics for conflict resolutionaries would guarantee higher levels of responsibility and accountability than now. It would ensure collaborative arrangements with groups such as the Red Cross and others empowered to deal with complex and violent humanitarian emergencies.

4. A fourth area that would help both theorists and practitioners lies in the area of distilling information and heightening coordination, especially in field situations. Just as good military operations require effective command, control, communication, and intelligence systems, so too do those designing processes for dealing with violent conflicts. Intelligent information about the

parties to the conflict, detailed awareness of its sources, and a sound nonethnocentric appreciation of the cultural framework surrounding the conflict are all critical to successful outcomes. Success also requires high linguistic competence on the part of intervenors, clearer maps of the field and identification of roles within it, and high levels of reality-based optimism about what conflict resolution can or cannot deliver.

Finally, and somewhat paradoxically, conflict resolution will discover its own distinctive niche in the field not by separating itself from the painstaking processes of democratization, building civil society, and leadership and management training, but by joining with those engaged in these activities and working out what distinctive role conflict-resolution professionals might play in them. Thus, the structural prevention of violent conflict requires conflict resolutionaries joining forces with socioeconomic- and political-development specialists and thinking through what conditions are essential for the advancement of human security as opposed to state and national security.

The World Bank, for example, notes that fifteen of the twenty least-developed countries in the world have been involved in major violent conflicts; and over half of all low-income countries have been involved in major evil conflicts during the past fifteen years.[15] Major development institutions are appalled at the ways in which decades of cumulative development investment has been wasted through the destruction of infrastructure, capital flight, and the squandering of human capital through hundreds of thousands of casualties and permanent emigration.

It is in relation to these sorts of issues that there should be a strategic marriage between collaborative analytical problem-solving workshops and specific peacebuilding processes, especially those connected to a wider variety of economic- and social-development initiatives.

Interactive problem-solving methods might be used to combine the development and conflict-resolution discourses, since these methods result in (1) identification and analysis of the problem; (2) joint shaping of ideas for solution; (3) influencing the other side; and (4) creating a supportive political environment.[16] These are not only critical backdrops to deeper understandings of the dynamics of the conflict; they are all absolutely critical to the development of a successful peacebuilding strategy as well.

Conclusion

The world clearly needs some new ways of thinking about old problems and new ways of acting if we are going to survive through the twenty-first century. This is why the future of peace and conflict studies is inextricably linked to global survival and a rigorous quest for what the United Nations Development Program calls *human security*. This is the security that is the right of all human beings. It is not state nor ethnic security, but a security aimed at protecting all peoples and it can only be achieved if political and economic institutions make it a priority.

The challenge facing peace and conflict studies, therefore, is to think of new ways of doing politics and of building moral conventions that will generate safe action spaces for all peoples to begin solving the big problems that afflict the globe. One of the reasons for doing this is the perception that adversarial politics (from the microcosm of the family to the community, national, and international levels) are proving more dysfunctional than functional.

Peace and conflict studies need to articulate some philosophical justification for the development of collaborative and analytic problem-solving processes as an alternative to more coercive and forceful processes. Conflicts in the Caucasus and other parts of the former Soviet Union are salutary reminders of the potency of ethnically based identities and the disastrous consequences of diverse politicians and military actors manipulating ethno-nationalist sentiments in order to maintain power and control. When ethnically based politics are activated in countries with weak or illegitimate political regimes and the groups concerned have adopted armed strategies or terrorism to assert their collective identities, then authoritarian and repressive responses are highly probable. If these conditions overlay adverse economic and social conditions, there is a very high probability of coercive politics and violent conflict. Thus, the central challenge for conflict analysts and resolutionaries is how to ensure that negative elements are preempted and transformed into virtuous rather than vicious cycles.

In the first place, we need to start looking for what Elise and Kenneth Boulding call "signals of peace" or what Jim Wallis calls "Signs of Transformation."[17] These are nonviolent opportunities for creative solutions in moments of tension and in relation to all social and political problems. It also means working to ensure that "Community" becomes the moral foundation for economics, diversity, justice, and reverence for the whole of creation.[18]

In these processes it is absolutely vital that problems/conflicts are dealt with as early as possible, when they are relatively tractable. This suggests that we need to devote more attention to developing early warning of potential problems and crises and develop the will to start addressing them before they go critical. Thus, when we discern yawning gaps between rich and poor (with no prospect of immediate or short-term amelioration), we should take this as an indicator of potential conflict sometime in the future. Similarly, when we see identity groups, epistemic communities, and opinion leaders engaged in divisive, polarizing processes, this is a signal that a problem may be brewing and that it may require some problem-solving intervention.

Perhaps most importantly we need to teach everyone how to resolve conflicts and problems in a nonviolent and creative fashion. This is a major challenge for education but it goes to the heart of the argument in this chapter. Only when peace and security become everyone's business and not just the business of the defense professionals will we be able to ensure global security and participatory governance. Only then will we understand how human rights are advanced by the evolution of a strong global ethic and economic justice. Only then will we understand how and why cultural diversity is critical to human survival.

At its best, conflict resolution/transformation is about personal and collective empowerment. It underlines the consciousness of the possibilities that lie in seemingly impossible and desperate situations. It is about generating options where there seem to be none, about radical dialogical engagement with those who seem to be enemies. It is about conquering threat-based systems of governance with institutions that rest on persuasion and consensuality. It is about generating socioeconomic and political situations conducive to realizing the full potentialities of the human spirit. At its best, it helps us explain what is happening within the Caucasus and more importantly how negative processes might be transformed into positive ones.

Kevin Clements was appointed secretary-general of International Alert in January 1999. He was the Vernon and Minnie Lynch Chair of Conflict Resolution at the Institute for Conflict Analysis and Resolution at George Mason University from 1994 to 2000, and director of the institute from 1994 to 1999. Dr. Clements has been a regular consultant to a variety of organizations and individuals on disarmament, arms control, and conflict resolution. He has also written numerous books and papers on conflict transformation, peacebuilding, preventive diplomacy, and development.

Notes

1. I am using the terms *conflict resolution* and *conflict transformation* interchangeably. Conflict transformation has more favor with theorists and practitioners at present because it underlines the fact that conflicts are never finally resolved, only reframed, altered, or changed so that nondestructive relationships can be developed. The reality is, however, that there is considerable confusion within the field about the meanings of terms such as *conflict management, conflict resolution,* and *conflict transformation.* They are often used very loosely and interchangeably and sometimes refer to exactly the same strategies.

2. See Gareth Morgan, *Images of Organization,* London: Sage Publications, 1996. Especially relevant here is chapter 6, "Interests, Conflict and Power," pp. 141–194.

3. See, for an important example of this perspective, Lawrence Susskind and Jeffrey Cruikshank, *Breaking the Impasse.* New York: Basic Books, 1987.

4. E Wayne Nafziger, Frances Stewart, and Raimo Vayrynen (eds.), *War, Hunger and Displacement: The Origins of Humanitarian Emergencies,* vol. 2. Oxford: Oxford University Press, 2000, p. 2.

5. See PIOOM Newsletter, 1994, pp. 20–21 for an excellent map plotting "Wars and Armed Conflicts in 1993."

6. The idea of "negative" and "positive" peace was originally the work of Johan Galtung. For more on this, see his "Violence, Peace and Peace Research," *Journal of Peace Research* 6 (3), pp. 167–191. He also developed the concept of "structural violence," which is violence perpetrated against individuals by institutions and social structures.

7. See Kenneth Boulding, *The Three Faces of Power,* London: Sage Press, 1993, for an analysis of the positive and negative impact of different types of power on social, economic, and political stability.

8. COPRED, *Global Directory of Peace Studies Programs,* Fairfax, UK: COPRED, 1997.

9. I am grateful to my former graduate assistant, Monika Jakobsen, for her analysis and classification of diverse conflict-resolution programs within North America.

10. Nafziger, Stewart, and Vayrynen (eds.), *War, Hunger and Displacement,* vol 2, p. 20.

11. Ronald Fisher, *Interactive Conflict Resolution.* Syracuse: Syracuse University Press, 1997.

12. John Burton, *Conflict Resolution: Its Language and Processes.* Lanham, MD: Scarecrow Press, 1996.

13. See Peter J. Carnevale and Dean G. Pruitt, *Negotiation in Social Conflict,* Buckingham: Open University Press, 1993. For a presentation of conflict theory from the communications perspective, see Joyce Hocker and William Wilmot, *Interpersonal Conflict,* Dubuque, IA: Wm. C. Brown, 1991.

14. C. Mitchell, *The Structure of International Conflict.* London: MacMillan, 1981, p. 19.

15. Steven Holtzman, *Post Conflict Reconstruction.* Washington, DC: Social Policy and Resettlement Division of the World Bank, 1996.

16. Herbert C. Kelman, "Negotiation as Interactive Problem Solving," *International Negotiation* 1, pp. 99–123.

17. Elise Boulding and Kenneth Boulding, *The Future: Images and Processes.* London: Sage Publications, 1995, p. 202; Jim Wallis, *The Soul of Politics.* New York: Harcourt Brace and Company, 1995, p. 175.

18. Ibid., Wallis, pp. 175–177.

9

Toward National Infrastructures for Peacebuilding

Guido de Graaf Bierbrauwer and Paul van Tongeren

Now that—finally—conflict prevention and peacebuilding have been recognized and accepted as legitimate and important activities, it is time to "mainstream" them. That means incorporating these instruments into policies and programs at all levels—intergovernmental, governmental, in the private sector, and among NGOs. At present, conflict prevention and peacebuilding activities are at various levels of development among the member states of the European Union. Significant gaps exist that impede a successful and comprehensive program to intervene effectively to prevent conflict and create the conditions for durable peace in the aftermath of conflict. What is needed is an "infrastructure" that will help build the community, provide the skills, and make possible successful conflict prevention and peacebuilding activities. In addition, there is a need for coordination of these activities. The EU has clearly expressed its support for the concept of conflict prevention and peacebuilding. It is now time to move beyond good intentions to meaningful action.

Conflict prevention, or as we prefer to put it, peacebuilding and the prevention of violent conflicts, has grown out of its infancy. Recently, the European Union, the United Nations, and the Group of 8 all voiced their belief in the need to do more to reduce the potential for violence and to support mechanisms to ensure lasting peace.

The G-8 communiqué for the Okinawa 2000 meeting called for the promotion of a "Culture of Prevention." In a joint report to the Nice European Council in December 2000, Secretary General/High Representative Javier Solana and External Relations Commissioner Christopher Patten stated that "preserving peace, promoting stability and strengthening international security world-wide is a fundamental objective for the Union, and preventing violent conflict constitutes one of its most important external policy challenges."[1] In June 2001 in Göteborg, the European Council endorsed the EU

Programme for the Prevention of Violent Conflicts, an initiative of the Swedish EU presidency.

In practice, this means that a great step forward has been taken at the policy and strategic level. International governmental organizations (such as the UN, EU, and World Bank), regional intergovernmental bodies (the Organization for Security and Cooperation in Europe and the Organization of African Unity), and subregional organizations (the Economic Community of West African States and the Southern Africa Development Community) have created small units to analyze early warning signals in order to respond with policy options for preventive action and/or reaction. More and more international NGOs have become active in the field of conflict prevention and peacebuilding, and their role is increasingly acknowledged and appreciated. A number of research institutions analyze conflict dynamics and study the lessons learned from earlier experiences in conflict intervention.[2]

Conflict Prevention at the National Level

Along with the intergovernmental approach embodied in the EU Common Foreign and Security Policy, we believe that at the national level, member states have an equally important role to play in conflict prevention and peacebuilding. Based on such factors as a common history, trade agreements, or long-term development projects, many EU governments have long traditions of bilateral contacts with countries where there is significant risk of conflict. Several countries recognize conflict prevention as an integral part of their foreign policy and are exploring ways to incorporate conflict prevention strategies into their foreign, development, security, and economic policies. In most cases where a conflict-prevention policy has been articulated, the role of civil society is recognized, and the need for cooperation and coordination is emphasized.

Shortcomings in Implementation

However, the mechanisms to ensure effective implementation of these strategies do not exist. One reason for this is that in comparison to the human-rights, development cooperation, or environmental movements, the field of conflict prevention and peacebuilding is still relatively new and is still developing. At this moment, most of the countries are just at the beginning of this process of integrating conflict-prevention and peacebuilding measures into all relevant policy sectors (foreign policy, trade, development cooperation, humanitarian aid, etc.)—that is, the process of *mainstreaming* conflict prevention, although the extent to which this has occurred differs considerably among the EU member states.

Consequently, in most EU countries, there are clearly some major gaps. These include:

- *A lack of early warning mechanisms (or effective warning mechanisms where they do exist).* To identify rising tensions and emerging conflicts, mechanisms are needed to pick up and analyze signals.

- *A lack of good up-to-date, ongoing conflict analysis.* To translate the early warning signals into concrete policy options for intervention, day-to-day analysis of conflict dynamics is needed.
- *A lack of expertise and capacity to do the analysis and to carry out the policy options,* both within the governmental apparatus and within NGOs. In continental Europe, it is hardly possible to study conflict prevention and peacebuilding at an academic level.
- *No overview of who is doing what in this field.* An overview is not only needed to avoid duplication or competition, but also to identify the gaps in this field.
- *A lack of interdisciplinary networks and forums,* connecting academics, civil servants, and practitioners. This could be helpful to share experiences and views from different angles.
- *Inadequate monitoring and evaluation of interventions.* Only recently has more attention been paid to the actual impact of our interventions and the "do no harm" approach (described in Mary B. Anderson's *Do No Harm: How Aid Can Support Peace—Or War*) grown in importance and influence.
- *Insufficient financial support.* More money is needed to make possible the implementation of all kinds of projects supporting the prevention of violent conflicts, reconciliation, and postconflict peacebuilding.

An Infrastructure for Conflict Prevention and Peacebuilding

Most of these gaps could be filled by making use of existing governmental structures, academic institutions, and NGOs, although for some of these activities new organizations may be necessary. In order to avoid gaps or duplication of activities—in other words, to have both an *integrative* and *coherent* approach toward conflict prevention and peacebuilding—a framework or infrastructure is needed. Especially for those Western countries actively involved in conflict regions through various forms of intervention, including development cooperation, humanitarian aid, and political support for peace processes, the establishment and/or institutionalization of conflict-prevention and peacebuilding measures is needed in all sectors and at all levels within the governmental structures as well as the NGOs. An infrastructure that incorporates state and nonstate actors would facilitate a clear division of labor, which is an absolute precondition for effective actions aimed at the prevention of violent conflict. And of course, a parallel infrastructure must also be established in the conflict zones.

Elements for a Conflict-Prevention Infrastructure

Below we try to outline some suggestions of what such an infrastructure would look like. The list of objectives and concrete activities is neither complete nor definitive. It is meant to provide some food for thought. Before starting to name the different elements of our suggested infrastructure, we would like to make some prefatory remarks. First, as mentioned before, the level of

Itum-Kale, Chechnya, near the Georgian border:
Prayers at traditional meeting of Chechen elders.

development in building conflict-prevention measures differs significantly among the various EU countries. Some countries already have quite extensive conflict-prevention policies and practices in place. Second, a better balance between conflict prevention and conflict management is needed. Finally, not all functions necessarily have to be fulfilled in all countries. In some cases it might be more efficient to have one overarching "European" agency, or a division of labor between different countries. For example, it is not at all clear that every country needs an early warning mechanism.

Pillar 1: Building the community. To transform a culture of reaction to a culture of prevention, the field of conflict prevention and peacebuilding requires broad public support. To build this support, awareness-raising activities, lobbying, and the exchange of information are needed. Concrete activities in this respect could be:

1. Raising awareness of the possibilities and importance of conflict prevention and peacebuilding in the public and among politicians, by means of educational activities, documentaries, and movies.
2. Streamlining of the public information process—acting as an information clearinghouse, by providing overviews of "who's who" and "who's doing what" in this field—locally, nationally, and internationally—along geographic as well as thematic lines. This entails providing easy access to information on conflicts, literature, sources, and resource persons via databases on the Internet.

3. Stimulating the creation of networks and forums by bringing together civil servants, nongovernmental organizations, academics, and research institutes on a regular basis. Regular seminars could be held to develop the network and discuss strategies toward particular countries, regions, or issues of concern. This could be useful in translating theory into practical policy options.

Pillar 2: Building the capacity for conflict prevention and peacebuilding. In order to have the capacity to react properly and to improve the quality of our actions, more attention should be paid to building up the capacity in the field of conflict prevention and peacebuilding. Over the last few years, a wide range of conflict-prevention and peacebuilding programs and activities in conflict zones has been developed. These should be examined and exposed, and conclusions can then be drawn from these experiences, for example, on the role and impact of aid (conflict impact assessment), the role of "local capacities for peace," and the role of the media in peacebuilding. Governmental and nongovernmental institutions (especially those in the field of international affairs, development cooperation, humanitarian aid, trade, etc.) that are active in conflict-prone areas should invest in in-house experience to incorporate conflict-prevention and peacebuilding measures into their policies and practices (mainstreaming conflict prevention). In the last few years, a similar process has occurred with human-rights and environmental issues.

Activities to improve capacity in the field of conflict prevention and peacebuilding are:

1. Introducing university programs and training on conflict prevention, peacebuilding, and reconciliation. In most of the countries in continental Europe, it is still virtually impossible to study conflict prevention, resolution, and related subjects at the university level. More programs at universities on conflict prevention and resolution, mediation, and training should be introduced. Besides this, training for civil servants and NGO personnel involved in conflict situations is needed.

2. Establishing expert pools and resources banks. Experiences of postcrisis situations, such as those in Kosovo or Rwanda, proved that, besides policemen, lawyers, and judges, there is a great need for experts in the field of democratization, election monitoring, training in mediation and peaceful conflict resolution, education, etc. Experience has proved, also, that these sorts of experts are very difficult to find, especially on short notice. For this reason, expert pools and resource banks should be created "as a civilian standby mechanism for the UN and other international agencies conducting field operations."[3]

3. Stimulating early warning–early action networks/systems. NGOs are frequently at the forefront when it comes to receiving early signals of growing tensions in a region. A desk that collects this information, producing up-to-date analyses of conflicts and giving policy-oriented assessments of actors, the mechanisms that trigger violence, escalation scenarios, and the options for

action, would be useful to translate the early warning into much-needed early action. This would be especially true if these options for action would be passed through to, for example, the disciplinary forums described above.

4. Analyzing lessons learned and best practices. It is often acknowledged that the field of conflict prevention and peacebuilding is in need of greater coherence, and that it lacks an integrated body of knowledge. One specified task of the aforementioned clearinghouse function is the gathering and analysis of the lessons learned from practitioners, academics, NGOs, and governments. For the field in general, it is of utmost importance to collect these lessons learned, restructure them, and formulate well-framed and well-structured common lessons. Furthermore, it is important to inform not only the conflict-prevention field, but also the non-conflict-resolution world about these lessons learned.

Pillar 3: Operational activities. Ultimately, this is of course the most important pillar. The goal of the infrastructure should be to stimulate and to be supportive of the people who want to prevent the escalation of violence and to transform conflict and potential conflict into durable peace. Current crises prove the necessity of more operational organizations specialized in conflict resolution in conflict zones.

The list of possible programs or activities aimed at conflict prevention and peacebuilding is endless.[4] Examples of these kind of activities include: programs aimed at reforming the security sector, disarmament, demobilization, and reintegration programs; training and education in human rights and democratization; training of local peacebuilders, journalists, and women's organizations; advocating and strengthening the roles these groups can play in conflict prevention and peacebuilding; facilitating dialogue and mediation; supporting the implementation of justice and peace commissions, and so on, limited only by imagination and available resources.

Organizational Hubs

Ideally, the various activities and structures described above can be realized by an array of specialized organizations. But in all well-considered discussions of conflict prevention and peacebuilding, and in official governmental papers, coherence and coordination constantly appear as key words. It is therefore important to establish independent centralized "hubs" that can serve as coordinating bodies for prevention and peacebuilding. These hubs would be the repositories of knowledge and information concerning all actors and actions, and would have the capability to share this information with others as required. These "spiders" in the web would be very helpful in building coalitions for joint action.

National platforms for conflict prevention or peacebuilding, such as the German Platform for the Peaceful Management of Conflicts, the Irish Peace and Reconciliation Platform, the UK-based Conflict, Development and Peace Network or the Finnish Citizens' Security Council could or already do play roles as national hubs on conflict prevention and peacebuilding. These (NGO) platforms or networks differ greatly among themselves, but they all seem to have certain common objectives and to be engaged in similar activities that would enable them to occupy the central position envisioned: the sharing of information, public relations/education, lobbying and advocacy, advisory support and training, and networking.

It must be said, however, that national platforms often suffer from limited capacity because they lack the financial resources they require. Most of the activities mentioned here are typical "core-funding activities," and in this era of project funding, securing adequate funding for them is difficult.

Another example of such a hub, but with quite a different approach, is the recently established Swiss Center for Peacebuilding. This center was created by the Swiss government and the Swiss Peace Foundation after broad consultation with Swiss peace and development NGOs. The center is funded by the Swiss government.

The objective of the center is to support the constructive role of Switzerland in settling international conflicts. This presupposes a coherent Swiss peace policy. The center has a unique "in-between role": it is expected to promote and exploit synergies between the various actors involved in peacebuilding—governmental and nongovernmental, national and international. The center also aspires to develop cooperation among Swiss NGOs, to promote their cooperation with international NGOs, and cultivate their links to official Swiss policy. The following sorts of activities are foreseen:

- Platform and facilitator. The center will provide a platform for the exchange of experiences and information and act as a facilitator with regard to the common resolution of problems by its partners in the area of peacebuilding. It will link its partners to relevant international actors.
- Information and documentation. The center will gather information and documentation related to peacebuilding, hold events, and produce publications for specific target groups.
- Analysis and advice. The center will offer its partners services such as conflict analysis and strategy advice for peacebuilding interventions, and will collect information on lessons learned in civil peacebuilding.

Conclusion

The field of conflict prevention and peacebuilding is on the move. We can celebrate the long-awaited breakthrough—there is now wide acceptance and support for the notion that we can and must do much more to prevent violent conflicts. Not only the NGO community, but also national governments and international governmental forums such as the UN, G-8, and the EU express in their policy papers a belief that more could and should be done. But it is now time to implement the recommendations made in those policy papers, and to mainstream conflict prevention: to incorporate conflict prevention and peacebuilding measures into all their policies and practices, and to come to both an integrated and coherent approach.

Because the EU Common Foreign and Security Policy is intergovernmental, all member states have an equally important role to play in conflict prevention and peacebuilding. In most of the EU countries, however, there are clearly some major gaps in this field. A top priority for EU member states—at the governmental level as well as in the NGO community—would therefore be for each country to examine the state of its own affairs in the field of conflict prevention and peacebuilding. And, after this, consider the following questions: Who is doing what? Where is the expertise? Is there any coherence in our policy and practice? Where are the clear gaps in the field? A next step would be to set priorities, and to draw up a national action plan to meet these priorities. An infrastructure for conflict prevention and peacebuilding may be helpful in this respect. In this article we have offered some suggestions about what such an infrastructure might look like. The list of objectives and concrete activities within this infrastructure is neither complete nor definitive, but it could serve as a framework outlining the objectives to be defined and tasks to be carried out nationally, and it could facilitate collaboration and a division of labor.

An important stimulus for the idea of national infrastructures can be found in the EU Programme for the Prevention of Violent Conflicts, which was endorsed by the European Council in Göteborg in June 2001. It states: "Member States are encouraged to develop national action plans to increase their capabilities for conflict prevention." We hope the member states will take up this challenge.

Paul van Tongeren is the founder and executive director at the European Centre for Conflict Prevention and Guido de Graaf Bierbrauwer is the center's project coordinator for lobbying and advocacy. The European Centre for Conflict Prevention is an independent nongovernmental organization. Its overall objective is to contribute to prevention and/or resolution of violent conflicts in the international arena. The center also acts as the secretariat of the European Platform for Conflict Prevention and Transformation and initiates, coordinates, and implements its activities. Apart from that, the center has specific networking and awareness-raising objectives focused on the Netherlands.

Notes

1. In *Improving the Coherence and Effectiveness of European Union Action in the Field of Conflict Prevention.* Report presented to the Nice European Council by the secretary general/high representative and the Commission, December 2000.

2. See M. Lund, G. Rasamoelina (eds.), *The Impact of Conflict Prevention Policy: Cases, Measures, Assessment, Yearbook 2000.* Ebenhausen, Germany: Conflict Prevention Network, Stiftung Entwicklung und Politik, 2000.

3. Mandate of the Canadian resource bank Canadem, a rapid-reaction mechanism for the UN, OSCE, other international organizations, NGOs, and the Canadian government, to identify skilled Canadian civilians. It includes experts in human rights, democratization, rule of law, peacebuilding, administration/logistics, security, and reconstruction.

4. To illustrate the important role civil society can have in conflict prevention and peacebuilding, the European Centre for Conflict Prevention published *People Building Peace—35 Inspiring Stories from Around the World* in 1999. The book includes descriptions of actions initiated by churches, women's organizations, youth organizations, the media, and the corporate sector, to promote peace and conflict resolution in all sorts of situations around the world.

10

Preventing Violent Intrastate Conflicts: Learning Lessons from Experience[1]

Michael Lund

Since the early 1990s, a series of new intrastate conflicts has erupted, such as in Somalia, Yugoslavia, Tajikistan, Rwanda, and Chechnya. The human suffering, destruction, diplomatic and peacekeeping travails, and financial costs these conflicts have caused have persuaded a growing number of international leaders and organizations that it is more humane and cost-effective to try to keep these horrible and costly wars from arising in the first place. For many laypeople and even international professionals, the idea that the civil and other wars that they read about in the newspapers are usually preceded by relatively peaceful conditions of socioeconomic and political competition and associated tensions, and that the sources of potential violent conflict can be deliberately addressed at this stage, is very new. Conflict prevention is certainly not yet a household word. However, for growing numbers of international professionals scattered across many organizations, the notion of stopping such wars before they start is no longer novel.

If one focuses only on the well-publicized instances when not enough was done to keep simmering conflicts from escalating, such as Rwanda and Kosovo, one could easily get the erroneous impression that conflict prevention is hardly being done at all. But this misperception occurs because most preventive activities are either simply not known about outside limited professional circles, or they are not labeled preventive action as such. It is useful, therefore, to briefly survey some of the recent developments in conflict prevention and disseminate that information, as this volume and the European Centre for Conflict Prevention (ECCP) seek to do. A more complete picture of these developments might help boost the morale of those hoping or laboring for more effective prevention. They can demonstrate to isolated decisionmakers and practitioners that they are actually not alone, but part of a larger and growing international enterprise whose overall contours have not been pointed out.

Looking first at the extent to which conflict prevention has become a focus of concern and discussion, conflict prevention has never been more salient on the international policy agenda than at present. Numerous intergovernmental and NGO international conferences and study groups have taken up the subject in Europe, North America, Africa, and Asia. Several institutes have sponsored research on it. Conflict prevention is now frequently urged in the policy declarations of major governments, the UN, the EU, and many regional bodies. In 2000, it was the topic of a UN Security Council discussion for the second time and a priority of the G-8 Okinawa Summit. In 2001, the successive Swedish and Belgian presidencies of the European Commission made it a priority. In June of that year, it was the focus of a report of the UN secretary general.

But the recent interest in prevention of violent conflicts has gone beyond talk, research, and exhortatory official statements. It is being practiced more and more through a variety of concrete efforts—usually little publicized and not always explicitly referred to as such—in Eastern Europe, Africa, Latin America, and Asia. In addition, the UN secretariat, the European Commission, regional intergovernmental bodies (e.g., the OSCE, OAU, OAS) and subregional bodies (e.g., the Southern African Development Community, Inter-Governmental Authority on Development, and the Economic Community of West African States) have created mechanisms with small units that assign a few staff to look for early warning signs and consider preventive responses.[2] Such mechanisms have been used to respond to a few threatening situations arising in particular countries, with some at least partial successes such as Congo-Brazzaville (1993), Guatemala, Peru, and Venezuela. Other preventive efforts have had significant impacts, such as in the new Baltic states and Macedonia (at least from 1992 to 2001). NGOs have sprouted up that are specifically dedicated to advocacy, analysis, and action in conflict prevention, such as ECCP, the Forum for Early Warning and Early Response (FEWER), and the International Crisis Group. These organizations are forwarding country situation reports to governmental bodies, often accompanied by prevention policy recommendations.[3] Also noteworthy is the recent recognition in discussions of postconflict peace operations, that international programs must address basic causes of conflict through fundamental peacebuilding activities—indeed, nation building—in order to prevent the reemergence of violence.[4]

Furthermore, the procedures entailed in doing early warning and identifying and implementing appropriate preventive responses are beginning to be "mainstreamed" in the regular ongoing operations at the country-mission level of the European Commission, the UN, and most major bilateral donor agencies, through the development of conflict policies, special units, practical analytical tools, and training in early warning and preventive policy responses.[5] A series of week-long training workshops since January 1999 has "graduated" over nine hundred desk officers from all the major UN agencies, each of whom has been introduced to issues in conflict analysis and the range of possible preventive responses.[6]

This mainstreaming activity stems from the concept, not accepted even a few years ago, that conflict prevention is not a specific policy sector in itself nor a single method of intervention. Ideally, it is a policy and bureaucratic "culture of prevention," which cuts across and pervades to some degree a wide range of major policy sectors and organizations that can be involved. Such sectors include diplomacy and interactive conflict or dispute resolution (thus the declining usage of the too-narrow term "preventive diplomacy"). It also could include economic development, democracy building, human rights, military affairs, environment, education, health, agriculture, and so on, as well as commercial activities such as international trade, finance, and natural-resource development. Thus, the notion has been widely accepted of a large policy "toolbox" on which preventive action potentially can draw. It also should involve, whenever possible and advisable, actors within the affected countries themselves. In sum, conflict prevention is becoming understood as ideally a multifaceted orientation or stance of responsiveness that is taken toward the conditions in particular places that often precede the emergence of violent conflict.

More broadly, one could argue that the international normative climate in which conflicts are perceived and discussed is changing. An imperative seems to be gaining very gradual acceptance—tacitly and inconspicuously—that regards it as a moral *obligation* to engage early to keep wars from breaking out. As each successive bloody crisis has hit the headlines, there is less heard about how they were inevitable tragedies resulting from age-old animosities (and thus something the international community cannot do anything about). Instead, more doubts seem to be publicly voiced that perhaps the calamity could

Split, Croatia: Mir Sada peace demonstration

have been avoided, and questions are asked about what went wrong and who is responsible.

Both UN Secretary-General Kofi Annan and U.S. President Clinton publicly acknowledged in 1998, for example, that their bureaucracies could have acted earlier to prevent the Rwanda genocide in 1994. Parliamentary official public inquiries have been made in France and Belgium into the roles that their governments may have played in neglecting or worsening that horrendous human calamity. A legal suit has even been brought by some families of victims of the Rwandan genocide against the UN secretary general for failing to prevent it. Evidently, the moral and legal stakes are being raised just a bit for well-positioned international actors, who now may be held more accountable for purported lapses of duty on their presumed conflict-prevention watch ("Daddy, what were *you* doing *before* the war?"). Despite some dramatic failures of prevention, or perhaps because of them, a new international norm may be attaining more legitimacy: If violent conflicts are not inevitable and can often be prevented with a reasonable amount of effort, international actors are morally bound to act to do what is possible wherever particular situations could very likely lead to massive violence.

In sum, conflict prevention, while clearly not mature, is no longer in its infancy. It has reached adolescence. Nine years have passed since UN Secretary-General Boutros Boutros-Ghali called in Agenda for Peace for "preventive diplomacy" toward conflicts such that as in Yugoslavia, and it is seven years after the genocide in Rwanda. It could be debated whether the amount of attention that conflict prevention is getting in the year 2001 is remarkable, or pitiful. But it is clear that the idea and practice have achieved wider acceptance.

Four Continuing Issues

Despite the unheralded progress that the field of prevention of violent conflict has made in the last decade, significant gaps obviously remain to be filled. Certain basic concerns need further attention in order for the field to advance further. These concerns are:

1. *Causation:* What are the underlying and immediate sources of violent, destructive conflict, and what warning signs indicate its emergence?
2. *Political will*: How can concerned people and specific organizations obtain sufficient political support and resources from publics, governments and bureaucracies to undertake timely and effective preventive action?
3. *Effectiveness*: What kinds of preventive action actually work in specific contexts?
4. *Organization*: How can procedures and policies for anticipating and responding to possible conflicts be operationalized in the regular functioning of international and domestic governmental and nongovernmental organizations, and how can separate actions be done in a more concerted way?

Although it certainly requires further research, consolidation, and refinement, a disproportionate amount of time and timber has been used up on question 1.[7] The field is very long on studies of the problem of intrastate conflicts in terms of their incidence and the diagnosis of their causes. A great deal of hand-wringing is also done over question 2, under the theme of the "lack of political will," almost to the exclusion of the other issues. Question 3 is much less examined, however. The field is very short on the identification of effective preventive-policy prescriptions that are also actually implementable. A crucial need is learning more about what kinds of actions and methods are effective in preventing armed conflicts, and under what conditions, and then applying those lessons. How specific programs may impact on political conflicts, individually and together, so as to reduce their potential for eruption or escalation is not yet well understood. Question 4, the intrabureaucratic and interbureaucratic organization of ongoing bilateral and multilateral preventive responses to emerging conflicts, is also in great need of attention.

The following sections take up questions 3 and 4, respectively. First, we look at the challenge of *effectiveness* by identifying several important decisionmaking levels in the international system at which prevention activity is now operating, and then summarizing some lessons that are being learned about what is effective at one such level. Then we address the challenge of *organization* by suggesting how to incorporate the lessons being gathered about effective conflict prevention into country-specific processes of decisionmaking and implementation that are beginning to be carried out by development agencies, foreign ministries, and multilateral organizations. This includes the challenge of encouraging synergy among different agencies and actors who have potential contributions to make to preventing a conflict.

Accountability for Effectiveness

Adolescence implies that one is old enough to have taken some individual initiative and to have had some impact on the world. By the same token, adolescents can do damage. But with that might come also an increasing self-awareness that they need to take responsibility for their mistakes and to learn from them (perhaps this occurs in late adolescence!). Something like this greater accountability is emerging in the conflict-prevention field.

Up until the last year or so, a conventional wisdom was that "the problem is not early warning but lack of political will to respond." Though sufficient political will is of course still lacking, now there is also a dawning realization that the problem is not merely getting *some* response to early warnings. It is also getting an *effective* response. It is no longer sufficient merely to take just any preventive action ("Do something, quickly!"). Practitioners are increasingly expected to get tangible results in both potential-conflict and postconflict situations toward the ultimate goal of a sustainable peace.

This new pressure for more effective prevention has been stimulated by evidence that existing international policies and actions inevitably get implicated in the course of conflicts and their outcomes, and often can worsen the situation.[8] The interest in more effective preventive action has been building for some time due to developments such as:

- Errors of judgment in prevention decisionmaking, such as conferring diplomatic recognition on Croatia in 1991 without guaranteeing Serb security, and failing to vigorously enforce aid conditionalities regarding human-rights abuses in Rwanda in 1993–1994, following the Arusha Accords
- The "Do No Harm" debate, which raised the question of whether humanitarian aid can often abet conflicts, such as by hosting Hutu Interhamwe militants in the refugee camps of eastern Zaire from 1994 to 1997, after their exodus from Rwanda. This concern in crisis areas is spilling over into conflict-prevention discussions.
- Funding agencies and foundations, wondering whether their money is being well-spent, have commissioned evaluations of prevention or related programs. The findings in some instances reveal strengths but also serious limitations of frequently used and well-meaning types of initiatives, such as NGO Track II diplomacy.[9]
- Evidence that the unqualified championing of major and rapid reforms in highly polarized societies, such as promoting democracy and minority rights through majoritarian elections, may increase the risks of violent backlash by factions who see themselves losing.[10]
- Doubts over the necessity of the peace enforcement military intervention in Kosovo.

These examples show that recent prevention failure has not only involved lack of action, but sometimes ineffective action. Policy errors have occurred in countries where international actors are already present on the ground carrying out programs, not places where they have yet to arrive. So if prevention failure involves not only acts of omission, but acts of commission, the challenge for the UN, EU, NGOs, and other international actors is not simply taking timely action, though timing is of course still crucial. The action taken must also be appropriate to and effective in the country context where it is applied. These actors not only need to respond toward incipient conflict situations more promptly; they also must respond more intelligently. The problem is not only political will, but also political wisdom.

How then can the agencies, resources, and policies already available to transitioning countries specifically be applied more effectively for conflict prevention? In essence, the question of conflict-prevention effectiveness is: What methods, programs, policies, and actions can achieve peaceful transition—and under what conditions? In response to the growth of conflict prevention activity, several researchers began in the early 1990s to gather policy-relevant lessons from actual prevention experience through variously rigorous methods of quantitative, case-study, and evaluation research.[11] More recently, donors and other funders are beginning to take an interest in "learning lessons" and identifying "best" or "good" practices in prevention. However, the findings from these accumulating studies have been scattered and diverse, so they have not been consolidated or disseminated to the locations where they might be applied. Supply and demand have yet to meet in any significant way. But lessons are being put on the shelf.

Drawing Lessons for Different Levels
of Preventive Action in the International System

One reason why relatively little progress has been made in applying the existing experience in conflict prevention—for the gap between existing knowledge and application—is that the lessons being gathered have not been codified in a unified classification scheme that indicates where they apply in terms of levels and types of prevention activities and how they pertain to choices that are within the control of particular practitioners. A common frame of reference is lacking in which to classify findings so they can be communicated to relevant users of this advice, and can be further tested and accumulated by researchers. Such a catalogue would enable the many differing actors who can influence a conflict situation to consult prevention guidance that applies to *them*. Without such a framework, the business of deriving and offering lessons from preventive activity is like reading tea leaves or seeing shapes in the clouds in the sky—almost anything can be stated to anyone about any facet of the subject.

Where and how can international actors try to learn systematically how to respond more effectively to specific potential conflict situations? About what kinds and aspects of prevention activity should "lessons" be gathered? To make significant headway in understanding what works in conflict prevention, we need to find useful handles on the question. To gather lessons about what works and why, with the hope of informing practitioners about new situations they may face, some way is required for identifying and classifying the major alternative forms of preventive activity at the different levels of preventive action. Using these units of activity as our units of analysis, we can observe those forms in as many of their actual applications as possible to see what effects they have and if patterns are evident when one form of action is chosen instead of another.

Conflict-prevention lesson learning can become more systematic and thus useful if we recognize that the governmental and nongovernmental efforts that are impacting positively or negatively on conflict and peacebuilding are being carried out at several rather distinct decisionmaking locuses: global, regional, national, and local. Examples of potential conflict prevention action at these different levels would be, respectively:

- The international criminal court, or international regulation of illicit small arms
- A regional embargo on arms traffic, or regional economic sanctions
- A national political debate, a multilateral preventive deployment
- A rural village development project

Because preventive action can take place at all of these differing levels, the question "What is effective?" also needs to be raised and answered at each of these levels. Tackling the question of effectiveness can be done from different perspectives, depending on where the inquirer is found in terms of his or her level of decisionmaking and implementation (e.g., at the department level, the project level) as well as the substantive policy concerns of their agency. Each of these perspectives would provide different kinds of (although not necessarily ultimately contradictory) advice.

We begin to construct a learning framework below by charting the terrain of the main forms of conflict-prevention activity. The following list identifies some major levels and units of preventive action, about which prevention lessons are being, or can be, gathered.

Major Levels of Preventive Action for Lesson Learning

International Standard Setting:
A Priori Norms, Standards, Goals, or Requirements Set for Countries
This level of collective action involves worldwide or regionwide legal and normative norms and principles that define standards with regard to human rights, rule of law, democratic government, the environment, etc. The standards are not formulated solely for particular countries that face conflicts at a given moment in time, but are a priori standards that seek to encourage or enforce adherence to certain ideal institutions and government behavior. These ideals are widely seen as effective measures of structural conflict prevention—especially before any violent expressions of conflict on such issues are imminent. The standards are agreed to mainly by states, written up in international conventions and treaties, and then promoted, assisted, or enforced by international bodies (e.g., OSCE standard setting, international human-rights conventions and the ongoing UN human-rights treaty bodies, international humanitarian law, the EU Lome Convention goals for democracy).

Constitutional and Territorial Governance Structures
These are overall institutional arrangements that can be adopted by states in order to define the prerogatives and relationships of the various parts of their central and local governments: federalism, autonomy, decentralization, parliamentary and presidential systems, and so on. These arrangements tend to persist for long periods of time and are considered to channel political life in ways that can help prevent violent conflicts in certain conditions.

Time-Sensitive Interventions into Specific Situations

Policy instruments. Another promising approach to learning what works is to focus on the comparative effectiveness of the several different generic methods or policy techniques—the major distinct policy instruments—that various actors have used, or can use, to try to influence the causes and dynamics of specific conflicts that are unfolding in particular places at particular times (e.g., human-rights observers, conditional aid, media professionalization, Track II diplomacy, conflict resolution training, preventive deployment, special envoys, etc.).[12]

A conflict-prevention instrument is the general technique reflected in various programs and projects or initiatives through which UN agencies or other parties engage a potentially violent conflict situation with the intent of reducing its underlying causes or conflict dynamics, or of strengthening the capacities of actors to manage tensions peacefully. Operating roughly within sectoral or functional areas, these are generic types of preventive interventions or policy tools that can be initiated at the global, national, or local levels and are applied to particular conflicts at particular points and for limited periods of time. Such instruments tend to embody differing kinds of incentives, disincentives, and other means to influence a conflict. They may be carried out in several locations in a conflict arena and usually require several actors at several levels to implement them.[13]

Such preventive instruments or measures can be examined where they have been applied in order to identify whether and how they have helped to prevent a conflict by influencing its course and sources. By observing many instances of particular preventive instruments in action, gradually we can gather lessons about which types work in what types of situations, and why. A crucial dimension in this analysis of the performance of generic instruments is the identification of the kinds of contextual conditions that tend to be associated with successful impacts and the conditions that consistently constrain their implementation and effectiveness. These conclusions can then be collected methodically in a central place and disseminated. Whenever some decisionmaker is considering how to respond to a specific situation in which violent conflict may threaten, this body of experience can then be reviewed, as an aid to deciding which particular preventive measures might be most appropriate and effective, and when and where.

Multi-instrument engagements. Multi-instrument engagements refer to the combination of programs that a peace operation or other multilateral mission, including NGOs, have initiated with regard to a particular potential or past intrastate conflict. They are maintained there over a certain period of time until international third-party involvement is deemed no longer needed. These engagements usually apply several kinds of preventive instruments (e.g., political dialogue, police training, electoral assistance, civil-society projects, etc.).

Individual Agencies' Programs and Projects
Some foreign or host governments and multilateral organizations, or their specific agencies, have taken an interest in how their own set of programs and projects in a developing country perform in conflict-prevention terms. The unit of analysis here may include a single program or groups of programs. Perhaps the smallest unit of collective activity that can be intended explicitly

to have its own prevention impacts would be individual projects (e.g., one or more radio programs developed by a peace radio studio).

Overall, the differing units of prevention activity defined above comprise the parts of a de facto international conflict-preventive system that are potentially and sometimes interlinked. Cumulatively, this system is currently affecting particular conflicts positively or harmfully in myriad ways. What is ultimately needed is to improve the overall efficacy of this system by imbuing more of its many levels and forms with the values and criteria of the "culture of prevention."

Lessons from Research on Country-Level Multi-Instrument Engagements

In response to the recent increase in explicit prevention activity, some researchers have looked at cases of intrastate potential or actual violent conflicts in order to identify elements that appear to be associated with the (unheralded) "successes" and the (more publicized) "failures" (although most outcomes are not simply one or the other). These studies have focused on the multiactor, multi-instrument preventive engagements in situations of potentially violent conflict. The appendix to this chapter pulls together some of the generalizations that have been synthesized from these case studies.

Though useful as policy guidance because they are based on existing systematic research, generalizations about all these units of analysis—instruments, multi-instrument engagements, etc.—still need to be considered as preliminary hypotheses that additional analysis can test further. Some are presented here in a structured outline in which lessons can be accumulated in an ongoing database, which is currently under development. This database thus can be tested further and continuously refined, and its findings continuously disseminated to those decisionmakers who can make best use of these lessons. Presented in this way, case studies can provide the basis for policy guidelines to effective conflict-prevention practice for would-be conflict preventors.

Applying Lessons from Experience

Although findings such as those in the appendix are accumulating, they have yet to be significantly disseminated to or discovered by practitioners, boiled down, and utilized to inform decisionmaking. Thus, they are not really being "learned" by the very organizations to which they pertain. Lessons of this kind that are distilled out of many instances of actual experience at the country and other levels of practice need to be reconnected to the actual routines and established processes of decisionmaking and implementation, for then they might be considered when specific conflicts are being addressed.

Formulating Country-Specific Prevention Strategies

To the extent possible, it is desirable for several agencies to apply several kinds of preventive instruments that are appropriate to a given potential conflict situation in some concerted fashion. One of the central lessons that has emerged from recent experience in countries where prevention efforts have either succeeded or failed—as indicated in the appendix—is that to build a strong socioeconomic and political environment in which violent conflict is unlikely and violence can be stemmed, several kinds of preventive measures need to be applied in a complementary fashion, thus requiring several actors to be involved. To be optimally effective and have multiplier effects, individual preventive measures should be implemented as the parts of a broader multisectoral strategy that includes a mix of several such preventive measures. This strategy should address the particular configuration of factors that are contributing to potential violent conflict in the specific country involved.

What is needed to arrive at such a country-specific strategy is a process of conflict diagnosis, selection of options, implementation, and evaluation that allows the lessons about effective prevention to become applied during the standard operating procedures of governmental and nongovernmental bureaucracies. This can be done within individual organizations, but it is ideally conducted among several organizations in a joint fashion.

Fortunately, as mentioned above, the process of mainstreaming early warning and prevention responses is already beginning among all major multilateral and bilateral development agencies (although less so perhaps among their colleagues in foreign ministries).[14] One example is found in the UN secretariat, where an interagency prevention team meets regularly to monitor potential trouble spots and recommend appropriate action. At the country level, every major donor and multilateral organization has established some regular process of drawing up country-specific development-assistance plans. But so far, the latter procedures often are not oriented explicitly to conflict sources or peace capacities. The ideal steps in developing effective country-level prevention strategies are essentially the following.[15]

Conflict analysis. The initial steps structure the problem and identify specific objectives.

Step 1: Identify the sources of potential conflict ("What is the Problem?")

The first task is to identify the nature of the conflict situation by pinpointing as clearly and explicitly as possible the main risk factors and conflict dynamics that could produce violent conflict and conflict escalation in the country of concern. Each local conflict situation is different in its details and nuances. Various early warning systems and analyses of general causes of intrastate conflicts can be synthesized into a checklist of possible factors that can be applied to specific country contexts in order to identify the sources of potential conflict in that setting.

Because the source of violent conflicts is multilayered, suggesting that violent conflicts arise out of several ingredients, this diagnosis will likely reveal a particular configuration of underlying structural, as well as more proximate and triggering factors. The analysis should seek to interpret how and why these conflict causes are interacting. The extent to which immediate factors are prominent will reveal the stage of escalation the conflict is in. The various sources should be ranked in terms of short-, medium-, and long-term priorities in order to sequence actions in some relation to the risks that have the most potential for resulting in bloodshed and destruction.

A similar analysis should look not only at these negative risks or threats ("causes of conflict"), but also for the existing countervailing capacities and positive opportunities that may be helping in the country to regulate conflict so it does not become violent ("causes of peace"). The balance between negative and positive factors provides some basis for judging the extent to which the situation requires external preventive action.

Step 2: Identify entry points and objectives

This involves first identifying possible *entry points, leverage points,* or *angles of attack* that can be taken with regard to each of the identified sources of conflict. These options will tend to appear in several policy sectors, suggesting where actions are needed to prevent eruption or escalation of conflict. All key sectors should be examined. These entry points can be translated into corresponding objectives that preventive action is intended to achieve in relation to the sources of conflict they are addressing.

Prevention analysis. The middle steps match specific preferred preventive measures to the identified conflict causes and existing peace capacities, generate an array of possible options, try to forecast the likely outcomes of each choice, and finalize the most promising options.

Step 3: Identify an array of possible preventive measures to achieve the objectives ("What is appropriate to do?")

Consider various plausible programmatic means or activities ("preventive measures," "policy tools," "instruments") for achieving the various objectives. Lists of possible instruments, such as UN mechanisms, can be used to stimulate brainstorming. They should include all the explicitly preventive as well as other sectoral programs.

Step 4: Do prior appraisal of the likely effectiveness and implementability of preventive measures (prospective evaluation—"What will these work in *this context?*")

Regarding those preventive measures that have been tentatively identified, this task asks the question "Will they be effective in *this* context?" Using clearly identified peace and conflict impact criteria, they should each be screened for their likely effectiveness in contributing to limiting violence, building peace capacities, or alternatively, worsening aspects of the conflict. This task can be aided by consulting information about the past performance of given proposed instruments, such as the respective advantages and disadvantages that are synthesized in the preventive-measures profiles.

Consideration obviously also has to be given to the preferred preventive measures' actual feasibility or implementability, in light of the availability of and constraints on UN political, human, and financial resources, and whether the local context in which they would be implemented is sufficiently favorable or too difficult.

Step 5: Identify a preferred total mix or combination of preventive measures

This involves identifying the overall set of measures that will be required to address all the major sources of the conflict, and thus are ultimately needed for effective conflict prevention—the various blocks that are needed to construct a stable peacebuilding. This task can be aided by consulting the lessons of successful prevention from structured case studies of the ingredients of effective multipreventive-measure country strategies, using those ingredients as a checklist to see what key overall ingredients ideally may need to be in place. The constraints affecting specific situations will often require trade-offs or compromises between equally worthy but conflicting values and thus will require arriving at unique and imperfect responses to difficult moral dilemmas.

Preventive action. The last steps deal with recruiting various actors for integrated implementation strategies, taking concrete action, and assessing the results.

Step 6: Organize implementation ("Who does what, and when?")

This involves getting specific agreement on who will do what, and when. It is put here, although it must actually start at the earliest possible stage. The several lead and other contributing UN departments and agencies that have the mandate and resources required to implement each specified measure and to work together to apply the array of desired preventive measures need to work out action plans for implementing the individual measures. The optimal timing, order, or sequencing for implementation of the individual measures need to be tentatively planned. Mechanisms need to be established for achieving as much concertation as possible, so as to ensure complementarity and avoid contradictions. Arrangements need to be made to engage other actors to address the sources of conflict and implement corresponding preventive measures that the UN cannot undertake, such as regional organizations, governments, NGOs, and other donors.

Step 7: Monitoring and evaluation ("How can we do better?")

This involves measuring the actual results of the implementation of the individual measures and their aggregate impacts on the various sources of the conflict. It requires ongoing monitoring of implementation and after a reasonable time, assessing the impact of preventive measures implemented in terms of their achievement of their respective corresponding objectives and any unwanted negative outcomes.

Step 8: Strategy modification or termination

This concerns identifying how the actions that are part of the strategy could improve to the extent they have not reached their objectives, or whether the job has been completed sufficiently for reduced involvement and fuller engagement of other local or international actors. The implementation of the measures has to be adjusted where events warrant, and a determination made of whether the criteria for effectiveness in securing operational objectives have been met. Follow-up/transitional arrangements with local, national, and international partners are required for clean withdrawal of assistance.

Organizing Strategies:
Joint In-Country Planning and Implementation

The various contributions to prevention that can be made by various actors need to be brought closer together. As many relevant actors as possible are often needed to prevent specific conflicts. Together, their contributions can form multifaceted strategies that are tailored effectively to the particular needs of specific potential conflict situations.

Some organized process is then needed that follows the steps above in order to apply the lessons from experience in strategies that fit particular potential conflict situations. This process should not be simply bilateral but multilateral. As one can see in the appendix , one of the key lessons from conflict-prevention successes is that multiple actors and their respective policy instruments and political influence are needed to steer any given unstable country toward peaceful progressive change. To the extent the country situation is difficult to influence, what is ideally needed is for many actors to join others in collaborative assessments and country-specific conflict-prevention strategy development.

This cannot be done in a rigid, hierarchical way, for no international agencies have effective mandatory controls over any others. But much more effort can be exerted informally to put the country desk officers at the headquarters level in differing agencies in touch with each other. In addition, the respective development staffs at the field level should engage informally with each other in joint analyses of each host country's conflict vulnerabilities and peacebuilding opportunities. Joint inventorying could be done of how the mix of instruments that these organizations might already be operating in a country, or that could be introduced, might be modified and amplified to achieve more effective leverage over emerging tensions that could turn destructive. While not obligatory or coerced, such joint consultation might over time encourage more complementary in-country programs. This is one concrete operational step that could help to spread the "culture of prevention."

Actually, major donor agencies are beginning to talk to each other informally through consultations sponsored by the OECD Development Assistance Committee Task Force on Peace, Conflict, and Development and the Conflict Prevention Network organized by the World Bank. Nevertheless, when it comes to operationalizing concerted conflict-prevention strategies on the ground, there seems to be little cross-agency consultation even within the same governments or international organizations present. Even among the most prevention-oriented organizations there persists an understandable but ultimately short-sighted tendency to ask for lessons of effective prevention that are packaged only in terms and forms that are specific to their particular organization's programs and procedures. International NGOs such as FEWER and International Alert are stepping forward to stimulate such country-level exercises in specific sites such as Georgia and Kenya, in the hopes of encouraging donors, the UN, the EC, the OSCE, and host governments and local NGOs to engage in collaborative assessment and response.[16] Ultimately, this convening function might be handled by UN resident coordinators or special representatives, EU country delegations, or key NGOs who could take the initiative and act as convenors and facilitators.

Conclusion:
Where There's A Way, There Might Be More Will

Putting more emphasis on examining recent prevention experience to understand what is effective in prevention, and then incorporating these lessons into existing country-level programming procedures conducted on some roughly joint basis, will not by themselves dramatically change the existing political priorities at the top levels of decisionmaking. But these steps might embolden various actors focused on particular countries to take a preventive initiative when they have the opportunity. They also can build up a basis for sounder policymaking at the level of high policy as conflict-prevention advocacy increasingly garners more serious and detailed attention. In the meantime, knowing that there are plausible and tried methods on the shelf for addressing potentially violent conflict situations may actually help to increase individual decisionmakers' comfort levels. They may begin to feel more confident that they can exercise political will, individually and multilaterally, without taking huge risks.

In any case, better analysis is essential for when there would be more political will. Publicity and lobbying do not automatically lead to more effective prevention decisions. In fact, the popularization of the awareness of conflicts and of the promise of conflict prevention might sometimes worsen policy decisions, just as responding to public sentiments during humanitarian crisis interventions has led to unwise choices in some instances. More political will needs to be accompanied by solid analysis of various policies' likely consequences, so that it can inform how various agencies' regularized procedures apply the range of prevention activities to developing countries' problems.

Appendix

Key Ingredients of Effective Multi-Instrument
Country-Level Preventive Engagements

Recent case-study findings suggest that serious intrastate political tensions and issues will tend to be addressed peacefully, rather than escalate into violence, to the extent that the following ingredients are present.[17]

Features of the Preventive Engagement Itself

When?

1. Timely early action is taken as tensions are emerging, but before, rather than following, significant use of violence, or immediately after initial outbreaks.
2. Engagement prioritizes the various goals of preventing violence (security, "peace"), managing issue disputes, and transforming overall institutions

and societies (e.g., political and social justice)—i.e., "direct" and "structural" prevention—in contextually appropriate mixes and sequences. Such prioritization generally recognizes that when behaviors and actions immediately threaten major loss of life and destruction, they need to be deterred or stopped before more fundamental structures of power and socioeconomic advantage are addressed. Also, short-term crisis management needs to be followed by actions that credibly tackle more fundamental issues.

What?

3. Early action is robust, rather than halfhearted and equivocal, by exerting vigorous positive and negative inducements specifically on the major potentially conflicting parties' leaders and their mobilized rank and file.
4. Early action thus brings an appropriate mix of sufficiently vigorous (conditional) "carrots," (unconditioned) support, actual or potential "sticks," negotiating "tables," and other modes of influence to bear on the several most important short-term and long-term sources of potential conflicts—the key "fronts" in which conflicts are being played out.
5. Early action does not solely promote the cause of the weaker parties in the conflict but also addresses the fears and insecurities of dominant parties.
6. Support and protection is provided to established governing formal institutions of the state, to the extent that they incorporate the leaders of the main contending communities in power sharing in rough proportion to their distribution in the population, rather than buttressing an exclusionary governmental structure or, alternatively, an antistate political opposition. Responsible autonomous organs of the state and within the security forces are assisted to provide public services professionally. This enables the state to host a process of give-and-take politicking over public policy and constitutional issues and to carry out business for the benefit of the general population.
7. Opportunities for joining regional security alliances and trade cooperation also create an overall climate of support for building liberal peaceful states.
8. Outside formal government, a broad-based "constituency for peace" is built up over time that cuts across the society's main politicized identity groups, is not solely interested in politics, is primarily interested in business and other peaceful pursuits and can generate wealth, and that thus has a vested interest in political stability and social prosperity.
9. A politically active but independent and cross-cutting civil society is encouraged to unify major identity groups. Peaceful people-power campaigns are supported through training opposition leaders in nonviolent tactics and nonincendiary rhetoric, but that also exert significant

pressure on incumbent leaders to take peaceful, responsible actions or retire from office.

Who?

10. Preventive engagements are implemented by a sufficient number and kind of governmental and nongovernmental actors so as to provide the range of needed instruments (mediation, deterrence, institution building, etc.) and resources to address the leading sources of the conflict. In the process, these actors form a "critical mass" that symbolizes a significant international commitment to nonviolent change. Rarely can any single actor or action prevent serious violent intrastate conflicts.
11. The engagement is supported politically and in other ways, or at least tolerated and not blocked or undermined by major *regional* powers and/or major *world* powers.
12. The engagement is generally viewed as legitimate by its being carried out under the aegis of the UN or a regional multilateral organization involving the states affected.

How?

13. The early multifaceted action is concerted and consistent among the major external actors, rather than scattered or contradictory.

Features of the Regional, National, and Local Contexts

Where?

14. Past relations between the politically significant groups have been peaceful in the recent past, rather than violent.
15. The major identity groups in society groups do not differ in multiple societal and cultural respects and have considerable everyday interaction; are not highly conscious of their respective identities or organized into separate political movements, parties, or governmental machinery; and have a relatively accepted balance of social power between them.
16. The dominant government structure permitted some participation by both groups simultaneously (power sharing), but was not rigidly divided between them, and the incumbent leaders on at least one side are not insecure and do not accentuate the existing ethnic divisions through provocative statements and policies.
17. Moderate leaders from each of the contending communities are in positions of significant authority and in regular contact as they carry out the public's business, and they show some progress in carrying out public policies that benefit all communities, including providing for physical security.

18. The countries and societies in which the groups lived have considerable diplomatic and economic ties and direct engagement in domestic issues by major international bodies.

19. The following regional actors adjacent or close to the immediate arena of conflict are neutral to an emerging conflict or actively promote its peaceful resolution, rather than supporting one side or another politically or militarily:

- neighboring states
- refugee communities

20. The diasporas of the parties to a conflict that reside in major third party countries also support peaceful means of resolution, or at least are not highly mobilized behind their respective countrymen's cause. Thus, they do not aid and abet coercive or violent ways to pursue the conflict and lobby their host governments to take a partisan stance toward the conflict.

Michael S. Lund is senior associate, Management Systems International, Inc. (MSI); professorial lecturer at the Johns Hopkins School of Advanced International Studies (SAIS); and senior associate, the Center for Strategic and International Studies, all in Washington, D.C. He is the author of Preventing Violent Conflicts *(U.S. Institute of Peace, 1996), coauthor of* Peacebuilding and Conflict Prevention in Developing Countries: A Practical Guide, *prepared for the European Commission (1999), coeditor and contributor to* The Impact of Prevention Policies, 1999/2000, *Yearbook of the Conflict Prevention Network (Nomos Verlagsgesellschaft, 2000), and author of other articles and chapters in the conflict field.*

Notes

1. This chapter derives in part from a chapter in Fen Hampson and David Malone (eds.), *From Reaction to Prevention: Opportunities for the UN System in the New Millennium,* a project of the International Peace Academy, Boulder, CO: Lynne Rienner Publishers, forthcoming in 2001; a paper by Michael Lund prepared for the conference "Facing Ethnic Conflicts: Perspectives from Research and Policy-Making," Center for Development Research, University of Bonn, 4–16 December 2000; and the volume *The Impact of Conflict Prevention Policy: Cases, Measures, Assessments,* by Michael Lund and Guenola Rasamoelina (eds.), which was the Yearbook for 2000 of the Conflict Prevention Network, Stiftung Wissenschaft und Politik, Ebenhausen, Germany: Nomos Verlagsgesellschaft.

2. ASEAN is also addressing conflict prevention informally through the Asian Regional Forum, largely under the rubric of interstate military confidence-building measures.

3. What one book described a decade ago as the "emerging global watch" seems to be taking some form, albeit slowly and in a scattered and patchy way. See B. G. Ramcharan, *The International Law and Practice of Early Warning and Preventive Diplomacy: The Emerging Global Watch,* Dordrecht, Netherlands: Martinus Nijhoff, 1991.

4. The idea that conflicts typically evolve eventually through early nonviolent, violent, and postviolent stages or phases and thus have a "life cycle" or history was implied in the UN Charter's Chapters VI and VII. It is developed more explicitly in Michael Lund et al., *Preventing and Mitigating Violent Conflicts: A Guide for Practitioners,* Creative Associates International Inc., 1997, viewable at <www.caii-dc.com/ghai>. Differing

stages of conflict (e.g., emergence, escalation, de-escalation, reconstruction, and reconciliation/resolution) have been adopted as an organizing framework by recent textbooks in the conflict field. See, for example, Louis Kriesberg, *Constructive Conflicts: From Escalation to Resolution,* Lanham, MD: Rowman and Littlefield, 1998; Hugh Miall et al., *Contemporary Conflict Resolution,* Cambridge, England: Polity Press, 1999.

5. Developments within major donor governments are surveyed in Manuela Leonhardt's chapter in Lund and Rasamoelina (eds.), *The Impact of Conflict Prevention Policy,* and in Guenola Rasamoelina, *Conflict Impact Assessment of EU Development Cooperation with ACP Countries: A Review of Literature and Practice,* London: International Alert and Saferworld, 2000. An example of an analytical tool is Michael Lund et al., *Peacebuilding and Conflict Prevention in Developing Countries,* Conflict Prevention Network, Stiftung Wissenschaft und Politik, 1999, prepared for country desk officers of the European Commission. A manual on conflict prevention is also being prepared for UN agencies. An earlier primer on conflict analysis and prevention prepared for USAID development practitioners is Lund et al., *Preventing and Mitigating Violent Conflict.*

6. Indeed, conflict prevention is now so trendy that, as it is discovered more and more widely, many programs that were once described as "conflict resolution" or "conflict management" have been relabeled "conflict prevention" or its synonyms, in a bandwagon process. This ascendancy may or may not reflect genuine diffusion of the prevention idea. With so much existing activity now being lumped under conflict prevention, there is a risk it will lose its distinctive value-added meaning. The popularization of prevention discourse seems to have led to some re-muddling of a vital distinction—that between *proactive efforts* that act before significant violence has arisen at all, and *reactive efforts* taken after violence has significantly escalated and armed conflict has ensued. To keep things straight, a core definition of conflict prevention would refer to: any structural or intercessory means to keep intrastate or interstate tensions and disputes from escalating into significant violence and use of armed force, to strengthen the capabilities of parties to possible violent conflicts for resolving their disputes peacefully, and to progressively reduce the underlying problems that produce those tensions and disputes.

7. In the present volume, this question is addressed primarily in the conflict surveys in Part 2.

8. See, for example, Peter Uvin, *Summary Report to the DAC Task Force on Peace and Development,* Paris: Development Assistance Committee, OECD, p. 4.

9. See, for example, Gunnar M. Serbe, Joanna Macrae, and Lennart Wohlgemuth, *NGOs in Conflict—An Evaluation of International Alert,* Bergen: Christian Michelson Institute, 1997. See also the findings of Michael Lund et al., "The Effectiveness of Civil Society Initatives in Controlling Violent Conflicts and Building Peace: A Study of Three Approaches in the Greater Horn of Africa," Management Systems International Inc., 2001, viewable at <www.usaid.gov>.

10. See, for example, Ben Reilly, "Voting Is Good, Except When It Guarantees War," *Washington Post,* 17 October 1999, p. B2. For a discussion of the risks of assuming, without careful contextual assessment, that the widely endorsed liberal goals of human rights, market-oriented economic reform, democratization, rule of law, civil society, and good governance will ipso facto prevent conflicts in unstable transitioning countries, see the section entitled "The Liberal Solution as Problem" in my chapter in Hampson and Malone (eds.), *From Reaction to Prevention.*

11. The earliest research of this nature includes Hugh Miall, *The Peacemakers: Peaceful Settlement of Disputes Since 1945,* New York: St. Martin's Press, 1992; Gabriel Munuera, *Preventing Armed Conflict in Europe: Lesson from Recent Experience,* Paris: Institute for Security Studies, June 1994; and Michael S. Lund, *Preventing Violent Conflicts,* Washington, DC: United States Institute of Peace, 1996.

12. The UN Charter refers to many diplomatic preventive measures, especially in Chapter VI. The present chapter's appendix lists many more such measures.

13. A small but growing field of analysis is evaluating the effectiveness of such instruments. Instruments such as mediation, negotiations, and sanctions have received libraries of attention, although not usually from a prevention perspective. A recent book that does probe the prevention value of negotiations is William Zartman (ed.), *Preventive Negotiations,* Lanham, MD: Rowman and Littlefield, 2001. Very little has been done on the wide range of other possible preventive measures. Work that has begun to do the latter, however, includes David Cortright (ed.), *The Price of Peace: The Role of Incentives in International Conflict Prevention,* Lanham, MD: Rowman and Littlefield, 1998; Milton J. Esman, "Can Foreign Aid Moderate Ethnic Conflict?" *Peaceworks* (13) (Washington, DC: US Institute of Peace, March 1998); Peter Harris and Ben Reilly (eds.), *Democracy and Deep-Rooted Conflict: Options for Negotiators*, Stockholm: Institute for Democracy and Electoral Assistance, 1998; and David Carment and Patrick James (eds.), *Peace in the Midst of Wars: Preventing and Managing International Ethnic Conflicts,* Columbia: University of South Carolina Press, 1998. A USAID-funded study under the Greater Horn of Africa Peacebuilding Project at Management Systems International, Inc., evaluated the peace and conflict impacts of peace radio, traditional local-level peace processes, and national Track II political dialogues in five countries. See Lund et al., *The Effectiveness of Civil Society Initiatives.* Earlier rudimentary efforts to apply various criteria to evaluate the conflict-prevention capacities and limits of nineteen diverse prevention policy instruments are found in Lund et al., *Preventing and Mitigating Violent Conflicts;* and Michael Lund, "Impacts of Development Aid as Incentives or Disincentives in Reducing Internal and Inter-state Conflicts: A Review of Findings from Documented Experience," an unpublished report to the Development Assistance Committee, Task Force on Peace, Conflict and Development, OECD, 1998. The case studies in Mary Anderson, *Do No Harm: How Aid Can Support Peace—Or War,* Boulder, CO: Lynne Rienner Publishers, 1999, and subsequent studies organized and analyzed by Ms. Anderson and her associates at Collaborating for Development Associates, Inc., are also very relevant. Some products are putting instrument assessments into forms that can be used by country desk officers and other practitioners. See, for example, the brief assessments of election observers, human-rights observers, and other instruments in Lund et al., *Peacebuilding and Conflict Prevention.* A prototype manual of UN "preventive measures" such as fact-finding missions, humanitarian aid, and local community economic development has been prepared for the Framework Team in the UN secretariat.

14. For recent developments, see the overview by Manuela Leonhardt in Lund and Rasamoelina (eds.), *The Impact of Conflict Prevention Policy.*

15. This list draws in part on "Policy Planning for UN Preventive Action: Nine Step Process Outline," Early Warning and Preventive Measures, United Nations Staff College, 2000, and other sources. Earlier discussions of the steps in tailoring country-specific strategies are found in Michael Lund, "Policymaking and Implementation," chapter 4 in *Preventing Violent Conflicts: A Strategy for Preventive Diplomacy,* edited by Michael Lund, Washington, DC: U.S. Institute of Peace, 1996; and Michael Lund, "Developing Case-Based Conflict Prevention and Peacebuilding Strategies from Recent Experience in Europe," chapter 2 in *Preventing Violent Conflict: Issues from the Baltics and the Caucasus,* edited by G. Bonvicini et al., Baden-Baden: Nomos Verlagsgesellschaft, 1998.

16. See, for example, Andrew Sherriff and Njeri Karuru, "Methodology for Conflict-Sensitive Planning for NGO, INGO, and Donor Operations in Kenya," draft prepared for the International Alert and Centre for Conflict Research, September 2000.

17. This synthesis draws from, among others, Miall, *The Peacemakers;* Munuera, *Preventing Armed Conflict in Europe;* SusanWoodward, *Balkan Tragedy: Chaos and Dissolution After the Cold War,* Washington, DC: Brookings Institution, 1995; Lund,

Preventing Violent Conflict; Peter Wallensteen (ed.), *Preventing Violent Conflict: Past Record and Future Challenges,* Uppsala, Sweden: Uppsala University, Department of Peace and Conflict Research, 1998; Michael Lund, Barnett R. Rubin and Fabienne Hara, "Learning from Burundi's Failed Democratic Transition, 1993–96: Did International Initiatives Match the Problem?" in *Cases and Strategies of Preventive Action,* edited by Barnett Rubin, New York: Century Foundation Press, 1998; Raimo Vayrinen et al., *Inventive and Preventive Diplomacy,* Notre Dame, IN: Joan Kroc Institute, University of Note Dame Press, 1999; Michael Lund, "'Preventive Diplomacy' for Macedonia, 1992–1997: Containment Becomes Nation-Building," and other chapters in *Preventive Diplomacy in the Post Cold War World: Opportunities Missed, Opportunities Seized and Lessons to Be Learned,* edited by Bruce Jentleson, Lanham, MD: Rowman and Littlefield, 1999; Michael Lund, "Why Are Some Ethnic Disputes Settled Peacefully, While Others Become Violent? Comparing Slovakia, Macedonia, and Kosovo," in *Journeys Through Conflict,* edited by Hayward Alker et al., Lanham, MD: Rowman and Littlefield, forthcoming in 2001. Special note should also be made of an outstanding book forthcoming in 2001 by Barnett Rubin, tentatively titled "The Politics of Preventive Action," which includes four case studies.

PART 2

Surveys of Conflict Prevention and Peacebuilding Activities

II

WESTERN EUROPE

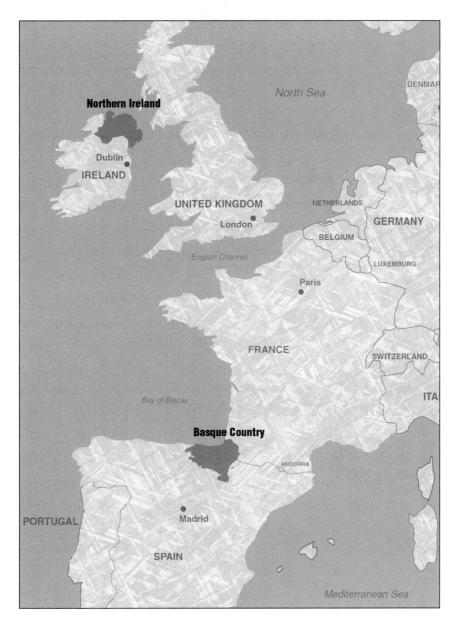

11.1

Northern Ireland: Painstakingly Slow and Small Steps to Bring About Change

Mari Fitzduff & Liam O'Hagan

Northern Ireland, the northeastern section of the island of Ireland, was created in 1921 as a result of the partition of Ireland. Northern Ireland, which is also referred to by some as the six counties, the north of Ireland, or Ulster, has endured a period of civil conflict from 1969 until the present. In the main, unionists want Northern Ireland to remain within the United Kingdom, and nationalists want to relocate Northern Ireland within the Republic of Ireland. Most unionists are Protestant, and most nationalists are Catholics. The situation has stabilized in recent years with a peace process resulting in the signing of the Belfast Agreement on Good Friday, 10 April 1998. Historic breakthroughs since then have been the birth in 1999 of the Northern Ireland Assembly and the long-awaited announcement of the IRA in October 2001 that it had started the process of disarmament.

The partition of Ireland that took place in 1921 was a logical outcome of the British attempts since the twelfth century to achieve dominance in Ireland. One key feature of these attempts was the use of "plantations" of settlers on the island as a means of control. Large tracts of Irish land were confiscated and then given to British soldiers who had fought in Ireland or to groups of people who wished to improve their lot, economically or religiously, by relocating to Ireland. Many of these people and their families eventually integrated their lives with the lives of the native Irish. Others, however, mostly those who came from Scotland and England to settle in the north of the island in the seventeenth and eighteenth centuries, retained their religious and political distinctiveness. These were Protestant farmers whose religion was the result of the recent Reformation, which had divided Christendom and in particular the British Isles, where only the island of Ireland remained loyal to Roman Catholicism.

Throughout the centuries, insurrections and rebellions by the native Irish against British rule had been common. Pressure on the British government to grant independence to the island continued to increase, and after World War I

Northern Ireland
Population: 1,688,600 (1998)
Conflict related deaths:
app. 3,665 (since 1969)
Conflict related casualties:
over 40, 000 (since 1969)

Britain agreed to limited independence. The pressure for Home Rule in Ireland had been firmly resisted by Protestants in the north who wanted to maintain the union with Britain. They feared their absorption into a united, mainly Catholic Ireland, where they believed their religious freedom would be restricted. Protestants also feared the poorer economic state of the rest of the island, compared to their own relatively prosperous region. Most Catholics living in the northern region, who were the descendants of the indigenous people who had been displaced by the settlers through the plantations, wanted independence from Britain and a united Ireland.

The unionists threatened to use force if they were coerced into a united Ireland and began to mobilize private armies against such an eventuality. In an effort at compromise, the then prime minister of Britain, Lloyd George, insisted that the island be partitioned into two sections: The six counties in the northeast would remain part of the United Kingdom while the other twenty-six counties would gain independence. Each state would have its own parliament. The decision to partition the island led to bitter civil conflict between those nationalists who accepted partition and those who rejected it.

At the time of partition in 1921, Protestants/unionists had a two-thirds majority in the region. The first prime minister of Northern Ireland, Sir James Craig, described the state as having "a Protestant Parliament for a Protestant people." This contrasted sharply with the Catholic ethos of the Republic of Ireland. The state effectively discriminated against Catholics in housing, jobs, and political representation. Membership of the Orange Order, a wholly Protestant society that was often essential for progress in politics and business, was forbidden to Catholics. Unionists dominated most local councils. Many unionists believe that such discrimination arose because many Catholics did not want to cooperate with the new state, and because unionists felt that the very existence of their state was threatened by what they saw as a subversive minority.

The ghettoization of society, wherein the two communities often had little contact with each other and discrimination prevailed, provided the main focus for the civil-rights campaigns of the late 1960s. These campaigns, which drew massive support from Catholics in Northern Ireland, were inspired by a worldwide nonviolent movement for civil rights to secure rights to votes, jobs, and services. The civil-rights movement drew a hostile response from the Protestant state, which saw it as a threat to its existence. The eruption of violence on the streets, and the full-scale movement of populations in urban areas into separate Protestant and Catholic communities, led to the formation of local vigilantes that in turn led to the resurgence of paramilitaries in local communities.

The Irish Republican Army (IRA) is the descendant of the most forceful military group that had fought for independence for the whole of the island of Ireland in 1921. By the end of 1969, following the resistance by the unionist government to the civil-rights campaign, the IRA had begun to regroup, and by early 1970 its members were confronting British troops who had arrived on the island to assist with riot control. The violence of the IRA grew into extensive bombing campaigns directed against civilian, public-utility, and military targets. Support for the IRA increased in August 1971 when, in an attempt to curb the escalating violence, internment (imprisonment) without trial was introduced. Hundreds of Catholics were wrongly imprisoned and internment helped to increase significantly Catholic support for the republican paramilitaries. In January 1972 support for the IRA was further increased when British soldiers opened fire on a demonstration by nationalists in Derry, killing thirteen men, an event that was to become known as "Bloody Sunday." The official inquiry concluded that the shooting had "bordered on the reckless" and a new inquiry into this incident is presently taking place in the city of Derry/Londonderry.

The threat of the use of force by the Ulster Volunteer Force (UVF), a Loyalist paramilitary group, in the early 1900s was a consistent factor in the opposition to home rule for Ireland. In the 1960s, a modern version of the UVF was formed. Loyalists were worried by the tentative civil-rights reforms for Catholics suggested by the prime minister of Northern Ireland and recruitment to the ranks of the Loyalist paramilitaries was substantially increased when violence erupted onto the streets in 1969. There was rioting between Catholic and Protestant areas of working-class Belfast almost every night. In the early 1970s, bombings by the IRA became a feature of daily life as businesses in the city center were targeted. There was frequent sniper fire from Protestant areas into Catholic areas and vice versa. Loyalist paramilitary tactics mainly consisted of bombing Catholic pubs and targeting Catholics for murder, and they often justified their killings on the basis that their targets were actively involved in the IRA, although these claims were rarely substantiated.

Throughout the state's history the actions of both Republican and Loyalist paramilitaries have provided most of the horrific headlines in Northern Ireland through their use of bombings, shootings, racketeering, and community intimidation in order to secure political leverage for their cause. The attempt at political agreement in 1974, where there was a power-sharing executive, was destroyed by the actions of Loyalist paramilitaries. The campaign of violence by Republican and Loyalist paramilitaries, with attempts at containment by both the police and army, lasted until the cease-fires of 1994 when the IRA announced "a complete cessation of military operations" followed by the announcement of a Loyalist cease-fire by the Combined Loyalist Military Command. By this stage, Republicans had developed an alternative way to fight for their political goals and Sinn Fein, widely acknowledged as being the political wing of Republicanism and the IRA, was crucially brought on board of the peace negotiations by leader Gerry Adams. In the 1990s, Loyalist paramilitary groups too began to develop their own political wings—the Progressive Unionist Party (PUP) and the Ulster Democratic Party (UDP). These were eventually to play a significant and positive role in the discussions leading up to the Belfast Agreement.

In addition to the representatives of Republican and Loyalist paramilitaries, these negotiations involved the other main political parties. The largest unionist political party in Northern Ireland is the Ulster Unionist Party (UUP). Led by David Trimble, the UUP is something of a broad church in terms of views but is generally seen as a representation of "mainstream unionism." The second main unionist party, the Democratic Unionist Party (DUP) is presently led by Ian Paisley. The party have refused to "negotiate with terrorists" but have strategically remained involved in the process. They are critical of any perceived compromise by Trimble and the UUP.

The Social Democratic and Labour Party (SDLP) is led by John Hume, although deputy leader Seamus Mallon was put forward as Northern Ireland's deputy first minister in 1999. The SDLP is a constitutional nationalist party and represents the middle ground in nationalist thinking. Although they want a united Ireland, they are committed to constitutional politics and nonviolence. Two other parties of note are the Alliance Party of Northern Ireland (APNI), led by Sean Neeson, and the Northern Ireland Women's Coalition (NIWC), led by Monica McWilliams. The APNI is a mainstream party that, although taking a pro-union stance, attempts to appeal to both sides of the community by encouraging cooperation and compromise within Northern Ireland. The NIWC is a relatively new party, having been formed in 1996, and has provided an important middle ground for dialogue among women and, just as importantly, for other political parties.

Conflict Dynamics

It is generally agreed that the paramilitary cease-fires and the current peace process were developed from a combination of factors. First, there was the realization by both the IRA and the British army that the war could not be won militarily, and the decision by the IRA to develop politics, through its political party Sinn Fein, as an alternative way to fight for its political goals. The SDLP played an important role in bringing Sinn Fein into the political process by engaging with them in pursuing common nationalist political goals by peaceful means. The cease-fires were developed through a combination of political dialogue processes that included British government secret contacts with the IRA, SDLP dialogue with Sinn Fein to see if common nationalist goals could be pursued together peacefully, and Sinn Fein and Loyalist contacts with the Dublin government.

Another important factor was the changing social and economic context in which many of the discriminations against Catholics were addressed, and in which a legal and social infrastructure to address issues of inequality, equality, and respect for diversity began to be developed. Alongside this there was an increased willingness by many within civic society—for example, among business, trade union, and community groups—to actively engage in the process of contact and political leverage for peace. As the process began to gain momentum, the development of some new (albeit small) political parties by the Loyalists, and by the NIWC, enabled some new thinking on the political landscape. Finally, a changing international context was an important factor in helping to facilitate the peace process. The proactive involvement from the U.S. government, and many U.S. businessmen and politicians, as well as assistance with developing peace processes from South Africa, are all cited as being important.

After almost two years of political talks, the negotiations that resulted in the Belfast Agreement were finally concluded on Good Friday, 10 April 1998. The agreement was approved by Northern Ireland's main nationalist political parties and most of the unionist parties. At the same time, the governments of the United Kingdom and the Republic of Ireland signed an international agreement. The Belfast Agreement involved constitutional change in the Republic of Ireland resulting in the ending of its territorial claim to Northern Ireland. At the same time, it recognized the right of self-determination on the basis of

North Belfast: Loyalist wall painting

consent, north and south, to bring about a united Ireland, subject to the agreement and consent of a majority of the people of Northern Ireland. The agreement also involved the setting up of cross-border bodies with executive powers, the establishment of a Northern Ireland Assembly based on power sharing, and the early release of paramilitary prisoners. The agreement was subsequently endorsed by referenda in Northern Ireland and the Republic of Ireland on Friday, 22 May 1998. In December 1999 a legislative assembly of both unionist and nationalist politicians was finally set up to share power in Northern Ireland, with ministers and committee members drawn from both sides of the political divide.

Thirty years of conflict have left deep scars in the community. In total there were over 3,600 deaths as a result of the conflict, most of which occurred in the early and mid-1970s. Civilians accounted for more than half of the fatalities. Most of those killed, 91 percent, were male and a majority of deaths, 53 percent, were of people under thirty years of age. Catholics were the majority of those killed (43 percent), as opposed to approximately 30 percent who were Protestant. Most of the fatalities, 59 percent, were inflicted by Republican paramilitaries, 28 percent were killed by Loyalist paramilitaries, and 11 percent by the security forces. In the majority of these killings, no one was convicted. Given the population of Northern Ireland—1.5 million people—it has been estimated that the number of people closely associated to those who were killed or injured is about half the population. It has been a huge price to pay for the inability of the people of Northern Ireland to resolve their differences peacefully.

Official Conflict Management

The governments of Britain and Ireland have been the most important international players in the Northern Ireland context. Direct rule was imposed on Northern Ireland by the British government in March 1972. The intensity of sectarian violence resulted in the deployment of the British army on the streets in Northern Ireland, where they have remained to this day. Throughout this period successive British governments have adopted varying means to manage the conflict. Among these, the British government has developed secret contacts with the IRA, while Sinn Fein and Loyalists have also done likewise with the Dublin government.

Dialogue between the British and Irish governments has often been seen as contentious, particularly by unionists. The dialogue was significantly helped by the fact that the Anglo-Irish Agreement of 1985 afforded the Republic of Ireland a consultative role in the affairs of Northern Ireland for the first time. It was also helped by the Framework Document of 1995 that committed both governments to addressing the internal relationship between the Northern Irish parties, a new all-Ireland relationship, and a review of the relationship between Britain and Ireland. Cementing a formal role for the Republic of Ireland has been an important factor in the current peace process.

The persuasion and support of both the British and Irish government was an important factor in the eventual establishment of the Belfast Agreement.

The United States has been an important player at various times in the conflict. During the 1990s, the United States was of substantial assistance in helping to develop and secure dialogue and peace. The United States had gradually developed a perspective that was able to take account of the needs and fears of unionists as well as nationalists. In the 1990s, spurred by the interests of the Irish vote in the United States, politicians began to focus on ways of ending the violence. U.S. congressmen and people from the business community visited Ireland to persuade the IRA of the need to end the military campaign, and to engage with the unionist community. Such assistance was particularly exemplified by the assistance of Senator George Mitchell, who acted as chair of the talks process for almost two years and whose efforts were invaluable to its success.

Developments in Northern Ireland must also be understood within an increasingly important European context. The continued expansion and development of the European Union have been used by some—for example, John Hume of the SDLP—as a means of recontextualizing the situation in order to envisage a so-called postnationialist society. External assistance offered by the EU was also of significance. When the cease-fires were declared in 1994, the EU decided to help to underpin the peace by allocating £250 million to help build upon the economy and establish peace. Such funds have been useful, as their criteria for distribution included in many cases the need for communities to work together on funding decisions. Such processes ensure that communities can no longer continue to be unaware of each other's social and economic needs, and have in many cases provided very useful training for future collaborative government at both local and regional levels.

In addition, many people have looked to the example of South Africa, and from the mid-1990s there were many initiatives that helped civil society and politicians to learn from the lessons of South Africa.

Multi-Track Diplomacy

Community Relations Commission and Council

When civil violence broke out in 1969 in Northern Ireland, the British government set up a ministry for community relations and a Community Relations Commission, charged with the promotion of policies that would improve community relations. The commission decided to adopt as its main strategy the initiation of local community-development programs across Northern Ireland, based on the belief that communities that lacked self-confidence were more likely to relate aggressively to one another. Although the commission only survived a few years, the process of community development remained an important method of facilitating communication within communities, and between government and communities, and this process continued to underpin many programs that were initiated and funded in the decades that followed.

Subsequently, in 1987, a Central Community Relations Unit was set up, which was located at the heart of government, and in 1990 an independent body, the Community Relations Council, was established to address issues of policy, training, and funding for community-relations work. Consequently, there was a significant expansion of the number of groups working at peace-building, which was facilitated by a hugely increased financial investment in such work. By 1998, the number of civic groups engaging in contact work and developing programs and training to address issues of cultural diversity, justice work, cooperation on social and economic issues, single-identity work, "neutral" venue work, education work, anti-sectarian and anti-intimidation work, trade union work, political dialogue, and mediation work had increased significantly (from 40 in 1986 to 150 in 2000).[1]

Mediators

Throughout the conflict there have been many hundreds of initiatives aimed at achieving contact, or shuttle diplomacy between the participants to the conflict. Shuttle diplomacy is where a mediator tries to increase understanding of differing perspectives through sequential conversations with the participants, rather than through contact between them. Indigenous mediators undertook most of these initiatives, although there were some very useful interventions by people from outside of Northern Ireland and particularly by some who came from a Quaker or Mennonite tradition. Such mediators tried to provide safe and unthreatening opportunities for politicians to look at issues of mutual concern such as social issues, or the economy, the conflict in Northern Ireland, or conflicts elsewhere. Training for such mediation was developed by many civic organizations, and such training provided a pool of people, many from difficult local communities, who were capable of defusing many social and political hostilities, and seeking agreements on many contentious issues.

Initiative 92: Community Consultation
In 1992 a major civil-society program, called Initiative 92, asked local communities and other interested bodies and individuals to express their views about ways forward for the future for Northern Ireland on a political, economic, and social level. Although condemned by most politicians (who initially saw it as irrelevant or threatening), the initiative was a significant success in achieving its objective of stimulating discussion. It received over five hundred submissions from people and groups in Northern Ireland, many of which had been developed on a cross-community basis, and it held public workshops at which various contributors were given an opportunity to expand on their ideas. The submissions were eventually contained in a huge ideas book for Northern Ireland called the *Opsahl Report*. Many of these ideas were to prove fruitful in eventually generating the Belfast Agreement.

Academics
During the 1990s, academics and others who were committed to constructive dialogue processes were very useful in organizing workshops for politicians and others to meet in places like the United States or South Africa in order to address issues of conflict resolution. These conferences often provided opportunities for relationships to form between the politicians, which were difficult to form at home in Northern Ireland given the restricted nature of society and the watchful eyes of the media. In addition, they also provided many opportunities for participants to learn from others elsewhere about what had been useful in constructing peace.

Churches
Although the churches themselves had in the main contributed little to dialogue processes, there were some exceptions. In addition to the work by some members of the Catholic clergy in opening up and developing dialogue with Sinn Fein in order to end violence, confidential workshops were held over a period of several years in the mid-1990s between Sinn Fein and members of the Protestant/unionist clergy. These were very useful in developing understanding between the parties. In addition, there were some Christian groups such as Corrymeela and Cornerstone who were very involved in facilitating contact and dialogue between opposing communities even during very difficult times of the conflict.

District Councils
Northern Ireland has twenty-six local councils that have, with varying degrees, exemplified the hostility that has pervaded much of Northern Ireland's public life. However, in 1990, a district council community-relations program was developed that was eventually established within all councils, despite resistance by many of them. Each of the twenty-six district councils now has at least one full-time community-relations worker addressing coexistence needs

in its local area. As their programs have had to ensure an overall commitment from what are often very divided councils, their existence has marked a substantial sign of progress in the field. Such programs involved contact work, cooperative economic development programs between the communities, cultural events that exemplified cultural diversity, mediation, problem solving, and political discussion workshops.

Business Community

A late, but effective, newcomer to the peace process was the business community, who began, in the mid-1990s, to cooperate with each other and with the trade unions to see if a more strategic approach could be put in place that would put pressure on both Republican and Loyalist paramilitaries to end their campaign of violence. They also publicly encouraged all parties to get involved in political negotiations. Groups such as the Chamber of Commerce, the Confederation of British Industry, the Institute of Directors, and the trade unions involved themselves in dialogue with Sinn Fein and the Loyalist parties, often on issues of the economy. Their influence was very helpful, particularly as it also put pressure on the political parties to enter into serious dialogue.

Cultural Traditions Group

For the entire period of the existence of Northern Ireland, expressions of cultural and political identity have been contentious. However, much of this has now changed—mainly due to the work of the Cultural Traditions Group, a group of academics, practitioners, and policymakers drawn from both the nationalist and unionist communities, which was set up in 1989 to address issues of culture and division. Together they addressed the hostility about the use of the Irish language, which was illegal in certain circumstances, ensured that broadcasters diversified their programs to represent all cultures, and undertook very extensive programs to ensure that the varying aspects of music and symbolism became much less contentious.

Policing

A particular area where issues of diversity were exceptionally critical was in the area of policing. The Royal Ulster Constabulary (RUC) has been a largely Protestant force, with a participation rate of only 6 percent of Catholics by 1994. In 1993, the RUC, in cooperation with the Community Relations Council and various NGOs such as Mediation Network and the Understanding Conflict Trusts, began to develop programs to deal with issues of sectarianism among the force, and to encourage a greater respect and understanding for the differing cultural and political traditions in Northern Ireland. Such training is now an integral part of the initial training of all recruits entering the force, and has also been introduced as part of the in-service training of established police personnel.

Civil Society and New Leaders

The program of community development that began in the 1970s began to pay significant political dividends in the 1990s. In the absence of local democracy, such work had provided for community participation in governmental consultation processes about social, economic, and political issues. By the 1990s, however, it had also helped to generate a new breed of "community" politicians. They developed Loyalist, Republican, and feminist thinking in a way that significantly enriched the political mix of parties who were eventually able to sign the Belfast Agreement. Parties such as the PUP, the NIWC, and Sinn Fein all have considerable experience at community and social politics. Such work also provided them with fruitful contacts gained from their collective experience in addressing local social issues together, and such experience will be useful for the social and economic tasks that face them as representatives in the new Assembly.

"YES" Campaign
Politicians often find it hard to deliver on political agreements because politicians are usually the people who find it the hardest to develop policies of diversity in the face of the fears of their electorates. Thus there is often a need for a constituency for such validation to be developed by their electorates. This can enable or permit them to move with energy on such policies, and here NGOs and others can play a crucial part. Such was the case in Northern Ireland where the work of the NGOs was crucial in developing processes of dialogue, models of training, and constituencies for political agreement both during the pre-agreement phase of the peace process and afterward. The "YES" campaign was a cross-community, cross-party campaign organized by civil-society leaders to secure its endorsement of the Good Friday agreement reached by the politicians in 1998.

Prospects
Northern Ireland is still very much in a state of transition. There is hope, as witnessed through the development and working of the various mechanisms of government. Local politicians have been given opportunities to deal with everyday political issues. The majority of people within Northern Ireland are still supportive of the peace process and there remains much goodwill. There are, however, a number of difficult issues that remain crucial to the future of Northern Ireland. The most difficult of these has proved to be the decommissioning of arms by the paramilitaries. Although agreed as part of the process in the Good Friday agreement, the modalities for such have proved to be the most difficult stumbling block in implementing the agreement. Linked to decommissioning is the issue of the demilitarization of British armed forces, which is of particular importance for Republicans.

The reform of policing was to prove almost equally difficult. From the time of its creation in Northern Ireland, the RUC police force has been seen as not only consolidating the divisions, but as largely representing and supporting the unionist, Protestant majority. The figure for Catholic participation in 1994 was 7 percent. The Patten Report of 1999 (commissioned under the terms of the Belfast Agreement to make recommendations for future policing within

Northern Ireland) made many recommendations about the need to change the nature of the composition of the police force so as to ensure the inclusion of more Catholics. It also recommended many changes to the structures of accountability of the police so as to ensure more overall community responsibility for policing strategy, as well as making recommendation about changing the name and symbols of the police force so that they could be seen as neutral. In addition, a new independent Police Ombudsman has been appointed to oversee complaints about policing. Many of these changes were to prove difficult for many unionists, and agreement on their implementation has taken far longer than expected. However, in autumn 2001, the main nationalist party, the SDLP, agreed, for the first time in history, to take up their positions on the newly formed Policing Board. This agreement should significantly advance the capacity of the police to become a much more representative body, with a capacity to be seen to be serving all communities equally.

Significant advances have been made in housing, employment, and other areas, but much remains to be achieved. There is a problem of long-term unemployment, particularly among Catholics (who are still twice as likely to be unemployed as Protestants), and in ensuring Catholic equality at the most senior levels of the civil service. The danger is that advances for the Catholic community can be perceived as deficits for the Protestant community in a "zero sum" game that does little to foster cooperation. At some point, Northern Ireland also has to deal with its past and the grievances of those who have suffered have to be acknowledged. It is a difficult balance, for while Northern Ireland has to deal with its past it has too often been held hostage to this past.

Finally, parades have been an important feature in Northern Ireland society since the eighteenth century as a means of commemorating and celebrating key historical events, particularly in the Protestant community. For many, they fulfill a social, political, and religious role. The actual number of annual parades has been increasing steadily and substantially over the past ten years, with 1995 seeing a total of 3,500 parades throughout Northern Ireland (an increase of 43 percent from 1986). Opposition to Loyalist parades from Catholic residents' groups has also increased and the "Drumcree" parade has been a focal point for varying degrees of civil unrest in recent years.

Should the Belfast Agreement and the institutions of government fail, the likelihood is that some type of informal joint authority between the British and Irish governments will be established. Relations between the British and Irish governments have improved to the extent that such an eventuality is not inconceivable, and their continuing cooperation is likely to be the most positive force that will sustain and develop peace in the future.

Recommendations

The current peace process, for all its flaws, needs to be supported and nurtured if it is to achieve longevity and lead to a stable future for Northern Ireland. In many ways its very contradictions are a representation of the problems of Northern Ireland society.

The international context has been cited previously. This support is important in the future but at the same time Northern Ireland has to take responsibility for its own future. A situation where all sides have equality of opportunity and a real stake in society is to be encouraged. In this regard it is important that "gains" for one section of the community are not equated as "losses" by the other. This is important if it is to achieve the legitimacy, both internally and internationally, that can see it prosper in the medium to long term.

The money that has come to Northern Ireland through the European Union Special Development Programme for Peace and Reconciliation has been important in helping to stabilize the situation in Northern Ireland. Community work, prisoners' groups, and victims' groups have all been developed through this input. There is a danger that much of this work will be lost as the money dries up. It is important that this does not happen, as grass-roots work from the bottom up is a significant engine for change. Of course, such work is not sufficient on its own and sectarianism retains a grip on large sections of the community. Distrust has been reinforced by the fact that it was possible for many people from one side of the religious-political divide to live, study, pray, work, and socialize almost completely apart from people of the other side of the divide. This situation will not be changed overnight, and it is only by a series of painstakingly slow and small steps that change can come about.

Resources

Reports

Central Community Relations Unit, Northern Ireland Office, *Training for Community Relations Work,* by Marie-Therese Fay, Mike Morrissey, and Marie Smyth, 1998.

Centre for the Study of Conflict, University of Ulster

Clashing Symbols? by Clem McCartney, Belfast, 1994.

Community Relations and Local Government, by Colin Knox and John Hughes, Coleraine, Institute of Irish Studies, Queen's University, 1997.

Community Relations Council, *Annual Reports 1990–99,* by Community Relations Council, Belfast, 1997.

Her Majesty's Stationery Office, "Disturbances in Northern Ireland: Report of a Commission Appointed by the Governor of Northern Ireland," Cameron Report, Belfast, 1969.

INCORE, University of Ulster

Mapping Troubles Related Deaths, by Mari Fitzduff, Derry Londonderry, 1989.

Past Imperfect: Dealing with the Past in Northern Ireland and Societies in Transition, edited by Brandon Hamber, Derry Londonderry, 1998.

Policy and Planning Unit, Northern Ireland Office, *A Typology of Community Relations Work and Contextual Necessities*, Belfast.

Other Publications

A Citizens' Inquiry: The Opsahl Report, by Andy Pollak. Dublin, Lilliput Press, 1993.

A Farewell to Arms? From "Long War" to Long Peace in Northern Ireland, by Michael Cox, Adrian Guelke, and Fiona Stephen. Manchester, Manchester University Press, 2000.

Beyond Violence: Conflict Resolution Processes in Northern Ireland, by Mari Fitzduff. Tokyo, United Nations University, 1996.

In Search of a State: Catholics in Northern Ireland, by Finnoula O'Connor. Belfast, Blackstaff Press, 1993.

Lost Lives: The Stories of the Men, Women, and Children Who Died as a Result of the Northern Ireland Troubles, by David McKittrick, Seamus Kelters, Brian Feeney, and Chris Thorton. Edinburgh, Mainstream Publishing, 1999.

Multiparty Mediation: Northern Ireland as a Case Study, by Paul Arthur. In Chester A. Crocker, Fen Osler Hampson, and Paula Aal P (eds.), *Herding Cats: The Management of Complex Mediation,* Washington, D.C., United States Institute of Peace, 1992.

Northern Ireland: A Political Directory 1968–1999, by Sydney Elliott and W. D. Flackes with John Coulter. Belfast, Blackstaff Press, 1999.

Northern Ireland's Troubles: The Human Costs, by Marie-Therese Fay, Mike Morrissey, and Marie Smyth. London, Pluto Press, 1999.

Northern Protestants: An Unsettled People, by Susan McKay. Belfast, Blackstaff Press, 2000.

Paths to a Settlement in Northern Ireland, by Sean Farren and Robert F. Mulvihill. Buckinghamshire, Colin Smythe Limited Publishers, 2000.

Peacemaking Strategies in Northern Ireland. Building Complementarity in Conflict Management Theory, by David Bloomfield. London, Macmillan Press Ltd., 1997.

Rethinking Unionism: An Alternative Vision for Northern Ireland, by Norman Porter. Belfast, Blackstaff Press, 1998.

Scorpions in a Bottle—Conflicting Cultures in Northern Ireland, by John Darby. London, Minority Rights Publications, 1997.

"Striking a Balance: The Northern Ireland Peace Process," by Clem McCartney. *Accord, An International Review of Peace Initiatives,* Issue 8, Conciliation Resources, 1999.

The Churches and Inter Community Relationships, by Duncan Morrow. Coleraine, Centre for the Study of Conflict, University of Ulster, 1994.

The Politics of Force: Conflict Management and State Violence in Northern Ireland, by Fionnuala Ní Aoláin. Belfast, Blackstaff Press, 2000.

Selected Internet Sites

www.incore.ulst.ac.uk/cds/countries/nireland.html (the INCORE Conflict Data Service: Country Guide for Northern Ireland)

www.cain.ulst.ac.uk/ (the Conflict Archive on the Internet [CAIN] site)

www.northernireland.gov.uk/ (government of Northern Ireland)

www.nio.gov.uk/ (Northern Ireland Office)

www.paradescommission.org/ (Northern Ireland Parades Commission)

www.community-relations.org.uk/community-relations/ (Community Relations Council)

Resource Contacts

Paul Arthur, University of Ulster, e-mail: paul@incore.ulst.ac.uk

Maggie Bierne, Committee on the Administration of Justice, Belfast, e-mail: webmaster@caj.org.uk

Richard English, Queen's University of Belfast, e-mail: politics@qub.ac.uk

Tanya Gallagher, Peace and Reconciliation Group, Derry Londonderry, fax: +44 (0) 28 71 377009

Bronagh Hynds, Ulster People's College, Belfast, e-mail: upc@cinni.org

Neil Jarman, Community Development Centre, Belfast, e-mail: info@cdcnb.org

Avila Kilmurry, Northern Voluntary Trust, Belfast, e-mail: info@nivt.org

Paul O'Connor, the Pat Finucane Centre, Derry Londonderry, e-mail: pfc@www.serve.com

Chris O'Halloran, Belfast Interface Project, e-mail: bip@cinni.org

Organizations

Equality Commission for Northern Ireland
Andras House
60 Great Victoria Street
Belfast
BT2 7BB
Tel.: +44 (28) 90 500600
Fax: +44 (28) 90 331544
Email: cbradley@equalityni.org
www.equalityni.org/

Northern Ireland Human Rights Commission
Temple Court
39 North Street
Belfast
BT1 1NA
Tele.: +44 (28) 9024 3987
Fax: +44 (28) 9024 7844
Email: nihrc@belfast.org.uk
www.nihrc.org/

Data on the following organizations can be found in the Directory section:

Committee on the Administration of Justice
Community Development Center
Community Relations Council
Co-operation Ireland
The Corrymeela Community
Democratic Dialogue
The Glencree Centre for Reconciliation
Horizon Project
INCORE
Irish Peace and Reconciliation Platform
Kilcranny House
Meath Peace Group
Mediation Network
Nonviolent Action Training Project
Peace and Reconciliation Group
Peace Pledge Ireland Campaign

Mari Fitzduff is currently professor of Conflict Studies, and director of INCORE (Initiative on Conflict Resolution and Ethnicity). From 1990–1997 she was director of the Community Relations Council in Northern Ireland. The Council works with government, statutory bodies, trade unions, the media, businesses, and community groups developing policy, programs and training to address issues of conflict in Northern Ireland. In addition to her work in Northern Ireland, Mari Fitzduff has also worked as a program consultant on projects addressing conflict in the Middle East, Sri Lanka, the Basque country, and the CIS States. Her publications include Beyond Violence—Conflict Resolution Processes in Northern Ireland, *published as part of the United Nations series on Conflict and Governance, and* Community Conflict Skills, *a source book of theory and skills for program development in conflict resolution.*

Liam O'Hagan is the research development officer at INCORE. Among his roles at INCORE, he is responsible for the Internet service The Conflict Data Service and he edits Ethnic Conflict Research Digest. *He is also researching a project on demilitarization in*

Northern Ireland that is being carried out by INCORE and the Bonn International Center for Conversion. He is a graduate of the Queen's University of Belfast and the University of Wales at Aberystwyth.

Note
1. Single-identity work is done within a community to increase confidence building prior to contact/cooperative work. Neutral venue work addresses the need to develop physical meeting places that are acceptable to both communities, and is much needed in Northern Ireland where most local venues are sectarian. Anti-sectarian work examines exclusion and discriminatory processes by groups and individuals against other groups, and develops programs to address these phenomena, i.e., reviewing the cross-community nature of staff and management, patrons, choices of holidays, and cultural practices within institutions that are alienated from one or another community. Anti-intimidation work includes addressing the difficulties of divided workplaces where contentious issues of flag flying and discrimination have frequently resulted in violence and sometimes in murder, and furthers the implementation of staff policies and training to deal with such intimidation.

11.2

Spain and the Basque Conflict: Still Looking for a Way Out

Gorka Espiau Idoyaga

When Spain returned to democracy in 1975, it inevitably took on some of the problems that had not been solved (or had been created) during the preceding forty years of dictatorship under Generalísmo Franco. One of the most persistent problems has been the precarious relationship between the central government in the capital, Madrid, and the regions that strive for self-government. The most notable region is known as the Basque Country. Since 1958, a nationalist group calling itself ETA has waged an increasingly violent campaign for Basque independence. Initially, it was met with brutal repression, but with the advent of democracy the government's response to violent Basque nationalism has been the carrot-and-stick approach. Separate talks between ETA and the government have twice been accompanied by cease-fires. Recently, the violence has escalated once again but in spite of this, there is some optimism, albeit extremely cautious, about a nonviolent outcome. Meanwhile, the overwhelming majority of the people in the Basque Country have made it clear that they want the violence to stop.

Euskal Herria, Euskadi, or *País Vasco:* These are the local and Spanish terms that are normally used to refer to the land and its people who live there, on the coast of the Bay of Biscay and the northern and southern slopes of the western Pyrenees that separate Spain and France. About one-fifth of the Basque territory lies in France; the rest is located in Spain and divided into two units, the Basque Autonomous Community and Navarre. The people of the Basque Country share a language, a history, and a culture all their own. Euskara, the Basque language, is said to be one of the oldest pre-Indo-European languages in Europe.

Basque nationalism was born in the early twentieth century. The area already had a long tradition of administrative and mental autonomy, but there had never been a real nationalist sociopolitical movement until then. Basque nationalism was still growing when the Spanish Civil War broke out in 1936.

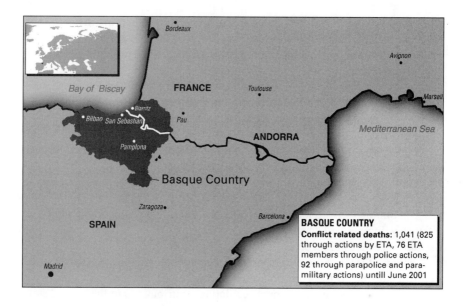

BASQUE COUNTRY
Conflict related deaths: 1,041 (825 through actions by ETA, 76 ETA members through police actions, 92 through parapolice and paramilitary actions) untill June 2001

The autonomous government of the time, made up of Basque nationalists, republicans, and socialists, fought against the coup d'état of the fascist army led by General Francisco Franco. The civil war ended with the victory of the Fascist rebels, and a dictatorship was put in place that was to last for forty years. During this period, a very strong repression took place against any Basque-identifying sentiment: language, culture, self-government, and so on.

Franco died on 20 November 1975. His death gave way to the monarchy of Juan Carlos I de Borbón. The new head of state appointed a government that was charged with transforming the Spanish political regime into a Western-style democracy. The challenges for the new dispensation included dealing with claims for basic democratic freedoms, amnesty for political prisoners, and the demands for sovereignty from the nations within the state, particularly Catalonia and the Basque Country. Both had been in the front line of the political struggle during Franco's regime.

A new Spanish constitution was approved in a referendum on 6 December 1978. Spain was constituted as a democratic state under the rule of law; it assumed parliamentary monarchy as its political form and recognized and guaranteed the right to autonomy of its nationalities and regions. As far as the Basque Country was concerned, the constitution protected and respected its historical rights, but obviously within the framework of the constitution.

The constitution, however, did not succeed in satisfying the claims of the more hard-line Basque nationalists, whose amendments to the new constitution had been rejected. With regard to the referendum, they proposed abstention or a vote against. In the event, 38.66 percent of Basques voted for the constitution and the rest either voted against it (11.21 percent) or abstained (46.61 percent). The key to this rejection lay, according to the critics, in the fact that the right to self-determination of the different nations that make up the Spanish state had not been recognized. An additional bone of contention was that according to the constitution the army was tasked with guaranteeing the territorial integrity of Spain—the army, had, after all, produced Franco.

Later, a system of self-government was negotiated for the three territories that were to become the Autonomous Community of the Basque Country. A similar status was arranged for the region of Navarre. These two statutes certify the administrative distinction of the Basque territories within the Spanish state. This decision continues to give rise to controversy because despite the fact that most citizens in Navarre express a Navarrese and Spanish sense of identity, there is a large minority that considers itself Navarrese and Basque.

The Statute of Autonomy of Gernika and the Ley de Amejoramiento Foral (Law Developing the Charter) for Navarre established the official status of the Basque and Spanish languages, as well as the local powers and institutions: the parliaments, the governments, and their presidents. Among the powers that were transferred to the Autonomous Community at the time, the following stand out: the economic agreement regulating contributions to the central state exchequer after collecting the main taxes directly, the autonomous police force, the creation of the Basque radio/TV station, and education and health systems. This effectively meant one of the highest levels of self-government in Europe. At the same time, the "Additional Disposition of the Statute" laid down that the acceptance of the autonomous system "does not imply that the Basque People would renounce any rights they may have by virtue of their history."

All Basque political parties took part in the negotiation except the pro-independence left, which recommended abstention because they considered the content of the statute insufficient. But this time, 53 percent of the citizens voted in favor, and 41 percent abstained.

Conflict Dynamics

Euskadi Ta Askatsuna (ETA; "Basque Country and Freedom") was formed in December 1958. It was born out of discontent among certain nationalist sectors with what they considered a passive attitude by moderate nationalists in defending Basque culture. It was also aimed against the Franco dictatorship. Initially, it was a political group that restricted its activity to propaganda. Slowly, however, violence became part of its methodology. ETA's first actions were limited to bombs, robberies, and sabotage that only caused damage to property. The police arrested ETA members on several occasions. The first death as a result of an action by ETA occurred on 2 August 1968. During the time of the Franco dictatorship, the ETA action that caused the greatest repercussion was the attack that killed Admiral Luis Carrero Blanco, president of the Spanish government and virtual successor to Franco.

The state responded likewise. Many ETA members died and were arrested during this period and the repercussions did not end when Franco died. One notable event was the kidnapping by the Grupos Antiterroristas de Liberación

(GAL; "Antiterrorist and Liberation Groups"), a paramilitary police organization, of the Basque exiles Joxi Zabala and Josean Lasa in October 1983. Their bodies, with signs of brutal torture, were finally found in the spring of 1995. During this period, senior figures in the Spanish Ministry of the Interior were involved and a total of twenty-seven people were killed as a result of its armed operations.

In the course of the 1970s and 1980s, there were a series of tentative initiatives and contacts between ETA and the Spanish government. First, there was the publication of the so-called Koordinadora Abertcale Socialista (KAS; "Nationalist and Socialist Movement") alternative in 1975. This was a document detailing minimum requirements established by the Basque pro-independence left, which had to be met if they were to accept a process of reform in the Basque Country. The first contacts date from this time.

From 1977 onward, there were sporadic talks between ETA and the Spanish government. There were initial talks between ETA *político militar* (a branch of ETA) and the government. These conversations were to conclude in a process of negotiation whereby ETA *político militar* would disband in September 1982, and its prisoners and exiles would be allowed to reintegrate into society. ETA *militar* was to continue its activity. There were no immediate results, but contacts were renewed in 1984–1985, although they failed to achieve any tangible results. In 1986, ETA and the Spanish government again held talks, a fact that was not made known until 1987 when Txomin Iturbe, the official representative of ETA in Algiers, died. The new representative, Eugenio Etxebeste ("Antxon"), picked up the contacts, which were only then publicly confirmed. Discernible results came two years later, in 1989, when ETA declared a fifteen-day unilateral cease-fire, followed by the first official meeting between the ETA delegation, headed by Antxon, and the Spanish government, represented by the secretary of state for security. The cease-fire was extended and during this period five meetings took place in Algiers. However, discrepancies on the content of the communiqués published by the two sides, which had previously been agreed, led to the breakup of the conversations and the collapse of the cease-fire.

Simultaneously, a political process was unfolding in Spain itself, resulting in the Pact of Ajuria-Enea. It was signed on 12 January 1988 by all the political parties with parliamentary representation, including all the Basque nationalist parties but except the pro-independence left. The document's full name is "Agreement for the Normalization and Pacification of Euskadi," but it became known as the Pact of Ajuria-Enea. The pact set out to establish a single strategy and give an image of unity and cohesion in the face of the violence of ETA, which was not involved in this process. It was based on the defense of the Statute of Autonomy, the need and the importance of police work in the eradication of violence, and the possibility of a solution through dialogue, provided that the will to abandon violence could be demonstrated. The pact also reflected the recognition that there was indeed an unresolved dispute between the Basque people and the Spanish state.

After the failure of the talks between ETA and the socialist government in Algiers in January 1989, the Spanish government deported six Basque exiles to the Dominican Republic, among them the three representatives in Algiers with whom it had been conducting a dialogue. The three were Eugenio Etxebeste, Belen González, and Ignacio Arakama, who are now in Spanish prisons and continue to be considered by ETA as their official interlocutors for any attempt at dialogue. But in the period between 1990 and 1992, both sides continued to sound each other out. These contacts once again passed into the political domain, with the restart of conversations between nationalist parties in the summer of 1992. However, these conversations did not achieve the hoped-for results.

In March 1992 the leadership of ETA was arrested in Bidart, the biggest setback ever for the organization. ETA's leadership was dismembered and it necessitated a radical change in the organization's negotiating strategy. The change became evident with the appearance of the so-called Democratic Alternative. This document contained a new proposal for negotiations that envisaged two different scenarios: one between ETA and the Spanish state, and the other among the political players in the Basque Country. The proposal stated that, once the first stage was passed (in which the Spanish state "should recognize the right to self-determination and the territorial unity of the Basque Country, and guarantee respect for what the Basque people decide democratically"), ETA would announce a "cease-fire." This would then clear the way for a "democratic process in which Basque citizens would decide on all aspects related to the organization and the future of the Basque Country."

Alberto Arzoz/Panos Pictures

Weekly vigil by relatives of ETA prisoners
in front of a local government building in Pamplona

But before any moves toward more dialogue or even an agreement were achieved, there was to be another violent phase in the conflict. In November 1993, the shooting of Joseba Goikoetxea, a sergeant in the Basque police force, was interpreted as another step in the strategy of ETA of attacking the Basque nationalist majority, which had stated it was against violence. These differences within the nationalist world, which had existed for as long as ETA, would increase with time. Other major events were the actions carried out in 1995 against the conservative Partido Popular (PP): the shooting of Gregorio Ordoñez, the president of the PP in Gipuzkoa, in January of that year and the failed attempt on the life of its president, Jose María Aznar. The assassination of the local councillor of the PP, Miguel Angel Blanco, brought thousands of citizens out onto the streets in protest. These events showed, yet again, that the majority of society (both nationalist and non-nationalist) rejected the use of violence as a means of political action. In 1995, representatives of ETA met Alfonso Pérez Esquivel, the 1980 Nobel Peace Prize winner, and asked him to act as interlocutor with the Spanish government. Esquivel accepted and exchanged messages with the deputy interior minister, Margarita Robles. The first tentative moves toward dialogue were again under way.

Then, on 12 September 1998, an important political milestone was reached. Four Basque political parties, together with some trade unions and social movements, signed the Declaración de Lizarra in which they adopted a methodology to solve the conflict similar to that used in the Irish peace process. Immediately afterward, on 16 September, ETA declared a unilateral, unconditional, and indefinite cease-fire. These events opened up the process of change or transition in the Basque situation from one of chronic, violent conflict toward a possible situation of peace and consensus. After some initial months of confusion, contact was made between members of ETA and Spanish-government spokesmen.

However, there was strict political division over the Lizarra Declaration. There were two groups. One was represented by the parties that signed the declaration, the other by those who did not. These divisions basically persist until the present day. In broad terms, the first group thinks that the "Basque problem" is a political problem. The peace process should therefore be accompanied by another process of dialogue and agreements that would eventually provide a response to the conflict. In the final stage, the will of the majority of the Basques, expressed freely, clearly, and democratically, should be respected. This group has also reproached the Spanish government for its entrenched position and lack of a political agenda, which has not contributed anything to the peace process.

The second bloc, led by the government, is of the opinion that peace basically means a definitive surrender by ETA. For them, the conflict is nothing less than the very fact that ETA exists. Once this organization has disappeared, they believe, any other problems can and should be solved within the already existing political and institutional channels and within the limits of the Spanish constitution and the Statute of Autonomy. This group has criticized the first group for trying to obtain political advantages for nationalism in exchange for peace.

This political split around the peace process has been rendered more serious by the cancellation of the cease-fire in December 1999. ETA based its move on the "absence of political progress" and started a violent offensive against politicians, journalists, businesspersons, intellectuals, members of the judiciary and armed forces. This took the form of the killing of notable figures such as socialist leader Fernando Buesa and university professor Ernest Lluch. A climate of political noncommunication and "fronts" emerged, fed by continuous polarization and controversy. Anything to do with the Basque conflict, whether it be a central or secondary issue, has meant an intense, noisy, and bad-tempered controversy. Dialogue, previously quite common, is now almost nonexistent between the political forces of both tendencies.

Official Conflict Management

There have been attempts and strategies to bring this situation to an end. Basically, all of them come under one of the following three models: "the security solution," "force," and "nonviolence and dialogue." The first two have been dominant. In the last thirty years, the official stance of the different governments on the Basque problem has been to defend a law and order solution to the situation. However, this strategy has been inefficient in finishing off an organization that has proven able to regenerate itself. At the same time, the use of violence by ETA, apart from ignoring the desire for nonviolence expressed by most Basque citizens, prevents a normal dialogue on underlying political issues. As a result, the conflict is maintained within its present parameters.

The third way, nonviolence and dialogue, has hardly had a chance to succeed, and any attempt has always been partial and incomplete. The first example of this was the Ajuria-Enea Pact, in which all political parties, including the ruling party, took an active part. In recent years, however, the meetings arising out of this pact have resulted in a succession of arguments and disagreements as a result of the different interpretations the political parties have made of the pact. Some have emphasized political unity, support for security measures, and isolation of the nationalist left. Others have defended an interpretation of the pact that would allow dialogue to take place and bring about a political solution to the problem. A complicating factor is the lack of compliance on the part of the Madrid government with the Statute of Autonomy. For these reasons, the pact is currently unworkable.

The second and best example of this third model was the attempt at a peace process that began with ETA's cease-fire. It began in September 1998 and has shown a positive partial result: sixteen months without any political killings and an unprecedented expectation of peace. Enthusiasm and hope were clearly present in Basque and Spanish society. This opportunity, however, has been lost for the time being. In the words of a senior church figure very familiar with the conversations between the government and ETA, "the intransigence of one side and the impatience of the other" have conditioned any progress.

As far as the two main political parties are concerned, the Partido Popular, which is currently in power, or the Partido Socialista, which was in power at the time of the Ajuria-Enea Pact, share a fairly hard-line position. But there are some clear differences of approach: the Partido Socialista does not deny the political nature of the conflict, is not unwilling to undertake a bilateral or multilateral dialogue, and is in favor of introducing changes in penal policy, which the current Spanish government is not adopting. Although the official version has historically denied "the existence of a political problem and the possibility of dialogue with the terrorists," various attempts at dialogue or negotiation with ETA took place. It is clear that the Partido Popular is not prepared to go this far. When it came to power in 1996, the channels of communication that had been open thus far were closed, be it temporarily.

Multi-Track Diplomacy

The Basque Country has an extensive network of associations working in the fields of peace and the promotion of human rights. International NGOs do not carry out specific programs in this area. The Basque conflict has been historically considered as an internal problem of the Spanish state, and has been analyzed exclusively from a security angle. As a result, the work done to transform the Basque conflict from a social and political perspective has not been able to garner support at the international level. Still, one of the main reasons for optimism is surely this great variety of associations, as well as the commitment by most Basque people, expressed in several demonstrations and reflected in almost all opinion polls, to find a democratic solution based on the end of violence and dialogue without limits or exclusions.

Gesture for Peace in the Basque Country

Coordinadora Gesto por la Paz de Euskal Herria (Gesture for Peace in the Basque Country) was born in 1986 with the aim of expressing Basque society's rejection of the use of violence as a political tool. Its main contribution lies in the area of the mobilization of society, characterized by silent demonstrations in many places in the Basque Country every time any death arising from the conflict occurs. At the beginning of the 1990s, it took on a high profile because it channeled the Basque people's call for nonviolence to a considerable extent. It now complements this work with specific contributions in areas related to the humanization of the conflict and Education for Peace.

Elkarri

Elkarri, the social movement for dialogue and agreement, was born on 20 December 1992. Its main activity lies in furthering the process of dialogue without exclusion to bring about the transformation of the Basque conflict, carrying out what it defines as "social mediation." Its work focuses on awareness campaigns, and greater knowledge and activity within society regarding the matters that sustain the conflict, and the search for its democratic transformation. Among its main initiatives, the following are worthy of mention: the Conference on the Future of Navarre, Local Forums for Dialogue and Agreement, and the

Social Initiative for a Peace Conference for the Basque Country, whose main objective is to facilitate public and unofficial dialogue between the different political parties and civil society.

Gernika Gogoratuz

Gernika Gogoratuz (Center of Peace Studies) mainly works in the area of research and training in dealing with conflicts. Its mission consists of the recovery and dissemination of historical memory, and activities aimed at providing scientific backup for efforts made in search of peace. Its activities have mainly focused on the annual organization of the International Seminar of Culture and Peace of Gernika, and the promotion of its documentation center.

Denon Artean

Denon Artean is a group that works with victims of violence in the city of San Sebastián. It has various support and assistance programs for people affected by ETA's operations. It is one of the promoters of the Association of Victims of Terrorism in the Basque Country (Covite) and the Basta Ya ("We've had enough") platform.

Senideak

Senideak (the Association of Relatives of Basque Prisoners) focuses its work on support for people who have a relative in jail related to the conflict. Senideak condemns situations in which people's human rights have been infringed in prisons, works on the political level against the prisoner dispersal policy, and provides humanitarian aid for prisoners and their relatives.

Prospects

The Basque conflict is now in a transition period between the end of a cycle of confrontation and the start of a cycle of solution. Like any other transition period toward a peace process, it is contradictory. The old ways have not completely died out and the new ways have not been born yet. The best example to explain this apparent contradiction is the existence of a strongly structured civil society that demands nonviolence and political dialogue without exclusions. What is especially important is that this defense of dialogue occurs separately from political preferences and the feeling of identity. In comparison to similar conflict situations, analysts understand that society is ready for a peace process that involves the parties giving something up along the way. This reality represents the future, but at present it has to exist alongside elements from the past that can be seen in violence and the lack of communication at a political level.

Among the positive elements, three factors stand out. First, the hope and willingness of the Basque people are exemplary. The extreme tension observed at the political level is not reflected at the grass-roots level. People have a reconciliatory attitude toward the future and are showing signs of disappointment at the strained political climate. This is shown time and again in the mass demonstrations that follow each political murder. It was also reflected in the results of the 2001 elections in the Basque Autonomous Community, which were focused on the debate for dialogue as a means of transforming the conflict. Moderate nationalism (antiviolence) emerged on top and electoral support for ETA's ideas diminished considerably. Social, economic, church, and civic figures are raising critical voices in representation of society, which is actively showing itself to be in favor of nonviolence and dialogue.

The second positive factor is the idea of all-party talks. It does not seem likely that this forum will be constituted in the short term, mainly as a result of ETA's operations and the denial of political dialogue by the Madrid government. Nevertheless, it offers hope for the future in that it provides an opportunity for transformation. In this respect, the Social Initiative for a Peace Process, presented in 2001, stands out. It has received the support of over 50,000 people in Basque society, in the form of signatures and a financial contribution. The objective of this conference is to set up a forum of political parties to reach basic agreement on the principles and procedures for dialogue.

There is a third, very important element that is having a great impact on the Basque conflict in its current form. Many people in the Basque Country are aware of the international trend toward solutions to violent conflicts through dialogue (e.g., South Africa and Northern Ireland). The peace process in Ireland has without any doubt had the greatest effect on this conflict. It is a conflict within the European Union and has similar elements to the Basque conflict: the search for a suitable legal and political framework for a society that is complex in terms of its expression of identity, the effects of violence, the relationship between community and territory, the problems of the victims and political prisoners, etc. This reality, and the close relationship that some political forces have maintained with the main protagonists of the Good Friday Agreement, mean that the Irish peace process is the one factor that has most accelerated the change of attitude of Basque political parties toward a willingness to find a solution through dialogue.

Administrative problems remain. Twenty years after the Statute of Autonomy was approved, its application and development are still subjects of political controversy. More than thirty powers (or "competences") are still claimed by the Basque government and parliament. They have not been transferred. Among them is the management of social-security contributions. In this context, laws that were aimed at creating an opportunity for social peace through the consolidation of the self-government of the Basque Country have not achieved the objective of transforming the conflict.

The Basque peace process is faced with two major obstacles to its progress. One is ETA, whose continuing operations do not respect the majority will of Basque society for nonviolence. The other is the lack of a political agenda from the Spanish government. ETA's activities represent an offensive against human rights and normal coexistence. This is met head on by the other side, which persists in its refusal to enter political dialogue on underlying matters and the basic rules of coexistence that could be accepted by people of different opinions within the Basque Country.

The spiral of violence and noncommunication feeds itself continuously. Violent attacks and police operations take place in succession. The former will never succeed in gaining the stated objective (independence) because of the overwhelming imbalance of forces and the lack of majority support from the people. The latter are insufficient in themselves to prevent further violent actions and are incapable of bringing about a lasting peace. Given that this is a conflict with deep political roots, a law-and-order approach does not offer definitive results. The short-term outlook is, therefore, one of indefinite impasse, unless new political initiatives can rescue the process from its present stagnation. The challenge lies in achieving a negotiation phase; otherwise, the current deadlock could take the process to a situation in which violence spirals, creating a risk of irremediable social division.

Recommendations

The thinking about conflicts in general has, over time, produced very clear results. There is detailed knowledge of which factors and actions prolong, worsen, and stagnate the problem: violence and the refusal to enter into dialogue. There is also a conviction about which factors can transform the situation and stimulate its positive development: nonviolence and political dialogue without exclusion. In the Basque case, it is a matter of attempting a political process similar to the one that led to the Good Friday agreements in Stormont-Belfast, in the Northern Ireland case. As regards the future, there are several priorities on which efforts should be concentrated to overcome the present state of affairs in the Basque process toward peace:

General

1. *Dialogue.* It is essential to promote dialogues from this moment on, with the aim of comparing the different points of view. Inclusive talks are considered fundamental to bringing about convergence and solutions to the underlying problems. We talk of a forum, although it should be situated within a flexible methodology in which, for example, there would be a specific talking circle for the Basque Autonomous Community, another for Navarre, and so on. Other appropriate forms of dialogue could be attempted, provided they do not exclude any political current.

2. *Promote a culture of reconciliation and participation.* The peace process requires that the search for dialogue and agreement should not only take place among the political elite but also in society at large. It is therefore essential to preach and practice a culture of reconciliation, understood as the development of abilities and skills in society to solve its conflicts in a positive way, without violence but through dialogue and respect for the various sensitivities and opinions. Moreover, the network of associations in the country can encourage people to participate and get social consensus that already exists at the grass-roots level across to the politicians, something the present political debate does not reflect.

3. *Reaching an agreement on the definition of the conflict.* It is necessary to make progress toward a convergent definition of the nature of the Basque conflict. Work should be done on establishing a "bridging" definition that expresses the antagonistic visions of the conflict. There is, at present, no basic agreement on the political rules of the game or, to be more specific, on the area and framework of decision. This basic consensus is the basic constituent of an integrated coexistence and a prerequisite in order to guarantee the normal opposition of the plurality of identities, projects, and political expressions. To achieve this, an extra effort at political dialogue and consensus on everyone's part is required in order to correct the lack of legitimacy that the current political framework presents.

4. *Humanization.* The consolidation of this process requires measures that will humanize the conflict. In addition to being imperative from the humanitarian and justice angles, these measures would contribute toward generating the climate of trust and tranquillity essential for the success of a peace process. There are three priority fields in which these measures can be implemented: dialogue and consensus around the treatment of victims in the peace process, the modification of the penitentiary policy so that the dispersion of prisoners is brought to an end, and finally an end to violent acts and sabotage in the streets.

5. *Making an intellectual effort to explore new and emerging concepts.* Sovereignty, interdependence, self-government, or self-determination are controversial concepts that are arising from different experiences and events in the world, and that can be approached from the angle of the transformation of conflicts. Many intellectuals and experts feel that it is possible to find new readings, interpretations, and applications of the ideas and concepts found in various constitutional frameworks. This involves proposing a new, shared starting point. Taking legal instruments in current codes as a basis, formulas can be found that refer the process of dialogue to the will of citizens, expressed freely and democratically.

Government
The government in Madrid could make a stronger contribution to the progress and consolidation of a peace process through support for the two driving forces that could consolidate it most effectively: (1) inclusive talks and (2) the humanization of the conflict. It should be involved in establishing a political agenda on the matter. Many observers regret the absence of an active, positive policy by the Spanish government. In this sense, the peace process in North Ireland is a point of reference that should be followed very closely.

The European Union
The transformation of a process such as the one in the Basque Country requires help and facilitation from the outside. The international community, governments, and institutions can help in bringing the Basque conflict into the realm of a peace process and democratic solution. Various peace movements in the Basque Country have emerged with the following proposals:

- Approach the Basque problem as a European matter. The Basque case *is* a European problem. The priority of the citizens of this part of Europe is pacification and normalization. Europe is asked to do something about it, if only for this reason.
- Prepare a European, suprastate position on pacification. This requires a critical and constructive look at the problem and the possible solutions to it. The vision of the Spanish state, as a direct part of the problem, is very important, but it should not be the only one. Its information and proposals are surely biased and based on its own past experience. Other points of view, both popular and political, should complete the European definition of the Basque case.
- Promote anything that can change things democratically, that is, initiatives based on nonviolence and dialogue without exclusions. The intervention of the European Community in the Basque peace process should be made specific, either publicly or privately. It should consist of the commitment of political resources that would be compatible and establish a synergy with the most constructive dynamics of the sociopolitical players who are directly involved.

Resources

Publications

Basque Politics and Nationalism on the Eve of the Millennium, by W. Douglass, C. Urza, L. White, and J. Zulaika. Basque Studies Program Occasional Papers Series No 6, University of Nevada, Reno.

Basque Politics: A Case Study in Ethnic Nationalism, by W. Douglass. Basque Studies Program, University of Nevada, Reno.

Dirty War, Clean Hands: ETA, the GAL and Spanish Democracy, by Paddy Woodworth. Cork: Cork University Press, 2000.

Militar en ETA, edited by Moneo Alcedo and Miren Hamburu. San Sebastian: Haranburu Editors, 1996.

Negotiating with ETA: Obstacles to Peace in the Basque Country, 1975–1988, by Robert P. Clark. Reno, University of Nevada Press, 1990.

"Political Autonomy and Conflict Resolution: The Basque Case," by Jose Manuel Castell and Gurutz Jauregui. In Kumar Rupesinghe and Valery A. Tiskhov (eds.), *Ethnicity and Power in the Contemporary World,* Tokyo, United Nations University Press, 1996.

The Basque History of the World, by Mark Kurlansky, New York, Walter & Company, 1999.

The Making of the Basque Nation, by Marianne Heiberg. Cambridge, Cambridge University Press, 1989.

Selected Internet Sites

www.cities.com/bastayaonline (Basta Ya)

www.elkarri.org/aldizkaria.html (Elkarri magazine)

www.euskadi.net/estudiossociológicos (Sociology Studies Group of the Basque Government)

www.euskadi.net/pakea (Peace Initiatives of the Basque Government)

www.eustat.es (Eustat. Servicio de Estadística del Gobierno Vasco)

www.ibs.lgu.ac.uk/forum/newtimes.htm (online access to a selection of articles)

www.incore.ulst.ac.uk (INCORE guide to Internet sources on conflict in the Basque
   Country)
www.lizarra-garazi.org (Lizarra Agreement)
www.manos-blancas.uam.es (Manos Blancas)
www.nodo50.org/pazeh (documents of interest on the Basque conflict)
www.unr.edu (University of Reno, Nevada)
www.usuarios.tripod.es/FOROERMUA (Foro de Ermua)

Resource Contacts
Jesus Herrero Arranz, Gesto por la Paz, e-mail: gesto@kender.es
Juan Gutierrez, Gernika Gogoratuz, e-mail: gernikag@sarenet.es
Gorka Espiau Idoyaga, Elkarri, e-mail: bizkaia@elkarri.org
Mario N. López Martínez, Subdirección del Instituto de la Paz y los Conflictos, e-mail:
   mariol@ugr.es
Christopher Mitchell, Institute for Conflict Analysis and Resolution, e-mail: cmitchel@
   gmu.edu

Organizations
Denon Artean
Zabaleta 1 2º
Donostia 20002
Tel.: +34 (94) 342 7200
Fax: +34 (94) 329 2188

Senideak
Plazaberri 2
Hernani 20120
Tel.: +34 (94) 333 5900
Fax: +34 (94) 333 5901

Data on the following organizations can be found in the Directory section:
Assembly of Cooperation for Peace
Campus for Peace
Centro de Investigacion para la Paz
Gernika Gogoratuz
Gesto por la Paz de Euskal Herria
Instituto de la Paz y Los Conflictos
Justiticia i Pau
Movimiento social por el diálogo y el acuerdo, Elkarri
Seminario de Investigacion para la Paz

---

*Gorka Espiau Idoyaga is the International Affairs Coordinator of the Social Movement
for Dialogue and Agreement in the Basque Country, Elkarri. A graduate in social sciences and media studies from the University of the Basque Country, he is currently
preparing his doctoral thesis on the subject, entitled "New Formulas of Sovereignty
as a Method of Transforming Conflicts: The Basque and Irish Cases." He works as an
international analyst for several Basque, Spanish, and international media, and has
participated as a speaker in the main universities that study the Basque conflict. At
present he is a senior member of the management team for the Peace Conference for
the Basque Country.*

12

EASTERN MEDITERRANEAN

12.1

Cyprus:
A Civil Society Caught Up in the
Question of Recognition

Oliver Wolleh

Following the Turkish invasion in 1974, Cyprus was divided into two by and large ethnically homogenous parts. The potential for societal actors to transform the conflict has been severely limited because the actors on each side of the divide refuse to extend recognition to the other, and each avoids any contacts that could suggest "implicit recognition." Avoiding indirect recognition of the other's legality makes any cooperation between institutions and interaction between people problematic, if not impossible. A political solution is unlikely as long as both parties adhere exclusively to their legal frameworks and do nothing to create the conditions for any meaningful confidence-building measures. However, the more frequent efforts of societal actors to initiate peacebuilding projects and the acceptance of Turkey as a candidate for EU membership give some reason for optimism. On the other hand, allowing the Greek part of the island to enter EU membership could provoke a fierce Turkish reaction and create another crisis.

The relationship between Greeks and Turks on Cyprus began in the sixteenth century when the Ottoman Empire conquered the island, ruled at that time by the Venetians. Greek Orthodox Christians and Muslims inhabited all parts of the island, though the two communities remained quite separate, with little intermarriage and little coeducation. Apart from the Greek Orthodox and Turkish Muslims, there have always been groups of Maronites, Armenians, and Jews on the island.

During the three hundred years of Ottoman rule peaceful coexistence prevailed. When the British landed in 1878, they formally ended the Ottoman rule and, in 1925, Cyprus became a British Crown Colony.

Colonial rule gave rise to nationalist movements that led to the independence of the island. Nationalism also engendered political visions that were incompatible with the multiethnic character of Cyprus, with its mixed settlements. At the beginning of the 1930s, the clerical and political elite of Greek Cypriots formed a movement with the aim of uniting Cyprus with the "Greek

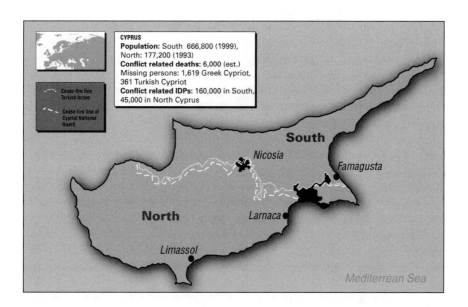

CYPRUS
Population: South 666,800 (1999),
North: 177,200 (1993)
Conflict related deaths: 6,000 (est.)
Missing persons: 1,619 Greek Cypriot,
361 Turkish Cypriot
Conflict related IDPs: 160,000 in South,
45,000 in North Cyprus

Cease-fire line
Turkish forces

Cease-fire line of
Cypriot National
Guard

South

Nicosia

Famagusta

North

Larnaca

Limassol

Mediterrean Sea

Motherland." However, the British government was not prepared, for strategic reasons, to relinquish the island and blocked what was known as the Enosis Plan by Greece and the Greek Cypriots. As a result of the Greek *enosis* movement and the subsequent rise of Turkish nationalism after the collapse of the Ottoman Empire, the idea of dividing the island into two ethnic units (*taksim*) developed within the Turkish Cypriot community. Another vision was the integration of the whole island with Turkey, or to divide the island and to unite it politically with Greece and Turkey respectively.

In 1955, the Greek Cypriot underground movement Ethnilci Organosis Kyprion Agoniston (EOKA; "National Organization of Cypriot Fighters") began the armed struggle for *enosis* against British colonial rule. In response to the armed struggle, the British used the Turkish Cypriot units against the EOKA as the Turkish community on the island opposed the union with Greece. During this time, apart from Turkish Cypriot police units, the first Turkish armed underground organizations such as Volkan and later Tòrk Mukavemet Tesil–li (Turkish Resistance Organization) were formed. With support from Turkey and the permission of the British colonial administration, they took up the fight against EOKA. As a consequence, the relations between the communities worsened significantly. Negotiations in Zurich and London in 1959 and 1960 between Great Britain, Greece, and Turkey led to the independence of Cyprus. This was considered a compromise. All three states became guarantors of the new Republic of Cyprus (RoC). However, in 1960 the majority of the island population and its political leadership found themselves in a state that did not correspond to their original political ideas. Under these circumstances, the young republic's complicated, very detailed, and clearly bicommunal constitution was very difficult to implement.

In 1963, President Makarios attempted to implement thirteen constitutional changes to overcome the internal constitutional crisis and political stalemate. On the Turkish Cypriot side, this was perceived as an attempt to change the constitutionally based distribution of power and thus triggered violent intercommunal fighting, during which about one thousand Turkish and two hundred Greek Cypriots were killed. The crisis led to the resignation of the Turkish Cypriot members of the government and to the formation of Turkish enclaves. In 1964, the previously mixed communities were divided politically and administratively. The physical separation of the communities and intercommunal violence led to the involvement of the UN Security Council and the deployment of the UN Peacekeeping Force in Cyprus (UNFICYP). This phase of the conflict is particularly painfully imprinted in the collective memory of the Turkish Cypriot community since their enclaves were partly besieged by Greek Cypriots; 361 Turkish Cypriots who vanished at the time have never been found. Following the division, the remaining Greek Cypriot administration gradually became the internationally accepted representative of the RoC.

After the military coup in mainland Greece in 1967, the demand for *enosis* among the island Greeks increasingly lost political support, but the Greek Cypriot government and the developing Turkish Cypriot administration in the enclaves were unable to resolve the constitutional crisis.

On 20 July 1974, Turkish troops landed in response to a coup against president Makarios, supported by the Greek Junta, with the aim of *enosis*. During the two-staged invasion approximately 45,000 Turkish Cypriots fled from their enclaves to the north of the island controlled by the Turkish army, while 160,000 Greek Cypriots fled to the south. To this day, 1,619 Greek Cypriots, including civilians, are still missing. Since 1974, between 30,000 and 35,000 Turkish troops have been stationed in the north. The United Nations has demanded their withdrawal in numerous resolutions.

In 1975, the Turkish Cypriots declared the Turkish Federal State, and in 1983 the Turkish Republic of Northern Cyprus (TRNC), but to date Turkey is the only country that has extended recognition.

Conflict Dynamics

The status quo on Cyprus is marked by a geographical separation of the Turkish and Greek ethnic groups into ethnically homogeneous areas. A buffer zone controlled by UNFICYP divides the Greek Cypriot southern part of the island from the Turkish northern part. There are very few direct lines of communication between these two parts, nor any official economic relationships.

For the Greek-Cypriot community, the Cyprus question is mainly viewed as an international problem related to the Turkish invasion and occupation. The intercommunal level of the conflict has been downplayed or completely denied. As a consequence, the complete withdrawal of Turkish troops and the unrestricted return of refugees are the central demands of the Greek Cypriots. The settlement by mainland Turks is also a contentious issue.

The Turkish Cypriots, on the other hand, emphasize the intercommunal character of the conflict and insist on their right to self-determination as an ethnic group. The coup against Makarios and the taking over of the government by the notorious EOKA terrorist Nicos Sampson are considered to have been a fundamental threat to the Turkish Cypriot community. According to this interpretation, Turkey intervened to enforce peace. For that reason the Turkish Cypriot side pleads for a presence of Turkish troops and settlers and, at the very most, only very limited resettlement of Greek Cypriots. Both sides are supported unconditionally by their "mother countries," Greece and Turkey.

A key factor in understanding the dynamics of the Cyprus conflict, both on the level of formal negotiations and at the level of civil society, is the status of the RoC and of the TRNC.

Since the Turkish Cypriot community has abandoned the state institutions of the RoC, the state is controlled, for all practical purposes, by island Greeks. According to the Greek Cypriots, the RoC has never ceased to exist, a position that corresponds to the international legal position. Based on this, the Greek Cypriot government claims to be the sole and rightful representative of Cyprus. This claim is refuted by the Turkish Cypriots on the grounds that the Constitution of 1960 was rendered invalid with the withdrawal of the Turkish Cypriots from all state institutions.

For their part, the Turkish Cypriots have made every effort to achieve equal status. In international negotiations and practical dealings concerning the Cyprus conflict, two linked demands are raised repeatedly: either the Greek Cypriots downgrade their claim to be the sole representatives, or the status of Turkish Cypriots is upgraded. So far, the Greek Cypriots have rejected all attempts by the island Turks to upgrade their status. This was the case in 1975 at the declaration of the Turkish Federal State and at the unilateral declaration of independence of the TRNC in 1983. The island Greeks consider their status as the sole representatives of the recognized government as their only advantage compared to the military superiority of Turkey and its support of the island Turks. To abandon this status in order to enter into open negotiations is generally considered unacceptable.

Decades of separation have cemented the rift between the communities. The economic gap between the North and the South has widened to the disadvantage of the north. Apart from the embargo imposed by the island Greeks, there is also an EU embargo on the North, which severely limits the North's ability to export. In 1994, the embargo was tightened by the European Court of Justice after an application by the Greek Cypriot government.

When the Greek Cypriot government applied for EU membership, this created additional controversy. Since 1990, when the EU approved the application of the Cyprus government for membership, the TRNC has been invited to participate as part of the official Cypriot delegation at the acceleration talks. However, the North has stated that it will only participate as an independent political unit or state and not as a part of the RoC.

In addition to this, the 1990s were characterized by renewed nationalism on the island. This was apparent in the growing militarization of the Cyprus conflict (especially in the S-300 missile crisis), the Unitary Defense Dogma of Greece and the RoC, the threat of war with Turkey, and an increasing buildup of arms on both sides.

Official Conflict Management

The Turkish invasion of 1974 caused the UN's involvement in the conflict to change. In Resolution 353 (1974), the Security Council asked all member states to preserve the sovereignty, independence, and territorial integrity of Cyprus. Furthermore, it demanded an end to the military intervention and the withdrawal of foreign military personnel to the extent that their presence was unjustified by international agreements. Following that, a framework for negotiation was developed that gave the Secretary-General an important role to initiate negotiations described as "intercommunal talks" on the basis of his "good offices." Within this framework of negotiations, the representatives of the two communities could ostensibly face each other on equal footing.

There have been numerous attempts by succeeding UN secretaries-general to start negotiations, but none of them has led to a solution. However, some intercommunal negotiations have achieved moderate success. In 1977 and 1979, both sides agreed on a "bicommunal," "bizonal," and "federal" solution, but the positions of both parties regarding the actual implementation of this formula diverge widely. While the Greek Cypriots and the mainland government in Athens aim for a federation with a strong central government in which the Turkish population has a minority status, the Turkish Cypriot government strictly rejects the legal status as a minority. Instead it pleads for a model with a relatively weak central government and a strong federal state. This difference of opinion has not changed, except that during the 1990s it was discussed under the headings of "federation" and "confederation"—terms that then were highly charged with emotion.

In spite of the differences that remain, the results of the 1977 and 1979 intercommunal negotiations marked a milestone, since both communities at least formally abandoned their original purely nationalistic concepts (*enosis* and *taksim*). For the Greek Cypriot side, and for large parts of their population in particular, the willingness to accept a federation is considered a major compromise.

Another controversial issue, apart from the authority of the "federal government," is the proportional participation of the population in federal institutions. While the Greek Cypriot negotiators plead for a distribution of 80:20 according to the size of the respective communities, the Turkish Cypriots invariably demand an equal representation (50:50) and/or veto power. The size of the envisioned political units is also a matter of controversy.

One of the most detailed and influential moves during the negotiations was initiated by the then UN Secretary-General Boutros Boutros Ghali. He suggested a comprehensive framework of agreements with the aim of creating a holistic base to find a solution to the Cyprus conflict. The "Set of Ideas" made suggestions on all controversial issues discussed above. It also contained map-making proposals for the shape of political units. However, it did not lead to any concrete results, and in the end the Secretary-General blamed Turkish Cypriot representative R. Denktash for having rejected its basic premise.

After the "Set of Ideas" had failed, the UN aimed for the implementation of confidence-building measures. These included a drastic reduction in the number of the Turkish military units, a reduction of the Greek Cypriot defense budget, bicommunal contacts on the expert level, cooperation in questions such as the water supply (which is a problem for both sides), the reopening of the international airport at Nicosia (which has been closed since the invasion), and the return of the uninhabited town of Varosa. In spite of some hopeful developments in the beginning, these negotiations, too, did not lead to any positive results, as each side insisted on an indirect acknowledgement of its respective legal position.

This caused the suspension of the intercommunal negotiations, and they only started again in 1997 in New York. Neither the New York talks nor their continuation in Switzerland in the summer of 1997 produced a breakthrough. Rather, the Turkish Cypriot positions hardened during this time as they now demanded an explicit recognition of the TRNC as a state and proposed a confederation as the ultimate solution. Renewed negotiations beginning in 2000 have not led to any solutions as of the summer of 2001. The fact that the Turkish Cypriot side is now insisting on official recognition and that the negotiations are taking place in separate rooms give no reason for optimism.

Multi-Track Diplomacy

The potential for bicommunal projects initiated by NGOs in the North as well as in the South is severely limited because of the mutual nonrecognition of the official actors. This absence of social cooperation is rooted in the desire to avoid any "implicit recognition."

The results of this are that the vast majority of bicommunal encounters and projects are informal, such as in dialogue and discussion groups, or at cultural and musical events organized by private persons. Any cooperation, for example, between students and professors of different universities is almost impossible because both institutions operate according to the laws of "their" states and receive funds from "their" respective governments. The Greek Cypriots fear that any official contact would indirectly legitimize the existence of the TRNC. As a consequence, the island Greeks are usually only prepared to participate in informal contacts. The Turkish Cypriot side also avoids implicit recognition, but in a different form, as the basic existence of a Greek Cypriot state is not questioned. Island Turks will generally avoid anything that indirectly acknowledges the existence of the RoC with its claim of sovereignty over the entire island. For that reason, they are open to informal meetings and avenues of cooperation when both sides act as legally equal partners. The problem of recognition also has consequences for the movement of people. Island Greeks find it especially difficult to cross over into the North as they are

Greek Cypriot soldier looks over buffer zone
toward Turkish-occupied Northern Cyprus (August 1996)

either denied entry or have to fill out forms in order to enter the North. These are interpreted as an implicit recognition of the northern state and are therefore avoided. The majority of contacts happen in the UN-controlled buffer zone.

One of the most important social peacebuilding initiatives is associated with the Conflict Resolution Trainer Group. Through its network of facilitated bicommunal follow-up groups, a process of dialogue and encounters has been created that, since the events of 1974, is unique in its intensity and extent. The trainer group consists of thirty Greek and Turkish Cypriot members and can be defined as an internal grass-roots structure aiming to initiate a range of peace-building projects. Between 1994 and the end of 1997, the trainer group implemented a multi-track diplomacy approach and founded twenty-five bicommunal follow-up groups, initiated several projects, and arranged visits to the other side for citizens.

The bicommunal trainer group first began to take form in 1993 and took over two years to establish. It was the result of cooperation between committed Cypriots as well as of foreign actors. It began as two separate groups in the two communities (monocommunal phase) and developed into a group that met and acted on a bicommunal basis.

Initially, the training of the Cypriots in conflict resolution was carried out by members of the Institute for Multi-Track Diplomacy and the National Training Laboratories, which formed the Cyprus Consortium together with the Conflict Management Group from 1994 onward. This project was sponsored by the Cyprus Fulbright Commission and funded by the U.S. Agency for International Development through Amideast. Apart from local training, the Cyprus

Consortium also carried out a number of workshops with students and potentially influential partners in the United States. Over the years, the trainer group has also been supported by several Fulbright scholars.

In the first phase, several follow-up bicommunal groups were formed by the trainer group: the Educators Group, the Citizens Group, the Federation and EU Studies Group, Peace Concert, the Cultural Evening Planning Group, the Letters to the Other Side Group, the Technology for Peace Project Group, the Management Group, the Women's Group, Young Political Leaders, Young Business Leaders, Students I, and the Lawyers Group. The bicommunal follow-up groups usually meet every two to three weeks and consist of between five and thirty persons.

In the summer of 1996, all bicommunal activities came to a complete halt. In August 1996 three Greek Cypriots lost their lives in violent clashes within three days. These incidents caused an outcry among the Greek Cypriot community. Because of demonstrations on the Greek Cypriot side, meetings of the bicommunal groups were impossible. Furthermore, the Turkish Cypriot authorities closed off all crossings to the southern part of the island. The blockade of the meetings by the Turkish Cypriot authorities lasted until March 1997, and could only be lifted after intervention by foreign embassies and the United Nations. The influence of the Turkish Cypriot group members on their government was not sufficient. When there was access to the buffer zone, it again led to a whole series of projects and the formation of numerous new groups. During the second phase, groups such as the Citizens Group II-VII, the Students Group II, the Co-Villager Project, Youth Encounters for Peace, Young Environmentalists, the *Hade* magazine, the Artists Group, the Federalism Group, and the Environmental Group were founded. In addition, new forms of "cross visits" (visits crossing the de facto border) took place. Inspired by the success of the groups, the United Nations also started major bicommunal events in the buffer zone and "cross visits" to religious sites on both sides of the island.

The foundation of a common, bicommunal NGO has been on the agenda of the Conflict Resolution Trainer Group for a long time but has not come to fruition, as the affiliation of an NGO with one of the two legal systems implies recognition of this particular state. The funding of bicommunal projects on the Turkish Cypriot side has turned out to be especially difficult because, on account of their nonrecognized status, the Turkish Cypriot groups have had no access to international funding.

Despite these obstacles, the trainer group did develop a network of informal citizens' groups. Coordination was very difficult because of the heterogeneity of those groups and because it would have provoked a counterreaction. The aims of this multi-track approach were to promote conflict-resolution training and to initiate a "deep dialogue" between the group members characterized by the steps "listening—understanding—acknowledging." For many Cypriots, the first encounter and consequent exchange between people of different communities is an important intellectual and emotional event. For the first time there is an opportunity to listen to the point of view of the other community in regard to historic events of the conflict as well as in regard to contemporary issues. These activities have led to a major learning process and resulted in a more balanced view of the past, a less negative image of the other community, and increased understanding and trust. Moreover, it has given hope to people that some day reconciliation can take place.

In December 1997 the Turkish Cypriot government used the decision of the EU not to accept Turkey as a candidate for membership as a pretext for a renewed blockade of all bicommunal activities in Nicosia by refusing to grant exit permits to its citizens at the local checkpoints. This blockade was to last until the EU summit in Helsinki in February 2000. Since then, the situation has improved slightly. Still, the restriction of movement is one of the main obstacles to the implementation of a comprehensive multi-track diplomatic approach. There is a meeting place in the bicommunal village of Pyla in the buffer zone to which the access has not been blocked by the Turkish Cypriot authorities. But as it is fairly difficult to reach, it is of only limited use for continuous group work. Despite its remote location, Pyla developed throughout the first half of 2001 into a meeting space for an increasing number of bicommunal citizens' groups. However, with the increased number of bicommunal activities, the Turkish Cypriot authorities also started restricting access to the village of Pyla. The problem of restricted movement applies not only to the multi-track groups of trainers but also to a number of other initiatives past and present.

The Doob Group, for example, which was funded by L. W. Doob in the 1980s, had to stop when its members launched common projects. Similarly, the initiative Citizens for Democracy and Federation in Cyprus, founded in 1989, failed when, after only a few meetings, its Turkish Cypriot members were no longer able to obtain passes.

The development of bicommunal groups was only made possible because of the support of the Cyprus Fulbright Commission, the U.S. Embassy, the United Nations, and other embassies. The establishment of the Westminster Group, named after an event sponsored by the Westminster Foundation in 1993, was only possible because its members were able to meet in the building of the British High Commission and could rely on its support.

The potential of small NGOs or groups to safeguard their freedom of movement is clearly limited on Cyprus. Those who are able to afford it prefer to meet on foreign soil. In 1997, an Initiative of Businessmen was founded by the Greek Cypriot C. G. Lordos and the Turkish Cypriot V. Chelik. During meetings in Athens, Istanbul, and Brussels (1997), two lists of projects were discussed. The group gained international attention because of the participation of Richard Holbrooke, who had organized the meetings in Brussels as well as encounters in Oslo (July 1998) and Istanbul (December 1998). When the group meets in Nicosia these days, they are facilitated by a representative of the International Peace Research Institute, Oslo. Though their project lists resemble each other, they have had little success in reaching agreement on implementation because of the problem of mutual recognition.

Another initiative relying on meetings abroad is the summer camp project with Cypriot adolescents in the United States (Seeds of Peace) financed by the Fulbright Commission. Since 1997, there have been two or three such camps per year during which the young people are partly looked after by members of the trainer group and are trained in communication and conflict resolution. Back on Cyprus, they hold fairly regular weekend meetings in the village of Pyla. The activities of these youth groups have increased since the beginning of 2000. In the same vein, a number of left-wing youth organizations have organized numerous meetings outside Cyprus.

Politically influential groups, on the other hand, are able to guarantee more or less regular encounters on the island itself. The representatives of the political parties, for example, meet regularly for talks in the buffer zone. They are facilitated by the Slovak Embassy, but safeguarding freedom of movement is not an issue. Two further long-standing initiatives are meetings of left-wing Greek and Turkish Cypriot trade unions as well as the cooperation of both municipalities in Nicosia within the Nicosia Master Plan.

Since 1995 there have been several bicommunal trade union conferences in the buffer zone. Apart from this, a number of subgroups have been established that have published declarations in which the organizers advocate a future federal constitution, as well as common employment standards and social structures following the resolution of the conflict.

The Nicosia Master Plan is the oldest example of bicommunal cooperation on Cyprus. Since 1979, the municipalities of North and South Nicosia have cooperated on sewage and water-supply issues. After its launch, the project, which mainly consists of meetings of experts (e.g., architects, doctors, etc.), was extended. Originally supported by the United Nations Development Progam, the United Nations High Commission on Refugees (UNHCR) took over as the lead party in 1986. The funds, mainly from the United States, were distributed by the UNHCR to bicommunal projects. When the UNHCR had to stop its activities on Cyprus, this function was taken over by the United Nations Organization for Project Services (UNOPS) in 1998. In contrast to the UNHCR, the UNOPS is free to fund NGO projects and has already financed extensive training in mediation in both communities, a mediation center, and a management center in the South, as well as the bicommunal choir. UNOPS also co-funds a research project carried out by the Cyprus Peace Centre in the South that deals with the attitudes and perspectives of the other community. UNOPS, with its annual budget of US$10 million, is a powerful funding agency on Cyprus. It is also fairly accessible to Turkish Cypriots and aims to promote a societal exchange at all levels.

Prospects

The decision of the EU to grant Turkey the status of an official EU candidate has shaken up the structure of the Cyprus conflict considerably. Since Helsinki (in February 2000), the Cyprus question has, more than ever, become a European problem as Greece, Turkey, and the Greek Cypriots refer to the EU rules as their common denominator. Turkey is more and more often confronted with demands that it really can't afford to ignore to resolve the conflict peacefully.

At the same time, the traditional nationalistic social patterns of both communities are increasingly under pressure. According to the political culture of the EU, neither the Greek Cypriot demand for a central government nor the Turkish Cypriot model of two ethnically and politically separate states offers an acceptable solution.

It is unlikely that the EU will formally recognize the TRNC as an independent state. It can be hoped, though, that the EU succeeds in convincing both sides that unification of the island is impossible within the legal framework of the RoC as it exists now, or by unifying the RoC with the TRNC. A future united Cyprus will have to have a constitution going beyond the existing ones. If the negotiations can be focused on a "third" legal way, then a common legal basis can develop, even during the transitional phase, on which the civil-societal actors will be able to act without touching on the question of implicit recognition.

At present, the idea of rapprochement is more acceptable in the Greek Cypriot population than ever before. There is a fear, however, that in pursuing this approach they might lose the only trump cards they believe they possess in the conflict with the North.

Recommendations

At the end of 2001, the conditions for a comprehensive multi-track diplomatic approach to the Cyprus problem are difficult and complex. Because of the controversial question of recognition, any cooperation that goes beyond dialogue and encounters is hardly possible between state and nonstate organizations. As long as the political leaders on each side are unable to agree on a common legal framework, the inner societal actors themselves lack the legal framework for pursuing other and more extensive forms of cooperation and exchange. At present, both civil societies lack their most characteristic tool: the freedom to enter into contracts. Furthermore, the opportunities for informal encounters of civil-societal actors are also restricted. The repressive measures, especially by the Turkish Cypriot authorities, with respect to bicommunal contacts, limit the possibilities for free exchange between persons willing to enter into a dialogue. Turkish Cypriots alone have restricted freedom of movement and access to the buffer zone.

The chances that societal actors can be assured of bicommunal encounters as a way of launching common projects and engaging in planning activities depend on the political assertiveness of groups and organizations in the North. One way of exerting pressure on the Turkish Cypriot authorities is for the international community to challenge violations of civil rights in the North.

Today, both Cypriot societies have an extensive and well-qualified pool of experienced trainers and facilitators at their command, in part because of the years of training given by foreign actors. Foreign actors should now focus less on conflict-resolution training and more on fulfilling a function as an "institutional bridge" for Cypriots and NGOs willing to cooperate. Foreign NGOs can (nominally) become initiators of bicommunal projects without touching on the question of recognition. This model would give Turkish Cypriots (in co-operation with their Greek Cypriot counterparts) better access to international funding (e.g., by the EU) where that access has been severely limited because of their status as citizens of an internationally unrecognized state. However, within the moment of Cyprus's EU membership the political and legal parameters of societal actors will change significantly. It is very likely that the RoC will become an EU member within the first round of expansion in 2004.

Most probably the Cyprus problem will not be solved by then. There is a serious danger that the Turkish reaction on an EU-membership for the Greek-Cypriot part will be extremely fierce. Annexation of the TRNC or even a blockade of the island might be possible. It is also expected that the northern authorities will end all bicommunal activities, thus removing possibilities for citizens to meet in the buffer zone. Under these conditions, it is important to make stronger use of multi-track strategies, which focus on civil-society development in the North and South. The Greek-Cypriot government needs to create and open up avenues for Turkish Cypriots living in the North toward the EU and their fellow Greek Cypriots. This strategy, however, will remain under serious constraints if no way is found to loosen up the concept of implicit recognition and its restrictive consequences for civil society. Nevertheless, at the end of 2001 there are small but optimistic signs that the Cyprus government is beginning to explore this avenue.

Resources

Newsletters and Periodicals
Cyprus Bulletin, Press and Information Office, Republic of Cyprus
Cyprus Mail, Greek Cypriot English-language daily
Cyprus Today, Turkish Cypriot English-language daily
Cyprus Weekly, Greek Cypriot English-language weekly
Hade: Bi-Communal Magazine
Kibris-Northern Cyprus Monthly, TRNC Ministry of Foreign Affairs and Defense, Public Information Office
The Cyprus Review

Reports
Berghof Research Center for Constructive Conflict Management, *Local Peace Constituencies in Cyprus: Citizens' Rapprochement by the Bi-Communal Conflict Resolution Trainer Group,* by Oliver Wolleh, Berghof Report No. 8, Berlin, 2001.

Other Publications
Cyprus, A Country Study, edited by E. K. Keefe et al. Washington, D.C., American University, 1980.
Cyprus: A Regional Conflict and Its Resolution, edited by Norma Salem. New York, St. Martin's Press, 1992.
Cyprus: The Failure of Mediation and the Escalation of an Identity-Based Conflict to an Adversarial Impasse, by Ronald J. Fisher. *Journal of Peace Research* 38, no 3, 2001.
Cyprus: The Need for New Perspectives, edited by Clement H. Dodd. Huntington, England, The Eothen Press, 1999.

Sovereignty Divided: Essays on the International Dimensions of the Cyprus Problem, by Michael Moran. Nicosia, CYREP, 1999.
The Cyprus Conspiracy, by Brendan O'Malley and Ian Craig, London and New York, I. B. Tauris, 1999.
The Rise and Fall of the Cyprus Republic, by Kyriacos C. Markides. New Haven, CT, Yale University Press, 1977.

Selected Internet Sites
www.americanembassy.org.cy/bicommun.htm
www.fulbright.org.cy (Cyprus Fulbright Commission)
www.peace-cyprus.org

Resource Contacts
Nicos Anastasiou, local conflict resolution trainer, e-mail: nicosiew@spidernet.co.cy
Benjamin Broome, professor at the Arizona State University, e-mail: bbroome@asu.edu
Maria Hadjipavlou, local conflict resolution trainer, e-mail: mariat@zeus.cc.ucy.ac.cy
Tumer Hali, Bureau of Bi-Communal Reconciliation and Strengthening of Civil Society, e-mail: tumerh@hotmail.com
Niyazi Kizilürek, professor at Cyprus University, e-mail: niyazi@ucy.ac.cy
Eleni Mavrou, AKEL (Communist Party of Cyprus), e-mail: emavrou@akel.org.cy
Servgül Uludag, local conflict resolution trainer, e-mail: servgul@europe.com

Data on the following organizations can be found in the Directory section:
Conflict Management Group
Cyprus Peace Center
Institute for Multi-Track Diplomacy
Women's Civic Initiative for Peace

Oliver Wolleh is a political scientist and associated researcher at the Berghof Research Center for Constructive Conflict Management, Berlin. Dr. Wolleh completed his Ph.D. on track-two strategies on Cyprus in 2000. His special interests include preventive and postwar peacebuilding, the complement between societal and governmental processes, and conflict-resolution and mediation training. His regions of interest include Cyprus and the Caucasus.

12.2

Turkey:
At the Crossroads

Mensur Akgün

A cursory reader of Turkish politics will have undoubtedly seen the above title on several different occasions. It is, however, quite likely that this overused, overburdened metaphor will not be utilized anymore in the future, not only because of academic efforts to find other, less exploited concepts, but also because Turkey will indeed have "crossed the road" and become a fully democratic society without the stigma of a questionable record on human rights. Despite existing problems at present, there is hope for a solution. This hope stems from Turkey's prospective EU membership. However, human-rights abuses and democratic deficiencies are not the only problems Turkey faces today. Cross-border issues such as the one with Greece in the Aegean and its dispute with Syria over water also need to be addressed.

This chapter is an attempt to describe most of Turkey's violent and potentially violent problems, including Partiya Karkeren Kurdistan (PKK; "Kurdistan Workers Party") separatism, the Kurdish question, and international disputes

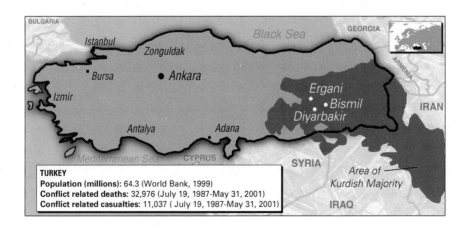

TURKEY
Population (millions): 64.3 (World Bank, 1999)
Conflict related deaths: 32,976 (July 19, 1987-May 31, 2001)
Conflict related casualties: 11,037 (July 19, 1987-May 31, 2001)

liable to lead to friction with its neighbors, such as the water issue with Syria and its jurisdictional disputes with Greece. Other conflicts will be touched upon as the need arises, but the main emphasis will be given to the Kurdish question throughout.

One can easily trace back the origins of the Kurdish question to the early nineteenth century. When the Ottoman Empire began to crumble, new states were formed on the former territories of the empire based on nationality. In reaction to that, the "Young Turks" began to embrace nationalism as a unifying concept—a decision that has had repercussions in modern times. To the extent that "Turkishness" was glorified and statehood was reduced to mere ethnicity, and where other identities flourished, conflicts erupted. As one of the leading scholars of Turkish politics aptly claimed, the prevalence of tribal politics, personal piety, educational standards, level of economic development, and social conservatism have also contributed to the conflict dynamics.[1]

The first Kurdish "rebellion" of relatively modern times took place at Süleymaniye, a district of contemporary Iraq, in 1806, and with some intervals lasted about thirty years. During the same period, other clans also raised their voices against the Sublime Porte, the place of political power for Turkey's imperial past, and riots continued throughout much of the nineteenth century. The final major uprising of the century lasted about three years, from 1878 to 1881. The region was then relatively calm until the end of World War I. The common feature of all riots in this period was their strong tribal and religious content overshadowing the ethnic component.

At the end of the war, the abortive peace treaty signed at Sevres between the defunct Istanbul government and the Allied powers provided for a commission to draft a scheme of local autonomy for the predominantly Kurdish area east of the Euphrates, south of Armenia, and north of Syria and Mesopotamia, with the intent of self-determination. But after the end of the war of independence waged in Anatolia, that treaty was never implemented. Instead, a new peace treaty was signed that defined Turkey within borders that have changed little since that time.

The two major rebellions of the republican era were the Sheikh Said rebellion of 1925 and Dersim (Tunceli) rebellion of 1937. Despite similar ethnic appeal, the origin of the current conflict, causing the suffering of thousands of people, is rather recent and largely a function of the organization of the PKK, established by a group of young leftists in Ankara during the 1970s. The leader of the group from the very beginning was Kurdish political-science student Abdullah Öcalan, born in the province of Urfa in 1948.

After fleeing to Syria in 1979, Öcalan began using camps in the Bekaa Valley, Lebanese territory under Syrian control, and launched attacks on Turkish police stations and similar targets in the southeastern provinces north of the border with Syria and Iraq. Öcalan's presence in Syria has complicated Turkey's relations with this country and delayed the solution of a water-rights dispute in the Euphrates-Tigris basin.

In fact, relations with Syria have almost always been problematic. Successive Syrian administrations could never accept Turkey's annexation of its former Hatay district in 1939 through plebiscite and via horse trading involving the mandatory power, France. Syrian maps still depict this part of Turkey as Syrian territory. Although causing occasional public outcries in Turkey, this sociopsychological drama was not taken very seriously by the Turkish authorities even during the heyday of the PKK, when the Syrian support for the organization became a point of contention in the water dispute.

There is no explicit demand for restitution on record from the authorities in Damascus. Given the other problems Syria faces, it is highly unlikely that there will be one in the future. The only real issue, which has strained relations or might strain them in the future, is the water issue. Syria, together with Iraq, has opposed virtually all of Turkey's development projects in the Euphrates-Tigris basin because Damascus claims that those installations will reduce the quantity of water flowing to Syria and Iraq. As early as the 1960s, Syria tried to hinder the development of the Keban and Karakaya dams. Today Damascus continues to raise objections to the Gòney Dogn Anadolu Projesi (Southeast Anatolian Project) with which Turkey is attempting to develop a network of twenty-two dams in the mainly Kurdish-populated areas of the country.

Nonetheless, relations between the two countries have developed at an unprecedented speed since Öcalan's departure from Syria in October 1998. The newly elected president, Ahmet Necdet Sezer, went to Damascus to take part in Hafiz Assad's funeral as his first "official" foreign trip. Before this historic trip, an agreement had been signed between the two countries on 20 October 1998 in Adana, Turkey. For the first time, the Syrian government designated the PKK a terrorist organization and pledged not to allow the organization to operate on its territory. The water dispute seems now to be reduced to a mere technicality and Ankara is keenly interested in finding an equitable solution to the problem.

However, Öcalan's expulsion from Syria strained Turkey's relations with Italy and Greece. Although Öcalan's first stopover was Moscow, the Russian authorities were quick to deport him in order to maintain amicable relations with Turkey. He was later detained in Italy on charges of using a false passport. Italy's treatment of Öcalan and Rome's reluctance to extradite him led Turkey to impose economic sanctions. In the end, Turkey's reaction compelled the Italian authorities to abandon Öcalan and he had to leave Italy for an unknown destination.

Öcalan mysteriously vanished, but later turned up and was captured in Kenya on 16 February 1999, and was taken back to Turkey by the Turkish secret service. It was later revealed that he was first transported from St. Petersburg to Athens and spent two nights there before moving on to the Greek embassy in Nairobi. But contrary to the expectations, the embarrassment felt by the Simitis government in Greece, and the resignation of hard-liner foreign minister Theodoros Pangalos soon led to a new phase in bilateral relations between Greece and Turkey.

Although the risk of military confrontation between Greece and Turkey has been significantly reduced in recent years, the possibility of a political crisis remains. Avoidance of any future crisis requires acknowledgement of the problems, particularly in the Aegean, where the major ones can be summarized as competing claims concerning territorial waters, delimitation of the continental shelf, militarization of the Eastern Aegean islands, disputes over airspace, and disagreements over so-called gray areas where there is no agreement on exact maritime boundaries.

If one were to classify the problems hierarchically, the conflicting claims to territorial waters would definitely be at the top. Under the present six-mile rule, Greece holds approximately 43.5 percent of the Aegean Sea, while the corresponding figure for Turkey is 7.5 percent. The remaining 49 percent is high seas. According to the Turkish authorities, "Should the territorial sea be extended to 12 miles as Greece advocates, the Greek territorial sea in the Aegean will increase to 71.5% whereas Turkey's territorial sea will only increase to 8.7%."[2] The area defined as high seas would be reduced to just 19.7 percent. Such an extension would enable Greece to have direct control over nearly three-quarters of the Aegean. Moreover, Turkey's current 126.5-kilometer front on its west coast would be reduced to 11.9 kilometers.

Greece, on the other hand, believes that it has the right to extend its territorial waters to twelve nautical miles in accordance with the Convention for the Law of the Sea (LoS) and notes that this right is exercised by the vast majority of coastal states throughout the world, including Turkey. In response to the Greek parliament's ratification of the LoS on 31 May 1995, the Turkish parliament bluntly declared that any move on the part of Greece to extend its territorial waters beyond the six-mile limit would be perceived as an act of war (*casus belli*). Athens argues that Turkey is attempting to blackmail Greece to give up a legal right emanating from an international treaty and is violating Article 2(4) of the UN Charter.[3]

With respect to the continental-shelf dispute, the positions of the parties are also hardly compatible. Following a semiscientific research attempt by Turkey in 1973 on the Aegean continental shelf in response to similar unilateral actions by Greece, the dispute came to the attention of the international community, and since then has been considered by Greece to be the sole problem between the two countries. On 10 August 1976, Greece appealed to both United Nations Security Council and the International Court of Justice (ICJ). The Security Council, in its Resolution 395 (25 August 1976), called upon the parties "to resume direct negotiations over their differences" and asked them "to do everything within their power to ensure that these result in mutually acceptable solutions."[4] Two weeks later, the ICJ rejected the Greek request for interim protective measures. The Court decided that areas beyond territorial waters were "areas in dispute."[5]

On 11 November 1976, Turkey and Greece signed an agreement in Bern and assumed the obligation to refrain from any unilateral initiative or act concerning the Aegean continental shelf. Although the Bern Agreement is still valid and its terms continue to be binding for both countries, they nevertheless tried to avoid the terms of the agreement in at least in two instances. In 1981, Greece started seismic activities and planned drilling operations in the disputed areas of the Aegean continental shelf, and Turkey reciprocated in 1987. A violent end to the serious crisis that followed Turkey's move was barely averted with the meeting of the two prime ministers in Davos, Switzerland, in January 1988. The issue is dormant at the moment and does not present any imminent threat for the security and stability of the region.

With the exception of the airspace-related problems, the others can be considered as auxiliary issues. They can easily be settled after reaching a compromise on the borders of the territorial waters of the Aegean. Some of them are kept on the agenda either to prove the aggressiveness of the other side or for future use as bargaining chips. Even the airspace problem is a rather trivial issue based on an unprecedented claim of sovereignty by Greece extending four miles beyond the limits of its territorial waters. Turkey has, however, occasionally challenged these limits. In return, the Greek air force has intercepted Turkish aircraft.

Conflict Dynamics

The Kurdish Question

The capture of Abdullah Öcalan and his revelations unavoidably caused a decline in the support enjoyed by the PKK organization domestically and internationally. The PKK is now reduced to a force confined primarily to the mountains of northern Iraq. There has not been a single major assault since they retreated from Turkey in September 1999 in compliance with Öcalan's orders. Still, the PKK is considered by the authorities as a threat to the integrity of the country and the security of the mostly Kurdish-populated regions. For the settlement of this problem, Ankara seems to follow a double track. On the one hand, the same heavy-handed policies are pursued against the insurgents, while on the other, leniency is shown toward the local population.

As acknowledged even by the authorities in Ankara, for final resolution of the problem, Turkey needs to tackle it from a different angle and recognize the "cultural rights" of the Kurds. Although there are no legal barriers to the participation of the Kurds in the economic, political, and social life of the country, ethnic identities are only recognized in the private sphere and almost never allowed to spill over into the public or political arena. The constitution and the Act on Political Parties prohibit ethnic and religious parties even when they don't advocate violence. Education and TV broadcasting in Kurdish are de jure banned. Yet three of Turkey's ten presidents were of Kurdish origin and Kurd representation in the parliament is larger than the Kurdish proportion of the population.

Despite the recent changes, freedom of expression is severely restricted in Turkey under the constitution and numerous laws. Particularly, Article 312 of the criminal code and the Act for the Prevention of Terrorism are in desperate need of revision. Not only the Kurds, but almost anyone can be summoned to prosecutor's office and sued for views expressed on ethnic and religious affairs. In March 2000, for instance, the mayor of Istanbul, Recep Tayip Erdogan from

"Demokrasi" is a pro-Kurdish Turkish-language newspaper published in Istanbul with a circulation of around 12,000 copies a week. Three of its predecessors were closed down by the state, but only after dozens of pro-Kurdish journalists were murdered and arrested, and the premises bombed (April 1997).

the Virtue Party (religious), was sentenced to ten months' imprisonment for quoting a poem written, ironically enough, by the author of the national anthem. As long as these rules and practices persist, the Kurdish-Turkish problem will remain on the agenda. However, at present, because of Turkey's candidacy to join the European Union, major reforms are under way and a package of thirty-four amendments to the constitution—concerning freedom of thought, prevention of torture, freedom of association—was adopted on 3 October 2001.

Relations with Syria

Syria officially claims that the Euphrates and Tigris rivers are "international water courses" and "shared resources." The waters of these rivers must be shared among the riparian states according to a fixed quota. Such a quota should be determined by a simple "mathematical calculation" based on declared demands of each riparian country. First, the capacities of the rivers are to be calculated, then water shared according to the stated figures. If the total demand exceeds the water potential, the exceeding amount should be proportionally deducted from the demand of each riparian state.[6]

Turkey, on the other hand, believes that the idea of "sharing the common resources through a mathematical formula" represents a complete contradiction of the principle of "equitable utilization" that is the core of the codification exercises in this field. Because Syria's arable landmass represents only 48 percent of the total contemplated to be irrigated, it believes that it is uneconomical and inequitable to utilize scarce water resources to irrigate infertile lands at the expense of the fertile lands of the southeastern Anatolia.[7]

Despite these divergent views, there have been various discussions with respect to water disputes between Syria and Turkey. Still, it has so far been impossible to reach a compromise accommodating the interests of both countries. With the settlement of the PKK score, Turkey is more likely to consult Syria and take into account the interests expressed by Damascus. At least there is no further need to talk of water as an instrument of influence.

Greek-Turkish Relations

In June 1999, Turkish foreign minister Ismail Cem and Greek foreign minister George Papandreou instructed their respective ministries to initiate a process of consultation and joint work on bilateral issues. One month later, Turkish and Greek joint committees started a dialogue. As a result of this dialogue, nine agreements on promoting cooperation in several fields, ranging from environment to combatting terrorism, have been concluded during the exchange of official visits by foreign ministers Cem and Papandreou in January-February 2000.

As has often been pointed out, the rapprochement between the Turkish and Greek NGOs after the devastating earthquakes each suffered in 1999 provided another incentive to the diplomatic efforts for improvement in bilateral relations. The endorsement of Turkey's EU candidacy on 10 December 1999 at the Helsinki Summit also enhanced the spirit of cooperation. Athens and Ankara now collaborate on a wide range of issues, so much so that the Greek and the Turkish armed forces have taken part in joint exercises such as the one held in Greece between 20 May and 10 June 2000. However, despite the public and diplomatic rapprochement, the positions of the parties have not yet changed with respect to the Aegean disputes, and have even hardened with respect to Cyprus. Ankara's urge for dialogue on the Aegean issues has not yet been reciprocated by Athens. Greece continues to maintain a "one problem-single solution" policy, while Turkey is seeking an "equitable negotiated settlement."

Official Conflict Management

Turkey has never recognized the PKK as a legitimate partner for any sort of political bargaining. The Turkish authorities flatly refused mediation attempts even during the peak of the problem. Therefore, there are no known instances of official conflict-management endeavors. On the other hand, the Kurdish issue has always been on the international agenda and usually tackled as a human-rights problem. The European Parliament, the European Union, the Parliamentary Assembly of the Council of Europe, the United Nations High Commissioner for Human Rights, the European Committee for the Prevention of Torture, and the Organization for Security and Cooperation in Europe, as well as several Western governments, have all criticized human-rights violations in Turkey and suggested ways to eliminate them.

The institution with the greatest influence over the Turkish government is no doubt the European Union. Turkey is seeking full membership in the organization and is therefore receptive to the suggestions made in EU circles. Even the recognition of the competence of the European Court of Human Rights in 1987 to receive individual petitions with regard to human-rights abuses is related to Turkey's application for the EU membership that year. Since 1999, the European Commission has been producing progress reports about Turkey and specifying the deficiencies in the human-rights regime on the basis of the Copenhagen Political Criteria. In November 2000, the European Commission issued the Accession Partnership Document in which the EU specified all its short- and medium-term demands, including TV broadcasting and education in Kurdish.

Official conflict-management attempts in Greek-Turkish relations, on the other hand, are nearly as old as the Cyprus question. Since the dispute first appeared on the UN General Assembly's agenda in 1954, the UN has played a conflict-management role between the two countries. But since December 1963, the UN Security Council has been actively involved with the Cyprus issue and, though indirectly, with Greek-Turkish relations. A UN peacekeeping force is almost permanently stationed on the island and representatives of the successive secretaries-general visit Cyprus regularly. For the settlement of the problem, several rounds of talks have been completed without any tangible results. Yet, these talks and the papers produced by the UN staff have helped in keeping the conflict from escalating.

The UN Security Council, together with the ICJ, has played a more direct conflict-management role in the Aegean when Greece unilaterally resorted to these two international bodies on 10 August 1976 to complain about Turkey's alleged violations of its sovereign rights. Although the result was not at all satisfactory for the applicant country, the decision taken by both organizations again facilitated the de-escalation of the conflict.

Another international organization that showed keen interest in the Greek-Turkish relations has been NATO. The organization is actively involved in settling the differences between the two countries in order to avoid paralyzing the alliance's southern flank. NATO officials have tried to induce military confidence measures and to mediate between the parties. However, the major role in conflict management has usually been played by the United States, as in the case of the Imia/Kardak crisis in 1996 regarding sovereignty over islands in the eastern Aegean.

Contrary to the Greek case, there is no ongoing mediation attempt regarding the problems between Syria and Turkey. In October 1998, Egypt's president, Hosni Mubarak, and Iran's foreign minister, Kamal Kharazi, intervened when crisis was imminent after Turkey's unambiguous demand from Syria. They were able to defuse the tension and settle the problem as Turkey wished. Since then relations have noticeably improved without any need for third-party intervention. The likelihood of another crisis is remote at present.

Multi-Track Diplomacy

Of the three problem areas discussed here, the one offering the most fertile ground for NGO involvement has always been Greek-Turkish affairs. The parties to the conflict were usually receptive to third-party involvement and its influential figures have been generally inclined to take part in workshops on the issue. Moreover, the target could be clearly defined and the legitimacy of the venture has rarely been questioned. There have been innumerable meetings among NGOs, business leaders, students, academicians, women, journalists, historians, municipalities, rescue teams, and "intellectuals" from both sides of the Aegean in recent years. Greek and Turkish peace activists have also had meetings in Cyprus on various occasions.

Greek and Turkish branches of the Helsinki Citizens Assembly played a leading early role in the cultural rapprochement and in diffusion of the tension after the Imia/Kardak incident in 1996 at a meeting held in Naphlion, where the participants denounced the role played by the media in the escalation of the crisis. But their effort suffered from the familiar problem of inadequate financial resources and the Naphlion meeting could not be reciprocated in Turkey.

Nevertheless, the intensity of the activities increased in the following years. Delegations of women from both countries formed a network (WIN-PEACE) aiming at consolidation of relations between Greece and Turkey during their four days of talks on the Greek island of Kos and the nearby Turkish town of Bodrum in May 1998. Seven months before, another important nongovernmental activity was the meeting of the business leaders in Thessaloniki for a conference organized to honor Atatürk and Venizelos for their efforts to improve relations in the 1930s.

However, with most of the workshops, meetings, and concerts there was much common sense but no long-term strategic planning. The participants enjoyed talking about the common characteristics linking the two cultures together. Intentionally or unintentionally, the problems were avoided. Instead, names of particular dishes and drinks were uttered in these very friendly gatherings. Under the heavy atmosphere of an impending crisis, even that kind of human touch had an impact on the relations, especially when these meetings were transmitted to the general public through the media. But the press from both sides has been mostly indifferent to these unofficial civic proposals and thus unwilling to publicize them.

During some of these activities, substantive issues were in fact discussed. But the remedies produced have been either irrelevant for resolving the problems concerned or had such a long-term perspective that their results would only be felt by future generations. In this respect, the most popular themes of the Greek and Turkish NGO meetings during the 1990s were such themes as "the image of the other" and "rewriting history books."

Another deficiency of these meetings was their irrelevance to decision-making circles. The results of these activities were usually ignored, if not despised, by the authorities. The participants very rarely had access to political and diplomatic channels. Those having access had little influence. Of course there were and are some exceptions. One of them is the Greek-Turkish Forum, which was established by a group of retired diplomats and generals, as well as active journalists and academics from both sides with the blessing of the respective governments and the financial and organizational support of British-based RUSI (Royal United Services Institute).[8]

The group is in constant contact with the foreign ministries of the two countries and produced a substantial report on the Aegean problems with viable policy suggestions. In March 2000, the group sent a memorandum to EU officials in Brussels and the ministers of foreign affairs of Greece and Turkey. The Greek-Turkish Forum recognized the importance of delimitation of the continental shelf, the delimitation of continental waters and airspace, and the militarization of certain Greek islands as problem areas in the Aegean, and suggested a concrete procedure to settle the differences. According to this group, the countries can follow a two-stage approach with respect to the continental-shelf dispute.

During a first stage, the countries are advised to negotiate for a predetermined duration to reach agreement on some or all substantive issues, or to submit disputes to the ICJ. Any settlement reached at this stage will be formally confirmed by relevant agreements, while any issue not settled will then be submitted to the ICJ. The underlying premise, as the group claims, is that both parties—meaning Turkey, in fact—will have accepted the jurisdiction of the ICJ. With respect to territorial waters and airspace-related problems, the group also suggests a legalistic approach and advises consulting the ICJ. With respect to the militarization issue, the Greek-Turkish Forum believes that progress in other areas will reduce its importance to Turkey.

This procedural approach, although developed in close contact with the respective foreign ministries, is very much tilted toward the Greek position, but it also reflects Turkish interests. Even if not accepted as a course of action to settle the disputes, it provides some ideas about the roles that third parties can play. In fact, prospective third parties are also capable of finding viable solutions focused on the substance of the issues. There are plenty of academics working in the field and recommending compromise formulas on a wide range of issues of concern in Greek-Turkish relations.

In addition to that, the business communities in both countries have always been eager participants in conflict-resolution endeavors. The Foreign Economic Relations Board of Turkey, with its business councils, and the Turkish Industrialist and Businessmen Association are actively involved in Greek-Turkish affairs. The thriving think tanks such as the Turkish Economic and Social Studies Foundation (TESEV) and Avrasya Stratejik Arastirmalar Merkezi (Eurasian Strategic Research Center) in Turkey and Hellenic Foundation for European and Foreign Policy in Greece also provide valuable venues for conflict-resolution attempts. They organize workshops and conferences and facilitate contacts not only among Greek and Turkish diplomats and politicians but also among Armenians, Azeris, and Turks.

On 17 February 2001, for instance, TESEV organized a conference on the "Search for Stability in the Caucasus" with the intention of assisting conflict settlement in the region. The conference brought together officials and civic participants from Azerbaijan, Armenia, Georgia, Iran, Russia, Turkey, and Ukraine. Representatives from the European Union, the Organization for Security and Cooperation in Europe, Britain, France, Germany, and the United States also took part in the deliberations. In his opening remarks, Foreign Minister Ismail Cem emphasized that Turkey could play a mediating role in the region's conflicts.[9] Despite earlier objections to Cem's proposal from the Armenian side, the first tangible results of this endeavor were seen in July 2001 with the establishment of a Reconciliation Commission whose aim is to find ways to settle problems between Armenia and Turkey stemming from the different interpretations of the human tragedy experienced in 1915.[10]

As might be expected, contacts between Turkey and Syria at the civil-society level are rather limited due to the lack of significant civil society in Syria. The driving forces of the current rapprochement between the two countries have been the harsh realities of the region and Turkey's decision not to tolerate Öcalan's presence in Syria any longer, despite its risks. Damascus did not want to further jeopardize relations with Ankara and decided to settle the differences through negotiations instead of resorting to blackmail. Currently (as of late 2001), preparations are under way for Syrian president Bashar al-Assad (son and successor to Hafaz) to visit Turkey. According to Syrian authorities, this visit will mark a radical change in relations.[11] If it does take place, there will be little room or need for prospective third-party intervention in the conflicts between the two countries.

When it comes to the Kurdish issue and the PKK, the role played by many international and domestic NGOs has been problematic on many occasions. The effective and functional NGOs were those that were involved in monitoring human-rights abuses in Turkey.

Amnesty International, with its reliability and reputation, played an important role in the modification of Turkey's policies toward its citizens. Human Rights Watch, with its influence in the U.S. Senate, has been a factor to be taken into account by the Turkish authorities. Also, among the civic networks, PRIO has contributed positively to settlement of the problem. Since neither the authorities nor the PKK was willing to tolerate deviation from its own views and ranks, very few domestic NGOs were able to play a constructive role in this long-lasting conflict, but the Foundation for the Research of Societal Problems (TOSAM) is definitely among those few.

TOSAM has collaborated with U.S.-based Search for Common Ground in an attempt to establish common principles for peaceful coexistence in Turkey. Kurdish and Turkish members of the group produced a joint analytical paper. However the paper and the accompanying principles could not be widely debated. Finally, the Turkish branch of Helsinki Citizens Assembly has also played a moderating role through city twinning and summer-school projects, with the support of EU funds.

Prospects

The Greek-Turkish problems and the Kurdish question are highly likely to endure. They are prone to remain on the domestic and international agendas until Turkey's membership to the EU is realized. If Turkey can fulfill the requirements of the Copenhagen Criteria and settle the differences with Greece both in Cyprus and in the Aegean, then it can theoretically obtain full member status. But this theoretical possibility by no means guarantees membership. The enlargement of the EU, pending membership of Cyprus (under the Greek Cypriot government), and shifts in the political environment in Germany, as well as several other unforeseen developments, could have disastrous consequences with respect to Turkish ambitions.

As long as these eventualities exist, it will be extremely difficult to convince the decisionmakers in Turkey to compromise on what they see as their vital national interests. However, a solution to the Kurdish question short of autonomy and decentralization (not to mention federalism) is in sight. With proposals to permit broadcasts and education in the mother tongue as part of the national program prepared by Turkey to qualify for EU accession, changes in the policies of the government and the legal structure of the country are beginning to take form. Besides, political representatives of the Kurdish groups, in particular the Peoples Democracy Party (mainly Kurdish), are actively supporting the ongoing democratization process and Turkey's EU bid. What's more, in January 2001 Kurds and Turks protested for the first time hand in hand the assassination of Diyarbakir's police chief Gaffar Okan, allegedly by the Turkish Hizbullah.

On the other hand, prospects for a solution of the Greek-Turkish differences are not as bright as the Kurdish issue. The Cyprus question is likely to effect relations. Turkey and the Turkish side in Cyprus will most probably not consent to a settlement without a right of self-determination unless a timetable is given to Turkey for full EU membership. Such resistance will unavoidably disrupt the Greek-Turkish rapprochement and have adverse repercussions on EU-Turkish relations. Potential third-party interlocutors are therefore very much needed for EU-Turkish relations as well.

Still, to be fair, the prospects for a final settlement are brighter than they have ever been. The media on both sides of the Aegean seem to have benefited from the Imia/Kardak experience of 1996. They are less likely to stir up public opinion and escalate otherwise routine incidents of sovereignty claims. Third-party interventions designed to bring Greece and Turkey to the negotiating table to talk about the Aegean issues could well yield positive results, which is likely to also help in efforts to resolve the Cyprus problem. After all the Cyprus problem is nothing more than a clash of Greek and Turkish nationalism on a small island.

Recommendations

Turkey's political culture is not particularly receptive to third-party intervention concerning what it regards as domestic affairs from either governmental or nongovernmental circles, and "foreign" NGOs are viewed with suspicion.

Those who are willing to contribute to the solution of the Kurdish question are strongly advised to find reliable and respectable domestic counterparts. They are also advised to study the case they are dealing with in more detail and realize that the task at hand is not one of separation but of coexistence.

Moreover, attempts to manufacture a wider Kurdish platform, as suggested by some outside observers with the intention of creating a negotiating partner following the demise of the PKK, can only be counterproductive for settlement of the problem. Instead, third parties may try to encourage Turkey to find a judicial solution by establishing a solid constitutional foundation wherein the rights of every ethnic identity is protected. For instance, Ankara might be persuaded to sign the Framework Convention on Minorities and the Charter for Regional or Minority Languages.

With respect to international affairs, Turkey is more receptive to third-party intervention. Retired ambassadors, generals, and even active officials taking part in various conflict-resolution attempts are numerous. The authorities seem to be learning the intricacies of multi-track diplomacy and becoming increasingly more self-confident. They are well aware of the possibilities presented by second-track efforts and are willing to use such efforts to achieve their goals. Needless to say, these tendencies help to create a hospitable environment for third-party intervention, as long as such interventions are focused on the resolution of an international (rather than domestic) dispute.

Resources

Publications

A Changing Turkey: Challenges to Europe and the United States, by Heinz Kramer. Washington, DC, Brookings Institution Press, 2000.

Contemporary Turkish Politics: Challenges to Democratic Consolidation, by Ergun Ozbudun. Boulder, CO, Lynne Rienner Publishers, 2000.

"Human Rights and Democratization in Turkey in the Context of EU Candidature," by Chris Rumford. *Journal of European Area Studies* 9, no. 1, 2001.

Islam and Society in Turkey, by David Shankland. Huntingdon, England, The Eothen Press, 1999.

Middle East Review of International Affairs (MERIA), Quarterly publication available at: http://meria.biu.ac.il.

The Emergence of Modern Turkey, by Bernard Lewis. London, Oxford University Press, 1986.

The Kurdish Question and Turkey: An Example of a Trans-State Ethnic Conflict, by Kemal Krisci and Gareth Winrow. London, Frank Cass, 1997.

"The Kurdish Question in Turkish Politics," by Svante E. Cornell. *Orbis* 45, no. 1, 2001.

"The Land of Many Crossroads: Human Rights and Turkey's Future in Europe," by Aslan Gündüz. *Orbis* 45, no. 1, 2001.

"Turkey," by Kemal Kirisci. In J. Hampton (ed.), *Internally Displaced People: A Global Survey.* Global IDP Survey. London, Earthscan Publications, 1998.

Turkey in the Middle East: Oil, Islam and Politics, by Alon Liel. Boulder, CO, Lynne Rienner Publishers, 2001.

Turkey in World Politics: An Emerging Multi-Regional Power, edited by Barry Rubin and Kemal Kirisci. Boulder, CO, Lynne Rienner Publishers, 2001.

Turkey's Kurdish Question, by Henri Barkey and Graham Fuller. Carnegie Commission on Preventing Deadly Conflict. New York, Rowman & Littlefield Publishers, Inc., 1998.

Turkey's Transformation and American Policy, edited by Morton Abramowitz. New York, Century Foundation Press, 2001.
Turkish Politics and the Military, by William Hale. London, Routledge, 1994.

Selected Internet Sites
www.amnesty.org/web/ar2001.nsf/webeurcountries/TURKEY?OpenDocument
   (Turkey's section of the Amnesty International Annual Report 2001)
www.eurasianews.com (Eurasia Research Center web site service)
www.greekturkishforum.org (Greek Turkish Forum web site)
www.members.tripod.com/~dimos/grtr.html (Greek-Turkish Peace & Cooperation links
   web site)
www.ntvmsnbc.com/news/ENGLISH_Front.asp (reliable news portal)
www.turkey.org (Official website of the Embassy of the Republic of Turkey, Washington, DC)
www.turkiye.net/sota/sota.html (Web site from research foundation dedicated to the research and analysis of the Turkic World)

Resource Contacts
Nimet Beriker Atiyas, professor of Conflict Resolution and International Relations, Sabanci University, Turkey, e-mail: beriker@sabanciuniv.edu
Henri Barkey, professor of International Relations, Leigh University, USA, e-mail: hbarkey@sprynet.com
Kemal Kirisci, professor at Department of Political Science, Bogazici University, Turkey, e-mail: kirisci@boun.edu.tr
Taciser Ulas, TESEV, Turkey, e-mail: taciser@tesev.org.tr

Data on the following organizations can be found in the Directory section:
Conflict Analysis and Resolution Programme at Sabanci University
TOSAM
Turkish Economic and Social Studies Foundation

Mensur Akgün graduated from Middle East Technical University (Ankara), continued his studies at the University of Oslo and the University of Bosphorus (Ph.D.). He worked at Marmara University (1992–2001) and currently works at Istanbul Kultur University. He has authored various papers, reports, and a book on issues concerning Turkish foreign policy.

Notes
1. Philip Robins, "Turkey and the Kurds: Missing Another Opportunity," in *Turkey's Transformation and American Policy,* edited by Morton Abramowitz. New York: Century Foundation Press, 2001.
2. For the official Turkish position on the Aegean disputes see: www.mfa.gov.tr/grupa/ad/ade/adeb/default.htm.
3. For the official Greek position on the Aegean disputes see: www.mfa.gr/foreign/bileteral/relations.htm.
4. See: www.un.org/documents/sc/res/1976/scres76.html.
5. See: www.icj-cij.org/icjwww/decisions/isummaries/igtsummary760911.html.
6. For the Syrian position see: www.mfa.gov.tr/grupa/ad/adg/adgc/Chap2b.htm.
7. For the standard view of Turkey's Ministry of Foreign Affairs, see: www.mfa.gov.tr/grupa/percept/i2/i2-6.htm, and also www.mfa.gov.tr/grupa/ad/adg/default.htm.
8. See: www.greekturkishforum.org.
9. For further information see: www.tesev.org.tr/eng/caucasusdevam.php.
10. See *New York Times,* 10 July 2001.
11. See *Yeni Gündem,* 28 February 2001.

13

SOUTHEASTERN EUROPE

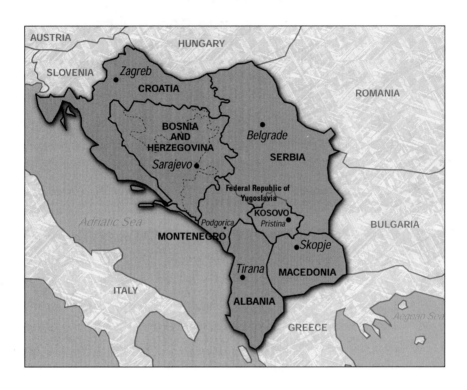

13.1

Regional Introduction: The Tragic Consequences of Nationalism in an Ethnically Heterogeneous Region

Raymond Detrez

Since the fall of the communist regimes in the Soviet Union, Eastern Europe, and the Balkans, the Balkan Peninsula has received far more than its fair share of attention, primarily because of the tragedy of nearly constant war in the former Yugoslavia. It has often been said that the Balkan wars are simply more of the same—that the various ethnic groups inhabiting the Balkans simply can't get along and that the wars of the past decade are simply a continuation of centuries of conflict and animosity. But in fact, under the domination of the Ottoman Turks, peaceful coexistence among the diverse ethnic groups was the rule. With the disintegration of the Ottoman Empire, and the growing influence and interference of Western powers, the notion of "nation-state" took hold. As the various groups began to pursue their nationalist aspirations, conflict increased. It was held largely in check by the authoritarian regimes that dominated the political scene throughout half of the twentieth century. With the collapse of communism, however, the consequences of nationalism in Southeastern Europe have been painful and tragic.

The Balkan Peninsula is the easternmost of the three major southern European peninsulas. To the west and south, seas that form part of the Mediterranean surround it. The Black Sea is located in the east. The northern geographical border of the Balkan Peninsula is formed by the Kupa River (originating near Rijeka on the Dalmatian Sea) and the Sava and the Danube rivers, but there are sound historical and cultural-historical arguments for including Romania within the Balkan states too.

For the most part, the Balkans are a mountainous area. Only the valleys, the low hills, and the few plains are suitable for agriculture (wheat, fruits, vegetables, wine). In the high mountains, only sheep breeding and forestry are viable. Raw materials and energy sources are relatively scarce. Although the region abounds in water (in recent years the ecological balance has been threatened by an increasing drought), only a few rivers are navigable, of which the Danube and the Sava are the most important. Road transport is difficult due to the irregular terrain. These geographic features put a severe constraint on the region's economic possibilities.

Partly due to massive migrations, the Balkans have been ethnically heterogeneous since classical times. In antiquity, Greeks, Illyrians, and Thracians inhabited the peninsula. The Illyrians are thought of by the Albanians as their ancestors, while the Thracian tribes of the Dacians and the Ghetes were Latinized and evolved into the Romanians, north of the Danube, and the Vlachs south of it. The Slavic invasions of the sixth and seventh centuries left a lasting mark on the peninsula, and it has remained predominantly Slavic. Before the nineteenth century, except for some short periods, all the peoples of the Balkans lived within large, multinational empires: the empire of Alexander the Great, the Roman Empire, the Byzantine Empire, and the Ottoman Empire. The Byzantine influence, from the start of the fourth century until the fall of Constantinople in 1453, was of exceptional importance, as it led most people in the region to embrace Orthodox Christianity. The Ottoman period, from the end of the fourteenth century to the Balkan wars in 1912–1913, resulted in a substantial immigration of Turks from Anatolia and the spread of Islam, mainly in Bosnia and Albania.

Due to the large internal demographic mobility (seasonal labor, nomadic cattle breeding, dissemination through population growth, mass migration, migrations due to wars and riots) and massive spontaneous and occasionally forced conversions, significant ethnocultural diversity has developed. Ten very different Indo-European languages are spoken in the Balkans: Albanian, Greek, Romanian and Vlach (two Roman languages), Croat, Bosnian, Serb (formally called Serbo-Croat), Slovenian, Macedonian, and Bulgarian (six Slavic languages). To the Indo-European family also belong Romani (the language of the Roma gypsies) and the languages of the small Armenian and Sephardic Jewish minorities. Turkish, nowadays spoken only in enclaves in Bulgaria, Greece, and of course Turkey, and Hungarian, spoken in the Vojvodina (northern Serbia), are the only non-Indo-European languages in the Balkans. Bilingualism and polylingualism were very common phenomena.

In addition to Orthodox Christianity and Islam, Roman Catholicism is present in the northwest of the peninsula (Croatia and Slovenia) and in Northern Albania. The Ottoman administration granted a large degree of autonomy to the various religious communities (millets), which allowed the peoples of the Balkans to live according their own traditions and at the same time screened them from Islamization.

Languages and religions have appeared in all possible combinations. One can still find, for example, Bulgarian-speaking Muslims (Pomaks) as well as Turkish-speaking Christians (Gagauz). Remarkably, the various ethnocultural identities, far from being well defined, have gone through all sorts of changes. Identity, with language and religion as core components, has often depended on certain collective interests, and has been smoothly exchanged for another where expedient.

Despite this diversity, there was a large degree of cultural unity in the Balkans. This manifested itself, for example, in the very similar grammatical structure of the Balkan languages, in the numerous common aspects of popular culture, and in a shared moral value system characterized in particular by honor, collectivity (extended family, region, and by extension nation), generosity, and "machismo." Furthermore, the religious contrasts were less pronounced than would appear at first sight. At the level of popular religion in particular, many forms of religious syncretism existed.

Contrary to popular perceptions, the Balkans is neither a region of centuries-old ethnic hatred, nor an area that has historically experienced extraordinary levels of violence. The ethnic contrasts and conflicts that seem so very typical of the Balkans today in fact originated in the Westernization of Balkan society from the end of the eighteenth and through the nineteenth centuries. The economic expansion of Western Europe into the Balkans, and the role the region came to play in the economic and political power struggles among European powers (including Russia), resulted in the introduction of new technologies and new ways of thinking, including the idea of the nation-state. This soon came to be understood exclusively as an ethnically independent national state, or one that was as ethnically homogeneous as possible. In a region as ethnically heterogeneous as the Balkans, such a state was not feasible without ethnic cleansing, genocide, or in the most civilized of cases, population exchanges and forced assimilation of minorities. Furthermore, the realization of ethnically homogenous national states caused tensions and conflicts with neighboring states, which felt entitled to claim certain territories inhabited by their conationals (irredentism).

The major peoples of the Balkans considered the pursuit of national independence as the restoration of the situation that had existed prior to the Ottoman domination. They wished to restore their medieval state to its largest territorial dimensions. Due to the many overlaps alone, this would have caused innumerable territorial conflicts between the Balkan countries. This ambition provided the foundation for "imagined" states such as Greater Bulgaria, Greater Serbia, or the restored Byzantine Empire (the "Great Idea" of the Greeks). Of these, however, only Greater Albania is based on ethnic reality, as the Albanians did have a state of their own of considerable size in the Middle Ages. Moreover, the Balkan peoples wished to restore the ethnocultural homogeneity of their former "state," although it had never actually existed. This led to a politics of ethnocultural homogenization, to which mainly Islamic communities, and in particular the Turks, fell victim. The cause of restoring the former homogeneity was served especially through their expulsion.

Thus, during the nineteenth century the modern Balkan states were created: Greece and Serbia around 1830; Bulgaria, Montenegro, and Romania in 1878; and Albania in 1912. After the Second Balkan War in 1912, Macedonia, claimed by Bulgaria, Greece, and Serbia, was divided between the three irredentist powers. Bulgaria was left the smallest part. At that time, most of the Slavs in Macedonia considered themselves Bulgarians, but a growing number had developed a Macedonian national consciousness. However, in Greece and Serbia they were not recognized as Bulgarians, nor as Macedonians, but subjected to forced assimilation. Bulgaria supported these Macedonians, who believed Macedonia should be part of Bulgaria. During the two world wars, it tried to annex parts of the region. In 1999, the Bulgarian government officially acknowledged the existence of a separate Macedonian language, and implicitly of a separate Macedonian nation. However, historians, linguists, and other scientists (among whom were many amateurs) continue to decry as an injustice the situation whereby Macedonia has remained outside the borders of the Bulgarian state and the Slavs in Macedonia have been "denationalized."

The creation of the independent Balkan states occurred during military confrontations and was often accompanied by ethnic cleansing. During the implementation of the peace accords, recourse was taken to population exchanges: minorities were exchanged (for example between Bulgaria and Greece, between Bulgaria and Turkey, and between Greece and Turkey, all in the 1920s). This operation resulted in a number of states that were ethnically homogeneous, or claimed to be so, and pursued policies with little or no consideration for minorities.

After World War I, Yugoslavia (until 1929 the Kingdom of Serbs, Croats, and Slovenes) was the only state in the Balkans that was still truly multiethnic or multinational. Romania also had many minorities, but the Romanians made up the overwhelming majority, while the preponderance of the most numerous of peoples in Yugoslavia, the Serbs, was far less pronounced. The Serbs, who regarded themselves as the creators of Yugoslavia, considered Yugoslavia to be "their" state. The 1921 Constitution was democratic indeed, but created an extremely centralized state. The minorities policy pursued was no worse than in other countries. Yet the government did make the lives of the Albanians, whom it considered a danger because of Albanian irredentist claims on Kosovo, such a misery that many of them emigrated. Problems arose mainly where the Serbs treated peoples with a developed national consciousness as minorities rather than equals.

In the nineteenth century, the Croats in the Habsburg Empire had advanced the idea that Croats, Serbs, and even Slovenians made up one South Slavic people (Yugoslavism), speaking one language (Serbo-Croat). As such, they claimed that they had the right to a separate federal state within the Habsburg Empire, comparable to Hungary, which had gained a status of relative autonomy in 1867. The most important cultural difference between Croats and Serbs—the Croats were Catholics with a cultural and political orientation toward Central Europe, while the Serbs were Orthodox with a stronger orientation toward Russia—was minimized. There were other opinions too, laying emphasis on a Croat ethnic nationalism and the singularity of the Croat language, and working for independence from the Habsburg Empire. At the beginning of the twentieth century, the notion took root that the Habsburg South Slavs would be best served by forming one state with the Kingdom of Serbia, which had developed into a regional military power. This state was expected to give the Croats some sort of autonomy.

In independent Yugoslavia, the Croat political and intellectual elite felt, justifiably, discriminated against. Serbs occupied nearly all senior positions in the state. This gave a strong impulse to the development of a pure Croat, ethno-national consciousness. Moderate Croat politicians fought for autonomy, the more radical ones for independence. Some of the more radical Croat nationalists fell under the spell of fascism and during World War II collaborated with the Axis Powers within an Independent Croat State.

The Bosniaks (Bosnian Muslims), who felt an allegiance to Istanbul and the Islamic world, were caught between Serbs and Croats. At the end of the nineteenth century, the development of a Bosnian national consciousness was strongly supported by the Austrian government, which sought to isolate Bosnia from Croatia and Serbia. The process of national awakening of the Bosniaks reached a climax in 1969, when Tito recognized the Bosniaks, though as Muslims in the ethnic sense, as a distinct nation.

Between the two world wars, internal ethnic tensions and claims of neighboring countries to Yugoslav territory haunted Yugoslavia. In order to end this situation, after World War II the communist government under Tito gave Yugoslavia a federal structure. Although communist Yugoslavia deserves praise for guaranteeing and indeed respecting the cultural rights of the ethnocultural communities in Yugoslavia, ultimately the Yugoslavian experiment failed. From a historical point of view, one could argue that the most recent wars in the former Yugoslavia have completed the process of state formation that began in the early nineteenth century. Today, states that consider themselves ethnic nation-states (with the exception of still "multinational" Bosnia-Herzegovina, and in the future perhaps Macedonia) also exist in the western Balkans. The way these states have been established demonstrates once again that in the Balkans, ethnic nation-states are not feasible without dramatic violations of civil and human rights.

Political Transition

This process of state formation in Yugoslavia coincided with, and is partly caused by, the transition that swept through the whole of communist Eastern Europe, and which also caused states to disintegrate elsewhere. The transition has two aspects: the political shift from a dictatorial regime, with power tightly held by the Communist Party, to a parliamentary democracy with a multiparty system; and in the economic sphere, by the shift from a centrally led, planned economy, in which most or the most important companies were state-owned, to a free-market economy with private enterpreneurship. In the Balkans, this transition was made in a situation of poverty and restricted economic opportunities, which exacerbated the negative social consequences.

The new democracy can be held partially responsible for the ethnic tensions and conflicts that manifested themselves, particularly in Yugoslavia. The introduction of the multiparty system led to the development of several parties, a few of which played the nationalist card. Some former communist parties resorted to nationalism—Slobodan Milosevic's Serb Socialist Party being the most notorious example—but the "democratic" opposition parties were also prone to nationalist rhetoric. As a result, minorities and neighboring countries were portrayed as threats against which the party in question could offer protection. This tendency was further complicated by the existence of ethnic parties, which often presented themselves as "human-rights parties" but were exclusively concerned with protecting the interests of a particular ethnic group. Because of the widespread practice of clientism, large segments of society, sometimes even complete ethnic communities, seemed to depend on such parties. The fate of the party politicians seemed to be critical for the fate of the whole community—a situation that fostered political extremism. The result was that even in the new democratic system, political behavior was dominated by ethnic affiliation. Accordingly, a sense of membership, first and foremost as a member of a civil society, remained underdeveloped.

The "free" media played a similar role. Within a few years of Tito's death in 1980, the media had been liberalized, which made it possible for the Serb press to conduct a campaign of hatred against the Albanians in Kosovo. In the absence of any responsible legislation—every restriction on the absolute freedom of expression was branded "communist"—the Yugoslav republics at the end of the 1980s had virtually no restrictions on arousing ethnic hatred. It can be argued that the war in Yugoslavia began as a media war, first in Serbia with respect to the Albanians in Kosovo, and subsequently in other republics, especially with respect to Serbia. In other Balkan countries, ethnic minorities were attacked mainly in extreme right-wing publications (the Hungarian minority in Romania, for example). The Roma minority, however, was branded the scapegoat even in quality papers and journals. In many of the Balkan countries, radio and television still have to free themselves of state interference. Often, the independent magazines are owned by financial groups with close relations to politicians. The government sometimes takes measures against opposition newspapers and magazines, in the form of legal actions against "slander," levying a variety of taxes, hampering distribution, among other tactics. There have also been cases of journalists being molested and even murdered.

Nationalism has also become the dominant ideology outside the countries of the former Yugoslavia. The reaction against communism in education up to university level, in the media, and in the arts often boils down to the rehabilitation and adoration of the "national identity," in which the negative image of "the Other" has a prominent place. Whereas the arts have to propagate the national identity, the humanities are considered as instruments for defining and protecting this national identity. Critical self-reflection and the ability to put one's self in the opponent's position so as to understand his point of view are absent; the opponent is by definition *mala fide*. A further illustration is the tendency to solve current political disputes by referring to the past, or to seek guidance from historical situations and events in political actions. Thus the perception of problems that involve Muslims is still shaped by the Ottoman oppression of the Balkans, which ended at least ninety years ago. Most of the time, the comprehensive and "lived" knowledge of the national past, often present even among the common people in the Balkans, is a mythological representation of the national past. The few dissident historians in the Balkans who draw a more realistic picture are perceived as practically betraying the nation.

Throughout the recent period of conflict in the Balkans, most intellectuals have played a very negative role. Those who committed crimes against humanity were primarily members of militias and soldiers acting in the service of politicians, but historians, philosophers, writers, and journalists provided the ideology that gave these crimes a moral legitimacy. It is not enough to point out works with a clearly inflammatory character. A sympathetic postmodern discourse on "identity," "otherness," and "belonging" has often created an atmosphere of understanding and tolerance with regard to these aggressive nationalist publications that verges on complicity. It is no coincidence that in societies in which manliness, not to say machismo, has such an important role, it was mainly women who brought charges against the nationalist madness.

Nor have the churches in the Balkans always played a constructive role in the political developments over the last decade. Through a combination of historical circumstances, the churches in the Orthodox world have developed into national churches that do not recognize a supranational head comparable to the pope in the Catholic Church, but strongly identify themselves with the nation as an ethnic community and with the national state. The Greek constitution was promulgated in the name of the Holy Trinity, and the Greek Orthodox Church recently fiercely opposed the government's proposal to no longer mention religious affiliation on identity cards. The Bulgarian constitution explicitly states that "Eastern Orthodox Christianity is the traditional religion in the Republic of Bulgaria." The church likes to manifest itself as a politically impartial keeper of the people, but does in fact assume a political role. Even a critical attitude with regard to worldly power is more often than not dictated by a virulent nationalism. That was the case in Greece with regard to the problem of the Greek minority in southern Albania and the question of the final name of the Former Yugoslav Republic of Macedonia (FYROM). In Serbia, too, the Orthodox Church has played an equally dubious role, and in Croatia, the Croat church has also strongly identified itself with Croat nationalism. These nationalist tendencies are in part an outgrowth of the position of religion under communism. At that time, religious leaders—Catholic, Muslim, and Orthodox—were repressed and humiliated. Church attendance declined quickly. After the fall of the communists, the churches sought to gain respectability and influence and to that end adopted a nationalist posture, in which they presented themselves as "keepers" of the nation. The fact that Bosniaks, Croats, and Serbs saw religion as an important component of their national identity contributed to the religious revival.

The role played by the various diasporas in the political developments should also be noted. Greece has been the source of a large migration extending back into ancient times, and Greeks are present on all continents. The Albanians have a large diaspora in Turkey, the United States, and a few Western European countries (Belgium, Germany, and Switzerland). Many Croatians whose social position had been compromised in the eyes of the communists because of their cooperation with the fascist regime of the Independent Croat State left Croatia after World War II. Over the last fifty years, the Balkans have witnessed frequent political emigrations, and Yugoslavia, in particular, also experienced a large emigration of workers to Western Europe. In general, those in the diasporas adopt far more extreme political positions than those who are left behind. This is related to certain political grudges, mainly held by political emigrants, linked to the fact that they have a very distorted image of the situation in their former homeland, and to the fact that they run a low risk in case of armed conflicts. It is known that Croat and Albanian emigrants played a significant role in the current events in Yugoslavia. Nationalist parties, but also armed organizations, were often financially dependent on their conationals in the diaspora. Consequently, the diaspora was able to influence the political aims of these organizations. In some cases, such as in the case of Gojko Susak of Croatia, individuals from the diaspora performed important political functions as well. And in the case of the Kosovo Liberation Army, most of its funds were provided by those in the Albanian diaspora. Furthermore, emigrants are well placed to influence the policy of foreign powers through lobbying. The Greek diaspora in particular was very active in relation to the controversial name of the Republic of Macedonia.

Economic Transition

The political transition was accompanied by an economic transition. Although its evolution was slow and difficult and had far-reaching negative consequences such as inflation, industrial closures, unemployment, a decline in social services, and impoverishment, it caused relatively few severe social tensions and conflicts. Apart from massive strikes, there were no incidents of social unrest. At present, after the initial declines, most Balkan countries are displaying a slow improvement at the macroeconomic level, but the social situation continues to be deplorable. The privatization of public enterprises has played a crucial role here. Profitable public enterprises often fell into the hands of the former communist nomenclature. Sometimes, profitable businesses were represented as being unprofitable by communist managers in order to keep their prices low. Unprofitable businesses sometimes continued to receive government subsidies to prevent shutdowns and massive layoffs, but the subsidies often disappeared into the managers' pockets. Foreign buyers and investors paid more attention to their own commercial interests than to rehabilitation of the local economy. They were attracted by a well-educated work force, low wages, and the absence of a strict social and environmental legislation. Although the Balkan countries had no other option than to attract foreign buyers and investors, this often aroused nationalist sentiments. The sale of businesses to foreign investors was depicted as a sell-off of national resources.

The worst effect of the economic transition was the emergence of an illegal commercial circle. In fact, many so-called illegal transactions could not, strictly speaking, be so described, since there existed no governing legislation, but the legal void presented plenty of opportunities for malicious practices. Smuggling, in particular, increased sharply, in part because of repeated embargos against Yugoslavia, which has been an important trading partner for many Balkan countries. Some of the criminal activities have revolved around the well-known "Balkan Connection"—a drug-trafficking route along which heroin from Pakistan is brought to the West through Bulgaria, Macedonia, and Albania. One consequence of the UN embargo against Yugoslavia in the first half of the 1990s was that, with effective monitoring difficult, trafficking along the Bulgaria-Macedonia-Albania route increased significantly. The Balkan Connection is reported to be dominated by Albanians. As many politicians are also involved in illegal transactions, one can speak of a "mafia" in the true sense of the word. Governments have been powerless to cope with the mafia, and eradicating mafia activities has proved to be just as difficult as eliminating that other social disease resulting from poverty—corruption.

For a long time, joining the European Union was considered to be the best solution to the many economic problems. However, although the situation on the macroeconomic level has improved considerably, the failure to realize a palpable improvement in the standard of living has generated widespread Euro-skepticism. Major problems remain, as the Balkan countries find it extremely difficult to meet EU norms. The vague prospect, recently offered by the Stability Pact for Southeastern Europe, of accelerated entry into the EU has not fundamentally changed this attitude, in spite of the respective govern ments' enthusiasm. The Stability Pact has proved not to be, as was hoped for, a kind of Marshall Plan for the Balkans.

International Involvement

Being a region of little economic importance, the Balkans would have attracted little international attention had the Organization for Security and Co-operation in Europe (OSCE), the EU, and the UN not been forced, quite unprepared, to deal with the region because of the wars in Yugoslavia. These wars posed a threat to European security and challenged the Western world's belief, which arose after the collapse of communism, in its own ability to cope with regional conflicts and to force dissident states to adjust to a "New World Order" imposed by the United States. The attention, of course, was directed at Yugoslavia, while, for a long time, the other Balkan states were almost completely neglected, even though their vulnerable economies suffered considerably from the sanctions imposed on Yugoslavia. The governments of Bulgaria, Romania, and Macedonia were forced to comply with the policies of the UN, and later NATO and/or the United States, despite the considerable moral support among local populations for the Serbian cause. This support was inspired largely by aversion to the Muslim Albanians and by the fear of separatist movements among the minorities in their own countries.

During the successive wars in the former Yugoslavia, extensive aid programs had already been established. In the first instance, these programs existed primarily to provide relief food aid, clothing, temporary shelter, and the like. Later, aid was diversified and acquired a more systematic or institution-alized character. It included the delivery of machinery for the reconstruction of homes, education for refugee and minority children, relief of people suffering from war traumas, programs for the reintegration of refugees, and so forth. Many of these projects were implemented by NGOs. On a more institutional-ized level, economic and financial aid has also been distributed, mainly in order to facilitate a smooth economic transition, ameliorating the social con-sequences of economic transition, for example, by expanding a workable sys-tem of social security. This kind of aid is offered to all Balkan countries, not just the former Yugoslavia.

Despite its failures as a mediator and lack of a strong consensus on mili-tary intervention, it seems that the EU can still play an important role. The prospect of EU membership—and to a lesser extent, NATO membership—makes candidate countries in the Balkans especially keen to conform to the European political and economic norms. This has already led to better treat-ment of ethnic and religious minorities and to improved relations with neigh-boring countries. The Stability Pact for Southeastern Europe, launched in June 1999, strives in the first instance to increase the stability in the region by pro-moting democracy and human rights, economic development, and security. In particular, the Balkan countries have been pushed to more regional consulta-tion and cooperation. For the time being, most projects are still at the stage of good intentions. Alongside that and albeit vaguely worded, the Stability Pact offers the prospect of an accelerated accession to the EU.

International involvement in Balkan affairs has been mainly limited to Western involvement. The support of Islamic states, in the form of financial aid to Muslim communities or "Muslim states," has been largely exaggerated by Islamophobes among the Balkan Christians and abroad. Neither should Russia's support to Slavic and Orthodox brother nations, in particular Serbia, be overestimated. In fact, Russia's actions were mainly inspired by its desire to continue to play the diplomatic role of a superpower and by its fear of the extension of NATO's influence in the region. Nothing can be compared to the overwhelming and often rather unfathomable and headstrong performance of the United States in the Balkan region. Attention should also be directed to Greece, which has invested considerable energy in serving as the EU's politi-cal and cultural bridgehead in the Balkans, though not to the exclusion of the pursuit of its own real or perceived national interests.

Without any doubt, the Balkans remain a trouble spot within Europe. Never-theless we should avoid stigmatizing the whole area because of the conflicts that arose in only some parts of only one Balkan country. Today, countries such as Bulgaria, Romania, and even Albania are far more democratic than they were ten years ago. They have free-market economies, their citizens can travel more freely and meet each other, they treat their minorities better than before, and they are trying very hard to integrate themselves into the European eco-nomic and military institutions. Albeit with varying degrees of success, the for-mer Yugoslavian states have evolved in the direction of modern constitutional states, despite all their conflicts. Before condemning the Balkans, we should be aware that the cause of the problems—the idea of the ethnic nation-state—was imported to the Balkans from the West.

Raymond Detrez (born in Antwerp, Belgium, in 1948) studied Eastern European Languages and History at the University of Ghent (1967–1971) and specialized in Bulgarian Philology at the University of Sofia (1971). In 1986 he obtained his Ph.D. with a thesis on the autobiography of Grigor Parlicev—the forgotten Greek poet Grigorios Stavridhis—and the development of national consciousness in the Balkans. He is currently a professor of Eastern European and Modern Greek history at the University of Gent. He has published numerous books and articles on Balkan history, minority policies, and nationalism in Southeastern Europe.

13.2

The Collapse of Tito's Yugoslavia

Raymond Detrez

During the 1990s, the multiethnic Yugoslavian state virtually disintegrated. Though the rivalries between ethnic groups did play a role in the collapse of Yugoslavia, the process was far more complex than that. The death of Tito (who had played a crucial role in maintaining the unity of the Yugoslav federal state), an unworkable federal structure, economic differences among the constituent units of Yugoslavia, and the national aspirations of the various ethnic groups all played a part, as did more general economic deterioration in Yugoslavia and widespread corruption. External factors were also important, particularly the end of the Cold War, which fundamentally changed the dynamics of relations in Europe. When declarations of independence did occur, followed by violent conflict, the international community attempted, both through diplomacy and by means of military intervention, to establish peace and stability. The results have been uneven, and true stability has not yet been achieved.

The collapse of Yugoslavia is the result of a variety of factors. Among them, the various historical factors—age-old ethnic hatred, cultural differences (the "clash of civilizations"), national myths, the artificiality of the Yugoslav state, etc.—seem the less decisive, however attractive they may seem to be as "explanations." The most plausible interpretations of the collapse of Yugoslavia are related to the country's federal structure in the postwar period.

The Yugoslav communist state dealt with two concepts of its people: Yugoslav civil nationhood, based on loyalty to the Yugoslav communist system (with its two pillars of self-government and nonalignment), and ethnic nationhood. According to this approach, communist Yugoslavia was organized as a federal state, in which the major ethnocultural communities acquired a considerable extent of territorialized political autonomy. Nations (*nacije, narodi*)—ethnocultural communities that had their nation-state within the borders of Yugoslavia—were considered to be constituent peoples and were assigned a republic of their own: Slovenes, Croats, Serbs, Montenegrins, Macedonians.

The Bosniaks (called Muslimani or "Muslems in the ethnic sense" in the former Yugoslavia) were a nation too, but shared their republic, Bosnia-Herzegovina, with Serbs and Croats. Nationalities (*nacionalnosti*, *narodnosti*) were ethnocultural communities that had a state of their own outside Yugoslavia—Albanians, Hungarians, Bulgarians, Italians, and others—and were actually considered as minorities. If sufficiently numerous and living in compact masses, they were assigned an autonomous province. Both autonomous provinces—the "Albanian" Kosovo and the "Hungarian" Vojvodina—were geographically and institutionally incorporated within the Republic of Serbia. According to the introduction to the 1974 Yugoslav Constitution, nations had the right to secession, whereas nationalities did not. The latter provision was consistent with international law concerning the limited extent of the right to self-determination (excluding the right to secession) minorities have, and had a rather hypothetical character as long as Yugoslavia was a solid state.

Formal Autonomy

Until the end of the 1960s the autonomy enjoyed by the Yugoslav federal units (republics and autonomous provinces) was merely formal. Decisions were made by the leadership of the very centralized League of Communists of Yugoslavia (LCY), which possessed a monopoly on power as the only legal party. The majority of the LCY members were Serbs, the capital of Yugoslavia was also the capital of the Republic of Serbia, and Serbs in the federal units other than Serbia were often overrepresented in local and federal governmental and party institutions. As a result, the dominance of the LCY was perceived by the non-Serbs in Yugoslavia as a resumption of the prewar Serb hegemony. This perception was even reinforced by the fact that the communist government tended to collectively stigmatize Croats and Albanians for their collaboration with the German and Italian occupiers during World War II, discrediting their demands—justified or not—for more cultural rights.

However, the Serbs too, in spite of their dominant position, increasingly felt victimized by the postwar federal structures. Tito's aim was to create a more balanced federation by establishing the federal units of Macedonia, Montenegro, and Bosnia-Herzegovina, as well as the autonomous provinces on what was seen as former Serbian territory (or in the case of Bosnia-Herzegovina, partly Serb territory). This was considered by the Serbs as an attempt to reduce the impact the Serbs should rightfully have on federal decisionmaking as the largest community in Yugoslavia. While the other Yugoslav peoples lived in their respective own states (federal units), the Serbs alleged they were deliberately dispersed over several federal units, which weakened their position. (In fact, only in the case of Slovenia and the Slovenians were the political and the national units congruent.) By the end of the 1960s, as the federal units started to gradually acquire greater autonomy, this problem became even more acute: Yugoslavia, the multinational state that the Serbs perceived as theirs, grew weaker, while the Yugoslav federal units grew stronger and increasingly acquired the features of self-contained ethnic nation-states. All these developments weakened not only the central power, but also the Serb communities in Croatia, Bosnia-Herzegovina, and Kosovo.

Radical Federalization

The relative democratization and quite radical federalization of the Yugoslav state was wrested from the LCY under the pressure exerted by protest movements in a number of federal units. The most important was the 1967 Croat Spring, headed by prominent members of the Croat League of Communists and leading intellectuals. The main issues were the position of the Croat language, which was particularly vulnerable because of the great similarity between Croat and Serb, and the poor economic and social conditions in Croatia, for which "Belgrade" was blamed. "Belgrade" stood for the Serbs, the Communists, and the Yugoslav government. When in 1971 the Croat activists posed a challenge to the entire Yugoslav federal construction by demanding that the internal borders between the federal units be changed in order to incorporate some Croat-inhabited regions in the neighboring republics into Croatia, Tito intervened and had the leaders of the Croat Spring arrested and sentenced to long prison terms. Subsequently, he gave in to a great number of the demands of the reformers.

The 1974 Constitution finally established a new federal organization in the Yugoslav state. The parliaments and governments of the federal units acquired large, statelike responsibilities in all fields of political, economic, social, and cultural life. The actual differences between republics and autonomous provinces were practically nonexistent. Since the reforms were, in most cases, the outcome of compromises reached to satisfy all the federal units involved, the legal arrangements were often marked by ambiguity. For instance, the Serb government retained a voice in Kosovan affairs since Kosovo was still, albeit nominally, a part of the Republic of Serbia, and simultaneously, representatives of Kosovo in the federal government—nearly all of whom were ethnic Albanians—participated in decisionmaking concerning the Republic of Serbia. This and similar situations raised fierce disputes over areas of responsibility, poisoning the good relations that were supposed to be advanced by the federal structure.

The extension of the responsibilities of the federal units inevitably led to the weakening of the governmental institutions. The LCY remained the only permitted political party in Yugoslavia and the main unifying entity, but since it had been given a federalized structure itself, party members and officials were inclined to favor the interests of their own units above those of the federation as a whole. The federal units increasingly tended to act as autarchic states, considering each other more as rivals than as partners. The fact that all decisions on the federal level had to be taken unanimously, which necessarily resulted in bargaining and concessions, contributed to the rivalry and resentment as well. Frustrations grew as every federal unit had the idea the others were better off. The perception of the federal unit as a nation-state or a fatherland led to the transformation of disagreements on purely technical matters into clashes of national interests, which gave a particular emotional impetus to all negotiations.

Growing Tensions

Tensions between the federal units increased in the late 1970s as a result of the deteriorating economic situation in Yugoslavia. A crucial issue was the transfer of financial resources from the economically better-performing northern republics Slovenia and Croatia to the less prosperous southern units of Montenegro, Kosovo, and Macedonia, with the aim of eliminating the economic and social discrepancies in Yugoslavia. As Western loans became scarce, the northern federal units grew reluctant to continue giving financial support to the southern ones. The southern units, for their part, demanded more extensive aid, arguing that the northern republics owed much of their prosperity to the cheap raw materials they obtained from the south. In Slovenia and Croatia this debate on economics was later to be accompanied by a barely concealed racist discourse, presenting the peoples in the north as diligent, efficient, and frugal—that is, "European"—and the peoples in the south as lazy, inefficient, and prodigal—that is, "Balkanic." In Serbia, by the way, a similar discourse emerged regarding the Albanians in Kosovo and the Moslems in general. Of course, the economic performance had to do with historical circumstances rather than with intellectual capacity, but the essentialist theories did not fail to stir up emotions.

The increased autonomy of the federal units enabled the local governments to carry out a policy favoring the interests not only of the federal unit as a territory, but also of the dominant nation (or ethnic majority) at the expense of the other ethnocultural communities living in the federal unit. The Serbs outside Serbia proper (the Republic of Serbia without the two autonomous provinces) considered themselves as the main victims of this situation. For instance the requirement, imposed by the Albanian-dominated Kosovan government, that applicants for certain jobs in Kosovo should have a basic knowledge of the Albanian language disadvantaged the Serbs, who usually spoke no Albanian. Of crucial importance was the special attention paid to the observance of the so-called ethnic key. This distribution code required a fair representation of all ethnocultural communities in public offices (governmental institutions, the army, the party), both on the level of the federation and of the federal units. The ethnic key was particularly important in federal units with an ethnically heterogeneous population. Until the end of the 1960s, systematic neglect of the ethnic key had resulted in Serb overrepresentation. From the beginning of the 1970s on, the ethnic key was applied more scrupulously and the representation of most of the ethnocultural communities slowly but steadily evolved to more fair proportions, especially within the federal units. On the federal level, however, there continued to be a striking underrepresentation of the nationalities—as opposed to the nations—particularly Albanians. Serb overrepresentation remained overwhelming in the army and the police forces, although even there, according to the general tendency, it tended to decline.

The application of the ethnic key reduced the job opportunities of the Serbs and was considered by many of them as a kind of discrimination.

The scrupulous implementation of the ethnic key looked even more threatening to the Serbs (and to others) in combination with certain demographic developments, particularly the spectacular growth of the Bosniak population in Bosnia and the Albanian population in Kosovo. In 1948, the Bosniaks made up 30.7 percent of the total population of Bosnia-Herzegovina, and the Serbs 44.3 percent. In 1991 the Bosniak share in the total population had increased to 43.7 percent and the Serbian share had declined to 31.4 percent. The implementation of the ethnic key in these circumstances would limit the job opportunities of the Serbs even more. The same happened in an even more dramatic way in Kosovo, where the Albanian population grew from 67 percent of the total population in 1961 and probably exceeded 90 percent by 1991. While non-Serbs applauded the painstaking implementation of the ethnic key and the undoing of Serb overrepresentation, the Serbs themselves became more and more resentful of it. To be sure, Croats in Bosnia-Herzegovina and Macedonians in Macedonia also felt (and feel today) uncomfortable with the growth of the Bosniak population in Bosnia-Herzegovina and Albanian population in Macedonia.

The ethnic key was a fair solution to many problems that might arise in a multiethnic society, but it had two negative consequences: it forced Yugoslav citizens to constantly take into account or point out their ethnic origins, which finally hampered the formation of a civil nation; and any failure to adhere to the ethnic key incited strong feelings of solidarity among the members of the "duped" ethnic community, which only exacerbated the feelings of rivalry among the ethnic communities.

In spite of all these problems, the regime had managed to inspire in most members of all ethnic communities a certain degree of loyalty to the Yugoslav communist state. Yugoslavia enjoyed considerable international esteem; Yugoslav citizens had a relatively high standard of living, especially compared to the citizens in the neighboring communist countries; the Yugoslav regime was rather liberal as long as the Yugoslav communist system itself was not seriously questioned, and finally, Yugoslav citizens could freely travel abroad. Most Yugoslavs had no difficulty combining allegiance to the Yugoslav civil nation with allegiance to their respective ethnic nations, in an order depending on one's own preference. Those to whom ethnicity was not so important could register themselves as "Yugoslavs," without mentioning any ethnic affiliation. Such was the pattern among many party officials and professional soldiers, and also many of the children born to one of the about 1.4 million mixed marriages.

After Tito

The death of Tito deprived the Yugoslavs of an authoritarian but charismatic leader who had always succeeded in maintaining the precarious balance across the very divergent territorial, economical, social, political interests of the different ethnic communities. Tito's death coincided with a deep economic and social crisis in Yugoslavia. It became obvious that the Yugoslav standard of living was based on Western loans and capital imported by Gastarbeiter (guest workers), rather than on sound economic performance. Besides, there was the moral crisis of the Yugoslav communist system itself. Widespread corruption among the highest party officials, the obvious inability of the government to cope with the economic problems, and the inefficiency of the economic system itself, increasingly described at great length in the liberalized media, caused citizens to lose their confidence in the Yugoslav communist system. The transition to parliamentary democracy and a free-market economy by the end of the 1980s finished Yugoslav communism, but also involved further economic instability and social malaise.

The end of the Cold War also meant the end of the particular role the non-aligned Yugoslavia had played in the postwar world and of the preferential treatment by the Western powers it had enjoyed. Yugoslavia's utility as a factor in the balance-of-power system had disappeared, as had the fear that a local conflict could escalate and provoke a conflict between NATO and the Warsaw Pact.

The vacuum caused by the loss of Yugoslav civil nationhood was filled by a radicalized allegiance to the ethnic nation, from which the individual expected protection against instability, impoverishment, and discrimination. Once the power monopoly of the LCY had been abolished and a multiparty system introduced, former communist politicians and new "democratic" ones equally resorted to nationalism, bidding for the voters' favor. The new nationalist parties, once in power, controlled everything, just like the LCY had done before. The former Communist Party's malevolent tradition of patronage was continued, offering to the new nationalist parties the opportunity to mobilize huge masses of followers whose social positions were very much dependent on the electoral successes of their leaders, who believed they were threatened by other ethnic communities, and who were prepared to take up arms to defend their real or imagined interests. Respected intellectuals and historians, in particular, willingly delivered messages laden with nationalist ideology that dehumanized the adversary and instilled in the members of their own nations the ruthlessness of the wronged in order to ease their consciences when it came to looting, ethnic cleansing, rape, and murder.

Nearing Catastrophe

The signs of the nearing catastrophe, which can be traced back to the beginning of the 1980s, remained unnoticed or were inadequately assessed abroad. Albanians in Kosovo had demanded that their autonomous province be given the status of a republic as early as 1981, with the hope that republic status would provide relief from their economic and social backwardness. Slovenes and Croats wanted to solve the economic crisis by extending the autonomy of the federal units and turning Yugoslavia into a confederation. Stronger federal units and a weaker central government would also have enabled them to reduce their economic support of the south, or to make it conditional. Serb leaders insisted the crisis be solved by restoring centralized authority to better cope with the economic problems. The smaller southern republics of Montenegro and Macedonia were in favor of extending the federal units' responsibilities, but at the same time feared that weakening of centralized power could jeopardize the financial support provided by the federal government to their economies.

Although a moderate re-centralization could have been justified (since radical federalization had rendered Yugoslavia more or less ungovernable), the fact that it was Serbia that insisted on such a move made it unacceptable to the others. They recalled the Serbs' hegemonic policy in the interwar period and Serb dominance in the first decades after World War II. In addition, they were alarmed, quite understandably, by the aggressive Serb nationalism that had become fashionable in the Serb media during the 1980s, and especially by the ominous "Memorandum"—an inventory of complaints and demands—Serb intellectuals had issued in 1986. It should be emphasized, however, that separatism, especially in Kosovo, Slovenia, and Croatia, was also a strong force in and of itself, and would have emerged even without the challenge of reemerging Serb nationalism. Yugoslavia's disintegration was very much the corollary of the decades-long erosion, resisted by the Serbs, of the central, federal institutions. Actually, there was a spiral movement in which Serb centralism and non-Serb separatism mutually reinforced each other.

Initially, overt Serb nationalism was aroused in 1981 by riots in Pristina/Prishtinë and ensuing unrest in Kosovo. The riots were provoked by the deplorable social situation in Kosovo, especially by the high unemployment rates and the declining preferential treatment of the Serbs. The reaction of the security forces and the judiciary was extremely harsh and actually increased the tensions even more. The Serb media started accusing the Albanians of systematically harassing and intimidating Serbs in order to encourage them to leave the province and create an ethnically pure Albanian Kosovo. In 1989 and 1990, the new Serb leader, Slobodan Milosevic, a former communist and rather opportunist proponent of the radical Serb nationalist line, drastically limited the autonomy of both autonomous provinces, Kosovo and Vojvodina, depriving them of all statelike jurisdiction. Although the extent of autonomy left was still considerable according to international standards, the Albanian ministers, who constituted a qualified majority in the parliament, refused to implement the new 1990 Constitution, since it was imposed by street violence and police intimidation. Instead, they voted a new Kosovan constitution of their own and in 1991 proclaimed the independence of Kosovo. International recognition failed to materialize. In Vojvodina, on the other hand, the parliament decided to make the best of the limited autonomy still conferred under the 1990 Constitution.

Breaking Up

It was not just in Kosovo and Vojvodina that the followers of Milosevic carried out a kind of coup d'état and brought Milosevic's men to power; the same thing occurred in Montenegro, so that representatives of Kosovo, Vojvodina, and Montenegro voted in support of the Serb positions in the federal government, making any legislative initiatives offered by the Slovene and Croat representatives totally futile. This new situation, following the many frustrations of the previous years, led to the decision by Slovene and Croat representatives to break with the LCY, and subsequently with the Yugoslav federation itself. On 25 June 1991 they unilaterally proclaimed their independence.

At this point, the Serb leaders too were prepared to give up the federation and split. The problem, however, was determining the borders of the new states. Should they correspond to the existing internal borders between the republics (the autonomous provinces were not taken into consideration), or should new borders be drawn coinciding with the ethnic borders? Both options could be justified, although the latter was nearly unrealizable because of the ethnic heterogeneity of many regions, particularly Bosnia-Herzegovina. The final choice was inspired not by reasons of principle, but by mere opportunism. Each budding state opted for the solution that was most favorable to it, without much regard for consistency. Only the Slovenes and the Macedonians, having no minorities in other Yugoslav republics, chose the first option unconditionally. Milosevic was prepared to fight in order to impose the second option, which would unite all Serb-inhabited territories into one state (called Greater Serbia), while simultaneously and quite inconsistently insisting that the overwhelmingly Albanian Kosovo should remain within the borders of Serbia. The Croat leader Franjo Tudjman supported the maintenance of the existing Croat state borders, but nonetheless quite overtly supported the annexation of Croat-inhabited West-Herzegovina by Croatia.

Peter Banker/Panos Pictures

Zagreb: protest wall

During the ten-day war in Slovenia in June-July 1991, the Yugoslav National Army, the most stubborn defender of the crumbling Yugoslav federation, made a last attempt to save the federation by military force. After that attempt failed, and the Slovene and Croat soldiers defected, the Yugoslav army finally became an exclusively Serb army. Henceforth it would join with the local Serb armed forces, first in Croatia and later in Bosnia, in an attempt to establish Greater Serbia—a project that implied, for geographic and strategic reasons, that many regions with a Serb minority and even without Serbs would also become part of Greater Serbia.

In 1990, the local Serb community in Croatia had demanded a separate autonomous province, which was to remain a part of Croatia as long as Croatia remained in Yugoslavia. The autonomous province would secede from Croatia if Croatia were to secede from Yugoslavia. Resorting to military violence and massive ethnic cleansing, the Serbs created four autonomous provinces in Croatia, which were united in the Serb Republic of Krajina (SRK), an independent ministate seeking unification with Yugoslavia. The SRK was finally abolished in late summer 1995 when the Croat army invaded it and expelled most of the local Serbs.

In Bosnia-Herzegovina, three nations lived alongside each other: Bosniaks, Croats, and Serbs. The Bosniaks had been officially recognized by the Yugoslav government as a nation in 1969, but many Croats and Serbs continued to consider them as a religious and not an ethnic community. The Bosniaks, as a nation, insisted on the same rights to self-determination and secession as Croats and Serbs did. The problem, however, was that each of the three nations in Bosnia wanted to implement its respective right to self-determination in a totally different way.

Until 1991, the Bosniaks had been in favor of preserving the Yugoslav state. However, as soon as Slovenia and Croatia were internationally recognized on 15 January 1992 and finally left the federation, the Bosniaks and Bosnian Croats felt threatened by the Serbs in the new, completely Serb-dominated Yugoslavia. The Bosniak leaders wanted Bosnia to secede from Yugoslavia and to become an independent state. The Bosniak view was implicitly based on the idea that, since the Croats had acquired a state of their own and the Serbs lived in Yugoslavia, which was increasingly Serb, Bosnia, though multinational, should become a Bosniak state.

The Bosnian Serbs followed the example of the Serbs in Croatia: they established a number of autonomous regions that were to secede from Bosnia-Herzegovina and constitute an independent state, eventually to be attached to Yugoslavia. Thanks to their military superiority and to large-scale ethnic cleansing, the Serb local armed forces, supported by the Yugoslav army, succeeded in bringing about 70 percent of Bosnia under the control of their "independent" Serb Republic (Republika Srpska [RS]).

Although some Croat politicians believed the international community would support the cause of Croatia's territorial integrity more vigorously if Croatia clearly demonstrated that it was prepared to respect the territorial integrity of Bosnia, President Franjo Tudjman was in favor of annexing the overwhelmingly Croat West-Herzegovina. In 1993, he encouraged the Herzegovian Croats to establish the Croat autonomous province of Herceg-Bosna, which was eventually to join Croatia. The more scattered Croats in Central Bosnia did not back this move. These ambiguities explain a great deal of the vicissitudes of the war in Bosnia. In some regions, Bosniaks and Croats fought as allies against the Serbs and expelled the Serb population; in other regions, Bosniaks and Croats were enemies and expelled each other. Moreover, their relations underwent many changes as the war proceeded, depending on the Serb advance, which encouraged their alliance, and on international pressure to reconcile.

Although Croat and Serb nationalist leaders in Bosnia, Croatia, and Serbia were adversaries wherever the borders of their coveted territories overlapped, they were in general agreement that the best solution to the Bosnian question was to divide Bosnia between Croatia and Serbia. This solution, however, was unacceptable to the Bosniaks and to the international community. The latter had already recognized the independence and the territorial integrity of the Bosnian state in April 1992. The 1995 Dayton Accord maintained the Bosnian state, but assigned an ethnically homogenous entity to the Bosnian Serbs, with Bosniaks and Croats sharing the same entity. However, the Croats in particular have continued to insist on an entity of their own.

Throughout the duration of the wars in Croatia and Bosnia-Herzegovina, the Kosovan question remained unresolved. The international community supported a solution that would restore or even extend the former autonomy of Kosovo within the borders of Yugoslavia. This, however, was not viewed as an option by either the Serbs or the Albanians. After more than half a decade (1991–1997) of Kosovar nonviolent resistance under the leadership of the Kosovan president, Ibrahim Rugova, a bloody war between the Kosovan Liberation Army and Serb military forces in 1998, massive NATO air strikes against Yugoslavia in 1999, and the establishment of an international protectorate in Kosovo, the parties involved and the international community have moved no closer to settling the conflict. However, the election of Vojislav Kostunica as president of Yugoslavia and the fall of Milosevic in October 2000 resulted in the international community showing more understanding for the Serb point of view.

The Republic of Macedonia proclaimed its independence from Yugoslavia in autumn 1991. Although the Badinter Arbitration Committee considered that Macedonia met all the requirements to be recognized as an independent state, the international community for many years refused to confer recognition because of the objections of Greece. The latter feared that the new republic had territorial claims to northern Greece, and insisted that a Slavic state could not call itself Macedonia because of the name's associations with the historical heritage of Greece. In September 1995 a compromise was reached, opening the way to normal diplomatic relations. Henceforth, the new state was officially called Former Yugoslav Republic of Macedonia (FYROM).

The Albanian minority—an estimated 30 percent of the total population—proved to be more of a threat to the survival of Macedonia. Moderate Albanian leaders' demands included the recognition of Albanian as a second official language, fair representation in public services, and a federal organization of the state, but the majority of Macedonians have not been inclined to concede much more than cultural autonomy. In March 2001, clashes between Albanian rebels and Macedonian forces broke out in the neighborhood of Tetovo. The situation was contained, but remained explosive. In August 2001 a Western-brokered peace deal was signed, largely meeting the Albanian demands.

Finally, as result of the Yugoslav leader Milosevic's authoritarian and failing rule, an independence movement emerged in Montenegro as well. The decisive April 2001 elections clearly revealed the deep divisions within Montenegrin society on this subject. The international community had covertly encouraged the Montenegrin separatist Milo Djukanovic when Milosevic was still in power, but it subsequently proved to be more reluctant to recognize Montenegro's independence than Kostunica himself. The secession of Montenegro might inspire the Serbs in the Bosnian RS to secede as well and the final disintegration of Yugoslavia would render obsolete a solution to the Kosovan question, in which Kosovo became a kind of federal unit within a very loose Yugoslav federation.

International Involvement

During the years following the collapse of Yugoslavia, the international community had an ongoing involvement in the region. It is to this involvement that we now turn our attention. Immediately after the Yugoslavian National Army (YNA) entered Slovenia in June 1991, the European Union (then European Community) mediated the Brioni Accord, which postponed the Slovenian declaration of independence. The European Union was less successful in its mediation of the conflict in Croatia, where the YNA, in cooperation with local militias, occupied the Krajina and parts of Slavonia and carried out ethnic cleansing. After the international recognition of Slovenia and Croatia in January 1992 and the cessation of the fighting in Croatia, UN and EU representatives negotiated an agreement with the Croat and Serb parties. The agreement allowed the Krajina to be controlled by a UN Protection Force (UNPROFOR), which was charged with demilitarization of the region and organizing the return of the refugees (and was nicknamed FUNPROFOR because of its failure to do so).

At the time of the conflict in Bosnia-Herzegovina, the EU and UN tried to reach a solution at the International Conference on the Former Yugoslavia. Paying lip service to ethnocultural pluralism, they actually looked for a double compromise: between the political and territorial ambitions of the parties involved on the one hand, and between political and moral principles and the military reality in the field on the other. The Vance-Owen Plan and the Owen-Stoltenberg Plan, named after the representatives of both organizations, provided for the preservation of the territorial integrity of the Bosnian state and simultaneously for the establishment of very autonomous entities (resembling federal units) assigned to ethnic majorities. The Dayton Peace Treaty of December 1995, forced upon the recalcitrant Serbs after a UN military intervention and an action of the Croat and Bosnian army, accorded with those plans. It created a weak state, giving extensive authority to two entities (Bosniak-Croat and Serb) that are apparently unwilling to cooperate with each other. Dayton ended the war, but created a situation that made international military presence (*in casu* the Implementation, and later the Stabilization Force) indispensable. Bosnia was rapidly demilitarized and normalized, but the Bosnian institutions still function awkwardly.

Similarly in Kosovo, where the Albanians had already declared independence in 1991, diplomatic mediation did not lead to a solution. Here, military intervention was agreed to, mainly under U.S. pressure, more quickly than in Bosnia-Herzegovina. This was carried out by NATO, without an explicit UN mandate. The objective was to end the brutal Serb military retaliations. In June 1999, the intervention ended with the establishment of a UN protectorate in Kosovo, but left the future of Kosovo unclear. According to UN Resolution 1244, Kosovo would "enjoy a substantial autonomy within the Federal Republic of Yugoslavia." In practice, all kinds of measures by the representatives of the international community strengthened the Albanians in Kosovo on the assumption that Kosovo would become independent. That was a realistic possibility, as long as Slobodan Milosevic, loathed by the West, was president of Yugoslavia. Since the fall of Milosevic in October 2000 and the start of Vojislav Kostunica's presidency, the international community has appeared to be more sympathetic to the Serb position. Whatever the case, in Kosovo a long-term military presence looks indispensable. The implementation of the military aspect of the various accords, especially with regard to demilitarization, the respect of demilitarized zones, and the like, seemed to have proceeded smoothly. Nevertheless, as the events in Macedonia in spring and summer 2001 showed, full demilitarization had clearly not been achieved: the Albanian National Liberation Army was able to smuggle in weapons from Kosovo on a large scale. The implementation of the civil aspect—the rehabilitation of a regularly functioning society—has proven to be much more difficult, and so far there has been no truly convincing success in this area.

One may hope that, despite the fact that international intervention did not really succeed in resolving the political and social problems, it may at least have provided some moral and material relief, served to restore mutual trust, and encouraged a willingness between the afflicted communities to work together. In this respect, NGOs in particular have a crucial role to play.

Some Moral Considerations

In considering the developments in Yugoslavia, it can be said, in general, that the international community has pursued an inconsistent policy, has made choices of principle without regard for the consequences in one case, and has failed to follow its own principles in favor of realpolitik in another. To the warring parties concerned, this policy has given the impression of arbitrariness or partiality. For example, in considering the legitimacy of secession, a "rigorous" interpretation justifies secession only if there is a "good cause" in the form of persistent and severe violations of human rights—a situation not prevailing in 1991 in Slovenia and Croatia. And here, both countries were recognized immediately. But despite the fact that these kinds of violations were occurring in Kosovo, the country is still awaiting international recognition of its independence. In contrast, a liberal interpretation of the legitimacy of secession states that it is justified when the majority of the population in a given region or entity demands it. And here, too, Kosovo qualifies, but then so too do the Croat and Serb areas of Bosnia-Herzegovina.

The war in Yugoslavia has also caused a very sizable refugee problem. The number of internal and external refugees (displaced persons and refugees) during the conflicts in Croatia and Bosnia-Herzegovina was estimated at 4 million. During the air strikes in Kosovo and Serbia, more than half a million people left Kosovo—mainly Albanians. In Croatia, most of the Croat refugees have returned. The prospects for the return of the Serbs chased away from the Krajina in summer 1995 were held out, but practical constraints (homes that were destroyed or occupied by others, intimidation, the threat of arrest because of real or supposed war crimes) have persuaded the refugees that they should stay in Serbia for the time being. The Dayton Accord stipulated that refugees would return to the places from where they were evicted, but as yet this has not happened. Even within the Bosniak-Croat entity, the return, for example, of Bosniak refugees to areas with a predominantly Croat population has thus far proved very problematic. In Kosovo, the return of Albanian refugees proceeds smoothly, facing only material problems such as destroyed houses and local infrastructures. The Serb refugees have not been enabled to return. Serbs who were expelled from Croatia, Bosnia-Herzegovina, or Kosovo are still in Serbia. At present they number some half a million.

The extent of violence—atrocities, rape, torture, and massacres—may not have been higher than in other wars, but it was extensively described by journalists and shown on TV, often for propaganda purposes. Nevertheless, ethnic cleansing, in particular, was perpetrated on such a scale that it verges on genocide. The rape of women (and men) was used as a tool of ultimate humiliation and destruction of human dignity. The massacres of able-bodied men (as in Srebrenica) may have been perpetrated primarily to serve military aims, but that fact does not render them less a violation of international conventions or less repulsive.

The UN War Tribunal in The Hague is expected to meet the moral and juridical norms that are currently observed by the international community by condemning the guilty. Besides that, these convictions should contribute to an improvement of the relations between the various ethnic communities in the former Yugoslavia itself. These convictions would make clear who did *not* commit crimes, and thus prevent communities from being denounced collectively for such crimes. Convictions in one's own country and pronouncements of Truth and Reconciliation Commissions could have an even more valuable effect of collective reflection and repentance. However, such exercises are unlikely when indicted war criminals are extradited or "sold" in exchange for financial aid. It has been argued that the arrest and/or extradition of certain important persons can only aggravate the tensions and impede the process of democratization, since some of the accused are considered heroes in their own countries. On the other hand, it is generally believed that, with the extradition of Milosevic in July 2001, the arrest of the other indicted war criminals, which seemed to have been shelved for a long time, will gain a new impetus.

However, the dark period following the collapse of Yugoslavia will not draw to a close with the conviction of war criminals or with the establishment of normalized diplomatic relations. It can only occur with the democratization of the ex-Yugoslav states and the development of a sound civil society in each of them.

Raymond Detrez (born in Antwerp, Belgium, in 1948) studied Eastern European Languages and History at the University of Ghent (1967–1971) and specialized in Bulgarian Philology at the University of Sofia (1971). In 1986 he obtained his Ph.D. with a thesis on the autobiography of Grigor Parlicev—the forgotten Greek poet Grigorios Stavridhis—and the development of national consciousness in the Balkans. He is currently a professor of Eastern European and Modern Greek history at the University of Gent. He has published numerous books and articles on Balkan history, minority policies, and nationalism in Southeastern Europe.

13.3

Policy Recommendations: Have the Courage to Set Far-Reaching Goals

International Crisis Group

Building on its experience of five years of field-based analysis, the International Crisis Group (ICG) makes recommendations as to how to best move forward in the Balkans. Among its recommendations is the call for the international community and local actors to have the courage to define clear final and future status goals for the communities and republics at issue. It advises, for instance, to let Montenegro develop into an independent state if that is what its citizens decide they want and urges that "conditional independence" be closely explored as a possible solution for Kosovo.

Slobodan Milosevic has gone, but he has left behind him a bitter legacy of death, destruction, and distrust in the Balkans. His democratic overthrow was a watershed, but the potential for renewed conflict in the region remains dangerously high. Across the Balkans, security and stability continue to be undercut by lingering nationalism, fragile and unresponsive government institutions, underperforming economies, undelivered justice, and the issue of refugees who have not been able to return to their homes. Breaking the cycle of violence in the region will require shattering the hold on power of narrow and often antidemocratic political elites, and accelerating difficult transitions to lasting political and economic reform.

Because the potential for renewed conflict remains clear, it is vital that the international community take comprehensive and forward-looking action to address the sources of underlying tensions in the region, including final status issues. The Balkans are not doomed by history or character to suffer perpetual conflict. Lasting peace is possible with practical steps, everyday actions, and the will of the people to achieve it.

So what can or should foreign actors do?

Few tasks are more central or profound for the international community than peacefully guiding processes to resolve status issues in Kosovo and Montenegro, enforcing the Dayton Accords in Bosnia vigorously so as to create the

209

conditions for ultimate acceptance of a more viable post-Dayton governance structure, and maintaining the integrity of Macedonia while achieving political rather than military solutions that address the political and cultural concerns of ethnic Albanians. While policymakers often wince at the complexity and intractability of these issues, such fundamental structural challenges are the great unfinished business that Yugoslavia's dissolution set in motion.

To ignore these issues or to reason that they are better left for another day is to risk pouring gasoline on the lingering fires of nationalism in the region. There is simply no way for these societies to emerge from chronic instability until some order and rationality is brought to their fundamental legal and institutional structures. The time has come to peacefully, transparently, and democratically resolve final-status issues in keeping with the rule of law and relevant international mandates. If the international community shirks this admittedly difficult work, history will not be kind to it.

Credible Presence in the Region

The international community will have to approach its work within a general strategy to break the economic and political power of extremists. Broad economic restructuring, designed to generate tangible economic benefits in the near term, will be crucial. Efforts to restore the rule of law, bring perpetrators of war crimes to justice, build better-functioning public institutions, and return refugees to their homes will be essential as well.

All this requires international engagement that is built around foresight, prevention, and a willingness to aggressively counter nationalist forces. Indeed, having already tried a far more reactive, cautious, and timid approach to the Balkans throughout much of the 1990s—with poor results—the international community has clear incentive to take a more proactive stance.

This has a number of practical ramifications. NATO should maintain a credible presence in the region, supported by all of the alliance's nineteen members, and should not shy away from being prepared to use its military muscle for preventive purposes. The international community should encourage its high representative in Bosnia and the UN Mission in Kosovo to exercise their mandates aggressively. The generous international assistance to the region should continue, but it should also be more clearly tied to meeting specific benchmarks such as meaningful economic reform, cooperation with the International Criminal Tribunal for the Former Yugoslavia, and full implementation of the Dayton Accords.

Both the EU and the Stability Pact will need to more closely focus their activities on a narrower range of issues where meaningful progress can be made in generating jobs and economic growth within the context of lasting reform.

Greater Clarity

With regard to the final status of Kosovo, the profound gulf between Belgrade and Pristina has led many in the international community to assume that the issue remains too explosive to tackle in the near term. However, substantial progress toward building a viable economy, deradicalizing the province, and stabilizing the wider regional neighborhood will be virtually impossible unless greater clarity is brought to the fundamental legal and constitutional framework in Kosovo.

In addition to establishing without delay the system of self-government within Kosovo as provided for in UN Security Council Resolution 1244 adopted after the Kosovo war, the international community should organize an "international meeting" and hold consultations in Kosovo on principles that might constitute the foundations for a final political settlement.

The most appropriate status for Kosovo to emerge from such consultations may be "conditional independence," which could involve preconditions (e.g., minority-rights protection) that would have to be satisfied before all the benefits of recognition (e.g., UN membership) were granted; the permanent renunciation of some measures (e.g., territorial expansion); and a period of some type of international trusteeship, during which certain veto powers would limit Kosovo's sovereignty.

Common Interests

The international community should no longer discourage Montenegro from seeking independence if that is what the people of Montenegro demonstrate they wish through their political processes. Concerns about moves toward independence triggering internal conflict, negative impacts on Serbia and in Kosovo, and domino effects in Bosnia and elsewhere, have all been overstated. The departure of Montenegro from the Federal Republic of Yugoslavia would not mean the latter's automatic dissolution as a legal entity. There are a number of constitutional models available through which Montenegro and Serbia could retain some of their traditional ties and advance common interests. For its part, the international community should help Montenegro and Serbia to find a mutually satisfactory basis for this new relationship. The approach until now, seeking to pressure Montenegro into drawing back from independence, has been both unconstructive and ineffective, and has discouraged Belgrade from engaging in meaningful dialogue.

With regard to Serbia, the international community should call on Belgrade to change a range of policies that are unacceptable, including its policies toward ethnic minorities, support for extremist elements in both Bosnia and northern Kosovo, and the detention of large numbers of ethnic Albanian "political prisoners." The international community should closely condition financial assistance on Serbia's ability to meet clear benchmarks with regard to economic and democratic reform, and cooperation with the Hague Tribunal and international efforts in Bosnia and Kosovo. If the standards are met, the EU and the United States should initiate a comprehensive economic-assistance strategy for providing the Federal Republic of Yugoslavia desperately needed technical assistance to rapidly reform the old socialist economic laws and carry out privatization.

Overarching Concerns

ICG holds that all entities in the Balkans it is now engaged in—Serbia, Montenegro, Kosovo, Bosnia, Macedonia, and Albania (as well as Croatia)—share a
number of common problems and challenges that need to be addressed. Five
broad issues deserve particular consideration: unsatisfied nationalism, unresponsive government institutions, underperforming economies, undelivered
justice, and refugees and displaced persons.

Dealing with these overarching concerns remains fundamental to preventing conflicts in the Balkans. Obviously these issues must be addressed within
a local context. However, there is also merit in analyzing broader themes from
a regional perspective to gain more comprehensive insight into the situation in
the Balkans today.

Unsatisfied Nationalism

The fear and insecurity surrounding the breakdown of communist Yugoslavia
set the stage for rabid nationalism in the 1980s and 1990s. In a climate of dissatisfaction and deep uncertainty brought on by economic crisis and the disintegration of communist rule, political leaders seized upon appeals to nationalism as a powerful mobilizing tool. This is not to say that nationalist
aspirations and grievances were not keenly felt. However, these sentiments
were whipped up and manipulated by leaders for their tactical political purposes at the extraordinarily high cost of precipitating a bloodbath.

Today, effectively undermining destructive nationalism requires addressing the underlying causes of the fear and insecurity that have been exploited
by nationalist leaders. Croatia offers an interesting example in that regard.
Having won its independence, it reestablished control over its territory through
the military campaigns against the Serb-controlled regions in 1995 and
through the United Nations Transitional Administration in Eastern Slavonia,
which ended in 1998. While the right wing in Croatian politics, including the
late president Franjo Tudjman himself, did not give up its obsession with the
lands inhabited by ethnic Croats in Bosnia, territorial claims against Bosnia
never had widespread popular support. After 1995 a more normal, healthy political environment began to evolve in which the nationalist right led by Tudjman and the Croatian Democratic Union (HDZ) was progressively less able to
mobilize the population against international pressure for democratic reform
as the price of European integration. Following Tudjman's death in December
1999, the HDZ was heavily defeated in elections early in 2000.

A number of major issues concerning territorial claims and political status
in the region remain unresolved, inflamed by nationalism and economic hardship. Each offers the clear potential for renewed conflict. All will be daunting
to resolve. In each case there is a clear need for a democratic dialogue to peacefully resolve outstanding issues of territorial claims and political status. Changes
to established borders should only be made by mutual agreement. Under no circumstances should ethnic cleansing be rewarded. The relationship between
majority and minority populations within any entity should be reciprocal and

unconditional. Full individual rights and protection before the law should be guaranteed to the minority, with respect paid to its collective identity and culture; the minority, thus protected, owes the larger entity respect for both its laws and its identity. The international community should play an active role in advancing political status and rights issues, including hosting and facilitating talks, and also by offering economic incentives and, where appropriate, security guarantees.

Unresponsive Government Institutions

Across the Balkans, problem after problem can be traced back to public institutions that fail to provide for the economic, legal, and security needs of citizens. Almost all state institutions in the Balkans are fragile, a large number are corrupt, and a great many are discredited. Throughout much of the region, antidemocratic forces maintain a stranglehold over political, military, and economic power. Breaking this legacy is crucial to reducing tensions and preventing conflict.

While international assistance has produced a patchwork of projects to address a variety of problems at different stages using different means, the essential challenge is almost invariably the same, that of institution building. For example, the continuing strength of stridently nationalist parties in some parts of the Balkans, such as Bosnia, often reflects the weakness and lack of credibility of state structures, particularly in providing basic security.

More effective and integrated institutions are needed at the larger European level, at the inter-entity level, and within each of the entities ICG is involved with in the Balkans. Ultimately, not all countries in the Balkans need, or want, the same kind of institutions. As the experience of the United Nations Interim Administration Mission in Kosovo demonstrates, particularly with regard to dictating the pace of establishing democratic institutions, many Western impositions will be resented and undermined. Assistance through provision of models and mentors may be more effective, with one recent example being the EU's help to the Balkans in drafting a standard regional Investment Compact through the Stability Pact mechanism.

To succeed, the process of institution building will have to be owned by local communities. Institution building must take account of peculiarities in constitutional as well as economic circumstances in each location.

Regarding security institutions, a number of practical and commonsense steps can be pursued. It is clear that a considerable gulf exists between rhetoric and practice with regard to military matters in the region. Over time, force levels should be reduced and the internal security and paramilitary forces that have been so abusive over the last decade should be disbanded. Support for training and professionalization through NATO's Partnership for Peace can augment Organization for Security and Cooperation in Europe (OSCE) efforts and help return these militaries to the role of national defense and away from explicitly political agendas.

As justice and policing go hand in hand, the training of local forces should be a central goal in the security arena. International supervision of these police forces should be maintained. The European Union has made improving its ability to support civilian police efforts a central goal for strengthening its crisis-management capabilities. By 2003, EU member states hope to be able to volunteer up to five thousand police officers in a regional crisis. These are welcome steps. However, much more still needs to be done, and sooner than 2003, to develop professional local police forces. General precepts need to be backed up with specific, practical help for institution building. In Bosnia, for instance, much effort has been devoted to training and equipping border police. This program should pay dividends in increasing state revenues, improving control over sovereign territory, reducing crime and smuggling, and establishing better relations between the Bosnian communities.

Corruption, which weakens many Balkan institutions, is another problem that the international community could help to reduce. The starting point in this regard needs to be new laws. However, the rule of law is discredited by the Balkan habit of passing legislation that is not fairly and honestly applied but rather often designed just to impress donors. Ensuring that the law is applied fairly and rigorously means making sure that officials are sufficiently well paid that they do not regard taking bribes as essential to their livelihood. The international community, where it has the power, and local governments should sack corrupt or partial judges and vigorously prosecute corrupt firms and officials, not least for the demonstration effect.

Underperforming Economies

None of the Balkan economies has made an effective transition from state-dominated economic control to market management. Indeed, many have gone backward. Unless the peoples of the Balkans themselves address these issues, assisted by the international community, there is no realistic prospect of attracting major investment or sustaining growth.

Broader integration within the European Union will remain a mirage without major institutional reforms. Most of the people of the Balkans are eager to take their place in Europe. However, such Europe-wide cooperation will work only if those involved from the outside—funding agencies, investors, lenders, consultants, and government officials—know that they can rely on the institutions being developed.

Failure to improve economic conditions or move forward with broader integration into Europe would be a recipe for continued tensions, extreme nationalist policies, and potential conflict. Above all, the governments in the region need to recognize how serious their problems are. That involves avoiding any temptations to convince themselves that they can be completely bailed out in the short term by donor assistance, in the medium term by quick-fix remedies (poorly designed privatization, for example), and in the longer term by affiliation with the EU. External support will certainly be helpful. But the necessary reform momentum ultimately has to come from within.

Privatization, while not a panacea, will be the key to reform efforts. The process of privatization will reduce the scope for arbitrary, capricious, and corrupt government-party interventions in business management. But Balkan governments need to make sure that they fix a fair price for their assets, particularly in circumstances where their value may have been understated. They need to carefully manage the pace and scope of privatization, avoiding either a "fire sale" to cronies or a process so disruptively slow it undercuts the momentum for reform.

Undelivered Justice

Reliable, impartial, and timely delivery of justice is another key to progress in the Balkans. The quality of justice, especially in settlement of property claims and dispute-settlement procedures, is one crucial variable in determining prospects for foreign investment. Perceived ethnic or nationalist bias in the judicial systems reinforces the fears and hatreds that fuel unsatisfied nationalism.

The essential problem with the judicial systems lies not so much in the enactment of appropriate laws as in making sure those laws are applied fairly. Balkan governments too often introduce new laws as though this in itself will reform their systems of government. In too many cases, those laws are notional only, contradict other legislation, are undermined by administrative discretion, and are not policed rigorously.

A number of steps can be taken to strengthen the judicial system, including removal of corrupt judges, more-objective processes for the appointment and dismissal of judges, and better training for judges and advocates.

The issue of war criminals remains far more contentious and complicated. Bringing war criminals to court goes to the heart of international law, morality, and the ability to assign blame for Europe's worst atrocities in the second half of the twentieth century. Only by bringing the perpetrators of such acts to justice can the stigma of collective guilt begin to be lifted from the peoples of the region, allowing them to embrace a larger and more lasting sense of reconciliation. The role of the Hague Tribunal is crucial in this respect, and a number of measures to strengthen its effectiveness should be considered.

First of all, the international community should take great care not to let its enthusiasm for recent democratic progress in Serbia lessen its commitment to seeing Belgrade cooperate with the tribunal. Croatia in particular, which has cooperated to a considerable extent with the tribunal, would be deeply angered if the international community instituted a double standard.

The International Criminal Tribunal for the Former Yugoslavia could make greater progress by using available procedures to try selected war-crimes suspects in the region itself, with proceedings fully translated and locally transmitted. With a substantial portion of its proceedings moved from The Hague to local settings, the tribunal might develop much greater legitimacy in the eyes of the general ex-Yugoslav public.

The tribunal could also be strengthened by the international community standing firm and consistent in imposing penalties for noncooperation with it. The tribunal should be allowed to expand its number of experienced judges so that it can hold more trials simultaneously.

Unreturned Refugees

Of the 3 million internally displaced persons and refugees created by war in the Balkans, only 38 percent have been able to return to their former homes. The 1.9 million people remaining displaced throughout the region, and in third countries, constitute a serious impediment to broader stability.

The prospect of improved relations among the successor states of the former Yugoslavia has opened up new opportunities for the remaining refugees and displaced people who wish to return, but various administrative and political obstacles remain. Personal security, as in almost all refugee situations, remains the largest impediment to large-scale returns. Despite the presence of peacekeeping forces, many individuals are rightly concerned that they may still be targets of intimidation and violence. The current state of property laws across much of the Balkans has also prevented higher rates of return. Attempts by returnees to use the courts to evict temporary occupants (often themselves refugees) from their homes and regain property have often ended in frustration.

In some areas, returns have shown a promising increase, even in some hard-line areas in Bosnia and Croatia. Unfortunately, the United Nations High Commission on Refugees (UNHCR) has often lacked funding to facilitate individuals. Given the emphasis that the international community has placed on preserving the multiethnic character of communities in the Balkans, it would be a tragedy if it failed to deliver the relatively modest financial support needed to assist displaced individuals willing to brave returns.

The goal of preserving and restoring multiethnic societies has been a cornerstone of Western policy in the Balkans. Except within Bosnia, Western policymakers rightly refused to reward "ethnic cleansing" by redrawing maps along ethnic lines. However, while some groups want to return, and others cannot return, yet others may opt to stay in their areas of displacement. Peace has come too late for some refugees who are well integrated into their new local communities and for a variety of reasons, including economic factors, wish to stay there. This, for example, is the case for a significant proportion of Bosnian Croat refugees in Croatia, as well as many of the 500,000 or more internally displaced persons and refugees in the Federal Republic of Yugoslavia. For those who fall into these categories, normalization of citizenship laws will need to be the principal motor for integrating them into the community. In Croatia, most such persons have been granted citizenship. In the Federal Republic of Yugoslavia, recent amendments to the citizenship law will impact on the legal status of this significant case load. It is important to stress that integration in the host country cannot include long-term occupation of someone else's home. Lead agencies such as the UNHCR should continue to earmark donor funds to support local integration.

Where indicted war criminals have been arrested by, or have surrendered to, the Hague Tribunal, refugees have subsequently returned home. More aggressive pursuit of indicted war criminals, and efforts to disband paramilitary groups, would greatly improve the prospects for refugee return.

Western Capitals

Some of the recommendations made here go well beyond the present cautious international consensus. But the test, according to ICG, is not what is currently acceptable in the diplomatic marketplace but what will contribute to lasting peace. As has been said earlier, the Balkans are not doomed to suffer perpetual conflict. Making steps toward lasting peace requires sustained attention by the international community, particularly the Western capitals, in order to build on the foundations that have been laid at high cost. Few tasks are more important than peacefully resolving final-status issues in the Federal Republic of Yugoslavia (Kosovo, Montenegro, Serbia), putting Bosnia on a sounder constitutional footing, and ensuring that military conflict yields to political dialogue in Macedonia.

Note

This chapter is an authorized summary of the ICG-Balkans book-length Report No. 108, "After Milosevic: A Practical Agenda for Lasting Balkans Peace," dated 2 April 2001. As such, it reflects the situation in the region in early spring of 2001.

13.4

Albania:
From Anarchy to
Kanun Politics and Society

Albana Shala & Daniel Chavez

For almost five decades Albania had the most autarchic dictatorship in postwar Europe. After the fall of the communist regime in 1991, the country embarked on a radical program of market reforms with profound social and political impacts, and in 1997 the state experienced a virtual meltdown. About two thousand people were killed in the social and political upheaval triggered by the collapse of pyramid investment schemes. Given pervasive developmental problems and the weakness of state institutions, despite some grounds for optimism regarding political stabilization, the establishment of a stable and resilient peace in Albania, located as it is in a conflict-ridden region, remains highly unlikely in the immediate future.

When Albania opened its doors in 1991, the world discovered a landscape of widespread poverty, due to the country's isolation, heavy military spending, and an archaic and rural-based economy. In 1990, the residents in rural areas accounted for 64 percent of the country's population. The demise of the old regime led to the manifestation of long-repressed tensions loosely based on traditional alliances. When the violent crisis erupted in 1997, some media coverage portrayed these tensions as the real cause of the conflict, with frequent references to the north-south cleavage, and even to a purported ethnic divide between the *ghegs* (northern people) and the *tosks* (southern people). Differences do exist between the different regions of Albania—as well as between urban and rural areas, and between highlands and lowlands. However, unlike other contemporary conflicts, the essence of internal disturbances is not primarily linked to ethnic, regional, cultural, or religious divisions, but to the flaws and contradictions inherent to the economic and political transition.

Albania experienced two periods of acute internal conflict in the 1990s. On the first occasion, the "years of anarchy" of 1990–1992 were characterized by political violence and social disorder accompanying the fall of the communist regime. Following the elections of May 1996, denounced as irregular by independent analysts, Albania was once again on the road to social and political violence.

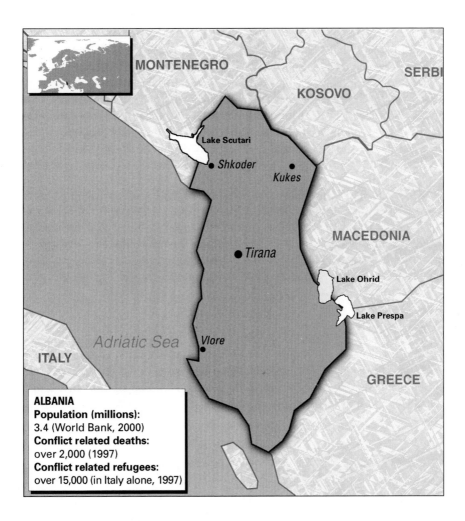

ALBANIA
Population (millions):
3.4 (World Bank, 2000)
Conflict related deaths:
over 2,000 (1997)
Conflict related refugees:
over 15,000 (in Italy alone, 1997)

Seeking political benefits, the government of the Democratic Party (DP) allowed the rise of pyramid investment schemes. In 1996 these get-rich-quick plots "infected" most of the social tissue. It is estimated that close to $1.5 billion were invested in companies offering monthly interest rates ranging from 10 to 25 percent, while the average monthly income was around $80. About a fifth of the population invested in the schemes. People sold their homes to invest the proceeds, and emigrants working in Greece and Italy transferred additional resources to the schemes back home. The opposition lacked an alternative economic policy and the population was satisfied with the unexpected wealth. The authorities were conscious of the risks, and even forced the governor of the National Bank to stop warning investors. International agencies were also aware of the danger, but the IMF waited until October 1996 to issue an admonition.

In December 1996 the whole system began to crumble. Having been assured of the legality of the schemes, the people lost confidence in the government. On January 1997, angry investors threw the first stones. As protests spread across the country, the Socialist Party (SP, former communists) attempted to take control of civil discontent. The government responded with a policy of violent repression and the deployment of the military. As the situation worsened, the government declared a state of emergency and cut off Albanian communications, banning radio and press and taking control of TV stations. The offices of the biggest newspaper, *Koha Jone,* were burned down by the secret police.

Between March and April, Albania descended into anarchy. Foreign "war correspondents" contributed to the rise and spread of the conflict by presenting images of violence and destruction, and drawing maps of a country allegedly divided between "North" and "South." The government lost control of most of the country. Many public buildings and private businesses were damaged or destroyed, and practically every state function was severely hampered. The cities of Vlore, Gjirokaster, and Sarande were run by self-styled "Salvation Committees," where SP leaders had some influence, but with politics in fact subject to the interests of competing criminal gangs.

In the meantime, Western governments appeared more concerned with the threat of massive emigration and the rising importance of Albania as a center for European criminal networks than with political conflict. As the crisis spun out of control, the Organization for Security and Cooperation in Europe (OSCE) sent former Austrian prime minister Franz Vranitzky as an envoy to

Tirana:
Demonstration against the scandal involving pyramid funds (Jan. 1997)

negotiate an agreement between the president and the opposition. Both sides agreed to a government of national reconciliation under a socialist prime minister, as well as to early elections and the request for a multinational stabilization force. By then, images of insurrection and the exodus of refugees had become a constant in prime-time international news.

The Western European Union (WEU) and NATO declined to intervene. Italy and Greece, the states primarily affected by the Albanian crisis, proposed an EU operation, but were only able to achieve an ambiguous commitment for the provision of emergency humanitarian aid. The lack of regional solidarity moved Italy to pursue crisis management unilaterally, and to seek United Nations authority. In late March 1997, the UN Security Council approved the deployment of an Italian-led coalition, codenamed Alba (Italian for "dawn"). Some 7,000 soldiers from nine countries participated in the first conflict management mission conducted in Europe by a military force composed exclusively of Europeans.

The parliamentary elections of June 1997 ultimately led to the restoration of a degree of political stability (though of a delicate nature) that has been maintained in the intervening years. The most dangerous threat to this stability emerged in September 1998, when a failed coup staged by the DP exposed the fragility of Albania's democracy.

In late 1998, the Kosovo conflict and the growing influx of refugees created a new crisis for the government, threatening internal security and stretching administrative capacity. During 1998–1999, as many as 460,000 refugees flooded into Albania. The majority were accommodated with local families, but 300 camps or shelter sites were established throughout the country to house the overflow of refugees. Most Kosovars returned home toward the end of 1999. In the past two years, Albania's political development has once again been challenged by regional instability after the uprising of ethnic Albanian militants in neighboring Macedonia. The government and the people of Albania have managed to remain relatively neutral in this conflict.

Conflict Dynamics

Weak governance capacity threatens to undermine Albania's socioeconomic and political recovery. References to rising criminality, governmental corruption, permanent political tensions between the two opposing parties, and the destabilizing effect of armed conflict in neighboring countries have been constant in practically every policy report on Albania since 1997. Looking back, the events of 1997 cannot be attributed solely to the sudden loss of savings. The roots of the conflict lay in the generalized disenchantment with the economic and political transition. Even before the upheaval, the government had taken control of the electronic media, law enforcement agencies, and the judiciary with persistent disregard for human rights, democracy, and public affairs.

Approximately two thousand Albanians lost their lives in the unrest from March through June 1997. Most of the casualties originated in the arming of the population. Official statistics from the Ministry of Defense, as reported in a 1999 United Nations Development Program (UNDP) paper, indicate that during the first two weeks of March, 656,000 weapons of various types were looted from army depots, together with 1.5 billion rounds of ammunition, 3.5 million hand grenades, and 1 million land mines.[1] To date there are no exact figures on the total number of casualties and weapons looted during the crisis, and nobody seems to know how many arms are still missing. However, most analysts agree that the events of 1997 left deep scars on the face of public order, as many arms ended up in the hands of criminal gangs or in the illegal trade associated with Kosovo and other armed conflicts throughout the Balkans.

Besides the dramatic impact in terms of the loss of human lives, the violent social upheaval of 1997 eroded much of the economic and social achievements Albania had made during the early years of transition. Regardless of the quality and nature of earlier gains, the macroeconomic indicators showed that after a sharp contraction between 1990 and 1992, the GDP had increased by around 9 percent annually for four consecutive years between 1993 and 1996. The official unemployment rate had been halved to 12 percent in 1996, per capita consumption had recovered, and inflation had fallen from 240 percent per year in 1992 to only 6 percent in 1995. Immediately after the crisis, the GDP declined 7 percent, inflation reached over 40 percent, and the exchange rate depreciated by one-third. Albania's GDP per capita at the end of 1997 had fallen to US$735. At its height, the nominal liabilities of pyramid schemes reached 50 percent of the GDP. Poverty, already endemic in the country, rose significantly as result of the crisis, according to a 1998 World Bank report.[2]

In the aftermath of the upheaval, good progress was made toward restoring macroeconomic stability and advancing structural and institutional reforms, as acknowledged by the EU, the World Bank, and other donors. However, the donor community cautioned that further progress is at risk unless Albania addresses its structural weakness, enhances governance and rule of law, and improves the functioning of public administration and the judiciary.[3]

During the past three years (1998–2001), Albania has tried to restore some semblance of political stability. The general elections of 1997 were considered acceptable and satisfactory under the circumstances. In November 1999 the Albanian citizenry adopted by referendum a new constitution that provided for the establishment of an ombudsman and other legal measures for the protection of human rights.

In October 2000, Albania held local elections, and despite some irregularities and isolated incidents of political violence, the OSCE reported that they represented "significant progress" toward meeting international standards. Parliamentary elections took place in June 2001. However, this latest parliamentary election turned into a political marathon that lasted almost two months, as there was a need for extra rounds in nearly 40 percent of the electoral districts and demands of reruns posted by the opposition. The winning force was the ruling Socialist Party and its allies. Ilir Meta was reelected as prime minister after harsh debate within the party. Despite the peaceful nature of the electoral campaign, the opposition Democratic Party is still boycotting the parliament. OSCE and other international organizations are demanding the complete functioning of a legislative power including the opposition, as well as the creation of a political space for further discussion and consensus building. This is unlikely to work, and if it does could run the risk of undermining the role of the parliament.

After the crisis, the SP-led government also broadened the freedom of the media. State television and radio tend to provide more balanced reporting of national news. Nevertheless, the opposition has reacted to allegedly biased information and harassment of media loyal to the DP. In general, most of the press is still loyal to competing political interests, and further efforts are required for the development of alternative/independent media and the depolarization of reporting.[4]

Despite postcrisis improvements, a decade after the fall of communism Albanian party politics remain pervasively confrontational and based on loyalties to personalities (namely Sali Berisha of the Democrats and Fatos Nano of the Socialists) rather than on ideological profiles. Both the DP and the SP leaderships are unlikely ever to accept the legitimacy of a government led by the other, resulting in perpetual political instability. Not surprisingly, Albanian citizens have become largely apathetic about national politics.

Albania's institutions were seriously challenged in September 1998 after the assassination of Azem Hajdari, a senior DP member of parliament. The political nature of the murder was never proven, but the opposition used this opportunity to organize a coup against the SP-led coalition. The coup failed, but within weeks the prime minister resigned and a new government was appointed. Ever since, the opposition has blamed the government for the killing of several DP members, as well as for police harassment and the dismissal of public workers for political reasons. Many of these claims have some credibility, but in the present Albanian context it is difficult to precisely delineate the border between politics and crime.

Throughout the past decade internal problems have been compounded by regional and global conflicts. Since 1994, foreign intelligence services have highlighted the threat that Albania could be transformed into an Islamic terrorist center—and have even alleged that Osama Bin Laden had established a presence in the country. During the Kosovo crisis, the Kosovo Liberation Army (KLA) used Albania as a permanent base, raising fears about Albania becoming embroiled in some form of military confrontation with Yugoslavia. International observers reported that during the Kosovo crisis, northeastern Albania was effectively under the military control of the KLA, resulting in border skirmishes between the Yugoslav army and the guerrillas.[5]

Even before the Kosovo crisis it was feared that Tirana could become a base for the instigation of pan-Albanian initiatives. The "national question" regarding the future status of Albanians living throughout the Balkans could become a permanent source of conflict in the region. The international press renewed this threat after the outburst of warfare in Macedonia in March 2001.

However, only a handful of extremists in Albania are still demanding modifications of existing national borders. At the moment of this writing, the Macedonian government and ethnic Albanian representatives seem to have reached a feasible agreement. The Albanian foreign minister, Paskal Milo, greeted the signing of Macedonia's framework agreement supporting the territorial integrity of Macedonia, while denouncing destabilization and ethnic violence. The Albanian government also rejected Macedonian accusations for supporting the "Albanian terrorists." The role of Albania during the Macedonian crisis has been acknowledged by NATO, which recognized the efforts of the Albanian government for securing peace and stability in the region.

Official Conflict Management
The conflict of 1997 revealed a postdictatorial state without adequate capacity to govern. The inability—or unwillingness—of the government to enforce its own laws allowed the pyramid schemes to mushroom to enormous proportions. The schemes contravened the banking law, but the judiciary did not take any action to prevent further damage. Since the crisis, several programs supported by various international agencies have aimed at the reconstruction of the judiciary, but its foundations are still shaky due to continued political instability, limited resources, political pressure, inexperienced and untrained personnel, and widespread corruption.

Postcrisis progress in internal security is also uncertain. The crisis of 1997 resulted in a drastic increase of every type of criminality, and in particular violent crime. In the absence of an effective legal and police system, families, gangs, and even politicians refer to a renewed and bastardized form of the archaic laws of the Kanun [6] as the moral justification for the escalation of cold-blooded assassinations. Moreover, Albania is now a major launchpad for drugs and economic migrants and asylum seekers coming from outside the Balkans and moving into Western Europe. A recent study estimates that more than 25 percent of young men of the eighteen to twenty-five age group are engaged in criminal activities.[7]

Police officers remain largely untrained and often unreliable, notwithstanding the support of the international community in the provision of training, advice, and equipment. The police are affected by, and also part of, Albania's culture of widespread corruption and human-rights violations. International aid toward improving the police levels of competence and combating crime is constrained by the restricted mandate granted to the Western European Union Multinational Advisory Police Element—the key international agency active in this field. This mandate excludes all participation in enforcement operations.

The role of international agencies is currently crucial in Albania. The country has had nine cabinets in a decade, and political tensions often reach dangerous levels. Albania is divided around two politicians, despite the common authoritarian past of both Berisha and Nano as members of the (communist) Labor Party. In this scenario, there is practically no political debate in the parliament regarding public policy and administration. As one Western diplomat interviewed for this survey put it, "The OSCE and other agencies are the real government and opposition in Albania."[8]

It was only after 1991 that the country joined the "international community." Since then, Albania has become a member of OSCE, the Council of Europe, NATO's Partnership for Peace, and just recently, the WTO (World Trade Organization). The EU has stated that it sees Albania as a potential candidate for future membership, and has created an EU/Albania Steering Group to pursue the negotiation of a Stabilization and Association Agreement. Eventually, Albania could benefit from regional policy initiatives such as the Stability Pact for Southeastern Europe—a multinational and multisectoral program established after the Kosovo conflict.

During the past four years, OSCE has been the paramount external actor in Albania. OSCE started to work in Albania in April 1997 in coordination, inter alia, with the Council of Europe, as the agency in command of the stabilization strategy. The mandate included advising and assisting the Albanian authorities with democratization issues, the development of free media, the promotion of human rights, and the preparation and monitoring of elections. During the Kosovo conflict, OSCE helped to organize the responses to the refugee crisis, and has maintained monitoring posts on Albania's borders with Kosovo, Montenegro, and Macedonia ever since. OSCE also chairs the Friends of Albania (FOA Group), an informal platform for countries and organizations active in providing financial support, technical assistance, and other forms of aid. Since September 1998, FOA has become the principal forum for donors' coordination and international monitoring of economic and political reform in Albania.

A social response to economic and political crisis has been emigration. This practice has increased dramatically since the upheaval of 1997. The impact of migration is twofold. On the one hand, it has been good for the economy, as emigrants' remittances represent approximately one-fifth of the GDP, almost twice as much as revenues from exports. On the other hand, many of the emigrants are highly educated people, urgently needed in Albania for social and political development. During 1990–1999 about 40 percent of the overall number of professors and scientific researchers abandoned the country.[9]

Multi-Track Diplomacy

A decade after the fall of the communist regime, and four years after the crisis of 1997, Albania is still trapped in a transitional phase. It is searching for a way out of its deep economic, social, and political difficulties without a clear sense of direction, and with a weakened social capital to sustain whatever policy the almost powerless government may choose. "Civil society" in Albania is a synonymous for NGOs, since there are no significant social movements or relevant community-based organizations. During the transition Albanian society shifted towards a new stratification, consisting of a newly wealthy bourgeoisie, impoverished peasants and workers intending to emigrate, small entrepreneurs, and emigrants. Albania was not able to develop a true middle class, a group which could be a key contributor to social and political stability.[10]

There are currently between 400 and 800 NGOs in the country, of which approximately 200 are active. The strongest are youth and women's organizations, and those engaged in advocacy and civic education. In general, the NGO sector remains highly dependent on the donor community. While there was a broadening of participation in NGOs during the Kosovo crisis, little has been done since then to strengthen the sector's capacity to serve a broader constituency. The impacts and sustainability of NGOs were further constrained after much of the funding shrank as the Kosovar refugees left.[11] In fact, since their appearance in the early 1990s, Albanian NGOs have been subject to ongoing crisis resulting from both a lack of resources and the polarization of the political scene. Still, under the most difficult conditions—those of spring 1997—NGOs were quick to organize new projects for the pacification of the country. These projects included public awareness and preparation for the elections, and public debates on the collection of weapons and public security concerns. Women's NGOs were particularly active throughout the crisis.

At present, the coordination between international entities and Albanian NGOs is problematic. The official discourse of Western agencies stresses the concept of "local involvement," meaning that the objectives and characteristics of each intervention should be locally determined and should involve local human resources, local leadership, and committed local NGOs. In reality, the power divide is clear. Many Albanian NGO practitioners interviewed for this survey referred to the example of the recent Kosovo crisis, when hundreds of foreign humanitarian workers landed in the country to organize the response to the influx of refugees and treated local organizations as secondary agents without significant responsibilities.

Local NGOs identify the rising social exclusion as a major potential source of conflict. They feel that programs implemented by UN agencies, the World Bank, the EU, and other international entities have failed to address the needs of wide segments of the population in critical distress. They argue for vigorous external intervention running in parallel with the creation of accountable and responsive structures, both official and nongovernmental. External assistance in devising and implementing such a strategy is made critical by the weakness of central and local governments and Albania's meager fiscal resources.

The traumatic transition from communism to a criminalized market economy increased social conflict. In the countryside, the majority of violent disputes originate over land and water rights. After the abolition of collective ownership of the land, pre-1994 owners reclaimed their properties in a context of an acute shortage of productive land, high demographic growth, and dissolution of law and order. In the cities, conflicts arise as result of overpopulation and rapid urbanization following the granting of internal freedom of movement. However, social conflict resolution is not a priority area for either Albanian NGOs or governmental bodies.

One of the few organizations working in this field is the Albanian Foundation for Conflict Resolution and Reconciliation of Disputes. This organization was founded in December 1995 by a group of experts in the fields of social sciences and jurisprudence. It works toward the resolution of conflicts emerging among individuals and social groups on account of economic, property, or family disputes, as well as around problems inherited from the authoritarian Albanian past, especially in terms of intolerance and the recent revival of blood feuds. The foundation also runs volunteer-based "mediation centers" actively involved in decentralized conflict prevention focused on public awareness and resolution of disputes. According to the foundation's records, most of the conflicts solved by mediation between January and December 2000 concerned property (33.7 percent) and criminal (25.5 percent) disputes.

A few other local organizations and individuals based in the northern city of Shkodra run reconciliation programs among families subject to blood feuds. The return of interfactional conflict and traditional revenge is putting young men at increased risk of violence as they arm themselves to protect their families or communities. A 1999 survey by an Albanian NGO indicated that 50 percent of teenagers responded that they respected the Kanun and would be willing to engage in vendettas, and concluded that thousands of young Albanian men are forcibly locked at home under the threat of revenge.[12]

A significant initiative toward pacification of the country is the ongoing Weapons for Development program run by the UNDP in coordination with local NGOs and CBOs (community-based organizations). The program developed after a exploratory mission concluded in June 1998 that a weapons-buying program was not feasible in Albania, mainly for economic reasons, and proposed instead a weapons collection program with development initiatives benefiting communities as a whole. The program began with a pilot project in the Gramshi district south of Tirana, and after this proved successful, expanded to four other districts. Currently, the UNDP and potential donors are evaluating its expansion into a nationwide program.[13]

Another initiative specifically focused on conflict prevention has been the development of a National Early Warning System (NEWS), building on and following a Bulgarian project launched in 1997. The UNDP and several Albanian research-oriented NGOs—principally the Institute for Contemporary Studies—have promoted the construction of a model for monitoring events or processes indicative of potential conflict. This model would be based on a series of social, economic, and political indicators such as income, labor indexes, macroeconomic environment, political and institutional stability, ethnic relations, and personal security. NEWS was conceived of as a system to provide input to the Albanian government, civil-society organizations, and international agencies to assist in decisionmaking processes. However, in spite of the successful publication of a yearly report for 1999 (UNDP-ICS, 2000),[14] this important project has not yet secured enough funding to assure its long-term sustainability.

Prospects

Albania remains the most backward country in Europe in terms of economic development and physical and social infrastructure, akin to the poorest and conflict-ridden areas in the world. Not surprisingly, the aforementioned NEWS survey (see note 14 below) showed that the population has mixed opinions about the future and the recent past. The most sensitive issues are family income and crime, while there seems to be almost no concern for conflicts of an ethnic or religious nature. Regarding the public perception of state institutions, the survey found that most Albanians support the strengthening of the army and the police after the 1997 upheaval, but that confidence in the judiciary, political parties, and the parliament continues to decline.

Nevertheless, most of the population, as well as practically every local NGO and international agency in the country, agree that the chaos of 1997 will never be repeated. The material conditions that triggered the crisis of 1997 are no longer present. Unlike 1997, a massive and sudden impoverishment is not a current menace, since most people have already lost their savings. And more important, as the NEWS survey showed, the Albanian people have thought over the consequences of violence and institutional collapse.

Over the long term, Albania's stabilization will not be secured unless the issue of rising social exclusion is addressed. The events of 1997 showed how political interests could manipulate vulnerable social groups. Responding to social needs is not only imperative for national development, but also for the stability of other countries in the region that receive a massive influx of Albanian immigrants, many of whom become associated with—or are exploited by—organized crime.

In brief, the prospects for conflict prevention and conflict management in Albania are highly dependent on the nature and extent of the involvement of external forces and institutions. The profound fragility and limited accountability of public institutions contribute to the recurrence of conflict. A coherent and purposeful strategy agreed to by the several and highly influential international agencies is essential in this case.

Recommendations

The key Albanian challenge is the reconstruction of an accountable, efficient, and transparent state. Most international agencies agree that Albania needs to make substantial progress in this area in order to move forward in social, economic, and political terms. This is not an easy task. The main question is how to develop further trust in the state among the Albanian people, who moved in a few years from an authoritarian state to the collapse of public institutions. The reconstruction of trust should be built upon family and local loyalties that already exist, but in ways designed to promote broader networks of interdependence and trust.

Recurring recommendations in policy reports, from the perspective of conflict prevention and with the objective of furthering Albania's integration into European structures, refer to the improvement of public order. This should be accomplished by combatting crime and fighting corruption; the deepening of institutional reforms, mainly by securing the independence of the judiciary; and the improvement of macroeconomic indicators with international support. However, the last Albanian Human Development report argues that concentrating on these reforms at the expense of poverty reduction programs could leave the country exposed to more instability in the future.

Last but not least, external and internal efforts should focus on the reconstruction of Albanian politics, including moving away from the present situation of permanent confrontation and absence of debate. The establishment of a civil society based on modern and strong state institutions will not be achieved until Albanians are encouraged to shift away from political loyalties associated with personalities, and toward loyalties to democratic and accountable political institutions.

Resources

Newsletters and Periodicals

Bulletin–Newsletter, trimonthly newsletter published by the Albanian Human Rights Group

Pajtimi (Reconciliation), quarterly sociological, juridical, and cultural journal published by the Center for Conflict Prevention.

Reports

ICG, *Albania: State of the Nation,* ICG Balkans Report No. 87, Tirana/London/Brussels, 2000.

UNDP, *Albanian Human Development Reports,* various years.

World Bank, *Albania. Filling the Vulnerability Gap,* by H. la Cava and R. Y. Nanetti, Technical Paper No. 460, Europe and Central Asia Environmentally and Socially Sustainable Development Series, Washington, DC, 2000.

Other Publications

Albania's Road to Democracy: A Fascinating Country in Transition, by L. Jenkins, L.A.K. Musha, and D. Molnar. Tirana, ORT/USAID, 1998.

The Albanians: A Modern History, by M. Vickers and J. Pettifer. Albany, New York University Press, 2001.

The First Decade and After: Albania's Democratic Transition and Consolidation in the Context of Southeast Europe, edited by F. Tarifa and M. Spoor. The Hague, CESTRAD/Institute of Social Studies, 2001.

Selected Internet Sites

www.dds.nl/pressnow/albania.html (Press Now, Albanian media links)

www.osce.org/albania (OSCE, Albania)

www.seerecon.org/Albania/Albania.htm (Economic Reconstruction and Development in South East Europe, Albania)

www.undp.org.al/ (UNDP, Albania)

Resource Contacts

Elsa Ballauri, executive director of the Albanian Human Rights Group, e-mail: elsa @abissnet.com.al

Daniel Chavez, Ph.D. candidate, Institute of Social Studies, the Netherlands, e-mail: chavez@iss.nl

Rasim Gjoka, executive director of the Albanian Foundation for Conflict Resolution and Reconciliation of Disputes, e-mail: gjoka@frd.tirana.al

Kozara Kati, director of the Albanian Center for Human Rights, e-mail: kozi@ahrdc.
tirana.al
Vladimir Malkaj, project officer, UNDP Albania, e-mail: vladimir.malkaj@undp.org
Fron Nazi, New York–based writer and analyst on Albanian and Balkan affairs, e-mail:
nfron@aol.com
Albana Shala, project officer, Press Now, the Netherlands, e-mail: shala@pressnow.nl

Organizations

Albanian Centre for Human Rights (Qendra Shqiptare për Të Drejtat e Njeriut)
Rr. Kont Urani, Nr. 17
Tirana, Albania
Tel.: +355 (42) 30630
Fax: +355 (42) 39363
E-mail: kozi@ahrdc.tirana.al

Albanian Helsinki Committee (Komiteti Shqiptar I Helsinkit)
Rr. Sami Frasheri Pall. 20/1, Hyrija B, Ap. 21
Tirana, Albania
Tel/Fax: +355 (42) 33671
E-mail: helsinki@ngo.org.al
www.ihf-hr.org/albhc.htm

Albanian Human Rights Group (Grupi Shqiptar i të Drejtave të Njeriut)
Rr. Dëshmorët e 4 Shkurtit
P. 7/1, Sh. 2, Ap 1
Tirana, Albania
Tel/Fax: +355 (42) 51995
E-mail: elsa@abissnet.com.al
www.ahrg.org

Society for Democratic Culture (Shoqata per Kulture Demokratike)
Rr. Hamid Shijaku, Pall. 6, Shk. 1, Ap. 3
Tirana, Albania
Tel.: +355 (42) 27674
Fax: +355(42) 30350
E-mail: monda@ndial.tirana.al

UNDP (United Nations Development Programme. Mission in Albania)
Rr. Dëshmoret e 4 Shkurtit
Tirana, Albania
Tel.: +355 (42) 33148
Fax: +355 (42) 34448
E-mail: registry.al@undp.org
www.al.undp.org

Data on the following organizations can be found in the Directory section:
Foundation for Conflict Resolution and Reconciliation of Disputes
Institute for Contemporary Studies

---

*Albana Shala studied Foreign Languages, Law, and Development Studies in Albania
and the Netherlands. Currently she works as project manager for Press Now, a Dutch
foundation supporting media development in the Balkans. Daniel Chavez is a Ph.D.
candidate at the Institute of Social Studies in the Netherlands. He has worked as a free-
lance researcher in South and Central America and Albania.*

Notes

1. UNDP, *Albanian Human Development Report 1998.* Tirana: United Nations Development Program, 1999.

2. World Bank, *Albania Beyond the Crisis: A Strategy for Recovery and Growth.* Report No. 18658-ALB. Washington, DC: World Bank, 1998.

3. Friends of Albania Group, *Final Conclusions of the 5th International Conference of the Friends of Albania Group.* Brussels: FOA Group, 2 March 2001.

4. Albana Shala, "Why Independent Media Should Be Supported in Countries in Transition," in Albana Shala (ed.), *Free Press in South-Eastern Europe: Top Priority,* Amsterdam: Press Now, 1998.

5. ICG, *The State of Albania,* ICG Balkans Report No. 54. Tirana: International Crisis Group, 1999.

6. The *Kanun of Lek Dukagjini* (S. Gjecov and L. Fox [eds.], *Kanuni I Lekë Dukagjinit: The Code of Lekë Dukagjini,* New York: Gjonlekaj Publishing Co., 1989) is a compilation of customary law established in the fifteenth century. This northern Albanian code, heavily repressed by the communist regime, has been transmitted orally through generations as a legal set concerning almost every social practice: birth, death, marriage, land and property administration, hospitality, and the resolution of blood feuds.

7. G. La Cava and R. Y. Nanetti, *Albania. Filling the Vulnerability Gap.* World Bank Technical Paper No. 460. New York: World Bank, 2000.

8. During the crisis of 1997 some independent Albanian analysts argued that the international community had played an active role in the unfolding of the conflict. According to Fron Nazi (N. Nazi,. "Albania: West's Blind Eye To Berisha's Abuses Fostered Crisis," London: IPS, 5 March 1997, available at: http://www.oneworld.org/ips2/mae/albania.html), "the West was willing to forsake civil rights in Albania for the sake of maintaining regional stability, while Berisha was willing to forsake the same to preserve his own power under the guise of a so-called communist threat."

9. UNDP, *Albanian Human Development Report 2000.* Tirana: United Nations Development Program, 2001.

10. UNDP, *Albanian Human Development Report 1998.* Tirana: United Nations Development Program, 1999.

11. USAID, *The 2000 NGO Sustainability Index for Central and Eastern Europe and Eurasia.* Washington, DC: United States Agency for Intenational Development, 2001.

12. Eureka, *Survey Report.* Tirana: Independent Social Center Eureka, 1999.

13. Offering development projects in exchange for arms is an innovative approach. The only examples comparable to this Albanian program are the provision of sewing machines in Mozambique, or the offering of jobs or training attempted in some other countries. Most buy-back programs failed because they rather create new arms trade with weapons coming from other places rather than reducing the weapons among the civilian population. Food-for-weapons programs have failed as well by not creating great incentives for returning arms (UNDP, *Weapons for Development: Report of the UNDP Mission for an Arms Collection Pilot Program in the Gramsh District, Albania,* Tirana: United Nations Development Program, 1998).

14. UNDP-ICS, *National Early Warning for Albania.* Tirana: United Nations Development Program and Institute for Contemporary Studies, 2000.

13.5

Bosnia and Herzegovina: Trying to Keep the Country Together

Yannick du Pont

*More than five years after the war, reconciliation, economic develop-
ment, refugee return, and institutional reform are moving ahead at a
very slow pace and at high cost in Bosnia and Herzegovina. Without
strong international presence, the country would still break up. International political and military presence will be necessary for decades
more to come and the development of a stronger civil society will
most likely take as long as that. Nevertheless, local conflict transformation organizations exist and are growing stronger.*

Bosnia and Herzegovina is situated in the center of the old Yugoslav territory.
It is bordered by Croatia to the west, Serbia to the east, and Montenegro to the
southeast. Its population is traditionally ethnically mixed with 44 percent
Bosnian Muslims (Bosniaks), 31 percent Bosnian Serbs, 17 percent Bosnian
Croats, and 8 percent others, according to the 1991 census.

The conflict in Bosnia should be understood as an escalated political conflict between ethnonationalist elites drawing upon popular fears based on an
unresolved past. As communism never dealt with the atrocities of World War
II, but rather repressed a debate on them, this left ample room for abuse by the
new ethnic elites that rose at the end of the 1980s. Their rise was facilitated by
a strong downturn in the economy at the time.

In November 1990, the first postcommunist elections were held in Bosnia
and Herzegovina. Although all established in the year of the elections, the three
main nationalist parties representing the three main ethnic groups attained an
overwhelming victory. Bosnian Muslims voted mainly for the Party of Democratic Action (SDA), Bosnian Croats for the Croatian Democratic Union (HDZ),
and Bosnian Serbs for the Serbian Democratic Party (SDS). This victory is in
part a result of their de facto electoral alliance against the former League of
Communists, which transformed itself into the Social Democratic Party (SDP).

After their electoral victory, the SDA, HDZ, and SDS formed a governmental coalition in November 1990. All levels of government, central and otherwise,

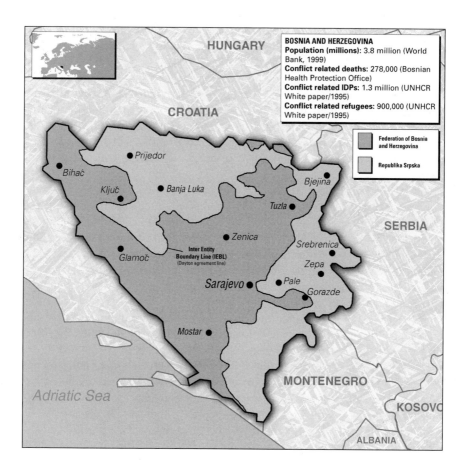

BOSNIA AND HERZEGOVINA
Population (millions): 3.8 million (World Bank, 1999)
Conflict related deaths: 278,000 (Bosnian Health Protection Office)
Conflict related IDPs: 1.3 million (UNHCR White paper/1995)
Conflict related refugees: 900,000 (UNHCR White paper/1995)

in virtually all locations were divided up between the three coalition partners. Friction between them started to develop from the very beginning.

The three nationalist parties were fast to develop a tight grip on the armed forces, police, judiciary, humanitarian aid, media, economy, and other crucial sectors of society in their own territorial sectors within Bosnia and Herzegovina.[1] The new ethnonationalist elite kept escalating ethnic tensions, using mass media to carry their message, while gaining support from various groups in society such as religious leaders and intellectuals.

Schools and universities started to differentiate curricula and to promote intolerance. As a result, three totally independent understandings of the conflict developed. Significant parts of influential groups in society, such as the church and academia, contributed to the escalation of tension. Various religious leaders (Orthodox, Catholic, and Muslim) supported the ethnic-nationalist political leaderships and thereby legitimized their rule. Also, many academics played an escalating role in the conflict. Many took active positions in ethnic-nationalist parties or promoted ethnic hatred through doubtful "academic" publications. Although some independent, alternative media and progressive religious leaders and intellectuals were active throughout the conflict, they failed to draw the mass appeal that would have been necessary to stop the vicious circle of escalation.

Meanwhile, the increasing nationalism in neighboring Serbia and Croatia strongly increased tensions in Bosnia and Herzegovina. The institutionalized nationalism of Tudjman and Milosevic further encouraged ethnic-nationalist politicians within Bosnia and Herzegovina to pursue their path of escalation. They also got direct support from the nationalist Croatian and Serb leadership.

In March 1991, Tudjman and Milosevic met secretly in the town of Karadjordjevo, where they discussed the partitioning of Bosnia and Herzegovina. Under this external and internal pressure, Bosnia and Herzegovina gravitated to war.[2] Within Bosnia and Herzegovina, tension increased, especially between the SDA and HDZ on the one side, and the Serb-led SDS on the other side. Whereas the SDS wanted to remain within a future Yugoslavia, the SDA and HDZ opted for independence of the republic. SDS leader Karadzic increased tension by organizing a referendum and in November 1991 the Bosnian Serbs overwhelmingly voted to remain in a common state with neighboring Serbia and Montenegro. The tension built up further, when subsequently, on 9 January 1992, Serb deputies of the old Bosnian Assembly adopted a separate constitution and thereby attempted to create a new state called the "Serbian Republic of Bosnia and Herzegovina."

On 15 January 1992, Croatia and Slovenia were internationally recognized as independent states. Bosnia and Herzegovina now had to choose between independence or staying in a rump Yugoslavia under the control of Serbia. Faced with this dilemma, the Bosnian parliament, on 25 January 1992, adopted a plan to hold a referendum on the sovereignty of the republic, a session that was boycotted by the Bosnian Serb parties. In the referendum, held from 29 February through 1 March, 99.4 percent of those voting (63 percent) voted for independence. It was mostly Bosniaks and Bosnian Croats who voted. The vast majority of Bosnian Serbs (who comprised 31 percent of the population) boycotted the referendum on a call by the SDS. The leader of the largest Bosnian Serb party (SDS), Radovan Karadzic, declared that "we will not accept an independent Bosnia and Herzegovina." The Bosnian Serbs still wanted to remain part of Yugoslavia. However, on 3 March 1992, the Bosnian government in Sarajevo declared independence. Subsequently, the Bosnian Serbs declared the independence of a Serbian Republic of Bosnia and Herzegovina on 25 March 1992. Throughout the war, the SDS hoped to continue the integration of the areas under its controls with neighboring Serbia, Montenegro, and Serbian-controlled areas in Croatia (Krajina and eastern and western Slavonia), in effect creating a "Greater Serbia."

Bosnia and Herzegovina was recognized as a sovereign state by the EU and the United States on 6 and 7 April 1992, respectively. The Sarajevo government was recognized as its legitimate representative. It was in this month that the SDS leadership, supported by the Yugoslav National Army, in conjunction with the Serbian regime, started fighting in Bosnia and Herzegovina on a large scale. The ill-prepared local territorial defense forces of the Bosnian government (part of which had already been dismantled by the Yugoslav National Army) attempted to mount some resistance. The police force was also used for this purpose. Strongest resistance came from the Bosnian Croat paramilitary formations, supported by the regular Croatian army.

The war would last three-and-a-half years and lead to enormous atrocities. Europe had not experienced such atrocities since World War II, and many had hoped that those would never occur again. The death toll among civilians was high. One of the worst episodes of the conflict was the fall of the UN-protected enclave of Srebrenica. As a report of the UN Secretary-General on the fall of Srebrenica put it: "Srebrenica is the largest massacre since the Second World War, with a death toll in the thousands, possibly as high as 8,000. The great majority of those who were killed were not killed in combat . . . The fall of Srebrenica is shocking because the enclave's inhabitants believed that the authority of the United Nations Security Council, the presence of UNPROFOR peacekeepers, and the might of NATO air power, would ensure their safety."[3]

Another tragic aspect of the Bosnian war has been the widespread rape and sexual assault on women and men, which according to a UN report published in December 1994 has been strategically used in campaigns of ethnic cleansing. Rape and sexual assault were reported in 162 detention centers as well as outside these centers. The report concludes, inter alia, that "a systematic rape and sexual assault policy exists . . . one factor in particular that leads to this conclusion is the large number of allegations of rape and sexual assault which occur in places of detention."[4]

Conflict Dynamics
Not long after the international recognition of Bosnia and Herzegovina, on 5 July 1992, the Bosnian Croats proclaimed their own quasi-state under the name Herceg-Bosna. Its aspiration was an eventual union with the independent state of Croatia. One of the first substantial international plans to resolve the conflict, the Vance-Owen Peace Plan, was presented on 2 January 1993, but like many other diplomatic initiatives, failed to stop the war.

In February 1993, the Croat-Muslim allies started fighting each other and by summer 1993, this developed into a war. During this conflict, regular army units of the Croatian army took part in the fighting. This military conflict officially ended with the creation of an unstable Muslim-Croat federation on 18 March 1994. The so-called Washington Agreement brokered by the United States, contained a preliminary agreement for a confederation with Croatia proper.

On 4 August 1995, the Croatian army started a successful offensive, covertly supported by the United States. Croatian forces swiftly took control of all territory in the Croatian Krajina, which had earlier been declared autonomous by local Serbian leaders. This opened the way for a large-scale offensive in Bosnia and Herzegovina, especially since on 1 September, NATO air strikes were launched against Bosnian Serb forces. In mid-September, a combined operation by Croatian, Bosnian-Croat, and Bosnian government forces started, again with political backing from the United States. Within weeks, the Bosnian-Serb army lost control over 15 percent of Bosnia-Herzegovina's territory.

Peace negotiations started in Dayton, Ohio, and on 21 November 1995 a General Framework Agreement was announced and subsequently signed in Paris on 14 December. The so-called Dayton Accords recognized Bosnia and Herzegovina as a sovereign state but divided it into two entities; the Republika Srpska (Serbian Republic), with 49 percent of the territory, and the Bosnian-Croat Federation (Bosnia and Herzegovina) with 51 percent of Bosnian-Herzegovinian territory.

In the first post-Dayton elections of 1996, the main three nationalist parties overwhelmingly won the elections and continued to wage war by political means. To date, the deliberate policy of the international community to hold elections frequently to accelerate the erosion of support for hard-line nationalist politicians has largely failed.[5] The same nationalists not only overwhelmingly won the first postwar 1996 elections, but remained in control of the largest parties in the subsequent 1997 and 1998 elections. It took until the municipal and general elections of 2000 before one of the three main ethnic parties would seriously lose support. This happened when the SDP obtained a victory over the SDA.

A very worrying development is the escalation of tension between the international community and the political party of Croatians, HDZ. In October, prior to the general 2000 elections, the HDZ together with some smaller Croat parties formed the Croat National Congress, which organized a referendum on the same day as the national elections. The Bosnian Croat electorate was hereby asked whether "Croats should have their own political, educational, scientific, cultural and other institutions on the entire territory of Bosnia and Herzegovina." The referendum was declared illegal by the OSCE, but went ahead as planned. According to the HDZ, over 70 percent of the registered Bosnian Croats voted, with 99 percent supporting the question asked in the referendum. This raised tensions between the international community and the HDZ.

The HDZ and its allies formed the so-called Croat Self-Government on 3 March 2001. Days later, the high representative removed the president of the HDZ, Ante Jelavic, from his post as Croat member of the Bosnian presidency. This tension was further aggravated when shortly after, NATO soldiers, UN security forces, Western auditors, and local financial police moved against the bank Hercegovacka Banka, allegedly a key source of financing for nationalist Bosnian Croat institutions and the HDZ party. This action caused widespread violence throughout Bosnian Croat majority areas in the federation. This situation was still far from resolved at the writing of this chapter and was expected to continue to pose a significant threat to the stability of Bosnia-Herzegovina.

Official Conflict Management

In Bosnia and Herzegovina, four civil and one military international organization played a key role in conflict management. The civil organizations being the Office of the High Representative, the Organization for Security and Co-operation in Europe, the International Police Task Force, and the International War Crimes Tribunal for the former Yugoslavia. The military organization keeping the peace in Bosnia is the NATO Stabilization Force, which succeeded the highly criticized United Nations Protection Force. No official domestic conflict-management organizations exist at this point. In the future, however, a commission on truth and reconciliation might be established.

In February 1992, the United Nations Protection Force (UNPROFOR) was established by the UN Security Council. It was based in Sarajevo and its peacekeeping role in Croatia was extended to Bosnia and Herzegovina on 30 May 1992 under the enforcement provisions of Chapter VII of the UN Charter. During the conflict, the mandate of UNPROFOR was extended time and again. Being the largest and most expensive peacekeeping force deployed by the UN, its main problem was connected to its mandate that allowed it to keep a peace that did not exist. It had no peace-enforcement possibilities. The force was also hindered by a suffocating bureaucratic UN decisionmaking process.

As had been laid out in the Dayton Accords, UNPROFOR was succeeded by the NATO-led Implementation Force (IFOR). IFOR had a maximum strength of 60,000 troops from thirty-five countries and was mandated to supervise the military side of the Dayton agreement. Unlike UNPROFOR, it was mandated to use force to achieve its objectives, had the necessary means to use that military force, and was operating under a far swifter NATO command. In 1998, IFOR was renamed the Stabilization Force (SFOR) and reduced to 36,000 troops.

Maria Söderberg/Panos Pictures

Mostar: UN troops in patrol

The Office of the High Representative (OHR) was mandated under Dayton to oversee the implementation of the civil aspects of the agreement and to coordinate the activities of the civilian organizations and agencies operating in the country. The high representative has no authority over SFOR. The OHR is the main civilian force keeping the Bosnian state together, and has imposed the most important state laws, such as those on the flag, coinage, passports, and the central bank.

The second most important international organization involved in conflict management in Bosnia and Herzegovina is the Organization for Security and Cooperation in Europe (OSCE). On 30 April 1992, Bosnia and Herzegovina was accepted as a member of the OSCE. OSCE's main role in Bosnia and Herzegovina started after the signing of the peace agreement in 1995. The UN Mission to Bosnia and Herzegovina received three main tasks: supervising elections, monitoring and reporting on human-rights issues, and negotiating and implementing confidence- and security-building measures and arms control. The OSCE has been widely criticized for its conduct of the 1996 elections, which legitimized the rule of the three nationalist parties that obtained a major victory.

The International Police Task Force (IPTF) monitors and advises the local police. It "aims to restructure and reform the local police to create democratic and professional police forces which are multi-ethnic, effective, transparent, impartial, accountable, representative of the society they serve, and which will facilitate the return of refugees and displaced persons."[6] It keeps local police officials under scrutiny and selects new officers from especially underrepresented ethnic and gender groups, and encourages the return and voluntary redeployment of experienced police officers. It is conducting training programs, for instance, in human rights, organized crime, drugs, crowd control, and major-incident management.

Another international organization worth mentioning here is the International War Crimes Tribunal for the former Yugoslavia (ICTY), which was established in May 1993 and has its seat in The Hague, Netherlands. Although it was slow to start, the tribunal has grown fast over the recent years and has succeeded to bring in a number of high-ranking suspects, including Slobodan Milosevic. To date, however, many important indicted war criminals remain at large. Reluctance of NATO to support the ICTY on the ground have made more widespread arrests infeasible. The extent to which the ICTY will succeed in bringing at least the most important war criminals (Karadzic, Mladic) to court is considered to be of crucial importance for establishing a sustainable peace as will be the acceptance of the court by all ethnic groups in the country. At present, the ICTY is perceived by especially the Bosnian Serb and Bosnian Croat leadership as biased, which inhibits its ability to serve as a conflict-resolution actor.

Multi-Track Diplomacy

Local civil society in Bosnia and Herzegovina is slowly developing. Although not all local NGOs are efficient and have an impact, several larger, well-developed local NGOs exist. Most of them are oriented on humanitarian issues, and many also work indirectly on conflict transformation. A significant number of local organizations choose postconflict transformation as their core activity.

During the communist era, Yugoslavia had no political or humanitarian NGOs other than state-sponsored associations that operated under government control. The years preceding the war were characterized by increasing political freedoms, and nongovernmental sociopolitical organizations started to develop in Bosnia and Herzegovina. In the years after 1989, many political groups appeared on the scene, such as the Association for a Yugoslavian Democratic Initiative (UJDI), the Anti-War Campaign Sarajevo, the Helsinki Citizens Assembly, the Citizens Forum of Croats in Bosnia and Herzegovina, and the People's Front. Various women's organizations were actively involved in the field of conflict prevention and conflict resolution as well.

Many of them had mixed ethnic membership and called for moderation of politics in a period of escalating nationalism. Roundtable discussions were organized, petitions circulated, and press conferences held. Activities were mostly concentrated in the larger towns. They were often initiated by political parties, especially the social democratic–oriented parties SDP and the Union of Bosnian Social Democrats.

At that time, most of these local NGOs were ignored by both national and international policymakers. The initiatives were often taken by intellectuals or on a very local grass-roots level, and failed to gain mass support. When the war broke out, so-called Humanitarian Service Delivery Associations were established. They rapidly outnumbered sociopolitical initiatives and engaged themselves with issues such as displaced persons, war victims, humanitarian aid, and reconstruction. From early on, the local NGO sector was concentrated in the larger cities and set up by the urban middle class.

It is difficult to precisely determine the number of local and international associations and humanitarian organizations in Bosnia and Herzegovina today. Different sources provide different figures. The International Council of Voluntary Agencies (ICVA) lists 173 international and 365 local NGOs in its 2000 directory. It should be noted, however, that by far not all existing initiatives are listed. In general, the number of NGOs is decreasing, mostly directly related to the decrease of international funding. Many international NGOs are "localizing" their efforts by transforming themselves into local organizations.

Some of the oldest, best-organized local NGOs, such as the Forum of Tuzla Citizens, Circle 99, and the Helsinki Committees, focus their activities on political advocacy. Through public campaigns, round tables, publications, and the like, they try to influence both government policymakers and public opinion.

The Forum of Tuzla Citizens, founded in 1993, received extensive support from citizens in Tuzla in support of its main objectives of building interethnic trust and preserving a multinational and multireligious society in Bosnia-Herzegovina. The forum organizes debates, roundtable discussions, and poster campaigns. Another important advocacy NGO is Circle 99, founded in 1992. Based in Sarajevo, it is run by the local Association of Independent Intellectuals, which rejects nationalism and supports a multicultural country. Recently, it published a full-page pamphlet in national newspapers, making clear policy recommendations to the newly elected government.

The Helsinki Committees in Sarajevo and Bijeljina, founded in 1995 and 1996 respectively, constantly monitor the human-rights situation, but do not shy away from joining or initiating political advocacy work. They often operate in a concerted effort with other organizations.

Most NGOs belong to broader cooperation structures. Two clear examples of these umbrella organizations are Citizens Alternative Parliament, founded in 1996, and the Alternative Ministers Council. The Citizens Alternative Parliament strives for a multiethnic state with autonomous, free, independent, and equal citizens and has thirteen member NGOs throughout Bosnia and Herzegovina. The Alternative Ministers Council is active in political circles and has both social-democratic parties and NGOs amongst its members.

A good example of a well-organized women's NGO is Medica Zenica. This organization provides professional multidisciplinary support to women, with a focus on traumatized survivors. It has provided support to rape victims in the Bosnian war and employs, inter alia, a score of doctors and psychologists. It has also engaged itself in political and policy-oriented advocacy work. For example, Medica is engaged in producing and spreading knowledge on the conflict and conflict resolution, publishing articles, and organizing seminars. It has its own information and documentation center.

Another level on which conflict-transformation NGOs are active is on the level of training and seminars. Three organizations worth mentioning in this respect are the Center for Nonviolent Action, the Nansen Dijalog Centar, and the hCa Youth Network.

The Nansen Dijalog Centar Mostar is part of the Nansen Network of Dialogue (NDC) operating Balkan-wide. It organizes workshops, seminars, round-table meetings and open discussions on peaceful conflict resolution as well as on the development of democratic processes and civic society in the region. Together with NDC Sarajevo, Banja Luka, Osijek, Montenegro, Belgrade, Pristina, and Skopje, it forms an expanding network of interdependent and cooperating offices. Each office is operated by ethnically mixed staff.

Established in early 1997, the hCa Youth Network aims to bring together youth from around Bosnia and Herzegovina in joined events. It consists of over one hundred local NGOs. The network publishes its magazine *TNT*, aimed at stimulating cooperation between youth groups from both entities. The hCa Youth Network organizes seminars, conferences, and nonviolent conflict-resolution training.

The Center for Nonviolent Action (CNA) organizes seminars in nonviolent conflict transformation. It supports other groups that are interested in organizing similar seminars. CNA puts its major focus on training NGO activists, teachers, media, and political-party representatives. Its network extends throughout the entire former Yugoslavia.

Other organizations active in the field are, amongst others, Protector, Open Society Institute, the Office for Human Rights, Zene Zenuma, Center for Civic Initiatives, and the International Multi-Religions and Intercultural Center.

A related but different sort of local organization is the Association of Citizens "Truth and Reconciliation," led by Jacob Finci, the leader of the Jewish community in Bosnia and Herzegovina. This association is lobbying for the establishment of an official state commission for truth and reconciliation. The association is comprised of representatives of leading conflict-resolution NGOs (such as the Forum of Tuzla Citizens, Circle 99, and the Helsinki Committee). The idea of a truth and reconciliation commission was initially launched by the U.S. Institute of Peace in 1997, but has developed into a local initiative. Since its conception, the ruling nationalist parties, although paying lip service to the idea, have never seriously supported the proposal in practice. The International Criminal Tribunal for former Yugoslavia is a supporter of the establishment of a truth and reconciliation commission.

The establishment of the Inter-Religious Council of Bosnia and Herzegovina dates back to October 1996, when for the first time since the war the World Conference on Religion and Peace brokered a meeting between the four principal leaders of the Jewish, Islamic, Catholic, and Orthodox religious communities in Bosnia and Herzegovina. The interreligious council, officially launched in June 1997, promotes religious tolerance and understanding. Jacob Finci was elected its first chairman. He was succeeded in 1999 by Cardinal Vinko Puljic, the Roman Catholic archbishop of Sarajevo. The establishment of the council was supported by the U.S. Institute of Peace. Although not extremely active, the council has an important moral weight and strong symbolic value.

Challenges for Local NGOs

One of the most important threats to local NGOs is the absence of proper NGO legislation. NGOs cannot register to operate throughout Bosnia and Herzegovina, but only in one of the entities. The law does not distinguish between mutual and public benefit organizations, which is of vital importance for tax-deductible financial contributions and access to government grants and contracts. The norms that regulate the economic, income-generating activities of NGOs are also lacking or inappropriate. The absence of a proper legal framework seriously impedes the development of a sustainable NGO sector and frustrates the role of NGOs as actors of conflict resolution. It is most disturbing that although the OSCE and OHR have been working with local NGOs since as early as 1997 on drafts for such a law, it has not been passed as of yet.

At present, most local NGOs are underresourced and rely heavily on international funding. With the dwindling of this international funding, local organizations are finding it increasingly difficult to secure the resources necessary for their survival. Especially in the absence of a legal framework providing financial benefits, the poor state of the local economy, and the lack of international investors (and thus sponsors), observers fear for the sustainability of many local NGOs.

Another obstacle for local NGOs is their relationship to international NGOs and governmental international organizations. Some internationals are said to have adopted what is described as paternalistic behavior toward local

NGOs. As many local NGOs rely on international funding, their agendas for action are often dictated by donor priorities. In some instances, this turns them into the role of cheap service-delivery organizations.

Local NGOs also have to improve themselves before they can expect to become an important factor in Bosnia and Herzegovina and to be taken seriously by international and local actors. Especially, coordination and cooperation between them could be improved. They have not been able, for example, to strongly unite behind a new NGO law and lobby for its passage. Too often, local organizations see each other as competitors over scarce funding, instead of as strategic partners.

Prospects

Recent violence in the Bosnian Croat majority areas continue to pose a threat to the stability of the country. It is clear that the process of democratization and the implementation of the Dayton Accords has made only limited progress. There are, however, also reasons for careful optimism.

In day-to-day life, things are slowly improving. Local NGOs in conflict transformation and resolution have been growing stronger. The citizens of Bosnia and Herzegovina can travel freely throughout the country. The number of refugees returning is increasing. On the political level, progress can be observed as well. The 2000 municipal and national elections in Bosnia and Herzegovina have shown increasing support for moderate parties. Bosnia and Herzegovina, for the first time since the end of the war, has a nonnationalist government in both entities and at the national level.

In neighboring Croatia and Serbia, important political changes have occurred as well during 2000. In both countries, the leadership that has been actively engaged in the recent ethnic-nationalist wars has been replaced by more moderate ones that better respect the territorial integrity of the Bosnian state.

Within Bosnia and Herzegovina, however, strong obstacles still exist to a better future for the country. The recent violence in many Croatian majority areas and the weak position of the new nonnationalist government are major obstacles.

Recommendations

It is absolutely clear that the international community will have to stick to the implementation of the Dayton Peace Accords and will have to step up its efforts to make it work. To put the Dayton agreement up for renegotiations, as has been advocated by some, would cause too much unrest and is unrealistic at this time. In the long term, however, it will surely require alterations.

The international community will have to keep dealing with the nationalist political parties HDZ, SDS, and SDA if it wants to see policy implemented in practice. It will not be an option to simply ignore their existence, as they still wield very strong influence throughout the country and are backed by very large proportions of the population.

The international community needs to be patient and should not move ahead too fast, or move too far beyond the Dayton framework, as this would play into the hands of the nationalist parties and could actually bolster their support. It will therefore be crucial for the success of the international community to recognize that the reality on the ground cannot be changed overnight, but that a persistent and continued, longer-term international presence will be required.

Following are some other concrete measures necessary for boosting stability and peace in the country:

- Full implementation on all levels of the decision of the constitutional court of Bosnia and Herzegovina on the equality of three constituent peoples and all the citizens in the entire territory of the state. The constitution of Bosnia and Herzegovina should be reformed to bring it into line with the international conventions on human rights and freedoms
- Establishment of a truth and reconciliation commission for Bosnia and Herzegovina, closely working together with such commissions in Croatia and Yugoslavia
- Reform of the educational sector—screening of educational curricula for inciting of hatred against other ethnic groups
- Continued support for independent media and strict enforcement of regulations that forbid hate speech
- Reduction of the military forces in the country in both staff and equipment
- Development of a clear long-term strategy of entry of Bosnia-Herzegovina into the Council of Europe, NATO's Partnership for Peace, and the European Union
- Passage of laws against violence and discrimination against women

Resources

Newsletters
Review of Free Thought (periodical), Circle 99, Sarajevo.

Reports and Articles
International Crisis Group
 After Milosevic: A Practical Agenda for Lasting Balkans Peace, Brussels, April 2001.
 Bosnia: Reshaping the International Machinery, November 2001.
 Is Dayton Failing? Bosnia Four Years After the Peace Agreement, Balkans Report no. 80.
International Council of Voluntary Organisations (ICVA), *Directory of Humanitarian and Development Agencies Operating in Bosnia and Herzegovina,* Sarajevo, 2000.
International Helsinki Federation for Human Rights, "Human Rights in Bosnia and Herzegovina," from *Human Rights in the OSCE Region: The Balkan, the Caucasus, Europe, Central Asia and North America,* Report 2001 (events of 2000).
Kvinna till Kvinna Foundation, *Engendering the Peace Process. A Gender Approach to Dayton—and Beyond,* Anna Lithhander (ed.), Halmstad, 2000.

NGO Information Support Center Sarajevo (CIP), *Directory of Local Non-Governmental Organisations in Bosnia and Herzegovina,* first English edition, Sarajevo, December 1998.
United States Institute of Peace, Bosnia's Next Five Years: Dayton and Beyond, Special Report, 3 November 2000.

Other Publications
Balkan Tragedy: Chaos and Dissolution After the Cold War, by Susan Woodward. Washington, DC, Times Books, 1995.
Bosnia: A Short History, by Noel Malcolm. New updated edition. London, Papermac, 1996.
"Civil Society and Peacebuilding in Bosnia and Herzegovina," by Roberto Belloni. *Journal of Peace Research* 38, no. 2, 2001.
Guidelines for Laws Affecting Civic Organisations, by Zeke Volkert. New York, Open Society Institute, 1997.
In Search of Politics: The Evolving International Role in Bosnia and Herzegovina, European Stability Initiative Discussion Paper, Berlin, 1 November 2001.
Peace Journey: The Struggle for Peace in Bosnia, by Carl Bildt. London, Weidenfeld & Nicolson, 1998.
The Space Between Us: Negotiating Gender and National Identities in Conflict, by Cockburn. London, Zed Books, 1998.
To End a War, by Richard Holbrooke. New York, Random House, 1998.
Yugoslavia and After: A Study in Fragmentation, Despair and Rebirth, edited by D. A. Dyker and I. Vejvoda. Harlow, UK, Longman Publishing Group, 1996.
Yugoslavia's Bloody Collapse: Causes, Course and Consequences, by Christopher Bennett. London, Hurst & Company, 1995.

Selected Internet Sites
www.crisisweb.org (International Crisis Group)
www.icva-bh.org/eng/ (International Council of Voluntary Agencies)
www.iwpr.net (Institute for War and Peace Reporting)
www.ohr.int (Office of the High Representative in Bosnia and Herzegovina)
www.oscebih.org (OSCE mission in Bosnia and Herzegovina)
www.ric.com.ba (Repatriation and return of refugees and displaced persons in Bosnia and Herzegovina)

Resource Contacts
Roberto Bellioni, research fellow, University of Denver, U.S., e-mail: rbelloni@du.edu
Goran Bozicevic, MIRAMIDA, Croatia, e-mail: goranb@zamir.net
Ivana Francovic, Center for Nonviolent Action Sarajevo/Belgrade, e-mail: cna.sarajevo@gmx.net
Zdravko Grebo, director, Law Center, University of Sarajevo, e-mail: zdravko@soros.org.ba
Jan ter Laak, Netherlands Helsinki Committee, e-mail: jtl@wxs.nl
Jasna Malkoc, head of the Democratisation Department, OSCE Belgrade, e-mail: JMMalkoc@yahoo.de
Vladimir Maric, Nansen Dialogue Center Mostar, e-mail: vladimir@ndcmostar.org
Slavko Santic, secretary, Circle 99, Sarajevo, e-mail: cna.sarajevo@gmx.net
Vehid Sehic, president, Forum of Tuzla Citizens, e-mail: tz@bih.net.ba
Miriam Struyk, Interchurch Peace Council, The Hague, e-mail: mstruyk@ikv.nl
Dubravka Zarkov, the Netherlands, e-mail: d.zarkov@chello.nl

Organizations

Association of Citizens "Truth and Reconciliation"
Ante Fiamenga 14b, 71000 Sarajevo
Tel.: + 387 33 663 473
Fax: + 387 33 454 230
E-mail: kip@bosnia.ba
www.angelfire.com/bc2/kip/engleski.html

Forum of Tuzla Citizens
Hazi Bakirbega Tuzlica no. 1
75000 Tuzla
Tel./Fax: + 387 35 251279/ 250702
E-mail: forum_tz@bih.net.ba
www.forumtz.com

Helsinki Citizens' Assembly Banja Luka
Jevrejska 87
Banja Luka
Tel.: + 387 51 358479
Fax: + 387 51 358479
E-mail: hcalido@inecco.net, hcabl@blic.net
www.hcamreza.org

Helsinki Citizens' Assembly Sarajevo
Human Rights House of Sarajevo
Antie Fijamenga 14b
71000 Sarajevo
Tel./ Fax: + 387 33 666372
E-mail: hca-sa@bih.net.ba

Helsinki Citizens' Assembly Tuzla
Hazi Bakirbega Tuzlica no. 1
75000 Tuzla
Tel./Fax: + 387 35 250481
E-mail: hcatuzla@bih.net.ba
www.hcamreza.org

Helsinki Committee for Human Rights in BiH
Ante Fijamenga 14b
Sarajevo
Tel.: + 387 33 230809/ 231852
Fax: + 387 33 230811/ 230809
E-mail: info@bh-hchr.org
www.bh-hchr.org

Helsinki Committee for Human Rights in RS
Brace Gavrica 6
Bijeljina
Tel.: + 387 55 472851/ 401532
Fax: + 387 55 401821
E-mail: helcomm@inecco.net

International Council of Voluntary Agencies (ICVA)
Obala Kulina Bana 4
71000 Sarajevo
Tel.: + 387 33.210201

Fax: + 387 33.668297
E-mail: icva@bih.net.ba
www.icva-bh.org/eng/

International Multi-Religious and Intercultural Center (IMIC)
Obala Kulina Bana 39
71000 Sarajevo
Tel.: + 387 33 440904/ 232310
Fax: + 387 33 446937
E-mail: zajedno@bih.net.ba

Nansen Dialog Centar Mostar
Mile Budaka 123 A
88000 Mostar
Tel.: + 387 36 327459
Fax: + 387 36 327458
E-mail: office@ndcmostar.org
www.ndcmostar.org

Protector
Buhotina 14-71217
Rakovica, Sarajevo
Tel.: + 387 66 136 110
Fax: + 387 33 404 848
E-mail: protector_sarajevo@yahoo.com
www.protector.com.ba

Data on the following organizations can be found in the Directory section:
Abraham
Center for Nonviolent Action
CIRCLE 99 Sarajevo
Human Rights Office Tuzla
United Nations Volunteers PIP
Women's Association Medica-Zenica
Youth Center Gornji Vakuf
Zene Zenama

Yannick du Pont studied International Relations and Sociology at the University of Amsterdam. Presently he is chairperson of the Dutch NGO Academic Training Association, which supports higher-education reform and conflict transformation through education in Southeast Europe.

Notes

1. Allcock, John B., Marko Milivojevic, and John J. Horton, *Roots of Modern Conflict: Conflict in the Former Yugoslavia,* Denver: ABC-CLIO, 1998; and Jan Ballast and Martin Roedbro, ECMM preelection special report *An Overview of the Bosnia and Herzegovina Political Spectrum,* 1 September 1998. D. A. Dyker and I. Vejvoda (eds.), *Yugoslavia and After: A Study in Fragmentation, Despair and Rebirth,* Harlow, England, Longman Publishing Group, 1996, p. 99.

2. The classification of the war in Bosnia and Herzegovina as either "civil war" or "war of aggression" is still very much dividing public opinion. Besides taking a stance on the emotional guilt issue, it is important to note that the issue has at its core an important international political dimension as well. Whereas it is possible to have an international intervention in a "war of aggression," or "international conflict," a "civil

war" excludes the possibility of such an intervention. In the early days of the war, the SDS leadership was portraying the conflict as a civil war, whereas the SDA/HDZ government was promoting to have it accepted as an international one.

3. UN Document A/54/549, 15 November 1999, *Report of the Secretary-General Pursuant to General Assembly Resolution 53/35/ The Fall of Srebrenica.*

4. *Rape and Sexual Assault,* UN Security Council Report (Annex IX of Report S/1994/674/Add.2) (vol. V), 28 December 1994. Final report of the United Nations Commission of Experts, established pursuant to Security Council Resolution 780 (1992), under the chairmanship of M. Cherif Bassiouni. To be downloaded from http://www.ess.uwe.ac.uk/comexpert/ANX/IX.htm.

5. *Report on the Conformity of the Legal Order of Bosnia and Herzegovina with the Council of Europe Standards,* AS/But/Bosnia and Herzegovina (1999) 1rev., Strasbourg, 7 January 1999, p. 39.

6. http://www.unmibh.org/unmibh/iptf/index.htm.

13.6

Croatia:
Struggling with Unresolved Postwar Issues

Katarina Kruhonja, Milan Ivanovic & Ivan Stanic

The war in Croatia was comparatively short but fierce. It took several years following the climax of the conflict before a postconflict normalization and reconciliation process could begin—the Dayton peace agreement on Bosnia-Herzegovina and the peace agreement with local Serbs on peaceful integration of Eastern Slavonia. Croatian society is still facing difficulties related to the transition from communism to a pluriform democracy, and to unresolved postwar issues including the prosecution of war criminals, cooperation with the International Criminal Tribunal for the former Yugoslavia, the return of Serb refugees, the protection of minority rights, and trust building and reconciliation.

Before war broke out in Croatia, it was one of the six republics of the Socialist Federal Republic of Yugoslavia, the country established under Tito. The population consisted of the following nationalities: 78 percent Croats, 12 percent Serbs, 10 percent others (Yugoslavs, Hungarians, Italians, Muslims, etc.).

Ever since the Middle Ages, Croatia, situated along the buffer zone that separated the Austrian-Hungarian Empire from the Ottoman Empire, has struggled to maintain its cultural, national, and political identity. Its history of instability and struggle is reflected in the comment of an old man from a village in the eastern part of Croatia, who pointed out that in his whole life he had never moved from his birthplace, but he had lived in six different states. First he lived in the Kingdom of Slovenians, Croatians, and Serbs (1918–1929), founded after the fall of the Austrian-Hungarian Empire, and then he became a citizen of the Kingdom of Yugoslavia (1929–1941), a parliamentary kingdom that evolved into a dictatorship under the Serbian royal family Karadjordjevic. After that, he lived in the Independent State of Croatia (1941–1945) under a Croatian fascist government, the Ustasha regime, followed by the Socialist Federal Republic of Yugoslavia (1945–1992), the socialist regime established by Tito. In the last decade of the twentieth century, his country was the Serbian Autonomous Region of Krajina (1992–1996), the

248

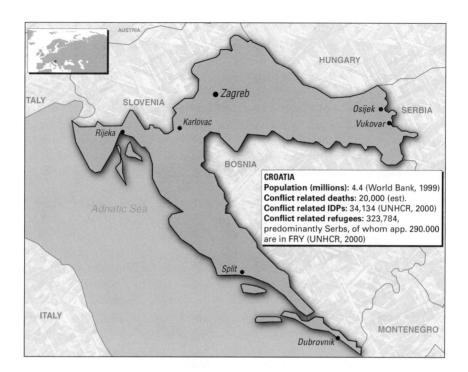

CROATIA
Population (millions): 4.4 (World Bank, 1999)
Conflict related deaths: 20,000 (est).
Conflict related IDPs: 34,134 (UNHCR, 2000)
Conflict related refugees: 323,784,
predominantly Serbs, of whom app. 290.000
are in FRY (UNHCR, 2000)

self-proclaimed Serbian autonomous region within the territory of the Republic of Croatia. Since 1996 he is an inhabitant of the Republic of Croatia, a multiparty democratic state, internationally recognized since 1992 following the disintegration of Socialist Federal Republic of Yugoslavia.

The recent war in the former Yugoslavia is perceived as being related to unresolved disputes of World War II and conflicts of interest between world superpowers. Part of the Croatian political elite struggling against the dictatorship of the Karadjordjevic family in the Kingdom of Yugoslavia took advantage of the momentum following a military defeat of the Yugoslav kingdom by Germany in 1941 to establish an independent state. Nazi Germany supported the establishment of the Independent State of Croatia (NDH), also known as the fascist Ustasha regime. The majority of the Croatian population did support independence, but not the actual regime of the NDH, which adopted a fascist ideology and persecuted Jews, Serbs, Roma, and its political opponents, the communists.

An antifascist movement led by Marshall Tito fought against German occupation and the fascist regime of the NDH, as well as against the Chetniks, armed Serbian nationalists aiming to restore the Kingdom of Yugoslavia. At the same time, Tito's movement had a political agenda of its own—to take power and build a communist regime. These overlapping agendas were never worked out and even today cause different interpretations of history within Croatian society.

At the end of World War II, the Allies tried to resolve these conflicts by forming a new state, the Socialist Federal Republic of Yugoslavia. Within this state Croats were granted the right to establish their own republic, Serbs the right to continue to live in Yugoslavia, and the communists to take political power. Tito's regime, espousing a so-called socialism with a human face, was built on the principle of "Brotherhood and Unity," but remaining tensions between different political approaches were actually kept under control by political repression. In the late 1980s, the political and economic instability of post-Tito Yugoslavia, followed by the collapse of the communist power bloc, led to political change and, eventually, to the disintegration of the Socialist Federal Republic of Yugoslavia.

The disintegration of the republic did not happen peacefully for a number of reasons. The Milosevic regime in Serbia stirred up nationalism, fueled by an identity crisis resulting from the collapse of a collective communist identity, painful memories from World War II, and the influence of political emigration. There was a lack of democratic structures and a democratic tradition, and no clear, authoritative voice opposing war. Churches abstained from trying to contribute to a nonviolent transition of society, independent media were virtually nonexistent, and last but not least, there is a perception that the attitude of the international community in the early stage of the conflict led to the parties opting for war.

The primary cause of the war was the disintegration of the Socialist Federal Republic of Yugoslavia, coinciding with the declaration of Croatian independence, and set against the background of Serbian policy. For Milosevic's regime, the only way to transform the federation was by pushing for a "Greater Serbia," which meant reestablishing the borders and adopting a policy of ethnic homogenity, achieved by carrying out, in various ways, ethnic cleansing.

The independence of Croatia, based on the political program of a single nation-state, raised the issue of the political rights of Serbs in Croatia. In addition, the Croatian Democratic Union (HDZ), as the leading exponent of Croatian nationalism, tried to implement a nationalist program with the goal of building an ethnically homogenous state, and asserting hegemony in Bosnia. As a result, the rights of minorities in Croatia, and the division of Bosnia along ethnic lines, also became points of contention.

Parties to the conflict in Croatia were the Croatian police and military and, at the beginning of the conflict, some paramilitary groups on one side, opposed by the Yugoslav army, local rebel Serbs, and paramilitary troops from Serbia.

The war between Croatia and Serbia or the Former Republic of Yugoslavia was never officially proclaimed, and Milosovic's regime never formally annexed the self-proclaimed republic of the Serbian Krajina, but because of the involvement of the Yugoslav army, from the Croatian point of view the war had an international dimension.

At the beginning of 1992, when an unconditional cease-fire was signed, 30 percent of Croatian territory was under Serbian control, with the Yugoslav army serving to enforce Serb authority, causing massive, forced migrations of the population. This led to polarization and mutual intolerance between the Croats and Serbs within the part of Croatia still under the control of the Croatian government, and frequent human-rights violations against Serbs including, in particular, illegal evictions, firings, harassment, and physical assaults.

Conflict Dynamics

After the disintegration of the Communist Party of Yugoslavia in 1990 and the establishment of new political parties, the first multiparty elections in Croatia (then still a federal republic within Yugoslavia) took place on 22 April and 6 May 1990. The HDZ of Franjo Tudjman won the elections, partly because of its nationalistic rhetoric and anti-Milosevic and anti-Serb rhetoric.

The rather substantial Serbian minority in Croatia expressed deep concern after the victory of HDZ. It refused to participate in the new government and announced a referendum for the autonomy not only for the predominantly Serb-inhabited areas of Croatia (northern Dalmatia and the eastern part of Lika), but also for those areas where Serbs were not a majority such as eastern and western Slavonia. In August 1991 Serbs put up roadblocks around Knin, a small town in northern Dalmatia. The Croatian government responded by sending two police helicopters, which were intercepted by Yugoslav army planes and forced back. The Yugoslav army now surfaced as a third party in the conflict. It captured all the weapons that were in Croatian possession and started to arm Serbian civilians. Consequently, Croatia intensified its efforts to obtain weapons for its police and military forces. Simultaneously, civilians, particularly members of HDZ, started purchasing weapons for themselves illegally.

Meanwhile, on the political level, there were numerous meetings of the republics' presidents to discuss the future of the federal Yugoslav Republic. Croatia and Slovenia shared a goal of complete decentralization. Serbia and Montenegro insisted on elections that would be conducted according to the principle of one-person one-vote, which would assure centralization. Macedonia and Bosnia tried to push models for themselves that would strike a balance between the two extremes. In addition to official meetings of the republics' presidents, Milosevic and Tudjman held a secret meeting with a secret agenda in Karadjordjevo in 1991.

Despite the meetings, the tensions in Croatia intensified. After the first road blockades in Knin, similar actions were taken in other regions where Serbs were dominant. The situation deteriorated when Slovenia and Croatia decided to hold referendums on independence. The Croatian referendum took place on 19 May 1991, with 94 percent of the votes cast favoring independence. The Croatian parliament proclaimed the independence of Croatia on 25 June 1991, the same day as Slovenia. Two days later the Yugoslav army made a show of force by launching a military operation in Slovenia. The conflict in Slovenia ended within a week, with the Yugoslav army retreating. Soon after that, the international community called a meeting in Brioni, attended by three

European representatives and all of the Yugoslav republics' presidents except for Milosevic. The participants adopted a resolution that Croatia and Slovenia would put the implementation of their independence declarations on hold for three months. But instead of bringing peace, this delay resulted in increased violence, followed by all-out war in Croatia.

In late 1991 the war zones were still restricted to those areas in Banija, northern Dalmatia, and eastern Slavonia where Serbs constituted the over-whelming majority. Until the end of 1992, all parts of Croatia (except for the northern and western regions) as well as the big towns of Osijek, Vinkovci, Vukovar, Karlovac, and Dubrovnik were subjected to heavy attacks by the Yugoslav army, which had intervened under the pretext that it wanted to create a buffer zone between the two parties.

The fall of Vukovar in November 1992 and the attack on Dubrovnik marked important turning points in the conflict, as they led to the active inter-vention of the international community. In January 1992, the Republic of Croatia achieved international recognition, and a cease-fire was signed. At that time, 30 percent of Croatian territory was under Serbian control, with the sup-port of the Yugoslav army. Forced migrations were imposed on the civilians in these areas, with some 300,000 internally displaced persons, predominantly Croats and other non-Serbian inhabitants.

Official Conflict Management

There were several aspects to the involvement of the international community in the Croatian conflict. The European Union became involved on the official level in summer 1991 when three European representatives participated in Brioni, along with the presidents of Croatia and Slovenia and the Yugoslav presidency. The meeting ended with the so-called Brijuni declaration, which demanded an immediate end to the war in Slovenia and asked for a three-month delay enacting the Slovenian and Croatian independence proclamations. Two months later, while the fighting continued, the European Council of Min-isters appointed Lord Carrington as the coordinator of a Yugoslavia peace con-ference, which first met on 7 September 1991. On 15 January 1992, the EU recognized Croatia as an independent state. The EU also contributed to moni-toring operations—the so-called Monitoring Missions in the Republic of Croa-tia—as did the OSCE.

UN involvement included the deployment of peacekeeping units. On 25 September 1991, the UN imposed an arms embargo against Yugoslavia, and shortly afterward, on 8 October 1991 appointed Cyrus Vance as the Secretary-General's personal envoy for Yugoslavia. After the fall of Vukovar, he called a meeting in Geneva, attended by Tudjman, Milosevic, and the Yugoslav defense minister, Kadijevic. An immediate cease-fire was agreed to, but it was not im-plemented. However, all warring sides expressed a wish for a quick beginning to UN peacekeeping operations in the former Yugoslavia, and in January 1992, in Sarajevo, Vance supervised the signing of a successful cease-fire.

On 21 February 1992, in accordance with the Vance Peace Plan, the UN Security Council adopted Resolution 743, which established UNPROFOR, the UN force in Croatia. It was deployed in four so-called UN Protected Areas (UNPAs), which included the 30 percent of Croatian territory controlled by the Serbs.

The main aims of UNPROFOR were to end the fighting in Croatia, to ensure the peace and security needed for negotiation of an overall settlement of the crisis, to monitor and protect human rights, and to create the conditions for the peaceful return of displaced persons. Nonetheless, Croats and non-Serbs living in the UNPROFOR zone were subject to human-rights abuses, and in 1993 there were several incidents of cease-fire violations by Croatian military forces.

During UNPROFOR's mandate, the Croatian government continued its military buildup, preparing for a new round of fighting. On 12 January 1995, President Tudjman announced that the UNPROFOR mandate would not be restored after its expiration date of 30 March, arguing that UNPROFOR had failed to restore Croatian authority in Serb-controlled territories.

Subsequently, on 31 March 1995, the UN Security Council created terms for deployment of a transformed peacekeeping operation—the United Nations Confidence Restoration Operation—to facilitate implementation of all relevant Security Council resolutions.

Only a month later, on 1 May 1995, Croatia launched a sudden military operation under the code name "Flash," followed by the "Storm" offensive, and recaptured the Serb-controlled areas in the self-proclaimed Republika Srpska Krajina, except for the Eastern Sector (eastern Slavonia, Baranja, and western Sirmium).

Negotiations on the status of this Eastern Sector led to the signing of the Basic Agreement on the region of eastern Slavonia, Baranja, and western Sirmium in November 1995. The Basic Agreement stated that the region would be reintegrated into the Republic of Croatia. To implement this agreement, a new UN mandate was created—the United Nations Transitional Administration for Eastern Slavonia (UNTAES). The UNTAES was deployed from January 1996 until January 1998, and has been widely regarded as one of the most successful, comprehensive peace-support missions in Croatia over the past decade, and one of the most successful of its kind in the world.

Multi-Track Diplomacy

In 1990, Amnesty International and Helsinki Watch were the first international organizations to warn of the increasing nationalism of the Milosevic regime. Unfortunately, their early warnings had no effect, and had no impact on civil society.

In fact, civil society at that time was quite underdeveloped. Since the early 1980s, only a few environmental groups and feminists had been active. Those actors within civil society did not have sufficient influence to prevent the outbreak of war, but they did play a crucial role in the further development of civil society in an environment characterized by national homogenization, prewar euphoria, and the war itself. While almost all national forces were focused on state independence, these civil initiatives raised the question of the content of that project: What kind of society and state are going to be developed?

The Antiwar Campaign Croatia (ARK), founded in July 1991, had the primary role during this initial period. A handful of people, members of a local prewar social-movement organization, published a charter in which they declared themselves against war, and in favor of nonviolent conflict resolution and the preservation of lines of communication across ethnic and republic boundaries as a precondition for postconflict peacebuilding. They lobbied for passage of a conscientious-objector law as a basis for refusing military service. They focused on proactive long-term peace projects, direct involvement with war victims, peace education, voluntary work in refugee camps, among other things. Individuals and small groups were empowered and a network was built up. ARK has since grown into a national network of more than twenty civil groups active throughout Croatia, including the Volunteer Project Pakrac, the Centre for Direct Human Rights Protection, the "Small Step," the Centre for Peace Studies, the Centre for Women's Studies, and Women's Network. Through organic organizational development, without international pressures put on its structure or programming, ARK has become an example of indigenous development of civil society in Croatia, supported by continuity of the sort of activism exemplified by Marina Skrabalo during the previous decade.

The Centre for Peace, Nonviolence and Human Rights (CPO) in Osijek is an organization playing a role in strengthening civil society in the war-torn area of eastern Slavonia. The center was founded in 1992, in an environment directly affected by war. The group joined ARK and also got support from numerous peace activists and groups throughout Europe. Based on permanent education and empowerment of its members, CPO developed a multifaceted, integrated approach to postwar peacebuilding and community recovery in ethnically divided local communities. The group combines psychosocial support to the injured population (displaced persons and refugees, women and children, ex-soldiers), cross-community activities, and peace education with direct opposition to human-rights violations against the remaining citizens of Serbian nationality. CPO also contributed to development of various NGOs in the region and to cross-border cooperation with peace initiatives and organizations operating in the area under Serbian control and in Serbia proper, such as the Association for Peace and Human Rights Baranja; the Centre for Peace Vukovar; Youth Peace group Danube, Vukovar; PRONI Centre for Youth Workers Education; the recently founded Institute for Peace Research; and Education Vukovar, Group 484, Belgrade, Association for Tolerance. The contributions of all these organizations to the peace and integrative processes in eastern Slavonia are significant and recognized by local communities, the wider community, local governments, and international organizations such as the OSCE and the UN.

Another important field of work for NGOs in Croatia has been the protection and promotion of human rights. In Split in 1992, the local organization Dalmatian Solidarity Committee (DOS) opposed the illegal evictions and other human-rights violations of Serbs living in parts of Croatia under the control of the Croatian government. Evictions were being carried out by state institutions such as the military housing committee and military and civil police. DOS in Split, CPO in Osijek, ARK in Zagreb, and a whole range of other organizations opposed these practices in Split, Osijek, Zagreb, Pula, and Karlovac. Shortly thereafter, the Civic Committee for Human Rights and the Croatian Helsinki Committee took over the central role in the campaign against human-rights violations in Croatia.

The Croatian Helsinki Committee (CHO) was founded in Zagreb at the end of March 1993 as a chapter of the International Helsinki Federation for Human Rights. It became the most influential forum for the protection of human rights in Croatia. In cooperation with the International Helsinki Federation and other international organizations, CHO campaigns at the national and international level for adherence to international standards for human-rights protection in the Republic of Croatia, and specifically, for equal rights for all Croatian citizens without regard for ethnicity, religion, social status, or politics. CHO's program includes monitoring activities, the publishing of its findings, press releases, the organization of seminars and panel discussions, educational publications, and direct legal assistance in ten regional offices. The organization has also recorded crimes in those areas then accessible to CHO, especially after the "Flash" and "Storm" military operations.

Because of their activities, CHO and other human-rights, peace, and women's organizations were marginalized or exposed to frequent attacks by state media and high-ranking officials. Although claims were made that civil society, multiparty democracy, and minority rights would be tolerated, those who attempted to put their principles into practice were accused of being enemies of the nation. But at the same time, as Marina Skrabalo claims, the government paradoxically welcomed various supranational (UN peacekeeping forces, UNHCR), regional (EU monitors, OSCE), international (various NGOs such as IRC), and other state (USAID, Norwegian People's Aid) and private (Open Society Institute) development enterprises, organizations, and programs. This enabled the development of a civil society and opposition.

Parallel with the end of the UNTAES mandate and the reintegration of the whole territory under the control of the Republic of Croatia, the influence of independent media increased. They took over the key role in "deconstruction" of the HDZ regime. After the parliamentary elections in 2000, the ten-year rule of the HDZ regime was ended and replaced by a broad opposition coalition. Civil society played a significant role in the election campaign. One hundred and forty NGOs participated in Coalition Glas '99, a group urging citizens to go to the polls. A women's network was especially efficient and well organized.

Paul Stubbs and some other researchers of the civil scene in Croatia also point to a negative aspect of interaction between international and local NGOs. Some of the negative consequences of donations and politics-driven interventionism include the uncontrolled influx of huge amounts of money for short-term projects, which has triggered rapid growth of local groups. These groups have been forced to professionalize too rapidly. When international assistance was reduced after 1995, many of the local NGOs, as well as local workers in international NGOs, struggled to reduce their size, identify new donors, or even reregister to suit the local environment better. In such circumstances, competition dominates and long-term planning and development of common strategies suffer. Investment into capacity building is insufficient.

During 1999, the government established the Government Office for Cooperation with NGOs. It has been active, in a very cooperative and supportive way, serving as a link between the government and NGOs.

In addition to those organizations described here that deal with the protection of human rights, peacebuilding, and the development of civil society, organizations that grew out of the war itself—such as war veterans, disabled people, and widows—played a role during and after the conflict. Most of them represent interests of war victims, but they were used by the HDZ government as an instrument of political manipulation. Today they represent an important part of a radical right-wing bloc that organizes demonstrations celebrating the "dignity" of the patriotic war. They are among the most formidable opponents to the new government.

The Role of NGOs in UN Peacekeeping Operations—UNTAES

The first experience from which important lessons were learned was the Volunteer Project in the then divided city of Pakrac, western Slavonia (UNPA zone). The project was initiated during 1993 by ARK jointly with MOST

Howard Davies/Panos Pictures

Serbs waiting at a UN checkpoint in Lipik, to visit their families. The town marked the border between Serbian-occupied Croatia and Croatian territory administered by the UNPROFOR force.

(Bridge) from Belgrade. It was a community-based peacebuilding project implemented by international volunteers in cooperation with different local and international organizations. Along the road, very good cooperation with UNPROFOR's civil service was cultivated, which contributed to the willingness of UNTAES to cooperate with international and local NGOs. Indeed, UNTAES has been widely regarded as one of the most successful UN peace-support missions. The operation was characterized by very good cooperation from the conflicting parties, a clear and time-limited mandate, sufficient resources, support from NATO and OSCE, and excellent cooperation with local and international NGOs.

In Eastern Slavonia and Baranja, NGOs have been cooperating since 1994 to boost cross-border communication and peaceful coexistence. Until 1995—until the ratification of the peace agreement and the beginning of the UNTAES mandate, that is—more than 1,100 persons from both sides met on neutral ground in Hungary. In order to use the political framework provided by UNTAES as efficiently as possible, ten organizations from Croatia and three organizations from Serbia joined to form the Coordination of Peace Organizations for Eastern Slavonia, Baranja, and West Sirmium. Around one hundred representatives from these organizations received UN accreditations, entered the region, worked with people, organized visits, engaged in dialogue, and provided people with information and legal help. A large number of international NGOs were also active in the region during that period.

After the end of the UNTAES mandate in 1998, in spite of all that had been achieved, the sustainability of the process remained an issue. The two-year mission helped mainly with the integration of the territory, institutions, and that part of the Serbian population that decided to stay in Croatia, but the Croat population did not return, and therefore the process of rebuilding trust could not be started. There was a danger that people's fear, mistrust, and anger, encouraged by nationalistic leaders, might lead to the completion of the process of ethnic division and, indeed, of ethnic cleansing. The situation demanded a proactive response. In the early post-UN period, many local organizations worked intensively in that area. Among other things, five more regional offices were opened to provide human-rights monitoring and legal assistance, ten INFO clubs and five youth clubs were also opened, and a network of peace teams was set up in five local communities with high risk of interethnic conflict.

An external impact assessment of the peace teams shows that such initiatives have helped the process of integration. Also, research done on the national level shows that citizens of eastern Slavonia, although most severely affected by the war, are still most open to the processes of reconciliation. Hopefully, this experience will contribute to even better cooperation in the future between international peacekeeping forces and local and international NGOs in postconflict peacebuilding.

Prospects

The end of the UNTAES mandate on 15 January 1998 was celebrated throughout Croatia as the end of the war and a definite victory. However, it took time to open a new chapter and to raise some other issues at the national level. The circumstances in which the parliamentary elections in January 2000 (and later the presidential elections) were held were colored by the illness and death of president Tudjman, a crisis for the HDZ regime, and an extremely difficult economic situation in the country. The great response of the voters in the elections and the victory of the opposition parties' coalition was an unmistakable signal that Croatian society desired change, particularly economic and social change, as well as an end to corruption and economic crime.

However, apart from the difficulties related to transition, Croatia still bears the burden of postwar hardships. The most important obstacles to the new practice related to protection of human and minority rights are obstruction of administration, local government, and the situation in judicature. Further, in order to proceed along the road to European integration, thus facilitating economic recovery, the new government could not avoid raising several issues that were not at all certain of popular support: the issue of processing war crimes, cooperation with the International Criminal Tribunal in The Hague, and the return of the refugees currently residing in the Federal Republic of Yugoslavia (FRY) and Bosnia-Herzegovina. In fact, these issues were not raised during the course of the election campaign. At present they serve to polarize a Croatian political and social scene that is highly unstable. But this polarization itself is indicative of an important change in the society as compared to the period of HDZ rule. At that time, the marginalized civil society and the independent media were the only and loudest opponents and critics of the notion of peace based on an ethnically and ideologically "clean" Croatia. But support within Croatian political culture for an ethnically pure nation has now practically vanished. At the same time, the extreme right has strengthened its positions "defending the dignity of the war," criticizing the government's economic and social policies, and using ideological confrontation as a strategy. The fear of the revival of communism is being fueled and the governing Social Democratic Party is often accused of being communist itself.

In the case of the war, the main argument is that none of the military actions that took place during this defensive war was illegitimate, i.e., that ethnic cleansing was not a goal; that war crimes per se could not be committed during a defensive war; that the International Criminal Tribunal and national "traitors" intend to discredit heroes as being war criminals. U.S. antiterrorist policies in the case of Afghanistan are used by the extreme right as an argument that the Western powers have double standards.

Unfortunately, the wide coalition that constitutes the Croatian government has shown itself to be very unstable. There are more discussions going on among coalition partners than efficient actions taking place. Unclear goals, restrictive social policies, and poor results in recovering the economy, as well as dealing with economic crimes, have seriously affected how the citizens perceive the competence of their rulers. The question of early (and untimely) elections is increasingly discussed.

According to assessments carried out by the international community, Serb refugees who fled to FRY and Bosnia-Herzegovina have not returned to Croatia in sufficient numbers. Up to mid-2001, 80,000 of a total of 300,000 registered refugees had returned. The conditions necessary for the return of the refugees have not been met. Remaining issues include problems related to tenant rights (discriminatory legal provisions are still in effect), obstacles in realization of the rights to property and rebuilding, unresolved issues concerning immigrants from Bosnia-Herzegovina, poor economic conditions, and social and emotional barriers including fear, anger, and revenge.

Unlike the rest of the former Krajina, the situation in eastern Slavonia and western Sirmium (former UNTAES regions) is somewhat better. Displaced persons have been gradually returning (although the process is rather slow and does not involve a significant number of young people) and there has not been further significant emigration of Serbs from the region. Grave interethnic incidents are rare, although the population in the region is burdened with unresolved traumas, tensions, and a lack of trust. People live beside each other under the strain of increasing economic hardship and unemployment.

Social tensions continue to increase throughout the country. The economic-stability program has caused a further increase in unemployment, the suspension of some benefits for ex-soldiers and special categories of citizens, and fear of falling wages in the public sector. In such circumstances, voter turnout was low for local elections, and consequently the ruling coalition achieved poorer results. A change in the local autonomy law resulted in a significant level of decentralization, but the new law did not decrease the number of local administration units. So existing human resources are inadequate to fill all positions with competent personnel in the local administrative units that do exist.

One year after the elections there is talk about the silence of the civil scene in Croatia. One of the reasons behind that is surely a certain degree of fatigue, but also the altered circumstances to which the Croatian population still must adapt. The new government has changed the rhetoric. NGOs are no longer seen as internal enemies of the state. However, institutional ways for NGOs and the government to cooperate are yet to be developed.

Further democratization of the society in Croatia will depend, among other things, on whether and in what way civil actors cooperate and coalitions develop within the civil scene, as well as on the nature of dialogue and cooperation that takes place between civil society and government. The intensity of cooperation at the subregional level among NGOs to build civil society, common security, and reconciliation will also play an important role.

With the victory of the opposition and the end of HDZ rule, Croatia came to be viewed as a partner of the international community contributing to stability in the region and encouraging positive change in the neighboring countries.

Recommendations

In order to build a sustainable, peaceful future, Croatian society has to deal with both the unresolved postwar issues and the postsocialist transition issues. It is important to understand the ways in which these two areas are interdependent and to build on that understanding.

The authors consider that priorities for building a sustainable peace include the following:

1. Securing the conditions for the return of refugees
   a. Further improvements in legislation, speeding up of legal proceedings, and securing implementation of valid verdicts
   b. Implementation of trust-building measures on the local community level
   c. Use of community development as the main peacebuilding strategy in ethnically mixed communities—instrumental approach to reconciliation through joint community development projects

2. Dealing with war crimes—two parallel complementary processes

   Track I:
   a. Strengthen national judiciary in order to process persons suspected of war crimes
   b. Cooperate with the International Criminal Court for the former Yugoslavia in The Hague

   Track II:
   a. Start a public discussion leading to the establishment of a truth commission by the parliament of the Republic of Croatia
   b. Establish links, even joint development of comparable concepts and methodologies, between Commission on Truth and Reconciliation in FRY, the soon-to-be-established commission in Bosnia-Herzegovina, and, eventually a similar body in Croatia

3. Expanding the notion of security to embrace a concept of peacebuilding. In order to avoid conditions in which the concept of security extends only as far as joining the Partnership for Peace or NATO, the concept of peacebuilding has to be included in
   a. National Defense Strategy
   b. National Development Strategy

4. Political stabilization through
   a. Grouping and profiling of political parties
   b. Development of management capacties of local governments
   c. Securing participation of minorities in local government
   d. Strengthening civil society by improving managerial capacities and forming coalitions within the NGO scene

5. Development of a culture of tolerance, dialogue, and dealing with conflicts, particularly enhancing the role of churches in a social dialogue.

6. Protection of social rights (European Social Charter) has to be an important part of a strategy of transition of the economy.
7. Creating a basis for reconciliation and common security in the region (e.g., opening business channels, cooperation on missing persons, prosecuting suspected war criminals, fighting organized crime, creating a book and newspaper distribution network, cultural exchanges, cooperation among civil society organizations)

Resources

Reports

Article 19, *Forging War—Media in Serbia, Croatia and Bosnia and Herzegovina*, by Mark Thompson. 1994.

Centre for Conflict Resolution, University of Bradford, *From Conflict Resolution to Transformative Peacebuilding: Reflections from Croatia*, by A. B. Fetherston, Working Paper 4, April 2001.

Centre for Transition and Civil Society Research/Agency Argument, *Media & War*, edited by Nena Skopljanac Brunner, Stjepan Gredelj, Alija Hodzic, Branimir Kristofic, Zagreb/Beograd, 2000.

UNHCR

I Choose Life: Post-War Peace Building in Eastern Croatia, edited by Katarina Kruhonja, Osijek, 2001.

Provisional Statistics on Refugees and Others of Concern to UNHCR for the Year 2000, Carnegie Endowment for International Peace.

Towards Reconciliation—Impact Assessment, by Jessica Jordan, Marina Skrabalo, Jasenka Pregrad, Osijek, 2000.

Unfinished Peace, Report of the International Commission on the Balkans, Washington, DC, Centre for Peace, Nonviolence and Human Rights, 1996.

Other Publications

Balkan Tragedy: Chaos and Dissolution After the Cold War, by Susan Woodward. Washington, DC, Brookings Institution, 1995.

East Central Europe: Paradoxes and Perspectives, by Jody Jensen and Ferenc Miszlivetz. Szombathely, Savaria University Press, 1998.

Selected Internet Sites

www.aimpress.org/dyn/trae/trae-zag.htm (Alternative Information Network created in 1992 by independent journalists)

www.bosnia.org.uk (The Bosnian Institute in London)

www.crisisweb.org (International Crisis Group)

www.gewi.kfunigraz.ac.at/csbsc/guide/Croatia.htm (Centre for the Study of Balkan Societies and Cultures at the Department for Southeast European History University of Graz, Austria)

www.incore.ulst.ac.uk (INCORE guide to Internet sources on conflict and ethnicity in Croatia)

www.iwpr.net (Institute for war and Peace Reporting)

www.nacional.hr/Default.en.asp (Croatian weekly)

www.uzuvrh.hr (Government's Office for Cooperation with NGOs)

Resource Contacts

Biserka Milosevic, Program for Promotion and Protection of Human Rights, Osijek Centre for Peace, e-mail: czmos@zamir.net

Vesna Terselic, Centre for Peace Study, Zagreb, e-mail: cms@zamir.net
Nenad Zakosek, professor at the Faculty of Political Science, University of Zagreb,
    e-mail: nzakosek@zamir.net

Organizations

Centre for Peace, Legal Advices and Psycho-Social Assistance
Sundučićeva 22
32000 Vukovar, Croatia
Tel.: + 385 32 441 417
Fax: + 385 32 441 416
E-mail: centar-za-mir@vk.tel.hr
www.members.nbci.com/cfpeace/

Civic Committee for Human Rights
Ulica grada Vukovara
35, 10000 Zagreb, Croatia
Tel.: + 385 1 6171 530
Fax: + 385 1 6171 530
E-mail: goljp@zamir.net

Croatian Helsinki Committee for Human Rights (CHC)
Trg Drage Iblera 9/5
10000 Zagreb, Croatia
Tel.: + 385 1 4812 322
Fax: + 385 1 4812 324
E-mail: glas@open.hr
www.open.hr/com/hho/

Dalmatian Solidarity Committee
Šetaliste Bačvice 10
PO BOX 248, 21000 Split, Croatia
Tel.: + 385 21 345 966
Fax: + 385 21 361 655
E-mail: dos.st@st.tel.hr
www.tel.hr/dalmatinski-odbor-solidarnosti/index.htm

HOMO—Association for Protection of Human Rights and Civil Liberties
Josepine Martinuzzi
23, 52100 Pula, Croatia
Tel.: + 385 52 505 976
Fax: + 385 52 505 976
E-mail: homo@pu.tel.hr
www.zenskestranice.hr/nevladi/homo.htm

Serbian Democratic Forum (SDF)
Berislavićeva 10/2
10000 Zagreb, Croatia
Tel.: + 385 1 4872483
Fax: + 385 1 3777032
E-mail: zagreb-sdf@sdf.hr
www.sdf.hr

Data on the following organizations can be found in the Directory section:
B.a.B.e.
Center for Education and Counseling of Women

Center for Peace Studies
Centre for Peace, Nonviolence and Human Rights–Osijek
MIRamiDA Centar–Regional Peace Building Exchange
Vukovar Institute for Peace Research and Education

The authors are associated with the Centre for Peace, Nonviolence and Human Rights– Osijek, which was founded in May 1992 by a number of intellectuals in response to the war experience, and as a way to help preserve a nucleus of civil society resistant to the ethnic, religious, political, or ideological divisions imposed by the war. Today it has more than one hundred members and a number of local and international volunteers working on protection and promotion of human rights, peace education, and community recovery and peacebuilding in multiethnic local communities in war-torn areas of Croatia.

Katarina Kruhonja is a medical doctor and one of the founders of the center. She currently serves as the center's president, and is a member of the Executive Board of Pax Christi International. In 1998, she was awarded The Right Livelihood Award, also known as "The Alternative Nobel Prize." Milan Ivanovic, an economist and sociologist, has been a member of the center for many years and has been involved in projects on democratization and civil society. Ivan Stanic is a medical doctor and a volunteer at the Centre for Peace.

13.7

Macedonia:
Extreme Challenges for the
"Model" of Multiculturalism

Sally Broughton & Eran Fraenkel

Macedonia, long considered the model of a multicultural society and conflict prevention, has been in crisis since spring 2001. After outbreaks of violence in March 2001 in Tetovo and along the Macedonian/ Kosovo border, the country has plunged into political and social crisis. Mistrust between Macedonians and Albanians has never been higher. The general public's cynicism about politics has skyrocketed. As all political parties struggle with difficult issues such as possibly changing the constitution or adopting an official second language, individual politicians are trying desperately to gain strength from clinging to their ethnically defined power bases. Despite the turmoil among political elites and shooting in the hills, the majority of citizens—Albanians and Macedonians[1]—still prefer nonviolent coexistence. Unfortunately, most fear speaking up. Consequently, whether this unspoken desire can prevent the country from collapsing remains to be seen. If a stable peace will be brought about by the NATO disarmament of Albanian rebels, followed by the acceptance of some amendments to the constitution by the Macedonian parliament, also remains to be seen.

Despite attempts by various rebel groups and even treaties declaring it an autonomous entity under the Ottomans, Macedonia was not given political recognition until 1944 when it was made a constituent republic of Yugoslavia. Macedonia as a republic of Yugoslavia had the same borders as it has now. It was as a constituent republic of Yugoslavia that the Macedonian identity was recognized. Literary standards were set for the Macedonian language, grammar books were published, and education was allowed in Macedonian as well as other languages of the republic such as Albanian, Turkish, and Serbian.

Macedonia was the only republic to leave Yugoslavia without bloodshed. The Yugoslav army withdrew from Macedonia in 1991, taking with it all military equipment in the republic.

Since 1991, Macedonia has been a parliamentary democracy, in which Macedonians and Albanians share power. Macedonia was considered a model

MACEDONIA
Population (millions): 2.0
(World Bank, 1999)
Conflict related deaths:
some 50 soldiers and
policemen untill the end
of 2001. Casualties Albanian
rebels unknown.
Conflict related IDPs: 25,000
(est., UNHCR, 2001)
Conflict related refugees:
65,000 in Kosovo, 6,000
in Serbia (UNHCR, 2001)

of effective conflict prevention and pluralism in the midst of ethnic conflict because members of all ethnic groups in Macedonia continued to participate in government and state institutions. There was no significant violence among the country's ethnic groups. Albanians and other minorities not only participated side by side in parliament, but also in the educational system, the military, and other state institutions.

Despite an apparently functioning pluralistic society and government, Macedonia has faced conflicts that arose from the question of whether the republic should be defined as a unitary or binational state, with its respective accompanying institutions. Unlike other ex-Yugoslav states (Serbia particularly), Macedonia did not inherit a political conflict with its Albanian population. Again, unlike Croatia or Serbia, Macedonia has been attempting to accommodate its Yugoslav legacy, essentially by retaining the previous structures that guarantee its minorities' political, social, and cultural rights. But whereas in the former Socialist Federal Republic of Yugoslavia competing nationalities were restrained by socialist ideology, in independent Macedonia this is not the case. Albanians and Macedonians have been struggling with conflicting sentiments about their civic versus ethnic identities. Albanians accuse Macedonians of imposing a unitary Macedonian ethnopolitical character on the state. Macedonians, in turn, equate most Albanian demands for self-determination with irredentism. Smaller minorities such as Turks and Roma accuse the Macedonians and Albanians of ignoring their needs. Although all ethnic communities continue to participate in the government and political discourse, each community fundamentally suspects the intentions of the other.

Macedonia has weathered several crises: the attempted assassination of president Gligorov (1995); the operation since 1997 of a paralegal Albanian university outside Tetovo; the violent removal by police of Albanian flags from Tetovo and Gostivar city halls (1997). Until February 2001, Macedonia's greatest crisis was the influx of 360,000 Kosovar refugees (March–June 1999). The Kosovo war compelled Macedonia's citizens to ask whether they primarily identified with their "ethnic community" regardless of political borders, or with their country including its ethnic, religious, and linguistic diversity. Since the violent events within Macedonia's borders, which began in February 2001, this question has become even more important. Conflicting political, economic, and social answers to this question continue to challenge conflict-prevention efforts in Macedonia.

At issue is whether Macedonia is a nation-state with an ethnic Macedonian majority and minorities enjoying protected rights; or whether it is a multicultural, civic state. Language rights (native-language education, or the right to use Albanian in parliament); decentralization of government and empowerment of municipal administrations; proportional parliamentary representation versus majority rule; accusations of cronyism, bribery, and black marketeering—all these issues are rooted in a basic mistrust between Macedonia's constituent communities and the assumption that any concession would be taken as a pretext for ulterior political or territorial ambitions.

When comparing life in independent Macedonia with life in former Yugoslavia, most Macedonians see a "golden cage." They have a state, but one poorer than the former Yugoslavia. Macedonia issues passports, but Macedonians face visa restrictions when trying to travel abroad. Despite positive World Bank and IMF assessments of the government's monetary policies, Macedonians feel they become more and more impoverished. Just as in other former communist countries, Macedonia suffered from a collapse of its state industries. Macedonia's economic development was further hampered by a Greek blockade that lasted more than two years, and also suffered from the international embargo against its number-one trading partner, Serbia. While the majority of the population lost purchasing power during the past ten years, Macedonia has seen the rise of a new elite that derived its wealth from smuggling (breaking the Greek embargo or busting the sanctions against FRY) as well as from corrupt privatization of state-owned property.

To some extent, Macedonia's political and social conflicts have been shaped by these economic conditions. Since 1994, unemployment has hovered officially around the 30 percent mark, but unofficially it is closer to 50 percent. During the Kosovo war, unemployment rose to 70 percent. An unfavorable tax environment, underdeveloped regional trade, unreliable banking institutions, far-reaching corruption, and questionable privatization have discouraged major foreign investments. Officially a free-market economy, Macedonia still needs to eliminate nepotism and corruption, which would open the way to entering the world market. Promises made by the current coalition government about economic recovery and massive foreign credit or investments, as well as promises of Western aid following the Kosovo war, have not materialized. There is little reason to believe they will.

These economic factors aggravate tensions between the mainly urban Macedonian and largely rural Albanian communities. Macedonians, having worked mostly in "socially owned" and now privatized or defunct enterprises, have borne the brunt of Macedonia's economic downturn. Albanian villagers also suffered. The agricultural sector is far from thriving, primarily due to loss of markets and harsh visa regimes limiting the number of seasonal workers finding temporary employment abroad. Nonetheless, Macedonians are convinced that Albanians have flourished at their expense. They believe that the money made by Albanians is used to support illicit activities ranging from arms smuggling to high-level bribery. Albanians, on their part, criticize the government's inattention to rural needs, including underinvestment in rural infrastructure, poor rural health care, etc. They present the neglect as ethnically based discrimination. Consequently, even legitimate requests by either community have become highly politicized. For example, Macedonians look at rural Albanian land tenure and family size and accuse Albanians of a demographic war meant to out-populate and expel them from western Macedonia. Conversely, Albanians interpret the recent electoral law reshuffling electoral districts as manipulation intended to disenfranchise them in districts where they used to be the majority.

Macedonia, in short, is a country in transition but unsure of where exactly it is going. Macedonia faces pressure from both the international community and domestic armed groups urging the country to complete the transition very quickly. Despite establishing institutions of a participatory and representative democracy, Macedonian citizens are still locked in bitter domestic disputes over political legitimacy and national identity. These disputes are becoming even more complicated by continual infighting among political elites, who repeatedly use nationalist causes to divert attention from their personal incompetence and to hide their refusal to consider realistic political solutions that do not enhance their own political careers. These dynamics have convinced the general population that many of Macedonia's politicians would prefer war than to relinquish their grip on power. Should this happen, the majority of people in Macedonia, who clearly had opted to avoid bloodshed, may have little choice.

Conflict Dynamics

Seen from a wider perspective, the crisis in Macedonia is, more than other disputes in the region, a direct heritage of the collapse of Yugoslavia. Based on the Soviet nationalities model, in the former Yugoslavia Macedonia was a republic and Macedonians were part of a constituent nation. Kosovo was not a republic, and Albanians were only tacitly recognized as a nation, despite the fact that they were twice as numerous as the Macedonians.

After independence, Macedonia continued this model of Macedonians being the constituent nation while most others, including Albanians, were considered a minority.[2] Albanians, however, categorically reject this majority/ minority paradigm and its implicit power relations. Albanians have demanded coequal status with Macedonians, including the institutionalization of all Albanian cultural and political features. In other words, they want a binational state. On the regional level, however, ethnic Macedonians are a minority surrounded in part by an Albanian majority and, on the other side of the border, by Greeks, Bulgarians, and Serbs whose governments each in their own way negate the existence of the Macedonians as a nation.

Greece continues to object to the use of "Macedonia" in the name of the country and, after imposing a trade embargo for more than two years, was able to convince Macedonia to change its flag. Bulgaria until recently officially claimed that Macedonian is merely a dialect of Bulgarian. The two countries signed an agreement in early 1999, but the Macedonian public dismissed it, arguing the document did not sufficiently affirm the Macedonian language. Serbia and some other Orthodox Christian countries still refuse to recognize the Macedonian Orthodox Church. Though Albania recognized Macedonia very quickly, the future of Kosovo is still undetermined. With the final status of their Albanian neighbors in Kosovo up in the air, Macedonians still fear developments there could result in Albanian expansionism.

Macedonians are at best reluctant, or at worst terrified, to negotiate with Albanians inside Macedonia, believing that their existence and identity are at stake. Even if Albanian claims of loyalty to Macedonia are sincere, Macedonians fear the Albanian birthrate might result in Albanians becoming the majority community.

This mutual mistrust was stirred up during the Kosovo war (1999). Kosovo's internal problems have challenged Macedonia since 1991. During the war, many Macedonians feared that Kosovo's independence would encourage irredentism among Macedonia's Albanians because of historical connections between Albanians in both countries and Albanian dissatisfaction with conditions in Macedonia. Similar irredentism accusations were expressed against Albania. But Kosovo was perceived as being the major threat to Macedonia's integrity. When Kosovo refugees began crossing into Macedonia in July 1998, before the waves of March–June 1999, Macedonians feared a permanent demographic shift. Not only could Macedonia be drawn into a war with Yugoslavia against its will, but this war also increased the number of Albanians in Macedonia. Just as the sociopolitical collapse in Albania (1997) highlighted differences between Macedonia and Albania, the Kosovo war underscored differences between Kosovar and Macedonian Albanians. Ties with Kosovo notwithstanding, the war illustrated that Macedonian and Yugoslav internal political and social dynamics differ fundamentally. Macedonia's Albanian political leaders took a firm stand during the war to protect Macedonia's interests, keeping Albanian emotions under control despite recurrent provocations.

Following the war, Albanians also rallied behind the primary Macedonian party, Internal Macedonian Revolutionary Organization (VMRO), to secure the election of its presidential candidate, Boris Trajkovski. Macedonian politicians have therefore accrued political "debts" that the Albanians have been collecting since.

Tetovo: Albanian area of town

Although central Albanian demands (e.g., recognizing Albanian as a second official language) have not been met, the governing coalition has opted for compromises that, ironically, have escalated intraethnic tensions. For example, Macedonia accepted the establishment of a private university offering education in Albanian, Macedonian, and English as an alternative to the unrecognized "University of Tetovo." This, and the tentative permission to use Albanian in parliament, for instance, has created intraethnic tension. Albanian opposition leaders blame the governing Albanian party for selling out Albanian national interests by reneging on the recognition of Tetovo University. Macedonians blame the VMRO for abandoning their national interests by making any concessions to Albanians.

Dissatisfaction of Macedonia's Albanians with their political leadership intersected with the fallout from the 1999 Kosovo war when armed Albanians calling themselves the National Liberation Army (UÇK in Albanian) launched an insurgency in Macedonia in February 2001. Starting along Macedonia's border with Kosovo, the violence spread to villages near Tetovo, Kumanovo, and eventually Skopje. The Macedonian parties in the government initially claimed the UÇK came from Kosovo and aimed to create a Greater Albania/Kosovo. Though they have recanted this to some extent, they still believe the UÇK to be driven by Albanian expansionism. Macedonian Albanians point to domestic grievances as the war's cause and deny any connection to Kosovo.

Unable or unwilling to respond decisively militarily, and under immense international pressure to respond "proportionately," Macedonia's parliamentary parties formed a "Grand Coalition." During a period of two months, this coalition attempted to reach domestic political consensus on issues annexed by the UÇK, such as rewriting the constitution to remove references to any one people. Failure to reach a consensus, however, has created an upsurge of both spontaneous and suspiciously organized violence by ethnic Macedonians, who maintain the government and international community have colluded against them. Such popular perceptions are supported by continuous quarrels in which each party leader, irrespective of his or her ethnicity, assumes the role of national savior and accuses his rivals of bad faith if not treason. Policy has been replaced by posturing. Remedies previously considered to be beneficial (early parliamentary elections or intervention by NATO) now are seen as nearly pointless or as outside meddling with ulterior motives.

These conflicts within the government and the escalating rhetoric of ultimatums and threats have eroded whatever trust emerged between Macedonians and Albanians following the Kosovo war. The average person does not consider citizenship versus national identity, or individual versus group rights, to be the basic issues at stake. Rather, politicians, media figures, and even intellectuals are now framing the dispute as an interethnic conflict, leaving people increasingly fearful that war may be the only alternative to impending political and social anarchy.

On 13 August 2001 a peace agreement was signed in Macedonia, and NATO began a thirty-day deployment to disarm ethnic Albanian rebels. In November 2001 the Macedonian parliament passed the amendments to the constitution agreed upon in August. However, the facts that there was such intense fighting leading up to the peace deal, and that harsh conditions were set by the Macedonian government and the ethnic Albanian rebels to stick to it, mean the period following the agreement is as volatile as that preceding it. There is little trust or even expectation of peace by either Macedonians or ethnic Albanians, and a heavy burden will fall on the international community.

Official Conflict Management

The first international intervention in Macedonia was by the United Nations Preventive Deployment Force (UNPREDEP; originally called UNPROFOR), a United Nations peacekeeping force that was relocated to Macedonia from Croatia in 1992. The mandate of UNPREDEP was to monitor Macedonia's borders with Yugoslavia and Albania, strengthen the security of the country, and report on any potential threats to stability in Macedonia. UNPREDEP was perceived as a stabilizing force by most people in Macedonia and was considered to have an impact not only on the security of Macedonia vis-à-vis its neighbors, but also on the internal situation. Despite the fact that many viewed it as the UN's most successful peacekeeping mission, UNPREDEP's mandate ended in 1999 and was not extended, due to a veto from China in the UN Security Council.

During its intervention in Macedonia, the UN worked very closely with the OSCE Spillover Mission to Skopje, whose role also included monitoring and reporting. Gradually the OSCE began to take a more active role. Max van der Stoel visited Macedonia more than fifty times between 1993 and 2001 as the OSCE High Commissioner on National Minorities to work to defuse tensions on specific issues. Van der Stoel focused most of his energies on dialogue about higher education for minorities in Macedonia and strongly supported the adoption of a new law on higher education that opened the way to establishing the South East European University. On 11 February 2001, after more than a year of negotiations, construction work officially began to build this university. The university will be a private, financed by international donors that will offer education in Albanian as well as Macedonian, in addition to a variety of other European languages. The university is intended to address the problem of higher education in the Albanian language in Macedonia. This issue has been at the top of political debate since the early 1990s when the new borders and subsequent closing of the university in Pristhina severely restricted the opportunities for Albanians to study in the Albanian language. Albanian-language sections were added to the pedagogical faculty at the university in Skopje, but this did not meet the demand for higher education in the Albanian language. In 1997, several professors opened a private university in Tetovo, but the Macedonian government never recognized this institution. The South East European University opened its doors in November 2001. There was still opposition to it among some Albanians who feel it should be sponsored by the state, and among some Macedonian who feel it should not exist at all. It remains to be seen whether or not the university will really ease the extreme tension that exists around the issue of higher education.

After the outbreak of violence in Macedonia in 2001, the EU, NATO, and other Euro-Atlantic institutions redoubled their efforts to maintain stability in Macedonia. During and immediately after the crisis in Tetovo, Javier Solana, George Robertson, Chris Patten, and other heads of European and Euro-Atlantic institutions repeatedly visited Skopje. These efforts continued as fighting spread to Kumanovo and villages around Skopje. The European Union appointed Francis Leotard as its special representative, while the United States appointed James Pardew as special envoy for the republic. Their message is that the Macedonian government merits support, but they also demand that pressing interethnic issues be resolved. Both Leotard and Pardew supported President Trajkovski's efforts to promote political dialogue, which resulted in a framework agreement that included changes in Macedonia's constitution, restructuring of police, and disarmament of the UÇK, among other things. The actual details of the changes to the constitution and restructure were left to be worked out within the Macedonian parliament.

NATO has sent mixed signals regarding its willingness to become engaged in Macedonia. Initially, NATO cracked down on illegal movement across the border and on suspected UÇK members in Kosovo. NATO's involvement peaked in June 2001 with the evacuation of UÇK insurgents and their weapons from the villages of Arachinovo and Nikushtek, both near Skopje. This action, which was the result of negotiations between the Macedonian government and the UÇK under the auspices of the EU, resulted in a mass demonstration in Skopje by Macedonians who demanded the resignation of President Trajkovski. After the signing of the framework agreement, NATO oversaw the voluntary disarmament of the UÇK and collected the required weapons within the one-month time limit given to the operation. Continued shooting around Tetovo suggests that this was not completely effective, or that the UÇK has somehow resupplied.

Macedonia's internal conflicts are directly influenced by external developments, both regional and within individual neighboring states. The international community considers integration into regional and European institutions the only sustainable basis for Macedonian and regional stability in the long term.

Perhaps the most touted instrument for this process is the Stability Pact (SP) for Southeastern Europe. The SP's intentions are to create sustainable peace, prosperity, and stability for Southeastern Europe through economic and sociopolitical development of all countries in the region. The SP was set up to coordinate all bilateral and multilateral development initiatives through its three working tables: Democracy and Human Rights, Economic Development, and Security. Though the SP's impact in these three areas is still uncertain, people in the region concur that it has created a new atmosphere of regional cooperation. The SP serves as a framework through which countries in Southeast Europe can reach the status of a candidate members of the EU.

Regional integration has been boosted through an initiative launched by the Stability Pact called the South East Europe Cooperation Process (SEECP). This SEECP includes all Yugoslav successor states (except Slovenia), as well as Albania, Romania, Bulgaria, and Greece. The SEECP has facilitated several meetings of heads of state. It also arranged multilateral and bilateral meetings on the ministerial level. At the latest SEECP meeting of heads of state, Macedonia signed the long-awaited border agreement with Yugoslavia and a higher-education agreement with Albania. SEECP's most powerful moment occurred in March 2001, when Albania used its presidency to call on all member states to condemn the violent action by Albanian groups in Macedonia. Such regional solidarity, in light of ethnic ties, bodes well not only for Macedonia but for the region as a whole.

Macedonia also made a big step towards integration into Europe when it signed the Stabilization and Association Agreement with the European Union on 8 April 2001. This agreement codifies Macedonia's desire to be part of the EU and outlines what reforms it should implement in order to get closer to EU membership. The Stabilization and Association Agreement also obligates the EU countries to assist Macedonia in these reforms and work toward stability in the region. The agreement may serve as a useful instrument for necessary reforms on interethnic issues that may arise from the intragovernmental negotiations.

Multi-Track Diplomacy

Civil society is a contentious concept in postcommunist states, including Macedonia. Unfortunately, Westerners routinely fail to recognize the discrepancies between civil-society "ideals" and Balkan socioeconomic realities. Again, Macedonia is no exception. The fundamental obstacle is society's ability to afford the time and resources that Western-style civil society requires. Coming from debates whether NGOs create civil society or civil society creates NGOs, one salient point prevails: civil society creates conditions allowing NGOs to emerge and function; reciprocally, NGOs reinforce the vitality of civil society. In Macedonia, neither condition yet prevails.

The social and financial preconditions for a vital nongovernmental sector are alien in Macedonia. Self-help traditionally is mostly embedded in family structures. Many NGOs are Yugoslav vestiges, meaning they are "of" but not "for" citizens. Additionally, the average Macedonian is too preoccupied with survival to have time and energy available for voluntary work in an NGO. A 23 percent tax on philanthropic contributions, intended to prevent money laundering through nonprofit organizations, doesn't help NGOs either. Frequent examples of questionable financial management contribute to general public skepticism about the integrity of NGOs and thus their importance in developing Macedonia's civil society.

The overall NGO environment is hazy, since no tradition exists of civic activism outside governmental control. NGOs' role in society is therefore ambiguous. The media are apathetic toward NGOs and NGOs are equally disinterested in educating the media. Rarely do NGOs and the media cooperate on issues of broad public concern. Generally, politicians tend to be dismissive of NGOs. Likewise, NGOs do not try to communicate constructively with politicians.

To jump-start democratization, international donors have allocated money to seed NGOs, ostensibly stimulating civil society. To Macedonians, however, the NGO sector represents employment opportunities for individuals already having skills. Rather than promoting cohesion around common causes—including conflict prevention—NGOs seem to have become competitors, struggling for funds in order to keep their members employed. As a result, Macedonia has hundreds of NGOs—ecology associations, women's groups, groups for the advancement of particular minorities, and many others—but few effective ones. Furthermore, unlike international organizations, whose staffs tend to be ethnically mixed, most local organizations are monoethnic.

Macedonia's local and international NGO community assist in preventing conflict in two ways. Some NGOs specifically focus on interethnic relations and try to reduce tension among different ethnic groups in Macedonia. Others focus on development, advocacy, ecology, or other areas, and indirectly improve interethnic relations by promoting inclusion and equal participation of different ethnic groups in their work.

The Nansen Dialogue Center (NDC) in Skopje, which functions essentially as a local NGO although it is part of a regional network, is a multiethnic

organization that facilitates dialogue projects and conflict analysis and resolution training for young people and children. CIVIL, another multiethnic
group in Skopje, promotes human rights and peaceful coexistence, conducts
community dialogue sessions and debates, and runs media campaigns for
peace. In Gostivar, an ethnically mixed city, the Interethnic Programme Gostivar (IPG) works specifically on interethnic cooperative projects. IPG attempts
to counter the separatist trend in the NGO community by devising activities
between organizations such as women's groups or sports clubs, which tend to
be monoethnic. Multikultura and the Youth Information Center, both in
Tetovo, work on building tolerance and awareness of interethnic issues among
high school students of different ethnic backgrounds.

The Macedonian Center for International Cooperation (MCIC) is considered the most stable and well-established local NGO in Macedonia. MCIC
bridges the gap between NGOs that specifically focus on interethnic relations
and those that positively influence interethnic relations while working toward
other goals. MCIC mainly focuses on development, such as support for rural
infrastructure and capacity building. It is also engaged in direct humanitarian
aid to refugees or others in need. MCIC's evenhanded and inclusive approach
fosters interethnic cooperation as a by-product. In addition, MCIC designed a
public-service campaign using the slogan "Celo e koga ima se" (literally,
[something is] complete when it has [consists of] everything). This campaign
intends to directly encourage tolerance and support for a multicultural society.

Although most women's organizations are monoethnic and many have a
tendency to be highly politicized, one group, ANTIKO, a network of women
from across the country, stands out from the rest. ANTIKO's mission is to empower women, especially young women, through seminars on economic integration, health issues, fighting prejudice, and other issues relevant to women
in Macedonian society. ANTIKO's leadership represents Macedonian, Albanian, Turkish, Bosniak, and Roma women and tries to reach women of all the
communities. Its work contributes to increased understanding and unity among
women of different ethnic backgrounds.

The Center for Civic Initiative (CCI) in Prilep was founded to promote
democracy and citizen involvement in creating positive social change. CCI's
project ranges from educating children in children's rights to providing educational services for refugees and creating resource centers and training programs for other NGOs. CCI's project participants are ethnically mixed, resulting in cooperation among individuals from different ethnicities. CCI also
works regionally. One of its most significant partners is the Albanian Center
for Human Rights in Tirana.

During and after the outbreak of violence in February 2001, more than
one hundred NGOs signed various appeals for peaceful resolution and nonviolence. Nonetheless, the NGO community did not launch a movement, nor did
it display unity or undertake significant action for a peaceful solution. Some
organizations did react individually to the crisis. NDC and CIVIL began a series of dialogue session with citizens of Tetovo, whereas IPG produced a video

spot for broadcast on local television that encourages building a positive future. Most organizations either remained silent or became further politicized. With a few exceptions, local NGOs in Macedonia have yet to become a major factor in conflict prevention.

Though historically Macedonia has hosted relatively few international NGOs (INGOs), this situation has changed since the Kosovo war and refugee crisis of 1999. Most international organizations focus directly on humanitarian assistance, economic development, or democracy building. Generally, INGOs both employ and serve members of different ethnic groups. Whether they are training local government officials, supporting microenterprise development, or building local NGO capacity, INGOs indirectly facilitate contact and cooperation among Macedonia's different communities.

Only a few INGOs work directly on conflict prevention and interethnic relations. Search for Common Ground in Macedonia (SCGM), which aims to improve interethnic cooperation, communication, and understanding, is the best-known organization. SCGM works closely with the Ethnic Conflict Resolution Project at the University of St. Kiril and Methodius on a variety of projects in the Macedonian education system. Educational programs teach skills for multicultural awareness and cooperation or for conflict resolution. SCGM also has a long history of implementing cooperative media projects in print and broadcast media including collaborative projects among media outlets throughout the region. SCGM produces *Nashe Maalo,* the award-winning children's television series that focuses on multicultural literacy, tolerance building, and skills for conflict resolution.

In cooperation with several local NGOs, UNICEF is implementing a project called Babylon that brings children from different ethnic backgrounds together for educational and social activities. These common activities are intended to decrease children's prejudices and mutual fear while encouraging their communication and friendship. The Dutch chapter of the peace organization Pax Christi also works with local organization, particularly NDC, CIVIL, and ANTIKO. Pax Christi provides support and training to local organizations and organized a peace concert. It also set up a bilingual radio station with its local partners.

Local and international NGOs that seem to have the most impact on interethnic relations in Macedonia are those employing a multiethnic staff and, by doing so, are inclusive and nondiscriminatory in implementing their activities. In Macedonia, where most NGOs are politicized, monoethnic, and many would even say corrupt, local and international organizations have an imperative to demonstrate both by their structure and programs that NGOs can function positively in a multiethnic environment.

Prospects

The outbreak of violence in Tetovo in March 2001 brought swarms of international journalists and analysts expecting the "Third Balkan War." Even though the violence has abated, most experts predict a bleak future for Macedonia.

Graham Fuller, writing in the *Los Angeles Times* (22 March 2001), argues that
the Albanian minorities in Macedonia, Serbia, and Montenegro are intrinsi-
cally unstable, and that Albanian and Macedonian ethnic and religious differences will eventually cause these ethnic groups to separate. This view, which
we consider to be fatalistic and oversimplistic, is surprisingly popular among
Western analysts. Many, like Paul Gastris in *Slate* (2 February 2001) and
Simon Jenkins in the *Times* (21 March 2001) blame NATO for permitting violence to become an effective and even rewarded model in the Balkans. Gastris predicts that the recurrence of violence and a strong reaction from the
Macedonian government will compel Macedonia's Albanian population to take
up arms. Many who predict that war in Macedonia is still inevitable are also
convinced that NATO will have no choice but to deploy forces to stop the violence, thereby creating another Kosovo-like protectorate.

Local analysts are not much more optimistic. Saso Ordanovski in *Forum*
(30 March–12 April 2001) primarily blames crime in the region and in the government for the crisis, which has been portrayed as an interethnic crisis. He predicts some kind of "half solution" among government officials so that corruption
and criminality can continue to increase the rift between Macedonians and Albanians and between the population and its governing institutions. According to
him, this rift will widen until some spark—elections or another violent incident—ignites a full-scale violent conflict. Kim Mehmeti, writing for the *Institute
for War & Peace Reporting* (21 March 2001) suggests that Macedonia has a
chance to avoid large-scale violence if its leadership commits itself to a real dialogue on interethnic issues; the alternative is a violent split of the country.

Recommendations
Many ideas for changes are floating about the political discourse in Macedonia. Most Western analysts have joined the general call for greater EU, U.S.,
and NATO intervention. For some, this takes the form of a NATO-led military
intervention. For others, including Balkans expert Tim Judah, the answer is
continued political pressure, the use of Western economic clout both to create
jobs and encourage all sorts of regional cooperation, from free trade areas to
local visa-less travel. Political pressure, according to most analysts, means
pushing the Macedonian government to ratify the peace plan that includes
changes to the constitution (eliminating references to ethnicity), and further
integration of Albanians into state structures.

The International Crisis Group (ICG), in Report 113, recommends pres-
suring Greece to accept the constitutional name of the Republic of Macedonia,
and to put pressure on the international community to design a final status plan
for Kosovo. It also calls for sending "a strong and explicit message that Albanian extremists will not be allowed to split the country along ethnic lines."

Analyzing the 13 August 2001 agreement, ICG argues that NATO cannot
limit its mission to thirty days. It must be prepared to do more than collect
arms that are voluntarily given to it. It must seal the border with Kosovo and
should provide the security assurance required to see the 13 August agreement

through to parliamentary ratification and implementation. And it must be prepared to use all necessary force to make that assurance real.

Mirjana Najcevska of the Institute for Social, Political and Juridical Research, in her article "Now It Is Time to Work" (*Multiethnic Forum,* April 2001), recommends a combination of both intense legal and judicial reform and a "gradual affirmation of a civic identity in all aspects of public life while allowing room also for ethnic identification." Najcevska maintains that legal reform must reflect the general will of the people and that in the process democratic process must be upheld.

Saso Klekovski, executive director of the MCIC, also believes that systemic reforms are necessary to build peace in Macedonia. According to him, while our ethnic problems are seen through the media in terms of gun battles in the mountains between the State military units and the extremists, we urgently need to look beyond these pictures to uncover the social injustice and poverty that sparked this conflict. Also, in order to achieve social justice Macedonia must have a sound economic base.

It is not enough to build trust between the Macedonian and Albanian people in Macedonia. Confidence must be generated in the country's governing institutions and the politicians who occupy them. The population needs to see reduced corruption and criminal behavior, elevated professionalism, and increased communication with the public. A strategic, visionary process must deal with the current dissonance between civic and ethnic identity. Macedonia needs to go back to the drawing board and decide through an inclusive and constructive process what kind of country its people want.

Resources

Reports
International Crisis Group
The Last Chance for Peace, Balkan Report 113, 20 June 2001.
The Macedonian Question: Reform or Rebellion, Balkan Report 109, 5 April 2001.
Macedonia's Name: Why the Dispute Matters and How to Resolve It, Balkan Report 122, 10 December 2001.
The Politics of Ethnicity and Conflict, unnumbered Report, 30 October 1997.
U.S. Institute for Peace, *The Future of Macedonia: A Balkan Survivor Now Needs Reform,* Special Report, March 2001.

Other Publications
Making Peace Prevail: Preventing Violent Conflict in Macedonia, by Alice Ackerman. Syracuse, NY, Syracuse University Press, 2000.
Nations in Transit: 1999–2000, edited by Adrian Karatnycky et al. New Brunswick, CT, Freedom House, 2001.
Peacebuilding in Macedonia: Searching for Common Ground in Civil Society, by Malvern Lumsden. Oslo, Norway, International Peace Research Institute, 1997.
The Macedonian Conflict: Ethnic Conflict in a Transnational World, by Loring Danforth. Princeton, NJ, University Press, 1995.
The New Macedonian Question, by James Pettifer. London, Palgrave, 2001.

Toward Comprehensive Peace in Southeast Europe: Conflict Prevention in the South Balkans, Center for Preventive Action, Council on Foreign Relations. New York, Twentieth Century Fund Press, 1996.

Vigilance and Vengeance: NGOs Preventing Ethnic Conflict in Divided Societies, edited by Robert Rotberg. Washington, DC, Brookings Institution Press, 1996.

Who Are the Macedonians? by Hugh Poulton. Indianapolis, Indiana University Press, 2000.

Selected Internet Sites

www.crisisweb.org (International Crisis Group)

www.delsol.net/~trufax/news/top_balkan_news.html (News on Macedonia from around the world)

www.iwpr.net (Institute for War & Peace Reporting)

www.mango.org.mk (Information on NGO activities and commentary on situation in Macedonia)

www.mia.com.mk (Macedonian Information Agency)

www.ok.mk (Articles and Local Analysis)

www.seecp.gov.mk/general_info.htm (South East European Cooperation Process)

www.stabilitypact.org (Stability Pact for South Eastern Europe)

Resource Contacts

Victoria Ayer, National Democratic Institute, Skopje, e-mail: ndi@mol.com.mk

Frosina Georgievska, Swiss Agency for Development and Cooperation, Skopje, e-mail: frosina.georgievska@sdc.net

Blerim Koljali, Center for Refugees and Forced Migration Studies, ISPPI, Skopje, e-mail: isppi@isppi.edu.mk

Mirjana Najcevska, Institute for Social, Juridical and Political Research, Skopje, e-mail: isppi@isppi.ukim.edu.mk

Saso Ordanovski, Forum, Skopje, e-mail: forum@unet.com.mk / info@forum.com.mk

Bekim Ymeri, Local Government Reform Project, Skopje, e-mail: Bekim_ymeri@dai.com

Organizations

Center for Multicultural Understanding and Cooperation
91000 Skopje
Macedonia
Tel./Fax: +389 02 130 407

CIVIL
Vasil Dglavinov 16
DTT Paloma Bijanca 3rd floor, nr. 13
91000 Skopje
Tel./Fax: +389 2 220 522
E-mail: civil_macedonia@yahoo.com

Multikultura
JNA bb (The Municipal Building)
Tetovo
Republic of Macedonia
Tel./Fax: +389 44 335 448
E-mail: multikultura@hotmail.com

Pax Christi
M.H. Jasmin 16 -1/49

Skopje
Tel.: +389 70 274759
E-mail: paxmak@netscape.net

Youth Information Center Tetovo
JNA 14
Tetovo
Tel.: +389 44 350 280
Fax: +389 44 331 423
E-mail: mic_sreten@yahoo.com
www.mkinter.net/mic

Data on the following organizations can be found in the Directory section:
Center for Balkans Co-operation
Center for Civic Initiative
Ethnic Conflict Resolution Project
Inter-Ethnic Program Gostivar
International Centre for Preventive Activities and Conflict Resolution
Macedonian Center for International Co-operation
Nansen Dialogue Center Skopje
Roma Centre of Skopje
Search for Common Ground in Macedonia

Sally Broughton is deputy director of Search for Common Ground in Macedonia and has been working in Skopje since January 1998. Eran Fraenkel has been executive director of Search for Common Ground in Macedonia since September 1994. He has been visiting the Balkans since the 1970s and spent several years conducting research in Macedonia and other countries in the region.

Notes

1. In this chapter, "Macedonians" refers to those people who are ethnic Macedonians. "Albanians" refers to ethnic Albanians living in Macedonia and not citizens of Albania unless otherwise identified. Other terms, such as "citizens of Macedonia" or "people in Macedonia," will be used to refer to all people living in Macedonia regardless of ethnic background.

2. The Yugoslav taxonomy had three levels: nation/*narod* (Macedonians and others who had republics named for them); nationality/*narodnost,* who had political entities or states outside the borders of Yugoslavia (Albanians, Turks, Hungarians, etc.); and ethnic community/*zaednica,* who had no political representation anywhere (Roma, Jews, etc.).

13.8

Moldova:
Peace Organizations
Search for Lasting Settlement

Jos Havermans

Violent conflict in Moldova has its roots in the carving up of the country and its predominantly Romanian-speaking people by the Russian and Ottoman empires. Official conflict management succeeded in negotiating a cease-fire, but did not come close to a resolution. A handful of NGOs helped to unblock the peace process as well as to shape it.

In August 1990, as the communist Soviet Empire was in dissolution, the former Soviet republic of Moldova, situated in between Romania and Ukraine along the Dniestr River, declared independence. The new state quickly gained international recognition. The postcommunist leadership in Moscow also accepted Moldova's secession. However, a considerable part of the inhabitants of a specific region of the new republic, the stretch of Moldovan territory across the Dniestr called Transdniestr, was unhappy with Moldovan independence. They staged protests.

Transdniestr's inhabitants are mostly of ethnic Russian origin and find it hard to sympathize with the desire of Moldovans to form their own state (or to reunite with Romania, as many Moldovans would favor) and cherish their own cultural identity. The Moldovan majority, on the other hand, shared bitter memories of the Soviet era, during which their cultural and ethnic identity was denied and suppressed. The Moldovans, therefore, felt little urge to accommodate the wish of the Russian minority, which for the most part had settled in Transdniestr in the 1940s, to stick to self-rule, or at least a fargoing form of autonomy in the Transdniestr region.

The dispute evolved into violent conflict in the late summer of 1991, when clashes occurred between Moldovan government forces and Transdniestr militia, which were allegedly advised and supported by members of the Russian army's fourteenth regiment, a unit with its home base in Transdniestr. Most of the fighting took place in the Transdniestr region and along the banks of the Dniestr River, with most bridges connecting Transdniestr with the Moldova

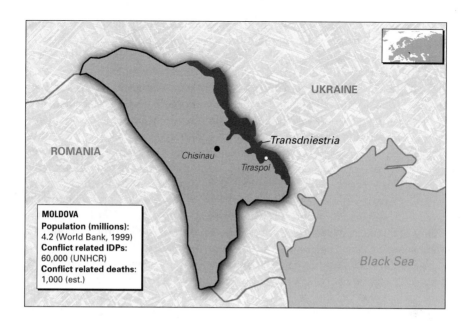

MOLDOVA
Population (millions):
4.2 (World Bank, 1999)
Conflict related IDPs:
60,000 (UNHCR)
Conflict related deaths:
1,000 (est.)

mainland destroyed. The most violent stage of the conflict was reached in April 1992 in the city of Bender on the heartland of Moldova. About one hundred armed fighters were killed on both sides.

Both official and nongovernmental interventions contributed to stop the violence. Officials of the ministries of foreign affairs of Russia, Romania, Ukraine, and Moldova, countries whose interests were directly involved in the conflict, formed special commissions that started to work on a settlement. These talks led to an agreement on a cease-fire in April 1992, followed by an agreement signed in July 1992 in Moscow by Moldovan president Mircea Snegur and Russian president Boris Yeltsin, stipulating a special status for the Transdniestrian region, to be elaborated later. The agreement also provided for the establishment of a so-called tripartite Joint Control Commission manned by representatives of Moldova, Transdniestr, and Russia, earmarked to work out an agreement on how to prevent further violence. This initiative resulted in the deployment of peacekeeping forces composed of Russian, Moldovan, and Transdniestrian troops. In 1997, Ukraine was invited to send observers as part of the peacekeeping mission.

In addition to arrangements for halting military confrontation, efforts were made to reach a long-term political agreement. The OSCE played an important role in this respect. In 1994, Moldova and Transdniestr formed groups of experts consisting of lawyers, experts in international law, and historians, who started to elaborate proposals for the solution of the conflict. OSCE representatives participated in these groups as mediators. The interaction between the participants of the expert groups is said to have changed from a direct confrontation to a cooperative attitude. Gradually, mutual understanding developed that the conflict should be solved within the framework of continued integrity of the Republic of Moldova. The most difficult and persisting problem is the extent of autonomy that will be allowed to the Transdniestr region.

NGOs work to reduce mistrust between the two conflicting parties, both on the level of political leaders as the general population. The Northern Ireland–based NGO Moldovan Initiative Committee of Management, in collaboration with academic institutes such as the Centre for Conflict Analyses of the University of Kent (UK) and the German Berghof Research Center for Constructive Conflict Management, worked to build up conflict-resolution knowhow in Moldova and is often consulted when negotiations on the higher political level reach a stalemate. Workshops were organized where negotiators from both sides could meet, followed up by a study tour to Northern Ireland. Many of the ideas that evolved from these activities were incorporated into the final series of peace agreements between the two sides.

The Joint Committee for Democratization and Conciliation (JCDC), a local NGO run by people from both the Moldova and Transdniestr communities, has taken a number of initiatives aimed at bridging the gap between the opposing parties on both sides of the Dniestr River. It organizes a festival of folk music on both sides of the river, and initiated the "Bridge of Trust" project, a mutual ecological program for the preservation of the Dniestr. JCDC puts much effort into bringing younger generations of the two opposing entities together, saying it may take another generation to find a final settlement for the conflict.

Resources

Selected Internet Sites
www.home.moldpac.md/~savelkin/frontpage.htm (Joint Committee for Democratization and Conciliation)
www.iatp.md (Viitorul Foundation, Moldovan NGO)
www.ifes.md (International Foundation for Election Systems)
www.moldova.org (Moldovan government site)
www.soros.md (Soros Foundation)

Data on the following organizations can be found in the Directory section:
InfoTAG
Institute for Public Policy
Joint Committee for Democratization and Conciliation

Jos Havermans is a senior journalist based in the Netherlands. He specializes in international affairs.

13.9

Federal Republic of Yugoslavia: A State in Search of Its Future

Filip Pavlovic & Franklin de Vrieze

The following text is a brief introduction to the Federal Republic of Yugoslavia (FRY), which consists of the republics of Serbia and Montenegro and two nominally autonomous provinces, Kosovo (under UN control) and Vojvodina. FRY was created in 1992 after the dissolution of the Socialist Federal Republic of Yugoslavia (SFRY), a state that had been composed of six republics (Slovenia, Croatia, Bosnia-Herzegovina, Serbia, Montenegro, and Macedonia) and two autonomous provinces (Kosovo and Vojvodina). This chapter is intended to inform the reader about the process and nature of FRY's creation and how the state is organized and constitutionalized. It is also intended to enhance understanding of the following surveys on Serbia, Montenegro, and Kosovo, which focus on the conflict dynamics in each of these territories.

To understand the process of creation of the Federal Republic of Yugoslavia, one needs to take into consideration the basis and interests upon which it is constructed. On 11 April 1992, in the twilight hours of the Socialist Federal Republic of Yugoslavia and against a backdrop of war looming or already under way in Croatia and Bosnia, the two republics of Serbia and Montenegro announced the formation of a joint independent state, the FRY. Besides historical, ethnic, and cultural ties between two member states, there were practical and pragmatic geopolitical reasons for a quick process of forming a joint state. The first was the fact that FRY insisted that it was the successor to SFRY, which had ceased to function at that time. The second reason was a nonofficial but direct involvement of Serbia and Montenegro in the wars in Croatia and Bosnia and Herzegovina. FRY was recognized as a state by the European Union in 1996 and in November 2000 by the United Nations and the United States.

Government

Administrative Divisions
The two republics of Serbia and Montenegro and the two nominally autonomous provinces of Kosovo, currently under UN control, and Vojvodina administratively compose FRY. The legal system is based on a civil law system.

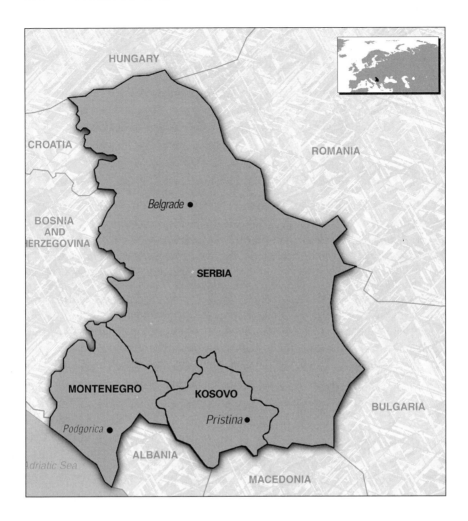

Legislative Branches

The bicameral Federal Assembly consists of the Chamber of Republics and the Chamber of Citizens. The Chamber of Republics contains forty seats, distributed among twenty Serbian and twenty Montenegrin representatives. Members serve for four years. Until the constitution was amended in 2000, these forty seats were distributed on the basis of party representation in the two individual republican assemblies in Montenegro and Serbia. Seats were filled on a proportional basis to reflect the composition of the legislatures of these two republics. Following two events in Montenegro, namely the split in the ruling Democratic Party of Socialists and the electoral victory of Milo Djukanovic in 1997, Serbia has effectively barred Montenegro from its constitutional right to delegate deputies to the Chamber of Republics, as of 1998.

The Chamber of Citizens has 138 seats. One hundred and eight seats are occupied by Serbians, half of whom are elected on the basis of simple constituency majorities, and the other half through proportional representation. Thirty seats are for Montenegrins, six of whom are elected on the basis of simple constituency majority, and the other twenty-four through proportional representation. Members also serve four-year terms.

Judicial Branch
Judicial branches are the Federal Court and Constitutional Court; the Federal Assembly elects judges for nine-year terms.

The Constitution
In March 1992 the socialists of Serbia and Montenegro, who were in power at the time of the collapse of the SFRY, announced the preparation of the new constitution of FRY. The constitution that changed the social structure and introduced a market economy was written in only twenty days. Both the Chamber of Republics and the Chamber of Citizens debated the federal constitution draft until late at night on 23 April. There were numerous objections on the part of the opposition, not only relating to the content but also to the manner in which the draft constitution was presented at the incomplete Federal Council with its delegates' mandates expired. Still, the proposal was adopted.

The process had also been criticized in other quarters, including legal experts. Bones of contention included its hasty composition, the incomplete formulation—-indeed, there are many omissions—and the fact that the process had taken place under the dictate of only one party. In sum, it was said that the new Yugoslavia has been created "behind closed doors."

Since its adoption, the 1992 Constitution has been amended on several occasions, two of which stand out because they had radical consequences when brought before parliament in the course of the year 2000. The consequences ran counter to those planned by the Socialist Party of Serbia and the Serbian Radical Party, which were still in power at the time. The first one was that Slobodan Milosevic lost the direct presidential elections. This had been introduced following an amendment that moved the presidential elections out of the Federal Assembly. The second was the announcement of the beginning of the separation process of Montenegro from Yugoslavia. This was associated with changes in the election procedures for the Chamber of Republics. Instead of being chosen from the ranks of the republican assemblies, as was the case until then, representatives were to be elected directly.

The notion that the FRY constitution is largely "a dead letter on paper" is confirmed by the fact that the constitution of Serbia has never been reconciled with it. There are also numerous regulations of the former SFRY that were never balanced with the 1992 Constitution but are still in effect.

Composition of the Population
The FRY is a very heterogeneous community. Together with Serbs and Montenegrins, members of more than twenty ethnic groups, which make up almost 33 percent of the total number of citizens, live in its territory. According to the 1991

census, the composition of ethnic groups is as follows: Serb, 62.6 percent; Albanian, 16.5 percent; Montenegrin, 5 percent; Yugoslav, 3.4 percent; Hungarian, 3.3 percent; and other, 9.2 percent. The proportion of religion groups is: Orthodox Christians, 65 percent; Muslims, 19 percent; Roman Catholics, 4 percent; Protestants, 1 percent; and other, 11 percent. Despite the fact that the constitution of the FRY assumes that all citizens are equal and recognizes and guarantees freedoms and rights established by the acts of international law, FRY was a stage of disputes, conflicts, and violence on interethnic and interreligious bases.

Economy

The swift collapse of the Yugoslav federation in 1991 has been followed by highly destructive warfare and the breakup of important interrepublic trade flows. Output in Serbia and Montenegro dropped by half in 1992–1993. Like the other former Yugoslav republics, it had depended on its sister republics for large amounts of energy and manufactured products. Wide differences in climate, mineral resources, and levels of technology among the republics accentuated this interdependence, as did the communist practice of concentrating industrial output in a small number of giant plants. The breakup of many of the trade links, the sharp drop in output as industrial plants lost suppliers and markets, and the destruction of physical assets in the fighting all have contributed to the economic difficulties of the FRY. One singular factor in the economic situation of Serbia was the continuation in office of a government that was primarily interested in political and military mastery, not economic reform. Hyperinflation ended with the establishment of a new currency unit in June 1993; prices were relatively stable from 1995 through 1997, but inflationary pressures resurfaced in 1998.

The economic boom anticipated by the government after the suspension of UN sanctions in December 1995 has failed to materialize. Government's mismanagement of the economy is largely to blame and the heavy damage to Serbia's infrastructure and industry by the NATO bombing during the war in Kosovo has added to problems. To this can be added the sanctions that continued to isolate Belgrade from international financial institutions, an investment ban and asset freeze imposed in 1998, and the oil embargo imposed during the NATO bombing. All of these remained in place until democratic changes took place in Serbia in October 2000.

The breakup of trade links between Serbia and Montenegro in 1998–2000 followed political disputes between two member states. The Montenegrin government refused to work under jurisdiction of the Federal Customs Management. At the same time, the Serbian government has established custom control checkpoints on the administrative border. New economy reorientation and promised reforms are challenged by an extremely hard economical situation, especially in social services, energy, health care, and industrial branches.

Grim Reality

One of the most important consequences of the actions of the regime that was removed from power in September 2000 is the utter devaluation of the meaning and credibility of the institutions in FRY. The manner in which the regime of Slobodan Milosevic has used and manipulated these institutions is in many ways noticeable even today. The actual centers of power were not identical to the official ones, and sometimes the two were even in conflict.

There were numerous occasions when Milosevic, as president of the republic, was directly and obviously influencing decisionmaking processes at the federal level. The nomination, election, and later replacement (after a bitter power struggle) of Milan Panic, FRY's first prime minister, and Dobrica Cosic, the first president of FRY, were very clear examples.

While Slobodan Milosevic was president of Serbia (until 1997), the focus of financial investment and modernization was the republican Ministry of Internal Affairs (MUP), and after he had been elected president of FRY, the larger part of the budget was being set aside for the federal Yugoslav army. This trend intensified before, during, and after the NATO bombing.

The fate of the institutions such as the federal police, national bank, federal customs management, and federal secretary of information is crucial. Focusing on the police, one can see that since 1993, when the republican police illegally took possession of the Federal Police Headquarters building, this institution has not functioned properly and has been completely deprived of its meaning. The same can be said of the other important federal institutions. After the democratic changes in Serbia, the relations inside the federation have not altered significantly, but certain conditions for their institutional and qualitative changes have been made. A long and difficult process of regaining trust in the institutions of the system has been initiated. The extradition of former president Milosevic to the International Criminal Tribunal for the former Yugoslavia in The Hague on 28 June 2001 caused a federal government crisis, supposedly leading to new elections and/or a revised FRY constitution.

The Future

It would be wrong to say that the Federal Republic of Yugoslavia is a nonexistent country. It is recognized by the United Nations, the United States, the European Union, Russia, the International Monetary Fund, the Stability Pact for South Eastern Europe, and other important international actors. The shift in Belgrade's position away from claiming to be the only successor state of the SFRY and toward accepting being one of the successor states is significant. Final agreement regarding the assets of the former SFRY was reached on 25 May 2001. The agreement covers property, foreign exchange reserves, archives, pensions, and other national proprietary concerns.

The time of challenges has clearly come; the context of the Yugoslav republic is (and will be) reshaping and changing. The constitution, laws, and regulations that have been written and designed according to the aspirations of former governments in Serbia and Montenegro will have to be modified. Is there strength, wisdom, and willingness to reshape FRY in accordance to modern world's needs and standards? The answer to this question is the same as the answer to that other frequently asked question: whether FRY, as such, is still a going concern.

Filip Pavlovic was born in Belgrade, Serbia/Yugoslavia, where he also studied philosophy. He is editor in chief of the magazine Kulturtreger *and cofounder and president of the steering board of the NGO Fractal. He was involved in several projects and conferences oriented toward confidence-building measures between Serbia-Kosovo and Serbia-Montenegro. From January 2000 to June 2001, he was initiator and program coordinator of the EU-Serbia program "From Exclusion to Integration."*

Franklin de Vrieze has been following developments in the Balkans on a professional basis since 1992. He facilitated a five-year dialogue project between Albanian and Serbian political parties and NGOs on behalf of Pax Christi. He is currently working for the OSCE Mission in Kosovo.

13.10

Kosovo:
Civil Society Awaits a
Chance for Reconciliation

Franklin de Vrieze

After a decades-long political conflict and the war of 1998–1999, Kosovo is trying to recover and to build a democratic and stable society. The period of self-rule will be an important test in building institutions and establishing rule of law. However, ongoing security problems are continuing to threaten all efforts to leave the period of conflict behind. An internationally facilitated dialogue on the final status of Kosovo seems unavoidable.

Taking into account the long history of tensions around Kosovo—since Tito's rule of the former Yugoslavia and long before—the origins of the most recent stage of the conflict have to be understood in terms of the new wave of nationalism in the 1970s and 1980s in the former Yugoslavia. Kosovo, since 1974 one of the eight constituent units of the Yugoslav federation but formally a province within the Republic of Serbia, became a rallying point during the rise to power of Slobodan Milosevic. The removal of autonomy from Kosovo and Voijvodina in 1989 was a key moment in a series of events leading to demands for independence from other republics.

The revocation of Kosovo's autonomy initiated an increase in human-rights abuses and discriminatory government policies designed to put Serbs in most key positions in the province, inhabited by a majority population of ethnic Albanians. However, it would be a mistake to see the Kosovo crisis during the 1990s as a human-rights issue only. Both Kosovo-Albanian politicians and the Serbian government agreed that more was at stake.

Once the Yugoslav federation fell apart, the right to self-determination became the central demand of Kosovo-Albanian politicians, leading to a declaration of independence in 1991. Serbia denounced what it perceived as separatism and insisted upon respect for the territorial integrity of the newly formed Federal Republic of Yugoslavia (FRY) of which the Republics of Serbia and Montenegro became the two constituent parts.

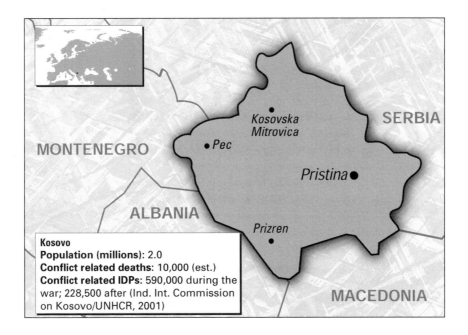

Kosovo
Population (millions): 2.0
Conflict related deaths: 10,000 (est.)
Conflict related IDPs: 590,000 during the war; 228,500 after (Ind. Int. Commission on Kosovo/UNHCR, 2001)

In order to achieve independence, Kosovo-Albanian leader Ibrahim Rugova, elected in 1992 as "President of the Republic of Kosovo," opted for a two-way strategy: building a parallel society and internationalizing the Kosovo question. The parallel society was aimed at implementing the desired independence by ignoring Serbian state institutions as far as possible and building its own institutions, in particular in the fields of education, health care, and political institutions. Internationalizing the Kosovo question resulted in international sympathy for the nonviolent approach of Rugova and the parallel system.

Serbian authorities insisted Kosovo was an internal affair and rejected any formal mediation in the conflict (until mid-1998). They hoped that the parallel system would get exhausted and that the Albanian community would accommodate with the status quo. The status quo was also advantageous for Milosevic in the sense that his party gained almost all parliamentary seats due to the Kosovo-Albanian boycott of political life in Serbia. Both parties ignored each other, assuming time was on their side.

During the end of 1996 and the beginning of 1997, Milosevic was under heavy pressure from three months of demonstrations by Serbian opposition and students demanding him to accept his defeat in local elections. However, the main Serbian opposition parties did not have fundamentally different opinions on the status of Kosovo within Serbia and FRY—with the exception of recognizing the need for foreign mediation.

In Pristina, Rugova was confronted with increasing criticism for the perceived lack of results of the strategy of nonviolence. The exclusion of the

Kosovo question from the Dayton negotiations and the diplomatic recognition of FRY in 1996, before any progress was made on the Kosovo question, led a growing number of Kosovars to conclude that violence was the only way to attract international attention.

In an effort to win time and to avoid the difficult issue of the status of Kosovo, on 1 September 1996 Belgrade and Pristina agreed to reopen all school and university premises for Albanian students. However, the failure to implement the education agreement, negotiated by the Italian-based Sant Egidio Community, directed the Independent Student Union of the University of Pristina to organize massive nonviolent protests for the unconditional return of university premises. It became clear Rugova's party, the Democratic League of Kosovo (LDK), was no longer in control of Kosovar Albanian political life. The violent suppression by Serbian police forces of student protests indicated that the possibilities of more active nonviolent resistance in Kosovo was exhausted. The step-by-step approach in settling different aspects of the conflict also seemed to have failed.

Frequently attacking police units in Kosovo, the Kosovo Liberation Army (KLA) made public appearances at funerals of its fighters and sympathizers from November 1997 on, attracting tens of thousands of people. Serbian forces accelerated their actions. Serbian civilians were armed and paramilitary groups entered Kosovo from Serbia. On 28 February 1998, heavily armed Yugoslav forces attacked the Drenica area and killed KLA leader Adem Jashari and fifty-eight other inhabitants of the villages. This turned out to be a turning point for public opinion in Kosovo. While openly confronting Serbian police control, KLA declared "liberated territories" within central Kosovo.

While on the Albanian side KLA actions were increasingly judged as legitimate acts of self-defense, Serbian authorities became even more determined to destroy terrorism. After the war, KLA leader Hashim Thaçi acknowledged attacks were sometimes aimed at provoking a Serbian response and endangering local population, since this would increase chances of foreign military involvement in the conflict.

From February 1998 until March 1999 the domestic and international political agenda was dominated by the fighting on the ground. While the international community was paying little attention to the Kosovo conflict during its earlier phase, media coverage of civilian casualties and internally displaced persons initiated intensive international mediation, the so-called coercive diplomacy, or diplomacy with the threat of force. After increasing pressure in October 1998, U.S. diplomat Richard Holbrooke and Slobodan Milosevic reached an agreement that included the deployment of the OSCE Kosovo Verification Mission. It helped to ease tensions between October and December 1998 and facilitated the survival of local populations throughout the winter.

The killing of forty-five Albanians in Raçak in January 1999 became another turning point in the conflict. Although forensic reports indicate that these people had been shot from a short distance, it remains in dispute whether they were civilians or combatants. Clearly, the Raçak events contributed to the indictment against Slobodan Milosevic and other Serb officials by the International Criminal Tribunal for the former Yugoslavia (ICTY). It also functioned as a galvanizing moment to unite European and U.S. allies behind a last effort to find a diplomatic solution: the Rambouillet negotiations.

During these negotiations, crucial parts of the political proposals and the prospect of the deployment in Kosovo of an international military implementation force—with NATO at its core—remained unacceptable for Belgrade. After the Albanian delegation unilaterally signed the Rambouillet texts and with the aim to force the Serbian delegation to do the same, NATO started a bombing campaign against the FRY that lasted from 24 March until 10 June 1999. Yugoslav and Serbian forces, paramilitaries, and criminal groups committed war crimes and organized a campaign of ethnic cleansing in Kosovo, which overwhelmed neighboring Macedonia and Albania. Actually, two simultaneous military confrontations took place: a continued armed conflict between Yugoslav army, Serbian police, and paramilitaries on one hand, and KLA on the other hand; a war between NATO and Yugoslav/Serbian forces.

One could claim the first armed conflict has never been officially terminated (no cease-fire). The second war had been concluded by the Kumanovo agreement on the withdrawal of FRY forces and authorities and start of the Kosovo Force (KFOR) and United Nations Interim Administration Mission in Kosovo (UNMIK) rule in Kosovo. After the changes in Belgrade and following the cooperation with NATO in South Serbia, Belgrade politicians are considering whether to join NATO's Partnership for Peace Program.

Conflict Dynamics

After intense negotiations between the representatives of the United States, the European Union, and Russia, the UN Security Council adopted Resolution 1244 on 10 June 1999, setting out the guidelines for the international community's response to the postwar situation in Kosovo. UNSC 1244 endorsed an interim administration in Kosovo that established its internal structure along four pillars: humanitarian affairs (UNHCR), civil administration (UNMIK), democratization and institution building (OSCE), and economic development (EU). UNSC 1244 also mandated the international security presence (KFOR) with the responsibility for establishing a secure environment for all citizens of Kosovo and the international organizations working in Kosovo and for providing appropriate control of the borders/boundaries of Kosovo. One of the points from UNSC 1244 that aroused a lot of comments was the combined commitment to "substantial autonomy and meaningful self-administration for Kosovo" together with "respect for the sovereignty and territorial integrity of FRY."

After the summer of 1999, Kosovo was characterized by a high level of crime and aggression against the non-Albanian population, primarily Serbs. As a result, the remaining Serb population in Kosovo is now living in isolated enclaves in the north of Kosovo and in Mitrovica.

While in the beginning the violence was perceived as isolated attacks by individuals looking for revenge, UNHCR and OSCE judged in February 2001

that the pattern of violence had changed, that attacks became more highly organized, coordinated, and carefully targeted than was previously the case. The
violence includes unlawful occupation of minority-owned properties and so-
called strategic sales. This can be defined as a practice whereby the minority
owners of property located within strategically important areas are induced to
sell their property, as part of what appears to be an organized campaign. This
inducement to sell may be linked to threats of or actual violence. In the area of
Kosovo Polje/Fushe Kosove, numerous cases have been documented by OSCE.
In Mitrovica, property disputes involve both Serb and Albanian people unable
to regain their property in the other part of the town.

In spite of the presence of 37,000 armed soldiers, international governmental organizations seemed unable or insufficiently prepared to stop ethnically motivated violence and organized crime, which has shaken the confidence of the minority groups and has created frustration and confusion among
the common Albanian population. While international political leaders increasingly blamed Kosovar Albanians for the ongoing climate of insecurity,
they couldn't manage to establish the mechanisms of security, i.e., an effective
police and justice system, which they were bound to do under the UN mandate. While pointing at the culture of silence of locals in relation to crime,
UNMIK too often did not include local capacities in combatting crime.

The highly deficient judiciary stems from a lack of international judges
and independent local judges who cannot be pressured, lack of well-guarded
prison facilities, and lack of uniform penal legislation. Since the UN international police were not very effective in combatting crime, one can claim that
an international police force would be more effective if set up by a regional
organization such as OSCE or EU. In so doing, police would be recruited from
a smaller number of countries, while today they are brought in from all over
the world, with widely varying cultural backgrounds and professional skills.
Giving more responsibility to the local police force, trained at the Kosovo Police School in Vucitrn/Vushtri, in investigation and other police work could
also contribute to a better security situation.

On 21 June 1999, NATO and KLA signed an agreement on the demilitarization of KLA, but it is widely believed that a big share of the weaponry has
not been handed over to KFOR. A number of KLA individuals were incorporated into a civilian agency for emergency help and reconstruction, the Kosovo
Protection Corps (KPC). Despite objection from KFOR and other representatives of the international community, leading figures within KPC seemed to
perceive this protection corps as the foundation of a future army of an independent Kosovo.

The main political factors on the Kosovo-Albanian side are Ibrahim Rugova and his Democratic League of Kosovo, Hashim Tahçi and the Democratic Party of Kosovo (the main political party emerging from the KLA), and
Ramush Haradinaj (former KLA commander now heading the Alliance for a
Better Future of Kosova). All parties strongly advocate international recognition of an independent Kosovo, with international rule as an intermediate

Teun Voeten/Panos Pictures

Djakovica: Man holding the burnt driver license of his brother, who was shot down by Serbian paramilitaries (June 1999)

phase. In the weeks and months leading up to the Kosovo local elections on 28 October 2000, violent attacks or threats against journalists and political activists, mainly from LDK, took place. Leading Kosovo-Albanian opinion makers such as Veton Surroi clearly spoke out against the violence, including the violence against minority groups.

On the Serbian side, the Serb National Council in Gracanica, under the leadership of Bishop Artemije (and until end of 2000, also Father Sava Janjic), was challenged by Serb politicians from Mitrovica headed by Oliver Ivanovic. While the Gracanica-Serbs were generally more favorable to cooperation with UNMIK in order to achieve their aims of return of Serb refugees and protection of Serb civilians and cultural monuments, the lack of progress on these matters became an obstacle for the Mitrovica-Serbs to fully cooperate with UNMIK structures. Ivanovic recently lost his influence to Momcilo Trajkovic, FRY President Kostunica's representative in Kosovo, and Marko Jaksic, his representative in Mitrovica. At the beginning of July 2001, Nebojsa Covic, who successfully mediated in the crisis in southern Serbia, was appointed head of the Serbian government coordination team for Kosovo. Father Sava Janjic was one of the very few Kosovo Serb opinion makers admitting mistakes and past crimes against Albanians while appealing for tolerance and protection for Serbs in Kosovo.

The divided city of Mitrovica remains a focal point for renewed tensions and conflict. After a high number of atrocities committed during the war,

Albanians moved to a large extent to the south, while Serbs—also from other parts of Kosovo—moved to the north of the city, which is north of the Ibar River. So-called bridge watchers and remnants of the security forces of Serbia increased tensions toward Albanians trying to visit relatives in the north. Albanians are claiming that KFOR policy contributed to the division of the city, while the international community is stressing that security and the people's right to return to the original place where they lived remain its first preoccupation.

The electoral defeat of Slobodan Milosevic and the inauguration of Voijislav Kostunica as new FRY president have had a major impact on developments in Kosovo. As long as Kosovar Albanians are still imprisoned in Serbia (while hundreds of Serbs, Albanians, and others are also still missing), Kosovo-Albanian political leaders remain very reluctant toward a dialogue with Belgrade. At the same time, the international community has become engaged in active partnership with the new Belgrade, discussing all issues, including Kosovo.

The crisis in southern Serbia and the support coming from Kosovo for the Liberation Army of Presevo, Medveda, and Bujanovac (UCPMB) brought the European Union even closer to Belgrade's concerns. NATO mediated a ceasefire between Yugoslav and Serbian forces on the one hand and armed Albanians on the other, leaving space for a political agenda on eliminating the discrimination of local Albanians in southern Serb society. NATO gave the green light for Yugoslav forces to return to the Ground Safety Zone around Kosovo. Hundreds of UCPMB fighters welcomed the deal to leave for Kosovo and escape persecution in Serbia.

The origins of the crisis in Macedonia are complex. Addressing the concerns and fears of both Macedonians and Albanians will probably be a long process at both the political level and within the society. A link to the Kosovo question could be found in the connections between the National Liberation Army (NLA; UCK in Macedonia), underground circles in Kosovo, and the Albanian diaspora operating from Zurich and Pristina. Some Albanians from Macedonia joined UCK in Kosovo during 1998–1999. After the war they felt no longer welcome or safe in Macedonia and stayed in Kosovo. Some of them returned to Macedonia to join NLA, since integration in Kosovar society didn't succeed as hoped.

Official Conflict Management

Important official conflict management initiatives within Kosovo are related to the efforts to include leading Albanian and Serbian politicians in governing Kosovo. In order to fulfil the UNMIK mandate to develop "provisional democratic self-government institutions," Dr. Bernard Koushner, special representative of the UN Secretary-General (SRSG), created the Kosovo Transitional Council (KTC). The weekly KTC meetings have consultative and advisory functions, hoping to bring about a process of dialogue and peacemaking among the political leadership of Kosovo.

On 15 December 1999, UNMIK established the Joint Interim Administrative Structure (JIAS), a body involving representatives of a broad cross section of Kosovar society. From this body evolved the Joint Interim Administrative Council, which functions as an executive body. Twenty departments or ministries have been established, each of which is controlled by two heads, one international and one local. The creation of these structures were accompanied by the dissolution of all parallel structures, including the Kosovo Provisional Government headed by Prime Minister Hashim Thaçi and Ibrahim Rugova's function as president of the Republic of Kosovo.

Frustration among local populations about the constraints on self-rule indicated a need for much greater involvement and responsibility of Kosovars at all levels of governance. SRSG Koushner judged that a first step would be local elections on 28 October 2000, as a means for Kosovo to improve its democratic credentials. The campaign of Albanian political parties focused more on mechanisms to implement independence than on the local issues of how to run a community. UNMIK tried to preempt postelection violence with a visit from U.S. diplomat Richard Holbrooke, who persuaded the five largest political parties to sign a joint statement agreeing to recognize the ballot results. LDK gained a convincing victory following voter dissatisfaction with the "revolutionary behavior" of the ex-KLA leadership, who had forcibly gained political and economical advantages after the war. However, Albanian parties saw these elections more as a warm-up exercise for the real "battle": parliamentary elections in November 2001.

A particular form of official conflict management had to do with Yugoslav and Serbian elections on 24 September and 23 December 2000. While the international community agreed that Kosovo is part of FRY, it was not eager to organize the September elections in Kosovo, since it had no confidence at all that the Yugoslav presidential and parliamentary elections would be free and fair. Moreover, any direct involvement of UNMIK in these elections could considerably increase tensions with the Albanian majority population. Finally, they decided not to object if the Yugoslav state were to organize the elections in the Serbian parts of Kosovo, but outside of official buildings. With the Democratic Opposition of Serbia ready to defeat Milosevic also on the republican level on 23 December 2000, UNMIK decided to facilitate Kosovo Serbs participating in these elections, while the Serbian election commission dropped all Albanians from the voters list.

Despite UNMIK's aim to hand over policy and management responsibilities to both Albanian and Serbian politicians in Kosovo, there has been considerable criticism of the approach of the international community in Kosovo. After the war, international officials took over almost all official Yugoslav positions of authority, leaving local Albanian or local Serb expertise aside in developing legislation, managing institutions, and analyzing problems. The local co-heads in UNMIK departments have very little policy influence and often no access to all documents. Also, after the local elections of 28 October 2000, international administrators kept crucial competences. There are growing demands for accountability for internationals governing Kosovo, demands stemming from Kosovar political parties, elected representatives, and the UN ombudsperson, Marek Antoni Nowicki.

A particular form of official conflict management has to do with the question of ongoing displacement of minority populations. The primary motivation for such emigration is fear for physical security as well as restrictions on freedom of movement and limited access to basic services and employment prospects. The UNHCR has worked on promoting the creation of conditions conducive for refugee return. With representatives of the Kosovo Serbs, they reached a consensus on a "Framework for Return 2001," the basic principles upon which to base further activities linked to the potential return of Kosovo Serbs. The UNHCR has embarked on a series of consultations with prominent Kosovo Albanians to solicit their views on how to proceed. Roma, Ashkaelia, and Egyptian communities also faced displacement. As a result of the Humanitarian Round Tables with representatives of these three communities, UNHCR negotiated a Platform of Joint Action (April 2000), which initiated direct talks with officials of the JIAS, including Kosovo-Albanian politicians and intellectuals. While Kosovo Albanians have returned to the province in huge numbers, the question of Kosovo Albanians returning to locations where they constitute a numerical minority, such as the towns of Mitrovica and Strpce, still demands special attention.

As part of a larger anticrime effort aimed a taking out of circulation the huge quantity of weaponry, which remained in Kosovo nearly two years after the conflict, UNMIK launched a weapons amnesty campaign between 1 May and 3 June 2001. KFOR continues to forcibly confiscate weapons and weapon depots.

Since the international community in Kosovo is no longer a mediator but an active player in the field, with its own interests to have its mission accomplished without casualties, it becomes clear that official conflict management is developing along three lines: (1) between the international community itself and the local population, (2) between local Albanians and Serbs, and (3) between the Albanian representatives and Belgrade, who are not yet at the beginning of any meaningful dialogue.

On 17 November 2001 members of all of Kosovo's communities voted for a new Kosovo Assembly, bringing to an end the ten-year-old separated, parallel political systems Albanians and Serbs were entrenched in. The OSCE mission in Kosovo has delivered upon its commitment to provide safe and convenient access to the electoral process to all voters and communities.

Rugova's LDK gained 46 percent of the votes, Thaci's PDK got 25 percent, AAK got 8 percent, and Coalition Return 11 percent. Since none of the parties got a majority in the 120-seat Assembly, a coalition government is unavoidable. The new transitional Kosovo authorities will be responsible for most policy areas, while SRSG remains the guarantor for respect for the UNSC 1244 provisions and the overall security policy. However, many political analysts expect growing tensions between UNMIK and the Kosovo institutions over the issue of the final status of Kosovo. The parties in the governing coalition will be challenged to deliver progress in the fields of economic recovery, establishing a social and health security system, improving education standards, and diminishing poverty. This challenge will be all the more pressing with new municipal elections ahead for the end of 2002.

Multi-Track Diplomacy

Semiofficial Dialogue
During a long-standing conflict or under new political circumstances, NGOs can play a distinctive role by bringing together key political players in a neutral and informal atmosphere.

The Project on Ethnic Relations (PER) of Princeton University in the United States organized Serb-Albanian semiofficial roundtable discussions in 1997. In December 2000, in Skopje, PER organized a significant conference— "Albanians as Majorities and Minorities: A Regional Dialogue"—that became the first face-to-face meeting between the Kosovo-Albanian leadership and members of the new government in Belgrade. Belgrade authorities reiterated Kostunica's offer to meet Rugova to discuss the situation in Kosovo. Kosovo Albanians indicated it was too early for that, referring to the general elections after which the new Kosovar institutions would have a full mandate to conduct talks with Belgrade and all actors. Kosovo-Albanian and Kosovo Serb leaders agreed that full protection of the rights of minorities in Kosovo must be provided.

Based upon a detailed proposal, the rights of Serbs were the topic of an in-depth discussion in Prishtina on 21 December 2000, organized by the Kosova Action for Civic Initiatives (KACI). KACI's proposal was exceptionally concrete in describing rights for minority groups in the fields of language, parliamentary representation, administration and judiciary, culture, and religion.

The U.S. Institute for Peace (USIP) brought together all relevant Kosovo-Albanian and Serb political and community leaders in July 2000 at Airly, Virginia. They adopted a "Pact Against Violence" covering such subjects as elections, media, civil society, security, refugee return, and areas for priority attention for the international community. In March 2001, USIP brought together Kosovo's newly elected mayors, deputy mayors, and municipal assembly members, calling for the adoption of a legal framework for Kosovo-wide institutions and establishment of an independent ombudsman.

From 1995 until 1999, Pax Christi Flanders and The Netherlands facilitated a dialogue program between Serbian and Albanian political parties, NGOs, and student associations involving representatives from twenty organizations. Meetings on points of common interest between the two groups, visits to Belgrade and Prishtina by people from the other community, and an exploration and comparison with the political process in Northern Ireland were the main elements of the program. After the war, the cooperation with Northern Ireland continued, this time with the different communities from Kosovo.

Local Civil Society in Kosovo

Efforts to stabilize and improve life in Kosovo will have to focus on different types of associations, broader than the classical NGOs, including human-rights groups, humanitarian organizations, women's and youth organizations, educational and cultural organizations, professional associations and unions, and minority-rights associations, among others. As was the case in other areas of the former Yugoslavia, civil-society organizations (CSOs) mushroomed in the wake of the dissolution of Yugoslavia in 1989. After the revocation of Kosovo's autonomy, organizations and networks in the fields of human rights, health, education, and rights for women, youth, and students were established. This parallel, well-organized infrastructure facilitated basic community services and advocated the interests of the Albanian population. They also provided unity and discipline, which were crucial under the conditions of repression. However, structures that served well during this time of repression are not necessarily well suited to a new situation of institution building, democratization, and developing pluralism.

Also in the 1990s, several NGOs emerged calling for peace and tolerance among Kosovars and between Albanians and Serbs. Nansen Group, Post-Pessimists, Albanian Youth Action Pjeter Bogdani, and others facilitated contacts among young people from the different communities. Their efforts, often with the support of international NGOs, were unable to influence the rising violence escalating to war. Today, while CSOs and individuals within the ethnic communities may discuss the need for tolerance, most Kosovars agree reconciliation on a wider scale must wait. Consequently, multiethnic CSOs are a rarity in Kosovo today. The realization of a large number of widely spread interethnic projects seems unrealistic in the short run. Civil-society building will have to take its starting point in the separate communities, and then see what local civil-society networks can gradually build upon to stimulate and support community building around Kosovo to ease tensions between members of different ethnic communities.

The collapse of the former Yugoslav federation, ten years of isolation in Kosovo, the war, and the return of groups of Kosovar refugees are heavily affecting social and economical life in today's Kosovo. The erosion of the middle class, serving in their functions as teachers, doctors, engineers, civil servants, et al., has been evident since the conflict. The middle class, as one of the main carriers of a democratic society, realizes very few options for active involvement in the improvement of social and economic life. The need for defining a much wider understanding of CSOs beyond the role of classical nonprofit NGOs will be crucial for these forces to be mobilized. Nearly half of the NGOs started since 1998, and many only first constituted themselves after registration at UNMIK began in mid-December 1999.

From an almost uncountable number of CSOs, we would like to give the following short overview of local CSOs.

Organizations assisting the NGO sector. The Kosovo Foundation for Open Society is an active link to the Soros Network that supports local civil-society initiatives, including cultural groups and media. The Kosovo Civil Society Foundation primarily concentrates on information and data collection, capacity building of local NGOs, and civil education programs. The Association for Democratic Initiatives is dealing with NGO development, media, and youth centers. Kosova Action for Civic Initiatives organizes cultural and educational programs, round tables, and, as an independent policy think tank, monitored local elections on 28 October 2000.

Human-rights organizations. During the last ten years, the Council for Defence of Human Rights and Freedoms has been one of the major sources on human-rights violations in Kosovo. After the war, the organization is carefully developing new skills and awareness of minority questions. The Kosovo Helsinki Committee is a branch of the International Helsinki Federation for Human Rights in Vienna. The Humanitarian Law Fund from Belgrade has also an office in Prishtina.

Humanitarian aid associations. The Mother Theresa Association was the main institution in the parallel health system. Up to the time of this writing, it cooperates with international humanitarian organizations. Also the Red Cross of Kosovo and a number of recently founded local humanitarian associations are also active. In north Mitrovica and in the Serbian enclaves, the Yugoslav Red Cross are continuing to work.

Women's organizations. The Centre for the Protection of Women and Children is the main organization for women's concerns, implementing health programs, legal and psychological counseling, and assisting refugees. Kosovo Women Initiative is working with people form different ethnic backgrounds. Also, the Kosova Albanian Women's League and several newly established organizations are active.

Youth and student organizations. The Independent Students Union of the University of Prishtina played a major political role prior to the war. Also, the Post-Pessimists, Albanian Youth Action Pjeter Bogdani, Hapi i Ri and Youth of Prizren, Millennium in Kamenica, and numerous other youth organizations are active throughout Kosovo. Kosovo Initiative for Democratic Society is the Prishtina branch of the Nansen network. The Forum in Prishtina has emerged as a strong actor in the fields of media (magazines and TV programs), NGO-training and computer courses, monitoring election campaigns, and initiating protests against domestic violence. The Forum initiated the Kosovo-wide "Boll Ma!" campaign.

Educational and cultural associations. Since 1994, the Association for Unity and Diversification Against Separation Mitrovica is working on civic culture and education in the city of Mitrovica. It is in charge of a local radio station and is conducting regular public debates. The Kosovo Education Centre, linked to the faculty of philosophy in Prishtina, develops activities that also include non-Albanian schools.

Professional associations and unions. The Union of Independent Trade Unions of Kosovo, established in 1990, is currently reshaping its programs and approach in close cooperation with international trade-union organizations. A future effort at labor legislation, to be issued by UNMIK, is at the core of the discussion.

Minority-rights associations. There are a considerable number of minority-rights groups emerging at different locations in Kosovo. Given the security problems, their activities are quite limited. Turks and Bosniaks gather in Prizren. Roma groups are now divided into Roma, Ashkali, and Egyptians. In Pristina, the Civic House and Radio Contact are strong (although threatened) promoters of ethnic tolerance.

The OSCE Mission in Kosovo, Department of Democratization, established a number of NGO field offices to encourage local civil society. With a shrinking OSCE presence in Kosovo, these field offices are now being handed over to the local communities.

In 2000 and 2001 the Kosovo Civil Society Foundation did research on the actual needs of local CSOs and came up with the following recommendations. There is continued need for skills and management training of CSO activists and organizations staff. This training has to happen at the local level, by local trainers, through Kosovar civil-society organizations.

Part of the relevance of CSOs in Kosovo rests on their ability to address pressing issues of society through the formation of strong equal partnerships with international NGOs. At the community level, outside of the major cities, it can be difficult to establish such partnerships. Moreover, a growing number of international NGOs are leaving Kosovo without keeping resources for the locals to take over.

Given the enormous problems of social and economical development, including the integration of young people, there is a need to build local social and economical expertise to develop employment opportunities. The mobilization of professional networks and associations will become more relevant.

The development of policy-oriented NGOs or independent think tanks is of critical importance for civil society to realize its potential in bringing about an accountable and transparent governance in Kosovo. To date, this domain has been left to international organizations or institutions. Local policy-oriented NGOs or independent think tanks such as KACI can play an active role in the sensibilization of politicians and public opinion in terms of the issues involved in the Stability Pact and the perspective of European integration, rather than in terms of conflict scenarios.

International NGOs in Kosovo
The presence and activities of the big international NGOs in Kosovo cause mixed reactions. While they have realized a quick recovery from war damages

in the fields of infrastructure, shelter, and humanitarian needs, many Kosovars fear their presence will have a significant negative impact on the development of civil participation and Kosovar self-reliance. Sometimes they tend to bring together people around running projects rather than around values. With their tremendous resources and comparatively high salaries for local staff, they might create new, unrealistic norms that will be hard to keep once international assistance shifts away from Kosovo. The salary policy of the international community in Kosovo might also distract qualified people from their local organizations or professions to fulfill a supportive or administrative role with the international organizations, supposedly trying to strengthen local civil society.

Moreover, and to ensure that international assistance does not feed into, exacerbate, or prolong the conflict, humanitarian and development agencies commissioned a report on what more they could do to minimize intercommunal violence or to promote interaction between communities in Kosovo. The report *Do No Harm* (20 November 2000) initiated lively debate among international workers in Kosovo about the so-called ghettoizing of minorities. One of the dilemmas indicated is: "Despite the best of intentions, providing special structures and assistance efforts to minorities may be counter-productive and potentially dangerous in the short term if it fuels or inflames pre-existing resentments, competition over scare resources, perceptions of bias, or anger among members of neighboring or surrounding communities. Special structures or assistance efforts may inadvertently become flashpoints."[1] Of course, this dilemma will rarely be sufficient grounds for discontinuing assistance programs for people in need. However, it does call for more creativity and heightened sensitivity to intercommunal dynamics in the areas where ethnic Albanians and minority groups intermingle or adjoin.

Conflict Management and Peacebuilding Initiatives
Next to reconstruction and humanitarian work, a number of international NGOs are specifically focusing on peacebuilding initiatives.

Following its eight-year-long activities in the region after the Kosovo war, the Balkan Peace Team (Germany/Netherlands) started an interethnic youth center in Dragash. It is now taken over by a consortium of NGOs including the forum Civil Peace Service (Germany).

Pax Christi (Flanders and the Netherlands) and the forum Civil Peace Service facilitate a peacebuilding program comparing and contrasting Kosovo and Northern Ireland, including Albanians, Serbs, and Bosniaks. Pax Christi is developing a yearly Kosovo Peace Week. Interchurch Peace Council (Netherlands) supports a community-building program in Mitrovica.

United Methodist Committee on Relief is developing numerous peace initiatives, including radio stations, multicultural sports festivals and drama classes, a newsletter with Serb and Albanian input, etc. Activities take place in Gjilane and Mitrovica.

The International Rescue Committee, Catholic Relief Service (CRS), and American Refugee Council are developing peacebuilding programs in the areas where they have also deployed their humanitarian programs. CRS is working with Parent and Youth councils, regional Justice and Peace commissions, and different training courses. CRS also encourages interreligious dialogue in Kosovo.

Partners for Democratic Change established a Kosovar branch, focusing on community mediation for family and social disputes, building democracy at the local level, and training on change and conflict management.

Bol Ma! (Albanian for "Enough"), a broad campaign initiated by The Forum against domestic violence, was started from within the Kosovo-Albanian society in May 2001. It is a public-awareness campaign with the aim to initiate a public debate about all kinds of violence and to increase cooperation between local populations and police forces in combatting crime. Given the massive response from Kosovar youth and the activities in most cities and in a growing number of villages, Bol Ma! can be considered the first Kosovo-wide and postwar Albanian initiative for nonviolence and change of public atmosphere in Kosovo. Although not active in non-Albanian areas, this campaign is of critical importance since it provokes an inter-Albanian reflection and dialogue on responsibility for violence.

Prospects

The prospect of a functioning Kosovar assembly and executive branch has put new emphasis on the question of the status of Kosovo. Blocked between the determination of the Albanian population not to accept Belgrade's rule over Kosovo and UNSC 1244 reaffirming the territorial integrity of the FRY, former SRSG Koushner expressed his belief that to try to define Kosovo's final status could create more problems that it solves. Therefore, the extension of the actual provisional status formed the basis of the discussions on the legal framework, enabling the holding of Kosovo-wide parliamentary elections on 17 November 2001. These elections will take place according to an electoral system of proportional representation and with the requirement that all parties should have a list with one-third of the candidates being women.

After months of debates, the new SRSG, Hans Haekkerup, signed the "Constitutional Framework for Provisional Self-Government" on 15 May 2001. Kosovars voted for a national assembly with 120 seats. Ten of those are reserved for Serbs and ten for Kosovo's other minorities. The assembly will elect a Kosovar president. He in turn will nominate a prime minister who will form a government. Two ministerial posts must be reserved for a representative of the Kosovo Serbs and one other minority group. Kosovo's government will then begin to run the province.

Significantly, UNMIK will still be responsible for justice, law and order, and the Kosovo Protection Corps. SRSG Haekkerup will be able to veto anything that he considers to be in contradiction with UNSC 1244.

Kosovo-Albanian leaders wanted the constitutional framework to contain a clause promising a referendum on independence. Not only did they not get it, but also the "provisional" arrangements have no time limit. The Rambouillet texts that the Kosovar-Albanian delegation signed in March 1999 stipulated that the interim government for Kosovo would have lasted for three years before the question of the final status would be addressed. Now that is no longer the case. This is now put off until "an appropriate future stage," as Haekkerup put it.

Hashim Thaci, head of the Democratic Party of Kosovo, stated that the constitutional framework "holds hostage the issue of independence." Also, Ibrahim Rugova and Ramush Haradinaj, the other two main Albanian leaders, disapproved the lack of a referendum on the provision. However, none of them boycotted the elections, since they consider the "Constitutional Framework" as a document enabling holding the general elections, after which the new parliament would start debating the issue of a real constitution and the final status of Kosovo. However, Kosovar publicist Veton Surroi advocates focusing on Kosovo's development as a functioning and civic state rather than on its international recognition. The self-rule period could be used to build the institutions, go through a process of internal consolidation, establish rule of law, and in this way prepare for eventual statehood.

Prior to the signing of the "Constitutional Framework," Haekkerup met FRY president Kostunica several times. However, Kosovo Serb leadership failed to include a veto mechanism into the text. Haekkerup reaffirmed UNMIK's guarantees for equal rights of different communities. He stated that a veto right for the Serb community would result in a complete stalemate in the work of the assembly. On 5 November 2001, UNMIK and FRY authorities reached an agreement on concrete measures to improve living conditions for Kosovo Serbs. Consequently, Belgrade called Kosovo Serbs to vote for "Coalition Return," the Kosovo-Serb entity to be represented in the Kosovo Assembly.

While it is reasonable to expect that Belgrade will not return to Kosovo in a ruling capacity, it is also obvious the international recognition of Kosovo as an independent state is not on the agenda in the foreseeable future. The extent to which this protracted transitional status succeeds in generating economic wealth and progress will determine its chances of success, along with continued participation of the major political actors. Since the "Constitutional Framework" will be the law until "an appropriate future stage," local Albanians and Serbs will be challenged to try to find a *modus vivendi* for living next to each other. If they fail, they might face a conflict without end.

However, future developments will also be influenced by the outcome of debate on reshaping relations between Serbia and Montenegro, in particular following the transfer of Slobodan Milosevic to The Hague. If Montenegro would become an independent state or an internationally recognized subject within a Serb-Montenegrin confederation, the present "provisional" status of Kosovo might become even more tenuous.

Nebojsa Covic, head of the Serbian government coordination team for Kosovo, advocates the creation of an Albanian and Serbian entity within Kosovo, following the Bosnia and Herzegovina principle. With Kosovo remaining one single unit under UN patronage, the Albanian entity would be protected by international forces and the Kosovo Protection Corps, while the Serbian entity would be protected by FRY security forces. He considers it a move to gain ten years of peace necessary for economic recovery and state consolidation in Serbia, ahead of the inclusion of Southeast Europe into the EU. International officials reject any idea that might lead to a possible division of Kosovo.

Recommendations

In its report *After Milosevic* (26 April 2001) the International Crisis Group (ICG) proposed that the international community facilitate an orderly process that can produce a final political settlement. In order to move the present situation forward, the report mentions the "possibility of negative guarantees" being given to the Kosovo Albanians. Under these guarantees, the Kosovo Albanians would never again be subjected to the uninvited presence of Serb military or police personnel, since it might be easier to reach agreement about how things will not be done than how they will be done. ICG notes that the option of a loose association between independent sovereign states, in which members would cooperate as much as they perceived to be in their common interest, might be a type of relationship that could serve as a model for Kosovo's or Montenegro's relation to Serbia.

ICG supports the International Independent Commission on Kosovo, headed by Richard Goldstone, in its proposal for "conditional independence." Based upon an agreement between the international community, the Albanian majority, and the minorities, Kosovo would become self-governing outside the FRY but within an international framework. The international community would take responsibility for protection of minorities and would also integrate Kosovo into a more effective stability pact.

In any case, long-term international involvement in Kosovo seems to be inevitable financially, security-wise, and politically. In order to avoid a situation in which "coercive diplomacy" toward almost all partners in the region becomes necessary, local ownership of political developments is needed. The prospect of European integration for Kosovo, Serbia, and Montenegro, with open noncriminal borders, might eventually give perspective.

Other recommendations include:

- Additional resources and training should be provided to the Kosovo police service to allow it to take primary police responsibilities in Kosovo by 2002.
- Vigorous investigation and prompt action should be taken against members of the Kosovo Protection Corps found to engage in improper activities.
- UNHCR and OSCE should continue its efforts to facilitate dialogue at local and provincial levels on the position of local Serbs, Roma, and Ashkaeli.
- UNMIK should increase its efforts to establish a functioning judicial system by deploying more foreign judicial personnel, increasing the

salary of local judges, devoting more resources to local judicial personnel and infrastructure, and introducing European criminal and civil law codes. Also, salaries of members of the Kosovo Police School could be increased.

- In order to contribute to a process of recognizing and reconciling, a Balkan-wide regional truth and reconciliation commission could be established.

Resources

Reports
ICRC, *Book of Missing Persons in Kosovo,* 2nd edition, 11 April 2001.
Independent International Commission on Kosovo, *Kosovo Report,* Oxford University Press, 2000.
Independent International Commission on Kosovo in cooperation with the Olof Palme International Center and Global Reporting, *The Follow-up of the Kosovo Report: Why Conditional Independence?* Solna, 2001.
International Crisis Group
  After Milosevic. A Practical Agenda for Lasting Balkans Peace, ICG Balkans Report 108, Prishtina/Brussels, 26 April 2001.
  Kosovo: A Strategy for Economic Development, ICG Balkans Report 123.
  Kosovo Report Card, ICG Balkans Report 100, Prishtina/Brussels, 28 August 2000.
IWPR
  Kosovars Forge Democracy, by Shkëlzen Maliqi, IWPR's Balkan Crisis Report No. 190, 27 October 2000.
  Albanian Extremists Pose Regional Threat, by Shkëlzen Maliqi, IWPR's Balkan Crisis Report No. 224, 7 March 2001.
OSCE, *Kosovo/Kosova as Seen as Told: An Analysis of the Human Rights Findings of the OSCE Kosovo Verification Mission,* October 1998 to June 1999, ODIHR, Warsaw, 1999.
OSCE and UNHCR, *Report on Kosovo Minorities: Anyone Can Become a Victim,* 3 April 2001.
The Transnational Foundation for Peace and Future Research, *Kosovo/a Independent? Perhaps, but What Matters Is How,* TFF Press Info 106, 4 December 2000.

Other Publications
Civil Resistance in Kosovo, by Howard Clark. London, Pluto Press, 2000.
Kosovo and the Challenge of Humanitarian Intervention, by Albrecht Schnabel and Ramesh Thakur (eds). Tokyo, United Nations University Press, 2000.
Kosovo: An Unfinished Peace, by William G. O'Neill. International Peace Academy Occasional Paper Series, Lynne Rienner Publishers, 2002.
"Self-Determination in Kosovo Will Take Much Determination," by Steven Erlanger. *New York Times,* 1 February 2001.
Winning Ugly—NATO's War to Save Kosovo, by Ivo H. Daalder and Michael E. O'Hanlon. Washington, DC, The Brookings Institution, 2000.

Selected Internet Sites
www.aimpress.org (AIM Press Agency)
www.albanian.com (Albanian Daily News)
www.alb-net.com (Kosova Crisis Center)
www.b92.net (B-92 news station)

www.civpol.org/unmik (United Nations International Police in Kosovo)
www.crisisweb.org (International Crisis Group)
www.egroups.com/group/balkanhr/fullinfo.html (The Balkan Human Rights List)
www.euinkosovo.org (European Union's Commitment to Kosovo)
www.greekhelsinki.gr (Balkan Human Rights Pages)
www.iwpr.net (Institute for War and Peace Reporting)
www.kforonline.com (KFOR Online)
www.kosova-info-line.de/APP (Association of Political Prisoners)
www.un.org/peace/kosovo (United Nations Mission in Kosovo UNMIK)
www.voiceofroma.org (Voice of Roma)

Resource Contacts
Yll Bajraktari, The Forum, e-mail: ylli@ipko.org
Sally Broughton, Search for Common Ground in Macedonia, e-mail: sallyb@sfcg.org.mk
Mient Jan Faber, Interchurch Peace Council, The Hague, e-mail: mjfaber@ikv.nl
Alan Frisk, Catholic Relief Services, Kosovo, e-mail: alan_kosovo@hotmail.com
Lulzim Peci, Kosovo Civil Society Foundation, e-mail: lulpeci@yahoo.com
Arben Qirezi, independent political commentator, Prishtina, e-mail: arbale@yahoo.com

Organizations
In Kosovo
Humanitarian Law Center
Tel.: +381 38 528 270 / +381 63 210 534
E-mail: kkosovar@Eunet.yu

Kosovo Civil Society Foundation
Tel.: +381 38 43.904 / +377 44 141.993
E-mail: lulpeci@yahoo.com

Kosovo Initiative for Democratic Society
Nansen Dialogue Center
Tel.: +381 38 24 650
E-mail: kids_pri@hotmail.com
www.nansen-dialog.net

NGO and Radio Mitrovica
Tel.: +381 28 29 905 / +377 44 146233
E-mail: r_Mitrovica@yahoo.com

International
Catholic Relief Service, CRS
Justice and Peace Program
Tel.: +377 44 500 695

Forum Civil Peace Service
Tel.: +49 228 981 4515 / +377 44 130 773
E-mail: forumZFD@t-online.de

Partners for Democratic Change
Center on Change and Conflict Management in Kosovo
E-mail: lshammond@hotmail.com / pdci@ix.netcom.com
www.partners-intl.org

Project on Ethnic Relations (PER)
Voice of Roma
www.voiceofroma.org

United Methodist Committee on Relief
Tel.: +381 38 549 187
Fax: +381 38 549 189
E-mail: umcor@gbgm-umc.org
http://gbgm-umc.org/umcor

Data on the following organizations can be found in the Directory section:
The Forum
Kosova Action for Civic Initiatives (KACI)

Franklin de Vrieze has been following developments in Kosovo on a professional basis since 1992. He facilitated a five-year dialogue project between Albanian and Serbian political parties and NGOs on behalf of Pax Christi. He is currently working for the OSCE Mission in Kosovo.

Note
1. Gregg Hansen, "Minorities Alliance Working Group, Kosovo," paper published by the Do No Harm Project, 2000.

13.11

Montenegro:
Splitting the Federation—
a Split in Society?

Robert Stallaerts

The rise to the top of Milo Djukanovic as president of Montenegro, and the ensuing conflict with former president of Yugoslavia Slobodan Milosevic, led to increasing tension in the relationship between the Serbia and Montenegro. Although the immediate threat of military intervention has receded with the fall of Milosevic, the relationship between the two federal partners has never been repaired. Prolonged political uncertainty about Montenegro's future could further polarize and radicalize the different sides. There is also a danger that the continued domination of the political agenda by the status issue could result in a loss of momentum in government reform efforts. But these risks can be avoided and various initiatives are under way to break the deadlock.

The issue of independence is a source of great tension and potential conflict both within Montenegro itself and between Montenegro and Serbia as parts of the Federal Republic of Yugoslavia (FRY). Much of the polarization of Montenegrin society can be ascribed to the problem of double identity. Related interests of economic and political power, status, and position are also undoubtedly factors in this conflict, but partisans of the conflict themselves refer to a recurrent pattern in Montenegrin history. Consequently, this history is relevant insofar as it feeds the people's need for an identity, even if ideology and the media use very selective devices when constructing stories about identity. We cannot simply dismiss this search for identity as an irrelevant process of mystification or a form of easy self-justification.

There are two traditions in Montenegrin history that provide the background and reference points for protagonists in today's conflicts. The first is the tradition of the native homeland that in its romantic vision extends back in time to Dioclea or Duklja, an Illyrian settlement that later fell under Byzantine influence. Much later, the center of Montenegrin ancestry and pride was located in the mountainous region of Cetinje, an area that more or less preserved its autonomy within the Ottoman Empire. As a result, an independent

MONTENEGRO
Population: 680,158 (2000)
Conflict related IDPs: 40,832 from Kosovo in summer 1999. In May 2001 this number had fallen to 32,000, in addition to the remaining 14,418 Bosnian and Croatian refugees (UNHCR).

Montenegrin state was finally recognized at the Congress of Berlin in 1878. According to this view, the Montenegrin identity was formed around the idea of a state that had developed slowly by grouping together various autonomous local tribes. But this was also subject to a second interpretation. As the region around the center of Cetinje expanded, some tribes with strong ties to the Serbian lands were incorporated. As more and more elements of Serbian culture were integrated, Montenegrins increasingly identified themselves with Serbs and eventually even called themselves "the best of the Serbs." From then on, the two tendencies were always present in the political and cultural life of Montenegro.

In the first decade of the twentieth century, for example, King Nikola of Montenegro promoted a dynastic party called the True People's Party (*pravasi*). In fact, this was largely a reaction against the foundation of another party, the People's Party (*klubasi*) by deputies who were critical of the regime. The members of this last organization sympathized with Serbia, and even proposed renaming the Montenegrin assembly the "Serb National Assembly of the Principality of Montenegro" and relocating the capital from Cetinje to the interior.

A second expression of this dualism survives into the present. During World War I, King Nikola went into exile and in 1918 the Montenegrin lands fell under the control of pro-Serbian military forces. The Serbian politician Nikola Pasic intended incorporating Montenegro into the new Kingdom of Serbs, Croats, and Slovenes by annexing Montenegro to Serbia. However, local Montenegrin forces, with little or no connection to King Nikola, joined together to resist the proposed annexation. They had the right to participate in elections for the deputies to the special Great National Assembly, the body that was to decide on the political future of Montenegro. Their list of candidates was printed on green paper, and henceforth they were known as the Greens (*ze-lenasi*). The pro-Serbians voted on white lists and became known as the Whites (*bjelasi*). In elections characterized by intimidation and fraud, the Greens were outvoted by the pro-Serbian Whites in 1918. For a while the Greens resorted to armed resistance but, lacking coordination and discipline, they were easily contained by the Serbian or Yugoslav progovernment forces, and the Greens soon turned into a reformist force, more or less harmless to the new rulers of Yugoslavia. During World War II, history would repeat itself. In fact, in each crisis of Montenegrin society, the same basic pattern of conflict appears.

The political attitudes of President Milo Djukanovic can also be partly explained with reference to this historical background. Though he began his political career in the Communist Party, he made an easy switch from the pro-Serbian camp and the so-called universal values of communism to a genuinely Montenegrin stance. Djukanovic's political choices once more reveal the basic contradiction that runs throughout Montenegrin history. The bipolar structure in politics was in fact revived in the 22 April 2001 elections, where the two main coalitions clearly represented the familiar historical positions. The problems of holding a referendum can be seen as the recurrence of a long historical process.

Conflict Dynamics

The roots of the present conflict can be traced to the moment when its main protagonists, Milo Djukanovic and Momir Bulatovic, came to power. At the end of 1989, Slobodan Milosevic instigated the so-called antibureaucratic revolutions in all the members of the Yugoslav federation. The governing communist cadres were lambasted and finally driven out of power by mass demonstrations. In Montenegro, the government was overthrown in January 1989. Following an extraordinary congress of the Communist Party, Momir Bulatovic and Milo Djukanovic were chosen president and general secretary of the party. This put them in a position to assume the posts of president and prime minister of the Republic of Montenegro after the communists were victorious in the first multiparty elections at the end of 1990.

Both leaders were strong supporters of Milosevic's policies during the breakup of Yugoslavia. Slovenia and Croatia went for independence and the Socialist Federal Republic of Yugoslavia (SFRY) was declared to have been dissolved by the Arbitration or Badinter Commission, a body installed by the European Community at the Yugoslavia Peace Conference that started in mid-1991. The EC Arbitration Commission defined the criteria for recognizing the independence of the new successor states of the SFRY. The Montenegrin leaders agreed to form the new Federal Republic of Yugoslavia with Serbia in a decision that came into force on 27 April 1992. FRY was confirmed by a referendum in Montenegro.

In May 1992, the UN Security Council installed an economic embargo against the FRY, holding it responsible for the outbreak of war in Bosnia-Herzegovina. In July 1993, a minor disagreement between the Montenegrin government and the FRY was made public when it distanced itself from the federal decision to ban Conference on Security and Cooperation in Europe (OSCE) monitors from further activity in Kosovo. In September 1993, President Momir Bulatovic was attacked by demonstrators favoring independence. The impact of the economic sanctions had clearly strengthened pro-independence groups and Bulatovic himself tried to acquire more equal relations and a clearer profile for Montenegro vis-à-vis Serbia.

The first real cracks in the Serb-Montenegrin front appeared during the Dayton Peace Conference at the end of 1995. Bulatovic disagreed with Milosevic on the position of Montenegro, but gave in at last. Then, however, Djukanovic took over the criticism, leading ultimately to a dispute between Djukanovic and Bulatovic. The dissent between the two Montenegrin leaders gradually increased and eventually resulted in a break. In 1997, Bulatovic left the leading Democratic Party of Socialists (DPS, the transformed Communist Party) to establish a new party. In the same year, Djukanovic marked a definitive break with the Milosevic regime when he characterized Milosevic as a throwback to an earlier political era. Djukanovic's "For a Better Life" coalition adopted a strong Western, reformist profile and won a convincing victory in the elections of 1998. This effectively forced Bulatovic to assume an even more pro-Serbian position and Milosevic consequently selected him as federal prime minister. Strains and difficulties further increased at the federal level. The delegation of the new Montenegrin deputies to the federal parliament was not ratified by Belgrade. Ratification was refused because the Montenegrin law had been changed and in place of proportional representation, a homogeneous representation of the new Montenegrin governing coalition had been sent to the federal parliament. The existing deputies, mainly supporters of Momir Bulatovic, remained in place.

On these grounds, Djukanovic rejected all further collaboration with the Yugoslav federation and ignored all the decisions of its organs. The conflict gradually developed into an economic war between Belgrade and Montenegro, and at times military intervention even seemed a possibility.

In order to reformulate Montenegro's relations to Serbia, in August 1999 the Montenegrin government adopted a platform proposing a loose confederation of two equal partners. The two republics as two sovereign states—without implying official international recognition of independence or a seat for each in the UN—would share some decisionmaking in areas as foreign policy, defense, and security. However, consultations with Belgrade about this confederation proposal yielded no significant results. An official answer to the proposals was never received.

A further reason for Djukanovic to maintain a noncooperative, if not to say obstructive, attitude toward the federation was Milosevic's decision to change the 1992 Constitution on 7 July 2000. Not only did Milosevic hereby clear a path to a possible further term as president, he also significantly reduced the competencies of the Montenegrin unit. The principle that both states were entitled to equality of treatment was seriously threatened and existing minority guarantees were abolished.

For this reason, Djukanovic refused to take part in the September 2000 federal elections. This again had the unfortunate consequence that the party of his opponent Bulatovic, supported by Milosevic, won nearly all the Montenegrin seats in the federal parliament. When Milosevic lost the elections in October 2000, his Montenegrin partner, the Socialist People's Party (SNP), was still firmly in power and even delivered the federal prime minister, Zoran Zizic. Even when Zizic had to resign on the coalition problems surrounding the cooperation with the War Crimes Tribunal in The Hague, he was followed up by his party colleague Dragisa Pesic. The federal institutions remained within the hands of the Montenegrin opposition politicians. This is the main reason why Djukanovic and the ruling government parties of Montenegro wanted direct negotiations with the Serbian government and Yugoslav president Kostunica.

After several informal and official meetings, it was finally concluded on 26 October after an official meeting between Montenegrin partners and Kostunica that the short dialogue on the highest political level had not moved the parties from their respective standpoints, as laid down in their earlier platforms. Now, ultimately the citizens of Montenegro themselves had to decide in a referendum on the fate of the Yugoslav federation. Djukanovic officially declared the referendum should be held in April 2002.

There are at least four other potential conflict threats of major importance to Montenegrin society. First is the problem of the relation between Orthodox churches in Montenegro, which is in fact closely related to the main conflict. Second, there could be problems with the Muslims of the Sandzak, as they are divided over both the Serbian and Montenegrin parts of this region. The third major problem is the expected resistance of the oligarchic elites to economic reform and political democratization. Fourth, it is still a big matter of dispute—again largely along opposition and government lines—whether there is a problem of "Macedonization." Is there really a threat of an armed uprising of Albanians in Montenegro?

Official Conflict Management

Before the parliamentary elections of 22 April 2001, there was no official domestic conflict management beyond the unproductive dialogue about two radically different proposals of the Serbian and Montenegrin partners in the Yugoslav federation. International diplomacy was limited to close observation of the moves of the protagonists, and displayed little initiative beyond issuing some cautious warnings, especially to the Montenegrin president, Milo Djukanovic.

The latest Montenegrin proposal on the relations between Serbia and Montenegro advances nothing less than a loose cooperation between two independent and internationally recognized states. Recognition implies a seat in its own right at the UN General Assembly, according to the Montenegrin Independence Proposal of 29 December 2000. It also implies the establishment of its own army and the creation of autonomous republican decisionmaking power in matters where no common ground can be found at the level of the federation, in fields such as foreign policy, foreign trade, and common monetary policy. Institutionally, the proposal foresees only one chamber of parliament, which has to be composed on a strict parity basis. Moreover, one of the partners of the government coalition, the Social Democrat Party (SDP), even expressed reservations about creating the function of a president for the federation.

Federal president Vojislav Kostunica reacted to this statement of aspirations by proposing a minimal, functional federation in the Minimal Functional Federation Proposal of 10 January 2001. In his view, the following competencies are (if useful) to be commonly shared: defense and foreign security, foreign policy, and competencies regarding a common market and a convertible currency. In order to secure the equality of the two federal units, the Kostunica proposal refers to the establishment of a system of multiple balances and a bicameral adoption of all federal decisions, on the basis of an absolute majority in both chambers: the Chamber of Republics and the Chamber of Citizens. The first has an equal number of deputies from the federal units, the second represents the interests of citizens on the base of "one citizen, one vote." However, in order to secure representation of the smaller (Montenegrin) unit in all decisions and commissions, an exception can be adopted from the purely quantitative principle. Moreover, the joint state of Serbia and Montenegro should have a president and a federal court. The president should chair the Supreme Defense Council. The government should comprise, under the prime minister, five federal ministers: justice, defense, roreign relations, finance, and transportion.

Shortly before the 22 April elections, Kostunica rejected the offer of Djukanovic first to secede and then to reconstruct a loose union of independent states.

Given the divergence of the two proposals, it was no surprise when, on 17 January 2001 in Belgrade, a confrontation between Montenegrin president Milo Djukanovic, Serbian prime minister Zoran Djindjic, and federal president Vojislav Kostunica only resulted in the conclusion that "there were high unbridgeable differences of opinion," offering no space for a compromise.

However, Kostunica later declared he would respect "the will of the people," meaning that if Montenegro held a referendum after the elections, he would not object to a peaceful separation. This of course contrasts to the threats of the Milosevic period, though even Milosevic himself once declared that he would not go so far as an armed intervention.

The radical formulation of the independence proposal had an unexpected side effect. It caused a deep rift in the Montenegrin governing coalition "For a Better Life." The National Party (NS, Narodna Stranka) left the government, which in turn led to the new elections of 22 April. In the talks with Serbia, the NS stuck to the August 1999 confederation proposal as a point of departure for the regulation of the relations between Serbia and Montenegro. This proposal prescribed an outcome without the need for the outright independence of Montenegro. According to the vice president of the NS, it was in fact Djukanovic who had stubbornly rejected any comprise on this point. Djukanovic's attitude was however approved by the direction of his own party, the DPS.

Thus, the Djukanovic government only made superficial attempts to come to terms with the new Serbian government. Probably the dynamics of the conflict had already forced the parties too far apart. On the one side, the isolation during the Milosevic period had strengthened the Montenegrin consciousness that the country could function effectively as an economically and politically autonomous state. Furthermore, Djukanovic and his party seemed convinced that their power base could be extended by the radicalization of the political scene. The role of Montenegrin emigrants is probably significant in this respect. Montenegrin organizations in both the United States and Australia strongly supported independence.

Of course, it is also true that the international community had always supported Djukanovic in his rebellion against Milosevic. But once this problem was tackled, international diplomacy preferred to restrain Djukanovic from initiatives that may have endangered the stability of the region.

With the results of the 22 April elections, the conflict entered a new phase. The pro-independence coalition, "Victory Belongs to Montenegro," of Djukanovic's own DPS, and the SDP gained a tense victory over the opposition bloc, "Together for Yugoslavia," containing the SNP, the NS, and the Serbian People's Party (SNS). The media and most politicians in Serbia—not least Kostunica—supported the defeated bloc, and especially the SNP. The federal minister of internal affairs, Zoran Zivkovic, remarked that Montenegrins would require passports in Serbia and that workers and students could have problems. In fact, the elections were seen as a first test for a referendum and, on the basis of most polls, much stronger support had been expected by the governing party. As a result of the elections, the Liberal Alliance assumed a decisive role, and as the Liberals were traditionally the staunchest defenders of Montenegrin independence, Djukanovic has no choice other than to further his initiative for independence, as he indeed announced immediately after the elections. He was in an uncomfortable position. The internal opposition had grown and both Belgrade and the international community are unanimous in rejecting unilateral steps and advising dialogue. As noted above, shortly before the elections, Kostunica had already rejected Djukanovic's offer "first to divorce and then to remarry" by creating a loose union of independent states. Some sources even reveal that his party materially supported the Montenegrin opposition, once Momir Bulatovic had left the SNP.

Before and after the April elections the EU sent delegations to Montenegro to support the dialogue between the two republics. They demanded that no unilateral steps be taken. The EU still advocated a "democratic Montenegro within a democratic FRY." Nevertheless, according to the EU it is ultimately up to the people of Montenegro to decide on their future. After the Montenegrin elections, Kostunica brought together a working group to rewrite the

Yugoslav attitude toward the Montenegrin problem. However, the new document scarcely departed from the earlier Kostunica position of a functional federation. After some informal and some cancelled official meetings—at times conditioned by rather unreal demands of who should or who should not attend the meeting—and following a three-hour discussion, Kostunica and Djukanovic concluded on 26 October 2001 that their standpoints were not coming closer. A referendum in Montenegro was to decide ultimately on the fate of the Yugoslav Federation.

Multi-Track Diplomacy

According to the Center for the Development of Nongovernmental Organizations, at the end of 2000 there were more than 800 registered nongovernmental organizations in Montenegro, although only 30–50 of these were active participants in civil-society development. In an analysis of the nongovernmental profit sector in Montenegro in December 1999, the center pointed to the danger of the government and political parties usurping NGO activity. Funding policies are even deemed essential under the new law on NGOs.

Here, some NGOs are described that have attempted to find a solution for the future status of Montenegro.

The Montenegrin Helsinki Committee for Human Rights

This committee has recorded its opinion in two recent documents. In a supplement to the OSCE report of 2000, its president, Slobodan Franovic, analyzes the development of the relations between Montenegro and Serbia and criticizes denial of rights to Montenegrins. A second document concentrates more specifically on the actual relations between Serbia and Montenegro. This is a joint declaration of the Serbian and Montenegrin, as well as the international section, of the International Helsinki Federation for Human Rights. The earlier statements are reformulated in two recommendations to the international community: respect strict neutrality and the will of the majority of the people of Montenegro.

Youth Cultural Center Juventas

From 22 to 24 January 2001, a conference titled "Montenegrin-Serbian Dialogue—How to Go On" was organized by the Youth Cultural Center (Omladinski Kulturni Centar) Juventas in Podgorica. This continued a conference called "Dialogue as a Method for a Nonviolent Conflict Resolution Between Montenegro and Serbia," which was held in November 1999 and organized in cooperation with the Open Society Institute of Montenegro and international partners. The conference brought together politicians and law professors from both Serbia and Montenegro before an NGO public. Despite the divergent political standpoints, at the end a declaration was issued on the "minimum conditions that must be met in order to have the crisis in relations between Montenegro and Serbia resolved in a nonviolent and democratic procedure." Only this, it said, will contribute to the stabilization of the region. The seven-point declaration expresses the opinion of the representatives of some twenty-five NGOs.

ANIMA-Kotor, Group Most, and the Nansen Dialogue Center

In cooperation with the Danish Center for Conflict Resolution, ANIMA-Kotor and Group Most of Belgrade have set up the dialogue workshops "Let's Talk Together" since 1999. Their aim is to revive the NGO network in Serbia and Montenegro.

The Montenegro arm of the Nansen Dialogue Center has also offered programs to develop a dialogue between communities. It is incorporated in a network that encompasses centers all over the former Yugoslavia, including Belgrade. From 21 to 24 June 2000, it organized a seminar in cooperation with its Belgrade equivalent and the Norwegian Nansen Academy on "Dialogue in the Relations Between Montenegro and Serbia." A round table on "The Attitudes of Young People About the Juridical Status of Montenegro" was held in February 2001.

The Democratic Forum for Human Rights and Inter-Ethnic Relations

The Democratic Forum for Human Rights and Inter-Ethnic Relations has also dealt with Montenegrin and Serbian relations. It has organized round tables gathering together a number of Montenegrin and Serbian academics to discuss the future of these relations.

The Center of Human Rights of Belgrade

Formed as an expert team for the reformulation of the relations between Serbia and Montenegro, the Center of Human Rights of Belgrade has subsequently found that the cooperation of some Montenegrin experts could not be obtained, as their Serbian partners would not abandon their preconceptions.

Reflections on the NGOs' Initiatives

The primary intentions of these initiatives appear excellent, but again no practical ways to resolve the conflict are really devised. While some initiatives propose radical (but contrasting) propositions, most NGO initiatives seem only to foster dialogue at a more or less preliminary and nonbinding level.

Of course, the primary decisionmakers in these matters are politicians and the electorate, albeit somewhat monitored by international diplomacy. While NGOs can do much to influence the atmosphere and the thinking about the problem, they mostly reach only a very restricted group of people. So far, in their opposition to the Milosevic regime, NGOs have stressed the basic right of Montenegrins to decide on their own fate and the need to develop the rule of law with a full guarantee of human rights. This is clearly reflected in the Montenegrin Helsinki Committee for Human Rights. However, a more complex and consensual strategy is perhaps in order. A first step toward this was taken by the Juventas conference. But is this enough? Can this attitude be made operational?

Prospects

Montenegrin authorities remain committed to independence. However, the hopes of the republic's ruling parties that the election of April 2001 would bring a comfortable victory, followed swiftly by a referendum and independence, were not realized. The narrow victory for the pro-independence parties only confirmed the depth of divisions over the republic's status. Plans for a referendum have been postponed until early 2002. With some difficulty, the pro-independence ruling parties formed a minority government. However, the lack of a broad consensus on the status issues or on the rules and conditions for a referendum make it difficult to press ahead with plans for independence under current circumstances.

The OSCE-ODIHR (Office for Democratic Institutions and Human Rights) was mildly critical of the technicalities of the April elections, and reflection on the February 2001 referendum law made some suggestions about ways the referendum could be made more reliable and public.

More important politically were the critical remarks of the Yugoslav Constitutional Court on the Montenegrin referendum law. The court's main criticism relates to voting eligibility. Some form of local "Montenegrin nationhood" is required. At present, only persons resident in Montenegro for more than two years can vote. This excludes a lot of refugees temporarily resident in Montenegro, but more importantly it also excludes the Montenegrins living in Serbia. Especially these votes—given that U.S. and Australian Montenegrin emigrants are generally in favor of independence—would support the political

Niksic, Montenegro's second city:
Graffiti says, "I love Montenegro" (April 2000)

option of parties who defend a stronger common bond with Yugoslavia. Eliminating these voters would create a strong bias in favor of the independence option. Additionally, there is the problem of whether a simple minority may decide the question. Of course, there are other guarantees. In order to accept the results of the referendum and change the constitution, parliament requires a two-thirds majority. The election results showing the complete polarization of the country have probably destroyed any temptation to ignore these requirements on the grounds that all this legislation was created under illegitimate political conditions. A new referendum law proposal, mainly worked out by the Liberals and Social Democrats, was presented in November 2001 to the parliament. OSCE-ODIHR earlier interpreted the new law proposal as a regression in comparison to the February 2001 Montenegrin referendum law, as the propositions on a qualified minority had here disappeared. In fact, only 50 percent plus one of the effective votes would be sufficient in this new proposal, while in the February law, 50 percent plus one of the registered voters was needed.

While in the short run there is little risk of serious conflict in Montenegro, prolonged political uncertainty could further polarize and radicalize the different sides. There is also a danger that the continued domination of the political agenda by the status issue could result in a loss of momentum in government reform efforts. But these risks can be avoided and various initiatives are under way to break the deadlock. Serbian government officials have stated that Montenegrins should decide on their future as soon as possible, so that Serbia's own development will not be held hostage to the indecision of its federal partner. Belgrade's impatience has been heightened by difficulties with its Montenegrin coalition partner at the federal level, the Pro-Yugoslav SNP, particularly over cooperation with the International Criminal Tribunal for the former Yugoslavia in The Hague, which the SNP opposes. The view increasingly gaining ground in Serbia is that a federation that is boycotted by the ruling Montenegrin parties and whose survival hinges on an alliance with Milosevic's recent allies, the SNP, is not worth preserving.

Western intervention to ease the economic conditions both in Serbia and Montenegro should, however, soften positions and increase the chances of a peaceful resolution of the conflict. In the middle of October 2001, the Europeans once more confirmed this position. Kristina Galjak reiterated in the name of Javier Solana, the European Council's high representative for the Common Foreign and Security Policy, that no sanctions or pressure were to be imposed on the Montenegrin government in its way to independence, on condition that all processes would proceed democratically and in full dialogue with all concerned partners.

Recommendations
In one of its recommendations during a Montenegro discussion meeting on 12 February 2001, the European Stability Initiative (ESI) tried to deconstruct the domino theory. The independence of Montenegro need not automatically lead to drastic changes in the other parts of the federation and could even contribute

to the stability of the Balkan region. If the principal external actor, the European Union—in transatlantic consensus with the United States—simply rejects the independence idea, it would probably only defer the question and the outcome could be the same, though more acrimonious.

In another recommendation, the ESI suggested shifting attention from the independence question to substantive content discussions and how to make proposals operational. As a starting point, the European Commission could propose the creation of a genuine single market on the European Union model.

A third recommendation further emphasizes the need to convince Montenegrins to study the functional links of such a proposal on the independence decision. A final recommendation points to the possibility of supranational institutions that could link the countries to the European Union.

The International Crisis Group (ICG) states in its different reports that the independence of Montenegro should no longer be discouraged, as it has been by the international community. Instead, the international community should make a long-term commitment to assisting reforms in Montenegro, emphasizing the work of building the capacity of Montenegrin institutions to implement reforms, especially in areas concerning more transparent government. The Montenegrin authorities, on the other hand, should seek a resolution to the status issue through dialogue within Montenegrin society, among the political parties, as well as with Belgrade. To overcome the political deadlock, the equal rights of all citizens, including members of ethnic minorities, should be respected by all political parties, institutions, and the media.

Stojan Cerovic, writing for the U.S. Institute of Peace, likewise concludes that because of the broader interregional consequences, international concern, if not mediation, is needed. Much more than the viability of Montenegro or the FRY (e.g., the foreclosing of the possibility of Kosovo functioning as a third republic) is at stake, he says.

Of course, these recommendations should not be accepted unconditionally, but must be validated and reevaluated in the light of the actual processes in Montenegro and Serbia and between them.

Resources

Reports
Center for European Policy Studies, "President Kostunica's Proposal for the Reconstruction of Yugoslavia," Brussels, *Europa South-East Monitor* issue 19, January 2001 (www.ceps.be).
European Stability Initiative
    Montenegro Discussion Meeting: Sovereignty, Europe and the Future of Serbia and Montenegro—A Proposal for International Mediation, Discussion Paper, 12 February 2001, Berlin (www.esiweb.org)
    "Montenegro Should Clarify Its Relations with the Republic of Serbia," Vienna, 2001 (www.ihf-hr.org).
    Rhetoric and Reform. A Case Study of Institution Building in Montenegro 1998–2001, International Helsinki Federation for Human Rights (www.esiweb.org).

International Crisis Group
  After Milosevic: A Practical Agenda for Lasting Balkan Peace, Brussels, ICG
    Balkans Report No. 108, 2001.
  Montenegro: Settling for Independence? ICG Balkans Report No. 107, 28 March
    2001.
  Resolving the Independence Deadlock, ICG Balkans Report No. 114, 1 August 2001.
  United States Institute of Peace, *Serbia and Montenegro: Reintegration, Divorce or
    Something Else?* Special Report, April 2001.

Other Publications
Analyses: Non-Governmental Non-Profit Sector in Montenegro Today, December 1999,
  CDNGO (www.crnovo.cg.yi/analize.1uk.htm).
*Assessment of the Draft Referendum Law for Conducting Elections in the Republic of
  Montenegro,* Warsaw, OSCE-ODIHR, 22 January 2001.
Montenegro: La Rebellion Albanaise, Theme Fetiche des Antidependantistes, Sead
  Sadikovic, Le Courrier des Balkans, 4 October 2001.
"Referendum Law on the State Status of the Republic of Montenegro" (draft), OSCE-
  ODIHR, Warsaw, 5 November 2001.
Serbia and Montenegro: Reintegration, Divorce or Something Else? by Stojan Cerovic.
  Washington, DC, U.S. Institute for Peace, 2 April 2001.
The Case for Montenegro's Independence, U.S.-Montenegrin Policy Forum Report,
  Center for Strategic and International Studies, 20 July 2001.
*The Union of Serbia and Montenegro: Proposal for the Constitutional Reconstruction
  of FRY,* by Bosko Mijatovic, Dragobljub Popovic, and Slobodan Samardzic. Bel-
  grade, Center for Liberal-Democratic Studies, 2000.

Selected Internet Sites
www.incore.ulst.ac.uk (INCORE guide to Internet sources on conflict and ethnicity in
  Serbia and Montenegro)
www.iwpr.net (Institute for War and Peace Reporting)
www.montenafax.com (Montenafax)
www.montenegro.rog/religion.html (Montenegrin church and religion site)
www.usip.org/library/regions/montengro.html (U.S. Institute of Peace Library, Montenegro Web Links)

Resource Contacts
Raymond Detrez, State University, Ghent, e-mail: Raymond.Detrez@rug.ac.be
Jelica Novakovic, University of Belgrade, e-mail: jnovlop@EUnet.yu
Daliborka Uljarevic, Nansen Dialogue Centre, Montenegro, e-mail: dali2003@hotmail.
  com

Data on the following organizations can be found in the Directory section:
Association for Culture of Peace and Nonviolence
Center for Democracy and Human Rights

*Robert Stallaerts studied at the Economic Institute of Belgrade and presented a doc-
toral dissertation on the economy of the former Yugoslavia at the University of Ghent,
Belgium. He is the author of several Dutch-language publications on former Yugoslavia (on the collapse of the state, and on poetry and literature) and the* Historical
Dictionary of the Republic of Croatia *(Metuchen, NJ: Scarecrow Press, 1995).*

13.12

Serbia:
A New Beginning Taking Shape

Maria Teresa Mauro, Dragan Lakicevic,
Zoran Lutovac & Danijel Pantic

Serbia is trying to recover from the disastrous Milosevic period. One of the most pressing internal-security problems for the republic is the situation in three ethnically heterogeneous regions: Sandzak, Vojvodina, and the southern part of the country. The region comprising southern Serbia, Kosovo, and the northwestern part of Macedonia probably represents the most delicate rim of ethnic and political instability in Europe today.This crisis can only be resolved gradually, applying the step by step approach. The conflict in southern Serbia is connected with the Kosovo crisis and unresolved major issues concerning the future of ethnic communities living in the region. The interest of the international community and NGOs is to defuse the ethnic tensions and create conditions for a normal life in all the communities. The first steps have been taken, but without intensive international support and goodwill from both sides this goal will be impossible to achieve.

The Republic of Serbia is formally a part of the Federal Republic of Yugoslavia (FRY), which came into being on 27 April 1992 by an act of unification of the republics of Serbia and Montenegro. This act had been preceded by the breakup of the Socialist Federal Republic of Yugoslavia (SFRY). In the period from 1991 to 2000, Serbia (both as a part of the SFRY and FRY) was involved in four large-scale violent conflicts: in Slovenia, Croatia, Bosnia, and Kosovo. This, coupled with the breakup of the SFRY, international sanctions, a major refugee crisis, the NATO bombing campaign, corruption, and mismanagement of the economy, have brought the Republic of Serbia into a disastrous economic situation. It is difficult to precisely determine how much each of these factors contributed to the economic collapse of the country. However, the direct costs caused by UN sanctions are estimated at US$36 billion and the losses caused by the NATO bombing at tens of billions. Under the minimum "consumer basket" criterion, the national standard for gauging poverty, 2.8 million people in central Serbia and Vojvodina lived below the poverty line in 1999.

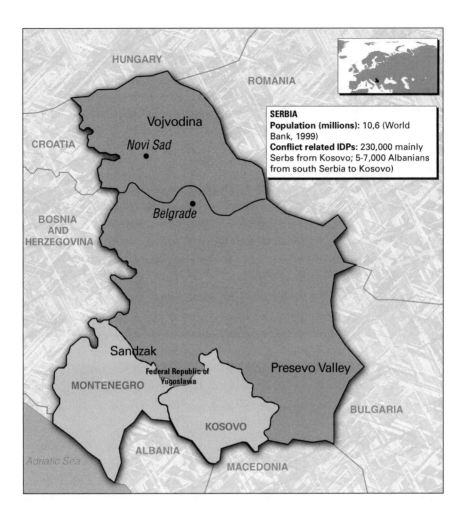

SERBIA
Population (millions): 10,6 (World Bank, 1999)
Conflict related IDPs: 230,000 mainly Serbs from Kosovo; 5-7,000 Albanians from south Serbia to Kosovo)

During the past ten years, Serbia has been shaken by numerous financial frauds and scandals. According to research carried out by Transparency International, FRY occupies second place on the "world's most corrupt countries" list. After the fall of President Milosevic, the new authorities in Serbia have set as their primary task the establishment of a state of law and the fight against corruption.

During the wars in Croatia, Bosnia, and Kosovo there was a steady growth in the narcotics trade, as well as money laundering. Two large pyramidal banks were under the direct sponsorship of the people associated with the Milosevic regime. Several hundred thousand people have been defrauded by the banks. Paramilitary units, which were engaged in the war in ex-Yugoslavia, were organized by criminals and secret services. To what extent the secret services were involved in illegal activities is also evidenced by the recent discovery of large quantity of heroin (500 kilograms) found in the vault of Commercial

Bank in Belgrade, which was rented by the Security Department of Serbia. One may speak of organized crime involving about 35,000 people. The extent of this mafia's influence, which was directly connected to Milosevic and other high state functionaries, could be seen in their attempts to assassinate leading political figures.

Generally speaking, the Balkans have a tradition of religious intolerance. There is a "powerful" presence of religion in politics and a dearth of modern theological concepts. The religious factor was decisive in the formation of most nations in this area—Catholicism in the case of Slovenes and Croats, Eastern Orthodoxy in the case of Serbs, and Islam in the case of Bosniaks. The apparent religious tolerance during the communist regime rested on the strong pressure exerted by the government, which was geared toward two goals: (1) suppressing latent nationalist passions and (2) precluding any alternative form of political action. With the breakup of the unity among national political oligarchies, religion became the key for national homogenization and thus an active factor in sociopolitical divisions. Thus, as of 1987 there was a growing rapprochement between the Serbian Orthodox Church (SPC) and the regime in Serbia. This link was also politicized: the SPC openly defended the idea of "Sacred Serbian Land" in Kosovo. Through public declarations, it took the side of Serbs in Croatia and Bosnia-Herzegovina. For quite some time now, the SPC has been in a canonic dispute regarding the capacity of Macedonian and Montenegrin churches to rule themselves. These disputes have a purely political connotation, because the activities of these nonrecognized churches evince anti-Serbian political sentiments and Montenegrin separatism.

There are two regions in Serbia that, due to their heterogeneous ethnic composition, manifest high sensitivity in intraethnic relations: Sandzak and Vojvodina.

Sandzak is the traditional name for the region encompassing the southwest of Serbia and northern Montenegro. It covers an area of 8,887 square kilometers, populated by 420,000 inhabitants, of which there are 257,000 in the Serbian part and 162,000 in the Montenegrin part. According to the 1991 census, 54 percent of them call themselves Muslim (this group lives in Montenegro) or Bosniaks (these are Muslims living in the Serbian part). In the early 1990s, some extremist statements were made by one Sulejman Ugljanin of the Democratic Action Party for Sandzak. He declared that Sandzak must have political autonomy within Serbia or else it would join Bosnia-Herzegovina, its "motherland." Statements such as these were used as arguments by Milosevic to conduct an aggressive policy during the war in Bosnia-Herzegovina, systematically intimidating the Bosniak population and applying other repressive measures, including political arrests and the deployment of paramilitary forces. There was a mass exodus from Sandzak to Bosnia, but estimates differ substantially (between 40,000 and 75,000). A certain number of Sandzak Muslims actively took part in the war in Bosnia against Bosnian Serbs. This has affected the strong intraethnic tensions in this region.

With the new democratic government in Belgrade, these tensions have greatly subsided, especially with the appointment of Rasim Ljajic (born in

Sandzak) as federal minister of intraethnic relations. New conflicts and tensions in the Sandzak region could arise from a possible separation of Montenegro from the Yugoslav Federation. If this happens, Sandzak would become split between two new states. The more or less homogenous Bosniak population would be divided: Bosniaks would become an tiny ethnic minority, accounting for 2.5 percent of the population in Serbia (in Montenegro they consist of 14.5 percent of the population and are actively supporting an independent Montenegro). This could mean that Bosniaks would be marginalized even more: becoming citizens of two sovereign states could substantially reduce their possibility of expressing and preserving their own national identity and culture, and of communicating with their families who would find themselves living in another state.

The region of Vojvodina covers an area of 21,506 square kilometers. It extends mostly on the plains in the north of Serbia. Vojvodina has slightly over 2 million inhabitants (according to the 1991 census), 56.8 percent of whom are Serbs, 16.9 percent Hungarians, 8.7 percent Yugoslavs, 3.2 percent Slovaks, 2.2 percent Montenegrins, 1.9 percent Romanians, 1.2 percent Roma, 0.9 percent Ruthenians, and 0.9 percent Macedonians. This variegated ethnic structure is the result of large waves of colonization that took place during several centuries. Each of these peoples developed their linguistic, religious, and cultural individuality, but they communicated and cooperated among themselves. Until the breakup of Yugoslavia, Vojvodina used to be one of the most tolerant and ethnically mixed areas in Europe. During the recent wars in ex-Yugoslavia, there was an influx of a large number of refugees from Croatia and Bosnia and an exodus of Croats and Hungarians. As a result, the present intraethnic structure is considerably changed. Back in 1988, Milosevic forced the provincial government leaders to resign by using Serbian national discontent and manipulating mass rallies. A year later, amendments to the constitution of the Socialist Republic of Serbia reduced Vojvodina's legislative, administrative, and judiciary powers. A national homogenization of the Serbian population mediated by Belgrade aggravated intraethnic relations to some extent, further exacerbated by the war with Croatia. A few NGOs took to defending those who refused to participate in the war. These were primarily ethnic Hungarians.

The decade of war and the isolationist policy of the Milosevic regime was experienced by the majority of Vojvodina citizens as economically devastating, breeding corruption and crowding out any understanding for the position of minorities. No wonder that in the post-Milosevic era sharp tensions remain between the demands of Vojvodina's political parties for an ever greater autonomy than the one that was abolished, and the absence of any readiness on the part of the new parties in power in Belgrade to meet those demands. The problem in Vojvodina today is of a social nature (although recently some interethnic incidents have been reported). Poverty, slow and insufficient reforms, unchecked corruption and theft, bankrupt factories, and diminished agricultural production make Vojvodina a vulnerable area. If there is no fast economic recovery, it is only a matter of time before another form of general discontent will manifest itself—ethnic, territorial, or otherwise. The recent decision of the

Hungarian government to allow ethnic Hungarians living in neighboring countries (Romania, Slovakia, and Yugoslavia) to enjoy the same sociopolitical benefits as its own citizens can easily lead to an increasing homogenization of Hungarians in Vojvodina and their possible demands for a new status. That might imply the deterioration of the traditionally tolerant intraethnic relations in this province.

In Serbia, there is the unresolved question of the province of Kosovo and the armed conflict in southern Serbia. After the NATO intervention and the withdrawal of the federal army and the Serbian police from Kosovo in June 1999, the former province became a sort of protectorate under the administration of the UN Mission in Kosovo (UNMIK) and the NATO force KFOR. They represented the international community, which could do little to prevent ethnic cleansing and acts of violence. Although the Kosovo issue is not the main subject of this chapter, it must be said that the unstable political situation in that region, revenge of former National Liberation Army (UCK) personnel toward Serbian and other communities, and the uncertain future political status of Kosovo may be seen as relevant factors contributing to making Serbia unstable.

Conflict Dynamics

The secession of the Republic of Slovenia led to the first armed conflict on the soil of ex-Yugoslavia between the federal army and the territorial defense units of Slovenia in June 1991. (It is useful to note here that there is virtual unanimity that the federal army represented exclusively the interests of the regime in Serbia.) This conflict took place exclusively on the territory of Slovenia and it ended after a couple of weeks with relatively little material damage and about sixty dead, mostly soldiers of the federal army.

The war between Serbs and Croats affected one-third of Croatia and lasted from 1991 to 1995. The dispute arose when the Croatian parliament declared an independent and sovereign Croat state (25 June 1991). Subsequently, the Serbian population in the region of Kninska Krajina and in parts of Slavonia, who wanted to remain in Yugoslavia, organized an armed rebellion. The conflict in Croatia led to mass expulsions of people, large-scale destruction, and human casualties. It ended with a blitzkrieg and the expulsion of Serbs from said areas. Neither Serbia nor FRY officially took part in these conflicts, although they provided ideological, military, and material support.

The multiparty elections in Bosnia-Herzegovina in 1990 resulted in the division of power between three nationalistic parties: the Bosnian Muslim Party for Democratic Action (SDA), the Croat Democratic Union (HDZ) and the Serbian Democratic Party (SDS). When on 15 October 1991 the SDA and the HDZ delegates in parliament adopted a memorandum declaring Bosnia and Herzegovina a sovereign state, the SDS took the decision to hold a plebiscite. The Serbs in Bosnia-Herzegovina voted to remain in Yugoslavia. Then, on 6 April 1992, the European Community (which mediated in the dispute) recognized Bosnia-Herzegovina as an independent state. In response, the assembly of the Serbian people in Banja Luka declared the independence of the Serbian republic of Bosnia-Herzegovina. That resulted in violent armed clashes between Serbs, Muslims, and Croats. With the Dayton Accords of 21 November 1995, Bosnia-Herzegovina was declared a federation, consisting of Bosnia, Herzegovina, and the Republika Srpska (RS). Again, FRY did not take part in this war in an official capacity. It did provide major military, diplomatic, and material aid to the Serbs. Soldiers and officers of the army of the FRY fought in Bosnia with Republika Srpska military symbols on their uniforms.

Internal Conflicts

From 1991 to 2001, Serbia was characterized by parallel violent conflicts and tensions developing on two mutually interwoven levels. On one hand, there was a conflict between the regime and the democratic opposition. On the other, there was a conflict with the ethnic Albanian community in Kosovo, which took various forms and phases. The Milosevic regime used and abused interethnic tensions and conflicts to maintain its power. It projected discontent toward other ethnic groups and it told the Serbian people that they were being threatened by a "hostile environment."

The accumulated discontent of the citizens of Serbia with the foreign and internal policy of Slobodan Milosevic and his party became manifest in mass protests that on a few occasions brought the country to the brink of civil war. On 9 March 1991 in Belgrade, Vuk Draskovic, the leader of the largest opposition party, organized a rally against the information monopoly of the ruling party. Tens of thousands of people clashed with the police. After Draskovic was arrested, the regime sent Yugoslav army tanks into the streets. Students and citizens protested for several days, but the regime managed to contain the protests. Two people were killed.

Although the protests continued from year to year and the number of protesters grew steadily, the disunity among the Serbian opposition, coupled with the charisma of Slobodan Milosevic, the media blockade, and systematic election fraud committed by the regime, frustrated democratic change. When after the November elections for local self-government in 1996 the regime tried to annul the results in the districts in which the opposition had won, mass demonstrations of 1 million people and more were staged all over Serbia. The demonstrations lasted three months, shaking all structures of society to the core and turning the majority of public permanently against the regime. This crisis was mediated by the former prime minister of Spain, Felipe Gonzales, on behalf of OSCE. He pressurized the regime in Belgrade to acknowledge the election results. In this way, the opposition in Serbia for the first time had a chance to manage finance and the local media, which was to be of crucial importance for its victory at the elections in September 2000.

The crucial reasons for the collapse of the Milosevic regime are the following:

- Military and diplomatic defeat in all wars that he waged (Croatia, Bosnia and Herzegovina, Kosovo)

- Economic devastation of the country resulting from the war policy, sanctions, and the failure to introduce economic reforms
- Unification of the opposition parties, proper organization of the election campaign, and effective election monitoring
- Readiness of Serbia's citizens to push through their electoral will even at the cost of confrontation with the police and the army

Kosovo and Southern Serbia

The conflict in Kosovo erupted in the middle of the 1990s and culminated in 1998–1999. Several international organizations and governments (Contact Group—France, Italy, Great Britain, Russia, and the United States—the EU, and the OSCE) tried to mediate, but after Yugoslavia refused to sign the Rambouillet Agreement, which allowed the deployment of 28,000 NATO soldiers in Kosovo and made FRY withdraw its military and police forces, NATO launched a bombing campaign. The bombing of FRY lasted from 24 March to 10 June 1999. This action was terminated by UN Security Council Resolution 1244 and the deployment of a multinational force led by NATO.

The Presevo Valley area in southeast Serbia is composed of the municipalities of Presevo, Bujanovac, and Medvedja, which border the provinces of Kosovo and Macedonia. The majority is Albanian, but there are also Serbs as well as Montenegrins and Roma living in the municipalities. The crisis in the south of Serbia revealed itself in conjunction with and in the aftermath of the NATO campaign, when a significant number of Yugoslav/Serb forces were concentrated there. The first publicly known series of attacks on the Serbian police forces started after the NATO campaign. Albanians linked the escalating violence to the redeployment of Yugoslav/Serb security forces, engaged in the Kosovo war until June 1999. Serbs are prone to associate the violence with the result of local elections in Kosovo, which were held under UNMIK auspices. The results showed that Rugova and his Democratic League of Kosovo still held an unassailable majority and that various UCK leaders had not won much confidence among the Kosovo Albanians. The violent actions and other armed incidents could therefore be explained in two ways: as an expression of the desire of Albanian extremists to draw the attention of the international community to the Kosovo problem, and as a demonstration before both the international community and fellow countrymen that the UCK was still in charge, regardless of the Kosovo election results.

The low-intensity conflict lasted till spring 2001. After the fall of Milosevic's regime, the West started to change its views on Serbia and Yugoslavia, which pushed the Kosovo problem largely into the background.

In the meantime, the armed clashes along the administrative border with Kosovo were not favorable for Belgrade, either at the international or the domestic level. The new government was concerned that such incidents could harm its newly found popularity at home and abroad. However, this government reacted in a manner that set it immediately apart from Milosevic's regime. It did not use excessive force, but tried to eliminate the causes of the conflict in cooperation with the international community and involve the Albanians in the process.

The newly elected authorities in Yugoslavia set up the Federal/Republican Coordination Body led by Serbian deputy prime minister Nebojsa Covic and comprising the federal minister of national and ethnic communities, Rasim Ljajic, as well as representatives of the Yugoslav army and the Serbian Ministry of Interior. To promote stability, the Coordination Body drafted and circulated the "Program for the Solution of the Crises" created by the activities of the Albanian extremists groups in southern Serbia. The program envisaged what might be termed a "gradual and conditional" approach. The Albanians presented their platform: "Platform for the Prevention of the Armed Conflicts and Crises Solutions in Presevo, Bujanovac and Medevedja Region." The Albanian platform insisted on the "demilitarization of Presevo, Bujanovac and Medevedja by withdrawing Serbian forces and placing the region under International supervision."

The international community welcomed Belgrade's attitude in seeking a peaceful solution to the crises and condemned the behavior of armed Albanians.

The damage resulting from the events in the south of Serbia is both indirect and direct. First of all, there is the misery of human casualties, destruction of properties, and people fleeing their homes. Also the obstruction of traffic on the international motorway Belgrade-Nis-Sofia-Salonika was a big problem: this highway is of an exceptional importance not only for Serbia but for the neighboring countries as well, particularly Greece, Macedonia, and Bulgaria.

The indirect damage refers to spreading political instability, thus creating an obstacle for the authorities to tackle economic issues, and particularly to attract foreign investments.

A cursory glance into the official Serb and Albanian platforms shows gaps between them. The Albanian side sees the resolution of the conflict through obtaining a "special status" of the area under international supervision. They recommend the withdrawal of Serbian police and the federal army as a condition for a peaceful settlement. In newspaper interviews, local Albanian political leaders have advocated their right for a referendum to be held to shape their own future. The Serbian government also advocates the assistance of the international community, expecting from it a guarantee of the sovereignty of the existing state (UNSC Resolution 1244) and the keeping in check of Albanian extremists who endanger the peace. It offers integration of the Albanian community into the common state, guaranteeing human rights according to the highest international standards, and its integration into security and municipal structures.

Official Conflict Management

The Republic of Serbia, first as a part of the SFRY, and then of the FRY, has been one of the key factors in the development of the Yugoslav crisis right from the beginning. That is why the international community (in particular, the EU, OSCE, UN, and United States) directed the bulk of its activities toward

Serbia. However, the regime in Serbia interpreted these activities as interference in the internal affairs of the (already disintegrated) Yugoslav state. In that sense, the Serbian regime reluctantly accepted the mediation of leading international organizations and governments in the conflicts in Croatia, Bosnia-Herzegovina, and Kosovo. On the other hand, FRY/Serbia was one of the signatories of all relevant documents (Dayton Accords, Military and Technical Agreement, etc.) foreseeing the inclusion of international organizations in the resolution of the crises in the area, notably NATO and the UN.

The UN Department of Peace Keeping Operations (DPKO) and other UN agencies such as UNHCR, UNICEF, and WFP have maintained an international presence in the FRY throughout the crisis affecting Yugoslavia. The UN provided diplomatic, information, and humanitarian assistance. The OSCE was allowed to set up a mission in Serbia covering Kosovo, Sandzak, and Vojvodina, from September 1992 to June 1993. Its basic objectives were to promote dialogue among ethnic communities, to collect information on the infringement of human rights, and to protect minority rights. Following the overthrow of the Milosevic regime, additional international organizations have been allowed to open their offices and operate throughout the territory of Yugoslavia. UNMIK has established a liaison office; OSCE has a mission; and the Council of Europe, NATO, the European Union Monitoring Mission, the European Agency for Reconstruction, the UNDP, World Bank, the IMF, and a number of international humanitarian organizations, all have offices in FRY.

Conflict Management in Southern Serbia

The case of southern Serbia reveals how a concerted effort of international and national actors including national NGOs can bring about a peaceful resolution, fragile as it still is.

To tackle the low-intensity conflict in southern Serbia was of paramount importance given the detrimental consequences an extended crisis would have created for the Serbian opposition, which had just replaced the Milosevic establishment, and the international actors that could have suffered retaliations and further instability in Kosovo. The UN, through its specialized agencies (UNHCR, UNICEF, WHO, WPF), and several international NGOs were present in the area throughout the conflict, but their intervention was ad hoc and purely humanitarian. Their main tasks were to provide humanitarian assistance to refugees, displaced persons from Kosovo, and social cases. Although their presence contributed to the containment of a certain degree of sociopolitical tension, it was clear that the solution should also be pursued on the political/security terrain. In this context and with a view to raise awareness, the UN special envoy for the Balkans, Carl Bildt, visited the area and met with local officials. The first significant diplomatic/political initiatives were initiated following the victory of the democratic forces in September 2000.

In November 2000 the European Union deployed monitors in the area. Their task was to monitor political and security developments and facilitate contacts among the parties. In mid-December of the same year, UNHCR deployed staff in Vranje. In March 2001 the U.S. State Department also established a presence there. However, NATO, in conjunction with the EU, took the lead in facilitating a solution to the crises and conducted shuttle diplomacy between Serbian authorities and Albanian officials to engineer and facilitate a peaceful end to the extremists' armed actions and a dialogue between the parties. As a result, a cease-fire agreement was signed that entered into force on 12 March 2001. Despite a number of reported incidents, the cease-fire is still holding (as of this writing).

Meanwhile, as of 13 March the Yugoslav army has been allowed to gradually and conditionally redeploy in the area. The redeployment was concluded on 31 May. No major incidents were reported and on all accounts both the army and the Serbian police acted professionally.

The deteriorated situation in Macedonia is a source of concern. At the moment of this writing, some 6,000 Albanian refugees from the country have taken refuge in southern Serbia. Though they have been absorbed by the local population, given the strong ties between Albanians in the Presevo Valley and in Macedonia, they represent an additional burden to the already precarious socioeconomic situation in southern Serbia, considered one of the poorest areas in the whole of Serbia.

In February 2001 the UN deployed an assessment mission to southern Serbia. Fifteen UN agencies and other international organizations participated. The mission found that the legacy of past systematic human-rights discrimination, coupled with economic disparities, is still prominent. The structural underdevelopment and inadequate institutional capacities further complicate the situation. The mission has suggested that confidence-building measures should be promoted immediately to help consolidate the peace process. Since June 2001 the UN has established an Inter-Agency Southern Serbia Support Office in Vranje. It focuses on developing a common strategic framework to include human-rights monitoring, promoting and supporting confidence-building measures (i.e., disarmament, demobilization, etc.), capacity building and quick-impact projects for employment, economic recovery, and development of the area. Priority is given to the municipalities of Presevo, Bujanovac, and Medvedja, with a view to extend the geographical coverage. The OSCE has established a multiethnic police academy where Serbs, Albanians, and members of other communities are jointly trained. As of November 2001, the OSCE has also established a "contact office" in Bujanovac. Furthermore, the Council of Europe is in the process of locating an international staff member in the office of the Federal Ministry of National and Ethnic Communities. In July 2001, the ministry opened an office in Bujanovac with the task of collecting information on human-rights violations.

Albanian representation in governing institutions remains one of the most problematic aspects of today's situation in southern Serbia. This is especially the case in the Bujanovac and Medevedja municipalities. However, the results of the election held in Kosovo in November 2001—where Serbs took part and moderate Albanian political parties were victorious—may indicate that ethnic communities are developing an allegiance with democratic values rather than exclusively with their own ethnic group.

Multi-Track Diplomacy

Until 1990 there were around 19,000 different nonprofit organizations in Yugoslavia, but they were neither independent nor served as promoters of civil society. Their main aim was to promote the communist regime and to organize the society according to the prevailing ideology. They worked under direct state control and, among other things, assisted the state in molding human activities according to prescribed shapes. In that sense, the real civil society with a network of genuine independent nongovernment organizations started in 1990, when the free association and organization of citizens was legalized. In FRY in the last ten years, 1,344 new NGOs have been registered. A major increase in the number of NGOs occurred after the mass civil protests, when most of the students and youth organizations were established. After 1997, improvements in the NGO sector could be perceived: there was more coherence in their actions, strengthening of their financial status, and expansion of their networks and their influence on broader public opinion. Besides major cities, where most NGOs have been concentrated, new NGOs appeared in the majority of the towns all over the country, especially in those where the opposition came to power after the 1996 local elections in Serbia.

It is necessary to point out that the development of civil society in FRY was anything but normal because of the policies emanating from the Milosevic regime, most of the population suffered under the UN, U.S., and EU economic, diplomatic, and cultural sanctions. These circumstances were highly unfavorable for the spreading of universal ideas of free society, independence, freedom of thought, and reform in line with a modern Europe.

The policy of the Milosevic regime had been based on the concept of the total mobilization of the masses and the manipulation of nationalistic feelings. From the very beginning, it was inimical to all independent organizations that promoted universal values and nonviolent policies. The NGOs that directed their activities to opening the channels of communication with the representatives of ethnic communities and the West, with whom the Serbian state was virtually at war, were constantly accused of being traitors, foreign spies, or agents. The state expressed its displeasure with their work not only through official media and constant accusations, but also by imposing administrative difficulties in the process of their registration, and sometimes by threats to their members.

NGOs were playing a double role. They were involved in peace initiatives concerning ethnic communities, against whom the regime waged a war (Croats, Bosnian Muslims in Bosnia and Herzegovina, Albanians in Kosovo). They were also engaged in the fight against Milosevic. In the first case, there have been dozens of initiatives serving as a bridge between different ethnic groups. Important to mention here are the Soros Foundation, Center for Anti-War Action, Belgrade Centre for Human Rights, Group 484, Humanitarian Law

Belgrade, Serbia: Women in Black demonstrate against the war every Wednesday in the Trg Republika or "Republic Square" (Sept. 1995)

Center, Helsinki Committee for Human Rights in Serbia, Women in Black, and the Belgrade Circle. Since their establishment, women's NGOs have most actively participated in antiwar campaigns and set the general tone of protests. Women in Black developed a network of organizations covering most of Serbia that in addition to antiwar actions were working on general education and the promotion of women's rights. Although they were not in a position to stop the conflicts, such NGOs played a very important role in showing alternative policies, in contrast to the policies of the ruling parties. This served the purpose of dismantling the prejudice that there is no need for communication and open talk with one's enemies. NGOs helped in the process of reintroducing the feelings of universal solidarity toward all innocent people who had been suffering as victims of ethnic wars.

Together with the opposition political parties, NGOs organized a pro-election campaign and convinced the majority of the citizens of Serbia that it was possible to replace the dictatorship of Milosevic in a peaceful, democratic way, by getting people out to vote in the greatest possible number. This must rank among their biggest successes. The most prominent role was played by young activists from Otpor (Resistance) who persuaded the youth of the country to actively participate in political life. A coalition of NGOs encompassing Civic Initiatives and the European Movement in Serbia lead a broad "get out the vote" campaign, advocating that citizens (the young, women, peasants, men) could change politics for the better by casting their vote. CESID, supported by a number of other NGOs, organized the monitoring of the vote counting. In sum, NGOs have helped enormously in combatting Milosevic and his regime in a peaceful manner, preventing a very real possibility of a catastrophic civil war. And they have proven that they have significant capacity to mobilize citizens around important political issues.

Finally, a word on the media. The long duration of the Milosevic regime to a large extent relied on its full control over the media, especially of those exerting the greatest influence—the electronic media. That is why the role of a free media was of utmost importance: Radio B92 (later renamed Radio Free B92) and the city's TV channel, Studio B, for years were the only beacons of free expression and objective information.

Multi-Track Diplomacy in Southern Serbia

The UN office in Vranje serves as a focal point for southern Serbia. It works closely with other international NGOs that also have offices in the area, such as USAID/OTI, ICRC, Médecins Sans Frontières (Belgium, Switzerland and Greece), and with those that have ad hoc programs but not a permanent presence, such as Care International, Cooperazione e Sviluppo, Cooperazione Italiana, Catholic Relief Service, HELP, IFRC, Médecins du Monde (Greece), Oxfam, Save the Children, Swiss Agency for Development and Cooperation/ Swiss Disaster Relief, and European Agency for Reconstruction, among others.

In the conflict zone itself, it is hard to establish proper institutional mechanisms capable of dealing with existing problems. For objective reporting, investigation, and resolution of human-rights problems, there are budding local institutions and NGOs. But they need strong and urgent support. The existing NGOs have little capacity and training, but they are in a learning process. For example, UNDP has launched and NGO capacity-building program.

The Council of Human Rights in Bujanovac regularly reports on the human-rights situation among the ethnic Albanian population to the established governmental coordination body and to relevant international organizations. Reportedly, the property rights of the Albanian population are challenged, since the Yugoslav army still occupies a school and a shoe factory. On the other hand, the coordination body has set up a fund to compensate those whose property had been looted or damaged during the conflict.

A parallel Initiative Board for Human Rights Protection operates for the Serb population, and was set up in Bujanovac in January 2001. It is concerned with the general insecurity of Serbs (especially those living in enclaves in Kosovo), kidnappings, and cultural heritage (i.e., churches, etc.).

The Multi-Ethnic Center in Medvedja was recently set up by a group of young Serbs, Gorans, Roma, and ethnic Albanians. They intend to work with the youth. As of 1 July 2001 and with the support of UNICEF, the center hoped to be publishing a newsletter in Serb, Albanian, and English.

The European Movement in Serbia organized a conference for political representatives and civil society delegates from both sides, as well as NGO representatives from Sandzak and experts from UN and UNMIK. The conference was held in Krusevac, on 2 and 3 February 2001. The conference was meant to be an initiative for multiethnic cooperation as a precondition for a better future. Both sides put on the agenda the unresolved problems that endanger the common lives of ordinary people. The result of the conference is the "Krusevac Declaration," which states that any political solution would be extremely complex and that any quick and efficient solution that would satisfy all sides concerned in the conflict can hardly be achieved.

Otpor has established a branch office. It is promoting actions to break ethnic-motivated barriers. It distributes humanitarian aid and provides legal advice. It plans to open an internet café. Like elsewhere in Serbia, it is focusing on young groups.

The Atmosphere and Potential for a Serbian Civil Society

Generally, in Serbia there is a distinction between urban and rural environments. In the major cities the values of a pluralistic society prevail. In that sense, urban areas are being included in dynamic changes proper to a modern society faster and easier. Individuals are left with a much larger maneuvering space for independent action and decisionmaking. Civil-society networks, branching out from these centers, are slowly covering ever larger areas.

Rural areas continue to be largely "closed societies": they are chronically enslaved to patriarchal values, customs, and prejudices, and their inhabitants are prone to subordination. No allowance is made for alternative ways of behavior. In this case, the activities of the NGOs sector in these areas are facing many obstacles and are often misunderstood; they are just taking the first steps in the process of establishing the rudimentary elements of a civil society. This requires patience and understanding the mentality of the local population. No wonder then that on the rims, such as southwest Serbia, the space for a civil society is very narrow and hard to develop.

A closer look at the zone of armed conflict itself, i.e., at the towns and villages where incidents occur, would show not only local communities divided along ethnic lines, but also poor conditions for the development of a civil society. This is due to cultural and economic factors, as well as to the Kosovo crisis. Very few NGOs try to cope with the problems of the divided society and those that do hardly keep their positions nonpartisan. This is not surprising after so many years of one-sided propaganda. NGOs mostly promote the views of political parties of their own ethnic group and seldom make mutual contacts. This is due to all kinds of pressure, including threats to individuals by the local political authorities and widespread public opinion that it is best not to meddle with the "opposite side." The Albanian community is especially very homogenous traditionally, and has a rigid vertical structure; sometimes it threatens the lives of individuals who break common expectations and rules of conduct. This basically works like a parallel system of control and should not be overlooked.

In these closed societies, events such as those in Kosovo, the Presevo Valley, and northwest Macedonia breed ethnic homogenization and the rise of xenophobic feelings. These are areas where women do not play a significant role in public, social, or economic life. It is hard to expect any significant improvement in the future, as it has proved difficult to break old customs, especially in this delicate situation.

Therefore, it is difficult both for the international community and NGOs to rebuild bridges between sharply divided societies that in many ways breed opposing hopes. So there is a need for support of local NGOs by strengthening the networks that already exist in larger cities in southern Serbia. Some backing may be needed for the Albanian side from NGO networks in Kosovo. International NGOs should find a way to combine civic energies from both sides and work toward some common end. Only through such a cooperation there is a hope for strengthening the civil sector.

Prospects

If the situation in southern Serbia reescalates, it could represent a major obstacle to economic recovery and political stability, given the fact that the defeated extreme-nationalist forces in Serbia direct the blade of their criticism toward the incapability of the new authorities to cope with extremism and to find rapid solutions for socioeconomic problems. On the other hand, the international community, especially the United States, has made financial aid and investments conditional on a restrained attitude of the Yugoslav/Serb security forces and full cooperation with International Criminal Tribunal in The Hague.

There are indications that Albanian extremists living in southern Serbia, in coordination with the Albanians living in Kosovo and probably in Macedonia, want to impose a different status on the municipalities populated mainly by Albanians in southern Serbia, and to consider that territory as their own. On the other hand, by allowing the Yugoslav armed forces to return, the international community has clearly made it known that they are extending great trust to the new government in Serbia. Negotiations between the two parties remain the only rational possibility, but to accomplish this it is necessary for the two sides in the dialogue to see all positions regarding the key issues in the dispute.

Thanks to the truce signed by the Yugoslav/Serb authorities and Albanians living in southern Serbia, facilitated by NATO/EU representatives, peace is holding, but is still fragile.

Recommendations

The following are three main recommendations for facilitating peacebuilding in Serbia:

- Assistance of leading international legal and economic institutions in the readmission of Serbia and the Federal Republic of Yugoslavia into their full membership
- Full cooperation with the International Criminal Tribunal in The Hague and extradition of the indicted persons accused of crimes against humanity

- Active participation of international institutions in the resolution of all intraethnic relations/conflicts

Regarding the current crisis, it is necessary for both parties in the conflict to bear in mind the following facts. One of the causes of the present crisis in southern Serbia is certainly discrimination of Albanians during Milosevic's regime. Another cause of the crisis are the extreme political demands of some Albanian politicians in the Presovo Valley for a special status based on territorial claims that occurred even before 1999 when the Kosovo conflict exploded. Their aspirations are connected with the aspirations of Albanians in Kosovo, who call this territory "Eastern Kosovo" and who wish to annex it into the future "independent" state of Kosovo.

Some aspects of the crisis could be eliminated by the governments of FRY and Serbia. Others could be eliminated only with the help of the international community, which should exert pressure on some Albanians politicians to give up their territorial claims toward this area, and to curb the illegal flow of money, arms, and people.

If it is in the interest of the international community and Yugoslavia to promote peace, stability, and prosperity, decisive steps should be taken toward easing tensions between ethnic communities. It is of vital importance to create an institutional framework (law, police, public services, education system, media, etc.) which would be trusted by all. In that sense international, regional, and local NGOs might be of great help. The presence of interested agencies (UN, EU, etc.) and donor-funded programs might help in the recovery process in southern Serbia and elsewhere. Local NGOs need external experts and resources to become more successful in their efforts. Local administration needs urgent institutional reforms and decentralization at the municipal level. Without help both from the Serbian government and foreign agencies, it will be impossible to upgrade public services.

In order to ensure a viable multiethnic community, it is essential to begin a series of economic projects that would involve people from both ethnic communities and provide regional and local NGOs with logistical and technical help in upgrading their capacities.

Resources

Newsletters and Periodicals
Centers for Pluralism, newsletter
Europe Plus, newsletter of the European Movement in Srebia, Belgrade (monthly)
New Balkan Politics (www.newbalkanpolitics.org.mk)
Policy Advocate, Center for Management (available on CD-ROM), Belgrade

Reports
Council on Foreign Relations Task Force Report, *Promoting Sustainable Economies in the Balkans,* by Steven Rettner and Michael B.G. Froman, New York, 2000.

International Crisis Group
> *Peace in Presovo: Quick Fix or Long Term Solution?* Balkans Report 116, August 2001.
> *Serbia's Transition: Reforms under Siege.* Balkans Report 117, September 2001.
> *Report of the UN Inter-Agency Assessment Mission to Southern Serbia,* March 2001.

United States Institute of Peace, *Whither the Bulldozer? Nonviolent Revolution and the Transition to Democracy in Serbia.* Special Report, August 2001.

Other Publications

A System for Post-War South-East Europe: Plan for Reconstruction, Openness, Development and Integration, by Michael Emerson. Brussels, Center for European Policy Studies, Working Document No. 131, May 1999.

EU Enlargement: Yugoslavia and Balkans, edited by European Movement in Serbia and Ekonomika Politica and Economski, Belgrade, 1998.

Preparing Yugoslavia for European Integration, edited by Jelica Minic. Belgrade, European Movement in Serbia, November 2000.

Serbia After Milosevic, by Nebojsa Covic. Belgrade, Liber-press, 2001.

The Albanians, by Miranda Vicker. London-New York, I. B. Taurus, 1997.

The Balkans, by Misha Glenny. Great Britain, Granta, 1999.

The Stability Pact for South Eastern Europe: Potential, Problems and Perspectives, by Rafael Biermann. Bonn, Center for European Integration Studies, C 56, 1999.

War in the Balkans: Consequences of The Kosovo Conflict and Future Options for Kosovo and the Region, by International Crisis Group. Brussels, ICG Balkans Report No. 61, April 1999.

Selected Internet Sites

www.balkan-info.com (Balkan Information Exchange)
www.copri.dk (Copenhagen Peace Research Institute)
www.emins.org (European Movement in Serbia)
www.gov.yu (Government of the Federal Republic of Yugoslavia)
www.iwpr.net (Institute for War and Peace Reporting)
www.kossovopress.com (Kosovo Press)
www.mup.sr.gov.yu (Ministry of Interior of Serbia)
www.southeasteurope.org (South-East Europe Online)
www.transnational.org (Transnational Foundation for Peace and Future Research)
www.unorg/peace/kosovo/pages/kosovo.htm (UNMIK)
www.yuembusa.org (Federal Ministry of Foreign Affairs)

Resource Contacts

Sonja Biserko, president of Helsinki Committee for Human Rights in Serbia, e-mail: bisrkos@EUnet.yu

Igor Djoric, Multiethnic Center, Medvedja, e-mail: mecmedvedja@ptt.yu

Fischer Gerard, adviser, UNMIK, Pristina, e-mail: gfis422800@aol.com

Alija Halilovic, Civic Forum, Novi Pazar, e-mail margina@EUnet.yu

Saip Kamberi, president, Committee for Human Rights, Bujanovac, e-mail: haipk@yahoo.com

Dragan Lakicevic, project manager, Ethnic Relations Program, European Movement in Serbia, Belgrade, e-mail: lakicevi@EUnet.yu

Goran Lapcevic, Local Council of EPUS, Krusevac, e-mail: lapac@ptt.yu

Bratislav Lazarevic, CeSID, Bujanovac, e-mail: batabiro@ptt.yu

Zoran Lutovac, M.A. Research Fellow, Institute of Social Sciences, Belgrade, e-mail: lutovacz@net.yu

Maria Teresa Mauro, political officer, UN Liaison Office, Belgrade, e-mail: mtmauro@EUnet

Srdjan Milivojevic, Otpor Branch in Bujanovac, www.zivot.zajed/no.org.yu
Zoran Milovanovic, City Home, Leskovac, e-mail: zojavid@ptt.yu
Behlul Nasufi, president of the Center for Multicultural Education, e-mail: behlulnasufi
    @yahoo.com
Shoko Noda, UNDP, Belgrade, e-mail: shoko.nodo@undp.org.yu
Danijel Pantic, secretary-general, European Movement in Serbia, Belgrade, e-mail:
    emins@eunet.yu
Sead Skrijelj, Center for Multi-Ethnic Dialog, Novi Pazar, e-mail: cemed@infosky.net
Biljana Vankovska, Transnational Foundation for Peace, Skopje, e-mail: biljanav@
    sonet.com.mk

Organizations
Centre for Anti-War Action
Mačvanska 8
11 000 Belgrade, Yugoslavia
Tel/Fax: +381 11 344 17 37
E-mail: caa@caa.org.yu

Helsinki Committee for Human Rights in Serbia
Zmaj Jovina 7
11000 Belgrade, Yugoslavia
Tel.: +381 11 637 542: 637 116
E-mail: biserkos@EUnet.yu
www.helsinki.org.yu/

Otpor (Resistance)
K. Mihajlova 49
11000 Belgrade, Yugoslavia
Tel.: +381 11 637 500
www.otpor.com

Data on the following organizations can be found in the Directory section:
Belgrade Center for Human Rights
Center for Free Elections and Democracy
Center for Psychological Growth and Development Encouragement
European Movement in Serbia
Group MOST
Humanitarian Law Center
PROTECTA
TRAIL Association
URBAN-IN

Dragan Lakicevic is author of five books in the domain of political philosophy and current events in the Balkans, and numerous articles and papers in various journals. Danijel Pantic (M.A. in law) is secretary of the European Movement in Serbia. He is the author of numerous articles concerning the European Union and the transition to democracy. Zoran Lutovac (M.A. in political science) is employed at the Insititute for Social Science in Belgrade. He is an expert on ethnic relations and a distinquished member of several governmental and nongovernmental organizations. Maria Teresa Mauro works as a political officer at the United Nations Labor Organization (UNLO) in Belgrade. She is temporarily concerned with the improvement of ethnic relations between Albanians and Serbs in southern Serbia. The views expressed here are her own and not necessarily those of the UNLO.

14

RUSSIAN FEDERATION

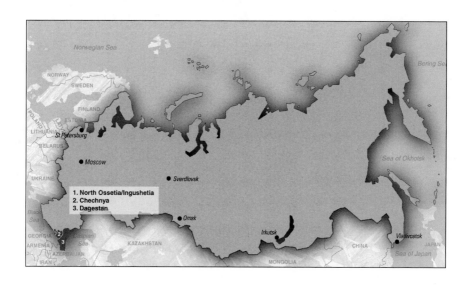

14.1

Regional Introduction: Post-Soviet Russia Redefines Its Interests

Anna Matveeva

Post-Soviet Russia, which emerged from the USSR almost by default, has too weak a sense of national cohesion to form a distinct identity. With a population of 150 million, the largest country in the world even after the Soviet collapse, Russia embarked on a dramatic journey during which it has transformed its political and economic life, and created a new identity for its people. In the Caucasian and Central Asian regions, Russia has been the dominant force since Tsarist times and has had to make some major adjustments in its relations to the newly created independent states. However, Russia's own security and internal development are still so deeply influenced by the fate of its neighbors that it will continue to be a key player in these troubled regions.

The End of Seventy Years of Communist Rule

After the defeat of the Russian Empire in World War I a splinter group of socialists (known as Bolsheviks and led by the exiled Lenin) seized control on 25 October 1917 and empowered the soviets as the ruling councils. The Union of Soviet Socialist Republics was created. A few months later, the Bolshevik Party was renamed the Communist Party. The brutal rule of Josef Stalin (1924–1953) strengthened Russian dominance of the Soviet Union at a cost of tens of millions of lives. The Soviet economy and society stagnated in the following decades until General Secretary Mikhail Gorbachev (1985–1991) introduced *glasnost* (openness) and *perestroika* (political and economic reform) in an attempt to modernize communism. In 1988 he shocked the world by holding elections to transfer power from the Communist Party to a new parliament. However, his initiatives inadvertently released counterforces. The failed August 1991 *putsch* against Gorbachev marked the coup de grace for the Soviet Union. In December 1991 the USSR broke up into fifteen independent republics. Boris Yeltsin became the first president of the Russian Federation, by far the largest and the most powerful of the fifteen.

After the collapse of the USSR, an atmosphere of naïve hope and inflated expectations prevailed in both the East and the West. In the former Soviet Union, people believed that prosperity and freedom could be quickly achieved following the removal of the communist system. Meanwhile, many in the West possessed strong faith in the ability of free-market and democratic practices to foster long-term stability. Both were disappointed. Since then, the Russian Federation has struggled in its efforts to build a democratic political system and market economy to replace the strict social, political, and economic controls of the communist period. Ten years later, pessimism and disillusionment are widespread among the elites and ordinary people in the Russian Federation.

The Yeltsin Regime

President Boris Yeltsin had two principal aims in guiding the emergence of the new Russia: first, to turn the country into a true democracy and, second, to replace the centrally planned economy with a capitalist model based on the free market and private ownership. A "shock therapy" program was introduced in January 1992 under the guidance of the young acting prime minister, Yegor Gaidar. The strategy had two pillars: liberalization of prices and the privatization of state industries. For most people, the immediate effect of these measures was a dramatic decline in living standards.

The Russian parliament became a stronghold of opposition to Yeltsin's policies. The government was accused, first of betraying the ordinary citizens who, instead of the promised prosperity, became impoverished, and second of abandoning the 25 million ethnic Russians who found themselves living in countries that were once part of the USSR. The parliamentary majority forced Yeltsin to sideline Gaidar and nominate as premier the centrist Victor Chernomyrdin, formerly the Soviet fuel and energy minister.

This step failed to reconcile the executive and the legislature and in March 1993 the struggle intensified. In response to the paralysis of power created by the "war of laws," Yeltsin declared emergency rule. In September 1993 the president, in violation of the existing constitution, dissolved the parliament and announced that elections would be held to two houses of a new body, the Federal Assembly. The parliament refused to obey, and 180 deputies barricaded themselves inside the parliamentary building, the so-called White House. Yeltsin ordered the army to bring tanks and to bombard the building. More than a hundred people were reported to have died as a result.

On the back of his victory over the parliament, Yeltsin then pushed through a new Russian constitution that was put to a nationwide plebiscite and won a dubious majority. The constitution set out new electoral legislation: the State Duma, the lower house of the Federal Assembly, was to consist of 450 deputies, half of them elected in single-member constituencies and the remaining half to be formed on the basis of party lists. The Federation Council, the upper house, was to be composed of independent candidates representing 89 constituent units, or "subjects" of the Russian Federation. The new constitution also vested most political power in a presidency that was tailor-made for Yeltsin, and greatly restricted the powers of the new State Duma.

However, the results of the December 1993 Duma elections were disappointing for the Yeltsin camp: the progovernment Russia's Choice Party gained only 15 percent of the vote, while the Liberal Democratic Party of Russia, a right-wing nationalist party led by Vladimir Zhirinovsky, a master of political public relations, won 22.8 percent. The reformed Communist Party led by Gennagy Zuganov also performed well. The results took the Yeltsin leadership and the Western powers by surprise and showed them both to be out of touch with the realities of Russian life.

The period from 1995 onward saw the emergence of a close-knit group of Yeltsin loyalists who were to become his "kitchen cabinet." Alexandr Korzhakov, Yeltsin's chief bodyguard, and Anatoly Chubais, the first deputy premier, responsible for the privatization of state assets, played prominent roles in the political intrigue. The evidence of Yeltsin's declining health and increasing signs of his weakness to alcohol raised doubts about the president's capacity for office. With the disastrous military intervention in Chechnya, Yeltsin's popularity ratings dropped below 10 percent.

In the run-up to the 1996 presidential elections it was thought likely that Yeltsin would be replaced either by Zuganov, the Communist Party leader, or by the retired general Alexandr Lebed, the commander of the Russian 14th Army in Moldova. This prospect alarmed the so-called oligarchs—powerful business tycoons—who came to shape Russian politics in the second half of the 1990s. With their power based on control of important economic assets such as oil and gas reserves acquired on the cheap in behind-the-scenes privatization deals, good relations with the government and the ability to manipulate it were vital for continued success. Their concerted effort in organizing Yeltsin's electoral campaign was crucial to his election victory, securing him 53.8 percent of the vote, compared with 40.3 percent for Zuganov.

Following the victory, Yeltsin withdrew from public politics, and Chernomyrdin appeared to step into his shoes. Moscow divided into a number of camps, headed by various oligarchs, while younger reform-oriented politicians tried to ensure that momentum for reform was not completely lost. Battles within the political community became still more poisonous when most of the prominent players acquired control over mass-media outlets to promote their own interests and denigrate their opponents.

At the beginning of 1998, Yeltsin returned to his duties and embarked on a string of reshuffles that wreaked havoc on the government's policies. Attempts to identify a successor and a desire to fight corruption in the government were cited as possible explanations for these shake-ups. In March 1998 the president dismissed Chernomyrdin and his entire government and appointed a young, unknown figure, Minister of Fuel and Energy Sergei Kirienko, in Chernomyrdin's place.

Kirienko was immediately confronted with the threat of economic collapse in Russia, largely owing to the combined effects of the drop in world oil prices and the Asian financial crisis. The government's wage arrears to federal employees gave rise to increasing political unrest. In August 1998 the ruble was devalued, precipitating the worst financial crisis of the Yeltsin era. The market was paralyzed by liquidity shortages, share prices plunged, and Russia defaulted on its foreign loans. In the weakest moment of his entire rule, the president was forced by the Duma to agree to the appointment of a compromise candidate, Foreign Minister Yevgeny Primakov, as premier.

Contrary to international expectations, Primakov's period in office saw improvements in the Russian economy and in political stability. This was a result of Primakov's stable rule, an increase in the world oil price, and the devaluation of the ruble, which encouraged domestic production.

In 1999, the widely popular Primakov initiated a campaign against corruption that extended to the heart of the Russian political system. Ultimately this was to jeopardize the security of the "Kremlin Family"—the all-powerful grouping around the ailing president. Additionally, the State Duma came close to impeaching Yeltsin in May 1999.

The president acted quickly and decisively. Having abruptly dismissed Primakov, who offered no resistance, he appointed Sergei Stepashin, the interior minister, to his post, only to dismiss him in turn three months later. This time Yeltsin appeared to have identified a successor for his own retirement—the relatively unknown Vladimir Putin, a former KGB officer who had spent most of his career in Soviet external intelligence and who headed the Federal Security Service (FSB) at the time of his nomination to the premiership. Yeltsin made it clear that he wanted Putin to take over from him as president.

Yeltsin voluntarily relinquished power to clear the way for the new leader, resigning early, on 31 December 1999. During his presidency, Russia developed, through violent political battles and dubious palace intrigues, into a democracy that, although flawed, seemed to be functioning. Political parties remained weak, but democratic institutions had taken root. Elections of federal and regional levels of power had become standard practice.

However, the Yeltsin rule left the economy in a state of disarray. Although cleared of much of the communist baggage, it still lacked a new market infrastructure. Corrupt practices, patronage networks, and organized crime filled the vacuum. Moreover, the transition period had taken its toll on ordinary Russians, leading to a demographic crisis: life expectancy dropped dramatically to 58.9 years for men. The population began to fall by 500,000 per year, and even the influx of ethnic Russians from other former Soviet republics could not reverse this decline.

In the social sphere, one positive phenomenon was the development of the civil society, a continuous tradition from the dissident movement of the Soviet era that was largely disrupted—and created anew—in other newly independent states. Russia's NGOs grew in numbers and influence, and began to spread across professional and age groups. Geographically, however, they are concentrated in the big cities and in the northern part of the country.

Russian mother looking for her son. Lydia Andreevna, from Novo-Cheboksary in the Urals, in the Chechen schoolhouse where she has lived for four months. She abandoned her job and home to come and search for her son Vallodiod, a conscript missing in action, but receives no help from the Russian government (Spring 1995).

In short, the first Russian president gave freedom to most Russians, prosperity to some, and security to nobody. He also left a great deal of work to be done by his successor.

The Putin Leadership

When appointed to the premiership, Putin seemed to struggle to come to terms with the huge responsibility of his new role. As a career civil servant with no political ambition for leadership, he rose to the presidency with no explicit political agenda. Nor did he appear to be driven by a lust for power for its own sake. Putin landed in the top job almost by default, trying to adapt to it as much and as quickly as he could.

The Russia he inherited was already longing for the kind of leadership personified by Vladimir Putin. The state he came to govern was chaotic and demoralized; poorer, weaker, and less influential in the world than during the previous ten years. A deep sense of national humiliation and insecurity possessed the nation. The desire for a sensible political order, stability, and growing prosperity in place of revolutionary change and sacrifice for the sake of bright future, was widespread across the country. Putin's personal qualities created a favorable contrast with those of Yeltsin: he was young and robust (forty-seven at the time of the election) and his reputation was unsullied by allegations of corruption and nepotism. Nor was he ashamed of the past, unlike

Yeltsin whose political career was built on the rejection of his own, and his country's, Soviet past.

Putin's presidential campaign, explicitly endorsed by Yeltsin, was greatly helped by an outbreak of Chechen rebel activity, which he decisively moved to suppress with the enthusiastic approval of most Russians. The second campaign in Chechnya, unlike the first, proved popular among the Russian public, and Putin's opinion-poll ratings soared. The December 1999 Duma elections were won by the pro-Putin forces, and Yedinstvo (Unity), a party created specially as Putin's electoral vehicle, performed unexpectedly well despite its short spell in existence. Putin's political rivals, such as the Fatherland–All Russia alliance of former premier Primakov and Moscow mayor Yurii Luzhkov, and the Communist Party, received a clear signal that neither had a chance of winning the presidency in the forthcoming presidential elections.

In March 2000, Putin was elected as the second Russian president with 53 percent of votes cast, defeating his nearest rival, Gennady Zuganov (29 percent). His electoral slogan, "Dictatorship of the Law," appealed to longings for a strong hand to reestablish the rule of law and combat crime and brought him astounding popularity. On assuming the presidency in May 2000, Putin reappointed many of the key figures from Yeltsin's last government, such as the prime minister, Mikhail Kasyanov. The government is divided into the economic bloc, controlled by the premier, and the security bloc, controlled directly by the president. The Yeltsin loyalists whom Putin kept in their jobs for a year dominated the latter. Observers speculated that such personnel policy constituted part of a promise given by Putin to the first president: personal guarantees against prosecution for the members of Yeltsin's inner circle and a commitment to keep key figures of the security bloc intact for a year. In the government reshuffle of March 2001, when Sergei Ivanov, Putin's most influential supporter, replaced Igor Sergeev as the defense minister, Putin demonstrated that he had now become his own man.

The priorities of the Putin regime differ from those of Yeltsin, but its challenges are no less formidable. They include restoring order within the federal and regional systems of government, overcoming social and economic backwardness, and national revival. Putin has followed the Russian tradition of putting the state at the center of the reform process, seeing a strong state as the guarantor of individual rights and freedoms. For the first time in Russian history, this task is being facilitated by a cooperative relationship between the executive and the Duma, where Putin enjoys a working majority.

The most spectacular undertaking of Putin's first year was his fight against the oligarchs. Also, the Putin's leadership succeeded in reinstating its control over Gazprom, the flagship of the Russian economy. It would be a mistake, however, to see Putin's hand behind every move in these cases—some of them have embarrassed him.

Economic performance has improved during Putin's time in office. Initial conditions were favorable. High oil prices provided spare cash for the government to invest in public services and pay wages and pensions on time. The devaluation of the ruble encouraged domestic output, and consequently budget revenue. Since 1999 inflation has been reduced to modest levels. The proportion of transactions conducted in cash, rather than by means of barter, rose, as has tax collection. The government was able to pursue a successful strategy for preserving a semblance of international financial respectability: it defaulted on its "inherited" Soviet-era debt, but continues to service its post-Soviet debt almost unaided by new Western lending. Economic policymaking has also improved since Yeltsin's presidency: Minister of Economic Development and Trade German Gref and presidential economic adviser Andrei Illarionov have introduced a sound package of reform measures and enjoy presidential backing.

Nevertheless, much still remains to be done. There has been little progress on banking reform. Banks tend to operate as the financial arm of an enterprise or conglomerate. The state is still tightly intertwined with business. The reform of the giant "natural monopolies," such as Gazprom and United Energy System, is only starting with considerable caution. Putin himself is under no illusion that the recent relative economic boom is a substitute for restructuring. In his own words, "Unless we start being active today, including implementing structural reforms, tomorrow we may enter a long period of stagnation."

After over a year in office, the new regime has showed some determination to make Russia a better place to live. By being an active and engaged president, Putin has restored the authority of the office. His regional reforms, prosecution of oligarchs, and moves toward economic restructuring are all signals of a renewed energy in the Kremlin. In his annual message to Russia's Federal Assembly in April 2001, Putin set out an ambitious, liberal agenda of economic, political, and judicial reform.

However, the biggest concern is the boost given to the security services under the new president, who himself originates from the security milieu. Their resurgence has been felt most sharply in the outlying regions, especially in the turbulent Northern Caucasus, rather than at the federal level, where the record is more mixed. Putin has also shown a personal vulnerability to criticism. The national NTV saga, during which Gazprom called in its loan through which the TV channel was financed, led to a scandal over the channel ownership and personnel appointments. It also called into question the ability of the new regime to tolerate public criticism and the future of free media in Russia.

Whether these moves should be attributed to the temporary difficulties of growth and learning, or point to a more alarming scenario, remains to be seen. So far, most Russians seem prepared to give the president the benefit of the doubt.

Specific Issues

Center-Periphery Relations
The Russian Federation is far more monoethnic than the USSR: 83 percent of the population is ethnic Russian. The federal structure based on ethno-territorial

federalism was inherited from the Soviet era. In a drive to preserve the territorial integrity of the federation, in spring 1992 Moscow introduced a Federation Treaty that consisted of three sets of agreements reflecting the unequal distribution of power between various federation subjects. The ethnic republics received the greatest degree of autonomy, which caused resentment among the territorial regions.

The 1993 Constitution sought to reduce the shift of rights to the republics. The republics lost their sovereign title, but retained most of their rights, i.e., presidency, parliament, constitution, language policy, and state symbols. In fact, many regions acquired similar powers to those enjoyed by the ethnic republics and the strongest leaders managed to sign power-sharing treaties with Moscow.

In the ensuing power struggles between the center and periphery in the first half of the 1990s, the regional elites were the principal winners. Their power was further strengthened in 1996 when in return for their support for Yeltsin in the presidential race, the regional and republican leaders became members of the Federation Council. Such "asymmetric federalism" was exercised through a number of agencies, most importantly through the presidential administration. The current president, Putin, was at one time in charge of regional affairs in the administration, which helps to explain why, later, streamlining center-periphery relations was to become one of his priorities.

The Ministry for Regional and Nationalities Policy, which was the subject of numerous reorganizations throughout the 1990s, was formally charged with implementing policies, but its real power largely depended on the standing of whoever was its head at the time. Gradually it came to be regarded as a backwater ministerial appointment. The Ministry of Finance, which deals with federal transfers from the central budget to the regions, as well as the Ministry of Transport, which controls the electricity grids and ground infrastructure, were much more important players. Finally, after the first war in Chechnya, the FSB emerged as the agency most actively engaged in the North Caucasus. Institutional and personal confusion prevailed at the top, enabling the regional bosses to fish in these murky waters.

On coming into office, Putin's major political initiative was an effort to restore authority throughout the country by streamlining center-periphery relations. The president moved to reorganize the system of presidential representation in the regions by creating seven federal districts (groups of regions) to which his envoys were appointed. The new representatives were to strengthen the president's authority in the periphery by ensuring that federal institutions in the regions answered to the center rather than to the regional leaders, and by bringing regional legislation into line with federal. However, the implementation stumbled across the resistance of powerful regional elites. The second move was the reform of the Federation Council in order to make the regional leaders cede to representatives the seats they had previously occupied themselves. The third move amended framework legislation to give the president the legal instruments to dismiss regional leaders and get the principle of federal intervention established.

Crime and Corruption

Corruption and crime are major obstacles to Russian social and economic development. Both are closely linked to the weak rule of law. A dramatic rise in violent crime has accompanied Russia's market transformation: for instance, according to the Russian Statistical Agency, the number of murders and attempted murders per annum doubled from 1990 to 1997, reaching a total of 29,300. Assassinations of business and political figures are common. It is estimated that some 80 percent of businesses pay protection money to racketeers. Drug addiction and drug smuggling from East to West is a new and a growing concern. Russian organized crime has emerged as a major force on the international criminal scene, building links with criminal organizations around the world.

Russia also suffers from endemic official corruption reaching deep into the fabric of the government and commerce. The diversion of state funds to private ends, the extraction of bribes, and the manipulation of sensitive information for financial gain are all rife. This malaise also affects law-enforcement agencies and the courts.

Relations with International Organizations

Relations with NATO and with the international financial institutions, especially the International Monetary Fund (IMF), have dominated Russia's engagement with multilateral international organizations. In June 1994 Russia joined NATO's Partnership for Peace program, which provided for closer military consultation, but opposed the entry of the Czech Republic, Hungary, and Poland into the alliance. In May both parties signed the Founding Act on Mutual Relations, and a Permanent Joint Council based at NATO headquarters in Brussels was created. Having grudgingly accepted the East European states' ascension to NATO, Russia vehemently opposes incorporation of the Baltic states.

Russian-NATO relations were tested by the NATO air strikes in Kosovo in 1999, which were vocally opposed by Russia. In June, however, Russian mediation was instrumental in persuading the Yugoslav leadership to accept a peace plan. Russia declared itself ready to send peacekeeping troops to Kosovo, but not under NATO's command. The last episode of the campaign was marked by the Russian troops' dash to seize the airport in Pristina shortly before NATO troops crossed into Kosovo. Some observers read into it a desire to establish a separate sector as a safe haven for Serbs. Others saw it as a brilliant piece of political entertainment, when the Russian foreign minister, apparently kept in the dark, described the incident as an "unfortunate mistake," while Yeltsin promoted the commander in charge of the operation.

The Russian political voice in the UN, although reduced from the days of the USSR, is still powerful since, as an heir to the Soviet Union, it has inherited a permanent seat at the Security Council. The Organization of Cooperation and Security in Europe (OSCE) was favored by the Russian political establishment, which sought to promote it as the leading forum to deal with security in Europe in an effort to counterbalance NATO's influence. OSCE also facilitated negotiations on withdrawal of Russia's troops from Georgia (2001) and Moldova (2002), to which Russia committed itself at the Istanbul summit in November 1999. OSCE played a successful conflict-prevention role during the recent deterioration of Russian-Georgian relations (2000) when it deployed an observer mission to monitor the Chechen sector of the Russian-Georgian border. Cooperation with the Assistance Group on Chechnya has been more controversial: during the first campaign, Russian politicians suspected the group of legitimizing the rebel leadership, and during the second campaign sought to keep it at arm's length.

Russia was admitted to the Council of Europe in 1995, in the midst of the first war in Chechnya. The organization then suspended the rights of Russia's parliamentary delegation to the Parliamentary Assembly (PACE) in 2000 during the second war, which were reinstated later in 2001. Russia's relationship with the European Union has been expanding on many levels, with the long-term commitment to supplies of Russian gas to the European markets lying at the heart of such cooperation. Russia's relations with the West were dramatically altered by the 11 September 2001 attacks on the United States. President Putin was the first leader to phone George Bush to express his unequivocal support and offered help in the struggle against terrorism. Russia transformed into a Western ally. Despite domestic pressures from the military and political establishment, Moscow engaged in intelligence sharing with the United States, opened the doors to the U.S. presence in Central Asia, and provided technical support for operations in Afghanistan. Soviet experience of intervention in Afghanistan also became useful under the new circumstances. Putin expects tangible benefits for Russia to emerge from cooperation with the West. The most important ones are an agreement on strategic missile defense and Russia's relationship with NATO, the acceptance of Russia as a member of the World Trade Organization, an easing of trade restrictions, and more understanding of Russia's actions in Chechnya.

The Commonwealth of Independent States

In the Yeltsin era, relations with the former Soviet republics that became the newly independent states fell between the remit of foreign and domestic policy. Although politicians of all levels publicly stated their commitment to engage with the management of these new relationships, in reality there was little desire to shoulder the task.

The Commonwealth of Independent States (CIS) was established in December 1991 with a mandate to provide an intergovernmental framework for the multilateral cooperation of its twelve members—all former Soviet republics, with the exception of the Baltic states. In reality, it proved a weak body, as its founding members did not share the same goals for its future. The intention of some (for example, Ukraine) was to use the organization to effect a peaceful divorce from the USSR. Others, for instance, Kazakhstan, hoped that it would provide a framework for economic, military, and political integration on a new and more equitable basis. Both groups, however, feared Russian hegemony. The result of such a mixture of motives was that the CIS has divided into an inner core of states that desire closer ties (Armenia, Belarus, Kazakhstan, Kyrgyzstan, Tajikistan, and Russia), and a group that has formed their own alliance, GUAM (Georgia, Ukraine, Azerbaijan, and Moldova). Uzbekistan shifts between the two, depending on its domestic needs, and Turkmenistan has opted for "neutrality." Following October 2001 fighting in Abkhazia, Georgia threatened to leave the CIS in an effort to distance itself from Russia.

Under President Putin the Russian rhetoric on the subject of the CIS has accelerated, but its meetings are low-profile. The new leadership's commitment to multilateral forums is waning, and it increasingly prefers to deal with CIS member states on an issue-by-issue, country-by-country basis.

Policies Toward the South Caucasus and Central Asia

Since Tsarist times, Russia has been the dominant force in the Caucasian and Central Asian region. It is also the power that has had to adjust the most to the independence of the new states. Under President Yeltsin, Russian actions were largely characterized by a syndrome of postimperial disengagement, leading to an odd mixture of imperial temptations, pursuit of the new opportunities, and inability to comprehend evolving changes.

President Putin has radically altered the image and substance of Russian leadership in the region, having embraced a more realistic and modernized definition of Russian interests. Still, Russia can never be indifferent to developments there. Its own security and internal development can still be influenced by the fate of its neighbors, particularly if that fate includes state collapse, ethnic violence, and regional conflicts that could spill over into Russia itself. Russia is a key continuing player in the region, though no longer in the lead role.

For Russia, the current issues appear as follows.

The threat of Islamic fundamentalism. All leaderships of the Muslim states of the region fear the influence of fundamentalism from abroad, which is shared by Russia since is has a sizeable Muslim population. The recent insurgencies in Uzbekistan and Kyrgyzstan, together with links to fighters in Chechnya, feed such perceptions. In the view of the Central Asian regimes, rightly or wrongly, Russia is the only power that can address their security concerns, since their own armies are too weak and there are slim hopes that the West is ready to commit forces to the region. In 2001, discussions on steps to combat anticipated incursions of Islamic rebels led to an agreement to create a rapid-deployment force to carry out operations in Central Asia. China also became a part of these security arrangements, and Moscow started to beef up its military forces in the region. The new U.S. role in the region and efforts to eradicate the Al Qaida network gave boost to this priority.

Caspian energy resources. Russia is one of the Caspian littoral states and the government is determined that Russia should have a share of the Caspian Sea's resources and control the transportation of those resources to their markets. The United States is equally determined that alternative routes should also be used, and that no routes should go via Iran. In November 1999 the presidents of Azerbaijan, Georgia, and Turkey agreed on a legal framework for the construction of an oil pipeline from Baku via Tbilisi to the Turkish terminal at Ceyhan. However, it is still not clear who will pay the considerable costs of construction and when it will begin. Meanwhile, Russia, in partnership with other players, has built the Caspian Pipeline Consortium (launched in 2001) to take Kazakh oil to the Black Sea port of Novorossyisk, and completed the Dagestan bypass of the Baku-Novorossyisk pipeline for the sake of avoiding Chechnya. These steps have ensured a continuous Russian role in the Caspian "great game."

Presence of Russian peacekeeping troops and its military bases. The future of the 25,000 Russian troops stationed in Tajikistan is not yet clear. The original purpose of their deployment was the sealing of the border with Afghanistan. There is, however, little pressure on them to leave. Russian forces have become largely indigenized at the lower ranks, with ethnic Tajiks flocking to Russian service for the better pay and provisions.

The situation is different in Georgia, which initially agreed to the presence of the Russian military bases and border guards in return for Russia's help in incorporation of Abkhazia back into Georgia. Since it has become evident that such hopes are unlikely to materialize, pressure on Russia to withdraw its troops has mounted. Russian border guards left Georgia in 1999 and the closure of the bases is under way.

Anna Matveeva is a program manager at Saferworld (on small arms and security). She previously worked as a research fellow at the Royal Institute of International Affairs (Chatham House, London) and program head at International Alert (London). As a scholar specializing in issues of conflict and the politics of post-Soviet Eurasia, she has authored publications such as The North Caucasus: Russia's Fragile Borderland *(London: RIIA, 1999) and academic articles, and undertook projects for organizations such as the International Peace Academy, EastWest Insititute, Minority Rights Group, and the Heinrich Böll Stiftung.*

14.2

Chechnya:
Drive for Independence
or Hotbed for Islamic Terrorism?

Anna Matveeva

Chechnya is a territory in the Russian Federation that has sought since 1991 to break away from Moscow's rule. It experienced a first military intervention by federal troops between 1994 and 1996, which ended in a Russian defeat and loss of control over the republic. Spillover of criminality from Chechnya, rise of Islamism, attacks on Dagestan, and several bombings in Moscow and in the North Caucasus, blamed on Chechen militants, prompted the Russian leadership to launch a second campaign in 1999. That war has continued, having assumed a character of a "holy war" and attracted Islamic fighters from abroad, including those from the Al Qaida network. Although more successful militarily, the war has not succeeded in resolving the political issue of Chechen independence. The Russian leadership, however, started to make a distinction between the separatist drive and terrorist threat to its territory emanating from Chechnya. This may form a basis for a solution, if Russia allows Chechnya to secede and a Chechen leadership could ensure that Chechnya does not threaten its neighbors. Although the West has generally supported Russian aims and found common interest in fighting Islamic terrorism, it has condemned its military methods. The OSCE was involved in facilitating peace negotiations during the first war, but the deteriorated security situation in Chechnya and Russia's unwillingness to cooperate have made further engagement problematic.

The Chechens are the largest ethnic group in the North Caucasus. In 1922, the Chechens were granted their own "autonomous oblast" (AO), but in 1934 it was merged with the Ingush AO, where Chechens were in the majority (57 percent). In 1943, Chechens and Ingush were deported to Central Asia, accused of collaboration with the German troops. The republic declared independence from Russia in November 1991 and adopted a constitution in March 1992. The independence movement was led by the Chechen National Congress, whose

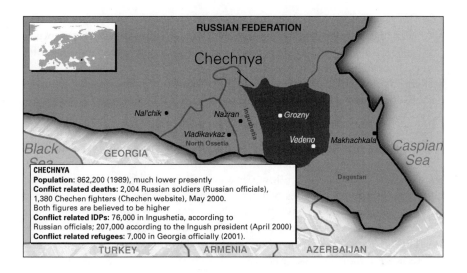

RUSSIAN FEDERATION

Chechnya

Nal'chik •   Nazran   • Grozny

Vladikavkaz •
North Ossetia   Vedeno   Makhachkala

Black   GEORGIA   Caspian
Sea

CHECHNYA
Population: 862,200 (1989), much lower presently
Conflict related deaths: 2,004 Russian soldiers (Russian officials),
1,380 Chechen fighters (Chechen website), May 2000.
Both figures are believed to be higher
Conflict related IDPs: 76,000 in Ingushetia, according to
Russian officials; 207,000 according to the Ingush president (April 2000)
Conflict related refugees: 7,000 in Georgia officially (2001).

Dagestan

TURKEY   ARMENIA   AZERBAIJAN

prominent member, former air force general Djohar Dudayev, became president of Chechnya in 1991. Following the declaration of independence and violence between supporters and opponents of the Chechen National Congress, Russian federal troops were sent to restore order but, owing to Chechen resistance and the refusal of the Russian Supreme Soviet to sanction the use of force, the troops were withdrawn. By June 1992 all Russian troops had left the republic, leaving behind a large stock of arms. The Ingush decided to distance themselves from the Chechen secessionist drive and left the dual-nationality republic.

On 10 December 1994, the Russian federal powers started the first military intervention into Chechnya, which became the largest war in the former Soviet Union. President Dudayev led the Chechen resistance to the Russian advances that culminated in the ill-fated storming of Grozny, massive loss of life, indiscriminate bombardment, and the destruction of most economic and social infrastructure in the republic. Crushing defeats by the federal forces vastly outnumbered limited military successes, while spectacular acts of hostage taking in Budennovsk and Kyzlyar demonstrated how vulnerable to the Chechen attacks the neighboring territories are.

Although the Federal Security Service (FSB) eventually succeeded in killing Dudayev, this failed to undermine Chechen resolve, and in summer 1996 the war intensified. After the storming of Grozny by the Chechen forces in August 1996, Moscow decided to retreat. The first war ended with the signing of the Khasavyurt Accords, which established the cessation of hostilities and committed the parties to delay the decision on political status for five years. Russian troops were withdrawn from the breakaway territory. The Treaty on Peace and the Principles of Mutual Relations between the Russian Federation and the Chechen Republic of Ichkeria—a no-use-of-force agreement—was signed in May 1997.

The postwar parliamentary and presidential elections took place in January 1997 and brought to power Aslan Maskhadov, chief of staff and prime minister in the Chechen coalition government, for a five-year term. The Islamic Republic of Ichkeria was proclaimed in 1998 and the *sharia* system of justice was introduced. Maskhadov tried to concentrate power in his hands to establish authority, but failed to create an effective state or a functioning economy. The situation gradually slid out of the control of the government, and the republic descended into chaos. The war and lack of economic opportunities left large numbers of heavily armed and brutalized "unemployed warriors" with no occupation but further violence. A growing epidemic of kidnappings, robberies, and murders of fellow Chechens and outsiders, most notably the beheading of four employees of British Granger Telecom in 1998, put an end to possibilities of outside investment. Maskhadov proved unable to guarantee the security of the oil pipeline running across Chechnya from the Caspian Sea. Illegal oil tapping and acts of sabotage deprived his regime of crucial revenues and exasperated his allies in Moscow.

Various opposition groups emerged around prominent field commanders. In August 1998, Shamil Basaev, hero of the Chechen resistance and a powerful warlord, broke off all relations with the Maskhadov government and requested the parliament and the *sharia* court to impeach Maskhadov for "treason," by which they meant his pragmatic approach to relations with Moscow. Several armed clashes between Maskhadov loyalists and oppositionists took place around the strongholds of rebellious commanders. At the same time, Islamists (dubbed by their opponents as Wahhabis) who had emerged in Chechnya during the first war started to proliferate and clash with the adherents of traditional Sufism. The presence of foreign Islamist fighters and the financial means they had to attract recruits added fuel to the existing tensions and created new fault lines in an already fragmented republic.

From the end of the first war, the border territories of the Russian Federation had progressively suffered from escalating crime stemming from Chechnya. Killings, kidnappings, and looting of property and cattle made social and economic activities virtually impossible, and led to the establishment of various local self-defense units. The regional and republican administrations increased their pressure on Moscow to seal the border with Chechnya with proper installations and border troops, and on several occasions they closed the border unilaterally. The culmination came after August 1999, when Chechen field commanders in opposition to Maskhadov led an offensive by Chechen and Dagestani militants into the highlands of Dagestan, where they clashed with the local rogue armies and with Russian troops.

Following the intervention in Dagestan, Moscow was subjected to a bloody terrorist campaign that killed over three hundred people and was blamed by the Russian government on the Chechen terrorists. This prompted Russia to bomb Chechnya, thus triggering the beginning of the second full-scale war in October 1999. The bombing spelled the end of the wait-and-see policy pursued by Moscow over the previous three years, which had implied the peaceful reintegration of Chechnya into the Russian state.

After the Russian federal troops suffered a humiliating defeat at the hands of the Chechen guerrillas in the first campaign, it seemed unlikely that the Russian establishment would be willing to intervene a second time, but the dynamics of the situation on the ground made Russian inaction impossible. The presidential campaign in Russia, emphasizing the resurgence of Russian power and the revival of the military, also required a good cause to fight for.

Conflict Dynamics

The second campaign differed from the first one in a number of respects. For one thing, the neighboring regions and republics, apart from Ingushetia, were supportive of the federal troops and hostile to their Chechen neighbors. Second, Russian propaganda, emphasizing Chechen terrorism and the victory in Dagestan, had the effect of boosting morale. Third, the Chechen fighters were far less internally united. Maskhadov, caught between militants and the Russians, proved unable to unite the Chechen nation to fight either the Russians or the Chechen warlords. Despite his legitimacy as the elected president of Chechnya—his term of office expired in January 2001—Maskhadov had little to bring to the negotiating table, since his authority over Basayev and Khattab was minimal, and the two in effect tried to assassinate him in the interwar period. And finally, ordinary Chechens were less enthusiastic about fighting than they had been during the first war. Military victory then had failed to bring peace and prosperity; on the contrary, after three years of lawlessness and economic devastation, the relative stability enjoyed by their North Caucasian neighbors has begun to seem more attractive.

The mobilization declared by Maskhadov was met with less enthusiasm than before, and the popular response seemed to be to flee rather than to fight. In the opinion of Ruslan Aushev, president of Ingushetia, Russia's major mistake was its failure to try to mobilize the Chechen people to fight on Moscow's side against the terrorists. If only Moscow could have capitalized on popular fear and resentment of warlordism, Chechnya's political incorporation would have been less traumatic.

During September 1999, the Russian military undertook air attacks against Chechnya combined with efforts to seal off the borders between Chechnya and the rest of Russia. The intervention by the ground troops started in October, causing a wave of civilians to the flee to neighboring Ingushetia, as well as widespread suffering. The initial Russian tactics were not to engage in frontal attacks, but to encircle the larger towns where fighters were suspected to be based and negotiate surrender if possible, or to bomb the area into submission otherwise. Progress into the lowlands was better than expected, but efforts in February to capture Grozny, the capital of Chechnya, proved difficult. Russia kept 80,000 troops in Chechnya, with the 15,000-strong 42nd Motorized Infantry Division, headquartered in Khankala, forming the backbone of the Russian military advances. Additional troops were stationed in the neighboring republics along the perimeter of Chechnya.

The Russian military managed to gain partial control over the eighty-kilometer Chechen-Georgian border, maintaining a presence in the disputed

Martin Adler/Panos Pictures

Grozny, in front of the presidential palace: Valentina Krasnentiya, age 82, shows a photo of her daughter who has been missing for months

sector so as to control mountain paths leading to Chechnya. This border was a source of constant friction in Russian-Georgian relations. Russian commanders claimed that the Georgian government turned a blind eye to the penetration of mercenaries and the flow of arms to the Chechen fighters through its territory. Russia also accused the Taliban movement in Afghanistan of sending fighters to Chechnya and training the Chechen Islamist guerrillas, and threatened to launch air strikes against the Taliban similar to those carried out by the United States following the bombings of its embassies in Africa. Evidence of links between the Taliban and Chechen Islamists have emerged with the launch of the U.S. operations in Afghanistan.

Security in the Russian-controlled areas has been constantly undermined. The Russian forces have been repeatedly hit by Chechen ambushes, mainly in the southern mountains, and in May 2000, two high-ranking Russian administrators were killed in a terrorist attack in Grozny. In March 2001 three terrorist acts took place in Stavropol *krai* (territorial area) and Karachaevo-Cherkessi, killing twenty-three. The Middle East–style suicide attacks have made the Russian troops even more suspicious of Chechen civilians. Ambushes of Russian convoys in Ingushetia have shown that the Chechen fighters cross under the guise of refugees, which has led to even stricter control of the border and misery for the civilians who tried to flee to safety.

Moscow's main challenge in Chechnya is how to rule the republic effectively. The Security Council, the main federal body in charge of Chechnya, has produced many plans but little clarity. Instead, policy intentions have been articulated by President Putin in his interviews at home and abroad, in which he accepted the possibility of Chechen independence as long as it does not serve as a launching pad for attacks on Russian territory. Operational policy has been expressed through personnel appointments.

In this area, two concerns prevailed among the Russian leadership: the quest to create an indigenous Chechen administration that would enjoy at least some respect among the local population, and the effort to ensure tight financial control over expenditures for reconstruction in order to avoid a repetition of the large-scale theft of federal money allocated to Chechen reconstruction in 1996–1997. After the first war, Chechnya emerged as a financial "black hole," where federal funds intended for reconstruction were often embezzled. For instance, the Russian procurator's office unsuccessfully tried to trace $1.5 billion believed to have ended up in Swiss bank accounts. The ultimate aim of the Putin administration is to funnel reconstruction funds from the federal budget through a closely controlled native Chechen administration that enjoys a degree of respect both in Chechnya and in Moscow. This financial responsibility is to be shared with the presidential representative to the federal region of Southern Russia and the North Caucasus; the current representative is Victor Kazantsev, who served as the commander of the federal troops in Chechnya until April 2000.

In February 2000, Moscow proclaimed an official end to the hostilities, marking the beginning of a period of postconflict reconstruction. But in reality, full control was never extended to the Chechen highlands. Attempts to create a pro-Moscow Chechen administration were only partially successful. The Russian authorities were forced to disarm pro-Moscow Chechen militia because of their unruly behavior and to distance themselves even from those Chechen leaders with whom they thought they could cooperate.

Mufti Akhmed-haji Kadyrov, a religious authority, appeared to be the only person who could be trusted. In June 2000, President Putin created a new Temporary Administration of Chechnya directly responsible to the Russian authorities and appointed Kadyrov as its head. Kadyrov is no Moscow puppet, unlike the Russian-backed administrations of the period of the first war, but had been a fighter on the Chechen side in the first war against Russia. He is also known as a staunch opponent of the Wahhabi version of Islam that has served as a source of inspiration for so many of the fighters in the second Chechen war. The Kadyrov administration was supposed to replace an earlier administration led by Nikolai Koshman, but confirmation of Kadyrov's status took over a year, and only in January 2001 did President Putin sign a decree establishing a system of executive power. He also appointed Stanislav Ilyasov, a Dagestani from Stavropol *krai*, as prime minister.

Local administrations in villages and towns have been created, led by loyal Chechens, often those who spent most of their lives in Moscow. The FSB gradually replaced the Ministry of Defense (MoD) as the main agency in charge of operations in Chechnya. It looked to Chechens who had problems with the law, promising them amnesty from prosecution if they agree to cooperate. In this way, the FSB has achieved leverage over some wealthy Chechen businessmen and their family networks, and manipulates them accordingly. Such local governments are backed by the authority of the Russian military administrations, where the commander in charge provides troops not only to maintain security, but also as a work force to restore essential civilian installations.

In an effort to preserve a semblance of normality, in 2000 Moscow organized by-elections for the Russian State Duma; at the time of the parliamentary elections (December 1999), those elections had not taken place because of the war. Aslan Aslambekov was elected as an minister of parliament from Chechnya. The next step would be to organize the election of a chief executive of the republic, but as of mid-2001, this has not yet occurred.

At the beginning of 2001, the Putin leadership made a decision to reduce the MoD force level from 80,000 to 15,000 over the next few years and to move operational control from the MoD to the FSB. However, after an initial withdrawal of 5,000 troops, it was decided at the 5 May 2001 meeting between Victor Kazantsev, Sergei Ivanov (the newly appointed minister of defense), Nikolai Patrushev (director of the FSB), and Boris Gryzlov (minister of interior) that the security situation was still turbulent and that a large-scale withdrawal was premature.

Currently, military operations focus on attacks on the Islamist Wahhabi leadership, especially the forces of Shamil Basayev and Emir Khattab, and attempts to eliminate or capture these two commanders, whose presence is viewed as essential to the resistance. Since being driven from the cities, the Chechens have shifted their tactics toward small-scale ambushes and attacks using land mines. The brutality, indiscipline, and corruption of the federal troops remains a major impediment to any political settlement in Chechnya. Federal operations involve widespread instances of indiscriminate bombardment, random killings, rape, and torture that the Russian authorities seem powerless to stop, and which have cost them dearly in the eyes of the ordinary people.

Official Conflict Management

The flimsy moral grounds used to justify intervention led Moscow to adopt a conciliatory stance in the aftermath of war. This also brought political moderates into key positions in negotiations with Chechnya. After the first Russian withdrawal in 1996, Russian officials had decided that Maskhadov was a moderate figure with whom they could deal on a pragmatic basis. He was expected to shelve the question of formal independence, while asserting the territory's de facto separation from Russia.

These assumptions proved false. Russian-Chechen dialogue was suspended after the kidnapping of Valentin Vlasov, presidential representative in Chechnya, in May 1998. The murder of Akmal Saidov, a staff member of the Russian delegation to Chechnya in September 1998, made the federal politicians even less willing to talk. The kidnapping of Deputy Interior Minister Gennadii Shpigun in March 1999 halted negotiations with Moscow completely. The moral high ground that Chechnya occupied during the war with Russia has been severely undermined by the beheadings of foreigners, public executions, and kidnappings of aid workers.

Since the beginning of the second war, Moscow has publicly refused to talk to Maskhadov, though behind-the-scenes contacts have continued. Finding a partner with whom to negotiate poses a real dilemma for Moscow. Maskhadov remains the nation's leader for the majority of ordinary Chechens, especially for those who fled the republic. The Russian Public Commission for Chechnya, headed by the State Duma Committee Chairman Pavel Krasheninnikov, met with the members of the Maskhadov government in May 2000 with the intention of entering into talks with him. However, his authority over the resistance fighters is minimal and he cannot make concessions on their behalf. Alliances and enmities between leaders are based more on personal relationships and opportunism than on political or ideological positions. Broadly, four kinds of warlords exist: Islamists, who fight more on religious than on ethnic grounds and enjoy external backing; heroes of the Caucasian wars of the 1990s who failed to adapt to civilian life; outright criminals who have been behind most of kidnappings; and local leaders concerned with security in their own area and driven primarily by local interests.

Kadyrov appealed to the Chechen field commanders to restore peace and stability, and expressed his readiness to talk to Maskhadov, despite the fact that Maskhadov failed to condemn the criminal activities of the warlords. In May 2000, general Troshev made a radical peace proposal when he suggested that a referendum should be held on whether Chechnya should remain part of the Russian Federation. Moscow also took steps to organize a loyalist Chechen political movement—the Union of Citizens for the Chechen Republic as a Democratic Rule-of-Law Within the Russian Federation (Solidarity)—to unite those Chechens who think that Chechnya's future lies with Russia.

Despite Western criticism of the campaign and its uncertain prospects, the second Chechen war has brought huge dividends at home. For the first time since the Soviet breakup, the feeling of national humiliation has been replaced by a belief that Russia is able to project power. The war in Chechnya also served as a launch pad for Vladimir Putin, then prime minister, to be promoted as a successor to president Boris Yeltsin. The military campaign costs $262 million each month, but high oil prices made it sustainable for the budget.

The Western Reaction

The West is in a difficult position vis-à-vis the second war in Chechnya. Russian territorial integrity, security of the North Caucasus, and the fight against Islamism all mitigate against a condemnation of Moscow's actions, let alone punishment of Russia in a tangible way. In the words of Javier Solana, "We are pragmatic and need a permanent dialogue with Russia." As the war progressed and the roles of foreign militants became more obvious, Western governments became more sympathetic to Moscow. The West could only criticize Russian military methods rather than the whole rationale for the intervention.

With so many well-documented accounts of brutality by the federal forces, the West could not accept Russia's methods, but since Maskhadov had virtually no control over the "independent warriors," Russia viewed any advice to negotiate with Maskhadov as impractical and the West had no other concrete proposals to offer.

The OSCE and the Council of Europe took the lead in dealing with both wars, while the UN was involved only on the humanitarian side through its High Commission on Refugees. The decision to establish an OSCE Assistance Group to Chechnya was made by the Permanent Council on 11 April 1995 after intense consultations in the wake of visits to Grozny and Moscow by a personal representative of the OSCE chairman-in-office. The group took up its duties on 26 April 1995. In December 1998, due to the deteriorating security situation in the region, the international staff of the group was withdrawn to Moscow.

The Assistance Group did contribute positively to Russian-Chechen negotiations during the first war. After the war it continued to maintain its presence in order to monitor transition to civilian rule and the establishment of political institutions, but lost rapport with the Chechen leadership due to its commitment to the principle of territorial integrity. With the beginning of the second campaign, the OSCE stepped up its activities and Knut Vollebaek, the OSCE chairman-in-office, conducted talks with presidents Maskhadov and Aushev. The November 1999 Istanbul summit acknowledged Russian territorial integrity and offered its assistance in the renewal of political dialogue. In return Moscow promised to permit Vollebaek to visit the region and eventually agreed to renew the OSCE mission in the Russian-controlled area of Chechnya. The intention was to locate the mission in Chechnya with the focus on humanitarian relief, but in May 2000 Russia refused to extend the mandate of the Assistance Group because of a disagreement on ambassadorial extraterritoriality and the rights of Chechen staffers to carry weapons. The Assistance Group then opened an office in Znamenkoye (northern Chechnya) on 15 June 2001, manning it with local staff of the group. The conditions for the return of international personnel to Chechnya, mainly concerning security requirements, are at present being negotiated with the Russian authorities.

The OSCE made another significant contribution to peace during the second campaign. Following the Russian claims that foreign fighters and Chechen guerillas entered Chechnya over the Georgian border, which led to a sharp deterioration in Russian-Georgian relations, the OSCE deployed an observer mission in February 2000 to monitor the movement across the border. The operation has been an example of a success in conflict prevention between two states, and Russia has appealed to the OSCE to extend the operation to cover the entire Russian-Georgian border. The issue is currently under consideration, but it is unlikely that the operation will cover the Dagestan sector because of the costs involved.

The Council of Europe (CoE) was mainly active during the second campaign, sending fact-finding missions to the region and advocating protection of the human rights of Chechen civilians. In April 2000, the Parliamentary

Assembly of the Council of Europe (PACE) voted to suspend Russian membership, as well as the voting rights of Russia's delegation, but this failed to gain the approval of the ministerial committee. PACE chairman Lord Russell-Johnston has been engaged in ongoing dialogue with Aslan Maskhadov, to the annoyance of the Russian presidential team. Under pressure from the UN Human Rights Commissioner and the CoE, Russian authorities established the position of human rights commissioner for Chechnya in April 2000 to work with the CoE experts.

Since then, the situation has started to improve. In January 2001, PACE approved a resolution submitted by Lord Judd that noted "encouraging, although limited progress." Positive developments included the beginning of reestablishment of the judicial system, including the establishment of local courts and police stations. It subsequently voted to readmit the Russian delegation to the full membership. At the same time, in April 2001, PACE published a report on crimes against civilians committed by the Russian troops.

International humanitarian agencies were active during the first Chechen campaign, but gradually withdrew or reduced their operations after killings and kidnappings of their workers, most notably the murder of six International Committee of the Red Cross (ICRC) expatriate staff members in 1996. By the beginning of the second campaign, no agency had a presence in Chechnya. The main remaining agencies in the region were UNHCR, Médecins sans Frontières, and ICRC, which have distributed aid to those republican authorities who appealed for help, and in particular the government of Ingushetia, which has accommodated over 200,000 IDPs.

The attitude of the Russian leadership and public at large regarding international activities has been one of suspicion. The Russians were puzzled by the contrast in Western reaction to the first and the second campaigns, noting that Russia was admitted to the Council of Europe in the midst of the first war, but suspended from the council because of the second campaign. Following NATO actions in Kosovo which many Russians interpreted as a dress rehearsal for peace-enforcement operations in Russia, the West lost moral credibility, and humanitarian concerns were interpreted as a desire to undermine their country.

Multi-Track Diplomacy

Prior to the outbreak of the first war, it was very difficult to attract international attention to problems in Chechnya, as International Alert discovered when it undertook a fact-finding mission to the republic in 1992 and sought to raise the issue. But the war quickly brought the republic into international focus, and the international presence prompted the development of local civil groups. This first war period was also marked by genuine cooperation between Chechen and Russian civil-society actors, such as the Committees of Soldiers' Mothers.

After the end of the first war in Chechnya, the security situation rapidly deteriorated, which impeded any international involvement. Consequently, the region became a "no-go" area for both foreigners and many Russians. The start of the second war in October 1999 made it virtually impossible for outside parties to intervene to establish peace because of the dangers on the ground and suspicions of the Russian secret services. Cooperation between Russian and Chechen NGOs also declined, largely because those Chechens who were prepared to work with Russians were looked upon with suspicion in their own society, and Russian propaganda influenced the attitudes of Russian NGOs. At the same time, the capacities and the confidence of the Chechen NGOs have increased significantly. Most NGOs had to move to Ingushetia at the beginning of the second war because of the security situation, but have returned to Chechnya since.

Facilitating Political Dialogue

The Conflict Management Group (CMG) has a long record of peace intervention in Chechnya. At the height of the first war in 1995, it established working relationships with the Russian Security Council and the Chechen presidential team. This enabled CMG to bring parties to the conflict to the Hague Peace Palace conference in 1996, where CMG proposed to delay the decision on the status of Chechnya pending a referendum in ten to fifteen years' time. The proposal was rejected by both parties at the time, but the settlement signed later in the year was based on that model. In May 1997, CMG arranged a second meeting that included influential political figures from both sides, such as Chechen vice president Vakha Arsanov and Russian oligarch Boris Berezovsky.

This initiative was followed up by a series of meetings in 1997–1998 in Moscow, Grozny, and Tatarstan, where CMG has been involved over a number of years in conflict-prevention activities. It was hoped that the Tatarstan example might help the Chechen leadership to adapt their expectations to the reality of the situation, and to enter into real bargaining with Moscow. Deteriorating security, lack of funding, and escalating infighting within the Chechen leadership group made it difficult to keep up the initiative, however. Plans have been drawn up to attempt to renew the project, pending funding, and also to capitalize on the willingness of the parties to talk, since their relationship is much worse now than during the first war.

General Alexander Lebed, current governor of the Krasnoyarsk *krai*, who served as Security Council secretary at the time, played a crucial role in ending the first campaign, having negotiated the end of hostilities with Aslan Maskhadov. He continued his efforts to bring peace to the region and created a peacemaking mission for the North Caucasus to facilitate dialogue between Chechnya, its neighbors, and the Russian authorities. Despite some initial promise, this initiative gradually came to a halt, since Lebed's political career failed to take off on a national scale and he became absorbed in power struggles in Krasnoyarsk. Moreover, Lebed was regarded as a traitor by the local Russians whose interests he failed to acknowledge while negotiating Russian withdrawal with Maskhadov.

In June 2001, the Forum on Early Warning and Early Response (FEWER), in cooperation with the Institute of Ethnology and Anthropology (Russia), Peace Mission in the North Caucasus (Russia), and the Netherlands Institute of International Affairs (Clingendael), organized a meeting on "Post-Conflict Reconstruction in Chechnya" in Stockholm. The aim of the meeting was to develop the Peace Reconstruction Initiative for Chechnya, drawing on local knowledge of the situation and the expertise of international representatives. The meeting was the second in a series of three roundtable meetings, the first having been held in Pyatigorsk in December 2000. The goals were to inform the international community about the situation in Chechnya and to discuss the issues of security and economic development.

Progress was impeded, however, by the fact that the postconflict situation in Chechnya has not yet begun, despite Russia's official claims to the contrary. In the absence of a political dialogue between the federal authorities and the representatives of the Chechen authorities on the future of Chechnya, work on reconstruction and security lacks the necessary foundation to proceed.

Humanitarian Work

In 1995, the Centre for Peacemaking and Community Development (CPCD) was established as a grass-roots organization and registered as an NGO both in Russia and the United Kingdom. It maintains its presence in Moscow, Chechnya, Ingushetia, and Kabardino-Balkaria, and works to support local capacities for peace. This involves projects with groups and individuals in the fields of human rights, peacemaking, community development, and humanitarian assistance. In Chechnya it cooperates with such organizations as Laman Az (Voice of the Mountains) and the Union of North Caucasus Women, a women's group working in community development and peacemaking.

The main project in the North Caucasus is the Little Star children's rehabilitation center in Grozny, opened in May 1997. In July 1997, two British psychologists working in the Little Star center, Camilla Carr and Jon James, were kidnapped, held for fourteen months in Chechnya, and later freed for ransom; since then, Little Star is staffed by local therapists. CPCD also provides humanitarian relief for the displaced in Ingushetia, and is involved in rehabilitation programs for traumatized children and essential reconstruction work. When the second war began, CPCD, together with Laman Az, set up a grain mill in the Chechen village of Sernovodsk to provide this service at low cost or for free for those in need.

NGOs that moved to Ingushetia when the second war began have now begun to return to Chechnya. One Laman Az group that went to Ingushetia and launched its humanitarian operations from the neighboring republic returned to Grozny to reopen its office, and currently operates in Chechnya. As the security situation has allowed, CPCD relief work has also gradually returned to Chechnya, where it works in close cooperation with the UNHCR and the Norwegian Refugee Council (NRC). The Caucasus Refugee Council, a Vladikavkaz-based Russian NGO, is engaged in humanitarian work with 5,670 families of IDPs from Chechnya in Ingushetia. Humanitarian and human-rights work has also been undertaken by Women of Don, a Rostov-on-Don-based Russian NGO.

The Danish Refugee Council (DRC) has maintained a presence in Stavropol *krai* providing humanitarian aid to IDPs from the first war who arrived in the *krai* in 1995–1996. DRC maintained cooperation with the regional authorities, assisting in forming policies toward migration issues and accommodation of the new entrants. Since the start of the second war, DRC and NRC, which has maintained a presence in the Southern Caucasus, have moved to supply relief aid to the new IDPs from Chechnya. DRC hosted weekly NGO meetings in Nazran (Ingushetia) to coordinate their activities.

The Cultural Centre of Vainakhs of Stavropolie was involved in delivering humanitarian aid to vulnerable groups in Chechnya, both Chechens and Russians, during the interwar period. Following the beginning of the second war, Kharon Deniev, its head, was appointed by the DRC as its local staff member responsible for distribution of humanitarian aid to Chechen IDPs in Ingushetia.

Advocacy and Human Rights

In Russia, the first Chechen campaign was marked by widespread opposition to the war, a significant antiwar movement, and cooperation between Russian and Chechen organizations. By the start of the second campaign, however, the atmosphere had changed, especially as a result of the kidnapping of Russian journalists who had provided coverage sympathetic to the Chechen cause during the first war. Though these journalists were freed for ransom, the attitude of the mass media changed. In 1999, civil society in Russia largely supported the intervention, if not the particular methods employed by the military. However, initial prowar enthusiasm subsided as casualties among Russian soldiers mounted, and human-rights groups consolidated their efforts to protest against the war.

The Anti-War Committee is a forum of Russian human-rights groups protesting against the war in Chechnya. Its members include the Memorial Human Rights Centre, the Union of Committees of Mothers of Russian Soldiers, the Russian Human Rights Network, the Antimilitarist Radical Association, the Young People's Human Rights Centre, Movement Against Violence, the Democratic Union Party, the Centre for Development of Democracy and Human Rights, the Anarchist Antiwar Movement, and other groups and individuals. The goal of the committee is to demonstrate publicly that not everybody in Russia agrees with the war in Chechnya. The committee organizes a variety of activities such as rallies, meetings, and publications.

The Union of Committees of Mothers of Russian Soldiers (renamed Committee of Soldiers' Mothers of Russia) is a humanitarian organization dedicated to the plight of Russian military personnel. It is involved in advocacy activities against the war, submits open letters to the Russian president, counsels the families of the affected servicemen, and takes up individual cases of violations of the human rights of soldiers.

The London Information Network on Conflicts and State-Building, a London-based NGO with an office in Tbilisi, has been involved in Chechnya since the end of the first war, and has organized meetings throughout the 1990s both in London and in the region to promote international conflict-resolution efforts. At the beginning of the second war, it organized a visit of a group of Laman Az members who went to Georgia and from there paid international visits to raise public awareness of the situation in Chechnya and to advocate President Maskhadov's position.

The Cultural Centre of Vainakhs of Stavropolie *krai* has been involved in monitoring human-rights violations related to the North Caucasian diasporas and raising public awareness of interethnic peace in Stavropol *krai* in the interwar period. It has worked with the regional authorities to monitor interethnic relations in the *krai* and especially on the border between Stavropol *krai* and Chechnya.

Quaker Peace and Service (QPS) was active during the first war in mobilizing Russian and Chechen civil-society groups to advocate peace and protest against the war. It organized a peace march from Moscow to Chechnya in an effort to generate publicity and appeal directly to the Russian troops. However, the fact that it attempted to unite very diverse social and political groups that otherwise had little in common with each other undermined the public message it sought to project. Work with the women's groups was one of its most effective undertakings.

Young People's Programs
CPCD has facilitated a Young People's Peacebuilding Network in the North Caucasus, sponsored by the EU Technical Assistance to the CIS (TACIS) program, providing individuals and local groups with training in alternatives to violence, and with e-mail communication facilities. Four youth meetings and two seminars have been held since its establishment. Laman Az is one such Chechen youth group working closely with Assa in Ingushetia, the Caucasus Forum, and CPCD.

Promotion of Citizen Security
The legacy of two wars in Chechnya has left the territory heavily mined, but there are few maps of the minefields. Land-mine awareness is a serious concern. CPCD is engaged in the International Campaign to Ban Land Mines through its partner organization, the Human Rights Investigation Bureau. Laman Az members have also played an active role in the mine-clearing program and have initiated a land-mine training program for the local staff members. In 1997, Laman Az conducted surveys of the Achkoi-Martan and Urus-Martan regions of Chechnya in an effort to identify the mined areas and in 2000 undertook a project to raise awareness of mines and unexploded ordnance among IDPs in Ingushetia and the inhabitants of Chechnya, acting as an implementation agency for the UNHCR. The project focused especially on children in cooperation with UNICEF.

Early Warning

International Alert (IA) has been involved in peacebuilding activities since 1992, having sent the first fact-finding mission to the republic to assess the mounting tensions. Unfortunately, early warning failed to influence decision-makers in the West who at the time believed in the democratic credentials of the Yeltsin regime.

The Forum on Early Warning and Early Response started its Caucasus program in 1997 and provides early-warning reports on Chechnya that can be found on FEWER's website (see Resources).

Training and Capacity-Building

In 1995, a Dutch charity, Chechen Relief, set up the Agency for Rehabilitation and Development (ARD), an NGO in Chechnya. ARD taught local trainers and schoolteachers to work with affected children, young people, and women and help with their psychosocial rehabilitation after the first war. Since autumn 1997, it has no longer been possible for foreigners to go to Chechnya, but a training seminar was held in Piatigorsk (southern Russia). ARD also established itself as an NGO in Ingushetia, and since the start of the second war most of its members work in an IDPs camp in Chechnya. Roswitha Jarman, an independent British consultant working in the Caucasus, was involved with both the CPCD and ARD.

The CPCD offers training in the fields of community development, peacebuilding, and humanitarian work, and links local NGOs with partners outside the region. It was instrumental in helping many local groups to get established. Laman Az sought to consolidate the Chechen NGO sector prior to the second war and organized a conference in Grozny where all NGOs could meet and learn about each other. It also worked as a capacity development center for less-developed NGOs since Laman Az had an established office in Grozny. DRC also worked intensively to provide training in project management and community development for IDPs and in capacity-building for the local NGOs.

Chechen civil activists have been also involved in a number of multilateral pan-Caucasian undertakings. In 1998 when the Caucasus Forum of NGOs was founded with assistance from the IA, Chechen NGOs participated and benefited from capacity-building assistance provided by the forum. In 2000, Ambassador Heidi Tagliavini, personal representative of the Austrian OSCE chairperson-in-office for missions in the Caucasus, and Freimut Duve, the OSCE representative on freedom of the media, launched a book project entitled *Caucasus—Defense of the Future,* containing essays by Caucasian writers. The project was aimed at promoting dialogue among representatives of intelligentsia in the Caucasus.

Paula Gutlove from Cambridge, Massachusetts, organized a training seminar in autumn 1998 on "Health as a Bridge to Peace" in Piatigorsk for Chechen, Russian, North Ossetian, and Ingush participants, financed by the World Health Organization, and a follow-up meeting in spring 2000.

Concluding Remarks

The efforts of INGOs (international nongovernmental organizations) have strengthened cross-ethnic and cross-clan solidarity in Chechnya and promoted civic values as an alternative to networks based on family and ethnicity. Apart from providing valuable humanitarian assistance, they have empowered local groups, especially women's groups that otherwise might not have been able to operate in an increasingly male-dominated environment. They also played a significant role in providing access for the Chechens to wider international networks, publicity opportunities, and funding.

At the same time, the Russian authorities have grown increasingly suspicious of western INGOs, believing that they engaged in conflict-resolution activities in Chechnya in order to facilitate its formal secession from Russia. At times, the attitudes and behaviors of INGOs could have been interpreted in such a light, and even if they did not constitute formal policy, they raised expectations on the Chechen side that there was a substantial constituency in the West that was willing to support independence.

Reports and appeals by Western human-rights INGOs failed to resonate with the Russian authorities and the wider public. Since the beginning of the second war they have been viewed in Russia as an indication of obliviousness to the killings and kidnappings of Russian and Chechen civilians prior to the second war. Also, they are seen as having a greater interest in criticizing the Russian state than in protecting human rights, irrespective of political concerns.

During the second campaign, the activities of international agencies in the North Caucasus have acted as an irritant to the FSB, which has suspected them of spying and interfering in Russian internal affairs. The agency has not always accepted their humanitarian mandates and has interpreted their peacebuilding efforts as attempts to obstruct the federal authorities' efforts to maintain order. CPCD was one such NGO, seen by the FSB as detrimental to stability. Another example involves those members of Laman Az who received training from the Berghof Research Center in Germany on raising land-mine awareness; in response, the Russian press accused Germany of training Chechen terrorists.

Prospects

The situation as it now exists offers little reason for optimism in Moscow, as it is difficult to bring such a secessionist war to an end. Reaching a compromise will be more difficult now after extreme violations of human rights by both sides and the emergence of an Islamic movement with broad international links.

In the opinion of presidential aide Sergei Yastrezhembsky, the Russian authorities view the prospects as follows: the Chechen conflict cannot be resolved solely by military means, but the transition to a political phase requires the end of the military operation. The political process in Chechnya will evolve more rapidly after the Chechen resistance is neutralized. A further obstacle to the political phase of conflict resolution is that there is no single figure within the Chechen diaspora who could unite all Chechen clans and districts and take responsibility to rid Chechnya of links with international Islamic terrorists.

Maintaining security will remain a major challenge. While the military campaign in the mountains may continue for years, the Russian-controlled areas are not secure either; Russian forces will likely face prolonged guerrilla war and terrorist attacks. As Russia has a conscript army, this may increase opposition to war by a Russian public unwilling to sacrifice its sons for the sake of conquering a remote territory. In such a situation, even if the Russian government proves relatively conciliatory and the majority of the Chechen population does not side with the insurgents, it could take years for the guerrillas to reconcile themselves to integration into the Russian Federation.

Moscow's relationship with its citizens of Chechen nationality is also problematic. What Moscow called the "fight against terrorism" turned into a wave of xenophobia against Chechens and Caucasians in general. The achievements of the Soviet era in creating indigenous professional classes and infrastructure have been severely undermined, and reintegration into the social environment will be slow and painful. Until a new leadership, untarnished either by a "Moscow puppet" image or by links with criminal warlords, emerges in Chechnya, the population will remain confused and torn between the two camps.

The longing for independence has not receded among those Chechens who are not fighting the federal troops at present. It is only that they are largely unwilling to align themselves with the Islamists, and regard their *jihad* as dominated by foreigners. As Kadyrov himself stated, fighting Moscow did not advance the Chechen struggle to achieve independence, and "we have to chose another route." Moscow did finally begin to make a distinction between criminality and separatism, and assumed a more relaxed stance on the issue of the Russian Federation's territorial integrity. During the first war, the predominant concern in the Yeltsin circle was that Chechnya would be the first republic to break away and that other republics would follow suit, until Russia disintegrated as the USSR had disintegrated. By contrast, the Putin leadership views Chechnya as an exceptional case that is not representative of any general separatist aspirations. The Russian leadership finally started to make a distinction between foreign-backed Islamic terrorism and a pro-independence drive on behalf of ordinary Chechens, which may be far less threatening to Russia than Moscow previously assumed. As it is easier to govern in the conditions of voluntary compliance than coercion, the desire to hold onto Chechnya at all costs may be diminishing in Moscow. Security of the North Caucasus however, remains a top priority.

Recommendations

The most realistic—and dignified—solution to Russian-Chechen relations would be an independent Chechnya, recognized by Moscow, that would not serve as a destabilizing factor for the rest of the North Caucasus. This, however, is a long-term goal, unrealizable until the last Wahhabi is driven out of Chechnya and tangible concessions are made to the Chechen aspirations for independence. Still, some practical steps can be taken in this direction, such as negotiating a power-sharing agreement with Moscow that will give Chechnya a great deal of autonomy. This can only be done when the Kadyrov government is more securely established.

There are, however, some legal foundations to build upon: a draft power-sharing agreement was negotiated between the Chechen parliament and Moscow in December 1992. President Dudayev opposed the agreement and used his opposition to undermine his legislature. Moscow has since offered to renegotiate the agreement a number of times, and it may be worth considering.

There is a consensus among internationals on the need to provide humanitarian relief for the foreseeable future, but this is complicated by the inability of foreign aid workers to operate freely in Chechnya. In such a situation, the aid is most effectively distributed through local NGOs and community leaders, assuming they are properly trained and organized. Strengthening their local capacities has been undertaken, but the need for more work still exists. It is hoped that as local NGOs become more developed, it will, in time, be possible for them to make a transition from relief to development work or to actual conflict-resolution activities.

In the present circumstances of the Russian-Western rapprochement, it is important that the brutality of the Russian troops and police forces in Chechnya does not go unnoticed and Moscow is held accountable for human-rights abuses. After the 11 September 2001 attacks, the Western leaderships made it clear that they recognize that Russia has a real cause and that Chechen terrorism does exist. This, however, does not imply that the Russian forces should denigrate themselves to the same methods and cause even more suffering than Chechnya has already had. In the long run, this will be only beneficial for Russia.

Resources

Newsletters and Periodicals
Contemporary Caucasus Newsletter, University of California, Berkeley
Crisis in Chechnya, Radio Free Europe/Radio Liberty, Prague, Czech Republic
FEWER Reports, London
Monitor & Prism, Jamestown Foundation, Washington, DC
WarReport, 1995–98, Institute for War and Peace Reporting, London

Reports
Amnesty International, *Russian Federation/Chechen Republic: Humanity Is Indivisible,* Open Letter to the United Nations from the Secretary-General of Amnesty International, EUR 46/38/99, November 1999.
Human Rights Watch, *Chechnya: A Renewed Catastrophe,* available at http://www.hrw.org/campaigns/russia/chechnya.
Strengthening Democratic Institutions Project, *The Caucasus and the Caspian,* Seminar Series vols. I–III, Cambridge, MA, Harvard University, 1996–1998.
United Nations High Commissioner for Refugees, *North Caucasus Update,* June 2000.

Other Publications
Chechnya: A Small Victorious War, by Carlotta Gall and Thomas de Waal. London, Pan
  Books, 1997.
Chechnya: Tombstone of Russian Power, by Anatol Lieven. New Haven and London,
  Yale University Press, 1998.
*No War in the Caucasus: Secessionist Conflict in Chechnya, Abkhazia and Nagorno-
  Karabakh,* by Edward W. Walker. Cambridge, MA, Harvard University Press, 1998.
The North Caucasus: Russia's Fragile Borderland, by Anna Matveeva. London, RIIA,
  1999.

Selected Internet Sites
www.amina.com (Chechen Republic On-line, Chechen website in English)
www.cdi.org (Center for Defense Information, USA)
www.chechengovernment.com (Maskhadov website, in opposition to Kavkaz-Tsentr)
www.hro.org/Human Rights On-line (the Russian human-rights network)
www.iwpr.net (IWPR's Caucasus reporting service, Institute for War and Peace Reporting, London, UK)
www.kavkaz.org (Kavkaz-Tsentr, Chechen website in Russian)
www.rferl.org (Crisis in Chechnya, by the Radio Free Europe/Radio Liberty)

Resource Contacts
Tom de Waal, e-mail: tomdewaal@hotmail.com
Chris Hunter, Center for Peacemaking and Community Development, e-mail: peace-
  centre@glasnet.ru
Anatol Lieven, Carnegie Center, Washington, D.C., e-mail: alieven@ceip.org
Arthur Martirossian, Conflict Management Group, e-mail: martiros@cmgroup.org
Anna Matveeva, expert on the Caucasus, London, e-mail: sophiamat@ukonline.co.uk
Gevork Ter-Gabrielian, International Alert, London, e-mail: gtergabrielian@interna-
  tional-alert.org
Anna Zelkina, SOAS, e-mail: az4@soas.ac.uk

Data on the following organizations can be found in the Directory section:
In Chechnya
  Caucasus NGO Forum
  Center for Peacemaking and Community Development
  Center for the Study of and Management of Conflict (Institute of Ethnology and An-
    thropology)
  Don Women's Union
  Mission Peace in North Caucasus
  Union of the Committee of Soldier's Mothers of Russia

International
  Conflict Management Group
  Danish Refugee Council
  FEWER
  International Alert
  International Federation of Red Cross and Red Crescent Societies
  Médecins Sans Frontières
  Quaker Peace and Service

*Anna Matveeva is a program manager at Saferworld (on small arms and security). She
previously worked as a research fellow at the Royal Institute of International Affairs
(Chatham House, London) and program head at International Alert (London). As a*

scholar specializing in issues of conflict and the politics of post-Soviet Eurasia, she has authored publications such as The North Caucasus: Russia's Fragile Borderland *(London: RIIA, 1999) and academic articles, and undertook projects for organizations such as the International Peace Academy, EastWest Insititute, Minority Rights Group, and the Heinrich Böll Stiftung.*

14.3

Dagestan:
Sustaining a Fragile Peace

Anna Matveeva

Dagestan is an autonomous republic within the Russian Federation, populated by over thirty distinct ethnic groups. Intergroup competition for power and resources makes conflict prevention the main preoccupation of the republican authorities. The multitude of different but interrelated conflicts constitutes the main constraint to conflict resolution. Spillover of instability from neighboring Chechnya, proliferation of radical Islamism, and violent crime contribute to the precarious security situation. While the involvement of international NGOs has been modest, Dagestani and Russian authorities have managed to sustain a fragile peace. Still, issues related to the conflicts remain unresolved and the regional security setting adversely affects peace prospects.

Dagestan, the largest of the North Caucasian autonomous republics of the Russian Federation, is situated on the western coast of the Caspian Sea. The republic's most distinct feature is its ethnic diversity: it is made up of a total of thirty-four ethnic groups of either Caucasian or Turkic origin. None of the ethnic groups constitutes a clear majority, or occupies a dominant position, although the main rivalry is between lowlanders and highlanders. The main groups include Avars (28 percent), Dargins (16 percent), Kumyks (12.9 percent), Lezgins (12.2 percent), Russians (6 percent), Laks (5 percent), Chechens (4.5 percent), Tabassarans (4.5 percent), Azerbaijanis (4.5 percent), and Nogais (2 percent). The majority are Sunni Muslims and the political culture remains highly conservative.

Interethnic tensions place a strain on Dagestan's social stability. There is competition over scarce lands between lowlanders and highlanders. Migration and the concomitant conversion of pasturelands to agricultural use threatens the lowlanders and their traditional economy and way of life. The Nogais and Kumyks are a shrinking minority in their homelands and have claimed that the ethnic group to which a territory historically belongs should be legally

RUSSIAN FEDERATION

DAGESTAN (Russian Federation)
Population (millions): 2.1 (1998)

Ingushetia

Grozny   Khasavyurt

Nal'chik
Vladikavkaz

North Ossetia   Chechnya   Makhachkala

Dagestan

Caspian
Sea

GEORGIA   Derbent ●

TURKEY   ARMENIA   AZERBAIJAN

recognized as the owner of its land. In their turn, the mountain ethnic groups have argued that their original enforced migration was to lands that were depopulated, and which they invested effort in cultivating. In response the Dagestani constitutional court issued a decision that ethnic groups have no rights to own land or allocate its use, this being the responsibility of the state through the Peoples' Assembly (a republican parliament).

As a result, land tenure is a controversial issue, and is regarded through the prism of the various ethnic groups' claims rather than that of individual rights. The Dagestanis voted against land privatization in a referendum in 1992, fearing that the implementation of a successful land division would provoke interethnic tension (the region had no tradition of individual landownership). Conflicts over land assigned for the use of one ethnic group within the traditional area of another have already led to serious clashes.

Four groups living in the border areas of Dagestan—the Lezgins, the Russians, the Chechens, and the Nogais—have their ethnic kin across the border. Cross-border tensions often involve such separated minorities, especially in the first three cases, when the size of the groups is relatively large.

Some 250,000 Lezgins live in southern Dagestan while there are 177,000 in northern Azerbaijan. After the breakup of the USSR, when the border with Azerbaijan became international rather than administrative, Lezgins found themselves a divided people. The Lezgin issue is caught up in the uneasy relationship between Russia and Azerbaijan, which, unlike Dagestan, does not acknowledge that the division of the Lezgins by the international border presents a problem.

Azerbaijan's reluctance to join the Commonwealth of Independent States (CIS) in 1992–1993 and its refusal to permit Russian border guards to police the Azerbaijani-Iranian border have contributed to a tightening of the

Azerbaijani-Russian border regime. The situation was aggravated by the first war in Chechnya. The border with Azerbaijan was closed by Russia in December 1994, and controls and customs were introduced. The establishment of border controls came as a shock to the local population. In April 1996 the regime was relaxed and local residents, mainly Lezgins, were allowed to cross the border freely. After signing the Khasavyurt Accords, which ended the conflict with Chechnya, the Russian government opened the border and recruited local conscripts to serve as border troops. Since 1996 the Dagestani authorities have taken a more proactive approach, exchanging official visits with Azerbaijan, signing a Treaty on Friendship and Cooperation, and supporting efforts at border delimitation.

Tensions between Lezgins and Azeris began in 1992, but reached a peak in mid-1994, a time of heavy casualties on the Karabakh front and Lezgin resistance to conscription in the Azerbaijani army. Violent clashes occurred in Derbent, Dagestan, and in June in the Gussary region of Azerbaijan. In Dagestan in 1991 the Sadval political movement had called for the creation of an independent Lezgistan. The Dagestani authorities never supported this claim and it was officially rejected in April 1996 at the sixth congress of Sadval. However, the fear of assimilation as a result of what they saw as Azerbaijan's Turkic nationalist policies and the perception of a threat to their survival as a distinct community remained powerful. Unlike other Dagestani ethnic movements, Sadval and its splinter groups were not led by powerful individuals, and their direct political influence is limited. A Lezgin splinter group organized a meeting in Derbent in October 1998 to demand the creation of a Derbent autonomous region within the Russian Federation, but outside Dagestan.

Akki Chechens live in lowland Dagestan on the border with Chechnya and are estimated to number some 100,000, but many believe the actual numbers are higher. In 1944, they were deported to Central Asia along with other Chechens, and since their return have aspired to resettlement in their historical homelands in the Novolak and Khasavyurt region. These lands are now occupied by Laks and Avars who were forcibly resettled in these territories from the mountains. Tensions center around the disputed villages of Leninaul and Kalininaul and the question of resettlement of the Laks and Avars, should they be persuaded to move from the villages. These disputes have been recently overshadowed by Dagestani suspicions about where the Akki Chechens' loyalties lie.

Prior to the first Russian intervention in 1994, the attitude of the local Chechens and Dagestani population as a whole toward the Dudayev regime in Chechnya was largely negative; his independence claim was regarded as unrealistic, and the breakdown of law and order clearly obvious in a republic that was suffering from the disruption of railway traffic caused by frequent robberies in Chechnya. This attitude has changed since the beginning of Russian military intervention, when Dagestan accommodated the displaced Chechens. Some Dagestani young men volunteered to fight against Russia in Chechnya on religious grounds. As the fighting escalated, the war started to affect the border areas of Dagestan directly, and caused local resentment toward Russian federal troops.

The anti-Chechen feeling was provoked by the taking of 3,000 people hostage in 1996 in Kyzlyar by a group of Chechen fighters led by Salman Radyuev, but this was overshadowed by the brutality of the Russian retaliatory assault. In 1996 the influential Dagestanis facilitated the first meeting between Aslan Maskhadov, later to become president of Chechnya, and Alexandr Lebed, the secretary of the Russian Security Council, leading to the signing of the Khasavyurt Accords in August 1996 in Dagestan, ending the war. This, however, failed to bring peace dividends to Dagestan, since lawlessness in Chechnya produced more destabilization than did the straightforward conflict between the separatist republic and Russian federal power.

The Russians are a diminishing minority in Dagestan, with a steady pace of emigration to more ethnically homogeneous regions of the Russian Federation. There is no official pressure on Russians to leave, and measures are in fact taken to encourage them to stay. In reality, however, all the important economic and socially prestigious positions, as well as viable political appointments, are being filled by indigenous groups. Moreover, many Russians used to work in the numerous defense enterprises in the region, but with the collapse of heavy industry and a shift in economic activity to the trade and service sectors, many Russians have lost their jobs. Their ability to adapt to the new situation has also been restricted by the absence of extended family networks and lack of investment capital. Russians more readily consider emigration, as few have roots in the North Caucasian republics and some have places to return to in other parts of Russia.

The existence of criminal networks organized around ethnic affiliations is a distinct feature of Dagestani social culture. Local mafias are based on a core kinship group with a powerful, often young and ruthless individual in the center of it, surrounded by a group of supporters from whom he commands strict loyalty. Groups normally secured start-up capital from criminal activities, but gradually moved into other areas, including legitimate businesses. Presently, the North Caucasus rates highest in the Russian Federation for violent crime and terrorist acts. Political terrorism, assassination attempts, and kidnappings have become frequent occurrences in Dagestan. The death of sixty-nine people as a result of the bombing of an apartment block in Kaspiisk near Makhachkala in 1996 and about seventy in Buinaksk in 1999 were just the most publicized of many such acts of violence. Most of the acts of terrorism are not a direct result of the groups attempting to gain power in the republic, but rather violence among elites that is a part of a political bargaining process in Dagestan. The kidnapping of civilians has become a virtually unpunishable offense unless the victim's family can afford to embark on a vendetta, and hostages are freed without ransom only when local ethnic leaders intervene. Currently, since the beginning of the second Russian campaign in Chechnya, the situation regarding kidnappings has markedly improved.

Conflict Dynamics

While relations between Dagestan and Moscow have improved and the situation around the Lezgin community has de-escalated since 1996, and the morale of the Russians has improved with the commitment of the Putin government to protect their rights, the war in Chechnya and Islamic extremism remain extremely dangerous sources of potential conflict.

The Chechen-Dagestani border has been the scene of major tensions since the signing of the Khasavyurt Accords. After years of cross-border violence, looting, and kidnappings, Dagestanis' initial sympathy toward the Chechens during the first war has turned into fear and animosity. In August 1999, field commanders in opposition to President Maskhadov in Chechnya led an offensive by Chechen and Dagestani militants into the highlands of Dagestan. Their proclaimed goal was to establish government by Shari'a (Koranic) law in Dagestani territory and to end colonial rule by Russia. However, having suffered defeat in confrontation with detachments of Dagestani fighters and Russian federal troops, the militants retreated to Chechnya. A Russian assault in September on the Islamist strongholds in central Dagestan provoked a second wave of attacks from across the border. The September fighting resulted in another setback for the Chechen fighters.

Apart from religious zeal, there were more mundane reasons for the Chechen attacks. Unification with Dagestan—which has over 2 million citizens, access to the Caspian Sea, and a much longer border with Azerbaijan—would have created a new Chechen-Dagestani state with improved chances of surviving as an independent entity. The Russians would be denied the opportunity to cut the Chechen sector of the Baku-Novorossiisk pipeline, excluding the republic from oil transit, since the bulk of it goes through Dagestan. The Chechen tactics have been to exploit three political tools: to use the Akki Chechens, their ethnic kin across the border, to start an anticolonial struggle against Russian domination, and to call for a holy war to create an Islamic state. Chechens, who themselves fought under the nationalist banner, have failed to realize that there is no anti-Russian separatism in Dagestan, but that, on the contrary, anti-Chechen sentiment is widespread. Far from attracting support, the Chechen attacks provoked fury among Dagestanis, who were quick to set up self-defense units and demand weapons. The authorities reluctantly accepted this. Ethnic "barons" led small, but decisive private forces who fought alongside the Russian federal troops. Thus the events in Dagestan together with bombing raids on the apartment blocks in Moscow led to the second Russian military intervention into Chechnya in October 1999.

As a result, when Russia's second military intervention in Chechnya started, Dagestan did not allow ethnic Chechen refugees to enter its territory, and agreed to only receive people of Dagestani ethnic groups fleeing Chechnya, such as the Nogais, Kumyks, and Avars. The refugees were screened because of a fear of infiltration. Reprisals have been carried out against the Akki Chechen community of Dagestan for their collaboration with Basayev and Khattab. Laks and Avars, who had been resettled in the villages of deported Chechens, and were intimidated throughout the 1990s by Chechen threats to expel them from their historical Chechen homeland, were particularly active. They also feared that the Chechens wanted these lands back in order to detach

Khasavyurt, Dagestan:
Chechnyan refugees

them from Dagestan and join them to Chechnya. Anti-Chechen sentiment has
led to the expulsion of all Chechens who do not hold permanent residence permits and to the disarmament of Dagestani Chechen paramilitary groups.

Such developments were further aggravated by the rise of Islamism—an
ideology aimed at gaining power to establish a system of government based on
Islam—in Chechnya and Dagestan. Dagestan is one of the most religiously devout areas in the former Soviet Union and the birthplace of the Islamic Revival Party in 1990. In 1998 three settlements proclaimed an independent Islamic territory ruled by Shari'a law, where Dagestani (and Russian federal)
laws were not applicable. Links with Chechen Islamist militants were established, and preparations made for a long struggle against the Russians and
against secular Dagestanis. It was claimed by the Russian government that this
was facilitated and financed by international agents of radical Islam. The
Russian and Dagestani authorities tolerated the rebellious Islamic territory for
a year, and probably would have continued their policy of accommodation but
for the Chechen cross-border attack in August 1999. Irrespective of whether
the Dagestani Islamists supported the Chechen guerrillas militarily, their political links were well known. The Islamists mounted ferocious resistance to
the Russian advances, but suffered a defeat.

The second war in Chechnya was a serious setback for Islamism in Dagestan. The internal chaos in Chechnya is the worst advertisement for the Islamist cause, and a relatively stable Dagestan has little sympathy for the

Islamists. The Islamists in Dagestan are more feared and hated than before, and are regarded as siding with the Chechen enemy, with the result that society is more openly split along religious lines. Traditional believers have a genuine hatred for the radicals, whom they view as enemies of stability. The Spiritual Board of Muslims of Dagestan, the official clerical institution, has undergone consolidation and leads the struggle against real or perceived Islamists.

The Islamist external links to the Middle East and to the wider radical Islamist movement are a further point of irritation. These links include a few hundred volunteers of Arab, Turkish, and Afghan origin who began arriving in Chechnya during the course of the first war and whose numbers have increased in Chechnya and Dagestan since. The authorities dubbed them "Wahhabis," although few of them are actual Wahhabis, who were followers of the teachings of the eighteenth-century Arab preacher Mohammed Abd al-Wahhab. One genuine Wahhabi is identifiable—the Chechen field commander Habib Abdurrahman Khattab, an Arab of Saudi origin, who came to Chechnya reportedly after fighting with the *mujahedeen* in Afghanistan and forged links with the Dagestani Islamists. The combined influence of Middle Eastern aid and the prestige of their disciplined and fanatic ideology has won the Islamists recruits among disaffected Dagestani youths and provoked ferocious resentment among the more traditional Sovietized population.

Recently, there has been an improvement in the crime situation, since it has become more difficult for kidnappers to hide their victims in Chechnya. Still, the ongoing war in Chechnya and presence of Islamist sympathizers in Dagestan remains a challenge. The Russian federal troops regularly report incidents of seizure of Wahhabi literature, and of arms and communication devices being moved to Chechnya through Dagestan. On one occasion, Afghanis have been detained in the republic while crossing borders. The Dagestan Security Council has stated that the threat of terrorism continues to be acute. It claims that the Chechen field commanders made a decision to intensify the war by taking it to the neighboring territories, including Dagestan. The Security Council also stressed that a threat to security comes from within Dagestan from the ongoing presence of Wahhabis in the republic.

Local disputes for power and money are still often settled by force. Kinship networks and proliferation of weapons feed into the local business culture, making it difficult to break out of the vicious circle.

Official Conflict Management

The Dagestan authorities' chosen conflict-management strategy was to adopt constitutional and political arrangements that reflect the peculiar ethnic and social composition of the republic, and the commitment to preserve interethnic peace by reducing the scope of political rivalry among groups. Dagestan is the only region of the Russian Federation where the head of the republic is not elected directly by a popular vote, but rather by a two-level, indirect procedure. The supreme authority in the republic is vested in the State Council, which consists of representatives of the fourteen major ethnic groups (those which have a written language) and is elected by the Constitutional Assembly for a period of four years. The position of chairman of the State Council can be occupied by a representative of a single ethnic group for a period of four years and then has to be given up in favor of another group. The chairman of the State Council, Magomedali Magomedov (a Dargin), is de facto the acting president of the republic. According to the constitution, the terms of office cannot be extended. This provision for a collective presidency was introduced after an attempt to establish a presidency soon after the breakup of the USSR. This was thrice rejected by referenda in 1992, 1993, and 1999 because of the fear that it would put one ethnic group in a dominant position. The prime minister is also a member of the State Council and therefore precluded from being of the same ethnic origin as the chairman.

However, this commitment to the principle of a four-year period in power for representatives of each ethnic group has proven to be halfhearted. Magomedov's term of office was first extended in 1996 for two years, and then in 1998 Magomedov succeeded in pressing the deputies into passing a constitutional amendment to abolish altogether the provision that the chair of the State Council should be changed in favor of another ethnic group. Magomedov was voted in for a second term in July 1998. This in effect meant the power balance was secured in favor of the Dargins, the second ethnic group, especially after election of Said Amirov, a prominent Dargin, to the important position of mayor of Makhachkala.

At the same time, systems have been developed to encourage cross-ethnic voting. The electoral system is designed to ensure that the balance between the ethnic groups in the assembly mirrors that in the population. According to electoral law, sixty-five constituencies are classified as multiethnic and are allocated to candidates from only one ethnic group living in the constituency. Only members of that ethnic group (not necessarily living in the constituency) could compete against each other, but all the registered electorate, irrespective of ethnicity, vote in the constituency. The government determined which ethnic group would be allocated which constituency, and an arrangement broadly accepted as fair was worked out. Constituencies regarded as monoethnic had an ordinary open-candidate system.

The ministry for nationalities and external relations of Dagestan is vested with the responsibility for overseeing the affairs of nationalities and ensuring that multiethnicity is sustainable. It is a relatively powerful body compared to its Russian counterpart. In Dagestan, however, the ministry assists in promoting the cultural and educational rights of ethnic groups rather than addressing interethnic relations or providing strategies for conflict-prone zones. Still, the minister himself does serve as a special envoy in situations where tensions arise.

A Security Council was introduced in Dagestan in August 1996 to "combat organized crime and promote national security." Its powers and functions are mainly directed toward fighting the impact of instability in Chechnya, but it remains a fairly weak body, highly dependent on the political standing of its head at any given moment.

Russian Government

Since 1991, Moscow policymakers have been searching for solutions to the problems of governance in Dagestan. In the period between the two Russian-Chechen wars in 1999, Moscow's perception of the region was that it had developed into a gangster stronghold where crime was feeding ethnic tensions, and into a bastion of radical and increasingly militant Islamism. The policy undertakings included a mixture of steps to combat crime and corruption, buying off the republican elite by providing federal subsidies to the republican economy, and attempts to mediate between the Islamists and the republican authorities. The commitment of Boris Yeltsin's regime to the North Caucasus in general and to Dagestan in particular appeared halfhearted.

Such attitudes have rapidly changed since the Chechen attacks on Dagestan in 1999, the appointment of Vladimir Putin as prime minister under Yeltsin, and then his election as president of Russia. The Dagestanis' loyalty to Moscow, resistance to the Chechen attacks, and popular support given to the Russian federal troops have persuaded the new regime in Moscow that the North Caucasus is not a lost cause and that there is no threat of separatism. On the contrary, the Dagestanis look to Moscow to provide protection from Islamist threats. The new Russian regime was quick to strengthen its standing in Dagestan, while the republican authorities managed to benefit from Moscow's renewed attention to the republic. The improved economic situation has enabled Moscow to increase subsidies to Dagestan and start building a pipeline bypass around Chechnya through the Dagestani territory, thus creating local jobs. The authorities' position vis-à-vis the ethnic barons has been strengthened and they have gradually obtained the upper hand, so that the leaders of various ethnic factions are less inclined to compete for power.

Multi-Track Diplomacy

The great majority of nonstate activities in Dagestan parallel ethnic affiliations and in practical terms coalesce around national fronts and movements of ethnic groups. The collapse of Soviet (civic) identity and the absence of overarching national identity on the basis of which internal coherence could have emerged, strengthened the divisions in the Dagestani society. National movements, formed during the late 1980s, had passed their peak by the mid-1990s, but have fulfilled the important functions of putting ethnic groups' claims on the governmental agenda and serving as platforms for emerging leaders. These powerful individuals, often ruthless, shadowy businessmen, rely on their ethnic, clan, and regional kinship networks among whom they command loyalty and for whom they can negotiate with the authorities and with the leaders of other groups when conflicts arise. Outside this ethnically stratified framework, nonstate initiatives such as NGOs or intellectual groupings are limited. This "ethnic democracy" has little in common with the Western notion of "civil society," but in the absence of strong civic bonds, ethnic ties serve a function in providing a social support network.

A more mundane reason for the slow development of NGOs in Dagestan has been limited international involvement and difficulties in accessing Western funding. Nevertheless, some initiatives have taken place. The Center of Social and Psychological Rehabilitation and Culture of Peace was recently established in Derbent (southern Dagestan), facilitated and sponsored by the United Nations Educational, Scientific and Cultural Organization. Masliat, an NGO with a mandate to facilitate conflict prevention and resolution and work toward social consolidation in Dagestan, was set up in November 1993. It publishes a newsletter of the same name, but the impact so far has remained limited.

Women as Peacemakers

Following the deterioration of women's social standing after the communist collapse, with women increasingly pressured to withdraw from running for elected office, and the Dagestani government's introduction of special "women only" electoral districts where only women can compete against each other, women's groups have started to organize themselves on a small scale since the mid-1990s. They mainly address the needs of the most deprived families among the displaced, as the NGO Materinskii Ochag (Motherly Hearth) does, for example, in Khasavyurt. Some of them have been involved in peacebuilding activities; an example is the organization of a seminar on "Dagestan: a Center of Peacemaking" undertaken in Makhachkala by the Don Women's Union.

Conflict-Prevention Fieldwork

International Alert (IA) has been involved in conflict prevention in Dagestan throughout the 1990s. In the early period IA organized three pan-Caucasian seminars in conflict-resolution training attended by individuals from Dagestan, and in 1995 set up a fact-finding mission to assess the situation and design a program of conflict-prevention measures. IA worked in close partnership with the ministry of nationalities of Dagestan and with local administrations in the conflict-prone regions of the republic. IA regarded conflict prevention as the strengthening of the local capacity to govern effectively, and the facilitation of cross-ethnic solidarity while recognizing the different needs of individual groups. In 1996 and 1997 it implemented five problem-solving seminars in Dagestan on such issues as local government in multiethnic areas, ethnic disputes about land distribution, and the situation regarding the Chechen and Lezgin communities in border areas of the republic. The seminars aimed at bringing together the representatives of the authorities from the local and republican levels, as well as members of the People's Assembly and representatives of the society, such as individuals from ethnic movements and journalistic and academic circles. A fact-finding mission to Azerbaijan followed in 1997 to assess the impact of the community division on the Azeri Lezgins and to recommend further conflict-prevention measures. In 1997, IA organized an educational trip by Dagestani administrators to the United Kingdom to familiarize them with the experience of power devolution and the survival of a minority culture in Wales. Deterioration of the security situation in 1998–1999 precluded further fieldwork, but in 2000 IA returned to Dagestan to take part in the women's peacemaking initiative.

Academic Initiatives and Early Warning
In February 1997, Rabelais University of Tours, France, and the Academy of Civil Service of the Russian Federation (Moscow) held an EU TACIS–sponsored international seminar on "Activities of Bodies of State Power and Local Self-Government in Conditions of Social and Regional Conflicts." The seminar was preceded by a site visit. The local partners were Kurban Bulatov, Dagestan deputy procurator general (who was murdered in 1999), and Vice Premier Ilyas Umakhanov.

The Conflict Resolution in the Post-Soviet States Project, pursued jointly by the Institute of Ethnology and Anthropology (Moscow) and Conflict Management Group (Harvard University), established the Network on Ethnological Monitoring and Early Warning of Conflicts in the early 1990s to provide early warning and discuss possible action. The project produces the *Bulletin,* published quarterly in Russian and English with regular entries on Dagestan written by local analysts, which plays an important role as a source of information. Since 1998, FEWER also runs a website containing early-warning reports on Dagestan.

Multilateral Undertakings
Representatives from Dagestan have taken part in various multilateral undertakings, either pan-Caucasian or involving the North Caucasians only. The Center for Peacemaking and Community Development (CPCD) has engaged Dagestanis in its Young People's Peacebuilding Network, sponsored by the EU TACIS program, providing individuals and local groups with training in alternatives to violence, and with e-mail communication facilities. Four youth meetings and two seminars have been held since its establishment in 1999. The Caucasus Forum of NGOs, founded in 1998 at the initiative of IA, also includes Dagestani representatives among its members.

A few Dagestanis participated in the Peace-Making Mission for the North Caucasus, established by General Lebed, ex-secretary of the Russian Federation Security Council, in order to facilitate dialogue between Chechnya, its neighbors, and the Russian authorities. Still, with Lebed's political demise, the mission gradually came to a halt.

Humanitarian Assistance
International humanitarian organizations have been involved in Dagestan since the start of the first Russian-Chechen war, providing relief aid to the Chechen IDPs who crossed into the neighboring republic. ICRC (Red Cross/Red Crescent) and Médecins Sans Frontières were the first to arrive, in December 1994, followed by UNHCR and UNICEF in January 1995, the International Organization for Migration (IOM) in February, and the World Food Program in

March. IOM was first to withdraw in September, following the murder of its expatriate worker in Chechnya, and most other organizations halted their operations inside Chechnya after the murder of six ICRC workers in 1996. The French NGO Equilibre got involved in spring 1995, but closed its operations in August 1997 when four of its workers were kidnapped and taken to Chechnya. A similar fate befell the Hungarian Interchurch Organization, which halted its activities in November 1997 after two of its staff members were taken hostage in Chechnya. Non-Violence International, a Moscow-based Russian NGO, remains actively involved in humanitarian work in Dagestan, mainly in the Khasavyurt region, helping those affected by the 1999 violence in the border areas.

Initially, INGOs were discouraged from becoming involved in Dagestan because of its remote location, conservative political culture, and difficult social environment. Moreover, Dagestani authorities were cautious about international engagement, fearing that disproportional activities might open up dormant wounds. A Western organization unwittingly offended Dagestani sensitivities in the time of a crisis; this negatively impacted the work of the others. Involvement of various U.S. Protestant missionaries in Dagestan made the authorities suspicious that Western actors might have a hidden agenda behind the conflict-resolution front. After 1997, with the proliferation of kidnappings of foreigners and deteriorating security situation, Dagestan became virtually off-limits for international engagement. Worsening relations between the Russian Federation and the West made Dagestanis increasingly see conflict-prevention activities as a weapon of Western neo-imperialism.

Prospects

The war in Chechnya has a very serious impact on security in the border areas in Dagestan, since the Chechen militants and their Islamist supporters in Dagestan periodically raid the territory and engage in fighting against the local self-defense groups and Russian soldiers. This low-key guerrilla campaign may continue for years, distracting the government and population from attention to investments to meet other needs.

To a significant degree, the prospects for stability in Dagestan depend on the success of the policies of the Russian government to strengthen the state and deliver on the law-and-order agenda, as well as on particular ways chosen to achieve such goals. Currently, it is likely that the reassertion of control by the center over developments in its constituent parts will be implemented. In the Dagestani context, this may mean that the law-enforcement function can be taken out of the hands of the republican authorities and administered directly from Moscow, and control over the movement of nationals from the Islamic countries will be reinforced in order to prevent the penetration of Islamist missionaries. The border regime with Azerbaijan is also likely to be tightened, and the division of the Lezgin community will acquire the features of permanence. In such conditions, it will be increasingly difficult for INGOs to engage in conflict-prevention activities in Dagestan even if the security situation improves, since the Russian state is growing suspicious of foreign organizations and their intentions. Deterioration of the Russian-Western relations, war in Chechnya, and improved standing of the security services (with which the current Russian president was once affiliated) mean that Western NGOs' efforts immediately become the focus of attention from local FSB branches.

The important factor that will continue to affect peace and stability in Dagestan is the ongoing conflict in Chechnya. Even if the Russian federal troops achieve a substantive degree of control over the Chechen territory, some spillover of the instability into the border areas of Dagestan is inevitable. The Dagestani Islamists, although having suffered a defeat in 1999, nevertheless are believed to operate underground, and future attacks cannot be ruled out. The Islamist challenge, together with the proliferation of weapons from across the Chechen border, is likely to replace intergroup rivalry as the main security threat.

Recommendations

Out of multiple challenges to stability in Dagestan, two present the most immediate danger: the resentment of the local Chechen community by the rest of Dagestanis and the spread of Islamism. Both are difficult for the outside intervenors to tackle, albeit for different reasons. Recent violence in the areas where ethnic Chechens live and the continuing war across the border make access difficult, and the republican authorities are wary that the outsiders may make the situation worse, or that they may be kidnapped or killed. Conflict-prevention measures with regards to Islamism are difficult to develop and implement because of a lack of knowledge of the essential nature of the challenge, i.e., whether it is a homegrown response to social change or provoked by international agents of radical Islam. So far, analysis has been based on either very remote or highly politicized sources, and as yet there is no real in-depth understanding of the Islamist challenge.

Future conflict-prevention strategies will need to be implemented with the knowledge and cooperation of federal and republican authorities; otherwise obstruction is inevitable. Close cooperation with the authorities may limit the flexibility NGOs might wish for, but it can also improve access to crucial players and provide a degree of protection. Over the longer term, when the war in Chechnya has ended and the law-and-order situation improves, it could be possible to design a comprehensive package of conflict-prevention and development policies to address the multiple needs of Dagestani society.

Resources

Newsletters and Periodicals
Bulletin of the Network on Ethnological Monitoring and Early Warning of Conflicts, Conflict Resolution in the Post-Soviet States Project, IEA/CMG, published quarterly in Russian (by Moscow University) and English (by Harvard University)
Caucasus Report, Radio Free Europe/Radio Liberty, Prague, Czech Republic
Contemporary Caucasus Newsletter, University of California, Berkeley

EWI Russian Regional Report, EastWest Institute, United States, weekly
FEWER Reports, London
Monitor & Prism, Jamestown Foundation, Washington, DC
WarReport, 1995–98, Institute for War and Peace Reporting, London

Reports
International Alert
> *Dagestan: A Situation Assessment Report,* by Clem McCartney, 1996.
> *The Lezgins: A Situation Assessment Report,* by Anna Matveeva and Clem McCartney, 1997.
> Strengthening Democratic Institutions Project, *Russia's Tinderbox: Conflict in the North Caucasus and Its Implications for the Future of the Russian Federation,* by Fiona Hill, 1995.

Other Publications
Conflict and Catharsis: Developments in Dagestan Since September 1999, by Robert Ware and Enver Kisriev. London, Nationalities Papers, 2000.
"Political Stability and Ethnic Parity: Why Is There Peace in Dagestan?" by Robert Ware and Enver Kisriev. In M. Alexeev (ed.), *Center-Periphery Conflict in Post-Soviet Russia: A Federation Imperiled,* New York, St. Martin's Press, July 1999.
Russia's Soft Underbelly: The Stability of Instability in Dagestan, by Edward W. Walker. Berkeley, Working Paper Series, Berkeley Program in Soviet and Post-Soviet Studies, winter 1999–2000.
The North Caucasus: Russia's Fragile Borderland, by Anna Matveeva. London, RIIA, 1999.

Selected Internet Sites
www.eawarn.ru (Network on Ethnological Monitoring and Early Warning, Institute of Ethnology and Anthropology, Russian Academy of Sciences, and Conflict Management Group, Harvard University)
www.fewer.org (Forum on Early Warning and Early Response, London)
www.rferl.org (Radio Free Europe/Radio Liberty Newsline, daily news and analysis)
www.socrates.berkeley.edu/~bsp (Berkeley Program in Soviet and Post-Soviet States)

Resource Contacts
Enver Kisriev, Institute of History, Archaeology and Ethnography, Dagestan Research Center, Russian Academy of Sciences, e-mail: enver@datacom.ru
Anna Matveeva, expert on the Caucasus, London, e-mail: sophiamat@ukonline.co.uk
Clem McCartney, consultant in conflict resolution and community development, e-mail: C.McCartney@ulst.ac.uk
Edward Walker, Berkeley Program in Soviet and Post-Soviet Studies, University of California, Berkeley, e-mail: eww@socrates.berkeley.edu
Robert Bruce Ware, Southern Illinois University, Edwardsville, e-mail: rware@siue.edu

Data on the following organizations can be found in the Directory section:
Local
> Caucasus NGO Forum
> Center for Peacemaking and Community Development
> Mission Peace in North Caucasus

International
> FEWER
> International Alert

International Federation of Red Cross and Red Crescent Societies
Médecins Sans Frontières

Anna Matveeva is a program manager at Saferworld (on small arms and security). She previously worked as a research fellow at the Royal Institute of International Affairs (Chatham House, London) and program head at International Alert (London). As a scholar specializing in issues of conflict and the politics of post-Soviet Eurasia, she has authored publications such as The North Caucasus: Russia's Fragile Borderland *(London: RIIA, 1999) and academic articles, and undertook projects for organizations such as the International Peace Academy, EastWest Insititute, Minority Rights Group, and the Heinrich Böll Stiftung.*

14.4

North Ossetia/Ingushetia: A History of the Expulsion and Resettlement of People

Anna Matveeva

The conflict between two North Caucasian groups in the Russian Federation—the Ingush and the North Ossetians—is rooted in the history of the Stalin-era deportations of 1943. Violence erupted over the jurisdiction of the territory from which the Ingush were deported and was then allocated to North Ossetia instead. In 1992 the Ossetians drove Ingush returnees out of the republic. Efforts to resolve the conflict were pursued by the Russian government through its offices on the ground. A change of leadership in North Ossetia brought new impetus into the conflict-resolution process, but interethnic resentment between the communities proved too deep for real progress. War in Chechnya and conflict in South Ossetia, Georgia, produced further obstacles to the resolution of conflict.

Both North Ossetia and Ingushetia are autonomous republics within the Russian Federation in the North Caucasus. Christian Ossetians are of ethnic Iranian origin. The republic historically has been the stronghold for Russian advances into the Caucasus. North Ossetia is the most urbanized and industrialized of the North Caucasian republics. Ossetians live divided over North and South Ossetia. South Ossetia is a breakaway republic of Georgia. At present, the two Ossetian communities are separated by the international border between Russia and Georgia.

Muslim Ingush are a northeastern Caucasian group. Ingushetia is the newest and the second-smallest republic of Russia, created in 1992 as a result of the Ingush separation from the dual-nationality republic of Chechno-Ingushetia. Although the Ingush and the Chechens are two closely related groups, collectively known as Vainakh, the Ingush chose not to follow the Chechen drive for secession and opted for a peaceful divorce.

The Ingush/North Ossetian conflict, which was the first incident of large-scale intercommunal violence within the Russian Federation, erupted in 1992 over the issue of jurisdiction over the Prigorodny region, the area from which

RUSSIAN FEDERATION
North Ossetia

NORTH OSSETIA/INGUSHETIA (Russian Federation)
Population: 663,000 (North Ossetia), 303,000 (Ingushetia)
Conflict related deaths: 583 (in 1992)
Conflict related IDPs: 40,300 Ingush (1992), just a few thousand have returned
Conflict related refugees: 37,700 in North Ossetia, incl. 28,100 from Georgia.

Nal'chik
Vladikavkaz
Nazran
Ingushetia
Chechnya
Makhachkala
Caspian Sea
Black Sea
GEORGIA
Dagestan
TURKEY   ARMENIA   AZERBAIJAN

the Ingush were deported in 1943 by the Stalin regime. This region, historically Ingush territory, was populated by Cossacks between the 1820s and the 1920s, at which point the Cossacks were deported and the Ingush returned. After the Ingush returned from the Stalin-era deportation in 1957, Prigorodny stayed a part of North Ossetia. The Ingush made every effort to return to the territories they regarded as their historical homeland, but faced problems obtaining residence permits. The Soviet system, however, carried out some affirmative-action programs for the Ingush.

The Ingush justify their claim to Prigorodny by the decision the USSR Supreme Soviet adopted in November 1989 and by Articles 3 and 6 on territorial rehabilitation of the Law on the Deported Peoples, adopted in April 1991.

The period between November 1991 and October 1992 saw increased armament by both sides. Violence erupted in October 1992, when the North Ossetian special police force killed three Ingush, and the Ingush self-defense units advanced toward Vladikavkaz, the capital of North Ossetia. Within a few days Russian federal troops intervened on the North Ossetian side and, supported by the North Ossetian National Guards and special police force, drove the Ingush out of the republic.

Since then tensions have remained, but major violence has been avoided. The situation was aggravated in summer 1997, during which twenty-nine people were killed, and Ruslan Aushev, president of Ingushetia, appealed to the Russian leadership to introduce direct presidential rule on the territory of Prigorodny. Protest meetings in North Ossetia called for reinstallment of the self-defense units. Then President Akhsarbek Galazov threatened that North Ossetia would break away from Moscow rule. A number of terrorist attacks took place. Tensions were exacerbated by statements made by the Chechen leaders that in the event that the North Ossetian leadership failed to bring peace to the republic, Chechnya would dispatch an armed unit to restore order.

Official relations improved somewhat during the second half of 1997, when a number of legal obstacles were removed. On 15 October 1997 a Joint Action Program was signed, earmarked to facilitate the return of internally displaced persons and improve interethnic relations. The program envisions repatriation of the Ingush to all places of previous settlement, including Vladikavkaz, and not only to the villages of Prigorodny, as had been provided for in the past. The legal relationship is currently determined by the Treaty Regulating Relations and Cooperation between the Republic of North Ossetia-Albania and the Republic of Ingushetia, signed in September 1997.

The Ossetian side, following recommendations by the Office of the Russian Federation Presidential Representative, has abolished one law and three other items of legislation that obstructed the repatriation. On the other hand, the constitution of the Republic of Ingushetia still contains Article 11, which claims "the return of the territory of which Ingushetia was illegally deprived."

The election of Alexandr Dzasokhov in January 1998 as president of North Ossetia was welcomed by the Ingush side, not least because he was not associated with the conflict. Initially, prospects for resolution of the conflict seemed good. Direct dialogue between the leaders was established after Dzasokhov took office. For the first time the leading North Ossetian politician put political weight behind the repatriation program, and initiatives to improve the psychological atmosphere were pursued by the Ossetian side. However, as repatriation was transformed from a political slogan into imminent reality, the fragility of the high-level dialogue became apparent. Popular resistance on the Ossetian side intensified, while the Ingush grew increasingly impatient. This led to a wave of kidnappings and killings in summer 1998 and to a general deterioration of the security situation. A breakdown in high-level communication followed when in June 1998 Aushev openly accused Dzasokhov of siding with the nationalists.

Conflict Dynamics

Throughout the 1990s, the popular anti-Ingush sentiment on the Ossetian side only hardened, and all high-level measures to resolve the conflict were generated under pressure from Moscow. The main obstacles to repatriation remain the same, despite the efforts to overcome them. The degree of ethnic resentment between the communities has not diminished and high-level dialogue failed to generate grass-roots support. The slogans of the "impossibility of mutual coexistence with the Ingush" on the Ossetian side and "reconstruction of the territorial integrity of Ingushetia within the 1944 borders" on the Ingush side persist, even if discouraged by the authorities. Returnees often live in segregated communities; in villages where the Ingush have returned, the two parts of a village usually avoid communication with each other and intercommunal violence, such as the burning of houses, often occurs.

Neither side is satisfied with the pace of the return of internally displaced persons. The Ingush consider it to be too slow, while the Ossetians think things proceed too rapidly. An Agreement on Measures for the Return of Internally

Displaced Persons was signed in March 1993 in Kislovodsk, but the Ingush side blamed the North Ossetian leadership for a lack of commitment to its implementation. Proliferation of weapons and the existence of local armed groups on both sides does not help either side to feel secure. The Ingush complain about the absence of security guarantees for the returnees, who doubt the capacity of the North Ossetian police forces to effectively protect them. The Ossetians claim that they fall victim to the Ingush bandits who reportedly penetrate the region among the returnees. The continuous presence of refugees from South Ossetia, 9,000 of whom are estimated as living in houses belonging to displaced Ingush in Prigorodny, produces further disincentive for repatriation.

The gravity of these obstacles was revealed during the second half of 1998, when leaders on both sides took real steps toward full-scale repatriation, marked by the organized return of five Ingush families in March 1998. Violence started in June 1998 with a series of killings and kidnappings, and retaliation undertaken by each side exacerbated the situation. A joint Ingush-Ossetian patrol in the village of Mayskoye was attacked by Ingush terrorists, killing five Ossetians. In response, local Ossetians held Ingush returnees hostage and set fire to 140 Ingush houses.

The two republics came very close to an all-out war. Fortunately, further bloodshed was averted when federal troops were called in to protect the Ingush in North Ossetia—1,250 federal Interior Ministry troops were stationed in Prigorodny, in addition to 1,000 republican Interior troops already deployed there, making this one of the most militarized areas in the Caucasus. For a time, the border between the two republics was closed. The Ingush leadership appealed to Moscow to place the region under direct federal control, and the North Ossetian leadership came under severe domestic criticism for putting Ossetian lives at risk for the sake of Ingush repatriation.

The dialogue resumed in October 1998 when both sides again pledged to work toward conflict resolution, although after the recent bitter experience the Ossetian commitment to progress seemed to be halfhearted.

The escalation of violence in and around Chechnya in 1999 started to increasingly affect neighboring Ingushetia. Chechnya now emerged as the top security priority, sidelining the Prigorodny dispute. President Aushev, the most prominent of the North Caucasian leaders, maintained an independent stance both toward Chechen field commanders and policymakers in Moscow, and attempted to mediate between the two sides. Since then, his relationship with the new Russian government has deteriorated, largely because Ingushetia passed laws that were perceived to be inconsistent with the federal constitution. This concerned the legitimization of customs such as polygamy and bride kidnapping.

The beginning of the second war in Chechnya imposed a heavy burden on tiny Ingushetia since it became the main recipient of over 200,000 Chechen refugees. The Chechen war also adversely affected the prospects for resolution of the conflict with the Ossetians, whose resistance to repatriation of the Ingush mounted further. The Ossetians claimed that Chechen terrorists were likely to enter the republic disguised as returning Ingush in order to avenge for North Ossetia's agreement to deploy Russian federal missile-launching facilities to bomb Chechnya. A number of appalling terrorist actions, such as a bomb explosion in the Vladikavkaz central market killing fifty people, or cutting the throats of Ossetian civilians, made the population blame the Chechens rather than the Ingush for such actions. Irrespective of the validity of such perceptions, they are strongly felt and impede any possible peace initiative.

Official Conflict Management

The North Ossetian/Ingush conflict was the first example of the Russian federal authorities' management of an interethnic conflict. Initially, the Russian Ministry for Nationalities was in charge of managing the deteriorating relations between the two communities. But after the outbreak of violence the ministry was sidelined and the presidential entourage took over. The presidential officials decided to render military support to the Ossetians.

Following the military phase, a civilian body was created to supervise the situation on the ground. In October 1992, a special federal structure—the Interim Administration in the State of Emergency Zone—was created as a body of the Russian federal government. When the state of emergency was abolished in September 1996, the Interim Administration was transformed into the Office of the Russian Federation Presidential Representative (ORFPR). This was done in an attempt to streamline center-periphery relations and put them under the control of the presidential administration. However, the staff was mainly made up of Russian military officers.

The ORFPR has adopted a more proactive stance since the appointment of Vladimir Kalamanov as its head in December 1997. It took steps to facilitate a high-level dialogue and took efforts to build confidence. The federal authorities also took the initiative to open accounts for all registered IDPs, in order to allow them to use federal financial assistance in ways they find appropriate. They could chose to use the assistance to either return or for settlement in a new place. As a former academic from the diplomatic service, Kalamanov, compared to his predecessors, who had military backgrounds, implemented more imaginative initiatives and was prepared to take more risks. He hoped such an approach might break the deadlock. However, it was alleged that during his time in office corruption increased and that machinations with the money accounts of the IDPs proliferated.

In the mid-1990s, Moscow's policies consisted of providing positive incentives for the respective leaderships to make concessions. In return for the willingness to accommodate the returning Ingush, North Ossetia was allocated the right to produce tax-free vodka and emerged as the vodka haven in the Russian Federation. It also acquired the right to control customs on the border with Georgia, with virtually no revenue reaching the Russian federal budget. In 1995, North Ossetia signed a power-sharing treaty with Moscow providing for preferential treatment.

Ingushetia, in its turn, acquired the status of a free economic zone in 1994, and became a tax haven for the North Caucasus and southern Russia. Since the Ingush claimed that after separation from Chechnya they suffered from the lack of an urban center in their republic, Moscow allocated subsidies to Ingushetia to build a new capital, Magas, and a new airport.

Gradually, the responsibility for dealing with the North Ossetian–Ingush conflict was transferred from the Ministry of Defense and Ministry for Nationalities to the Interior Ministry. Moscow's reaction to the September violence 1998 was to dispatch Sergei Stepashin, Russian Interior minister, to the region to mediate between the two sides. The Russian Federal Migration Service initiated a survey among the Ingush IDPs in order to determine how many people were prepared to wait until they could return and how many would be willing to be resettled elsewhere in Russia.

The survey, well-intentioned as a policy-planning measure, provoked a hostile Ingush reaction. The Ingush interpreted it as a decision by the federal government to preserve the existing situation and to give up on repatriation. They also felt that the social atmosphere in Russia was unfavorable for resettlement, due to the alleged rise in anti-Caucasian sentiment. In September 1998, Aushev proposed a status of condominium for Prigorodny, including a joint control of the area, but this idea was rejected both by Moscow and Alexandr Dzasokhov. Before the start of the war in Chechnya, federal policy consisted of efforts to persuade the North Ossetian and Ingush leaders to sign a twenty-year moratorium on the territorial dispute. Moscow also planned to provide funds to restore damaged housing. Troops stationed in the region were intended to serve as a deterrent to the renewal of violence.

Multi-Track Diplomacy

Both North Ossetia and, to a lesser degree, Ingushetia have experienced the involvement of international organizations since the early 1990s. This involvement produced the first impetus for the establishment of local NGOs, mainly in the fields of relief and conflict prevention/resolution. However, the number of NGOs is still modest and growing at a slow pace. Both societies are mainly organized around family and clan lines, structures that provide them with social support. Outside these networks, any activities independent of the state have little space to develop. Traditional bonds also provide a much-needed sense of belonging for communities in the time of trouble. At the same time, they are an obstacle for civic ties to emerge.

In the early 1990s the Peace Research Institute in Oslo (PRIO) became involved in facilitating problem-solving workshops between representatives of the two divided communities. In 1994–1995, the Coordinating Committee for Conflict Resolution Training in Europe (renamed Committee for Conflict Transformation Support) organized two meetings between young people from both sides in partnership with the Quaker Peace and Service (QPS). The meetings enabled people-to-people contacts and helped to overcome some of the stereotypes held vis-à-vis the other group.

The Caucasus Refugee Council has been facilitating dialogue aimed at creating good neighborly relationship between the Ossetian and Ingush communities. It undertakes meetings to bring together representatives of particular social or professional groups from the two republics. Young journalists from North Ossetia and Ingushetia work together to provide information for the intercommunal dialogue.

LINKS (formerly VERTIC) organized a joint study visit for North Ossetian and Ingush representatives to Britain, including a trip to Northern Ireland, to familiarize them with the relevant experience of successes and failures of the conflict-resolution process in another country. The Vladikavkaz Centre of Ethnopolitical Studies has been involved in research and analysis of the issues of conflict. Alexandr Dzadziev, senior research fellow of the center, is also the expert on the North Ossetian–Ingush conflict for the Network for Ethnic Monitoring & Early Warning of Conflicts (EAWARN). Dzadziev has acted as an adviser to the Office of the Presidential Representative on conflict-resolution matters and was involved in the organization of meetings with the Ingush side.

Multilateral Contacts and Training

The Centre for Peacemaking and Community Development (CPCD), which was established in 1995 as a grassroots organization with offices in Moscow, Chechnya, Ingushetia, Dagestan, and Kabardino-Balkaria, works to strengthen local capacities for peace. Its activities include projects with groups and individuals in the fields of human rights, peacemaking, community development, and humanitarian assistance and provision of training in these fields. CPCD renders humanitarian relief to the displaced and vulnerable people in Chechnya and Chechens in Ingushetia. It also runs rehabilitation programs for traumatized children.

International Alert (IA) has been involved in peacemaking activities in the region since 1992 initially via cooperation with the Institute of Ethnology and Anthropology, the director of which was the former nationalities' minister engaged with the conflict. Later, in 1993–1994, IA organized three training seminars in conflict resolution for Caucasian policymakers and civil-society actors. These seminars were attended by a number of North Ossetians. One of the seminars, in Nalchik, involved participants from both sides. In 1998, when the Caucasus Forum of NGOs was founded under the auspices of IA, representatives of both sides were incorporated into a larger pan-Caucasian network on a more permanent basis. In 2001 the Caucasus Forum moved its office to Vladikavkaz, and the Caucasus Refugee Council became its lead agency.

In autumn 1998, Paula Gutlove from Cambridge, Massachusetts, organized a training seminar on "Health as a Bridge to Peace" in Piatigorsk, attended by Chechen, Russian, North Ossetian, and Ingush participants. The project was financed by the WHO. A follow-up meeting was held in the spring of 2000.

The Conflict Management Group (CMG) has been involved in the region since 1992 in partnership with the Institute of Ethnology and Anthropology

(IEA). Since CMG was actively involved in the resolution of conflict in South Ossetia, it made efforts to incorporate the North Ossetians into the dialogue together with their ethnic kin from across the border. The rationale for such a regional framework was that the ties between the two Ossetian communities are strong and North Ossetia has a stake in a resolution of the conflict in South Ossetia, as it has to host Ossetian refugees from Georgia.

In 1996, two British Quakers, John Lampen and Peter Jarman, together with lieutenant Robin Chisnall from the British Ministry of Defense, ran a three-day training seminar on peacekeeping in disputed territories in Vladikavkaz. The seminar was attended by paramilitary troops responsible for security in the Prigorodny district. The training was funded by the British Foreign Office and the Ministry of Defense.

Organizations representing the peoples deported from the North Caucasus during the Stalin era (Chechen, Ingush, Balkar, and Karachai), conducted their own initiatives. In April 2001, a Congress of the Repressed Peoples was held in Magas (Ingushetia). It called on the Russian federal authorities to fulfil their commitment to the Law on Repressed Peoples, which they claimed Moscow failed to respect.

Humanitarian Efforts

The Caucasus Refugee Council (CRC) is a North Ossetian NGO originally established by the UNHCR Vladikavkaz office and the Norwegian Refugee Council. Following the kidnapping of its representative, the UNHCR closed its office and the CRC took over its local functions. The CRC is still supported from a distance by the UNHCR, which maintains an office in Stavropol *krai*. Currently, CRC has offices in Vladikavkaz and Nazran and offers humanitarian aid to 6,000 families of displaced people who fled fighting in Chechnya. It also provides free legal advice for the IDPs with regard to their legal rights. CRC was planning to expand its operations into Chechnya as soon as the security situation allows.

In Ingushetia, the Association for the Protection of Rights of Deported Peoples (ADEPT) represents the interests of the Ingush as displaced people. The association was established under the sponsorship of Mukharbek Aushev, a member of the State Duma from Ingushetia and senior manager at Lukoil, a major Russian oil company. ADEPT mainly operates from its Moscow headquarters.

A Dutch charity, Chechen Relief, set up the so-called Agency of Rehabilitation and Development (ARD). This organization started its activities in Chechnya but also started to operate in Ingushetia. ARD trained local trainers and schoolteachers to work with affected children, teenagers, and women in order to be able to help with the psychosocial rehabilitation of these affected groups. Since the start of the second war in Chechnya, most of its members worked in an IDP camp. Roswitha Jarman, an independent British consultant working in the Caucasus, was involved both with the CPCD and ARD. Roswitha and Peter Jarman pursued activities, but mainly focused on peace

North Ossetia: Displaced Ingush man

education and psychosocial counseling in Ingushetia and North Ossetia. They were also involved in bilateral seminars aimed at confidence-building measures, especially in the disputed Prigorodny district of North Ossetia.

Youth Organizations

Assa, an independent organization of young people, is one of the most active NGOs based in Ingushetia. It participates in the Caucasus Forum and pursues projects aimed at establishing contacts between youth groups elsewhere in the Caucasus. Laman Az from Chechnya is their main counterpart.

CPCD helped to establish the Young People's Peacebuilding Network in the North Caucasus, an initiative that is also sponsored by the EU-TACIS program. It provides individuals and local groups with training in alternatives to violence. It also helps them to set up and use e-mail communication facilities. Four youth meetings and two seminars were held since its establishment.

The United Nations of Youth Foundation (UNOY), a global network of young peacebuilders, held two regional conferences for young peacebuilders from the Caucasus in 1994 and 1996 entitled "Peacebuilding in Caucasia." During a UNOY Global Youth Peace Conference in May 1999, regional working groups were held for Caucasian youth leaders. These conferences put much effort in training young people in techniques of nonviolent conflict resolution, diplomatic negotiation, reconciliation, networking, and setting up common projects. The UNOY has a partnership relation with the Centre for

Peacemaking and Community Development, which provides regional expertise and contacts.

Women Peacemakers

Many women's groups originated from the soldiers mothers' movement developed during the first war in Chechnya. The Council of Social Organizations of Ingushetia, led by Leila Tsoroeva, is one of these groups, covering a wide agenda. The Union of North Caucasus Women is a women's group working in community development and peacemaking fields in Ingushetia and Chechnya. It cooperates with CPCD.

The IEA pursues the project on "Conflict Resolution in the Post-Soviet States" in cooperation with the CMG. It maintains a network of regional experts (EAWARN) who contribute to the Early Warning Bulletins. IEA and CMG contribute to the bulletins, organize training events for the network members, and target Russian and international policymakers to promote early action. The Forum on Early Warning and Early Response (FEWER) started its Caucasus program in 1998 and also provides early-warning reports and training for the regional actors.

International interest in the Ossetian-Ingush conflict has diminished over the past years, probably because little progress has been made despite the efforts made by the official conflict-management bodies and third parties. Also, other conflicts required attention.

Deterioration of the security situation in the region, a consequence of the war in Chechnya, also became an obstacle to international involvement. The kidnapping of a UNHCR expatriate worker in 1998 had a detrimental effect, while other organizations suffered similar disasters. The region became a "no-go" area for foreigners, as well as for many Russians. The start of the second war in Chechnya in October 1999 made peace interventions into North Ossetia/Ingushetia virtually impossible because of the dangers on the ground. In addition to security problems, the Russian authorities grew increasingly suspicious of foreign NGOs, as Moscow apparently believed their representatives might be spying on the Russian military.

Prospects

The future of Ingushetia is closely related to the outcome of the second war in Chechnya. The longer the war continues, the bigger the chance that Russian troops in Ingushetia will be the subject of Chechen attacks. Some spillover of instability would then be inevitable.

A similar risk affects North Ossetia, since it is the bastion of the Russian military presence in the North Caucasus. The Russian government is more concerned with the current war in Chechnya than with the old Ossetian-Ingush problem, and new Chechen refugees are a more pressing issue than the Ingush ones. In such a situation, it is unlikely that any progress will be made before the Chechnya crisis is settled.

Two points of view on the future of the conflict exist. One holds that Aushev was effective in communicating Ingush grievances to the Russian government, which in turn was prepared to engage in some conflict-resolution measures. This involvement may have averted the worst violence. If this is to change and the Ingush find themselves in a powerless position with a Moscow deaf to their concerns, the Ingush may start a sustained campaign of violence to draw attention to their situation. The counterargument is that the dispute will dissolve gradually because, without any clear progress on the political level, individuals will start to make more practical choices, such as finding a new home in Ingushetia or resettle elsewhere in Russia.

Recommendations

It does not seem feasible to plan practical conflict-resolution measures in North Ossetia/Ingushetia until the war in Chechnya comes to an end. It would be very useful, however, to reflect on the lessons learned from the Russian experience regarding North Ossetian–Ingush conflict management. The federal government tried different approaches at different times, and there is rich material to study in order to be able to plan future strategies. A research paper into the methods employed and the rationale for them based on interviews with practitioners both on the Russian side and with the representatives of the international humanitarian organizations who were involved in the area, would be a useful tool.

More should be done in terms of reducing interethnic resentment on a village level. Efforts in this field have been neglected throughout the 1990s, despite the ORFPR's initiatives. However, unless basic security settles in, it will be impossible to undertake measures on the ground. Since the Russian government is increasingly sensitive to the activities of foreign organizations in its conflict areas, it would be advisable to form a partnership with a Russian group and to maintain good relations with the authorities.

Resources

Newsletters and Periodicals

Bulletin of the Network on Ethnological Monitoring and Early Warning of Conflicts, Conflict Resolution in the Post-Soviet States Project, IEA/CMG, published quarterly in Russian (Moscow University) and English (Harvard University)

Contemporary Caucasus Newsletter, University of California, Berkeley

EWI Russian Regional Report, EastWest Institute (U.S.), weekly

Monitor & Prism, daily news and analysis, Jamestown Foundation, Washington, DC

WarReport, 1995–98—Institute for War & Peace Reporting, London/UK

Reports

Danish Refugee Council, *Conflict and Forced Displacement in the Caucasus: Perspectives, Challenges and Responses,* edited by Tom Trier and Lars Funch Hansen, Copenhagen, 1999.

Human Rights Watch, *The Ingush-Ossetian Conflict in the Prigorodny Region,* April 1996.

Strengthening Democratic Institutions Project, *Russia's Tinderbox: Conflict in the North Caucasus and Its Implications for the Future of the Russian Federation,* by Fiona Hill, 1995.

Writenet (UK), *Refugees and Internally Displaced Persons in North Ossetia and Ingushetia,* by Egbert Wesselink, March 1994.

Other Publications

The Mind Aflame: Ethnicity, Nationalism and Conflict in and After the Soviet Union, by Valery Tishkov. Thousand Oaks, CA, Sage Publications, 1997.

The North Caucasus: Russia's Fragile Borderland, by Anna Matveeva. London, RIIA, 1999.

Selected Internet Sites

www.eawarn.ru (Network for Ethnic Monitoring & Early Warning of Conflicts)

www.fewer.org (Forum on Early Warning and Early Response)

www.iews.org (EastWest Institute, Russian Regional Report)

www.iwpr.net (Institute for War and Peace Reporting, Caucasus reporting service, London)

www.rferl.org (Radio Free Europe/Radio Liberty Newsline, daily news and analysis)

Resource Contacts

Alexandr Dzadziev, Vladikavkaz Centre of Ethnopolitical Studies, North Ossetia, e-mail: sandro@osetia.ru

Lars Funch Hansen, program coordinator, Danish Refugee Council, e-mail: lars.funch. hansen@drc.dk or lars_funch_h@hotmail.com

Christopher Hunter, Centre for Peacemaking and Community Development, e-mail: peacecentre@glasnet.ru

Peter and Roswitha Jarman, independent consultants on the Caucasus, e-mail: jarmans @gn.apc.org

Anna Matveeva, expert on the Caucasus, London, e-mail: sophiamat@ukonline.co.uk

Gevork Ter-Gabrielian, International Alert, e-mail: gtergabrielian@international-alert.org

Valery Tishkov, director, Institute of Ethnology and Anthropology, Moscow, e-mail: tishkov@orc.ru

Organizations

The Union of Human Rights, Humanitarian and Other Nongovernmental Public Organizations
Karabulak Street 36-39
386231 Jabaguieva
Republic of Ingushetia
Tel.: +7 8312 340488
E-mail: friend@sinn.ru

Data on the following organizations can be found in the Directory section:

Local

    Caucasus NGO Forum

    Caucasus Refugee Council

    Center for Peacemaking and Community Development

    Center for the Study of and Management of Conflict (Institute of Ethnology and Anthropology)

    Don Women's Union

    Mission Peace in North Caucasus

International
   Conflict Management Group
   FEWER
   International Alert
   LINKS
   Peace Research Institute in Oslo (PRIO)
   Quaker Peace and Service

Anna Matveeva is a program manager at Saferworld (on small arms and security). She previously worked as a research fellow at the Royal Institute of International Affairs (Chatham House, London) and program head at International Alert (London). As a scholar specializing in issues of conflict and the politics of post-Soviet Eurasia, she has authored publications such as The North Caucasus: Russia's Fragile Borderland *(London: RIIA, 1999) and academic articles, and undertook projects for organizations such as the International Peace Academy, EastWest Insititute, Minority Rights Group, and the Heinrich Böll Stiftung.*

15

SOUTHERN CAUCASUS

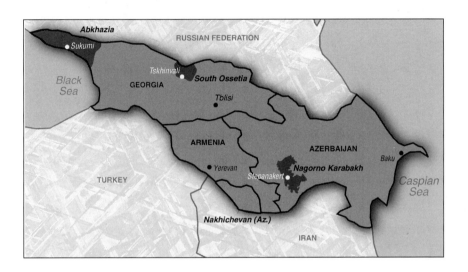

15.1

Regional Introduction: Struggling to Find Peace

Jonathan Cohen

The dominant images of the Caucasus in the past decade have been violent conflict, social and economic disarray, and the prospect that the extraction and export of oil might transform the region. While the region remains little known and less understood by the outside world, it has long inhabited a strategic geographic location both as a buffer zone and a bridge between regional powers and cultural traditions. This has informed the identities and international orientation of the states and peoples of the Caucasus, which presents a diverse and often fluid ethnic, cultural, and linguistic mosaic.

In the aftermath of the collapse of the Soviet Union in 1991, Armenia, Azerbaijan, and Georgia emerged as new states only to experience a decade of armed conflict and economic misery that overshadowed the high expectations that came with independence. Apart from an interlude of limited independence from 1917–1921, Russian rule had defined life and borders in the Caucasus for two centuries, as a result of wars of conquest in the nineteenth century and Soviet rule in the twentieth. With the demise of this rule, political structures and economic practices that had long conditioned peoples' lives were undermined and long-suppressed aspirations unleashed. Hostility within and between communities degenerated into wars in Abkhazia, South Ossetia, and Nagorno Karabakh that have yet to be resolved. The Caucasus also experienced a number of coups accompanied by wider civic conflict. Ethnic difference was central to much of this, but it would be wrong to call these "ethnic conflicts." They were instead a consequence of elites and societies grappling with past grievances and present insecurities, changing power constellations, and access to resources in the context of a disintegrating empire and were very much political power struggles. Recognizing the broader issues behind conflicts in the Caucasus helps to explain why they have so far not been resolved and why democracy and development in the region remain a weak insurance against further conflict.

State and Nation Building

The ebbing of the nationalistic fanaticism of the early 1990s allowed greater concentration on state and nation building in Armenia, Azerbaijan, and Georgia as the decade progressed. The needs of nation building have often complicated the coherence of state building, particularly in Azerbaijan and Georgia where the very diversity of ethnic groups has been a major cause of the current fractured statehood and has often given rise to prejudicial policies against minorities. All the newly independent states have struggled to control and administer their territory. Georgia and Azerbaijan in particular have failed to establish a monopoly on the use of force as a prerequisite for the defense of the realm and hence statehood. In addition to the challenges posed by violent conflicts, the extent of criminality also undermines state coherence.

While the formal structures of democratic systems have been put in place—presidents, parliaments, constitutional courts, and multipartyism—question marks loom over the degree to which democratization is entrenched. Legislatures remain relatively weak within strong presidential systems that suffer from a lack of accountability. Although general and local elections have been held, they have been flawed by tampering and outright manipulation. The credibility and administration of law is fragile. Governance remains bedeviled by corruption and malpractice. The operation of patronage networks in exercising much political and economic power does not bode well if the ritual of democracy is to become more substantive. There has been no democratic change of government in the region since independence and with presidents Aliev (Azerbaijan) and Shevardnadze (Georgia) aging, political succession is an increasingly worrisome issue.

Politics has generated pluralistic debate, but societies are only partially coming to terms with the notion that democracy in multiethnic societies means participation in decisionmaking by diverse groups airing different views. Accepting conflict, as opposed to violence, as part of social and political life is a threatening notion to weak states. Ways in which difference (ethnic or otherwise) is handled will have a significant impact on whether or not more democratic processes can be consolidated or will rather be subsumed to a persistent authoritarianism.

This applies even more to Abkhazia, Nagorno Karabakh, and South Ossetia than to the recognized states. Since the establishment of cease-fires, these entities have entrenched their positions. While they have worked on establishing the institutions of statehood, politics remains more restrictive. Despite the appearance of more authoritarian regimes, it would be mistaken to assume that there is no political debate. Rather, it is more circumscribed, with participants reluctant to expose disagreement to their opponents. There are also fewer legal constraints upon the conduct of political activity, making it more prone to the maneuvering of powerful individuals. Pluralism, democratization, and the development of civil societies have been less important goals than survival and political consolidation. Solidarity has been central to survival, but leaderships have to balance the integrity of their political positions with the aspirations of populations, which on the one hand might be motivated by the same political ends, but on the other seek greater options for participation and material well-being. The bottom line is that despite several years of de facto sovereignty for Abkhazia, Nagorno Karabakh, and South Ossetia, the international community shows no inclination to recognize their status formally.

Economics: Dismal Reality or Hope for Change?
The socioeconomic ramifications of the conflicts will remain for years to come, even if political accords can be reached. Each of the conflicts generated humanitarian crises. Out of a South Caucasian population of about 15 million, over a million people have been displaced. As a result, isolation and marginalization scars the lives of whole generations, not just of those displaced but also of those living in areas where the social infrastructure has been unable to cope with the influx of displaced people and those living in areas where political isolation has curtailed economic opportunities. This blight is compounded by the painful and incomplete transition from communism to democracy and free-market capitalism.

Economic indicators show a regionwide development crisis: radical deindustrialization, growing unemployment, shrinking consumption, swathes of the population living below the poverty line, and out-migration (generally in search of better work opportunities) amounting to as much as 20 percent of the region's population. Reduced life expectancy and birthrates indicate the gravity of the situation. While new economic elites have emerged and economic activity has undergone a dramatic reconfiguration, in rural areas monetary economies are faltering. Conflict and political antipathies have diminished intraregional trade just at the time when the economies have become more open to trade.

Nevertheless, the chaos of the early 1990s has been overcome, and largely as a result of the prospect of Azerbaijani oil fuelling change, the risk takers of international investment are slowly being attracted. However, ineffective tax collection has imposed major constraints on the exercise of power. The control exerted by mafia-type organizations on business reflects on the market less as a civilizing mechanism than as one generating inequality and quick, but rarely clean, wealth. Certainly the wealth generation that has occurred has not yet been transferred into reinvestment into the productive capacities of any of the countries.

In the war-torn regions, economic reconstruction has occurred at different rates. Progress is most advanced in Nagorno Karabakh, where the existence of a secure border with Armenia, the largesse of a wealthy diaspora, and the expropriation of materials and equipment from occupied territories in Azerbaijan have contributed to the renovation of much of the economy. In South Ossetia, links to North Ossetia provide an important outlet, while trade with Georgia is in fact both a sign of relative progress in the peace process as well as a confidence-building measure encouraging further progress. In Abkhazia, there is little productive industry because the physical infrastructure devastated by war has yet to be reconstructed and much of the agricultural bounty of what was a supremely fertile region has gone to waste. The trade that does exist is either of a subsistence kind or controlled by mafia-type organizations.

Economic and political isolation resulting from the imposition of blockades and trade restrictions as crude means of leverage generates siege mentalities, self-reliance, and antagonism that reduces the propensity not only to compromise but to make any form of contact with antagonists. Yet there are constituencies (black marketeers, local monopolists, border guards, troops, and militia members) who benefit from thinly regulated economies across conflict divides. They are unlikely to promote resolutions that might undermine their scope for graft. Economic and ethnic relationships between entrepreneurs and criminals are blurred when profits are to be made, whether this relates to Abkhaz and Georgians trading across the Inguri River or Armenians and Azeris meeting in the Sadakhlo market in Georgia.

The long-term viability of the economies of the conflict-ridden zones remains questionable. The economic benefits from peaceful cooperation (such as the Inguri hydroelectric dam, or ambitious regionwide plans such as the Transport Corridor Europe Caucasus Asia [TRACECA], let alone pipelines) have yet to provide a sufficient incentive to conflict resolution. This suggests that despite recognition that peace would enable trade and transport links to be reconstructed (within the region and to surrounding markets), the prospect of economic development on its own is not a sufficient temptation to encourage communities to compromise their long-term political goals, despite the costs. In this light, spurring economic development should not be seen as the carrot that will make peace agreements happen, but rather as the cement that can hold them in place.

Civil Society: Preparing the Way for Peace?

Although an ill-defined notion, much emphasis has been placed on civil society by Western donors searching for an antidote to ethnic nationalism and as an aid to democratization. Central to this understanding of civil society as a motor for social change has been the promotion of NGOs. To a certain extent these have begun to meet social needs not met through official channels, because of policy, political constraints, or the dearth of resources. In Georgia, more than elsewhere, NGOs have begun to engage dynamically in dialogue with the authorities.

Yet despite the proliferation of NGOs, the salaries they generate, and the extensive sphere of their activities, their influence is limited. Their activity has been confined primarily to cities and rarely spreads to rural communities. More significantly they are dependent on external financial support, which leaves them vulnerable to the vagaries of international donors. The fragility of democratic institutions exacerbates this vulnerability, as does the failure of a free and open media to take root. Crude censorship is not frequent, but generally the only dynamic media are supported by international agencies or are close to the NGO sector. Civic actors striving for peaceful solutions are politically weak and the majority of the regions' population is grappling with economic hardship rather than political change. Institutions supporting participatory democracy and the rule of law have not, despite considerable progress in recent years, consolidated democracy in terms of the creation of a free and open political space. Whether civil society would be able to resist political reversals is uncertain. This is especially important given the creeping disillusion with Western values that is emerging alongside a revival of nationalistic tendencies in response to frustrations at the depth of socioeconomic disarray and the flawed nature of regimes that the West has supported with too little conditionality.

Civil-society voices are also emerging in Abkhazia, Nagorno Karabakh, and South Ossetia, although they face greater constraints. The fact that people here want to see a widening of civic space, more democracy, and a peaceful resolution to conflicts does not, however, mean that they are willing to compromise on their political aspirations.

This presents a challenge. Communities have been in turn mobilized by war and rendered passive by the socioeconomic burdens of transition. The lack of public information and debate about progress in or constraints on negotiation processes suggests that politicians and societies are divorced from one another. The space for compromise or the abandonment of animosities cultivated by the media and nationalistic political leaders is limited. Paradoxically, while pushing through unpopular compromises could be easier for less democratic leaders, the leaders tend not to be strong enough to risk doing this. In this light, NGOs and civic actors that have worked to build bridges across conflict divides, widen the discussions about matters of conflict resolution and visions for the future within their own societies, and create a social readiness for settlement assume an ever more important role as agents of social change. This is especially important given the lack of trust in politicians and politics throughout the region. However, civic organizations are not themselves political decisionmakers, but rather opinion formers.

No War No Peace
Cease-fires that have now held for several years have been punctuated by periodic bouts of heightened tension and actual hostilities. While none of the parties to the conflicts seem inclined toward a renewal of outright war, it would be premature to say that all have categorically ruled out the prospect of resolution through military engagement. Constituencies exist, particularly within the countries more disaffected with the status quo (Azerbaijan and Georgia, which advocate recourse to military options), but it is hard to envision that these could be decisive. However, as long as vocal groups harbor aspirations of victory, or at least resolution on their terms without consideration of the needs and fears of opponents, compromise will be difficult to achieve.

Despite the attempts to mediate in the region (by the Organization for Security and Cooperation in Europe and the United Nations; through the bilateral and multilateral involvement of a number of states; through bilateral contact at high levels; and through the role of a number of "second track" and civic initiatives by international and local NGOs) there has been little substantive progress toward political settlements. It is a misnomer to call these frozen conflicts since there are always dynamics at play that suggest some actors or interests are fluid. The difficulty for those intervening or for internal actors pushing for resolution is to identify the malleable issues and underlying interests and to design constructive means to work with the potential for change.

South Ossetia has shown more promise of resolution. But any settlement there seems tied to the Abkhazia conflict where, despite the signing of framework agreements early in the peace process, there has been little meaningful trading of benefits and concessions, and as a result the irreconcilability in the public positions of the parties has not been dented. UN efforts to interject new ideas have encountered this intransigence as well as an unbending Russian position, such that a UN position paper on the distribution of competencies under preparation for almost a year has yet to see the light of day.

In the first half of 2001 efforts to resolve the conflict over Karabakh, led by the cochairs of the Minsk Group, raised expectations for a settlement. However, following a meeting in Florida, the Armenian and Azeri presidents returned home for consultations, and although the detail of any proposed agreement was kept out of the public domain, opposition figures were openly discussing the option of resuming hostilities and there was certainly no outspoken public support for compromise. As a result, the momentum has, for the time being, abated. The problem remains an inability to sell hard choices back home.

The chapters on Georgia and Nagorno Karabakh that follow provide analysis of the conflicts and the interventions of international organizations in seeking resolution. The complexity of the conflicts partly explains the lack of success in reaching sustainable solutions. Difficulties in coordination, negotiating mandates, and often cautious diplomacy, in the face of a multiplicity of actors and precarious balances of power, have constrained the way in which mediation has operated in the different conflicts. The remainder of this chapter looks at the factors motivating intervention by states and what light this sheds on the challenges of the peace processes and hence prospects for the future.

The Inner Circle: Russia, Turkey, and Iran
Historically, the power and influence of Russia, Turkey, and Iran, in various incarnations, has ebbed and flowed across the region. This has left a legacy of overlapping and conflicting interests that do not necessarily facilitate conflict resolution or stable development despite each being aware that instability in the Caucasus has its costs at home.

Russia's roles in the generation of the conflicts and in attempts to resolve them have been the most complex. Conditioned by a loss of empire, new constraints on strategic and economic interests, concerns about Russian minorities, and the possible expansion of NATO or at least GUAAM (the mutual support grouping created in 1996 by Georgia, Ukraine, Azerbaijan, and Moldova, joined by Uzbekistan in 1999) as opposed to the Russian Federation's Commonwealth of Independent States' security framework, Russia has displayed a tendency to pursue vital interests through often heavy-handed means. The multiplicity of institutional actors pursuing policies in the region (including the president, ministries of Foreign Affairs and Defense, border guards and the State Duma) has hindered the emergence of a coherent approach and made Russian policy vulnerable to accusations of partiality. Russia's ability to act as a peacemaker or peacekeeper in the longer term could be diminished by the lack of capacity to provide economic investment. However, economic interests (particularly export routes for the hydrocarbon resources of the Caspian region) and instability in the North Caucasus mean that the Caucasus remains one of Russia's main security priorities.

Following the cease-fires, which Russia brokered, there was a decline in Russia's capacity to influence events as the states began to assert their independence and become involved in an ever more complex web of bilateral and multilateral international relations. This coincided with the first of two Chechen wars in the 1990s, both of which have drained Russia's financial and political capital and imposed a particular strain on relations with Georgia. Since President Putin's accession to power, Russia's negligent approach to the region has been replaced with more rigorous measures, such as cutting off gas to Georgia or the introduction of a visa regime for Georgia, but not Abkhazia or South Ossetia, although these have been accompanied by indications that Russia is introducing more subtle and accommodating policies as well.

Attitudes toward Russia vary from perceptions of benign patronage in Armenia to Machiavellian intrigues in Georgia. The military-bases issue is a good litmus test, as well as having strategic significance. Armenia holds onto bases as part of its national security, whereas Georgia strongly opposes continued basing rights, even though populations living in regions where some of the bases are located oppose their removal (mainly on economic grounds). The distrust generated by Russia's roles will in itself be an important legacy of how the South Caucasian states choose to engage with Russia in the foreseeable future. Nevertheless, regional stability will require all stakeholders to be engaged. Russia remains the regional hegemony. It operates as a facilitator in the UN- and OSCE-mediated peace processes (often being concerned to restrict or at least control international mandates), as a mediator in bilateral and trilateral relations with the parties, as a troop contributor to the Commonwealth of Independent States Peacekeeping Force and UN Observer Mission in Georgia (UNOMIG) in Abkhazia, and as a state seeking to promote its national interest. Russia will continue to be a key player with the ability to sabotage peace processes if not to resolve the conflicts.

For Iran and Turkey, the emergence of three independent states, and their subsequent conflicts, on their borders created opportunities and threats. Their rivalry in the region was initially based on the false premise that the influence of Russia was in terminal decline. While this has not been the case, the Caucasian states themselves have not been the passive objects of external intervention. Furthermore, their initial ambitions overstretched their capacities, resulting in them playing more modest roles while attempting to promote their own interests.

Turkey's penetration into the Caucasus has historically been an obsession in Russia; therefore, its strengthening of relations with Azerbaijan and Georgia has prompted caution in Moscow. Support to Azerbaijan has posed a particular threat to Armenia, where attempts at normalization have been hampered not only by the Karabakh conflict but also due to the genocide debate. Downplaying grandiose ideas of a renewed Turkish sphere of influence stretching into Central Asia, Turkey has increasingly focused on promoting its commercial interests, its role in pipeline routes, and its contribution to international efforts to foster peace and security (conscious of ramifications with its Kurdish population).

Iran's position tends to be more pragmatic and flexible than its external image suggests. Closer relations with Armenia than with Azerbaijan reflect the fact that oversimplified interpretations of religious affiliations should not disguise geopolitical interest or imperial legacy. In Azerbaijan, there are perceptions of Iran as a historical overlord that is ambivalent about its independence, while the issue of a substantial Azeri population in northern Iran, which prompted Azeri nationalists to call for a reunification of historic Azerbaijan in the early 1990s, cautions Iranian policy. Iran has provided an important economic outlet for Armenia and has used this relationship and common interests with Russia (particularly demarcation of the Caspian and a less enthusiastic attitude to the West) to alleviate its diplomatic isolation, in particular in regard to its relations with the United States.

The Outer Circle: The United States and Europe

Before 1994, Western policies in the region sought to enhance political stability through state building and democratization, to promote market reforms, and to support the sovereignty of the states vis-à-vis Russia. These limited aims did not justify a significant political, let alone military, involvement. Energy interests came to the forefront after the signing of the so-called Contract of the Century to export Caspian oil in September 1994. Policies toward the region were reconceived, with pipeline politics at their heart, especially for the United States. It can be argued that the potential oil wealth to be derived from the region has exaggerated its strategic significance given that while Caspian oil is important for the West, it is not vital to Western security. The United States has been very wary of assuming a security role, partly due to the logistical difficulties this would entail but also due to the priority of integrating Russia into an international cooperation framework. However, balancing relations with Russia, the influence of the oil lobby and the Armenian diaspora, as well as troubled relations with Iran, has created constraints that have not always been conducive to fluent policymaking.

European states individually and collectively have been less proactive than the United States. Policy has generally lacked a developed political agenda, let alone conflict-resolution planning for the region. Instruments such as Partnership and Cooperation Agreements, aid and development programs such as TRACECA, INNOGATE, Technical Assistance for the Commonwealth of Independent States (EU TACIS), and the European Community Humanitarian Office (ECHO) have been used to exert leverage, with almost a billion euros being invested in the Caucasus since 1991. But often-ambitious plans, while contributing to change, have been undermined by bureaucratic implementation and have not produced striking outcomes nor led to the region being embraced by Europe. In the late 1990s, this did begin to change as the EU developed more-assertive policies. Furthermore, the stated long-term goal of the Caucasian states to join the EU should provide future leverage. This implies exporting a certain model of economic and political life. But it is questionable to what extent Russia and Iran want this, or how far this is feasible within the states for at least a generation. Acceptance of the three states into the Council of Europe is a sign of Europe's commitment to the Caucasus. However, this poses a challenge since at times advocacy of human rights and deep-rooted democratization have been relegated below supporting stability and sovereignty, and in so doing risked breeding contempt for these values.

A more dynamic European involvement has also contributed to increased discussion of proposals for a regional stability pact. The notion may have met criticism in regard to the unlikelihood of Western investment (financial or political) on the same scale as in the Balkans, because of Russia's hesitance and in regard to persuading states that have only recently gained independence to relinquish aspects of their sovereignty. Nevertheless, there is a clear demand for regional thinking as indicated by frequent allusions by political leaders and civil-society actors to the need for solutions to conflict and developmental issues that assume a regional dimension. One challenge will be that Caucasian experience of shared sovereignty (federal and autonomous relations under Soviet rule) has left very a negative legacy. Another will be how to engage the North Caucasus in any long-term solution to the region's tensions, given that Russia is very protective regarding how this region relates to international forums.

Challenges on the Road to Peace

Resolving conflicts in the Caucasus is not only about mediation or negotiation processes. To limit the search for peace to the domain of official diplomacy is to ignore the fact that sustainable peace requires economic development, social justice, and legal frameworks that can accommodate conflicting relationships.

Political elites in the Caucasus have pursued a dangerous game, often encouraged by external political actors, of creating states without meaningful politics and permeated by paternalism and clientalistic networks. Personalities and not policies are at the heart of politics. The narrow focus on democracy as an institutional arrangement distracts attention from wider definitions in terms of the real distribution of power, socioeconomic rights, and accountability in society. The underperformance of institutions is not as damaging for the long term as the absence of a wider culture of democracy. Although the political climate throughout the South Caucasus, including within the unrecognized entities, has been changed by the experience of the past decade, there have been few signs of statesmanship or the promotion of reconciliation within societies (let alone with regard to the so-called enemies). Nowhere is democracy sufficiently entrenched to allow the creativity of leadership that might overcome the ongoing political impasse.

A number of challenges need to be addressed and preconceptions confronted if coherent political communities characterized by a consolidation of democracy rather than cycles of violent conflict are to evolve. Reframing needs to recognize that resolution is complicated by conflicting perceptions of political principles, above all territorial integrity and self-determination. Mediators have operated from the basis that any outcome other than territorial integrity has been proscribed, but the international community's commitment to territorial integrity presents the prospect that the parties that effectively won the wars will lose the peace. Whether it is possible to reconceptualize and reinvigorate perceptions of political relationships in such a way that parties can be convinced that they have not lost what they fought for or that security priorities are not compromised is questionable. But this will be critical to the achievement of nonviolent settlements that are neither fragile nor short-lived.

There is a deep fear of federal-type solutions to the conflicts. To an extent, discussion of this is a case of closing the barn door after the horse has bolted—federal solutions that might have interested the "separatist" parties prior to the violent conflicts are now less attractive. But there is a reluctance to move beyond the abstract level and explore the detail of what the long-term implications for political representation and financial accountability, social and economic policy, policing, and foreign policy could be. Exploring power-sharing mechanisms is of importance beyond the current unresolved conflicts. The existence of compact ethnic communities contiguous with state borders in Javakheti and the Lezgin and Talysh regions in Georgia and Azerbaijan, respectively, is perceived to present a threat to territorial integrity and therefore it is feared that any steps to devolve power could precipitate this. There is also a tremendous need to rethink structures of governance at central and local levels (regardless of unresolved conflicts). Given the incompetence and corruption—sometimes perceived and often real—of so much of the governance in the Caucasus, this will be no easy task. These issues are especially pertinent as the demands of state and nation building collide with processes of economic interdependence and globalization.

If progress toward peace is to be attained, ideals of multiethnicity and cultural diversity must be reinvigorated. It is, however, hard to envisage a settlement based on these ideals being realized in Nagorno Karabakh or parts of Abkhazia, where a comfortable political cohabitation of Armenians and Azeris or Abkhaz and Georgians in the near future is unlikely. The psychological inheritance of the wars cannot be ignored in the search for resolution. A generation is growing up without having known Georgian or Azeri rule (despite the fact that this was a very different type of rule, more Soviet than anything else, prior to the conflicts) and therefore with little inclination to effect compromises that could reintroduce such political relationships. The knowledge of what this rule might constitute is sparse and characterized by perceptions of undemocratic practices and a continuation of ethnically prejudicial approaches that are not attractive.

The fact that communities live beyond one another's orbit makes reconciliation, which will be a component of political settlements in the long run, problematic. Conflicting perceptions of justice in terms of history, atrocities committed during the war, and the needs of marginalized and displaced people make compromise difficult. Finding ways to process the past that will lead to mutual understanding rather than recrimination will not be easy. Holding the perpetrators of wartime atrocities to account will be costly in political and financial terms.

The mass return of the displaced is impeded because of the absence of political agreements, security concerns, and economic factors, but it is inextricably linked to conflict resolution. The reconstruction and rehabilitation of war-affected areas can only be limited without political normalization. International humanitarian assistance has been essential in providing a safety net for the displaced. Agencies have had to negotiate the dilemma that integrating the displaced within Azerbaijan and Georgia is a highly political act because it implies that they may not eventually return to the homes from which they were displaced. Yet not integrating them risks their marginalization in IDP and refugee camps and has often meant their exclusion from elementary social provisions such as health care and educational opportunities, as well as political life.

A tendency to blame outsiders for many of the predicaments that the region faces often influences political debate, and often with good reason. Nevertheless, directing blame to the crude manipulations or efforts to exert influence by others is also a convenient way to shift responsibility from one's own actions. This tendency is accompanied by an expectation that peace and development can be delivered by external factors—be it NATO, Russia, or the United States. Oil production and transportation exemplify such thinking. Oil might lubricate development that could mesh together a regional interdependence making conflict resolution worthwhile for enough actors, but it could bring as much conflict as harmony. Furthermore, while it gives the Caucasus a new strategic relevance, this is not as great as many in the region might think. The West will continue to be preoccupied with the Balkans and the Middle East, and after "September the 11th" Afghanistan and its surrounds, among other regions, above the Caucasus.

The existence of vested interests, the lack of trust, the psychological heritage of separation that is accumulating, and the lack of sufficiently strong or motivated peace constituencies within societies will continue to make it difficult to turn war fatigue into peace hunger. For politicians and people to engage profoundly with the above challenges will require time. But the expectation (whether believed or simply used as political rhetoric) that problems can be resolved quickly is a factor that has undermined progress since the establishment of cease-fires. It is arguable on whose side time lies in each conflict—economic and social problems, out-migration, and democratic deficits afflict all societies in the region to the extent that none can comfortably afford perpetual instability. The scale of the challenges, the lack of material resources, and responses that have frequently lacked strategic coherence have at times threatened the existence of the states themselves. Nevertheless, while the multitude of problems persist the region has muddled through without a return to war in the past seven years. Crisis has become part of the political fabric and fragile stability. This, however, is no insurance against deterioration nor compensation for the millions of people enduring great hardship in comparison to their former economic well-being.

Jonathan Cohen is Caucasus program manager at Conciliation Resources, a London-based NGO where he is involved in peacebuilding and dialogue projects primarily in regard to the Georgia/Abkhazia conflict. He previously served as deputy director of the Foundation on Inter-Ethnic Relations in The Hague, working with the OSCE High Commissioner on National Minorities.

15.2

Georgia: Peace Remains Elusive in Ethnic Patchwork

Anna Matveeva

In the early 1990s, Georgia survived a number of great upheavals that overshadowed its newly won independence. Conflict in South Ossetia and in Abkhazia led to violence and the flight of many Georgians from conflict zones. The situation in Georgia has stabilized since, but neither the political status of the breakaway territories nor the return of the displaced have been resolved, despite intensive international involvement. The UN took the lead in resolution of the Abkhaz conflict while the OSCE concentrated on South Ossetia, with international NGOs pursuing many second-track initiatives. Attacks of Georgian paramilitaries on Abkhazia have upset the fragile progress made both by leaderships and NGOs, making resolution of the conflict in Abkhazia more difficult than ever.

Abkhazia (12.5 percent of territory of the Republic of Georgia) is situated on the Black Sea coast, stretching along the Caucasian mountains and bordering Russia in the north. For Georgia, it is a valuable territory. The former Soviet Riviera, it contains half of Georgia's coastline, including the best resorts, rich agricultural resources, a major power station, and rail and road links to Russia. Demography played a vital role in a small-scale but brutal war in Abkhazia, with a high degree of intercommunal violence. Because of the influx of Georgians since the 1920s, the Abkhaz were a minority in their own homeland. Numbering just 93,000, they constituted just 1.8 percent of Georgia's population in 1989, and 17 percent of population of Abkhazia, with the remainder consisting of ethnic Georgians, accounting for 45 percent, and Armenians and Russians, accounting for a further 30 percent.

Georgian-Abkhaz interethnic relations deteriorated after 1988, as did relations between the central government in Tbilisi, the Georgian capital, and Sukhumi, the capital of Abkhazia. Cultural and language rights became the first focus of dissension, with a power-sharing dispute to follow. The main fighting took place in 1992–1993. Following civil strife in Georgia proper and

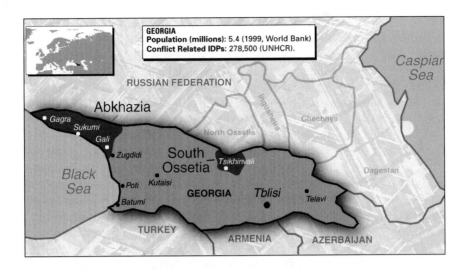

GEORGIA
Population (millions): 5.4 (1999, World Bank)
Conflict Related IDPs: 278,500 (UNHCR).

the overthrow of the nationalist president Zviad Gamsakhurdia, power was assumed by an unstable coalition of paramilitary leaders, most notably Tengiz
Kitovani and Jaba Ioseliani. They invited Eduard Shevardnadze, the former
first secretary of the Georgian Communist Party and later the Soviet foreign
minister, to head the state in the hope of securing international recognition and
domestic legitimacy. In August 1992, the Georgian State Council ordered
Georgian troops, comprised primarily of paramilitaries led by Kitovani, to
enter Abkhazia to ensure railroad safety and rescue officials allegedly kidnapped by Zviadists. Their entry was accompanied by wanton violence and
human-rights abuses against Abkhaz and other non-Georgian civilians. Although Shevardnadze denied sanctioning the march on Sukhumi that led to
full-scale war, he subsequently endorsed it.

In response to the Georgian attack, the Abkhaz, joined by most non-
Georgians, mobilized support from ethnically related peoples of the North
Caucasus, with Chechen fighters playing an important part in boosting military morale. The Abkhaz also benefited from Russian military support channeled through the Russian bases in Abkhazia. Initially the Abkhaz lost most of
the territory to the Georgian troops, but in March 1993 managed to fight back
and in June they launched a counteroffensive during which atrocities were perpetrated by Abkhaz troops. Their advance culminated in a decisive victory in
September. The Georgian population fled from most of Abkhazia. In November 1999, the Abkhaz leadership proclaimed formal independence.

The conflict in Abkhazia is rooted both in the legacy of the Soviet nationalities policy and in the rise of ethnic nationalism during the demise of the
USSR. The Soviet administrative arrangements were a source of grievance for
both sides. Soviet policy granted political status to major nationalities within
the Soviet state and ranked them in a hierarchical federal system. In the Soviet
ethno-federal construction, the union republics had the highest status, followed

by the autonomous republics in the second rank. Abkhazia was created as a separate union republic in 1921, but was joined with Georgia in a confederate union treaty later the same year. Abkhazia's status was downgraded in 1931 as a result of its incorporation into the Georgian union republic as an autonomous republic. The Soviet legacy continues to dominate mind-sets. The Abkhaz saw Stalin's Georgian nationality reflected in the post–World War II migration of large numbers of Georgians into Abkhazia. Meanwhile, despite the small Abkhaz population, Georgians were wary of preferential treatment accorded to the Abkhaz.

The political culture of the region is characterized by an exclusive ethnic nationalism and profound skepticism of autonomy structures. Since the late 1980s, actors on both sides have exploited to their political advantage opportunities presented by *perestroika*, greater freedom, and unprecedented geopolitical change. While Georgians were concerned with Russian domination and sought to break away from Russia's rule, the Abkhaz were driven by the fear of assimilation into the Georgian nation and the future viability of their community. Both sides attempted to elevate their political status: the Georgians by seeking outright independence from the Soviet Union, and the Abkhaz by demanding union republic status and status within the USSR equal to the Georgians. Cultural claims and interpretations of history brought intellectuals to the forefront of political battles, including the Abkhaz leader Vladislav Ardzinba, a historian, and Georgian ex-president Gamsakhurdia, a Soviet dissident. The proliferation of Georgian militias led to a collapse of political authority over coercive forces. The Abkhaz retaliated by forming their own militias and forging links with the Confederation of Caucasian Peoples, which mobilized volunteers for the Abkhaz cause.

Russia played a controversial role in the conflict, with various parts of the Russian establishment supporting different sides. Parts of the Russian military and security structures and parliamentarians rendered assistance to the Abkhaz, but the Russian military also helped Shevardnadze to defeat his opponents in Georgia, evacuating him from the battlefield in Abkhazia. During the conflict, the Russian foreign ministry and the military high command acted as mediators between the parties, while individual military regiments pursued their own political and business agendas on the ground.

Conflict Dynamics

Since 1993, the internal political situation in Georgia has greatly improved. President Shevardnadze has managed to rid himself of unruly allies and consolidated his regime. As a result, the Georgian leadership is able to pursue a more coherent policy toward conflict on its territory. Still, Georgia painfully feels the loss of Abkhazia, and the leadership has attempted to bring it back under Georgian sovereignty in one form or another. To achieve this, Georgia has used three political tools: (1) imposition of economic restrictions on Abkhazia within a CIS framework enforced by Russia, (2) involvement of the Western powers to provide a counterbalance to Russian influence, and (3) tacit support for Georgian guerrillas groups such as the White Legion and the Forest Brothers, operating in the border zone. These policies have brought mixed results. Sanctions have only reinforced a siege mentality among the Abkhaz and radicalized their stance, and were mostly abandoned by Russia in 1999 when Georgian-Russian relations deteriorated and the second war in Chechnya began.

The internationalization of conflict-resolution efforts has paid off, bringing Georgia into the spotlight of the international community and enabling it to attract aid and investment. Guerrillas do put pressure on the Abkhaz, since they penetrate as far as Sukhumi and inflict casualties on the Abkhaz militias, but the Abkhaz militias respond with punitive raids, often indiscriminate, on Georgian returnees in the border area. Tensions escalated in May 1998 when fighting broke out in the border region of Gali, resulting in the expulsion by the Abkhaz troops of Georgian paramilitaries and some 40,000 Georgian returnees.

Little progress has been made at bilateral negotiations. Two major issues continue to stand out: the question of the future political status of Abkhazia and the return of Georgian internally displaced persons (IDPs). Prior to the outbreak of hostilities, the Abkhaz leadership sought to conclude a federal power-sharing agreement with Tbilisi, but since the war they've insisted on internal sovereignty within a loose confederation, or outright independence. Tbilisi wants Abkhazia to recognize that it is a subordinate part of the Georgian state while guaranteeing self-rule and noninterference in Abhazian internal affairs.

The Abkhaz maintain that unification in a single state does not provide any assurance that Georgia will maintain its obligations in the long run. They claim that if they disband their armed units, they will be unable to defend themselves if more nationalistic forces should gain power in Georgia. Furthermore, unification will be followed by a mass influx of Georgians, who might commit atrocities in revenge, and would gradually come to outnumber the Abkhaz, making them once again a minority in Abkhazia. Democratic processes will work in favor of the Georgians since they will have a numerical majority, and there will be no superior arbiter to ensure the Abkhaz rights. This has led the Abkhaz leaders to assert that they must never again allow themselves to become a minority—with a clear implication that they will not accept a return to their prior subordinate position.

The Abkhaz suspect that returnees will be a fifth column preparing the way for Georgian reconquest and have kept the rate of return to a trickle (UNHCR-assisted return has amounted to 311) by vetting returnees, but have not interfered with unofficial spontaneous return to the Gali region. A unilateral Abkhaz initiative to permit return to Gali was announced in 1999, but Georgia was prevented from providing security. Those who return do so at their own risk and find themselves at the mercy of Abkhaz militias operating in the border area and Georgian paramilitaries chasing them out. Since Gali is Abkhazia's prime agricultural region, gangs from both sides practice racketeering and deprive farmers of much of their income in return for dubious protection. The

Leo Erken/Panos Pictures

Sukhumi, Georgia/Abkhazia: Karina Dirapetyan is Russian. Her husband was Armenian. He died while fighting on the Georgian side. His brother, married to an Abkhazian woman, was fighting on the Abkhazian side. The family, including Ukrainian members, lives together in two little flats in Sukhumi (1994).

security situation in the Kodori Valley and the Gali district remains precarious. In December 2000, two UN military observers were kidnapped and held hostage in the Kodori Valley, and in January 2001 a remote-controlled mine explosion was directed at the CIS peacekeeping force (PKF). In April 2001 a wave of killings and hostage taking on both sides brought the parties to the brink of renewed hostilities.

Many IDPs are concentrated in Tbilisi and its suburbs or in Western Georgia close to the Abkhaz border. They form an outspoken lobby, with their own parliament, government-in-exile, and links to the paramilitaries operating in Abkhazia. The Georgian leadership sponsors the government-in-exile for two political ends: to put pressure on the Abkhaz side and to perpetuate the polarization of refugees so as to maintain the issue of the right of return. Some observers perceive that the Georgian government intentionally keeps IDPs in limbo, although after seven years of exile a policy to assist them in adapting to their new circumstances would probably be preferable.

Since late 1999, the World Bank and the UN Development Program (UNDP) started to pursue a new approach to the IDP situation to help them adjust to their new circumstances, without excluding the possibility of return. UNHCR has adopted a modified approach by targeting assistance to improve the situation of IDPs in their current places of residence, and to improve relations between the IDPs and the local population by increasing the transfer of resources to the regions under strain.

War and the collapse of the Soviet economic system have inflicted painful consequences on both sides, but Georgia has been able to attract international aid and investment, and has started to overcome the economic chaos that developed in the early 1990s. In Georgian-Abkhaz relations, mutual economic interests sometimes prevail over political confrontation; for instance, cooperation over the Inguri dam and hydroelectric power plants, vital for both sides, has progressed smoothly. Citing this example, the Abkhaz claim that there is no need to agree on status and restore relations to ensure progress in the economic field.

The predominant discourse on the Abkhaz side is that there is no desire to enter a common state with Georgia. The common perception is that if incorporated into Georgia, the Abkhaz have a lot to lose, such as security and dominant political position. Since the end of the war, the political regime in Abkhazia has undergone consolidation. President Ardzinba has managed to concentrate power within formal institutions and ensure functioning political process, although restrictions on internal democracy and free media are increasingly felt. Ethnic Abkhaz are dominant in both the political and commercial arenas. The economic viability of the breakaway regime has also improved. Rich agricultural land and ad hoc trade links with Russia and Turkey have ensured survival, and vacationers have started to return to the Black Sea resorts. Following Russia's introduction of the visa regime with Georgia in December 2000, which exempts Abkhazia and South Ossetia, incorporation of these territories into Russia's economic and social space has proceeded further.

Trade and economic restrictions contributed to the development of a criminal and national-resistance economy, and to the proliferation of smuggling and black-market activities. Attracting foreign investment is difficult, but international aid has helped to improve the situation for a reduced population.

Some observers express the view that the solution to the problems in Abkhazia is not related exclusively to reaching a settlement on the political status with the Georgian government, but also to finding new ways of ensuring sovereignty for all people living on the territory of Abkhazia and redefining relations between different ethnic communities irrespective of political status.

The two Russian wars in Chechnya have had an impact on developments in Georgia. During the first war, the Russian military needed to ensure President Shevardnadze's support against the Chechen fighters and especially his consent to use Georgian territory for air strikes on Chechnya. In return for this, the Russian military were prepared to close the Russian-Abkhaz border and to impose restrictions on the movement of Abkhaz males. However, in the interwar period Georgian-Chechen relations improved greatly while relations with Russia deteriorated. The beginning of the second war was marked by the opening of Russia's border with Abkhazia in retaliation for the lax border controls over the Chechen sector. Meanwhile, the security situation in the Kodori Valley and in Gali deteriorated throughout 2001 as kidnappings and killings of locals became frequent occurrences and Russian peacekeepers and UNOMIG personnel were targeted by Georgian paramilitaries. Tensions culminated in the October 2001 attacks in the Abkhaz territory by Georgian and Chechen fighters, the latter having been moved by the Georgian Interior Ministry from Pankassi Valley, where they concentrated escaping war in Chechnya. An UN-OMIG helicopter was shot down and nine people died as a result. The Abkhaz mobilized and fought back, forcing the attackers to flee, while Georgia accused Russia of assisting the Abkhaz side in carrying out retaliation air strikes on the Georgian territory. The outcome was a political crisis in Tblisi, when the president dismissed his entire government and the parliamentary speaker amidst protests, and the Abkhaz requested membership in the Russian Federation.

Official Conflict Management

Shevardnadze's reputation attracted much international attention to the conflicts in Georgia, since they were interpreted as a testing ground of Russian neo-imperialism. However, intergovernmental organizations only became actively involved in Georgia in the postconflict phase by facilitating negotiations, monitoring the cease-fire, and providing delivery of various aid programs and serving to counterbalance the Russian influence.

The United Nations assumed the prime responsibility for resolution of the conflict in Abkhazia and since 1992 has worked in an uneasy partnership with Russian official mediators. In December 1993, talks between the Georgians and the Abkhaz under Russian and UN auspices resulted in the signing of a memorandum of understanding. The Georgian government had requested a multinational UN peacekeeping force. This was not endorsed by the UN, given peacekeeping problems in the former Yugoslavia, and a Russian force under the CIS mandate was agreed upon. In May 1994, agreements were reached on a cease-fire (Moscow Treaty) and on deployment of a CIS PKF to be monitored by a UN observer mission (UNOMIG). This force has remained in place ever since, with some 1,500 (Russian) peacekeepers (the PKF) and 137 UNOMIG officers (figures as of July 2000) patrolling a twenty-four-kilometer-wide security zone. The UNOMIG mandate is based on the right of return for all IDPs and preservation of territorial integrity of Georgia within the 1991 borders. UNOMIG has restricted its operations because of poor security in the conflict zone. Consequently, its impact is limited compared to the resources committed to the operation. UNOMIG presence was designed to ensure the impartiality of the Russian peacekeepers, but in reality does little to dispel Georgian allegations about PKF partiality.

Throughout the mid-1990s, the Abkhaz leadership was subjected to pressure to make concessions, first by the Russian government joined by the UN, and later by Western governments. Russia closed its land border with Abkhazia in late 1994 and imposed a naval blockade in response to the imposition of sanctions by the CIS in 1996. Moscow played a significant negotiating role and its bouts of shuttle diplomacy have borne fruit in a series of high-level meetings between Georgian and Abkhaz officials. This culminated in a major step forward in August 1997 when Shevardnadze and Ardzinba met in Tbilisi and signed an agreement renouncing the use of force.

Still, the role of Russia has given grounds for discontent on both sides. The Georgians accuse the PKF of failing to fulfill its mandate and secure the return of the displaced, lax imposition of border controls, and Russia of reluctance to complete its withdrawal, scheduled for 2001, from its military base in Gudauta (Abkhazia). Tbilisi has several times threatened to refuse to extend the PKF mandate, complaining that both Abkhaz territorial gains and the displacement of ethnic Georgians are perpetuated by the presence of the PKF. Well-equipped Georgian paramilitaries have targeted Russian peacekeepers in the Gali region, killing about sixty. The Abkhaz also have reason for discontent. They believe that the PKF is not doing enough to protect them from Georgian guerrillas and assert that contingents of North Caucasian volunteers would be more effective. Russia's support for Georgian territorial integrity and the sanctions it continues to impose on Abkhazia provoke resentment, but since Russia is the only Abkhaz ally, criticism is restrained.

In 1993, the UN Secretary-General designated Swiss diplomat Eduard Brunner as special representative of the Secretary-General (SRSG) to mediate between the parties. Brunner's approach was to tackle the issue of political status first and encourage the parties to sign a peace settlement. In 1997 Yevgeny Primakov, the then Russian foreign minister, played a crucial role in arranging the high-level meeting between the Georgian and Abkhaz officials, and an agreement mediated by both Moscow and the UN appeared to be close, but negotiations broke down at the last minute.

Liviu Bota, a Romanian diplomat who succeeded Brunner in 1997, tried an indirect approach leaving the issue of status aside and concentrating on more practical issues. He initiated the Geneva process, a series of meetings to negotiate political issues involving the parties and various international mediators. An action program was adopted by the end of 1997. Three working groups were set up for the prevention of a resumption of hostilities, the return of the displaced persons, and economic rehabilitation. A coordinating council was established and undertook many useful initiatives. Further meetings took place in Athens and Istanbul, supported by high-level delegations of Georgians and Abkhaz to each other's capitals, with the hope of creating a process in which the relationship could be rebuilt and progress in particular areas achieved, so as to facilitate subsequent progress on political status. Economic assistance was designed to provide an additional incentive for peace. The UNDP sent a needs-assessment mission to Abkhazia in February 1998, and a number of donors, including the United States and the EU, committed funds to reconstruction and assistance programs conditioned on progress toward a political settlement. This initiative failed after the May 1998 events in Gali when external agencies realized that parties were not prepared to move beyond their entrenched positions.

Bota facilitated internationalization of the conflict-resolution efforts, making it less of a Russian-led process. He also promoted the role of the Friends of the Secretary-General on Georgia, a self-appointed group consisting of the United States, the United Kingdom, France, Germany, and Russia, since such a mechanism had achieved successes in other conflicts. The Friends of the

Secretary-General were recognized as official observers to the Geneva process in November 1997, but were greeted from the start with distrust by the Abkhaz because of their fundamental position on the territorial integrity of Georgia.

Neither of these approaches has so far had much success in achieving a negotiated settlement, but this can hardly be blamed on the UN, given the wide differences over the issue of status between conflicting parties and the lack of any real military threat. Rather, UN activities have helped to prevent more serious confrontations from erupting, forced the parties to reflect on the consequences of their actions in light of the international situation, and contributed positively to the management of the conflict and cease-fire.

The chairmanship of SRSG Dieter Boden reinvigorated the coordination-council process and provided impetus for the resumption of the work of Working Groups I and III. Nevertheless, a solution to Abkhazia's political status remains elusive. Still, there is some reason for hope following the March 2001 Yalta political dialogue. The sides issued a joint statement and signed a Program of Action for Confidence-Building between the Georgian and Abkhaz parties. The Annex to the program specifies concrete steps to be undertaken within the program's framework.

The Yalta meeting was notable in yet another respect: each official delegation included three representatives of the NGO community, which has had the effect of elevating the status of NGOs in the two regions. Still, the Yalta meeting had only limited impact, since ultimately neither side excludes the possibility of a resumption of military action.

The UN Human Rights Office in Abkhazia (HROAG) monitors and reports on human rights as part of the UNOMIG. The HROAG trains educators, the media, NGOs, the judiciary, and law-enforcement bodies. The International Committee of the Red Cross (Red Cross/Red Crescent) also plays an active role in the protection of the civilian population, with a special emphasis on vulnerable groups, by informing the authorities regarding cases of discrimination. UNHCR conducts limited protection monitoring in areas of return.

OSCE's function has been to support UN efforts, but the organization came to be viewed negatively by the Abkhaz following the Budapest 1994 and the Lisbon 1996 Summit decisions when the OSCE mentioned "ethnic cleansing" by the Abkhaz without expressing concern over Georgian intervention in Abkhazia. The establishment of the UN/OSCE Human Rights Office in Sukhumi in 1996 was initially viewed in such a light. The situation changed after the December 1998 Oslo Ministerial Council meeting when the OSCE increasingly engaged with officials, NGOs, and the media on the Abkhaz side. At present, it provides small grants to Abkhaz NGOs.

Although not directly engaged in conflict resolution, the European Union has been active in the region through its Technical Assistance to the CIS (TACIS) program, renamed EuropeAid. It has provided funds for the reconstruction of the Inguri dam and support for development of civil society, including dialogue between Georgian and Abkhaz NGOs.

Any potential role for NATO in the Caucasus is a highly charged political issue, especially in view of NATO actions in Kosovo. Georgians hope that closer links with NATO, which their leadership promotes, will lead the alliance to enforce a peace deal in Abkhazia as desired by Georgia, despite the fact that NATO has given no indication of its readiness to do so. The Abkhaz are apprehensive of such involvement, but hope that Georgia's close relations with NATO will provoke Russia to be more supportive of Abkhazia. This in effect has happened since Russia's second war in Chechnya.

The Council of Europe accepted Georgian membership in 1999. Since then it has created the Venice Commission for discussions on the status of Abkhazia. The first meeting took place in February 2001 in Pitsunda, Abkhazia, and a second one should take place in Tbilisi.

Initiatives have also been taken by the Georgians and the Abkhaz themselves, such as the Bilateral Coordination Commission headed by Executive Director Zurab Lakerbaia, who is half Georgian and half Abkhaz.

In November 2000 a joint assessment mission visited the region, led by the UN, with the participation of OSCE, including the Office for Democratic Institutions and Human Rights, and the Office of the High Commissioner on National Minorities, the Council of Europe, and the European Commission. The ICRC and UNHCR sent observers. The purpose of the mission was to evaluate conditions for the return of refugees and IDPs.

Multi-Track Diplomacy[1]

In the early 1990s, development of civil society in Georgia including the conflict regions was influenced by ethnic politics and efforts to cope with the consequences of violence. As a result, a culture of tolerance was slow to develop. The Soviet legacy of state domination was significant, since there was scant understanding about the role of the third sector and its relationship to the state. A tradition of independent agents of society was largely absent, while the state regarded NGOs with suspicion and NGOs themselves easily became politicized. This was especially true with NGOs voicing opposition views on politically contentious issues, such as political status and the return of IDPs.

Since independence, sentiments have changed substantially. Prior to the outbreak of armed conflicts, societies were receptive to mobilization projects aimed at realization of national goals, but when wars and massive suffering followed, the lesson most people took away was that individual survival was more important than the pursuit of political goals. The societies became more inward-looking as the standard of living declined and the sense of disillusionment impeded the development of civil society, although Western policymaking entities provided external impetus and financial support for the growth of local NGOs.

Since independence, Georgia has been a cause célèbre for international involvement in the former Soviet Union. Many international humanitarian organizations are present in Georgia and their activities range from organizing the return of displaced persons to supplying emergency aid and assistance to the most vulnerable groups among the displaced, and strengthening capacities of local NGOs. For the small territories of Abkhazia and South Ossetia, Western involvement in conflict-resolution activities has been huge compared to conflicts elsewhere in the CIS. Whether this occurred because the international community was hopeful that conflict resolution had more prospects in Georgia, or to Shevardnadze's leadership efforts to bring the issue into high profile, or because of the proximity to Europe and appeal of the place and its people, Abkhazia and South Ossetia emerged as a great opportunities for testing multi-track approaches.

On the positive side, this has meant that local NGOs have had a chance to consolidate their capacities and to acquire skills. Their efforts have been directed toward areas that the international community regarded favorably, and certain values that international community saw as positive have been cultivated. There is, however, a risk that an agenda will be imposed from outside, and that projects have been tailored to match the requirements of international donors. Moreover, involvement in the third sector has been a way for many intellectuals and academics to find new roles for themselves—and family members as well—in the area of conflict analysis and resolution after previous jobs ended along with the dissolution of the USSR. As a result, there is considerable skepticism on both sides about the other's intentions.

At the same time, where outright hostility between the parties to conflict precluded legitimate commercial links or social interaction, NGOs provided the only communication channels available. Still, constraints on their operations were also significant. Georgian interference with telephone lines out of Abkhazia in 1995–1998 made communication between NGOs on both sides difficult, and restrictions on movement for the Abkhaz and tensions in the border area prohibited direct contacts on the ground. Initially, logistical problems created suspicion between local NGOs, but the situation did improve when better interaction was possible and personal relationships were gradually rebuilt. NGOs in Abkhazia, as in other breakaway entities, faced another hurdle, in view of the general apprehension of international organizations, all of which adhere to the notion of the territorial integrity of Georgia. NGOs easily become susceptible to accusations that they've lost touch with their national agendas.

Bilateral Contacts Between NGOs

International NGOs (INGOs) played a significant role in opening up channels for dialogue between the conflicting parties, having facilitated a number of direct contacts between the opponents. In many cases, without the support of INGOs these initiatives could not have developed. International Alert (IA) has been involved in conflict-resolution activities in Abkhazia since 1992, and in February 1996 facilitated an informal meeting between Georgian and Abkhaz NGO representatives at the conference in Moscow that started the development of the long-term program of confidence-building measures in the Georgian-Abkhaz conflict. The initiative is funded by EU TACIS and laid the foundation for the emergence of the Caucasus NGO Forum (see below).

From 1 to 5 June 1996, International Alert facilitated the first meeting between Georgian and Abkhaz NGO and policymaking communities. The International Center on Conflict and Negotiations (ICCN), the best-developed Georgian NGO working in the conflict-resolution field, was IA's partner on the Georgian side at the initial meeting and in the following Georgian-Abkhaz confidence building projects. The Abkhaz partners in this project were the Civic Initiative–Person of Future Foundation. Its founders were a part of the Abkhaz political establishment. Although they participated in the NGO activities in their individual rather than official capacities, they had better access to the key political actors and decisionmakers in Abkhazia. In 1997, IA facilitated a bilateral meeting between Georgians and Abkhaz NGOs in Yerevan on overcoming mutual stereotypes. It continues with its confidence-building program, focusing on three strategic priorities—women, young, people, and ex-combatants—and has brought Georgian and Abkhaz NGO representatives to an internship program in London.

United Nations Volunteers (part of the UNDP), has done extensive work among the IDP community and with Abkhaz NGOs. It played a prominent role in the establishment and development of contacts between the divided communities and in facilitating access to Abkhazia for other INGOs. Martin Schümmer, Paata Zakareishvili (who has done pioneering work in conflict resolution with Abkhazia partners), and Batal Kobakhia from the Centre of Humanitarian Programs (CHP) all made major contributions.

Paula Garb from the University of California at Irvine, whose early work in Abkhazia addressed environmental and development issues, later addressed the role of citizen diplomacy options for postconflict settlement, helping to initiate a series of bilateral meetings in Russia. The "academic" nature of this work was key, since the Abkhaz were reluctant to engage in bilateral dialogue with the Georgian side by the late 1990s. In subsequent meetings, discussions have moved from academic to policy issues.

In 1997 a dialogue process was initiated by the Berghof Research Center for Constructive Conflict Management, the Austrian Study Center for Peace and Conflict Resolution, and United Nations Volunteers (UNV) that involved civic activists, officials, and politicians. After a break of three years, this dialogue process was reinvigorated by Berghof and Conciliation Resources and in 2000 and 2001 five informal dialogue meetings have been organized for officials from Georgia and Abkhazia.

Russian organizations, namely the Institute of Ethnology and Anthropology (IEA), led by its director Valery Tishkov, Glasnost Foundation under the chairmanship of Sergei Grigoriants, and individuals such as Viktor Popkov from the NGO Omega, promoted dialogue interventions in the early 1990s. They were, however, inevitably perceived by the Georgian side as Russian-biased.

Other organizations involved in promoting dialogue were VERTIC (LINKS/Caucasus Links at present), which organized a Georgian-Abkhaz meeting on environmental issues in 1996, and the Institute of Conflict Analysis and Resolution of George Mason University, which made an effort to bring together Georgian and Abkhaz parliamentarians in the United States in 1997.

However, from fairly early on the Abkhaz demonstrated an increasing reluctance to take part in bilateral contacts with the Georgian side. Their argument was that these contacts would lead nowhere if the ultimate goal of such projects was the reintegration of Abkhazia back into Georgia. Subsequently, the Abkhaz preference for multilateral contacts gained momentum.

Multilateral Contacts and Training

There is no shortage of multilateral projects in the South Caucasus. At the same time, constraints exist on the ability of local actors to pursue multilateral undertakings without the involvement of international groups, since such activities normally have a political undertone, however subtle, or are perceived as such. For instance, South Ossetian and Circassian organizations maintain contacts with Abkhaz NGOs for activities such as citizen education and sport exchanges, but this is greatly facilitated by their common political agenda. By the same token, this political filter is often applied to the links between Georgian, Chechen, and Azerbaijani NGOs.

The HCA was one of the first organizations to establish a network of local NGO offices through its Transcaucasia Dialogue movement, begun in 1992. In Georgia HCA branches include a national office in Tbilisi and branch offices in Kutaisi and Telavi. The HCA branches have served as umbrellas for civic initiatives and new NGOs that lack legal status and organization. In 1996 the International Helsinki Citizen's Assembly (HCA) established a regional structure with a Dutch Interchurch Peace Council (IKV) liaison officer based in Tbilisi and Baku. The HCA South Caucasus Commission on refugees/IDPs was initiated by the IDP Women's Association from Tbilisi. The commission responded to the 1998 Gali crisis by fostering regional cooperation on social-psychological rehabilitation and protection of social, economic, and political rights.

In 1998, IA facilitated the confidence-builidng meeting at which the participants decided to establish the Caucasus NGO Forum, an international undertaking providing for pan-Caucasian interaction. In part, the creation of a multilateral platform was a response to the Abkhaz's reluctance to continue bilateral meetings with the Georgians. The forum is a network uniting about fifty local peacemaking organizations from the North and South Caucasus and provides an opportunity to take into account the broader Caucasian context, its interrelated conflicts, linkages, and alliances. For instance, it enabled a dialogue between Georgians on one hand, and Circassians and Chechens who supported the Abkhaz, on the other. The forum has focused on programs for women, youth, and ex-combatants, and organized a peacebuilding mission to Karachaevo-Cherkessia to calm down local passions and make local actors realize the bitter lessons of the Georgian-Abkhaz conflict.

LINKS and its partner Caucasus Links have pursued a multi-track approach in the Caucasus, working with prospective young leaders and professionals and extending links between different ethnic groups.

Participants from the Caucasus attended conferences and courses in conflict resolution in a wide variety of Western organizations. The Center for

International Development and Conflict Management at the University of Maryland has been involved in the Caucasus since 1994, and in 1995 brought together individuals from various hot spots in the South Caucasus for a four-month program of NGO training.

The ICCN implements "Peace Education and Conflict Management Training," which is to continue into 2004. ICCN is also involved in the South Caucasus Network for Civil Accord in partnership with eight NGOs from the region.

The Brussels-based Centre for European Policy Studies (CEPS) has launched an initiative for the Stability Pact for the Caucasus where conflict resolution in Georgia is a central tenet.

Reintegration of Displaced Populations and Conflict Prevention

In societies affected by large-scale displacement, the displaced persons represent a source of future conflict—a recruitment base for those who seek to achieve settlement by force. Many of the displaced are confused about the current situation and whether their best solution is to adapt to the new environment or to await their return home. At the same time, IDP groups play an active role in peace initiatives, since they consist of those people most affected by the conflict.

The IDP Women's Association pursues important work in and around Tbilisi, and also in the Zugdidi and Kutaisi regions of Western Georgia where many IDPs are concentrated. It has worked with CHP (Abkhazia) on a joint project to send children from both sides to the holiday camps. ICCN in Georgia has been undertaking a "Program of Training in Conflict Resolution Skills and Methods," sponsored by the Norwegian Refugee Council (NRC), which played a significant role working with the displaced in Georgia. ICCN runs seminars and conflict-resolution workshops in Tbilisi and ten other regions where concentrated settlements of IDPs are located. This work is important in mitigating tensions and improving the atmosphere in the community, but has not yet reached out to the radical and vocal IDP political structures.

Local NGOs also work closely with international organizations and INGOs in relief provision. They do valuable work in improving morale, such as sending children from displaced families to summer camps, working with especially vulnerable groups, and increasing awareness of existing opportunities for help and empowerment. For example, Assist Yourself in Georgia has recently compiled an information packet for IDPs providing information on the rights of IDPs, and on governmental structures and aid agencies offering information on employment and training opportunities.

Demobilization and Reintegration of Ex-Combatants

Separatist entities experience a very great need for the demobilization and reintegration of ex-combatants into civilian life or into the proper armed forces. Some are handicapped and psychologically traumatized, and the resources to help such vulnerable groups are extremely limited, while others never surrendered their weapons, do not hold proper jobs, and easily become engaged in crime and drug taking.

In Abkhazia, CHP renders medical and psychological assistance to ex-combatants and assists veterans' organizations. The CHP also has a rapid-response capacity to deal with veterans' problems. In 1999, the Caucasus Forum organized a meeting of ex-combatants in the Caucasus to build bridges between them and to promote their capacity to act as peacemakers. In May–June 2001, it facilitated an ex-combatants' conference entitled "Behavioral Norms in Caucasian Conflicts and Wars: Traditions and Current Practices."

Initiatives Among Particular Social Groups

The Centre for Human Rights and Support for Democracy in Abkhazia is engaged in developing women's capacities to act as peacemakers, and organizes women's bilateral and multilateral projects. It was involved in organizing a women's conference in Abkhazia in October 1999. CHP provided psychological rehabilitation for war-affected women in Abkhazia and undertook projects on sending women and children from both sides for treatment and rehabilitation.

In the Caucasus, contacts and trust are more easily established between young people than among the older generations, despite the fact that many young men have been involved in the fighting. Georgian NGOs such as Multinational Georgia have been taking steps to promote contacts among young people. This includes training seminars for young leaders and meetings of young journalists. The Academy for Educational Development (U.S.) brought children from both sides to summer camps in the United States and in the region, while the United Methodist Committee On Relief (UMCOR) set up youth houses for the young people in Tbilisi, Zugdidi, and Sukhumi.

The Foundation for the Development of Human Resources facilitated a bilateral Georgian-Abkhaz meeting of elderly people in Sochi. This is especially noteworthy since this was one of very few dialogue meetings organized without intervention by the external actors.

Mass Media and Information Exchange

Many INGOs have been active in the promotion and development of independent media. For example, Conciliation Resources (CR), in collaboration with UNV concentrated on capacity-building activities in Abkhazia, running training seminars for journalists and and NGOs. CR sought to pursue media and public awareness work across the conflict divide, having facilitated a visit of a Georgian journalist to Abkhazia and vice versa. A Georgian and an Abkhaz journalist who traveled together then made a joint radio program on the Georgian-Abkhaz conflict. CR also facilitated a series of TV discussion programs, undertaken by Studio Re, a Georgian NGO.

The Caucasus Media Support Project, funded by the Swiss Federal Department of Foreign Affairs, has been engaged in a project to promote regional dialogue among journalists in the South Caucasus, to facilitate more balanced reporting and make travel to the opponent's territory possible. Between 1997 and 2000, twelve conferences and training seminars were held, involving over two hundred participants from local print and broadcast media.

Between 1995 and 1998, the Institute of War and Peace Reporting (IWPR) published *WarReport,* a magazine that originally covered the conflicts in the Balkans and also later covered the Caucasus. It incorporated local voices into the debate, and drew on the local media networks. In 1999 IWPR launched an on-line service on the Caucasus.

Although the exchange of information has been established, it is not without problems. For instance, the Abkhaz side excluded *Nuzhnaia Gazeta* ("The Needed Newspaper"), the most popular Abkhaz daily, but also one critical of the authorities, from its official list of publications destined for the exchange with the Georgian side. The Abkhaz Information Ministry also limits distribution of the Georgian media to a tightly knit group of confidantes. Caucasus Home, a Georgian NGO, has played a valuable role here by supplementing the halfhearted efforts of officialdom. In summer 2001, ICCN started to produce *The Peace Times,* a new peacebuilding bimonthly magazine in Georgian.

Cross-Border Visits and Exchanges

South Ossetia has unrestricted interaction with Georgia, but Abkhazia remains officially off-limits to Georgians. UNV played a vital role in providing links between two divided communities and in facilitating visits by Georgian and Abkhaz representatives to each other's territory. Batal Kobakhia from Abkhazia and Paata Zakareishvili from Tbilisi were the first to achieve this breakthrough. Subsequently, five representatives of the Georgian NGOs visited Abkhazia to participate in the South Caucasian NGO Conference on Migration held in Pitsunda.

In autumn 1999 the head of Assist Yourself, a representative from the displaced community who is half Georgian and half Abkhaz, was invited by the Abkhaz women's organizations to take part in a conference in Pitsunda. She was able to convey the problems and feelings of the displaced Georgians to the Abkhaz side. In November 1999, LINKS facilitated a conference on "Self-Determination in Conditions of Interdependence" organized in partnership with the National Human Rights Committee of Abkhazia, which was attended by Georgian representatives. A number of other significant cross-border visits and exchanges have also taken place, usually organized with travel assistance by the UN. In 2000, the Caucasus NGO Forum organized a women's conference in Tblisi in partnership with the Caucasus House, in which representatives of Abkhaz NGOs took part.

Research and Public Debate

Research and analysis occupy a prominent place in the activities of many NGOs. Much of the published research is on issues of conflict, but in some cases, it tends to provide historical justification for claims and actions of different sides. The other, more practical field of research is that of polling and population surveys. In Abkhazia, for instance, a sociological research group of the Civic Initiative Foundation conducted several surveys focused on demography and migration.

In Georgia, the Caucasian Institute of Peace, Democracy and Development (CIPDD) plays a leading role in debate and research on politics, security, and monitoring of the interethnic situation. ICCN also helps promote intellectual debate on political issues and conflict resolution.

Initially, Western reporting and debate on the Georgian-Abkhaz conflict appeared to primarily reflect the Georgian perspective on the conflict due to the international isolation of Abkhazia. In the early 1990s, however, Abkhazia's profile was raised by the Unrepresented People's Organization, which sent a fact-finding mission to Abkhazia and served as an advocate for the Abkhaz position.

Since then the situation has changed considerably. In 1997, Bruno Coppieters of Vrije Universiteit of Brussels, together with colleagues from CIPDD, the Institute of Ethnology (Moscow), and the Centre for Human Rights and Support for Democracy (Abkhazia), organized two conferences in Brussels presenting the Georgian and Abkhaz perspectives on the conflict and addressing the issue of federalism and the principle of shared sovereignty. The aim of the project was to inject new ideas drawn from relevant European experience into the Georgian-Abkhaz search for a solution. Georgian and Abkhaz participants visited Switzerland and Belgium to be exposed to comparative federal experiences. A third project was started in the summer of 2000 on the foreign policies of federal states entitled "Federalization, Foreign Relations and the Georgian-Abkhaz Conflict." Here, the focus is on a model of foreign policymaking in a federal framework largely based on the Belgian ethno-federal experience.

In 1999 CR published *A Question of Sovereignty: The Georgia-Abkhazia Peace Process*, which includes contributions by Georgian, Abkhaz, and international authors. Another project, led by Paula Garb on the effectiveness of citizens' diplomacy, resulted in a publication with contributions from Georgian and Abkhaz participants.

Enhancement of Local Capacities for Peace
In the context of the Georgian-Abkhaz conflict, civil-society actors in Abkhazia are at a disadvantage compared to their Georgian counterparts. Some INGOs have attempted to assist Abkhaz NGOs to find an identity and a social role independent of their potential partners in Georgia. UNV has helped to start many local projects in Abkhazia aimed at postwar rehabilitation, the promotion of a culture of peace, and the emergence of independent media. Both IA and the Berghof Foundation have engaged in activities to advance conflict-resolution skills in Abkhazia.

Since early 1998, CR has concentrated on capacity-building work in Abkhazia by providing training on conflict management, strategic planning, and international relations to NGOs, academics, and official actors in Abkhazia.

Currently CHP in Abkhazia functions as a resource center for other NGOs and conducts training in conflict resolution, in partnership with international NGOs and independently. In 1999, CHP was responsible for running a small-grants competition in Abkhazia aimed at building the capacity of the local NGOs.

Early Warning

Many local and international groups are engaged in the early-warning activities. For instance, ICCN runs a project on early warning and dissemination of information regarding potential tensions in Georgia, such as the situation in Ajara. The Conflict Resolution in the Post-Soviet States Project, pursued jointly by the Institute of Ethnology and Anthropology (Moscow) and Conflict Management Group (Harvard University) established the Network for Ethnic Monitoring & Early Warning of Conflicts in early 1990s to provide early warning and foster discussion of possible action. The Project produces the *Bulletin,* published quarterly in Russian and English, including entries on Georgia. Since 1998, the Forum for Early Warning and Early Response (FEWER) has published online reports on early warning and conflict prevention in Georgia.

In June 1999 the EastWest Institute launched an initiative, together with FEWER, on "Early Responses to Early Conflict Warnings in the Caucasus."

Children's Needs and Psychosocial Rehabilitation

With support from the U.S. Agency for International Development (USAID), UMCOR established a youth house in Sukhumi to serve the needs of vulnerable children. Programming includes language, art, and music classes, a journalism program, and computer training, as well as psychosocial rehabilitation.

Enhancement of Citizen Security

Activities for enhancing the security of citizens are mainly taken up by international organizations together with the respective governments, INGOs such as the Halo Trust, and local actors, mainly CHP. These involve land-mine awareness, repair of schools and other public buildings damaged by war, and human-rights monitoring. The Halo Trust completed a comprehensive mine survey in March 2000 and continues the mine-clearing of priority sites, with plans to expand its operations in the near future. ICRC assists victims of mine accidents with health care services (including surgery) and a workshop to produce artificial limbs.

Concluding Remarks

INGOs working on the Georgian-Abkhaz conflict make positive contributions in a number of ways: by providing the breakaway Abkhaz regime with a voice to counterbalance the statist perspective advanced by the IGOs, thus limiting the effect of international isolation; by establishing the infrastructure and promoting the spirit of bilateral contacts, making direct dialogue between senior

Georgian and Abkhaz politicians possible; and by beginning the process of social rapprochement between the divided communities, enabling personal relationships to be gradually reestablished, and facilitating links between Tbilisi and Sukhumi intelligentsia.

Such contacts have been instructive in outlining the best practices of multinational states elsewhere and making parties to the conflict think through the alternatives to the current deadlock. All these efforts have contributed to a growing realization that in isolation, neither diplomatic nor civil-society efforts can resolve the conflict. Furthermore, civil-society contacts have built solidarity and respect between civil actors from the opposite sides: for example, the fact that a group of Georgian intelligentsia published a statement in the Georgian press calling for a peaceful resolution of conflict in Abkhazia produced a powerful resonance in Abkhaz society.

In Abkhazia the main achievement of the three years of bilateral interaction is the establishment of the channels of communication with Georgian representatives of civil society. Remarkably, these channels withstood the impact of the spring 1998 events in the Gali region. The positive outcome of the sustained dialogue has been that the relations between individuals have been restored. As one respondent put it, "each society now has a small number of people who do not suffer from stress when meeting people from the other side."

Nonetheless, civil-society initiatives toward peace involve a relatively small segment of the population that does not appear to be growing significantly. In the opinion of Ghia Anchabadze, those people who take part in the Georgian-Abkhaz dialogue should spread their new understanding of the existing realities to their wider community. Anchabadze identified this as the main future task for the Georgian NGOs—a task thus far unfulfilled, as they do not yet have sufficient influence in their communities.

As Batal Kobakhia said in June 2001, one result of the Georgian-Abkhaz dialogue in Abkhazia had been that the enemy image of the Georgian side became less intense and more diffuse. People in Abkhazia stopped getting angry at the actual fact of interaction with the Georgians, or of children being sent together to the holiday camps, and do not pay much attention to Georgian visitors to Abkhazia, even those from the IDP community. The NGO activities also give the Abkhaz authorities greater latitude for action within the Abkhaz community, bridging the gap between the political dialogue and social attitudes. Still, a gap exists between progress achieved on Georgian-Abkhaz NGO cooperation and the deterioration of the overall political environment, as a negotiated settlement now seems more remote than ever.

NGO representatives from the separatist states who cooperate easily with their counterparts from the opposite side have not abandoned their political positions, such as the commitment to independence, and sometimes name such contacts as "peace enforcement" for civil society. Nevertheless, despite criticism at home, the Abkhaz NGOs remain committed to contacts with their Georgian counterparts. Their argument is that since the conflict happened with the Georgians, relationships should be restored first and foremost with them.

The Abkhaz NGOs feel that civil-society initiatives provide greater flexibility in terms of issues and concerns that they can address, in contrast to the official negotiations where Georgia has the upper hand. At the same time, there is a reluctance on the Abkhaz side to face the problem of the displaced ethnic Georgians from Abkhazia, and INGOs have failed to persuade the Abkhaz to acknowledge this issue.

Beyond that, it is difficult to determine the impact of the civil-society initiatives. Second-track diplomacy is regarded as a slow process and it may be unrealistic to expect quick fixes to result from it. Expectations of what civil-society initiatives can achieve have to be moderated, since key decisions are being made at the level of political negotiations. Many observers believe that the time perspective applied to the first-track diplomacy is inapplicable for the second-track interventions, and that a longer-term view is more appropriate. Successes and failures in the Georgian-Abkhaz peace process should be regarded in this light. For instance, NGOs elaborating alternative peace solutions confront difficulties because NGOs have thus far failed to muster enthusiasm for their efforts from political leadership or to seriously engage the governments in their peace efforts. The predominant perception is that the political leadership on both sides doesn't trust their own NGOs/civil representatives.

Some local and international observers still feel that this process has been aggravated by the conflicting relations within the INGO community stemming from competition for fame and funds, and institutional and personal rivalries. Researcher Susan Allen Nan confirms that the apparent competition between international conflict-resolution specialists desiring to claim credit for conflict-resolution progress discourages locals attempting to work with internationals. Georgian and particularly Abkhaz participants in conflict-resolution efforts have lost patience with the seemingly endless stream of efforts in which they are asked to participate. Abkhaz sometimes participate in such workshops only to ensure that Georgian IDPs from Abkhazia will not attempt to represent Abkhazia there. However, Nan also finds that in some instances the multiple conflict-resolution efforts directed at the Georgian-Abkhaz conflict do indeed complement each other, building a stronger peace process together than the sum of their individual initiatives.

Prospects

The lack of political progress is a source of frustration on the Georgian side. The policy of the Abkhaz leadership is to maintain the status quo, since in any peace settlement their status will likely be reduced. Much attention has been directed toward Abkhaz leader President Ardzinba and his role as the major stumbling block to postconflict progress. However, there is a growing realization that personalities matter only so much: for instance, the appointment of Anri Jergenia as the new prime minister of Abkhazia in 2001 produced no impact on the Abkhaz stance toward Georgia. So far, the Georgian leadership has been unable to move the Abkhaz from their position by means of negotiations or by offering economic incentives, and a more confrontational approach has emerged throughout 2001. It is more difficult for representatives of Georgian civil society to argue for reconciliation, as it goes contrary to the developments on the ground and actions of the Georgian authorities.

Currently, both sides are affected by the change in the geopolitical situation following the attacks on the United States and ensuing Russian-U.S. rapprochement and deterioration of Russian-Georgian relations. It is becoming increasingly difficult for the Georgian leadership to exploit geopolitical rivalries between Russia and the United States to their advantage. First, Russia has been transformed into a Western ally. Moreover, Moscow's claim that Georgian negligence has enabled the growth of international terrorism has sounded more credible in the light of the October 2001 attack on Abkhazia and evidence of the presence of Arab instructors and training camps in Pankissi. Second, there is an increasing realization that substantial international, especially U.S., aid to Georgia has done little to enable internal transformation, but encouraged dependency and corruption instead.

In Georgia, the internal atmosphere has become increasingly radicalized, as the government crisis looms large and even Shevardnadze's own political future has been put into question by growing opposition to his corrupt and inefficient rule and uncertainty regarding the continuation of Western support.

The Georgian government's sponsorship of the attacks on Abkhazia and support for the Chechen fighters, the existence of which had been previously denied, made a discouraging impact on the international engagement in Georgia. Doubts have been raised about the commitment of external actors to the region for some time. The SEF Forum, for instance, noted that there is waning interest by external actors that is reflected in diminished involvement, a trend that is likely to continue. In this situation, overestimation of both the readiness of the external actors to take action and the available options open to them to exert influence may result in disillusionment and dashed expectations. The conference's opinion was that as a result of disappointments, both the United States and the EU would review their original motivation for action. They will continue to provide some resources for the peace process, but the longer the negotiating processes and blockades continue, the more their interest will decline.

One has to add that since most international attention is likely to be directed toward involvement in Afghanistan and Central Asia, the priority of the South Caucasus will be diminishing. Moreover, hopes for a visible progress, characteristic for the 1990s, gave way to pessimism and expectation of a Cyprus-style deadlock.

The SEF Forum, as did many other commentators, concluded that Russia's role is key. Meanwhile, Russian-Georgian relations have deteriorated steadily since Vladimir Putin came to power in Moscow. Georgia's inability or unwillingness to secure its border with Russia over the Chechen sector, its lack of control over the criminal situation in Pankissi Valley and subsequent spillover of instability, the introduction of the visa regime for the Georgian citizens and exemption of Abkhazia and South Ossetia from it, and Russia's efforts to preserve its military bases in the minority-populated areas of Georgia, have all contributed to escalation.

These tensions culminated in the aftermath of attacks on Abkhazia when the Georgian parliament voted for the termination of the PKF mandate and the withdrawal of the peacekeepers. Shevardnadze threatened to take his country out of the CIS. These threats caused little fear in Moscow: Putin personally announced that he would consider removing Russian peacekeepers and said that Georgia should approach the UN to handle the cease-fire issue. Moscow also indicated that it would not oppose Georgia's leaving the CIS and would pull out its troops from the Gudauta base by the end of 2001. Apparently, Russia's interest in Georgia, including its conflicts, diminishes, while security of its southern border remains of primary importance.

To sum up, a strategy for solving political conflicts could not be defined from outside the region. The local and regional actors bear the main responsibility for their conflict and for its resolution. Meanwhile, neither Georgia nor Abkhazia is ready for a serious compromise: Georgia will not accept a "peace of the winners," and Abkhazia is not prepared to relinquish the Georgian-populated Gali region, which may prove a security risk impossible to control.

Recommendations

Parties to conflict often take an attitude that their conflicts can be resolved for them by outside powers. Sometimes the behavior of Russia and the West in the Georgian-Abkhaz context sends messages that can be interpreted in such a light. An alternative view to this is that the conflicts have local roots and are better understood by the local people who share the same historical and cultural legacy. According to this view, it is up to the Georgians and the Abkhaz to find a solution.

If the trend toward confrontation on the ground continues, it will be counterproductive for INGOs to work against such a powerful current, as neither they nor their local partners have any leverage over the radical actors. Instead, it would be more helpful to concentrate on moderation of public attitudes and the development of effective governance than on conflict resolution as such, and to engage in only a limited number of projects so as to avoid confusion. It would be useful if INGOs work toward encouraging a sense of realism among the Georgian society and help it to come to terms with the postwar situation and its actual outcome. This may help both the elites and the population to accept the fact that the past is irretrievable and make steps to rescue what can be saved. Such a task, however, may be too radical and unpopular for INGOs to engage in.

What may be more feasible is to discourage competition among Western NGOs, to introduce a code of conduct, and to ensure coordination of their activities by an outside body. Since it is impractical for the INGOs to regulate themselves, it would be better for international donors or IGOs to assume such a role with the additional benefit of providing logistical support where necessary.

The SEF Forum identified some starting points for strengthening peace efforts. These include promotion of an intensive debate on the various concepts of federalism and the ways in which such notions may be enshrined in future constitutional arrangements between Georgia and Abkhazia; incorporation into the overall peace process of measures aimed at building new confidence and encouraging reconciliation; and a more active role for Russia in mediation. The forum also noted that success in the peace process is only possible with synergy between first-track and second-track initiatives, since these initiatives are interdependent.

The SEF Forum stressed that in order to achieve success, peace initiatives must win support from broader segments of the population and address their concerns. The key challenge to civil-society initiatives is to include a broader spectrum of actors in their activities, and to provide stimulus at the political level. In this respect, there is a great need for more professionalism within the NGO sector. Local NGOs can increase their effectiveness by becoming more transparent about the ways they operate and the projects they pursue, by making more use of the media in raising awareness and by redoubling their efforts to disseminate balanced information. The following recommendations concerning outside support were made:

- Involvement of external groups can improve the reputation and degree of acceptance of the work of the local NGOs, especially if the latter are faced with hostility and defamation on account of their work for reconciliation.
- Appropriate "division of labor" between international organizations and INGOs should be ensured: while IGOs can play a special role in maintaining pressure on the governments to involve forces working for peace and take up mediation functions, INGOs can open up additional channels and provide more space for arguments to be made by playing a facilitative role and serving bridge functions between the parties to conflict.
- When selecting local partners, the donor community should try to ensure that local groups have been in existence for some time, have developed participatory structures and have been involved in practical activities.
- INGOs should abstain as much as possible from introducing their own political agendas into peace work.

One of the key tasks of peace work is to empower the particularly vulnerable sections of population and to build up their capacities. For such purposes, integrated schemes are needed that include both the IDP population and the local population in order to break through the isolation of the IDPs. Short-term measures aimed at improvement of the housing situation and the creation of jobs must be expedited. These measures need not conflict with the longer-term goal of IDP return.

Many participants at the SEF Forum recommended the development of a comprehensive approach to the whole Caucasus region and creation of a Stability Pact for the Caucasus along the lines of the Pact for Southeastern Europe.

In fact, such a pact has been advocated by the CEPS, which set up the CEPS Task Force in January 2000. The pact has developed a conceptual paper entitled "Stability Pact for the Caucasus in Theory and Practice." Following the publication of a first document in May 2000 proposing a comprehensive stability pact for the Caucasus, members of the CEPS Task Force traveled to the three states of the South Caucasus and to Nagorno Karabakh, Abkhazia, Ajara, and South Ossetia. In September 2000, CEPS organized a conference together with the Armenian Center for National and International Studies on "Prospects for Regional and Transregional Cooperation and the Resolution of Conflicts."

The proposed stability pact process includes systemic and constitutional aspects, with suggestions on how to overcome the transitional problems of weak states and reconcile conflicting principles such as independence and territorial integrity, or the choice between federation and confederation. Particular consideration is given to how a Caucasus stability pact could serve the interests of Russia as the region's key player, together with enhanced cooperation with the EU over the "Southern Dimension" concept.

A joint EastWest Institute and FEWER conference (Brussels, January 2000) on early warning and early action in the Caucasus concluded that in conflict prevention, warnings should be issued about the possible side effects of intervention since too much international involvement can raise unreasonable hopes and send the wrong signals to local actors. Overly enthusiastic conflict-prevention measures can do more harm than good, bearing in mind that the Georgian state has managed to sustain a fragile peace in Ajara and Javakheti. This might precipitate conflict in either region or elsewhere in Georgia when it is subject to a sudden increase in attention. There is a general mind-set, especially in Abkhazia, that there is no reward for peace. Violence may be perceived as a means for receiving both more international attention and the necessary resources for reconstruction and reform.

* * *

South Ossetia: Waiting for a Final Settlement

Georgia is a multiethnic country and other areas of actual or potential tension exist within its territory. While each of them has its unique background, political actors in the conflict areas look at each other and especially at the developments in Abkhazia, the most significant conflict, to see what kind of settlement will be achieved there in the end, and level their demands accordingly. This is particularly relevant for the conflict in South Ossetia.

Conflict in South Ossetia unfolded along similar lines as in Abkhazia, with mutually exclusive claims to the territory and the Ossetian fear of assimilation into the Georgian nation at its heart. South Ossetia is much smaller than Abkhazia, with a population of about 60,000. In Soviet times, South Ossetia was established as an autonomous region (*oblast*) within Georgia. While Ossetians were ruled from Tbilisi and separated from the rest of the Ossetian people, the main bulk of whom live in the Russian Federation, the Georgians considered that South Ossetians were in a privileged position vis-à-vis other regions of Georgia. In the period of *perestroika* (1989–1991) Georgians started to assert the primacy of Tbilisi's authority and Georgian language and culture.

The actual conflict is largely associated with a resurgence of Georgian nationalism under President Gamsakhurdia. In August 1990, South Ossetia issued a declaration of sovereignty and demanded recognition from Moscow as an independent subject of the USSR. Tbilisi retaliated by abolishing South Ossetia as a distinct administrative entity in December 1990. Fighting erupted at the end of 1990 between Ossetian and Georgian militias and the national guard, and resulted in expulsion of the Georgians from Tskhinvali, the region's capital, who then besieged and bombarded the city from surrounding hills.

The fighting continued after Gamsakhurdia's fall from power and the Ossetians, supported by North Caucasians, gained the upper hand in 1992. Population exchanges took place: Ossetians from other parts of Georgia moved to South or North Ossetia, and most ethnic Georgians left South Ossetia, although four Georgian-populated villages remain. A cease-fire was signed in June 1992 to be supervised by a combined Russian, Georgian, and Ossetian peacekeeping force under a Joint Control Commission (JCC) with North Ossetia represented, together with Russia and the parties to conflict. The JCC also serves as a forum for ongoing discussions between the parties.

In South Ossetia, unlike Abkhazia, the issue of repatriation is not so important, since both sides accepted de facto population exchanges and some Georgians managed to return. There is also less sense of ethnic resentment, and people are free to travel and engage in commerce. Gradually, links between North and South Ossetians have cooled off, and the South Ossetian leadership has learned to play a balancing act between its ethnic kin in Russia and the Georgians.

Such developments, however, have not brought any progress on the issue of political status. Ossetians maintain that they will settle for the same status as is eventually agreed upon with Abkhazia, while Georgians offer the wide-ranging autonomy. From a practical point of view, the conflict is almost resolved: both sides agree that the resumption of hostilities is unlikely and cooperation on economic matters is ensured. However, the Georgian government would like to gain control over the Ossetian military highway, the main commercial artery connecting Georgia with Russia, and to generate revenue from customs, but the Ossetians are reluctant to submit to this demand.

The OSCE took the lead in conflict management in South Ossetia. An OSCE mission was established in late 1992, and in March 1994 its mandate was extended to monitor peacekeeping operations. Relations between OSCE monitors and peacekeepers were good, and it was agreed in February 1997 that hostilities had subsided to a level that allowed a reduction in the peacekeeping and monitoring activities.

Negotiations were held under Russian auspices and supported by the OSCE mission with the JCC providing a forum for the discussion of practical matters. In May 1996, the parties signed a memorandum on refraining from the threat of force, solving the refugee problem, and gradual demilitarization. Various UN agencies, most notably UNHCR and UNDP, and the EU provided humanitarian and reconstruction aid, as well as investments in human-resource development and conflict-resolution meetings and training.

Harvard University's Conflict Management Group (CMG) has facilitated unofficial "one and a half track" meetings between officials and political leaders. Much fruitful work was done with the Georgians and Ossetians in low-key bilateral seminars with external experts and study visits. CMG has been working in Georgia since 1995 to facilitate informal brainstorming and joint problem solving among senior officials and negotiators from Georgia and South Ossetia. Four meetings have been held since April 1995, resulting in an easing of tensions and cooperative efforts on practical matters, such as IDP return, restoration of basic services, and economic development.

At the fourth brainstorming meeting a Joint Steering Committee, composed of Georgian and Ossetian participants in the CMG meetings, was established to create an informal forum parallel to the official negotiation process. This group continues to meet, and has also conducted a survey of public attitudes and media in Georgia and South and North Ossetia. The ICCN from the Georgian side was involved in conflict resolution in South Ossetia in cooperation with CMG and NRC. The latter has facilitated relief efforts in South Ossetia since 1996, and in 1997 the UNHCR and NRC started to work together on the reconstruction program for returnees. It was involved in conflict-resolution activities through the CMG/NRC Georgia-South Ossetia Dialogue Project, in which NRC provided important support to CMG. LINKS also played an active role in conflict-resolution activities in South Ossetia.

The prospects look brighter for South Ossetia than in Abkhazia because the conflict-resolution process has already yielded results on the ground with a sense of local ownership. Interethnic relations have greatly improved and normal human interaction has been largely restored. Economic incentives, lack of a large displaced community in Georgia, and conciliatory policies of the Georgian government under Shevardnadze have all contributed to the easing of tensions. Economic and social initiatives have taken root and cooperation can continue on a pragmatic basis bypassing the unresolved status problem. At the same time, the exemption of South Ossetia from the Russian visa regime has the effect of advancing South Osetia's integration into the Russian economic and social space.

* * *

Resources

Newsletters and Periodicals
Abkhazian Newsletter, International Documentation and Information Centre for Abkhazia/ the Netherlands

Caucasus Report, Radio Free Europe/Radio Liberty, Prague, Czech Republic
Contemporary Caucasus Newsletter, University of California, Berkeley
FEWER Reports, London
Monitor & Prism, daily news and analysis, Jamestown Foundation, Washington, DC
Moscow News, Russian weekly, also published in English with regular updates on the
  Caucasus
WarReport (1995–1998), Institute for War and Peace Reporting, London
Working Paper Series, Berkeley Program in Soviet and Post-Soviet Studies, University
  of California, Berkeley

Reports
Amnesty International, *Amnesty International 1999 Annual Report on Georgia,* London, 1998.
Conciliation Resources, "Question of Sovereignty: The Georgia-Abkhazia Peace Process," *Accord: International Review of Peace Initiatives,* issue 7, 1999.
Human Rights Watch/Helsinki
  HRW World Report 1999, Georgia, Human Rights Developments.
  Georgia/Abkhazia: Violations of the Laws of War and Russia's Role in the Conflict,
    Human Rights Watch Arms Project, vol. 7, no. 7, March 1995.
United Nations Development Program, *United Nations Needs Assessment Mission to Abkhazia, Georgia,* Working Group III, March 1998.
United Nations, Reports of the Secretary General concerning the situation in Abkhazia, Georgia. Latest: 19 January 2000.

Other Publications
A Question of Sovereignty: The Georgia-Abkhazia Peace Process, edited by J. Cohen. London: Conciliation Resources, 1999.
Contested Borders in the Caucasus, edited by Bruno Coppieters. Brussels, VUB Press, 1996.
Managing Conflict in the former Soviet Union: Russian and American Perspectives, edited by A. Arbatov, A. H. Charles, and L. Olson. Cambridge, MA, CSIA and MIT Press, 1997.
No Peace, No War in the Caucasus: Secessionist Conflict in Chechnya, Abkhazia and Nagorno-Karabakh, by Edward W. Walker. Cambridge, MA, Harvard University, 1998.
The New Caucasus: Armenia, Azerbaijan and Georgia, by Edmund Herzig. London, RIIA/Pinter, 1999.

Selected Internet Sites
www.ceps.be/Research/Caucasus (Centre for European Policy Studies, a full text of the Stability Pact for the Caucasus can be downloaded from it)
www.eurasianet.org (Central Eurasia Project of the Open Society Institute)
www.fewer.org (Forum on Early Warning and Early Response)
www.iwpr.net (Caucasus reporting service, Institute for War and Peace Reporting)
www.poli.vub.ac.be/publi (Caucasian Regional Studies, Vrije University of Brussels, in Russian and English)
www.rferl.org (Radio Free Europe/Radio Liberty Newsline)
www.socrates.berkeley.edu/~bsp (Berkeley Program in Soviet and Post-Soviet States)
www.soros.org/caucasus (Soros Foundation)

Resource Contacts
Jonathan Cohen, Conciliation Resources, e-mail: j.cohen@c-r.org
Bruno Coppieters, Vrije University of Brussels, e-mail: Bruno.Coppieters@vub.ac.be
Paula Garb, Global Peace and Conflict Studies, e-mail pgarb@uci.edu

Edmund Herzig, University of Manchester/RIIA, e-mail: edmund@bnn.dircon.co.uk
Julia Kharashvili, IDP Women's Association (Tbilisi), e-mail: julia.kharashvili@undp. org.ge
George Khutsishvili, ICCN, Tbilisi, e-mail: iccn@access.sanet.ge
Arthur Martirossian, Conflict Management Group, e-mail: martiros@cmgroup.org
Anna Matveeva, expert on the Caucasus, London, e-mail: sophiamat@ukonline.co.uk
Susan Allen Nan, e-mail: sallenn@emory.edu
Ghia Nodia, chair of the board, Caucasian Institute for Peace, Development and Democracy, Tbilisi, Georgia, e-mail: ghian@caucasus.net
Dennis Sammut, LINKS, London, e-mail: dennissammut@hotmail.com
Gevork Ter-Gabrielian, International Alert, London, e-mail: gtergabrielian@international-alert.org
Marten van Harten, independent consultant, e-mail: harten16@ zonnet.nl
Edward Walker, Berkeley Program in Soviet and Post Soviet Studies, University of California, Berkeley, e-mail: bsp@socrates.berkeley.edu
Paata Zakareishvili, e-mail: paatazak@access.sanet.ge

Organizations

In Georgia
Norwegian Refugee Council
19A Tabukashvili Street
380086 Tblisi
Tel.: +995 32 923 162/64
Fax: +995 32 982 564
E-mail: res.rep_georgia@access.sanet.ge
http://www.nrc.no

In Abkhazia
Foundation Civic Initiative, Man of People Foundation
9 Zvanba Street
Sukhum(i), Abkhazia, Georgia
Tel.: +995 88 122 2 41 37 / 88 122 27162
E-mail: dianapp@yahoo.com

International
Global Peace and Conflict Studies
University of California, Irvine
717, Social Science Tower
Irvine, CA 92697-5100, USA
Tel.: +1 949 824 1227
Fax: +1 949 824 1544
E-mail: pgarb@uci.edu

Data on the following organizations can be found in the Directory section:

In Georgia
Assist Yourself
Association of IDP Women
Caucasian Institute for Peace, Democracy and Development
Caucasus Links
International Center on Conflict and Negotiation
Partners-Georgia
South Ossetian Center on Humanitarian Initiatives and Research

Union Public Movement Multinational Georgia
United Nations Association of Georgia

In Abkhazia
Association of Women of Abkhazia
Center for Humanitarian Programmes

International
Austrian Study Center for Peace and Conflict Resolution
Berghof Research Center for Constructive Conflict Management
Center for European Policy Studies
Conciliation Resources
Conflict Management Group
East West Institute
Evangelische Akademie Loccum
FEWER
Helsinki Citizens Assembly
Interchurch Peace Council
Institute of Conflict Analysis and Resolution
Institute of Ethnology and Anthropology
Institute of War and Peace Reporting
International Alert
LINKS
United Nations Volunteers

Anna Matveeva is a program manager at Saferworld (on small arms and security). She previously worked as a research fellow at the Royal Institute of International Affairs (Chatham House, London) and program head at International Alert (London). As a scholar specializing in issues of conflict and the politics of post-Soviet Eurasia, she has authored publications such as The North Caucasus: Russia's Fragile Borderland *(London: RIIA, 1999) and academic articles, and undertook projects for organizations such as the International Peace Academy, EastWest Insititute, Minority Rights Group, and the Heinrich Böll Stiftung.*

Note

1. Some of the information in this section draws on research carried out for the joint EWI/FEWER Project on Mapping Local Capacities for Conflict Prevention in the Caucasus.

15.3

Nagorno Karabakh: A Straightforward Territorial Conflict

Anna Matveeva

The conflict in Nagorno Karabakh, an Armenian-dominated territory in Azerbaijan, is the oldest of the post-Soviet conflicts, dating back to 1988. Russia and the OSCE have been active as mediators. Multi-track efforts by international and local groups reached their peak in the mid-1990s, but were unable to break the stalemate. Hopes for a long-term resolution are based on a new round of international effort by the United States and Russia.

The conflict in Nagorno (or "Mountainous") Karabakh, a predominantly ethnic-Armenian area in the territory of Azerbaijan, involves the Armenian struggle for Karabakh and the ethnic violence that followed suit, and played a crucial role in the proliferation of conflicts elsewhere in the USSR and in its subsequent demise.

In the late 1980s, *perestroika*'s freedom allowed Karabakh-Armenian ethnic grievances to be expressed. These included the perceived Azerbaijani policy of denial of cultural rights to the Armenians, resettlement of ethnic Azeris into Karabakh that led to the shift in demographic balance (Armenians made up 94 percent of the population in 1921, reduced to 76 percent in 1979), and suspicion that the region was starved out of resources because of its Armenian composition. Irrespective of the fairness of these arguments, these were deeply felt Armenian concerns. The desire for the region to be transferred from Azerbaijani to Armenian jurisdiction was at the heart of the ethnic dispute.

Armenians in the Union Republic of Armenia wholeheartedly supported their ethnic kin in Karabakh, and issued an appeal to the Soviet leadership in Moscow and then Soviet leader Michael Gorbachev himself to submit to the Armenian demands. With the appeals for transfer firmly rejected, the Karabakh Committee of nationalist-minded intellectuals was formed, which included the first president of independent Armenia, Levon Ter-Petrosyan, and most of the future key political figures. The old Soviet elite jumped on the bandwagon of the struggle for Karabakh. In 1988 the Armenian Supreme

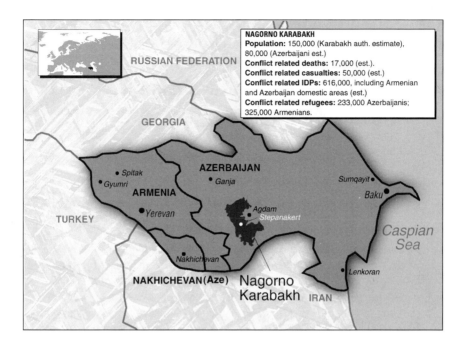

NAGORNO KARABAKH
Population: 150,000 (Karabakh auth. estimate), 80,000 (Azerbaijani est.)
Conflict related deaths: 17,000 (est.).
Conflict related casualties: 50,000 (est.)
Conflict related IDPs: 616,000, including Armenian and Azerbaijan domestic areas (est.)
Conflict related refugees: 233,000 Azerbaijanis; 325,000 Armenians.

Soviet, under intense public pressure, had to support the Karabakh Soviet's (local assembly) call for unification with Armenia. Karabakh proclaimed independence in 1991 rather than unification with Armenia in order not to undermine the latter's international standing, and remains a secessionist territory, unrecognized officially even by the Armenian government.

In February 1988, ethnically motivated killings occurred in Sumgait, Azerbaijan, when, unprecedentedly in Soviet history, Armenians were killed by mobs for the sole reason of belonging to an adverse ethnic group. Moscow's failure to react and exercise justice further escalated the conflict.

Further killings of Armenians took place in Baku in 1990. The late and inefficient deployment of ill-prepared Soviet troops only added fuel to the tensions. Some 200,000 Armenians (340,000 according to Armenian sources) fled Azerbaijan, mostly to Armenia, but also to Russia. The Armenian side learned the lesson that their security, as well as the future of Karabakh, was in their own hands. The formation of paramilitary groups began. The Karabakh self-defense army eventually developed into the best fighting force in the former Soviet Union. Fighting initially erupted in Karabakh. As a result, 47,000 Karabakh Azeris were forced to flee. Starting in November 1988, anti-Azeri demonstrations in Karabakh and Armenia led to escalation of interethnic tensions and, subsequently, the expulsion of 185,000 Azeris and 11,000 Muslim Kurds from Armenia in 1989.

Throughout the Soviet period, Moscow supported the Azerbaijani authorities against Armenian secessionists, and dispatched arms and Interior Ministry troops for pacification operations against Armenian villages in and around Karabakh. In 1989 an administration was set up to rule Karabakh directly from Moscow and mediate between the two sides. Still, de facto power belonged to the members of Karabakh Committee. In July 1992, the State Defense Committee was set up by the Karabakh Armenians to concentrate all political and military power in a single authority. The Azerbaijani side, supported by Soviet troops, enjoyed military success until spring 1992, when it controlled nearly half of Karabakh. Armenians gained an upper hand in 1992, taking the strategic Lachin corridor that connects Karabakh with Armenia, and the important points of Shusha and Khojaly.

In summer 1992, the Azeri side managed to fight back, retaking most of Karabakh. The Armenian counteroffensive of the winter of 1992–1993 led to more Armenian territorial gains—Agdam, Fizuli, Jebrail, Kelbaijar, Kubatly, and Zangelan. In winter 1993–1994, the Azeri side made the last push, which resulted in a disastrous defeat, after which the May 1994 cease-fire was signed. Between 500,000 and 600,000 Azeris fled their homes. In July, Armenia, Karabakh, and Azerbaijan committed themselves to a cease-fire that generally held despite minor exchanges of fire between sides.

Post-Soviet Russia, by contrast, supported the Armenian cause, partly because Russian democrats struggling against Soviet bureaucrats in Moscow forged links with the Armenian Nationalist Movement (ANM). Supplies of Russian weapons to the Armenian side, as revealed in spring 1997, amounted to about $1 billion, and included tanks and long-range missiles. They constituted a vital contribution to the Armenian victory.

The conflict is a straightforward territorial dispute. In the 1920s, Stalin sought rapprochement with Turkey and tended to support Azerbaijani claims laid on the Armenian-populated lands of Karabakh, as well as of Nakhichevan where the population was approximately half Muslim and half Armenian. These political ambitions collided with Armenian aspirations to bring together historical homelands where Armenians still constituted a majority. The genocide of 1915, when an estimated 1 million Armenians were killed by forces of the Ottoman Empire, made a tremendous impact on Armenian national identity and helped to form a revanchist agenda. The religious aspect—Christian Armenians fought Azeri Muslims—had limited significance since both parties fought for an explicit ethnoterritorial agenda.

The ANM, created in 1989, emerged as a powerful vehicle of national mobilization and state building in virtually monoethnic Armenia. In Soviet times, de facto transfer of power from communists to the nationalists had already occurred, manifested in its confrontation with Moscow in 1990–1991 when the ANM enjoyed huge domestic support. Levon Ter-Petrosyan was elected in October 1991 as the first president of Armenia following the declaration of independence. It played a crucial role in the transition to independence, maintenance of stable government, and the incorporation of paramilitaries into an organized armed force.

By contrast, Azerbaijan suffered from intense political turmoil in the early years of independence and from the worst fighting on the Karabakh front. Its first president, Ayaz Mutalibov, a reformed communist, was forced to resign

Armenian war-invalid. The village of Shusha used to be partly inhabited by Azeri, now only Armenians live there (1996).

following the massacre of Azeri civilians in Khojaly in February 1992. The Azerbaijani Popular Front (APF) came to power, and Abdulfaz Elchibey, its leader, was elected president in 1992. APF failed to take a firm grip on the political process, and created instead a chaotic government unable to deliver basic law and order. Losses on the Karabakh front, increased authoritarian tendencies, and Elchibey's policy of rapprochement with Turkey alienated him from much of the Azerbaijani population. In 1993, a successful coup against APF, led by a rogue colonel, Surat Husseinov, with covert support of the Russian military based in Azerbaijan, resulted in the defeat of the APF. However, the fruits of Husseinov's military coup were quickly monopolized by Heidar Aliev, a man with a long history of survival under different political regimes. Aliev is a former Soviet KGB general, chairman of the Azerbaijani KGB, then the communist leader of Azerbaijan and member of the Politburo. So he returned to his old job, but this time as the leader of an independent state. His authoritarian and highly personalized rule pulled the country from chaos to stability, but democracy was sacrificed on the way.

Conflict Dynamics

There is consensus in Armenia about the status of Nagorno Karabakh: it is a part of Armenia and sooner or later the outside world will have to come to terms with the existing situation. In practical terms, Armenia already has formed a common state with Karabakh. Military and political figures from Karabakh, including president Robert Kocharian, hold key positions in Armenia. The enclave is well connected to the republic via a highway built with

Armenian diaspora money, it uses Armenian currency, and Armenian youths usually serve half of their military conscription term in Karabakh. The struggle for the ethnic cause also strengthened the Armenian national identity. Armenia's military superiority and seizure of strategic positions around Karabakh mean that the risk of a new war is low. The Armenian diaspora financed a program of economic reconstruction in Karabakh, thus enabling the region to avoid the worst realities of postwar devastation.

Armenia, however, has to pay a price for its military gains. From 1989 on Azerbaijan has imposed a blockade of road, rail, and energy links with Armenia, supported by Turkey, which also closed its borders. The blockade caused severe economic problems for Armenia and led to an acute energy crisis in 1992–1993. Armenia retaliated with the closure of its border with Nakhichevan, an Azerbaijani enclave in Armenia separated from the mainland.

Currently, the mutual blockade is most damaging to Armenia since it lost a direct connection to Russia, its powerful strategic ally. However, it still enjoys links with Iran, where the Armenian diaspora is historically strong, and via Georgia with Russia. Continuous Armenian fears that Georgia might restrict Armenian transit seem hardly viable since ethnic Armenians populate the Georgian region of Javakheti, posing a constant threat of secession that the Georgian authorities are eager to prevent. Armenian transit also brings customs revenue and transit fees into the Georgian treasury.

Another Armenian fear was its exclusion from the development of Caspian Sea energy-generating resources, which were expected to exclusively benefit energy-rich Azerbaijan. By 2000 these fears had diminished, since the Azerbaijani resources proved to be exaggerated, and the interplay of business and politics resulted in delayed investment and poor economic performance. Azerbaijani oil revenues are also expected to be far from sufficient on the short term to arm and recruit a mercenary force capable of posing a threat to the Karabakh army.

Each Azerbaijani president started his career with attempts to make military progress in Karabakh, and by appealing for Turkish technical and training support, which was rendered in part. Heidar Aliev even invited Afghani *mujahedeen,* with disastrous consequences. Since then, diplomatic efforts have been focused on exerting international pressure on Armenia and using the prospect of rich Caspian oil revenues for political purposes. Following the Kosovo crisis, Aliev moved to exploit the growing rift between Russia and the West, and sought a rapprochement with NATO. These are, however, long-term policy undertakings unable to materialize in the short run, while Russia's second war in Chechnya and Aliev's old age put more pressure to find a quick solution.

Negotiations center on the following issues. First, Armenia insisted on accepting Karabakh as a party to the conflict, a demand eventually accepted by Azerbaijan. Second, there are arguments in favor of either phased or package settlements. In 1997, Baku authorities and President Ter-Petrosyan, under considerable international pressure, accepted the OSCE proposal for a phased settlement, but that was rejected by the Karabakh authorities and the majority of Armenians. Ter-Petrosyan, who already ruled in an increasingly authoritarian way, was accused of national betrayal. He was forced to resign in February 1998 under pressure from key political and security barons whose careers were built on the struggle for Karabakh.

Prime Minister Robert Kocharian, the former leader of Nagorno Karabakh, was elected president in March 1998 and improved the democratic credentials of the regime. His position on Karabakh, however, is less comforting for the international community. Although Kocharian reaffirmed the Armenian commitment to peaceful settlement and met with President Aliev, the essence of his position is that Armenia and Karabakh can develop economically without a settlement and Armenia will not have to suffer from international isolation more than it has already done in 1992–1993. So far, this position has proven viable, since the economic situation in Karabakh is better than in its neighboring Azerbaijani regions. Whether it is sustainable in the long run depends on how the government manages the domestic economy and whether it is successful in fighting corruption. It is also dependent on aid from the diaspora and the pace of the development of power-generating capacity in Azerbaijan.

Official Conflict Management
Since independence, Armenia has been subjected to significant international pressure to make concessions on the Karabakh issue. So far, these efforts have brought little, or even negative, results.

Between 1988 and 1994, the Karabakh conflict had been subject to mediation by a variety of international actors, including Russia, Turkey, Iran, Kazakhstan, and Western countries and international organizations. Finally, in May 1994 Russia succeeded in brokering a cease-fire that left Armenian forces in control of 15 percent of Azerbaijani territory. In July, Armenia, Azerbaijan, and Karabakh committed themselves to maintaining the cease-fire while seeking a negotiated settlement under Russian mediation. OSCE promised to deploy peacekeeping troops to supervise the situation, but disputes over whether required conditions on the separation of forces were met, as well as the composition of the international force, prevented this from happening. Russia volunteered to provide a peacekeeping contingent, but this proposal was rejected by Azerbaijan, which was suspicious of Russia's neutrality. The cease-fire generally held since without an external presence.

The OSCE Minsk Group was set up in January 1992 as the main international vehicle for resolution of the Karabakh conflict. Initially, the Minsk Group's work has been hampered by disagreements with Russia, which, being a member of the Minsk Group, still pursued unilateral initiatives. As a result, Russian and Western proposals kept undercutting each other and enabled parties to the conflict to play off international mediators against each other, until Russia acquired permanent cochairmanship of the group in December 1994. Under pressure from Azerbaijan, the Minsk Group cochairs at the OSCE Lisbon summit submitted a proposal in December 1996 for a framework of settlement of the Karabakh conflict based on the territorial integrity of Azerbaijan and providing for the "highest degree" of autonomy for the Karabakh Armenians within Azerbaijan. The Armenians vetoed the proposal and it was read as the "Chairman-in-Office" statement. The summit was a diplomatic victory for Azerbaijan, but in the Armenian view it has set back the peace process, disrupting the quiet diplomacy between presidential advisers from both sides. Armenians were convinced that Azerbaijan was using its oil weapon to force the United States to take Baku's side.

When energy-resource development and foreign direct investment in Azerbaijan started to materialize in 1996–1997, the profile of the Minsk Group changed. An oil lobby emerged in the West to act as a counterbalance to the Armenian diaspora and the Caspian Sea area acquired more international significance. The post of Caspian Coordinator was established in the U.S. Department of State. Because of changing context, new Russian foreign minister Yevgenii Primakov and the new U.S. secretary of state, Madeleine Albright, each made more effort to advance the resolution of the Karabakh conflict. New commitment to the region also resulted in improved cooperation within the Minsk Group when in 1997 the United States and France joined Russia as cochairs. The group submitted successive proposals for a phased settlement consisting of two elements. The first one provided for the withdrawal of the Armenian forces from the occupied territories, deployment of an international peacekeeping force, repatriation of the Azeri IDPs, and lifting the blockade. The second one provided for the preservation of Azerbaijan's territorial integrity and a de facto self-governing status of Karabakh. By autumn 1997, Baku and Levon Ter-Petrosyan had accepted the plan as the basis for negotiation, but it was rejected by both political elites and society at large in both Armenia and Karabakh. When Ter-Petrosyan publicly endorsed the plan and attempted to pressure the Armenian political establishment into concessions, this set in motion the train of events that forced his resignation in February 1998.

Robert Kocharian, who succeeded Ter-Petrosyan, has little incentive to be accused of betraying Karabakh by entering into concessions, if avoidable. Moreover, time, the weaker-than-expected economic performance of Azerbaijan, and reinforced Russian commitment to Armenia make the position of the Armenian leadership look more sustainable that it seemed in the mid-1990s. The main issues of contention are as follows:

• The status of Karabakh. Baku has stated that it is prepared to grant the highest degree of autonomy to Karabakh without elaborating what this means in practice. Karabakh and Armenia reject any vertical subordination to Baku and insist on real sovereignty.

• Armenian withdrawal from Azerbaijani territory outside Karabakh, which the Armenian side regards as a guarantee of Karabakh security and as a bargaining chip. In principle, the Armenia side accepts the eventual return of most of the occupied territories, but is in practice reluctant to relinquish them before the final settlement is signed.

• Security of Karabakh. The Armenian side insists on strong security guarantees in compensation for a withdrawal from the territories it currently holds. It demands the right to retain its own security forces, long-term presence of international peacekeepers, and the permanent maintenance of the Lachin corridor to enable unrestricted communication with Armenia. A complex lease arrangement for Lachin proposed by the Minsk Group has so far proved unconvincing.

• Return of refugees and IDPs, especially to Shusha. Baku insists that Azeri IDPs should be allowed to return to Shusha, a predominantly Azeri town at the time the conflict broke out. From the Armenian perspective, Shusha is an ancient Armenian homeland of great symbolic significance. Shusha is situated on a strategic height overlooking Stepanakert, the Karabakh capital, and served as a launching pad for the Azeri side for bombarding Stepanakert in 1992.

• Schedule for resolving the crisis. The Minsk Group has advocated a phased approach, claiming that it will be impossible to tackle difficult issues, such as status, before some confidence-building measures have been implemented. The Armenian side argued that this would provide a unilateral advantage to Azerbaijan since it will be the Armenian side that is required to give up territory at the first stage and endanger its security. Instead, it insists on a "package" solution that will incorporate all major issues in a single settlement.

The first two years of the Kocharian government have not brought any significant changes in the negotiation process. Throughout 1999 there were indications that Aliev and Kocharian had started to take steps forward on the political settlement, meeting at international forums for undisclosed discussions, but the October 1999 shootings in the Armenian parliament and the subsequent turmoil in the Armenian ruling establishment disrupted the initial progress. Internal struggles on both sides have intensified and shifted the focus of both the elites and the population at large from the Karabakh issue to the immediate political battles. The November 1999 OSCE Istanbul summit did not make any substantive statements on the Karabakh issue.

In early 2001, the Karabakh peace talks gained significant momentum, culminating in the Key West summit (3–7 April), at which the leaders of Azerbaijan and Armenia met for intensive negotiations under the auspices of the OSCE. As cochairs of the OSCE Minsk Group, the United States, Russia, and France were mediators at the talks. The Key West meeting was a result of the two presidents' direct dialogue during over fifteen bilateral meetings conducted in recent years, and managed to establish a relationship of trust. Joint investigations of cease-fire violations and confidence-building measures along the line of contact also helped them to get to know each other better. International pressure was very important: French president Jacques Chirac met with the two presidents under the auspices of the Minsk Group, which was followed by concerted efforts by the U.S. and Russian leaderships. This demonstrated a rare example of cooperation and goodwill between the major external players.

Time is also an important factor as the status quo is negative for both countries. President Aliev is aging and prefers to sign a peace settlement during his term of office rather than leave such a political burden to his successor, especially if his son is to replace him. Aliev understands that every leader who succeeds him would be less capable of making a significant compromise. For President Kocharian, the effects of isolation, a by-product of the conflict, are a powerful brake on economic progress, resulting in a slow pace of development and the depopulation of the country over which he presides.

The contours of a possible deal are unclear. *The Economist* (London) speculated that it was shaping up as follows: Azerbaijan receives back six of the seven occupied regions and an internationally protected road, linking it to the isolated enclave of Nakhichevan. In return, Karabakh and the adjacent Lachin corridor will be granted self-governing status, implying its de facto independence.

Both presidents returned from Florida to hold consultations with their political allies. However, since Key West, developments on this front have been discouraging. Consultations with the domestic constituencies only seemed to have hardened the leaderships' positions. Given this, a planned follow-up meeting in Geneva in mid-June has been called off. The current obstacles are that the two sides live in deep isolation from one another, that public opinion in both countries is skeptical or even hostile toward a peace settlement, and that the two presidents—while close on many issues—are reluctant to make further concessions.

The major obstacle to a successful peace settlement remains entrenched public opinion on both sides. The two presidents seem to be "ahead of their populations" in their understanding of the need for compromise. A British journalist and publicist on the Caucasus, Tom de Waal identifies four key reasons why the presidents, apparently so keen to reach a solution, find themselves unable to take their societies with them.

1. Both leaders believe that a tough stance at home will win them more at the negotiating table. While Aliev tries to put pressure on international mediators to do more for Azerbaijan, Kocharian may be calculating that a little brinkmanship with the aging Aliev could force more concessions out of him.

2. The presidents find it easier to imagine a peace settlement in Florida than back home. Publics in the region are critical of the internationals, and the United States in particular, for "rushing" the process. The potential danger is that the two leaders might sign onto something that they cannot deliver.

3. Their respective personalities easily explain such attitudes. Neither man is a democrat. Aliev is a former Politburo member who has rigged all the elections he has held since coming to power. Kocharian was the wartime leader of the Karabakh Armenians. Both men energetically pursued the "military option" over Karabakh in 1993–1994. For them, the popular will presents a potential threat and they would rather manipulate it than engage in dialogue.

4. Most importantly, there is a fear of loss of power, as has already happened to Ter-Petrosyan, the first Armenian president. For both men, self-preservation would seem to be the highest goal, higher than peace and prosperity. Ultimately, both men may decide that the cost of signing a peace agreement is too high and that they could be swept away by the storms of protest it arouses.

Multi-Track Diplomacy

In the early 1990s, development of civil society in the Caucasus has been influenced by ethnic agendas and by efforts to cope with the consequences of violence. As a result, a culture of tolerance was slow to develop. The Soviet legacy of state domination was significant, since confusion prevailed over what the third sector is and how it relates to the state. A tradition of independent agents of society was largely absent, while the state regarded NGOs with suspicion and NGOs themselves easily became politicized. At times, many acted as the covert opponents of the regime.

After independence, popular moods changed substantively. Prior to the outbreak of armed conflicts, societies have been greatly affected by mobilization projects aimed at realization of national goals. Wars and massive suffering followed suit. The lesson most people learned was that individual survival is more important than any political initiative. The societies became more inward-looking as the quality of everyday life took a sharp downturn.

At the same time, Western aid targeted toward the development of the third sector, the presence of international humanitarian organizations, and periodic threats to democracy created new impetus for local groups to develop. However, few of them take up issues of resolution of the Karabakh conflict, although there is a wide proliferation of NGOs in Armenia and, to a lesser extent, in Azerbaijan. About sixty local NGOs exist in Karabakh itself. By the same token, compared to conflicts in Georgia, the Nagorno Karabakh dispute attracted peace efforts of international NGOs on a much more modest scale. Moreover, international humanitarian NGOs in Karabakh experienced severe constraints on their presence, since their mandate to operate was conditioned on approval from Baku, which Karabakh Armenians found unacceptable. As a result, only the International Committee of the Red Cross and Médecins Sans Frontières managed to establish permanent missions in Karabakh.

Those local and international groups who are involved in conflict resolution pursue the following range of activities.

Bilateral Contacts

Given the high degree of interethnic tension and a general lack of desire by the parties to engage in dialogue, few bilateral meetings have happened so far. The Helsinki Initiative 92 (HI-92) organized two meetings with representatives of Azerbaijani NGOs in 1994 and in 1995, bringing ethnic Azeris to Stepanakert. In 2000, Karen Ohajanian, the organization's head and a Karabakh minister of parliament, visited Baku to take part in preparations for the next International

Helsinki Citizen's Assembly (HCA) meeting in Baku. The visit was widely covered by the Azeri mass media.

The Swiss-based Caucasus Media Support Project played a crucial role in promotion of bilateral contacts. Important achievements were the trips of Azerbaijani journalists to Armenia (October 1997) and Karabakh (September 1998) and of Armenians to Azerbaijan (July 1999). Journalists met with leading politicians and this made the fact of such contacts more acceptable in the societies in conflict. For instance, Mark Grigorian, president of Cooperation and Democracy (C&D), visited Azerbaijan in July 1999, meeting President Aliev and Azeri senior officials. His articles about the trip were printed in both the Armenian and Azeri press.

LINKS is another INGO to embark on a series of bilateral measures. Apart from working on a number of pan-Caucasian initiatives aimed at development of good governance practices, in 2000 it undertook a mission to Karabakh to hold talks with the Karabakh leadership and its political rivals on future conflict-resolution strategies. Relevant discussions have been held on the Azeri side as well.

Two German foundations, namely the Friedrich Naumann Stiftung and the Friedrich Ebert Stiftung organized meetings of representatives from the South Caucasus in Sofia and Istanbul, attended mainly by politicians from both sides. Subsequent meetings in Yerevan and Baku were designed to facilitate dialogue between journalists. The Azerbaijan Foundation for the Development of Democracy was the Azeri partner for this project.

Multilateral Contacts and Training

The Transcaucasia Dialogue movement of the HCA, a project in community mobilization, was one of the first to start pursuing multilateral initiatives in the Caucasus. It has been supporting a network of civic initiatives, namely HCA local branches in Armenia, Azerbaijan, and Karabakh, since 1992. This built relationships of trust between individuals from different sides of the conflict and helped to protect local activists from domestic political pressures. Some of its most active members are HI-92 and the Human Rights Center of Azerbaijan (HRCA), which position themselves within the broader HCA movement. Both take part in wider networks and all-Caucasian peacemaking efforts, and HRCA also provides early-warning reports for INGOs such as FEWER.

In November 2000, the HCA General Assembly was held in Baku, bringing together six hundred participants, including over forty Armenians, twelve of them from Karabakh, with personal security guarantees from President Aliev, which were offered as a goodwill gesture for promoting Azerbaijan's entry into the Council of Europe. At the initiative of Arzu Abdualayeva, who was elected as new cochair of HCA International, an appeal for dialogue between Cultures and Civilizations was launched, with the purpose of fostering civil society in the Southern Caucasus. The assembly was facilitated by International Alert. A fringe subconference was held, addressing the issues of human rights, regional economic cooperation, religious dialogue, and youth projects. Currently, preparations for an Armenian-Turkish exchange of writers and intellectuals by Armenian and Turkish HCA committees are under way.

International Alert (IA) has been involved in the Karabakh conflict through the activities of the Caucasus Forum, a network of Caucasian NGOs active in conflict resolution. The aim of the forum was to provide an ongoing space for dialogue on conflict resolution and to incorporate the broader Caucasian context into particular peace efforts. The forum also gives an opportunity for civil-society representatives from Azerbaijan, Armenia, and Karabakh to maintain contacts and discuss their situation in a more relaxed atmosphere of pan-Caucasian dialogue. The latest of the Caucasus Forum events took place in Tsakhkadzor (Armenia), where the participants decided to proceed with projects in the core dimensions of the forum's peacebuilding activities, such as women, youth, journalists, and ex-combatants' programs.

The Norwegian Refugee Council was involved in a regional project in the South Caucasus aimed at networking and strengthening regional capacities to deal with conflicts.

Much international effort was dedicated to the provision of conflict-resolution training. Participants from Armenia and Azerbaijan have attended training courses together with participants from other conflict zones from around the world in a number of U.S. organizations, such as George Mason University. In 1995 the Center for International Development and Conflict Management at the University of Maryland has hosted individuals from each of the hot areas in the South Caucasus for a four-month program of NGO training.

In May 2001 a workshop entitled "Stability and Peace in the Caucasus: The Case of Nagorno Karabakh" was organized by the Development and Peace Foundation at the Evangelische Akademie Loccum. The workshop sought to bring together the official representatives of all sides, civil-society actors, and international mediators and international NGOs. Still, locals were vastly outnumbered by internationals: out of 146 participants, 29 were Azeri and 16 Armenian. The presence of international mediators such as Carey Cavanagh and Vladimir Kazimirov provided an extra clout, and the fact that the workshop happened shortly after the Key West meeting heightened the international interest.

The conference discussed the interrelationship between the confidentiality of the peace process on one hand, and the isolation of civil societies and the general public from high-level peace initiatives on the other. It warned that this might result in a huge gap in understanding between the top political leaderships and their respective societies, when and if the agreement is made. The participants also noted a deepened understanding by the international community of the issues surrounding the Karabakh conflict, such as the attitudes and perceptions of the genocide on the Armenian side and the deficiency of existing international law. The conference has also exposed a range of opinions within the Azeri and Armenian communities, who were prepared to discuss them in an open forum, marking a substantial change from the earlier uniformity and increasing the number of avenues for compromise.

In 2000, the Centre for European Policy Studies formed a task force for the Stability Pact for the Caucasus under the leadership of Michael Emerson. The task force published two reports in May and October 2000 outlining the concept of the plan. The second report was a substantial refinement of the first, benefiting from a summer of consulting the leaders of the secessionist regions.

The Stability Pact offers an alternative paradigm for political and territorial arrangements in the Caucasus in opposition to the Westphalian concept of nation-states that does not appear to be able to bring peace and development to the region. It is based on the analysis of the way the evolution of the EU has gone. The Stability Pact argues that these alternative strategies are of fundamental importance for the future of Europe. In a Europe with fuzzy frontiers, the EU's voluntary offer to export its policies for application to its neighbors, thus reducing perceptions of exclusion (although still limiting participation in key political bodies), is emerging as a key issue. It may be called the neomedieval empire, i.e., one with a set of peripheral associates rather than an EU that becomes a clear-cut European neo-Westphalian state. This is a major aspect of the emerging "future of Europe" debate, but one that has not yet been brought out sufficiently clearly. This attachment to conventional self-determination may need to change if the stability of the European periphery is to be achieved.

Based on such thinking, it advocates conflict resolution based on fuzzy constitutional settlements for Karabakh and Abkhazia. Both cases would see political solutions closer to confederalism than federalism for Azerbaijan and Georgia in relation to the secessionist entities. The option of secession would, however, be excluded. Power structures would be essentially horizontal rather than vertical, with very thin union structures. Asymmetric relations would be provided, notably in the case of Karabakh with co-ethnic Armenia. Refugees and IDPs would be able to return to such areas as the Azeri provinces occupied by Armenian forces and the southern region of Abkhazia. This will be supported by a new regional security order in which the settlements of the conflicts would see monitoring and enforcement by military units from OSCE member states under an OSCE umbrella.

In 2000, Ambassador Heidi Tagliavini, personal representative of the Austrian OSCE chairperson-in-office for missions in the Caucasus, and Freimut Duve, the OSCE representative on freedom of the media, launched a book project, *Caucasus: Defence of the Future,* containing essays by Caucasian writers. The project was aimed at promoting dialogue between representatives of the intelligentsia in the Caucasus.

Working with the Displaced

In Armenia, the conclusion that displaced Armenians will not return to Azerbaijan was arrived at fairly early on, and efforts to integrate new arrivals were made from the beginning. They were mainly state-driven with some international input. By contrast, in Azerbaijan, where the IDP and refugee population is much larger and where hopes for return still exist, local NGOs played more prominent roles. For example, the Baku-based NGO Hayat deals primarily with delivering humanitarian and development assistance to the vulnerable groups, most notably IDPs from Nagorno Karabakh. Hayat is engaged in the Migration Sector Development project, the regional initiative facilitated and funded by the International Organization for Migration that also involves Georgian, Armenian, and North Caucasian NGOs. Hayat conducts research into problems facing vulnerable groups and provides training and capacity-building seminars for local NGOs dealing with migration issues.

The Danish Refugee Council, working in Azerbaijan on the grassroots level, has focused on long-term peacebuilding and the creation of new possibilities for the IDP community. Its programs focused on the Fizuli and Sumgait regions, providing training in skills for prospective returnees.

Mass Media and Information Exchange

One area where significant progress has been made is the development of contacts between journalists and the facilitation of information exchange. This goal also fit in with a broader agenda of development of free media in the Caucasus pursued by many Western organizations. An important role has been played by the Caucasus Media Support Project, funded by the Swiss Federal Department of Foreign Affairs. The project has aimed to create a regional dialogue between journalists in the South Caucasus, to facilitate more balanced reporting and enable travel to the opponent's territory. Between 1997 and 2000, twelve conferences and training seminars took place in various locations in the Caucasus involving over two hundred participants from local print and broadcast media. Bulletins were produced in Russian and English.

In May 2001, seven journalists undertook a unique trip, crossing for the first time the front line between Azerbaijanis and the Armenians of Karabakh. The trip was organized by the American, French, and Russian cochairs of the Minsk Group. They designed a route that took in the sections of the population that are most affected by the stalemate: in Azerbaijan, displaced people; in Armenia, people suffering because of the economic isolation of their country. They also want to open up three routes across the Line of Contact that can be used by aid agencies and mediators. In 2000, they made two crossings of the Armenia-Azerbaijan frontier, which has also been closed. This third crossing was the most sensitive because it took place in what is the internationally recognized territory of Azerbaijan.

The Institute of War and Peace Reporting (IWPR) published the periodical *WarReport* from 1995 to 1998, making efforts to incorporate local voices into the English-language publication. It also pursued the Transcaucasian Media Training, Human Rights and Information Project, in development of independent mass media in the Caucasus, and published the *Media Caucasica* quarterly magazine in which C&D was involved. In 1999, IWPR started an on-line service on the Caucasus.

Promotion of Public Debate

One venue for public debate are press clubs. The Yerevan Press Club, cofinanced by the EU's Poland and Hungary Action for Rehabilitating the Economy and TACIS programs, acts as a forum for debate on issues of democracy and security, and also undertakes media monitoring in Armenia. Journalists participating in the Yerevan Press Club have been involved in contacts with their Azeri counterparts. Stepanakert Press Club, modeled on the Yerevan club, was established in Karabakh with a similar agenda. Baku Press Club operates in Azerbaijan.

The Caspian Studies Program at the JFK School of Government and the Berkeley Program in Soviet and Post-Soviet Studies at the University of California–Berkeley act as such centers of debate and discussion in the United States. For example, the Caspian Studies Program organized a panel discussion on "Negotiations on Nagorno Karabakh: Where Do We Go from Here?" soon after the Key West talks. The discussion was led by Ambassador Carey Cavanaugh, U.S. special negotiator for Nagorno Karabakh and NIS Regional Conflicts, and OSCE Minsk Group cochair, who sought to generate international support for the momentum for change.

Exchanges of War Prisoners

Despite the fact that active combat ended in 1994, exchanges of war prisoners and information on missing persons remains a burning problem. The HCA branches both in Armenia and Azerbaijan played an active role lobbying for the restoration of human interaction and reduction in ethnic resentment. As a practical measure, they were engaged in exchanges of prisoners of war and Anait Baiandur (Armenia) and Arzu Abdullaeva (Azerbaijan) won the Olof Palme Peace Award for their efforts. HI-92 is also actively engaged in exchanges of prisoners of war, hostages, and missing persons. Zinvori Mair (Society of Soldiers' Mothers), an Armenian grassroots NGO, was engaged in lobbying activities as well as practical issues of human-rights protection and prisoner exchanges.

Enhancement of Democracy and Human Rights

Many local NGOs that were originally established with a human-rights mandate, such as HI-92, founded in August 1992 as a civil-society reaction to the events in Khojaly, later broadened their focus to include democracy building and issues of conflict resolution. As a result, two agendas—fight for democracy and human rights, and resolution of conflict—go hand in hand and are often pursued by the same individuals. This also refers to NGOs such as HRCA or C&D. HRCA is the most established human-rights organization in Azerbaijan. The main activities are focused on human rights and minorities by monitoring and distributing information, and on direct engagement in the protection of citizens' rights by visiting prisons and trials, liaising with political parties, and putting pressure on the government to adhere to human-rights standards. The Institute of Peace and Democracy (Baku) is engaged in the protection of human rights and women's and young people's civil movements. It publishes *Azerbaijani Press on Human Rights and Democratic Freedoms,* which provides a summary of the mass-media monitoring on human-rights issues, but is also involved in the conflict-resolution agenda. The institute has a group on conflict studies that focuses on internal conflicts, but also monitors international developments.

In Armenia, C&D was involved in mass-media monitoring since 1996 and took part in ensuring fair coverage of the parliamentary elections there in 1999. It has compiled an English-language *Elections' Guide for Journalists* and established the elections' website.

Humanitarian Assistance

Given the difficulty for international humanitarian organizations to operate in Karabakh, the presence of those few that did was extremely important for the local people, both practically and psychologically. For example, Christian Solidarity Worldwide, founded on the initiative of Baroness Caroline Cox, has been involved in providing humanitarian assistance to the Armenians in Karabakh since 1990. This aid has taken the form of international public diplomacy in support of the Karabakh Armenians and of medical assistance, such as the building of a rehabilitation center in Stepanakert for persons paralyzed as result of the war, provision of medical supplies, and support to educational facilities, including organizing student exchanges.

Women as Peacemakers

Some peace initiatives were taken by women's organizations either as a part of a Caucasian regional effort, such as the Transcaucasian Women's Dialogue, or within their own political entities. In Azerbaijan, the Association for Protection of Women's Rights is one of the most vocal and active organizations involved in civil-society building and conflict resolution.

Concluding Remarks

There is no single convincing explanation as to why the conflict in Nagorno Karabakh attracted far less conflict-resolution professionals than similar conflicts in Georgia. A number of factors appear to have played a role.

First, international NGOs implicitly did not believe that progress in Karabakh could ever be made and felt that the Armenian position was fully entrenched. Second, interethnic hostility was so intense that few people of substance would be willing to participate in a bilateral dialogue with the opposite side. Such sensation was indirectly fueled by the Armenian diaspora, which in the beginning of 1990s supplied finance for the Karabakh struggle, and later found itself opposing the oil lobby in the West that advocated Azerbaijani interests. Third, the nature of civil society on both sides produces obstacles. In Armenia and partly in Karabakh, military victory and relative security led to the feeling that as far as Armenians are concerned, the issue has been resolved and peace is a reality. Azerbaijan should rather concentrate on assimilation of the displaced and economic development than on the pursuit of unrealistic goals.

In Azerbaijan, authoritarian control by the state left few local NGOs genuinely independent. Those that survived concentrated on the struggle for internal democracy and human rights as the most pressing issues. Fourth, international

NGOs found the social environment difficult to cope with, and after many initial approaches resulted in frustration, initiatives were not taken any further.

Finally, the needs of the Karabakh Armenians appear to be different from those of the Abkhaz and Ossetians, who take an active part in conflict-resolution initiatives. While the Abkhaz have to break through international isolation and gain access to foreign donors, the Karabakh Armenians can travel freely on Armenian passports and appeal for money to the Armenian leadership and diaspora organizations. As a result, there is a lack of popular belief in the validity of peacebuilding efforts; the only issues that provoke popular interest are the exchange of prisoners of war and a search for missing persons. Armenian intellectuals are interested in the theory of conflict resolution, but only as far as it can justify the Armenian claim on Karabakh. Azerbaijani intellectuals feel that they have no other option but to follow the presidential line on Karabakh, and their space for an independent initiative is more limited.

Prospects

Throughout the 1990s, negotiations have not brought much tangible result. Neither side was prepared to enter substantive bargaining, but rather conducted "negotiations about negotiations." Presently, the situation is changing, and there are signs that the conflicting sides are more committed to making some progress. The Azeri leadership probably feels that Azerbaijan's position cannot be strengthened any further; on the contrary, there is a real risk that it could weaken. First, Azerbaijan's oil resources have proven to be more limited than expected. Second, the president is aging and might not survive much longer. In the event of his death and subsequent infighting for the leadership position, the Karabakh issue could become a platform for a bid for power. Renewed fighting with potentially disastrous consequences for Azerbaijan cannot be ruled out. Therefore, a settlement of the Karabakh conflict is best concluded soon, while President Aliev is still in power. Third, from the Azerbaijani point of view, Russian help, as promised by President Putin, could be very useful in order to reach a negotiated settlement.

The internal political situation In Armenia became volatile following the October 1999 assassinations in parliament. Prime Minister Vazgen Sarkssian was killed, together with six other politicians, including the parliamentary speaker. An attempt was also made to kill President Arkadii Gukasyan of Nagorno Karabakh.

While Aliev's political and physical survival is an acute, but short-term, concern, the general political and social framework is a more important durable factor. Consensus among the general public in Armenia and in Karabakh that the conflict is already resolved and no action is necessary is extremely difficult to change. During election campaigns, the conflict in Karabakh is hardly mentioned while economic and social issues dominate the political agenda. Armenia does not suffer from the blockade as much as Abkhazia does, and so far the effects of the international condemnation have proved minimal. Refugees from Azerbaijan have been resettled in Armenia and have no desire to go back to Azerbaijan. Moreover, less developed and more authoritarian Azerbaijan does not appear an attractive alternative for the Karabakh Armenians who can rely on financial and political support of the Armenian state and diaspora. At the same time, the Azerbaijani army currently is unable to pose a serious military threat to force the Armenian side into concessions.

To sum up, there are no real pressures for the Armenian side to give up its territorial gains and claim on Karabakh. The argument can be made that Azerbaijan's interests are better served by allowing Karabakh to secede, while regaining the occupied territories and reaching an acceptable compromise on the Lachin corridor. However, such a political burden proved too heavy even for such a mighty leader as President Aliev.

Participants of the Wilton Park Conference concluded that although there was reason for some optimism, due to an improved cooperation between the co-chairs of the Minsk Group, the potential for escalation still remains. An insecure new president seeking to reinforce his position through a military victory could unleash renewed fighting. The other danger, in the Key West conference's view, is that the approach of a peace settlement that would require compromises on both sides, may prompt hard-liners to embark on policies to sabotage a peace deal. Anxiety also exists about the potential public reaction to compromises. The Azeri and the Armenian presidents, well aware of the political realities faced by their countries, are more able to agree on the outlines of a future peace settlement than to justify such a settlement to their respective constituencies.

As De Waal notes, there is an unhappy paradox at the heart of the Karabakh peace process. Two essentially undemocratic leaders are pursuing a peace settlement. They have apparently come close to achieving one. They understand that a peace deal is best for their countries, yet they are reluctant to engage their societies in the process. Clearly there are reasons why undemocratic leaders, as in Armenia and Azerbaijan, can actually do more in a peace process. The political base they need to consult with is narrow. They have to worry less about elections. They can simply ignore the nationalist consensus that still grips their respective publics. Equally, it is pointless to wait for more democratic leaders to emerge, which could take a generation—and is, in any case, more likely to be a consequence of peace than a cause of it. Still, the lack of trust between authoritarian leaders and their publics is the biggest problem for the Caucasus in general and the Karabakh peace process in particular.

Recommendations

Many of the activities of international NGOs have been targeted toward the development of free media and the facilitation of contacts between journalists from both sides of the conflict. With much work done, it may be worth turning their attention to other potential areas and tools. However, to achieve such a goal, it will be useful to reflect on the past record of multi-track conflict-resolution activities and assess the lessons learned. This may help to determine whether it is wise to pursue conflict-resolution efforts any further, or whether the political and social environment in both Armenia and Azerbaijan is not conducive to real progress and the international community should rather concentrate on maintaining open channels of communication until changes in domestic or international settings occur.

The start of the second Russian-Chechen war demonstrated the fragility of a "no war, no peace" situation and the freezing of conflicts, which in Karabakh seem an entrenched status quo. There are warning signs that renewed hostilities on the ground may not be ruled out. In such a context, early warning and low-key confidence-building measures may be appropriate steps to undertake.

Despite the long history of the Karabakh conflict, society in Azerbaijan has not yet had a chance to process the recent traumatic experience and come to terms with the new situation. A deep feeling of national humiliation appears to have settled in, and neither promises of an oil boom nor efforts to blame the military defeat in Karabakh on Russia currently pursued by the ruling establishment have helped in overcoming such sensations of a nation in distress. International actors, therefore, are urged to help Azerbaijanis to feel more like proud and confident citizens who can take responsibility for their own affairs rather than expecting, or apprehending, an externally generated solution.

International organizations, as well as the West and Russia, should take care not to push leveraged mediation too far, since it has produced negative impacts in the past and can do so in future. A cautious approach may be more appropriate than excessive zeal. As the Caspian Studies Program warns, failure to achieve peace in this recent round of negotiations could easily collapse into a situation of war between Armenia and Azerbaijan. This would be a worse scenario than the current stalemate. Energy development in Azerbaijan will receive an enormous setback, as international companies will be reluctant to invest in a country at war. The Karabakh conflict may become a platform for emerging rivals for the presidency.

The Caspian Studies Program concentrated on recommendations as to which action is to be taken by the international community in the postconflict stage, talking about the signing of the Karabakh peace settlement as an "almost done deal." It recommends, for instance, one concrete action: resettlement of Azerbaijani IDPs in some or all of the occupied districts that are outside of the disputed territory of Nagorno Karabakh under Armenian occupation. However, Carey Cavanagh, speaking at Chatham House in May 2001, noted that it is unrealistic to hope that all IDPs would return to their original settlements, given the choice, and that the Dayton peace process showed that once interethnic coexistence is brutally interrupted, restoration is not that easy.

The Caspian Studies Program further stresses that since the OSCE is likely to be the leading agency in the postconflict period, it should make a particular effort to be well prepared for the challenges ahead. In the past, the OSCE has repeatedly suffered from understaffing, and in some cases the quality of deployed personnel was not on par with the high demands of the job. The OSCE should encourage member states to identify their citizens who are qualified and willing to serve on a field mission and to hire appropriate experts on the open market. Similarly, the UN needs to decide which of its agencies will take the lead role. Once designated, this agency should develop a clear contingency plan that will allow for a timely response. It is especially important that the agencies identify a sufficient number of motivated and well-qualified workers for the mission.

As part of international settlement efforts, the involved sides should strive for sustained cooperation and coordination. Within this framework,

1. International organizations should coordinate future rehabilitation programs. There is a need to decide on the lead agencies for rehabilitation and development projects and to secure joint planning with clearly delimited responsibilities.

2. The United States should use the positive dynamics of cooperation with Russia to make the decisive breakthrough. The current cooperative position of Russia should be appraised, while at the same time contingency planning should be carried out in case Russia's policies in the region change.

3. In order to help President Aliev promote a peace settlement in Azerbaijan, the U.S. Congress should cancel Section 907(a) of the Freedom Support Act. In the interim, the executive should waive or reinterpret the limitations to the extent that is legally possible.

The international community should be ready to address other issues too. Parts of the occupied territories are mined, but many of the minefields are not properly documented. The international community should assist Azerbaijan in the speedy marking of the minefields, followed by demining. Countries with expertise in this field should be sought out and encouraged to contribute to this humanitarian effort. It will also be necessary to repair and rebuild at least the land communication links between Azerbaijan and the occupied territories, so that the return of IDPs and economic revival can proceed.

Moreover, the UN and the OSCE need to improve the caliber of specialists who occupy operational posts, perhaps by recruiting some experts from outside their organizations' framework. To date, appointments of leading personnel have often been plagued by interstate politics, where candidates have been chosen by citizenship before any other quality.

International agencies await a clear signal from the OSCE that a settlement is likely to materialize before they launch needs-assessment missions, and thus have not conducted formal estimates. The World Bank should take the lead and provide direct access to funding for Azerbaijan and Armenia, as well as mobilize additional financial resources and seek to attract private investors. Under the coordinated leadership of the OSCE, international agencies should start working out the responsibility for sharing strategies in financing and implementation of the rehabilitation and development programs.

De Waal draws up recommendations with an idea in mind that the settlement is still some way away. He suggests taking existing elements of the framework agreement and incorporating them into a "phased" or "step by step" plan, in which some of the thornier problems (such as security issues and the status of Karabakh itself) are postponed until later. The Armenians could, for example, give up some occupied territory, while Azerbaijan and Turkey could open up some communications with Armenia, perhaps through the Azerbaijani enclave of Nakhichevan, which is also suffering from economic isolation.

The participants in the Loccum conference stressed that since the societies are not prepared for a peace deal, civil-society contacts and multi-track diplomacy are needed to prepare the ground for implementation of a peace agreement. There was a strong shared view among the participants that starting up a peace process without respective civil societies being ready for it, both psychologically and practically, can be detrimental. It was emphasized that the decisions that the international actors make about the peace process should be accomplished in an inclusive way, engaging the local stakeholders in the decisionmaking process.

Resources

Newsletters and Periodicals
Azerbaijan Press on Human Rights and Democratic Freedoms, Institute of Peace and Democracy, Baku, Azerbaijan
Caspian Studies Program Reports, John F. Kennedy School of Government, Harvard University
Caucasus Report, Radio Free Europe/Radio Liberty, Prague, Czech Republic
Contemporary Caucasus Newsletter, Working Paper Series, Berkeley Program in Soviet and Post-Soviet Studies, University of California, Berkeley
Monitor & Prism, Jamestown Foundation, Washington, DC
Moscow News, Russian weekly, also published in English with regular updates on the Caucasus
WarReport (1995–1998), Institute for War and Peace Reporting, London

Reports
Amnesty International
   1999 Annual Report on Armenia, London, 1998.
   1999 Annual Report on Azerbaijan, London 1998.
United Nations High Commissioner for Refugees
   2000 Armenia Program
   2000 Azerbaijan Program

Other Publications
Conflict, Cleavage and Change in Central Asia and the Caucasus, edited by Karen Dawisha and Bruce Parrot. Cambridge, Cambridge University Press, 1997.
Humanitarian Action in the Caucasus: A Guide for Practitioners, by Greg Hansen. The Thomas J. Watson Jr. Institute for International Studies, Humanitarianism and War Project. Providence, RI, Local Capacities for Peace Project, 1998.
No Peace, No War in the Caucasus: Secessionist Conflict in Chechnya, Abkhazia and Nagorno-Karabakh, by Edward W. Walker. Cambridge, MA, Harvard University, 1998.
Pride of Small Nations, by Suzanne Goldenberg. London, Zed Books, 1994.
Russia's Policies in the Caucasus, by Pavel Baev. London, RIIA, 1997.
State Building and the Reconstruction of Shattered Societies. Berkeley, University of California at Berkeley Program in Soviet and Post-Soviet Studies, April 1999.
The New Caucasus: Armenia, Azerbaijan and Georgia, by Edmund Herzig. London, RIIA/Pinter, 1999.

The Transcaucasus in Transition: Nation-Building and Conflict, by Shireen Hunter. Washington, DC, Center for Strategic and International Studies, 1994.

Transcaucasia, Nationalism and Social Change: Essays in the History of Armenia, Azerbaijan and Georgia, by Ronald Grigor Suny. Ann Arbor, University of Michigan Press, 1996.

Selected Internet Sites

www.ceps.be/Research/Caucasus (Centre for European Policy Studies)

www.iwpr.net (Institute for War and Peace Reporting, London)

www.poli.vul.ac.be/publi (Caucasian Regional Studies, Vrije University of Brussels, in Russian and English)

www.rferl.org (Radio Free Europe/Radio Liberty Newsline, daily news and analysis)

www.socrates.berkeley.edu/~bsp (Berkeley Program in Soviet and Post-Soviet States)

www.soros.org/caucasus (Chronology of events in the Transcaucasus)

Resource Contacts

Vicken Cheterian, CIMERA, e-mail: vicken.cheterian@cimera.org

Thomas de Waal, e-mail: tomdewaal@hotmail.com

Mient Jan Faber, Interchurch Peace Council, e-mail: mjfaber@ikv.nl

Mark Grigorian, Cooperation and Democracy, e-mail: markos@media.am

Edmund Herzig, University of Manchester/RIIA, e-mail: edmund@bnn.dircon.co.uk

Zhanna Krikorova, e-mail: zhanna@arminco.com

Arthur Martirossian, Conflict Management Group, e-mail: martiros@cmgroup.org

Anna Matveeva, expert on the Caucasus, London, e-mail: sophiamat@ukonline.co.uk

Karen Ohajanian, Helsinki Initiative-92, Stepanakert, e-mail: karandje@hca.nk.am

Dennis Sammut, LINKS, London, e-mail: dennissammut@hotmail.com

Gevork Ter-Gabrielian, International Alert, London, e-mail: gtergabrielian@international-alert.org

Marten van Harten, independent consultant, e-mail: harten16@zonnet.nl

Edward Walker, Berkeley Program in Soviet and Post Soviet Studies, University of California, Berkeley, e-mail: eww@socrates.berkeley.edu

Arif Yunusov, Institute of Peace and Democracy, Azerbaijan, fax: 009 99 412 94-14-58

Organizations

In Armenia

Cooperation and Democracy
7 Saryan Street
Yerevan 375002, Armenia
Tel.: +37 42 27 21 19, 58 11 65 or 58 75 36
E-mail: markos@media.am

Norwegian Refugee Council Yerevan
50 Khanjian Str.
Tekeyan Center
Yerevan, Armenia
Tel.: +374 1 57 17 21
Fax: +374 1 57 46 39
E-mail: admin@nrc.am
www.nrc.no

In Azerbaijan
Norwegian Refugee Council-Baku
Norway House, Boyuk Quala Street 40
Icheri Sheher

Baku, Azerbaijan
Tel.: + 994 12 98 81 25 / 92 8
Fax: + 994 12 92 69 19
E-mail: nilsnrc@intrans.az
http:www.nrc.no

International
Norwegian Refugee Council
Grensen 17
P.O. Box 6758 St. Olavs plass
0130 Oslo, Norway
Tel.: (47) 23 10 98 00
Fax: (47) 23 10 98 01
E-mail: nrc-no@online.no

Data on the following organizations can be found in the Directory section:

In Armenia
  Armenian Center for National and International Studies
  Armenian Sociological Association
  Armenian Young Lawyers' Association
  Conflict Resolution Center of Armenia
  Democracy Union
  Fund Against Violation of Law
  Nagorno-Karabakh Committee of "Helsinki Initiative-92"
  Union of Non-Governmental Organizations of Shirak Region
  Yerevan Press Club

In Azerbaijan
  Azerbaijan Human Rights Resource Center
  Azerbaijan Young Lawyers' Union
  Committee of Democracy and Human Rights
  Human Rights Centre of Azerbaijan
  Institute of Peace and Democracy
  Resource Centre on National Minorities
  Society for Humanitarian Research

International
  Center for European Policy Studies
  Cimera
  Evangelische Akademie Loccum
  Friedrich Ebert Stiftung
  Helsinki Citizen's Assembly
  Institute for War and Peace Reporting
  International Alert

Anna Matveeva is a program manager at Saferworld (on small arms and security). She previously worked as a research fellow at the Royal Institute of International Affairs (Chatham House, London) and program head at International Alert (London). As a scholar specializing in issues of conflict and the politics of post-Soviet Eurasia, she has authored publications such as The North Caucasus: Russia's Fragile Borderland *(London: RIIA, 1999) and academic articles, and undertook projects for organizations such as the International Peace Academy, EastWest Insititute, Minority Rights Group, and the Heinrich Böll Stiftung.*

16

CENTRAL ASIA

16.1

Regional Introduction:
A Host of Preventable Conflicts

John Schoeberlein

Following the collapse of the Soviet Union a decade ago, observers within Central Asia and abroad predicted that numerous conflicts would break out in the region between irreconcilable forces that had been held in check under Soviet rule. Conflict arising from ethnic tensions, Islamist militancy, or social upheaval has not proven to be as inevitable as many supposed. Apart from a devastating but relatively short civil war in Tajikistan, a decade of independence in the region has largely been characterized by peace. However, many signs now point to rising conflicts both within and between states—conflicts that are in no way inevitable, but rather arise from the regional leadership's policies, which have failed to address points of tension and in many cases have instead exacerbated them. More farsighted leadership and engagement from the international community will be required to avert the increasing tensions and the outbreak of proliferating regional conflict and chaos.

The demise of the Soviet Union in 1991 resulted in the softening of once virtually hermetic boundaries that separated Central Asia from Iran, Afghanistan, and China. At the same time, the emergence of five independent states now outside of Russia's direct control has resulted in the appearance of increasingly sharp lines of fragmentation, both between the Central Asian states and within each one. Soviet Central Asia had been relatively seamless, with virtually no significant tensions between the Soviet republics and few apparent internal political and social rifts. The Soviet system, for all its inefficiencies and injustices, did not foster ethnic clashes, while it did further the formation of a stable equilibrium of regional power elites. It also established a form of authority that was almost universally considered legitimate despite a distinct social hierarchy of access to privilege and power. Contrary to the predictions of some, the Soviet Union did not retreat from Central Asia due to radical discontent or violent resistance.

Independence came to the Central Asians peaceably, almost without their even trying for it. If there was much less violence than some expected in the early years of independence, the region has nevertheless been extremely unstable. Potential causes of violent conflict are very present and threaten to increase. Though in 1997 Tajikistan achieved a peace accord ending its five-year civil war, the country is still very much under the sway of the military commanders and factions that emerged during the war. Also, the wartime fighting forces have yet to be fully demilitarized, and military clashes and frequent assassinations remain a feature of life in the country. Much worse is the situation in Afghanistan, which has suffered nearly a quarter century of continuous civil war. Here, in the five years of fighting since the emergence of the Taliban movement with Pakistan's support, the Northern Alliance was defeated in all but a tiny fraction of the country's territory, saved only by the support they received from Russia, Iran, and others. The intervention of the U.S.-led coalition at the end of 2001 has dramatically reversed the balance between the Northern Alliance and the Taliban, and while it is too early to tell whether a stable new government will emerge to unite disparate elements within Afghanistan, it is clear that many years and considerable foreign assistance will be required in the best-case scenario to reestablish the institutions of government in a country devastated by a quarter century of continuous war. In the absence of stability over the near term, the threat of spreading violence, corrupting contraband trade, and refugees will continue to emanate from Afghanistan for a long time to come. Developments in western China (Xinjiang, or Eastern Turkistan) also pose a threat to Central Asia as an aggrieved Uyghur population there conducts a militant insurgency supported by a network that extends into Central Asia and Afghanistan. Like other discontented groups in the region that have been driven underground by lack of democratic avenues for pursuing their interests, Uyghur activists who see their homeland being overrun numerically and economically by Han Chinese are building links across borders that provide an economic base for insurgency, and provide weapons and training for antigovernment activities.

In spite of this regional instability, during the first years of independence there was relatively limited conflict in and between the other four Central Asian states—Uzbekistan, Turkmenistan, Kyrgyzstan, and Kazakhstan. As compared with the Caucasus, which emerged from Soviet domination with a series of devastating wars and has since undergone periodic changes of government, in these four Central Asian countries the same heads of state that came to power in the last years of the Soviet Union have remained. They have presided over remarkably peaceful development. In the *perestroika* period that culminated in the collapse of the USSR, there had been numerous incidents of intercommunal violence across the region. The worst of these included a pogrom in 1989 carried out against Meskhetian Turks in Uzbekistan, which resulted in hundreds of deaths and the exodus of 100,000 Meskhetians from the region. In summer 1990, even more severe violence broke out in southern Kyrgyzstan in clashes between the Uzbek and Kyrgyz communities, which resulted in perhaps a thousand deaths (the official figures are generally considered unreliable, but some confidential sources within the security apparatus put the number of deaths as high as 6,000). By contrast, no incident even remotely comparable has occurred since 1991 apart from the civil war in Tajikistan, and for a number of years it appeared that Central Asia could undergo the transition to independence with remarkably little turmoil.

The last several years have seen a sharp change in the prospects for peace in the region. This change traces to failures in leadership—largely avoidable—in two key areas: governance and the economy. In governance, the leaders have opted for authoritarianism, carrying out systematic efforts to eliminate all means for the popular will to be expressed through institutionalized political pluralism. In the economy, the leaders have pursued somewhat different paths, but in every case they have failed to establish a legal regime that would protect market development—foreign investment, entrepreneurship in the productive economy, or small-time local trader—from predatory government officials and stifling corruption. Instead, the leaders themselves all appear to be tightly enmeshed in a patronage system that favors cronies and powerful families, first and foremost their own. The rampant unemployment and deepening poverty, combined with a pervasive sense of resentment toward a narrow, rapacious, and self-absorbed elite, together with the absence of legitimate means to mobilize opposition, is prompting a growing segment of the population to support radical and violent means to oust the current regimes. The number of people ready to use violence remains comparatively small. However, there is a growing danger that the element of violence could severely disrupt the delicate balance that exists in the society and, as in Tajikistan, bring about an irreversible chain of events with devastating ramifications.

In addition to fostering internal tensions, the leaders in some of the countries have adopted a confrontational stance and aggressive policies toward their neighbors that could turn existing interstate conflicts over such vital issues as access to water and transportation corridors into confrontations and possibly even war. There have been a series of very serious incidents already between Uzbekistan and Tajikistan involving armed incursions from the territory of one country into the other. For example, in 1998, insurgents led by Mahmud Khudayberdiev entered Tajikistan from Uzbekistan, seeking to wrest the northern part of the country from government control. In 1999 and the following years, there have been annual campaigns by the Islamic Movement of Uzbekistan emanating from the territory of Tajikistan. In every case, the country where the insurgents originate denies supporting them, but the country victimized by these incursions considers that their neighbor's support is undeniable. These and other tensions have led to an increasing militarization of the borders and military buildup in general, and there are growing fears that insurgencies, water disputes, internal disorder, or disputes over borders could lead to escalating armed clashes between the Central Asian states.

Other aspects of the postindependence social and political environment have the potential for fostering social tensions and conflict as well. A critical factor is the decline of education, which was at a relatively high level during Soviet times. Now many children and youth are no longer getting access to education on all levels, with declining literacy and ensuing consequences for the economy and for interethnic communication. There have been considerable setbacks also for women, who were extensively engaged in the economy and the public sphere during Soviet times. Now there has been a resurgence of "conservative" values on the official and popular levels that press for women to withdraw from these spheres, and the genereal economic decline has driven women out of many aspects of the economy. At the same time, in many communities, there has been an increasing need to rely on women despite these trends, since their contributions to the household economy have grown more vital as resources become strained and men grow increasingly scarcer due to migration.

The development of civil society varies greatly among the Central Asian countries, with some governments—notably Kyrgyzstan and Kazakhstan—allowing considerable latitude for the activity of NGOs while others often view them as antigovernment by nature—especially Turkmenistan and Uzbekistan. In all cases, however, there is a great need for an expanded role for nongovernmental actors as the governments show themselves as increasingly unable to fill social-welfare functions that the state fulfilled during Soviet times. Nongovernmental actors have the potential to play an important role in conflict prevention and mitigation, but so far there is only limited NGO capacity, not only because of governmental interference in many countries, but also because of their weak institutional development, weak links with popular constituencies, and lack of ability to mobilize resources apart from sources in international aid organizations.

A key problem for all countries in Central Asia is the lack of strong linkages between the population and their governments. Weakly developed democratic institutions mean that people have few means of influencing the policies of their governments. The widespread corruption undermines the people's trust and diminishes the sense of loyalty that is vital if all are to work together to overcome social tensions and other challenges facing the region. Unfortunately, where popular support is lacking, the governments have often sought to force the populations' cooperation by coercive means, much as they did during Soviet times. The risk is that such coercive control cannot be effective in the current globalizing environment, and popular discontent will increasingly be channeled into radical and underground movements.

Five Different Paths Toward the Same Place?

Each of the Central Asia countries has followed a somewhat different path of development since independence, due to differing circumstances, cultures, and proclivities of the leaders. Two countries—Kyrgyzstan and Tajikistan—are constrained by extremely poor resources, even including agricultural land due to their mountainous terrain. Kazakhstan is blessed with some of the world's richest oil resources, Turkmenistan has an abundance of natural gas, and Uzbekistan is able to gain considerable export earnings from gold and cotton.

Yet despite their resources, none of these richer countries have committed needed resources to bring the poorest segment of the population out of severe poverty. Kazakhstan has been very progressive in introducing market reforms, whereas governments in Turkmenistan and Uzbekistan retain tight controls over the economy, and Kyrgyzstan and Tajikistan have very little indeed to export. In all five countries, the general perception is that only a narrow elite is benefiting from economic independence and many people long for Soviet times, characterized by substantially greater prosperity and generous state social services.

Turkmenistan is the quietest—and possibly the most explosive—of the Central Asian countries. President Saparmurat Niyazov has pursued a policy of "neutrality," avoiding military or other alignments with other countries, but in effect, this has amounted to keeping the country under an iron hand and sealed off from the world at large. He has promoted a Stalinesque personality cult and has provided virtually no latitude for the development of civil society and none for political pluralism. The discontents of the poor and of large ethnic minorities such as the Uzbeks are effectively suppressed by fear and repression. The country consists of a series of enclave or oasis populations distributed around the Qara-Qum desert, which occupies the country's heart—enclaves inhabited by diverse clan and ethnic groups. Niyazov maintains control of these by handpicking the leadership and demanding absolute loyalty. There is much anticipation of the struggle for control of the country after Niyazov's term of office, which he has made a lifetime presidency, comes to an end. Since power is personalized, there are no institutionalized mechanisms for mediating the struggle for power, and it is probable that the succession struggle will be violent. Niyazov's policy of neutrality and isolation has indeed led to generally peaceable relations with Turkmenistan's neighbors. Some significant tensions have never-the-less arisen on the border with Uzbekistan as both countries have engaged in unilateral actions to determine where the border should run. Some parts of this border are inhabited on both sides by Uzbek communities, which once had intensive interactions and now are perceived as a security threat and subjected to persecution by the Turkmenistan government. Still Niyazov, for all his megalomania in relation to his own country, does not appear to have ambitions for a role of regional domination, and the greatest threat of conflict comes from tensions within the country—temporarily thoroughly suppressed, but it is impossible to know for how long.

In Uzbekistan, the situation is much more complex. While the government of President Islam Karimov shows not much more affinity for political pluralism, the country by its nature has more diverse bases for power and opposition. Uzbekistan consists of a series of regions, represented by elites whose power was balanced in a careful equilibrium through Soviet times. These regions include, notably, the Ferghana Valley, the country's most populous and agriculturally rich region; Tashkent, the capital; and Samarqand, from where Karimov originates. After Karimov came to power, he steadily consolidated his control in a struggle especially with the Tashkent elite, and through careful manipulation of patronage and alliances, he gradually marginalized competing regions and achieved overwhelming dominance. In this "success," meanwhile, lie tremendous tensions whereby such groups as the powerful Ferghana Valley elite see their interests as severely eroded.

The tensions have greatly worsened since the mid-1990s, when the government began a campaign to eliminate Islamic groups and organizations that were not directly under its control. Islam, which had flourished as an organizational force following the lifting of Soviet-era controls under Gorbachev, was increasingly perceived as the only viable institutional basis for opposition to the regime. It indeed became so following Karimov's banning and suppression immediately after independence of all of the secular opposition groups that had emerged in the *perestroika* era. These campaigns against "unofficial" Islam have led to thousands of arrests and widespread police abuse of elements of the population that were not previously politicized, but rather were focused on religious observance. Religious activity itself has been treated as a marker of disloyalty to the regime, and these efforts at suppression have gone far to politicize religion and to antagonize the population against the regime. While militants remain very few in number, they are gaining in force and popular support. Some of those fleeing possible arrest in Uzbekistan are joining the Islamic Movement of Uzbekistan (IMU). For the past three years, IMU has made its ambition of toppling the Karimov regime known through clashes each summer with security forces and guards on the borders of Kyrgyzstan and Uzbekistan.

These very limited skirmishes, involving a couple of thousand guerilla fighters, will not threaten broader stability in the region, despite the significant though limited support they have received from outside Islamist forces, including the Taliban. With the Taliban virtually routed now, some of the Islamist forces targeting other parts of Central Asia have undoubtedly been dealt a setback, but it is quite probable that Islamists will continue to find support among former *mujahedeen* groups in Afghanistan. Support from outside is not the most important factor, meanwhile, and the internal discontent that has fueled support for militancy is likely to grow stronger, adding support to militants operating out of Afghanistan and elsewhere. Of much greater significance meanwhile are the underground Islamist movements within Uzbekistan—most notably the Hizb ut-Tahrir, or "Party of Liberation." Though they espouse nonviolence, Hizb ut-Tahrir is equally bent on ousting the *faqir* ("nonbeliever") regime of Karimov, and their rapidly growing popularity, fed mainly by the government repression, makes this ambition increasingly credible. Perhaps the greatest danger of violent conflict comes from the possibility that discontented elite elements who have been marginalized by Karimov's consolidation of power could form an alliance of convenience with Islamist forces in making a bid for power. It is possible that such an alliance indeed lies behind the massive car bombings that shook Tashkent in February 1999, severely damaging a number of monuments to the prestige of the current regime.

The government of Uzbekistan has raised the alarm, pointing to threats of instability coming from outside forces and international Islamist networks and thereby evoking some resonance from states such as Russia and the United States, who see themselves as sharing this enemy. However, the key sources for the growing potential for violent conflict actually come from within the country and even within the regime.

In Tajikistan, large-scale violent conflict is already a feature of the post-Soviet experience. Independence came to Tajikistan at a time when the communist leadership was weak and the opposition had gained considerable organizational strength and popular support. Therefore, unlike in any of the other Central Asian countries, there was a threat to the continuity of power of the communists. The opposition received a strong impetus from the backlash against hard-liners following the attempted coup against Gorbachev in August 1991. Mass demonstrations led to the replacement of the Tajik Communist Party first secretary and president, Qahhar Mahkamov, who had made the mistake of aligning himself with the coup plotters. Though the opposition failed to elect its candidate in the presidential election later that year, the standoff, which persisted through spring 1992, led ultimately to the formation of armed groups. The decisive moment came when the new president, Rahman Nabiev, distributed weapons to a crowd of his supporters, creating the Presidential Guard that eventually was to grow into the fighting force that came victorious out of the civil war.

Many factors contributed to the escalation of fighting. A decisive factor was the flow of weapons from the Russian army through illegal sales, probably to both sides, as the result of the chaos and lack of discipline that affected the army at the time of the collapse of the Soviet Union. Another was the previous existence of tensions between regional groups, which became the sides in the conflict as it progressed—chiefly, the Kölabi who eventually won the war and the Gharmi who formed the core of the militant opposition, though a number of other groups were also important. For example, Pamiris, who differ from the main Tajik population by language, religion (they are predominantly Ismaili Shiites), and physical appearance, became the victims of ethnic cleansing as the Kölabi fighters took control of the capital Dushanbe. Within the space of a few weeks, what had been mild antagonisms turned into mortal opposition as entire villages were destroyed thanks to effective demagoguery and the availability of firepower. Within half a year, about 50,000 people were killed and roughly a fifth of the country's population was displaced. The next five years saw ongoing battles in the region near Afghanistan where the opposition forces took refuge and learned much about guerilla warfare from the Afghan *mujahedeen*.

Ultimately, a power-sharing agreement was concluded in 1997 that resulted in a divvying up of portfolios and economic assets between the combatants of the war. The country remains under the control of commanders from both sides, though increasingly President Emamali Rahmanov has consolidated power on the model of other Central Asian authoritarian leaders. The current tensions in Tajikistan are far greater than before the war, though the war-weariness of the population may provide some insurance against any widespread outbreak of violence. Despite the direct experience with war, the prospects for new conflict may be as great in Tajikistan as anywhere in Central Asia. The rise to power of the Kölabi fighters has meant that other regions have been subject to widespread appropriation of assets at gunpoint and a patronage system like elsewhere in Central Asia but here enforced by violence and frequent assassinations, thus stifling economic development and generating strong resentments among other groups. A particularly volatile element of the population is the former fighters, many of whom retain their weapons, for whom peace has meant no jobs and the end of profitable pillaging. One consequence of the peace accord was the emergence of the only pluralist political system in Central Asia, where even the groups that the government likes the least have been allowed to participate. However, as Rahmanov consolidates his power, he and his supporters are working to reduce pluralism. In fact, though the opposition were assured 30 percent of government positions in the peace agreement, that promise was never fulfilled and a number of those who did get positions have been turning up dead.

Kyrgyzstan, in the early years of independence, seemed to be following a distinctly democratic path with wide latitude given for the development of opposition parties, independent media, nongovernmental organizations, and generally the features of a burgeoning civil society. The leaders of neighboring countries argued that democracy led to chaos, and insisted that a measure of authoritarianism was essential to avoid developments as in Tajikistan. President Askar Akaev of Kyrgyzstan, meanwhile, insisted that his people in fact were politically mature enough to implement democracy, and events bore this out in that tensions and violence in Kyrgyzstan were no greater than in any neighboring country. Yet at the same time as it was proceeding quickly with market reforms, Kyrgyzstan has supported flourishing corruption and has become the most highly stratified country in the former Soviet Union, with two-thirds of the population living in poverty while a narrow elite enjoys conspicuous wealth. Flagrant corruption on the part of those close to the president and increasing criticisms from independent voices of Akaev's record have prompted him to cope with growing opposition by stripping the judiciary and parliament of their powers and by assuming increasingly authoritarian control. Where previously a flourishing party system allowed for relatively effective popular participation, now the leaders of the strongest opposition parties are regularly faced with criminal charges or thrown in jail in order to prevent their winning elections. All of the media outlets that have been most critical of the government have been shut down, and leaders of some of the most influential NGOs have been intimidated or beaten up by people widely presumed to be members of the security services. The government works in many ways to restrict the activities of Islamic groups, as in Uzbekistan and elsewhere (though less actively), and the consequences are to increase the feeling of persecution among devoted Muslims and the support that groups such as Hizb ut-Tahrir receive in Kyrgyzstan as well.

Kyrgyzstan, like its neighboring countries, is heavily divided by regionalism, ethnic tensions, politicized Islam, and elite privilege and cronyism. Many of these issues coalesce in the Ferghana Valley region of southern Kyrgyzstan, where there is a very large Uzbek minority who have been systematically excluded from power and experience and fallen under the scrutiny of the security services particularly intensely because of their greater devotion to Islam. Uzbeks are generally outside of the patronage networks that allow one to get a job in law enforcement or the judiciary. Meanwhile, they do well for themselves in agricultural production and the markets, which has sometimes led to resentment from less well-to-do Kyrgyz. The narrowing of effective political participation and growing alienation from what is seen as a highly privileged, corrupt, and unjust regime has resulted in increasingly militant views among a segment of the population, including Kyrgyz as well as Uzbeks. Here as elsewhere, authoritarianism is pursued in order for the current leader to hold onto power, but it has the effect of increasing the likelihood of conflict. This potentiality has begun to manifest itself increasingly in confrontation with the government, usually in demonstrations in response to economic hardship, arrests of religious activists, and actions against opposition leaders.

In Kazakhstan, too, there has been increasing tension toward authoritarianism on the backdrop of some greater leeway for the development of markets and civil society. There is some hope that with its tremendous oil resources, the government will have the capacity to ensure the well-being of its broader population, though there is little sign of sharing the wealth so far. Kazakhstan, like its neighbors, is very regionally divided, with some western regions holding most of the oil resources, southern regions being very poor and oriented more strongly toward Islam, and the north having an overwhelmingly Russian population.

In the country as a whole, Kazaks make up the largest group by a slim margin. Kazakhstan was previously seen as relatively immune to the influences of radical Islam since observance of the religion had widely diminished or disappeared in much of the country, yet here too it is increasingly forming the foundation for underground mobilization. While the presence of large numbers of Russians makes the country potentially vulnerable to pressures and interference from Russia, President Nazarbaev has successfully pursued a policy of inclusion, at least on the level of state ideology. On the level of everyday life, meanwhile, many Russians see no future in a country where Kazaks are actively promoted over other nationalities. Those with the youth and skills required to resettle and find employment in Russia have left Kazakhstan in large numbers, severely damaging the country's economy but releasing some of the internal pressures, at least temporarily. With rampant corruption and growing perceptions of inequity, Kazakhstan is also not immune to the tensions that have the potential of tearing the region apart.

Prospects

The comparison with Iran prior to the revolution is very pertinent to Central Asia. Iran descended into violence and revolution, not because of a lack of resources, but rather because of the perception of inequity linked to authoritarian rule, increasing social stratification, resentment of the West's support for the dictator, and the regime's suppression of forms of Islam that it saw as potentially threatening. All of these conditions exist increasingly in Central Asia. Nevertheless, the leadership everywhere seems to find hope in shoring up their position by increasing repression, and many in the West seem determined to make the same mistake as they made in Iran, supporting undemocratic rule, and ultimately sowing distrust of Western involvement among the wider population.

There is a broad array of factors that could lead to the sparks that provoke wider conflict: ethnic tensions, regional imbalances, interstate disputes over resources and borders, and the state-driven radicalization of Islam, among others. Each of these issues must be addressed to avoid increasing tensions and the eventuality of widespread violent conflict. None of these issues can be resolved if the underlying problems of economics and governance are not adequately addressed. Without effective democratic institutions, the governing elite will be unresponsive to the needs and interests of the wider population. Without curtailing patronage, corruption, and cronyism, even the resource-rich countries will remain highly stratified and unreliable for investment, and in the poorer countries the broad population will grow increasingly desperate and angry.

The increased interest that the West now shows in Central Asia in connection with the war in Afghanistan represents both challenges and opportunities. There is ground for hope that there will be the commitment that is required to build stronger economies and democratic systems. Yet there is also the risk that Western engagement will be led by the kind of security support to undemocratic regimes that has increased polarization and radicalization and promoted anti-Westernism in other countries such as Iran, Egypt, Palestine, and Algeria. Western military leaders have found it convenient to pursue close relations with the government of Uzbekistan, for example, which could lead to a closer dialogue and greater influence on economic and political reform processes, but could also have the effect of reducing the pressure to democratize and could even intensify the tensions that have existed between Uzbekistan and its neighbors, with Western support unwittingly encouraging aspirations for a regionally dominant role. International calls for the kinds of reforms that are essential in order to reduce the chances of tensions and conflict have already become weaker as leaders focus on tightening regional security through military and other similar means.

John Schoeberlein is a political anthropologist and director of the Forum for Central Asian Studies at Harvard University (since 1993). He also heads the International Crisis Group's Central Asia Project (since 2000), serves as president of the Central Eurasian Studies Society, and led the United Nations Ferghana Valley Development Programme focusing on regional conflict prevention (1998–1999). His research focuses on issues of identity, including nationalism, Islam, ethnicity, community organization, and conflict.

16.2

Policy Recommendations: Some Strategies for Stability

Anara Tabyshalieva

The five nations of Central Asia have had a difficult time since gain-
ing independence in 1991. They have been plagued by violence, po-
litical instability, and economic hardship, and despite some progress
towards the development of democratic institutions, and despite enor-
mous potential from the exploitation of natural resources, the risks of
continued political instability, ethnic violence, and even interstate
conflict remain. Complicating factors are the burgeoning drug trade
and the threat posed by religious extremists. The events of 11 Sep-
tember 2001 and the U.S. antiterrorist action in Afghanistan seriously
changed the security situation in post-Soviet Central Asia. Internally,
democratic institutions and civil society need to be further developed.
External actors can contribute by addressing the severe poverty in the
region, and by working with governmental and nongovernmental ac-
tors to build conflict-prevention and conflict-resolution structures.

In the Soviet era, unrest in Central Asia (Uzbekistan, Kazakhstan, Tajikistan, Kyrgyzstan, and Turkmenistan) was managed and held in check through the highly centralized political structure. Although the Kremlin's propaganda of proletarian internationalism played a somewhat positive role in achieving rapprochement among ethnic groups, it did not provide any mechanism, free from paternalist ideology, guardianship, and strict control from the center, for natural cooperation based on mutual economic interests and horizontal links. The Central Asian states entered the postcommunist era suffering from sharp economic decline and experiencing ethnic and political divisions, a legacy of ethnic and religious violence and Soviet border demarcation.

The five relatively homogeneous states of Central Asia have been unable to prevent conflict in the region. Experts argue that the Central Asian region is sitting on a time bomb that could explode at any moment. International terrorism, violent religious extremism, organized crime, poverty, and drug trafficking represent increasing challenges to the security of Central Asia. Underdevelopment and deprivation, poor governance, overpopulation, scarcity of water, and environmental stress greatly contribute to underlying sources of conflict in Central Asia. The essential differences with regard to cultural backgrounds, level of political and economic development, and degree of transformation and democratization in the five Central Asian states will increase. There are also different perceptions with respect to a conflict-prevention agenda in Central Asia among governments, international organizations, nongovernmental organizations, and scholars. In some cases conflict-prevention measures are perceived by Central Asian governments as a challenge to a state's sovereignty and an opportunity to muzzle any opposition within the country.

Preventing Religious Extremism and Terrorism
Events of 11 September 2001 and the actions of the antiterrorist alliance in Afghanistan opened a new chapter on the security and geopolitical balance of power in the Central Asian region. All five states expressed a readiness to help the alliance; Uzbekistan offered military bases for the U.S. armed forces against Afghanistan. In response, the Taliban leaders declared a *jihad* against Uzbekistan authorities. Soon after, the Taliban regime crumbled but there is still the risk of retaliation by the Islamic Movement of Uzbekistan (IMU) or former Taliban fighters in Central Asian states. One of the most serious fears is that the man-made water reservoirs could be a target of terrorist attacks. All Central Asian countries unprepared for refugee influx have different policies toward refugees. Moreover, Uzbekistan and Turkmenistan have closed their borders to them and stay away from regional cooperation on this issue. Afghan refugees become a Central Asian issue and can be resolved only at a regional level.

Other religious extremists of Hizb ut-Tahrir intend to boost their activities aimed at overthrowing the constitutional order in the Central Asian states. The influence of radical and militant Islam in the Central Asian states and their neighbors poses a number of structural challenges to the region's stability. The emergence of such groups should certainly be viewed in the broader context of global trends, such as the rise of international terrorism and increasing poverty in the region. Meanwhile, Central Asian governments may use the "war against terrorism" as an excuse to further undermine respect for human rights and religious freedom.

There is an alarming tendency to equate Islam with extremism just because a small group of young people are motivated by religion to engage in activities fomenting social unrest, and use religion to justify their terrorist activities. Anti-Islamic propaganda and the oversimplification of the current religious situation in Central Asia may lead to flawed decisionmaking. One evidence of that is the increasing deportation of citizens of neighboring states, mainly traders, and the tightening passport and visa regime that restricts people's movement within Central Asia. Although all Central Asian leaders declare common goals and concerns over terrorism, each country has its own agenda and is engaged in rivalry with its neighbors. The Washington-Tashkent alliance is changing the role of Uzbekistan in the region. For Uzbekistan, it might be a slippery slope not only in the form of further repression of zealous Muslims and other religious believers, but in continuing land-mining and a hurried demarcation of borders with weaker countries such as Tajikistan and Kyrgyzstan. The U.S. engagement in Central Asia is also a serious test for Russian influence in the region.

It is clear that in the Central Asian security arena, small and poor countries are more affected than others; Tajikistan and Kyrgyzstan could strengthen their independence. International and local experts suggest consultations and negotiation with the external opposition in Uzbekistan. Local actors such as governments, NGOs, or regional organizations may be able to deal with small-scale crises with mediation, conciliation, and assistance with negotiations. Central Asian states should encourage joint actions involving the international community focusing on conflict resolution in Afghanistan. The West may also support intervention to end conflict at whatever stages of development such conflicts have reached.

Development of Civil Society

There is an urgent need to enhance the capacity and expertise of NGOs in long-term conflict prevention. All governments in Central Asia are still suspicious of nonstate actors. Therefore they are reluctant to grant a monitoring or "intelligence" function to NGOs working together in a network, even though such a network could provide an effective early warning service and might also serve to direct attention to emerging issues. NGOs in Central Asia can also play important roles in actually intervening in conflict situations to ease tensions, and to provide mediation and facilitation functions. Increasing regional cooperation among state officials and NGOs would be extremely beneficial in progressive political and democratic reforms, including the strengthening of the rule of law, good governance, and respect for human rights.

Joint programs between Central Asian and Western grassroots organizations are of particular value. It is important to cooperate in the area of conflict prevention and human rights. It is only by embracing the idea of universal human rights that ethnic or subethnic group interests can be transcended in the region. The donors and international organizations could use their influence to encourage improvements in legislative procedures and to facilitate moves toward truly law-abiding civic societies that would replace autocratic governmental structures headed by territorial-based clans or families. The work of NGOs in intervening to resolve disputes should be improved, as well as their capacities to provide policy-relevant information and analysis.

There is a real need for effective monitoring and systematic research in the Ferghana Valley, shared by three states. Monitoring, in and of itself, acts as a stabilizing factor in Central Asia. It allows ethnic and social interests to be manifested and leads to reduced tension. The participation and attention of external parties would induce more responsible attitudes from stakeholders on conflict-related issues. To prevent the recurrence of violent conflict in Central

Asia, more research on the causes of such conflicts needs to be conducted, and the necessary theoretical models need to be created to help analyze future eventualities.

The open-minded and well-educated people in nongovernmental and governmental sectors are eager to participate in critical discussions on the problems of democratization and conflict prevention. They may monitor conflict and provide early warning and insight into situations in Tajikistan, the Ferghana Valley, and other areas; provide a neutral forum where key stakeholders can discuss factors contributing to destabilization of the social, ethnic, and religious situation; initiate mediation between conflicting parties (for example, between the IMU and the government of Uzbekistan); initiate education and training for conflict resolution and conflict prevention; advocate press freedom and initiate media activities; monitor elections and prevent electoral violence; and warn of potentially violent situations.

More effective participation of women in the male-dominated decision-making and security processes in Central Asia is essential. Protection, assistance, and training for refugee women, internally displaced women, and children in need of international protection must be articulated and advocated. The gender aspect in the conflict-prevention agenda should not be neglected.

Responding to Poverty

The burden of unresolved economic problems is increasing ethnic and social tension, and could lead to open clashes. Many believe that economic development will reduce interethnic and religious tension. But without radical improvements in the socioeconomic situation, which are highly unlikely in the near future, there is little reason for optimism. Such change is dependent on the manifestation of political will in the Central Asian states. In the light of recent Afghanistan crises and U.S. engagement in Central Asia, the governments of the region must redirect their meagre funds from social needs to defense and security issues. Unemployment and cross-border trade are primary issues to be addressed. The top priority for a policy toward Central Asia should be job-creation programs. Active microcredit programs to small and medium-size farms are one effective way to respond to unemployment and social tension. A majority of the unemployed are young people; a family-planning policy could also lead to stabilization in population numbers and stop uncontrolled growth. The concept of ethnic cleansing remains embedded in the collective consciousness of some groups, and could become a grim reality if the economic and social situation in the region deteriorates. The threat of separatist and ethnic violence exists in all the Central Asian states; the monoethnic upper echelon must learn to listen to the voices of national minorities to prevent both discrimination based on ethnicity and actual ethnic conflict.

Fostering Regional Cooperation for Conflict Prevention

The end of Soviet rule has given new impetus to changing relationships within and among Central Asian states. In this new situation, as these republics deal with each other for the first time without strict control from Moscow, they must invent a way to live next to each other. The development of new horizontal relations has been uneven and incoherent. Regional efforts to cooperate for the sustainable development of Central Asia are often fragile and not adequate to combat a process of disintegration. Despite the geographic and economic interdependency of the Ferghana Valley states, this tendency toward continuing disintegration continues to plague the region.

Interstate frictions over trade, custom fees, borders, water and energy distribution, old debts, and different levels of democratic and economic reforms may only increase. The Central Asian states have failed to make their national currencies mutually convertible, using U.S. dollars in trade. The problems of resources, especially the shortage of water, seem to be the most serious issues confronting this huge area. Other problems include the absence of developed economic concepts of cooperation, lack of cooperation in food security, and inadequate mechanisms to implement the numerous agreements among the Central Asian states. Despite numerous meetings and declarations of the Central Asian politicians, a cold war over custom fees with both an economic and political character is assuming new unpredictable forms.

There are many sites subject to dispute along the borders of the Central Asian states. Experts believe with further deterioration of the irrigation systems and mismanagement of the water distribution systems, the number of local conflicts will increase. Environmental problems are also a serious threat to stability in Central Asia. The leaders of the five Central Asian republics still have a unique opportunity to develop truly effective (cooperative as opposed to competitive) regional organizations centered on the management and use of regional water supplies. Conflict over natural resources, especially water and land, is, in addition, complicated by different styles of political leadership in the post-Soviet era and different levels of economic development in each country. In such a conflict-prone environment, it is clear that entirely new forms of regional cooperation are required to avoid the kind of flare-ups that have occurred in the Ferghana Valley and in Tajikistan. It is vitally important to build the capacity of regional governmental and nongovernmental organizations to deal with conflict prevention at various levels.

The emergence of intergovernmental organizations such as the Central Asian Economic Union (CAEU) provides a positive example of cooperation. Security, water and energy management, transport and communication, customs checkpoints, and mutual payments will all be addressed by the CAEU. The conflict management role of the CAEU could be strengthened. The Central Asian states should create a mechanism for making common decisions, focusing on common ecological and environmental problems. Obvious common interests such as road construction and drug control will remain the most potentially fruitful avenues for regional coordination in Central Asia. For example, all Central Asian countries could benefit if these landlocked states were to establish a consortium for the creation of transcontinental connections.

Attacking Narco-Trafficking

The total value of the drug trade in Central Asia is not known, but probably now constitutes the largest national income stream in Tajikistan and is close to that in Kyrgyzstan. Both opposition and official branches of the Tajik government receive money from the drug trade, as do some law enforcement officers, customs officials, and military officers in other countries, according to local informants. It is not primarily an urban phenomenon, but occurs mostly in the mountainous rural areas where other economic alternatives are scarce. The drug trade is fueled by the poverty prevailing in the most neglected regions. The Ferghana Valley is a center of such activity.

Presently, large numbers of people all across Central Asia are involved in the production and trafficking of narcotics, and state structures seem powerless to prevent this kind of "regional cooperation" and "ethnic accord." During severe downturns in the regional economies, more and more people turn to growing opium poppies and cannabis. The growing power of the "Mafia network" means that criminals will increase their influence in political and economic decisionmaking throughout the region. The accumulation of revenue and weapons from the operation of these criminal networks could be a serious threat to ethnic stability in the Ferghana Valley, the site of considerable narcotics transshipment. If the Central Asian states and international community are serious about eliminating drug trafficking and drug use, they must address the economic issues that have resulted in the mass involvement of unemployed people in this business. In affected regions, local governmental and nongovernmental stakeholders, and international actors should work together to attack the worldwide network of the narco-mafia.

Reinforcing the Peace Process in Tajikistan

The war in Tajikistan, one of the world's poorest countries, was the most destructive in the region. Tajikistan's government is still unable to assert control over parts of its territory, with private paramilitary groups operating within some parts of Tajikistan or from across the borders with Kyrgyzstan and Uzbekistan. The peace process in Tajikistan is an encouraging example of how to overcome a military conflict involving divergent interests within one society, and to gradually establish a culture of peaceful political cooperation. Tajik society still needs to recover from the consequences of the civil war, and to now address with determination the issue of the postconflict reconstruction and rehabilitation processes in order to provide a basis for stable reforms. Job-creating programs in Tajikistan can contribute to stabilization of the situation and the integration of military men into postconflict reconstruction. The uncontrolled presence of small arms and light weapons, inherited from the civil war in Tajikistan, hampers security in the country as well as in the neighboring states of Kyrgyzstan and Uzbekistan. Tajikistan should disarm and integrate the paramilitary groups in order to prevent the proliferation of small arms and light weapons. It is clear that because of the weakness of the government and economy, Tajikistan is not able, on its own, to tackle the consequences of the war, such as the illegal paramilitary groups, the accumulation of arms, drug trafficking, a porous Afghan-Tajik border, and many other problems that should be resolved by appropriate collective measures. The international community should provide assistance in designing appropriate collective measures to address these problems.

Anticipating Militarization of the Caspian Subregion

The interest of the Western countries in the oil and gas resources of the Caspian Basin is great, and the natural resources in Central Asia are also bound to become increasingly important to China and India. One can expect growing competition among regional as well as several extraregional players for access to the vast oil and gas reserves thought to be in the Caspian Sea Basin. Among the major obstacles to the use of the Caspian oil and gas resources is a dispute over the existing Caspian Sea legal regime and the divergent approaches to its resolution supported by the various Caspian Sea states (Azerbaijan, Iran, Kazakhstan, Russia, and Turkmenistan).

Transportation of oil and gas from the Caspian Basin to outside consumers passing through Russia is another problem. An inevitable conflict of interests among the littoral states is developing, spurred in part by growing involvement of the United States, Russia, and some European and Asian countries. Moreover, the security of oil and gas transportation routes passing across or located close to zones of local conflict is increasingly dependent on the resolution of these conflicts.

Some experts predict an increase in the militarization of the Caspian Basin countries, which would lead to further interstate tensions in the subregion. The profits from the oil industry could benefit a small, privileged elite. Those oil dollars could also lead to further arms proliferation, and nobody excludes the possibility that new conflicts among the Caspian Basin states could develop. Clearly, the completion of pipelines in the future will result in a very different political and economic situation, as well as a new security climate in the whole Central Asian region.

Increasing External Aid and International Intervention

The millions of dollars invested by the West in technical assistance and building democratic institutions in Central Asia have not been wasted. All five states are full-fledged members of the Organization for Security and Cooperation in Europe (OSCE). They have adopted the OSCE commitments and the region is an integral part of the OSCE space. Although Central Asian governments have failed to implement many of the recommendations with respect to fair elections that have been offered by the OSCE and other international organizations, the nations of Central Asia have made some slow progress in the field of democratic reform in the last ten years.

Recent conflicts in the region indicate that the United Nations, the OSCE organizations, and other international actors need to be better equipped to practice conflict-prevention activities in the Central Asian region. At the same time, in the context of conflict prevention, the OSCE needs to cooperate with other multilateral institutions. International and regional organizations can help in building the institutional framework for electoral systems, party systems, legislative structures, government, and NGOs. However, institutional competition between international organizations, and a lack of cooperation or coordination among these organizations, are important impediments to conflict prevention in the region. The governments of the Central Asian states should stimulate donor activity on conflict prevention in the region.

The UN, Bretton Woods Institution, OSCE, and other international organizations should deal more systematically with the regional dimension of the conflict-prevention agenda in Central Asia, fostering economic and political reforms. The painful lessons in Tajikistan, Afghanistan, and the Ferghana Valley have brought the structural deficiencies of the international organization to light. To prevent conflict in Central Asia, the international community should give more priority to a conflict-prevention agenda and set up a coalition of key actors, to include governmental and nongovernmental actors, scholars, religious leaders, and other prominent persons. The international and local communities should learn more from recent experience and reinforce their awareness, build coalitions, and design their agenda within a broader regional context of conflict prevention. The international organizations and donor countries could provide robust support for conflict prevention, contributing more to regional cooperation in Central Asia among governmental and nongovernmental actors. Conditionality could be more widely used to encourage adherence to democratic and economic reforms, respect for human rights, religious freedom, protection of minority rights, and the encouragement of regional cooperation.

It is likely that Russia, the United States, China, and Japan will remain engaged in Central Asian conflict prevention. Still, there is no outside power sufficiently interested in the region to make major investments in its security. Their interests are often very limited, focusing on the potential of this region to cause instability in "more important" areas through the drug trade or the spread of Islamist radicalism.

The effectiveness of conflict-prevention efforts depends to a large extent on the actions undertaken by many key actors on their own and in collaboration with other key actors. But it would be wrong to embrace a one-size-fits-all approach to conflict prevention in Central Asia. Of course no single measure can completely eliminate tensions in the region and prevent conflict, but it is possible to counteract and drift toward destabilization, to minimize the risk of ethnic cleansing, and in so doing, to save the lives of potential victims. However, compared to the level of instability and economic hardship, the current efforts of the various stakeholders to improve the situation and prevent conflict are woefully inadequate. The Central Asian region can serve as an incubator for a more peaceful future if proper efforts are made, or it can become a place of disaster for the millions of people who live there.

Anara Tabyshalieva is director of the Institute for Regional Studies (an NGO in Kyrgyzstan). She was a senior fellow at the United States Institute of Peace, a visiting scholar at the UN University in Tokyo, and Dorothy Cadberry fellow at Selly Oak College in Birmingham. She has a number of publications, including The Challenge of Regional Cooperation in Central Asia: Preventing Ethnic Conflict in the Ferghana Valley *(1999) and* Faith in Turkestan *(1993).*

16.3

The Ferghana Valley: In the Midst of a Host of Crises

Randa M. Slim

The borders of the three countries within the Ferghana Valley were artificially drawn between 1924 and 1936 by the Soviet authorities in Moscow, with Tajiks, Uzbeks, and Kyrgyz living on all sides. This is one of at least six major sources of present tension in the valley. Most international attention focuses on the threat of Islamic extremism. However, official attempts at conflict management through repressive measures and crackdowns against Islamic groups and civil society organizations are fueling rather than dampening people's anger and frustration. Effective conflict prevention might still push the Ferghana Valley away from the precipice to which it is now heading.

Throughout Central Asia's history, the Ferghana Valley provided an important center for merchants trading with China and the Mediterranean. A branch of the Great Silk Road linking China to the Middle East, the Mediterranean, and Europe passed through the Ferghana Valley. Initially part of the Timurid empire, after Timur's death the Ferghana Valley became a single political unit under the Kokand Khanate from the late sixteenth to the midnineteenth century. Tsarist Russia's advance into Central Asia by the midnineteenth century was fueled by "expansionist imperial policy, ambition to rule the entire continent east of Moscow, and unrelenting economic pressure from merchants, bankers, and industrialists."[1] Russian merchants were interested that Moscow secured supplies of Central Asian cotton. With the Bolshevik revolution and the introduction of Soviet rule into Central Asia, the social and political relations in the region were fundamentally altered. Prior to their assuming control of the region, people in Central Asia identified themselves in terms of their region and locale, religious practices, and family or clan. The Soviet policies in the region "precipitated nationalities from a range of less codified identities that had existed before, giving them their own distinct literary languages written in variants of the Cyrillic alphabet."[2] Borders were artificially drawn in such a way that Tajiks, Uzbeks, and Kyrgyz were found on all sides. This enabled the

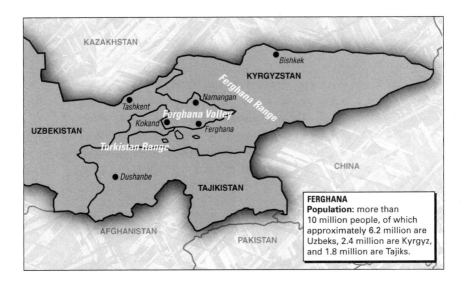

FERGHANA
Population: more than
10 million people, of which
approximately 6.2 million are
Uzbeks, 2.4 million are Kyrgyz,
and 1.8 million are Tajiks.

Soviet authorities to continuously be called upon by the people in the region to help them manage conflicts that were bound to emerge as a result of these artificial divisions.

Home to more than 10 million people, the Ferghana Valley is divided among three Central Asian republics: Uzbekistan, Tajikistan, and Kyrgyzstan. About 60 percent of the valley's territory lies in Uzbekistan (4.3 percent of Uzbek territory), 25 percent in Tajikistan (18.2 percent of state territory), and the remaining 15 percent in Kyrgyzstan (42.2 percent of state territory). The Ferghana Valley lies in the heart of the Tien-Shan range with the Syr-Darya River flowing through it. It is 350 kilometers long and 100 kilometers wide. There are seven administrative provinces in the valley—three are Uzbek (Andijan, Ferghana, and Namangan), three Kyrgyz (Batken, Osh, and Jalal Abad), and one Tajik (Sughd, formerly Leninabad). Complicating the boundary issue in the valley is the presence of five small enclaves.

From the beginning, the Muslim people of Central Asia deeply mistrusted the Soviet ideology. Islam arrived in Central Asia in the eighth century and has since then played an important role in the cultural, social, and political development of the Ferghana Valley. In February 1918, the Basmachi Muslim rebel movement was created in the aftermath of an aggression by Soviet troops against the population of Kokand. The Basmachis were local military groups also led by *mullahs* who tried to overthrow Soviet rule and the old regional political elites in the name of an Islamic Turkistan. The Basmachi rebellion lasted until 1924 in most of Central Asia and was sustained in many parts of the Ferghana Valley until 1928. In 1991, following the collapse of the Soviet Union, the different states of Central Asia declared their independence and later introduced their national currencies.

Today, the Ferghana Valley remains the part of Central Asia with the highest level of Muslim observance. Although the level of knowledge of Islamic theology and *shari'a* is quite limited among the general population, this has been increasing in the last several years. Seventy-five years of Soviet rule and constant attempts at suppressing Islam have in a small way paid off. What now remains strong in the valley is a ritualistic form of Islam. The Ferghana Valley is also the region in Central Asia that suffered most from independence, due to the imposition of territorial borders in an area that was economically interwoven during the Soviet times. As noted by an International Crisis Group report, "What were once internal administrative borders, across which flowed lively social and economic exchange and across which individual collective farms or villages had expanded, became new national borders."[3]Acute conflicts over water and land resources, old ethnic rivalries, and steep decline in people's living standards make this region most prone to violence.

This is a quick review of some of the conflicts that have occurred in the past thirteen years, 1989–2001.

1989
Ethnic clashes occurred in the Uzbekistan part of the valley between ethnic Uzbeks and Meskhetian Turks. Meskhetian Turks belong to a small ethnic group deported from the Caucasus to Uzbekistan by Stalin. One hundred and three people died and over a thousand were reported wounded. The pretext for the fighting was a quarrel in the local market in the Kuvasay bazaar in the Ferghana district over the price of strawberries. Most of the Meskhetian residents had to flee the valley back to Russia and other Central Asian countries.

Ethnic clashes also occurred in Samarkandek (on the Kyrgyzstan part of the valley) between Tajiks and Kyrgyz over land distribution and water allocation. Several people were killed and injured. Violent tensions have also occurred between Tajik refugees and local Kyrgyz residents in the Batken province. Tensions erupted over water allocation.

1990
Riots occurred between Kyrgyz and Uzbeks in Osh and Uzgen, Kyrgyzstan. Hundreds were killed. The causes of this conflict involved control over land and housing, the underrepresentation of ethnic Uzbeks in local and regional authority structures (while Uzbeks at the time made up 29 percent of the region's population), and demands for greater Uzbek autonomy as it relates to preservation of Uzbek culture and language.

1991–1992
The conflict involved a takeover of the Namangan regional administration by an unofficial militant organization called Adolat. The takeover was a protest by the local devout Muslim group against the official clergy's decision to endorse Islam

Karimov's presidential candidacy. A wave of arrests followed the takeover and most of Adolat's supporters fled to Tajikistan, Afghanistan, and Iran.

1996–1998

A series of riots, protests, and eventually a military coup attempt occurred in Leninabad (recently renamed Soghd), Tajikistan. In May 1996, violent demonstrations were held in Khujand and Öra-Teppa demanding the removal of unpopular local officials. In April 1997, prison riots occurred in Khujand prison that led the deaths of a large number of prisoners. On 30 April 1997, Tajik president Imomali Rakhmonov was injured along with seventy others in an assassination attempt in Khujand. In November 1998, rebels led by ethnic Uzbek leader Mahmud Khudoiberdiev crossed into Leninabad from Uzbekistan, seized control of the security installations in Khujand, and occupied a regional airport in Chkalovsk. The main reason behind these events was the growing dissatisfaction by the Khujandis over the Kölabi-run government's attempts to undermine the northern region's traditional role in Tajikistan's political life. The Tajik government accused Uzbek president Islam Karimov of supporting the rebels.

A series of assassinations of police and local officials in Namangan, in the Uzbekistan sector of the valley, led to a massive crackdown in Namangan and Andijan including hundreds of arrests of suspected Islamic terrorists. The Uzbek government charged "foreign-trained Wahhabis" with responsibility for the assassinations.

1999

In August 1999, rebels crossed from Tajikistan into the Batken district in Kyrgyzstan, kidnapped foreign nationals, and engaged in clashes with the Kyrgyz and Uzbek troops. It is now believed that the rebel group included members of the Islamic Movement of Uzbekistan (IMU), an Uzbek opposition Islamic group and former Tajik opposition fighters. They demanded a free corridor through the territory of Kyrgyzstan to Uzbekistan. The rebels eventually released the hostages after obtaining a ransom.

On 16 February 1999, six car bombs targeting Uzbekistani government facilities exploded in different parts of Tashkent, Uzbekistan's capital, killing sixteen persons and wounding more than a hundred others. Uzbek official circles blamed the attacks on the IMU. The government used these bombing incidents as an excuse to launch a crackdown on the militants in the Ferghana Valley. Eleven people were sentenced to death and more than 120 others received long prison sentences. Despite the official version for these incidents, it is now strongly believed these bombings were part of an internal power struggle in Uzbekistan, and were aimed at shoring up the influence of one clique in the ruling elite.

In November 1999, clashes occurred in Yangiabad, in the Uzbekistan part of the Ferghana Valley. A group of fifteen to twenty gunmen also believed to be members of the IMU killed six people in clashes with the Uzbek security and Interior Ministry troops in the mountainous areas around Angren. The gunmen were killed. Violence erupted over water allocation between Tajik refugees and local Kyrgyz residents in the villages of Chet-Kyzil and Bai-Karabak in the Batken province.

2000

Violent tensions occurred in Samarkandek, Kyrgyzstan, over housing and land allocation pitting Kyrgyz against Tajik villagers.

In August 2000 small units of IMU rebels raided small villages over a wide area along the Uzbek, Kyrgyz, and Tajik borders. The rebels are now believed to be stationed in parts of Tajikistan and the highlands of southern Kyrgyzstan.

2001

Under pressure from the international community, Tajikistan expelled the IMU militants from Tavildara in the Karategin Valley where the group had reportedly been based for several years. The militants along with their leaders were escorted to Afghanistan.[4]

Skirmishes have occurred in July between Kyrgyz government forces and IMU militants. That summer's raids were occurring nearer to Kyrgyz-Uzbek border regions, and indicate a shift in IMU tactics.[5] IMU members seem now to have settled among the local population in these border areas inside Kyrgyzstan.

Conflict Dynamics

The three countries sharing the Ferghana Valley are in the midst of a host of crises. A legitimacy crisis undermines the people's confidence in their leaders' ability to represent their interests in a fair and inclusive manner. An economic crisis worsens that prevents these countries' leadership from meeting the basic needs of their population, thus giving way to the rise and eventual dominance of an informal or shadow economy. A security crisis, which causes these governments to divert scarce resources away from the development field and toward the military sector, still plagues the area's government. And finally, a mounting crisis of traditional values that have always governed these societies and by which traditional methods of decisionmaking in communities such as the council of elders have worked is of growing concern. These crises present the background against which we must view and analyze past and potential future conflicts in the Ferghana Valley. As Lubin and Rubin note, conflicts in the Ferghana Valley were "caused less by ethnic animosities than by a mix of elements—economic, social, political—embedded in a complex political and ethnic strata that formed the fault lines along which these conflicts eventually exploded."[6] Most analysts focus on seven sources of tension in the valley: borders, overpopulation and "creeping migration," water, unemployment, Islamic militant groups, ethnicity, and a criminal cluster including drug trafficking, corruption, and organized crime.

Borders

Stalin drew the borders in the region in the 1920s, based on political and economic considerations and without respect for ethnic balance (many different groups were deported by Stalin, which complicated the border issues). These lines had little practical impact for most of the valley's residents when they were all part of the Soviet Union. Overnight with independence, these lines became the international borders of three sovereign countries, thus disrupting the ordinary flow of people, goods, and trade in the Ferghana Valley. Numerous border posts have been established between the different parts of the valley. As the United Nations Development Program/International Labor Organization social-policy review paper (1995–1996) noted, "The borders, being artificial, created ethnic groups and nationalities, not the other way around, and these divisions were perpetuated when the five Central Asian republics became independent. Where once there was unity, today there is national division and rivalry, at least potentially."

In response to growing IMU activity, Uzbekistan has imposed a visa regime and moreover mined its borders. Kyrgyzstan has also mined its borders with Tajikistan and blown up mountain passes in order to make them impenetrable by IMU militants. These actions make people's daily lives extremely difficult. They disrupt trade routes and hamper cross-border economic activities. By February 2001, it was reported that border mines had killed thirty civilians along the Tajik-Uzbek border. Border guards' abusive behavior and corruption indirectly foment interethnic tensions as blame for their behavior is displaced on neighboring villages of similar ethnic backgrounds. Local leadership in the valley is pushing their respective national government to take tough stands on the border issues and is applying increasing pressure on them to solve this problem.

There are also currently a number of border disputes among the three countries sharing the different parts of the valley that need to be addressed within some forms of multilateral or bilateral official mechanisms. There are close to 140 unresolved border disputes between Uzbekistan and Kyrgyzstan. In April 2001, reports of a land swap between the two countries, enabling Uzbekistan to establish a land corridor to its Sokh enclave located in Kyrgyzstan's Batken district, drew ire from the local population and antagonized the Kyrgyz parliament.[7]

Overpopulation and "Creeping Migration"

With a young and rapidly growing population in a small region with limited arable land, the Ferghana Valley faces tremendous demographic pressures. The highest population density in Central Asia is now found in the valley—up to 250 inhabitants per square kilometer compared with the average of 14 inhabitants per square kilometer in Central Asia. Observers are witnessing a rural exodus to Osh in Kyrgyzstan, especially from the Batken province and among ethnic Kyrgyz who reside in Tajikistan, to Khujand in Tajikistan from the Jirgatal and Murghab regions, and to Andijan, Ferghana, and Namangan provinces in Uzbekistan. There is also a brain drain in the valley as Russians and Russian-speaking residents are emigrating to Russia and other Commonwealth of Independent States countries due to unemployment and deteriorating living conditions in the valley.

Competition for land is also rising as a result of demographic pressures. This problem is most acute in the case of Kyrgyzstan. This competition is taking on an ethnic dimension. There is a "creeping migration" phenomenon as Tajik citizens cross borders and try to purchase land and build houses on Kyrgyz farmland. They usually buy the land from Kyrgyz farmers only to discover later that the sale was illegal. This has lately caused a number of small-scale violent clashes in southern Kyrgyzstan among Kyrgyz and ethnic Tajiks who live in these border communities. Similar problems are arising among ethnic Uzbeks and Kyrgyz in the Osh region. In the Uzbekistan part of the valley, it is being claimed that land is being reallocated to Uzbeks to the disadvantage of ethnic Kyrgyz and Tajiks who live in the area.

Water

Water is a cause of many of the small-scale conflicts that are currently unfolding in the valley, especially between northern Tajikistan and southern Kyrgyzstan. During Soviet times, the different parts of the valley were made interdependent through a infrastructural network of water, energy, and transportation lines. The three countries "often have contrary needs for scarce water supplies: Kyrgyzstan uses one of the main rivers, the Syr-Darya, for energy production, but Kazakhstan and Uzbekistan need the water for irrigation of their large cotton and fruit crops."[8] In 2000, agricultural production fell by 30 percent due mainly to limited water resources. Though water allocation is discussed each year in bilateral summits and agreements, the latter are often violated. Most water reservoirs are season-regulated and 90 percent of their water is for irrigation. Both Tajikistan and Kyrgyzstan, while water-rich, are dependent on imported electricity from Uzbekistan and Turkmenistan. This dependence has created many tensions among the three countries. On 23 July 2001, President Akayev of Kyrgyzstan signed a new law, "On the Interstate Use of Water Installations, Water Resources and Hydro Facilities in the Kyrgyz Republic," seeking to impose charges on countries such as Uzbekistan for Kyrgyz water usage. This new law will further weaken the already frail relationship between Kyrgyzstan and Uzbekistan.

Water scarcity is further exacerbated by the inefficient use of water in farming in the valley—the malfunctioning and in some cases totally destroyed drainage system and irrigation channels built by the Soviet Union. This has led to periodic flooding, rising water tables, and increased soil salinity, thus directly contributing to increased ethnic tensions among border communities.

Unemployment

Unemployment is high in the Ferghana Valley, particularly among youth. The collapse of the Soviet Union had a major impact on the economies of Central

Asia, mainly in depriving the region of its network of suppliers and distributors and markets that used to be scattered throughout the former Soviet Union. Many industries in the valley are now idle. According to unofficial reports, the unemployment rate in the Batken province in the Kyrgyz part of the valley runs from 50 to 80 percent. It is estimated that 35 percent of the workforce in the Uzbekistan part of the valley is unemployed, including the majority of those under the age of twenty-five. An unemployed and hungry youth is readily attracted to popular movements and ready to engage in criminal and violent activities. It has been reported that the unemployment problem has taken on an ethnic character. For example, in the Kyrgyzstan part of the valley, it has been observed that the rate of unemployment is higher among ethnic Uzbeks than Kyrgyz residents.[9]

Islamic Militant Groups

Islam has always been an inalienable part of the Central Asian culture, and more so in the Ferghana Valley. Although the Soviet Union tried over seventy-five years of its rule to co-opt local clergy and control them, underground Islamic networks that survived the Soviet times have now come to the surface and are playing a major role in the growth of militant Islamic groups in the valley. The two largest underground opposition Islamic movements known to be currently operating in the valley are the Islamic Movement of Uzbekistan (IMU) and the Hizb ut-Tahrir (Islamic Liberation Party). They both appear to be pan-Islamists with a vision for creating an Islamic caliphate in the historical region of Turkestan based on *shari'a* law. They are ideologically influenced by the Wahhabi Islamic tradition of Saudi Arabia, though a leader of Hizb ut-Tahrir has recently claimed that though they agree on the goals, they differ with the Wahhabi movement over the means to achieve their goals. The latter believe in a guerrilla war and the creation of an Islamic army to do that while the former espouses a peaceful, long-term strategy of ideological work at the community level.

Hizb ut-Tahrir was founded in Palestine in the 1950s and remained underground during the Soviet times.[10] It operates in small five-man cells, is highly secretive, and believes in peaceful political change through a mass revolt against the Central Asian regimes, while not excluding the possibility of using violent means if repression continues. The party has growing support in Tajikistan, Uzbekistan, and Kyrgyzstan. Recently, more than twenty followers were sentenced to different prison terms in Khujand, Tajikistan. The IMU core leadership consists of former members of banned Islamic parties in Uzbekistan who had to flee the Ferghana Valley to Tajikistan, Afghanistan, and Iran in 1992 during the harsh crackdown on the opposition by Uzbekistan's government. IMU members fought with the United Tajik opposition during Tajikistan's civil war (1992–1997). When the Tajik civil war ended in 1997, the Uzbek fighters refused to lay down their arms, claiming that their goal now is to engage in an armed struggle to topple the Uzbek government and establish an Islamic state in Uzbekistan.

Until recently, it was believed that IMU members maintained their bases in eastern Tajikistan, from where it is convenient to pass into Kyrgyzstan and Uzbekistan. Following their incursions into the Batken region in Kyrgyzstan in 2000 and 2001, and under strong pressure from neighboring Central Asian states, the government of Tajikistan is reported to have expelled the IMU's leader and some of his followers, who were flown aboard Russian helicopters to Afghanistan. It is now clear that the IMU did receive some support from the Taliban in Afghanistan and it is reported that other funders included Osama bin Laden and private Islamic groups in Pakistan and Saudi Arabia.[11] As pointed out earlier, skirmishes in July 2001 between IMU and the Kyrgyz government forces point out that militants are now operating inside Kyrgyzstan. Strategically, this tactical shift indicates that the IMU leadership now regards Kyrgyzstan as a military objective in its own right, aiming to embroil it in a wider regional conflict. Many analysts tend to argue that Islamic militancy now represents the most serious threat to stability in the region. Others feel, however, that it is the harsh repressive regimes of Central Asia and the economic crisis in the region rather than Islamic militancy that are the real cause of instability in the region. Furthermore, an International Crisis Group report correctly argues that "the [Islamic] insurgency is a reflection of the economic hardships and discontent affecting a part of the population and a reaction to the severe crackdown on Islamic activities which has pitted observant but otherwise moderate Muslims against their state."[12]

Ethnicity

A gap exists between the ethnic divisions and the political boundaries in the Ferghana Valley. For example, 700,000 ethnic Uzbeks live today in southern Kyrgyzstan, 300,000 ethnic Kyrgyz reside in Uzbekistan, and more than 1.4 million ethnic Uzbeks live in Tajikistan. The threat of interethnic tensions is more likely in southern Kyrgyzstan. Osh residents still remember the 1990 clashes between ethnic Uzbeks and Kyrgyz. Close to 30 percent of Kyrgyzstan's southern provinces are non-Kyrgyz. The largest minority group consists of Uzbeks (close to 15 percent), while Russians and Tajiks make up about 2–3 percent each. Despite Kyrgyzstan's publicly touted efforts toward diminishing the importance of ethnicity, ethnic Uzbeks in their part of the valley believe they have been increasingly discriminated against in allocation of official position, access to redistributed land, and access to other employment opportunities in the private sector such as the bazaar. It is also an alarming trend that many of the resource-based conflicts in the valley, and in particular in the Kyrgyz-Tajik border communities, are being expressed along ethnic lines. It has been noted that there is "sufficient tension based on discrimination, differential access to resources and the memory of past conflict to make the reoccurrence of such clashes a distinct possibility."[13]

Criminal Cluster: Drug Trafficking, Corruption, and Organized Crime

Drug trafficking and criminal activities are some of the main factors contributing to present and future instability in the Ferghana Valley. Drug trafficking has grown as a business as the economy in the region has declined. Drought, the wars in Afghanistan and Tajikistan, and the absence of economic and social reforms have plunged the region into poverty. This phenomenon is aided by the informal economy known as the "shadow economy" that has developed over decades in the former Soviet sphere including Central Asia. The national governments in Kyrgyzstan and Uzbekistan claim that the drug trade is also funding the radical Islamic movements operating in the valley, including the IMU. There is yet no firm evidence to support this claim.

Drug cultivation, production, and transportation have started to create a culture of consumption in the valley, especially among the unemployed youth. Today's typical drug addict in the valley is aged between thirteen and twenty-two and is unemployed. More women are becoming drug addicts as they are being used as couriers. The fear is that the increasing drug business will in the future contribute to further corruption of the power and security structures in this region. On 2 March 2001, a former Tajik embassy official was convicted of carrying 68 kilograms of heroin.

There is an ongoing intense competition among various criminal groups for control of the best trafficking routes. According to Agence France-Presse, over a hundred new organized criminal drug-smuggling groups have sprung up in Tajikistan alone. One explanation for the murder of Tajikistan deputy interior minister Habib Sanginov on 11 April 2001 relates to intensifying competition among Tajikistan's drug lords. According to analysts, the greatest struggle now centers on the road running northeast from Tajikistan's capital, Dushanbe, connecting the Garm region with southern Kyrgyzstan.[14] At present, large numbers of people are involved in these activities and the local state structures throughout the valley seem helpless at this point in containing this trade. Though one analyst points out that the drug trade in the Ferghana Valley presents one of the few examples of "coordinated interethnic cooperation," one might speculate whether in the future competing drug gangs will engage in turf wars that might take on an interethnic character.[15]

Official Conflict Management

National governments sharing the Ferghana Valley have in the past used and are now using different strategies and tactics for tackling sources of tension in the valley. This section will focus on the official attempts to deal with three major sources of tension: the economy (including land and unemployment), water, and Islamic militancy.

On the economic front, all three states have officially embraced economic reform policies. However, the implementation of such policies has varied in practice from one country to another, and within each country from one region to another. As far as the Ferghana Valley is concerned, these economic reforms have had a negative impact. As noted by Lubin and Rubin, "Customs controls, the establishment of separate currencies, and differences in rates and means of economic liberalization are all policy decisions that tear at the fabric that has woven the valley together over the course of centuries."[16] The imposition of customs controls, especially by Uzbekistan, has impeded cross-border regional trade and exacerbated corruption and given border guards free reign to make people's lives very difficult.

Land privatization has proceeded slowly in both the Uzbek and Kyrgyz parts of the valley. In the Uzbek part of the valley, "privatized" collective farms are still required to produce cotton and wheat for sale exclusively to the state at well below market prices. In southern Kyrgyzstan, privatization has proceeded slowly given the history of the 1990 ethnic rioting in Osh over land allocation policies. There is a fear among Kyrgyz that ethnic Uzbeks will use their economic advantage to buy more Kyrgyz land, while Uzbeks fear that local officials in the valley will use the privatization process as a pretext to chase them out of prime agricultural land. The industrial sector is not faring better in the Ferghana Valley. Similar to the rest of Central Asia, industries (both primary and secondary) need to be overhauled and restructured. Local firms lack investment funds and an efficient infrastructure. Potential large-scale foreign investment is being withheld, especially in the Uzbek part of the valley, due to that country's restrictive economic policies. These economic woes are further compounded by the lack of good transportation links between the different regions in the valley and their respective national centers. It is fair to say that the valley's main economic activities remain centered on agriculture, and the sector is in bad need of reform.

As far as water reform is concerned, the major obstacles to effective management lie mainly in the lack of political will to tackle such a complex issue. This holds especially on the part of the regional and local authorities that derive much of their power from their control over water allocation in their respective localities. In addition, any successful attempts at dealing with water-based conflict will require an input of funds and expertise that are currently lacking in the region. These are necessary to overhaul a water supply system that is in sore need of restructuring and in some cases total rebuilding.

Conflicts over water resources manifest themselves in the valley at both the national and the regional/local levels. Some of the resource-based conflicts at the local level are in some cases amenable to a localized, affordable solution that need not involve the national authorities. Many of these conflicts over water have taken on an ethnic character at the local level. In southern Kyrgyzstan, many of the local conflicts over water pit Kyrgyz villagers against ethnic Tajiks or Tajik refugees living in Kyrgyzstan. They also involve border communities in southern Kyrgyzstan and northern Tajikistan. The potential of these local conflicts to escalate into widespread ethnic rioting in these parts of the valley is high, but are easily preventable with a site-specific, intercommunal, low-cost intervention. One of the few success stories in the Ferghana Valley has been a project funded by the Swiss Development Agency that focuses on local resource-based conflicts. This project will be presented in detail in the following section on multi-track diplomacy.

At the national level, water reform must be addressed within the framework of a multi-issue, multiparty negotiation process linking border, water, and energy issues. A multiparty process is essential due to the fact that the Amu Darya and Syr Darya basins go through all six countries in the region—Afghanistan, Kazakhstan, Kyrgyzstan, Tajikistan, Turkmenistan, and Uzbekistan. Due to the crisscrossed infrastructure links set up by the Russian Federation among its former republics in Central Asia, countries in the Ferghana Valley are interdependent in the supply of resources such as water and gas. Uzbekistan is totally dependent on Kyrgyzstan and Tajikistan for irrigation water, while the latter depend on their gas supplies from the former. Economic relations among the three countries have been lately the subject of tit-for-tat games over these resources. While bilateral swap agreements on water resources and energy (e.g., the agreement between Kyrgyzstan and Uzbekistan signed in December 2000) have averted major crises in the short term, they have proven to be dysfunctional in the long term due to complex political and economic problems between the upstream and downstream countries. Uzbekistan has imposed a gas embargo on Kyrgyzstan in winter 2000–2001 in order to coerce the latter into settling a territorial dispute over the Sokh enclave. To compensate for gas shortages, Kyrgyzstan diverted water resources into hydroelectric power generation, resulting in decreasing water supplies to Uzbek farms across the border.

A regional, integrative approach to dealing with resource-based conflicts has so far been rejected by Uzbekistan. The latter has also rejected international assistance in helping the countries reach consensus on a region-wide water management system. It fears that outside intervention will increase the bargaining power of the two weaker parties in this relationship, i.e., Kyrgyzstan and Tajikistan. Water is the one resource that gives Kyrgyzstan, and to some extent Tajikistan, leverage over its powerful neighbor. Uzbekistan's position has been that all Central Asia's water resources are "common wealth" that must be provided by the upstream countries, Kyrgyzstan and Tajikistan, at no cost. Kyrgyzstan has proceeded to defend its water resources. In March 2001, Kyrgyzstan declared that it was ready to provide 750 million cubic meters of water instead of the previously agreed-upon 2.3 billion cubic meters. Combined with the drought that has plagued the region for the last two years, this is having a devastating impact on Uzbekistan's cotton harvest. As stated earlier, President Akaev has signed on 23 July 2001 a law that seeks to impose charges for water usage in line with world prices. Both Tajikistan and Kyrgyzstan have proceeded to decrease their dependence on Uzbekistan for their energy supplies. The Kyrgyz government hopes to invest in the building of new hydropower stations over the next four years. The hope is that by 2005, Kyrgyzstan will produce enough electricity to meet its domestic needs. Tajikistan is making strong efforts to attract foreign investment in the hydropower sector. With its rich hydropower resources (presumed to have the eighth-highest concentration of such resources in the world), Tajikistan still relies on neighboring countries such as Uzbekistan to meet 20 percent of its energy needs. In order to attract investment into prospective hydropower projects, Tajikistan is considering a variety of options from joint ventures to direct investment. It has already transformed twenty-four power stations into joint stock companies, with the government holding all the initial shares. It has recently turned over the management of these shares to the Ministry of Power Engineering.[17] Enacting a new water management regime will be directly linked to the land privatization efforts. Unless farmers in the valley start using water more efficiently, any water management system will fail. Creating such incentives among the valley's farmers is tightly linked to a "real" land privatization effort by the government. So far, governments have seemed content to continue subsidizing the agricultural sector rather than privatize the land.

In dealing with the Islamic insurgency, the three countries sharing the Ferghana Valley differed in their assessment of the threat and consequently in their response to it. After fostering an Islamic revival in the 1990s following the Soviet collapse, Uzbekistan has recently come to perceive Islamic militancy as the most serious threat to its national security. Its official strategy for dealing with this threat has so far centered on repressive military measures. It has recently closed down more than nine hundred mosques in the Ferghana Valley region. Regional authorities regularly conduct house-to-house raids and mass arrests of groups of men who assemble in public. Government agents monitor mosques, even "official" ones, and men shave their beards for fear they will be labeled Islamic radicals. In Namangan, nearly everyone has a family member or friend who has been arrested. Recently, the Uzbek government has admitted that detention camps exist, though it is impossible to determine the exact number of detainees, believed to be in the thousands.[18] Recently, in Andijan more than three hundred people demonstrated in front of municipal administrations demanding that their relatives be released from jail.[19] In order to stem the cross-border IMU incursions, the Uzbek government has mined its borders with both Kyrgyzstan and Tajikistan, causing many civilian deaths. It has also imposed a strict visa regime that hampers cross-border trade in the valley. In March 2001, fifty ethnic Uzbeks holding Tajik citizenship and living in Uzbekistan were deported to the Tajik border on suspicion that they are IMU collaborators. In response to the August 1999 IMU incursion, Uzbekistan bombed territory in Tajikistan thought to be occupied by IMU followers, thus increasing the tensions that already existed between the two countries. Uzbekistan is still pursuing its policy of mining mountainous areas along the borders with Kyrgyzstan and Tajikistan, further indicating its intent to deal unilaterally with the IMU threat. Many observers believe that the increasing popularity of the militant groups in the valley, particularly of the IMU and Hizb ut-Tahrir, is as much a result of the government's repressive tactics and people's discontent with the region's economic decline.

Recent reports indicate that the IMU has changed its professed view of Kyrgyz territory as purely a corridor into Uzbekistan, and is now seeking to embroil Kyrgyzstan in a wider regional conflict. Kyrgyzstan's government has so far adopted a two-pronged approach to its interactions with the IMU: On the one hand, it has been building up its defense capabilities, while on the other, they made overtures to the IMU about negotiating a nonviolence pact.[20]

However, negotiation overtures came to a halt after a Kyrgyz military court sentenced two IMU fighters to death for their participation in the August 2000 raids. The IMU had warned of retaliation if the death sentences are carried out. Kyrgyzstan' policy toward Islamic activists has recently become more restrictive. Distinctions are being made between "official" Islam and the independent Muslim clergy. The latter are being closely monitored, especially in southern Kyrgyzstan. Following the 1999 incursions, a closer collaboration was established between the Kyrgyz Ministry for National Security and the Uzbek National Security Service. With the recent IMU incursions showing that the IMU is now operating inside the Kyrgyz territory, the Kyrgyz government is bound to increase its repressive tactics in southern Kyrgyzstan.

Tajikistan is the only country in Central Asia that has involved Islamists in its governing coalition. The 1997 peace accord between the government and the United Tajik opposition stipulated that 30 percent of the official posts be allocated to members of the opposition, which consisted mostly of Islamic Revival Party members. The current minister of emergencies, Mirza Ziyayev, is reputed to have fought alongside IMU leader Juma Namangani during the 1992–1997 Tajik civil war. There is now ample evidence that former United Tajik opposition militants have been involved with the IMU in the actual fighting in Kyrgyzstan and Uzbekistan. In May 2000, under pressure from its neighbors, Tajikistan expelled IMU fighters from its territories where they have been based for years. However, there are some in the Uzbek and Kyrgyz military who still believe that the IMU is utilizing bases in Tajikistan. Tajikistan's government is more threatened by Uzbekistan's policies than by the IMU. Uzbek raids inside Tajikistan in 1999 against IMU bases there killed civilians and damaged homes. Its strict visa regime has restricted Tajik citizens' travel throughout the region, given the fact that Tajikistan is almost exclusively dependent on Uzbekistan for transportation links to the outside world. Its mining of the borders has caused close to thirty civilian deaths in Tajikistan to date. Continuous accusations by the Uzbek president that Tajikistan is supporting the IMU is further exacerbating tensions between the two governments. Recently, he demanded that the Tajik government relieve its minister of emergency situations from his post on the grounds that he is a close ally of IMU leader Juma Namangani.[21] Tajikistan's government views the IMU's presence in Tajikistan as providing it with some leverage vis-à-vis the Uzbek government, which still harbors a dissident army officer, Mahmud Khudaiberdiyev, who attempted a coup in 1998 against the ruling elite. Both the Tajikistani government and the leadership of the Islamic Revival Party are now more worried about the activities of the Hizb ut-Tahrir in northern Tajikistan. A number of Hizb ut-Tahrir followers were captured in November 2000 and sentenced to terms in prison. Other followers of Hizb ut-Tahrir were recently captured in Dushanbe.

Due to different assessments in the three countries of the seriousness of the Islamic threat vis-à-vis their respective national security, multilateral regional attempts to counter this threat are likely to be limited. In June 2001, at a summit of the Shanghai Five, Uzbekistan joined the newly created Shanghai Cooperation Organization (SCO). In addition to Uzbekistan, SCO's members include China, Kazakhstan, Kyrgyzstan, Russia, and Tajikistan. One of the major aims of the SCO is to improve the regional response to radical Islam in Central Asia, including the creation of a regional antiterrorist center in Bishkek. However, recent statements by Uzbek president Karimov and Russian officials already attest to the difficulties facing the newly created organization.[22] The Uzbek president has expressed concern that the SCO should not become a Russian instrument to mount anti-U.S. initiatives in the region. Previous border demarcation agreements between China on the one hand and Kyrgyzstan and Tajikistan on the other are being reexamined, creating tensions among the three governments. Russia is becoming more concerned with Beijing's growing influence in the region and is concerned that the SCO might become a venue for China to pursue its ambitions in Central Asia. Furthermore, financial resources needed for the implementation of regional agreements such as the regional antiterrorist center have yet to materialize. A far more serious implication of the Islamic threat to the valley lies in the fact that it has provided the governments in the region the opportunity for diverting scarce governmental resources away from the developmental field and toward the security and military sectors.

Multi-Track Diplomacy

This section will focus on the efforts being undertaken by international governmental and nongovernmental organizations to manage some of the sources of tension in the Ferghana Valley. Few of these projects have involved cross-border partnerships, mostly due to Uzbekistan's resistance. Due to their mandate, some donor agencies, such as USAID, work mostly bilaterally with partners in the other states. Hence, they will find it hard to fund a regional project. Regional projects have so far been limited to two parts of the valley: southern Kyrgyzstan and northern Tajikistan. One or two projects are truly regional in their action plan and implementation policies in that they involve joint Kyrgyz-Tajik analytical and implementation teams. Southern Kyrgyzstan has benefited from much international aid and development assistance due to the fact that the Islamic insurgencies have hit it most in the past two years. Though many donor agencies now profess funding conflict-prevention projects, few are committed to the long-term agenda of a conflict-prevention program. To succeed, a conflict-prevention program cannot be subordinated to the three-to-five-year funding cycle of most development agencies. As correctly noted by Barnett Rubin, "The evolution of perceptions of Central Asia illustrates . . . a tendency to overemphasize operational prevention—intervention to halt escalation of violence—and under-emphasize structural prevention—establishing programs to strengthen fundamental factors that prevent conflict, such as governance and equitable development."[23] This section will discuss in brief the two projects that first brought the ideas of structural conflict prevention in the Ferghana Valley to the attention of Western policymakers, and then present four projects that promise much hope for long-term conflict prevention in the valley.

The United Nations—Ferghana Valley Development Program
This is the first international project to call for a comprehensive conflict-prevention approach in the Ferghana Valley. The project discusses three major challenges facing the Ferghana Valley: maintaining the interethnic peace and good community relations; promoting regional dialogue and cooperation on issues such as Islamic militancy and drug trafficking; and building regional institutions covering both the official and the civil-society sectors. The program called for a regional, trilateral program focusing on issues dealing with growth and sustainable development. The programmatic areas advocated by the program were five: (1) job creation and income generation; (2) establishing joint interethnic confidence-building measures; (3) regulation of cross-border trade and a related dialogue on the maintenance of transparent boundaries; (4) regional cooperation in the fields of language and education; and (5) revival of a common cultural heritage in the region. The program further advocated cross-border partnerships in the valley among NGOs and other civil-society organizations working in the region. The project officially began in August 1998, established its headquarters in Osh (Kyrgyzstan), and set up a bilingual website at <www.ferghana.elcat.kg>. Tajikistan and Kyrgyzstan participated in the program. The United Nations Development Program was the lead agency and funder in the countries where the program operated. Uzbekistan refused to participate in the program, and couched its refusal in terms of opposition to external conflict prevention in the valley. In reality, analysts now note that Uzbekistan's rejection of the program was due to its perception that this effort was a Kyrgyz attempt to intervene in Uzbekistan's affairs through international agencies.[24]

Center for Preventive Action (CPA) Project on the Ferghana Valley
The purpose of this project was to assess the potential for conflict in Central Asia by studying one of its most volatile areas and provide recommendations for policymakers on conflict prevention in the region. In addition to the interethnic schisms, this project's key premise focuses on "a range of economic, political, social, organized crime, environmental, security, and other factors that have long proved incendiary in this part of the world."[25] A project working group was assembled, chaired by former U.S. senator Sam Nunn, a very influential and widely respected policymaker, that included policy experts, business executives, journalists, national security experts, and members of the nongovernmental sector. A delegation of the working group traveled to the region in March 1997, visiting the Uzbek and Kyrgyz parts of the valley. Other members of the working group visited northern Tajikistan in May 1998. The working group report was issued in the form of a 1999 book titled *Calming the Ferghana Valley—Development and Dialogue in the Heart of Central Asia*. It recommended the following conflict-preventive measures in the valley: (1) creation of an information clearinghouse on the Ferghana Valley to assist both investment and foreign assistance; (2) promotion of cross-border civil-society initiatives in the fields of governance and human rights; (3) supporting efforts at regional intercultural dialogues; (4) focusing foreign development assistance

on cross-border regional projects while maintaining bilateral aid; and (5) promoting foreign direct investment in the valley by pressing Uzbekistan to relax its currency and border restrictions.

The UNDP and the CPA projects were critical in putting the Ferghana Valley on policymakers' agendas, especially in the West, and in promoting an active interest and eventually engagement by the donor community in the valley. Many of the ongoing development projects in the valley have adopted the principles and recommendations advocated by these first two initiatives. Following is a short description of four other projects that have much potential for regional conflict prevention in the Ferghana Valley.

Peace Promotion Program for Bordering Regions

This is one of the most ambitious, ongoing peace promotion programs, funded by the Swiss Agency for Development and Cooperation. It is a regional program involving a number of local NGOs in all three countries. It adopts a multifold strategy targeting the grass roots, and middle-level leadership in the region. This program includes a number of civil-society initiatives.

Cross-Border Conflict Prevention Project at the community level. Initiated in June 1999 and implemented by the Kyrgyz NGO Foundation for Tolerance International and Tajik NGO Ittifok, this program has offices in Batken and Leilek (southern Kyrgyzstan) and Isfara and Khujand (northern Tajikistan). It targets border communities that have manifested a potential for interethnic violence, and it promotes the prevention of such conflicts through:

- Application of consensus-building processes and the cultivation of the tradition of good neighborhood and mutual trust in managing emerging disputes
- Organization of joint educational, cultural, and social programs among neighboring communities
- Establishment and institutionalization of a regional network of community mediators who can help de-escalate local disputes
- Attracting public attention in the border communities to nonviolent methods of conflict resolution.

Goodwill Ambassadors Networks Project. This initiative's aim is to set up three national networks of unofficial diplomats in Uzbekistan, Tajikistan, and Kyrgyzstan. These unofficial networks promote conflict prevention through:

- Field visits to the Ferghana Valley, on the basis of which they can provide their former colleagues in the official sector with a more accurate analysis of the causes of conflict and sources of tension
- Sharing their experience with conflict management with the local leadership in the different communities, in the hope that this might help reduce the tensions

- Lobbying state authorities about the persistent problems
- Disseminating new ideas and approaches for conflict prevention and management in the decisionmaking bodies of the three countries

This project was initiated in June 2000 and has now established the three national networks. The networks have offices in Bishkek, Dushanbe, and Tashkent. The project is being funded in collaboration with the Peace-Building Section of the Swiss Ministry of Foreign Affairs.

Rehabilitation of physical infrastructure project. This intiative is being implemented by UNDP in Tajikistan and Kyrgyzstan through the United Nations Office for Project Services (UNOPS) and focuses on cross-border social infrastructure rehabilitation, mainly drinking water and irrigation.

Central Asia media support project. This initiative promotes a regional dialogue among journalists, holds training seminars for journalists from all three countries on producing balanced and accurate news on regional issues, and produces bulletins on subregional media issues. It is a joint collaboration between the Geneva-based CIMERA Network and the Osh Media Resource Center.

Preventive Development in the South of Kyrgyzstan Program

The overall objectives of this program are to support the government of Kyrgyzstan and local communities in the south, to identify the root causes of conflict, and take the necessary measures for conflict prevention. It was established by the UNDP and the government of Kyrgyzstan. Though only focusing on four municipalities in the Batken province in south Kyrgyzstan, it is hoped that in the future this program will extend to other areas in the south of the country as well as to Tajikistan. It involves a three-pronged approach:

1. Establish a preventive development center to be equipped with an early warning system.
2. Support community-based organizations in carrying out community-wide projects through microcredit programs. Community members will receive training in the creation and management of small business enterprises.
3. Strengthen the law-enforcing capacities of the Batken provincial police department through provision of equipment, training, and vehicles.

The International Crisis Group Central Asia Project

The International Crisis Group (ICG) is a private multinational organization committed to strengthening the capacity of the international community to understand and act to prevent conflicts. The ICG project contributes to crisis prevention in the Ferghana Valley through:

- Research and analysis on political and socioeconomic trends in the valley and in the region in general. It opened an office in Osh in October

2000 where its staff conducts field research involving a wide range of sources.

- Publications in the forms of regular briefings and analytical reports including practical recommendations for international decisionmakers. It has so far published five reports on Central Asia and one briefing.
- Lobbying decisionmakers and the international media to keep the former informed about events as they unfold in the region and to build momentum for international action to avert a surge of violence region-wide.

Organization for Security and Cooperation in Europe (OSCE)

The OSCE has held a number of training workshops for the purpose of disseminating information about conflict analysis and prevention. Such seminars include a human-rights training program for Kyrgyz border guards, and training in the field of interethnic relations targeting officials in provincial and local administrations in south Kyrgyzstan as well as major ethnic communities. Monthly early warning reports by local monitors trained and employed by the OSCE are sent to the OSCE Commissioner on National Minorities.

Prospects

When covering the Ferghana Valley, the Western media has placed much emphasis on the Islamic threat in Central Asia, which diverted attention away from the root causes of conflict in that region. The root causes lie in poverty, repressive measures being undertaken against opposition and civil-society groups, corruption in the official sector creating a total disconnection between the governors and the governed, and poorly maintained and badly built infrastructure networks in the region. Official policies that focus solely on the Islamic threat and neglecting the root causes previously mentioned further exacerbate tensions and will, if sustained in the long term, lead to conflict escalation.

Official attempts at conflict management through repressive measures and crackdowns against Islamic groups and civil-society organizations are fueling rather than dampening people's anger and frustration. Visa regimes and mining of borders are further exacerbating simmering social and political frustrations and daily increasing the risks of local outbreaks of violence. Following 11 September 2001, repressive measures against Islamic groups have been on the rise, especially in Uzbekistan. There are valid concerns among the human-rights community that increased cooperation between the United States and Uzbekistan would result in less U.S. scrutiny of Uzbekistan's human-rights record. In the past, the United States has been one of Uzbekistan's strongest critics on human-rights violations. In February 2001, the U.S. State Department reported that the Uzbek government's poor human-rights record worsened, primarily due to the iron-fisted assault on independent political and religious expression. But as cooperation between the two countries increased following the launching of the U.S.-led antiterrorism war, official disapproval in Washington over Uzbek human-rights violations has turned silent. In October 2001, the U.S. State Department chose not to designate Uzbekistan as one of the countries of particular concern. An intensification of the government crackdown on all forms of religious expression might lead to increased popular support for militant movements such as the Islamic Movement of Uzbekistan and the Hizb ut-Tahrir. It might also lead to consolidation of efforts among the two movements and further radicalization of those such as Hizb ut-Tahrir, who have until now espoused nonviolent forms of opposition to the Uzbek government.

Following the U.S.-led antiterrorism campaign, countries in the region, including the three sharing the Ferghana Valley, have imposed additional restrictions on population movements across borders and a crackdown on illegal migration. These new security measures mean more hardship for residents of the Ferghana Valley, impeding cross-border trade and visits. Farmers who have previously depended on cross-border trade are now trying to find new sources of income. People find it very hard to visit relatives in neighboring countries. Border soldiers are trying to supplement their meager salaries with bribes imposed on those who want to cross to neighboring villages. A black-market economy is flourishing, especially in border communities, as small-scale entrepreneurs try to resell scarce goods purchased at a lower price across the border. Local economies in the valley are suffering due to decreased cross-border trade. There is a fear in the valley that poor economic conditions, especially in places such as Osh in Kyrgyzstan, might foster renewed interethnic tensions between Kyrgyz and Uzbeks similar to the ones that occurred in 1990.

Governments in the region have also stepped up their crackdown on illegal migrants as of late September 2001. Kyrgyzstan, for example, deported three hundred undocumented foreigners, mostly Tajiks and Afghans. This behavior has increased interstate friction in the region. Until recently, the drug trade has provided some funding to the militant groups. It has also contributed to the increase in criminal behavior, especially among the youth. Drug addiction is also on the increase, further weakening the region's economy due to the diversion of human and financial resources away from more productive sectors such as agriculture and industry. It is hoped that one of the positive outcomes of the U.S.-led antiterrorism campaign is a termination of Afghanistan's drugs industry. If that were to happen, there would be an urgent need to inject funds into the valley to provide alternative jobs for youth who used to be engaged in drug trafficking and to provide drug rehabilitation and treatment for drug addicts. Otherwise these unemployed youth will become eager recruits to Islamic militant movements. The real threats in the Ferghana Valley remain rooted in internal factors, mainly economic deprivation, lack of employment opportunities, total distrust in their government's ability and/or willingness to improve their living conditions, and anger at their government's repressive measures. One of the few valid generalizations in the literature on social protests and collective mobilizations is that social, violent mobilization of groups occurs when aggrieved groups cannot work through established channels, such as political parties or civil-society groups, to communicate new claims into the political process of authoritative decisionmaking.[26] Other factors that contribute to success of violent mobilization efforts include the intensity of deprivation, the resources of the mobilizing actors, the militants' strategic skills, and the counterstrategies of the opponents, i.e., governments. All these factors apply to today's situation in the Ferghana Valley. These factors are further exacerbated by a feeling of hopelessness that is quickly spreading among the population. People do not believe anymore that their respective governments are fair, willing to be inclusive, able to relate to their people, and/or willing to reform themselves to become less corrupt and more accountable. History has shown us that when people feel they are pushed against the wall and they have nothing to lose, they usually resort to drastic and violent measures.

The Ferghana Valley is now at a critical juncture where effective conflict-prevention efforts might push it away from the precipice to which it is now heading. An effective conflict-prevention intervention must be multisector and multilevel, and focus on structural rehabilitation, institutional reform, and attitudinal and behavioral change. A multilevel approach will involve simultaneously the national governments, the regional/local leaderships, and the civil-society organizations. A multisector intervention will focus on making information more accessible, promoting participation in decisionmaking processes, reforming education, restructuring national and local economies, and promoting governance and decentralization of the decisionmaking process. Structural rehabilitation will involve overhauling and in some cases rebuilding the infrastructure networks that are currently at the root of many of the local ethnic tensions in the valley. Institutional reform aims at eliminating the corruption that is rampant in official circles at the national, regional, and local levels. Corruption has eroded people's trust in their government and contributed to the feelings of injustice that fuel people's support for the Islamic militant groups.

Attitudinal and behavioral change is often bypassed or paid lip service in institutional efforts at conflict prevention. However, sustainability of conflict-prevention efforts rests on the success of programs that aim at changing people's attitudes about others and the conflict in general. Specifically, this implies creating mechanisms for nonviolent adjudication of conflict at the community level, introducing different habits for dealing with conflict, changing people's attitudes toward the enemy however the latter is defined, and strengthening people's collaborative problem-solving capacities and skills.

Recommendations
An effective conflict-prevention strategy should focus on the following tasks:

• Governments and donor agencies working in the region must reinvigorate economic reforms, target immediate humanitarian support to those sectors of the population living in extreme poverty, and create jobs through the promotion of better investment environments. While continuing to push for reforms at the macro level, donor agencies must focus at the micro level on promoting and strengthening the capacities and resources of existing community-based organizations to become the engines of economic growth in their communities.

• Establish a joint expert committee from Tajikistan, Uzbekistan, and Kyrgyzstan to assess the impact of the travel restrictions and border controls recently established in the valley. This committee should be funded by the international community and provided with outside expertise and training. While these controls should continue in the short-term to be part of the security measures to counter terrorist and drug-trafficking activities, in the long term they might prove to be counterproductive if they continue to limit cross-border trade and fuel people's anger and frustrations due to the humiliations inflicted on them by the border guards.

• Judicial systems in each of the three countries are in need of serious reform. The judicial systems must be allowed to be truly independent from the executive structures; judges must be better trained and paid, and subject to stiff sanctions if they were to accept bribes. In the Ferghana Valley, people view the judicial system as corrupt, inefficient, and incapable of providing an impartial venue for channeling their grievances. In such a context, it is no wonder that people resort to violence.

• Efforts at reducing corruption in the administrative and security state structures must be strengthened. Such efforts could take the form of strict legal sanctions for those officials who accept bribes, electing rather than appointing local officials, new standards of personnel management to ensure an educated work force, transparent hiring practices to ensure that ethnic minorities are not discriminated against, and better pay for personnel to help them meet their family basic needs. In the Ferghana Valley, border and customs officers are most notable for their corrupt and humiliating practices.

• Establish a multi-issue, multiparty negotiation process to simultaneously address border, water, and energy issues in the valley. This process should be held under the aegis of a respected, impartial third party. In July 2001, a regional effort at dealing with energy issues paid off when representatives from the five Central Asian energy ministries signed a treaty in Bishkek forming a regional energy grid. This grid should foster efficient trading of power resources among the five Central Asian states and is likely to be of benefit to the Ferghana Valley energy problems. This approach should also allow more efficient production and distribution of power throughout the region and facilitate quick decisions about when and where to send surplus power.[27] However this regional treaty does not deal with the water issues in the region. Unlike energy, some governments in the region are neither ready nor willing to pay for water. In particular, Kazakhstan and Uzbekistan announced that they find the idea of paying for water to be "unacceptable" and a violation of international norms. The United States Agency for International Development has been pushing for a solution linking water and energy, which Uzbekistan has so far found unacceptable. An unofficial process involving trusted experts from the three countries, and moderated by international experts in these issues, could be promoted and funded by the international community.

• Governments in the region should abandon the repressive measures against their clergy, the political opposition, and members of the civil society.

They need take a look at the modern history of neighboring Iran and conclude that such measures did not help the shah in preventing the Islamic opposition from assuming power. There is a fear that U.S.-led efforts to counter terrorism in Afghanistan have led regimes in Central Asia to believe that all forms of oppression against their opposition, as long as the latter are labeled Islamist, would be accepted by the international community. The international community must send a strong message that such behavior is unacceptable. Islam is an integral part of Central Asian societies, and won't go away. Seventy years of communism failed to achieve that and any efforts by these three governments to suppress it will likely fail and eventually backfire on them. The donor community must push for a dialogue in each of these countries involving the government, the Islamic clergy, and the civil-society structures. However, it is extremely important that this dialogue not involve outside voices or "experts." Unless it is locally owned, initiated, and facilitated, such a dialogue will be labeled as a Western attempt at containing the Islamic revival movement in Central Asia.

• In addressing the structural causes of conflicts in the region, especially water-based disputes, donors must adopt a twofold strategy. In the long term, the Soviet-built irrigation and water supply networks must be totally overhauled. In the short term, they must focus on the localities where water-based conflicts have taken on an ethnic character and which, if not addressed, might provide the spark for region-wide interethnic violence. Needs-assessment teams including engineers and conflict-management specialists must work together in identifying those communities in the valley most at risk for this type of conflict. The Swiss Development Corporation has been most successful in following this strategy in its "peace promotion for bordering regions" project.

• Training in conflict-management techniques must be organized at all levels in the valley, involving the regional and local official leaders, community leaders, and civil-society organizations. These training workshops must focus on fostering in the participants skills of conflict analysis and collaborative problem-solving behavior. Conflict prevention is most successful if done quickly and locally. This requires certain skills and abilities: skills in conflict monitoring, conflict analysis, dispute system design, consensus building, negotiation and mediation, and strategic planning. Civil-society organizations and local experts in "conflictology" lack minimal expertise in this field. It is important that such training programs be designed for regional and local officials, members of traditional institutions such as the council of elders, local staff of nongovernmental organizations, teachers, and high school and university students. These local stakeholders can then provide a local cadre working to promote different attitudes about the "enemy" and new habits of collaborative problem-solving behavior.

• Free information flow is essential for equal opportunity, consensus building, and keeping the state structures accountable. Governments in the region must be pushed to honor the freedom of the press and combat the harassment of journalists.

• Drug addiction and consequently AIDS are on the increase in the different regions of the valley. Regional antidrug educational programs must target the at-risk communities, mostly involving unemployed youth. Young men and women get drafted into the business due to lack of other employment opportunities and the good pay. It is hoped that with increased attention focused on the region, more aid will flow into drug prevention programs and projects to create alternative sources of employment for the Ferghana Valley's unemployed youth.

Resources

Newsletters and Periodicals

Central Asia and the Caucasus–Journal of Social and Political Studies, Central Asia and the Caucasus Information and Analytical Center, Sweden

Central Asia–Caucasus Analyst, the Central Asia–Caucasus Institute of the Johns Hopkins University, the Nitze School of Advanced International Studies

Central Asia Monitor

Information Analytical Bulletin, International Centre Interbilim, Bishkek

Reporting Central Asia, Institute for War and Peace Reporting, London

The Central Eurasian Studies Review, the Central Eurasian Studies Society

Turkistan Newsletter, Research Center for Turkestan, Azerbaijan, Crimea, Caucasus and Siberia in the Netherlands

Reports

International Crisis Group's Central Asia Project

"Afghanistan and Central Asia: Priorities for Reconstruction and Development." *Asia Report* No. 26, 27 November 2001.

"Central Asian Perspectives on 11 September and the Afghan Crisis," briefing, 28 September 2001.

"Central Asia: Crisis Conditions in Three States," *Asia Report* No. 7, 7 August 2000.

"Central Asia: Drugs and Conflict." *Asia Report* No. 25, 26 November 2001.

"Central Asia: Fault Lines in the New Security Map," *Asia Report* No. 20, 4 July 2001.

"Incubators of Conflict: Central Asia's Localized Poverty and Social Unrest," *Asia Report* No. 16, 8 June 2001.

"Islamist Mobilisation and Regional Security," *Asia Report* No. 14, 1 March 2001.

"Kyrgyzstan at Ten—Trouble in the 'Island of Democracy,'" *Asia Report* No. 22, 28 August 2001.

"Recent Violence in Central Asia: Causes and Consequences," *Central Asia Briefing,* 18 October 2000.

"Uzbekistan at Ten—Repression and Instability," *Asia Report* No. 21, 21 August 2001.

Royal Institute for International Affairs, *Western Engagement in the Caucasus and Central Asia,* by Neil MacFarlane, 1999.

United Nations Development Program

Kyrgyzstan Human Development Report, 1998, 1999, and 2000.

Tajikistan Human Development Report, 1998, 1999, and 2000.

Uzbekistan Human Development Report, 1998, 1999, and 2000.

United States Institute of Peace, *The Challenges of Regional Cooperation in Central Asia: Preventing Ethnic Conflict in the Ferghana Valley,* by Anara Tabyshalieva, June 1999.

Other Publications

Calming the Ferghana Valley: Development and Dialogue in the Heart of Central Asia, by Sam Nunn, Nancy Lubin, and Barnett Rubin. New York, The Century Foundation Press, 1999.

Central Asia: Conflict, Resolution, and Change, edited by Roald Sagdeev and Susan Eisenhower. Chevy Chase, MD, Center for Post-Soviet Studies, January 1995.

Central Asia's New States: Independence, Foreign Policy, and Regional Security, by Martha Brill Olcott. Washington, DC, United States Institute of Peace, October 1997.

Civil Society in Central Asia, edited by M. Holt Ruffin and Daniel Waugh. Seattle, University of Washington Press, 1999.

Conflict, Cleavage and Change in Central Asia and the Caucasus, edited by Karen Dawisha and Bruce Parrott. Cambridge, Cambridge University Press, 1997.

Islam and Central Asia: An Enduring Legacy or an Evolving Threat? edited by Susan Eisenhower and Roald Sagdeev. Washington, DC, The Center for Political and Strategic Studies, June 2000.

Political Islam and Conflicts in Russia and Central Asia, by Lena Johnson and Murad Esenov. Stockholm, The Swedish Institute of International Affairs, 1999.

The New Central Asia: The Creation of Nations, by Olivier Roy. New York, New York University Press, 1999.

The Resurgence of Central Asia: Islam or Nationalism? by Ahmad Rashid. Karachi, Oxford University Press, May 1999.

Selected Internet Sites

www.camsp.osh.kg/ (Central Asia Media Support Project)
www.crisisweb.org/ (ICG's Asia reports are available at this site)
www.eurasianet.org/ (An Open Society Institute site that provides an independent source of news and analysis about Central Asia and the Caucasus)
www.fas.harvard.edu/~casww/ICG-CAP.html (The International Crisis Group's Central Asia Project website)
www.fas.harvard.edu/~cess/ (The website of the Central Eurasian Studies Society)
www.ferghana.elcat.kg/ (Ferghana Valley Development Programme)
www.fti.kyrnet.kg/ (The Foundation of Tolerance International, Ferghana Valley List-server Archive, by date)
www.icarp.org (Interactive Central Asia Research Project)
www.internews.ru/ (An independent news service that covers events in Central Asia)
www.iwpr.net/index.pl?centasia_index.html (Institute for War and Peace Reporting, Central Eurasia Resource Pages)
www.times.kg (Online version of the weekly English language newspaper *The Times of Central Asia*)

Resource Contacts

Vicken Cheterian, CIMERA, e-mail: vicken.cheterian@cimera.org
John Gely, Swiss Agency for Development and Cooperation, Tashkent, e-mail: johan.gely@tas.rep.admin.ch
Jonathan Goodhand, INTRAC, e-mail: intrac@gn.apc.org
Altaaf Hasham, Agha Khan Foundation, e-mail: akfgarm@atge.automail.com
Raya Kadyrova, Foundation Tolerance International, e-mail: fti@infotel.kg
Kamol Kamilov, Center of Youth Initiatives, e-mail: davron@cyi.khj.tajik.net
Irene Leibundgut, Swiss Coordination Office, e-mail: irene@swisscoop.kg
Rasoul Rakhimov, United Nations Office for Drug Control and Crime Prevention, e-mail: rakhimov@odccp.tojikiston.com
Elena Sadovkaya, Center for Conflict Management, e-mail: ccm@online.ru
John Schoeberlein, Forum for Central Asian Studies, Harvard University, e-mail: schoeber@fas.harvard.edu

Anara Tabyshalieva, Institute for Regional Studies, e-mail: ifrs@elcat.kg

Data on the following organizations can be found in the Directory section:

In Kyrgyzstan
  Foundation for Tolerance International
  Institute for Regional Studies
  Osh Media Resource Center

In Tajikistan
  Center for Youth Initiatives, Ittifok

International
  CIMERA
  International Crisis Group
  Office of the OSCE High Commissioner on National Minorities
  OSCE Office for Democratic Institutions and Human Rights
  United Nations Development Program
  United Nations Office for Project Services

Randa Slim (Dayton, Ohio, USA) focuses on consulting and training in the fields of conflict management and public participation. Since 1993, Slim has been a member of the Inter-Tajik Dialogue, an unofficial dialogue focusing on the conflict in Tajikistan. She is currently the principal consultant for the Inter-Tajik Dialogue civic initiative, a three-year project funded by a consortium of U.S. foundations. She is also a consultant for the Peace Promotion Project in the Ferghana Valley funded by the Swiss Agency for Development and Cooperation.

Notes

1. Ahmed Rashid, *The Resurgence of Central Asia—Islam or Nationalism?* Cambridge, Oxford University Press, 1994, p. 17.
2. Nancy Lubin and Barnett Rubin, *Calming the Ferghana Valley: Development and Dialogue in the Heart of Central Asia*, New York, The Council on Foreign Relations, 1999, p. 41.
3. ICG, "Central Asia: Crisis Conditions in Three States," *Asia Report* No 7, August 2000, p. 2.
4. Asad Sadulloyev, "SOS: Jaga Is Going Out," *Central Asian News* from Ferghana, 2 February 2001.
5. Arslan Koichiev, "Skirmishes Suggest IMU Is Changing Tactics," *Eurasia Insight,* 6 August 2001.
6. Lubin and Rubin, *Calming the Ferghana Valley*, p. 59.
7. Arslan Koichiev, "Batken Residents Furious over Secret Kyrgyz-Uzbek Deal," *Eurasia Insight,* 25 April 2001.
8. Anara Tabyshalieva, *The Challenges of Regional Cooperation in Central Asia—Preventing Ethnic Conflict in the Ferghana Valley,* Washington, DC, United States Institute of Peace, 1999, p. 26.
9. Lubin and Rubin, *Calming the Ferghana Valley,* p. 66; "Incubators of Conflict: Central Asia's Localised Poverty and Social Unrest," *International Crisis Group Report,* no. 16, 8 June 2001, p. 8.
10. Ahmed Rashid, "Confrontation Brews Among Islamic Militants in Central Asia," *Turkistan Newsletter,* 22 November 2000.
11. ICG, *Asia Report* No 14, p. 11; Rashid, "Confrontation Brews."
12. ICG, *Asia Report* No 14, p. 11.
13. ICG, "Central Asia: Fault Lines in the New Security Map," *Asia Report* No.

20, 4 July 2001, p. 6.

14. Gregory Gleason, "Tajikistan Minister's Murder Points to Drug-Route Conflict," *Eurasia Insight,* 16 April 2001.

15. Tabyshalieva, *The Challenges of Regional Cooperation,* p. 27.

16. Lubin and Rubin, *Calming the Ferghana Valley,* p. 79.

17. Daler Nurkhanov, "Tajikistan, Kyrgyzstan Seek to Bolster Power Generating Capacity, Break Energy Dependence," *Eurasia Insight,* 2 August 2001.

18. ICG, *Asia Report* No. 14, p. 7.

19. Musaev Bakhodir, "Uzbeks Losing Patience: Uzbeks Take to the Streets to Air Anti-Government Grievances," *Reporting Central Asia,* no. 47, 10 April 2001.

20. Arslan Koichiev, "Kyrgyz Soldiers Reportedly Clash with IMU Fighters," *Eurasia Insight,* 26 July 2001.

21. "Uzbek President Urges Tajik Authorities to Sack Opposition Minister," Voice of the Islamic Republic of Iran, via BBC Worldwide Monitoring, 12 August 2001.

22. "Russia Has Misgivings About Shanghai Cooperation Organization," *Eurasia Insight,* 20 June 2001.

23. Barnett Rubin, unpublished document, 2001, p. 36.

24. Ibid., p. 27.

25. Lubin and Rubin, *Calming the Ferghana Valley,* p. xii.

26. Herbert Kitschelt, "Social Movements, Political Parties, and Democratic Theory," *Annals of the American Academy of Political and Social Science,* no. 528, July 1993.

27. Gregory Gleason, "Mixing Oil and Water: Central Asia's Emerging Energy Market," *Eurasia Insight,* 27 August 2001.

16.4

Tajikistan:
From Civil War to Peacebuilding

Randa M. Slim & Faredun Hodizoda

Tajikistan, along with other former Soviet republics, declared its independence in September 1991. With a weak state structure, independence engendered a struggle for power and national identity resulting in civil war and the installation of an authoritarian regime run by former members of the Communist Party of Tajikistan. This war has resulted in thousands of deaths and thousands of refugees who have fled their country to neighboring Afghanistan, Pakistan, and Russia. In the conflict, the government and its allies were confronted by a loosely united Tajik opposition including Islamists, democrats, and nationalists. In April 1994, a United Nations mediation effort was launched for the purpose of bringing a lasting peaceful settlement to the conflict. This mediation effort lasted three years and ended on 27 June 1997 with the signing in Moscow of the General Agreement on the Establishment of Peace and National Accord in Tajikistan. Tajikistan is now in the midst of a postconflict peacebuilding phase that will determine the future sustainability of the 1997 general agreement.

The causes of the Tajik civil war are many. Some are rooted in the history of Tajikistan, some in the breakdown of the Soviet Union, some in regional politics, and some in the historical events that led to the establishment of today's Tajikistan. As Olivier Roy puts it, "Most of the difficulties of present-day Tajikistan are linked to the very definitions of what is Tajikistan and what is a Tajik."[1] Tajikistan appeared on the map in the mid-1920s, along with the other countries of Central Asia, when the Soviets territorially divided Turkestan, which they inherited from the tsars and the Emirates of Bukhara and Kokand. The present Tajik republic was first divided between the Soviet Republic of Turkestan (created in 1918) and the People's Republic of Bukhara (1920). Later, it became an autonomous region of the new Republic of Uzbekistan, then an autonomous republic in Uzbekistan (1925), and in 1929, a full Soviet Socialist Republic.

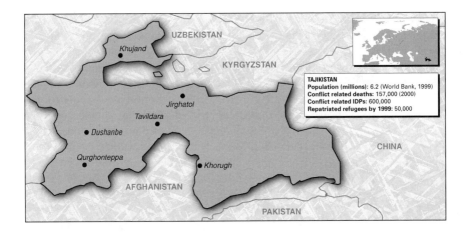

TAJIKISTAN
Population (millions): 6.2 (World Bank, 1999)
Conflict related deaths: 157,000 (2000)
Conflict related IDPs: 600,000
Repatriated refugees by 1999: 50,000

The 1920s division was not fair to Tajikistan. Only a small portion of the total Tajik population lived in the newly established state, and the Tajik's two most important intellectual and cultural centers, Bukhara and Samarkand, were placed within the borders of Uzbekistan. Instead, the small city of Dushanbe became the capital of the new republic. Stripping Tajikistan of its cultural centers undermined the formation of a Tajik intelligentsia and deprived Tajikistan of critical human resources for state building. It also hindered the development of a strong ethnic Tajik identity and strengthened the influence of local and regional affiliations on political loyalties, a phenomenon referred to by the Tajiks as *mahalgerai* ("localism"). Furthermore, a poorly developed transportation infrastructure reinforced the isolation of the different Tajik regions, impeding the establishment of relations among them.

Tajikistan was the center of the Basmachi resistance movement against the Bolsheviks and Soviet control of Central Asia in 1918–1928. A period of repression and collectivization followed that led to the depopulation and forced resettlement of certain groups in the republic. Stalin further insisted on staffing the Communist Party and the state apparatus with ethnic Tajiks. Thousands of Tajiks with limited Marxist education were enlisted in the party apparatus. The traditional regional networks of authority, power, and benefits soon infiltrated the Soviet power machinery in Tajikistan. The primary base of power for the new regime in the 1940s became the district of Khujand, renamed Leninabad. Though part of Tajikistan, the region had always been more closely linked by geography and trade to Uzbekistan than to the rest of Tajikistan. Throughout Soviet rule, the north was the economic powerhouse of Tajikistan, and the home of all republican Communist Party first secretaries from 1943 until independence in 1991. The Khujandis endorsed localism as the basis of their policy in Tajikistan and channeled the majority of their allocations from the central budget to industrial development in their province. During Soviet rule, northern Tajikistan prospered in comparison to the south, a tendency reinforced by a large-scale Soviet resettlement policy imposed to meet labor needs. Following World War II, many people from the Karategin Valley and Gorno-Badakhshan were moved into the southwestern province of Qurghan-Teppa, leading to tension and resentment on the part of the locals, mainly Kölabis, toward the newly settled groups. In the 1970s, the Communist Party leaders sought to broaden their political base and started involving people from the southern conservative district of Kölab, motivated, quite probably, by a desire to broaden their political base and forge an alliance with the south. Following the invasion of Afghanistan, elites from Gorno-Badakhshan were promoted by the Russian KGB in the ranks of the local KGB. Few political elites were recruited from other regions of Tajikistan.

The monopoly on political power exercised by the Khujand-Kölab alliance created much resentment among the intelligentsia of the other regions and led, with the advent of *perestroika*, to the formation of opposition movements. In 1991, these opposition forces included the Islamic Renaissance Party, the Democratic Party of Tajikistan, the La'li Badakhshon and Nosiri Khusraw societies, as well as forces loyal to the republic's official Islamic clergy. In 1991, they formed an opposition coalition with the aim of rooting out localism, uniting the nation, and building an independent democratic nation. With the exception of La'li Badakhshon and Nosiri Khusraw, which were regionally based nonpolitical associations, all other opposition forces operated as national parties.

Officially registered in December 1991, the Islamic Renaissance Party (IRP) called for the revival of the role of Islam in both political and everyday life. It declared Islam the guiding principle of the party while its immediate tasks involved establishing a legal and democratic state. Two other opposition parties were the nationalist Rastokhez Popular Movement and the Democratic Party of Tajikistan, an anti-Marxist reformist party calling for an end to totalitarianism and localism, and supporting democracy, a market economy, and a more equitable distribution of power.

In addition to these local actors, Russia and Uzbekistan played crucial roles in the developing conflict by taking sides with the governing coalition against the opposition. As Sergei Gretsky puts it, "It was outside interference that turned civic strife in Tajikistan into civil war." Russia's "Near Abroad Policy" aimed to (1) protect the interests of Russians living in those areas, (2) stop migration to Russia from those areas, and (3) maintain stability in neighboring regions, especially on Russia's southern borders. A variety of Russian interest groups, including officers in the Russian 201st Motorized Rifle Division based in Tajikistan, were able to make the argument inside the Kremlin that Russia must support the government coalition to prevent the spread of Islamic fundamentalism in Central Asia and an exodus of Russians from Tajikistan.

Two factors prompted Uzbekistan's leader, Islam Karimov, to back the Tajik government. *Perestroika* brought a revival of age-old rivalries between the Tajiks and Uzbeks, and with *glasnost* came demands in Tajikistan, Bukhara, and Samarkand for the return of these two intellectual and cultural centers to Tajikistan and for the protection of the rights of the Tajik population living in Uzbekistan. At the same time, Karimov faced domestic opposition and feared that any opposition success in Tajikistan might send the wrong message to the Uzbek opposition.

Conflict Dynamics

In February 1990, two weeks prior to Tajikistan's first parliamentary elections, violent riots erupted in Dushanbe, sparked by public anger in response to rumors that large numbers of refugees from the Armenian earthquake were to be rehoused in the capital. Blaming the Rastokhez Popular Movement for instigating the riots, the government banned opposition parties from the upcoming elections. In March 1990, those elections produced a Communist Party–dominated parliament. In December 1990, a multiparty system was adopted, and new political parties and movements were subsequently established, including the Democratic Party of Tajikistan and the IRP. In August 1991, after president Quahhar Mahkamov backed the coup attempt in Moscow, angry protesters in Dushanbe demanded his resignation. On 9 September 1991, the Tajik Supreme Soviet declared Tajikistan's independence and Mahkamov immediately resigned. He was replaced by Kadreddin Aslonov, who suspended Communist Party activities and froze its assets, but Aslonov was then ousted by parliament and replaced by former party first secretary Rahmon Nabiev.

However, after fourteen days of street protests, Nabiev stepped down and called for presidential elections. During the November 1991 elections, opposition parties including the Democratic Party and IRP, and the Rastokhez Popular Movement united and presented an opposition candidate, Davlat Khudonazarov,

Tajik refugees in North Afghanistan

who was defeated in what most observers considered to be seriously flawed elections. Former communists from the Khujand and Kölab regions were over-represented in the new regime under the leadership of Nabiev. Soon after, a series of repressive measures was implemented preventing opposition forces from assuming any role in the governing structure. In March 1992, opposition followers began a fifty-two-day rally in Shahidon Square. Pro-government forces responded with their own demonstrations and in May 1992, opposition and pro-government forces clashed violently, with the Russian military, still present in the country, supplying arms to the government. In an attempt to pre-vent further escalation of the conflict, President Nabiev put together a coali-tion government, the Government of National Reconciliation (GNR), with a third of the ministerial posts allocated to the opposition. But hard-line ele-ments, primarily from Kölab and Khujand, opposed the move and declared the new government to be invalid because it had not been approved by parliament. In mid-May 1992, the armed conflict shifted to the south, and by June fierce fighting had broken out across the country between the supporters of the coali-tion government and forces loyal to the old Soviet order. In September 1992, Popular Front militiamen broke through the blockade of Kölab and killed a large number of opposition supporters in the Qurghan-Teppa region, causing hundreds of thousands to flee to neighboring countries.

There followed a period of instability, during which President Nabiev was forced to resign. A government of "national reconciliation" was formed under parliament chairman Akbarsho Iskandarov, and the government survived a coup attempt. A the end of 1992, Iskandarov resigned and a new government was formed, headed by the chairman of the parliament, the Kölabi Imomali Rahmonov. With no representation from the opposition, this government was comprised almost exclusively of Kölabis and Leninabadi Communist Party members. It soon repealed all previous GNR legislation, banned opposition parties and newspapers, and merged Qurghan-Teppa and Kölab into the newly created Khatlon Province.

The Uzbek and Russian governments decided that their national interests were being jeopardized by the chaotic situation in Tajikistan, and agreed, along with the governments of Kazakhstan and Kyrgyzstan, to intervene with peacekeeping forces from the Commonwealth of Independent States (CIS). These forces included troops from the Russian 201st Motorized Rifle Division and additional troops from Uzbekistan, Kyrgyzstan, and Kazakhstan. In early December 1992, after days of brutal fighting, the Kölabi Popular Front troops, supported by Russian and Uzbek troops, entered Dushanbe. When Rahmonov was named head of state, a Kölabi headed Tajikistan for the first time in mod-ern history. Kölabi troops conducted a campaign of murder and terror against the pro-opposition Pamiris and Karateginis. This resulted in mass displacement of refugees into Afghanistan. Arrest warrants and death sentences were issued for the opposition leaders, who were blamed for the war. The opposition lead-ership fled to Moscow, Iran, and Afghanistan. During the period of March through August 1993, the government consolidated its power throughout the country. Opposition groups, now stationed in Afghanistan, launched an offensive across the Panj River from Afghanistan into southern Tajikistan, targeting both Russian and pro-government forces.

Between 1993 and the signing of the peace accords in June 1997, the opposition forces constantly skirmished with Russian border guards and pro-government forces. A number of cease-fire agreements were signed following the launch of UN-mediated negotiations in April 1994. During this period, the pro-government bloc was wracked by dissension, with a split between the Kölabi governing leadership and what came to be called the new or third force, the Khujandis, and a further split within the Kölabi camp itself. Although the Democratic Party of Tajikistan also splintered and differences emerged between the political and military wings of the opposition, overall relations within the opposition forces remained cooperative and civil.

The governing coalition was first forged in 1992 when the Khujandis, seeking military support, invited economic leaders and crime bosses from Kölab to join a coalition against the Islamic-democratic opposition. The Kölabis were rewarded when Rahmonov was named head of state in December 1992 and in the new government, the Kölabis were a majority. The Khujandis, who still maintained control over the important economic and security posts, assumed that once the opposition was taken care of, they could reinstate a Khujandi as head of state. But regional factors including a shift in Russia's policy toward Uzbekistan and its allies in the region disrupted their political calculations. Russia threw its support to Rahmonov and in 1993 Abdulmajid Dostiev, Rahmonov's first deputy, formed a pro-Kölab People's Party of Tajikistan. Rahmonov eventually forced the dismissal of his prime minister, Abdumalik Abdullajanov, a powerful Khujandi political leader. Most political and security officials in the province of Leninabad were sacked and replaced by Kölabis.

In November 1994, Rahmonov defeated his opponent, Abdumalik Abdullajanov, in a presidential election, and in February 1995 his supporters won an overwhelming victory in parliamentary elections. But because of both fraud and legislative restrictions, these elections were widely condemned by outside observers.

In May 1996, in the first significant sign of northern concern about the Kölabi-dominated government, there was serious unrest, including riots, in Khujand and Öra-Teppe, followed by the arrest and imprisonment without trial of hundreds of demonstrators. The riots were sparked by the murder of a prominent Leninabadi businessman, but soon developed into political protests over the disproportionate influence of Kölabis in Leninabad. In July 1996, Abdumalik Abdullojanov and two other prime ministers from northern Tajikistan, Abdujalil Samadov and Jamshed Karimov, formed the National Revival Movement, which constituted a "third force" in Tajik politics. In mid-April 1997, a protest in the Khujand prison involving the jailed leaders of the May 1996 riots was violently suppressed and it is estimated that more than 150 inmates died. These events culminated on 30 April 1997 in an assassination attempt on Rahmonov. Two people died in a grenade attack and seventy-three were injured, including the president. Using the attack as an excuse, the Tajik government immediately initiated a widespread crackdown on the "new" opposition in the Leninabad region, including arrests, beatings, and disappearances.

A similar split occurred within the Kölabi camp. The Kölabi militia, the Popular Front of Tajikistan, consisted of two major factions: Kölabi and Hisari. The Hisari group included units from districts with a substantial ethnic Uzbek population, where the communists had always enjoyed support. In 1993, the relations between the two factions turned sour when the government of Tajikistan declared its intention to form the armed forces of Tajikistan out of Kölabi units only. In May 1994, Kölabis and Hisaris battled each other just outside Dushanbe—an indication that localism prevailed not only at the regional level, but had also permeated the lower administrative echelons of the society to the district level.

The exiled opposition forces concentrated themselves in Afghanistan, Moscow, and Gorno-Badakhshan, with some troops operating in the Karategin Valley. The Islamic military forces, headed by Said Abdullah Nurwere, were located in Afghanistan, and consisted of forces loyal to the Muslim cleric Qazi Kalan A. Turajonzoda and IRP supporters. The political/secular opposition was based in Moscow. Now called the Coordinating Center of Tajik Democratic forces in the CIS, it united members of the Democratic Party, Rastokhez, different Pamiri groups, and other activists and intellectuals. Otakhon Latifi, former deputy prime minister of Tajikistan, headed the center. In July 1995, the various groups forming the opposition created the United Tajik Opposition, headed by Said Abdullah Nuri. The United Tajik Opposition (UTO) then became the main interlocutor for the opposition during negotiations.

Official Conflict Management

UN involvement in the Tajikistan war was initiated in September 1992 by the address of Uzbek president Islam Karimov to the UN Secretary-General, supported by Finnish president Mauno Koivisto. A mission visited Tajikistan in October, and then in January 1993 a small United Nations unit of political, military, and humanitarian officers was dispatched to monitor the situation on the ground. Ismat Kittani was appointed special envoy to Tajikistan in April 1993, followed in January 1994 by Ramiro Pirez-Ballon. Their efforts at promoting peacemaking bore fruit when both sides to the conflict agreed to come to negotiations in Moscow in April 1994. The special envoy chaired three rounds of talks, leading to a temporary cease-fire and the establishment of a joint commission to oversee its implementation. In December, the Security Council established the United Nations Mission of Observers to Tajikistan to monitor the implementation of cease-fire, maintain contact with the conflicting parties, and support the efforts of the UN Secretary-General's special envoy.

In February 1994, the Organization for Security and Cooperation in Europe also opened a permanent office in Tajikistan with a mandate to promote institution building, assist in establishing a constitution, organize democratic elections, and survey human-rights conditions. The mission was given the status of observer at ongoing UN-mediated talks.

The Inter-Tajik Dialogue on national reconciliation lasted until June 1997. From the beginning, they were held under the auspices of the United Nations. Representatives of Russia, Uzbekistan, Iran, Pakistan, Kazakhstan, Kyrgyzstan, Afghanistan, and Turkmenistan, with the OSCE and the Organization of Islamic Conference (OIC) participating as observers. The venue of the talks shifted among the capitals of the observer countries. Having these countries as observers helped mitigate the potential negative influence of some of the neighboring countries' policies on the domestic actors. Both Russia and Iran played important roles at critical junctures by persuading their allies to make necessary compromises.

The General Agreement on the Establishment of Peace and National Accord in Tajikistan (hereafter, General Agreement) is the name given to a package of nine documents that were signed in the course of eight rounds of negotiations between the delegations of the government of Tajikistan and the UTO, and numerous other meetings. The General Agreement stipulated a transition period of twelve to eighteen months during which all the protocols of the agreement were to be implemented. During the transitional period, the following provisions would be implemented:

- 30 percent UTO representation in government executive structures
- Voluntary and safe return of all refugees and internally displaced people
- Disbanding, disarmament, and reintegration of opposition forces into government power structures
- Reform of government structures
- Constitutional amendments
- Amendments to the law on elections, the law on political parties legalizing banned opposition and other political parties and movements, and the law on mass media allowing the functioning of free and objective mass media
- Full exchange of prisoners of war and other forcibly detained people
- Adoption of an Amnesty Law and an Act on Mutual Forgiveness
- Establishment of a Central Electoral Commission for conducting elections and referenda, with 25 percent UTO representation in its composition
- Setting the date for new parliamentary elections

The principal mechanism for the implementation of the General Agreement was the Commission on National Reconciliation (CNR). The CNR was established with equal representation from both sides (thirteen members each). The CNR chairman was the UTO leader, Said Abdullah Nuri, with the first deputy speaker of parliament, Abdulmajid Dostiev, as deputy chairman. Following the first plenary meeting in Moscow in July 1997, the CNR's mandate went into full effect on 15 September 1997, with a working plan prepared by its four subcommissions to complete the schedule of implementation within twelve to eighteen months. The four subcommissions respectively dealt with the protocols concerning political, legal, military, and refugee issues. Two subcommissions were headed by government representatives and two by UTO representatives. An expert group was also established in September 1997 to administer the Amnesty Law. Each subcommission and the expert group consisted of six members, based on equal representation of the government and UTO.

The main monitoring entity of the implementation of the General Agreement was the Contact Group (CG), consisting of eight states (Afghanistan, Iran, Kazakhstan, Kyrgyzstan, Pakistan, Russia, Turkmenistan, and Uzbekistan) and three international organizations (OIC, OSCE, and the UN) with the special representative of the UN Secretary-General serving as coordinator. In addition to its monitoring functions, CG provided expertise, advice, good offices, and recommendations on ways to ensure the parties' compliance with the General Agreement.

Multi-Track Diplomacy

The Inter-Tajik Dialogue

The Inter-Tajik Dialogue, which first met in Moscow in March 1993, was established to provide a forum for pro-government and pro-opposition Tajikistani citizens to come together and discuss the root causes of the Tajik conflict. The objective then was to see whether a group could be formed from within the civil conflict to design a peace process for their own country. The dialogue was conducted under the auspices of the Dartmouth Conference Regional Conflicts Task Force[2] by a subgroup organized by the U.S.-based Kettering Foundation and the Russian Center for Strategic Research and International Studies of the Institute of Oriental Studies in Moscow. A third-party team that included three Americans and three Russians facilitated the Inter-Tajik Dialogue. The meetings were alternately chaired by the Russian and American cochairs. The dialogue involved a core of eight to ten citizens of Tajikistan divided between the pro-government and pro-opposition camps. When the dialogue began, the majority of the pro-opposition members were in exile in Moscow. Two members of the dialogue group eventually became formal delegates to the UN-mediated negotiations.

The cochairs and the rest of the team members facilitated the discussions by setting the agenda at the beginning of every meeting, raising questions at critical times during the discussions, asking for clarifications about certain ideas and proposals when needed, helping to put down on paper the ideas articulated during the meeting, and (when emotions flared up) trying to help the participants deal constructively with their anger. At the end of every meeting, the U.S. team drafted a report and shared it with UN agencies and other interested official bodies in the United States and Russia.

During meetings between March and August 1993, participants discussed the origins and conduct of the civil war. They concluded in August 1993 by agreeing on the need to start a negotiation between the government and the opposition about creating conditions for the safe return of refugees. In January 1994, opposition participants came to the dialogue with the new platform for a United Tajik Opposition. Pro-government participants grilled them for over two days. The pro-government participants left the meeting feeling that the basis for negotiations now existed and promised to report the meeting discussions to the government. One month later, the government of Tajikistan accepted the special envoy's invitation to join UN-mediated peace talks. A high-level Tajikistani official later said, "After six meetings of the Dialogue, it was no longer possible to argue credibly that negotiations between the government and the opposition were impossible."

During meetings in March 1994, the dialogue participants produced their first joint memorandum, which recommended the creation of four working groups to focus on refugee, political, military, and economic issues—an idea that became part of the General Agreement. When official negotiations started in April 1994, the dialogue redefined its objectives as "designing a political process of national reconciliation for the country." They also addressed issues that caused stalemate in the official negotiations. In March 1995, the dialogue began using the idea of "a transitional period." The General Agreement adopted that concept to describe the twelve-to-eighteen-month postaccord phase during which the CNR would try to implement the provisions of the General Agreement. In May 1996, the Inter-Tajik Dialogue stated in a joint memorandum: "Participants believe that the primary obstacle to peace in Tajikistan is the absence of an adequate understanding on sharing power among the regions, political parties and movements, and nationalities in Tajikistan." Beginning in the summer of 1995, the dialogue repeatedly recommended the creation of a Consultative Forum for the Peoples of Tajikistan as a mechanism for bringing together different regions and political forces for deliberations on the kind of country they envisioned. Although the forum has never come into being, it was agreed in 1996 in a memorandum signed by President Rahmonov and UTO leader Nuri that such a forum should be created.

When the CNR was formed, four participants in the dialogue were members. In March 1993, the dialogue provided the only channel of communication across factional lines and relations were acrimonious. At the end of 2000, after twenty-nine meetings, the Inter-Tajik Dialogue was still meeting and had become what we call "a mind at work in the midst of a country making itself." Through these eight years, dialogue participants have played significant roles at all levels in a multilevel peace process that includes government negotiators, highly informed citizens outside government, and grassroots organizations.

There can be no doubt that the Inter-Tajik Dialogue played a role in the peace process in Tajikistan, but determining exactly what that role was illustrates one of the continuing problems in assessing the impact of unofficial dialogues. One of the lessons learned from the Tajikistan peace process, observes Gerd Merrem, former special envoy to Tajikistan and the official mediator at the UN-mediated Inter-Tajik Dialogue, is that "in a two-track approach, an NGO-facilitated dialogue between Tajiks on existing political and socio-economic antagonisms enabled these personalities within the polarized conflict to look beyond what separates them. This exercise, facilitated by a former U.S. official with skill and perseverance, has clearly facilitated compromise at the negotiation table."[3]

International Nongovernmental Organizations

International nongovernmental organizations (INGOs) played an important role in the promotion and then implementation of the peace agreement. The main ones are as follows.

The Aga Khan Foundation. The Aga Khan Foundation has focused its efforts in the early stages of the war on providing humanitarian assistance to the Ismaili population in the Gorno-Badakhshan province. Throughout the official negotiations, UN special envoys consulted frequently with His Highness Prince Karim Aga Khan on issues related to the peace process. The prince's visits to Tajikistan (in particular in May 1995) had a moderating influence on some of the negotiating parties. Since the signing of the peace accords, the foundation has launched an impressive array of long-term programs focusing on community-based economic development, a new humanities curriculum at Tajikistani universities, and support for civil society. They are also launching a Western-style Central Asian university with a main campus in Kharugh (Tajikistan) and satellite campuses in Kyrgyzstan and Kazakhstan.

United States Institute of Peace. The United States Institute of Peace organized a number of forums and study groups on the prospects for negotiations to end the Tajikistan conflict. It also published a report on the prospects for conflict and opportunities for peacemaking in the southern tier of former Soviet republics. In June 1995 it organized a forum on the conflict with U.S. ambassador to Tajikistan Stanley T. Escudero and former OSCE head of mission in Tajikistan Olivier Roy, later publishing its findings, and in June 1996, it hosted a discussion involving the Inter-Tajik Dialogue participants. Its contribution to the peace process has been in providing analysis and a forum for ideas.

International Committee of the Red Cross. The International Committee of the Red Cross (ICRC) played a significant role in implementing the agreement on prisoner exchange, which served an important confidence-building function. These agreements were reached during the third and fourth rounds of the official negotiations in late 1994 and 1995. The ICRC could assume this task because of its vast experience with such exchanges, and the respect it enjoyed among all parties to the negotiations. Beyond this role, it was also involved informally throughout the negotiation process in discussions on humanitarian issues.

Local Nongovernmental Organizations

NGOs are a relatively new phenomenon in Tajikistan. Since 1994, there has been a rapid increase in their activity and 415 NGOs representing a wide variety of interests (e.g., youth, civil society, education, women, health, social protection and poverty elimination, environment, culture, business training, mass media, science) have been established in the past five years.

Historically, civil society in Tajikistan is rooted in local institutions. Each Tajik rural community or village has a council called *mahalla* council where all local problems were discussed and wherever possible, solved by the people themselves.[4] The *mahalla* council is supplemented by informal meetings, forums, and small group conversations around common dinners held in a mosque where adult males gather, each bringing food.

Though useful in providing venues for people to get together and solve local problems, the *mahallas* could do little to bind the different regions of Tajikistan together. This local civic infrastructure reinforces the problem of localism by failing to provide sufficient incentives for common national or interregional collaboration and by shaping the average Tajikistani citizen's mind-set where the terms of reference are a narrow circle of relatives, neighbors and community members.

Many of Tajikistan's NGOs were established in 1997 following the signing of the General Agreement. Some of them, like the Oli Somon Cultural and Intellectual Foundation, were established during the war, but their effect on the course of events during the civil war was, in our opinion, minimal. They were hampered by fear of retaliation from the militia structures, lack of human and financial resources, lack of professional knowledge about the third sector and its role in a democratic society, and a weak legal framework to protect the integrity of their activities.

During the transition period (June 1997–February 2000), the local NGOs played a major role in the preelection process. In collaboration with the OSCE mission in Dushanbe, local NGOs trained by OSCE experts and staff organized hundreds of training seminars focusing on civic, gender, and human-rights topics. A network of thirteen local NGOs trained in the field of conflict resolution was organized by Counterpart Consortium, with financial assistance from the U.S. Agency for International Development. In our opinion, these two programs, targeting the entire country and focused on promoting skills and knowledge critical to the establishment of a nonviolent civic culture, have played a supporting role in the grassroots consolidation of the official agreements.

But Tajikistan's NGOs still suffer from a number of weaknesses:

1. The majority of NGOs (at least the more professional ones) are still concentrated in the two largest cities in the country, Dushanbe and Khujand. Few are established in small towns and in rural areas. The weak transportation and communication infrastructure as well as lack of local funding sources present the major obstacles to the emergence and sustainability of NGOs in rural areas.

2. All local NGOs in Tajikistan are far from being self-sustaining. They are still dependent on outside funding and the funders' priority areas mostly drive their programs. As funders change their funding priorities (from gender issues, to drug prevention, to HIV/AIDS prevention), local NGOs follow suit.

How to achieve local NGOs' long-term sustainability is one of the most challenging issues facing the donor community today.

3. Members of the intellectual and academic intelligentsia founded many of these organizations. The majority of their leaders are Russian-educated and lack real connections to the local strata of the society, especially to people living in rural areas. They have no close or ongoing relationship with the traditional civic networks and local *mahalla* councils. It is our opinion that the basis of civil society in Tajikistan are these *mahalla* councils, and unless NGOs shift their area of operation to these local units, their efforts at strengthening and building civil society will not be sustainable.

Prospects

The main task facing Tajikistan today is that of building a democratic civil society. The obstacles to this task lie in an unaccountable and centralized governing structure, unemployed ex-combatants, and the illegal drug trade.

According to the government of Tajikistan, the stipulations of the General Agreement have been implemented. In August 1999, the UTO announced that no further opposition military units existed—all had been disarmed and integrated into existing government units. That announcement led the government to lift the ban on opposition parties. On 26 September 1999, a referendum was held on constitutional amendments with about 73 percent supporting the proposed amendments. The constitutional amendments created a new two-chamber parliament where the parliamentarians would be no match for the executive branch since the presidential appointees in the upper chamber (eight members) and the members of the president's party in the lower chamber could effectively uphold any veto.

The presidential election was held on 6 November 1999. Though there was one other candidate on the ballot, President Rahmonov ran, in effect, unopposed, receiving close to 97 percent of the vote. Parliamentary elections followed in February 2000. Of the sixty-three seats in the lower chamber, the pro-presidential People's Democratic Party garnered thirty seats, the Communist Party thirteen, the Islamic Renaissance Party two, and a group of nonpartisan candidates believed to be pro-presidential garnered fifteen seats. Although the election process was not considered fair, it was the first multiparty election ever held in Tajikistan, with the Islamic Renaissance Party participating for the first time in the post-Soviet era. More importantly, the new parliament now includes some experts with strong intellectual and experiential credentials.

The CNR ended its work when the new parliament took office. However, international observers in Tajikistan judge that implementation of the General Agreement of 1997 has not really been completed despite a proclamation by the government to that effect. Most political observers do consider that the protocol on refugee issues has been successfully implemented. Both government and the UTO shared an interest, though for different reasons, in having the refugees return home.

Implementation of the military and political protocols has been less successful. The military protocol aimed both to integrate Tajikistan's many armed forces into a unified military and to promote decommissioning and demobilization. One could argue that the defeat of a November 1998 uprising in the Leninabad region was a test for the newly integrated armed forces. Nonetheless, former UTO commanders, though supportive of the peace process, are not satisfied with the current situation. Many of the integrated UTO units are poorly housed, clothed, and fed. An esprit de corps has failed to develop among the armed forces. Rank and file are still loyal to their former military commanders and many rank and file in the Tajik army did not even know the names of their formal commanding officers. A hostage-taking incident in June 2001, engineered by former Tajik opposition fighters, provides further support to this argument. Despite the progress made by the United Nations Mission of Observers to Tajikistan and United Nations Organization for Project Services in reintegrating ex-combatants, the government is now challenged to find salaried jobs for all ex-combatants.

The main task now facing Tajikistan is to build a democratic civil society. It must begin by building democratic institutions and democratizing the structures of power. Tajik political institutions are now more centralized than they were before. The president and his administration control the decision-making process with minimal influence from the legislative and judicial bodies. The decisionmaking process is far from transparent and is perceived to be corrupt. The president's party, People's Democratic Party (PDP), enjoys privileged access to government resources. In three recent by-elections, only PDP candidates were allowed to run, with opposition candidates barred on technicalities. The IRP is now suffering from a lack of resources. As one IRP senior official stated privately, "It is easier to fund the *kalashnikov* than to support political and social platforms." There is an ongoing internal debate between the hawks, who are still motivated by the *jihad* mentality, and the young Turks, who are calling for professionalization of IRP political activities. Today, three political parties dominate Tajikistan's political scene, though they do not enjoy equal stature and access to resources. The most prominent is the PDP. The two other parties with some support base are the Communist Party and the IRP. The Democratic Party is split into many factions, and many of its leading figures are now in government.

According to official statistics, the economy is on the road to recovery. According to the United Nations Development Program *2000 Human Development Report,* "Since 1997, the government has managed to achieve positive economic growth and an improvement in the well-being of the population." Yet Tajikistan still remains the poorest country in the CIS, with the lowest income per capita and more than 80 percent of the population living in poverty.

The illegal drug trade is undermining Tajikistan's moral fabric, pushing its youth into criminal activities, and infiltrating its governing and judicial bodies. Tajikistan is a major conduit for narcotics produced in Afghanistan. According to UN estimates, Afghanistan's poppy harvest in 2000 was about

3,000 metric tons, making the country the largest producer of heroin in the world. Despite official efforts to stop the flow of narcotics into Tajikistan, drug trafficking has been increasing, and Russian Federal Border Service guards patrolling part of the Tajik-Afghan border confiscated more than 1,300 kilograms of drugs, including 970 kilograms of heroin, in the first half of 2001. This amount exceeds the amount seized during all of 2000. A similar trend is seen in drug-related criminal activities, with major increases in the cultivation, use, and sale of narcotics. According to official statistics, 135,000 people are estimated to be drug addicts, representing about 2.3 percent of Tajikistan's population.

The process of nation building is just now beginning again after an abortive start in the nineteenth century. This process will be affected by regional events including military and political developments in Afghanistan and the ongoing power struggle in Uzbekistan. Following the 11 September 2001 events, and with the launching of the antiterrorism war in Afghanistan, the future of Tajikistan is likely to be affected by the new realities in the region. Following the assassination of the Northern Alliance's commander Ahmad Shah Masoud and the launching of the U.S.-led antiterrorism war, there were widespread fears in Tajikistan of a potential massive influx of refugees into the country. Such fears have so far proven to be unfounded. However, such fears are not completely eliminated. If, in the future, UN efforts to promote a multiethnic governing process in Afghanistan fail and the country once again plunges into interethnic and interfactional fighting, Afghan refugees might again head toward the Afghan-Tajik border. Any influx of refugees in Tajikistan in the short- to long-term future will threaten the fragile economic and political infrastructure of the country.

In October 2001, during a visit to the region by U.S. Secretary of Defense Donald Rumsfeld, Tajikistan agreed to grant basing rights to the U.S. military and to provide assistance to the U.S.-led coalition in intelligence gathering and various types of military-to-military cooperation. In return, Tajikistan's leadership was promised increased U.S. economic assistance, and now expects Washington's help in using its influence to help them to gain access to development aid offered by international financial institutions. However, unless the United States and other donor agencies tie future economic assistance to improved social and economic conditions, additional development funds might instead end up exacerbating popular frustrations. On the security front, destruction of the Al Qaida network by the U.S.-led coalition eliminated a major source of logistic and economic assistance for Central Asia's Islamic militants, including the Islamic Movement of Uzbekistan and Hizb ut-Tahrir; both movements have been active in Tajikistan. Without such support, it is still too early to say how these movements will react in the long term. In the short term, it is fair to say that they will cease their military and recruiting activities and wait to see how these events in Afghanistan shape up.

It is certain that the United States will expect from any future Afghan government, in exchange for its military support, an elimination of Afghanistan's drug industry. Ending Afghanistan's drug industry will have a dual impact on Tajikistan. On the one hand, Tajikistani youths who have in the past engaged in drug trafficking will now find themselves unemployed. Many of these young people are also drug addicts. Unless these young people are provided jobs and drug rehabilitation facilities, they can be a source of major trouble, including being recruits for Islamic militant groups in the future. On the other hand, this will assist ongoing efforts to put an end to the corruption and criminal activities that have infiltrated Tajikistan's society and leadership structures as a result of drug money. Well before 11 September, Russia has been reasserting its power in Central Asia. A Russian threat assessment in 1999 identified Central Asia as of vital importance for its security and economic well-being, and it is now seizing the initiative. Most importantly, until recently Moscow has seen the region as a bulwark against radical Islamic movements emanating from Afghanistan and Pakistan, and is, therefore, willing to commit considerable resources to securing the southern border. The Central Asian leaders agree with Russian president Putin on the need to stop the rise of militant Islam in the region. At a meeting of the Shanghai Five (Russia, China, Kyrgyzstan, Kazakhstan, and Tajikistan) in June 2001, all leaders, plus the Uzbek president, adopted a framework for cooperation in battling Islamic insurgency. The organization was then transformed into the Shanghai Cooperation Organization (SCO) with the addition of Uzbekistan. One of the major aims of the SCO is to improve the regional response to different problems connected with radical Islam. Such concerns have been heightened in the wake of 11 September. However, anti-insurgency efforts in the region have so far been hampered by a lack of coordination among the countries' security forces and by disputes among the members over borders and resources. It is safe to say that the course of future events in Tajikistan will be significantly influenced by the actions of these regional players. It is hoped that with increased attention focused on the region, more aid will flow into drug prevention programs and projects to create alternative sources of employment for the Ferghana Valley's unemployed youth.

Recommendations

The period between now and the next round of elections in 2004–2005 can be viewed as a new transition period for Tajikistan. As Tajikistan moves into this new transition phase, the following are priority tasks.

• Strengthening the continuing peace process and the public involvement in it. In particular, attention must now be paid to broaden the political base of the government both in terms of regional representation and opposition forces. The recent forays made by Hizb ut-Tahrir in Khujand attest to the feelings of marginalization that this region still feels. The regime has strengthened its position in the north and the secession scenario is less applicable today than it was in 1997. Any negative developments in north Tajikistan will in the future have an immediate and severe impact on border countries. The international community must convince the Tajik government, through the use of carrots and sticks, to truly implement a policy of inclusion embracing all political forces and movements in the decisionmaking processes. Laws on elections and political parties must be revised in order to enable wider participation.

• Strengthening the capacities of the parliament to perform its legislative duties well by establishing a training academy for the parliamentarians and their staff.

• Widening and deepening the process of democratization in the society by promoting democratic self-governing institutions via legislation to protect the role and function of entities such as *mahallas.*

• Facilitating development of a free and independent press by continuing to expand access to alternative sources of information through the granting of licenses for private radio and TV broadcasting stations.

• Encouraging professionalization of political parties. Parties also need to extend their reach beyond Dushanbe. Only the People's Democratic Party and the Islamic Renaissance Party have branches outside Dushanbe. Other parties must be encouraged to do so through adequate training and availability of resources, both of which could be provided by the international community.

• Advancing economic reform by broadening involvement of citizens in the economic life of the country.

• Military reform and preservation of the security of citizens with particular attention to integrating former soldiers into the economy. Close to 1,500 former UTO armed fighters are still in the Karategin Valley, unemployed and marginalized.

• Professionalization, with encouragement of the donor community, of the NGO sector. We estimate that less than 10 percent of the NGOs currently registered in Tajikistan have the necessary skills to engage in strategic planning and project design, and few of them are sustainable financially in the long term. It is time for the donors to recognize that quality and not quantity should be the rule of thumb in the development of a healthy civil-society sector. NGOs are not necessarily the best elements of a strong civil society. Community-based organizations, especially the ones developed and promoted by local *mahallas,* might be a more sustainable element in Tajikistan's civil society.

• The establishment of closer connections between citizens and government, that is, the building of "some sort of bridge" that government must not fear as a rival. Both government and NGOs must be involved in the building of a new national identity. Localism and regionalism are still prevalent in Tajikistani political life. Now might be the time to reintroduce the idea of a Consultative Forum of the Peoples of Tajikistan as a parallel power structure to involve representatives from all regions of Tajikistan, all ethnic groups, and representatives of civil society and of government.

• A whole array of activities must be promoted to deal with the growing drug problem and HIV/AIDS crisis.

• Lastly, the international community must send a strong message about its low tolerance for the criminalization of Tajikistani society through drug money. Different layers of Tajikistan's political, security, and economic structures are now involved in the narco-trafficking business. The international community could link future loans and economic assistance to the willingness of the government to rid its structures of elements that are known to be involved in the drug business.

Resources

Newsletters and Periodicals
Central Asia and the Caucasus, Journal of Social and Political Studies, Information and Analytical Center, Sweden
Central Asia–Caucasus Analyst, the Central Asia–Caucasus Institute of the Johns Hopkins University, the Nitze School of Advanced International Studies
Central Asia Monitor
Current History, some of its issues focused on Central Asia
Turkistan Newsletter, Research Center for Turkistan, Azerbaijan, Crimea, Caucasus and Siberia, the Netherlands

Reports
Conciliation Resources, *The Tajikistan Peace Process, Accord,* issue 10, 2001.
Human Rights Watch, *Conflict in the Soviet Union: Tajzhikistan,* July 1991.
International Crisis Group
  "Incubators of Conflict: Central Asia's Localised Poverty and Social Unrest," in *Central Asia: Fault Lines in the New Security Map,* July 2001.
  "Tajikistan: An Uncertain Peace." *Asia Report* no. 30, 24 December 2001.
The Civil War in Tajikistan: Causes and Implications, by Olivier Roy, December 1993.
The War in Tajikistan Three Years On, Special Report, November 1995.
United Nations Development Program, *Tajikistan Human Development Reports,* 1998, 1999, 2000.
United Nations Mission of Observers in Tajikistan, *General Agreement on the Establishment of Peace and National Accord in Tajikistan—What Does It Say?* September 1997.
United States Institute of Peace

Other Publications
A Public Peace Process, by Harold H. Saunders. New York, St. Martin's Press, 1999.
Central Asia and the Transcaucasia: Ethnicity and Conflict, edited by Vitaly V. Naumkin. Westport, CT, Greenwood Press, May 1994.
Central Asia: Conflict, Resolution, and Change, edited by Roald Sagdeev and Susan Eisenhower. Chevy Chase, MD, Center for Post-Soviet Studies, January 1995.
Central Asia's New States: Independence, Foreign Policy, and Regional Security, by Martha Brill Olcott. Washington, DC, United States Institute for Peace, October 1997.
Civil Society in Central Asia, edited by M. Holt Ruffin and Daniel Waugh. Seattle, University of Washington Press, 1999.
Islam and Central Asia, edited by Susan Eisenhower and Roald Sagdeev. Washington, DC, Center for Political and Strategic Studies, June 2000.
"Managing Conflict in Divided Societies: Lessons from Tajikistan," by Randa M. Slim and Harold H. Saunders. *Negotiation Journal* 12, no. 1, January 1996.
Tajikistan: Disintegration or Reconciliation? by Shirin Akiner, London: The Royal Institute of International Affairs, 2001.
The New Central Asia: The Creation of Nations, by Olivier Roy. New York: New York University Press, May 2000.

The Resurgence of Central Asia: Islam or Nationalism? by Ahmad Rashid. Karachi, Oxford University Press, May 1999.

The Subtlest Battle: Islam in Soviet Tajikistan, by Muriel Atkin. Philadelphia, Foreign Policy Research Institute, 1989.

The Tajik War: A Challenge to Russian Policy, by Lena Jonson. London, Royal Institute of International Affairs, 1998.

Selected Internet Sites

www.angelfire.com/sd/tajikistanupdate (The Tajikistan update includes sections on news, culture, discussion, analytical articles, and a message board)

www.crisisweb.org (International Crisis Group with reports on Central Asia online)

www.eurasianet.org/ (An Open Society Institute site that provides an independent source of news and analysis about Tajikistan)

www.fas.harvard.edu/~centasia (Perhaps the richest and most concentrated source of information on Central Asian studies worldwide)

www.friends-partners.org/~ccsi/nisorgs/tajik/taj (List of organizations in Tajikistan)

www.icarp.com/tajik.html/ (An online resource for original reference and curricular materials, analytical materials, and annotated links to Tajikistan and Central Asia)

www.incore.ulst.ac.uk/cds/countries/tajik.html (INCORE guide to internet sources on conflict and ethnicity in Tajikistan)

www.internews.ru/ASIA-PLUS (An independent news service in Tajikistan)

www.iwpr.net (Institute for War and Peace Reporting)

www.reliefweb.int/ (Reports from WHO, OCHA, IFRC, and other agencies on humanitarian disasters in Tajikistan from 1997 to the present)

www.rferl.org/bd/ta/index.html (Daily news, analysis and real audio broadcasts covering the developments in Tajikistan)

www.times.kg (Online version of the weekly English-language newspaper covering Central Asia)

www.un.org/dept/dpko/missions/unmot.html (Information on the United Mission of Observers in Tajikistan)

Resource Contacts

Abdelaziz Abdelaziz, Organization for Security and Cooperation in Europe, Dusti field office, e-mail: azizaziz@mail.com

Zuhra Halimova, Tajik Branch of Open Society Institute Assistance Foundation, e-mail: zhalimov@osi.tajik.net

Mirza Jahani, Agha Khan Foundation, e-mail: mirzajahani@atge.automail.com

Ibodullo Kalonov, Khujand Madreseh, tel: 3422 65236, 3422 64457

Shamsiddin Karimov, Global Training for Development Project, e-mail: shams@tajnet.com

Christine Kiernan, Internews, e-mail: kiernan@internews.ru

Abdugani Mamadazimov, National Association of Political Scientists of Tajikistan, e-mail: abdu@napst.td.silk.org

Parviz Mullojanov, Public Committee for the Promotion of Democratic Processes, e-mail: okpdv@tajik.net

Stephane Nicolas, ACTED, e-mail: stephane.nicolas@acted.org

Muzaffar Olimov, Sharq Center, e-mail: olimov@tajik.net

Randall Olson, Counterpart Consortium, e-mail: rolson@counterpart-tj.org

John Schoeberlein, Forum for Central Asian Studies, Harvard University, e-mail: schoeber@fas.harvard.edu

Hiroshi Takahashi, United Nations Tajikistan Office of Peace-Building, fax: 992 372 210159

Akbar Usmani, United Nations Development Program, e-mail: akbar.usmani@undp.org

Daniel Zust, Swiss Coordination Office, Dushanbe, e-mail: zud@sdc.tojikiston.com

Data on the following organizations can be found in the Directory section:

Asia Plus
Centre for Conflict Studies and Regional Research
Centre for Social Technologies
Fidokor
Foundation to Support Civil Initiatives
Manizha Information and Education Centre
National Association of Political Scientists of Tajikistan
Sharq Reserach and Analysis Center
Silk Road—Road of Consolidation
Sudmand
Tajik Center for Citizenship Education
Traditions and Modernity

Randa M. Slim (of Dayton, Ohio, USA) focuses on consulting and training in the fields of conflict management and public participation. Since 1993, Slim has been a member of the Inter-Tajik Dialogue, an unofficial dialogue focusing on the conflict in Tajikistan. She is currently the principal consultant for the Inter-Tajick Dialogue civic initiative, a three-year project funded by a consortium of U.S. foundations. She is also a consultant for the Peace Promotion Project in the Ferghana Valley, funded by the Swiss Agency for Development and Cooperation. Faredun Hodizoda is currently the national coordinator of the Goodwill Ambassadors project, funded by the Swiss Agency for Development and Cooperation. He holds a doctorate from the Rudaki Institute of Language and Literature of the Tajikistan Academy of Sciences.

Notes

1. Olivier Roy, *The Civil War in Tajikistan: Causes and Implications.* Washington, DC: United States Institute of Peace, 1993, p. 13.

2. The Dartmouth Conference, which began in 1960, is the longest continuous bilateral dialogue between Soviet (now Russian) and U.S. citizens. The regional conflicts task force was formed in 1981 to probe the dynamics of Soviet-U.S. interactions in such regional conflicts as those in southern Africa, the Middle East, and Afghanistan. It was cochaired until 1988 by Yevgeny Primakov and Harold Saunders. Gennady Chufrin succeeded Primakov in 1989. The task force has met every six months since August 1982. In 1992, the task force decided to conceptualize the process of dialogue that it learned through more than twenty meetings and to apply that process to one of the conflicts that had broken out on the territory of the former Soviet Union.

3. Gerd Merrem, "The Tajikistan Peace Process: UN Achievements to Date and Challenges Ahead," unpublished document, March 1999, p. 14.

4. Parviz Mullojanov, "Civil Society and Peacebuilding," in *Conciliation Resources: The Tajikistan Peace Process, Accord,* issue 10, 2001, pp. 60–63.

PART 3

Directory

Introduction to the Directory

The directory that follows contains profiles and contact information for more than 400 organizations in the fields of conflict prevention and peacebuilding across Europe and Eurasia.

The prime focus is on key organizations—governmental as well as nongovernmental (NGOs)—that are based and active in Europe and Eurasia. It also includes organizations with headquarters in the region but with activities outside of it. To make the picture as complete as possible, we have also included a selection of key organizations from North America that are involved in relevant projects in Europe and Eurasia.

The organizations are listed in the following order: organizations of the European Union, organizations of the OSCE, organizations of the United Nations, organizations presented in order of country of location. A selection of government agencies and ministries can be found in the appendix.

For larger international NGO networks, we have only included the profile of the headquarters' office and not a profile for each and every regional office. Consequently, for organizations like the International Helsinki Federation for Human Rights, the Helsinki Citizen's Assembly, and the Partners for Democratic Change, the reader is advised to contact the main office for country-specific information on their activities in the fields of conflict prevention and peacebuilding. However, there are a few exceptions to this selection criterion. We have included a small number of local offices in certain countries where few organizations exist in the field. This has been done in the interest of providing at least one "bridgehead" in almost all countries of Europe and Eurasia.

Because organizations in the fields of development cooperation and humanitarian aid have increasingly incorporated ideas of conflict prevention and peacebuilding into their prime mandate, we have also opted to include organizations that, at first sight, might not be seen as conflict prevention organizations.

The shaded box that appears at the upper right of each profile presents the organization's main activities in conflict prevention and peacebuilding.

The countries/regions in which the organization's activities are focused are presented above the organization's name.

A far as possible, the given number of staff and budget relates to the organization's specific activities in the field of conflict prevention and peace-building.

Additional information on some organizations may be found in the Resources sections that appear at the end of the survey chapters in Part 2. Some of this information has been omitted here due to space limitations.

Europe, Global

ACTION

EuropeAid Co-operation Office

The EuropeAid Co-operation Office's mission is to implement the external aid instruments of the European Commission. It is responsible for managing the full project cycle of most European Commission external assistance programmes. While the External Relations Directorate General, as part of the Common Foreign and Security Policy, has the primary responsibility for crisis management, it falls on the EuropeAid Co-operation Office to implement long-term conflict prevention and peacebuilding measures as part of the Commissions aid and development programs drawn up by the Development Directorate General.

European Commission
EuropeAid H/5 L41 7/52
Rue de la Loi, 200
1049 Brussels
Belgium

Tel: +32 (2) 299 1111
Fax: +32 (2) 299 6407
europaid-info@cec.eu.int
www.europa.eu.int/comm/europeaid/index_en.htm

Publications: European Initiative for Democracy and Human Rights, 2001.

Europe, Global

ACTION
ADVOCACY

External Relations Directorate General of the Commission

The External Relations Directorate General of the Commission (DG Relex), headed by Commissioner Chris Patten, is a new department of the European Commission. The DG Relex administers the TACIS program, which is aimed at sustaining reform and conflict prevention, in the CIS countries. It also administers the People to People Program,the overall objective of which is to help support the civil society for a sustainable peace in the Middle East. A crisis management unit has been established in DG Relex. The Commissioner works in close cooperation with the High Representative for the Common Foreign and Security Policy in the field of conflict prevention.

European Commission
200 Rue de la Loi
1049 Brussels
Belgium

tel +32 (2) 299 1111
maria.mcloughlin@cec.eu.int
europa.eu.int/comm/dgs/external_relations/index_en.htm

Contact: Maria McLoughlin, Head of Conflict Prevention and Crisis Management Unit
Number of staff: 8
Publications: Communication from the Commission on Conflict Prevention, 2001.

Europe, Global

Humanitarian Aid Office
of the European Commission

RESEARCH
EDUCATION
ACTION
ADVOCACY

The Humanitarian Aid Office of the European Commission (ECHO) is a service of the European Commission and it manages humanitarian aid provided by the EU to non-EU countries. Through its partners, it offers help to victims of both natural disasters and man-made crises. ECHO's mandate includes disaster preparedness by means of early warning systems and the financing of disaster prevention in high-risk areas. ECHO is active in all the world's major crisis zones including the Balkans and the northern Caucasus.

Rue de la Loi 200
1049 Brussels
Belgium

Tel: +32 (2) 295 4400
Fax:+32 (2) 295 4572
echo-info@cec.eu.int
europa.eu.int/comm/echo/en/index_en.html

Contact: Costanza Adinolfi, Director
Number of staff: 130
Budget: > $1,000,000

Publications: ECHO News, quarterly newsletter;
Country leaflets and thematic publications

Europe, Global

Office of the High Representative for the
Common Foreign and Security Policy

ACTION
ADVOCACY

Headed by Javier Solana Madariaga, the European Council's Office of the High Representative for the Common Foreign and Security Policy (CFSP) is one of the EU's main instruments for implementing its conflict prevention policies. The office aims to represent the EU externally and to develop a civilian crisis management capacity as well as initiatives to control small arms proliferation. In 1999, a security and defense policy for the EU was adopted, later followed by a decision to create a Rapid Reaction Force to assist in different conflict situations. It will be operational in January 2003. In 2001, Solana's office was involved in political discussions in both Macedonia and the Middle East in order to defuse the situation.

General Secretariat
  of the Council of the
  European Union
Rue de la Loi 175
1048 Brussels
Belgium

Tel:+32 (2) 285 8111
Fax: +32 (2) 285 8026
cristina.gallach@consilium.eu.int
www.consilium.eu.int

Contact: Cristina Gallach, Spokesperson of the High Representative for the CFSP

Europe, Global

Policy Planning
and Early Warning Unit

RESEARCH
ADVOCACY

Under the responsibility of the High Representative for the Common Foreign and Security Policy, the Policy Planning and Early Warning Unit (PPEWU) has the task of analyzing potential conflict situations and drawing the attention of member state governments to rising tensions at an early state. The unit is made up of national, EU, and Western European Union (WEU) civil servants and is part of the Council of Ministers' Secretariat in Brussels. It presents options for common strategies in foreign policy to the EU foreign ministers. The PPEWU increasingly consults with NGOs when writing policy papers.

General Secretariat of the
    Council of the
    European Union
Rue de la Loi 175
1048 Brussels
Belgium

Contact: Andre Gillissen, Press Officer
Number of staff: 20

Tel: +32 (2) 285 5430
Fax: +32 (2) 285 5570
press.office@consilium.eu.int

OSCE participating states

Office of the OSCE High Commissioner on National Minorities

ACTION
ADVOCACY

The Office of the OSCE High Commissioner on National Minorities has been established to identify and seek early resolution of ethnic tensions that might endanger peace, stability, or friendly relations between the participating states of the OSCE (Organization for Security and Co-operation in Europe). His mandate describes him as "an instrument of conflict prevention at the earliest possible stage."

The office was established in 1992 by the then Conference for Security and Co-operation in Europe. The former Netherlands Minister of State, Max van der Stoel, was appointed as the first High Commissioner. Rolf Ekéus was appointed as his successor in 2001.

Operating independently from all parties involved, the High Commissioner is empowered to conduct on-site missions and engage in preventive diplomacy at the earliest stage of tension. In addition to seeking first-hand information, the High Commissioner seeks to promote dialogue, confidence, and cooperation.

His role is to contain and de-escalate tensions, but he also functions as a "tripwire" who is responsible for alerting the OSCE. The High Commissioner is allowed to operate with the necessary independence. He does not require the approval of the Senior Council or of the state concerned. This independence is crucial to the timing of his involvement.

Although the title of this post sometimes creates the impression that the High Commissioner is intended to function as a national minorities ombudsman or as an investigator of individual human rights violations, this is not the case. He is the OSCE's High Commissioner on minorities and not for minorities.

The High Commissioner has been involved in minority issues in OSCE participating states such as Albania, Croatia, Estonia, Hungary, Kazakhstan, Kyrgyzstan, Latvia, Romania, Slovakia, the former Yugoslav Republic of Macedonia, and Ukraine.

P.O. Box 20062
2500 EB The Hague
The Netherlands

Tel: +31 (70) 312 5500
Fax: +31 (70) 363 5910
hcnm@hcnm.org
www.osce.org/hcnm

Contact: Walter Kemp, Senior Adviser

Publications: Report on the Situation of Roma and Sinti in the OSCE Area, 2000; *The Lund Recommendations on the Effective Participation of National Minorities in Public Life,* 1999; *The Hague Recommendations Regarding the Education Rights of National Minorities in Public Life,* 1999; *The Role of the High Commissioner on National Minorities in OSCE Conflict Prevention: An Introduction,* 1997.

OSCE participating states

RESEARCH
EDUCATION
ACTION
ADVOCACY

OSCE

Once a forum for talks between two highly polarized blocs, the intergovernmental Organisation for Security and Co-operation in Europe now aims to consolidate common values, build civil societies, prevent local conflicts, bring peace to war-torn areas, and promote a cooperative system of security.

The OSCE (known until January 1, 1995, as the Conference on Security and Co-operation in Europe [CSCE]) embraces a region that stretches from Vancouver to Vladivostok, comprising Canada, the United States, all the countries of the former Soviet Union, and the whole of Europe.

Early warning, conflict prevention, crisis management, and post-conflict rehabilitation have become a central part of the OSCE's responsibilities. Its ability to shoulder these tasks is a relatively new asset of the Organization and comprises an impressive list of institutions, field activities, and mechanisms, augmented by a great body of experience. Much of this has been brought together in the Conflict Prevention Centre at the Vienna Secretariat.

An important element of the OSCE's work is its long-term field missions to such countries as Bosnia and Herzegovina, Estonia, Georgia, and Tajikistan. In 1996, the OSCE's key role in fostering security and stability in all their dimensions was further elaborated at the Lisbon Summit, which stimulated the development of a common and comprehensive security model for Europe for the twenty-first century. This was adopted by the leaders of the OSCE participating states at the Istanbul Summit in November 1999 as the Charter for European Security.

The OSCE offers its participating states the constant possibility of entering into dialogue, by means of the permanent delegations to the OSCE in Vienna. Such discussions can have important functions as preventive diplomacy and early warning signals.

While the OSCE usually takes decisions by consensus, in some cases the support of a number of states is sufficient to dispatch missions to investigate situations of a human dimension or military nature. The receiving state is committed to accepting these missions.

In order to identify ethnic tensions that might endanger peace, stability, or relations between OSCE states, and to promote the early resolution of such tensions, the Organization has created the Institution of High Commissioner on National Minorities (see previous entry). The High Commissioner is empowered to conduct on-site missions and to engage in diplomacy at the earliest stages of tension.

OSCE Secretariat
Kärntner Ring 5-7
1010 Vienna
Austria

Tel: +43 (1) 5143 6180
Fax: +43 (1) 5143 6105
info@osce.org
www.osce.org

Contact: Keith Jinks, Public Information Officer
Number of staff: >4000 (including field staff)
Budget: >$1,000,000
Publications: The OSCE Handbook; The OSCE Newsletter; OSCE Human Dimension Commitments: A Reference Guide, 2001.

Balkans, Central Asia, Caucasus, Eastern Europe

OSCE Office for Democratic Institutions and Human Rights

EDUCATION
ACTION

The Office for Democratic Institutions and Human Rights (ODIHR) is the principal institution of the OSCE responsible for the human dimension, and it works to help OSCE's participating states fulfill their commitments to human rights, democracy, and the rule of law. The ODIHR observes elections, monitors the human rights situation in OSCE countries, and carries out some one hundred assistance projects in the fields of rule of law, gender, prevention of trafficking, migration/freedom of movement, civil society, Roma and Sinti issues, and freedom of religion. The work of ODIHIR in these fields is seen as a contribution to conflict prevention.

Aleje Ujazdowskie 19
00-557 Warsaw
Poland

Tel: +48 (22) 520 0600
Fax: +48 (22) 520 0605
office@odihr.osce.waw.pl
www.osce.org/odihr

Contact: Eric Rudenshiold, Head of Democratisation Section
Number of Staff: 80
Budget: > $1,000,000
Publications: ODIHR monthly electronic newsletter; Election Reports; Various thematic publications on democratization and human rights issues

Global

DPKO Lessons Learned Unit

RESEARCH
ACTION
ADVOCACY

The Lessons Learned Unit of the Department of Peacekeeping Operations (DPKO) was set up in April 1995 in order to develop structural mechanisms to collect and analyze information on the various missions being fielded by the United Nations and to recommend ways of improving their effectiveness. The unit seeks to avoid duplicating similar work being done within the UN or elsewhere. Instead it attempts to bring these separate initiatives together. A resource center gives access to books, documents, and other material. One research topic is the former Yugoslavia, where UNPROFOR is stationed.

UN Department of Peace Keeping Operations
One United Nations Plaza
Room S-927
New York, N.Y. 10017
USA

Tel: +1 (212) 963 3745
Fax: +1 (212) 963 1813
peace-keeping-lessons@un.org
www.un.org/depts/dpko/lessons

Global

Office for the
Coordination of Humanitarian Affairs

RESEARCH
ACTION
ADVOCACY

The UN Office for the Coordination of Humanitarian Affairs (OCHA) is mandated to coordinate UN assistance. It is also committed to conflict prevention through advocacy efforts and humanitarian policy development. OCHA discharges its coordination function primarily through the IASC, with the participation of humanitarian partners such as the Red Cross Movement and NGOs. At present, OCHA maintains 32 field offices in Africa, Asia, and Europe including the Integrated Regional Information Network (IRIN). Instrumental in implementing its conflict-prevention goal is its leading role in the UN Framework for Coordination Team, an interagency body that identifies countries at risk and promotes appropriate preventive and preparedness measures.

Palais des Nations
1211 Geneva 10
Switzerland

Tel: +41 (22) 917 1234
Fax: +41 (22) 917 0023
ochagva@un.org
www.reliefweb.int/ocha_ol

Contact: Ramesh Rajasingham, Humanitarian Affairs Officer

Publications: OCHA News; Guiding Principles on Internal Displacement, 1999; *OCHA Orientation Handbook on Complex Emergencies,* 1999.

Global

UNESCO's Culture of Peace Program

RESEARCH
EDUCATION
ACTION
ADVOCACY

UNESCO's Culture of Peace Program (CPP) is based on the principles established in the UN Charter and on respect for human rights, democracy, and tolerance, the promotion of development, education for peace, the free flow of information, and the wider participation of women as an integral approach to preventing violence and conflicts, and efforts aimed at the creation of conditions for peace and its consolidation. In working with a wide range of partners, UNESCO aims to advance a global movement for a culture of peace. This includes, for example, organization of regional or international seminars and the mobilization of projects.

7 Place de Fontenoy
75352 Paris 07 SP
France

Tel: +33 (1) 4568 1319
Fax: +33 (1) 4568 5521
cofpeace@unesco.org
www.unesco.org/cpp

Contact: Francoise Riviere, Director

Publications: Culture of Peace, newsletter; *Conflict Resolution: New Approaches and Methods,* 2000; *World Directory of Peace Research and Training Institutions,* 2000; *Human Rights of Women: A Collection of International and Regional Normative Instruments,* 1999.

Global

United Nations Department of Political Affairs

RESEARCH
ACTION

The United Nations Department of Political Affairs (DPA) provides advice and support on all political matters to the Secretary-General relating to the maintenance and restoration of peace and security. DPA monitors, analyzes, and assesses political developments throughout the world; identifies potential or actual conflicts in whose control and resolution the United Nations could play a useful role; recommends to the Secretary-General appropriate actions in such cases and executes the approved policy; and assists the Secretary-General in carrying out political activities decided by him and/or mandated by the General Assembly and the Security Council in the areas of preventive diplomacy, peacemaking, peacekeeping, and post-conflict peacebuilding.

UN Plaza
DPA Policy Planning Unit
Room S-3780
New York, NY 10017
USA

Contact: Tapio Kanninen, Chief Policy Planning Unit

Tel: +1 (212) 963 5118
Fax: +1 (212) 963 5065
commond@un.org
www.un.org/depts/dpa

Global

United Nations Development Programme

EDUCATION
ACTION
ADVOCACY

Over the past several years the United Nations Development Programme (UNDP) has come to place greater emphasis on conflict prevention. The Emergency Response Division sees poor governance as a major factor in the development of man-made crises, so it works on capacity building for good governance nationally and internationally by means of preventive development and training. Among other things, the Programme provides electoral assistance, support for judiciaries, and public-sector management. UNDP's core goal of supporting sustainable human development is in itself a strong foundation for the prevention of conflict in the long term.

304 E. 45th St.
New York, NY 10017
USA

Tel: +1 (212) 906 5324
Fax: +1 (212) 906 5364
aboutundp@undp.org
www.undp.org

Contact: Robert Piper, Deputy Director Emergency Response Division

Publications: Transition 1999: Regional Human Development Report for Central and Eastern Europe and the CIS, 1999; *Central Asia 2010: Prospects for Human Development,* 1999; *The New Yalta: Commemorating the 50th Anniversary of the Declaration of Human Rights in the RBEC Region,* 1999; *Poverty in Transition?* 1998.

Global

United Nations
High Commissioner for Refugees

ACTION

In recent years the United Nations High Commissioner for Refugees (UNHCR) has increased its emphasis on conflict prevention, although it has no special department exclusively responsible for this. The High Commissioner is mandated to take action in situations of severe human rights violations and is expected to alert governments and other agencies. The work of the Reintegration and Local Settlement Section is sometimes described in terms of peacebuilding activities, such as ensuring the reintegration of returning refugees and displaced people. The focus of the organization changes from year to year, depending of the patterns of displacement.

94 rue de Montbrillant,
1202 Geneva
Switzerland

tel :+41 (22) 739 8111
fax: +41 (22) 739 7367
cdr@unhcr.ch
www.unhcr.ch

Contact: Niels Harild, Head of UNHCR reintegration and local settlement section

Publications: Refugees, quarterly magazine; *The State of the World's Refugees,* UNHCR global report

Global

United Nations
Institute for Disarmament Research

RESEARCH
ACTION
ADVOCACY

The United Nations Institute for Disarmament Research (UNIDIR) was established in 1980 for the purpose of undertaking independent research on disarmament and related problems, particularly international security issues. It aims to provide the international community with diversified and complete data, and to assist ongoing negotiations on disarmament, particularly on nuclear armaments, by means of factual studies and analyses. Among other activities, UNIDIR is currently running a project on peacebuilding and practical disarmament in Africa, and contributes to the monitoring and evaluation of mine action programs.

Palais des Nations
1211 Geneva 10
Switzerland

Tel: +41 (22) 917 3186
Fax: +41 (22) 917 0176
plewis@unorg.ch
www.unog.ch/unidir

Contact: Patricia Lewis, Director

Publications: Disarmament Forum, quarterly journal; *Illicit Trafficking in Firearms: Prevention and Combat in Rio de Janeiro Brazil,* 2001; *Peacekeeping in Africa: Capabilities and Culpabilities,* 2000; *Tactical Nuclear Weapons: Options for Control,* 2000; *The Small Arms Problem in Central Asia: Features and Implications,* 2000.

Global

United Nations
Institute for Training and Research

RESEARCH
EDUCATION
ACTION

,The United Nations Institute for Training and Research (UNITAR) is an autonomous body within the United Nations with a mandate to enhance the effectiveness of the UN through training and research. UNITAR provides training to diplomats and negotiators in such areas as international affairs, the environment, and finance (debt, economic management and public administration). The Institute also conducts research to innovate training and capacity-building approaches. Together with governments, NGOs, and other UN agencies, it customizes training programs that meet a country's needs.

Palais des Nations
1211 Geneva 10
Switzerland

Tel: +41 (22) 917 8577
Fax: +41 (22) 917 8047
trisha.riedy@unitar.org
www.unitar.org

Contact: Connie Peck, Principal Coordinator, Programme in Peacemaking and Preventive Diplomacy

Number of staff: 4
Budget: > $1,000,000

Global

United Nations
Office for Project Services

ACTION

United Nations Office for Project Services (UNOPS) offers the international community a broad range of services, from overall project management to the provision of single inputs. It became a separate UN organization in January 1995. The Geneva-based Rehabilitation and Social Sustainability (RESS) Division implements social and economic initiatives aimed at preventing conflict and supporting peace and reconciliation, currently in some 20 war-torn societies. Examples include the implementation of peace agreements, rebuilding of societies, reintegration of refugees, project design, and organization of development activities.

RESS Headquarters
11-13 chemin des Anemones
1219 Chatelaine
Geneva
Switzerland

Tel: +41 (22) 917 8384
Fax: +41 (22) 917 8062
christopheb@unops.org
www.unops.org

Contact: Jean Christophe Bouvier, Chief RESS division & Geneva Office

Number of staff: 1,200
Budget: > $1,000,000

Publications: RESS Approach, magazine published twice a year; *RESS Operational Guide for Substantive Management of Rehabilitation Programmes*

Global

United Nations Volunteers Program

EDUCATION
ACTION

The General Assembly of the UN created the United Nations Volunteers program (UNV) in 1970 to serve as an operational partner in development cooperation at the request of UN member states. It works through the UNDP's country offices around the world. Each year, some 5,000 volunteers of over 150 nationalities serve in developing countries. They work in technical, economic, and social fields, including support of human rights and electoral and peacebuilding processes. Of these volunteers, 22 percent are active in Europe and the CIS countries. The UN Volunteers program was also designated the focal point for the International Year of Volunteers 2001 by the UN General Assembly.

Postfach 260 111
53153 Bonn
Germany

Tel: +49 (228) 815 2000
Fax: +49 (228) 815 2001
hq@unv.org
www.unv.org

Contact: Sharon Capeling-Alakija, Executive Coordinator

Number of staff: 120

Budget: > $1,000,000

Publications: UNV News, bi-annual magazine.

Albania

Foundation for Conflict Resolution and Reconciliation of Disputes

RESEARCH
EDUCATION
ACTION

The Albanian Foundation for Conflict Resolution and Reconciliation of Disputes (AFCR) aims at contributing to the democratization of Albanian society through mediation and reconciliation of conflicts and disputes arising among individuals and social groups. It has set up nine mediation centers in Albania where workshops are held in order to strengthen community-based mediation processes in Albanian society. The AFCR also works to educate youths and students on the concepts and practices of conflict prevention and resolution.

Him Kolli, nr 23/1
Tirana
Albania

Tel: +355 (42) 48 681
Fax: +355 (42) 32 739
gjoka@albaniaonline.net

Contact: Rasim Gjoka, Executive Director

Number of staff: 20

Budget: $100,000–$500,000

Publications: Reconciliation Magazine

Albania

Institute for Contemporary Studies

RESEARCH
ACTION

The Institute for Contemporary Studies (Instituti për Studime Bashkëkohore) is an independent institute for public policy research. The Institute's main objectives are to assist the development of human capacities that relate to the process of policy formulation, offer policy alternatives, assist expansion of public involvement in the policy formulation process, and to make public the ideas and alternatives proposed. The Institute is currently cooperating with the UNDP on a National Early Warning System (NEWS) intended for monitoring processes indicative of potential conflict.

Rr. Vaso Pasha, 7
Tirana
Albania

Contact: Artan Hoxha, Research Director
Number of staff: 3

Tel: +355 (42) 47 146/51 010
Fax: +355 (42) 34 868
ics@isb.icc-al.org
www.ics-al.org

CIS countries, Europe, Middle East

Armenian Center for National and International Studies

RESEARCH
EDUCATION

The Armenian Center for National and International Studies (ACNIS) conducts research on a comprehensive agenda of foreign and public policy as well as regional cooperation and conflict resolution issues. The organization conducted the International Conference on "Prospects for Regional and Transregional Cooperation and the Resolution of Conflicts" organized by ACNIS with the support of the OSCE, on September 27–28, 2000, in Yerevan, Armenia.

Vazgen Sargsian Street 4
Yerevan 375010
Armenia

Tel: +374 (1) 528 780/580 877
Fax: +374 (1) 524 846/151 801
root@acnis.am
www.acnis.am

Contact: Hrach Hakobyan, Director
Number of staff: 6
Budget: < $25,000

Publications: Center News, newsletter; *Ichkeria: Independence with No Demand, in Russian,* 2000; *Conflicts and Mediations for Their Settlement: A Look at the Intermediatory Attempt to Regulate the Karabagh Conflict, in Russian,* 1999; *Authority and Opposition in Azerbaijan: Traditions, Interrelations and Prospects, in Russian,* 1999.

South Caucasus

Armenian Sociological Association

RESEARCH
ACTION

The mission of the Armenian Sociological Association (ASA) is to conduct research, produce publications, and hold conferences and meetings on social and political issues. Its program in the field of conflict prevention is the "Trans Caucasian Common Migration Space," which is aimed at the creation of an NGO network for conflict resolution progress. Main activities under the program are conferences in hotpoints of TransCaucasus, Baku, Yerevan, Tbilisi, Stepanakert, Sukhum, and Tskhinval.

Aram Street 44
Yerevan 375010
Armenia
_____
Tel: +374 (1) 530 571/530 822
Fax: +374 (1) 530 521
gevork@sci.am
www.asa.am

Contact: Gevork Poghosyan
Number of staff: 5
Budget: < $25,000

Publications: Ethnic Processes and Migration in the Caucasus: Ethno-regional Policy of Armenia and Georgia, 1999; Eurasian Dispossessed NGOs and Human Security, 1999; Ethnic Groups and Migration, 1999; Caucasian NGOs on Migration Sector, 1998.

Armenia

Armenian Young Lawyers Association

RESEARCH
EDUCATION
ACTION

The mission of the Armenian Young Lawyers Association (AYLA) is to unite and direct the efforts and potential of members of the network organization to promote democratic development and the rule of law in Armenia. Major activities of the programs are dedicated to the institution of asylum and strengthening of national capacities including protection of the rights of refugees (in partnership with UNHCR).

Bagramayan Street 2/3a
Yerevan 375000
Armenia
_____
Tel: +374 (1) 560 539/540 199
Fax: +374 (1) 580 299
aylainformcentre@armpac.com; ayla@armpac.com

Contact: Karen Zadoyan, Director
Number of staff: 5
Budget: < $25,000

South Caucasus

Conflict Resolution Center of Armenia

RESEARCH
EDUCATION
ADVOCACY

The Conflict Resolution Center of Armenia (CRCA) aims to promote the principles of cooperation and non-violence, to protect minority rights, and to work for the prevention and peaceful resolution of conflicts in the political culture of Armenia. Special attention is paid to the Nagorno-Karabakh conflict and the situation in the Georgian subregion of Javakheti, populated mainly by ethnic Armenians. The Center produces publications and develops joint programs with regional NGOs with a similar profile.

Marshal Baghramyan
Avenue 24G
Yerevan 375019
Armenia
_____

Tel: +374 (1) 583 382
nhovanes@sci.am

Contact: Nikolay Hovhannisyan, Director

Number of staff: 4

Budget: < $25,000

Publications: The Karabakh Conflict: Factors, Criterias and Variants of Its Solution, 1999; *Ethnopolitical Conflicts in the Transcaucasus: Their Roots and Solutions,* 1997.

Caucasus

Democracy Union

RESEARCH
EDUCATION
ACTION

The Democracy Union aims to strengthen democracy and the rule of law. The NGO conducts research,produces publications, and runs educational programs in the field of conflict prevention and resolution, both at the theoretical and practical levels. The programs focus on the Caucasus and are in partnership with NGOs in Georgia, Azerbaijan, and internationally with the International Fellowship of Reconciliation (IFOR). The program aims to train representatives of border regions of Armenia in mediation, negotiation, and peacebuilding.

Nalbandian Street 17, apt. 4
Yerevan 375010
Armenia
_____

Tel/fax: +374 (1) 565 680
sshah@arminco.com

Contact: Samvel Shahinian, Director

Number of staff: 3

Budget: $25,000–$100,000

South Caucasus

Fund Against Violation of Law

RESEARCH
EDUCATION
ACTION
ADVOCACY

The main goal of the Fund Against Violation of Law is to help spread international humanitarian law and human rights principles in Armenia and the South Caucasus, harmonizing inter-ethnic relations in the region and promoting democratic reforms in Armenia. The organization has a department exclusively responsible for conflict prevention/resolution work in the region called the Aspect Group. The Fund's main program,"The Karabakh knot," studies legal aspects of the Karabakh problem.

Arshakunyants Street 6
Yerevan 375023
Armenia
_____
Tel: +374 (1) 582 819/568 272
Fax: +374 (1) 582 819
favl@intarnet.am

Contact: Michael Aramyan, President
Number of staff: 2
Budget: < $25,000

South Caucasus

Nagorno-Karabakh
Committee of "Helsinki Initiative-92"

EDUCATION
ACTION

The Nagorno-Karabakh Committee of "Helsinki Initiative-92"s (Lernayin Gharabaghi "Helsinkyan Nakhadzernutyun-92" Komite) mission includes civil-society building; conflict transformation; human rights protection; democracy development; and youth, migration, gender, and environmental issues. Its main program is the "Creation of a House of Peace in Nagorno-Karabakh ." The program aims to coordinate the activities of Karabakhi NGOs with other peace initiatives in the Caucasus, to establish a resource center for free information exchange, training courses, seminars, psychosocial, and post-conflict rehabilitation. The NGO is based on volunteer work and has no stable budget.

Tumanian Street 15
Stepanakert N/A
Nagorno-Karabakh
Armenia
_____
Tel: +374 (1) 421 252
Fax: +374 (1) 151 894/151 000
karandje@hca.nk.am; anna@umcor.am

Contact: Karen Ohanjanyan, Coordinator
Number of staff: 5

Armenia, Caucasus

Union of Non-Governmental Organizations of Shirak Region

EDUCATION
ACTION
ADVOCACY

The Union of Non-Governmental Organizations of Shirak Region (UNGO) is a network of 30 NGOs that deals with human rights, gender, children, refugees, disability, and national minority issues. The Union's mission is to assist in strengthening democracy and developing the NGO sector in the Shirak region of Armenia. It aims to set up close links among governmental, nongovernmental, and international organizations. Its main program focuses on the creation of an educational, consultative, and psychological resource center for refugees, national minorities, and disabled people. The NGO carries out migration studies in the Shirak region, and produces publications and media programs on human rights.

Vazgen Sargsyan Street 8, , Apt. 4
Gyumri 377510
Armenia

Tel: +374 (41) 30205/34157/32497
Fax: +374(41) 30205
revival@shirak.am

Contact: Mkrtich Tchartaryan, Chairman
Number of staff: 7
Budget: < $25,000
Publications: Booklet on migration investigations in Armenia, 2000; Cooperation of NGOs and self-governmental institutions in the book *Women and Development, Rights and Opportunities.*

South Caucasus

Yerevan Press Club

RESEARCH
EDUCATION
ACTION
ADVOCACY

Objectives of the Yerevan Press Club (YPC) include international and regional cooperation between journalists and NGOs for peace and integration; development of media legislation; and establishment of conditions for a free, responsible, and professional media. The focus of YPC's activities is on developing the combined efforts of journalists, media, and NGOs for peacebuilding and integration in the South Caucasus. Main projects include "The South Caucasus Network for Civil Accord," "Karabagh Conflict in the Mirror of Media and Public Opinion in Armenia, Azerbaijan and Mountanous Karabagh," and "The Role of Media in Overcoming Regional Conflicts and Eliminating the Enemy Image."

Mesrop Mashtots Avenue, 39/12
Yerevan 375009
Armenia

Tel: +374 (1) 530 067/533 541
Fax: +374 (1) 537 662/151 685
boris@ypc.am
www.ypc.am

Contact: Boris Navasardian, President
Number of staff: 17
Budget: $100,000–$500,000
Publications: Press Club, newsletter.

Alps/Adriatic Region

Alpen-Adria-Alternativ

The Alpen-Adria-Alternativ is a non-governmental organization that works for peace, ecology, intercultural encounters, and development of democracy and sustainable development. Its primary field of activity is the Alps-Adriatic Region, the area between Italy, Hungary, Bavaria, and Bosnia. One objective is the development of a network of environmental, peace, and cultural organizations in the region. In addition, Alpen-Adria-Alternativ is involved in a variety of projects with organizations throughout Europe. The projects are primarily pedagogic and academic with a focus on peace education, intercultural learning, and youth participation.

Rathausgasse 8
9500 Villach
Austria

Tel: +43 (4242) 22 864
Fax: +43 (4242) 238 396
alpen-adria-alternativ@netway.at
www.a3a.at

Contact: Bettina Gruber, Vice Chairwoman

Number of staff: 2

Budget: $25,000–$100,000

Publications: Alpe Adria Magazine, newsletter.

Former Republic of Yugoslavia, Southern Caucasus, Africa

Austrian Study Center
for Peace and Conflict Resolution

RESEARCH
EDUCATION

The Austrian Study Center for Peace and Conflict Resolution (ASPR) aims to contribute to peace and peaceful conflict resolution, and to promote practical ideas for peace, including its developmental and environmental aspects.

To further help advance its goals, ASPR established the European University Center for Peace Studies (EPU) in 1988. EPU, an NGO with UNESCO status, concentrates on university-level programs and courses in peace research and peace education designed mainly for post-graduate students who aspire to or have started careers in such fields as science, education, government, culture, economics, and international management.

Since 1993 ASPR and EPU have provided the infrastructure, staff support, and expertise for the International Civilian Peace-Keeping and Peace-Building Training Program (IPT), the first program in this area to provide training to professionals from a variety of cultural, organizational, and professional backgrounds. It aims to create a pool of civilian professionals who are available for civilian peacekeeping and peacebuilding on a stand-by basis. Four-week courses, partly dedicated to a specialization of choice (e.g., mediation and election assistance) are offered several times a year. Other training programs and courses include:

- Project Preparation, Implementation, and Conflict Management for Bosnia and Herzegovina
- Rebuilding the Multi-Ethnic Society in Eastern Slavonia, Baranja, and Western Sirmium
- Summer Academy on OSCE
- Preventive Diplomacy and Peacebuilding in Southern Africa.
- Mission Preparation Training for the OSCE (in cooperation with the Berghof Center for Constructive Conflict Management, the Constitutional and Legal Policy Institute, and the Diplomatic Academy Vienna)

ASPR also carries out research. Among its main focuses are European peace politics, peace education, the peace movement, NGOs, and social movements. These and other studies produce a steady flow of publications. ASPR also co-organizes an annual State of Peace conference, which it hosts every other year.

Rochusplatz 1 (Burg)
7461 Stadtschlaining
Austria

Tel: +43 (3355) 2498
Fax: +43 (3355) 2662
aspr@aspr.ac.at (ASPR);
   w.suetzl@epu.ac.at (EPU)
www.aspr.ac.at

Contact: Arno Truger, Deputy of the Executive President
Number of staff: 4 at HQ
Budget: $500,000–$1,000,000
Publications: Friedenserziehung konkret, Schulpraktische Handreichungen zur Friedenserziehung (Concrete Peace Education), journal; Dialog: *Beiträge zur Friedensforschung* (Dialogue: Contributions to Peace Research); *Friedensforum* (Peace Forum), bimonthly newsletter.

Global

International Helsinki Federation for Human Rights

RESEARCH
EDUCATION
ACTION
ADVOCACY

The International Helsinki Federation for Human Rights (IHF), a non-governmental and not-for-profit organization, seeks to promote compliance with the human rights provisions of the Helsinki Final Act in the OSCE member states. The Federation organizes seminars and workshops to debate issues concerning ethnic tension and democracy, and publishes reports and study results. IHF has representative committees in 37 OSCE member states. A series of confidence-building activities have taken place over the last few years and are planned to continue.

Wickenburggasse 14/7
1080 Vienna
Austria
_____

Tel: +43 (1) 408 8822
Fax: +43 (1) 408 8822-50
office@ihf-hr.org
www.ihf-hr.org

Contact: Aaron Rhodes, Executive Director

Number of staff: 12

Budget: < $25,000

Publications: Religious Intolerance in Selected OSCE Countries in 2000, 2001; *Religious Freedom in Southeastern and Central Europe,* 2001; *Human Rights in the OSCE Region: The Balkans, the Caucasus, Europe, Central Asia and North America,* 2001; *A From of Slavery: Trafficking in Women in OSCE Member States,* 2000.

Global

International Institute for Peace

RESEARCH
ACTION

The International Institute for Peace (IIP), an NGO with consultative status at ECOSOC and UNESCO, conducts research and disseminates the results in order to contribute to the maintenance and strengthening of peace. The IIP carries out studies on interdependence as a strategy for peace and on the economic, social, and political transformation of Central and Eastern European countries. The Institute has worked out a number of suggestions concerning the restructuring of the United Nations and the role of the UN and regional organizations in peacekeeping and conflict resolution. It also studies the effects of ethnic conflicts over arbitrary borders.

Möllwaldplatz 5/2
1040 Vienna
Austria
_____

Tel: +43 (1) 504 6437
Fax: +43 (1) 505 3236
iip@aon.at

Contact: Peter Stania, Secretary General

Number of staff: 7

Budget: $25,000–$100,000

Southeastern Europe, Africa, Asia

Ludwig Boltzmann Institute of Human Rights

RESEARCH
EDUCATION

The Ludwig Boltzmann Institute of Human Rights (Ludwig Boltzmann Institut für Menschenrechte, BIM) is an academic human rights research and service institution based in Vienna, Austria. The Institute was founded in 1992 under the umbrella of the Ludwig Boltzmann Society, a leading Austrian research association. The primary focus of the Boltzmann Institute is research in the field of human rights, on both the national and the international level. The BIM staff is also engaged extensively in human rights teaching and training, and hosts a public human rights library.

Hessgasse 1
1010 Vienna
Austria
_____
Tel: +43 (14277) 27 420
Fax: +43 (14277) 27 429
bim.staatsrecht@univie.ac.at
www.univie.ac.at/bim

Contact: Hans Tretter, Director
Number of staff: 15
Budget: < $25,000
Publications: Temporary Protection in Europe,
2000; *The Legal System of Bhutan,* 2000.

Azerbaijan

Azerbaijan Human Rights Resource Center

ADVOCACY

The Azerbaijan Human Rights Resource Center works for the protection of human rights in Azerbaijan and promotes free information exchange. It also supports and promotes new NGOs in the provinces of Azerbaijan. It offers information and newsletters via email.

Sh. Badalbeyly Street 41
Baku 370014
Azerbaijan
_____
Tel/fax: +994 (12) 954 459
mmehtiyev@rc-hro.baku.az

Contact: Mehti Mehtiyev, Director
Number of staff: 10
Budget: < $25,000

Azerbaijan

EDUCATION

Azerbaijan Young Lawyers' Union

The main goal of Azerbaijan Young Lawyers' Union (AYLU) is to study and to educate the public in human rights, while focusing particularly on the legal problems of the transitional times. The AYLU has a department of conflict resolution, which is chaired by Elmari Mamishev.

D.Alieva Street 251
Baku 370010
Azerbaijan

Tel/fax: +994 (12) 988 804
aylu@azeronline.com

Contact: Ramil Avez Iskanderov, Director
Number of staff: 2
Budget: < $25,000

Azerbaijan

RESEARCH
ACTION
ADVOCACY

Committee of Democracy and Human Rights

The basic mission of the Committee of Democracy and Human Rights is to promote democratic development and civil society building in Azerbaijan. The Committee provides free legal consultation/assistance to all the citizens of Azerbaijan whose rights have been infringed and disseminates information on the victims of the Karabakh conflict. The organization has established the Karabakh Commission. Conflict prevention/resolution activities have been implemented in the "Refugees and Human Rights" program.

Azerbaijan Avenue, 37
Baku 370000
Azerbaijan

Tel/fax: +994 (12) 981 117
ganizadehc@azerin.com

Contact: Chingiz Ganizadeh
Number of staff: 5
Budget: < $25,000

Caucasus

Human Rights Centre of Azerbaijan

RESEARCH
ACTION
ADVOCACY

The best known human rights NGO in Azerbaijan, the Human Rights Centre of Azerbaijan (HRCA) monitors the general human rights situation in Azerbaijan, and provides human rights education and early warning of conflicts. HRCA administers the dissemination of information in the CIS via about thirty mailing lists, as well as its website. The majority of publications are available in Russian. The NGO has been active in the NGO Working Group on Conflict Prevention in CIS (CISCONF).

Bashir Safaroglu Street 150
Baku 370000
Azerbaijan

Tel: +994 (12) 977 026
Fax: +994 (12) 977 026/947 550
eldar@azerurotel.com; hrca@mail.az
www.koan.de/~eldar

Contact: Eldar E. Zeinalov, Director
Number of staff: 3
Budget: $25,000–$100,000

Publications: Daily bulletins via email; reports on human rights and migration issues.

Caucasus

Institute of Peace and Democracy

RESEARCH
EDUCAITON

The mission of the Institute of Peace and Democracy (IPD) is to democratize public consciousness, educate the population in law-based statehood, protect human rights in Azerbaijan, and conduct peace and security studies in the region. The IPD has a Department of Conflict and Migration Studies with a "Culture of Peace" (2000-2001) program. The IPD has organized international conferences and training sessions on peace and conflict resolution, facilitated Azerbaijani-Armenian negotiations, published textbooks for university students in Azerbaijan, as well as produced video-films in the field of conflict resolution. In 2001, a project on a Caucasus stability pact was started in cooperation with the Armenian Legal and Political Research Centre.

Shamsi Badalbeily Street 38, apt. 2
Baku 370014
Azerbaijan

Tel/fax: +994 (12) 941 458
root@ipd.baku.az
www.ipd.co.hypermart.net

Contact: Dr. Leila Yunus, Director
Number of staff: 5
Publications: Textbooks for universities in Azerbaijan; joint Azeri-Armenian articles on how to solve the Nagorno Karabakh conflict.

South Caucasus

Resource Centre on National Minorities

RESEARCH
EDUCATION

The Resource Centre on National Minorities (RCNM) is dedicated to protecting the rights of national minorities. It has worked on warning and prevention of inter-ethnic conflicts, and the role of NGOs in the Karabakh conflict resolution. The RCNM prepared a database of NGOs dealing with national minorities and conflict resolution, and newsletters on national minorities issues in South Caucasus. The RCNM is one of the founders of the Network of NGOs of National Minorities in South Caucasus (about 80 members).

121-82, Mir-Jalal St.
Baku 370147
Azerbaijan
_____

Tel/fax: + 994 (12) 988 804
nadir_kamaladdinov@hotmail.com;
rcnm@clee.co-az.net
www.rcnm.org

Contact: Nadir Kamaladdinov, Director
Number of staff: 4
Budget: < $25,000

CIS Countries

Society for Humanitarian Research

RESEARCH
EDUCATION
ACTION

The Society for Humanitarian Research (SHR) is dedicated to help strengthen the third sector, to promote civil society values, and to develop human rights principles. Its main conflict prevention activity is the current program of monitoring the forced migration situation in Azerbaijan. The target groups in the program are local NGOs, migrants, and mass media.

May Street 28
Baku 370000
Azerbaijan
_____

Tel/fax: +994 (12) 987 022
avaz@azeurotel.com
www.mg.klever.net/~shr

Contact: Avaz Hasanov, Director
Number of staff: 11
Budget: < $25,000

Belarus
Civic Society Center

The Civic Society Center (Centar Supolnasc—CSCSC) in Minsk promotes civil society in Belarus through its support of various civic initiatives as well as through conducting educational programs. In recent years the Center has been particularly involved in coalition building, which it sees as an effective tool for preventing internal political conflicts. This NGO serves as an umbrella for pro-democratic organizations that want to meet each other, organize their own training schemes, or enhance cooperation. A database is maintained of most NGOs and informal groups throughout the country.

P.O. Box 208
Minsk, 220040
Belarus

Tel/fax: +375 (17) 263 9990
supolnasc@user.unibel.by
www.cacedu.unibel.by/cscsc/infa.htm

Contact: Vincuk Viacorka, Director
Number of staff: 12
Budget: < $25,000

Publications: Supolnasc newsletter, bi-monthly publication.

Belarus
Human Rights Education Center

The mission of the Human Rights Education Center is to work on conflict prevention, resolution, and mediation by means of education in the field of human rights. Founded in 1997, it trains teachers and youth in Belarus and seeks to disseminate information on human rights as well as law. Activities of the Center include conferences and workshops, databases, and publication of newspapers. It is part of a human rights NGO-network in Eastern Europe.

Rusianova 8
P.O. Box 93
Minsk-141, 220141
Belarus

Tel: +375 (17) 263 7184
Fax: +373 (17) 263 7274
hrytsuk@ns.iboch.ac.by

Contact: Valery Hrytsuk, Director
Number of staff: 1
Budget: < $25,000

Central and Eastern Europe, Great Lakes Region

ADVOCACY

APRODEV

APRODEV (Association of World Council of Churches related Development Organizations in Europe) represents 15 European development aid agencies to the European Union and aims to strengthen cooperation between its members. It is concerned mainly with promoting people-centered development, by means of influencing decisionmaking processes and facilitating access for member organizations to the European Union institutions and to information. The association works in the fields of development cooperation, European aid policies, food security, humanitarian aid, gender, trade and civil society, and conflicts and development.

174 rue Joseph II
1000 Brussels
Belgium

Tel: +32 (2) 234 6840
Fax: +32 (2) 231 1413
www.aprodev.net

Contact: Rob van Drimmelen, General Secretary

Number of staff: 4

Publications: Peace in Guatemala, 1997; *Peace and Reconciliation in Sudan: An Example of How APRODEV Agencies Are Involved in Peace Brokering,* 1997; *Peace, Reconciliation and Conflict Prevention,* 1997.

Balkans, Greece, Turkey, Caucasus

RESEARCH
EDUCATION
ACTION
ADVOCACY

Association des Etats Généraux des Etudiants de l'Europe

The Association des Etats Généraux des Etudiants de l'Europe (AEGEE), a network of more than 250 European cities that was established in 1985, aspires to a Europe of peaceful cooperation where no barriers separate people. The peace projects of AEGEE are usually targeted at students. The AEGEE's special focus is on the Balkan region where conferences, seminars, film festivals, and a Peace Summit has been organized. Lately the attention of AEGEE has also been directed toward the situation in the Southern Caucasus. Projects are implemented by working groups or affiliated organizations.

P.O. Box 72
B-1040 Bruxelles-Etterbeek 1
Belgium

Tel: +32 (2) 245 2300
Fax: +32 (2) 245 6260
info@aegee.org
www.aegee.org

Contact: Dijan Albayrak, Peace Academy Programme Manager, Turkey

Caucasus, Europe

Centre for European Policy Studies

RESEARCH
ACTION
ADVOCACY

The Centre for European Policy Studies (CEPS) provides decisionmakers, inside and outside government, with analysis of European affairs. Additionally, it provides a forum for discussion about European integration and creates networks of leaders committed to the development of European integration and co-operation as well as security issues. The Centre's conflict prevention activities include policy research, advice on conflict resolution and regional integration, publications, and conferences. The conflict prevention program focuses on the Caucasus. CEPS is involved in the development of a Stability Pact for the region.

Place du Congres 1
1000 Brussels
Belgium

Tel: +32 (2) 229 3911
Fax: +32 (2) 229 4151
info@ceps.be
www.ceps.be

Contact: Michael Emerson, Senior Research Fellow
Number of staff: 6
Budget: $100,000–$500,000
Publications: CEPS News, electronic newsletter; *A Stability Pact for the Caucasus,* 2000; *Perspectives on the Future of the Caucasus after the Second Chechnya Conflict,* 2000.

Baltic States, Eastern Europe, Africa

Centre for Peace Research
and Strategic Studies

RESEARCH

The Centre for Peace Research and Strategic Studies (CPRS) of the Catholic University of Leuven has research and development programs on concepts related to conflict prevention. Research is being conducted on the issues of missed opportunities, democratic peacebuilding, field diplomacy, cost/benefit-accounting and conflict-profiteering, early warning of genocidal conflict dynamics, and peace architecture. The Centre is also working on a system for conflict impact assessment in Burundi.

Van Evenstraat 2B
3000 Leuven
Belgium

Tel: +32 (16) 323 257
Fax: +32 (16) 323 088
luc.reychler@soc.kuleuven.ac.be

Contact: Luc Reychler
Budget: $100,000–$500,000
Publications: Cahiers van Centrum voor Vredesonderzoek, bulletin; *Conflict Prevention and Democratic Peacebuilding,* 1997; *The Art of Conflict Resolution,* 1994.

Great Lakes Region of Africa

Centre for the Study of the Great Lakes Region of Africa

RESEARCH
ACTION

The Centre for the Study of the Great Lakes Region of Africa is a research and documentation center dedicated to gathering and processing information about countries in the Great Lakes Region to promote accurate assessment and monitoring of conflict in the area. The Centre, which is a part of the University of Antwerp, was founded in 1994, just prior to the Rwandan genocide. It favors multidisciplinary activities integrating economics, political and social science, and law in its analyses. It also serves as a consultant to NGOs, governments, and international institutions.

IDPM
Middelheimlaan 1 C
2020 Antwerp
Belgium
_____
Tel: +32 (3) 218 0662
Fax: +32 (3) 218 0666
gralac@ua.ac.be

Contact: Filip Reyntjens, Director

Number of staff: 8

Budget: $100,000–$500,000

Publications: L'Afrique des grands lacs: Yearbook; series of working papers, in French and English.

Africa, Middle East, Southeast Asia

Centre for Third World Studies

RESEARCH
EDUCATION

The Centre for Third World Studies (CTWS), part of the Faculty for Political and Social Science at Gent University in Belgium, concentrates its activities on contemporary political problems of the Third World. It conducts both scientific and policy-oriented research, organizes conferences, and publishes articles and books. Early warning systems, conflict prevention, and sustainable development have been major focuses for research. Special attention was given to the regions Southern Africa, the Middle East, Central Africa, and Southeast Asia.

Universiteitstraat 8
9000 Gent
Belgium
_____
Tel: +32 (9) 264 6915
Fax: +32 (9) 264 6997
ruddy.doom@rug.ac.be
ctws.rug.ac.be

Contact: Ruddy Doom, Dean of the Faculty of Political and Social Sciences

Number of staff: 11

Publications: Resignation or Revolt? Socio-Political Development and the Challenges of Peace in Palestine, 1998; *Early Warning and Conflict Prevention,* 1995.

Global

European Centre for Common Ground

The European Centre for Common Ground (ECCG) is a Brussels-based, international, non-governmental organization that works with European institutions, governments, and other NGOs in the field of international applied conflict transformation.

Since 1982, with its sister organization, Search for Common Ground (see separate entry), ECCG has developed ongoing projects around the world that seek to incorporate the principles of co-operative and preventive action into the lives of people in areas of extreme tension or violence.

With offices in Africa (Angola, Burundi, Liberia, Sierra Leone), the Balkans (regional office in Macedonia), the Middle East (regional office in Jordan), Ukraine, the United States, and Indonesia, and projects in Cyprus, Greece, Turkey, Belgium, the Democratic Republic of Congo, and Rwanda, ECCG uses well-known conflict resolution techniques such as mediation and facilitation, as well as less traditional methods such as radio, television, and drama production—aimed at both children and adults. Common Ground radio production studios, Studio Ijambo in Burundi, and Talking Drum Studio in Liberia received the 1998 ECHO Radio and Television awards.

The ECCG is convinced that today's problems – whether ethnic, ideological, or economic—are too complex and interconnected to be settled on an adversarial basis. The earth is simply running out of space, resources, and recuperative capacity to deal with wasteful conflicts. It believes that NGOs can play a key role in complementing and supplementing the works of governments and international organizations.

ECCG's decentralized structure and emphasis on working locally is based on its recognition that staff members living on the scene are better equipped to oversee programs than people in remote headquarters.

Common Grounders function as "social entrepreneurs" who design and implement ways to reframe issues and solve problems. The ECCG has developed tools such as: roundtable and policy co-ordination forums; pro-active mediation; conflict resolution institution-building; training workshops; publication of newsletters and books; television and radio programming; and joint action projects.

Rue Belliard 205
1040 Brussels
Belgium

Tel: +32 (2) 736 7262
Fax: +32 (2) 732 3033
eccg@eccg.be
www.sfcg.org/eccg.htm

Contact: Sandra Djuvara Melone, Executive Director

Number of staff: 10 at HQ, 250 worldwide (including SFCG)

Budget: > $1,000,000

Publications: Coexist International Magazine, in partnership with Association for International Coexistence (AIC); *Bulletin for Regional Cooperation in the Middle East,* in partnership with Search for Common Ground (SFCG).

Global

ADVOCACY

European Peacebuilding Liaison Office

A growing awareness among a number of NGOs that they needed a focal point to address the European Union on the conflict prevention and peacebuilding activities of the institutions of the EU led to the establishment of the European Peacebuilding Liaison Office (EPLO) in January 2001.

Its most important task is to keep some seventeen member organizations updated about the EU's conflict prevention and peacebuilding policy. In this way NGOs can learn more quickly and in greater detail about the developments in European approaches and can therefore react more promptly to decisions. But EPLO also works in the other direction. It aims to improve EU awareness of the contribution NGOs can make to conflict prevention and peacebuilding and informs EU decisionmakers about activities of its members. At the same time EPLO facilitates the lobbying of its members, which are all European, as it seeks ways to improve the effectiveness and co-ordination of NGOs themselves.

To this end the Office provides its members with information on EU structures and policies, and gives updates on developments, including details of the EU's instruments for conflict prevention and transformation. EPLO assesses EU-funded peace building programs, and provides the platform with systems for monitoring and sharing information on current NGO activities. In addition, EPLO aims to foster EU-NGO cooperation, their primary mandate.

EPLO works only on behalf of its members. Services available to its membership include conferences and workshops. The first EPLO event was a conference, at the end of 2000, on non-military aspects of EU Conflict Prevention and Crisis Management. Members also regularly receive a newsletter, which contains information on EU policies, project, and budget lines as well as contact details of relevant EU officials working on conflict prevention, and information on members' projects.

Rue Beillard 205
1040 Brussels
Belgium

Tel: +32 (2) 282 9421
Fax: +32 (2) 282 9424
schneider-eplo@tiscalinet.be
www.eplo.org

Contact: Heike Scheider, Coordinator

Number of staff: 1

Budget: $25,000–$100,000

Balkans, Central Asia, Africa

EDUCATION
ACTION

Field Diplomacy Initiative

The Field Diplomacy Initiative (FDI) is working toward sustainable peace based on the belief that fieldwork is essential for peacebuilding, and the involvement of people in the peace process of vital importance. It strives for a more cost-effective peace policy and greater accountability from policymakers, and questions current fragmented, piecemeal approaches to peacebuilding and conflict resolution. Founded in 1997, FDI has been involved in briefing and debriefing of election monitoring teams; training programs for human rights and election monitoring; research; and consulting on development programs addressing conflict management, democratization, and human rights.

Laar 8
2140 Antwerp
Belgium
_____
Tel/fax: +32 (3) 235 2419
info@fdi.ngonet.be
www.fdi.ngonet.be

Contact: Luc Reychler, Chairman
Number of staff: 2 + 3 interns
Budget: $25,000–$100,000
Publications: Field Diplomacy Initiatives in Burundi and Cameroon; Peacebuilding: A Field Guide

---

European Union, Balkans, Africa

RESEARCH

Group for Research and Information on Peace and Security

The Group for Research and Information on Peace and Security (GRIP or Groupe de recherche et d'information sur la paix et la sécurité) is an independent research institute studying issues related to defense, security, and disarmament. GRIP works to contribute to a better understanding of security-related issues, and in doing so endeavors to enhance European and global security. GRIP's activities include two notable programs focused on conflict prevention and management: "European Union and Conflict Prevention," and "Arms Transfers and Light Weapons." Much of the Institute's attention has been directed at the Balkans and Africa.

Van Hoordestraat 33
1030 Brussels
Belgium
_____
Tel:+32 (2) 241 8420
Fax: +32 (2) 245 1933
admi@grip.org
www.grip.org

Contact: Bernard Adam, Director
Number of staff: 16
Budget: $100,000–$500,000
Publications: L'Union Européenne et la prévention des conflits africains, 2000; Post-Cold War Conversion in Europe: Defence Restructuring in the 1990s and the Regional Dimension, 1999; La guerre Congo-Kinshasa: Analyse d'un conflit et transferts d'armes vers l'Afrique centrale, 1999.

Balkans, Africa, Asia

International Crisis Group

The International Crisis Group (ICG) is a private and multinational organization committed to strengthening the capacity of the international community to anticipate, understand, and act to prevent and contain conflict.

ICG's approach is grounded in field research. Teams of political analysts, based on the ground in countries at risk of conflict, gather information from a wide range of sources, assess local conditions, and produce regular analytical reports containing practical recommendations targeted at key international decisiontakers.

ICG's reports are distributed widely to officials in foreign ministries and international organizations and made generally available at the same time via the organization's internet site. ICG works closely with governments and those who influence them, including the media, to highlight its crisis analysis and to generate support for its policy prescriptions. The ICG Board—which includes prominent figures from the fields of politics, diplomacy, business, and the media—is directly involved in helping to bring ICG reports and recommendations to the attention of senior policymakers around the world. ICG is chaired by former Finnish president Martti Ahtisaari. Former Australian foreign minister Gareth Evans has been president and chief executive since January 2000.

ICG's international headquarters are in Brussels, with advocacy offices in Washington, New York, and Paris. The organization currently operates in three broad program areas (Africa, Asia, and the Balkans) and has field projects in eighteen crisis-affected countries and regions: Algeria, Burundi, Rwanda, the Democratic Republic of Congo, Sierra Leone, and Zimbabwe in Africa; Burma/Myanmar, Indonesia, Kyrgyzstan, Tajikistan, and Uzbekistan in Asia; Albania, Bosnia, Kosovo, Macedonia, Montenegro, and Serbia in Europe. ICG is soon to establish a fourth regional program in Latin America. In addition, issues-reports are also produced which combine original research on themes relating to preventing and containing conflict, drawing on ICG's in-country experience in crisis zones. ICG raises funds from governments, charitable foundations, corporations, and individual donors.

149 Avenue Louise, level 16
1050 Brussels
Belgium

Tel: +32 (2) 502 9038
Fax: +32 (2) 502 5038
icgbrussels@crisisweb.org
www.crisisweb.org

Contact: Gareth Evans, President and Chief Executive

Number of staff: 58

Budget: > $1,000,000

Publications: After Milosevic: a Practical Agenda for Lasting Balkans Peace, 2001; *The Macedonian Question: Reform or Rebellion,* 2001; *Central Asia: Islamist Mobilisation and Regional Security,* 2001; *The European Union Crisis Response Capability: Institutions and Processes for Conflict Prevention and Management,* 2001; *Sierra Leone: Time for a New Military and Political Strategy,* 2001.

Africa, Colombia

International Peace Information Service

RESEARCH
ADVOCACY

The International Peace Information Service (IPIS) is an independent study and information service that is geared at an international public of journalists, researchers, NGOs, and (inter-) governmental institutions. Its large collection of specialized journals, monographs, and other documents can be consulted at the IPIS Library. The collection covers topics such as military security and strategy, the arms race, privatization of security, mercenaries, and related subjects. IPIS research focuses on processes of state collapse, privatization of security, and war financing. Current research projects include the diamonds-for-arms trades and Belgian arms production. Most publications are written in Flemish/Dutch.

Italiëlei 98 A
2000 Antwerp
Belgium

Tel: +32 (3) 225 0022
Fax: +32 (3) 231 0151
ipis@skynet.be
users.skynet.be/ipis

Contact: Johan Peleman, Executive Manager

Number of staff: 12

Budget: $100,000–$500,000

Publications: Central Africa Minerals and Arms Research Bulletin, periodical in 2001; *IPIS–Informatief,* quarterly newsletter in Dutch; *Aspects of Corporate Security in a Colombian Context: Contracting Kidnap Response and Deterrence Services,* 2000; *Angola's War Economy: The Role of Oil and Diamonds,* 2000; *The Arms Fixers: Controlling the Brokers and Shipping Agents,* 1999.

Europe

International Security Information Service, Europe

RESEARCH
ADVOCACY

The International Security Information Service, Europe (ISIS Europe) provides factual information and analyses on issues of international defense and security to European parliamentarians, the European Council, Commission officials, and other interested parties in this field. It aims to improve the transparency of EU developments in security and defense policy and encourage the development of EU conflict prevention capacities. The service brings together EU policymakers and NGOs in monthly seminars on aspects of European security policy and organizes annual conferences in the European Parliament. The 2000 conference addressed how the EU could move beyond reaction to preventive action in response to violent conflict.

Rue Stévin 115
1000 Brussels
Belgium

Tel:+32 (2) 230 7446
info@isis-europe.org
www.isis-europe.org

Contact: Catriona Gourlay, Director

Number of staff: 3

Budget: $500,000–$1,000,000

Publications: European Security Review, bi-monthly journal on security issues in Europe; *Cluster Bombs: the Case for New Controls,* 2001; *International Security in the Early Twenty-First Century,* 2000.

Global

Médecins Sans Frontières

Médecins Sans Frontières (MSF) is an international humanitarian aid organization that provides emergency medical assistance to populations in danger in more than 80 countries. In carrying out humanitarian assistance, MSF is also mandated to raise awareness of crisis situations. MSF acts as a witness and will speak out about the plight of populations in danger for whom it works. MSF has headquarters for field operations in France, Switzerland, Luxembourg, Spain, the Netherlands, and Belgium. A further 14 sections, from Sweden to Australia, support operations in the form of representation, recruitment of field volunteers, fundraising, and information.

39, rue de la Tourelle
1040 Brussels
Belgium

Contact: Rafael Vila Sanjuder, Secretary General

Tel: +32 (2) 280 1881
Fax: +32 (2) 280 0173
office-intnl@brussels.msf.org
www.msf.org

Europe

NGDO-EU Liaison Committee

The NGDO-EU Liaison Committee represents European NGOs in the institutions of the European Union in Brussels and facilitates cooperation among European NGOs. The Liaison Committee helps European NGOs raise public awareness of EU relations with the South and provides a channel for the views of civil society in the South to be heard in Europe. The Committee aims to contribute to the formulation and monitoring of EU development cooperation, emergency assistance, conflict prevention, and other policies that have a bearing on the EU's relations with the South.

10 Square Ambiorix
1000 Brussels
Belgium

Contact: James Mackie, Secretary General
Publications: Liaison News, monthly newsletter.

Tel: +32 (2) 743 8760
Fax: +32 (2) 732 1934
sec@clong.be
www.oneworld.org/liaison

Global

EDUCATION
ACTION
ADVOCACY

Pax Christi International

Pax Christi International is a Catholic peace movement working globally on a wide variety of issues in the fields of human rights, security and disarmament, economic justice, and ecology. In dealing with resolution of violent conflict, Pax Christi in most cases opts for solidarity work with victims. In other cases, mediation efforts are undertaken. Specific activities are dialogue projects with young people in former Yugoslavia and educational projects on minorities in Eastern Europe. On a theoretical level the movement has organized seminars. Pax Christi has representation in a number of intergovernmental organizations.

Oude Graanmarkt 21
1000 Brussels
Belgium

Tel: +32 (2) 502 5550
Fax: +32 (2) 502 4626
www.paxchristi.net

Contact: Etienne de Jonghe, International Secretary

Number of staff: 3

Publications: Pax Christi, monthly newsletter; *An Inside View on Shell's Human Rights Policy,* 1998; *Pax Christi Campaign on Light Weapons and Child Soldiers,* 1998.

Europe

RESEARCH
ACTION
ADVOCACY

Quaker Council for European Affairs

The Quaker Council for European Affairs (QCEA) is a religious-based organization that works on the causes of conflict and their peaceful resolution. QCEA focuses primarily on the policies of the European institutions, governments, and NATO. QCEA monitors developments in arms trade policies and regulations, the Rapid Response Force and Rapid Response Mechanisms of the European Union, missile defense, human rights, economics, and trade. QCEA works with the Quaker United Nations Offices in Geneva and New York as well as the world-wide network of Quaker International Affairs Representatives to monitor the impact of European policies and practices.

50 Square Ambiorix
1000 Brussels
Belgium

Tel: +32 (2) 230 4935
Fax: +32 (2) 230 6370
qcea@ngonet.be
www.quaker.org/qcea

Contact: John Welton, QCEA Representative and Head of Office

Number of staff: 4

Budget: $100,000–$500,000

Publications: Around Europe, monthly newsletter; *Renegotiation of the Lomé Convention,* 2000; *European Social Policy,* 2000.

Global

Service Civil International

ACTION

Service Civil International (SCI) is a voluntary organization with consultative status with UNESCO and the Council of Europe. The aims are to promote peace, international understanding and solidarity, social justice, sustainable development, and respect for the environment. There are several international working groups: East-West (GATE); Africa, Youth and Unemployment (YUGWG); Balkan region (SALVA); Latin America (Abya Yala); Refugee issues; Women's issues; Environment and Development; and Peace and Human Rights. Traditionally SCI works with special work camps to help projects that need outside support until they can become independent. Service Civil has 33 branches in Europe, Asia, Africa, and North America.

International Secretariat
St-Jacobsmarkt 82
2000 Antwerpen
Belgium

Tel: +32 (3) 226 5727
Fax: +32 (3) 232 0344
sciint@sciint.org
www.sciint.org

Contact: Isabelle Vandenbergen, International Coordinator

Publications: IS Newsletter.

Balkans, Global

VOICE

ADVOCACY

VOICE (Voluntary Organisations in Cooperation in Emergency) is a network of more than eighty European NGOs that are active in the field of humanitarian aid, including emergency aid, rehabilitation, disaster-preparedness, and conflict prevention. The overall purpose of VOICE is to foster links between these NGOs and to facilitate their contact with the European Union. It aims to contribute to a humanitarian policy based on solidarity, effectiveness, and high quality. Its goal is to provide NGOs with opportunities for discussion and collaboration, together with services for their humanitarian action.

46, Rue Dejoncker
1060 Brussels
Belgium

tel +32 (2) 541 1360
fax +32 (2) 543 9953
voice@clong.be
www.oneworld.org/voice

Contact: Katherine Schick, Director
Publications: VOICE newsletter
Focus Balkans, newsletter.

Global

Vrede

People who actively participated in the resistance movement established Vrede (peace) just after World War II. The organization is particularly active in the fields of European security, defense policy, and gender. Through seminars, conferences, and publications the organization aims to contribute to social justice and arms reduction worldwide. Sustainable peace is promoted in terms of strengthening democracy, solidarity, emancipation, and social integration. The "Jan Verwest" Library, advisory work, and lectures contribute to this. Vrede participates in a range of coalitions in Belgium.

Galgenberg 29
9000 Gent
Belgium

Tel: + 32 (9) 233 4688
Fax: +32 (9) 233 5678
vrede@vrede.be
www.vrede.be

Contact: Georges Spriet, Secretary General
Number of staff: 3
Budget: $100,000–$500,000
Publications: Vrede, bimonthly magazine in Dutch on peace and international politics; *Vredescahiers,* quarterly booklet in Dutch.

Bosnia and Herzegovina, Balkans

Abraham

Abraham (Association for Inter-Religious Peace Work) is a non-profit, non-governmental organization that aims to contribute to conflict prevention and/or resolutio, and peace making through inter-religious peace work. Working on a number of broad issues including inter-religious dialogue, Abraham also organizes basic training sessions in non-violent conflict transformation for believers in co-operation with Oekumenischer Dienst (OeD) Wethen, Germany and CNA Sarajevo. Valuable projects are also inter-religious seminars and the "Abraham"—magazine for culture of inter-religious dialogue. Abraham has working relations with variety of local and international NGOs, but also with the Orthodox Church, Catholic Church, and Islamic community in Sarajevo.

Bistrik medresa 21
71000 Sarajevo
Bosnia and Herzegovina

Tel: +387 (33) 237 052
Fax: +387 (33) 537 339
ibrahime@bih.net.ba

Contact: Fetahovic Abdulah, Deputy Director
Number of staff: 2 office staff, 15 active members
Budget: $25,000–$100,000
Publications: Abraham-Brief, bulletin in German; *Abraham,* monthly magazine for culture of inter-religious dialogue.

Former Yugoslavia

Center for Nonviolent Action

RESEARCH
EDUCATION
ADVOCACY

The Center for Nonviolent Action (CNA—Centar za nenasilnu akciju) is a non-governmental and non-profit organization whose basic goals are peace-building, the development of civil society, cross-border co-operation, and promotion of nonviolence.

The CNA is mainly active in organizing and implementing training seminars in nonviolent conflict transformation and in supporting groups and individuals who wish to do this kind of work. CNA seminars draw together people from all parts of Bosnia and Herzegovina, Croatia, Yugoslavia (Serbia, Montenegro, Kosovo), and Macedonia, and hence they facilitate networking and communication between people from different areas whose channels of communication have been interrupted by the war. These seminars thus actively support the process of prejudice reduction and communication. The CNA team is also drawn from different countries in this region. CNA training in nonviolent conflict transformation aims to encourage citizens to search for ways to develop and protect social values such as human rights. It strives toward a model of active citizenship in which individuals are ready, skilled, and aware of their own responsibility, power, and strength to influence the society they live in. The participants in the training sessions are primarily people involved in NGO activities, political parties, media, teachers, and similar professional groups. The CNA also holds training sessions in non-violence with other target groups, which are seen as potential "multipliers." CNA organizes and conducts a six-month Training for Trainers program for people who already have basic training in non-violent conflict transformation and who are interested in further education in this field. In 2001 CNA opened an office in Belgrade. CNA is open for co-operation with all individuals and groups who share their goals, basic convictions, and commitment to nonviolence.

Bentbasa 31
71000 Sarajevo
Bosnia and Herzegovina

Tel/fax: +387 (33) 440 417
cna.sarajevo@gmx.net
www.nenasilje.org

Contact: Nenad Vukosavljevic and Ivana Franovic

Number of staff: 7

Budget: $100,000–$500,000

Publications: 3-month reports, in English and Bosnian/Croatian/Serbian languages; *Nenasilje?,* training manual for nonviolent conflict transformation for work with adults, in Bosnian/Croatian/Serbian languages, 2000; training documentation and materials.

Bosnia and Herzegovina, Southeastern Europe

EDUCATION
ACTION
ADVOCACY

CIRCLE 99 Sarajevo

The Association of Independent Intellectuals CIRCLE 99 Sarajevo (Asoci-jacija nezavisnih intelektualaca KRUG 99 Sarajevo), one of the oldest NGOs in the country, is focusing on political advocacy work. Through public campaigns, round tables, and publications, it tries to pressure government policy-making and influence public opinion. All its members oppose the nationalism of the leading political parties and support a multi-cultural country. It has published a full-page announcement in national newspapers making clear policy recommendations to the newly elected government.

Vrazova 1
71000 Sarajevo
Bosnia and Herzegovina

Tel/fax: +387 (33) 217 854/200 155
ekrugpen@bih.net.ba

Contact: Slavko Santic, General Secretay
Budget: $25,000–$100,000
Publications: Review for Free Thought, quarterly electronic newsletter.

Bosnia and Herzegovina

EDUCATION
ACTION

Human Rights Office Tuzla

The Human Rights Office Tuzla (Biro za ljudska prava Tuzla) is a non-profit organization involved in human rights education and advocacy, as well as the monitoring of the human rights situation. The Office has a specific training and advisory program for returnees, preparing and empowering them for their return. The overall goal of the program is to change the hostile attitude of the returnees toward the state entity and the inclusion of returnee population into the reconciliation process in Bosnia andHerzegovina.

Fra Stjepana Matijevica 3
75000 Tuzla
Bosnia and Herzegovina

Tel/fax: +387 (35) 250 504
biroy@bih.net.ba

Contact: Branka Rajner, Executive Director
Number of staff: 2 staff, 2 volunteers
Budget: < $25,000

Bosnia and Herzegovina

United Nations Volunteers PIP

UNDP/UNV Assistance to Promote Community Based Confidence-building Measures in Bosnia and Herzegovina (PIP, Projekt Izgradnje Povjerenja) is an initiative that aims to contribute to the overall growth of a settled and healthy functioning society characterized by respect for difference, tolerance, inclusivity, and acceptance of itself and its recent history through the process of confidence building with young people. UNV PIP operates numerous programs for empowering youth in Bosnia and Herzegovina, such as youth confidence building workshops, Confidence Building Fund projects implemented by workshop participants, radio programs for youth, and other activities.

Osmana Krupalije 26
71000 Sarajevo
Bosnia and Herzegovina

Tel: +387 (33) 205 868/470 692
Fax: +387 (33) 458 665
lmesbah@undp.ba
www.bihyouth.net

Contact: Laurent A Mesbah, Project Coordinator

Number of staff: 10

Budget: $100,000–$500,000

Publications: Project press releases; UNV PIP brochure; youth radio program; *Peace Garden Training Manual; Confidence Building Training Manual;* database of local workshop facilitators.

Bosnia and Herzegovina

Women's Association Medica-Zenica

RESEARCH
EDUCATION
ACTION
ADVOCACY

Media-Zenica aims to provide adequate help for the women and children that have been traumatized by the violence in the war and in the post-war society as well as to work toward a life without violence for women and their families. To reach its aims, Medica-Zenica applies a humanistic, holistic, and respectful approach toward women and children; works to raise women's self-consciousness; provides support for the reaching of economic independence through professional training; informs and educates about traumas, violence and women's human rights; as well as builds on the network of supporters to survivors of the war and the post-war violence.

Mokusnice 10
72000 Zenica
Bosnia and Herzegovina

Tel: +387 (32) 280 311/286 566
Fax: +387 (32) 28 710
medica@bih.net.ba

Contact: Marijana Senjak, Director
Number of staff: 6
Budget: < $25,000

Bosnia and Herzegovina

Youth Centre Gornji Vakuf

EDUCATION
ACTION

The Youth Centre (Omladinski centar) Gornji Vakuf is an organization in which children and young people participate in creating educational programs, in order to learn and develop, thus bringing together two communities that have been separated by war. It offers a peace education program to four cities in Central Bosnia. The Centre works with schools, educational institutions, and youth organizations providing training and workshops in peaceful conflict resolution skills, thereby supporting reconciliation.

Bratstva i jedinstva 10
70240 Gornji Vakuf
Bosnia and Herzegovina

Tel/fax: +387 (30) 265 594
ocgv@gmx.net
www.centar.notrix.net

Contact: Jasminka Drino-Kirlic, Programme
Director
Number of staff: 6
Budget: < $25,000

Bosnia and Herzegovina

Zene Zenama

EDUCATION
ACTION
ADVOCACY

The primary objective of Zene Zenama is advocacy directed at ending all forms of discrimination, and in particular working for gender equality. Through its school of democracy program it aims to improve co-existence. It focuses on emotional and psychological support for women, and education (Organizational Development, Violence-free Communication and Conflict Resolution, Women Studies, Civil Society, and The Foundation of Politics). Zene Zenama has a self-understanding of an organization as a free space in which women think about their lives, the society they live in, and ways of being creative individuals.

Kosevo 32 / I
71000 Sarajevo
Bosnia and Herzegovina

Tel/fax: +387 (33) 213 737
zene2000@bih.net.ba

Contact: Memnuna Zvizdic

Number of staff: 13, approximately 80 volunteers

Budget: < $25,000

Southeastern Europe

Center for the Study of Democracy

RESEARCH
ACTION

The Center for the Study of Democracy (CSD) is an interdisciplinary public policy institute dedicated to the values of democracy and market economy. The Center tries to achieve its objectives of institutional reform and integration through policy research, process monitoring, drafting legislation, dissemination and advocacy activities, partnership building, and networking. One of CSD's special activities is an early warning report project, which monitors Bulgaria's stability. The Center cooperates with other Balkan early warning programs in the region.

1 Lazar Stanev str.
1113 Sofia
Bulgaria

Tel: +359 (2) 971 3000
Fax: +359 (2) 971 2233
csd@online.bg
www.csd.bg

Contact: Alexander Stoyanov, Director of Research

Number of staff: 55

Budget: < $1,000,000

Publications: Democratic Institutions, Rule of Law, Human Rights and Protection of Minorities, 1997.

Bulgaria, Balkans

Partners Bulgaria Foundation

RESEARCH
EDUCATION
ACTION
ADVOCACY

The mission of the Partners Bulgaria Foundation is to facilitate the ongoing process of democratic transition and the building of a civil society in Bulgaria primarily, by supporting various and unique relationships among people. It aims to popularize mediation as an alternative method for conflict resolution and offers training to that end. The Partners Bulgaria Foundation also aims at building sustainable structures for promotion of inter-ethnic and inter-sectoral cooperation, to facilitate ethnic conciliation, and to increase the effectiveness of minority groups in their work of improving the conditions of minority communities. The organization is part of the international network Partners for Democratic Change International.

67, Ljuben Karavelov
1000 Sofia
Bulgaria

Tel: +359 (2) 963 2677
Fax: +359 (2) 664 318
pdcmm@mbox.cit.bg
www.partners-bulgaria.dir.bg

Contact: Dr. Daniela Kolarova, Director
Number of staff: 9
Budget: $100,000–$500,000
*Publications: Peer Mediation Manual;
Alternative Dispute Resolution: A Handbook
for Students in Law.*

Global

Canadian Peacebuilding Coordinating Committee

ACTION
ADVOCACY

The Canadian Peacebuilding Coordinating Committee (CPCC) is a network of Canadian NGOs and institutes, academics, and other individuals from a wide range of sectors, including humanitarian assistance, development, conflict resolution, peace, faith communities, and human rights. CPCC has been working since 1994 to formulate policy and operational directions for Canadian NGOs involved in peacebuilding, in collaboration with other relevant actors. The network is engaged in a process of dialogue with a broad range of NGOs and institutes and the Canadian government to articulate Canadian directions in the area of peacebuilding, and to strengthen NGO and civil society input into peacebuilding policy and program development.

1, rue Nicholas Street no. 510
Ottawa, Ontario K1N 7B7
Canada

Tel: +1 (613) 241 3446
Fax: +1 (613) 241 5302
cpcc@web.ca
www.cpcc.ottawa.on.ca

Contact: Robin J. Hay

Croatia, Southeastern Europe

B.a.B.e.
Women's Human Rights Group

RESEARCH
EDUCATION
ADVOCACY

The B.a.B.e. (Be active, Be emancipated) Women's Human Rights Group is a strategic, feminist lobbying group working on the promotion and implementation of women's human rights on national, regional, and international levels. B.a.B.e. is engaged in training and advocacy and works on conflict prevention within the framework of the project Education for Women's Human Rights. Other projects include Women & Media, Legal Monitoring and Influencing Changes to Laws, Legal Hotline, and other various subprojects such as the 16 Days of Activism against Gender Violence.

Vlaska 79/III
10000 Zagreb
Croatia
_____
Tel/fax: +385 (1) 461 1686
babe@zamir.net
www.babe.hr

Contact: Martina Belic, Coordinator
Number of staff: 5
Budget: < $25,000

Croatia

Center for Education
and Counseling of Women

EDUCATION
ADVOCACY

The Center for Education and Counseling of Women (CESI) is dedicated to the advancement of the status of women and the building of a civil society by offering educational programs. CESI is actively involved in the "Intercultural links between women of different backgrounds" program that aims to ease tensions and to create the conditions necessary for dialogue, co-operation, and solidarity among women of different origins.

Krizaniceva 1/3
1000 Zagreb
Croatia
_____
Tel/fax: +385 (1) 461 1704
cesi@zamir.net
www.zamir.net/~cesi

Contact: Gordana Obradovic, Director
Number of staff: 2
Budget: < $25,000
Publications: CESI Tribunela, newsletter.

Croatia, Former Yugoslavia

RESEARCH
EDUCATION
ACTION
ADVOCACY

Center for Peace Studies

The Center for Peace Studies (Centar za mirovne studije—CMS) is a non-profit, non-governmental organization that aims to promote non-violence and social change, through education, research, and activism. It is one of over twenty member organizations engaged in issues of non-violence, women rights and human rights, gathered in the network Anti War Campaign Croatia. The CMS originated from a peace-building project (1993–1997) in Western Slavonia.

The CMS offers two main programs, Peace Studies and Peace Building, and acts as an exchange for information and support to peace groups and as the center for education of its own activists. The Center is dedicated to furthering the democratic transitional process of Croatian society in all its aspects. Working on networking between different initiatives in the region, the Centre contributes to the accumulation and deepening of knowledge, and to the development of local trainer capacity.

Rockfellerova 26
10000 Zagreb
Croatia

Contact: Vesna Terselic, Mirjana Radakovic
Number of staff: 5

Tel/fax: +385 (1) 468 3020
cms@zamir.net

Croatia

RESEARCH
EDUCATION
ACTION

Centre for Peace, Non-violence and Human Rights—Osijek

Promotion of nonviolence and encouragement of responsible participation of individuals in the process of social change is the mission of the work of the Centre for Peace, Non-violence and Human Rights—Osijek. The work is aimed toward the creation of a civil society based on a culture of nonviolence, respect of human rights, tolerance, and common security.

The Centre's work is focused on the Danube area, Baranja, Eastern and Western Slavonia in Croatia. The Centre has two main programs in the area of conflict prevention/resolution: the Peace Building and Community Development Programme aims at opening communication between polarized groups, strengthening the role of women, religious communities, and youth in the process of trust rebuilding and community development; the Peace Education and Psychosocial Development Programme is especially focused on providing support to youth.

Zupanijska 7
31000 Osijek
Croatia

Contact: Katarina Kruhonja, Marijana Mitrovic
Number of staff: 50-60
Budget: $100,000–$500,000
Publications: I Chose Life; Stories from Berak.

Tel/fax: +385 (31) 206 886/889/887
czmos@zamir.net
www.centar-za-mir.hr

4444444

Former Yugoslavia
MIRamiDA Centar

EDUCATION / ACTION

The MIRamiDA Centar, Regional Peace Building Exchange, provides a space where individuals, organizations, and institutions involved in peacebuilding at local, national, and global levels can exchange their experiences and support each other. The MIRamiDA Centar has only recently come into operation but it has a great potential to develop activities essential for these regions. Its priorities are peace education, training, and mediation. The well-known "MIRamiDA Basic" program works on empowerment for peacebuilding in (post) war areas at the grassroots level. The MIRamiDA Centar is a part of the Antiwar Campaign (ARK) network.

Stolarska bb
52429 Groznjan
Croatia

Contact: Goran Bozicevic, Director
Number of staff: 3

Tel/fax: +385 (52) 776 138
miramidac@zamir.net
www.miramida.org

Croatia, Southeastern Europe
Vukovar Institute for Peace Research and Education

RESEARCH / EDUCATION / ACTION / ADVOCACY

The Vukovar Institute for Peace Research and Education (VIMIO) is designed to contribute to the long-term process of conflict resolution, reconciliation, and deepening of inter-ethnic tolerance in the Croatian Danube Region, Croatia, and the region of Southeastern Europe.

For the sake of building peace, the Institute also carries out education and research. VIMIO is a connecting point for Croatian and foreign individuals and organizations seeking to draw lessons from experiences in conflict resolution, especially those gained in Eastern Slavonia.

VIMIO is also a communication and information center for governmental and NGOs working on peacebuilding. For that reason, the institute manages a peace library.

Ljudevita Gaja 3
32 000 Vukovar
Croatia

Contact: Biljana Kondic, President and Project Coordinator
Number of staff: 5
Budget: $25,000–$100,000

Tel: + 385 (32) 442 978
Fax: + 385 (32) 442 977
vimio@hi.hinet.hr
clik.to/vimio

Cyprus

Cyprus Peace Center

The Cyprus Peace Center has operated in Nicosia since 1991 as a not-for-profit organization and has no affiliation to any political party. Its general goal is to promote the ideal of peace and non-violence in Cyprus and the world through the organization of relevant activities, which aim at introducing a new mindset and skills in conflict analysis and dealing with differences.

The Peace Center was instrumental in introducing the values and principles of conflict resolution in the Cypriot communities. The Center works as a platform for hundreds of Turkish Cypriot and Greek Cypriot volunteers who get together to develop strategies of peace resolution and to articulate an alternative to the national discourses. Hundreds of individuals from both Cypriot communities have been trained in conflict resolution skills and today over sixty bi-communal groups exist on the island. Contacts with the Turkish Cypriot community are close, but for political reasons they can only be of an informal character.

Together with UNOPS, the Peace Center is studying bi-communal perceptions, belief systems, and future solutions in both communities. In 2001, the first comparative research study on both communities was carried out. A publication on all the research findings is planned for and it is intended to be used by policymakers, academics, and NGOs.

The Peace Center has also acted as the facilitator for other bi-communal groups that have not been able to form separate NGOs due to political obstacles. The Center acts as the intermediary to submit and sign grant proposals on their behalf to the UN or other international organizations. Such has been the case for the Bi-communal Choir and for bi-communal artist groups.

The Center has organized many public activities jointly with the University of Cyprus and the New Cyprus Association. Many of these activities aim at introducing the "other's perspective" to the Cyprus conflict.

P.O. Box 23817
1686 Nicosia
Cyprus

Tel: +357 (2) 436 940
Fax: +357 (2) 495 777
peaceccy@spidernet.com.cy

Contact: Maria Hadjipavlou, President and contact person for the Conflict Resolution Trainer Group

Number of staff: 230 volunteers

Budget: $100,000–$500,000

Cyprus

Women's Civic Initiative for Peace

RESEARCH
EDUCATION
ACTION
ADVOCACY

The Women's Civic Initiative for Peace is a coalition of the Women's Research Centre and the Patriotic Women's Union. Their aim is to create gender awareness, as well as work for change for peace and reconciliation among the communities in Cyprus.

c/o Women's Research Centre
19 Necmi Avkiran Street
Lefkosha Nicosia
Cyprus

Tel: + 90 (392) 227 5407
Fax: +90 (392) 228 3823
sevgululudag@hotmail.com

Contact: Sevgul Uludag, Director Women's Research Centre

Czech Republic

Civil Society Development Foundation

ACTION

The Civil Society Development Foundation (NROS) aims to promote the development of a civil society in the Czech Republic. It provides support to NGOs working in the fields of democratization, human rights, and minorities. NROS is principally concerned with awarding human rights grants and the entire budget is spent within the Czech Republic. NROS is part of the framework of the Phare Civil Society Development Program in East European countries.

Jeleni 15/196
118 00 Prague 1
Czech Republic

Tel: +420 (2) 3335 6173
Fax: +420 (2) 3335 4708
nros@nros.cz
www.nros.cz

Contact: Radim Burkon, Head of Grants Department
Number of staff: 3

Europe

ACTION

Helsinki Citizens' Assembly

The Helsinki Citizens' Assembly (HCA) is an international non-governmental organization working to promote the democratic integration of Europe from below, and to strengthen European civil society. Its 10,000 members comprise both international NGO's and individuals.

Established in Prague in 1990, the Assembly grew out of dialogues between independent citizens groups on both sides of the Cold War divide during the 1980s. Since 1990 the HCA has developed into a network of NGOs spread across most European countries that focuses on various local and regional issues in co-operation with the HCA International Secretariat. The Assembly's central office is currently in Prague (The HCA International Secretariat) while the other HCA groups who assist in the co-ordination of activities are based in France, the Netherlands, and Turkey.

The Assembly works with decisionmakers and ordinary citizens to provide a forum where every individual can present his or her concerns and opinions. It aims to establish links between individuals and organizations from different countries, to help citizens actively participate in democratic institutions, and to promote peaceful and productive dialogue at all levels.

The Helsinki Citizens' Assembly has been active in conflict regions, particularly the Balkans and the TransCaucasus, both in supporting and protecting local civic activists and in campaigning at an international level on their behalf. In October 2000 it organized a General Assembly in Baku attended by delegations from all the South Caucasian societies, which tried to build bridges between the different cultures and ethnic groups in the region.

The HCA is also active in Turkish, Moldovan, Crimean, and Southern Balkan conflict regions. Minority issues, particularly Roma and the Hungarian minority in Slovakia, are another concern. HCA places particular focus on young people, trying to involve them in inter-cultural, inter-religious, and inter-ethnic dialogue.

Veletrzni 24
170 00 Prague 7
Czech Republic

Tel:+42 (2) 2057 0642
Fax: +42 (2) 2039 7251
hca@hca.cz
www.hca.cz

Contact: Tomas Krasauskas, Executive Director

Number of staff: 5 at Prague office

Publications: The Collage, quarterly youth magazine; *The hCa Quarterly,* political discussion magazine.

Eastern and Central Europe, CIS Countries

RESEARCH
ACTION

Transitions Online

The Internet magazine, *Transitions Online* (TOL) covers all 28 countries of Central and Eastern Europe, the Balkans, and the former Soviet Union. It is dedicated to strengthening independent journalism by giving young, local reporters a change to build up experience in international journalism. TOL also fuels policy debate in countries in both the East and the West, with analysis of regional events. Conflict prevention activities are limited to monitoring and reporting on hotspots, especially in areas that are not well covered by the international press.

Chlumova 22
130 00 Prague 3
Czech Republic

Tel: +420 (2) 2278 0805
Fax: +420 (2) 2278 0804
transitions@tol.cz
www.tol.cz

Contact: Jeremy Druker, Director

Budget: $100,000–$500,000

Publications: Transitions Online, Internet magazine.

Europe, Baltic States, Asia, Middle East, Southern Africa

RESEARCH

Copenhagen Peace Research Institute

The Copenhagen Peace Research Institute (COPRI) is a government research institute pursuing activities to support and strengthen multidisciplinary research and stimulate debate on peace and security issues. Research topics include: Military Restructuring (MIL); European Security (EUR); Nordic-Baltic Security in a Transforming Europe (NORD); Intra-State Conflict: Causes and Peace Strategies (CONF); and Global Governance and Peace (GOV). CONF focuses on civil wars dominated by ethno-national, cultural, and economic aspects of struggles for power, and addresses conflict prevention and minority rights issues. The GOV program examines how changes in global governance structures influence peace and democracy.

Fredericiagade 18
1310 Copenhagen K
Denmark

Tel: +45 3345 5050
Fax: +45 3345 5060
www.copri.dk

Contact: Tarja Cronberg, Director

Number of staff: 15

Budget: $500,000–$1,000,000

Publications: Working papers; bulletins.

Caucasus

Danish Association for Research on the Caucasus

RESEARCH

The Danish Association for Research on the Caucasus (DARC) is a non-governmental, non-partisan forum for researchers and others interested in the Caucasus region. The aim of DARC is to provide high quality information on the Caucasus and to work with similar research organizations worldwide to create a common space where information on literature, people, and institutions of the Caucasus region is easily accessible. A broad range of publications is available on the DARC website.

Godthaabsvaenghet 12
2000 Frederiksberg
Denmark

Tel: +45 3819 6432
Fax: +45 3915 1508
faurby@private.dk
www.caucasus.dk

Contact: Ib Faurby, Director

Budget: < $25,000

Publications: The Failure of Conflict Prevention and Management: The Case of Chechnya, part I and II, 1999; Mountaineers, Racketeers and the Ideals of Modernity: Statebuilding and Elite-Competition in Caucasia, 1999; Oil in the Caspian Region and Central Asia: The Political Risk of the Great Game Continued, 1998.

Former Yugoslavia, Tibet, Caucacus

Danish Centre for Conflict Resolution

RESEARCH
EDUCATION

The Danish Centre for Conflict Resolution aims to promote understanding and develop competence in nonviolent conflict resolution in Denmark and abroad. In Denmark, its Neighbourhood Mediation Project helps people in urban housing areas to resolve their own conflicts, and The School Project promotes creative conflict management. Abroad, the Centre has been engaged in such activities as nonviolent training and empowerment projects in: India, working with Tibetan exiles; Russia, addressing conflict in the Caucasus; and Albania, Montenegro, and Bosnia. It has also established a cross-boundary conflict resolution network in the Balkans.

Noerrebrogade 32. 2
2200 Copenhagen N
Denmark

Tel: +45 3537 1052
Fax: +45 3537 9052
center@konfliktloesning.dk
www.konfliktloesning.dk

Contact: Palle Westergaard, Director

Number of staff: 7 at HQ, 25 in the field

Budget: $100,000–$500,000

Publications: The Art of Conflict Resolution

Europe

Danish Institute of International Affairs

The goal of the Danish Institute of International Affairs (DUPI) is to strengthen Danish research, analysis, and information activities on international relations and Danish foreign policy. Within its research branch, one of five main areas of study is "Security and Defence Studies," which includes research on topics such as civilian-military cooperation during peacekeeping operations, and security in Southeastern Europe. The Institute also participates in the education of researchers and provides funding for debate and information activities.

Nytorv 5
1450 Copenhagen
Denmark

Tel: +45 3336 6565
Fax: +45 3336 6566
dupi@dupi.dk
www.dupi.dk

Contact: Betel Heurlin, Research Director

Number of staff: 35

Budget: $100,000–$500,000

Publications: DUPI News, bi-monthly newsletter; *The European Security and Defence Policy: Rebalancing the Transatlantic Security Relationship,* 2000; *"War Is Never Civilised": Civilisation, Civil Society and the Kosovo War,* 2000; *Humanitarian Intervention,* 1999.

Balkans, CIS Countries

Danish Refugee Council

The Danish Refugee Council is a private independent organization providing assistance to people in war zones and to refugees attempting to build a new life in Denmark. The goal of the Danish Refugee Council is to protect refugees against persecution and to promote viable solutions to the problems they face. Among its activities, the Council provides information to the public on refugees, advice to asylum seekers, and assistance to refugees seeking to return to their homes. It is also engaged in refugee assistance projects in 15 countries around the world.

Borgergade 10
P.O. Box 53
2100 Copenhagen Ø
Denmark

Tel: +45 3373 5000
Fax: +45 3332 8448
drc@drc.dk
www.drc.dk

Contact: Ulla Godtfredsen, Policy Advisor

Publications: Legal and Social Conditions for Asylum Seekers and Refugees in Western European Countries, 2000; *Coming Home: A Survey of the Living Conditions of Refugees Repatriating to Bosnia and Herzegovina from Denmark between August 1994 and August 1997,* 1997.

Global

ADVOCACY

Danish United Nations Association

The Danish United Association (FN-forbundet) is a cross-political NGO working on ideas for the United Nations and global governance. They also informs Danish people about United Nations issues. Important themes are peace, environment, development, and human rights. Its members are Danish organizations and individuals. The Association has an active Youth Organization and provides educational information for schools. It organizes debates and publishes discussion papers, books, and videos on current international problems. The Association has observer status in the Danish delegation of the United Nations General Assembly.

Midtermolen 3, st. tv.
2100 Copenhagen
Denmark
_____

Tel: +45 3546 7373
Fax: +45 3546 7350
fnforbundet@una.dk
www.una.dk

Contact: Jørgen R. Madsen

Number of staff: 11

Publications: FN Bladet (UN Magazine), bimonthly newsletter in Danish.

Europe

EDUCATION
ACTION

European Negotiation and Conflict Resolution

European Negotiation and Conflict Resolution (ENCORE) is a branch of the Danish consultancy firm Nelleman Konsulenterne A/S. It is devoted to helping professionals and organizations to resolve conflicts through negotiation so as to serve the long-term interests of all parties involved. ENCORE's primary activity is to provide negotiation services to the Danish labor market, but it now also provides mediation and negotiation services internationally. ENCORE endeavors to put research and theory into practice in the fields of negotiation and dispute resolution by offering mediation training programs and negotiation skills workshops.

Sortemosevej 2
3450 Allerod
Denmark
_____

Tel: +45 4814 0466
Fax: +45 4814 1038
encore@nelkon.dk
www.nelkon.dk

Contact: Ib Ravn, international liaison

Number of staff: 11

Budget: > $1,000,000

Estonia, Russia

RESEARCH
ACTION
ADVOCACY

Estonian Institute for Human Rights

The Estonian Institute for Human Rights (EIHR) is a non-profit, non-governmental organization that is active in the internal human rights situation in Estonia and some foreign regions such as Chechnya. The Institute offers free legal help on human right issues (both in Estonian and Russian languages), distributes information, and deals with problems regarding prisoners and minorities. Another goal of the EIHR is to inform the world about the human rights situation in Estonia. International experts are invited to propagate human rights. The Institute promotes educational programs for young lawyers and law students with the help of foreign grants.

Tõnismägi 2
10122 Tallinn
Estonia
_____
Tel/fax: +372 6311 239
infor@eihr.ee
www.eihr.ee

Contact: Merle Haruoja, Secretary General

Number of staff: 4

Budget: $25,000–$100,000

Estonia, Baltic states

RESEARCH
EDUCATION
ACTION
ADVOCACY

Legal Information Centre for Human Rights

The Legal Information Centre for Human Rights (LICHR) is a public non-profit organization focused on human rights in Estonia. The Centre has four priorities: conflict prevention (through analyses of the situation and creating awareness); the creation of an Estonian society based on culture and standard human rights; the analysis of legislation with international instruments of human rights; and the provision of legal advice and aid to individuals and groups whose rights have been violated. The main aim is to co-operate with the government of Estonia as well as with independent institutions.

Nunne Street 2
10133 Tallinn
Estonia
_____
Tel: +372 646 4268
Fax: +372 646 4272
centre@lichr.ee
www.lichr.ee

Contact: Aleksei Semjonov, Director

Number of staff: 5

Budget: $25,000–$100,000

Publications: Estonia: Nation Building and Integration—Political and Legal Aspects, 2000.

Baltic Region

RESEARCH
EDUCATION

Åland Islands Peace Institute

The Åland Islands Peace Institute conducts research and offers educational programs focusing on security policy, autonomy and minority rights, and political relations in the Baltic Sea region. The Institute addresses issues in relation to each other that may more frequently be treated in isolation from each other. The Institute's Research Program is, to some extent, shaped by the unique character of the Åland Islands as a demilitarized, neutral, autonomous political entity. In its educational programs the Institute is also active in promoting conflict management through seminars and training programs.

P.O.Box 85
22101 Mariehamn
Finland

Tel:+358 (18) 15570
Fax: +358 (18) 21026
peace@peace.aland.fi
www.peace.aland.fi

Contact: Nils-Gustaf Eriksson, Leader of the Centre for Crisis and Conflict Management
Number of staff: 6
Budget: $100,000–$500,000
Publications: Human Rights of Minority Women: a Manual of International Law, 2000; *The Kaliningrad Puzzle: a Russian Region within the European Union,* 2000; *New Conflicts and Their Peaceful Resolution,* 1998.

Africa

EDUCATION
ACTION
ADVOCACY

KATU

KATU (Kansalaisten turvallisuusneuvosto, the Citizen's Security Council) is a conflict prevention forum and network consisting of some 50 Finnish NGOs. It collects and distributes information on conflict prevention, organizes educational programs in the field, offers policy recommendations, and carries out concrete conflict prevention projects. KATU is currently focusing its efforts on conflict prevention and resolution in Southern Africa and working with Southern African NGOs to establish an NGO-based conflict prevention network in Southern Africa for training, networking, and information exchange programs on conflict prevention issues related to the region.
c/o Finnish UN Association

Unioninkatu 45B
00170 Helsinki
Finland

Tel: +358 (9) 6220 1223
Fax: +358 (9) 135 2173
anne.palm@katu-network.fi
www.katu-network.fi

Contact: Anne Palm, Secretary General
Number of staff: 3
Budget: $100,000–$500,000
Publications: KATU Bulletin; Building Peace in Africa; Report of the Conference on the Role of International Cooperation in Conflict Prevention in Africa, 1999; *The Role of Youth in Conflict Prevention in Africa,* 1999; *Cooperation or Conflict: Ways of Managing Scarce Natural Resources in Africa,* 1999.

Europe

RESEARCH
EDUCATION

Tampere Peace Research Institute

The Tampere Peace Research Institute (TAPRI) is dedicated to research in fields related to maintaining and safeguarding peace, with special emphasis on the management and resolution of international and national conflicts. Founded in 1970, the Institute facilitates publications in the field of peace research and promotes national and international cooperation in peace research. Its present research activities focus on European security and change, on new forms of conflict and effective strategies for resolving them, and on the Mediterranean. Problems of peaceful change are the recurrent theme in all these activities.

University of Tampere
Åkerlundinkatu 3
33014 Tampere
Finland

Tel: +358 (3) 215 7696
Fax: +358 (3) 223 6620
unto.vesa@uta.fi
www.uta.fi/tapri

Contact: Tarja Väyrynen, Research Director

Number of staff: 15

Budget: $100,000–$500,000

Publications: Estonia and the EU: Integration and Social Security in the Baltic Context, 2000; *Individuals, Society, Ideologies: Tracing the Mosaic of Mediterranean History,* 2000; *Peace-building in the Great Lakes Region of Africa,* 2000; *Democratic Security Building: Cases from the Baltic and Black Sea Regions,* 2000; *A Better Peace: the OSCE in Europe,* 1996.

Global

EDUCATION
ACTION
ADVOCACY

Coordination SUD

Coordination SUD (Solidarity, Urgency, Development) is a platform of more than one hundred NGOs working in the field of development and solidarity. Some of these also focus on conflict prevention and peacebuilding. As part of its network activities, it organizes debates and sets up synergies among members. SUD provides support through training, workshops, publications, and missions.

14 Passage Dubail
75010 Paris
France

Tel: +33 (1) 4472 9372
Fax: +33 (1) 4472 9373
international@coordinationsud.org
www.coordinationsud.org

Contact: Nathalie Herlemont-Zoritchak, International Officer

Number of staff: 8

Budget: $100,000–$500,000

Publications: Les Nouvelles de SUD, monthly newsletter; *Albanian Associative Dynamics: Kosovo Crisis and the Strategies of French NGOs,* 2001; *Journée de travail sur la prévention des conflits,* 1997.

Europe

Council of Europe

EDUCATION
ACTION
ADVOCACY

The Council of Europe was created in 1949 with the aim to achieve greater unity between its members through common action in a wide range of fields. As accession to membership is subject to significant conditions in terms of human rights, democracy, and other fundamental freedoms; the integration into the Council of Europe is in itself a conflict-prevention and peacebuilding measure. In order to protect national minorities, the Council has created a program of "civil society confidence-building measures" intended to diffuse tensions. In close collaboration with other inter-governmental organizations, the organization is also contributing to post-conflict peacebuilding in Southeastern Europe and the Caucasus.

Directorate General of
 Human Rights—DG II
Secretariat of the Framework
 Convention for the Protection
 of National Minorities and
 of the DH-MIN
67075 Strasbourg Cedex
France

Tel: +33 (3) 8841 2963
Fax: +33 (3) 9021 4918
mark.neville@coe.int
www.coe.int

Contact: Mark Neville, Executive Secretary for the Directorate General of Human Rights

Publications: The Europeans, electronic newsletter; *A Partnership for Co-operation and Reconciliation in the Middle East,* 1998; *The Minority Question in Europe,* 1996.

Global

Groupe Urgence de Rehabilitation et Développement

RESEARCH
ADVOCACY

The Groupe Urgence de Rehabilitation et Développement (URD) is a platform of almost thirty French and international member groups that meets to discuss the relationships between conflict and development, and humanitarian disasters and development. The group was formed in 1993 after several organizations felt the need to exchange ideas and seek synergy with fellow NGOs on these issues. One of the Groupe's major commitments is to work for conflict prevention.

La Fontaine des Marins
26170 Plaisians
France

Tel: +33 (4) 7528 2935
Fax: +33 (4) 7528 2936
urd@urd.org
www.urd.org

Contact: Francois Grunewald, President
Number of staff: 4
Budget: $ 25,000–$100,000
Publications: Synthèse de Réunion, newsletter; *Responding to Emergencies and Fostering Development—The Dilemmas of Humanitarian Aid,* 1999.

Global
Institut de Recherche sur la
Resolution Non-violente des Conflits

RESEARCH
EDUCATION

The goal of the French Research Institute on Non-violent Conflict Resolution (IRNC), which was founded in 1984, is to perform trans-disciplinary scientific research work on the non-violent resolution of conflicts and to implement the means to communicate that research. The IRNC also organizes training sessions and seminars in France and abroad. In the past research has had an international focus, but currently attention is also being given to internal conflicts such as Kosovo and the former Yugoslavia.

14 Rue des Meuniers
93100 Montreuil
France

Tel: +33 (14) 287 9469
Fax: +33 (14) 857 9297
irnc@multimania.com
www.multimania.com/irnc

Contact: Jean Marie Muller andChristian Mellon

Publications: Alternatives Non-Violentes,
quarterly publication; *Vers une culture de non-violence,* 2000; *La non-violence expliquée à mes filles,* 2000.

Global
International Federation
of Human Rights

RESEARCH
EDUCATION
ADVOCACY

The International Federation of Human Rights (FIDH, by its French acronym), founded in 1922, was the first international human rights organization with a universal mandate to defend all human rights. It brings together 114 human rights organizations from 90 countries. Besides activities to prevent violations and support local civil society, FIDH sends missions of mediation and election monitors. It has consultative or observer status at the UN, UNESCO, Council of Europe, the African Commission for Human Rights and People, and at the International Labour Organization.

17, Passage de la Main d'Or
75011 Paris
France

Tel:+33 (1) 4355 2518
Fax: +33 (1) 4355 1880
fidh@ fidh.org
www.fidh.org

Contact: Antoine Bernard, Director
Number of staff: 20
Budget: > $1,000,000
Publications: The Letter of the FIDH, monthly newsletter; *Preparatory Commission for the International Criminal Court,* 2000; *Kirghizistan: Chronicle of a Rigged Election.*

Global

Internews Europe

EDUCATION
ACTION

Internews Europe is a non-profit organization that aims to support the independence of media from political or financial monopolies. Recent projects have included training television journalists in Central Asia who work for independent stations, providing technical assistance to radio personnel in Kosovo, the co-production of a videoconference in the Balkan countries, and the financing of a television series, portraying life in Algeria, made by Algerian filmmakers. Internews Europe is a member of Internews International, a network of fifteen similar organizations from around the world.

14, Cite Griset
75011 Paris
France
_____

Tel: +33 (1) 5336 0606
Fax: +33 (1) 5336 8341
johnson@internews.org
www.internews.org

Contact: Eric Johnson, Executive Director
Number of staff: 6
Budget: > $1,000,000
Publications: Internews Reports, annual newsletter.

Chechnya, Kosovo,
Guinea-Bissau, Sierra Leone, Sudan, East-Timor

Médecins du Monde International

RESEARCH
EDUCATION
ACTION
ADVOCACY

Médecins du Monde (MdM) is a humanitarian association, composed of eleven international delegations, which relies on the voluntary commitment of member health care providers. MdM originated from a split with Médecins Sans Frontières in 1980. Although humanitarian assistance, throughout the world and in France, is the main element in the mandate of Médecins du Monde, conflict prevention, resolution, and mediation also comprise a considerable part of their concern. The organization operates internationally in 212 projects in 56 countries, over half of which are involved in rehabilitation and development actions.

62 rue Marcadet
75018 Paris
France
_____

Tel: +33 (1) 4492 1515
Fax: +33 (1) 4492 9999
medmonde@medecinsdumonde.org
www.medecinsdumonde.org

Contact: Médrinal Eléonore, Executive Assistant
Publications: Médecins du Monde, quarterly publication aimed at donors; *Actualités,* monthly publication aimed at members and field workers.

Global

ACTION

Mouvement de la Paix

Since 1949 Le Mouvement de la Paix, or the French Peace Movement, has been fighting against nuclear weapons, nuclear testing, and the arms trade. It initiates petitions, campaigns, and demonstrations. The movement supports and participates in Abolition 2000, a global network aimed at eliminating nuclear weapons. Its National Council and Bureau comprise many personalities from cultural and scientific circles. The organization, which has more than three hundred local committees, is a member of the international Peace Bureau and the World Peace Council

139 Boulevard V. Hugo
93400 Saint-Ouen
France

Tel: +33 (1) 4012 0912
Fax: +33 (1) 4011 5787
ddur@francenet.fr
www.perso.wanadoo.fr/mvpaix-rennes

Contact: Dainel Duran, National Secretary

Publications: Combat pour la Paix.

Global

RESEARCH
ACTION
ADVOCACY

OECD/DAC Network on Conflict, Peace and Development Co-operation

The OECD/DAC (Organisation for Economic Co-operation and Development/Development Assistance Committee) Network on Conflict, Peace and Development Co-operation aims at improving development co-operation policies and promoting partnership within partner countries and between external actors such as other government departments, civil society institutions, NGOs, business communities, and the media. The Network will also contribute to enhancing policy coherence and encourage communication and networking. Participants will share best practices and lessons learned on the role of development co-operation and the use of conflict analysis for conflict prevention and peacebuilding.

2, rue André Pascal
75775 Paris Cedex 16
France

Tel: +33 (1) 4524 8200
dac.contact@oecd.org
www.oecd.org/dac

Contact: Francesca Cook, OECD/DAC Secretariat

Budget: > $1,000,000

Publications: Helping Prevent Violent Conflict: Orientations for External Partners, 2001; *Security Issues and Development Co-operation,* 2001; *The Influence of Aid in Situations of Violent Conflict: Incentives and Disincentives for Peace,* 2001.

Africa

ACTION

Panos Institute

The Panos Institute in Paris specializes in information and communication for sustainable development and has a focus on Africa. Together with sister organizations in different parts of Africa and in London, the Institute supports local media professionals with an aim to promoting ethical concerns, stimulating public debates, and increasing the security and enforcing the rights of journalists involved in covering conflicts. Its latest project is the Media for Peace program, which is an extension of a project in which workshops were given on the role of the media in conflict prevention and peacebuilding.

10, Rue du Mail
Paris 75002
France

Tel: +33 (1) 4041 0550
Fax: +33 (1) 4041 0330
panos.paris@wanadoo.fr

Contact: Françoise Havelange, Director
Number of staff: 5
Budget: $500,000–$1,000,000

Africa

ADVOCACY

SURVIE

SURVIE is a public pressure group working for change in French African policy. In particular, the organization works to move French foreign policy toward Africa in the direction of support for democratization and away from alleged ethnic favoritism in the Great Lakes District. SURVIE alerts French legislatures and the public opinion to assumed French financial support to governments in Africa that perpetrate or condone mass killings. In recent years, special focus has been on international financial crime and fiscal paradises.

57 Avenue du Maine
75014 Paris
France

Tel: +33 (1) 4327 0325
Fax: +33 (1) 4320 5558
survie@globenet.org
www.globenet.org/survie

Contact: Sharon Courtoux, Conflict Prevention Programme
Number of staff: 1
Budget: < $25,000
Publications: Billets d'Afrique, newsletter; *Les Dossiers Noirs de la Politique Africaine de la France,* publication series.

Global

Transcend

RESEARCH
EDUCATION
ACTION
ADVOCACY

Transcend is a network of invited scholars and practitioners working for peace and development through action, education/training, dissemination, and research. In its action programs it uses conflict transformation, actor empowerment, education, journalism, peacekeeping, and reconciliation as tools to achieve their aims. The network also carries out research on a number of topics in the field of conflict transformation and peacebuilding. Among other outcomes, manuals on various themes have been published. Transcend currently plans for a Peace University.

51 Bois Chatton
01210 Versonnex
France

Tel: +1 (609) 799 8319
Fax: +1 (609) 799 2581
transcend@transcend.org
www.transcend.org

Contact: Johan Galtung, Director
Publications: Peace Actor Empowerment, 2001; *Searching for Peace: The Road to TRANSCEND,* 2000; *TRANSCEND: 40 Years, 40 Conflicts,* 1999.

Caucasus

Assist Yourself

EDUCATION
ACTION

Assist Yourself helps IDP's (especially women) from Abkhazia adapt to new lives. The main program of the organization is the "Confidence Building between Georgians and Abkhazians" program that is carried out with the collaboration of the Caucasus NGO Forum. The program focuses on Georgia, Abkhazia, and other regions of the Caucasus and is scheduled to run over three years. The program's major activities include meetings and joint projects of the leaders of the women NGOs of the Caucasus. Local and international partners involved in the program include International Alert (London), ICCN (Tbilisi) Civic Initiatives, and Sukhumi.

Nutsubidze Plateau IV, build. 25, app. 4
Tbilisi 380083
Georgia

Tel: +995 (32) 226 588
Fax: +995 (32) 999 494
ay@ip.osgf.ge; forum@access.sanet.ge

Contact: Marina Pagava, Head of Organization
Number of staff: 7
Budget: $25,000–$100,000
Publications: Bridge, newspaper; *Restoring the Culture of the Peace in the Caucasus: The Human Solidarity Document,* together with the International Center on Conflict and Negotiation, Georgia.

South Caucasus

**EDUCATION
ACTION
ADVOCACY**

Association of IDP Women

The mission of the Association of IDP Women (IDPWA) is to promote equal opportunities for IDP women and members of their families in social, political, and economical spheres. Originally the Association focused on the areas directly involved in the Abkhazia conflict. Since 1999 the NGO has been co-leader of "Working together—networking women in Caucasus," a network of 24 women's NGOs from Georgia, Armenia, Azerbaijan, and Chechnya. This includes the leading organizations: the IDP Women Association (Georgia), the Association for Protection of Women's Rights (Azerbaijan), and Helsinki Citizens Assembly (Armenia). The main conflict prevention activity is the program of peace camps for teenager IDPs.

Kikodze Street 16
Tbilisi 380000
Georgia

Tel: +995 (99) 570 798
julia.kharashvili@unv.org.gr; idpwa@gol.ge
www.whitecrane.org.ge

Contact: Julia Kharashvili, Director
Number of staff: 4
Publications: The Children's Magazine.

Caucasus

**ACTION
ADVOCACY**

Association of Women of Abkhazia

The Association of Women of Abkhazia's (AWA) mission is to support gender development and the advancement of women, human rights promotion, civil society development, advocacy of the rights of ethnic and religious minorities, and participation in second-track diplomacy and other peace initiatives for Georgian/Abkhaz conflict resolution. Strategic planning is the responsibility of the organization's Coordinating Group. The AWA has no regular funding; the projects are implemented with support of occasional grants. Main AWA activities are, directly or indirectly, connected with conflict prevention and resolution. The most important program AWA is currently involved in is "Confidence Building in Georgia/Abkhazia with participation of the Caucasus NGO Forum."

25, Gogol Street
384900 Sukhum
Abkhazia
Georgia

Tel: +995 (122) 24 264/27 950
Fax: +995 (122) 22 887

Contact: Natella Akaba, Director
Number of staff: 5
Budget: < $25,000

Caucasus

Caucasian Institute for
Peace, Democracy and Development

RESEARCH
EDUCATION
ACTION
ADVOCACY

The Caucasian Institute for Peace, Democracy and Development (CIPDD) runs research programs in peacebuilding, human rights, and security studies, and promotes democratic values on the national and regional scales.

In recent years there has been a special emphasis on studying civil-military relations in Georgia. Its main activities focus on South Caucasus, especially on the Georgian/Abkhaz conflict. The main program, "Non-formal contacts of Georgian and Abkhaz officials," is coordinated by Paata Zakareishvili and aims at conflict transformation through better understanding of the opposite party's position. The project partners are the Foundation Civil Initiative—Person of the Future (Abkhazia), Berghof Research Center for Constructive Conflict Management (Berlin), and Conciliation Resources (London). Other important programs are "Educational set on Abkhaz-Georgian conflict" and "Aspects of the Georgian-Abkhaz Conflict."

The most recent activities focus on monitoring the situation in Javakheti, Kvemo-Kartli, and Pankisi (2000-2001). Through its affiliate organization "Studio Re" TV, the CIPDD provides discussions, documentary TV films, workshops, and publications.

M. Alexidze Street 1
P.O. Box 101
Tbilisi 380008
Georgia

Tel: +995 (32) 334 081
Fax: +995 (32) 334 163
cipdd@access.sanet.ge
www.cipdd.org

Contact: Ghia Nodia, Chairperson

Number of staff: 3

Budget: $100,000–$500,000

Publications: Society and Politics 2000, periodical; *The Conflict in Abkhazia,* 1999; *The Political System in Georgia (A Directory),* 1998.

Caucasus

ACTION

ADVOCACY

Caucasus Links

Through its activities, Caucasus Links aims to promote the idea of peaceful settlement of conflicts in the Caucasus; to assist in the process of state-building of the Caucasus states; to support the work of civil society; to assist in the promotion of human and minority rights and the values of mutual respect and tolerance; to support initiatives aimed at raising environmental awareness; and to make the Caucasus better known to the outside world. It's primary mandate is work in the field of conflict prevention/resolution, human rights, and democratic development. The organization's main partner organization is the UK-based organization LINKS (London Information Network on Conflicts and State-building).

Barnov Street 41
Tbilisi
Georgia

Tel: +995 (32) 292 399
Fax: +995 (32) 987 439
links@caucasus.net
www.caucasuslinks.org

Contact: Kakhaber Berodze, Director
Number of staff: 5
Budget: $25,000–$100,000

Caucasus

RESEARCH

EDUCATION

ACTION

ADVOCACY

Center for Humanitarian Programmes

The Center for Humanitarian Programmes is a non-governmental organization that promotes the development of a democratic society in Abkhazia based on the principles of equality, social justice, and participation. Through citizen diplomacy, it promotes confidence building between civil societies in the Caucasus with the aim of preventing conflict from becoming violent. Research has been carried out on the role of citizen diplomacy in the resolution of the Georgian-Abkhazian conflict. Part of its mandate is also to see to the needs of vulnerable groups in society such as women, children, the disabled, and ex-combatants.

36, Gogol St
384900 Sukhum
Abkhazia/Georgia

Tel: +995 (122) 25 598
Fax: 871 761 909 181 (satellite)
chpabkhazia@yahoo.com

Contact: Batal Kobakhia, Executive Director
Number of staff: 8
Budget: $25,000–$100,000

Caucasus

International Center
on Conflict and Negotiation

RESEARCH
EDUCATION
ACTION
ADVOCACY

Founded in 1992, and formed into an NGO with support from the John D. and Catherine T. MacArthur Foundation in 1994, the International Center on Conflict and Negotiation (ICCN) is a pioneering institution in the Caucasus in the fields of conflict prevention/transformation, conflict studies, peace education, and citizen diplomacy.

ICCN organized the first informal Georgian-Abkhaz group meetings along with International Alert and the Fund Civic Initiative—Person of the Future, Sukhumi, and Georgian-Osset (with Conflict Management Group and Norwegian Refugee Council). It is also responsible for the first nation-wide training program in conflict management specifically designed for IDPs and other conflict-affected groups (supported by Norwegian Refugee Council and Danish Refugee Council); the first and successfully tested multi-indicator-based empirical model for early warning of ethnic conflict in Georgia,and other initiatives in regional security and integration studies. ICCN is one of the foremost national centers for forced migration studies, and has established (sub) regional branches, and through its affiliate group CWN (the Caucasus Women's Research and Consulting Network, founded in 1997) has done research on hidden discrimination against women and gender stereotypes in Georgia (1999; available on ICCN web site) and also on trafficking in women (2000).

The most important of its ongoing programs include: "Peace education and conflict management training" (supported by Cordaid); "Confidence building between Georgians and Abkhaz" (in partnership with International Alert, London, and Fund Civic Initiative—Person of the Future, Sukhumi; supported by Tacis/ EuropeAid); and "South Caucasus network for civil accord" (in partnership with eight NGOs in Armenia, Azerbaijan and Georgia, coordinated by the British East-West Centre; supported by Tacis/EuropeAid). The Accord Club for Civic Dialogue opened at the ICCN head office in 2000 to promote democratic development and non-violent transition in Georgia. It contributed to the founding of the Caucasus NGO Forum in 1998.

Machabeli Street 5
Tbilisi 380005
Georgia

Tel: +995 (32) 999 987
Fax: +995 (32) 939 178
iccn@access.sanet.ge
iccn.tripod.com

Contact: George Khutsishvili, Founding Director and Chairperson

Number of staff: 18

Budget: $100,000–$500,000

Publications: The Peace Times, bimonthly journal since 2001; *Jincharadze, Paata and Kordzakhia, Irakli: Empirical Model for Early Warning of Ethnic Conflicts,* 2000; *Understanding Conflict,* 1998.

South Caucasus

Partners-Georgia

EDUCATION
ACTION

The mission of Partners-Georgia (Center for Change and Conflict Management) is to promote civil society and advance a culture of change and conflict management in Georgia and the South Caucasus region. The main program for conflict prevention/resolution is "Youth development." Another major activity is the "Academic Program in South Caucasus," which supports the development and integration of the conflict resolution field into the universities of the South Caucasus. Recent programs have focused on Georgia, Armenia, and Azerbaijan (1999-2000). Partners-Georgia is a member of the international network NGO "Partners for Democratic Change," which has its headquarters in San Francisco.

Griboedov Street 12
Tbilisi 380008
Georgia
_____
Tel: +995 (32) 995 452
Fax: +995 (32) 988 344
pdcgeo@access.sanet.ge
www.partners.ge

Contact: Sofiko Shubladze, Director
Number of staff: 6
Budget: $25,000–$100,000

Caucasus

South Ossetian Center on Humanitarian Initiatives and Research

RESEARCH
ADVOCACY

The main activities of the South Ossetian Center on Humanitarian Initiatives and Research are in conflict prevention/resolution/mediation, democratic development, capacity building, and mass media. The Center has participated in the programs conducted in South Ossetia by the Conflict Management Group (CMG) and in the Caucasus by the Caucasus NGO Forum.

Geroyev Street 14
Tskhinvali 383570
South Ossetia
Georgia
_____
Tel:+244 (42) 003/42 381
alan@caucasus.net

Contact: Alan Parastaev, Director
Number of staff: 5
Budget: < $25,000

South Caucasus

Union Public Movement Multinational Georgia

EDUCATION
ACTION
ADVOCACY

The Union Public Movement Multinational Georgia is an NGO for ethnic minorities in Georgia. Its mission includes peacebuilding, resolution of conflicts in the sphere of inter-ethnic relations, protection of civil liberties, and intercultural education in ethnic majority-minority relations focusing on the country's legislation. Its main program is the Multi-ethnic Resource Center on Civic Education in Georgia. The organization's team comprises representatives of different ethnic groups from NGOs such as The Union of Armenian Youth of Georgia, Association of Azerbaijaniani Youth of Georgia, The Union of Ossetians of Georgia "Phidat," International Foundation of the Jewish Heritage, and The Union of Ukrainian Women of Georgia to name just a few.

Rustaveli Avenue 37
Tbilisi 380008
Georgia

Tel: +995 (32) 998 790
Fax: +995 (32) 995 228
pmmg@caucasus.net;
    arnostep@yahoo.com
www.friends-partners.org/ccsi/nisorgs/georgia/pubmove.htm

Contact: Arnold Stepanian, Director
Number of staff: 5
Budget: $25,000–$100,000
Publications: Multinational Georgia, newsletter.

Georgia

United Nations Association of Georgia

RESEARCH
EDUCATION
ACTION
ADVOCACY

The United Nations Association of Georgia (UNAG) is a national non-governmental, non-profit, and non-partisan organization that was established to promote the ideals of the United Nations and assist in bringing the UN closer to people and people closer to the UN. It is a member of the World Federation of United Nations Associations (WFUNA), and thus co-operates in a multilateral framework. UNAG works with programs funded by donors or conducted in partnership with international organizations in the fields of human rights, transparency and good governance, and civic education. UNAG's main partners are IOM and UNHCR.

Dolidze Street 2
Tbilisi 380015
Georgia

Tel/fax: +995 (32) 335 216/332 516
una@una.ge
www.una.org.ge

Contact: Ramaz Aptsiauri, Secretary General
Number of staff: 3
Budget: < $25,000
Publications: UN Suggested Reading for Students; special leaflets on OSCE, EU, UN

Global
Action Committee Service for Peace

The Action Committee Service for Peace (AGDF), founded in 1968, is an association of 34 peace organizations that represents their members' concerns such as reconciliation and international co-operation, support and encouragement for initiatives working for justice, social security, and for environmental concerns. Ultimately, the AGDF aims to build a comprehensive concept of peace. The association is active in the fields of co-operation and information. It organizes seminars and courses, and undertakes fundraising and grant writing activities.

Blücherstrasse 14
53115 Bonn
Germany

Tel/fax: +49 (228) 24 999
agdf@friedensdienst.de
www.friedensdienst.de

Balkans
Balkan Peace Team International

The Balkan Peace Team (BPT) International is a project, sponsored by eleven member organizations, that provides day-to-day support for the work of peace and human rights advocates in the states of former Yugoslavia. BPT is an experiment in grassroots nonviolent intervention. At the invitation of local NGOs, BPT has placed international teams of volunteers in Kosovo, Croatia, and Serbia, where their encouragement and the reassurance of their daily presence has helped enable local activists to carry out their work. The teams sometimes arrange meetings between different ethnic communities, help with networking, and arrange workshops.

Ringstr. 9a
32427 Minden
Germany

Tel: +49 (571) 20 776
Fax: + 49 (571) 23 019
bpt@balkanpeaceteam.org
www.balkanpeaceteam.org

Contact: Dorie Wilsnack, Co-Coordinator
Budget: $100,000–$500,000
Publications: BPT Newsletter, quarterly report; *Reports from the Teams,* available via e-mail

Northern Ireland, Southern Africa, Horn of Africa

Bonn International Centre for Conversion

RESEARCH

The Bonn International Center for Conversion (BICC) is an international think tank dedicated to facilitating the processes whereby people, skills, technology, equipment, and economic resources can be shifted away from the defense sector and applied to alternative civilian uses. Through research and analysis, technical assistance and advice, re-training programs, publications, and conferences, it supports government and NGO initiatives on reducing military-related activities. BICC provides project management and consulting services in connection with the redevelopment of former military installations for civilian use, and maintains an information clearinghouse with extensive information on economic conversion issues.

An der Elizabethkirche 25
53133 Bonn
Germany
_____

Tel: +49 (228) 911 960
Fax: +49 (228) 241215
bicc@bicc.de
www.bicc.de

Contact: Kees Kingma, Researcher

Number of staff: 30

Budget: $100,000–$500,000

Publications: BICC disarmament and conversion studies; *BICC Bulletin,* quarterly newsletter; Conversion survey yearbooks.

Southeastern Europe, Caucasus, Sri Lanka

Berghof Research Center for Constructive Conflict Management

The Berghof Research Center for Constructive Conflict Management aims to strengthen civilian approaches to conflict management. The Center's key concern is the creation and promotion of peace constituencies in ethno-political conflicts.

These constituencies refer to the local or regional networks of individuals and institutions endeavouring to bring about permanent conflict transformation in crisis regions. External actors and institutions can assist the formation of peace constituencies by supporting local initiatives or by assuming mediating roles. It is the belief of the Center that tackling these issues requires closely coordinated activity in the areas of: action oriented research, support for local peace initiatives, network formation, and political consultancy.

The Center's research seeks both to analyze the conditions and characteristics of the long-term macro- and micro-social processes involved in creating peace, and to assess the effectiveness of particular approaches to intervention in current conflict resolution. Most of the Center's work is conducted in the form of action-research projects undertaken in collaboration with individuals and institutions in the field, and with other academic bodies.

Current activities include:

-"Berghof Handbook," a resource consisting of articles on state-of-the-art of conflict transformation.

-"Georgian-Abkhazian Dialogue," a project exploring the creation of channels of communication between the conflicting parties, in order to strengthen civil society in the region and establish a sustainable infrastructure of complementary conflict management initiatives.

-"Peacebuilding through Youth Work in Bosnia and Herzegovina," a joint project with the German development agency, Gesellschaft für Technische Zusammenarbeit (GTZ or German Technical Development Association), to support local initiatives for empowering youth and promoting reconciliation among young people in Bosnia and Herzegovina.

The Center has also been engaged in other projects in Southeastern Europe, including support for "South East European NGOs and the Stability Pact," a conference held in 2000 on networking in the region to further implementation of the Stability Pact, and support and evaluation of nonviolence training programs and networking activities of the Sarajevo-based Center for Nonviolent Action.

Altensteinstrasse 48a
14195 Berlin
Germany

Tel: +49 (30) 844 1540
Fax: +49 (30) 844 15499
info@berghof-center.org
www.berghof-center.org

Contact: Reiner Steinweg, Acting Director

Number of staff: 11

Budget: $500,000–$1,000,000

Publications: Berghof Handbook for Conflict Transformation, 2002; *Crisis Prevention and Conflict Management by the European Union: Concepts, Capacities and Problems of Coherency,* 2000; *South European NGOs for the Stability Pact,* 2000; *Effective Crisis Prevention: Challenges for German Foreign and Development Policy,* 1999.

Balkans, Turkey, East Africa, East Timor

Center for Education and Networking in Nonviolent Action

EDUCATION
ACTION

The Center for Education and Networking in Nonviolent Action (Kurve Wustrow) is a non-profit organization that focuses mainly on increasing the effectiveness of non-violent action by providing training for peace activists and networking opportunities among movements to share information, approaches, and expertise. Kurve Wustrow offers training in non-violent conflict transformation for group leaders in youth and social work, prepares for long-term volunteer placement, and offers certified training programs leading to qualifications for long term peace service. It cooperates with organizations in conflict regions.

Kirchstrasse 14
29462 Wustrow
Germany

Tel: +49 (58) 439 8710
Fax: +49 (58) 439 87111
www.kurvewustrow.org

Contact: Berndt Hagen, Director
Number of staff: 9
Budget: $500,000–1,000,000
Publications: Rundsrief, newsletter.

Africa, Global

Church Development Service

EDUCATION
ACTION
ADVOCACY

The Church Development Service (Evangelischer Entwicklungsdienst, EED) is an association of the protestant churches in Germany. It aims to strengthen capacities for peacebuilding and peaceful conflict management among the members of its own network and its partner organizations by linking organizations with a certain demand with experts in the respective field. It also facilitates information sharing and carries out political lobby work in Germany. The organization is currently focussing on the oil issue in Sudan and Chad/Cameroon as well as on the small arms trade.

Mittelstrasse 37
53 175 Bonn
Germany

Tel: +49 (228) 810 1220
Fax: +49 (69) 791 200 291
agked-bonn@geonet.de
www.eed.de

Contact: Angelika Spelten, Desk for Peace and Conflict Issues

Central, Eastern, and Southeastern Europe

ADVOCACY

Development and Peace Foundation

Founded on the initiative of former Chancellor Willy Brandt, the Development and Peace Foundation (Stiftung Entwicklung und Frieden—SEF) aims to contribute to preventive peace policy by fostering a political dialogue that helps ensure that global issues are tackled in a well-informed manner.

The Foundation seeks to make plain the links between development and peace, particularly in relation to developing countries; to demonstrate the interaction between the world economy, the global environment, and international security; to encourage dialogue in Germany and elsewhere about major global trends; and to stimulate the search for solutions that can be translated into practical policy.

The Foundation works to heighten public awareness around issues related to conflict resolution. Furthermore, it encourages and commissions research in its fields of interest. It cooperates closely with the Institute for Peace and Development, an associate body of the University of Duisburg that also provides academic back-up to the Foundation.

A basic aim of the Foundation is to build and consolidate global governance. In pursuit of this aim, it has chosen to focus on three key areas that are linked to each other and to the guiding theme of global governance: the creation of sustainable development structures; the creation of structures and institutions capable of fostering peace; and transformation in Central, Eastern, and Southeastern Europe.

The Foundation organizes conferences and workshops; addresses peace and conflict resolution issues, including the annual Development and Peace Foundation Symposium; and has been an active participant in the Policy Forum on Regional Conflict Management, in partnership with other organizations. It has an active publishing program, including publication of a newsletter, the "One World" series of collected essays, policy papers, and the biannual *Global Trends: The World Development in Figures and Facts,* in which questions of war and peace are dealt with extensively.

Gotenstrasse 152
53175 Bonn
Germany

Tel: +49 (288) 959 250
sef@sef-bonn.org
www.sef-bonn.org

Contact: Burkhard Könitzer

Budget: $100,000–$500,000

Publications: SEF News, newsletter; *Conflict Transformation: How International Assistance Can Contribute,* 1999; *Ecology, Politics and Violent Conflicts,* 1999.

Eastern Europe, Caucasus, Honduras, Kenya

EDUCATION
ACTION

Ecumenical Service Shalom Diaconate

Ecumenical Service Shalom Diaconate (Oekumenischer Dienst Schalomdiakonat) is an ecumenical Christian organization primarily engaged in nonviolent conflict management training and the supervision of peace workers. It offers a variety of courses and seminars at different levels. Its efforts are informed by inter-religious dialogue and intercultural teamwork. Members seek inspiration in the Christian tradition of nonviolence and are deeply committed to the vision that nonviolence can transform violent structures.

Mittelstrasse 4
34474 Diemelstadt-Wethen
Germany

Tel: +49 (56) 948 033
schalomdiakonat@t-online.de
www.schalomdiakonat.de

Contact: Christian Garve, Director

Number of staff: 4

Budget: $100,000–$500,000

Publications: International Basic Course in Non-violent Conflict Transformation, folder; *Schalom-Dienst,* newsletter in German*; Schalomdiakonat: Erfahrungen und Einsichten zur Gewaltfreiheit,* 2000; *Versoehnungsprozesse und Gewaltfreiheit,* 1999.

Europe, West Africa, Latin America

EDUCATION
ACTION

EIRENE

EIRENE (the International Christian Service for Peace) is an ecumenical peace and development organization working to promote peace and justice in both the North and South. It believes such change can be achieved mainly by changes in cultural values and living styles. EIRENE is engaged in human rights work, women's issues, conflict resolution training, and development work in Africa and Latin America; in programs to promote reconciliation in Ireland; in both humanitarian assistance and reconciliation programs in the Balkans; and in programs to assist groups on the social and economic margins elsewhere in Europe.

Engerser Strasse 74b
P.O. Box 1322
56503 Neuwied
Germany

Tel:+49 (2631) 83790
Fax: +49 (2631) 31160
fricke@eirene.org
www.eirene.org

Contact: Eckehard Fricke, General Secretary

Number of staff: 15

Budget: > $1,000,000

Balkans and Baltic states

European Centre for Minority Issues

RESEARCH
ACTION

The European Centre for Minority Issues (ECMI) is engaged in a range of activities to reduce the potential for conflict between minority and majority populations in Europe, particularly through early monitoring, study, and conflict-resolution efforts. The Centre conducts practice-oriented research; provides information and analysis to the academic community, the media, and the general public; and serves as a consultant with governments, inter-governmental organizations, and representatives of minority populations. The Centre is involved in the evaluation, further development, and implementation of standards of governance based on ethnic diversity and human rights.

Schiffbruecke 12
24939 Flensburg
Germany
_____

Tel: +49 (461) 141 490
Fax: +49 (461) 141 4919
info@ecmi.de
www.ecmi.de

Contact: Marc Weller, Director

Number of staff: 14

Publications: Evaluating Policy Measures for Minority Language in Europe: Towards Effective, Cost-effective and Democratic Implementation, 2000; Conflict Prevention in the Baltic States: The OSCE High Commissioner on National Minorities in Estonia, Latvia and Lithuania, 1999. Conflict in Kosovo: Failure of Prevention? *An Analytical Documentation 1992–1998,* 1998.

Eastern Europe, France, Austria, Italy, Magreb countries

European Institute
Conflict-Culture-Cooperation

EDUCATION

The European Institute Conflict-Culture-Cooperation (EICCC) is a nonprofit training institute. In the field of conflict prevention and resolution it offers two training programs for conflict resolution trainers: one on creative conflict resolution in Europe, and the other dealing with intercultural communication in German-speaking and French-speaking areas in Europe, as well as intercultural communication in Poland, the Czech Republic, and Slovakia. In the coming years the organization intends to extend the scope and length of its training programs. It also plans to found a European institute for intercultural communication and conflict resolution.

Hessestrasse 4
90443 Nürnberg
Germany
_____

Tel: +49 (911) 699 6294
Fax: +49 (911) 699 6295
karl-heinz.bittl@t-online.de
www.eiccc.org

Contact: Karl-Heinz Bittl (Germany) or Hervé Ott (France), Directors

Budget: $25,000–$100,000

Publications: CCC-info, newsletter.

Europe, Eastern Europe, CIS countries

European Migration Centre

The European Migration Centre (EMZ) aims to facilitate networking between European institutions working in the fields of migration and ethnicity. EMZ is engaged in international research as well as practical guidance for immigrant entrepreneurs in Berlin. EMZ maintains an extensive library and online data banks with statistics and literature on migration topics. EMZ strives to link research, practice, and politics in order to contribute to the implementation of a sustainable European migration policy, and endeavors to present a scientific basis for reasonable integration and immigration policies in publications and public programs.

Schliemannstrasse 23
10437 Berlin
Germany
_____
Tel: +49 (30) 4465 1065
Fax: +49 (30) 444 1085
emz@compuserve.com
www.emz-berlin.de

Contact: Jochen Blaschke, Director
Number of staff: 3
Budget: $25,000–$100,000

Publications: Migration: a European Journal on International Migration and Ethnic Relations, quarterly journal.

Southeastern Europe

European Stability Initiative

The European Stability Initiative (ESI) is a non-profit research and policy institute, established to assist international efforts to promote stability and prosperity in Southeastern Europe. It offers practical, independent, and timely analyses of international strategy and the impact of international programs. ESI has an active publications program and makes all of its materials accessible free of charge from its website.

Kiefholzstrasse 402
12435 Berlin
Germany
_____
Tel: +49 (30) 5321 4455
Fax: +49 (30) 5321 4455
esi@operamail.com
www.esiweb.org

Contact: Gerald Knaus, Executive Director
Number of staff: 6
Budget: $100,000–$500,000

Publications: Sovereignty, Europe and the Future of Serbia and Montenegro: A Proposal for International Mediation, 2001; *Turning Point— The Brussels PIC Declaration and a State-building Agenda for Bosnia and Herzegovina,* 2000; *Elections in 2000—Risks for the Bosnian Peace Process,* 2000.

Global

Evangelische Akademie Loccum

RESEARCH
EDUCATION
ACTION
ADVOCACY

Peaceful civilian settlement of conflict has in recent years been one of the main focuses of the Evangelische Akademie Loccum, a center of the Lutheran Church in Hannover. The center encourages the open-minded discussion of fundamental issues of our time; provides guidance to people searching for religious, cultural, social, and political direction; and fosters dialogue among people from all walks of life. The center has organized international workshops on peaceful conflict resolution in Europe and on the contribution of NGOs to conflict prevention, civilian conflict management, and post-conflict peacebuilding.

P.O. Box 2158
31545 Reiburg-Loccum
Germany

Tel: +49 (57) 66 810
Fax: +49 (57) 66 900
eal@evlka.de

Contact: Jörg Calliess, Director of Studies

Number of staff: 31

Budget: > $1,000,000

Publications: Peaceful Settlement of Conflict—A Task for Civil Society: Part 1: Possibilities and Instruments for Conflict Management in Cases of Ethno-National Tension, 1993; *Part 2: Third Party Intervention,* 1994; *Part 3: Cooperation Between Civil Society Actors and (Inter) governmental Institutions,* 1995.

Balkans

Federation for Social Defence

RESEARCH
EDUCATION
ACTION
ADVOCACY

The Federation for Social Defence (Bund für Soziale Verteidigung) promotes non-violent conflict resolution and social defense, human rights, and democratic development, and works for the abolition of armament and military forces. In Germany, the organization provides training in conflict resolution techniques, particularly for professionals working with young people, and peer mediation for school children. It is also one of five organizations that together run a four-month course for conflict transformation experts who prepare themselves for deployment abroad or in Germany. The Federation has been engaged in different project in the area of former Yugoslavia, among them the international Balkan Peace Team.

Ringstrasse 9a
32427 Minden
Germany

Tel: +49 (571) 29 456
Fax: +49 (571) 23 019
soziale_verteidigung@t-online.de
www.dfg-vk.de/bsv

Contact: Detlef Beck and Christine Schweitzer, Heads of Conflict Resolution Programs

Number of staff: 5

Budget: $25,000–$100,000

Publications: Quarterly newsletter.

Southeastern Europe

Forum Civil Peace Service

RESEARCH

The Forum Civil Peace Service (CPS—Forum Ziviler Friedensdienst) is an association of various German organizations sharing the goal of building and strengthening the instruments of nonviolent civilian conflict resolution, especially by creating an institutionalized body of well-trained conflict mediators. CPS places trained volunteers in areas of crisis and tension to work for conflict transformation and the prevention of violence, and works to support local people in building civil society, in which democratic participation and human rights are guaranteed. Currently, it focuses primarily on ethno-political conflict in Southeastern Europe.

Wesselstrasse 12
53113 Bonn
Germany

Tel: +49 (228) 981 4510
Fax: +49 (228) 981 4517
forumzfd@t-online.de
www.forumzfd.de

Contact: Helga Tempel and Heinz Wagner, Directors

Number of staff: 1

Budget: $100,000–$500,000

Europe, Magreb countries

Fränkisches Bildungswerk
für Friedensarbeit

EDUCATION

Fränkisches Bildungswerk für Friedensarbeit is a nonprofit training institute. In the field of conflict prevention and resolution it offers two training programs for conflict resolution trainers: one on creative conflict resolution in Europe and the other dealing with intercultural communication in German-speaking and French-speaking areas in Europe, as well as intercultural communication in Poland, the Czech Republic,and Slovakia. In the coming years the organization intends to extend the scope and length of its training programs. It also plans to found a European institute for intercultural communication and conflict resolution.

Hessestrasse 4
90443 Nürnberg
Germany

Tel:+49 (911) 288500
Fax: +49 (911) 9693812
karl-heinz.bittl@t-online.de

Contact: Karl-Heinz Bittl, Director

Budget: $50,000

Publications: FBF-news, newsletter; training materials.

Global

German Platform
for Peaceful Conflict Management

ACTION

In November 1998, the German Platform for Peaceful Conflict Management (PZK—Plattform Zivile Konfliktbearbeitung) was established in order to create a strong European infrastructure for peacebuilding activities. PZK is committed to the reduction of violence and peace promotion.

About fifty organizations are involved. The Platform is not a member organization, but a communal project of participating individuals, organizations, and institutions that maintain individual connections to the international NGO community and other actors in civic society. Participants originate from organizations in a wide variety of fields, including human rights, peace work, peace research, humanitarian aid, development co-operation, and church organizations.

The main goal of the network is to mutually support and strengthen participants' peacebuilding activities. Some of the network's important commitments are exchange of information, attracting support among the general public, and widening the constituency for peacebuilding. Participants also collaborate in lobbying activities as well as efforts to improve the theoretical and professional base of peacebuilding.

Consensus is a central principle in determining the actions and directions that the platform will take. The Platform's basic approach focuses on subsidiarity and a decentralized working structure. Participants do not engage in co-operation for the sake of it, but only if they see clear advantages and synergy in communal undertakings.

Secretariat:
Institut für Friedensarbeit und
   Gewaltfreie Konfliktaustragung
attn. Barbara Müller
Hauptstr. 35
55491 Wahlenau
Germany

Tel: +49 (6543) 980 096
bmuellerifgk@aol.com
www.konfliktbearbeitung.net

Contact: Barbara Müller, Coordinator
Budget: < $25,000

Global

Heidelberg Institute
for International Conflict Research

RESEARCH
EDUCATION

Heidelberg University's Institute of International Conflict Research (HIIK) was established in 1991 to pursue research, provide analysis, and maintain documentation of national and international political conflicts. The Institute maintains a comprehensive database, called KOSIMO (Conflict Simulation Model), on national and international political conflicts that have occurred since 1945. Conflicts are described by up to fifty-one characteristics, including type of conflict (international, civil war, coup d'état, for example) degree of violence, related sub-conflicts, mediation efforts, outcome, and other similar factors. The annual German-language *Konfliktbarometer* provides a succinct overview of global trends regarding conflicts and conflict management.

Institute of Political Science
University of Heidelberg
Marstallstrasse 6
69117 Heidelberg
Germany

Tel: +49 (6221) 542872
Fax: +49 (6221) 542896
info@hiik.de
www.hiik.de

Contact: Christoph Rohloff, Director

Number of staff: 20

Budget: < $25,000

Publications: Konfliktbarometer, yearly report; *Datenhandbuch nationaler und internationaler Konflikte,* 1994.

East and Southeastern Europe, Caucasus, Baltic states

Institute for Peace Research and Security
Policy at the University of Hamburg

RESEARCH

The Institute for Peace Research and Security Policy (Institut für Friedensforschung und Sicherheitspolitik an der Universität Hamburg, IFSH) was established in 1971 to carry out academic research on peace issues. Its goal is to promote balanced and innovative research, training, and teaching, and to publish its results. During the Cold War era, it focused especially on "common security" issues. More recently, it has focused on the establishment of structures for a "European Peace Order" and a pan-European Collective Security System. The Centre for OSCE Research (CORE) is part of the Institute. Increasingly, the Institute is turning its attention to conflicts of a more global nature.

Falkenstein 1
22587 Hamburg
Germany

Tel: +49 (40) 866 0770
Fax: +49 (40) 866 3615
ifsh@rrz.uni-hamburg.de
www.rrz.uni-hamburg.de/ifsh

Contact: Wolfgang Zellner, Deputy Director of the Centre for OSCE Research within the Institute

Number of staff: 35

Budget: $500,000–$1,000,000

Publications: OSCE Yearbook; Friedensgutachten, a state-of-peace yearbook.

Former Yugoslavia

Institute for Peace Work and Non-Violent Settlement of Conflict

RESEARCH
ADVOCACY

The Institute for Peace Work and Non-Violent Settlement of Conflict (IFGK—Institut für Friedensarbeit und Gewaltfreie Konfliktaustragung) is primarily a research organization engaged in the systematic analysis of nonviolent conflict resolution, informed by a firm commitment to the principles of active nonviolence. IFGK also provides counseling in nonviolent conflict resolution, carries out field studies, and develops and conducts action research. It has focused in particular on conflicts in the former Yugoslavia.

Hauptstrasse 35
55491 Wahlenau
Germany

Tel: +49 (6543) 980 096
Fax:+49 (6543) 500 636
bmuellerifgk@aol.com
www.ifgk.de

Contact: Barbara Müller

Budget: > $25,000

Publications: Vorbereitungen für die Zeit nach dem Krieg: Bericht für die Arbeitsgruppe Kosovo des Committee for Conflict Transformation Support, 1999; *Passiver Widerstand im Ruhrkampf: Eine Fallstudie zur gewaltlosen zwischenstaatlichen Konfliktaustragung und ihren Erfolgsbedingungen,* 1995; *Friedensbrigaden: Zivile Konfliktbearbeitung mit gewaltfreien Methoden,* 1995.

Global

Peace Research Information Unit Bonn

RESEARCH
EDUCATION

The Peace Research Information Unit Bonn (PRIUB) provides information and advice, and facilitates contacts on all matters concerning peace and conflict research. It maintains a database of hundreds of peace and conflict research organizations in Germany and elsewhere, and assists in putting scholars and institutions in touch with one another. The Unit also organizes workshops on peace and conflict issues for scholars, conflict resolution practitioners, politicians, activists, and the media; assists scholars in publishing research results; and serves as a bridge between academia and politics.

Beethovenallee 4
53173 Bonn
Germany

Tel: +49 (228) 356 032
Fax: +49 (228) 356 050
afb@priub.org
www.priub.org

Contact: Regine Mehl, Director

Number of staff: 4

Budget: $100,000–$500,000

Publications: AFB-INFO, bi-annual newsletter in English and German.

Global

Peace Research Institute Frankfurt

RESEARCH

The Peace Research Institute Frankfurt (PRIF or HSFK—Hessische Stiftung Friedens- und Konfliktforschung), founded in 1970, was the first peace research institute in Germany and remains the largest. It is primarily involved in research into the causes of violent conflicts, both internal and external, and the conditions of peace. Topics include arms control and disarmament, international organizations, development and democratization, and managing conflicts in democracies. PRIF's publications provide information to politicians and society about the conditions and decisions required to promote peace as a process of decreasing violence and increasing justice.

Leimenrode 29
60322 Frankfurt am Main
Germany

Tel:+49 (69) 959 1041
Fax: +49 (69) 558 481
Info@hsk.de
www.hsfk.de

Contact: Harald Müller, Director

Number of staff: 27

Budget: > $1,000,000

Publications: Positioning Europe as a Credible Actor in the "Ballistic Missile Defense Game": Concepts and Recommendations; Nuclear Weapons and Germans Interests: An Attempt at Redefinition; Switzerland: A Model for Solving Nationality Conflicts? 1999; *"Talk to them? No way!" Models of Dispute Settlement in Multicultural Urban Societies,* 1998.

Baltic states, Russia

Schleswig-Holstein Institute for Peace Research at Kiel University

RESEARCH

The Schleswig-Holstein Institute for Peace Research at Kiel University, SHIP (SCHIFF—Schleswig-Holsteinisches Institut für Friedenswissenschaften an der Universität Kiel) carries out fundamental and applied research, exploring both the opportunities for and the obstacles to building and maintaining peace, justice, and nonviolence in the international system as well as within society. SHIP takes an interdisciplinary, problem-oriented approach to peace research in cooperation with other academic institutions and carries out various public information programs. SHIP focuses on the Baltic Sea region, especially on non-military treatment of conflicts, conversion to a peace economy, and sustainable development.

Kaiserstrasse 2
24143 Kiel
Germany

Tel: +49 (431) 880 6330
Fax: +49 (431) 880 6333
wellmann@schiff.uni-kiel.de
www.schiff.uni-kiel.de

Contact: Christian Wellmann, Deputy Director

Number of staff: 2

Budget: $25,000–$100,000

Publications: Half Full or Half Empty? The OSCE Mission to Estonia and its Balance Sheet 1993–1999 (together with the European Centre for Minority Issues), 2000*; From Town to Town: Local Authorities as Transnational Actors, 1999; Preventive Diplomacy through Fact-Finding: How International Organizations Review the Conflict over Citizenship in Estonia and Latvia, 1997.*

Europe

Working Group on Peace Pedagogics at the Technological University of Berlin

RESEARCH
EDUCATION

The Working Group on Peace Pedagogics at the Technological University of Berlin (Arbeitsgruppe Friedenspädagogik, Technische Universität Berlin) conducts courses, seminars, and international workshops on conflict mediation, non-violence, and peace education. Current activities include research on gender aspects of conflict and a study of the International Workshops on Peace Education, as well as studies on holocaust education as a part of human rights education.

F.B. 02, Sekr. 3-7
Franklinstrasse 28/29
10587 Berlin
Germany

Tel: +49 (30) 3147 3144
Fax: +49 (30) 3142 1117
rathenow@tu-berlin.de

Contact: Hanns-Fred Rathenow

Number of staff: 4

Budget: < $25,000

Publications: Flügelschläge fur den Frieden (Wingbeats for Peace), biennial series.

Southeastern Europe

Andreas Papandreou Foundation

The Andreas Papandreou Foundation is an independent nonprofit organization. It aims to become an intellectual and creative center for communications and conflict resolution, scientific research, policy studies, training in democratic leadership, and similar activities.

The Foundation wants to achieve these goals through action-learning programs in the areas of education, international cooperation, and policy analysis within the European and global community. It undertakes problem-solving research on public policy. The methods employed are publication of books and studies, lectures by experts, and promotion of public dialogue.

83 Peiraios & Salaminos Street
105 53 Athens
Greece
_____

Tel: +30 (1) 322 0079
Fax: +30 (1) 322 0098
info@agp.gr
www.agp.gr

Contact: Nick Papandreou

Number of staff: 10

Budget: $100,000–$500.000

Mediterranean region, Caucasus, Europe, Middle East

Hellenic Foundation for European & Foreign Policy

The Hellenic Foundation for European & Foreign Policy (ELIAMEP), officially established in 1988, is an independent training and research institute, and serves as a foreign policy think tank in the European setting. It monitors, evaluates, and promotes awareness of political, economic, and security developments in the European Union, Southeastern Europe, the Black Sea, the Middle East, the Caucasus, and the Mediterranean Region. A research team undertakes research and training projects in the field of conflict prevention and early warning. Major activities are lectures and conferences, training, fact finding, and networking.

4, Xenophontos Street
105 57 Athens
Greece
_____

Tel: +30 (1) 331 5022
eliamep@eliamep.gr
www.eliamep.gr

Contact: Fotini Bellou, Conflict Prevention Analyst

Number of staff: 8

Publications: Journal of Southeast European and Black Sea Studies, three times a year; *The Southeast European Yearbook; Kosovo under International Administration: An Unfinished Conflict,* 2001; *Kosovo and the Albanian Dimension in Southeastern Europe,* 1999; *Avoiding Another Balkan War,* 1998.

Balkans, Southeastern Europe

RESEARCH
EDUCATION

Institute of International Relations

In 1989 a group of international relations scholars established the Greek Institute of International Relations (IRR) in Athens. Its objective is to advance understanding of issues in the fields of international politics, security, business, and economics, especially in the Balkan area and Southeastern Europe. The Institute seeks to generate new ideas and perspectives in its areas of competence through policy-oriented research programs, training activities, annual seminars on conflict resolution and other topics of international relations, as well as conferences and publications. The IRR also contributes to the dialogue regarding Greek foreign policy and security issues in Europe, the Balkans, and the Middle East.

3-5 Hill Street
105 58 Athens
Greece

Tel: +30 (1) 331 2325
Fax: +30 (1) 331 3575
idis@idis.gr
www.idis.gr

Contact: Dimitri Constas, Director
Publications: Cosmos, newsletter.

Southeastern Europe

RESEARCH
EDUCATION
ACTION

Mediterranean Women's Studies Centre

The Athens-based Mediterranean Women's Study Center (KEGME) is the co-ordinating NGO of the newly established "Balkan women's network for conflict prevention and democratization." Its main activity in this field is a program that aims to promote stability and good neighborliness in Southeastern Europe. It strives to empower women through education on democratic practices and human rights and training in conflict resolution and mediation processes, in order to enable them to play a key role in these fields as well as in their private domestic life.

115 Harilaou Trikoupi Street
114 73 Athens
Greece

Tel: +30 (1) 381 3968
kegme@hol.gr
www.kegme.org.gr

Contact: Eleni Stamiris, Director
Budget: $25,000–$100,000
Publications: Women's Dialogue for the Promotion of Stability, Human Rights and Peace in South-East Europe.

Central and Eastern Europe

European Roma Rights Center

RESEARCH
ACTION
ADVOCACY

The European Roma Rights Center (ERRC) is an international law organization that monitors the human rights situation of Roma and provides legal defense in cases of human rights abuse. The focus is mainly on Central and Eastern European countries, but it also deals with Western European countries on migration issues.

P.O. Box 906/93
1386 Budapest 62
Hungary

Tel: +36 (1) 413 2200
Fax: +36 (1) 413 2201
norka@errc.org
www.errc.org

Contact: Dimitrina Petrova, Executive Director

Number of staff: 20–25

Budget: > $1,000,000

Publications: Roma Rights Quarterly, newsletter; country reports.

Hungary

Hungarian Helsinki Committee

ACTION
ADVOCACY

The Hungarian Helsinki Committee monitors the enforcement of human rights protected by the European Convention of Human Rights, reports on the state of minority rights and the freedom of religion and expression in Hungary, provides free legal assistance to victims of human rights violations, and reports on such violations. A primary focus of the Committee is civilian oversight of law enforcement agencies through monitoring closed institutions and through assisting victims of human rights violations. Since 1994, the Committee has been actively involved in the field of providing free legal aid and representation to asylum seekers, refugees, and migrants.

József krt. 34.1/5
1085 Budapest
Hungary

Tel: +36 (1) 334 4575
Fax: +36 (1) 314 0885
helsinki@mail.datanet.hu
www.helsinki.hu

Contact: Ferenc K Szeg, President

Ireland, former Yugoslavia, Middle East, Central America, Africa

Centre for Peace and Development Studies

RESEARCH
EDUCATION

The non-political Centre for Peace and Development Studies endeavors to provide research evidence concerning conflict and its resolution, both in Ireland and in other countries throughout the world, which will contribute to an understanding of how conflicts develop and how they may be most effectively resolved. It supplies objective and reliable data to conflict resolution scholars, explores development issues in countries emerging from poverty and conflict, and studies top-down and bottom-up diplomacy as aspects of good governance. The Centre also offers a Masters program in Peace and Development Studies.

Foundation Building
University of Limerick
Limerick
Ireland

Tel: +353 (61) 202 633
Fax: +353 (61) 202 952
tracey.gleeson@ul.ie
www.ul.ie/cpds

Contact: Dominic Murray, Director

Number of staff: 9

Budget: $100,000–$500,000

Publications: Protestant Perceptions of the Peace Process in Northern Ireland, 2000; *Private Pain, Public Action: Violence Against Women in War and Peace,* 2000; *A Register of Cross Border Links in Ireland,* 1998.

Republic of Ireland, Northern Ireland, United Kingdom

Glencree Centre for Reconciliation

The Glencree Centre for Reconciliation is a membership-based, autonomous association of individuals committed to fostering mutual respect, tolerance, and understanding between individuals and groups in conflict, with a view to building peace and reconciliation within the island of Ireland, between Ireland and Britain, and beyond.

The Centre aspires to build a truly pluralist Ireland and strongly believes that new ways can be found to deal with conflict in a democratic society. Glencree, located in a tranquil setting in Ireland's Wicklow Mountains, is unique in Ireland in providing program facilities expressly devoted to peacebuilding and reconciliation issues.

Glencree's program is based on a conviction that peacebuilding is a process that encompasses an understanding of the nature of conflict and an exploration of the opportunities for resolving conflict without recourse to violence.

Current programs include the following:

Schools Peace Studies Programme—special Transition Year Peace Studies programs, which include action-based learning, listening exercises, group discussions, exercises to stimulate ideas and curiosity as well as challenge preconceptions and misconceptions, simulation exercises, and evaluation exercises.

Glencree Enquiry—an exchange program bringing together cross-border partnered groups of local church communities for discussions on sectarianism.

Political Workshops—sessions bringing together party activists from different political traditions to engage in political dialogue and get to know each other (held approximately every six weeks).

Political Training—training former combatants and other community activists in negotiation skills.

Youth Programme—workshops and exchanges for young people.

Women's Programme—A program of seminars and study visits allowing women to actively engage in peacebuilding.

L.I.V.E.—a series of workshops and a conference for victims and survivors of violence in Ireland, North and South, and Britain. L.I.V.E. also facilitates victim/perpetrator dialogue.

Glencree
Co. Wicklow
Ireland

Tel: +353 (1) 282 9711
Fax: +353 (1) 276 6085
www.glencree-cfr.ie

Contact: Ian White, Director

Number of staff: 6

Budget: > $1,000,000

Publications: Glencree Newsletter; "Emprisoned within Structures?" : The Role of Believing Communities in Building Peace in Ireland, 1998; *Northern Ireland: A Place Apart,* teaching material.

Africa, Asia, Central America, Europe

GOAL

GOAL is a development, rehabilitation, and emergency relief organization that targets the poorest and most vulnerable members of society, primarily in the developing world, to ensure that they have access to the fundamental needs and rights of life, such as food, water, shelter, medical attention, and literacy. GOAL runs programs in war-torn countries and regions aimed at post-war reconstruction and reconciliation. It also supports programs for street children, providing vocational training, family tracing, counseling, and re-integration assistance, in addition to basic services such as health care and shelter.

9 Northumberland Avenue
P.O. Box 19
Dun Laoghaire
Co. Dublin
Ireland

Tel: +353 (1) 280 9779
Fax: +353 (1) 280 9215
info@goal.ie
www.goal.ie

Contact: Neva Khan, Donor Liaison Officer
Number of staff: 25
Budget: > $1,000,000

Republic of Ireland, Northern Ireland

ACTION
ADVOCACY

Irish Peace and Reconciliation Platform

The Irish Peace and Reconciliation Platform is an ad-hoc grouping of nongovernmental organizations involved in managing, resolving, and transforming conflicts within the island of Ireland and between Ireland and Britain. The Platform provides opportunities for mutual support and will facilitate communication and co-operation between member bodies so as to enhance the capacities and effectiveness of the emerging peace and reconciliation group sector. The Platform aims to heighten public awareness and, where appropriate, inform governments of issues of vital concern. There are currently sixteen members in the Platform.

c/o Glencree Centre for Reconciliation
Co. Wicklow
Ireland

Tel: +353 (1) 282 9711
Fax: +353 (1) 276 6085
info@glencree-cfr.ie

Contact: Ian White, Chairman, Irish Peace and Reconciliation Platform
Publications: Peace-maker, 2000; *Peace Building in the Republic of Ireland,* 2000.

Republic of Ireland, Northern Ireland

Irish Peace Institute— Outreach Programme

EDUCATION
ACTION

The Irish Peace Institute, affiliated with the University of Limerick, explores the concept of peace and peaceful change at international, national, and regional levels, examining and working in particular to build peace, justice, and reconciliation on the island of Ireland. The Outreach Programme complements academic work at the Institute by means of North/South cooperation projects involving cultural, social, and community organizations and schools from both parts of the island. Activities include conferences, seminars, workshops, public lectures, debates, and concerts.

University of Limerick
Plassey
Limerick
Ireland

Tel: +353 (61) 202 768
Fax: +353 (61) 202 572
dorothy.cantrell@ul.ie
www.ul.ie/ipi

Contact: Dorothy Cantrell, Director Outreach Programme
Number of staff: 2
Budget: $100,000–$500,000

Northern Ireland, Global

Irish School of Ecumenics

EDUCATION

The Irish School of Ecumenics is an international academic institute within Trinity College, Dublin. It exists to promote through research, teaching, and outreach activities; the unity of Christians; dialogue between religions; and work for peace and justice in Ireland and abroad. Its recently completed research project, "Moving Beyond Sectarianism," examined the causes, expressions, and consequences of sectarianism in Ireland and provided insights and models for moving beyond it. The School offers a course on conflict resolution and nonviolence in its International Peace Studies program and in its Reconciliation Studies program and addresses conflict resolution through its Learning Together: Education for Reconciliation program in Northern Ireland.

Trinity College Dublin
Bea House, Milltown Park
Dublin 6
Ireland

Tel: +353 (1) 260 1144
Fax: +353 (1) 260 1158
isedir@tcd.ie
www.tcd.ie/ise

Contact: Cecelia Clegg, Coordinator Moving Beyond Sectarianism project
Number of staff: 8
Budget: $25,000–$100,000

Republic of Ireland, Northern Ireland

Meath Peace Group

The Meath Peace Group was established in 1993 after a peace rally in Slane, Co. Meath. It is a totally voluntary group, not attached to any political party or religious denomination. It aims to promote peace and the fostering of understanding, mutual respect, trust, cooperation, and friendship through dialogue between ordinary people in the North and South of Ireland. Study groups, workshops, and adult education are some of the tools used in order to reach the goals of the organization.

Parsonstown, Batterstown
Co. Meath
Ireland

Tel: +353 (1) 825 9438
Fax: +353 (1) 825 9261

Contact: Julitta Clancy, Contact person
Batterstown
Publications: Newsletter.

Africa, Latin America, Asia

ACTION

Trócaire

Trócaire was founded by the Bishops in Ireland in 1973 to respond to the needs and problems of the people of developing countries. The Catholic agency works in conflict-torn areas like the Great Lakes, Burundi, and Liberia: during the conflict, through relief and refugee activities, and after, by working on rehabilitation and development. Although it works mainly on development co-operation, it has extended its program involvement in conflict prevention and resolution through its own work and the work implemented by its partners.

169 Booterstown Avenue
Blackrock
Co. Dublin
Ireland

Tel: +353 (1) 288 5385
Fax: +353 (1) 283 3577
maryh@trocaire.ie
www.trocaire.org

Contact: Mary Healy, Emergencies Coordinator
Budget: $500,000–$1,000,000

Kosovo

Campagna per la Nonviolenza e Riconcialiazione in Kossovo

Campagna per la Nonviolenza e Riconcialiazione in Kossovo (Campagna Kossovo) is working to achieve a just and peaceful solution to the conflict in Kosovo through nonviolent action, and to support a multi-ethnic Kosovo as an alternative to its division into ethnic enclaves. Campagna Kossovo is a consortium of Italian NGOs and has worked in collaboration with the OSCE Democratisation Department on a series of workshops to promote inter-ethnic dialogue and nonviolent conflict resolution, as well as networking and communication among the various Kosovo communities.

Casa per la Pace c.a. 8
74023 Grottaglie (Taranto)
Italy

Contact: Etta Ragusa, Coordinator
Budget: $25,000–$100,000

Tel /fax: +39 (99) 566 2252
a.alba@areacom.it
www.peacelink.it/peacelink/kossovo/kosstart.htlm

Kosovo

Centro Studi Sereno Regis

Centro Studi Sereno Regis promotes nonviolent culture at all social levels through training activities in nonviolent conflict resolution, and advocacy of nonviolent conflict transformation, nonviolent popular defense, and a nonviolent economy. In recent times, the organization has focused in particular on the conflict in Kosovo, with a two-year program to train conflict resolution trainers, with the aim of achieving reconciliation among Kosovo's three main ethnic groups. The organization is also engaged in citizen diplomacy and mediation activities.

Via Garibaldi 13
10122 Torino
Italy

Contact: Nanni Salio, Director
Number of staff: 6
Budget: < $25,000

Tel: +39 (11) 532 0824
Fax: +39 (11) 515 8000
regis@arpnet.it
www.arpnet.it/regis

Global

Community of Sant'Egidio

ACTION

The Community of Sant'Egidio is a worldwide assembly of Christian Communities involved in conflict resolution and unofficial diplomacy. The Community was founded in Italy, and its 40,000 members are gathered in small groups, based in sixty countries. Though having a lay membership, the religious character of Sant'Egidio is an important part of its negotiation activities. The community has played a role in Mozambique, Algeria, Guatemala, and Kosovo. It promotes the international People of Peace movement whose 10,000 members are themselves partly fugitives or displaced people, and it tries to bring Europeans and immigrants together.

Piazza S.Egidio 3/a
00153 Roma
Italy

Tel: +39 (6) 585 661
Fax: +39 (6) 580 0197
info@santegidio.org
www.santegidio.org

Contact: Alessandro Zuccari, President
Number of staff: Mostly volunteers
Publications: Sant'Egidio, L'Évangile au-delà des frontières, Entretiens avec Dominique Chivot, 2001; *Sant'Egidio Rome and the World,* Andrea Riccardi in conversations with J.D. Durand and R. Ladous, 1999; *Vom Krieg zum Frieden, Mosambik: Geschichte einer ungewöhnlichen Vermittlung,* 1997.

Eastern Europe, Asia, Africa, Central America

COSPE

EDUCATION
ACTION

COSPE (Cooperazione per lo Sviluppo dei Paesi) is primarily engaged in development assistance, but about one third of its budget supports conflict prevention and resolution. COSPE has been engaged in programs addressing post-conflict rehabilitation of civil society in Rwanda, Angola, and Niger; has provided institutional support and training to organizations working on peace and human rights in Somalia, Rwanda, and Guatemala; and provided training to women and community-based organizations in Algeria, Albania, and the Palestinian territories. COSPE also works as an advocate in support of the rights of marginalized and oppressed peoples.

Via Slataper 10
50134 Florence
Italy

Tel: +39 (55) 473 556
Fax: +39 (55) 472 806
mc8008@mclink.it
www.cospe.it

Contact: Graziano Tonellotto, Secretary General
Budget: > $1,000,000

Europe

Ethnobarometer

Ethnobarometer is a joint project between the Italian Social Science Council (CSS), a non-profit research association based in Rome that does interdisciplinary and policy-oriented research, and the Centre for European Migration and Ethnic Studies (CEMES), which is based in the UK. They conduct and promote research and publish reports on ethnic conflict, providing objective and research-generated information to organizations that are engaged in conflict prevention/resolution. For the work, a network of European organization and institutions is used.

c/o CSS
Via Brescia 16
00198 Rome
Italy

Tel: +39 (06) 8540 564
Fax: +39 (06) 8417 110
cssroma@rmnet.it
www.ethnobarometer.org

Contact: Alessandro Silj, Secretary-General of CSS

Publications: Minority Politics in Southeast Europe, 2001; *Crisis in Kosovo: Reactions in Albania and in Macedonia at the Local Level.*

Eastern Europe, Latin America, Middle East

Interdenominational Peace Centre

The Interdenominational Peace Centre (Centro Interconfessionale per la Pace—Cipax) works to promote cooperation, information, and action to support the commitment of believers to justice and peace. Its major activity is education on peace and nonviolence. Founded in 1982, the Centre organizes conferences and develops videotapes and films designed to be shown in local communities. It facilitates dialogue among Muslim, Jewish, and Christian communities.

Via Ostiense 152
00154 Rome
Italy

Tel: +39 (6) 5728 7347
Fax: +39 (6) 5729 0945
cipax@romacivica.net
www.romacivica.net

Contact: Gianni Novelli, Executive Director
Number of staff: 4 at HQ, 10 in the field
Budget: $25,000–$100,000
Publications: Newsletter.

Europe

International School on Disarmament and Research on Conflicts

RESEARCH
EDUCATION

The International School on Disarmament and Research on Conflicts (ISO-DARCO) provides a forum for the discussion of international conflict issues and endeavors to bring together individuals with varying experiences and approaches on security issues for discussions focused on commissioned papers. ISODARCO invites participants from various professions and backgrounds, including traditional adversaries, and especially, young people, to take part in its discussions. So far, these discussions have addressed the main issues related to the nuclear arms race and nuclear weapons proliferation and other issues such as terrorism, energy, the environment, ethnic conflict, and Middle East security. ISODARCO has frequently published books based on the discussions it has organized.

c/o Dipartimento di Fisica
University of Rome "Tor Vergata"
Via della Ricerca Scientifica, 1
00133 Rome
Italy

Tel: +39 (6) 7259 4560
Fax: +39 (6) 204 0309
isodarco@roma2.infn.it
www.roma2.infn.it/isodarco

Contact: Carlo Schaerf
Number of staff: 1
Budget: $25,000–$100,000
Publications: Technology Transfer, 2000; *The Search for Stability in Russia and the Former Soviet Bloc,* 1997; *The Weapons Legacy of the Cold War,* 1997.

Global

International Training Programme for Conflict Management at the Scuola Superiore Sant'Anna

RESEARCH
EDUCATION

The International Training Programme for Conflict Management (ITPCM), a post-graduate program at the Scuola Superiore Sant'Anna, provides training for effective conflict management activities in the field, including civilian peacekeeping, humanitarian and refugee assistance, peace and democracy building, election monitoring and assistance, human rights monitoring, capacity building, and good governance. Graduates have served in Rwanda, Bosnia and Herzegovina, and Kosovo as human rights officers and election supervisors, and in Angola, Cambodia, Chechnya, Guatemala, and Nigeria providing humanitarian assistance and working on post-conflict reconstruction. ITPCM is also involved in research, consulting, and publishing activities.

Via Carducci 40
56127 Pisa
Italy

Tel: +39 (50) 883 312
Fax: +39 (50) 883 506
itp@sssup.it
www.itp.sssup.it

Contact: Nicola Naddi, Trainer Officer
Number of staff: 6
Budget: $25,000–$100,000
Publications: German and Italian Participation in Peace-keeping: From Dual Approaches to Co-operation, proceedings of the workshop "Towards a Future for Peace-keeping: Perspectives for a New Italian/German Co-operation," 1996.

Global

International University of People's Institutions for Peace

The International University of People's Institutions for Peace (IUPIP) offers training in people's diplomacy and nonviolence to enhance skills in nonviolent conflict resolution, to support human rights, and to promote nonviolence and a culture of peace. Programs have included focus on conflict transformation, human rights, and globalization for Israeli and Palestinian law students; and a three-week residential course on topics such as people's diplomacy and nonviolence for representatives of NGOs and grassroots organizations. IUPIP also supports research activities, publishes materials on conflict resolution issues, and maintains a library.

Palazzo Adami
Piazza San Marco 7
38068 Rovereto (TN)
Italy

Tel: +39 (464) 424 288
fax: +39 (464) 424 299
iupip@unimondo.org
www.unimondo.org/iupip

Contact: Giuliano Pontara, Director

Number of staff: 6

Budget: $25,000–$100,000

Publications: IUPIP Newsletter; "Alternatives," series of training and research materials; *Booklets for Peace.*

Balkans, Mediterranean region, Middle East, Central America

Italian Platform for Conflict Prevention and Transformation

The Italian Platform for Conflict Prevention and Transformation (Associazione per la Pace) was established in 1988 and works to address the causes of wars and to establish a more just and peaceful world. In pursuit of human rights, democratic development, and capacity building, Associazione per la Pace has most recently been engaged in "Jerusalem 2000," a program that resulted in 1000 Italian citizens traveling to Palestine and Israel in September 2000 to support grass roots efforts to bring peace to Israel and Palestine. The organization is also engaged in research on peace and conflict management issues.

Via Salaria 89
00177 Rome
Italy

Tel: +39 (6) 884 1958
Fax: +39 (6) 884 1749
info@assopace.org
www.assopace.org

Contact: Davide Berruti, Director
Number of staff: 5

Balkans, Southern Africa, Central America

EDUCATION
ACTION

Movimondo

Movimondo aims to contribute to the development of equitable relationships between North and South by cooperation and international solidarity, aspiring to meet basic human needs, and promoting democracy, human dignity, and social justice at the national, regional, and international level. Its priority areas of action include development co-operation, peacebuilding, emergency and humanitarian aid, refugees and displaced persons, and education.

Piazza Albania 10
00153 Rome
Italy

Tel: +39 (6) 5730 0330
Fax: +39 (6) 574 4869
info@movimondo.org
www.movimondo.org

Contact: Paolo Salvia, Head of Human Rights Unit
Number of staff: 2

Publications: After the War: Lectures on Human Rights, Democracy and Development in the Post-conflict Scenario, in Italian, 2000; *The Challenge of the Complex Crises in the International Co-operation: The Role of the NGOs and the Partnership between Institutions and Civil Society,* 2000.

Balkans

RESEARCH
ACTION

Observatory on the Balkans

Observatory on the Balkans (Osservatorio sui Balcani) works to support civilian society, NGOs, and institutions involved in cooperation projects and people's diplomacy activities in the Balkans region. It aspires to encourage reflection on, and contribute to the rebuilding of skills and potential in the region. The organization is primarily engaged in information gathering, monitoring as well as analysis, in order to provide the means for the interpretation of the situation in the Balkans and tools for intervention. Observatory on the Balkans is a project of the Peace Bell Foundation.

Palazzo Adami
Piazza San Marco 7
38068 Rovereto
Italy

Tel: +39 (464) 424 230
Fax: +39 (464) 424 299
segreteria@osservatoriobalcani.org
www.osservatoriobalcani.org

Contact: Mauro Cereghini, Director
Number of staff: 7
Budget: $100,000–$500,000

Italy

Research Center on Civilian Defense

RESEARCH
EDUCATION
ACTION

The Research Center on Civilian Defense (Centro Studi Difesa Civile) under-takes research on civilian defense and improving the capacity of society to resolve conflict nonviolently, and explores the feasibility of reducing the de-structive component of defense strategies. Research activities include studies for the Italian Ministry of Defense on the use of unarmed civilian peacekeep-ers, and for the Ministry of Foreign Affairs on confidence building at a com-munity level in international crisis situations. The Center also offers training programs on nonviolent conflict resolution and mediation services

Via del Balcone 13
06122 Perugia
Italy
_____
Tel: +39 (338) 170 5867
Fax: +39 (75) 573 2318
pacedifesa@libero.it

Contact: Francesco Tullio, President
Number of staff: 10
Budget: < $25,000

Global

Servas International

ACTION

Servas International is an association that works toward understanding and world peace and justice through person-to person contact. It operates through a network of some 13,000 Servas hosts around the world who are prepared to open their doors to travelers and offer them a view of their day-to-day life and culture. Besides this service, Servas also organizes youth camps and voluntary work as a means to foster greater understanding.

Peace Secretary
Via Sales, 3/11
16166 Genova
Italy
_____
Tel/fax: +39 (10) 372 4276
servas-int@geocities.com
www.servas.org

Contact: Bertrand Bailleul
Budget: < $25,000
Publication: Servas International Newsletter.

Global

International
Peace Research Association

RESEARCH
EDUCATION

The International Peace Research Association (IPRA) was founded in 1964 as the concrete result of a conference organized by the Quakers. It developed into an association with the principal aim of increasing the quantity of research focused on world peace and ensuring its scientific quality. Since its establishment in 1964 IPRA has held seventeen biennial conferences. IPRA promotes co-operation and national and international studies and teaching related to the pursuit of world peace. Its website offers a list of links to different European Peace Research Institutes.

Kodama Peace Research Office
Dept. of Humanities
Mie University
1515 Kamihama, Tsu
Mie 514-8507
Japan

Contact: Katsuya Kodama,
Secretary General

Publications: IPRA Newsletter.

Tel/fax: +81 (59) 231 9156
peace@human.mie-u.ac.jp
www.human.mie-u.ac.jp/~peace/secretariat.htm

Kazakhstan, Central Asia, CIS countries

RESEARCH
EDUCATION
ADVOCACY

Center for Conflict Management

The Center for Conflict Management (CCM) is a non-governmental organization that aims to contribute to the prevention and resolution of violent conflicts
in Kazakhstan and Central Asia, the development of civil society, and transformation of public consciousness.

The CCM operates within five spheres of work: educational programs; research and monitoring; promotion of non-violent conflict resolution, peace, tolerance, and institutional development of NGOs and development of co-operation
among NGOs working for conflict management and civic education; and practical activities in conflict management and prevention.

Since 1998 the CCM has organized annual Summer Schools on Conflict
Management for practitioners from Central Asia and the Caucasus, in partnership with the UK-based NGO Responding to Conflict. In 2001 the CCM conducted a Summer University on Conflict Studies for the university staff from
Central Asia and the Caucasus with the aim of introducing conflict studies at
university level. CCM staff has facilitated training on conflict resolution and
civic education in different countries of Central Asia.

The CCM is also involved in tolerance education and in addressing the issues of prejudice against ethnic minorities and refugees in Kazakhstan, which
includes educational seminars for different target groups, publications, and
awareness raising through the media.

In 1999 the CCM initiated the Central Asian Conflict Management Network, which unites around twenty active NGOs in the region. The network has
been established in the framework of the CIS NGO Working Group on Conflict Management in which the CCM has served as a lead agency, together
with International Alert (UK). The Working Group is supported by UNHCR.

The CCM is also active in the sphere of civic education. It is currently cooperating with the Ministry of Education in an effort to introduce civic education into the school curriculum.

The CCM is a co-founder of the Association of Conflict Researchers
(Russia). It has produced a database on conflict management organizations in
the CIS, which is available online.

Appt. 23, 57-V Timiryazev Street
Almaty 480090
Kazakhstan

Tel/fax: +7 (3272) 779 384
ccm@online.ru
www.ccm.freenet.kz

Contact: Elena Sadovskaya, President

Number of staff: 12

Budget: $100,000–$500,000

Publications: First Steps (Amnesty
International manual on Human Rights
translated from English into Kazakh), 2001;
Manual on Civic Education for Teachers,
2000; *Methods of Conflict Management and
Prevention Seminar Report,* 1998;
*Kazakhstan. Social Conflicts: Expertise,
Prognoses and Resolution Techniques,*
1997. Working with Conflict: Skills and
Strategies for Action (Responding to
Conflict book translated into Russian) 2001.

Kazakhstan

Center for Social Research

RESEARCH
EDUCATION

The Center for Social Research (CSR) is a local NGO that aims to contribute to the development of democracy in Kazakhstan through the study and analysis of social processes, development of practical recommendations, conducting seminars and training, and conveying the transformation of public awareness through mass media. The CSR is implementing a program on the eradication of violence through monitoring, roundtables, newspaper publication, dissemination of booklets, and radio programs at the grassroots level. The CSR cooperates with a number of local NGOs.

Office 442, 18 Sovetskoi Konstitutsii Street,
Karaganda 470074
Kazakhstan

Tel: +7 (3212) 754 607/734 875
maltabar@hotmail.com

Contact: Valentina Ukrainskaya,
Director
Number of staff: 10
Budget: < $25,000

Kazakhstan

Center for the Support of Democracy

RESEARCH
EDUCATION
ADVOCACY

Center for the Support of Democracy (CSD) is an NGO and a network whose mission is to provide information, consultancy, and research with the aim of strengthening constitutional democracy in Kazakhstan. The CSD is a member of the network of "democracy support centers" in Kazakhstan, financed by the National Democratic Institute (USA). In 2000 the CSD conducted research on ethnic conflicts and national identity in Kazakhstan. The CSD is planning to work on refugee issues by providing advice to refugee organizations.

Appt. 13, 2 Alalykina Street
Karaganda 470061
Kazakhstan

Tel: +7 (3212) 520 683
Fax: +7 (3212) 523 012/411 477
cad@nursat.kz

Contact: Marina Sabitova, Director
Number of staff: 5
Budget: < $25,000
*Publications: Mass Political
Consciousness,* 2000.

Kazakhstan

Dialogue

RESEARCH
EDUCATION
ADVOCACY

Dialogue is an Information and Communication Service that was established in August 1996 with the aim of contributing to the development of a multi-cultural society in Kazakhstan through research, education, and peacemaking activities. Dialogue has conducted a number of monitoring and expert assessments, including evaluation of inter-ethnic relations for the Assembly of Peoples of Kazakhstan and OSCE. Currently it is focused on media and community campaigns, such as development of the media dialogue between the state authorities and society on the issues of ethno-cultural needs of diasporas. Dialogue is engaged in the development of democratic mechanisms of ethno-cultural self-assertion of the Uzbek Diaspora in South Kazakhstan.

Office 10, 12-G Patrice Lumumba Street
Shymkent 486011
Kazakhstan
_____

Tel: +7 (3252) 537 028
savdial-shm@nursat.kz; savigsa@inbox.ru

Contact: Igor Savin, Director
Number of staff: < $25,000
Publications: Dialogue, bi-monthly bulletin, available on www.uko. nm.ru; *Multiculturalism and Prevention of Ethnic Conflict in Post-Soviet Kazakhstan, in Humanitarian Dimension: Culture, Politics, Economics,* a collection of "Materials of International Scientific-Theoretical Conference" (25–26 May 2001), in Russian 2001.

Kazakhstan

ZHARiA

RESEARCH
EDUCATION
ADVOCACY

ZHARiA (Women's Association of Development and Adaptation) works for the harmonization and adaptation of women to the undergoing reforms in the society and the defense of women's rights. ZHARiA runs the "Conflict: pro et contra" program, which aims at preventing inter-ethnic conflicts through education in the methods of conflict analysis and resolution. The project operates in Northern and Central parts of Kazakhstan. In the framework of the project, six seminars have been organized in 2000–2001. ZHARiA works in partnership with the Ministry of Culture, Information and Public Accord, as well as ethno-cultural centers, schools, and universities of Northern and Central Kazakhstan.

Appt. 38, 13 mikrorayon 2
Astana 473000
Kazakhstan
_____

Tel/fax: +7 (3172) 366 634
zharia@nursat.kz

Contact: Gulzi Nabieva, Director
Number of staff: 8
Budget: < $25,000

Kyrgyzstan

Adult Training Center, Osh affiliation

EDUCATION
ACTION

The Adult Training Center (ATC) is an NGO with a mission to contribute to the process of democratization in Kyrgyzstan through adult education, including civic education, professional education, and raising awareness on legal issues and interpersonal relations. The ATC is also involved in research in the sphere of adult education. The ATC organizes practical training on conflict prevention and tolerance education for the grassroots activists in Osh, Jalal-Abad, and Batken Provinces of Kyrgyzstan. In 1997–1998 the ATC tested an approach to early prognosis of conflicts, identification of the causes of inter-ethnic conflicts, and methods for their prevention.

205 Lenin Street, room 304
Osh 714000
Kyrgyzstan

Tel: +996 (3222) 55 780/55 621
Fax: +996 (3222) 55 621
atc-osh@mail.kg
www.atc.kg

Contact: Kambarbek Adyshev, Training Manager

Number of staff: 6

Budget: < $25,000

Publications: ATC Newsletter.

Central Asia

Bishkek Migration Management Center

RESEARCH
EDUCATION
ADVOCACY

The Bishkek Migration Management Center (BMMC) is an NGO and a network. The aim of the Center is to create the conditions and potential for developing an effective migration management system in Central Asian states. It re-registered and changed its name to the Regional Center on Migration and Refugee Issues.

The BMMC works for the protection of refugees in Central Asia through the improvement of legislation and procedures for granting refugee status. The program includes organizing seminars and drafting laws and regulations. The Center is involved in sub-regional consultations on the problems of Afghan refugees in Central Asia and in setting up a regional information exchange on migration and refugee issues through regular conferences.

The BMMC is part of the network of the International Organisation for Migration's (IOM) Centre of Technical Co-operation and the International Labour Organization's (ILO) Labor Migration Division. It also closely co-operates with the OSCE Office for Democratic Institutions and Human Rights.

139 Toktogula Street
Bishkek 720001
Kyrgyzstan

Tel: +996 (312) 663 290/663 370
Fax: +996 (312) 664 714
rcmr@elcat.kg
actp.www.rcmr.elcat.kg

Contact: Talaybek Kydyrov, Director

Number of staff: 10

Budget: $100,000–$500,000

Publications: Information bulletin; *Refugees in the Kyrgyz Republic; Problems of Russian Speaking Population in the Kyrgyz Republic; Research on Internal Registration of Citizens in the Kyrgyz Republic.*

Kyrgyzstan, Ferghana Valley

Center for Social Research of the National Academy of Sciences of the Kyrgyz Republic

RESEARCH
EDUCATION

The Center for Social Research (CSR) is an academic organization that is involved in research and educational activities. The CSR provides information for the EAWARN and FAST conflict monitoring projects, run correspondingly by the Institute of Ethnology and Anthropology of the Russian Academy of Sciences and Swiss Peace Foundation. The Center staff also publishes regularly in analytical bulletins.

265-A Chui Avenue
Bishkek 720071
Kyrgyzstan

Tel: +996 (312) 243 735
Fax: +996 (312) 243 647
nurbekcsr@freenet.kg

Contact: Nurbek Omuraliev, Director
Number of staff: 4
Budget: < $25,000

Kyrgyzstan, Tajikistan, Uzbekistan

Foundation for Tolerance International

EDUCATION
ACTION
ADVOCACY

The Foundation for Tolerance International (FTI) is a non-profit, non-partisan, non-governmental organization with a mission to prevent inter-ethnic conflicts. To achieve this, it aims to co-ordinate community-based activities and civil forums, which promote peace, tolerance, and conflict resolution strategies, and to support locally initiated solutions to regional inter-ethnic conflict. The Foundation has grown up over the last two years. Beginning as the Training Project in 1998, it now has several directions of work, which include a variety of projects in the field of conflict prevention, such as "Mass Media for Conflict Prevention Program," "Conflict Prevention through Support of Civil Initiative Program," and "Ambassadors of Goodwill in the Ferghana Valley."

Among those, FTI has worked on the resolution of resource related conflicts in the Batken oblast (province) of Kyrgyzstan. The project involved consensus building activities, mediation, and negotiation for local communities. In many of its project, the FTI works in partnership with Tajik NGO Ittifok Centre for Youth Initiatives. Other partners have included a range of local NGOs in Batken oblast: Osh State University (Kyrgyzstan), Teachers Association (Kyrgyzstan), Swiss Co-ordination Office, Delaware University (USA), and UNOPS.

Appt. 8, 116 Orozbekova Street
Bishkek 720040
Kyrgyzstan

Tel: +996 (312) 222 233/223 390/661 615
Fax: +996 (312) 222 233
fti@infotel.kg

Contact: Raya Kadyrova, Director
Number of staff: 32
Budget: $100,000–$500,000
*Publications: Salam Asia
Newsletter;* training materials.

Ferghana Valley, Central Asia

Institute for Regional Studies

RESEARCH
EDUCATION
ADVOCACY

The Institute for Regional Studies (IFRS, previously Kyrgyz Peace Research Center) is an NGO founded in November 1994. In order to provide a mechanism for effective changes in the society, a training program involving participants from the Central Asian countries is organized on the issues of conflict prevention and resolution. The Institute's activities are focused on facilitating a sense of citizenship among the people of the region, encourage participation in public life, and providing broad access to relevant information on democracy. The IFRS seeks to maintain inter-ethnic and religious peace by making recommendations to governmental bodies, international organizations, and local NGOs.

appt.105, 77 Toktogul Street
P.O. Box 1880
Bishkek 720021
Kyrgyzstan

Tel: +996 (312) 281 771
Fax: +996 (312) 280 635
ifrs@elcat.kg

Contact: Anara Tabyshalieva, Director

Number of staff: $25,000–$100,000

Publications: Central Asia: New Space for Cooperation, 2000; Man in the State, manual for schoolchildren, 2000; *Kyrgyzstan: Some Aspects of the Social Situation,* 2000; *The Challenge of Regional Cooperation in Central Asia, Preventing Ethnic Conflict in the Ferghana Valley,* together with the United States Institute of Peace, 1999; *Person and Law,* manual for schoolchildren, 1999.

Kyrgyzstan

Interbilim International Centre

RESEARCH
EDUCATION
ADVOCACY

The Interbilim International Centre is an NGO with a mission to strengthen non-governmental organizations and grassroots and community-based organizations that work with vulnerable and disadvantaged groups. Interbilim is engaged with data collection and research, is a provider of training for NGOs in Kyrgyzstan, and is active in lobbying. Although it has no special conflict-related program, Interbilim nevertheless responds to the emerging conflicts in the Kyrgyzstan by sending fact-finding missions to conflict areas, providing alternative information to the media and lobbying the government.

13/2 Razzakov Street
Bishkek 720040
Kyrgyzstan

Tel: +996 (312) 660 425/660 516
Fax: +996 (312) 664 434
ccpub@infotel.kg

Contact: Asiya Sasykbaeva,
Director

Number of staff: 14

Publications: Newsletter.

Central Asia

International Crisis Group, Central Asia Project

RESEARCH
ADVOCACY

The Central Asia Project was initiated by the International Crisis Group (ICG) in October 2000. The ICG strives to provide high quality advice and advocacy to help governments, international organizations, and the world community at large in preventing or containing deadly conflict. The Central Asia Project produces reports based on thorough field research on various aspects of the situation in Central Asia. The reports are available online. Please see also separate entry for ICG headquarters.

7 Michurin Street
Osh 714000
Kyrgyzstan

Tel:+996 (3222) 20 470/20 370/55 055
Fax: +996 (3222) 21 218
icgosh@crisisweb.org;
schoeber@fas.harvard.edu
www.crisisweb.org

Contact: John Schoeberlein, Director
ICG–Central Asia Project
Number of staff: 6

Publications: Central Asia: *Fault Lines in the New Security Map; Incubators of Conflict: Central Asia's Localised Poverty and Social Unrest; Central Asia: Islamist Mobilization and Regional Stability,* 2001; *Central Asia: Crisis Conditions in Three States,* 2000; *Recent Violence in Central Asia: Causes and Consequences,* 2000.

Kyrgyzstan

Osh Media Resource Center

ADVOCACY

The Osh Media Resource Center (OMRC) is a non-profit media development organization that aims to develop the independent media of southern Kyrgyzstan. The OMRC is a member of the Central Asian Media Support Project, which unites professional media associations from Uzbekistan, Tajikistan, and Kyrgyzstan. Through its primary mandate of working with journalists, the OMRC also addresses the issues of conflict. In May 2000 it organized a conference on "The Role of Mass Media in Post-Soviet Conflict Areas."

271 Kurmanjan Datka Street
Osh 714000
Kyrgyzstan

Tel: +996 (3222) 20 858
Fax: +996 (3222) 55 259
omrc2000@netmail.kg
www.camsp.osh.kg

Contact: Alisher Khamidov, Director

Central Asia

Spravedlivost Regional Human Rights Organisation

RESEARCH
ACTION

The mission of the Spravedlivost Regional Human Rights Organisation is to form an open multi-ethnic and multi-confessional society, and to establish the rule of law. Besides human rights defense work, Spravedlivost (Justice) focuses on ethnic and confessional monitoring, and trust-building measures among local communities in the Kyrgyz-Uzbek border regions. It analyzes the conditions of the ethno-cultural groups, provides regular reports based upon the ethno-confessional monitoring, and drafts suggestions on early warning for the authorities. The organization maintains a database on ethnic and cultural groups of the region, on non-customary confessions, and on the dynamics of dissemination of the radical Islam ideas.

27 Erkin-Too Street
Jalal-Abad 715612
Kyrgyzstan

Tel/fax: +996 (3722) 56 038
valery@elcat2.bishkek.su; opzo@mail.ru
www.spravedlivost.bishkek.su

Contact: Valery Uleev, Director and CANet Coordinator
Number of staff: 21
Budget: < $25,000
Publications: Rights for All, newsletter.

Kyrgyzstan

Youth Human Rights Group

RESEARCH
EDUCATION
ADVOCACY

The mission of the Youth Human Rights Group (YHRG) is to promote human rights and the rights of the children among Tajik and Afghan refugees in Kyrgyzstan. Its research into the situation, conducted in partnership with UNHCR and Save the Children (UK), provided a basis for future educational and practical work. The YHRG educational program for teachers includes a component of tolerance education and respect for diversity. The YHRG is also active in awareness-raising initiatives through dissemination of printed materials and production of radio programs, lobbying, and the provision of consultations on the existing legislation.

Appt. 8, 41-B Moskovskaya Street
Bishkek 720000
Kyrgyzstan

Tel: +996 (312) 681 370
Fax: +996 (312) 681 091
www.yhrg.elcat.kg

Contact: Maria Lisitsyna, Director
Number of staff: 8
Budget: < $25,000
Publications: Chaika (Seagull), quarterly bulletin; *The Covenant of the Rights of the Child in Drawings,* 2000; *Manuals on Teaching the Rights of the Child,* 1999; *Refugee Children in Kyrgyzstan,* 1998.

Central and Eastern Europe

Baltic Insight

Baltic Insight is devoted to research and practical work in the fields of human rights, conflict management, ethnic policies, and the integration of Latvia's society. Baltic Insight also promotes the use of modern information technologies for human rights and minority NGO activities to facilitate the establishment of civil society in Latvia. Its main project is the Minority Electronic Resources project (MINELRES), which provides an electronic forum for information and expert opinion exchange on issues pertaining to minorities and human rights in Central and Eastern Europe, as well as an online database devoted to various aspects of minority issues, situations, and rights in the region.

Brivibas 111-39
1001 Riga
Latvia

Tel/fax: +371 737 1770
minelres@mailbox.riga.lv
www.riga.lv/minelres

Contact: Boris Koltchanov, Director
Number of staff: 5
Budget: $25,000–$100,000

Latvia

Centre for
Non-Governmental Organisations

The mission of the Centre for Non-Governmental Organisations is to promote the development of a democratic and integrated civil society in Latvia. It directs special attention to what it calls "The Third Sector"—those institutions within society that operate neither for profit nor as part of the state. Its goal is to provide support to new NGOs and to encourage experienced and well-established NGOs to participate in building civil society. Its programs include information services, education, NGO support, and regional NGO development.

Lacplesa Str. 52/54–22
1011 Riga
Latvia

Tel: +371 728 3282
Fax: +371 728 9227
info@ngo.org.lv
www.ngo.org.lv

Contact: Kaija Gertnere, Director

Latvia

Latvian Centre for
Human Rights and Ethnic Studies

RESEARCH
EDUCATION
ADVOCACY

The Latvian Center for Human Rights and Ethnic Studies (LCHRES) is involved in human rights education, research on human rights and ethnic relations, advocacy, the provision of legal assistance to victims of human rights violations, and the promotion of dialogue. LCHRES places a special focus on minority rights and inter-ethnic relations, women's rights and gender issues, and human rights in closed institutions such as prisons, mental hospitals, and jails. One of its programs, "Coping with Extremism in a Democracy," monitors extremist groups and responses to them in society.

Alberta Street 13, 6th floor
1010 Riga
Latvia

Tel: +371 703 9290
Fax: +371 703 9291
office@humanrights.org.lv

Contact: Nils Muiznieks, Director

Number of staff: 10

Budget: $25,000–$100,000

Baltic states

Latvian Institute of International Affairs

RESEARCH
EDUCATION

The Latvian Institute of International Affairs was established in 1992 as a nonprofit foundation. The Institute organizes lectures, seminars, public debates, conferences, and exchange programs. It also conducts research on such topics as Baltic security within the context of Baltic Sea regional cooperation, EU and NATO enlargement, relations with Russia, and developments in Latvian society. The Institute maintains a specialized library and publishes extensively. Many of its publications are available to the public from its website.

Elizabetes iela 57
1050 Riga
Latvia

Tel:+371 728 6302
Fax: +371 782 8089
liialai@delfi.lv
www.lai.lv

Contact: Atis Lejins, Director

Number of staff: 8

Budget: $25,000–$100,000

Publications: Latvia's Foreign Policy within the UN Framework, 1999; *Baltic Security Prospects at the Turn of the 21st Century,* 1999.

Lithuania

Non-Governmental Organizations
Information and Support Centre

RESEARCH
EDUCATION
ACTION
ADVOCACY

The Non-Governmental Organizations Information and Support Centre's (NISC) mission is to strengthen Lithuanian NGOs by providing information, consultations, training, and technical assistance. It particularly promotes the role the NGO sector can play in the civil society. NISC is also involved in the PHARE and TACIS Democracy Programmes of the European Union.

A.Jaksto str. 9-301
2001 Vilnius
Lithuania

Contact: Vaidotas Ilgius, Director

Tel: +370 (2) 226 045
Fax: +370 (2) 618 782
nisc@pub.osf.lt

Global

Cercle de Coopération des ONG
de Développement de Luxembourg

ACTION

The Cercle de Coopération des ONG de Développement de Luxembourg (ONGD), is the national platform of NGOs in Luxembourg. The 57 member organizations of ONGD all focus on development co-operation issues, and increasingly on conflict prevention. In early 1998 it organized an international conference on conflict prevention and arms trade, connecting Luxembourg NGOs with international experts in these fields.

29, Rue Michel Welter
2730 Luxemburg
Luxembourg

Contact: Pit Prum, Coordinator
Number of staff: 4

Tel: +35 (2) 298724
Fax: +35 (2) 298725
cercle.ongd@handitel.lu
www.ongd.lu

Macedonia

Center for Balkans Co-operation

Center for Balkans Co-operation (LOJA) is part of the "Babylon" network that is spread through eight towns in the Republic of Macedonia and which provides children and young people from different ethnic and religious backgrounds with opportunities to exchange mutual experiences and to search for common ground. In a LOJA member's own words: "We are fighting for a better world and a normal life for our children. We will try to improve inter-ethnic relationships between the different nationalities in our region. Cultural revolution is one of our main aims, because we think that this section of modern life is forgotten."

Ohridska 12
1220 Tetovo
Macedonia

Tel/fax: +389 (44) 350 570
Tel: +389 (70) 524 539
cbcloja@yahoo.com

Contact: Bujar Luma, Director
Number of staff: 5
Budget: $25,000–$100,000

Macedonia

Center for Civic Initiative

The Center for Civic Initiative (CCI) is actively engaged in building a citizen's society with an accent on human rights. The organization aims to motivate the citizens of the Republic of Macedonia to take part in the processes of building a citizens' society and democracy and to become directly involved in the decisionmaking processes in Macedonia. It seeks to achieve this objective through citizen education and raising awareness of human rights. CCI co-operates with the Albanian Center for Human Rights.

Borka Taleski 228
7500 Prilep
Macedonia

Tel: +389 (48) 400 480/401 480
Fax: +389 (48) 25 125/418 319
ccimk@mt.net.mk
www.ccimk.org

Contact: Goce Todoroski, Executive Director
Number of staff: 9
Budget: $25,000–$100,000

Macedonia

Ethnic Conflict Resolution Project

RESEARCH
EDUCATION

The Ethnic Conflict Resolution Project (ECRP) in the Faculty of Philosophy at the Sts. Cyril and Methodius University, Skopje, was launched in January 1994. Its overall goal is to help citizens of the Republic of Macedonia take an active role in resolving seemingly intractable conflicts rooted in ethnic and other differences.

To achieve the main ECRP goal, various activities intended to contribute to changing people's understanding of conflict and cultural differences are undertaken:

Conflict: from looking at conflict as always being a destructive battle between incompatible interests, to perceiving it as a possibility for mutual growth and improvement of relationships which, besides interests, also involve needs, feelings, and values;

Cultural differences: from anticipating cultural differences as a source of competition that inevitably creates tensions and intolerance between different ethnic groups, to accepting them as a potential source of mutual growth through building relations of respect and interdependence.

So far ECRP activities have been concentrated in three major domains: developing educational programs and support literature, providing training in communication and conflict resolution, and conducting scientific research in the area of ethnicity and its impact on inter-ethnic relations in the country

The ECRP offers a variety of programs in the field of conflict resolution. These are: Conflict Resolution Games (for younger elementary school students); Understanding Conflicts (for elementary- and high-school students and teachers, as well as students' parents); Conflict Awareness (for undergraduate students who are studying to become psychologists, teacher-trainers, sociologists, and pre-school and primary-school teachers); Collaborative Negotiation and Mediation (for school psychologists and teacher-trainers). ECRP conducts research projects in the Ethnic Identity of Macedonians and Albanians in the Republic of Macedonia and the possibility of developing civic identity and Ethnic Stereotypes among Students at the Pedagogical Faculty in Skopje.

Institute for Social Political and
Juridical Research
Dane Krapcer 18
1000 Skopje
Macedonia

Tel/fax: +389 (2) 122 572
ecrp@mol.com.mk

Contact: Violeta Beshka, Director

Number of staff: 10

Budget: $25,000–$100,000

Publications: Ice-breaking Games, training manual, 2000; *Appreciating Differences,* training manual, 1999; *Ethnic Stereotypes Among Future Pre-School and Primary-School Teachers,* 1998; *Understanding Conflicts,* 1997; *Conflict Resolution Games,* training manual, 1996.

Macedonia

Inter-Ethnic Project Gostivar

RESEARCH
EDUCATION
ADVOCACY

The Inter-Ethnic Project Gostivar (IPG) is dedicated to improving inter-ethnic relations in the municipality of Gostivar and the entire Republic of Macedonia. The IPG works with different sectors such as the media, local government, and NGOs to bring together all ethnicities living in the municipality. Their main program is financial support for inter-ethnic activities carried out by local partners. The IPG is part of the Helsinki Citizens' Assembly and of the Citizens' Pact.

Braca Ginovski 6
P.O.Box 150
1230 Gostivar
Macedonia

Tel/fax: +389 (42) 218 289
ipgoffice@ipg.com.mk

Contact: Yllza Ademi, Director
Number of staff: $100,000–$500,000
Publications: Newsletter.

Macedonia, Balkans

International Centre for Preventive Activities and Conflict Resolution

RESEARCH
EDUCATION
ACTION

The International Centre for Preventive Activities and Conflict Resolution (ICPCR) is a foundation based in Skopje, Republic of Macedonia. Devoted to the general task of promoting education, research, and dialogue on prevention and conflict resolution, ICPCR is also working on promotion of interethnic and interreligious tolerance and understanding as well as legal reform in the country. The organization runs a program on Education on Conflict Prevention and Resolution aimed at young NGO activists and government employees.

University "Ciril I Methody"
Law Faculty
Krste Misirkov bb
1000 Skopje
Macedonia

Tel: +389 (2) 290 410
Fax: +389 (2) 290 411
icpcr@mol.com.mk; icpcr@icpcr.org.mk
www.icpcr.org.mk

Contact: Saso Georgievski, Director
Number of staff: 4
Budget: $25,000–$100,000
Publications: ICPCR Newsletter.

Macedonia, Serbia, and Kosovo, Balkans

Macedonian Center for International Co-operation

RESEARCH
EDUCATION
ACTION
ADVOCACY

The Macedonian Center for International Co-operation (MCMS) works on support and development of local and national initiatives for improving the sustainable development of human resources in Macedonia. The main body of the MCMS is concerned with conflict prevention/resolution is the Civil Society Group/Team for Mediation. One of its main programs is titled "Whole is when there is everything" and has long-term objectives of supporting the development of democratic processes, maintenance of national stability through reduction of inter-ethnic tensions among the population, and the promotion of positive values emerging from differences. The program includes audio-visual campaigns, workshops, and the distribution of printed materials.

Nikola Parapunov bb
1000 Skopje
Macedonia

Tel: +389 (2) 365 381
Fax: +389 (2) 365 298
mcms@mkinter.net; mcms@mcms.org.mk
www.mcms.org.mk

Contact: Saso Klekovski, Executive Director
Number of staff: 43
Budget: $100,000–$500,000

Macedonia

Nansen Dialogue Center Skopje

RESEARCH
EDUCATION
ACTION
ADVOCACY

The Nansen Dialogue Center in Skopje works with INGOs, NGOs, the youth wings of political parties, students, and children on programs aiming to further democracy development, human rights, and peaceful conflict resolution. Main activities are seminars, training sessions, and public meetings. The Skopje office is part of the Nansen Centre network with offices across the region of former Yugoslavia. Main co-operation partners are Norway-based institutes and organizations.

Sarski odredi 7
1000 Skopje
Macedonia

Tel: +389 (2) 296 000
Fax: +389 (2) 176 224
ndcskopje@ndc.net.mk
www.ndc.net.mk

Contact: Albert Hani and Alexander Pekovski, Coordinators
Number of staff: 7 staff, 18 volunteers
Budget: $100,000–$500,000
Publications: Dijalog, bulletin.

Macedonia

Roma Centre of Skopje

EDUCATION
ACTION
ADVOCACY

The activities of the Roma Centre of Skopje are focused mainly on the Roma population in Macedonia. It is concerned with improving the educational level of Roma, improving their social and economical situation, working on Roma women's emancipation, and collecting, sharing, and disseminating information. The Centre also works on improving and streamlining the cooperation between Roma NGOs and the local and state institutions. The Center organizes seminars and workshops on various topics for the members of Roma NGOs.

Ul. August Cesarec 3-4/2
1000 Skopje
Macedonia

Tel:+389 (2) 638 800
Tel/fax: +389 (2) 618 575
centar@mt.net.mk

Contact: Azbija Memedova

Number of staff: 4

Budget: < $25,000

Publications: The Pleasant Fiction: Human Rights of Romas in Macedonia.

Macedonia, Balkans

Search for
Common Ground in Macedonia

RESEARCH
EDUCATION
ACTION

Search for Common Ground in Macedonia is dedicated to improving and transforming the way people deal with conflict by encouraging a move from adversarial methods to co-operative action. It has a number of programs for conflict transformation based around television and radio, education, publishing, training, research, mediation, monitoring, and early warning.

The Conflict Resolution in Education program aims to integrate conflict resolution education and multicultural education into the Macedonian school system and introduce conflict resolution education into the educational system in Kosovo/FRY. This program has been developed and implemented in co-operation with the Ethnic Conflict Resolution Project of the University of Sts. Kiril and Methodius, Skopje. The program, Balkan Bridges: Co-operation and Dialogue through the Media aims to promote the pro-social and conflict reducing role of media rather than conflict escalation and to promote exchange of views among ethnic groups in Macedonia and the region. *Nashe Maalo* (Our neighborhood) is a curriculum-based television program for children ages 7–12 that aims to encourage inter-cultural understanding, conflict prevention through increased cultural awareness, and conflict resolution skills.

Orce Nikolov 63
1000 Skopje
Macedonia

Tel: +389 (2) 118 517
Fax: +389 (2) 118 322
sfcg@sfcg.org.mk
www.sfcg.org.mk

Contact: Eran Fraenkel, Director

Number of staff: 14

Budget: > $1,000,000

Publications: Multi-Ethnic Forum; *Karavan; Reporting Diversity;* training materials.

Moldova, Transdniestria

InfoTAG

The InfoTAG Information Agency is a media-oriented NGO that collects and disseminates information on the Moldova-Transdniestrian conflict and provides independent analysis of the ethno-political situation in Moldova and the settlement process. InfoTAG avoids political engagement with either of the parties to the conflict. It sees its role as that of a third party involved in early warning and post-conflict monitoring. InfoTAG regularly publishes analyses of current developments in Moldova and Transdniestria. It cooperates systematically with the Network of Ethnological Monitoring and Early Warning of Conflict, Moscow.

22 Pushkin Street
277 042 Chisinau
Moldova

Tel: +373 (2) 234 875/234 873
office@infotag.net.md

Contact: Alexander Tanase, Director

Publications: Regular news briefs and analytical reports.

Moldova, Transdniestria, Southeastern Europe, CIS countries

Institute for Public Policy

The Institute for Public Policy (Institutul de Politici Publice) is an independent, non-partisan and nonprofit organization, committed to the values of individual liberty, democratic society, rule of law, and free market economy. It was created by the Soros Foundation Moldova and the Euro Atlantic Centre Moldova in 2000. Through research, publications, policy recommendations, and public forums, the Institute provides political, business, media, and academic communities and leaderships with a deep analysis of public policy issues confronting the society in order to improve the policymaking process. The Institute runs a Conflict Management Programme that aims to solve the Transdniestrian conflict and to increase regional security.

28 Bulgara str.
2001 Chisinau
Moldova

Tel: +373 (2) 276 785
Fax: +373 (2) 270 527
oazu_nantoi@ipp.md
www.ipp.md

Contact: Oazu Nantoi, Director Conflict Management Programme

Number of staff: 6

Budget: $25,000–$100,000

Publications: The Legal Assessment of the Peace-Keeping Process in the Transdniestria Conflict Based on International Law Norms, in Romanian, 2001; *The Military Dimension of the Conflict Resolution in the Eastern Zone of the Republic of Moldova,* in Romanian, 2001.

Moldova, Transdniestria

Joint Committee for Democratisation and Conciliation

EDUCATION
ACTION

The Joint Committee for Democratisation and Conciliation (JCDC) (formerly known as the Joint Moldova-Transdniestrian Committee for Conciliation and Democratisation) draws its members from both conflicting sides and sees its primary task in supporting the process of conflict resolution and the prevention of escalation in Moldova and Transdniestria. It has initiated several programs for confidence building between the two communities and organized regular meetings between representatives of the respective administrations. The Committee is focusing on enhanced communications between the two sides, elaborating a human-rights program, and studying international conflict-management experiences. The Committee organizes seminars and workshops on conflict management with regional and international representation.

6 Botanica Veche Street, Apt. 103
277 062 Chisinau
Moldova

Contact: Vasile Sturza, Head of Commitee

Tel/fax: + 373 (2) 238 264

Global

ACT Netherlands

RESEARCH
EDUCATION
ACTION
ADVOCACY

ACT Netherlands (Action by Churches Together, Kerken in Aktie in Dutch) is part of a global ecumenical network of the World Council of Churches and supports hundreds of sister organizations all over the world. The struggle against injustice is its main concern. ACT Netherlands collaborates with local churches, women groups, labor unions, and human rights organizations. Its activities include fundraising for projects and informing the public. A new campaign is launched each year. In 2002 the campaign will be on food security.

Joseph Haydnlaan 2a
Postbus 456
3500 AL Utrecht
The Netherlands

Contact: Bea Stolte-van Empelen, Program Officer
Publications: Kerken in Aktie, newsletter.

Tel: +31 (30) 880 1456
Fax: +31 (30) 880 1457
info@kerkeninaktie
www.kerkeninaktie.nl

Eastern Europe, Africa, Latin America

RESEARCH
EDUCATION

Centre for Conflict Studies

The Centre for Conflict Studies (CCS) at the University of Utrecht was established at the end of 1999 and deals with the analyses of causes, dynamics, and consequences of international and intrastate violent conflict. It aims to increase our understanding of violent conflicts by using an interdisciplinary approach. CCS both examines the local dynamics of conflict as well as the problems related to international military and humanitarian interventions directed at the resolution of conflicts and post-conflict reconstruction. In addition, the CCS offers various courses at graduate level on issues such as peacebuilding, negotiation and mediation, and theories of conflict.

Kromme Nieuwegracht 66, room 1.05
3512 HL Utrecht
The Netherlands

Tel: +31 (30) 2536 443
Fax: +31 (30) 2536 024
conflict.studies@let.uu.nl
www.uu.nl/conflictstudies

Contact: Chris van der Borgh

Number of staff: 2

Europe, Central Asia, Africa

RESEARCH
EDUCATION

Centre for International Conflict Analysis and Management

An interdisciplinary institute at the University of Nijmegen, the Centre for International Conflict Analysis and Management (CICAM)—the former Peace Research Centre—is dedicated to the study of war and peace issues. It also conducts courses for undergraduate students. A central theme of investigation at CICAM is the feasibility of prevention and intervention in conflict situations by international and Dutch governmental and non-governmental entities. CICAM is also engaged in documentation and public information activities. It maintains a documentation center related to general issues of war and peace, as well as The Global Education Centre.

Thomas van Aquinostraat 1
P.O. Box 9108
6500 HK Nijmegen
The Netherlands

Tel: +31 (24) 361 5687
Fax: +31 (24) 361 1839
cicam@nsm.kun.nl
www.kun.nl/cicam

Contact: H.W. Bomert, Director

Number of staff: 12

Publications: Cahiers, yearbooks on peace and security, in Dutch.

Global

Cordaid

EDUCATION
ACTION
ADVOCACY

Cordaid (Catholic Organisation for Relief and Development) was established in 1999 following the merger of Bilance, Caritas Netherlands, and Memisa, three Catholic development organizations based in the Netherlands. Cordaid is engaged in all aspects of development cooperation including emergency aid, structural poverty alleviation, and health care. Cordaid views conflict prevention and reconciliation as integral themes within a more comprehensive development program. For example, in its programs to enhance disaster preparedness, it sees preparedness against "complex political emergencies"—and thus conflict prevention—as an integral component.

Lutherse Burgwal 10
Postbus 16440
2500 BK The Hague
The Netherlands

Tel: +31 (70) 313 6300
Fax: +31 (70) 313 6301
cordaid@cordaid.nl3
www.cordaid.nl

Contact: Ronald Lucardie, Policy Officer, The Department for Quality and Strategy

Number of staff: 285

Budget: > $1,000,000

CIS countries, Central America,
the Horn of Africa, Central Africa, Southeast Asia

Ethnic Conflicts Research Project

RESEARCH
ACTION
ADVOCACY

The Ethnic Conflicts Research Project (ECOR) is a network of experts and practitioners of conflict analysis, prevention, transformation, and resolution. ECOR studies multi-layered ethno-national conflicts, including the causes of ethnic conflicts and factors that help to prevent or resolve them. It has produced a survey of the global phenomenon of ethno-nationalism and is currently carrying out field research in four sensitive conflict regions. In 1994 ECOR helped to launch the Genocide Research Programme, which includes applications such as Genocide Alert, Genocide Prevention International, Responses to Genocide, and Genocide and Crisis in Central Africa.

Brachterhof 38
5932 XM Tegelen
The Netherlands

Tel/fax: +31 (77) 374 0290
ecor_cps@hotmail.com

Contact: Christian Scherrer, Director

Number of staff: 2 at HQ, 4 in the field

Budget: $100,000–$500,000

Publications: Genocide and Crisis in Central Africa, 2001; *Handbook on Ethnicity and State,* 3 volumes (in German: 1996–8; in English: 1998–99); *Ongoing Crisis in Central Africa: Conflict Impact Assessment and Policy Options,* 1998; *Intra-state Conflicts and Ethnicity: Types, Causes, Escalation and Peace Strategies,* 1997.

Europe, Global

European Centre
for Conflict Prevention

RESEARCH
ADVOCACY

The European Centre for Conflict Prevention (ECCP) is an independent NGO based in the Netherlands. Its mission is to contribute to prevention and resolution of violent conflicts in the world. The Centre acts as the secretariat of the European Platform for Conflict Prevention and Transformation (see next entry) and initiates, co-ordinates, and implements its activities. In addition, the Centre has specific networking and awareness-raising objectives focused on the Netherlands.

In its function as an information clearinghouse, the European Centre maintains the website www.conflict-prevention.net, one of the most comprehensive sources of information available regarding organizations and activities in the field of conflict prevention. The ECCP's Information Centre also maintains a large collection of material produced by other organizations, mainly NGOs, involved in the field.

The Searching for Peace Programme, part of the clearinghouse function, is aimed at analyzing conflict prevention efforts in the main violent conflicts of the world. The results are published in a series of books as well as on the website. A directory on the main local and international NGOs working in the field of conflict prevention and peacebuilding is included.

In line with ECCP's aim of raising awareness of the importance and possibilities of conflict prevention, People Building Peace is an ongoing project aimed at collecting and publishing inspiring stories of conflict prevention and peacebuilding, with special attention to civil society.

In its network capacity, the ECCP not only acts as the secretariat of the European Platform, but also as the secretariat of regular consultations between the Dutch Ministry of Foreign Affairs and Dutch NGOs active in the field of conflict prevention and peacebuilding.

On a regular base, the ECCP organizes roundtables and seminars on issues related to conflict prevention and peacebuilding. The organization has also taken an initiative to make conflict resolution part of the school curriculum. In 2000, the organization established a Special Chair of Conflict Prevention and Management at Utrecht University.

Korte Elisabethsheatt 6
P.O. Box 14069
3508 SC Utrecht
The Netherlands

Tel: +31 (30) 242 7777
Fax: +31 (30) 236 9268
info@conflict-prevention.net
www.conflict-prevention.net

Contact: Paul van Tongeren, Executive Director
Number of staff: 14
Budget: $500,000–$1,000,000
Publications: *Searching for Peace Series on Africa,* 1999; *Europe and Eurasia,* 2002; *Central and South Asia,* 2002; *Towards Better Peacebuilding Practice, Evaluation Practices, aand Aid and Conflict,* 2002; *Peace Studies and Conflict Resolution: An Overview of University Programmes and Training Courses in Europe,* 2001; *Conflict Resolution in Schools: Report of an International Seminar,* 2000; *People Building Peace: 35 Inspiring Stories from Around the World,* 1999.

Europe, Global

European Platform for Conflict Prevention and Transformation

The European Platform for Conflict Prevention and Transformation is an open network of over 150 key European and international organizations working in the field of the prevention and/or resolution of violent conflicts in the international arena. Its mission is to facilitate the exchange of information and experience among participating organizations, as well as to stimulate co-operation and synergy. The European Centre for Conflict Prevention (see previous entry) functions as the secretariat of the European Platform.

The main objectives of the Platform are:

• To raise awareness of the importance and possibilities of conflict prevention and resolution, through publications and media productions for a broad audience, and lobby activities aimed at governments and the European Union.

• To facilitate contact, networking, and information exchange between organizations active in the field of conflict prevention and resolution in Europe and other parts of the world (information clearinghouse).

In order to reach these objectives, the Platform produces the *Conflict Prevention Newsletter,* one of few general newsletters on the subject. It also organizes annual Platform-meetings where members come together to discuss relevant and timely issues.

Other examples of activities carried out by the European Platform include the support of national platforms and national infrastructures for conflict prevention/peacebuilding as well as the project on Lessons Learned, which is aimed at formulating common "best practices" taken from the field.

The Steering Group of the European Platform is composed of representatives from the Centre for Applied Studies in International Negotiations (Switzerland), the European Centre for Conflict Prevention (the Netherlands), the European Centre for Common Ground (Belgium), EAWARN (Russia), the Field Diplomacy Initiative (Belgium), the German Platform for Peaceful Conflict Management (Germany), International Alert (UK), KATU (Finland), the Life & Peace Institute (Sweden), and Saferworld (UK).

Secretariat:
European Centre for
   Conflict Prevention
P.O. Box 14069
3508 SC Utrecht
The Netherlands

Tel: +31 (30) 242 777
Fax: +31 (30) 236 9268
info@conflict-prevention.net
www.conflict-prevention.net

Contact: Paul van Tongeren, Executive Director, European Centre for Conflict Prevention

Publications: Conflict Prevention Newsletter, quarterly newsletter; *Preventing Violent Conflict: Opportunities for the Swedish and Belgian Presidencies of the European Union in 2001, European Platform, International Alert and Saferworld,* 2000; *Preventing Violent Conflict-Opportunities for the Spanish and Danish Presidencies,* 2002; *Saferworld International Altert, Intermon Oxfam G8 and Conflict Prevention: Turning Declarations into Action, European Platform, International Alert and Saferworld,* 2000; *Prevention and Management of Violent Conflicts: An International Directory,* 1998; Annual Reports.

Global

Hague Appeal for Peace

The Hague Appeal for Peace is an open network of civil society organizations that gathered for the first time in 1999, on the centenary of the First Hague Peace Conference. Its aim is to seriously raise questions as to whether humanity can find a way to solve its problems without resorting to arms. Their Hague Agenda for Peace and Justice for the 21st Century addresses root causes of war and cultures of peace; international humanitarian and human rights law; the prevention, resolution, and transformation of violent conflicts; disarmament and human security. The network also carries out a Global Campaign for Peace Education.

c/o The International Association
  of Lawyers Against Nuclear Arms
Anna Paulownasstraat 103
2518 BC The Hague
The Netherlands

Tel: +31 (70) 363 4484
Fax: +31 (70) 345 5951
hap@antenna.nl
www.haguepeace.org

Contact: Cecilia Nilsson, Department of Human Rights and International Humanitarian Law

Balkans, Turkey, Caucasus, Middle East

Interchurch Peace Council

The Interchurch Peace Council (IKV) addresses a wide range of peace and conflict resolution issues on behalf of Dutch Christian churches. IKV examines issues of war and peace and attempts to identify activities that can prevent or stop war and foster peace, reconciliation, and civil integration. Maintaining the involvement of society in general and churches in particular in issues of war and peace by stimulating discussion and activism is the Council's other main activity.

Together with other independent civic groups in Europe, IKV established the Helsinki Citizen's Assembly in 1990. It also took the initiative to build a network of civil society groups in Europe and the Arab: The Euro-Arab Dialogue (EAD). IKV programs include numerous activities focused on young people, many of which are carried out under the auspices of the Helsinki Citizen's Assembly.

P.O. Box 85893
2508 CN The Hague
The Netherlands

Tel: +31 (70) 350 7100
Fax: +31 (70) 354 2611
ikv@ikv.nl
www.ikv.nl

Contact: Mient Jan Faber, General Secretary
Number of staff: 15
Budget: > $1,000,000
Publications: Quarterly newletter; *Projecting Peace, Nuclear Arms, Humanitarian Intervention.*

Global

International
Fellowship of Reconciliation

ACTION

The International Fellowship of Reconciliation (IFOR) is a network of people believing in the power of non-violence to change the world. Its spiritual basis is fundamental to IFOR's work. The Fellowship has over 40 national groups on all continents (more than 55 countries) which respond to local needs. From IFOR's International Office, the IFOR Woman Peacemakers Program supports women's work for peace in a variety of ways.

Spoorstraat 38
1815 BK Alkmaar
The Netherlands

Tel: +31 (72) 512 3014
Fax: +31 (72) 515 1102
office@ifor.org
www.ifor.org

Contact: Susan H. Ross, Interim Coordinator, International Secretariat
Number of staff: 4 at HQ
Budget: $100,000–$500,000
Publications: Reconciliation International, newsletter, three issues per year; *Cross the Lines,* quarterly newsletter from Women Peacemakers Program; *Patterns in Reconciliation,* occasional paper series.

Global

International Peace Council
for States, Peoples and Minorities

RESEARCH
EDUCATION
ACTION
ADVOCACY

The International Peace Council for States, Peoples and Minorities is a non-profit organization led by a council of eminent persons from all parts of the world, which is dedicated to the prevention and resolution of violent conflicts between population groups and the states within which they exist. Where peace has been initiated, the organization helps to consolidate it. The Council exists to facilitate and empower state governments and the leadership of population groups worldwide to create the conditions for diverse communities to live in peace in an environment where they actively participate in a society, state, and region to which they belong.

Nassaukade 55
1052 CN Amsterdam
The Netherlands

mvanwalt@aol.com

Contact: Michael van Walt van Praag, Chairman
Number of staff: 3
Budget: $25,000–$100,000

Eastern Europe

Kontakt der Kontinenten

Kontakt der Kontinenten (KdK) is a training and conference center offering courses and training programs on issues including intercultural communication and international cooperation. It is increasingly emphasizing conflict management and prevention, and offers special training programs for those preparing to work in conflict areas, as well as courses for humanitarian relief workers. It also consults with NGOs on policy and practice with respect to peacebuilding strategies and conflict resolution. Conflict prevention and conflict resolution programs have been developed for target groups in Croatia, Bosnia, Romania, and Macedonia.

Amersfoortsestraat 20
3769 AS Soesterberg
The Netherlands

Tel: +31 (346) 351 755
Fax: +31 (346) 354 735
kdk@kdk-nl.org
www.kdk-nl.org

Contact: Wico Bunskoek, Director
Number of staff: 8
Budget: $500,000–$1,000,000

Global

Network University

The Network University (TNU) is a center for collaborative learning operating out of its base at the University of Amsterdam. TNU consists of a network of universities and additional outside experts and offers innovative online courses on a wide variety of topics, including the online courses "Transforming Civil Conflict" and "Post Conflict Development." TNU has also organized online debates on peace and conflict resolution issues. Detailed information on courses and fees is available at the Transforming Civil Conflict demo site www.netuni.nl/demos/tcc.

Gebouw Renault
Wibautstraat 224
PO Box 94603
1090 GP Amsterdam
The Netherlands

Tel: +31 (20) 561 8166
Fax: +31 (20) 866 1751
tcc@netuni.uva.nl
www.netuni.nl

Contact: Lambrecht Wessels, Course Director
Number of staff: 5
Budget: $25,000–$100,000
Publications: Electronic newsletter.

Central America, Sub Sahara Africa, and South Asia

Netherlands Institute of International Relations "Clingendael"

RESEARCH
EDUCATION
ADVOCACY

The Netherlands Institute of International Relations "Clingendael" in The Hague was established in 1983 by a merger of various Dutch institutes active in the field of international relations.

The overall objective of the Clingendael Institute is to promote a better understanding of international affairs among politicians, academicians, civil servants and diplomats, media, and the public at large. Special attention is devoted to Dutch foreign and security policy, the European Union, the United Nations, and other international organizations, and conflict and security issues in general.

The Institute derives income from courses, training, and contract research, and is furthermore subsidized by the Ministries of Foreign Affairs, Defence, and Education, Culture and Sciences.

The Institute and its staff are autonomous in that activities and views are completely independent of any public or private body

The Clingendael "Conflict Research Unit" (CRU) is part of Clingendael's research department and focuses on the study of intrastate conflict and conflict management, especially in the developing world. The CRU focuses in particular on the current gap between academic research and policy at a time when efforts to prevent and resolve violent conflicts are demanding new conceptual and analytical frameworks. The goal of CRU research is to develop innovative perspectives and policy approaches to intrastate conflict. This research is characterized by a systematic focus on the relationship between state and society, which is viewed as key to understanding the roots of conflict and the complexities of conflict resolution. Special attention is given to the ways in which power and resources are distributed and disbursed by the state.

An example of a CRU projects intended to provide policy advice is the "Coping with Internal Conflict Project," focusing on the political economy of internal conflict, power sharing, political military relations, resources, entitlements, and poverty-related conflict.

Clingendael 7
P.O. Box 93080
2509 AB The Hague
The Netherlands

Tel: +31 (70) 324 5384
Fax: +31 (70) 328 2002
tbouta@clingendael.nl
www.clingendael.nl/cru

Contact: Georg E. Frerks, Head of Conflict Research Unit

Number of staff: 5

Budget: > $1,000,000

Publications: Between Indifference and Naïveté: Dutch Policy Intervention in African Conflict, 2000; Conflict Prognosis: A Conflict and Policy Assessment Framework, Part Two, 2000; Conflict Prognosis: Bridging the Gap From Early Warning to Early Response, Part One, 1999; Conflict Prevention in the OSCE: An Assessment of Capacities, 1999; The Pretence of Peace-keeping: ECOMOG, West-Africa and Liberia (1990–1998), 1999.

Global

ADVOCACY

Novib

Novib (Netherlands Organization for International Development Cooperation) works for sustainable development by supporting the efforts of poor people in developing countries and by serving as their advocate in the North. Its three broad goals are to alleviate structural poverty, to educate the Dutch population on development issues, and to advance the interest of the poor in policy-making. Novib promotes dialogue in areas of conflict, lobbies in the international arena, undertakes fact-finding activities, and organizes conferences. It works closely with local counterparts and supports international groups such as International Alert and Synergies Africa.

Mauritskade 9
P.O. Box 30919
2500 GX The Hague
The Netherlands

Tel: +31 (70) 342 1621
Fax: +31 (70) 361 4461
info@novib.nl
www.novib.nl

Contact: Mario Weima, Human Rights Policy Advisor

Number of staff: 2

Budget: $25,000–$100,000

Publications: Conflict Management in Africa, 1997; *Country Assessment on Rwanda,* 1997.

Balkans, Colombia, Cuba, Middle East, Indonesia, Sudan

ACTION

Pax Christi Netherlands

Where violence reigns, Pax Christi seeks ways out of it. The organization invites opponents to meet, encouraging gestures of reconciliation. Pax Christi members visit those involved in or affected by armed conflict: victims and peace groups, socially committed religious movements, authors and other opinion leaders, and the warring parties, their politicians, and war-lords.

It has done so with the government and resistance movements in Colombia, with North and South Sudan, and with Serbs and Kosovar Albanians in former Yugoslavia.

At the request of the government of Colombia, Pax Christi Netherlands has played an important role in peace talks between the government and the armed resistance forces, and assisted in establishing a peace zone in Urab, near the community of San José. In 1997, a representative was sent to the diocese of San José, where he serves as an international observer and supports the initiative of San José. Pax Christi is also campaigning against the frequent kidnappings in Colombia.

Pax Christi has also supported peace efforts in Sudan and is closely involved in the so-called people-to-people peace process, a community-based process fostering dialogue and peace initiatives between conflicting communities in southern Sudan.

In former Yugoslavia, Pax Christi carried out a dialogue project from 1995 through 1999 in which some 20 Serbian and Kosovo Albanian organizations participated. Together with its partners, Pax Christi lobbied for a peaceful resolution to the Kosovo conflict and called attention to human rights violations in Kosovo. In 2000 Pax Christi initiated an exchange project between Kosovo and Northern Ireland, as well as the first annual Peace Week in Kosovo. It also initiated an inter-ethnic dialogue in Macedonia and launched a project entitled "Serbia-EU: From exclusion to integration." Pax Christi is working with project facilitators based in Serbia, Kosovo, and Macedonia.

In the Middle East, Pax Christi's focus is on the ongoing conflict in Israel and the Palestinian Territories.

P.O. Box 19318
3501 DH Utrecht
The Netherlands

Tel: +31 (30) 233 3346
Fax: +31 (30) 236 8199
paxchristi@paxchristi.nl
www.paxchristi.nl

Contact: Jan Gruiters, Director
Number of staff: 25
Budget: > $1,000,000
Publications: The Middle East Peace Process in Come: Some Policy Elements for the European Union and the USA, 1997; Bestemming onbekend (Destiny Unknown), interviews with refugees, 1997; *The Middle East Peace Process: Between Fighting Terrorism, Respect for Human Rights and Starting the Final Talks,* 1996.

Former Yugoslavia

Press Now

Press Now was established in 1993 to support independent media during the war in former Yugoslavia. Press Now is currently working in Albania, Bosnia and Herzegovina, Croatia, Macedonia, Serbia, Montenegro, Vojvodina, and Kosovo. Press Now provides support to media for short-term needs (paper, equipment, etc.) and for ongoing growth and improvement in journalistic quality and organization. Support includes both funding and training. Press Now also organizes public programs and campaigns to provide information to politicians, the press, and the general public in the Netherlands on the media in the Balkans.

Wibautstraat 3
1091 GH Amsterdam
The Netherlands

Tel: +31 (20) 596 2000
Fax: +31 (20) 596 2001
pressnow@pressnow.nl
www.dds.nl/~pressnow

Contact: Anique ter Welle

Publications: Independent Media in Former Yugoslavia and the Role of International Donors

Bosnia-Herzegovina: One Media Policy Under Three Banners?

Global

Unrepresented Nations and Peoples Organisation

EDUCATION
ACTION
ADVOCACY

One of the aims of the Unrepresented Nations and Peoples Organisation (UNPO) is to assist its 51 member nations, peoples, and minorities in preventing violent conflicts, or in resolving them through negotiations and political means. Through its Conflict Prevention Programme, UNPO provides training in diplomacy and conflict resolution, professional services, and advice relevant to these purposes. UNPO also encourages and facilitates dialogue between potential adversaries and carries out behind-the-scenes diplomacy.

Javastraat 40A
2585 AP the Hague
The Netherlands

Tel: +31 (70) 360 3318
Fax: +31 (70) 360 2246
unpo@unpo.org
www.unpo.org

Contact: Cathy Shin, Conflict Prevention Programme Coordinator
Number of staff: 16 at HQ

Budget: $100,000–$300,000

Publications: UNPO News, quarterly newsletter; *Nonviolence and Conflict: Conditions for Effective Peaceful Change,* 1998; *UNPO Monitor of the United Nations Working Group on Indigenous Populations,* 1997.

Caucasus, East and Southeastern Europe, Sub Saharan Africa

Centre for Conflict Management

RESEARCH
EDUCATION
ACTION

The Centre for Conflict Management (CCM) is an independent center for training, practice, and research focusing on the dynamic process of conflict management. CCM accepts that conflict is normal, unavoidable, and necessary, and embraces a vision where conflict's positive functions are maintained while the negative characteristics are managed in an effective and democratic way. The Centre is engaged in building practical competence and theoretical understanding in the field of nonviolent conflict resolution. Activities include workshops, forum evenings, and training programs for a diverse target audience including teachers, students, nonviolence trainers, and employees in humanitarian organizations and refugees.

Cort Adelers gate 18
P.O. Box 2778, Solli
0204 Oslo
Norway

Tel: +47 (22)129 920
Fax: +47 (22) 129 921
ccm@ccm.no
www.ccm.no

Contact: Graham Dyson, Executive Director
Number of staff: 10
Budget: $500,000–$1,000,0000
Publications: Foundations in Conflict Management: A Course Manual, in Norwegian, 2001; *Teacher's Guide to Human Rights Education,* 2000.

Balkans, Sub-Saharan Africa, Southeast Asia, Middle East

Chr. Michelsen Institute

The Chr. Michelsen Institute (CMI) is a private social science foundation working on issues of development and human rights, primarily in sub-Saharan Africa, Asia, and the Middle East. It carries out both basic and applied research. In its "Human Rights and Democratisation" program, CMI focuses on potential or actual conflict; the adequacy of conflict prevention mechanisms; the documentation of violations during conflict; humanitarian interventions to mitigate the effects of war; and post-conflict measures related to the settlement of injustices committed during conflict and the restoration of war-torn economies and societies.

Fantoftvegen 38
P.O. Box 6033
5892 Bergen
Norway

Tel: +47 (55) 574 231
Fax: +47 (55) 574 166
www.cmi.no

Contact: Gunnar Sørbø, Director

Number of staff: 59

Budget: > $1,000,000

Publications: The Institutional Impact of Aid Dependence on Recipients in Africa, 1999; *Humanitarian Assistance During Conflict in a Stateless Society: The State of Somalia,* 1999; *NGOs in Conflict: an Evaluation of International Alert,* 1997.

Global

Fafo Institute for Applied Social Science

The Fafo Institute for Applied Social Science runs the Program for International Co-operation and Conflict Resolution (PICCR). PICCR supports initiatives related to the search for peaceful solutions to conflict, such as third-party supportive diplomacy, facilitation, and negotiation. It is involved in research, dialogue, and learning initiatives related to effective international organizations. The Institute has organized a number of workshops with a focus on the creation of neutral space for inter-organizational dialogue. One of its core projects, the Peace Implementation Network (PIN) was established to explore the policies and practices of international assistance in support of the implementation of peace agreements.

P.O. Box 2947 Toyen
0608 Oslo
Norway

Tel: +47 (22) 088 600
Fax: +47 (22) 088 700
pisk@fafo.no
www.fafo.no/piccr

Contact: Mark B. Taylor, Programme Director PICCR

Number of staff: 2

Publications: The Conjurer's Hat: Financing Mechanisms in Support of UN Peace-building Missions, 2001; *Gendering Human Security: From Marginalisation to the Integration of Women in Peace-Building,* 2001; *Swords for Ploughshares: Microdisarmament in Transitions from Conflict,* 2000; *Command from the Saddle,* 1999.

Global

ACTION

First Week Foundation

The First Week Foundation is a non-profit organization founded in 1996. It is involved in projects addressing children and their welfare, especially in conflict areas; works to promote the Universal Peace Treaty; and is involved in additional health and development projects in the Chittagong region of Bangladesh. It supports the World Watch project, a computer-based early warning system. First Week's name is derived from its vision "that the first week of every calendar year will be a week of peace, celebrating the new opportunities at the beginning of the year."

Bragernes torg 13
P.O. Box 1147
3001 Drammen
Norway

Tel: +47 3289 4228
Fax: +47 3289 4224
first.week@bu.telia.no
www.first-week.com

Contact: Einar Michelsen, President
Number of staff: 2
Budget: > $1,000,000

RESEARCH
EDUCATION
ACTION

Former Yugoslavia

Nansen Dialogue

Nansen Dialogue is an umbrella of various projects that use dialogue as an important tool for conflict management. One of the projects is called Democracy, Human Rights and Peaceful Conflict Resolution, which started in 1995 and is operational in Former Yugoslavia. It is a joint project with the International Peace Research Institute of Oslo (PRIO) and aims to empower people who live in conflict situations to contribute to peaceful conflict transformation and democratic development with promotion of human rights. While this communication-training project has a clear educational purpose, an underlying goals are networking and to explore dialogue itself as a tool in conflict resolution.

Nansenskolen
Bjornstjerne Bjornsonsgate 2
2609 Lillehammer
Norway

Tel: +47 (612) 65 413
Fax: +47 (612) 65 445
dempro.2@online.no
www.nansen-dialog.net

Contact: Steinar Bryn, Project Director
Number of staff: 3
Budget: > $1,000,000
Publications: Dialogue in Practice: Reflections on a Dialogue Project with Serbs and Albanians from Kosovo, 2000; *PRIO/Nansen Dialogue: A Case Study of Democracy Training and the Balkan Dialogue Project,* 2000.

Eastern Africa, Horn of Africa, Latin America

ACTION

Norwegian Church Aid

Norwegian Church Aid (NCA) is an ecumenical, voluntary as well as independent organization whose aims include the promotion of fundamental rights and the improvement of living standards for the poor and oppressed, as well as the raising of consciousness among of those living in affluent societies. The promotion of human rights, peace, and reconciliation is one of NCA's nine strategic aims, and recently a new Department of Policy and Human Rights was created to strengthen and coordinate NCA's peace and reconciliation activities.

Sandakerveien 74
P.O.Box 4544 Nydalen
0404 Oslo
Norway

Tel: +47 2209 2700
Fax: +47 2209 2720
nca-oslo@nca.no
www.nca.no

Contact: Stein Villumstad

Number of staff: 10

Budget: $100,000–$500,000

Publications: Own the Aids Challenge, 2000; *Indigenous People: What, Why and How?,* 2000.

Africa, Middle East, China and Latin America

RESEARCH
EDUCATION
ACTION

Norwegian Institute of Human Rights

The Norwegian Institute of Human Rights (Institutt for menneskerettigheter) is a university institute devoted to research on human rights. Current research topics include global human rights protection; human rights protection and The Council of Europe; human rights and normative traditions; human rights and development; and human rights in Norway. The aim of the Institute is to contribute to the realization of internationally recognized human rights through a program of research, teaching, advice, international activities, documentation, and information. The library of the Institute is the largest collection of human rights literature in Norway.

Universitetsgata 22-24
P.O. Box 6832 St Olavs plass
0130 Oslo
Norway

Tel: +47 (22) 842 001
Fax: +47 (22) 842 002
admin@nihr.uio.no
www.humanrights.uio.no

Contact: Kristin Høgdahl, Project Director
Norwegian Resource Bank for Democracy
and Human Rights

Number of staff: 3

Budget: > $1,000,000

Balkans, Central and Eastern Europe, Russia, South Africa

Norwegian Institute of International Affairs

RESEARCH
EDUCATION
ADVOCACY

The Norwegian Institute of International Affairs (NUPI) undertakes research and disseminates information to the public on international affairs. One of its two primary research programs is its "Collective Security" program, which focuses on security theory, conflict prevention, and peace operations. An important element of the Collective Security program is NUPI's "UN Programme," which addresses conceptual questions concerning the UN and peace operations. NUPI is also responsible for coordinating a project entitled "Training for Peace in Southern Africa," which aims at building regional capacities for participation in peace operations.

Gronlandsleiret 25
P.O. Box 8159 Dep.
0033 Oslo
Norway

Tel: +47 (22) 056 500
Fax: +47 (22) 177 015
info@nupi.no
www.nupi.no

Contact: Torunn Tryggestad, Project Coordinator
Number of staff: 15
Budget: $100,000–$500,000

Publications: Forum for Development Studies, biannual publication; *Practical Disarmament,* 2001; *The Sanctions Debate: UN Sanctions in the 1990s,* 2001; *Gendering Human Security,* 2001. Gender Perspectives on Peace and Conflict Studies, 2000.

Global

RESEARCH

Norwegian Peace Alliance

The Norwegian Peace Alliance is a network of 18 Norwegian peace groups that works to advance cooperation and coordination among them. The Alliance's public information activities serve to inform the public and political authorities about peace issues and to increase knowledge among its members. The Alliance is also engaged in policy advocacy work. In the fall of 2000, it published "Peace is Possible," a collection of articles by prominent peace journalists describing examples of successful peacemaking. The Norwegian Peace Alliance is also involved in the development of a website (the Peace Academy and Internet Resource) with different resources on such issues as peace education, conflict prevention/transformation, and education.

Storg. 11, 5etg
0155 Oslo
Norway

Tel/fax: +47 (23) 010 300
norpeace@c2i.net
home.c2i.net/norpeace

Contact: Jorgen Johansen, Member of the Board
Number of staff: 3
Budget: < $25,000
Publications: Peace is Possible, 2000.

Global

Norwegian People's Aid

ACTION

Norwegian People's Aid (NPA) runs aid programs in over 30 countries based on the principles of solidarity, unity, human dignity, peace, and freedom. NPA sees peace not just as the absence of hostility but as a situation in which economic and social justice, human rights, and freedom from violence and gender-based discrimination are cherished and guaranteed. Conflict prevention, mine clearance, and mine awareness programs are among NPA's priorities; NPA has been involved in mine clearance and mine awareness programs in the Balkans, Southeast Asia, Northern Iraq/Kurdistan, and Southern Africa.

Storgata 33a
P.O.Box 8844
Youngstorget
0028 Oslo
Norway

Tel: +47 2203 7700
Fax: +47 2220 0870
npaid@npaid.org
www.npaid.org

Contact: Reiulf Steen, President

Publications: Strategy for Women: Gender Equality and Development; *Landmine Monitor Report,* 2000.

Global

Norwegian Refugee Council

EDUCATION
ACTION
ADVOCACY

The Norwegian Refugee Council (NRC) is a voluntary organization involved in refugee questions and international refugee work. For more than 50 years the organization has worked to provide humanitarian assistance to people fleeing from their homes and to defend their fundamental human rights. Together with the International Center on Conflict and Negotiation (Georgia), it has been undertaking a program of Training in Conflict Resolution Skills and Methods, working with the displaced in Georgia. NRC has also been involved in a regional project relating to the Karabakh conflict aimed at networking and strengthening regional capacities to deal with conflicts.

Grensen 17
P.O. Box 6758 St. Olavs plass
0130 Oslo
Norway

Tel: +47 (23) 109 800
Fax: +47 (23) 109 801
nrc-no@online.no
www.nrc.no/engindex.htm

Contact: Steinar Sørlie, Secretary General

Publications: På flukt, newsletter in Norwegian; *On Alert: Norwegian Assistance and Protection for Refugees; Protection of Children and Adolescents in Complex Emergencies,* with UNHCR and Save the Children Norway.

Global

PRIO

Founded in 1959, PRIO (the International Peace Research Institute, Oslo), is one of the oldest of its kind in the world. Its foundation and early influence were instrumental in projecting the idea of peace research.

PRIO disseminates information widely through courses, conferences, and seminars; visits by guest researchers; and school classes, and serves as a contact point between researchers in Norway and abroad. The Institute is responsible for a six-week summer course on Peace Research, held in cooperation with the International Summer School at the University of Oslo.

The work of PRIO is organized around four themes: the Conditions of War and Peace; Foreign and Security Policies; Ethics, Norms, and Identities; and Conflict Resolution and Peacebuilding. Together they express the institute's basic mission: to study the causes and consequences of peace and conflict through an inter-disciplinary approach.

The Conditions of War and Peace Program aims at understanding the origins of peace and violent conflict using both statistical methods and comparative case studies. The Program Foreign and Security Policies explores how political conflicts express themselves in state politics, how states are formed by internal conflicts, and how these states are developed within the framework of international organizations. The theme Ethics, Norms, and Identities is researched within the fields of ethics, political philosophy and theory, religious studies, social psychology, and social anthropology.

The program Conflict Resolution and Peacebuilding encompasses research, training and education, policy development, and the promotion of peace efforts around the world. It has a special Conflict Resolutions Training Program together with the Centre for Conflict Management.

PRIO is also active in the Norwegian Initiative on Small Arms Transfers (NISAT), a co-operative venture between PRIO and other Norwegian organizations that aims at reducing the flow of weaponry to conflict zones. PRIO is also engaged operationally in Colombia, the Balkans, and the Eastern Mediterranean region.

Fuglehauggata 11
0260 Oslo
Norway

Tel: +47 (22) 547 700
Fax: +47 (22) 547 701
info@prio.no
www.prio.no

Contact: Stein Tonnesson, Director

Number of staff: 60

Budget: > $1,000,000

Publications: Journal of Peace Research, bimonthly journal; *Security Dialogue,* quarterly journal; *Gender, Peace and Conflict,* 2001; *Environmental Conflict,* 2000; *The State of the World Atlas,* 1997.

Serbia, Kosovo

Educational Society for Malopolska

EDUCATION
ACTION

The Educational Society for Malopolska (MTO) works primarily with education. Their belief is that in order to create a responsible, democratic, and well functioning society, the youngest members of that society should be educated first. Among its activities, the workshop "Through Tolerance, to Democracy" is worth mentioning. It is aimed at increasing the knowledge about conflict prevention in Serbian schools. The organization also carries out training in conflict prevention and resolution methods for NGO leaders.

Limanowskiego 7
33-300 Nowy Sacz
Poland

Tel/fax: +48 (18) 444 2557
alader@pp.com.pl
www.mto.org.pl

Contact: Alicja Derkowska, Director
Number of staff: 2
Budget: > $25,000

Eastern and Central Europe, CIS countries

Karat Coalition

ACTION
ADVOCACY

The Karat Coalition is a regional coalition that works to ensure gender equality in the CEE/CIS countries. It monitors the implementation of international agreements and lobbies for the needs and concerns of women in the region. As far as women in armed conflicts are concerned, the organization has tried to establish a dialogue among representatives from different countries and ethnic groups involved in the conflicts of the Balkans. Furthermore, the Karat Coalition has tried to influence the international community on both governmental (especially UN and EU) and non-governmental level, proposing recommendations for resolving problems faced by women in armed conflict in the CEE region.

Franciszkanska 18/20
00-205 Warsaw
Poland

Tel/fax: +48 (22) 635 4791
karat@zigzag.pl
www.karat.org

Contact: Kinga Lohmann, Regional Co-ordinator
Budget: $25,000–$100,000
Publications: Women and Peace-Building: CEE Women's Recommendations for the Beijing +5 Review Process, 1999.

Poland, Central and Eastern Europe

EDUCATION
ACTION
ADVOCACY

"Never Again" Association

The "Never Again" Association (Stowarzyszenie 'Nigdy Wiêcej') was created in 1992 in response to the growing wave of racism and anti-Semitism in post-communist Poland. Its aims are to promote human rights and multicultural understanding and to contribute to the development of a democratic civil society in Poland. The 'Never Again' Association is particularly concerned with the problem of education against racial end ethnic prejudices among the young. They are targeted via music and football events. It is an independent, non-governmental organization.

P.O. Box 6
03-700 Warsaw 4
Poland

Tel: +48 (60) 364 7228
rafalpan@zigzag.pl
www.zigzag.pl/rafalpan

Contact: Marcin Kornak, Director

Budget: > $25,000

Publications: *'Nigdy Wiêcej' Magazine,* quarterly publication.

Mediterranean region, Africa

European Centre for Global Interdependence and Solidarity

The European Centre for Global Interdependence and Solidarity (formerly known as the North-South Centre) aims to provide a framework for European cooperation for the purpose of increasing public awareness of global interdependence issues and to promote policies of solidarity, in conformity with the aims and principles of the Council of Europe. The Centre is not involved in operational work, but encourages the policy dialogue on various issues, including conflict prevention in especially Africa and the Mediterranean countries, through conferences and publications.

Avenida da Liberdade 299-4
1250-142 Lisbon
Portugal
_____
Tel: +351 (21) 352 4954
Fax: +351 (21) 352 4966
nfo@nsc.coe.org
www.nscentre.org

Contact: Jos Lemmers, Executive Director

Number of staff: 5

Budget: $25,000–$100,000

Publications: The Interdependent, monthly newsletter; *Terraviva,* monthly newsletter; *Africa-Europe Civil Society Forum,* 2000; *The Protection of Human Rights in the Mediterranean,* 1999; *Intercultural Dialogue: Basis for Euro-Mediterranean Partnership,* 1999.

Global

Instituto de Estudos Estratégicos e Internacionais

RESEARCH

The Instituto de Estudios Estratégicos e Internacionais (IEEI) is an independent, non-profit organization dedicated to research and to the promotion of debate on international issues such as world peace (conflict, democratic transition, etc.), social development, human rights, integration and regional cooperation, foreign policy, defense, and security issues.

Its activities include not only the organization of various meetings, but also research projects and publications. Beyond programs in specific areas (Europe, Mediterranean, Latin America, sub-Saharan Africa, and Asia) IEEI organizes the annual Lisbon Conference, which generally focuses on European security and transatlantic relations.

Largo S. Sebastião 8
Paço do Lumiar
1600-762 Lisbon
Portugal
_____
Tel: +351 (21) 757 2701
Fax: +351 (21) 759 3983
ieei@ieei.pt
www.ieei.pt

Contact: Fernando Jorge Cardoso, Deputy Director

Number of staff: 20

Publications: "Lumiar Paper Series," research reports; *Estratégia,* bi-annual publication; *O Mundo em Português,* monthly publication.

Africa, Latin America

OIKOS

ACTION
ADVOCACY

OIKOS is a development aid organization working to increase international solidarity with the poor and restore peace in regions wracked by conflict. Its primary objective is to help local people with sustainable development through medium- and long-term projects, and to provide humanitarian aid to people affected by conflicts or natural disasters. OIKOS is also committed to advocacy and lobbying, both in Portugal and in the EU, through Eurostep. Development education is also an important objective, carried out through a network of schools and local associations in Portugal.

R. de Santiago 9
1100-493 Lisbon
Portugal

Tel: +351 (21) 882 3630
Fax: +351 (21) 882 3635
sec.geral@oikos.pt
www.oikos.pt

Contact: Luis de França, Chairman
Number of staff: 25
Budget: $500,000–$1,000,000

Romania

Civil Society Development Foundation

RESEARCH
EDUCATION
ACTION

The mission of the Civil Society Development Foundation (CSDF) is to strengthen democracy, support the development of civil organizations in Romania through promoting the active involvement of individuals in their communities, and to encourage non-profit organizations working on the improvement of the quality of life. One of its conflict resolution/prevention activities is a training program on mediation and negotiation. CSDF maintains a database on Romanian NGOs and publishes books and electronic newsletters.

Blvd Carol I, no. 78
Sector 2 Bucharest
Romania

Tel: +40 (1) 310 0177
Fax: +40 (1) 310 0180
office@fdsc.ro
www.fdsc.ro

Contact: Ancuta Vamesu, Executive Director
Number of staff: 3
Budget: < $25,000

Publications: Volunteer, weekly electronic publication; *Directory of Civil Society in Romania,* 2000.

Romania, Balkans

Ethnocultural Diversity Resource Center

EDUCATION
ACTION
ADVOCACY

The Ethnocultural Diversity Resource Center (EDRC) is one of the successor institutions of the Open Society Foundation Romania, Cluj Branch. Its mission is to contribute to the consolidation of democracy by improving Romania's inter-ethnic climate. EDRC programs consist of grant-giving activities; community-based interventions; policy research and documentation; and training of civil servants, police officers, and teachers working in multiethnic communities. EDRC is part of the Soros Open Network.

Tebei no.21
3400 Cluj-Napoca
Romania

Tel: +40 (64) 420 490
Fax: +40 (64) 420 470
info@edrc.osf.ro
www.edrc.ro

Contact: Levente Salat, Executive President
Number of staff: 3
Budget: $25,000–$100,000
Publications: Provinica, monthly newsletter; reports on Minorities Living in Romania; "Ethnocultural Diversity in Romania" series

Southeastern Europe

Foundation for Democratic Change

RESEARCH
EDUCATION
ACTION
ADVOCACY

The Foundation for Democratic Change (FDC) aims to develop a model of mediation and conflict resolution that is culturally appropriate for Romania, and to promote alternative dispute resolution. In 1999 the FDC decided to become actively involved in supporting the Stability Pact, and therefore to help constructing a Southeastern European Network of NGOs. Special activities in the field of conflict management include training programs in mediation, professional development of conflict resolution practitioners, a project supporting the Stability Pact, a third-party assistance program, and case studies.

1-3 Valter Maracineanu
P.O. Box 56-45
77750 Bucharest
Romania

Tel/fax: +40 (93) 314 3960
fdc@dnt.ro
www.fdc.ro

Contact: Anca Elisabeta Ciuca, President
Number of staff: 11
Budget: $100,000–$500,000

Romania

EDUCATION
ACTION
ADVOCACY

Liga Pro Europa

The programs of the Liga Pro Europa, implemented predominantly in Transylvania, are based on the promotion of the intercultural society, human rights and minority rights, civic education, and on preventing conflicts. For a short time after its establishment in December 1989, the League functioned as a forum for intellectual reflection on democracy and pluralism, but transformed into an activist group after inter-ethnic conflicts spread through the region. Activities involve observance of human and minority rights, analyses and studies, debates, workshops, education, and free consultations.

P.O. Box 1-154
4300 Tigru-Mures
Romania
_____
Tel: +40 (65) 214 076
Fax: +40 (65) 217 584
office@proeuro.netsoft.ro
www.proeuro.netsoft.ro

Contact: Szokoly Elek, Executive Director
Number of staff: 11
Publications: Newsletter of the Liga Pro Europa.

Southern and Eastern Europe

RESEARCH
EDUCATION
ACTION
ADVOCACY

Peace Action, Training and Research Institute of Romania

The Peace Action, Training and Research Institute of Romania (PATRIR) aims to link together scholars, grassroots activists, and critical thinkers active in the fields of peace work, peaceful conflict transformation, poverty, and human rights throughout Southern and Eastern Europe. The organization functions as a research institute, a training center, and a Romanian network. The core research programs, as well as the training programs, focus on peacebuilding and conflict transformation, non-violence and peace strategies, politics and governance, globalization, human rights and social and economic development, alternative defense, and security as well as ecological sustainability.

O.P.1-C.P. 331
Cluj-Napoca 3400
Romania
_____
Tel: +40 (64) 185 088
patrir@codec.ro
www.globalsolidarity.org

Contact: Kai Frithjof Brand-Jacobsen, Director

Romania

Resource Centre for Roma Communities Cluj-Napoca

EDUCATION
ACTION
ADVOCACY

The Resource Centre for Roma Communities Cluj-Napoca works on the improvement of living conditions of Roma communities in Romania. The Centre aims to support the efforts made by Roma communities, contribute to the fight against prejudice and discrimination, and to help improve the communication between Roma and non-Roma. The Centre are involved in the Roma Program initiated by the Soros Foundation. Activities organized through the Centre include providing information to the public, training and consultancy to Roma and non-Roma organizations, providing grants, and developing social policies and strategies for action for the Roma communities.

Tebei no.21
3400 Cluj-Napoca
Romania

Tel: +40 (64) 420 474
Fax: +40 (64) 420 470
fmoisa@romacenter.osf.ro
www.romacenter.ro

Contact: Florin Moisa, Executive President
Number of staff: 5
Budget: < $25,000
Publications: Educational Anti-racist Package for Intercultural Communication: Mediation and Conflict Negotiations, 2000.

Caucasus

Caucasus NGO Forum

ACTION

The Caucasus NGO Forum is a network in North and South Caucasus initiated by a group of participants in the Project of Confidence Building between Georgians and Abkhazians who signed the founding "Elbruss Declaration" in July 1998. The Forum rotates its main office once a year. In 1999–2000 it was based in Tbilisi, Georgia. Vladikavkaz, North Ossetia—Alania hosts the Forum office from summer of 2001. The principal objective of the Forum is the promotion of the culture of peace and peaceful resolution of conflicts through establishment of an effective communication network among the Forum participants and support for the capacity building of NGOs.

Kuybishev Street 15/1
Vladikavkaz 362000
North Ossetia–Alania
Russia

Tel: +7 (8672) 332 441/544 893/451 230
crc_vlad@ssc.ac.ru

Contact: Larisa Sotieva, Executive Secretary
Number of staff: 2
Budget: < $25,000

Russia

Caucasus Refugee Council

EDUCATION
ACTION

The main objective of the Caucasus Refugee Council, a charitable fund, is to provide help to refugees, IDPs, and other socially vulnerable people. The activities are primarily focused on conflict prevention/resolution, consultancy, development, and humanitarian assistance, mainly in the program of "Rendering help to Chechen IDPs residing in the Republic of Ingushetia." The organization actively co-operates with international organizations and is part of the Caucasus NGO Forum.

Kuybishev Street 15/1
Vladikavkaz 362000
North Ossetia—Alania
Russia

Tel: +7 (8672) 332 441/544 893/451 230
crc_vlad@ssc.ac.ru

Contact: Larisa Sotieva, Director
Number of staff: 8
Budget: $25,000-$100,000

Caucasus

Centre for Peacemaking and Community Development

ACTION
ADVOCACY

The Centre for Peacemaking and Community Development takes part in conflict-resolution initiatives in the Caucasus. The main objectives of the Centre's operations are nonviolent conflict management, human-rights monitoring, and the establishment of a reliable communication system between North Caucasian NGOs and international organizations, including email and personal exchanges. The Centre collects and disseminates analytical information about ethnopolitical developments in Chechnya. It also provides rehabilitation assistance to children who suffered during the Chechen war and emergency relief to refugees and displaced persons in the Caucasus.

P.O. Box 71
Moscow B 331
Russia

Tel: +7 (095) 240 0862/241 7770
peacecentre@online.ru

Contact: Chris Hunter, Director

CIS countries

Centre for the
Study and Management of Conflict

RESEARCH
EDUCATION
ACTION
ADVOCACY

The Centre for the Study and Management of Conflict was created in 1995 at the Institute of Ethnology and Anthropology, part of the Russian Academy of Sciences, which had been involved in conflict prevention and management since 1992. Its main activities are research on conflict issues and practical initiatives in the field of conflict prevention and management in the successor states of the USSR.

The Centre is running an independent project called Network for Ethnological Monitoring and Early Warning of Conflict (EAWARN; see separate entry) jointly with the Conflict Management Group at Harvard University. The Centre serves as a focal point and a clearinghouse for this network.

In addition to its newsletter, the Centre is updating and further developing a database covering a wide range of issues related to ethnic policies, conflict management, and early warning. The issues are analyzed from a socio-economic, political, demographic, and ethnological perspective.

Members of the Centre and its network have participated in high-profile practical initiatives on conflict resolution and conflict prevention such as the Russian-Chechen peace process and The Hague Initiative. The Centre collaborates with UNESCO, UNHCR, and other international organizations in their efforts to establish a reliable early-warning and early-response system in the post-Soviet political space. The Centre produces a wide range of theoretical publications as well as working papers on topics related to conflict management and early prevention strategies.

Many activities of other Centres and Departments within IEA are also of relevance to conflict prevention and management. Since 1989 the Centre on Interethnic Relations has published a long series of studies on ethnic movements and ethnopolitical situations. The Department of Ethnopsychology undertakes regular sociological surveys in conflict areas in Russia's republics and runs a project on Post-Soviet Ethnicity and Nationalism. The Department of Ethnic Ecology conducts studies on environment and conflict issues. Finally, the regional Departments of Central Asian, Caucasian and Siberian Studies carry out background research.

Leninsky Prospekt 32a
Moscow 117 334
Russia

Tel: +7 (095) 938 1747
Fax: +7 (095) 938 0600
tishkov@orc.ru
www.eawarn.ru

Contact: Valery Tishkov, Director

Number of staff: 11 at HQ, 32 in the field

Budget: $100,000–$500,000

Publications: Bimonthly newsletter; *Ethnicity, Nationalism and Conflict in and after the Soviet Union,* 1997.

Azerbaijan, Russia

Derbent Centre for
Social and Psychological Rehabilitation

The Derbent Centre for Social and Psychological Rehabilitation, a North-Caucasian NGO, works to prevent inter-ethnic, inter-confessional, and social conflict, to educate in the spirit of the culture of peace, and to provide psycho-social rehabilitation to conflict-affected populations such as forced migrants and ex-combatants. The Centre builds co-operative relations between town administrative authorities and population through the program "Derbent on the Way to the Culture of Peace."

Kobyakova Street 16   *Contact:* Tamara Osmanova, Director
Derbent 368600
Russia

Tel: +7 (87240) 25 640/272 84
Fax: +7 (8724) 25 640
nshirin@cityline.ru

North Caucasus

Don Women's Union

One of the most structured and active Russian network NGOs, the Don Women's Union's primary mandate includes conflict prevention/resolution, humanitarian assistance, promotion of human rights and democratic development, and psychological training and consultation.

The organization aims to promote women's role in public, political, economical, social, and cultural spheres. The main office of the regional organization in Rostov-on-the-Don, as well as the Union's divisions—Association of psychologists "ANIMA" and the Human Rights Committee devote attention to conflict prevention and resolution issues.

Among the most significant programs of the Union are three annually arranged sessions of the ongoing international conference "Women for life without war and violence!" The organization also serves as an information center for the conference. All programs are focused on the south of Russia and the North Caucasus. The program "Dagestan is a center of peace building" works toward consolidation of peace forces in Dagestan and the creation of a system aimed at the prevention of ethnic, social, and religious conflicts in the region.

The Don Women's Union comprises 25 organizations from the Rostov region's rural and urban areas. The Union is currently setting up a network of volunteer aids with a center in Novocherkassk.

Kalinin Street 88
Novocherkassk, Rostov Region 346404
Russia

Tel/fax: +7 (86 352) 31 936
donwomen@novoch.ru
home.novoch.ru/~donwomen

Contact: Valentina Cherevatenko, Director
Number of staff: 3
Budget: $25,000–$100,000

CIS countries

EAWARN

The mission of EAWARN (Network of Ethnic Monitoring and Early Warning) is to promote tolerance and accord, and to deliver independent expertise on minorities and conflict issues in Russia and other post-Soviet States.

In 1999, the EAWARN was legally constituted as a non-government organization embracing representatives of twelve states, with consultative status at the CIS Secretariat. In 2000, it established two regional branches—in the Volga and North Caucasus areas of Russia with a more regular mode of operation and with direct access to new federal district administrations. In previous years EAWARN operated in partnership with the Conflict Management Group (Cambridge, MA, USA) and with a grant award from the Carnegie Corporation (New York).

EAWARN has recently moved beyond applied research and training and is now involved in conflict prevention projects for mass media and government servants, and it is a beneficiary of the TACIS project on improvement of interethnic relations and promotion of tolerance in multi-ethnic Russia. The organization's annual budget and practically all activities are linked to conflict prevention/resolution. The main programs of the organization include production of a TV series, *Conflict and Accord in the North Caucasus,* which is devoted to conflict issues, and the further dissemination of this product through central and regional TV channels and educational institutions. EAWARN has hosted international conferences, "Chechnya from conflict to reconstruction" (Moscow, 2000), and "Restoration of culture in Chechnya" (2001). Every last week of October EAWARN conducts annual seminars on ethnic monitoring and early warning. EAWARN has published case study monographs of ethnological models based on 46 indicators and regularly publishes the bi-monthly *EAWARN Bulletin.*

Leninskii prospekt 32A
Moscow 117334
Russia

Tel: +7 (095) 938 0043/938 1815/938 1879
Fax: +7 (095) 938 0043
conrus@eawarn.tower.ras.ru
www.eawarn.ru

Contact: Valery A. Tishkov, Director

Number of staff: 5 at Moscow HQ; 42 EAWARN national/regional/local officers

Budget: $100,000–$500,000

Publications: EAWARN Bulletin, bi-monthly newsletter; Database on Ethnicity and Conflict in Post-Soviet States.

Russia

Forum

RESEARCH
EDUCATION
ACTION
ADVOCACY

The Forum, Center for Development and Peace Studies, is a network of practitioners and scholars working for democracy, peace, and development through action, training, dissemination, and empowerment. The Center supports effective policymaking and works together with groups, organizations, and individuals to lay the foundations for civil society. It also supports the reform of public administration and aims to develop creative and viable alternatives to violence. The network is present in all basic regions of Russia.

49-96, B. Nikitskaya, str.
Moscow 121069
Russia

Tel/fax: +7 (095) 332 1770
deos@cityline.ru
www.deos.narod.ru

Contact: Olga Vorkunova, Director

Publications: Forum—Stability Studies, journal, in Russian.

Russia

Human Rights Centre Memorial

RESEARCH
EDUCATION
ACTION
ADVOCACY

The mission of the Human Rights Centre Memorial (HRCM) is defending and monitoring human rights and legal counseling in the Russian Federation and other post-Soviet countries. Its main program, "Hot Spots," aims to monitor conflicts in the Northern Caucasus and the Moscow region. The partners in this program are Civic Assistance Committee, Common Action Round Table, Human Rights Watch, and Amnesty International. The organization maintain working relationships with other NGOs in the field, and in 2001 it opened a new web page, "The Caucasian Knot."

Malyi Karetnyi pereulok 12
Moscow 103051
Russia

Tel: +7 (095) 200 6506
Fax: +7 (095) 209 5779
memhrc@memo.ru
www.memo.ru

Contact: Oleg Orlov, President

Number of staff: 10

Budget: < $25,000

CIS countries

International Assembly
for Human Rights Protection

RESEARCH
ACTION
ADVOCACY

The International Assembly for Human Rights Protection works to co-ordinate human rights organizations in post-Soviet states with special focus on conflict prevention/resolution in the Kyrgyzstan and the Russian Federation. It supports existing organizations and establishes new organizations in the field of human rights, providing them with technical and legal consultation.

The Assembly organizes meetings, workshops, educational seminars, and aims to raise the awareness of governmental and non-governmental organizations, as well as the mass media toward human rights and liberties issues. The organization carries out expert assessments of legislative acts and projects.

Azovskaya Street 4
Moscow 117036
Russia

Tel/fax: +7 (095) 310 1683/126 1611
assambleya@mtu-net.ru

Contact: Mikhail Arutyunov, President
Number of staff: 30
Budget: < $25,000

Publications: The Russian Federation Passport System and Human Rights; The State, Ethnoi, Separatism and Human Rights.

North Caucasus

Mission Peace in North Caucasus

ACTION
ADVOCACY

The Mission Peace in North Caucasus is an NGO that works to mitigate the effects of war and prevent new sources of tension in North Caucasus. It participates in the liberation and rescue of hostages and missing persons and organizes seminars and workshops. The Mission has eleven regional branches in North Caucasus, Moscow, and St. Petersburg.

Ukrainskaya Street 56
Pyatigorsk 357538
Russia

Tel/fax: +7 (87933) 785 81
missionpeace@megalog.ru
www.chat.ru/~missionpeace

Contact: Alexander Lebed, Head
Number of staff: 6
Budget: $25,000–$100,000

Publications: Vestnik, newsletter; Database on missing persons returned by the Mission.

Russia

Nizhny Tagil
Human Rights Protection Center

ACTION
ADVOCACY

The primary focus of the Nizhny Tagil Human Rights Protection Center is human rights, advocacy, and democratic development. The organization is also involved in negotiations between parties to conflict who are in search of compromise. Further, it is implementing a project on the "Infringement of citizens' rights by local authorities." The organization has branch NGOs: Civil Democratic Center (Perm) and Public Organization for Protection of the Rights of Women (Tobolsk).

Lomonosov Street 6-20
Nizhny Tagil 622001
Russia

Tel/fax: +7 (3435) 416 802
mizol@uraltelecom.ru; hrntagil@glasnet.ru
www.glasnet.ru/~hrntagil

Contact: Mikhail Zolotukhin,
Director
Number of staff: 4
Budget: $25,000–$100,000
Publications: Human Rights Defender of the Ural, bulletin; *Worker's Word,* newspaper.

CIS countries

Research Center on Forced
Migration in the CIS and Baltic States

RESEARCH

The Research Center on Forced Migration in the CIS and Baltic States coordinates the work of the Independent Research Council on Migration in the CIS and Baltic States via discussions, research, and publications on migration problems in post-Soviet countries. Major activities include the monitoring and studying of migration processes in Central Asia and Kazakhstan, as well as the study of adaptation and integration of forced migrants in Russia, Georgia, and Armenia.

Nakhimovski Prospect 47
Moscow 117418
Russia

Tel: +7 (095) 124 2561
Fax: +7 (095) 718 9771
fmcenter@mail.ecfor.rssi.ru
www.demoscope.ru

Contact: Zhanna Zayonchkovskaya, Director

Russia

Union of the Committees of Soldiers' Mothers of Russia

ACTION
ADVOCACY

The Union of the Committees of Soldiers' Mothers of Russia (UCSMR) is widely known for its activities in protecting the human rights of conscripts, soldiers, and their parents, and for the promotion of democratic values. The Union has received four international awards for activities in the fields of peacebuilding and human rights. The Union coordinates over 80 legally registered member NGOs in Russia. The aim of the main program "The Second International Congress of Soldiers' Mothers" has been to stop the second Chechen war and to work out the peaceful and human rights oriented strategy for over 300 soldiers' mothers' NGOs in Russia and Europe.

Luchnikov Pereulok, Entrance 3
Moscow 101000
Russia

Contact: Valentina Melnikova, Responsible
Secretary

Tel: +7 (095) 928 2506
Fax: +7 (095) 206 8958

Slovakia, Central and Eastern Europe, Balkans

Partners for Democratic Change

EDUCATION
ACTION

The educational institution Partners for Democratic Change Slovakia (PDCS) is part of an international network of Partners educational centers in twelve countries of Central and Eastern Europe, the United States, (see separate entry for headquarters), and South America. PDCS provides educational, training, consultation, and facilitation services, mainly in Slovakia. Through its activities, PDCS encourages active participation of citizens in decisionmaking on issues of public interest and seeks out and supports co-operation among various groups of citizens and governmental and nonprofit organizations.

Sturova 13
811 02 Bratislava 1
Slovakia

Tel: +421 (2) 5263 3851
Fax: +421 (2) 5293 2215
pdcs@pdcs.sk
www.pdcs.sk

Contact: Dusan Ondrusek, Director

Number of staff: 15

Budget: $100,000–$500,000

Publications: Reader for Non-profit Organisations, in English, 2002; *Conflict Resolution: Handbook for Teachers and People Working with the Youth,* in Slovak.

Slovenia

Legal Information Center for NGOs

EDUCATION
ACTION
ADVOCACY

The Legal Information Center for NGOs (PIC—Pravno-informacijski center nevladinih organizacij) wants to strengthen the legal security and increase the independence and self-initiative of the civil society in the field of legal issues. PIC is focused on people in Slovenia including refugees, foreigners, marginalized groups, and asylum-seekers. PIC aims to establish a network of mediation services in Slovenia.

Metelkova 6
1000 Ljubljana
Slovenia
_____
Tel:+386 (1) 432 3358
Fax: +386 (1) 434 3181
pic@pic.si
www.pic.si

Contact: Tanja Benigar, Project Coordinator
Number of staff: 4
Budget: < $25,000

Slovenia, Southeastern Europe

Peace Institute

RESEARCH
EDUCATION
ACTION

The Peace Institute is a non-profit research organization dedicated to modern social and political studies and interdisciplinary research in the fields of sociology, anthropology, political science, and philosophy. The Institute combines academic research with practical education and strategic counseling services in various fields of politics and public activities. The Institute has many research centers on different issues. Among those, the Center for the Study of Violence and Conflict Resolution is responsible for conflict prevention/resolution programs, skill-building training, the development of a program for the resolution of disputes within Slovenia, and the promotion of mediating techniques and dialogues between various social, ethnic, and other minorities.

Metelkova 6
1000 Ljubljana
Slovenia
_____
Tel: +386 (1) 234 7720
Fax: +386 (1) 234 7722
info@mirovni-institut.si
www.mirovni-institut.si

Contact: Andreja Cufer, Project Coordinator
Number of staff: 3
Budget: < $25,000
Publications: Yugoslavia War, 1993.

Spain, Global

ACTION
ADVOCACY

Assembly of Cooperation for Peace

The Assembly of Cooperation for Peace (Asamblea de Cooperación Por la Paz) is a non-profit NGO that carries out activities in the fields of conflict prevention, development cooperation, and human rights. It supports democratic elements in the civil society, especially women's organizations, in their quest for peace and development. The organizations uses information as on of its prime tools to keep the national and international public opinion well informed and ready for action.

Santa Isabel nº 15, 2º dcha.
28012 Madrid
Spain

Tel: +34 91 468 15 76
Fax: +34 91 539 71 41
acpp@redestb.es
www.acpp.com

Global

RESEARCH
EDUCATION

Campus for Peace

Campus for Peace (C4P) is an initiative of the Open University of Catalonia and aims to bring knowledge about information technology to governmental and non-governmental organizations working in such fields as human rights, conflict prevention, and environment protection. This virtual city for peace wants to be an instrument for dialogue and co-operation by means of virtual communities (Intranets) and online training. Its website also provides a large database of participating organizations, including information on their activities and their resources.

Universitat Oberta de Catalunya
Diputació, 219
08011 Barcelona
Spain

Contact: Eduard Vinyamata, Rector's Commissioner

Tel: +34 (93) 253 2400
Fax: +34 (93) 453 9484
campuspeace@campusforpeace.org
www.campusforpeace.org

Global

Centro de Investigación para la Paz

RESEARCH
EDUCATION

Established in 1985, Centro de Investigación para la Paz (CIP) is a research and education institute that investigates international tendencies with special attention to armed conflicts and the actors involved and the effects of globalization on development. The Center also runs educational projects on peace and development, for example on children in armed conflicts. It publishes annual reports, including case studies, on militarization and other problems relating to war and peace. It also organizes seminars and courses for the media, NGOs, and teachers. CIP is part of the Asociación Española de Investigación para la Paz.

Duque de Sesto 40
28009 Madrid
Spain

Tel: +34 (91) 576 3299
Fax: +34 (91) 577 4726
maguirre@fuhem.es
www.fuhem.es

Contact: Mariano Aguirre, Director
*Publications: Construir la paz:
Una aproximación didáctica a la
reconstrucción posbelica,* 2000;
*Después la guerra: un manual para la
reconstrucción posbélica,* 1999; *Desarollo,
derechos humanos y conflictos,* 1998; *Ni
un solo niño en la guerra,* 1998.

Basque Country

Elkarri

EDUCATION
ACTION
ADVOCACY

Elkarri (Social Movement for Peace, Dialogue and Agreement) was established in 1992 as a grassroots movement. Their aim ever since has been to transform the conflict and violence situation in the Basque Country into a dialogue and agreement situation where the relationships and structures, which uphold the conflict and its violent manifestations, are changed on all levels of society. Their work, such as awareness-raising campaigns, is aimed at society, social agents, mass media, political parties, institutions, and all the actors in the conflict.

Arenal 5 of. 209
48005 Bilbao
Spain

Tel: +34 (94) 479 0316
Fax: +34 (94) 415 8003
bizkaia@elkarri.org
www.elkarri.org

Contac: Gorkia Espian, Coordinator
Number of staff: 16
Publications: Elkarri, monthly magazine;
*Meetings for Peace; Violence and Peace:
Tourism;* "Elkarrikasi," booklets on different
topics.

Basque Country, Northern Ireland,
Balkans, Latin America, South Africa

RESEARCH
EDUCATION
ACTION

Gernika Gogoratuz

Gernika Gogoratuz is a Peace Research and Conflict Transformation Center that contributes, through scientific reflection, to the creation of peace in the Basque Country, but also internationally. It works in the field of reconciliation through research and the organization of annual conferences on this subject. One of the Center's main objectives is to support and enrich the symbol of Gernika as town of peace and reconciliation. This city was bombed during the Spanish Civil War. The center, part of the worldwide Gernika Net, also teaches and trains people in conflict resolution.

Artekale, 1-1
48300 Gernika
Spain

Tel: +34 (94) 625 3558
Fax: + 34 (94) 625 6765
gernikag@gernikagogoratuz.org
www.gernikagogoratuz.org

Contact: Juan Gutierrez, Director
Number of staff: 5
Budget: $100,000–$500,000

Publications: Contruyende la paz:
Reconciliación sostenible en sociedades
divididas, 1998; Gernika y Alemania:
Historia de una reconciliación, 1998; Más
alla de la violencia: Procesos de resolución
de conflictos en Irlanda del Norte, 1998.

Basque Country

EDUCATION
ACTION
ADVOCACY

Gesture for Peace
in the Basque Country

Gesture for Peace in the Basque Country (Gesto por la Paz or Coordinadora Gesto por la Paz de Euskal Herria) was created in 1986 with the aim of expressing the Basque society's rejection of the use of violence as a political tool. Its main contribution lies in the area of the mobilization of society, characterized by silent demonstrations in many places in the Basque Country every time any death arising from the conflict occurs. At the beginning of the 1990s, it took on a high profile because it channeled the Basque people's call for nonviolence to a considerable extent.

P.O. Box 10.152
48080 Bilbao
Spain

Tel: +34 (94) 416 3929
Fax: +34 (94) 415 3285
gesto@kender.es
www.gesto.org

Contact: Isabel Urquijo
Number of staff: 2
Budget: $25,000–$100,000

Publications: Bake Hitzak (Words of Peace),
periodical.

Global

RESEARCH

Instituto de la Paz y los Conflictos

The Instituto de la Paz y los Conflictos, part of the University of Granada, engages in the inter-disciplinary analysis of the causes of violence and the necessary conditions for peace. It aims to promote a culture of peace, for which sustainable development and the satisfaction of basic human needs are prerequisites. Its primary goal is to create a team of researchers that concentrates on specific themes. The Institute co-operates with a small campus in Melilla in North Africa, where among other things the possibility of research is offered in bilingual and multicultural communities.

Rector López Argüeta s/n.   *Contact:* Francisco Muñoz
18071 Granada
Spain

Tel: +34 (958) 244 142
Fax: +34 (958) 248 974
eirene@goliat.ugr.es
www.ugr.es/~eirene

Global

RESEARCH
EDUCATION
ADVOCACY

Justicia i Pau

Justicia i Pau is a Barcelona based NGO whose activities are centered around the promotion of human rights and peace research. It focuses on topics such as poverty and opulence eradication, openness toward immigrants and the multicultural society, and the worldwide redistribution of those finances that came free after the reduction of armed forces. Lobbying, education, and publishing are the main activities of Justicia i Pau. The organization is part of the European Network against Arms Trade (ENAAT).

Rivadeneyra 6, 10a pl.   *Contact:* Joan Gomis, Director
08002 Barcelona   *Budget:* < $25,000
Spain

Tel: +34 (93) 317 6177
Fax: +34 (93) 412 5384
juspau@pangea.org
www.pangea.org/org/juspau

Global

 RESEARCH

Seminario de Investigación para la Paz

The research institute Seminario de Investigación para la Paz (SIP) wants to help constructing a peace culture by fostering multidisciplinary contributions to the many fields of peace research. SIP activities are carried out with the support of public and private bodies such as the autonomous regional government and the regional parliament of Aragón, and in cooperation with other institutions such as the University of Zaragoza. Research and education are mainly undertaken by professionals on a voluntary basis alongside their own commitments. SIP is a founding member of the AIPAZ network (Spanish Association for Peace Research).

Centro Pignatelli
P. de la Constitución, 6
50005 Zaragoza
Spain

Tel:+34 (97) 621 7217
Fax: +34 (97) 623 0113
sipp@seipaz.org
www.seipaz.org

Contact: Dr. Jesús María Alemany Briz, Director

Publications: La paz es un cultura, 2001; *Asia, escenario de los desequilibrios mundiales,* 2000.

Europa en la encrucijada, 1999; *Los conflictos armados: génesis, víctimas y terapias,* 1997.

Central Asia and the Caucasus

 RESEARCH

Central Asia and the Caucasus Information and Analytical Center

Central Asia and the Caucasus Information and Analytical Center (IAC) is a private center engaged in research on a range of topics related to social and political development in Central Asia and the Caucasus. One area of study is inter-ethnic conflict, including strategies for early prevention and settlement. IAC publishes the results of its research in its periodical, *Central Asia and the Caucasus,* which is accessible online. The organization has branches in the countries of Central Asia and the Caucasus, and in the United States, Russia, United Kingdom, Germany, Israel, Turkey, Iran, and Ukraine.

Rödhakegränd 21
974 54 Luleå
Sweden

Tel/fax: +46 (920) 620 16
murad@communique.se; murad@ca-c.org
www.ca-c.org

Contact: Murad Esenow, Director
Number of staff: 10
Budget: $100,000–$500,000
Publications: Central Asia and the Caucasus: Journal of Social and Political Studies, periodical in English and Russian versions.

Global

EDUCATION
ACTION

Christian Council of Sweden

The Christian Council of Sweden serves as a coordinating body for nearly all the churches of Sweden. It is committed to an ecumenical program for justice and peace, and has been involved in work for common and comprehensive security since the 1980s. The Council supports developments toward peace, democracy, and human rights in Sweden and internationally, with a special focus on education and training for Civilian Peace Service in the framework of Peace Team Forum (see separate entry), and the UN Decade on a Culture of Peace and Nonviolence for the Children of the World.

Starrbäcksgatan 11
172 74 Sundbyberg
Sweden

Tel: +46 (8) 453 6800
Fax: +46 (8) 453 6829
info@skr.org
www.skr.org

Contact: Margareta Ingelstam
Publications: Empowerment for Peace Service: A Curriculum for Education and Training for Violence Prevention, Nonviolent Conflict Transformation and Peacebuilding, 1997; *Learning to Work with Conflicts,* 1997; *Towards a Global Alliance of Peace Services,* 1994.

Colombia

RESEARCH
EDUCATION
ACTION
ADVOCACY

Civis

Civis is a Swedish NGO dedicated to supporting civil peacebuilding initiatives, especially in countries and areas with scarce resources. It supports the creation of resource centers for exchange of research, information, and experiences that favor democracy, conflict management, and peacebuilding. Civis considers the combination of research and theory necessary to reach these objectives. In its work it tries to constitute a link between the theoretical studies and practical reality. Main activities are project cooperation in Colombia, seminars, research, and lobbying in Sweden and Europe. Civis also keeps an open dialogue and exchange experiences with different organizations around the world.

Järntorget 3
413 04 Gothenburg
Sweden

Tel: +46 (31) 775 0944
Fax: +46 (31) 775 0941
civis@civis.nu
www.civis.nu

Contact: Barbara Lindell, Director
Number of staff: 6
Publications: Economía y Sociología de las Desigualdades: La Globalización y ONGD, 2001; *Marcos de legalidad y legitimidad de las ONG: Relaciones Estado-Sociedad; Tema: A quién pertenecen las ONGD?,* 2001; *El tercer sector: Entre el Estado y el mercado; Tema: ONG y tercer sector: Entre la acción pública y la acción privada,* 2001; *Local Conflict Resolution in a Colombian Context,* 1999.

Global

Department of Peace and Conflict Research at Uppsala University

RESEARCH
EDUCATION
ADVOCACY

The Department of Peace and Conflict Research at Uppsala University was established in 1971 to conduct research and offer courses in peace and conflict studies.

At present some 200 to 300 students are enrolled every academic year. The training offered includes an undergraduate and a Ph.D. program as well as advanced programs and special seminars. Several Ph.D. projects are in the field of conflict resolution, as well as interdisciplinary projects dealing with conflict resolution in West and Central Asia, Southern Africa, Southeast Asia, Cyprus, Northern Ireland, and Somalia.

There is one full professorship—the Dag Hammarskjöld Chair of Peace and Conflict Research. The first and present holder was appointed in 1985. There are now several associate and assistant professorships financed on a regular or temporary basis.

Research is basic to the Department. The teaching offered often reflects recent research or ongoing projects. This provides a link between undergraduate training and current research. Teaching is also provided by Ph.D. candidates and researchers engaged in research projects.

The research activities can be divided into two specific areas: first, the origins and dynamics of conflict, and second, conflict resolution and international security issues. In addition, there is considerable general work, including analysis of peace research itself as well as production of research-based educational materials.

The Department runs a Conflict Data Project. It continuously collects data on armed conflicts and has published statistics on major armed conflicts in the *SIPRI Yearbook* since 1988. As of 1993, a list of all armed conflicts appears in the *Journal of Peace Research*. This is a basic resource primarily for research. The Department also publishes a regular report of all armed conflicts.

Uppsala University
Box 514
751 20 Uppsala
Sweden

Tel: +46 (18) 471 0000
Fax: +46 (18) 695 102
info@pcr.uu.se
www.pcr.uu.se

Contact: Kjell-Åke Nordquist, Director

Number of staff: 33

Budget: > $1,000,000

Publications: States in Armed Conflict, annual publication; *Political Culture in Somalia: Tracing Paths to Peace and Conflict,* 2000; *A Century of Economic Sanctions: A Field Revisited,* 2000; *Gendering UN Peacekeeping: Mainstreaming a Gender Perspective in Multidimensional Peacekeeping Operations,* 1999; *Anarchy Within: The Security Dilemma between Ethnic Groups in Emerging Anarchy,* 1999.

Global

International Institute for Democracy and Electoral Assistance

RESEARCH
EDUCATION
ACTION
ADVOCACY

The International Institute for Democracy and Electoral Assistance (IDEA) is an inter-governmental organization that promotes and advances sustainable democracy and improves and consolidates electoral processes world-wide. Where other organizations stop after the first democratic election has been held, IDEA aims to help the country after the election to build a true, long-term, democratic state.

The Institute is helping the democratic process in countries such as Bosnia and Herzegovina, Burkina Faso, Burma, Guatemala, Indonesia, Mexico, Nicaragua, Nepal, Nigeria, and Romania. IDEA also prepares reports on the opportunities and constraints to democracy in numerous other countries. These reports are published in the "Capacity Building Series," which can be obtained from the Institute.

The formulation and promotion of acceptable standards and guidelines on electoral and democratic principles is an important activity of the Institute. It has produced "codes of conduct" for election managers and observers, and a similar code for political parties for campaigning during elections is on the way. IDEA has a special Conflict Management Program Team. It has published a handbook for would-be democracy builders in countries emerging from deep-rooted conflict and outlines options that negotiators can draw upon when trying to build democracy.

Strömsborg
103 34 Stockholm
Sweden

Tel: +46 (8) 698 3700
Fax: +46 (8) 202 422
info@idea.int
www.idea.int

Contact: David Bloomfield, Senior Executive, Democracy and Conflict Management Programme

Number of staff: 10

Budget: $500,000–$1,000,000

Publications: Democracy and Deep-Rooted Conflict: Options for Negotiators, 1998.

Former Yugoslavia, Eastern Europe, Middle East

RESEARCH
EDUCATION
ACTION
ADVOCACY

Kvinna till Kvinna Foundation

The purpose of the Kvinna till Kvinna Foundation (Woman to Woman Foundation) is to support long-term projects aimed at empowering women in general and providing assistance to traumatized women in particular. The organization supports projects designed to heal the wounds of war and ethnic conflict. It has been active in providing support for both the physical and psychological recovery of women who have been affected by war and conflict throughout the western Balkans and collaborates with women's organizations based in the region.

Tjärhovsgatan 9
116 21 Stockholm
Sweden

Tel: +46 (8) 702 9820
Fax: +46 (8) 643 2360
info@iktk.se
www.iktk.se

Contact: Kerstin Grebäck, Director

Number of staff: 16

Budget: $100,000–$500,000

Publications: Engendering the Peace Process: A Gender Approach to Dayton and Beyond, 2000.

Former Yugoslavia, CIS countries,
Middle East, South Africa, Central America

RESEARCH
EDUCATION
ADVOCACY

Olof Palme International Center

The Olof Palme International Center is a foundation for Swedish labor organizations working in the fields of peace, cooperation, and democracy. Member organizations include social democratic and cooperative organizations and trade unions. The Center's activities focus on international development cooperation and the formation of public opinion regarding international political and security issues. It supports partners all over the world and runs 200 aid projects, including several focused on conflict prevention. The Center organizes seminars, engages in public information activities, and networks with like-minded organizations.

Box 836
101 36 Stockholm
Sweden

Tel: +46 (8) 677 5770
Fax: +46 (8) 677 5771
info@palmecenter.se
www.palmecenter.se

Contact: Carl Tham, Secretary-General

Number of staff: 19

Budget: $500,000–$1,000,000

Publications: Newletter

Global

Life & Peace Institute

RESEARCH
EDUCATION
ACTION
ADVOCACY

The Life & Peace Institute (LPI) is an international ecumenical center for peace research and action. LPI's principal aim is to support the work of churches and others in the fields of peace, justice, and reconciliation. LPI cooperates with a wide variety of organizations such as academic institutions, church bodies, NGOs, and national and international governmental agencies.

LPI maintains a small staff in Uppsala, Sweden, but its primary activities take place in the field, where researchers, particularly from the South, carry out specifically commissioned projects. The three current research priorities are: the study of the role of religion in conflict and peace, human rights and economic justice, and nonviolent conflict transformation.

LPI also has a regional office in Nairobi, which coordinates the Institute's Horn of Africa program, including a network of trainers, field workers, and regional representatives in Somalia, Sudan, and elsewhere in the region.

Inspired by the grassroots peacebuilding initiatives developed in this program, LPI has in recent years increasingly focused on "action research." Research projects are developed in collaboration with partners in the field. The aims of these projects are to increase theoretical and conceptual understanding of conditions in specific conflict situations, in order to provide information to advocates, policymakers, and decisionmakers.

As part of its focus on religion and conflict and peace, LPI is engaged in research on the Holy Land, the former Yugoslavia, and fundamentalism as a threat to peace. The program on human rights and economic justice has examined, among other issues, the linkages between disarmament, debt, and development, and between militarization, economic penetration, and human rights in the Pacific region. In its focus on non-violent conflict transformation, study has been directed toward the role of third-party peace teams in conflict prevention and community-based peacebuilding work in Somalia and elsewhere.

Sysslomansgatan 7
P.O.Box 1520
751 45 Uppsala
Sweden

Tel: +46 (18) 169 500
Fax: +46 (18) 693 059
info@life-peace.org
www.life-peace.org

Contact: Claudette Werleigh, Conflict Transformation Programmes Director

Number of staff: 10 at HQ, 45 in the field

Budget: > $1,000,000

Publications: Horn of Africa Bulletin, a bi-monthly media review covering political, social, and humanitarian developments in the Horn of Africa; *New Routes,* a quarterly journal of peace research and action; *Building the Peace: Experiences of Collaborative Peacebuilding in Somalia 1993–1996,* 1998; *Linking Arms: Women and War in Post-Yugoslav States,* 1998.

Middle East, Global

Peace and Development Research Institute at Göteborg University

RESEARCH
EDUCATION
ACTION

Research at the Peace and Development Research Institute, Göteborg University, (PADRIGU) encompasses a broad range of topics: peace and conflict studies and the international system, conflict resolution, international political economy, and developmental studies. In 1997, the Peace College was established within the Institute by the Palestinian Fatah Youth and the Young Guards of the Israeli Labour party. The Peace College offers Israeli, Palestinian, and European students an MA in Peace and Development Studies with a special focus on the Israeli-Palestinian conflict. An additional goal is for young people, who may become the leadership of tomorrow, to have a better knowledge of each other and to develop personal contacts.

Brogatan 4
P.O. Box 700
405 30 Gothenburg
Sweden
_____
Tel: + 46 (31) 773 1000
Fax: +46 (31) 773 4910
info@padrigu.gu.se
www.padrigu.gu.se

Contact: Michael Schulz

Number of staff: 40

Publications: Peacekeeping through Democracy? Democracy and State Commitment to UN-Interventions 1991–99, 2000; *The New Regionalism and the Future of Security and Development,* 2000; *Social Capitals Impact on Boundaries, Ethnic Identity and Conflict Resolution: The Case of the Jerusalem Issue,* 2000.

Former Yugoslavia, Belarus, Moldova, Middle East

Peace Quest

EDUCATION

Peace Quest is youth-based organization working for peace, democracy, social justice, peaceful conflict resolution, sustainable and fair distribution of resources, and human rights. Peace Quest aims to deal with the causes of violence and to develop forms for conflict management, inspire young people to participate actively in society, work with other organizations outside Sweden in pursuit of its goals, and arrange activities such as seminars, training sessions, study tours, and voluntary work which unite theory and practice. For example, a current program works with youth in Israel/Palestine and Sweden to dispel commonly held stereotypes.

Lundagatan 56
117 27 Stockholm
Sweden
_____
Tel: +46 (8) 669 7520
Fax: +46 (8) 849 016
info@peacequest.se
www.peacequest.se

Contact: Joel Lindh, President

Number of staff: 1, others voluntary

Budget: $25,000–$100,000

Publications: Electronic newsletter; *Belarus: Europe's Last Dictatorship,* in Swedish, 2000.

Global

Peace Team Forum

Peace Team Forum is a network of Swedish-based non-governmental organizations. Its primary aims are to develop a capacity to prevent violent conflict, to manage conflict, to build peace in Sweden and the world, and to contribute more effectively to a non-military structure for European and international peace and security.

The Peace Team Forum is engaged in training and educational activities, policy consulting, research, data collection, and capacity-building for conflict-sensitive development and rehabilitation work.

The Peace Team Forum is currently involved in the following projects:

1. Training and Capacity-Building for a Culture of Peace and Nonviolence, which is being coordinated by the Christian Council of Sweden.
2. A Study of Swedish People's Organizations Involvement in Peacebuilding and Conflict Transformation, which examines what Swedish organizations are doing in terms of peacebuilding and conflict transformation in order to map the potential and develop strategies for future work. This project is coordinated by Forum Syd.
3. Peace and Conflict Impact Assessments in Development Cooperation of Swedish People's Organizations, which aims at mainstreaming a peace and conflict perspective into the planning, implementation, and follow-up of development and humanitarian projects at the headquarters' level of five Swedish NGO:s. This project is coordinated by Forum Syd, and is being undertaken in cooperation with U.S.-based Collaborative for Development Action;

Forum Syd
Contact: Anna Åkerlund
Box 15407
104 65 Stockholm
Sweden

Tel: +46 (8) 5063 7000
Fax: +46 (8) 5063 7099
anna.akerlund@forumsyd.se

Christian Council of Sweden
Contact: Margareta Ingelstam
Starrbäcksgatan 11
172 99 Sundbyberg
Sweden

Tel: +46 (8) 435 6800
margareta.ingelstam@skr.org

Global

SIPRI

SIPRI (The Stockholm International Peace Research Institute), best known for its authoritative yearbook on armaments, disarmament, and international security, is an independent international institute established more than 30 years ago to research problems of peace and conflict.

In its first two decades, SIPRI concentrated on questions of armaments, disarmament, and arms control; more recently it has broadened its agenda to include the study of conflicts, and international efforts to prevent, manage, and resolve armed conflicts.

SIPRI's research is conducted by an international staff recruited from various geographical regions and academic disciplines. Current research programs include Conflicts and Peace Enforcement; Conflict Prevention, Management, and Resolution; Arms Production and Military Expenditures; Arms Transfers; and Chemical and Biological Warfare.

SIPRI's Conflict and Peace Enforcement Project gathers data on major armed conflicts around the world, such as issues, combatants, costs in human terms, and outcomes. The project is also studying the reactions of external actors to violent conflict and the effectiveness of humanitarian military intervention. The Conflict Prevention, Management, and Resolution Project focuses on efforts to prevent disputes from turning violent, and activities to manage and resolve disputes that have resulted in armed conflict. It also collects and analyzes data on the many actors involved in inter- and intrastate conflict, and monitors multilateral peace missions.

These and other programs have resulted in the publication of over 150 books plus 32 editions of the yearbook, as well as the establishment of a range of open databases related to research activities. One such database provides information on multilateral peace operations. An annual public lecture is delivered in honor of the late Swedish Prime Minister Olof Palme. SIPRI cooperates with a wide range of international organizations and research institutions.

Signalistgatan 9
169 70 Solna
Sweden

Tel: +46 (8) 655 9700
Fax: +46 (8) 655 9733
esipri@sipri.se
www.sipri.se

Contact: Renata Dwan, Project leader conflict prevention, management and resolution

Number of staff: 4

Budget: > $1,000,000

Publications: SIPRI Yearbook; Preventing Violent Conflict: The Search for Political Will, Strategies and Effective Tools, 2000; Russia and Asia: The Emerging Security Agenda, 1999; Peace, Security and Conflict Prevention: SIPRI-UNESCO Handbook, 1998.

Central America, East Timor, Middle East

Swedish Fellowship of Reconciliation

RESEARCH
EDUCATION
ACTION
ADVOCACY

The Swedish Fellowship of Reconciliation (SweFOR) works to promote non-violent conflict resolution, mediation, human rights, democratic development, and capacity building. SweFOR is also engaged in data collecting and fact-finding activities, lobbying, peace monitoring, and educational and training activities, especially in the field of Small Arms in Central America. Its "Peace Service in Central America" program monitors developments in Chiapas State in southern Mexico, with the aim of protecting local inhabitants against violations of human rights. The organization has approximately three thousand individual members. SweFOR is working closely together with churches and church organizations and is co-ordinating the network "Parishes for Peace," with about 200 member parishes all over Sweden.

Ekumeniska Centret
172 99 Sundbyberg
Sweden

Tel: +46 (8) 453 6840
Fax: +46 (8) 453 6829
kristna.freds@krf.se
www.krf.se

Contact: Peter Brune, General Secretary
Number of staff: 4
Budget: $100,000–$500,000
Publications: Fredsnytt, quarterly newsletter.

Europe

Swedish Institute
of International Affairs

RESEARCH
ADVOCACY

The Swedish Institute of International Affairs is an independent organization providing information to the public and engaged in research on international political issues. It also provides a forum for debate on international issues and serves as a meeting place for academics, practitioners, journalists, and politicians. Its research activities encompass a range of topics, including numerous topics related to security, conflict resolution, and human rights. The Swedish Institute of International Affairs is active in organizing public lectures and conferences, and has an extensive publishing program.

Box 1253
Lilla Nygatan 23
111 82 Stockholm
Sweden

Tel: +46 (8) 696 0500
Fax: +46 (8) 201 049
info@ui.se
www.ui.se

Contact: Annika Björkdahl, Researcher
Number of staff: 40
Publications: Minorities in Turkey, 2001; *Future Challenges to Conflict Prevention: How Can the EU Contribute?* 2000; *Conflict Prevention: In Search of Political Will, Strategies and Effective Tools,* 2000; *A Failure of Conflict Prevention: The Yugoslavian Conflict,* 1998; *The Tajik Civil War: A Challenge to Russian Policy,* 1997.

Russia, Belarus, Europe

Swedish Peace and Arbitration Society

EDUCATION
ADVOCACY

The Swedish Peace and Arbitration Society (Svenska Freds) works to ease tensions in conflict areas, accelerate the pace of disarmament, promote economic conversion, and support the process of democratization. Much of its work focuses on European security policy and the international arms trade. It has also been involved in programs in Russia and Belarus supporting the development of democracy and civil society. In the former Yugoslavia, it is involved in the "Kvinna till Kvinna" (Woman to Woman) program to provide for the basic needs of women and children and encourage cooperation across ethnic lines.

Svartensgatan 6
P.O. Box 4134
102 63 Stockholm
Sweden

Tel: +46 (8) 702 1830
Fax: +46 (8) 702 1846
info@svenska-freds.se
www.svenska-freds.se

Contact: Christian Gustavsson, Project Manager

Number of staff: 7

Budget: $25,000–$100,000

Publications: EU Civilian Crisis Management Capability, 2001; *Secrecy Versus Transparency: Arms trade from the EU,* 1998; Country reports on arms trade.

Former Yugoslavia, Georgia, Burundi

Transnational Foundation for Peace and Future Research

RESEARCH
EDUCATION

The Transnational Foundation for Peace and Future Research (TFF) is dedicated to conflict mitigation, peace research and education, and studies of nonviolence. On the basis of nonpartisan field missions, TFF makes analyses and develops concrete peace proposals for use by politicians, media, humanitarian organizations, and others. Former Yugoslavia, Georgia, and Burundi have been among its geographical focuses. TFF also conducts courses and seminars, skills training, and lectures. Important research themes include conflict-mitigation theory, UN/NGO cooperation for peacebuilding, local peace plans, and reconciliation and reconstruction of war-torn countries.

Vegagatan 25
224 57 Lund
Sweden

Tel: +46 (46) 145 909
Fax: +46 (46) 144 512
tff@transnational.org
www.transnational.org
www.tff-store-and-donations.org

Contact: Jan Öberg, Director

Budget: $25,000–$100,000

Publications: TFF Pressinfo, electronic newsletter; *Peacebrowser,* electronic publication; *The UN Agenda for Peace Revisited,* 2000; *Violence Prevention, Postwar Reconstruction and Civil Society: Theory and Yugoslavia,* 1998; *Preventing Peace: Sixty Examples of Conflict Mismanagement in former Yugoslavia since 1991,* 1998.

Global

Center for Peacebuilding

RESEARCH
EDUCATION
ACTION
ADVOCACY

The Center for Peacebuilding (KOFF—Kompetenzzentrum Friedensförderung), founded with the support of the Federal Department of Foreign Affairs and Swiss NGOs, aims to support the constructive role of the country in settling international conflicts. It promotes synergies between the various actors involved and also wants to develop co-operation among NGOs in Switzerland and abroad. It contributes to the development of conceptual and operative coherence of Swiss peace policy by providing analyses, offering advice and training, and networking.

Gerechtigkeitsgasse 12
3000 Bern 8
Switzerland

Tel: +41 (31) 310 2727
Fax: +41 (31) 310 2728
koff@swisspeace.ch
www.swisspeace.ch

Contact: Tobias Hagmann,
Researcher/Programme Officer

Number of staff: 6

Budget: > $1,000,000

Publications: Newsletter; KOFF Peacebuilding Reports.

Global

Center for Security Studies and Conflict Research

RESEARCH
EDUCATION

The Center for Security Studies and Conflict Research is engaged in the study of Swiss security policy, international security, and conflict analysis. Its activities encompass research, teaching, and information services, including the International Relations and Security Network (ISN) and the Information Management System for Mine Action (IMSMA). The Center is engaged in basic research on the rise of violence and armed conflicts, the dynamics of conflicts, and the theory and practice of constructive conflict resolution. A current program is exploring the potential for enhanced cooperation among the nations of the Nile Basin.

ETH Zentrum/SEI
Seilergraben 45-49
8092 Zürich
Switzerland

Tel: +41 (1) 632 4025
Fax: +41 (1) 632 1941
postmaster@sipo.gess.ethz.ch
www.fsk.ethz.ch

Contact: Kurt Spillman, Director

Number of staff: 53

Publications: Bulletin on Swiss Security Policy, annual bulletin; "Studies of Contemporary History and Security Policy," series; "Zürich Contributions to Security Policy and Conflict Research," series of monographs.

Southeastern Europe, Sub-Saharan Africa

Centre for Applied Studies in International Negotiations

RESEARCH
EDUCATION

The Centre for Applied Studies in International Negotiations (CASIN) was established to assist leaders in government, business, and civil society, including negotiators and decisionmakers, in developing new approaches to governance, providing them with improved analytical, interactive, and problem solving skills, and broadening their comprehension of the global environment in which they operate. CASIN organizes professional training programs, issue and policy dialogues, informal negotiation sessions, and conflict management activities, and carries out studies and applied research under four thematic programs, including its "Programme on Governance," focused on negotiation, conflict management, and diplomacy.

7 bis avenue de la Paix
P.O. Box 1340
1211 Geneva 1
Switzerland

Tel: +41 (22) 730 8660
Fax: +41 (22) 730 8690
casinfo@casin.ch
www.casin.ch

Contact: Jean F. Freymond, Director

Number of staff: 4

Budget: $100,000–$500,000

Global

Centre for Humanitarian Dialogue

ACTION

The Centre for Humanitarian Dialogue (CHD), formerly known as the Henry Dunant Centre for Humanitarian Dialogue, is an international organization working for the promotion of humanitarian dialogue.

It facilitates dialogue among the principal humanitarian actors, stakeholders, and aid recipients to enhance understanding of acute and future humanitarian problems. Central to its mission are four guiding principles: partnership, transformation, common understanding, and dialogue.

CHD believes that more attention has to be paid to the priority accorded to the prevention of conflicts. To this end, its prime activity is to foster dialogue between parties in order to help reconcile their differences. The Centre focuses on building partnerships between humanitarian organizations and others who can improve the effectiveness of humanitarian action. In particular it reaches out to those whose motives are not humanitarian—who create or sustain conflict—in an effort to link them with those who are committed to the humanitarian movement. The Centre assembles international actors at conferences and meetings and helps to develop relationships.

The focus of recent meetings in which the CHD participated included support of the peace process in Colombia, the issue of development assistance and conflict, the small arms moratorium in West Africa, and strategies to promote stability in the Caucasus.

114 Rue de la Lausanne
1202 Geneva
Switzerland

Tel: +41 (22) 908 1130
Fax: +41 (22) 908 1140
info@hdcentre.org
www.hdcentre.org

Contact: Martin Griffiths, Director
Number of staff: 5

Caucasus, Central Asia, Balkans

CIMERA

RESEARCH
EDUCATION
ACTION

CIMERA works on the development of civil society in the Caucasus, Central Asia, and the Balkans, combining projects on governance with research activities. CIMERA focuses on media development by enhancing the professional skills of journalists. It also organizes cross-border cooperation among journalists, politicians, and policy experts. By encouraging collaboration among professionals in areas with conflict potential, and simultaneously confronting participants with a variety of viewpoints, CIMERA works to increase understanding of the fears and hopes of all parties, thereby to reduce the potential for conflict.

15 rue de l'Athénée
1205 Geneva
Switzerland

Tel: +41 (22) 347 2752
contact@cimera.org
www.cimera.org

Contact: Britta Korth, Project Director for Central Asia

Number of staff: 10

Budget: $100,000–$500,000

Publications: Media Insight Central Asia, monthly electronic newsletter; *Transcaucasus Media Bulletin,* output of the Caucasus Media Project (1997–2000); *Report on the Media Situation in Tajikistan,* 2000.

Africa

Femmes Africa Solidarité

EDUCATION
ACTION
ADVOCACY

Femmes Africa Solidarité (FAS) aims to foster, strengthen, and promote the leading role of women in the prevention, management and resolution of conflict in Africa. It acts as an advocate for African women, bringing their concerns to the attention of national, regional, and international bodies, and is engaged in tangible programs to enhance their capacities to assume and maintain their roles in leadership, decisionmaking, and especially, conflict resolution and peacebuilding. FAS focus primarily on conflict areas in Africa, including Liberia, Sierra Leone, Guinea, the Mano River Region, and the Great Lakes Region.

Case Postale 5037
1211 Geneva 11
Switzerland

Tel: +41 (22) 328 8050
Fax: +41 (22) 328 8052
info@fasngo.org
www.fasngo.org

Contact: Bineta Diop, Executive Director

Number of staff: 5 + 40 volunteers

Budget: $500,000–$1,000,000

Publications: FAS Advocacy News, bi-annual newsletter.

Europe, North America

RESEARCH
EDUCATION
ACTION

Geneva Centre for Security Policy

The Geneva Centre for Security Policy (GCSP) organizes and conducts advanced courses in international security policy for diplomats, military officers, and civil servants representing nations affiliated with the Partnership for Peace and/or NATO. Courses focus on the new challenges of the post-Cold War world, including issues such as new dimensions of security policy, crisis management, and conflict resolution. It also identifies relevant research topics, supports research on international security policy, organizes conferences and seminars on security issues, and facilitates contacts among experts in the field of security policy.

7 bis Avenue de la Paix
Case postale 1295
1211 Geneva 1
Switzerland

Tel: +41 (22) 906 1600
Fax: +41 (22) 906 1649
info@gcsp.ch
www.gcsp.ch

Contact: Fred Tanner, Deputy Director and Head of Academic Affairs
Number of staff: 36
Publications: Occasional papers.

Global

RESEARCH

Geneva International Peace Research Institute

The Geneva International Peace Research Institute (GIPRI) subscribes to the view that it is necessary to understand the nature of conflict in order to establish and maintain peace. Accordingly it is engaged in research and education on issues such as conflict prevention, resolution and mediation; human rights; democratic development; capacity building; peace; and disarmament. Each summer it organizes a French-language program addressing a range of peace and conflict resolution issues. GIPRI also publishes a variety of books and pamphlets on peace and security issues

7b, Avenue de la Paix
1202 Geneva
Switzerland

Tel: +41 (22) 730 8610
Fax: +41 (22) 730 8613
gipri@gcsp.ch

Global

International Committee
of the Red Cross

RESEARCH
EDUCATION
ACTION
ADVOCACY

The International Committee of the Red Cross (ICRC) is an impartial, neutral and independent organization whose exclusively humanitarian mission is to protect the lives and dignity of victims of war and internal violence and to provide them with assistance. It also endeavours to prevent suffering by promoting and strengthening international humanitarian law and universal humanitarian principles.

The ICRC's mandate has been conferred on it by the international community. This mandate has a two-fold legal base. On one hand, it is enshrined in the Geneva Conventions of 1949 and their Additional Protocols of 1977. Since their origin, the ICRC has taken initiative for and been closely associated to the development of these instruments of international humanitarian law. On the other hand, the ICRC's mandate is defined in its Statutes and the Statutes of the International Red Cross and Red Crescent Movement.

Considering its direct humanitarian involvement in conflict situations, the ICRC has indeed a great interest in all efforts that may be deployed to prevent conflict, promote a culture of peace, and prevent human suffering. Although its direct role in conflict prevention as such can only be limited, due to its primary concern to be present beside the victims and accepted by all the parties engaged in the conflict, the ICRC remains available to offer its good services to the parties to facilitate possible meetings between them for example. Moreover, the ICRC is firmly convinced that most of its activities, such as the promotion of the knowledge and respect of the international humanitarian law or the conduct of its operations of protection or assistance in the respect of its basic ethical principles, can contribute to a better resolution of an armed conflict or possibly to refraining nations from going to war.

19 Avenue de la Paix
1202 Geneva
Switzerland

Tel: +41 (22) 734 6001
Fax: +41 (22) 733 2057
webmaster.gva@icrc.org
www.icrc.org

Contact: Paul Grossrieder, Director General

Number of staff: 825 at HQ and 9,000 in the field (for all activities)

Budget: > $1,000,000 (for all activities)

Publications: The International Review of the Red Cross, quarterly magazine; *Strengthening Protection in War: a Search for Professional Standards,* 2001; *The ICRC and Civil-Military Relations in Armed Conflict,* 2001; *Cluster Bombs and Landmines in Kosovo: Explosive Remnants of War,* 2000; *War, Money and Survival, Forum Series,* 2000.

Global

International Federation of Red Cross and Red Crescent Societies

EDUCATION
ACTION

Conflict prevention is a priority implicit in the activities of the International Federation of Red Cross and Red Crescent Societies rather than a program area. Based on the Seven Fundamental Principles of the Red Cross and Red Crescent Movement and on explicit policy decisions by the governing bodies, the organization pursues the goal of preventing conflicts through the dissemination of knowledge, development of attitudes, providing fora for contacts, endeavouring to foster development, and providing assistance to direct and indirect victims of conflict. With 169 National Societies, the Federation is well placed to fulfil this mission.

P.O. Box 372
1211 Geneva 19
Switzerland

Tel: +41 (22) 730 4222
Fax: +41 (22) 733 0395
secretariat@ifrc.org
www.ifrc.org

Contact: Disaster Policy and Refugee Department

Number of staff: 270 at international HQ (for all activities)

Budget: > $1,000,000

Publications: Red Cross, Red Crescent, quarterly magazine; *Beyond Conflict: the International Federation of Red Cross and Red Crescent Societies, 1919–1994,* 1997; *Code of Conduct for the International Red Cross and Red Crescent Movement and Non-Governmental Organizations in Disaster Relief,* 1994.

Global

International Organisation for Migration

RESEARCH
EDUCATION
ACTION
ADVOCACY

The intergovernmental International Organisation for Migration (IOM) is the leading international organization for migration and is committed to the principle that humane and orderly migration benefits migrants and society. The department of the IOM responsible for conflict prevention is called the Emergency and Post-conflict Division. It has special expertise in the stabilization and development of communities and communal governance following the return of displaced persons in East Timor, but similar projects are being executed in Guatemala, Colombia, Kosovo, and Angola. Major activities herein are physical improvements and labor creation.

17 route des Morillons
P.O. Box 71
1218 Geneva 19
Switzerland

Tel: +41 (22) 717 9111
Fax: +41 (22) 798 6150
info@iom.int
www.iom.int

Contact: Hans-Petter Boe, Chief of Emergency and Post-conflict Division

Number of staff: 250

Budget: > $1,000,000

Publications: *International Migration,* bi-monthly journal; *IOM News,* quarterly newsletter.

Trafficking in Migrants, quarterly bulletin; *Migration and Health,* quarterly newsletter; *World Migration Report 2001.*

Global

ACTION

International Peace Bureau

The International Peace Bureau (IPB) claims to be the world's most comprehensive international peace federation. It is not strictly an organization for pacifists but also includes women's, youth, workers', religious, political, and professional bodies. The Bureau has 210 member organizations, both international (50 countries) and national. IBP supports peace and disarmament initiatives taken by governments and citizens. It acts as publishing house, a conference organizer, and gives logistic assistance to visiting NGOs in Geneva. Current priorities include nuclear weapons, conflict prevention, human rights, international humanitarian law, women, and peace as well as peace education.

41, rue de Zurich
1201 Geneva
Switzerland

Tel: +41 (22) 731 6429
Fax: +41 (22) 738 9419
mailbox@ipb.org
www.ipb.org

Contact: Colin Archer, Secretary General

Publications: IPB News, annual newsletter.

Georgia, Yugoslavia

International Research and Consulting Centre

RESEARCH
EDUCATION

The International Research and Consulting Centre of the Institute of Federalism at the University of Fribourg (IRCC) is an interdisciplinary center addressing issues of governance, human rights, and minority protection. The IRCC is currently working, in collaboration with the Swiss Agency for Development and Co-operation, on research projects covering the "Rule of Law and Decentralisation in a Multicultural Context" with the aim of establishing more just and equitable institutions of global governance. The Centre consults on issues such as federalism and co-operative government, decentralization, etc., and is involved in teaching activities, and networks with organizations worldwide on issues of federalism and decentralization.

Route d'Englisberg 7
1763 Granges-Paccot
Switzerland

Tel: +41 (26) 300 8160
Fax: +41 (26) 300 9684
federalism@unifr.ch
www.federalism.ch

Contact: Lidija Basta Fleiner

Number of staff: 5

Publications: Bulletin de législation, bi-montly newsletter in French and German.

Balkans

EDUCATION

Media Action International

Media Action International aims to promote more effective use of the media to help local populations in crisis situations and strengthen the role of information in humanitarian and development initiatives. It engages in a variety of activities to promote innovative exploitation of the media under challenging circumstances. For example, "Operation Lifeline Media" aims to promote more effective communication between the international aid community and crisis-affected populations. Its REACH project broadcasts educational radio programs in Afghanistan. Its *Qeshu Rini Qeshu* (Smile, Youth, Smile) is a radio program aimed at Kosovo Albanian youth.

Villa Grand Monfleury, 49
Versoix
1290 Geneva
Switzerland

Tel: +41 (22) 950 0750
Fax: +41 (22) 950 0752
info@mediaaction.org
www.mediaaction.org

Contact: Loretta Hieber, Director

Number of staff: 15

Budget: $100,000–$500,000

Publications: Information and Conflict: The Role of the Media, 2000; *Kosovo: the Creative Dimension of Humanitarian Aid,* 1999; *To Intervene or Not to Intervene, That is the Question,* 1998.

Global

Swiss Peace Foundation

The Swiss Peace Foundation (SPF) is an independent action-oriented peace research institute. Since its founding in 1988, it has developed into an internationally renowned institute for peace and conflict research.

The SPF program deals with prevention and transformation of armed conflicts. In view of current widespread wars and violent conflicts in the world, the Foundation focuses on establishing and further developing viable structures to resolve conflicts peacefully. The goal of its scientific and practical activities is a general and lasting reduction in organized violence between and within states.

Its basic research consists of various projects which examine causes of wars and violent conflicts and develop strategies for civilian management of conflicts either to prevent outbreak of violent conflicts or at least to reduce their impact on affected societies. An area of particular concern for SPF has always been the study of potential resource conflicts.

In the sphere of prevention, an important theme is the early warning of crises (early recognition of tensions and identification of windows of opportunities). The FAST project currently prepares periodic risk analyses in Central and South Asia (Tajikistan, Uzbekistan, Kyrgyzstan, Kazakhstan, Afghanistan, Pakistan, India) and Southern Africa (Angola, Mozambique, Madagascar, and South Africa). These aim to recognize potential crisis situations early enough and to provide decisionmakers with information and advice that has solid scientific backing.

SPF also sees itself as a forum permitting ongoing discussion within public and administrative, scientific, and political circles on questions of peace and security policy. The Foundation joins in shaping Switzerland's foreign and security policy in research, communications, and conception. With its analyses and reports as well as its regular publications and events, SPF contributes to developing informed political opinion on questions relating to peace and security policy. For information on the Center for Peacebuilding (KOFF), see separate entry.

Sonnenbergstrasse 17/19
CH - 3000
3000 Bern 7
Switzerland

Tel: +41 (31) 330 1212
Fax: +41 (31) 330 1213
info@swisspeace.ch
www.swisspeace.ch

Contact: Laurent Goetschel, Executive Director
Number of staff: 20
Budget: > $1,000,000
Publications: SPF Working Papers; FAST Country Risk Papers.

Global

Swiss Platform for
Conflict Prevention and Transformation

RESEARCH

The Swiss Platform for Conflict Prevention and Transformation is an open and informal network of more than 20 organizations that are based in Switzerland and involved in conflict prevention and resolution in the international arena. The Swiss Platform was launched in 1997 by the Centre for Applied Studies in International Negotiations (CASIN) and is affiliated with the European Platform for Conflict Prevention and Transformation. The primary objective of the Swiss Platform is to facilitate the exchange of information and experiences among interested organizations, and to stimulate cooperation and synergy among them.

c/o CASIN
7 bis avenue de la Paix
P.O. Box 1340
1211 Geneva
Switzerland

Tel: +41 (22) 730 8660
Fax: +41 (22) 730 8690
casinfo@casin.ch
www.casin.ch

Contact: Jean F. Freymond, Director
Budget: $100,000–$500,000

Balkans, Guatemala, Mozambique, Rwanda, Horn of Africa

War-torn Societies
Project International

RESEARCH
ACTION

Founded as a Swiss non-governmental organization in May 2000, the War-torn Societies Project International is the institutional successor body of the War-torn Societies Project (WSP). WSP was an experimental project of the United Nations (1994–1999) that sought to better understand the challenges of post-conflict reconstruction with a view to formulating recommendations to improve methods of international assistance. WSP used a methodology of research-based and consensus-oriented dialogue to facilitate the active involvement of local, national and international actors in peace-building processes. WSP International has a mandate to continue and further the work of WSP, including potential and ongoing conflict situations.

International Environment House
11-13 Chemin des Anémones
1219 Châtelaine, Geneva
Switzerland

Tel: +41 (22) 917 8593
Fax: +41 (22) 917 8039
info@wsp-international.org
www.wsp-international.org

Contact: Matthias Stiefel, Executive Director
Number of staff: 11 + 23 in the field
Budget: > $1,000,000
Publications: Rebuilding Somalia: Issues and Possibilities for Puntland, 2001; *From Conflict to Dialogue: The WSP Guatemala Way,* 1999; *War-torn Societies Project: The First Four Years,* 1999, *War-torn Societies Project in Practice,* 1999; *Rebuilding after War: Lessons from the War-torn Societies Project,* 1999.

Global

Women's International
League for Peace and Freedom

ACTION

The Women's International League for Peace and Freedom (WILPF) aims to educate, inform and mobilize women for action. It organizes meetings, seminars, and conferences to study issues and seek solutions to social, economic and political problems. It organizes campaigns to promote disarmament measures, to stop 'adventurism' and interventions. WILPF sends missions to countries in conflict and reports to its members and to the United Nations. It offers two one-year internships to young women to learn about the role of the United Nations in the fields of disarmament, development and human rights. International Secretariat

1, Rue de Varembe
C.P. 28
1211 Geneva 20
Switzerland

Tel: +41 (22) 733 6175
Fax: +41 (22) 740 1063
wilpf@iprolink.ch
www.wilpf.int.ch

Contact: Lohes Rajeswaran

Global

World Council of Churches

ACTION

The World Council of Churches (WCC) is an international fellowship of Christian churches, built upon encounter, dialogue and collaboration. It has a special Unit for Justice, Peace and Creation, which includes in its mandate the Program to Overcome Violence. The Program seeks to engage with churches, religious communities and others in a "journey of transformation," inspiring them to do more to build a culture of peace (with justice) at different levels of society and encouraging the churches to play a leading role in using non-violent means, such as prevention, mediation, intervention, and education.

P.O. Box 2100
1211 Geneva 2
Switzerland

Tel: +41 (22) 791 6111
Fax: +41 (22) 791 0361
info@wcc-coe.org
www.wcc-coe.org

Contact: Salpy Eskidjian
Publications: WCC News, on-line quarterly publication; *Echoes, on justice, peace and creation news,* on-line bi-annually publication; *Overcoming Violence,* on-line quarterly publication; *Uprooted People,* on-line quarterly publication.

Tajikistan, Central Asia

Asia Plus

RESEARCH

Asia Plus is an information agency that informs Tajik society and the international community about issues such as politics, economics, defense, law-making and others relevant to Tajikistan. The agency was established in 1995 and has since then been involved in data collecting, fact-finding, publishing and research activities. It has provided information support for the peace process in Tajikistan, with information being collected and disseminated at grassroots level.

35/1 Bokhtar Street, 8th floor
Dushanbe 734002
Tajikistan

Tel: +992 (372) 217 863/217 220/218 490
Fax: +992 (372) 510 136
info@asiaplus.tajik.net
www.asiaplus.tajnet.com

Contact: Umed Babakhanov
Number of staff: 25
Budget: $25,000–$100,000
Publications: Newsletter.

Tajikistan, Afghanistan, Central Asia

Center for Conflict Studies and Regional Research

RESEARCH
ACTION

The Center for Conflict Studies and Regional Research (CCSRR) is an NGO that deals with conflict prevention and resolution, as well as research in history, politics, conflicts, and related subjects. The CCSRR is currently implementing a program entitled "We are the Tajik citizens," together with the Center for Social Technologies (Tajikistan), which involves teaching students in conflict resolution skills, with the ultimate aim to contribute to sustainable peace in Tajikistan. Previously the Center has conducted research on "Tajik-Afghan borders and security issues in Central Asia" and organized a conference on "Afghan conflict and security issues in Tajikistan."

appt. 27, 35 Husseinzoda Street
Dushanbe 734025
Tajikistan
_____
Tel: +992 (372) 234 390
iskandar@ac.tajik.net

Contact: Kosimsho Iskandarov, Director
Number of staff: 25
Budget: < $25,000

Tajikistan

Center for Social Technologies

ACTION
ADVOCACY

The Center for Social Technologies (CST) is a local NGO that aims to develop and introduce progressive social technologies, including those on community-based conflict prevention and resolution. Currently the CST develops programs on education in conflict prevention for local communities in the border regions of Tajikistan. In partnership with the Center for Conflict Studies and Regional Research (Tajikistan) the CST is implementing the 'We are the Tajik citizens' program, which aims to develop conflict resolution skills among students from the cities of Dushanbe and Garm, by means of organizing meetings and producing radio programs.

appt.36, 17/2 Navoii Street
Dushanbe 734026
Tajikistan
_____
Tel: +992 (372) 373 057/231 497
cst@ac.tajik.net

Contact: Zilya Shomakhmadova, Director
Number of staff: 4
Budget: < $25,000

Tajikistan, Kyrgyzstan

Center for Youth Initiatives, Ittifok

Center for Youth Initiatives, Ittifok, is an NGO in Northern Tajikistan which aims to contribute to the development of civil society in the Republic of Tajikistan by means of efficient employment of youth potential through various educational and social programs.

Currently the Center's work focuses on two programs: "Conflict Prevention between Tajikistan and Kyrgyzstan" and "Reconciliation and Community Development." The "Conflict Prevention between Tajikistan and Kyrgyzstan" program aims to prevent interethnic conflicts in the border communities of Tajikistan and Kyrgyzstan through consensus- and trust-building activities, joint educational, cultural and social programs, development of a network of local mediators, and increasing public awareness on non-violent conflict resolution. The program targets the grassroots population in five border regions of these two countries. The program is implemented in partnership with the Foundation for Tolerance International (Kyrgyzstan). The "Reconciliation and Community Development" program is implemented in partnership with a number of Tajik NGOs and aims at promoting reconciliation in the Tajik society and providing assistance to communities in addressing various issues. The activities include problem identification, conflict resolution, and development of social partnership, family health and family law. The program is implemented in ten Tajik communities.

appt.35, 53 Lenin Street
Khujand 735700
Tajikistan

Tel/fax: +992 (3422) 67 318
davron@cyi.khj.tajik.net

Contact: Yusuf Kurbonhodjaev, Director

Number of staff: 15

Budget: $25,000–$100,000

Publications: Modules of the seminars for the community leaders and activists (including: Conflict introduction, Monitoring and Conflict Assessment, Process of Consensus building, Mediation, Negotiation), 2000; *ABC of Civil Education,* 1999; *Politics for People,* 1998.

Afghanistan, Tajikistan

EDUCATION
ACTION
ADVOCACY

Fidokor

Fidokor is a local NGO that provides social, legal and humanitarian assistance to vulnerable groups, and assists local NGOs in addressing social problems through supplying them with information. Fidokor also provides psychological and social rehabilitation to returnees and other victims of the civil war, as well as addresses the issues of poverty, thus contributing to the development of Peace Process in Tajikistan.

Currently the organization is involved in three programs: "Conflict Resolution and Tolerance Education," which aims to mitigate tension in the areas of mass return of refugees after the civil war; "The Coalition for Tolerance and Peace," which unites four local NGOs in their work on conflict resolution; and "Children are Our Future," which provides psychological and social rehabilitation to the returnees' children. In the framework of these programs Fidokor facilitates training seminars, produces publications and TV programs, organizes sports, social, and cultural events. All the three programs are implemented in the Khatlon region, the most volatile region in Tajikistan, and due to that the Fidokor head office has been recently moved to the city of Kurgan-Tube in the Khatlon region. Fidokor is working in partnership with field offices of international organizations, such as Counterpart Consortium, UNHCR, Mercy Corps International, as well as with a number of local NGOs.Previously Fidokor has also been active in the field of providing humanitarian assistance and rebuilding schools and hospitals after the civil war.

6 Lokhuti Street
Kurgan-Tube 735140
Tajikistan

Tel: +992 (3222) 24 191/25 664
shamsoro@vakhsh.tajik.net

Contact: Dilbar Halilova, Director

Number of staff: 12

Budget: $25,000–$100,000

Publications: Conflict Resolution and Tolerance Education, teachers' manual, 2000; *Conflict Resolution and Tolerance Education: Collection of Children's Essays,* 2000; monthly newspaper, in Tajik.

Tajikistan

Foundation to Support Civil Initiatives

EDUCATION
ACTION
ADVOCACY

The Foundation to Support Civil Initiatives (FSCI) is a local NGO established in June 1995. It provides assistance in the processes of democratic change and in the establishment of strong civil society in Tajikistan through the development of NGOs. Since 1996, the FSCI has been a member of the Public Council for National Peace and Accord, the process which is led by the Tajik President, Emomali Rakhmonov. In the framework of the program, in 1999–2000 FSCI conducted 36 training seminars on conflict prevention for the local population in the volatile southern regions of Tajikistan.

office 19, 73-A Shotemura Street
Dushanbe 734002
Tajikistan

Tel/fax: +992 (372) 215 857
root@tfsci.tajik.net; muazama@yahoo.com

Contact: Muazama Burkhanova,
Director
Number of Staff: 6
Budget: < $25,000
Publications: Civil Society,
information bulletin; *Conflict Resolution at Grassroots Level in Tajikistan,* training module.

Tajikistan

Manizha Information and Education Centre

EDUCATION
ACTION

The Manizha Information and Education Centre was founded in March 1999. It provides training for those involved in conflict management and prevention activities in Tajikistan. Manizha's work is currently focused on conflict management at workplaces and within families as well as prevention of interethnic conflicts. The latter involves peace and confidence building activities among different ethnic groups in Tajikistan. The program was implemented in partnership with local NGOs as well as with the Academy for Educational Development and CARE International. Manizha is a member of the Central Asian Network on Conflict Management and the Central Asian Network of Independent Media.

Appt. 5, 19/4 Nazarshoev Street
Dushanbe 734012
Tajikistan

Tel: +992 (372) 213 711/217 558
Fax: +992 (372) 217 559
iec_manizha@tojikiston.com

Contact: Alisher Rahmonberdiev,
Director
Number of staff: 16
Budget: < $25,000
Publications: Sozvezdie
(Constellation), newspaper.

Tajikistan

National Association
of Political Scientists of Tajikistan

EDUCATION
ACTION

The mission of the National Association of Political Scientists of Tajikistan (NAPST) is to facilitate the development of political science, to enhance the political culture of society, and to develop the international links of Tajik researchers in the field. It was founded in July 1994 and since then has actively researched and publicized the current situation in Tajikistan. NAPST holds a political discussion club "The process of peace-building in Tajikistan: problems and ways to resolve them," which gathers together politicians, the military, economists, and conflict researchers with the aim of discussing the post-conflict revival of Tajikistan and ways of addressing current problems.

7 Gorky Street
Dushanbe 734025
Tajikistan

Tel: +992 (372) 213 396
Fax: +992 (372) 347 035
abdu@napst.td.silk.org

Contact: Abdugani Mamadazimov

Budget: < $25,000

Publications: Parties and Movements of Tajikistan, bulletin; materials from the conferences.

Tajikistan, Afghanistan, Central Asia

Sharq Research and Analysis Center

RESEARCH
ACTION

The Sharq Research and Analysis Center was established with the mission of supporting democratic reforms, conducting basic and applied research, and establishing contacts with other researchers. Sharq has conducted research on "Conflict and Society in Tajikistan" (1996–99), "Political Parties and Elite in Tajikistan" (1996–99), "Political Islam" (1997–2000), "Migration in Tajikistan" (1997–2000). The Center provides information for the EAWARN and FAST conflict monitoring projects, run respectively by the Institute of Ethnology and Anthropology of the Russian Academy of Sciences (Russia) and Swiss Peace Foundation (Switzerland). In 1997–2000, Sharq staff worked as independent experts in the Inter-Tajik Dialogue in the framework of the Dartmouth Conference.

Appt. 9, 7 Bofand Street
Dushanbe 734042
Tajikistan

Tel: +992 (372) 218 370/218 995
Fax: +992 (372) 218 995
sharq@tajik.net

Contact: Muzaffar Olimov, Director

Number of staff: 15

Budget: < $25,000

Publications: Tajikistan on the Threshold of Changes, 1999; *Inter-Tajik Conflict: Pathway to Peace,* 1998.

Tajikistan

Silk Road—Road of Consolidation

RESEARCH

The National Foundation, "Silk Road—Road of Consolidation" was set up in August 1998 with the aim of consolidating the unity of the Tajiks and of facilitating the development of the newly independent state. The Foundation strives to revive, develop and enrich the national, historical, and cultural heritage of the Tajiks, and to reveal the importance of the Silk Road for people of the world. In July 1999 and 2000 the Foundation together with the Presidential Cabinet organized the first and second "Caravans of Peace and Consolidation."

7 Gorky Street
Dushanbe 734025
Tajikistan

Tel: +992 (372) 213 396
Fax: +992 (372) 344 973
silk@road.td.silk.org

Contact: Naimjon Yasinov, Director

Number of staff: 9

Publications: *Road of Consolidation,*
magazine.

Tajikistan

Sudmand

EDUCATION

ACTION

Sudmand is a non-governmental organization with a mission to contribute to the processes of societal transformations through educational programs. Sudmand is currently working on the 'Ties of friendship' project which aims to decrease tension in the relations of conflicting regions of Tajikistan (Kuliab and Pamir provinces). The project targets youth and involves such types of activity as seminars on conflict resolution and tolerance education, meetings with military servants, and a festival of youth friendship. Within this project Sudmand co-operates with the government of Tajikistan (Youth Committee), USAID, and Counterpart Consortium.

16 S.Safarov Street
Kuliab 735360
Tajikistan

Tel: +992 (3322) 34 988/22 692
Fax: +992 (3322) 34 988
sudmand@kulob.tajik.net

Contact: Dodarbek Saidaliev, Director

Number of staff: 9

Budget: < $25,000

Publications: Bo Rohi Vakhdat (Along the Road of Friendship), newsletter.

Tajikistan, Central Asia

Tajikistan Center
for Citizenship Education

RESEARCH
EDUCATION
ACTION

The mission of the Tajikistan Center for Citizenship Education (TCCE) is to initiate and develop a wide system of citizenship education in Tajikistan and to ensure a more active participation of Tajik citizens in the most acute political, social, and economical problems. Since its establishment, the TCCE has organized regular "Civic Forums" aiming at promoting civic education. Following the Tajikistan peace process TCCE embarked on the issues of post-conflict settlement and development as well as peace education. The Center co-authored the issue of Accord Bulletin on "Politics of Compromise: The Tajikistan Peace Process," together with Conciliation Resources (UK).

Room 2, 7 Gorki Street
Dushanbe 734025
Tajikistan

Tel/fax: +992 (372) 217 033
gula@nosirova.tajik.net; abdullaevk@irex-tj.org

Contact: Gulchehra Nosirova,
Director

Number of staff: 2

Budget: < $25,000

Publications: Regionalism and Unity of Nation, 1998.

Tajikistan, Central Asia

Traditions and Modernity

RESEARCH
EDUCATION

Traditions and Modernity (T&M) is a women's NGO whose mission is to help create a gender balance in all spheres of Tajik society through implementation of research and educational projects. In 2001 T&M launched a program entitled "Women, Conflict, Politics: Central Asia," in co-operation with UK-based NGO Women in Societies in Transition. The program aims to explore the relationship between women, conflict, and politics in Central Asia and to identify and implement appropriate strategies to improve women's rights and interests in conflict situations. T&M is part of the Women in International Affairs in Asia (WIIAA) and Vital Voices Global Partnership (VVGP) networks.

appt. 18, 84/5 Popov Street
Dushanbe 734013
Tajikistan

Tel: +992 (372) 218 959/244 915
akuvatova@yahoo.com; mnkhegai@yahoo.com

Contact: Margarita Khegai,
Director

Number of staff: 3

Publications: Women's and Gender Studies in Tajikistan, 2000; *Gender and Culture,* manual 1999.

Turkey, Global

Conflict Analysis and Resolution Programme at Sabanci University

RESEARCH
EDUCATION

The Sabanci University in Tuzla, near Istanbul, offers an MA program on Conflict Analysis and Resolution. The program is interdisciplinary within the Faculty of Arts and Social Sciences and dedicated to improve the understanding and resolution of contemporary violent conflicts. It combines macro level and micro level analysis, linking theory with practice. Special focal points of the program include conflict termination, interventions, civil society and conflict resolution as well as second track diplomacy.

Orhanli   *Contact:* Nimet Beriker
81474 Tuzla/Istanbul
Turkey

Tel: +90 (216) 483 9090
db@sabanciuniv.edu
www.sabanciuniv.edu

Turkey

TOSAM

RESEARCH
EDUCATION
ACTION
ADVOCACY

TOSAM (Toplum Sorunlarini Arastirma Merkezi or Center for the Research of Societal Problems), formerly known as TOSAV, promotes peaceful co-existence between communities—especially Turks and Kurds—by strengthening civic society, democracy and good governance. This is accomplished through training in conflict resolution and conflict resolution education, as well as by popularizing its "consensual document of mutual understanding": a statement of principles describing the framework of TOSAM's activities. It organizes regional meetings where local opinion leaders are brought together for discussion and broadcasts radio programs under the title of Democracy Radio.

Bagcilar mahallesi   *Contact:* Prof. Doguergil, President
2. sokak Villagül ap.
No 1/1
G.O.P. Ankara
Turkey

Tel: +90 (312) 447 1133
Fax: +90 (312) 446 8959
tosam@tosam.org
www.tosam.org

Turkey, Caucasus

Turkish Economic and Social Studies Foundation

RESEARCH
EDUCATION
ACTION
ADVOCACY

The Turkish Economic and Social Studies Foundation (TESEV) is an academic and non-governmental organization that has gradually expanded its range to include a more active interest in international affairs, with a particular focus on Turkey-EU relations and regional economic and security questions. Together with the Hellenic Foundation for European and Foreign Policy (ELIAMEP), it explores Turkish-Greek relations from a conflict prevention perspective. TESEV has also been involved in the Caucasus, organizing a Search for Stability in the Caucasus-conference in 2001 with the intention of assisting conflict settlement in the region.

Bankalar Cad. No:2 K:3
Karakoy Istanbul
Turkey

Tel: +90 (212) 292 8903
Fax: +90 (212) 292 9046
info@tesev.org.tr
www.tesev.org.tr

Contact: Taciser Ulas

Publications: Human Development Report for Turkey, annual publication; *Political Islam in Turkey and Women's Organizations,* 2000; *Political and Economic Cooperation and Integration in the Middle East: An Analysis of Turkey's Medium to Long-term Regional Policy,* in Turkish, 1998.

Ukraine

Interregional Association of Mediation Groups of Ukraine

RESEARCH
EDUCATION
ACTION
ADVOCACY

The Interregional Association of Mediation Groups of Ukraine is an association of independent and regional mediation organizations, established in order to promote mediation, education, facilitation as well as other effective and alternative non-violent methods of conflict resolution at all levels in Ukraine. The network also aims at strengthening the civil society and to support the democratic changes in the country. Members are Kiev Mediation Group, Crimean Republic Mediation Group, Odessa Regional Mediation Group, Tavricheskaya Mediation Group and Kharkov Regional Mediation Group.

c/o Odessa Regional Group of Mediation
Ak. Wiliamsa 54/3, apt. 84
65015 Odessa
Ukraine

Tel: +380 (48) 728 6290
Fax: +380 (48) 247 2881
orgm@paco.odessa.ua

Contact: Inna G. Tereschenko, Head of Council Odessa Regional Group of Mediation
Budget: $25,000–$100,000

Ukraine

Ukrainian
Conflict Resolution Association

RESEARCH
EDUCATION
ACTION

The Ukrainian Conflict Resolution Association (UCRA) is a non-governmental organization committed to combining the efforts of specialists in conflict resolution. It attempts to support them in studying, understanding, and predicting conflicts in ethnic, national, labor-management, and political areas. The focus is primarily on the Ukraine itself. The Association has working relationships with local NGOs and is part of a network consisting of fifteen Ukrainian organizations.

Marshala Bluhera 13-A-38
04128 Kiev
Ukraine

Contact: Professor Andriy Girnyk
Budget: < $25,000

Tel: +380 (44) 442 1842
hirnyk@bast.freenet.kiev.ua

Colombia

ABColombia Group

RESEARCH
ADVOCACY

ABColombia Group is a coordinated response by British and Irish agencies working in Colombia to the deteriorating situation in the country in which forced internal displacement has become a humanitarian and human rights emergency. ABColombia Group believes that the civilian population has the right not to be involved in the armed conflict and promotes a negotiated end to the armed conflict that includes the voice of civil society. Members are: CAFOD (Catholic Agency for Overseas Development), Christian Aid, Oxfam GB, Save the Children Fund UK, the Scottish Catholic International Aid Fund, and Trócaire.

35-37 Lower Marsh
P.O. Box 100
London SE1 7RT
United Kingdom

Tel: +44 (20) 7523 2374
Fax: +44 (20) 7620 0719
abcgroup@christian-aid.org

Contact: Madeline Church, Liaison Officer
Number of staff: 2
Budget: $25,000–$100,000
Publications: Colombia This Week, weekly news summary; *Colombia Forum,* bi-monthly journal; *Colombia Fact File.*

Africa

ACORD

RESEARCH
EDUCATION
ACTION
ADVOCACY

ACORD (Agency for Co-operation and Research in Development) is a broad-based, international consortium active in the field of development cooperation in Africa. It was set up as the operational arm of a group of European and Canadian NGOs to provide a practical response to drought in sub-Saharan Africa and grew into an operational NGO in its own right.

Since its establishment in 1976, ACORD has sought to combine development assistance and conflict resolution. Peacebuilding is one of the major aims of the consortium. It aims to help people cope with conflict and build peace. This involves joining with the people involved to analyze the causes and manifestations of conflict, helping them cope with crisis, and equipping them to face future crises and promote change.

Emphasis is placed on consolidating support for vulnerable communities and groups of people, and at the same time helping to build and reinforce within 17 country programs.

In its Rwanda program, ACORD has played a role in reconciliation and peacebuilding by bringing together different groups through communal activities. In Burundi the approach has been to create the conditions necessary for reconciliation, to organize income-generating activities, while a specific peace building activity included the training of local leaders to manage peaceful co-existence at a local level and training of individuals in rights and duties. Other peace projects were executed in Uganda, Somalia, Ethiopia, West Africa, Mali, Burkina Faso, and Southern Africa.

Empowering grassroots organizations and civic society characterize ACORD's approach. ACORD believes that communities themselves must identify problems and seek ways to solve them. Its own role should be complementary, while taking advantage of its international links. ACORD also carries out research and organizes seminars and workshops. All its work is underpinned by research.

Dean Bradley House
52 Horseferry Road
London SW1 2AF
United Kingdom

Tel: +44 (20) 7227 8600
Fax: +44 (20) 7799 1868
davidw@acord.org.uk
www.acord.org.uk

Contact: David Waller, Executive Director
Number of staff: 34
Budget: > $1,000,000
Publications: COPE (Consortium for Political Emergencies) Working Papers on Gulu District, Uganda, 19992000.

Africa, South Asia, Latin America

ActionAid

RESEARCH
EDUCATION
ACTION
ADVOCACY

ActionAid is dedicated to eradicating poverty by overcoming the injustice and inequity that cause it. With a view that conflict is a development issue, it is increasingly integrating conflict prevention and peacebuilding initiatives into its country programs. In the UK, it maintains an Emergency Unit with a "rights-based" approach to emergency humanitarian aid. The rationale is that the denial of human rights is a frequent cause of humanitarian crises, and therefore, realizing those rights in conflict areas should be the ultimate goal of any emergency intervention. There is also a point person working on lobbying activities related to conflict and peacebuilding.

Hamlyn House
MacDonald Road
London N19 5PG
United Kingdom

Tel: +44 (20) 7561 7561
Fax: +44 (20) 7272 0899
mail@actionaid.org.uk
www.actionaid.org

Contact: Roger Yates, Head Emergencies Unit

Number of staff: 15

Budget: $25,000–$100,000

Publications: Peacebuilding in Africa: Case Studies from ActionAid, 2001; Forced Displacement and Human Rights: Training Modules for Rights in Emergencies, 2001; Rights Based Approach in Emergencies: Setting the Scene, 2000; Rights Based Approach in Emergencies: Rights Based Analysis in Practice, 2000; An Assessment of Sanctions Against Burundi, 1999.

Africa

African Rights

RESEARCH
EDUCATION
ACTION
ADVOCACY

African Rights is an organization dedicated to issues of human-rights abuses, conflict, famine and civil reconstruction. It tries to give a voice to concerned Africans, as it believes any solutions to the continent's most pressing problems must be sought primarily among Africans.

The Rwanda project involves documenting abuses, detailing evidence against those responsible and providing support to survivors. Somalia is another focus of Africa Rights concern and it has opened an office with a program of human rights education and research. African Rights presses for more accountability from the international community in its operations in Africa.

P.O. Box 18368
London EC4A 4JE
United Kingdom

Tel: +44 (20) 7947 3276
Fax: +44 (20) 7947 3253
afrights@gn.apc.org
www.unimondo.org/africanrights

Contact: Rakiya Omaar, Director

Publications: Left to Die at ETO and Nyanza, 2001; The Conflict Cycle: Which Way Out in the Kivus? 2000; Rwanda: The Insurgency in the Northwest, 1998.

Balkans, Russia, Northern Ireland,
East and Central Africa, Middle East, Southeast Asia

Agenda for Reconciliation

Agenda for Reconciliation (AfR) is an international program of Initiatives of Change (formerly the Moral Re-Armament network), which is devoted to conflict prevention and other peacemaking initiatives within and between nations. Its work is based on the beliefs that durable peace depends on genuine processes of healing the past and that reconciliation is only possible where trust has been built. An international steering committee with its secretariat in London coordinates this work.

24 Greencoat Place
London SW1P 1RD
United Kingdom

Tel: +44 (20) 7798 6000
Fax: +44 (20) 7798 6001
www.caux.ch/afr

Contact: Peter Riddell, Secretary of the International Steering Committee

Number of staff: 150 activists

Budget: $100,000–$500,000

Publications: For a Change, periodical; Forgiveness: *Breaking the Chain of Hate,* 1999; *Conflict and Resolution,* 1998; *The Forgiveness Factor,* 1996; *Religion, the Missing Dimension of Statecraft,* 1994.

West Africa, Kenya, Uganda

EDUCATION
ACTION
ADVOCACY

Alliances for Africa

Alliances for Africa (AfA) is an African-led nongovernmental peace, human rights, and sustainable development organization. AfA works for progress in guaranteeing both civil and political rights on one hand, and economic and social rights on the other, by bridging a gap that it perceives between groups working for human rights and peace, and those working for economic development. Initiatives are designed to build strategic partnerships with local, national, and regional organizations, and to build capacity and alliances among local, national, regional, and international human rights, peace, and development agencies.

Unit 10, Aberdeen Centre
24 Highbury Grove
London N5 2EA
United Kingdom

Tel: +44 (20) 7359 1181
Fax: +44 (20) 7354 4900
iheoma@alliancesforafrica.org
www.alliancesforafrica.org

Contact: Iheoma Obibi, Executive Director

Number of staff: 5

Budget: $100,000–$500,000

Publications: "Rape as an Instrument of War," AfA On-Line Bulletin issue 4, 2000; *Sierra Leone: Protecting Human Rights under the African Charter on Human and People's Rights in Situations of Conflict in Africa: A Case Study,* 2000.

Global

Amnesty International

RESEARCH
EDUCATION
ACTION
ADVOCACY

With national sections in over fifty countries, Amnesty International is one of the world's leading human rights organizations. Apart from focusing on individual cases of human rights abuse, it also reports on systematic violations, offers recommendations on how to prevent these, and puts pressure on governments through public and lobby campaigns to heed them. For sudden escalations of human rights violations, such as are typical for violent conflict, the organization has a special crisis response team. AI's human rights education work also contributes to the prevention of violent conflict.

99-119 Rosebery Avenue
London EC1R 4RE
United Kingdom

Tel: +44 (20) 7814 6200
Fax: +44 (20) 7833 1510
information@amnesty.org.uk
www.amnesty.org.uk

Contact: The Campaigning and Crisis Response Programme

Number of staff: 320 at international HQ

Budget: > $1,000,000

Publications: Over 200 books, reports, and circulars in over a dozen languages annually.

Afghanistan

British Agencies Afghanistan Group

RESEARCH
EDUCATION
ACTION
ADVOCACY

The British Agencies Afghanistan Group provides a forum for a network of British agencies assisting Afghans both inside and outside Afghanistan and facilitates communication and cooperation among these agencies. It provides its members with information by monitoring developments, analyzing information, producing position papers, and interacting with other networks and agencies. It encourages its members and other NGOs to integrate peacebuilding into their development and assistance programs, and to adopt long-term community-based approaches to programming in conflict areas. The Group also consults with governments and international organizations on the situation in Afghanistan.

Refugee Council
3 Bondway
London SW8 1SJ
United Kingdom

Tel: +44 (20) 7820 3098
Fax: +44 (20) 7820 3107
peter.marsden@refugeecouncil.org.uk

Contact: Peter Marsden, Information Co-ordinator

Number of staff: 15

Budget: > $25,000

Publications: Afghanistan: Monthly Review.

Latin America, Somalia, Southern Africa, Southeast Asia

Catholic Institute
for International Relations

RESEARCH
EDUCATION
ACTION
ADVOCACY

The Catholic Institute for International Relations (CIIR) lends advocacy support to civil organizations and countries affected by internal conflict. The activities center on development, fact-finding, lobbying, policy advice, publishing and research. The International Cooperation for Development (ICD), the technical assistance program of CIIR, is active in eleven countries. ICD's development workers are recruited in Britain and other European countries as well as in the target country itself.

Unit 3, Canonbury Yard
190a New North Road, Islington
London N1 7BJ
United Kingdom

Tel: +44 (20) 7354 0883
Fax: +44 (20) 7359 0017
steve@ciir.org
www.ciir.org

Contact: Steve Kibble, Conflict Prevention Programme

Number of Staff: 1

Budget: $25,000–$100,000

Publications: Humanising Peace: The Impact of Peace Agreements on Human Rights: Lessons from Guatemala, Haiti and South Africa with Responses from Burma, Colombia and East Timor, 1999; *The People's Peace: Civil Society Organisations and Peace Processes in the South,* 1998; *The People's Conscience?: Civil Groups in the South African and Guatemalan Transitions,* 1997.

Global

Centre for Conflict Analysis

RESEARCH
EDUCATION

The Centre for Conflict Analysis (CCA) at the University of Kent is a network of researchers studying conflict theory who put their academic knowledge to practical use by holding problem-solving workshops on international/internationalized and intercommunal disputes. They also act as mediators and facilitators, usually keeping a very low profile. The Centre does not have a fixed budget, but depends on ad hoc funding for the workshops.

Department of Politics and
    International Relations
c/o Rutherford College
University of Kent at Canterbury
Canterbury CT2 7NX
United Kingdom

Tel: +44 (1227) 823 404
Fax: +44 (1227) 827 033
www.ukc.ac.uk/international

Publications: Electronic Journal of International Conflict Analysis; Approaches to Conflict and Cooperation in International Relations: Lessons from Theory for Practice.

Global

Centre for Defence Studies

RESEARCH
EDUCATION
ADVOCACY

The Centre for Defence Studies is part of the War Studies Group at King's College London, the largest concentration of expertise for security studies research and training in Europe. The purpose of the Centre is to act as a focus for research on a wide range of defense, conflict prevention, peacebuilding, and security issues. The work of the Conflict, Security and Development Group focuses on conflict resolution issues and since 1996, has been running the Complex Emergencies Programme to develop paradigms for early international response to complex emergencies, aimed at governments, NGOs, and the military in Southeast Europe and East and West Africa.

King's College
The Strand
London WC2R 2LS
United Kingdom

Tel: +44 (20) 7848 2946
Fax: +44 (20) 7848 2748
keith.britto@kcl.ac.uk
www.kcl.ac.uk/depsta/rel/cds/index.htm

Contact: Paul Cornish, Head of the Conflict, Security and Development Group

Number of staff: 10

Budget: > $1,000,000

Publications: Journal of Conflict, Security and Development, three times a year.

West Africa

Centre for Democracy & Development

RESEARCH
EDUCATION
ACTION
ADVOCACY

The Centre for Democracy & Development (CDD) is an African-led nongovernmental organization dedicated to policy-oriented engagement, research, advocacy, and training on questions of peacebuilding, the establishment of democratic structures, and economic development in West Africa. Its work is grounded in an appreciation of the practical problems that inhibit democratic reform, security, and stability in West Africa, and the need to strengthen civic organizations as well as local and national governments. CDD is preparing to launch a monitoring program called "Stability Monitor" to track threats to peaceful change and social transition.

Unit 6, Canonbury Yard
190 A, New North Road
London N1 7BJ
United Kingdom

Tel: +44 (20) 7288 8666
Fax: +44 (20) 7288 8672
cdd@cdd.org.uk
www.cdd.org.uk

Contact: Kayode Fayemi, Director

Number of staff: 23

Budget: > $1,000,000

Publications: Democracy & Development, bi-annual journal; *Nigeria: Democratising a Militarised Society,* 2001; *Mercenaries: An African Security Dilemma,* 2000.

Middle East, South Asia, China, Northern Ireland, Africa

Centre for the Study of Forgiveness and Reconciliation

RESEARCH
EDUCATION

The Centre for the Study of Forgiveness and Reconciliation is engaged in educational activities, research, and outreach with the goal of contributing to the deeper understanding and promotion of the processes of reconciliation and forgiveness. It is affiliated with Coventry University. A basic premise informing the work at the Centre is that within the context of struggles to achieve peace and reconciliation, the transformative power of forgiveness in such processes is not only underestimated but also under-researched. The Centre is currently preparing a Masters program in Peace and Reconciliation Studies.

Coventry University
Priory Street
Coventry CV1 5FB
United Kingdom

Tel: +44 (24) 7688 7448
Fax: +44 (24) 7688 8679
ea.rigby@coventry.ac.uk
www.coventry-isl.org.uk/forgive/

Contact: Andrew Rigby, Director

Number of staff: 4

Budget: > $25,000

Kosovo, Turkey, Sierra Leone, Sri Lanka

Children and Armed Conflict Unit

RESEARCH
EDUCATION
ACTION
ADVOCACY

The Children and Armed Conflict Unit works to improve the situation for children caught up in armed conflict and for those emerging from years of violence. The Unit has established a database of information and it conducts field visits to investigate the effects of conflict on children. The Unit has worked in Kosovo where it focused on juvenile justice. It has been working in Turkey where it is helping to set up a Child Rights Center and trains police officers in children's rights. The Unit is currently researching the situation in Sierra Leone and Sri Lanka.

Children's Legal Centre
University of Essex
Wivenhoe Park
Colchester, Essex CO4 3SQ
United Kingdom

Tel: +44 (1206) 873 483
Fax: +44 (1206) 874 026
armedcon@essex.ac.uk
www2.essex.ac.uk/c&acu

Contact: Rachel Harvey, International Children's Rights and Armed Conflict Programme Manager

Number of Staff: 3

Publications: Children and Armed Conflict Unit Review, newsletter.

Northern Ireland

Committee on the Administration of Justice

RESEARCH
ACTION
ADVOCACY

The Committee on the Administration of Justice (CAJ) is an independent non-governmental organization that seeks to secure the highest standards in the administration of justice in Northern Ireland by ensuring that the government complies with its responsibilities in international human rights law. CAJ's activities include publishing reports, conducting research, monitoring, and holding conferences. Its areas of work include prisons, policing, emergency laws, the criminal justice system, and the use of lethal force. It takes no position on the constitutional status of Northern Ireland.

45/47 Donegall Street
Belfast BT1 2BR
Northern Ireland
United Kingdom

Tel: +44 (28) 9096 1122
Fax: +44 (28) 9024 6706
webmaster@caj.org.uk
www.caj.org.uk

Contact: Maggie Beirne, Research and Policy Officer

Publications: Just News, monthly newsletter.

Northern Ireland

Community Development Centre

RESEARCH
ACTION
ADVOCACY

The Community Development Centre (CDC) is a community based independent organization working to develop local capacities for cooperative efforts to promote peace, progress, and prosperity in North Belfast, Northern Ireland, and to assist local communities in rebuilding relationships free of conflict, division, and mistrust. Its Community Bridges program is a conflict prevention, resolution, and mediation program drawing on models in South Africa, with the aim of responding to conflict and violence between Protestant/unionist and Catholic/nationalist communities in North Belfast. CDC also carries out research and organizes various training programs.

22 Cliftonville Road
Belfast BT14 6JX
Northern Ireland
United Kingdom

Tel: +44 (28) 9028 4400
Fax: +44 (28) 9028 4401
info@cdcnb.org
www.cdcnb.org

Contact: David Holloway, Co-ordinator Community Bridges Programme

Number of staff: 5 on the Community Bridges Programme

Publications: Stewarding Crowds and Managing Public Safety, 2000; *Independent Intervention,* 1999; *Drawing Back from the Edge,* 1999.

Northern Ireland

Community Relations Council

RESEARCH
EDUCATION
ADVOCACY

The Northern Ireland Community Relations Council was set up in 1990 as an independent charity to promote better community relations and the recognition of cultural diversity in Northern Ireland in order to enable a change towards a society free from sectarianism. The Council supports groups and individuals engaged in constructive work by means of advice and information. It also gives grants for projects in the fields of development cultural diversity and victim support.

6, Murray Street
Belfast BT1 6 DN
Northern Ireland
United Kingdom

Tel: +44 (28) 9022 7500
Fax: +44 (28) 9022 7551
info@community-relations.org.uk
www.community-relations.org.uk

Contact: Will Glendinning, Chief Executive

Budget: > $1,000,000

Publications: CRC News, periodical; *What Have We Learned?: Community Relations and Peace Building,* 2000; *Directory of Cross Community Church Groups and Projects in Northern Ireland,* 1999; *Dealing with Difference: A Guide to Peace, Reconciliation and Community Projects in Northern Ireland,* 1998; *Skills Guide for Community Relations Work in N. Ireland,* 1997.

Republic of Ireland, Northern Ireland

Co-operation Ireland

Co-operation Ireland tries to create mutual understanding and respect between the people of Northern Ireland and the Republic of Ireland. All program departments are engaged in promoting practical co-operation rather than conflict resolution in a narrow sense. Programs are in the fields of youth, education and community exchanges, economic co-operation, and media. Co-operation Ireland is an implementation body for the EU Special Support Program for Peace and Reconciliation. For the target groups—youth, grassroots movements, business and cultural groups—practical activities include exchanges, study visits, workshops, training, and research.

7 Botanic Avenue
Belfast BT7 1JG
Northern Ireland
United Kingdom

Tel: +44 (28) 9032 1462
Fax: +44 (28) 9024 7522
37 Upper Fitzwilliam Street
Dublin 2
Republic of Ireland

Tel: +353 (1) 661 0588
Fax: +353 (1) 661 8456
info@cooperationireland.org
www.cooperationireland.org

Contact: Garrett Casey, Media and Communications Officer

Number of staff: 50

Budget: > $1,000,000

Publications: Co-operation Ireland Newslink, newsletter; *Living with Change; Committed to Change; Forging Links,* 1999.

Balkans, Caucasus, Tajikistan, Fiji, Angola, Uganda, West Africa

RESEARCH
EDUCATION
ACTION
ADVOCACY

Conciliation Resources

Conciliation Resources (CR) is a non-governmental international service for conflict prevention and resolution seeking to provide sustained assistance to partner organizations and their initiatives at community and national levels.

This assistance can take the form of collaborative design and implementation of conflict transformation or peacebuilding strategies, support for seminars and workshops, training, and education for constructive conflict transformation, media training, or support for institutional development. In addition to the Accord Programme—which aims at providing practical tools for learning from peace processes—CR is supporting partner initiatives in vast number of countries around the world. CR also has a program on Media & Conflict in Africa, currently focusing on Nigeria, Sierra Leone, and Uganda.

In the South Caucasus, CR supports a wide range of initiatives within civil society (including the media) in Georgia and Abkhazia, as well as a semi-official dialogue process between representatives of the two sides. The program is aimed at breaking the deadlock in this frozen conflict by creating space at both governmental and societal levels and suggesting avenues towards a sustainable solution. It also tracks wider issues in the region, including Nagorno-Karabakh.

In the Balkans, CR works with a network of local groups from Albania, Kosovo, Macedonia, Montenegro and Serbia that conduct practical activities promoting regional peacebuilding and multi-cultural democracy. This work started before the Kosovo war as a dialogue project between Albanians and Serbs from Kosovo but has since widened to include groups and communities from the wider region.

The Accord Programme has had projects on the peace processes in Georgia/Abkhazia, Northern Ireland, and Tajikistan. An "education pack" of training and discussion materials is produced to accompany the Accord publications. Other project activities in these countries have included policy seminars, briefing meetings, and other initiatives to encourage the development of strategies that will consolidate the peace processes in the respective countries.

173 Upper Street
London N1 1RG
United Kingdom

Tel: +44 (20) 7359 7728
Fax: +44 (20) 7359 4081
conres@c-r.org
www.c-r.org

Contacts: Andy Carl, Co-Director; Jonathan Cohen, Program Manager Caucasus

Number of Staff: 10 in UK, 5 in Sierra Leone

Budget: > $1,000,000

Publications: Accord: An International Review of Peace Initiatives, a book series covering Liberia, Guatemala, Mozambique, Sri Lanka, Cambodia, Philippines/Mindanao, Georgia/Abkhazia, Northern Ireland, Sierra Leone, and Tajikistan available online and in print; *Sierra Leone Peace Process: Learning from the Past to Address Current Challenges,* 2000; *African Media and Conflict,* 1998.

Global

Conflict, Development and Peace Network

RESEARCH
EDUCATION
ACTION
ADVOCACY

Conflict, Development and Peace Network (CODEP) is a multi-disciplinary forum, established to bring together NGOs, consultants, academics, and donors working in development, human rights and peacebuilding with the aim of sharing knowledge and improving practice.

In particular, it aims to bring these specialists together to explore the causes of conflict and its impact on people, and to improve practice in peacebuilding, conflict resolution, and development work.

CODEP publishes an e-mail newsletter every other week, with information on upcoming conferences and workshops, recent publications and resources, and postings of job vacancies. The newsletter is available on request and back issues are accessible on the CODEP website. It organizes workshops and roundtable discussions on subjects related to security, development, and conflict resolution issues. Recent topics have included "Kosovo, the media and NGOs," "The role of faith organizations in peacebuilding and reconciliation," and "Strategic planning and southern partners." It has also established thematic working groups on a number of topics, and holds an international conference each year.

CODEP plans to augment its activities by making use of its website as a platform for networking and information exchange, and developing a database providing information on organizations, networks, academic institutions, government departments, individuals, and others active in the UK and globally on conflict, development, and peace issues.

6th Floor, Dean Bradley House
52 Horseferry Road
London SW1P 2AF
United Kingdom

Tel: +44 (20) 7799 2477
Fax: +44 (20) 7799 2458
mail@codep.org.uk
www.codep.org.uk

Contact: Kathleen Armstrong, Co-ordinator
Number of staff: 2
Budget: $100,000–$500,000
Publications: CODEP Newsletter.

Northern Ireland

Corrymeela Community

EDUCATION
ACTION

The Corrymeela Community is a dispersed community of people of all ages and Christian traditions who are committed to reconciliation through the healing of social, religious, and political divisions in Northern Ireland and throughout the world. Its activities take place in its residential center in Ballycastle. The Community is engaged in programs for schools, youth, community groups, families, and different churches. Corrymeela, in partnership with others, works toward the building of a society whose priorities are mutual respect, the partnership of all, and the sharing and stewardship of resources.

8 Upper Crescent
Belfast BT7 1NT
Northern Ireland
United Kingdom

Tel: +44 (28) 9050 8080
Fax: +44 (28) 9050 8070
belfast@corrymeela.org.uk
www.corrymeela.org.uk

Contact: Colin Craig, Programme Director
Number of staff: 35
Budget: > $1,000,000

Northern Ireland

Democratic Dialogue

EDUCATION
ACTION

Democratic Dialogue is a think tank designed to stimulate fresh approaches to the political problems of Northern Ireland, as well as addressing economic, social, and cultural questions. It forms networks with the voluntary sector, trade unions, intellectuals, the churches, and the political parties. Democratic Dialogue organizes Round Table debates, writes reports and tries to influence the governments in London and Dublin. It focuses on themes such as social exclusion, the position of women, reconstituting politics, and Northern Irelands' place in the European Union.

53 University Street
Belfast BT7 1FY
Northern Ireland
United Kingdom

Tel: +44 (1232) 232 228
Fax: +44 (1232) 233 334
dd@dem-dial.demon.co.uk
www.dem-dial.demon.co.uk

Contact: Robin Wilson, Director
Publications: "New Order: International Models of Peace and Reconciliation," Democratic Dialogue Report series, 1998.

Global

Department of
Peace Studies at Bradford University

RESEARCH
EDUCATION
ADVOCACY

The Department of Peace Studies at Bradford University was established a quarter of a century ago and has grown to be the largest university center for peace studies in the world.

The Department has developed a large undergraduate program leading to a BA Honors degree in Peace Studies with nearly 200 full-time students, but has balanced this with the development of a substantial graduate school and a doctoral program with around 50 research students. Together with 20 lecturers and research fellows, they work primarily in the following areas: international politics and security studies, development and peace, regions in conflict (especially former Yugoslavia, the Middle East, Africa and Latin America), conflict resolution, politics and society; international politics, and the environment.

The Department has a large publishing program, including publication of its regular newsletter three times a year and the Bradford Arms Register Studies (BARS) Project. The Strengthening of the Biological and Toxin Weapons Convention and Preventing Biological Warfare Project maintains a dedicated information service on Bradford University's website to more effectively disseminate information on the process of strengthening the Biological and Toxin Weapons Convention (BTWC) worldwide.

Further applied work in conflict resolution is conducted within the Department's Centre for Conflict Resolution. This Centre, an applied research unit within the Department, combines theoretical studies in peacekeeping, mediation, and conflict resolution with a range of practical programs, many of them concerned with training mediators and peacemakers in areas in conflict. Staff have worked in former Yugoslavia, Cyprus, Sri Lanka, and Uganda, and they have collaborated in mediation training for diplomats and a wide range of NGOs in Britain and overseas. The research and project work of the Centre is comprehensively described on its website at www.brad.ac.uk/confres. The Department has recently been recognized as a Rotary Centre for International Studies in Peace and Conflict Resolution.

Richmond Road
Bradford BD7 1DP
United Kingdom

Tel: +44 (12) 7423 5235
Fax: +44 (12) 7423 5240
n.lewer@bradford.ac.uk
www.brad.ac.uk/acad/peace

Contact: Nick Lewer, Head of the Centre for Conflict Resolution

Number of staff: 20

Publications: Newsletter; *Confronting Ethnic Chauvinism in a Post-War Environment: NGOs and Peace Education in Bosnia,* 2000; *Women, Gender and Peacebuilding,* 2000; *International Non-government Organisations and Peace-building: Perspectives from Peace Studies and Conflict Resolution,* 1999.

Caucasus, Great Lakes Region of Africa,
West Africa, Central and Southeast Asia, Central America

FEWER

FEWER (Forum on Early Warning and Early Response) is an independent global network of organizations committed to preventing conflict by providing early warning and informing peacebuilding efforts. FEWER's activities are led by its members. The network is composed of NGOs, UN agencies, and academic institutions who work together to exchange knowledge and experience in the field of early warning, conflict prevention, and conflict resolution. FEWER's motivation is strictly humanitarian. The services provided by FEWER are oriented toward the promotion of human rights, sustainable development, and peace. FEWER provides local perspectives on the causes and dynamics of violent conflict and peace building to different policymaking communities.

Old Truman Brewery
91-95 Brick Lane
London E1 6QN
United Kingdom

Tel: +44 (20) 7247 7022
Fax: +44 (20) 7247 5290
secretariat@fewer.org
www.fewer.org

Contact: David Nyheim, Director
Number of staff: 8
Budget: $500,000–$1,000,000
Publications: Development in Conflict: A Seven Step Tool for Planners (together with International Alert and Saferworld) 2001; *Conflict Analysis and Response Definition: Abridged Methodology* (together with the West Africa Network for Peacebuilding and the Centre for Conflict Research) 2001; *Conflict Prevention in the Caucasus: Actors, Response Capacities and Planning Processes* (together with the EastWest Institute) 2001; *Generating the Means to an End: Planning Integrated Responses to Early Warning* (together with CIPDD, EastWest Institute, International Alert, IEA-RAS-EAWARN and WANEP) 2000; *Thesaurus and Glossary of Early Warning and Conflict Prevention Terms* (together with PIOOM) 2000.

Cambodia, Angola, Liberia, Sierra Leone

RESEARCH
ACTION
ADVOCACY

Global Witness

Global Witness focuses on the links between the exploitation of natural resources and the funding of conflict and corruption. It seeks to try to break these links and change the current corporate and government practices, where they have resulted in an unregulated rush for resources. To achieve these aims Global Witness utilizes different lobbying techniques to achieve real and effective change. Global Witness' campaigns have, among other things, targeted the Khmer Rouge in Cambodia as well as the global multi-billion dollar diamond industry, forcing it to admit that it was party to the trade in conflict diamonds, a major casual factor of war.

P.O. Box 6042
London N19 5WP
United Kingdom

Tel: +44 (20) 7272 6731
mail@globalwitness.org.uk
www.globalwitness.org

Contact: Simon Taylor, Co-Director

Number of staff: 16

Budget: > $1,000,000

Publications: The Credibility Gap—and the Need to Bridge It: Increasing the Pace of Forestry Reform, 2001; *Conflict Diamonds: Possibilities for the Identification, Certification and Control of Diamonds,* 2000; *The Untouchables: Forest Crimes and the Concessionaires—Can Cambodia Afford to Keep Them?* 2000; *Chainsaws Speak Louder than Words,* 2000; *A Rough Trade: The Role of Companies and Governments in the Angolan Conflict,* 1998.

Ireland, Northern Ireland

Horizon Project

RESEARCH
EDUCATION
ACTION
ADVOCACY

The Horizon Project is an organization that brings together Irish students to promote mutual respect, trust, and friendship across religious and social divides. Horizon enables students in Irish schools to become aware of and to understand each other's culture. Each school involved, often together with other schools in the region, has its own projects. These could be cleaning a municipal park, learning sign language, or doing a project with deaf people.

"Crannagh"
234 Upper Lisburn Road
Belfast BT10 0TA
Northern Ireland
United Kingdom

Tel: +44 (28) 9060 5424
Fax: +44 (28) 9060 5423
horizonbel@admins.freeserve.co.uk
www.medialinx.co.uk/horizon

Contact: Eileen Patterson, Director

Number of staff: 2

Budget: $25,000–$100,000

Global

Humanitarian Practice Network

RESEARCH
EDUCATION

The Humanitarian Practice Network (HPN) is part of the Overseas Development Institute (ODI). HPN's objectives are to provide relevant analysis and guidance for humanitarian practice, as well as summary information on policy and institutional developments in this sector. Current areas of activity include work on issues of aid politics, policy and principles, accountability, evaluation, and natural disasters.

The Overseas Development Institute
111 Westminster Bridge Road
London SE1 7JD
United Kingdom

Tel: +44 (20) 7922 0331
Fax: +44 (20) 7922 0399
hpn@odi.org.uk
www.odihpn.org

Contact: Frances Stevenson, Coordinator

Number of staff: 4

Publications: *Humanitarian Exchange,* bi-annual magazine; *Operational Security Management in Violent Environments,* 2000; *The Political Economy of War: What Relief Agencies Need to Know,* 2000; *Humanitarian Mine Action: The First Decade of a New Sector in Humanitarian Aid.*

Northern Ireland, Basque Country,
Middle East, West Africa, South Africa, Southeast Asia

RESEARCH
EDUCATION
ADVOCACY

INCORE

A joint program of the United Nations University and the University of Ulster, the Initiative on Conflict Resolution & Ethnicity (INCORE) aims to integrate research, training, practice, policy, and theory, and to provide an international focus on ethnic violence.

Established in 1993, it is developing a systematic approach to understanding and resolving the problems of ethnic conflict. INCORE's approach includes a particular concern with two ethnic issues: how to successfully manage pluralism and how to reach a fair and stable settlement after a period of violence.

Currently, INCORES's research focuses mainly on post-conflict issues, issues of governance and diversity, and research methodology in violent societies. The INCORE Research Unit publishes the *Ethnic Conflict Research Digest* and organizes a biennial conference. It also operates the Ethnic Studies Network (ESN), an international network of 700 academics, students, and researchers in the field of ethnic conflict.

INCORE's Policy and Evaluation Unit was established in 1998 to examine, research, and analyze the ways in which conflict management research and practical lessons from past practice are currently utilized by policymakers, and to identify mechanisms that will enhance effectiveness in the field of conflict management. The Unit also addresses the issue of "best practice" in evaluating conflict interventions, and commissions and undertakes training and other development work for policymakers, diplomats, governmental organizations, and NGOs, and others to ensure the development of strategies and programs to address conflict.

Based in Northern Ireland, INCORE is also engaged in a variety of activities related to establishing a stable nonviolent civil society in Northern Ireland.

INCORE's Conflict Data Service, available on its website, provides current and historical information on all major on-going conflicts, theme sites on a variety of issues relevant to conflict, and information on conflict resolution institutions throughout the world.

Aberfoyle House
Northland Road
Derry/Londonderry BT48 7JA
Northern Ireland
United Kingdom

Tel: +44 (28) 7137 5500
Fax: +44 (28) 7137 5510
incore@incore.ulst.ac.uk
www.incore.ulst.ac.uk

Contact: Mari Fitzduff, Director

Number of staff: 10

Budget: $100,000–$500,000

Publications: Ethnic Conflict Research Digest, journal; *Hope and History: Study on the Management of Diversity in Northern Ireland,* 2001; *Assessment of UN Research Needs,* 1999; *Peacekeepers? Peacemakers? Women in Northern Ireland 1969–1995.*

Global

International Action Network
on Small Arms

ACTION
ADVOCACY

The International Action Network on Small Arms (IANSA) is a network consisting of international NGOs who make it their goal to prevent the proliferation and misuse of small weapons both by civilians and official users like policemen and the military. IANSA aims to bring the possession of small weapons under control and to combat illegal trafficking. The Network wants to make governments accountable for their decisions on licensing arms transfers and the availability of weapons to civilians. The Network publishes an electronic newsletter dealing with local efforts to come to terms with the small arms problem.

Box 422
37 Store Street
London WC1E 7BS
United Kingdom

Tel: +44 (20) 7523 2037
Fax: +44 (20) 7620 0719
contact@iansa.org
www.iansa.org

Contact: Sally Joss
Publications: IANSA Newsletter.

Global

International Institute
for Strategic Studies

RESEARCH

The International Institute for Strategic Studies (IISS) is a private, non-profit membership organization for the study of military strategy, arms control, regional security, and conflict resolution. The Institute aims to be a source of accurate, objective information on international strategic issues for politicians and diplomats, foreign-affairs analysts, international business, economists, the military, journalists, academics, and the informed public. IISS publishes the annual inventory of the world's armed forces (*The Military Balance*) and an annual survey about political and military trends (*Strategic Survey*).

Arundel House
13-15 Arundel Street
Temple Place
London WC2R 3DX
United Kingdom

Tel: +44 (20) 7379 7676
Fax: +44 (20) 7836 3108
iiss@iiss.org
www.iiss.org

Contact: Mats Berdal, Director of Studies
Number of Staff: 38
Publications: Adelphi Papers, monographic series in the strategic studies and defense fields; *The Military Balance,* yearbook; *Strategic Survey,* yearbook; *Strategic Comments,* online publication; *Survival,* quarterly journal.

Caucasus, Great Lakes region, West Africa, Sri Lanka

International Alert

RESEARCH
EDUCATION
ACTION
ADVOCACY

International Alert (IA) was founded in 1985 by a small group of scholars and human rights activists headed by Martin Ennals. It was born out of recognition that in many countries internal conflicts undermine efforts to protect individual and collective human rights and the promotion of sustainable social and economic development.

IA was founded as an action-based, non-governmental organization to contribute to the prevention and resolution of violent internal conflict. As part of the international humanitarian and human rights community, IA responds to the suffering of the victims or potential victims of war. IA seeks the consent and trust of parties to a conflict, and urges adherence to international humanitarian law and respect for human rights. IA believes that the protagonists in a conflict and the people it affects will be the primary actors in its resolution, and that sustained dialogue is the principal means to this end.

Together with different organizations and individuals, IA has worked to peacefully resolve many of the world's most intractable disputes that can be found in the following regions: Great Lakes Region of Africa, West Africa, the Caucasus Region of the Former Soviet Union, and Sri Lanka.

The Organization is also engaged in advocacy and policy analysis. This includes issues relating to: light weapons transfers; the impact of development aid; the impact of private military companies; and the role of woman in peacebuilding. IA is developing work, which looks at the role of corporations operating in conflict situations.

IA seeks to strengthen the ability of people in conflict situations to make peace by: facilitating dialogue at different levels of society in conflict; helping develop and enhance local capacities through funding or training; facilitating peace-oriented development work among local peacebuilding initiatives; and encouraging the international community to address the structural causes of conflict.

1 Glyn Street
London SE11 5HT
United Kingdom
_____

Tel: +44 (20) 7793 8383
Fax: +44 (20) 7793 7975
general@international-alert.org
www.international-alert.org

Contact: Martin Honeywell, Associate Director

Number of Staff: 40

Publications: The Business of Peace: The Private Sector as a Partner in Conflict Prevention and Resolution, 2000; The Privatization of Security and Peacebuilding: a Framework for Action, 2000; Equal Access to Education: A Peace Imperative for Burundi, 2000; Arms Watching: Integrating Small Arms and Light Weapons into the Early Warning of Violent Conflict, 2000; Code of Conduct for Conflict Transformation Work, 1998.

Balkans, Caucasus, Central Asia

RESEARCH
EDUCATION
ACTION
ADVOCACY

Institute for War and Peace Reporting

The Institute for War and Peace Reporting (IWPR) supports democratization and development in crisis zones by providing an international platform, professional training and financial assistance to independent media, human rights activists and other democratic voices, and publishing a variety of online reports. It works in partnership with many media organizations and human rights groups in widely dispersed locations including the Balkans, Caucasus, and Central Asia. It also maintains an office in The Hague, where it is engaged in a special project on the Yugoslav war crimes tribunal.

Lancaster House
33 Islington High Street
London N1 9LH
United Kingdom

Tel: +44 (20) 7713 7130
Fax: +44 (20) 7713 7140
letters@iwpr.net
www.iwpr.net

Contact: Alan Davis, Director of Programmes

Number of staff: 24

Budget: > $1,000,000

Publications: Balkan Crisis Reports; Caucasus Reporting Service; Reporting Central Asia.

Horn of Africa, Great Lakes region

RESEARCH
EDUCATION
ACTION
ADVOCACY

Justice Africa

Justice Africa is an organization that is grouped around five directors with many years of experience in grappling with the problems of democracy, human rights, humanitarian action and peace and security in Africa. Justice Africa has no single blueprint for successful work. Instead, it adapts its mode of operation to the demands of each situation. Justice Africa initiates and supports civil society activities for human rights, democracy and peace. It works with a network of African organizations, implements its own human right projects, and has a publishing and educational arm.

Lancaster House, 1st Floor
33 Islington High Street
London N1 9LH
United Kingdom

Tel: +44 (20) 7837 7888
Fax: +44 (20) 7837 8919
ja@justiceafrica.org
www.justiceafrica.org

Contact: Alex de Waal, Co-Director

Number of Staff: 5

Publications: African Arguments, journal; *Who Fights? Who Cares?: War and Humanitarian Action in Africa,* 2000; *The Phoenix State: Civil Society and the Future of Sudan,* 2000; *The Sudan Civil Project,* in Arabic, 1999.

Northern Ireland

Kilcranny House

EDUCATION
ACTION

Kilcranny House is a residential, educational, and resource center committed to addressing the divisions which exist between the people of Northern Ireland, and exploring nonviolence as a way of life and a means of working for change in society. Set in a rural environment, it provides a safe place for people from different communities in Northern Ireland to meet together. Kilcranny House offers programs dealing with issues such as conflict resolution, nonviolence, prejudice awareness, and the environment, and is also available to outside groups for use as a program center.

21 Cranagh Road
Coleraine BT51 3NN
Northern Ireland
United Kingdom

Contact: Anne Cummings, Project Co-ordinator
Number: < $25,000

Tel/fax: +44 (28) 7032 1816
info@kilcranny.thegap.com

Caucasus, CIS countries

London Information Network on Conflicts and State-Building

RESEARCH
EDUCATION
ACTION
ADVOCACY

The London Information Network on Conflicts and State-Building (LINKS) was set up in 1997. It organizes seminars, conferences, and workshops both in the target regions and in Europe. Training is held through seminars and in-house workshops designed specifically for NGOs, political parties, and governmental organizations. Besides the dissemination of information, the organization also runs projects. It is currently leading a number of projects in partnership with Caucasus LINKS, an independent NGO based in Tiblisi. Activities include the facilitation of dialogue, development of confidence-building measures, and training and support for grassroots activities.

Fifth Floor South
Buckingham House
Buckingham Street
London WC2N 6BU
United Kingdom

Contact: Paul Bergne, Co-Director
Number of Staff: 10
Publications: Democracy in Armenia: Crisis or Renewal?, 2000; *The Georgian-Abkhaz Peace Process: A New Role for the United Nations Observer Mission in Georgia?,* 2000; *Assessment of OSCE Work in the Caucasus,* 1999.

Tel: +44 (20) 7930 2001
Fax:+44 (20) 7930 1360
info@links-london.org
www.links-london.org

Balkans

Medact

ACTION
ADVOCACY

Medact is an organization of health professionals concerned about the health impacts of violent conflict, poverty, and environmental degradation. It was for five years an implementing partner in the Unicef program sending mental health professionals who gave help in the psychological rehabilitation of children and their families in the former Yugoslavia. Medact considers such activities as a form of conflict prevention in that they break the cycle of violence. Medact has organized conferences on conflict prevention, the health effects of conflict, and the role of health professionals in preventing violence and on improving the health of refugees and asylum seekers in the UK.

601 Holloway Road
London N19 4DJ
United Kingdom

Tel: +44 (20) 7272 2020
Fax: +44 (20) 7281 5717
gillreeve@medact.org
www.medact.org

Contact: Jack Piachaud, Chair of the Working Group on Violence, Conflict and Health
Number of staff: 9

Publications: Communiqué, newsletter three times a year; *Medicine, Conflict and Survival,* quarterly journal.

Northern Ireland

Mediation Network
for Northern Ireland

EDUCATION
ACTION

The Mediation Network for Northern Ireland, established in 1991, assists reconciliation in the country by supporting a culture in which conflict is dealt with constructively. It seeks to promote a culture of third-party intervention. The Network provides training in community relations, conflict intervention, and mediation. It also builds and maintains a corps of mediators, supports individuals and organizations in developing capacities for intervention in conflict, and provides mediative assistance in disputes.

10 Upper Crescent
Belfast BT7 1NT
Northern Ireland
United Kingdom

Tel: +44 (28) 9043 8614
Fax: +44 (28) 9031 4430
info@mediation-network.co.uk
www.mediation-network.co.uk

Contact: Brendan McAllister, Director
Publications: Mediation and Peace-Building, 2000; *Mediation: An Outline of its Application Lessons Learned,* 2000; *Encountering the Strange: Mediation and Reconciliation in Northern Ireland's Parades Conflict,* 1999.

United Kingdom

Mediation UK

EDUCATION
ADVOCACY

Mediation UK is a network of projects, organizations, and individuals interested in mediation. It serves individuals and projects involved or interested in constructive ways of settling conflicts. In addition, it provides information and referral services on mediation, and helps individuals and groups find mediation services, training, and practitioners. Mediation UK sponsors training events and workshops for professionals and volunteers, and organizes meetings and conferences.

Alexander House
Telephone Avenue
Bristol BS1 4BS
United Kingdom
_____
Tel: +44 (117) 904 6661
Fax: +44 (117) 904 3331
mediationuk@mediationuk.org.uk
www.cix.co.uk/~mediationuk

Contact: Tony Billinghurst, Director
Budget: $100,000–$500,000
Publications: Mediation, quarterly magazine; *Directory of Mediation and Conflict Resolution Services.*

Global

Minority Rights Group International

RESEARCH
ACTION
ADVOCACY

Minority Rights Group International (MRG) is a non-governmental organization working to secure rights for ethnic, religious, and linguistic minorities worldwide, and to promote cooperation and understanding between communities. MRG has over 30 years of experience promoting the rights of marginalized, non-dominant groups within society. MRG has four main activities: researching and publishing; advocacy to secure the rights of minorities; educating children and teachers on minority issues; and cooperative efforts with other organizations and activists who share its aims to build alliances, discuss ideas, develop skills, and further minority rights worldwide.

379 Brixton Road
London DW9 7DE
United Kingdom
_____
Tel: +44 (20) 7978 9498
Fax: +44 (20) 7738 6265
minority.rights@mrgmail.org
www.minorityrights.org

Contact: Alan Phillips, Director
Number of staff: 26
Budget: > $1,000,000
Publications: Outsider, newsletter; *World Directory of Minorities,* 2001; *The International Convention on the Elimination of All Forms of Racial Discrimination: A Guide for NGOs,* 2001; *Minority Rights in Yugoslavia,* 2000; *Batwa Pygmies of the Great Lakes Region,* 2000.

Northern Ireland, Republic of Ireland

Nonviolent Action Training Project

EDUCATION
ACTION

The Nonviolent Action Training Project (NAT) was established in 1988 under the auspices of the Fellowship of Reconciliation Ireland (FORI). NAT's main objective is to help groups explore imaginative, effective and nonviolent ways of working in the Northern Ireland context. NAT is founded on the premise that nonviolence and nonviolent tools and techniques can be successfully applied to a variety of conflict issues in Northern Ireland. All courses given are tailor-made to the needs of a group, and discussion takes place to explore exactly what is being sought. NAT provides various publications on nonviolence and nonviolent training.

16 Ravensdene Park
Belfast BT6 0DA
Northern Ireland
United Kingdom

Tel/fax: +44 9064 7106

Contact: Rob Fairmichael, Volunteer/Trainer

Number of staff: 1

Publications: Exploring Nonviolence.

Global

Oxfam GB

RESEARCH
EDUCATION
ACTION
ADVOCACY

As a development and humanitarian relief agency, Oxfam GB increasingly has to cope with conflict. Direct victims of conflict are enabled to survive by providing them with their basic needs. Support is given to grassroots community groups working to safeguard their rights, prevent violence, and rebuild their societies. Oxfam GB urges international decisionmakers to help prevent and resolve conflicts. It seeks to strengthen governmental and multilateral commitment to conflict prevention, resolution, and reconstruction. In 1997, the Cut Conflict Campaign was launched, calling on governments to curb the arms trade, bring war criminals to justice, promote peace through general aid, trade and economic policies, and uphold the rights of refugees.

274 Banbury Road
Oxford OX2 7DZ
United Kingdom

Tel: +44 (1865) 312 610
Fax: +44 (1865) 312 380
oxfam@oxfam.org
www.oxfam.org.uk

Contact: Suzanne Williams, Policy Advisor

Number of staff: 6

Publications: Building Sustainable Peace: Conflict, Conciliation and Civil Society in Ghana; Ending Violence Against Women: A Challenge for Development and Humanitarian Work; Listening to the Displaced: Action Research in the Conflict Zones of Sri Lanka; Post-War Reconstruction in Central America.

Global

Oxford Research Group

RESEARCH
ACTION
ADVOCACY

The Oxford Research Group is an independent team of researchers and support staff who combine rigorous research into nuclear decisionmaking with an understanding of the people who make those decisions. Their aim is to assist in the building of a more secure world without nuclear weapons and to promote non-violent solutions to conflict. Their work involves policy research, the promotion of accountability and transparency, facilitation of public debate, and the fostering of dialogue. They recently published a book containing stories of people resolving conflict.

51 Plantation Road
Oxford OX2 6JE
United Kingdom

Tel: +44 (1865) 242 819
Fax: +44 (1865) 794 652
org@oxfordresearchgroup.org.uk
www.oxfordresearchgroup.org.uk

Contact: Scilla Elworthy, Director

Number of staff: 9

Publications: War Prevention Works: 50 Stories of People Resolving Conflict, 2001; *Dialogue with Decision-Makers: Everyone's Guide to Achieving Change,* 2000; *Current Decisions Reports.*

Horn of Africa

Pastoral and Environmental Network in the Horn of Africa

RESEARCH

The Pastoral and Environmental Network in the Horn of Africa (PENHA) was established by a group of researchers, academics, and workers in the Horn of Africa to further development efforts in the region leading to self-reliance and peaceful co-existence. PENHA works to eliminate poverty among pastoralists in the Horn of Africa through the empowerment of communities, and the fostering of sustainable and dignified livelihoods based both on the keeping of livestock as well as other economic activities. PENHA is also involved in research, information exchanges, training, and publishing.

1 Laney House
Port Pool Lane
P.O. Box 494
London EC1N 7FP
United Kingdom

Tel: +44 (20) 7242 0202
Fax: +44 (20) 7404 6778
info@penhanetwork.org
www.penhanetwork.org

Contact: Zeremariam Fre, Director
Budget: $100,000–$500,000

Northern Ireland

Peace and Reconciliation Group

EDUCATION
ACTION

The Peace & Reconciliation Group (PRG) consists of a small number of people with different backgrounds—Nationalist, Unionist, British, and Irish—and who want to do something positive in a conflict situation. PRG sees the task of reconciliation as the rebuilding of confidence and understanding and the reduction of fear and tension at personal and community level. The Group believes that everyone has to play a part in making peace and making sure there is a working relationship with people at all levels. PRG organizes seminars and conferences on issues effecting the conflict and provides training in community relations issues.

18-20 Bishop Street
Londonderry BT48 6PW
Northern Ireland
United Kingdom

Tel: +44 7136 9206
Fax: +44 7137 7009

Contact: Tanya Gallagher, Co-ordinator

Number of staff: 5

Publications: Newsletter; training pack.

Colombia, Indonesia/East Timor, Mexico

Peace Brigades International

ACTION

Peace Brigades International (PBI) is an international nongovernmental organization that protects human rights and promotes nonviolent conflict transformation. PBI works in areas of violent conflict where local organizations committed to nonviolent social change are often under severe threat. This work is implemented by sending teams of international volunteers who undertake protective accompaniment, peace education, and independent observation and reporting. In order to deter the potential perpetrators of violence, their work is backed up by a broad international network of organizations and individuals. The aim of PBI's presence is to deter violence so that local organizations can carry out their work.

5 Caledonian Road
London N1 9DX
United Kingdom

Tel: +44 (20) 7713 0392
Fax: +44 (20) 7837 2290
pbiio@gn.apc.org
www.peacebrigades.org

Contact: Helen Yuill, Internal Communications Worker

Number of staff: 4 in HQ, 20 internationally

Budget: > $1,000,000

Publications: Unarmed Bodyguards: International Accompaniment for the Protection of Human Rights, 1998.

Ireland

EDUCATION
ACTION

Peace Pledge Ireland Campaign

The Peace Pledge Ireland Campaign was founded in 1989 to promote, directly and indirectly, ecumenical community events. It is based in Northern Ireland but functions across the boundary between Ulster and the Irish Republic. The Campaign is involved in organizing conferences, workshops, public information programs, and publishing activities. Since the signing of the Good Friday Peace Accord in Northern Ireland, the Campaign has worked to assist in the establishment of the new inter-communal governmental institutions.

8 Thornhill
Bangor BT19 1RD
Co. Down
Northern Ireland
United Kingdom

Tel: +44 (28) 9145 4898
Fax: +44 (28) 9127 4274

Contact: David Bleakley
Number of staff: 4
Budget: < $25,000

Global

RESEARCH
EDUCATION
ADVOCACY

Peaceworkers UK

The mission of the non-governmental Peaceworkers UK, established in November 2000, is to increase the pool of people trained and available for international peace work, and to increase the opportunities for civilian participation in international peace missions by the UN, OSCE, or NGOs. Second, it seeks to increase the availability of suitable training and placement programs in the UK. For the moment Peaceworkers UK is in the research stage, exploring, together with other UK organizations, the feasibility of developing a Civil Peace Service. The first pilot project is expected to be run in 2002.

162 Holloway Road
London N7 8DD
United Kingdom

Tel: +44 (20) 7609 2777
Fax: +44 (20) 7609 9777
info@peaceworkers.fsnet.co.uk
www.peaceworkers.fsnet.co.uk

Contact: Timmon Milne-Wallis, Director
Number of staff: 2
Budget: $100,000–$500,000

Bosnia and Herzegovina, Croatia, Georgia,
Northern Ireland, Afghanistan, Sri Lanka, Guatemala

RESEARCH
EDUCATION

PRDU

The academic Post-War Reconstruction and Development Unit (PRDU) specializes in research, consultancy and training of professionals in issues of the management and planning of reconstruction after war, humanitarian intervention in complex political emergencies, and post-war recovery. The Unit developed a one year MA in Post-War Recovery Studies to provide accessible, professionally relevant, multi-disciplinary training specifically developed to cover these areas of concern. The PRDU is part of the Department of Politics of the University of York.

Derwent College
University of York
Heslington
York YO10 5DD
United Kingdom

Tel: +44 (1904) 432 640
Fax: +44 (1904) 432 641
www.york.ac.uk/depts/poli/prdu

Contact: Roger MacGinty, Lecturer

Number of Staff: 11

Publications: *Revival*, newsletter; *Institutional Development of Southern NGOs: What Role for Northern NGOs?* 2000; *From Rhetoric to Reality: The Role of Aid in Local Peacebuilding in Afghanistan*, 1998; *Urban Triumph or Urban Disaster?: Dilemmas of Contemporary Post-war Reconstruction*, 1998; *Water under Fire*, 1997.

Eastern Europe, Sri Lanka, Middle East

EDUCATION
ACTION

Quaker Peace and Service

Quaker Peace and Service is a religious organization working mainly in the field of mediation citizen diplomacy and education on conflict prevention and resolution. Its International Relations Section has a special Reconciliation Program. It has a large number and variety of projects in Sri Lanka, Former Yugoslavia, Lebanon, and Northern Ireland. The Quaker United Nations Office Geneva deals with disarmament, the problem of child soldiers, refugees, and new international agreements on trade and development.

Friends House
173 Euston Road
London NW1 2BJ
United Kingdom

Tel: +44 (20) 7663 1053
miliusp@quaker.org.uk
www.quaker.org.uk

Contact: Bob Neidhardt, Conciliation Programme Coordinator

Global

Responding to Conflict

RESEARCH
EDUCATION
ACTION
ADVOCACY

Since its foundation in 1991, Responding to Conflict (RTC) has sought ways to support and extend the efforts of people engaged in resolving or ameliorating the situations of political and social conflict in which they live.

RTC therefore works with local and international NGOs and increasingly also with UN agencies, diplomats, government officials, and public service institutions. Using French, Spanish, and Russian as well as English, RTC provides a range of practical opportunities for individuals and organizations to reassess and redirect their programs, and facilitates the sharing of insights and experience across cultures and continents.

RTC's regular courses are "Working with Conflict," for practitioners in development, human rights, emergencies, and peacebuilding; and a workshop called "Strengthening Practice and Policy," for staff of international agencies with advisory or direct management responsibility for relief, development, rights, and peacebuilding programs.

In addition to the open program of courses, RTC staff are frequently invited by both local and international organizations to accompany them in working on situations of actual and potential conflict in different parts of the world. Wherever possible they share this work with colleagues in the region.

For a few years RTC and the Coalition for Peace in Africa (COPA) have been engaged in a joint project, "Linking Practice to Policy: a multi-level approach to peace-building." This project aims primarily to influence policy-makers of international agencies and governments. Initially, the project is concerned with documenting case studies of African peacemaking initiatives using video, sound, and photography as well as written material.

Responding to Conflict currently has a new three-year international program called Action for Conflict Transformation (ACTION) which focuses on capacity-building in conflict-affected areas. ACTION will bring together experienced practitioners who are catalysts for conflict transformation and peacebuilding in their own conflict-affected areas of the world. They work and learn together as an international team.

1046 Bristol Road
Birmingham B29 6LJ
United Kingdom

Tel: +44 (121) 415 5641
Fax: +44 (121) 415 4119
enquiries@respond.org
www.respond.org

Contact: Simon Fisher, Director

Number of Staff: 8

Publications: Working with Conflict: Skills and Strategies for Action, 2000.

Global

Richardson Institute for Peace Studies

RESEARCH

The Richardson Institute for Peace Studies, a research center within the Department of Politics and International Relations at Lancaster University, is involved in teaching and research on peaceful change and conflict resolution. It was the first peace research institute in Britain. It promotes an understanding of the conditions of peaceful change, researches and encourages the practical application of its work, and undertakes applied peacebuilding activities in areas of conflict or potential conflict. The Institute offers an Masters program in Conflict Resolution and a Bachelors in Peace Studies and International Relations.

Lancaster University
Lancaster LA1 4YF
United Kingdom

Tel: +44 (1524) 594 290
Fax: +44 (1524) 594 238
ri@lancaster.ac.uk
www.lancs.ac.uk/users/richinst/

Contact: Hugh Miall, Director

Number of staff: 3

Budget: $25,000–$1,000,000

Publications: Small Hearts and Big Minds: Prospects for Sustainable Peace in Sierra Leone; Central Asia and the Caucasus: Conflict and Security in the Post Soviet Space.

Europe, Africa

Saferworld

RESEARCH
EDUCATION
ACTION
ADVOCACY

Saferworld is an independent research group committed to alerting governments and educating the public about the need for more effective approaches to tackling and preventing armed conflicts around the globe. Saferworld conducts research on the causes that underlie armed conflict and, in consultation with experts, suggests steps governments can take.

The group was founded in 1989 following the end of the Cold War and in response to the changing nature of armed conflict. Throughout the world, the vast majority of wars are now fought within countries rather than between them and are dominated by the use of small arms. That is why Saferworld's main programs deal with conflict management and the arms trade

Saferworld wants to act as a catalyst for change through a wide network of parliamentarians, civil servants, academics, journalists, and NGOs. It publishes research reports targeted at key policymakers throughout Europe, the United States, and Africa. Saferworld aims to provide new information and fresh analyses. It stays in close dialogue with government officials, parliamentarians, and other opinion shapers.

Saferworld holds seminars, roundtables and other meetings, in order to bring together policymakers from different countries to help develop common approaches to specific conflict prevention and arms controls issues.

The research group is working with a program on small arms in South Africa (together with the Institute of Security Studies of South Africa) called "Tackling the Proliferation of Small Arms in Southern Africa." Saferworld monitors the EU Code of Conduct on Arms Exports and works with supportive governments to ensure further development of the Code. The Group examines the development of common measures for illicit arms trafficking, especially in Central and Eastern Europe. It is a member of the International Action Network on Small Arms (IANSA).

46 Grosvenor Gardens
London SW1W 0EB
United Kingdom

Tel: +44 (20) 7881 9290
Fax: +44 (20) 7881 9291
general@saferworld.demon.co.uk
www.saferworld.co.uk

Contact: Paul Eavis, Director

Number of Staff: 13

Publications: Transparency and Accountability in European Arms Export Controls: Towards Common Standards and Best Practice, 2000*; Prevention of Violent Conflict and the Coherence of EU Policies towards the Horn of Africa: Case Studies on Uganda, Djibouti and Ethiopia,* 2000*; Kosovo: the Crisis and Beyond,* 1999.

Global

Verification Research, Training and Information Centre

RESEARCH
EDUCATION
ADVOCACY

The Verification Research, Training and Information Centre (VERTIC) is an independent organization which aims to provide reliable information on compliance with international and intra-national agreements. It is also involved in negotiation, monitoring, and implementation of such agreements. VERTIC operates from the premise that the success of any agreement depends on an atmosphere of trust, best established when compliance or noncompliance can be verified. VERTIC has done extensive work in the fields of nuclear, chemical, biological and conventional weapons, and climate change. It is also involved in research, training, and dissemination of information.

Baird House
15-17 St. Cross Street
London EC1N 8UW
United Kingdom

Tel: +44 (20) 7440 6960
Fax: +44 (20) 7242 3266
info@vertic.org
www.vertic.org

Contact: Trevor Findlay, Director

Number of staff: 8

Budget: $500,000–$1,000,000

Publications: Verification Yearbooks: Arms Control, Peacekeeping and the Environment; Laying the Foundations for Getting to Zero: Verifying the Transition to Low Levels of Nuclear Weapons.

Global

Applied Conflict Resolution Organizations Network

ADVOCACY

The Applied Conflict Resolution Organizations Network (ACRON) is a network of over 22 organizations actively engaged in peacebuilding activities around the world. As an organization, ACRON seeks to enhance the effectiveness of international conflict resolution and peacebuilding activities by: promoting communication, coordination, and collaboration among applied conflict resolution organizations; increasing awareness of and funding for the field; and building bridges to other applied and academic organizations in related fields. ACRON members are mostly—but not exclusively—non-governmental US-based non-profit organizations. All have significant experience in the field of applied conflict resolution and peacebuilding.

c/o The Institute of World Affairs
1321 Pennsylvania Ave., SE
Washington, DC 20003
USA

Tel: +1 (202) 544 4141
nlaslett@iwa.org
www.acron.iwa.org

Contact: Neil Laslett, the Institute of World Affairs

Global

Association for Conflict Resolution

The Association for Conflict Resolution (ACR) is a professional organization dedicated to enhancing the practice and public understanding of conflict resolution. ACR represents and serves a diverse audience that includes more than 7000 mediators, arbitrators, facilitators, educators, and others involved in the field of conflict resolution and collaborative decisionmaking. The International Section seeks to make nonviolent dispute resolution processes more readily available to countries throughout the world. It seeks to honor global diversity by working with indigenous people to design and implement processes which best meet the needs of the culture, consistent with the goal of resolving conflicts with maximum equity for all parties.

1527 New Hampshire Avenue, NW third floor
Washington DC 20036
USA

Tel: +1 (202) 667 9700
Fax: +1 (202) 265 1968
info@acresolution.org
www.acresolution.org

Contact: Daniel Bowling,
Executive Director
Number of staff: 15
Budget: > $1,000,000
Publications: ACR Newsletter.

Global

Carter Center

The Carter Center works to advance peace and health worldwide. Founded in 1982 by former US President Jimmy Carter and Rosalynn Carter, the Atlanta-based Center focuses in its conflict resolution program on peaceful prevention and resolution of conflicts, primarily civil wars.

An array of associated programs reinforces the Center's conflict resolution work. These include activities to improve nations' capacities for sustainable development, promote, and protect human rights, and strengthen democracy. Through its Conflict Resolution Program (CRP), the Carter Center marshals the expertise of peacemakers worldwide to prevent and resolve armed conflicts around the globe. It is the base for the International Council for Conflict Resolution, a small body of internationally recognized experts and world leaders. They are engaged on an individual basis in ongoing CRP projects.

The CRP regularly monitors many of the world's armed conflicts in an attempt to better understand their histories, the primary actors involved, disputed issues, and efforts being made to resolve them. When a situation arises where President Carter has a unique role to play and specific conditions have been met, the CRP directly supports his intervention.

In order to make mediation more effective the Center fosters collaboration among individuals, NGOs, official agencies, and corporations. It tries to identify creative ways to address problems, seeks partners to implement solutions, and aims to build the internal capacity of countries to ensure continued growth and progress.

In 1994 President Carter and his Center brokered a four-month ceasefire in Bosnia and a pledge from all sides to resume peace talks. In Estonia an effort was made to ease tensions over citizenship and language issues by holding workshops for parties to work through their differences.

The Carter Center is part of Emory University, a selective private university in Atlanta. Private donations from individuals, foundations and corporations, and project support from international development-assistance agencies finance the Center.

Office of Public Information
453 Freedom Parkway
Atlanta, GA 30307
USA

Tel: +1 (404) 331 3900
Fax: +1 (404) 420 5145
carterweb@emory.edu
www.cartercenter.org

Contact: Ben Hoffman, Director of the Conflict Resolution Program

Budget: > $1,000,000

Publications: Carter Center News, biannual; Developing a Methodology for Conflict Prevention: The Case of Estonia, 1999.

Global

Collaborative for Development Action

The Collaborative for Development Action (CDA), headed by Mary B. Anderson, is a small consulting agency that works with nongovernmental organizations, governments, and UN agencies involved in humanitarian and development assistance.

The focus of CDA efforts with its collaborating partners is to support people's activities in developing peaceful and productive societies and economies. Incorporated in 1985, CDA has worked in over seventy-five countries to support local economic and social development. CDA has also worked on integrating gender analysis into the design and implementation for aid programs and on achieving sustainable public health and primary education systems.

Current projects include "Local Capacities for Peace Project" (LCPP); "Reflecting on Peace Practice Project"(RPP); "Corporate Options: Constructive Engagement in Conflict Zones" (CEP).

The LCPP seeks to identify ways in which assistance given in conflict settings may be provided so that, rather than exacerbating and worsening the conflict, it helps local people disengage from fighting and develop systems for settling the problems that prompt conflict within their societies.

In the RPP Project, all kinds of agencies collaborate in gathering experiences from their recent conflict-focused programs and identify what works and what does not work. The project will produce twenty-five field-based case studies of work in different areas of the world, in different conflicts, and different stages of conflicts.

The CEP Project helps companies clarify and manage the interactions of their corporate activities with conflicts. The approach involves a systematic and comparative examination of a range of corporate field operations designed to identify the patterns of interactions between business and conflict. This results in identification of management options and development of practical tools for achieving more constructive interactions with local communities that reinforce a climate of political and economic stability.

26 Walker Street
Cambridge, MA 02138
USA

Tel: +1 (617) 661 6310
Fax: +1 (617) 661 3805
mail@cdainc.com
www.cdainc.com

Contact: Wolfgang Heinrich, Project Coordinator Local Capacities for Peace Project

Number of staff: 6

Publications: Do No Harm: How Aid Can Support Peace- Or War, 1999; *Rising from the Ashes: Development Strategies in Times of Disaster,* 1998.

Global

Conflict Management Group

Conflict Management Group (CMG) was founded in 1984 to place into public practice an innovative approach to negotiation developed at Harvard Law School (HLS). CMG still has close working relationships with HLS. As an international nonprofit organization, CMG is dedicated to improving the methods of negotiation, conflict resolution, and cooperative decisionmaking as applied to issues of public concern.

CMG has many years of practical experience around the world in a variety of arenas including bilateral and multilateral diplomacy, border conflicts, and internal and ethnic strife. Among its activities are negotiation and conflict resolution training, consultation, and assistance in structuring and facilitating negotiation, mediation, and consensus-building processes and facilitation of inter-ethnic dialogue.

In Cyprus, CMG collaborated with the Institute for Multi-Track Diplomacy to provide joint conflict resolution training and dialogue facilitation to over 300 Greek and Turkish Cypriots. CMG has worked extensively in the former Soviet Union to address ethnic conflict through the establishment of a Network for Ethnological Monitoring and Early Warning on Conflict. CMG inaugurated the MOMENTUM program in several former Soviet Republics. The program is designed to assist young promising decisionmakers from the region to acquire the leadership skills necessary to turn their respective countries into more democratic and prosperous entities that can hold their place in the world politically and economically. CMG also developed a model program in the Great Lakes Region of Central Africa designed to strengthen the conflict management skills of civil society actors and prepare them to actively participate in the post-conflict reconstruction of their societies.

With the World Health Organisation (WHO), CMG formed a partnership to develop and provide practical advice, strategies, and operational tools to ensure the effective participation of developing countries in international negotiations, rule setting, and institutions. The project seeks to develop the capacity of developing countries to negotiate the advancement of the public health as an essential part of building human capital needed for real development.

The Roger Fisher House
9 Waterhouse Street
Cambridge, MA 02138
USA

Tel: +1 (617) 354 5444
Fax: +1 (617) 354 8467
info@cmgroup.org
www.cmgroup.org

Contact: L. Michael Hager, Executive Director

Number of staff: 10

Publications: Peace by Piece, quarterly newsletter; *Planning for Intervention,* 1999; *Preventing Conflict in the Post-Communist World,* 1996; *Beyond Machiavelli: Tools for Coping with Conflict,* 1996.

Global
Coexistence Initiative

The Coexistence Initiative believes in greater understanding between peoples and the settlement of conflicts without recourse to violence and it acts as a catalyst, driver, advocate, and clearinghouse for other institutions and individuals with the same beliefs. In order to reach its aims, the Coexistence Initiative works to set the agenda for coexistence at political and policy levels, create an international network, as well as heightening public awareness and involvement in the issue. The organization manages a Coexistence Resource Center, a gateway to coexistence material on the Internet as well as a source of valuable coexistence information.

477 Madison Avenue, 4th floor
New York, NY 10022
USA

Tel: +1 (212) 303 9445
Fax: +1 (212) 980 4027
info@coexistence.net
www.coexistence.net

Contact: Eric Nonacs, Executive Director

Number of staff: 4

Publications: The Coexistence Noticeboard, biweekly on-line periodical; *The Coexistence Chronicle,* on-line periodical.

Global
Eastern Mennonite University's Conflict Transformation Program

The Eastern Mennonite University's Conflict Transformation Program (CTP) comprises a Master of Arts degree in conflict transformation and the Institute for Justice and Peacebuilding (IJP). The IJP provides services in the form of training sessions, consultancies, peace-process design, conciliation, mediation, and action-oriented research. Through its links with partners in Africa and Latin America and with practitioners engaged in peacebuilding worldwide, IJP provides a connection between current practice and the academic program. CTP supports the professional development of individuals as peacebuilders and strengthens the peacebuilding capacities of the institutions they serve.

1200 Park Road
Harrisonburg, VA 22802-2462
USA

Tel: +1 (540) 432 4490
Fax: +1 (540) 432 4449
ctprogram@emu.edu
www.emu.edu/ctp

Contact: John Paul Lederach, Founding Director

Number of staff: 14

Publications: Footpaths, newsletter; *From the Ground Up: Mennonite Contributions to International Peacebuilding,* 2000; *The Journey Toward Reconciliation,* 1999; *Building Peace: Sustainable Reconciliation in Divided Societies,* 1998.

Central and Eastern Europe, Russia, Central Asia

RESEARCH
EDUCATION
ACTION
ADVOCACY

EastWest Institute

The EastWest Institute (EWI), founded in 1981, aims to defuse tensions and conflicts that threaten geopolitical stability in Eastern Europe. In the past the Institute has served as a security think tank and has supported the development of democracy, free enterprise, and European integration. In the near future the Institute wants to serve as a long-term strategic partner facilitating stability, economic development, and democracy with special attention for Russia, Trans-Caucasus, and Central Asia. The EWI provides information about economic and business developments, advises governments on reforms, and organizes conferences. EWI has offices in Brussels, Kiev, Prague, Moscow, and New York.

700 Broadway, 2nd floor
New York, NY 10003
USA

Tel: +1 (212) 824 4100
Fax: +1 (212) 824 4149
iews@iews.org
www.iews.org

Contact: John Edwin Mroz, President
Number of staff: 65
Budget: > $1,000,000
Publications: EW Insight, quarterly bulletin; *Russian Regional Report,* weekly survey.

Global

RESEARCH
EDUCATION
ACTION
ADVOCACY

Human Rights Watch

Human Rights Watch (HRW) is the largest human rights organization based in the United States. Its researchers conduct fact-finding investigations into human rights abuses in all regions of the world. Those findings are then published in books and reports every year to put the spotlight on abusive governments. HRW lobbies at the United Nations, the European Union, and in capitals around the world to urge changes in policy and practice. In moments of crisis, HRW provides up-to-the-minute information about conflicts. Refugee accounts, collected by HRW, helped shape the response of the international community to recent wars in Kosovo, Chechnya, and Afghanistan.

350 Fifth Avenue, 34th floor
New York, NY 10118-3299
USA

Tel: +1 (212) 290 4700
Fax: +1 (212) 736 1300
hrwnyc@hrw.org
www.hrw.org

Contact: Kenneth Roth, Executive Director
Publications: News releases; *Welcome to Hell: Arbitrary Detention, Torture, and Extortion in Chechnya,* 2000.

Global

Institute for
Conflict Analysis and Resolution

RESEARCH
ACTION
ADVOCACY

The Institute for Conflict Analysis and Resolution (ICAR) aims to advance the understanding and resolution of significant and persistent human conflicts among individuals, groups, communities, identity groups, and nations.

The ICAR community has close ties with a number of affiliated organizations, which play an important role in the field of conflict resolution, locally, nationally, and internationally. At the heart of the Institute's work is the systematic and ongoing analysis of the nature, origins, and types of social conflict and of the processes and conditions required for the co-operative resolution of conflicts.

The Institute pursues its mission through four major components. It offers M.Sc. and Ph.D. degrees in conflict analysis and resolution, as well as training and short courses for general and specialized audiences.

Enhancing the degree programs are three additional components: research and publication, a clinical and consultancy program, and public education. The research and publication component focuses on exploration of conditions which attract parties to the negotiation table, the role of third parties in dispute resolution, and the testing of a variety of conflict intervention methods.

A clinical program is offered to students through the Applied Practice and Theory Program and through consultant work with individual faculties, associates, and affiliate organizations.

Community outreach is accomplished through the publication of books and articles, public lectures, conferences, seminars, and special briefings on the theory and practice of conflict resolution. In all, ICAR can be considered one of the major institutes when it comes to linking theory and practice of conflict management.

George Mason University
Fairfax
Virginia 22030-4444
USA

Tel: +1 (703) 993 1300
Fax: +1 (703) 993 1302
icarinfo@osf1.gmu.edu
www.gmu.edu/departments/icar

Contact: Sara Cobb, Director

Publications: Culture and Conflict Resolution, 2000; *The New Agenda for Peace Research,* 2000; *Conflict Resolution: Dynamics, Process and Structure,* 2000.

Balkans, Cyprus, South Asia, Africa

EDUCATION
ACTION

Institute for Multi-Track Diplomacy

The mission of the Institute for Multi-Track Diplomacy (IMTD) is to promote a systems approach to peacebuilding and to facilitate the transformation of deep-rooted social conflicts. The Institute, chaired by Ambassador John W. McDonald, seeks to integrate different approaches in any given case of conflict transformation and identifies nine dimensions or "tracks": governmental; professional conflict resolution; business; private citizen; media; religion; activism; research, training and education; and philanthropy.

Each track in the system, the Institute says, brings with it its own perspective, approach, and resources, all of which must be called on in the peacebuilding process. The Institute assumes that individuals and organizations are more effective working together than separately and that ethnic and regional conflict situations involve a large and intricate web of parties and factors.

An example of one of the activities is the India-Pakistan Business and Conflict Resolution Program, which aims to increase awareness and to engage the business community in concrete peacebuilding initiatives in Southeast Asia. Another example of an IMTD activity is the International Negotiation Skills Training. The aim of this program is to empower elected political leaders and others involved in peacebuilding efforts with skills of effective communication and diplomatic protocol to give them better capabilities to negotiate. A third example is the Inter-Kashmir Dialogue and Negotiation Skills Workshop, a project that promotes citizen peace building in the region of Kashmir by bringing together concerned citizens from both sides of the Line of Control (LoC). And in IMTD's Dialogue Program, the Institute seeks to mobilize and engage communities affected by violent conflict to enter into the process of dialogue. IMTD has facilitated dialogues for Ethiopians, Eritreans, Somalis, Cubans, and Sudanese.

1819 H Street NW Suite 1200
Washington, DC 20006
USA

Tel: +1 (202) 466 4605
Fax: +1(202) 466 4607
imtd@imtd.org
www.imtd.org

Contact: Chris Bjornestad, Program Associate

Number of staff: 5

Budget: $500,000–$1,000,000

Publications: PeaceBuilder, newsletter; *The Need for Multi-Track Diplomacy*

Multi-Track Diplomacy: A Systems Approach to Peace.

Central and Eastern Europe, South Caucasus, Latin America

Partners for Democratic Change

Partners for Democratic Change (Partners) is an international non-profit organization committed to building sustainable capacity to advance civil society and a culture of change and conflict management worldwide. It pursues this mission through locally managed Centers for Change and Conflict Management.

Since 1989, Partners has provided communication, negotiation, and cooperative planning skills to thousands of civic, NGO, municipal, and national government leaders in nearly forty countries. The Centers work within communities and are currently located in Argentina, Bulgaria, the Czech Republic, Georgia, Hungary, Kosovo, Lithuania, Poland, Romania, Slovakia, and the United States. In the last two years Partners has grown both in terms of the creation of new national centers in Albania and Kosovo, and in the increase of regional work. It is also working in more difficult settings, such as South Caucasus and Latin America, than it has in the past.

All the Centers work in the field of conflict resolution/prevention through a number of programs and projects such as ethnic conciliation, mediation, women's leadership, environmental work, cooperative planning, police-community relations, disability rights, NGO development, intersectoral relations, good municipal governance, etc. Services include conferences and workshops, publications on such issues as mediation and education for tolerance, training manuals, and documentary films.

The Regional Partnership, based in Budapest, facilitates the exchange of expertise between Centers and the mobilization of international teams of experts. In developing new centers, Partners International (composed of its New York and San Francisco offices) works together with the Budapest office to ensure the transfer of expertise, using experienced trainers from various countries.

Partners International works directly with the Centers and Regional Partnership to continuously enhance the Center's skills, and develop and build the capacities of new centers. A research unit has been developed to keep the entire organization abreast of new methodologies, programs, and lessons learned.

823 Ulloa Street
San Francisco CA 94127
USA

Tel: +1 (415) 665 0652
Fax: +1 (415) 665 2732
pdci@ix.netcom.com
www.partners-intl.org

Contact: Brad Heckman, Director of International Programs

Number of staff: 125

Budget: > $1,000,000

Publications: Partners International Newsletter

Books and Training Manuals for specific countries

Central and Eastern Europe, Balkans, CIS countries

Project on Ethnic Relations

The Project on Ethnic Relations (PER) was founded in 1991 in anticipation of the interethnic conflicts that were to erupt following the collapse of communism. This non-governmental, non-profit organization conducts programs of high-level intervention and dialogue and serves as a neutral mediator in several major disputes in the region.

PER also conducts programs of training, education, and research at international, national, and community levels. In addition to its headquarters in the United States, PER maintains centers and representations in Bulgaria, Hungary, Poland, Romania, Russia, Slovakia, and Yugoslavia (both in Belgrade and in Pristina).

Its core activities are mediation with governments and ethnic leaderships, seeking solutions to inter-ethnic disputes. Another major activity is working together with strategic elites, opinion leaders, government officials, and professionals on projects dealing with ethnic conflict and to help them to obtain expert advice on peaceful resolution. A third strategic goal is to assist in the development of institutions that deal with ethnic conflicts.

Among PER's most notable achievements are the roundtable talks that it initiated in 1991 between the government of Romania and its large Hungarian minority. It led to the conclusion of a pact that provides for the use of minority languages in public administration, multilingual place signs, and regional decentralization, among other measures. PER's efforts also contributed to the original decision of the present Slovak government to form an inter-ethnic governing coalition. Furthermore, PER was the pioneer in working with Europe's large, complex Roman (Gypsy) minority to establish regular channels of communication with national governments and international organizations. The organization co-operates, among others, with the UN, the European Union, the OSCE, the US government, and governments of Eastern and Central European countries and of the former Soviet Union. PER has been granted consultative status at the Council of Europe.

15 Chambers Street
Princeton
New Jersey NJ 08542-371078
USA

Tel: +1 (609) 683 5666
Fax: +1 (609) 683 5888
per@per-usa.org
www.per-usa.org

Contact: Allen H. Kassof, President ; Livia B. Plaks, Executive Director; Alex N. Grigor'ev, Program Officer
Number of staff: 7 at HQ, 15 in field
Budget: > $1,000,000
Publications: Albanians as Majorities and Minorities: A Regional Dialogue, 2001; *State Policies toward the Roma in Macedonia,* 2001; *The Year 2000 Elections in Romania: Interethnic Relations and European Integration,* 2000; *Montenegro on the Brink: Avoiding another Yugoslav War,* 2000; *Vojvodina: The Politics of Interethnic Accommodation,* 2000.

Central and Eastern Europe,
Balkans, CIS countries, Central Asia

ACTION

Soros Foundations Network

To transform closed societies into open ones and to protect and expand the values of existing open societies is the common mission of the Soros Foundations Network. To this end, the various entities of the Soros foundations network fund and operate an array of activities dealing with the arts and culture broadly defined; the strengthening of civil society; economic development, and reform; education at all levels and in diverse subject areas; human rights, with special attention to the rights of marginalized groups; legal reform and public administration; media and information, including publishing and support for libraries; and public health. The Soros Foundations Network consists of thirty-two autonomous institutions established in countries or regions to initiate or support open society activities. Soros foundations are located primarily in the former communist countries of Central and Eastern Europe and the former Soviet Union, as well as South African, Haiti, and Guatemala.

The national foundations are independent entities with their own boards of directors, staff, program priorities, application guidelines, and grant making procedures. In addition to operating their own programs, the foundations award grants—principally to local organizations and individuals.

The Open Society Institute-Brussels is the representative office of the Soros Foundations Network in Western Europe. It acts as a liaison office to facilitate collaboration between the Soros Foundations Network and West European partners, including the various institutions of the European Union, bilateral donors, and nongovernmental organizations.

In 2000, the Soros Foundations Network's expenditures totalled $500 million.

400 West 59th Street   *Contact:* Mabel Wisse Smit, Director
New York, NY 10019
USA

Tel: +1 (212) 584 0600
Fax: +1 (212) 548 4679
www.soros.org/osi

Open Society Institute-Brussels
26 rue des Minimes
1000 Brussels
Belgium

Tel/Fax: +32 (2) 505 46 46

Global

Search for Common Ground

EDUCATION
ACTION

Search for Common Ground, in partnership with the European Centre for Common Ground (see separate entry), is an international nonprofit peace and conflict resolution organization. Its goal is to transform conflict into co-operative action.

Search for Common Ground believes in long-term commitment in conflict areas in which they work. Currently, there are fully operational offices in Angola, Burundi, Iran, Liberia, Macedonia, Middle East, Sierra Leone, Ukraine, and the United States.

Search for Common Ground is convinced that traditional adversarial approaches are increasingly irrelevant in dealing with today's conflicts. The organization encourages a new level of thinking based on a non-adversarial framework.

Over the years, the organization has developed a toolbox that includes twenty-four different tools for conflict resolution and prevention. These include such traditional methods and approaches as training, capacity-building, and convening adversaries for dialogue, as well as less standard methods such as TV and radio productions, investigative reporting, sports, culture, and music. The organization emphasizes use of electronic media. Its media division, Common Ground Productions, carries out numerous projects including a children's television series in Macedonia (Nashe Maalo, Our Neighborhood), a TV-series on African conflicts and their resolution for broadcast in Africa, radio stations in Liberia and Sierra Leone (called Talking Drum Studio) and in Burundi (Studio Ijambo).

Established in 1982, the organization has experienced rapid expansion since the early 1990s. The sister office, the European Centre for Common Ground, was opened in Brussels, Belgium, in 1995.

1601 Connecticut Ave. N.W.
Suite 200
Washington, DC 20009
USA

Tel: +1 (202) 265 4300
Fax: +1 (202) 232 6718
search@sfcg.org
www.sfcg.org

Contact: Susan Collin Marks, Executive Vice President

Number of staff: 250

Publications: Search for Common Ground Newsletter; Bulletin of Regional Cooperation in the Middle East.

Global

United States Institute of Peace

The United States Institute of Peace (USIP) is a federal institution created and funded by the Congress to strengthen the nation's capacity to promote the peaceful resolution of international conflict. The board of directors is appointed by the president of the United States and confirmed by the Senate.

The Institute meets its congressional mandate through an array of programs, including grants, fellowships, conferences and workshops, library services, publications, and other educational activities. It seeks to mobilize the best national and international talent from research organizations, academia, and government to support policymakers by providing independent and creative assessments of how to deal with international conflict situations by political means. Conceptual projects cover cross-cultural negotiation, coercive diplomacy, civilian-military relations, human rights implementation, and political violence. USIP facilitates resolution of international disputes through 'Track II' encounters among parties to conflicts and by preparing US negotiators for mediation work. Furthermore, international affairs professionals are trained in conflict management and resolution techniques, mediation, and negotiation skills. The Institute seeks to strengthen curricula and instruction in educational institutions and raise the level of awareness about the changing character of international conflict and nonviolent approaches to managing international disputes. It also tracks and evaluates the role of new information technologies as they transform international relations and therefore open new possibilities to facilitate prevention, management and settlement of conflicts.

USIP awards grants to support academic research, curriculum development, public education, and other programs in the United States and elsewhere. The Institute sponsors a number of Special Initiatives, which represent issues that are of special concern. The Balkan website links facilitate information sharing by all those involved in conflict management in the former Yugoslavia. Other initiatives deal with the rule of law, religion, and peacemaking and virtual diplomacy.

1200 17th Street NW,
Suite 200
Washington, DC 20036-3011
USA

Tel: +1 (202) 429 3828
Fax: +1 (202) 429 6063
usip_requests@usip.org
www.usip.org

Contact: Richard H. Solomon, President

Publications: Peace Watch Newsletter; Peace Works; Guide to IGO's, NGO's and the Military in Peace and Relief Operations, 2001; *The Tragedy of Russia's Reforms,* 2001; *Serbia and Montenegro: Reintegration, Divorce or Something Else?* 2001.

Uzbekistan, Central Asia

Association of Uzbekistan for
Sustainable Water Resources Development

EDUCATION
ADVOCACY

The mission of the Association of Uzbekistan for Sustainable Water Resources Development (AUSWRD) is to bring together water resource specialists to discuss the issues of water consumption and conflict in Central Asia. In 1996 the association contributed to the establishment of a group of independent experts from the six countries of the Aral Sea basin for discussing the conflict-related issues of the region. The Association also provides training to local community leaders in the border regions of Uzbekistan on addressing the issues of water consumption and conflict.

Office 208a, 39-G Kari-Niyazova Street
Tashkent 700 000
Uzbekistan

Tel: +998 (71) 169 4338
Fax: +998 (71) 234 4940
auswr@freenet.uz
www.freeyellow.com/members8/abdullaev/auswrd.html

Contact: Madina
Nazhimova,
Chairperson
Number of staff: 6
Publications: Quarterly
newsletter; *General
Strategies in Preven-
tion of Aral Sea
Problems,* 1996.

Uzbekistan, Central Asia

Union for Defence of the
Aral Sea and the Amudarya

RESEARCH
ACTION
ADVOCACY

The Union for Defence of the Aral Sea and the Amudarya (UDASA) is a union of people who strives to protect the sea and the rivers that nourish it with the aim of improving environmental conditions and fostering stability in the region. Being one of the oldest NGOs in the region, UDASA considers the issues of water consumption an important aspect of conflict prevention in Central Asia. UDASA has a wide network of contacts among environmental NGOs in Central Asia and world-wide.

8th floor, 41 Berdakh Avenue
Nukus 742000
Karakalpakstan
Uzbekistan

Tel: +998 (61) 217 7229
Fax: +998 (61) 224 0616
udasa@nukus.freenet.uz
www.cango.net.kg/homepages/uz/udasa/

Contact: Yusup
Kamalov
Number of staff: 3

Kosovo, Macedonia

Forum

RESEARCH
ACTION
ADVOCACY

The Forum works to rebuild a postwar Kosovo by advocating for opportunities for all citizens to actively participate in the development of a Kosovar civil society. It aims to provide a platform for the exchange and realization of ideas as well as to develop interest groups that would effectively lobby both local and international organizations working for conflict prevention and reconciliation in Kosovo. Recently, the Forum has carried out an anti-violence campaign among youth groups (Boll mal) as well as conferences on reconciliation.

Qendra Tregtare Kroni i Bardhenr.1
Rruga Ilaz Kodra
Prishtina
Kosovo

Tel/fax: +381 (38) 548 946
theforum@ipko.org
www.forumi.org

Contact: Yll Bajraktari, Director
Number of staff: 8
Budget: $25,000–$100,000
Publications: The Forum Magazine.

Kosovo, Macedonia

Kosova Action for Civic Initiatives

RESEARCH
EDUCATION
ACTION
ADVOCACY

The Kosova Action for Civic Initiatives (KACI), formed in May 1998, is a young research think-tank, and NGO support center, that aims to help the international community to understand the main segments of decision making in Kosovo related to recent political developments. It also functions as an action council for civic initiatives, suggesting ideas for the development of civil society and helps the already present initiatives to get known by international NGOs.

Nena Tereze 18A-7
38000 Prishtina
Kosovo

Tel: +381 (38) 518 157
Fax: +381 (38) 518 156
kaci@kohamail.net
www.kaci-kosova.org

Contact: Ylber Hysa, Executive Director
Number of staff: 3
Budget: < $25,000

Montenegro

Association for
Culture of Peace and Non-Violence

RESEARCH
EDUCATION

The goals of the Association for Culture of Peace and Non-Violence (ANIMA) are to facilitate and establish concretely the idea of cooperation and tolerance, peace and nonviolence, understanding and accepting differences. Anima is a part of two networks: MANS (Network for affirmation of nongovernmental sector) and FRESTA (Peace and Stability through Cross-Boundary Civil Society Collaboration).

Stari grad 329
85330 Kotor
Montenegro
Yugoslavia

Tel/fax: +381 (82) 322 860
Tel: +381 (82) 322 858
anima@cg.yu

Contact: Julijana Cicovic, Director
Number of Staff: 7
Budget: < $25,000

Montenegro, Yugoslavia, Southeastern Europe

Center for
Democracy and Human Rights

RESEARCH
EDUCATION
ACTION
ADVOCACY

The Center for Democracy and Human Rights (CEDEM) is an NGO and think tank that analyzes and encourages democratic transitions, protects human rights and international standards of human rights as well as working to strengthen civil society in Montenegro by analyzing main currents and trends in the region. Its partners in the field of conflict prevention/resolution include the following NGOs: the US Institute of Peace, International Crisis Group, European Stability Initiative, Center for European Policy Studies, Danish Institute for International Relations, and the Hellenic Foundation for European & Foreign Policy.

Mose Pijade 40
81000 Podgorica
Montenegro
Yugoslavia

Tel/fax: +381 (81) 623 091
cedem@cg.yu

Contact: Srdjan Darmanovic, Director
Number of staff: 3
Publications: Transition in Montenegro, quarterly publication.

Federal Republic of Yugoslavia

Belgrade Center for Human Rights

The Belgrade Center for Human Rights was established by a group of human rights experts and activists. The main purpose of the Center is to study human rights and humanitarian law and to disseminate knowledge about them. By these means, it intends to promote the development of democracy and the rule of law in the region. The Belgrade Center's younger associates, students at its human rights schools, are members of the Balkan Youth Network. Their goal is to use joint campaigns to build bridges to similar organizations in the region and to eliminate prejudice, xenophobia, and other adverse consequences of armed conflicts.

Mlatisumina 26-I
11000 Belgrade
Yugoslavia

Tel/fax: +381 (11) 308 5328
bgcentar@bgcentar.org.yu
www.bgcentar.org.yu

Contact: Professor Vojin Dimitrijevic, Director

Number of staff: 9

Budget: < $25,000

Publications: Human Rights in FRY: A Comprehensive Report for 2000, in Serbian and English, 2001; *The Rights to Nationality,* in Serbian, 1999; *Cultural Rights,* in Serbian, 1999.

Serbia

Center for Psychological Growth and Development Encouragement

The Center for Psychological Growth and Development Encouragement (Oak) is a small organization working for conflict prevention and the mental health of children and adults. Oak organizes and implements workshops on conflict prevention for children and young people. These workshops are based on "the Goodwill Classroom" program developed by psychologists from Belgrade's Group MOST.

Vinicka 21
18000 Nis
Yugoslavia

Tel: +381 (18) 716 151
hrast@bankerinter.net

Contact: Tatjana Pejcic Radisavljevic

Number of staff: 15 volunteers

Budget: < $25,000

Yugoslavia

Center for
Free Elections and Democracy

EDUCATION
ACTION

The Center for Free Elections and Democracy (Centar za slobodne izbore i demokratiju—CeSID) draws together citizens on the basis of mutual trust and tolerance in order to contribute to the establishment of the Rule of Law and the enhancement of democratic values and institutions in the Federal Republic of Yugoslavia.

CeSID promotes these values through its educational and research programs and by organizing voters to monitor elections. CeSID has organized workshops for elected representatives in local assemblies in Vojvodina helping them acquire the knowledge and practical tools necessary to help them resolve local conflicts of interest and needs in parliamentary bodies by helping them to respect political and cultural differences.

Bearing in mind that previously held elections in Serbia were seen as a source of great political tension, repression, and disintegration of institutions, CeSID intends not only to open a new space for building bridges between political opponents, by educating its activists, but also to make communication easier between main actors in the election process. This would prevent or at least significantly reduce numerous disputes and conflicts, which might occur during the pre-election (candidacy, submitting the electoral lists, electoral communication etc.), election and post election campaign in order to secure elections as a peaceful way of overcoming political differences. Thereby the road to new democratic changes would be opened. CeSID's activists will be engaged in the future in disseminating knowledge and skills on conflict prevention and resolution issues in their local communities addressing specific target groups in need (trade unions, displaced persons, political parties etc.).

Kralja Milutina 21
11000 Belgrade
Yugoslavia

Contact: Soraja Sokovic,
Regional Coordinator Vojvodina
Number of staff: 3

Tel: +381 (11) 334 2762
Fax: +381 (11) 334 2771
cesid@bitsyu.net: sokovicsoraja@hotmail.com
www.cesid.org

Yugoslavia

European Movement in Serbia

EDUCATION
ACTION
ADVOCACY

The European Movement in Serbia is a non-governmental network that promotes European values in the Federal Republic of Yugoslavia. It aims to create a democratic, multipartisan society that recognizes human rights and the importance of integration of Yugoslavia into the rest of Europe. Together with the UNDP, it runs an early-warning system that aims at harmonization of interests and ethnic reconciliation. It also organizes training workshops to improve dialogue skills among various actors.

Dure Jaksica 5/F
11000 Belgrade
Yugoslavia
_____
Tel: +381 (11) 303 0687
Fax: +381 (11) 630 281
emins@gunet.yu
www.emins.org.yu

Contact: Dragan Lakicevic
Number of staff: 4
Budget: < $25,000
Publications: Europe Plus, monthly bulletin.

Serbia, Montenegro, Kosovo

Humanitarian Law Center

RESEARCH
ACTION

The Humanitarian Law Center (HLC) regularly and systematically monitors and researches human rights violations in Serbia, Montenegro, and Kosovo. Since it was founded, the HLC has investigated cases of killings, disappearances, sexual abuse, discrimination, and other breaches of the international humanitarian law that occurred during the armed conflicts in former Yugoslavia. Although the HLC does not have a special department for conflict resolution activities, it plays an important role in conflict transformation process in this region. The HLC reports on its findings and recommendations by publishing books, bulletins, and reports.

Avalska 9
11110 Belgrade
Yugoslavia
_____
Tel/fax: +381 (11) 444 3944/444 1487
office@hlc.org.yu
www.hlc.org.yu

Contact: Natasa Kandic, Director
Number of staff: 20
Budget: $100,000–$500,000
Publications: Human Rights in Serbia and Montenegro; Human Rights in Former Yugoslavia from 1991 until 1995; Police against Civilian Protest in Serbia; Police Crackdown on Otpor; Abductions and Disappearances of Non-Albanians in Kosovo.

Former Yugoslavia, Balkans

Group MOST

RESEARCH
EDUCATION
ACTION

Group MOST (the Bridge), the association for co-operation and mediation, is a professional non-governmental, non-profit organization that pursues capacity building for democratic changes and peaceful resolution of social and ethnic conflicts in the region of Former Yugoslavia. Group MOST aims to develop and introduce an efficient, constructive approach to conflict management and apply these principles and skills to the public.

MOST has developed a number of conflict resolution programs. "The Goodwill Classroom" program aims to introduce the methods of non-violent conflict resolution into elementary and secondary schools in Yugoslavia. It was initiated in 1995, and consists of workshops for three age levels of students and also training for teachers who would like to implement this program. The "Peace Studies" program was launched in 1999 with the aim of providing peace education for university students and fostering co-operation between regional peace initiatives. MOST supports young NGO activists in developing and framing inter-culturally sensitive local actions. It also operates a program for young people from a deprived background which aims to develop, promote and spread the ideas of constructive dialogue and multiculturalism. During and after ethnic conflicts in the region, MOST has been working on establishing dialogue between conflicting sides (e.g. between young Serbs and Albanians from Kosovska Mitrovica).

MOST provides many workshops on different themes such as mediation, dialogue and negotiation, public debate and effective discussion, constructive inter-cultural discussion, co-operation and NGO management. MOST also publishes peace education books.

Kneza Milosa 28/10
11000 Belgrade
Yugoslavia

Tel/fax: +381 (11) 361 4346
Tel: +381 (11) 361 4991
most@most.org.yu
www.most.org.yu

Contact: Dr. Dragan Popadic, President of the Board

Budget: $25,000–$100,000

Publications: Introduction to Peace Studies, in Serbian and English, 2000; *Lessons in Democracy,* 1998; *The Wiser Does Not Give In: A Guide through Conflicts to an Agreement,* 1998; *Social Conflicts: Characteristics and Methods of Their Resolution,* 1997; *The Goodwill Classroom,* in Serbian, Albanian, and English, 1995.

South Serbia, Yugoslavia, Balkans

PROTECTA

EDUCATION
ACTION
ADVOCACY

PROTECTA (Center for civil society development—Centar za razvoj gradjan-skog drustva) aims to develop and upgrade civil awareness by working in the fields of democracy, culture, NGO development, humanitarian work, non-violent conflict resoluton, information exchange, and environmental issues. PROTECTA focuses on supporting NGOs and civic groups in South Serbia.

Generala Boze Jankovica 15
18000 Nis
Yugoslavia

Contact: Milan Stefanovic, Executive Director

Tel/fax: +381 (18) 523 499
protecta@bankerinter.net
www.protecta.org.yu

South Serbia

TRAIL Association

RESEARCH
EDUCATION
ADVOCACY

The promotion of multiculturalism, intercultural democracy, the culture of peace, and tolerance are the main goals of the TRAIL Association (Udruzenje TRAG). Most of the Association's activities focus on the part of South Serbia populated by Albanians and Serbs, and address the need to enhance communication and rebuild trust between the two communities. Trail organizes workshops that deal with the issues of communication skills, co-operation, ethnic prejudice, culture and tradition of respective groups.

Dusanova 90
18000 Nis
Yugoslavia

Contact: Mirjana Kristovic, President
Number of staff: 5
Budget: $25,000–$100,000

Tel: +381 (63) 402 535/(18) 25 609
Tel/fax: +381 (18) 353 857
info@trag.org.yu
www.trag.org.yu

Yugoslavia

URBAN-IN

URBAN-IN provides civic, cultural, and democratic education to citizens from Novi Pazar and Sandzak. Through its educational, cultural, and psychosocial programs it aims to encourage their creativity in building an open, democratic, civic society in which they can fully participate. URBAN-IN is also streaming toward improvement of the relations between majorities and minorities in Serbia and Montenegro. In co-operation with Group MOST from Belgrade it provides "the Goodwill Classroom" program for primary and secondary school students.

1. maja bb (T. C. Vakuf)
36300 Novi Pazar
Yugoslavia

Tel: +381 (20) 314 966
Fax: +381 (20) 313 966
urban_in@hotmail.com

Contact: Aida Corovic, Coordinator
Number of staff: 20–30 volunteers
Budget: $25,000–$100,000

Appendix 1:
Selected Government Agencies and Ministries

Austria
Department for Development Co-operation
Ministry for Foreign Affairs
Minoritenplatz 9
1014 Vienna
Austria

Contact: Ms. Sigrid Boyer
Tel: +43 (1) 531 154 494
Fax: +43 (1) 536 664 494
sigrid.boyer@wien.bmaa.gv.at

Belgium
Directorate-General for International Cooperation
Ministry of Foreign Affairs
Regentlaan torat 45/46
1000 Brussels
Belgium

Contact: Mr. Jan Vanheukelom, Senior Advisor
Tel: +32 (2) 549 0936
Fax: +32 (2) 512 2123
jvanheukelom@cabos.fgov.be

Canada
Canadian International Development Agency (CIDA)
200 Promenade du Portage
Hull, Quebec K1A 0G4
Canada

Contact: Susan Brown, Chief Peacebuilding Unit
Tel: +1 (819) 997 5006
Fax: +1 (819) 953 6088
info@acdi-cida.gc.ca
www.acdi-cida.gc.ca

Peacebuilding and Human Security Division (AGP),
Department of Foreign Affairs and International Trade

125 Sussex Drive
Ottawa, Ontario K1A 0G2
Canada

Contact: Mr. David Viveash
Tel: +1 (613) 992 7993
Fax: +1 (613) 944 1226
david.viveash@dfait-maeci.gc.ca

Denmark
Secretariat for the Peace and Stability Fund/FRESTA
Royal Danish Ministry of Foreign Affairs
Asiatisk Plads 2
1448 Copenhagen K
Denmark

Contact: Ambassador Michael Wagtmann, Head of FRESTA
Tel: +45 (33) 921 932
Fax: +45 (33) 921 816
fresta@um.dk
www.see.fresta.org

Finland
Department for International Development Co-operation
Humanitarian Assistance Unit
Ministry of Foreign Affairs
Katajanokanlaituri
00160 Helsinki
Finland

Contact: Mr. Glen Lindholm, Director General
Tel: +358 (9) 1341 6225
Fax: +358 (9) 1341 6324
glen.lindholm@formin.fi

France
Direction Génerale du Développement et Coopération Technique
Ministere des Affairs Etrangeres
20 rue Monsieur
Paris 75700
France

Contact: Ms. Mireille Guigaz
Tel: +33 (1) 53 693 000
mireille.guigaz@diplomatie.fr

Germany
Federal Ministry for Economic Co-operation and Development
Friedrich-Ebert-Allee 40
53113 Bonn
Germany

Contact: Mr. Hans-Peter Bauer, Director
Tel: +49 (228) 535 3112
Fax: +49 (228) 535 3815
bauer@bmz.bund.de

German Technical Development Association (GTZ)
Dag Hammarskjöld weg 1-5
P.O. Box 5180
65726 Eschborn
Germany

Contact: Bernd Hoffman, Head of Division
Tel: +49 (6196) 790
Fax: +49 (6196) 791 115
bernd.hoffmann@gtz.de
www.gtz.de

UN Peacekeeping and Crisis Prevention Desk
Federal Foreign Office
Werderscher Markt 1
10117 Berlin
Germany

Contact: Martin Fleischer, Head of Desk
Tel: +49 1888 170
Fax: +49 1888 173 402
poststelle@auswaertiges-amt.de

Ireland
Political Division/ International Security Policy Desk
Department of Foreign Affairs
80 St. Stephen's Green
Dublin 2
Ireland

Contact: Mr. Keith McBean, Director
Tel: +353 (1) 478 0822
Fax: +353 (1) 478 5923
keith.mcbean@iveagh.irlgov.ie

Italy
Policy Planning Unit
Ministry of Foreign Affairs
Piazzale della.Farnesina, 1
00194 Rome
Italy

Contact: Mr. Roberto Toscano, Head of Unit
Tel: +39 (6) 3691 2172
Fax: +39 (6) 323 6210
roberto.toscano@esteri.it

The Netherlands
Human Rights and Peacebuilding Department
Ministry of Foreign Affairs
P.O. Box 20061
2500 EB The Hague
The Netherlands

Contact: Ms. Marion Kappeyne van de Coppello and Ms. Susan Blankhart, Directors

Tel: +31 (70) 348 5001
Fax: +31 (70) 348 4486
dmv@minbuza.nl
www.minbuza.nl

Norway
Department for Human Rights, Democracy and Humanitarian Assistance
Sub-Department Humanitarian Assistance
Ministry of Foreign Affairs
P.O. Box 8114
0032 Oslo
Norway

Contact: Mr. Fredrik Arthur, Head of Division
Tel: +47 (22) 243 386
Fax: +47 (22) 242 734
fredrik.arthur@mfa.no

Sweden
Secretariat for Conflict Prevention,
Ministry of Foreign Affairs
103 39 Stockholm
Sweden

Contact: Mr. Ragnar Ängeby, Head of Secretariat
Tel: +46 (8) 405 1000
Fax: +46 (8) 723 1176
ragnar.angeby@foreign.ministry.se

Swedish International Development Co-operation Agency (Sida)
Sveavägen 20
105 25 Stockholm
Sweden

Contact: Per Byman, Programme Officer Department for Central and Eastern Europe
Tel: +46 (8) 698 5000
Fax: +46 (8) 208 864
info@sida.se
www.sida.se

Switzerland
Political Division/ Section for Peace Policy and Human Security
Federal Department of Foreign Affairs
Bundesgasse 32
3003 Bern
Switzerland

Contact: Mr. Peter Reinhardt, Head of Section
Tel: +41 (31) 322 3516
Fax: +41 (31) 323 8922
peter.reinhardt@eda.admin.ch

United Kingdom
Department for International Development (DFID)
94 Victoria Street

London SW1E 5JL
United Kingdom

Contact: Dr. Mukesh Kapila, Head of Conflict and Humanitarian Affairs Department
Tel: +44 (20) 7917 7000
Fax: +44 (20) 7917 0019
enquiry@dfid.gov.uk
www.dfid.gov.uk

United Nations Department
Foreign and Commonwealth Office
Whitehall
London SW1
United Kingdom

Contact: Mr. Stephen Pattison, Head of Department
Tel: +44 (20) 7270 2487
Fax: +44 (20) 7270 3680

Appendix 2:
Internet Resources

AlertNet

www.alertnet.org

This site was developed by Reuters in order to provide quick and easily accessible information to disaster relief organizations. It contains the latest news and reports from the field, which are compiled in a clear overview by country. The country profiles and relief resources guides on topics and regions are also useful.

Alternative Information Network (AIM Press Agency)

www.aimpress.org

This website offers news provided by a network of independent journalists in the former Yugoslavia and the Southern Balkans. The network is sponsored within the framework of the Stability Pact for the Balkans.

Balkan Human Rights Web Page

www.greekshelsinki.gr

Brings together the latest news and reports on special issues from different sources. Good overview of subjects filed by country or theme. The site also features an extensive list of links relating to human rights organizations.

Balkan Information Exchange

www.balkan-info.com

Sponsored by the U.S. Department of Defense, this site offers the latest news on the Balkans and in-depth articles, all in English as well as Russian, Albanian, Greek, and Serbian. There are special sections on KFOR, humanitarian aid, human rights, regional politics, reconstruction, culture, and diplomacy in the Balkans.

Berghof Research Center for Constructive Conflict Management

www.berghof-center.org

The most important asset of this site is the selection of high-quality articles that can be accessed. Large portions of the *Berghof Handbook* are included, which contain academic articles on various aspects of conflict management and transformation. Furthermore, various Berghof Reports and Occasional Papers can be viewed through this site.

Bonn International Centre for Conversion (BICC)

www.bicc.de

The main aim of the BICC is research on the conversion of military resources to civilian purposes. It publishes extensively on this issue and summaries of the articles and publications are available on the website. Most notably, these include the yearbooks of conversion survey as well as disarmament and conversion studies. The "What's New" section presents an update of the latest publications and events.

Carnegie Commission for Preventing Deadly Conflict
www.ccpdc.org
This website is valuable for its many online documents, including the extensive Final Report, published in December 1997, that presents the findings of the Commission's work over three years, the causes of conflict, and methods of preventing deadly conflict.

Carter Center
www.cartercenter.org
An important part of the Carter Center's activities are its Peace Programs. These include conflict resolution programs and human rights monitoring in various countries of the world. Descriptions of these programs can be found in the section on international activities. Speeches, news releases, election reports, and reports of Jimmy Carter's formal travels (trip reports) are easily accessible through this page.

Central Asia-Caucasus Analyst
www.cacianalyst.org
The Central Asia-Caucasus Analyst of the Central Asia-Caucasus Institute, an independent research and policy institution affiliated to Johns Hopkins University, is a biweekly briefing on important events in the region. It can be downloaded in PDF format. The site further includes field reports and "news bites."

Coexistence Initiative (CI)
www.co-net.org
This site is valuable for its compilation of links to publications and information on the subject of coexistence. The Coexistence Resource Centre compiles information on topical issues as well as training programs, jobs, events, experts, and resources. The coexistence library has links to related publications lists, news, and online libraries.

Conciliation Resources (CR)
www.c-r.org
The website of Conciliation Resources contains large selections from the Accord Series —excellent international reviews of peace initiatives in a certain country or region. The series includes reviews of initiatives in Tajikistan, Northern Ireland, and Georgia-Abkhazia. A collection of occasional papers can also be viewed online.

Conflict Prevention Network
www.swp-berlin.org/cpn
A particularly interesting feature of this website of the German Stiftung Wissenschaft und Politik is its special section on the European Union and conflict prevention. It contains official EU as well as related documents. There is also a section on conflict prevention bibliographies.

CRInfo
www.crinfo.org
The Conflict Resolution Information Source is a co-operation of various participants, sponsored by the William and Flora Hewlett Foundation. The site contains a wealth of information on conflict resolution and related topics, including on education and training, organizations, and networking. There are a variety of search engines and listings of subjects included, and for easy reference it is possible to browse by topic or key-

word. Especially valuable is the "Today's News" section in which the latest news is assembled from various sources and arranged by subject.

Eurasianet
www.eurasianet.org
This comprehensive site focuses on the latest news and analyses of current affairs and political and social developments. Additional features include newsmaker interviews with leading experts, book reviews, a discussion forum, and special sections on human rights, the environment, and election watch. Excellent resource pages by country are also included. This site is operated by the Central Eurasia Project of the Open Society Institute.

European Platform for Conflict Prevention and Transformation (EPCPT)
www.conflict-prevention.net
The website of EPCPT offers a host of valuable information on conflict prevention and peacebuilding. All of the Platform's publications appear online, most importantly the surveys on conflict prevention and peace building in Africa, Europe, Central Asia, and the Caucasus (with more regions to follow). These surveys (with regional as well as thematic focuses) provide comprehensive background information on the causes of a conflict and on the prevention and transformation activities that take place in relation to it, as well as on organizations working in the field. With a directory listing profiles of 475 organizations in the Africa publication alone, this site offers the most comprehensive directory of organizations available on the Internet.

EU Stability Pact for South Eastern Europe
www.stabilitypact.org
Information on the functioning of the Stability Pact, online access to constituent documents, conference papers, and speeches are provided on this site. Valuable information on Working Table III's Sub-Table on Defense and Security issues, including the subjects of non-proliferation , disarmament, security sector reform, small arms, and disaster prevention.

Forum on Early Warning and Early Response (FEWER)
www.fewer.org
This site offers comprehensive early warning reports on various regions in the world, including Central Asia and the Caucasus, and lists links to other valuable information and documents available on the web. Furthermore, there is a focus on documents on methodology development, conflict prevention, and small arms flows.

Heidelberg Insititute of International Conflict Research
www.hiik.de
Two unique projects set up by the Department of Political Science of the University of Heidelberg can be found at this site. First, there is the Conflict Barometer, which gives a concise annual update of the status of conflicts around the world. Secondly, there is the KOSIMO database, which contains 693 political conflicts since 1945. In a short overview, it describes these conflicts by using 28 variables on the background of a conflict, international diplomacy, transformation efforts, and so on.

INCORE
www.incore.ulst.ac.uk
The website of the Initiative on Conflict Resolution & Ethnicity contains a good, comprehensive collection of links and documents. The host of information is subdivided along various lines. There are regularly updated country guides, which provide a list of news sources, discussion groups, academic links, and NGOs by country. There is also

a list of peace agreements, an ethnic conflict research digest with bibliographies of recently published documents, and a list of thematic guides on subjects such as media and conflict and women and conflict. Furthermore, there is a database on subjects such as academic and training programs, organizations, and bibliographies.

Institute for War and Peace Reporting
www.iwpr.net
A professional collaboration of international and local journalists provide weekly in-depth analyses of events and issues on the Balkans, Caucasus, and Central Asia. The site contains valuable special reports and a comprehensive list of links to local media.

Interactive Central Asia Resource Project (ICARP)
www.icarp.com
This site offers an excellent portal to information on countries in Central Asia. It provides biographies and quick facts on a country, as well as a list of links to institutions, experts, bibliographies, and news sources. The site contains a valuable list of publications. ICARP does not have its own news sources but presents links to local news networks instead.

International Alert
www.international-alert.org
This site focuses on the projects run by IA, including those in the Caucasus. The site offers an extensive list of links as well as a collection of IA publications that can be downloaded in their full-text version. The site is a gateway to the international campaign to promote the role of women in peace building.

International Crisis Group
www.intl-crisis-group.org
This website is one the most resourceful and accurate sites about conflicts and conflict prevention. It is subdivided along the lines of ICG's projects, Africa, Asia, and Balkans. All ICG's policy reports (country specific and issue reports) are easily accessible and regularly updated. The Balkans Program section offers a compilation of breaking Balkan news from the leading news sources. Interesting, too, is the special section on news and reports on the EU and conflict prevention. A nice asset is the option to customize the home page according to the country or subject of the user's interest.

International Security Network (ISN)
www.isn.ethz.ch
The International Security Network website is a product of the Centre for Security Studies and Conflict Research in Switzerland. It is highly valuable for its links library and databases. The extensive "ISN Links Library" offers full-text publications by (inter-) governmental organizations, NGOs, and the media. These documents can be found by searches on countries/regions, subjects, and directories. Equally useful is the "FIRST Reference Database" (Facts on International Relations and Security Trends). This is a joint project with the Stockholm International Peace Research Institute and offers documents from research institutes around the world in the field of international relations and security. The site also contains a daily updated "Security Watch" section in cooperation with Reuters.

OSCE
www.osce.org
This valuable website offers not only general information on the OSCE's activities, but also their latest news, press releases, statements, a comprehensive calendar of events, and in-depth stories in the section "In Focus." The homepage of the Forum for Security

Co-operation offers documents on the military aspects of security. Country-specific information is accessible through the homepages of the mission headquarters.

Peace News
www.igc.org/igc/gateway/pnindex.html
Peace News is an initiative of the Institute for Global Communications. The site contains a "calendar on progressive activism," links to organizations, and a basic search engine for full-text documents on the web. The subscription to a weekly e-mail news digest is worthwhile.

Radio Free Europe/Radio Liberty Newsline
www.rferl.org
Daily reports on events in Eastern and Southeastern Europe, Russia, the Caucasus, and Central Asia are provided on this site. It is based on news gathered by the correspondents, services, and regional specialists of Radio Free Europe/Radio Liberty.

Red Cross
www.icrc.org
In addition to weekly ICRC news and an overview of regional operations, this site offers information and articles on various topics, including women and war, children and war, and humanitarian action in armed conflicts. There is also a large and informative section on international humanitarian law.

Relief Web
www.reliefweb.int
This site advertises itself as serving the information needs of the humanitarian relief community. It is indeed a valuable source for news on complex emergencies and natural disasters around the world. A comprehensive list of links by country provides a diverse range of subjects including country profiles, development, disaster history, politics, defense, refugees, and media. The site also features a large map center and the IRIN (Integral Regional Information Networks) news service that also covers Central Asia.

Soros Foundation
www.soros.org
The Soros Foundation is dedicated to promoting open societies. It has several national foundations, mainly in Central and Eastern Europe and the former Soviet Union. The websites of the national foundations, which can be accesses though the main site, offer background information and links on the social and political situation by specific country.

The Times of Central Asia
www.times.kg
This site offers daily news from the region as well as offering country guides and links. Full-text articles and news are available after registering.

UN Department of Peacekeeping Operations
www.un.org/Depts/dpko/dpko/cu_mission/body.htm
This site provides overviews and in-depth information on past and current peacekeeping operations.

UN Development Programme
www.undp.org
The country office websites offer news, documents, and publications on the development situation in specific countries and give overviews of development cooperation

projects and UNDP programs. Depending on the country and the set up of a country office site, peace building activities are also included. The home page presents a section on conflict and security and is also a portal for the sites of the UNDP offices around the world.

United States Institute for Peace (USIP)
www.usip.org
This site is invaluable for the large amount of reports and documents that can be accessed through it. The USIP Digital Library in International Conflict Management is being set up and includes a digital collection of peace agreements and truth commissions. The *Peace Watch Newsletter* and the Peaceworks series of reports on special subjects can all be found in full-text version. The site further hosts an overview of events in the peace research field, often including web casts, and a section "On the Wire," which contains interviews with experts.

World Bank
www.worldbank.org
Not focusing on conflict prevention and peacebuilding as such, the website of the World Bank offers valuable information on related subjects such as legal and judicial reform and poverty reduction. The frequently updated country statistics provide a useful source of information. In-depth information is given on some regional projects, such as post-conflict transportation and communication in the South Caucasus.

Selected Bibliography

Abdullaev, Kamoludin, and Catherine Barnes, *Politics of compromise: the Tajikistan peace process*. London: Conciliation Resources, 2001, 100 pp.

Ackerman, Alice. *Making peace prevail: preventing violent conflict in Macedonia*. Syracuse, NY: Syracuse University Press, 2000.

ACR Newsletter, Association for Conflict Resolution, Washington, DC.

Afghanistan Monthly Review, British Agencies Afghanistan Group, London.

Aggestam, Lisbeth, and Adrian Hyde-Pride (eds.). *Security and identity in Europe: exploring the new agenda*. Houndmills, UK: Macmillan, 2000, 270 pp.

Arnold, Hans. *Security for Europe through cooperation: counter-project to a policy of intervention*. Bonn: Stiftung Entwickelung und Frieden (SEF), 2001, 11 pp.

Around Europe, Quaker Council for European Affairs, Brussels.

Azerbaijan Press on Human Rights and Democratic Freedoms, Institute of Peace and Democracy, Baku, Azerbaijan

Balkan Crisis Report, Institute for War and Peace Reporting, London.

Barkey, Henri, Graham Fuller, and Morton Abramowitz. *Turkey's Kurdish question*. Lanham, MD: Rowman & Littlefield, 1998.

Bertsch, G., C. B. Craft, S. A. Jones,and M. D. Beck, M.d. (eds.) *Crossroads and conflict: security and foreign policy in the Caucasus and Central Asia*. London: Routledge, 1999.

BICC Bulletin, Bonn International Centre for Conversion, Bonn.

Biermann, Wolfgang, and Martin Vadset. *UN peacekeeping in trouble: lessons learned from the former Yugoslavia: peacekeepers' view on the limits and possibilities of the United Nations in a civil War-like conflict*. Aldershot, UK: Ashgate, 1999, 378 pp.

Birckenbach, Hanne-Margret. *Half full or half empty?: OSCE mission to Estonia and its balance sheet, 1993–1999*. Flensburg, Germany: European Centre for Minority Issues (ECMI), 2000, 86 pp.

BPT Newsletter, Balkan Peace Team International, Minden, Germany.

Brauch, Hans Günther, (ed.). *Euro-Mediterranean partnership for the 21st century*. Houndmills, UK: Macmillan, 2000, 477 pp.

Brewin, Christopher. *The European Union and Cyprus*. Huntingdon: The Eothen Press, 2000, 290 pp.

Briza, Jan. *Minority rights in Yugoslavia*. London: Minority Rights Group International (MRG), 2000, 32 pp.

Bulletin of the Network on Ethnological Monitoring and Early Warning of Conflicts, Conflict Resolution in the Post-Soviet States Project, IEA/CMG, Moscow and Cambridge, MA.

Burg, Steven L., and Paul S. Shoup. *The war in Bosnia-Herzegovina: ethnic conflict & international intervention*. Armonk, NY and London: M.E. Sharpe, 2000, 499 pp.

Campbell, David. *National deconstruction: violence, identity, and justice in Bosnia*. Minneapolis: University of Minnesota Press, 1998, 304 pp.

Carter Center News, Carter Center, Atlanta, GA.

Caucasus Reporting Service, Institute for War and Peace Reporting, London.

Central Asia and the Caucasus: Journal of Social and Political Studies, Central Asia and the Caucasus Information and Analytical Center, Luleå, Sweden.

Central Asia-Caucasus Analyst, The Central Asia-Caucasus Institute of the Johns Hopkins University/The Nitze School of Advanced International Studies, Washington, DC.

Cerovic, Stojan. *Serbia and Montenegro: reintegration, divorce or something else?* Washington, DC: United States Institute for Peace, 2001

Children and Armed Conflict Review, Children and Armed Conflict Unit, Colchester, UK.

Clark, Howard. *Civil resistance in Kosovo*. London: Pluto, 2000, 266 pp.

Cockburn, Cynthia. *Gender and democracy in the aftermath of war: women's organisations in Bosnia-Herzegovina*. Utrecht, Netherlands: Universiteit voor Humanisatiek (UVH), 2000, 36 pp.

Cockburn, Cynthia. *The space between us: negotiating gender and national identities in conflict*. London: Zed Books, 1998.

CODEP Newsletter, Conflict, Development and Peace Network, London.

Coexistence Noticeboard, Coexistence Initiative, New York.

Cohen, J. *Conflict prevention in the OSCE: an assessment of capacities*. The Hague: Netherlands Institute of International Relations Clingendael, 1999, 150 pp.

Cohen, Jonathan, (ed.). *A question of sovereignty: the Georgia-Abkhazia peace process*. London: Conciliation Resources, 1999, 100 pp.

Cohen, Jonathan. *Question of sovereignty: the Georgia-Abkhazia peace process. Accord: international review of peace initiatives,* vol. 7, 1999.

Conflict Prevention Newsletter, European Platform for Conflict Prevention and Transformation, Utrecht, the Netherlands.

Conflict Trends, African Centre for the Constructive Resolution of Disputes, South Africa.

Contemporary Caucasus Newsletter, University of California, Berkeley, CA.

Cooperation and Conflict, Nordic International Studies Association, Copenhagen.

Co-operation Ireland Newslink, Co-operation Ireland, Belfast and Dublin.

Coppieters, Bruno, David Darchiashvili, Natella Akaba (eds.). *Federal practice: exploring alternatives for Georgia and Abkhazia*. Brussels: VUB Press, 2000, 281 pp.

Coppieters, Bruno, Ghia Nodia, and Yuri Anchabadze (eds.). *Georgians and Abkhazians: the search for a peace settlement*. Cologne: Sonderveröffentlichung des Bundesinstituts für Ostwissenschaftliche und Internationale Studien, 1998.

Cornell, Svante E., *The land of many crossroads: the Kurdish question in Turkish politics*. Orbis, vol. 45, no. 1, 2001, pp. 31-46.

Cox, Caroline, and John Eibner. *Ethnic cleansing in progress: war in Nagorno Karabakh*. London: Christian Solidarity Worldwide (CSW), 1999, 52 pp.

Cox, Michael, Adrian Guelke, and Fiona Stephen. *A farewell to arms?: from "long war" to long peace in Northern Ireland*. Manchester, UK: Manchester University Press, 2000.

Crocker, Chester A. *Herding cats: multiparty mediation in a complex world*. Washington, DC: United States Institute of Peace Press (USIP), 1999, 735 pp.

Cross, Peter, and Guenola Rasamoelina, (eds.). *Conflict prevention policy of the European Union: recent engagements, future instruments*. Baden Baden: Nomos Verl; Stiftung Wissenschaft und Politik/Conflict Prevention Network (SWP-CPN), 1999, 229 pp.

CSS. *Ethnic conflict and migration in Europe: first report of the Ethnobarometer Programme.* Rome: CSS/CEMES, 1999, 329 pp.

Current History, Current History Inc, Philadelphia.

Daftary, Farimah. *Insular autonomy: a framework for conflict settlement?: a comparative study of Corsica and the Åland islands.* Flensburg, Germany: European Centre for Minority Issues (ECMI), 2000, 71 pp.

Dawisha, Karen, and Bruce Parrot (eds.). *Conflict, cleavage and change in Central Asia and the Caucasus.* Cambridge, UK: Cambridge University Press, 1997.

Debiel, Tobias, and Martina Fischer. *Crisis prevention & conflict management by the European Union: concepts, capacities an problems of coherence* (Berghof Report no. 4). Berlin: Berghof Research Center for Constructive Conflict Management, 2000, 33 pp.

Dimitrijevic, Nenad (ed.). *Managing multiethnic local communities in the countries of the former Yugoslavia.* Budapest: Local Government and Public Service Reform Initiative, 2000, 468 pp.

Dixon, Paul. *Northern Ireland: power, ideology and reality.* London: Macmillan, 2000.

Dodd, Clement H., (ed.). *Cyprus: the need for new perspectives.* Huntingdon: The Eothen Press, 1999.

Douglass, W.A., (ed.). *Basque politics: a case study in ethnic nationalism. Reno: Associated Faculty Press and Basque Studies Program, 1985. (Basque Studies Program Occasional Papers Series No. 2)*

DUPI News, Danish Institute of International Affairs, Copenhagen.

Dwan, Renata, and Oleksandr Pavliuk, (eds.). *Building security in the new states of Eurasia: subregional cooperation in the former Soviet space.* New York: M.E. Sharpe, 2000, 304 pp.

Ebel, Robert, and Rajan Menon, (eds.). *Energy and conflict in Central Asia and the Caucasus.* Lanham, MD: Rowman & Littlefield, 2001, 262 pp.

Eisenhower, Susan, and Roald Sagdeev, (eds.). *Islam and Central Asia.* Washington: Center for Political and Strategic Studies, 2000, 255 pp.

Emerson, Michael, and Daniel Gros, (eds.). *The CEPS Plan for the Balkans.* Brussels: Centre for European Policy Studies, 1999, 120 pp.

Ethnic Studies Network Bulletin, INCORE, Londonderry, Northern Ireland.

Europe Plus*, European Movement in Serbia, Belgrade, Serbia.*

European Centre for Conflict Prevention (ECCP). *People Building Peace: 35 Inspiring stories from around the world.* Utrecht, Netherlands: ECCP, 1999, 411 pp.

European Commission. Communication on conflict prevention. Brussels: European Commission, 2001.

European Journal of International Relations, Standing Group on International Relations, London.

European Security Review, International Security Information Service Europe, Brussels.

EWI Russian Regional Report, East West Institute, USA.

Farren, Sean, and Robert F. Mulvihill. *Paths to a settlement in Northern Ireland.* Buckinghamshir: Colin Smythe, 2000.

Fischer, Martina, and Giovanni Scotto, (eds.). *Southeast European NGOs for the Stability Pact.* Berlin: Berghof Research Centre for Constructive Conflict Management, 2000, 43 pp.

Fisher, Simon, et al. *Working with conflict: skills and strategies for action.* London: Zedbooks, 2000, 185 p.

Fitzduff, Mari. *Beyond violence: conflict resolution processes in Northern Ireland.* Tokyo: United Nations University, 1996.

Footpaths, Eastern Mennonite University, Harrisonburg, USA.

Francis, Diana. *Lessons from Kosovo—alternatives to war: the peace testimony in the twenty-first century.* London: Quaker Peace & Social Witness Department of the Religious Society of Friends (Quakers) in Britain, 2001, 20 pp.

Garb, Paula. "Ethnicity, alliance building and the limited spread of ethnic conflict in the Caucasus," in D. A. Lake and D. Rothchild (eds.). *The international spread of ethnic conflict: fear, diffusion, and escalation*. Princeton, NJ: Princeton University Press, 1998.

Glencree Center for Reconciliation Newsletter, Ireland.

Gourlay, Catriona, and Ciarán Donnelly, (eds.). *EU reconstructuring for conflict prevention and crisis management: conference report and comment, 22 November 1999—Brussels*. Brussels: International Security Information Service (ISIS), 1999, 40 pp.

Grin, François. *Evaluating policy measures for minority languages in Europe: towards effective, cost-effective and democratic implementation*. Flensburg, Germany: European Centre for Minority Studies (ECMI), 2000, 84 pp.

Gurr, Ted Robert. *Peoples versus states: minorities at the risk in the new century*. Washington, DC: United States Institute of Peace Press (USIP), 2000, 399 p.

Hade: Bicommunal Magazine, Cyprus.

Hamber, Brandon, (ed.). *Past Imperfect: dealing with the past in Northern Ireland and societies in transition*. Derry/Londonderry: University of Ulster, INCORE, 1998.

Harris, Peter, and Ben Reilly (eds.). *Democracy and deep-rooted conflict: options for negotiators*. Stockholm: International Institute for Democracy and Electoral Assistance (IDEA), 1998, 414 pp.

Helsinki Monitor: Quarterly on Security and Cooperation in Europe, Netherlands Helsinki Committee/International Helsinki Federation for Human Rights, the Hague.

Herzig, Edmund. *New Caucasus: Armenia, Azerbaijan and Georgi*. Cassell, 1999.

Hill, Christopher, and Karen Elizabeth Smith (eds.). *European foreign policy: key documents*. London: Routledge, 2000, 477 pp.

IANSA Newsletter, International Action Network on Small Arms, London.

Interdependent, European Centre for Global Interdependence and Solidarity, Lisbon.

International Crisis Group (ICG). *After Milosevic: a practical agenda for lasting Balkans Peace*. Balkans Report No. 108. Brussels: ICG, 2001.

International Crisis Group (ICG). *Is Dayton Failing? Bosnia four years after the peace agreement*. Brussels: ICG Balkans Report, 1999.

International Institute for Democracy and Electoral Assistance (International IDEA). *Advancing democracy in Slovakia through local self-governance: lessons learned from other European countries*. Stockholm: International IDEA, 2000, 108 pp.

International Migration, International Organisation for Migration, Geneva.

International Negotiation, Kluwer Law International, Cambridge, MA.

International Review of the Red Cross, International Committee of the Red Cross, Geneva.

International Security Information Service (ISIS). *Enhancing the EU's response to violent conflict: moving beyond reaction to preventive action: conference report and policy recommendations, 7–8 December—Brussels*. Brussels: ISIS, 2001, 47 pp.

International Studies Quarterly, International Studies Association, London.

IPRA Newsletter, International Peace Research Association, Mie, Japan.

Irvin, Cynthia, and Sean Byrne. *The politics and practice of external economic assistance in resolving protracted ethnic conflicts: lessons from Northern Ireland*. Fort Lauderdale: Nova Southeastern University, Department of Dispute Resolution, 2001.

Jegen, Mary Evelyn. *Sign of hope: the center for peace, nonviolence and human rights in Osijek*. Uppsala: Life and Peace Institute, 1996, 91 pp.

Jentleson, Bruce W., (ed.). *Opportunities missed, opportunities seized: preventive diplomacy in the post-cold war world*. New York: Carnegie Commission on Preventing Deadly Conflict, 2000, 431 pp.

Jordan, Jessica, Marina Krabalo, and Jasenka Pregrad. *Towards reconciliation: impact assessment*. Osijek: Centre for Peace, Nonviolence and Human Rights, 2000.

Journal for Strategic Studies, Frank Cass Publishers, London.

Journal of Conflict Resolution, Peace Science Society (International), London.

Journal of Conflict, Security and Development, Centre for Defence Studies, London.

Journal of Peace Research, Peace Research Institute, Oslo.

KATU Bulletin, Citizen's Security Council, Helsinki.

Kemp, Walter A., (ed.). *Quiet diplomacy in action: the OSCE high commissioner on national minorities.* The Hague: Kluwer Law International, 2001, 396 pp.

King, Charles, and Neil J. Melvin (eds.). *Nations abroad: diaspora politics and international relations in the former Soviet Union.* Boulder: Westview, 1998, 240 pp.

Knezys, Stasys, and Romanas Sedlickas. *The war in Chechnya.* College Station: Texas A&M University Press, 1999, 359 pp.

Korac, Maja. *Linking arms: women and war in post-Yugoslav states.* Uppsala: Life & Peace Institute, 1998, 75 pp.

Kramer, Heinz. *A changing Turkey: challenges to Europe and the United States.* Washington, DC: Brookings Institution Press, 2000.

Kruhonja, Katarina, (ed.). *I choose life, post-war peace building in Eastern Croatia.* Osijek: Centre for Peace, Nonviolence & Human Rights, 2001.

Large, Judith. *The war next door: a study of second-track intervention during the war in ex-Yugoslavia.* Gloucestershire: Hawthorn Press, 1996, 178 pp.

Lederach, John Paul. *Preparing for peace: conflict transformation across cultures.* Syracuse: Syracuse University Press, 1995, 133 pp.

Liel, Alon. *Turkey in the Middle East: oil, Islam, and politics.* Boulder: Lynne Rienner, 2001, 275 pp.

Lithander, Anna, (ed.). *Engendering the peace process: a gender approach to Dayton—and beyond.* Stockholm: The Kvinna till Kvinna Foundation, 2000.

Loughlin, John, and Farimah Daftary. *Insular regions and European integration: Corsica and the Åland Islands compared.* Flensburg, Germany: European Centre for Minority Issues (ECMI), 1999, 78 pp.

Lund, Michael S., *Preventing violent conflicts: a strategy for preventive diplomacy.* Washington, DC: United States Institute of Peace Press (USIP), 1996, 220 p.

Malfliet, Katlijn, and Wim Keygnaert. *The Baltic States in an enlarging European Union: towards a partnership between small states?* Leuven: Institute for European Policy, 1999, 179 pp.

Matveeva, Anna. *The North Caucasus: Russia's fragile borderland.* London: Royal Institute of International Affairs (RIIA), 1998.

McCartney, Clem. *Striking a balance: the Northern Ireland peace process.* London: Conciliation Resources, 1999, 107 pp.

McCormack, Gillian, (ed.). *Media and conflict in the Caucasus.* Düsseldorf: European Institute for the Media, 1999, 102 pp.

McSpadden, Lucia Ann, Joan Löfgren, and Halina Grzymala-Moszczynska (eds.). *Reaching reconciliation: churches in the transitions to democracy in Eastern and Central Europe.* Uppsala: Life & Peace Institute, 2000, 243 pp.

Mediation, Mediation UK, Bristol, United Kingdom.

Mediterranean Politics, Frank Cass Publishers, London.

Mertus, Julie A., and Judy A. Benjamin. *War's offensive on women: the humanitarian challenge in Bosnia, Kosovo, and Afghanistan.* Bloomfield: Kumarian Press, 2000, 157 pp.

Miall, Hugh, Oliver Ramsbotham, and Tom Woodhouse. *Contemporary conflict resolution.* Cambridge, MA: Polity Press, 1999, 270 pp.

Minic, Jelica. *Preparing Yugoslavia for European Integration.* Belgrade: European Movement in Serbia, 2000.

Ministry for Foreign Affairs, Sweden, Division for European Security Policy. "EU programme for the prevention of violent conflicts: endorsed by the Göteborg Council, June 2001." Stockholm: Ministry for Foreign Affairs Sweden, Division for European Security Policy, 2001, 11 pp.

Ministry of Foreign Affairs, FRESTA. "Peace and stability through cross-boundery civil society collaboration: final report on Fact Finding mission—South Eastern Europe." Ministry of Foreign Affairs, FRESTA, 2000, 134 pp.

Mirbagheri, Farid. *Cyprus and international peacemaking.* London: Hurst, 1998.

Moran, Michael. *Sovereignty divided: essays on the international dimensions of the Cyprus problem.* Nicosia CYREP, 1999.

Mungenast, Hendrik. *The Georgia-Abkhaz peace process: a new role for the United Nations Mission in Georgia.* London: Links, 2000, 40 pp.

Nachmani, Amikam. *Turkey and the Middle East.* Ramat Gan: Begin-Sadat Center for Strategic Studies, 1999, 29 pp.

Nan, Susan Allen. *Complementarity and coordination of conflict resolution efforts in the conflicts over Abkhazia, South Ossetia and Transdniestria.* Farifax, VA: George Mason University, 1999.

Nelson, Jane. *The business of peace: the private sector as a partner in conflict prevention.* London: International Alert (IA)/New York: Council on Economic Priorities (CEP)/London: The Prince of Wales Business Leaders Forum (PWBLF), 2000, 158 pp.

New Balkan Politics, Macedonia.

New Routes, Life & Peace Institute, Uppsala, Sweden.

North Caucasus Update, United Nations High Commissioner for Refugees, New York.

Northern Ireland Community Relations Council. *Dealing with difference: a directory of peace, reconciliation and community relations projects in Northern Ireland.* Belfast: Northern Ireland Community Relations Council, 1998, 144 pp.

ODIHR Newsletter, OSCE Office for Democratic Institutions and Human Rights, Warsaw.

Organization for Security and Co-operation in Europe (OSCE). *OSCE handbook,* 3d ed. Vienna: OSCE, 2000, 197 pp.

Ortakovski, Vladimir. *Minorities in the Balkans.* Ardsley: Transnational, 2000, 383 pp.

OSCE Newsletter, Organization for Security and Co-operation in Europe, Vienna.

Özbudun, Ergun. *Contemporary Turkish politics: challenges to democratic consolidation.* Boulder: Lynne Rienner, 2000, 174 pp.

Partners International Newsletter, Partners for Democratic Change, San Francisco, CA.

Pavkovic, Aleksandar. *The fragmentation of Yugoslavia: nationalism and war in the Balkans.* Houndmills, UK: Macmillan, 2000, 243 pp.

Pax Christi Newsletter, Pax Christi International, Brussels.

Peace by Piece, Conflict Management Group, Cambridge, MA.

Peace News for Nonviolent Revolution, Peace News Limited, London.

Peace Watch Newsletter, United States Institute of Peace, Washington, DC.

PeaceBuilder, Institute for Multi-Track Diplomacy, Washington, DC.

Pettifer, James. *The new Macedonian question.* London: Palgrave, 2001.

Popov, Nebojsa, (ed.). *The road to war in Serbia: trauma and catharsis.* Budapest: Central European University Press, 2000, 712 pp.

Poulton, Hugh. *Minorities in Southeast Europe: inclusion and exclusion.* London: Minority Rights Group International (MRG), 1998, 40 pp.

Poulton, Hugh. *Who are the Macedonians?* Bloomington Indiana University Press, 1995, 256 pp.

Rafael Biermann. *The Stability Pact for South Eastern Europe: potential, problems and perspectives.* Bonn: Zentrum für Europaeische Integrationsforschung, 1999, 46 pp.

Rakipi, Albert, (ed.). *Stability pact just around the corner.* Tirana: Albanian Institute for International Studies (AIIS), 2000, 168 pp.

Rashid, Ahmed. *The resurgence of Central Asia: Islam or nationalism?* Karachi: Oxford University Press/London: Zed Books, 1994, 278 pp.

Rattner, Steven, and Michael B.G.Froman. *Promoting sustainable economies in the Balkans: independent task force report.* New York: Council on Foreign Relations Press, 2000, 73 pp.

Reconciliation International, International Fellowship of Reconciliation, Alkmaar, the Netherlands.

Reporting Central Asia, Institute for War and Peace Reporting, London.

Review of Free Thought, Circle 99, Sarajevo.

Revival, Post-war Reconstruction and Development Unit, University of York, United Kingdom.

Reychler, Luc, and Thania Paffenholz (eds.). *Peacebuilding: a field guide.* Boulder: Lynne Rienner, 2001, 571 pp.

Riskin, Steven M., (ed.). *Three dimensions of peacebuilding in Bosnia: findings from USIP-sponsored research and field projects.* Washington, DC: United States Institute of Peace (ISIP), 1999, 54 pp.

Roma Rights Quarterly, European Roma Rights Center, Budapest.

Rosandic, Ruzica. *Grappling with peace education in Serbia.* Washinton, DC: United States Institute of Peace (USIP), 2000, 44 pp.

Roy, Olivier. *The new Central Asia: the creation of nations.* New York: New York University Press, 1999.

Rubin, Barry, and Kemal Kirisci (eds.). *Turkey in world politics: an emerging multiregional power.* Boulder: Lynne Rienner, 2001, 270 pp.

Ruffin, M. Holt, and Daniel C. Waugh (eds.). *Civil society in Central Asia.* Seattle: University of Washington Press, 1999, 331 pp.

Saferworld and International Alert. *Preventing violent conflict.* London: Saferworld/ International Alert, 2000.

Saunders, Harold H. *A public peace process: sustained dialogue to transform racial and ethnic conflicts.* New York: St. Martin's Press, 1999, 328 pp.

Schnabel, Albrecht, and Ramesh Thakur (eds.). *Kosovo and the challenge of humanitarian intervention: selective indignation, collective action, and international citizenship.* Tokyo: United Nations University Press, 2000, 536 pp.

Search for Common Ground Newsletter, Search for Common Ground, Washington, DC.

Security Dialogue, Peace Research Institute, Oslo.

Servas International Newsletter, Servas International, Genova, Italy.

Shankland, David. *Islam and society in Turkey.* Huntingdon, UK: The Eothen Press, 1999.

Solana, Javier, and Christopher Patten. "Improving the coherence and effectiveness of EU action in the field of conflict prevention," report presented at the EU summit, Nice, 2000

Stavrou, Nikolaos A., (ed.). *Mediterranean security at the crossroads: a reader.* Durham, NC: Duke University Press, 1999, 312 pp.

Survival, International Institute for Strategic Studies, London.

Tabyshalieva, Anara. *The challenge of regional cooperation in Central Asia: preventing ethnic conflict in the Ferghana Valley.* Washington, DC: United States Institute of Peace, 1999, 48 pp.

Tarifa, F., and M. Spoor (eds.). *The first decade and after: Albania's democratic transition and consolidation in the context of Southeast Europe.* The Hague: Centre for the Study of Transition and Development (CESTRAD)/Institute of Social Studies, 2001, 130 pp.

Terrett, Steve. *The dissolution of Yugoslavia and the Badinter Arbitration Commission: a contextual study of peace-making efforts in the post-cold war world.* Aldershot, UK: Ashgate, 2000, 395 pp.

Tiberghien-Declerk, Christine. *The conflict prevention capacities of the EU in the Caucasus.* London: International Alert/East West Institute/Fewer, 1999.

Tishkov, Valery. "Ethnicity, nationalism and conflicts," in *The mind aflame.* London: Sage Publications, 1997.

Tribunal Update, Institute for War and Peace Reporting, London.

Trier, Tom. *Inter-ethnic relations in transcarpathian Ukraine.* Flensburg: European Centre for Minority Issues (ECMI), 1999, 70 pp.

Truedson, Lars. *Future challenges to conflict prevention: how can the EU contribute?*, report from a seminar organized by the Swedish Institute of International Affairs, Paris, 22 September 2000. Stockholm: The Swedish Institute of International Affairs, 2000, 43 pp.

UNPO News, Unrepresented Nations and Peoples Organisation, the Hague.

VOICE Newsletter, Voluntary Organisations in Cooperation in Emergency, Brussels.

Walker, Edward W. *No peace, no war in the Caucasus: secessionist conflict in Chechnya, Abkhazia and Nagorno-Karabakh.* Cambridge, MA: Harvard University Press, 1998.

Walker, Edward W. *Russia's soft underbelly: the stability of instability in Dagestan.* Berkeley: University of California Press, 1999.

Waller, Michael, Bruno Coppieters, and Alexei Malashenko (eds.). *Conflicting loyalties and the state in Post-Soviet Russia and Eurasia.* London: Frank Cass, 1998, 258 pp.

Ware, Robert, and Enver Kisriev. "Political stability and ethnic parity: Why is there peace in Dagestan?" in M. Alexeev (ed.). *Center-periphery conflict in Post-Soviet Russia: a federation imperilled.* New York: St. Martin's Press, 1999, 288 pp.

White, Paul J. Primitive rebels or revolutionary modernizers?: the Kurdish National Movement in Turkey. London: Zed Books, 2000, 258 pp.

Wolfsfeld, Gadi. *The news media and the peace processes: the Middle East and Northern Ireland.* Washington, DC: United States Institute of Peace (USIP), 2001, 54 pp.

Wolleh, Oliver. *Local peace constituencies in Cyprus: citizens' rapprochement by the bi-communal conflict resolution trainer group,* Berghof Report No. 8. Berlin: Berghof Research Center for Constructive Conflict Management, 2001.

Woodworth, Paddy. *Dirty war, clean hands; ETA, the GAL and Spanish democracy.* Cork: Cork University Press, 2001.

Yerevan Press Club Bulletin, Yerevan Press Club, Yerevan, Armenia.

Subject Index

resolution/transformation, 84
Middle East, 75
Milosevic, Slobodan: *After Milosevic,* 305;
Amnesty International/Helsinki Watch warn
about, 253; antibureaucratic revolution,
311; Bosnia and Herzegovina, partitioning
of, 234; Bulatovic, disagreements with,
312; collapse of regime, reasons for the,
327–328; Constitution, changes to the,
312–313; coup d état pulled off by, 201;
defeat in local elections, 290, 295, 313;
International Criminal Tribunal for the
Former Yugoslavia, 208, 287, 304;
manipulation of government institutions,
286–287; Montenegro, 205; nationalism,
188–189, 250; nongovernmental
organizations, 332; Organization for
Security and Cooperation in Europe, 291;
overthrow of, 209, 327–328; privatization,
41; repressive acts, 292; Vance, meeting
with, 252; Vojvodina, 325; xenophobia, 48
Ministry for Regional and Nationalities Policy
in Russia, 349
Ministry of Finance in Russia, 349
Minority issues in Southeastern Europe:
citizenship and population, 44–45; High
Commissioner on National Minorities,
19–21; inclusion/exclusion: assimilation
and expulsion, 42–44; irredentism and
expansion, 41–42; overview, 39–41;
religion, 39–41, 45–47; representation and
education, 47–49. *See also*
Xenophobia/racism in Western Europe;
individual countries
Mitchell, George, 130
Moldova: GUAM Alliance, 352, 409;
independence for, 280; nongovernmental
organizations, 280–282; Organization for
Security and Cooperation in Europe, 21, 22,
281; resources, informational, 282; Russia,
relations with, 351; USSR, history and
legacies of the former, 33, 36, 280–282
Molotov-Ribbentropp Pact of 1939, 31
Monitoring and conflict prevention, 57, 60,
111
Montenegro: conflict dynamics, 311–313;
conflict management, official, 313–316;
creation of, 186; diplomacy, multi-track,
316–317; Helsinki Committee for Human
Rights, 316; historical background,
309–311; independence of, debate over the,
205; International Crisis Group, 211, 320;
nongovernmental organizations, 316–317;
Organization for Security and Cooperation
in Europe, 312, 318, 319; overview, 309;
prospects, 318–319; recommendations,
319–320; resources, informational,
320–321. *See also* Balkans, the; Yugoslavia,
Federal Republic of; Yugoslavia, the former
Moscow Treaty, 422

Multiethnicity/cultural diversity in Caucasus
region, reinvigorating ideals of, 413
Multi-instrument engagements and conflict
prevention, 107, 108, 113–116
Muslims: Balkans, the, 193; Bosnia and
Herzegovina, 232; Chechnya, 356, 359;
Cyprus, 156; Dagestan, 374, 378, 379–380;
minority issues in Europe, 39–43, 45–46;
Montenegro, 313; Nagorno Karabakh, 447;
Russia, 352; Serbia, 324; Wahhabi version
of Islam, 354, 356, 359, 371, 380
Mussolini, Benito, 42

Nabiev, Rahman, 476, 519–520
Nagorno Karabakh: bilateral contacts,
454–455; conflict dynamics, 448–450;
conflict management, official, 450–454;
democracy and human rights, enhancement
of, 459–460; diplomacy, multi-track,
454–461; economic issues, 406, 451;
humanitarian assistance, 460; international
community does not recognize, 406; media,
the, 455, 458; multilateral contacts and
training, 455–457; nongovernmental
organizations, 454–461; Organization for
Security and Cooperation in Europe, 22,
450–452, 457–459, 462–464; overview,
445–448; prisoner exchanges, 459;
prospects, 461–462; public debate,
promotion of, 458–459; recommendations,
462–465; refugees, 452, 457–458, 463, 464;
resources, informational, 465–467;
state/nation building, 405; Technical
Assistance for the Commonwealth of
Independent States, 10; USSR, history and
legacies of the former, 30
Namangani, Juma, 502
Nano, Fatos, 223, 224
Narimanov, Nariman, 30
Nashe Maalo, 275
Nationalism, 189–190, 212–213. *See also*
individual countries
Nationalist and Socialist Movement in Spain,
143
National Liberation Army (UCK) in
Macedonia, 269, 271–272, 326
National Organization of Cypriot Fighters,
157, 159
National Party (NS) in Montenegro, 314–315
Nation/state building in the Caucasus region,
405–406
Nativization policy and history/legacies of the
former USSR, 32
Navarre region in Spain, 142
"Negotiations on Nagorno Karabakh: Where
Do We Go from Here?", 459
Netherlands, 16, 19, 57, 298
Newly Independent States (NIS), 9
Nice European Council, 91
Nicosia Master Plan in Cyprus, 165

process, 485–486; power-sharing, 476–477, 518; regional conflicts, 472, 492; UN, 522; violence, 492. *See also* Central Asia, Ferghana Valley.
Taliban movement in Afghanistan, 358, 475, 481, 497
Technical Assistance for the Commonwealth of Independent States (TACIS). *See under* European Union
Ter-Petrosyan, Levon, 445, 447, 449, 450, 454
Tersk region and history/legacies of the former USSR, 30–31
Thaci, Hashim, 296, 303–304
Therapeutic model and conflict resolution/transformation, 80–83, 85
Time-sensitive interventions and conflict prevention, 106–107
Tito, Marshal, 188, 195, 197, 199–200
Training: Bosnia and Herzegovina, 240; Chechnya, 368; Georgia, 429, 431; Nagorno Karabakh, 455–457; North Ossetia/Ingushetia, 394–396
Trajkovski, Boris, 268, 271, 272
Transcaucasian Media Training, Human Rights and Information Project, 458. *See also* Armenia; Azerbaijan; Georgia
Trans-Causasian Federation in 1922, 30
Transdniestrian region in Moldova, 280–282
Transport Corridor Europe Caucasus Asia (TRACECA) Programme, 10, 11, 407, 412
Treaty of Amsterdam in 1998, 56, 57
Treaty on Friendship and Cooperation, 376
Treaty on Peace and the Principles of Mutual Relations between Russian Federation and the Chechen Republic of Ichkeria (1997), 355
Treaty Regulating Relations and Cooperation between the Republic of North Ossetia-Alania and the Republic of Ingushetia (1997), 391
Trimble, David, 127
Tudjman, Franjo: Bosnia and Herzegovina, partitioning of, 234; death of, 258; elections, first multiparty, 251; International Crisis Group, 212; privatization, 41; Vance, meeting with, 252; West-Herzegovina, annexation of, 202, 204
Turkey: Azerbaijan, relations with, 411; Caucasus region, complex role in the, 410–411; conflict dynamics, 173–175; conflict management, official, 175–176; diplomacy, multi-track, 177–179; Greece, relations with, 171–173, 175–178, 180; High Commissioner on National Minorities, 19; historical background, 169–171; minority issues in Europe, 42, 43; Nagorno Karabakh, relations with, 450; nongovernmental organizations, 179, 180–181; oil issues, 353; overview, 169; prospects, 180; recommendations, 180–181;

resources, informational, 181–182; "Search for Stability in the Caucasus," 179; Syria, relations with, 174–175; USSR, relations with former, 447. *See also* Cyprus
Turkish Republic of Northern Cyprus (TRNC), 158, 159, 161, 166, 167
Turkish Resistance Organization in Cyprus, 157
Turkmenistan, 352
Turkmen people, 31
Turks and history/legacies of the former USSR, 33

Ukraine: Commonwealth of Independent States, 351–352; GUAM Alliance, 352, 409; independence, political, 28, 37; Moldova, relations with, 281; Organization for Security and Cooperation in Europe, 22; "Search for Stability in the Caucasus," 179; USSR, history and legacies of the former, 31, 32, 34
Umakhanov, Ilyas, 384
Union of Soviet Socialist Republics. *See* USSR, history and legacies of the former
United Kingdom: Cyprus, 156–158; Dagestan, relations with, 383–384; Georgia, 423; High Commissioner on National Minorities, 19; Organization for Security and Cooperation in Europe, 16; Royal United Services Institute, 178; "Search for Stability in the Caucasus," 179; Serbia, 328; Verification Technology Information Centre, 12; xenophobia/racism in Western Europe, 52, 54, 56. *See also* Ireland, Northern
United Nations: Agenda for Peace, 73; Albania, 221, 222, 227; Balkans, the, 192; Bosnia and Herzegovina, 73, 235–237; Chechnya, 362, 363, 365; civilian crisis-management capacity, 5; conflict prevention, 91, 92, 100, 106, 112; conflict resolution, broad approach to, 73; Croatia, 205, 252–257; Cyprus, 158, 160–162, 165; Dagestan, 383, 384; Declaration on the Rights of Persons Belonging to National or Ethnic, Religious and Linguistic Minorities, 40; Department of Peace Keeping Operations (DPKO), 330; Development Program (UNDP), 86, 222, 227, 330, 420, 441; Educational Scientific, and Cultural Organization (UNESCO), 383; European Union, 3; Ferghana Valley Development Program, 504–505; Georgia, 410, 420, 422–425, 427; Greek-Turkish relations, 172, 175, 176; High Commissioner for Human Rights, 175; High Commission on Refugees (UNHCR), 165, 216, 292–293, 305, 330–331, 362, 365, 396, 398, 420, 425, 441; Human Rights Office in Abkhazia (HROAG), 424; Interim Administration Mission in Kosovo (UNMIK), 23–24, 213, 292, 295–298, 303, 305, 326, 330, 334;

Index of Organizations

Page numbers presented in bold type indicate an entry in the Directory.

821

About the
Searching for Peace Program

The Searching for Peace Program of the European Centre for Conflict Prevention (ECCP) consists of several regional projects. The ultimate aim of these projects is to contributue to a peaceful transformation of violent conflicts around the world by filling the gaps in information, communication, and coordination that exist in the fields of conflict prevention and peacebuilding. The Searching for Peace publication series is the result of an ongoing process involving research and regional seminars, as well as collaboration with local partners, practitioners, and prominent international scholars.

Searching for Peace in Europe and Eurasia is the second book in the series, following *Searching for Peace in Africa* (1999). Subsequent volumes will cover Central and South Asia, Southeast and East Asia, the Middle East and North Africa, and Latin America and the Caribbean.

About the Book

Searching for Peace in Europe and Eurasia offers much-needed insight into the possibilities for effective conflict prevention and peacebuilding throughout the region.

Presenting surveys of the violent conflicts in Europe, the Caucasus, and Central Asia, the contributors offer a unique combination of background information, detailed descriptions of ongoing activities, and assessments of future prospects for conflict resolution and peacebuilding. A major focus of their work is the efforts of regional organizations and NGOs to make civil society part of any peace process, and they thoroughly cover the activities of grassroots groups. A directory of more than 400 organizations working in the field of conflict prevention and peacebuilding in the region is also included.

More than 40 experts and organizations in Europe and Eurasia have collaborated in the compilation of this important work, which includes a foreword by Max van der Stoel (the former OSCE high commissioner on national minorities) and contributions by such prominent scholars and practitioners as Mari Fitzduff, Michael S. Lund, Valery Tishkov, Raymond Detrez, and Kevin Clements. The work was coordinated by the European Centre for Conflict Prevention, an NGO dedicated to contributing to the prevention and resolution of violent conflicts in the international arena.

Paul van Tongeren is founder and executive director of the European Centre for Conflict Prevention (ECCP), based in Utrecht. Hans van de Veen is senior journalist and coordinator of an independent network of journalists, Environment and Development Productions, based in Amsterdam. Juliette Verhoeven is coordinator of the ECCP s program on Europe and Eurasia.